THINGS WE SAID TODAY

pierian press 1980

THINGS WE SAID TODAY

The Complete Lyrics
and a Concordance to
The Beatles' Songs,
1962-1970

by Colin Campbell
and Allan Murphy

Notice

THE PIERIAN PRESS
5000 Washtenaw Ave.
Ann Arbor, MI 48104

I'm only sleeping.

(1) When I wake up early in the morning,
Lift my head I'm still yawning
When I'm in the middle of a dream
Stay in bed   float   upstream.

Please don't wake me no don't shake me
Leave me where I am I'm only
                              sleeping.

(2) Everybody seems to think I'm lazy
I don't mind I think they're crazy
Running everywhere at such a speed.
Till they find there's no need.

Please don't spoil my day
I'm miles away
And after all I'm only sleeping.

Keeping an eye on the world going by my window
Taking my time

(3) Lying there and staring at the ceiling
Waiting for a sleepy feeling

John Lennon

Contents

List of Illustrations ix
Acknowledgements x

Preface xi
Notes on Content and Use xv
From Romance to Romanticism:
    Analysing The Beatles' Lyrics xxi

Songs Included xxxiii
Songs Not Included xxxiv

Song Title Abbreviations xxxv
Chronological List of Songs xxxix

Complete Lyrics 1
Concordance 65

Appendix One: Contractions 365
Appendix Two: Prefixed Words 367

Alphabetical Word-frequency List 369
Numerical Word-frequency List 375

Listener's Guide to Songs 381
Song Index to Albums 383

PAPER BACK WRITER

Dear Sir (or Madam) (INTROD.)

Will you read my book. It took me years to write, will you take a look It's based on a novel by a man named Lear, and I need a job, so I want to be a paperback writer. RIFF TWICE

It's a dirty story of a dirty man, and his clinging wife doesn't understand. His son is working for the Daily Mail It's a steady job, but he wants to be a paperback writer. (INTROD) RIFF ONCE

It's a thousand pages, give or take a few, I'll be writing more in a week or two. I could make it longer, if you like the style, I can change it round and I want to be a paperback writer. RIFF.

If you really like it you can have the rights, and it could make a million for you overnight If you must return it you can send it here, but I need a break, and I want to be a paperback writer.

Yours Sincerely, Ian Iachimoe.

List of Illustrations

I'm Only Sleeping vi
Paperback Writer viii
Good Day Sunshine xiii
Blue Jay Way xiv
Help! xx
And Your Bird Can Sing xxxii
Yesterday xxxviii
For No-One xli
I Want To Hold Your Hand xlii
The Word 63
Lucy In The Sky With Diamonds 64
Eleanor Rigby 364
Michelle 366
Yellow Submarine 368, 382

Acknowledgements

We are grateful to both the Department of Sociology and Anthropology and The Faculty of Arts of Simon Fraser University for financial assistance with this project and, in particular, for bearing the postage and computation costs involved. We should also like to thank Jean Jordan of the Sociology and Anthropology Department and Reo Audette and Coleen Melsness of the computer terminal staff for their cooperation and generous assistance at various stages of the project. Above all, we are greatly indebted to Michel Begin who was a constant source of encouragement and inspiration. Finally, we should like to express our thanks to Thomas Schultheiss, both for his general enthusiasm when this project was first suggested and for his continuous and persistent efforts to obtain the necessary permissions. If George Martin is rightly known as "The Fifth Beatle" then Tom Schultheiss must surely be "The Third Author" of this work.

Preface

The idea for this work arose out of a conversation between the authors sometime in May 1976. At that time we were bemoaning the fact that no adequate "authorised" version of The Beatles' song lyrics was available which could be used as the basis for serious critical analysis. Although there were several works in print which were advertised as "The Beatles Lyrics," nearly all of them defined a "Beatle lyric" in a manner inappropriate for our purpose, frequently including songs performed but not written by The Beatles (such as *Long Tall Sally* and *Kansas City*) or written but not performed by them (such as *From a Window* and *World Without Love*). More importantly, these collections were never complete and commonly omitted songs if copyright permission proved difficult to obtain. This usually meant that George Harrison's songs were not included. Finally, the lyrics that were contained in these books showed all the signs of having been hastily put together and carelessly presented: obvious errors and inconsistencies were noticeable and it was clear that they could not be regarded as reliable sources. Subsequent experience did, in fact, endorse our initial suspicion of their accuracy. Clearly these books were inspired by commercial rather than scholarly considerations and could not serve as the basis for serious critical analysis.

The value of such an analysis seemed self-evident to us, whether its primary purpose was to unravel the mysterious excellence of The Beatles' songs or to shed light upon the fascinating cultural and social changes that characterised the decade of the nineteen–sixties. In either case, little could be done until the primary material was set out accurately and with an eye to its serious use. Having thus identified the need, what seemed inescapable was that we would have to meet it ourselves.

By a fortunate coincidence, Thomas Schultheiss of Pierian Press was, at that very moment in 1976, looking for new reference material on The Beatles to incorporate in a sequel to the highly successful book *All Together Now* and had, in fact, half–jokingly suggested to the authors of that work that they should consider a concordance to The Beatles' lyrics. He thus responded enthusiastically when we approached him with the idea for this work.

Many problems had to be overcome in the course of the four years which it has subsequently taken to bring this book into being. A central one has been the fact that for all but about six months of that time, the two authors have had to communicate with each other across a distance of 6,000 miles, a process made more difficult by clerical strikes and postal disputes at one end and by the burdensome demands of academic and administrative duties at the other. Only for brief periods of time was either author able to devote his energies to this project full-time. Although the initial work of transcribing lyrics onto coding sheets and feeding material into the computer was completed as early as the autumn of 1976, it transpired that the real work of correcting errors was only just beginning. This was necessarily a tedious business for the triple nature of the work (lyrics, concordance and word frequency lists) meant that any one error was repeated in three separate places. In addition, the fact that a format of one-lyric line per punched card was not adopted when the data was prepared subsequently caused considerable delays, for it meant that quite minor corrections frequently involved the recoding of a whole song. Hence both 1977 and 1978 were largely taken up with the work of correcting together with the resolution of various computer programming problems.

Delays were also caused by the difficulty of obtaining copyright permissions and at one time it looked as if not all The Beatles' lyrics would be included, a possibility which cast considerable doubt on the value of proceeding with the book. Obviously these problems were eventually overcome, although not without much anxiety and transatlantic correspondence; in 1979 we moved towards the final stages of preparing the computer print-outs and accompanying materials for publication.

The resultant work is unusual, if not unique, in at least two ways. Firstly, it consists of both The Beatles' lyrics and a concordance to them. Commonly, the work of poets or authors have been in print for many years and are issued in the form of "definitive" collections prior to the construction of a concordance. In this instance the two exercises have been collapsed into one and the publication of a definitive version of The Beatles' lyrics combined with the production of a concordance and word frequency lists. There were both advantages and difficulties in such a procedure. Although it meant that the lyrics could be prepared and organised with the construction of a concordance in mind, it also meant that the work involved would be double that facing anyone who adopted the more conventional approach of dealing with these tasks one at a time. Nevertheless it seemed worthwhile, for publishing the two together enables the reader to consult both the concordance and the lyrics to which it refers within the pages of one book.

Secondly, this work is unique, as far as we are aware, in being the very first concordance to deal with the lyrics of popular songs. Until now, concordances have commonly been prepared for the work of poets, writers or dramatists but not for lyricists or at least not for popular song-writers. What is more, it is very unusual indeed to prepare a concordance to refer to the work of artists who are still alive and hence capable of adding to their "collected works." However, it is because The Beatles, considered as a single entity, are not "alive" that this work is justified. It seems to us highly appropriate that, of all modern artists, they should be the occasion for such innovation.

The assumption underlying the construction of this concordance is that The Beatles are of scholarly interest as the creators of recorded songs and that, in consequence, critical analysis will focus upon the song-as-performed rather than upon the lyric or the music abstracted from this. The concordance is thus a means to this end and its publication does not imply that the authors hold the view that the lyrics can properly be considered apart from the music or that they should justifiably be regarded as poetry. There is bound to be a fundamental inadequacy attendant upon any analysis of lyrics that does not take into account the music that was intended to accompany them and this is especially true in the case of The Beatles. This fact is fully acknowledged and an analysis of the lyrics alone, no matter how detailed and penetrating, cannot possibly serve as a satisfactory substitute for a critical appraisal of the complete songs. However, the analysis of recorded popular songs is still a young discipline and attempts to consider words and music conjointly have, to date, dealt satisfactorily with only one half of the equation. It therefore seems more sensible to proceed through the less ambitious but more technically manageable procedure of considering the words and music separately so that at some later date a critical consideration of the integrated songs may take place on a more secure basis.

Even this limited aim is fraught with difficul-ties. It is not merely that the full meaning of the lyrics can only be understood in the context of the music and in conjunction with the manner of performance. It is that the division between music and lyrics is itself indistinct. Sung lyrics constitute musical sounds whilst music can have symbolic meanings at least as accepted and widely understood as words (consider the *Marseillaise* at the beginning of *All You Need Is Love*). Consequently it would be foolish to assume that the full meaning of a lyric is to be found by a consideration of its verbal and literary properties alone. Nonetheless, despite these difficulties, there is clearly much that a careful analysis of the lyrics can contribute to an understanding of the songs as a whole and it is here that the methods of conventional literary criticism have a role to play. The construction of a concordance is just such a technique and its use will hopefully extend our understanding of some of the best loved songs of our time.

Preceding the lyrics, the concordance, and the word lists are notes on the use of this work, together with a general introduction setting out some of the themes which a critical analysis reveals to be contained in The Beatles' songs. The former are there to help the reader make the most of the material contained in the book and should be consulted before referring to the concordance proper. The latter, entitled "From Romance to Romanticism," is intended as an exploratory discussion of the key question of the philosophy to be discerned in the lyrics and may be read as a self-contained essay independent of the accompanying material, whilst it also serves to illustrate how useful the concordance can be as an aid to critical analysis. Also included are various alphabetical and chronological supporting lists of songs included and not included, an abbreviations list, and a song index to The Beatles' albums. This work is thus presented in the hope that it may be of value to other serious students of The Beatles as well as of interest to their numerous admirers around the world.

Colin Campbell
Allan Murphy
June 1980

ROBERT FITZPATRICK ASSOCIATES

9229 SUNSET BOULEVARD. LOS ANGELES. CALIF. 90069
CRestview 1-4561

ROBERT FITZPATRICK, *President*

BLUE JAY WAY.
upon L.A.

There's a fog ~~the~~ . .
and my friends have lost their way.
"will be over soon" they said,
Now they've lost their way instead.
    please dont be long
        or else I'll be asleep.

_____

Well it only goes to show
and I told them where to go
ask a policeman on the street
there's so many there to meet.
    please dont be long

Now its past my bed I know
but I'd really like to go
soon will be the break of day
Sitting here in Blue Jay way
        please dont be long.

When I see you at the door
I'll know your worth waiting for
and the moment when you speak —
I know I'd wait here all week

Notes on Content and Use

On content

Songs Included

Things We Said Today includes the complete lyrics of all the songs written, recorded and released by The Beatles as a group between 1962 and 1970, beginning with the single release *Love Me Do/PS I Love You* in October 1962 and ending with the album **Let It Be** in May 1970. A complete list of the 184 song titles included, arranged alphabetically starting with *Across the Universe* and finishing with *You've Got to Hide Your Love Away*, follows the introductory material. For the sake of completeness, the titles of the instrumental *Flying* and the experimental *Revolution Nine* (counted in the total of 184) have also been included, even though there are no accompanying lyrics. Additional versions of the songs *All You Need Is Love, Revolution, Let It Be* and *Get Back* (see **Song Variants** below) have been treated here as separate songs, as has the reprise to *Sgt. Pepper's Lonely Hearts Club Band*, regarded merely as the closing chorus of the song by the sheet music publisher. For the purpose of this work, this makes a total of 189 distinct songs included.

Songs Not Included

Not included are songs which The Beatles recorded but did not write or songs which they wrote for other performers. Songs not composed by The Beatles appeared on all albums up to **Rubber Soul** (1965). Thereafter The Beatles only recorded their own compositions, with the exception of the occasional traditional song such as *Maggie Mae*.[1] Songs written and performed by John Lennon, Paul McCartney, George Harrison and Ringo Starr after the break-up of The Beatles in 1970 are not included. Also excluded are songs and versions of songs carried on various bootleg albums: some of these are merely recordings of live performances, and thus provide no new material; others consist of studio out-takes and thus usually contain slightly different versions of the songs which were eventually released; some also contain songs which have

never been released. Whilst this material is undoubtedly of interest and can, in some instances, throw light upon the processes by which a lyric came to have its final form, they do not represent the lyrics which The Beatles themselves approved for release or indeed the lyrics which the public have come to know and love. For these reasons, and also, it must be said, because of the legal difficulties involved, no bootleg material has been included.

What Is a Lyric?

A Beatles' lyric is defined here as those words and vocal sounds which are audible on officially issued Beatles' recordings. These lyrics thus differ from those which have been previously published, either in sheet music form, in compilations such as *The Beatles Lyrics Complete* (which, as a court was subsequently to confirm, was not complete)[2] or even as given on the record sleeves in the case of **Sgt. Pepper's Lonely Hearts Club Band**. As commentators have observed, these published lyrics frequently differ from each other and from that which is audible on the record, thereby giving rise to the problem of what should be regarded as the "authorised" version.[3] The position taken here is that the record itself contains the only true "authorised" lyric and hence all published lyrics must be judged against this standard. Where, therefore, there have been disputed or contradictory accounts of a lyric, attempts to resolve the issue have been made simply by carefully listening to what is sung. There

----

1. This does not mean, however, that other songs may not have been inspired by existing works. *Golden Slumbers*, for example, appears to have been taken from a poem by Thomas Dekker (see *Strawberry Fields Forever*, no. 20, p. 7) and is one of several instances where lyric lines derive from existing published works.

2. The book in question is *The Beatles Lyrics Complete*, published by Futura Publications Limited (London) in 1974. This firm was subsequently sued under The Trade Descriptions Act by school teacher Allan Bacon on the grounds that the book did not contain the song *Paperback Writer*. His complaint was upheld by a court in Fleetwood, Lancashire and the publishers were ordered to pay a fine of £ 25. The next edition of the book was simply called *The Beatles Lyrics*.

3. Some of these problems are raised in a discussion in *The Journal of Popular Culture* in 1969/70. See for example: Geoffrey Marshall, "On Taking The Beatles Seriously: Problems of Text," number 3, 1969 pp. 28--34; Neil V. Rosenberg, "Taking Popular Culture Seriously: The Beatles," number 4, 1970 pp. 53--56; and, George W. Lyon, Jr., "More on Beatles Textual Problems," number 4, 1970 pp. 549--552.

are, of course, limitations to this technique. Occasionally phrases remain impenetrably inaudible despite the most determined efforts and it may then become necessary to consult published sources. Even so, some particularly faint and distorted backing vocals are indecipherable. In addition, such a technique cannot solve the problems presented by homonyms and homophones or indeed questions of spelling and punctuation.

The use of the recorded lyric as the authorised one means that these lyrics differ from those previously published in the inclusion of all words and vocalisations that are audible. Rather than impose some arbitrary convention concerning what constitutes a lyric, all discernible words have been included (except where they are not by The Beatles), even where it is possible to claim that their inclusion was initially accidental. Hence the jokes, exclamations and snatches of conversation which frequently precede and follow the music in later Beatles' songs have been included as part of the lyric. This practice seems justifiable on the grounds that since those words were not erased one can only assume that they were intended to be heard. To have excluded them would have meant not only being untrue to the audible reality but have introduced difficult decisions concerning exactly where one should draw the line between the "real lyric" and extraneous comment.

These lyrics also differ from those which have been published previously in a second respect. This is in the extensive inclusion of vocalisations. As there is no clear line separating words from sounds made with the voice, an attempt has been made to incorporate all vocalisations into the lyric. The "yeah yeah" that was so characteristic of The Beatles does not represent a problem in this respect since it is merely a colloquial version of "yes yes." Exclamations are also clearly words and hence part of the lyric, but what is one to make of the "nah, nah, nah" at the end of *Hey Jude*? Is this merely vocalised music or could it possibly be a colloquialism? Given the difficulty of deciding such issues it seemed wiser to treat all vocalisations as if they were part of the lyric proper.

Authorship

The term "The Beatles' lyrics" is taken to refer to the words and vocalisations of all songs indigenous to the group no matter who has been formally credited with the authorship. Of the 189 songs included in the concordance, 162 are accredited to the names of John Lennon and Paul McCartney. A further twenty-two are acknowledged as creations of George Harrison whilst Ringo Starr is identified as the composer of only two songs. Two numbers -- *Dig It* and *Flying* -- are accredited to all four of them whilst *What Goes On* is listed as by Lennon and McCartney and Starr. The legal division of rights in various Beatles' songs naturally raises the question of how justifiable it is to treat the lyrics of all 189 songs as an entity. Perhaps a concordance of Lennon lyrics or McCartney lyrics might be more appropriate than one relating to the group? This is a reasonable argument and there is no doubt that such personal concordances would be very interesting. However, even if examination were to reveal considerable differences between the lyrical styles of the individual Beatles it would not affect the basic justification for treating all the lyrics as a single entity. This, as has already been suggested, is the fact that the basic art--form under consideration is not the lyric but the recorded song. As this is a product of all four of them there is some justification for deeming the lyric itself to belong to all "The Beatles."

In any case, there are grounds for doubting whether formal allotment of credit for lyrics which the designation of authorship represents actually corresponds, in detail, or in all cases, to reality. Although some lyrics do appear to have been entirely the product of one member of the group, many more resulted from collaboration. The extent and character of this collaboration was various and is not adequately reflected in the simple credit "music and lyrics by Lennon and McCartney." Unlike other famous song-writing partnerships there was no simple division between the composer and the lyricist: instead each contributed music or lyrics as the occasion demanded. What is more, the extent to which one of them contributed to a song begun by the other might vary from merely a word or phrase to an entire stanza. Given these complications it is not an easy matter to decide exactly who was responsible for which lyric or part lyric. It would appear that the identity of the lead singer is probably the best indication of whom the main lyricist might be, since the convention was that the one who knew the words best did most of the singing. In fact, the division of authorship for many songs is well established as it has been acknowledged by The Beatles themselves.[4]

However, to pursue questions of individual authorship in this way is to overlook the central and inescapable fact that binds these lyrics together: they were written by one or more individuals who were acutely conscious of their membership of a larger entity. No matter who wrote them, all these songs were written so that The Beatles could perform them. Although there has been ample evidence since 1970 that John, Paul, George and Ringo have

---

4. For details see, in particular, Jann Wenner, *Lennon Remembers*, Penguin Books, 1973, and Paul Gambaccini, *Paul McCartney In His Own Words*, Omnibus Press, 1976.

different tastes in music and styles of lyric writing, it seems quite clear that when they were members of the group they were extremely conscious of their identity as "a Beatle" and what that meant musically and lyrically. It is this common identity which is the thread that binds these lyrics together, and, transcending all individual variations, reveals itself as the distinctive "personality" known as The Beatles.

Discrepant Titles

There are at least three Beatles' songs which have been given slightly different titles in the United Kingdom and the United States. On the **Help!** album issued in the UK there is a song entitled *You're Going to Lose That Girl*, whilst on the US version of this album the song is listed as *You're Gonna Lose That Girl*. In fact, "gonna" and not "going to" is what The Beatles sing but there are several other songs where the titles do not reflect the colloquial expressions used. Of more interest is the fact that on the **Revolver** album issued in the US there is a song called *Love You To* whilst on the label of the UK album (but not on the cover) this song is given as *Love You Too*. As the title is not included in the lyric of the song there is little possibility of deciding from the context of use which of these it should be.

A similar problem occurs with the song *Dig a Pony* which appears under that title on the UK **Let It Be** album but is listed as *I Dig a Pony* on the US album. Although John does sing "I dig a pony" there is a sufficient pause between the "I" and the "dig" to suggest that it is not altogether unreasonable to make "Dig a pony" stand on its own. In the former case, the alternative title is indicated by the use of an oblique line, *Love You To/Too* whilst *Dig a Pony* is listed alphabetically under "I" and not under "D."

Song Variants

A second set of discrepancies arises from the fact that some songs were issued in more than one version, usually first as a single and then subsequently on an album. Although the lyrical differences are generally very slight (whilst musical differences are often considerable) and mainly concern variations in the introductions and fade outs to the songs, it does mean that it has been necessary to include these "variants" as additional songs. Songs which have two forms included are *All You Need Is Love, Get Back, Let It Be* and *Revolution* (this is the obvious case because the two versions have been distinguished by the different titles *Revolution* and *Revolution One*). As far as *All You Need Is Love* is concerned, the only difference is that the version which appeared on the **Magical Mystery Tour** album contains six more "Love is all you need" lines than does the version on the **Yellow Submarine**

album. In the case of *Revolution* and *Revolution One* there are slight differences in the introductions and endings as well as in the backing, but the most significant lyrical difference is the addition in the later version of the word "in" at the end of the two lines "But when you talk about destruction, Don't you know that you can count me out?", an addition which is important enough to significantly modify the overall sentiment expressed in the song. With *Get Back* the differences concern the introduction and fade out, the **Let It Be** version opening with studio talk and ending with the famous comment "And I hope we passed the audition" whilst the single release version ends with lines absent from the other version about Loretta's mother and her apparel. With *Let It Be* the longer version merely has lines 27 and 28 repeated. In each case the two versions have been appropriately identified and are arranged in order of release.

Line Arrangement

Given that the original material from which the lyrics are taken was in an aural and not a printed form, the imposition of a line arrangement was necessarily a difficult matter. Of course, in some instances the original hand--written lyrics were available and could be taken as a guide. However, even these are somewhat unreliable as it would appear that the limitations of paper size occasionally caused the composer to set his lyrics down in a form different from that which, ideally, he would have preferred. Hence in the event, the line arrangements chosen reflect a personal judgement of what corresponds best to the phrasing of the song, constrained in this case, by the limitations of the computer programme and the column format of the book.

Backing Vocals

Backing vocals are also included in addition to the main lyric line (at least in those instances where they are clearly discernible) and in order to distinguish between a backing which succeeds the lyric line from one which accompanies it, a system of single and double brackets has been used. Single brackets signify a backing subsequent to the main lyric whilst double brackets indicate a backing contemporaneous with it. In both cases the backing is most commonly a repeat of all or part of the main lyric line although this is less true of the later songs.

Alternate Words

In a few instances alternate words are recorded in the lyrics. These are shown separated by an oblique line. For example, line 17 of *I'll Get You* reads "When I'm gonna change/make your mind" whilst line seven of *Hello Goodbye* reads "I say hi!/high, you say 'lo/low." There are two reasons for this. In the first case the lead singers actually sing different words, presumably by mistake, whilst in the second case the homophonic nature of the words makes it impossible to be sure which of the two meanings is intended or indeed if they both are. Hence both alternatives are shown.

Stop Words

Not all the words which appear in the lyrics have been included in the concordance. Certain of the commoner words have been disregarded. Those not included are A, AN, AND, THE and 'N' (the latter as in rock 'n' roll).

Contractions and Prefixed Words

These, such as 'cos (for because) and 'cept (for except) together with prefixed words like "a--move" and "a--when" are listed separately in appendices immediately after the main concordance.

Derivative and Inflexional Forms

Variants and derivatives of standard words are listed alphabetically and no effort has been made to group together all words with the same stem.

Spelling

The audible reality demands that the colloquial form of spelling be used in many instances, e.g. "gonna" instead of "going to" and "wanna" instead of "want to." However, these words are not consistently sung in this fashion thereby giving rise to the inclusion in the concordance of both colloquial variants and the more conventional forms.

English rather than North American spelling has been preferred throughout in deference to The Beatles' origin and it is necessary to remember this when searching for a word.

Emotives and Vocalisations

An attempt has been made to record all discernible emotives and vocalisations, such as "oh," "aah," "yeah" and "ooo" and to represent these in print by letter combinations on an onomatopoeic basis. Clearly there are immense difficulties in such an exercise and it was very hard to record all of these as accurately or as consistently as we would have liked, especially when the vocalisations are added on to or blended in with a recognisable lyric word. The emotives have not been excluded from the concordance and hence it is possible to examine in detail the extent and character of their use in the lyrics.

Song Order

Within the concordance proper, references to keywords are listed chronologically by the earliest date of release of the song, whether this occurred in Britain or North America; the primary source for this release date information was the book *All*

Together Now by Harry Castleman and Wally Podrazik, together with their sequel called *The Beatles Again*. Where songs were released on singles and EPs prior to their appearance on long-playing albums, chronological order reflects the earlier release. Songs contained on the same album are listed in alphabetical order and are not in the sequence given on the record sleeve. As far as it is possible to determine, songs were released more or less as they were recorded (though not always as they were written), the principal exceptions being *You Know My Name (Look Up My Number)* which, although recorded in May 1967, was not released until March 1970, and the album **Let It Be** which, whilst recorded in January 1969, was not released until May 1970. Generally speaking, therefore, the song order corresponds to that in which they were recorded.

Computer Facts

All the computer work was carried out at the computing centre, Simon Fraser University, Burnaby, British Columbia between mid-1976 and early 1980. The data was sorted on an IBM system/370 model 155 computer with 3 million bytes of storage using an OS/MUT system with a release of 21.8. The language used was PL/1. All songs written, recorded and released by The Beatles were listened to and carefully transcribed on to coding sheets for card punching. This data was then fed into the computer and lyric print-outs and a concordance obtained. Alphabetical and numerical word frequency lists were also generated as a by-product of the concordance programme. The total material constituted 2,839 cards, that is 35,390 written words and 2,346 distinct words.

On use

The Concordance and How to Use It

A concordance is basically a word-finder with the words listed alphabetically as in a dictionary, but in place of a definition of the word there is a reproduction of the line or lines of the original song in which that word appeared. Thus, if you looked up the word "tulips" you will find the single line

TULIPS
Looking through the bent-backed tulips--
GLASSONION--5

indicating that the word only appears once in all The Beatles' songs and that is in line five of *Glass Onion*. However, most entries concern words that appear more than once. Where this happens within the lyric of one song the lines are given in the order in which they are sung. The word immediately above "tulips" for example, is "Tuesdays" which appears twice in the song *She Came in Through the Bathroom Window*. Hence the entry reads:

TUESDAYS
Tuesdays on the phone to me.--
SHECAMEINT--11
Tuesdays on the phone to me.--
SHECAMEINT--23

Where the same word appears in lines from different songs these are listed chronologically according to the release dates. Thus the word "Tuesday" in the singular appears in both *I Am the Walrus* and *Lady Madonna*, but the line from *I Am the Walrus* is given first because it was released in 1967 whilst *Lady Madonna* was issued in 1968, hence this entry is shown as:

TUESDAY
Corporation T--shirt, stupid bloody Tuesday--
IAMTHEWALR--5
Tuesday afternoon is never-ending--
LADYMADONN--14

Finally, when a word appears both several times in one song and in more than one song, these two principles are combined with all the lines from the same song listed together with the songs grouped by date of release. We can see this if we look up a word like "town."

TOWN
In the town where I was born--
YELLOWSUBM--1
Heading for home you start to roam then you're in town.--GOODMORNIN--8
Everywhere in town is getting dark--
GOODMORNIN--19
So one day he walked into town--
ROCKYRACCO--7

The arrangement of lines according to the words they contain in this fashion makes it possible to investigate many features of The Beatles' lyrics. In the first place, it means that it is easy to locate any specific word. If, for example, you remember that there is a reference to Edgar Allan Poe somewhere in one of The Beatles' songs, but you can't remember which song, then it only takes a second to look under the P's to find the line.

POE
Man you should have seen them kicking Edgar Allan Poe--IAMTHEWALR--27

indicating that the song in question is *I Am the Walrus* and the name is to be found in line twenty-seven.[5]

But the concordance can be used in a much more adventurous way to discover facts about The Beatles' lyrics. If, for example, you wanted to learn which colour appears most often in their songs then, by consulting the word frequency list and checking on each colour in turn, you would find that blue is mentioned most often -- thirty--five times -- closely followed by yellow with thirty--one. However, if you now look up both words in the concordance itself you will discover that "yellow" only appears in five songs and that the vast majority of references are to *Yellow Submarine* whilst the thirty-five references to "blue" cover a total of no less than seventeen different songs. Thus the word "blue" is much more widely used in the lyrics than is "yellow" even though this is not immediately apparent from the frequency lists. One reason for this, of course, is that "blue" can have two meanings referring either to the colour or to an emotional state of deep unhappiness. Consideration of the lines printed out in the concordance can reveal that in ten of the seventeen cases the word is clearly being used to refer to a mood whilst it is used in its more conventional sense in the remaining ten. What is more, as the lyric lines are listed chronologically it is possible to see that this pattern has changed over time with most of the "mood" uses of the word appearing in the earlier songs. What this examination also reveals, however, is that there are instances where this very ambiguity of meaning has been deliberately employed. In *Baby's In Black* for example, with the line "Baby's in black and I'm feeling blue" and in *Yes It Is* with "For red is the colour that will make me blue" and lastly in *Because* with "Because the sky is blue it makes me cry." Thus already this brief investigation into the use of colour words has revealed something of interest about the significant and changing use of the word "blue" as well as about The Beatles' exploitation of verbal ambiguity. However, there is no reason why one should stop there. One could, for example, continue by examining what kinds of objects are typically described as "blue" and in which contexts.

By using the concordance and word frequency lists together in this way and by referring where necessary to the original lyric, it is possible to discover a great deal about the character and content of The Beatles' lyrics. It is, however, necessary to remember that the investigation of more complex subjects or themes, such as, for example, loneliness, requires that one should also check synonyms and derivative forms of the key word. In this case, it would mean a consideration of such words as "alone" and "lonely" as well as "loneliness," together with associated phrases such as "on my own."

---

5. Alternatively, of course, the same information can be found by looking up "Edgar" or "Allan."

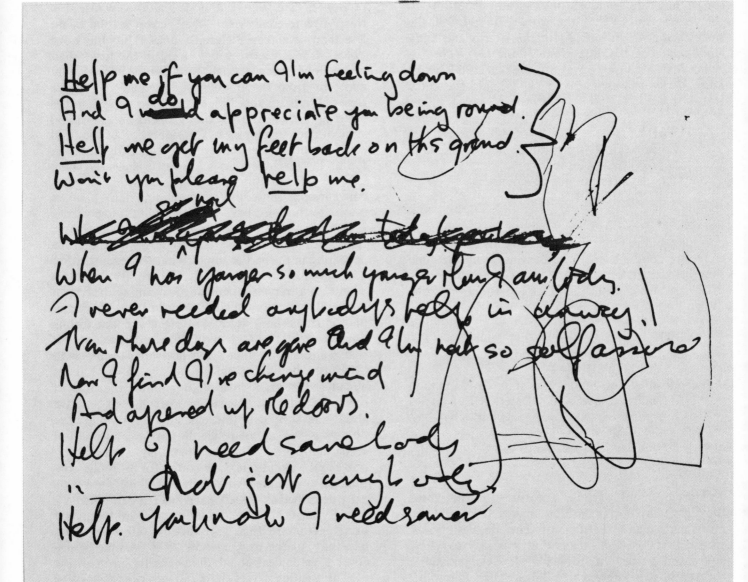

From Romance to Romanticism:
Analysing The Beatles' Lyrics

How should one go about the task of analysing and interpreting The Beatles' lyrics? What assumptions can one legitimately make concerning the nature and levels of meaning to be found in them or in their relationships to one another? It is clear that not everyone shares the same opinion on these questions, for at one extreme there are those conservative arbiters of public taste who would deny that any analysis or interpretation is required and assert that these lyrics, like those of most popular songs, are banal, trivial and not worthy of the treatment accorded works of art. Whilst at the other extreme, there are the "true believers" in The Beatles, their dedicated and devoted fans, for whom these lyrics constitute "sacred texts" and accordingly require a detailed and careful scrutiny in order to uncover their underlying "truths." Neither of these extremes, however, neither off-hand dismissal nor reverential deciphering, would seem an entirely reasonable response based as they are upon either uncritical denigration or worship. A more sober and balanced attitude would appear to be required, which, whilst recognising that The Beatles first made their reputation in the thoroughly commercial world of popular entertainment, nevertheless acknowledges that some of their later songs constitute powerful and effective works of art.

Pop Music or Art?

Three points are worth making in connection with the argument that The Beatles' lyrics do not warrant serious critical consideration. The first is that it is wrong to suppose that because some of the lyrics were reportedly composed in a random, haphazard and spontaneous manner, one should conclude that no valid or significant works of art were created. There is a long and respected tradition in the arts which considers creativity as less a matter of discipline or will than of instinct and intuition and regards the artist as a vehicle for creative forces which he experiences as arising "beyond" or "within" himself. From this viewpoint The Beatles' habit of improvising lyrics is no more strange than was Jackson Pollock's method of painting or John Cage's way of composing. The second point is that The Beatles' close association with rock'n'roll and the popular song should not cause us to imagine that their work must necessarily be seen as lying outside the elite Western artistic and cultural traditions. For although their combined experience of formal education was limited (John's period at art college being perhaps the only factor of significance), they

did educate themselves extensively during the critical years 1965–67 and one can find references to Edward Lear, Edgar Allan Poe, Allan Ginsberg and Shakespeare in their lyrics. There are, therefore, grounds for assuming that they were influenced by writers such as these. Finally, it would also be a mistake to assume that the frequent flippancy and humour characteristic of The Beatles both on stage and off (and indeed, not uncommonly in their lyrics) indicates that their songs could not be the work of serious artists, for, as has been noted, whilst "seriousness seeks to exclude play . . . play can very well include seriousness."[1] This does indeed appear to have been especially true of The Beatles, whose playfulness could be said to reveal the determination of a group of serious artists not to become solemn ones.

Circumstantial Comment or Textual Criticism?

Although concentrating on deciphering The Beatles' lyrics is undoubtedly mistaken, it does raise the difficult problem of exactly how one should approach the task of interpretation. Should one, for example, concentrate primarily on examining the songs themselves or should one turn instead to a consideration of the personal circumstances of the lyricist and the occasion on which the song was written? Should one, in effect, turn to an internal "textual" or an external, "circumstantial" mode of critical analysis? To date, most criticism of The Beatles' lyrics has been external rather than internal in form, focusing on the occasion upon which the song came to be written and relying heavily upon comments supplied by the lyricist himself. This approach sheds light upon the lyric to the extent that one learns when it was written, who contributed which lines, where the original idea came from and what, in general, the lyricist's intention might have been. Thus we know that the title for *Lucy in the Sky with Diamonds* came from a painting which John's son Julian did at school and that the lyric for *Mr. Kite* came from an old poster, whilst *Sexy Sadie* ostensibly refers to the Maharishi Mahesh Yogi.[2] It is on the basis of information of this kind that commentators frequently "interpret" The Beatles' songs. Thus one reads that *Penny Lane*

---

1. Johan Huizinga, *Homo Ludens: A Study of the Play Element in Culture*, Beacon Press, Boston (1950) p. 32.
2. Hunter Davies, *The Beatles: The Authorised Biography*, Heineman, London (1968).

is "about" a street in Liverpool, that *Eleanor Rigby* is "about" loneliness, whilst *Lucy in the Sky with Diamonds* is "about" drug experiences. These comments are then often linked with claims that The Beatles moved through "phases" such as "flower power" and "Eastern mysticism," so that individual songs are then additionally tagged as belonging to one of these periods. The effect of this style of criticism is to imply that there is no overall pattern or meaning to The Beatles' work but that they simply used whatever they came across as the basis for a lyric and, like sensitive reporters, had the happy knack of capturing in song what other people were feeling.

Yet this form of analysis is clearly inadequate. To learn what occasioned a work of art frequently contributes little or nothing to an understanding of the work as a whole. It certainly doesn't help one penetrate to the meaning of *Lucy in the Sky with Diamonds* to learn how John obtained the title any more than the fact that *Penny Lane* is a street in Liverpool helps one to understand the remarkable appeal of this lyric. It is, after all, what an artist does with his material which is significant, not where he obtains it. There are also reasons for feeling that the lyricists' comments on his intentions may be less valuable than they appear to be. The Beatles may not have been totally honest in this respect choosing to emphasise only one of the meanings contained in a lyric or indeed pretending that the lyric as a whole is lacking in meaning, either because they do not wish to appear pompous and alienate a section of their public or so that the song might be all the more effective for remaining unexplained. Then again, it is very possible that the lyricist was not fully aware of his motives and that subconscious factors, necessarily unrecognised by him, need to be considered. In addition, it is important to remember that no artist ever achieves exactly what he sets out to attain and that the end product is consequently both more and less than his intention. Finally, it is the songs' success, its power to delight and enchant us, which is of prime interest and here the composer may well be as mystified as any critic.

However, the central reason for deeming this style of criticism inadequate is that it fails to consider the songs of The Beatles as a whole or to view them as a consistent and coherent body of work in which individual songs must be understood both in their own right and in terms of complex relationships with each other. For these reasons the mode of criticism favoured here is an internal one, concerned primarily with the content, structure and relationship of the lyrics themselves, both as these are perceived within individual songs and more significantly, as these develop over time between them. Thus, although it is necessary to refer to the general circumstances in which The Beatles found themselves, it is the lyrics which are seen as providing the main clues to an understanding of their experience rather than the reverse.

How a Lyric Is Born?

Unlike such composer-performers of the nineteen-sixties as Leonard Cohen or Bob Dylan, The Beatles' lyrics cannot adequately be described as poetry set to music. Their primary and natural medium was the song and hence the lyrics are characterised by the fullest use of the possibilities which are unique to the sung word. Two of these, the use of homophones and accentuation, particularly need to be mentioned as they present special difficulties for the compilers of a concordance. When, in *Hello Goodbye*, Paul sings "I say high, you say low," should it be "high" or should it be "hi!"? Or should we, more properly, recognise that the ambiguity contained in the two words and their common sound is the very essence of the line's meaning and record it in print as "hi!/high"? However, if we do this then it becomes necessary to scan all the lyrics for homophones and decide which we consider to have been deliberately employed in this way. A similar problem arises through the variation in accentuation and phrasing which a singer can give to a lyric line. In *Blue Jay Way* George sings "Please don't be long, please don't you be very long" and he repeats this line several times, finishing the song by reiterating "Don't be long, don't be long." Somewhere in the course of singing these lines he shifts the accent so that it becomes "don't belong" another perfect meaningful phrase which is not inconsistent with the general sense of the song as a whole. In this case, we have incorporated the change in the printed version but it is very possible that other similarly accentuated shifts of meaning have been overlooked.

These examples serve to suggest how The Beatles' lyrics -- or at least some of the later ones -- may have come to be written. Mellers outlines the process by which a musical phrase of a few bars such as the "love, love, love" in *All You Need Is Love* is added to and developed until it constitutes a complete melody and something similar would appear to characterise the process of lyric composition.[3] Here too the starting point may be a single phrase or snatch of conversation such as "From Me to You," "Let It Be," "I'm Only Sleeping" or "Hello, Goodbye." Then the immanent verbal harmonies and resonances are developed through a process that approximates to free association drawing heavily upon the metric, rhythmic and alliterative

---

3. Wilfrid Mellers, *Twilight of the Gods: The Beatles in Retrospect*, Faber & Faber, London (1976) 102--4.

possibilities of the original.

In the early songs the key phrase is simply reiterated unchanged anything up to five or six times. But in the later ones it almost invariably goes through some form of development parallel to that taking place in the music. Thus in *Getting Better* the key phrase "It's getting better" is repeated many times but various suffixes and prefixes are added to make "I've got to admit its . . . " and " . . . since you've been mine," " . . . all the time" whilst there are also the qualifying insertions "so much" and "a little." In this way, the basic phrase becomes six different ones all expressing the same general sentiment but with varying nuances and qualifications. This process of development and elaboration of a basic phrase may proceed either on primarily verbal associations, as for example, John does in *Don't Let Me Down* when he goes from "she done me" to "She done me good," or more on the basis of rhythmic and alliterative ones, as would appear to be the case in *Hello Goodbye*. Here the starting sentence would appear to be "You say Goodbye and I say Hello." "Why" is then spawned through rhythmic association with "bye" leading to the line "I don't know why you say goodbye." "High" is produced by the same process and then following the oxymoron principle embodied in "Hello Goodbye" itself, "low" is set off against "high." "Go" which rhymes with the end of "Hello" brings "stop" with it in its turn. "No" is in turn associated with "Go" and brings "yes" along too. "Hello" then modulates to "hela" at the end of the song. In this way it is possible to claim that every single word in the lyric is derived either through rhythmic or oxymoronic association with one of the two words "hello" and "goodbye."

It was also possible for The Beatles to develop a lyric in a different way, that is by capitalising on the fact that there were four singers to call on. This meant that they could sing more than one lyric line at a time and hence weave two (or even more) verbal statements together. In the early songs the non-lead singers were merely called upon to provide a backing in the form of repetition of key words and exclamations especially the characteristic "yeah," "yeah." Only gradually did the lyric backing become different from the lead line (in *Girl* the backing is "tit, tit, tit . . . ") and only via a process of elaboration. In *I'm Down* the backing phrases "I'm really down" and "Down on the ground" don't appear at all in the lead line. Finally this culminates in two independent and alternative lyric lines characteristically engaged in a dialogue as occurs in *With a Little Help from My Friends*:

19   (Would you believe in a love at first sight?)
20   Yes, I'm certain that it happens all the time.

21   (What do you see when you turn out the light?)
22   I can't tell you but I know it's mine.

A similar question and answer format involving the blending of two lyric lines can be found in *Baby You're a Rich Man*, but this process reaches its fullest expression in *She's Leaving Home* where the skilful blending of the two lyrics creates both pathos and irony.

The Beatles: Two Groups or One?

Several different kinds of song can be found among the lyrics contained in this concordance. At one time or another, The Beatles tried their hand at the ballad, the blues, the calypso, the lullaby, the music-hall song and the nursery-rhyme. However, this experimentation is largely confined to the years after 1966. Before that date they wrote only one sort of lyric, and that was the kind associated with the popular romantic song. Approximately half the songs listed can be said to belong to this category. The lyrics of these possess several common features. Firstly, the lyric proper tends to be fairly short (c. 80–100 words), but this is compensated for by a considerable refrain element, not uncommonly as much as half the total. The lyric is constructed in a simple verse form, usually rhyming couplets, from what appear to be snatches of direct conversation, the language used being commonplace (often vernacular) and quite uncomplicated. *Love Me Do* is a good example of this type of lyric:

1   Love, love me do
2   You know I love you.
3   I'll always be true
4   So please love me do
5   Whoa-ho love me do
6   Love, love me do
7   You know I love you
8   I'll always be true
9   So please love me do
10   Whoa-ho love me do.

11   Someone to love, somebody new
12   Someone to love, someone like you.

These lines are then repeated and, together with two "yes, love me do"s at the end, constitute the total lyric.

Many of the later lyrics contrast sharply with this. There is generally a larger proportion of the lyric made up of original unrepeated lines: in a song such as *Mother Nature's Son*, for example, only the title phrase is repeated. The rhyming form is much more varied, and, in some cases, abandoned altogether in favour of the greater possibilities offered by free verse. Also the format is no longer purely conventional but is also reflective, self-revelatory or narrative, whilst the language is richer and more varied. *Blackbird* illustrates the extent of this change:

1   Blackbird singing in the dead of night
2   Take these broken wings and learn to fly.
3   All your life
4   You were only waiting for this moment
        to arise.

Whilst *Across the Universe* reveals how much closer to poetry (and correspondingly how far from the jingle form of *Love Me Do*), The Beatles' lyrics had become by the late '60's and early '70's:

1   Words are flowing out like endless rain
        into a paper cup
2   They slither wildly as they slip away
        across the universe.
3   Pools of sorrow, waves of joy
4   Are drifting through my opened mind
5   Possessing and caressing me.

These later lyrics also differ from the earlier ones in that the anonymous "you," "me," and "girl" are replaced by real and imaginary characters like Eleanor Rigby, Dr. Robert, Michelle, The Fool on the Hill and Bungalow Bill, whilst the greater care revealed in the construction of the lyrics suggests that an altogether deeper level of thoughtfulness lies behind them.

Clearly, the differences between these two lyric forms are considerable and correspond to an equally marked change in the accompanying music. It is a contrast which necessarily strikes all those familiar with the details of The Beatles' career and in itself constitutes the central problem in any attempted critical appreciation of their work. For it is not at all obvious why or even exactly how this transition occurred. Yet it is very tempting, as some commentators have done, to concentrate merely upon songs written after 1966, simply ignoring the first three years of The Beatles' career entirely. This is perhaps an understandable temptation, for a superficial acquaintance with The Beatles' songs gives rise to the impression that there were in fact two different groups. The first (roughly from 1963–66) nothing but a good rock 'n' roll band singing unremarkable romantic jingles in an extra-loud and somewhat raucous style. The other (from '66/67 onwards), a sophisticated and highly talented group of composer-lyricist-performers who could seriously be considered among the foremost artists of their time. This contrast is associated visually with a group of mopheads in suits in the first case and with long-haired bohemians in psychedelic dress in the second. Obviously, an acceptance of this image of The Beatles' career is going to raise considerable difficulties for the critic, for how is one to account for such a dramatic metamorphosis? It is, however, no solution to this problem to ignore or write off one of these images altogether. The Beatles were one group with one career and the problem of the relationship between the early and late songs must be faced up to and resolved. In reality, such a contrast is overdrawn and ignores both important continuities present in The Beatles' lyrics throughout the decade of the sixties and the fact that the later, admittedly very different, lyrics can be seen nevertheless as having developed out of those written before 1966. Indeed, only by viewing the songs of The Beatles as a whole and fully appreciating the nature of both the early and the later lyrics is it possible to understand their development from rock and rollers to talented artists.

The continuities largely arise from the fact that all the lyrics in this concordance can be considered as those of popular songs and hence generally correspond to the conventions governing that particular art-form: one which is largely distinguished from the art song by its mass appeal and from the folk song by its greater contemporary and urban relevance.[4] Although it is not easy to apply such neat categories to the work of The Beatles (and they did extend the possibilities inherent in this medium considerably), it was nevertheless as writers and performers of popular songs that they began their career and this fact clearly accounts for the general form and character of the early lyrics. For example, the regular verse-refrain structure of these songs is clearly derived from the then currently prevailing style. At the same time, the length of the lyric (usually between 200 and 300 words) was similarly determined by conventional expectations together with the additional limitation imposed by the playing time of a 78 rpm record. Finally the content and language of the lyrics was, at least initially, also set by the expectations of the public (or at least that relevant section of it) concerning what was appropriate for a rock and roll number. This meant that the language of the lyrics had to be the vernacular if the songs were to be in any real sense popular whilst romantic love was to be the predominant theme. Hence one can detect a fundamental continuity between the earlier and later lyrics in the primacy accorded the love song format and the extent to which lyrics are drawn directly from conversation. An analysis of word frequencies, for example, reveals that the personal pronouns "you" and "me" are among the most common and amount to nearly one-tenth of all words used.

---

4.   For a discussion of these categories see E. Lee, *Music of the People*, Barrie and Jenkins, London (1970).

In addition, it is important to note that The Beatles' lyrics never became heavily symbolic or allegorical, in the way, for example, that Bob Dylan's were. Although many people have claimed to find complex symbolism in The Beatles' lyrics, particularly drug-inspired symbols, there seems to be little support for this view. There is the occasional reference to that form of non-mundane experience which is typically associated with drug-taking and the use of phrases which appear in the argot of drug-takers (although not exclusive to them). But suggestions like those of Gary Allen's, who claims that "Norwegian Wood" is a British teenager's term for marijuana, or that "Strawberry Fields" was chosen as a title because of the common practice of planting marijuana plants in strawberry patches, are clearly nonsense.[5] An examination of word frequencies does not suggest that an elaborate symbolism of any kind can be found in The Beatles' lyrics, for "love" and "girl" are the only nouns which appear 100 times or more. Only if words with a frequency of fifty times or more are examined do nouns such as "home" and "sun" become prominent, suggesting the possibility that nostalgia and sun-worship might be central features of a Beatle philosophy. Hence there is little reason to assume that there is a "hidden" symbolism in the lyrics of The Beatles' songs. There is evidence, on the other hand, that there are meanings in the lyrics which, although clearly apparent, are not often recognised.

Not only is it necessary to recognise what the lyrics never became, it is also important to realise what they never were. For although the music of The Beatles clearly derives from the rock'n'roll tradition, this is less obviously true of their lyrics. In the early years they were clearly influenced by such established performers as Elvis Presley, Buddy Holly, Chuck Berry and Little Richard and commonly included songs like *Twist and Shout, Roll Over Beethoven* and *Kansas City* in their act. Yet a comparison of the lyrics of these songs with those which John and Paul wrote at this time reveals a considerable difference. For whilst the rock'n'roll culture which these songs epitomise commonly deals with such topics as dancing and male narcissism in addition to romantic love, there isn't a single Beatles' song out of the total of nearly sixty issued between October 1962 and July 1965 which is concerned with anything except boy-girl romance. There is no classic Beatles' number dealing with dance, for example, to stand comparison with *Twist and Shout* or to celebrate the male peacock response as with *Blue Suede Shoes*. Neither is there a lyric

which contains any of the male aggression or sexuality associated with Elvis Presley and later with *The Rolling Stones*. Thus although the music was loud and the accents broad, the lyrics were uniformly romantic if not at times sentimental. In this respect they would appear to have more in common with the popular songs of the period than the rock'n'roll or blues traditions, a view which is reinforced by the recognition that some of them actually embody the bourgeois norm of polite respectability. Consider for example, the plea, "please say to me you'll let me hold your hand" (*I Want to Hold Your Hand*).

It was therefore not merely as rock and rollers but as composers and performers of love songs that The Beatles first established their identity. Indeed their identity as creative artists rather than as a rock and roll group was exclusively linked to love songs. It is this fact which provides the key to an understanding of the subsequent development of their lyrics.

1965–67: The Crucial Years

The changes that occurred in The Beatles' lyrics between the years 1965 and 1967 coincided with several major changes that were taking place in their lives. For example, they gave up touring and spent more time in the recording studios. They met the Maharishi Mahesh Yogi and were influenced, at least for a while, by his brand of Hinduism. They started to make films, experimented with drugs, changed their appearance and, after the death of Brian Epstein, formed their own recording company to give themselves greater artistic freedom. It was clearly a period of thoughtfulness, experimentation and some uncertainty, if not doubt, for The Beatles, which, however, seems to have been largely resolved by 1968 and the success of *Sgt. Pepper's Lonely Hearts Club Band*.

Of the various explanations offered to account for the changes in their lyrics, two in particular are frequently mentioned: the influence of drugs and the example of Bob Dylan. As far as the second is concerned, there is evidence that in the winter of 1965 they compared their lyrics with his and found them wanting, consequently deciding that they would try harder in the future to "tell it like it is."[6] Drugs, however, only seem significant in that John and George tried LSD for the first time (unwittingly) in 1965, for, like most rock and jazz groups, The Beatles had made use of amphetamines since their Hamburg days. Neither event would appear, in itself, to be significant enough to be a cause of the change in The Beatles' lyrics, even if they did contribute to some degree to the character of the changes that occurred. A more accurate interpretation of this

5. G. Allen, "More Subversion Than Meets the Ear" in R.S. Denisoff and R.A. Peterson (eds.) *The Sounds of Social Change*, Rand McNally, Chicago (1972), p. 159.

6. Julius Fast, *The Beatles: The Real Story*, Putnam (1968) p. 192.

period would suggest that these events are less causes than consequences of the new, critical and exploratory mood of The Beatles. A mood in which they decided to find

> 19 ... the time for a number of things
> 20 That weren't important yesterday
> (*Fixing a Hole*)

and which requires some other, broader explanation.

The simple fact is that these changes were largely forced on The Beatles as a consequence of their phenomenal success. Touring had become a nightmare experience and was inimical to their development as musicians, whilst Beatlemania made any appearance in public a hazardous experience. Fame, as Paul recalled, can have its disadvantages:

> Fame is what everyone wants, but in the end it is only getting out of a parking fine because a bobby wants your autograph, or else being interrupted while you eat by a fifty-year-old American lady with a pony-tail.[7]

At the same time that the realisation was growing that there might well be more to life than the achievement of popular acclaim, The Beatles were experiencing more psychological stress and strain than they had ever done in their early years in Liverpool and Hamburg. The pressures which they endured were such that as John recalled "We had to grow up or we'd have been swamped."[8] However, the central problem for The Beatles at this time was to find a new aim and identity for themselves, a philosophy which would restore their sense of purpose. For it was not the inconveniences or pressures of success which threatened to swamp them so much as the fact that they had attained their life's ambition. This had always been simply understood as success as a rock and roll group, ambitiously, to be "bigger than Elvis," something which they had indeed achieved by 1966. Thus the problem now was, what next? How could The Beatles find a new goal, cope with the problems of fame, and yet remain loyal to their past?

The self-doubt and questioning which this problem prompted is very apparent in the lyrics of the period, especially in those written by John, whose style could perhaps be described as more explicitly confessional and self-revelatory than Paul's. The problem is recognised and stated in *Help!*, which is significantly the first Beatles' song dealing with a topic other than romantic love. Here the problems presented by fame are recognised, "help me get my feet back on the ground" and the feelings of doubt acknowledged "I'm not so self-assured," whilst the search for a new perspective on life is admitted "Now I find I've changed my mind and opened up the doors." The theme of doubt and uncertainty is then taken up in several later songs especially in the form of a crisis of identity. *Nowhere Man* for example, who "Doesn't have a point of view" and "Knows not where he's going to" is actually "a bit like you and me," whilst in *Got to Get You into My Life* there is the interjected line "What can I do, what can I be?" In *Strawberry Fields Forever* it is acknowledged that "It's getting hard to be someone" whilst in *Baby You're a Rich Man* The Beatles ask themselves the sixty-four-thousand dollar question, "Now that you know who you are, What do you want to be?" Before looking at the answer which they found for themselves and the way in which it constitutes a development of their earlier identity it is important to recognise how this period of self-doubt and questioning is intimately related to the process by which The Beatles made the transition from entertainers to artists.

In so far as it is possible to make a clear distinction between artists and entertainers there are two criteria which help in doing so. One is that works of art involve the elaboration and development of themes rather than their simple repetition (something very true of The Beatles' songs after 1966) whilst the other is that artists are concerned with serious or central questions rather than matters of minor importance. Clearly this period of self-doubt raised just such questions for The Beatles, as Hunter Davies records: "when the touring had to stop their concern was with themselves, what was the point of it all."[9] "What was the point of it all" embraced such questions as "what is the meaning of success?", "Who am I?" and "What is the meaning of love and life itself?" There can be no doubt that the achievement of material success had thrust these formerly neglected questions into the foreground. These are serious questions and The Beatles' consistent attempts to deal with them constitutes an important argument for claiming that they became artists in the years 1965--67.

This change was disguised because The Beatles had no desire to alienate their former public nor to identify themselves too closely with what was conventionally understood to be the serious art tradition. Thus they continued, even after this point in their career, to deny publicly that they were artists or that their songs should be considered works of art, preferring to reiterate that they were merely

7. Fast, op. cit., p. 195.
8. Rick Friedman, *The Beatles: Words Without Music*, Grosset (1968).
9. Hunter Davies, op. cit., p. 233.

"rock 'n' rollers." Clearly, they were being disingenuous in maintaining this position although it is possible that they may have erroneously believed that their association with rock and roll and the popular song necessarily excluded them from the serious art tradition.

As soon as The Beatles began to formulate answers to these basic questions and to develop their own philosophy of life they also began to urge it on others: they became, in effect, evangelists for their cause. This is very clear in such songs as *The Word, Strawberry Fields Forever, Fool on the Hill, Nowhere Man* and *Glass Onion*, even though one can also detect an ironic self-deprecation in these lyrics, as if the former rock 'n' rollers are mocking these serious-minded philosophers. However, as they gradually rediscover themselves and gain confidence in their new spiritual awareness they drop the more didactic and exhortative approach – exemplified in *The Word* and employed by George in *Within You, Without You* – in favour of demonstrating the truth and wisdom of their vision. Instead of attempting to tell us about the truth, with exhortations like "try to realise it's all within yourself" (*Within You, Without You*) or "Have you heard the word is love?" (*The Word*), they come to concentrate more and more upon showing us. As operators of the Magical Mystery Tour, The Beatles arrive to "take (us) away"; in *Strawberry Fields Forever* they offer to take us down to the Fields whilst in *Lucy in the Sky with Diamonds* it is newspaper taxis which arrive to "take us away." Again and again in the later songs the lyrics provide the same offer of transport as The Beatles become our guides to a better, truer vision of the world.

In order to show us what reality is truly like The Beatles have first of all to indicate that the normal way in which we live and perceive the world is wrong. That we are, in fact, "blind" to truth and unappreciative of the marvels which surround us. It is hence with sympathetic sadness and a touch of kindly exasperation that this message is presented in such songs as *She's Leaving Home, The Fool on the Hill* and *Nowhere Man*. The poor Nowhere Man cannot see "that the world is at his command" any more than the parents in *She's Leaving Home* can see what it is they have failed to do for their daughter. Most ordinary people are presented as "nowhere" men and women leading miserable lives in a dull, grey world, much indeed as life in Pepperland is portrayed under the Blue Meanies. An overwhelming feature of such an existence is that it is characterised by loneliness and The Beatles, in their personna as Sergeant Pepper's Lonely Hearts Club Band, feel a very special sympathy for "all the lonely people." Thus they plead with us to throw off

our blindness, to simply open our eyes and see the truth. Prudence, perhaps living up to her name, is slow to cast off her "nowhere" view of the world and has to be persuaded to "open up (her) eyes" and "come out to play" so that she can learn that she is "part of everything." (*Dear Prudence*).

Repeatedly The Beatles urge us to simply relax and let our senses work unhindered, to "let it out and let it in" (*Hey Jude*) or simply *Let It Be*, so that we might see, hear and feel the world directly. And, in case we are simply too hidebound to take their advice or too stupid to realise the wisdom of it, they are prepared to show us exactly how the world can be magically recreated through a total openness to sensory experience. This they do in *Penny Lane* where the very ordinariness of the everyday scene is transformed into something "very strange," – a vision -- merely by using one's senses to the full, by allowing Penny Lane to be "in my ears and in my eyes." The message is clear: all of us live in a street called Penny Lane. Yet to realise our blindness and open our eyes is really only the first step on the road to true enlightenment. For it is only when we have done that, that we are in a position to discover the "true point of it all," the purpose of life. There can be little doubt what The Beatles consider this to be, for it is "the word," "all you need" – "love."

Love Was All They Needed

In the period 1965–67 The Beatles were faced with the challenge of adapting, both individually and collectively, to the problems posed by phenomenal success and fame. As individuals they had become increasingly aware that success and wealth had their drawbacks and did not in themselves solve the problem of life whilst as a group they recognised the need for a new purpose now that their original aim had been obtained. It was thus against this background that they half-consciously, half-subconsciously turned to "love" for an answer. After all, "love" had served them well to date; a passionate feeling for the sensibilities of romantic love having been their primary stock-in-trade since the beginning of their rise to fame. Now they turned to "love" once again, but this time not merely as a means to worldly success but as the basis for a total and satisfying philosophy of life. In this they remained essentially true to themselves -- The Beatles always believed passionately in the power of love -- and merely extrapolated this faith from its restricted basis in the context of boy-girl attachments. Hence there was no dramatic metamorphosis from simple rock 'n' rollers to consummate artists but a process of development in which a faith in romanticism emerges from a faith in romance. The two stereotypes of The Beatles are thus bound together by the thread of "love" itself. The first was never abandoned but simply added to in such a way as to extend and deepen its meaning and significance.

The lyrics of The Beatles' early songs deal with all the various nuances of the primary romanticism of boy-girl relationships, at least, as far as these are perceived from the male standpoint. Many involve expressions of a lover's entreaties to the loved one (e.g., *Love Me Do, Please Please Me*) or of declarations of love and devotion (e.g., *From Me to You, All My Loving*). Some express gratitude for a love received (*Thank You Girl, I'll Cry Instead*) or simply celebrate the joys of love (*I Should Have Known Better, I'm Happy Just to Dance with You*). Equally numerous however, although interestingly enough not by any means as popular with the public at the time, are songs which deal with the darker side of romance. There is the fear that a love will not be returned (*If I Fell*) together with the total dejection of the spurned lover (*I'm Down, I'm a Loser*) and the misery of a lover betrayed (*Tell Me Why, What You're Doing*). Finally, there is the bitterness and even hatred that jealousy can bring (*You Can't Do That, Run for Your Life*).

An examination of these songs with the benefit of hindsight reveals that they do indeed contain, in embryo as it were, many of the themes which are central to the later romanticism. The delight and wonder associated with falling in love, for example, is clearly seen as the prototype for the later celebrations of more general "conversion" experiences. The concern with the intense personal loneliness of the abandoned or rejected lover becomes, in turn, the model for the later treatment of loneliness in general. Whilst the description of the unity experienced by lovers, that transcendence of separate individuality in the "oneness" of love, is itself the basis for the quasi-Eastern mysticism which appears from 1967 onwards. Indeed, there are few subjects treated in the later songs which are not presaged in this way The Beatles' handling of romantic love. Even the later rejection of materialism from the standpoint of a deep spiritual concern (see, for example, George's reference to "gaining the world and losing your soul" in *Within You, Without You*) is heralded in 1964 in the words "I don't care too much for money, money can't buy me love." (*Can't Buy Me Love*). The principal difference therefore between the lyrical content of the earlier and later songs is that the sentiments and attitudes contained in the earlier ones are taken out of the restrictive context of romantic love and extrapolated in a self-conscious fashion to life itself.

One example of this process of extrapolation can be found in the treatment of nostalgia, which is a central Beatles' theme. In the early songs home is simply the place where the loved one is to be found and the associated ideas such as security, peace, comfort and happiness are naturally linked with her presence:

15 When I'm home everything seems to be right
16 When I'm home feeling you holding me tight, tight, yeah.

(*A Hard Day's Night*)

The same sentiment can be found in *When I Get Home* and *It Won't Be Long* and *Wait*. However, Lennon's song *In My Life* displays a feeling for lost people and places which is only very loosely linked to romantic love and appears instead as a sensitive exercise in generalised nostalgia:

1 There are places I remember
2 All my life, though some have changed
3 Some forever, not for better
4 Some have gone and some remain.
5 All these places had their moments
6 With lovers and friends I can still recall
7 Some are dead and some are living
8 In my life I've loved them all.

This process becomes increasingly apparent in the songs that follow, with *Penny Lane* in particular, outstanding as a song built upon the celebration of recollected emotion. Finally, in *Golden Slumbers* and *Two of Us* only the pure distillation of nostalgia remains and there is little sign of any reference to romantic love.

A similar process is discernible if one examines the attitude towards nature and its use as a source of imagery. The early songs are almost completely devoid of images, the language used being sparse and direct as one imagines boy-girl conversation in working-class Liverpool to have been. Intentions, feelings and desires are baldly stated -- love me do, hold me tight, I feel sad, I wanna hold your hand -- but given force and colour by means of such exclamations as yeah! yeah! oh! and baby! A significant deviation from this pattern appears with *And I Love Her* which is the first in a recognisable line of McCartney love ballads with cha-cha rhythms. Even here the majority of the lyrics are simple and direct but it is the couplet, "Bright are the stars that shine, dark is the sky" which heralds a change.

Although the use of nature imagery had long been an accepted convention in both love poetry and the ballad this was its first use by The Beatles. One suspects that it had been deliberately eschewed up to this point because it was too closely associated with the trite sentimentality of the popular song and not regarded as part of the more vulgar rock and roll tradition with which they identified. A greater self-confidence, consequent upon success, was probably responsible for the abandonment of this inhibition. Whatever the reason, this form of imagery becomes more and more noticeable in the lyrics written during 1964 and '65 with lines like "My tears are falling like rain from the sky" (*I'm a Loser*) and "For tomorrow may rain so I'll follow the sun" (*I'll Follow the Sun*). Even so, it is still only employed sparingly and within the framework of a style of expression in which phrases are pruned of all but their most essential words as can be seen in the song called *The Word*:

> It's so fine, it's sunshine
> It's the word love.

In this way curtness is successfully pressed into service to limit the sentimentality which is otherwise inherent in the use of such stock nature images as rain and sun.

This progressive introduction of nature imagery occurs with at first phrases, then couplets and finally whole stanzas being interjected into the basic love lyric. The intention, however, does not seem to have been merely to embroider or add ornament to this so much as to find a class of symbols which could stand for the powerful emotional states which The Beatles wished to express. Hence although they came to make more and more extensive use of nature imagery they did not do so in the manner commonly associated with the popular song where it functions merely as a backcloth to enhance the drama of romance. Instead the images of the sun, the sky and rain have a power and existence in the lyrics which is independent of the messages of love. The impression given is that being in love and enjoying nature are experiences which are comparable in quality and intensity -- which is why they are associated -- but they are not therefore to be reduced one to the other. Because nature imagery has this independent existence in The Beatles lyrics it was possible for it to develop, in accord with the general principle of extrapolation, to the point of displacing the romantic message altogether. This is indeed what happens in the later "nature poems" such as *Good Day Sunshine, Blackbird* and *Mother Nature's Son*.

The early songs of The Beatles are dedicated to the powerful expression and celebration of the feelings and emotions associated with romance. Each song is built around one such emotion which is usually encapsulated lyrically in a simple phrase such as "I'm so happy when you dance with me" or "I feel fine." Gradually the range of material drawn upon to provide the emotional subject-matter of the songs is extended to include affection for people and places (*In My Life*), delight in nature (*Good Day Sunshine*), and compassion for lonely people (*Eleanor Rigby*). As this process continued in the years after 1966 the celebration of emotion and powerful feeling completely replaced any mere concern with the histrionics of lovers. Thus *I've Got a Feeling*, which can be seen as the end product of a process of extrapolation which started with *I Feel Fine*, catalogues a range of feelings, a "hard year," a "good--time" a "wet dream," etc., which are in no way especially associated with romance.

This process of extrapolation is the key to an understanding of the relationship between the early and later songs and central to the way in which The Beatles deepen and extend their comprehension of the concept of love. In the early songs, love is personalised and restricted since it is always associated with a lover. Thus the benefits of love, such as the overcoming of loneliness and attainment of happiness and security are necessarily inseparable from the acquisition of a person who can perform this role. At the same time, love is seen primarily as an exchange of affection between individuals and is necessarily destroyed if one party withdraws from the exchange. But love comes to be redefined in the later songs and seen less as a "shared high" than as a philosophy of life, an attitude which does not require reciprocation from another in order to survive, but can and indeed should be held toward all people and all living things. Love in this sense is also viewed as incompatible with the negative feelings of jealousy and bitterness which are inherent in romantic attachments. The song which clearly marks the turning point in this process of redefinition is *The Word*:

1 Say the word and you'll be free
2 Say the word and be like me
3 Say the word I'm thinking of
4 Have you heard the word is love?

There is nothing in this lyric to suggest that love is being thought of in the restricted context of boy-girl romance. Indeed, the usual personalised dialogue is absent and the "you" mentioned is clearly plural. What is suggested is that love is "the way" or answer to life's problems, an answer which has to be arrived at through a conversion experience ("In the beginning I misunderstood") and yet which has been widely expressed before in religion and the arts, ("Everywhere I go I hear it said,/In the good and the bad books I have read"). Obviously one cannot assume in relation to any of the songs written after this that whenever the word love appears it refers merely to boy-girl romance. This does continue to be the archetype of The Beatles' romanticism, the fundamental analogy for a philosophy of life, but love is now conceived as a general outgoing emotion applied to all kinds of people with whom one might not be "in love" (like Eleanor Rigby for example) or even to nature itself. Love is thus "the word" for a positive tenderness and openness toward the world.

The Beatles have faith in love because they see it as the power that can overcome all obstacles. This is the great theme of romanticism, that of a world made perfect through the power of love, and it is the explicit philosophy of The Beatles between 1966 and 1970.[10] This message of salvation is stressed over and over again, for "There's nothing you can do that can't be done" through love's power, everyone can be "saved" and "learn how to be you," "it's easy," "all you need is love."

Word Play and Irony

We have already seen that there are no hidden messages or "secret codes" in The Beatles' lyrics and that all that is required in order to penetrate their meaning is to listen carefully to what is being sung. This is especially necessary as far as the later songs are concerned, because here The Beatles increasingly employ irony, that is they appear to say one thing but actually say something different. Although there is no irony in the early songs there is an obvious element of word-play and punning which serves as the prototype for the later development of serious and complex ironic statements. Right from the beginning, Lennon and McCartney lyrics contain an obvious delight in the fun to be had from playing with words, as such titles as *Please Please Me, Eight Days a Week* and *A Hard Day's Night* suggest. Soon this is displaced by the self-conscious pun as with **Rubber Soul** (Sole) and **Revolver** (for a record which revolves), but there is still, at this stage, little more than a desire to make a joke. Only with *Help!* and the phrase "I've changed my mind" do we get a suggestion of the kind of penetrating exploitation of the ambiguity of common English expressions which is to come. The phrase can be taken, on the surface, to imply that a decision has been reversed. However, the subsequent line "And opened up the doors," together with the rest of the lyric and the context in which it was written, strongly suggest another meaning. This is that John has exchanged one "mind" for another in the process of gaining a new and very different view of the world. This is an example of the deliberate and self-conscious use of irony which is employed more and more by The Beatles in the years after 1966, especially by John. Other major examples would include the "words of wisdom" themselves "Let It Be," where the ambiguity and hence irony rests on the contrast between "let it alone" and "let it become"; the "nothing is real" from *Strawberry Fields Forever* with the implication that a true understanding of reality must start from a meditation experience in which one empties one's mind completely; "Well here's another place you can be" in

10. Lascelles Abercrombie, *Romanticism*, Martin Seeker, London (1926) p. 89.

Glass Onion with the attendant plea "Listen to me" just in case one has missed the point about "here" being the other place, and the delightfully ambiguous

> . . . it really doesn't matter if I'm wrong I'm right
> Where I belong I'm right where I belong

from *Fixing a Hole*.

The use of irony was The Beatles' way of solving the problems posed by success, in particular the problem of how to be popular and serious at one and the same time; of how to entertain and yet still make important statements. Irony helps because it makes it possible to say two different things at once leaving the listener with the choice of simply singing (unthinkingly) along with the words or penetrating, through reflection, to their deeper meaning. But the use of irony did much more than this. It also enabled The Beatles to take everyday expressions and breathe new life into them, in effect resuscitating clichés and adding surprising interpretations to stale phrases. In addition, the use of irony creates a dynamic tension within the lyric, a contrast between surface appearance and deeper meaning which gives that internal resonance and complexity characteristic of works of art.

A supreme example of this can be found in *Because*. At first sight it would appear that The Beatles have, if anything, reverted to their earlier delight in puns with such lines as "Because the world is round it turns me on" and "Because the wind is high it blows my mind" and the jokes themselves seem strangely obvious if not feeble. Yet the clue provided by the music suggests that The Beatles have perpetrated a double-bluff upon the growing body of fans who had previously penetrated their irony, for it isn't the not-so-hidden joke but the apparent meaning which The Beatles are endorsing so lyrically. *Because* is thus a beautiful paean to nature, thinly disguised as a joke.

In the very best of The Beatles' songs the most striking quality is the honesty, the authenticity of feeling, that sense of being absolutely true to emotional experience. This is a characteristic hall-mark of the earliest songs and continues throughout in numbers like *Yesterday, In My Life, Julia* and *The Long and Winding Road*, all of which are overwhelming in the power and poignancy of their emotion. But, in their later songs, The Beatles also attempt to transcend description and move toward analysis. Here their deep concern for honesty forces them into the ironic mode for only in this way can the essential ambiguity of truth be captured. Recognising that all intense emotion contains the seeds of its opposite and that any slogan or simple formula is bound to be a lie and hence a distortion of the nature of reality as we experience it, The Beatles are concerned to record the oppositions, tensions and transitions which characterise the life of feeling. Thus with "pools of sorrow" comes "waves of joy" (*Across the Universe*), with the "oh, no"s, the "Oh, yeah"s and the "in" with the "count me out" (*Revolution One*). In this way, The Beatles are led naturally into irony and then, as we have seen with *Because*, beyond it as they pursue emotions past the point of their exhaustion, turning the solemn into a joke and a joke into a hymn, day into night, hello into goodbye, man into woman, as they record the ebb and flow of emotional truth with a sense of authenticity as unerringly accurate as their musical ear.

The Hour of Feeling

The Beatles' obvious genius has caused them to be compared favorably with such outstanding composers as Beethoven, Schumann and Schubert.[11] However, it is usually the music and not the lyrics which people have in mind when making comparisons, and although their words have been commended they rarely receive the accolades accorded to the music proper. This is not so much because the lyrics are generally felt to be inferior to the music (listening to purely instrumental versions of The Beatles' songs one is acutely conscious of the lack of that vital ingredient), but more because of a general uncertainty over how they are to be judged. Should they be measured against the standard of popular song-writers like Rogers and Hart? Or against semi-classical ones like Gilbert and Sullivan? Or perhaps not in relation to song-writers at all but in comparison with earlier generations of poets? The problem has not properly been resolved and hence judgements on the quality of The Beatles' lyrics remain very tentative.

At the beginning of their careers, Lennon and McCartney themselves aspired to be like Goffin and King, at that time a highly successful popular song-writing partnership. However, it is clear that they soon transcended the limitations of this tradition and the content and style of the later lyrics owe more to poetry than entertainment. It is for this reason that the person who most readily comes to mind as a basic for comparison with The Beatles is Robert Burns. He was a song-writer with a supreme lyrical gift, a provincial artist who deliberately chose to work in the local or vernacular tradition and was as irreverent and convivial in his way as The Beatles were in theirs. Beautiful and simple love ballads like *And I Love Her* and *Yesterday* are surely in the same lyric tradition as *My Love's Like a Red, Red Rose*.

Yet The Beatles' art is too English for such a comparison to be particularly convincing and it does not, in any case, satisfactorily cover the developed romanticism of the later years. Here one is tempted to turn to a more philosophical and quintessentially English representative of The Romantic Movement, William Wordsworth. Although separated by apparently unbridgeable gulfs of time and tradition the romanticism of the former poet laureate and the most successful pop group of all time are nevertheless of a kind. In both cases it is rooted in a powerful remembrance of the past, especially of childhood and of the great sense of loss associated with its passing, such that *Tintern Abbey* and *Penny Lane*, *Intimations of Immortality from Recollections of Early Childhood* and *Strawberry Fields Forever* speak to the same human condition. Both too were filled with "the pleasure which there is in life itself" (*Michael*) and especially with the pleasure which nature offers, towards which they adopted a "mystical" or panpsychic attitude. One feels that Wordsworth, who was sensitive to the spirit which "rolls through all things" and who delighted so much in the setting sun, would have approved of such Beatles' nature hymns as *Good Day Sunshine, Here Comes the Sun* and *Because*. Both too perceived the virtue of a "wise passiveness" in which one allows oneself to be sensorily and emotionally "open" to the world around. The Fool on the Hill who sees "the sun going down" and "the world spinning round" clearly has no need of Wordsworth's injunction in *The Tables Turned* to "Come forth into the light of things, Let nature be your teacher." Both, in addition, share the typical romantic sympathy for the lonely and the outcast and also value that sleepy, dreamy state of reverie, that "vacant and pensive mood" so conducive to remembered visions. However, perhaps more than anything else, it is a belief in love which unites them. Wordsworth was speaking for the first generation of romantics when he declared in 1798 that

> Love, now a universal birth,
> from heart to heart is stealing;
> From earth to man, from man to earth:
> --It is the hour of feeling.
>
> (*To My Sister*)

But it was The Beatles who, one hundred and seventy years later, created the "hour of feeling" which was the nineteen–sixties, hence rekindling the romantic dream in the hearts of a new generation and making faith in love a powerful force in the world once more.

---

11. See Mellers, op, cit.

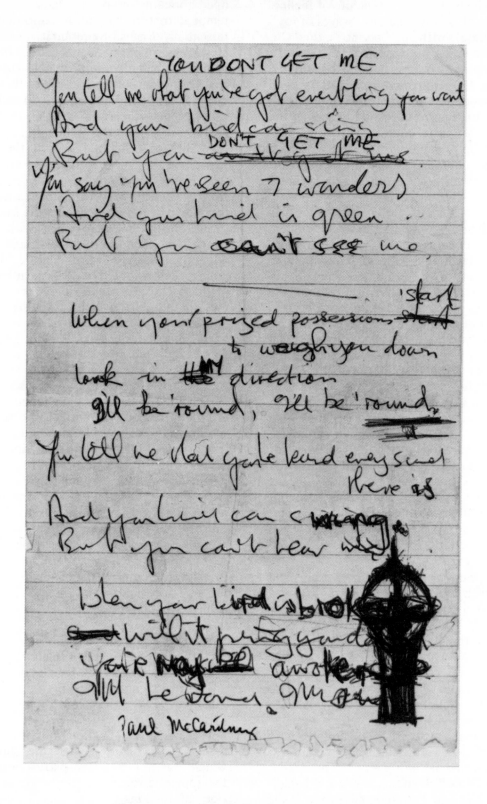

Songs Included

Only those songs *both written and recorded* by one or more of The Beatles in his role as a group member while under contract to EMI/Capitol are treated in this volume. Songs *written but not recorded* and songs *recorded but not written* by The Beatles (see listings below) are not included. A total of 184 distinct song titles (not counting different versions of songs) qualify for inclusion in this work; for our purposes, the number of songs analyzed as discrete entities when versions are counted reaches 189. Two songs of this total – *Revolution Nine* and *Flying* – do not figure in the lyrical analysis.

ACROSS THE UNIVERSE.
ALL I'VE GOT TO DO.
ALL MY LOVING.
ALL TOGETHER NOW.
ALL YOU NEED IS LOVE. (Two versions)
AND I LOVE HER.
AND YOUR BIRD CAN SING.
ANOTHER GIRL.
ANY TIME AT ALL.
ASK ME WHY.
BABY, YOU'RE A RICH MAN.
BABY'S IN BLACK.
BACK IN THE U.S.S.R.
THE BALLAD OF JOHN AND YOKO.
BECAUSE.
BEING FOR THE BENEFIT OF MR. KITE.
BIRTHDAY.
BLACKBIRD.
BLUE JAY WAY.
CAN'T BUY ME LOVE.
CARRY THAT WEIGHT.
COME TOGETHER.
THE CONTINUING STORY OF
    BUNGALOW BILL.
CRY BABY CRY.
A DAY IN THE LIFE.
DAY TRIPPER.
DEAR PRUDENCE.
DIG IT.
DO YOU WANT TO KNOW A SECRET?
DR. ROBERT.
DON'T BOTHER ME.
DON'T LET ME DOWN.
DON'T PASS ME BY.
DRIVE MY CAR.
EIGHT DAYS A WEEK.
ELEANOR RIGBY.
THE END.
EVERY LITTLE THING.
EVERYBODY'S GOT SOMETHING TO
    HIDE EXCEPT ME AND MY
    MONKEY.
FIXING A HOLE.
FLYING.
THE FOOL ON THE HILL.
FOR NO-ONE.
FOR YOU BLUE.
FROM ME TO YOU.
GET BACK. (Two versions)
GETTING BETTER.
GIRL.
GLASS ONION.
GOLDEN SLUMBERS.
GOOD DAY SUNSHINE.
GOOD MORNING, GOOD MORNING.
GOOD NIGHT.
GOT TO GET YOU INTO MY LIFE.
HAPPINESS IS A WARM GUN.
A HARD DAY'S NIGHT.
HELLO GOODBYE.
HELP!
HELTER-SKELTER.
HER MAJESTY.
HERE COMES THE SUN.
HERE, THERE AND EVERYWHERE.

HEY BULLDOG.
HEY JUDE.
HOLD ME TIGHT.
HONEY PIE.
I AM THE WALRUS.
I CALL YOUR NAME.
(I) DIG A PONY.
I DON'T WANT TO SPOIL THE PARTY.
I FEEL FINE.
I ME MINE.
I NEED YOU.
I SAW HER STANDING THERE.
I SHOULD HAVE KNOWN BETTER.
I WANNA BE YOUR MAN.
I WANT TO HOLD YOUR HAND.
I WANT TO TELL YOU.
I WANT YOU (SHE'S SO HEAVY).
I WILL.
IF I FELL.
IF I NEEDED SOMEONE.
I'LL BE BACK.
I'LL CRY INSTEAD.
I'LL FOLLOW THE SUN.
I'LL GET YOU.
I'M A LOSER.
I'M DOWN.
I'M HAPPY JUST TO DANCE WITH YOU.
I'M LOOKING THROUGH YOU.
I'M ONLY SLEEPING.
I'M SO TIRED.
IN MY LIFE.
THE INNER LIGHT.
IT WON'T BE LONG.
IT'S ALL TOO MUCH.
IT'S ONLY LOVE.
I'VE GOT A FEELING.
I'VE JUST SEEN A FACE.
JULIA.
LADY MADONNA.
LET IT BE. (Two versions)
LITTLE CHILD.
THE LONG AND WINDING ROAD.
LONG, LONG, LONG.
LOVE ME DO.
LOVE YOU TO/TOO.
LOVELY RITA.
LUCY IN THE SKY WITH DIAMONDS.
MAGICAL MYSTERY TOUR.
MARTHA MY DEAR.
MAXWELL'S SILVER HAMMER.
MEAN MR. MUSTARD.
MICHELLE.
MISERY.
MOTHER NATURE'S SON.
THE NIGHT BEFORE.
NO REPLY.
NORWEGIAN WOOD (THIS BIRD HAS
    FLOWN).
NOT A SECOND TIME.
NOWHERE MAN.
OB-LA-DI, OB-LA-DA.
OCTOPUS'S GARDEN.
OH! DARLING.
OLD BROWN SHOE.
ONE AFTER NINE-O-NINE.

ONLY A NORTHERN SONG.
P.S. I LOVE YOU.
PAPERBACK WRITER.
PENNY LANE.
PIGGIES.
PLEASE PLEASE ME.
POLYTHENE PAM.
RAIN.
REVOLUTION.
REVOLUTION ONE.
REVOLUTION NINE.
ROCKY RACCOON.
RUN FOR YOUR LIFE.
SAVOY TRUFFLE.
SGT. PEPPER'S LONELY HEARTS
    CLUB BAND. (and REPRISE)
SEXY SADIE.
SHE CAME IN THROUGH THE
    BATHROOM WINDOW.
SHE LOVES YOU.
SHE SAID SHE SAID.
SHE'S A WOMAN.
SHE'S LEAVING HOME.
SOMETHING.
STRAWBERRY FIELDS FOREVER.
SUN KING.
TAXMAN.
TELL ME WHAT YOU SEE.
TELL ME WHY.
THANK YOU GIRL.
THERE'S A PLACE.
THINGS WE SAID TODAY.
THINK FOR YOURSELF.
THIS BOY.
TICKET TO RIDE.
TOMORROW NEVER KNOWS.
TWO OF US.
WAIT.
WE CAN WORK IT OUT.
WHAT GOES ON?
WHAT YOU'RE DOING.
WHEN I GET HOME.
WHEN I'M SIXTY-FOUR.
WHILE MY GUITAR GENTLY WEEPS.
WHY DON'T WE DO IT IN THE ROAD.
WILD HONEY PIE.
WITH A LITTLE HELP FROM MY
    FRIENDS.
WITHIN YOU, WITHOUT YOU.
THE WORD.
YELLOW SUBMARINE.
YER BLUES.
YES IT IS.
YESTERDAY.
YOU CAN'T DO THAT.
YOU KNOW MY NAME (LOOK UP MY
    NUMBER)
YOU LIKE ME TOO MUCH.
YOU NEVER GIVE ME YOUR MONEY.
YOU WON'T SEE ME.
YOUR MOTHER SHOULD KNOW.
YOU'RE GOING TO/GONNA LOSE
    THAT GIRL.
YOU'VE GOT TO HIDE YOUR LOVE
    AWAY.

Songs Not Included

Songs written but not recorded by The Beatles.

BAD TO ME.
FROM A WINDOW.
GIVE PEACE A CHANCE.
GOODBYE.
HELLO LITTLE GIRL.
I DON'T WANT TO SEE YOU AGAIN.
I'LL BE ON MY WAY.
I'LL KEEP YOU SATISFIED.
I'M IN LOVE.
IT'S FOR YOU.
LIKE DREAMERS DO.
LOVE OF THE LOVED.
NOBODY I KNOW.
ONE AND ONE IS TWO.
STEP INSIDE LOVE.
THAT MEANS A LOT.
THINGUMYBOB.
TIP OF MY TONGUE.
A WORLD WITHOUT LOVE.

Songs recorded but not written by The Beatles.

ACT NATURALLY.
AIN'T SHE SWEET.
ANNA (GO TO HIM).
BABY, IT'S YOU.
BAD BOY.
BOYS.
CHAINS.
DEVIL IN HER HEART.
DIZZY MISS LIZZIE.
EVERYBODY'S TRYING TO BE MY BABY.
HEY—HEY—HEY—HEY!
HONEY DON'T.
KANSAS CITY.
KOMM, GIB MIR DEINE HAND.

LONG TALL SALLY.
MAGGIE MAE.
MATCHBOX.
MR. MOONLIGHT.
MONEY (THAT'S WHAT I WANT).
PLEASE MR. POSTMAN.
ROCK AND ROLL MUSIC.
ROLL OVER BEETHOVEN.
SIE LIEBT DICH.
SLOW DOWN.
A TASTE OF HONEY.
'TILL THERE WAS YOU.
TWIST AND SHOUT.
WORDS OF LOVE.
YOU REALLY GOT A HOLD ON ME.

Song Title Abbreviations

Release dates, composer credits and lead vocalist designations are derived from information contained in *ALL TOGETHER NOW; The First Complete Beatles Discography, 1961–1975*, by Harry Castleman and Wally Podrazik (Pierian Press, 1976).

SONG ID	SONG TITLE	RELEASE DATE	SOLE/PRINCIPAL COMPOSER(S)	LEAD VOCALIST(S)
ACROSSTHEU	ACROSS THE UNIVERSE.	May 8, 1970	Lennon	Lennon
ALLIVEGOTT	ALL I'VE GOT TO DO.	November 22, 1963	Lennon	Lennon
ALLMYLOVIN	ALL MY LOVING.	November 22, 1963	McCartney	McCartney
ALLTOGETHE	ALL TOGETHER NOW.	January 13, 1969	McCartney	McCartney
ALLYOUN/YS	ALL YOU NEED IS LOVE. (YS version)	January 13, 1969	Lennon	Lennon
ALLYOU/MMT	ALL YOU NEED IS LOVE. (45 & MMT version)	July 7, 1967	Lennon	Lennon
ANDILOVEHE	AND I LOVE HER.	June 26, 1964	Lennon/McCartney	Lennon/McCartney
ANDYOURBIR	AND YOUR BIRD CAN SING.	June 20, 1966	Lennon	Lennon
ANOTHERGIR	ANOTHER GIRL.	August 6, 1965	McCartney	McCartney
ANYTIMEATA	ANY TIME AT ALL.	July 10, 1964	Lennon	Lennon
ASKMEWHY	ASK ME WHY.	January 11, 1963	Lennon	Lennon
BABYYOUREA	BABY, YOU'RE A RICH MAN.	July 7, 1967	Lennon/McCartney	Lennon/McCartney
BABYSINBLA	BABY'S IN BLACK.	December 4, 1964	Lennon/McCartney	Lennon/McCartney
BACKINTHEU	BACK IN THE USSR.	November 22, 1968	McCartney	McCartney
BALLADOFJO	THE BALLAD OF JOHN AND YOKO.	May 30, 1969	Lennon	Lennon
BECAUSE	BECAUSE.	September 26, 1969	Lennon	Lennon/McCartney/ Harrison
BEINGFORTH	BEING FOR THE BENEFIT OF MR. KITE!	June 1, 1967	Lennon	Lennon
BIRTHDAY	BIRTHDAY.	November 22, 1968	Lennon/McCartney	McCartney
BLACKBIRD	BLACKBIRD.	November 22, 1968	McCartney	McCartney
BLUEJAYWAY	BLUE JAY WAY.	November 27, 1967	Harrison	Harrison
CANTBUYMEL	CAN'T BUY ME LOVE.	March 16, 1964	Lennon/McCartney	McCartney
CARRYTHATW	CARRY THAT WEIGHT.	September 26, 1969	McCartney	Lennon/McCartney/ Harrison/Starr
COMETOGETH	COME TOGETHER.	September 26, 1969	Lennon	Lennon
CONTINUING	THE CONTINUING STORY OF BUNGALOW BILL.	November 22, 1968	Lennon	Lennon
CRYBABYCRY	CRY BABY CRY.	November 22, 1968	Lennon	Lennon
DAYINTHELI	A DAY IN THE LIFE.	June 1, 1967	Lennon/McCartney	Lennon/McCartney
DAYTRIPPER	DAY TRIPPER.	December 3, 1965	Lennon	Lennon
DEARPRUDEN	DEAR PRUDENCE.	November 22, 1968	Lennon	Lennon
DIGIT	DIG IT.	May 8, 1970	Lennon	Lennon
DOYOUWANTT	DO YOU WANT TO KNOW A SECRET?	March 22, 1963	Lennon	Harrison
DRROBERT	DR. ROBERT.	June 20, 1966	Lennon	Lennon/McCartney
DONTBOTHER	DON'T BOTHER ME.	November 22, 1963	Harrison	Harrison
DONTLETMED	DON'T LET ME DOWN.	April 11, 1969	Lennon	Lennon
DONTPASSME	DON'T PASS ME BY.	November 22, 1968	Starr	Starr
DRIVEMYCAR	DRIVE MY CAR.	December 3, 1965	Lennon/McCartney	McCartney/Lennon
EIGHTDAYSA	EIGHT DAYS A WEEK.	December 4, 1964	Lennon/McCartney	Lennon/McCartney
ELEANORRIG	ELEANOR RIGBY.	August 5, 1966	Lennon/McCartney	McCartney
THEEND	THE END.	September 26, 1969	McCartney	McCartney
EVERYLITTL	EVERY LITTLE THING.	December 4, 1964	Lennon/McCartney	Lennon
EVRBDYMONK	EVERYBODY'S GOT SOMETHING TO HIDE EXCEPT ME AND MY MONKEY.	November 22, 1968	Lennon	Lennon
FIXINGAHOL	FIXING A HOLE.	June 1, 1967	McCartney	McCartney
FLYING	FLYING.	November 27, 1967	Lennon/McCartney/ Harrison/Starr	Instrumental
FOOLONTHEH	THE FOOL ON THE HILL.	November 27, 1967	McCartney	McCartney
FORNOONE	FOR NO-ONE.	August 5, 1966	McCartney	McCartney
FORYOUBLUE	FOR YOU BLUE.	May 8, 1970	Harrison	Harrison
FROMMETOYO	FROM ME TO YOU.	April 12, 1963	Lennon/McCartney	Lennon/McCartney
GETBACK/45	GET BACK. (45 version)	April 11, 1969	McCartney	McCartney
GETBACK/LP	GET BACK. (LP version)	May 8, 1970	McCartney	McCartney
GETTINGBET	BETTING BETTER	June 1, 1967	McCartney	McCartney
GIRL	GIRL.	December 3, 1965	Lennon	Lennon
GLASSONION	GLASS ONION.	November 22, 1968	Lennon	Lennon
GOLDENSLUM	GOLDEN SLUMBERS.	September 26, 1969	McCartney	McCartney
GOODDAYSUN	GOOD DAY SUNSHINE.	August 5, 1966	McCartney	McCartney
GOODMORNIN	GOOD MORNING, GOOD MORNING.	June 1, 1967	Lennon	Lennon
GOODNIGHT	GOOD NIGHT.	November 22, 1968	Lennon	Starr
GOTTOGETYO	GOT TO GET YOU INTO MY LIFE.	August 5, 1966	McCartney	McCartney
HAPPINESSI	HAPPINESS IS A WARM GUN.	November 22, 1968	Lennon	Lennon
HARDDAYSNI	A HARD DAY'S NIGHT.	June 26, 1964	Lennon	Lennon
HELLOGOODB	HELLO GOODBYE.	November 24, 1967	McCartney	McCartney
HELP	HELP!	July 19, 1965	Lennon	Lennon
HELTERSKEL	HELTER-SKELTER.	November 22, 1968	McCartney	McCartney
HERMAJESTY	HER MAJESTY.	September 26, 1969	McCartney	McCartney
HERECOMEST	HERE COMES THE SUN.	September 26, 1969	Harrison	Harrison
HERETHEREA	HERE, THERE AND EVERYWHERE.	August 5, 1966	McCartney	McCartney
HEYBULLDOG	HEY BULLDOG.	January 13, 1969	Lennon	Lennon
HEYJUDE	HEY JUDE.	August 26, 1968	McCartney	McCartney
HOLDMETIGH	HOLD ME TIGHT.	November 22, 1963	Lennon/McCartney	McCartney
HONEYPIE	HONEY PIE.	November 22, 1968	McCartney	McCartney
IAMTHEWALR	I AM THE WALRUS.	November 24, 1967	Lennon	Lennon
ICALLYOURN	I CALL YOUR NAME.	April 10, 1964	Lennon	Lennon
IDIGAPONY	(I) DIG A PONY.	May 8, 1970	Lennon	Lennon
IDONTWANTT	I DON'T WANT TO SPOIL THE PARTY.	December 4, 1964	Lennon	Lennon/McCartney
IFEELFINE	I FEEL FINE.	November 23, 1964	Lennon	Lennon/McCartney
IMEMINE	I ME MINE.	May 8, 1970	Harrison	Harrison
INEEDYOU	I NEED YOU.	August 6, 1965	Harrison	Harrison
ISAWHERSTA	I SAW HER STANDING THERE.	March 22, 1963	McCartney	McCartney
ISHOULDHAV	I SHOULD HAVE KNOWN BETTER.	June 26, 1964	Lennon	Lennon
IWANNABEYO	I WANNA BE YOUR MAN.	November 22, 1963	Lennon/McCartney	Starr

IWANTTOHOL	I WANT TO HOLD YOUR HAND.	November 29, 1963	Lennon/McCartney	Lennon/McCartney
IWANTTOTEL	I WANT TO TELL YOU.	August 5, 1966	Harrison	Harrison
IWANTYOUSH	I WANT YOU (SHE'S SO HEAVY).	September 26, 1969	Lennon	Lennon
IWILL	I WILL.	November 22, 1968	McCartney	McCartney
IFIFELL	I IF FELL.	June 26, 1964	Lennon	Lennon/McCartney
IFINEEDEDS	IF I NEEDED SOMEONE.	December 3, 1965	Harrison	Harrison
ILLBEBACK	I'LL BE BACK.	July 10, 1964	Lennon	Lennon
ILLCRYINST	I'LL CRY INSTEAD.	June 26, 1964	Lennon	Lennon/McCartney
ILLFOLLOWT	I'LL FOLLOW THE SUN.	December 4, 1964	McCartney	McCartney
ILLGETYOU	I'LL GET YOU.	August 23, 1963	Lennon/McCartney	Lennon/McCartney
IMALOSER	I'M A LOSER.	December 4, 1964	Lennon	Lennon
IMDOWN	I'M DOWN.	July 19, 1965	McCartney	McCartney
IMHAPPYJUS	I'M HAPPY JUST TO DANCE WITH YOU.	June 26, 1964	Lennon	Harrison
IMLOOKINGT	I'M LOOKING THROUGH YOU.	December 3, 1965	McCartney	McCartney
IMONLYSLEE	I'M ONLY SLEEPING.	June 20, 1966	Lennon	Lennon
IMSOTIRED	I'M SO TIRED.	November 22, 1968	Lennon	Lennon
INMYLIFE	IN MY LIFE.	December 3, 1965	Lennon/McCartney	Lennon
INNERLIGHT	THE INNER LIGHT.	March 15, 1968	Harrison	Harrison
ITWONTBELO	IT WON'T BE LONG.	November 22, 1963	Lennon	Lennon
ITSALLTOOM	IT'S ALL TOO MUCH.	January 13, 1969	Harrison	Harrison
ITSONLYLOV	IT'S ONLY LOVE.	August 6, 1965	Lennon	Lennon
IVEGOTAFEE	I'VE GOT A FEELING.	May 8, 1970	Lennon/McCartney	McCartney/Lennon
IVEJUSTSEE	I'VE JUST SEEN A FACE.	August 6, 1965	McCartney	McCartney
JULIA	JULIA.	November 22, 1968	Lennon	Lennon
LADYMADONN	LADY MADONNA.	March 15, 1968	McCartney	McCartney
LETITBE/45	LET IT BE. (45 version)	March 6, 1970	McCartney	McCartney
LETITBE/LP	LET IT BE. (LP version)	May 8, 1970	McCartney	McCartney
LITTLECHIL	LITTLE CHILD.	November 22, 1963	Lennon/McCartney	Lennon/McCartney
LONGANDWIN	THE LONG AND WINDING ROAD.	May 8, 1970	McCartney	McCartney
LONGLONGLO	LONG, LONG, LONG.	November 22, 1968	Harrison	Harrison
LOVEMEDO	LOVE ME DO.	October 5, 1962	McCartney	Lennon/McCartney
LOVEYOUTWO	LOVE YOU TO/TOO.	August 5, 1966	Harrison	Harrison
LOVELYRITA	LOVELY RITA.	June 1, 1967	McCartney	McCartney
LUCYINTHES	LUCY IN THE SKY.	June 1, 1967	Lennon	Lennon
MAGICALMYS	MAGICAL MYSTERY TOUR.	November 27, 1967	McCartney	Lennon/McCartney
MARTHAMYDE	MARTHA MY DEAR.	November 22, 1968	McCartney	McCartney
MAXWELLSIL	MAXWELL'S SILVER HAMMER.	September 26, 1969	McCartney	McCartney
MEANMRMUST	MEAN MR. MUSTARD.	September 26, 1969	Lennon	Lennon
MICHELLE	MICHELLE.	December 3, 1965	Lennon/McCartney	McCartney
MISERY	MISERY.	March 22, 1963	Lennon/McCartney	Lennon/McCartney
MOTHERNATU	MOTHER NATURE'S SON.	November 22, 1968	McCartney	McCartney
NIGHTBEFOR	THE NIGHT BEFORE.	August 6, 1965	McCartney	McCartney
NOREPLY	NO REPLY.	December 4, 1964	Lennon	Lennon
NORWEGIANW	NORWEGIAN WOOD (THIS BIRD HAS FLOWN)	December 3, 1965	Lennon	Lennon
NOTASECOND	NOT A SECOND TIME.	November 22, 1963	Lennon	Lennon
NOWHEREMAN	NOWHERE MAN.	December 3, 1965	Lennon	Lennon
OBLADIOBLA	OB-LA-DI, OB-LA-DA.	November 22, 1968	McCartney	McCartney
OCTOPUSSGA	OCTOPUS'S GARDEN.	September 26, 1969	Starr	Starr
OHDARLING	OH! DARLING.	September 26, 1969	McCartney	McCartney
OLDBROWNSH	OLD BROWN SHOE.	May 30, 1969	Harrison	Harrison
ONEAFTERNI	ONE AFTER NINE-O-NINE.	May 8, 1970	Lennon	Lennon/McCartney
ONLYANORTH	ONLY A NORTHERN SONG.	January 13, 1969	Harrison	Harrison
PSILOVEYOU	PS I LOVE YOU.	October 5, 1962	McCartney	Lennon/McCartney
PAPERBACKW	PAPERBACK WRITER.	May 30, 1966	McCartney	McCartney
PENNYLANE	PENNY LANE.	February 13, 1967	McCartney	McCartney
PIGGIES	PIGGIES.	November 22, 1968	Harrison	Harrison
PLEASEPLEA	PLEASE PLEASE ME.	January 11, 1963	Lennon	Lennon/McCartney
POLYTHENEP	POLYTHENE PAM.	September 26, 1969	Lennon	Lennon
RAIN	RAIN.	May 30, 1966	Lennon	Lennon
REVOLUTION	REVOLUTION.	August 26, 1968	Lennon	Lennon
REVOLUTONE	REVOLUTION ONE.	November 22, 1968	Lennon	Lennon
REVOLUNINE	REVOLUTION NINE.	November 22, 1968	Lennon	Experimental music
ROCKYRACCO	ROCKY RACCOON.	November 22, 1968	McCartney	McCartney
RUNFORYOUR	RUN FOR YOUR LIFE.	December 3, 1965	Lennon	Lennon
SAVOYTRUFF	SAVOY TRUFFLE.	November 22, 1968	Harrison	Harrison
SGTPEPPERS	SGT. PEPPER'S LONELY HEARTS CLUB BAND	June 1, 1967	McCartney	McCartney
SGTPEPPREP	SGT. PEPPER'S LONELY HEARTS CLUB BAND (REPRISE)	June 1, 1967	McCartney	McCartney
SEXYSADIE	SEXY SADIE.	November 22, 1968	Lennon	Lennon
SHECAMEINT	SHE CAME IN THROUGH THE BATHROOM WINDOW.	September 26, 1969	McCartney	McCartney
SHELOVESYO	SHE LOVES YOU.	August 23, 1963	Lennon/McCartney	Lennon/McCartney
SHESAIDSHE	SHE SAID, SHE SAID.	August 5, 1966	Lennon	Lennon
SHESAWOMAN	SHE'S A WOMAN.	November 23, 1964	McCartney	McCartney
SHESLEAVIN	SHE'S LEAVING HOME.	June 1, 1967	Lennon/McCartney	McCartney
SOMETHING	SOMETHING.	September 26, 1969	Harrison	Harrison
STRAWBERRY	STRAWBERRY FIELDS FOREVER.	February 13, 1967	Lennon	Lennon
SUNKING	SUN KING.	September 26, 1969	Lennon	Lennon/McCartney/ Harrison
TAXMAN	TAXMAN.	August 5, 1966	Harrison	Harrison
TELLMEWHAT	TELL ME WHAT YOU SEE.	June 14, 1965	McCartney	Lennon/McCartney
TELLMEWHY	TELL ME WHY.	June 26, 1964	Lennon	Lennon/McCartney
THANKYOUGI	THANK YOU GIRL.	April 12, 1963	Lennon/McCartney	Lennon/McCartney
THERESAPLA	THERE'S A PLACE.	March 22, 1963	Lennon	Lennon/McCartney
THINGSWESA	THINGS WE SAID TODAY.	July 10, 1964	McCartney	McCartney
THINKFORYO	THINK FOR YOURSELF.	December 3, 1965	Harrison	Harrison
THISBOY	THIS BOY.	November 29, 1963	Lennon	Lennon/McCartney
TICKETTORI	TICKET TO RIDE.	April 9, 1965	Lennon	Lennon
TOMORROWNE	TOMORROW NEVER KNOWS.	August 5, 1966	Lennon	Lennon
TWOOFUS	TWO OF US.	May 8, 1970	McCartney	McCartney/Lennon
WAIT	WAIT.	December 3, 1965	Lennon	Lennon/McCartney
WECANWORKI	WE CAN WORK IT OUT.	December 3, 1965	McCartney	McCartney
WHATGOESON	WHAT GOES ON?	December 3, 1965	Lennon	Starr
WHATYOURED	WHAT YOU'RE DOING.	December 4, 1964	Lennon/McCartney	McCartney
WHENIGETHO	WHEN I GET HOME.	July 10, 1964	Lennon	Lennon
WHENIMSIXT	WHEN I'M SIXTY-FOUR.	June 1, 1967	McCartney	McCartney

WHILEMYGUI	WHILE MY GUITAR GENTLY WEEPS.	November 22, 1968	Harrison	Harrison
WHYDONTWED	WHY DON'T WE DO IT IN THE ROAD?	November 22, 1968	McCartney	McCartney
WILDHONEYP	WILD HONEY PIE.	November 22, 1968	McCartney	McCartney
WITHALITTL	WITH A LITTLE HELP FROM MY FRIENDS.	June 1, 1967	McCartney	Starr
WITHINYOUW	WITHIN YOU, WITHOUT YOU	June 1, 1967	Harrison	Harrison
THEWORD	THE WORD.	December 3, 1965	Lennon/McCartney	Lennon/McCartney/ Harrison
YELLOWSUBM	YELLOW SUBMARINE.	August 5, 1966	Lennon/McCartney	Starr
YERBLUES	YER BLUES.	November 22, 1968	Lennon	Lennon
YESITIS	YES IT IS.	April 9, 1965	Lennon	Lennon
YESTERDAY	YESTERDAY.	August 6, 1965	McCartney	McCartney
YOUCANTDOT	YOU CAN'T DO THAT.	March 16, 1964	Lennon	Lennon
YOUKNOWMYN	YOU KNOW MY NAME (LOOK UP MY NUMBER)	March 6, 1970	Lennon	Lennon
YOULIKEMET	YOU LIKE ME TOO MUCH.	June 14, 1965	Harrison	Harrison
YOUNEVERGI	YOU NEVER GIVE ME YOUR MONEY.	September 26, 1969	McCartney	McCartney
YOUWONTSEE	YOU WON'T SEE ME.	December 3, 1965	McCartney	McCartney
YOURMOTHER	YOUR MOTHER SHOULD KNOW.	November 27, 1967	McCartney	McCartney
YOUREGONNA	YOU'RE GOING TO/GONNA LOSE THAT GIRL.	August 6, 1965	Lennon	Lennon
YOUVEGOTTO	YOU'VE GOT TO HIDE YOUR LOVE AWAY.	August 6, 1965	Lennon	Lennon

YESTERDAY

Yesterday, all my troubles seemed so far away.
now it looks as though they're here to stay
oh I believe in yesterday.

Suddenly, I'm not half the man I used to be
There's a shadow hanging over me
Yesterday came suddenly.

middle∘

Why she had to go, I don't know
she wouldn't say,
I said something wrong. now I long
for yesterday.....

Yesterday, love was such an easy game to
play
Now I need a place to hide away
oh I believe in yesterday

Chronological List of Songs

Songs included in this work are listed here by earliest date of release as derived from information contained in *ALL TOGETHER NOW; The First Complete Beatles Discography, 1961–1975,* **by Harry Castleman and Wally Podrazik (Pierian Press, 1976).**

OCTOBER 5, 1962 (UK) 45
  LOVE ME DO
  PS I LOVE YOU

JANUARY 11, 1963 (UK) 45
  ASK ME WHY
  PLEASE PLEASE ME

MARCH 22, 1963 (UK)
    Please Please Me LP
  DO YOU WANT TO KNOW A SECRET
  I SAW HER STANDING THERE
  MISERY
  THERE'S A PLACE

APRIL 12, 1963 (UK) 45
  FROM ME TO YOU
  THANK YOU GIRL

AUGUST 23, 1963 (UK) 45
  I'LL GET YOU
  SHE LOVES YOU

NOVEMBER 22, 1963 (UK)
    With The Beatles LP
  ALL I'VE GOT TO DO
  ALL MY LOVING
  DON'T BOTHER ME
  HOLD ME TIGHT
  I WANNA BE YOUR MAN
  IT WON'T BE LONG
  LITTLE CHILD
  NOT A SECOND TIME

NOVEMBER 29, 1963 (UK) 45
  I WANT TO HOLD YOUR HAND
  THIS BOY

MARCH 16, 1964 (US) 45
  CAN'T BUY ME LOVE
  YOU CAN'T DO THAT

APRIL 10, 1964 (US)
    The Beatles Second Album
  I CALL YOUR NAME
  LONG TALL SALLY

JUNE 26, 1964 (US)
    A Hard Day's Night LP
  AND I LOVE HER
  A HARD DAY'S NIGHT
  I SHOULD HAVE KNOWN BETTER
  IF I FELL
  I'LL CRY INSTEAD
  I'M HAPPY JUST TO DANCE WITH
    YOU
  TELL ME WHY

JULY 10, 1964 (UK)
    A Hard Day's Night LP
  ANY TIME AT ALL
  I'LL BE BACK
  THINGS WE SAID TODAY
  WHEN I GET HOME

NOVEMBER 23, 1964 (US) 45
  I FEEL FINE
  SHE'S A WOMAN

DECEMBER 4, 1964 (UK)
    Beatles For Sale LP
  BABY'S IN BLACK
  EIGHT DAYS A WEEK
  EVERY LITTLE THING
  I DON'T WANT TO SPOIL THE
    PARTY
  I'LL FOLLOW THE SUN
  I'M A LOSER
  NO REPLY
  WHAT YOU'RE DOING

APRIL 9, 1965 (UK) 45
  TICKET TO RIDE
  YES IT IS

JUNE 14, 1965 (US)
    Beatles VI LP
  TELL ME WHAT YOU SEE
  YOU LIKE ME TOO MUCH

JULY 19, 1965 (US)
  HELP!
  I'M DOWN

AUGUST 6, 1965 (UK)
    Help! LP
  ANOTHER GIRL
  I NEED YOU
  IT'S ONLY LOVE
  I'VE JUST SEEN A FACE
  THE NIGHT BEFORE
  YESTERDAY
  YOU'RE GOING TO/GONNA LOSE
    THAT GIRL
  YOU'VE GOT TO HIDE YOUR LOVE
    AWAY

DECEMBER 3, 1965 (UK) 45
  DAY TRIPPER
  WE CAN WORK IT OUT

DECEMBER 3, 1965 (UK)
    Rubber Soul LP
  DRIVE MY CAR
  GIRL
  IF I NEEDED SOMEONE
  I'M LOOKING THROUGH YOU
  IN MY LIFE
  MICHELLE
  NORWEGIAN WOOD
  NOWHERE MAN
  RUN FOR YOUR LIFE
  THINK FOR YOURSELF
  WAIT
  WHAT GOES ON?
  THE WORD
  YOU WON'T SEE ME

MAY 30, 1966 (US) 45
  PAPERBACK WRITER
  RAIN

JUNE 20, 1966 (US)
    Yesterday...And Today LP
  AND YOUR BIRD CAN SING
  DR. ROBERT
  I'M ONLY SLEEPING

AUGUST 5, 1966 (UK)
    Revolver LP
  ELEANOR RIGBY
  FOR NO ONE
  GOOD DAY SUNSHINE
  GOT TO GET YOU INTO MY LIFE
  HERE, THERE AND EVERYWHERE
  I WANT TO TELL YOU
  LOVE YOU TO/TOO
  SHE SAID SHE SAID
  TAXMAN
  TOMORROW NEVER KNOWS
  YELLOW SUBMARINE

FEBRUARY 13, 1967 (US) 45
  PENNY LANE
  STRAWBERRY FIELDS FOREVER

JUNE 1, 1967 (UK)
    Sgt. Pepper's Lonely Hearts
      Club Band LP
  BEING FOR THE BENEFIT OF
    MR. KITE
  A DAY IN THE LIFE
  FIXING A HOLE
  GETTING BETTER
  GOOD MORNING GOOD MORNING
  LOVELY RITA
  LUCY IN THE SKY WITH DIAMONDS
  SGT. PEPPER'S LONELY HEARTS
    CLUB BAND
  SGT. PEPPER'S LONELY HEARTS
    CLUB BAND - REPRISE
  SHE'S LEAVING HOME
  WHEN I'M SIXTY-FOUR
  WITH A LITTLE HELP FROM MY
    FRIENDS
  WITHIN YOU, WITHOUT YOU

JULY 7, 1967 (UK) 45
  ALL YOU NEED IS LOVE
  BABY, YOU'RE A RICH MAN

NOVEMBER 24, 1967 (UK) 45
  HELLO GOODBYE
  I AM THE WALRUS

NOVEMBER 27, 1967 (US)
    Magical Mystery Tour LP
  BLUE JAY WAY
  FLYING
  THE FOOL ON THE HILL
  MAGICAL MYSTERY TOUR
  YOUR MOTHER SHOULD KNOW

MARCH 15, 1968 (US) 45
  THE INNER LIGHT
  LADY MADONNA

AUGUST 26, 1968 (US) 45
  HEY JUDE.
  REVOLUTION

NOVEMBER 22, 1968 (UK)
    The Beatles LP
  BACK IN THE USSR
  BIRTHDAY
  BLACKBIRD
  THE CONTINUING STORY OF

BUNGALOW BILL
CRY BABY CRY
DEAR PRUDENCE
DON'T PASS ME BY
EVERYBODY'S GOT SOMETHING TO
    HIDE EXCEPT ME AND MY
    MONKEY
GLASS ONION
HAPPINESS IS A WARM GUN
HELTER-SKELTER
HONEY PIE
I WILL
I'M SO TIRED
JULIA
LONG, LONG, LONG
MARTHA MY DEAR
MOTHER NATURE'S SON
OB-LA-DI, OB-LA-DA
PIGGIES
REVOLUTION ONE
REVOLUTION NINE
ROCKY RACCOON
SAVOY TRUFFLE
SEXY SADIE
WHILE MY GUITAR GENTLY WEEPS
WHY DON'T WE DO IT IN THE
    ROAD?
WILD HONEY PIE
YER BLUES

JANUARY 13, 1969 (US)
    Yellow Submarine LP
ALL TOGETHER NOW
ALL YOU NEED IS LOVE
HEY BULLDOG
IT'S ALL TOO MUCH
IT'S ONLY A NORTHERN SONG

APRIL 11, 1969 (UK) 45
    DON'T LET ME DOWN
    GET BACK

MAY 30, 1969 (UK) 45
    THE BALLAD OF JOHN AND YOKO
    OLD BROWN SHOE

SEPTEMBER 26, 1969 (UK)
    Abbey Road LP
    BECAUSE
    CARRY THAT WEIGHT
    COME TOGETHER
    THE END
    GOLDEN SLUMBERS
    HER MAJESTY
    HERE COMES THE SUN
    I WANT YOU (SHE'S SO HEAVY)
    MAXWELL'S SILVER HAMMER
    MEAN MR. MUSTARD

OCTOPUS'S GARDEN
OH! DARLING
POLYTHENE PAM
SHE CAME IN THROUGH THE
    BATHROOM WINDOW
SOMETHING
SUN KING
YOU NEVER GIVE ME YOUR MONEY

MARCH 6, 1970 (UK) 45
    LET IT BE
    YOU KNOW MY NAME (LOOK UP MY
        NUMBER)

MAY 8, 1970 (UK)
    Let It Be LP
    ACROSS THE UNIVERSE
    DIG IT
    FOR YOU BLUE
    GET BACK
    (I) DIG A PONY
    I ME MINE
    I'VE GOT A FEELING
    LET IT BE
    THE LONG AND WINDING ROAD
    ONE AFTER NINE-O-NINE
    TWO OF US

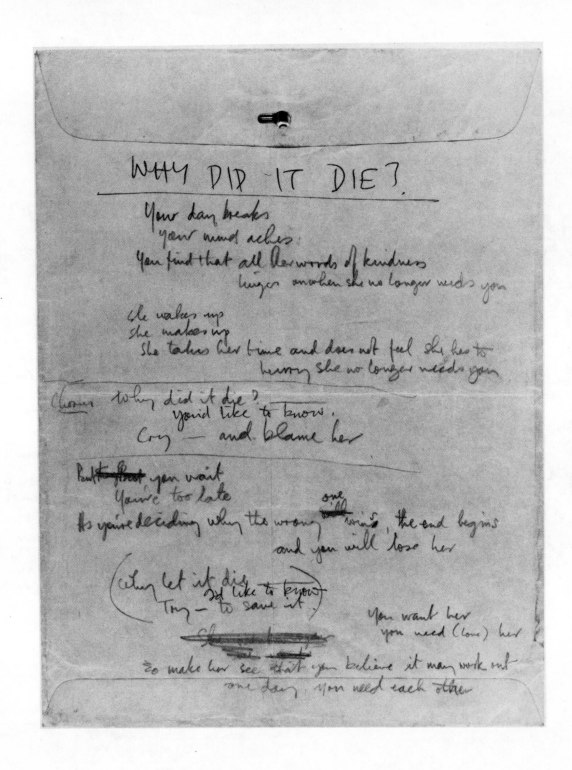

I WANNA ~~HOLD~~ YOUR HAND

Oh yea, I'll tell you something
I think you'll understand
When I say that something
I wanna hold your hand

Repeat twice
___

Oh please say to me
you'll let me be you man
And please say to me
you'll let me hold your hand

And when I touch you
I feel happy inside
It's such a feeling
~~that our love~~
    — I can't hide
    ~~I can't hide~~
___

An you got that something
I think you understand
When I feel that something
I wanna hold your hand
    —

Complete Lyrics

ACROSS THE UNIVERSE
by John Lennon and Paul McCartney

1 Words are flowing out like endless rain
     into a paper cup
2 They slither wildly as they slip away
     across the universe.
3 Pools of sorrow, waves of joy
4 Are drifting through my opened
     mind
5 Possessing and caressing me.

6 Jai Guru Deva OM.
7 Nothing's gonna change my world
8 Nothing's gonna change my world
9 Nothing's gonna change my world
10 Nothing's gonna change my world.

11 Images of broken light which dance before
     me like a million eyes
12 They call me on and on across the universe.
13 Thoughts meander like a restless wind
     inside a letter-box
14 They tumble blindly as they make their
     way across the universe.

15 Jai Guru Deva OM.
16 Nothing's gonna change my world
17 Nothing's gonna change my world
18 Nothing's gonna change my world
19 Nothing's gonna change my world.

20 Sounds of laughter, shades of life
21 Are ringing through my opened
     ears
22 Inciting and inviting me.
23 Limitless undying love which shines
     around me like a million suns
24 It calls me on and on across the universe.

25 Jai Guru Deva OM.
26 Nothing's gonna change my world
27 Nothing's gonna change my world
28 Nothing's gonna change my world
29 Nothing's gonna change my world.

30 Jai Guru Deva, Jai Guru Deva, Jai
     Guru Deva
31 Jai Guru Deva, Jai Guru Deva, Jai
     Guru Deva.

ALL I'VE GOT TO DO
by John Lennon and Paul McCartney

1 Whenever I want you around, yeah
2 All I gotta do
3 Is call you on the phone
4 And you'll come running home
5 Yeah, that's all I gotta do.

6 And when I, I wanna kiss you, yeah
7 All I gotta do
8 Is whisper in your ear
9 The words you long to hear
10 And I'll be kissing you.

11 And the same goes for me
12 Whenever you want me at all
13 I'll be here, yes I will
14 Whenever you call
15 Ya just gotta call on me, yeah
16 Ya just gotta call on me.

17 And when I, I wanna kiss you, yeah
18 All I gotta do
19 Is call you on the phone
20 And you'll come running home
21 Yeah, that's all I gotta do.

22 And the same goes for me
23 Whenever you want me at all
24 I'll be here, yes I will
25 Whenever you call
26 Ya just gotta call on me, yeah
27 Ya just gotta call on me
28 (Ooh) ya just gotta call on me
29 Mmm mmm mmm.

ALL MY LOVING
by John Lennon and Paul McCartney

1 Close your eyes and I'll kiss you
2 Tomorrow I'll miss you
3 Remember I'll always be true
4 And then while I'm away
5 I'll write home every day
6 And I'll send all my lovin' to you.

7 I'll pretend that I'm kissing
8 The lips I am missing
9 And hope that my dreams will come true
10 And then while I'm away
11 I'll write home every day
12 And I'll send all my lovin' to you.

13 All my lovin', I will send to you
14 All my lovin', darlin', I'll be true.

15 Close your eyes and I'll kiss you
16 Tomorrow I'll miss you
17 Remember I'll always be true
18 And then while I'm away
19 I'll write home every day
20 And I'll send all my lovin' to you.

21 All my lovin', I will send to you
22 All my lovin', darlin', I'll be true
23 All my lovin', all my lovin', ooo-ooo
24 All my lovin', I will send to you.

ALL TOGETHER NOW
by John Lennon and Paul McCartney

1 One, two, three, four
2 Can I have a little more?

3 Five, six, seven, eight, nine, ten
4 I love you.

5 A, B, C, D
6 Can I bring my friend to tea?
7 E, F, G, H, I, J
8 I love you.

9 Bom bom bom bom-pa bom, sail the ship
10 Bom-pa bom, chop the tree
11 Bom-pa bom, skip the rope
12 Bom-pa bom, look at me.

13 All together now (all together now)
14 All together now (all together now)
15 All together now (all together now)
16 All together now (all together now)
   (all together now).

17 Black, white, green, red
18 Can I take my friend to bed?
19 Pink, brown, yellow, orange and blue
20 I love you.

21 All together now (all together now)
22 All together now (all together now)
23 All together now (all together now)
24 All together now (all together now)
25 All together now (all together now)
26 All together now (all together now)
27 All together now (all together now)
28 All together now (all together now).

29 Bom bom bom bom-pa bom, ((Oh! boy)),
      sail the ship
30 Bom-pa bom, chop the tree
31 Bom-pa bom, skip the rope
32 Bom-pa bom, look at me.

33 All together now (all together now)
34 All together now (all together now)
35 All together now (all together now)
36 All together now (all together now)
37 All together now (all together now)
38 All together now (all together now)
39 All together now (all together now)
40 All together now (all together now)
41 All together now (all together now)
42 All together now (all together now)
43 All together now (all together now)
44 All together now
45 All together now! (wuh, yeah, wahoo!)

ALL YOU NEED IS LOVE (YS)
by John Lennon and Paul McCartney

1 Love, love, love
2 Love, love, love
3 Love, love, love.

4 There's nothing you can do that can't be
      done ((love))
5 Nothing you can sing that can't be sung
      ((love))
6 Nothing you can say but you can learn how
      to play the game ((love))
7 It's easy.

8 Nothing you can make that can't be made
      ((love))
9 No-one you can save that can't be saved
      ((love))
10 Nothing you can do but you can learn how
      to be you in time ((love))

11 It's easy.

12 All you need is love, all you need is love
13 All you need is love, love, love is all
      you need.

14 Love, love, love
15 Love, love, love
16 Love, love, love.

17 All you need is love, (wuh) all you
      need is love (hey)
18 All you need is love, love, love is all
      you need.

19 There's nothing you can know that isn't
      known ((love))
20 Nothing you can see that isn't shown
      ((love))
21 There's nowhere you can be that isn't
      where you're meant to be ((love))
22 It's easy.

23 All you need is love, all you need is love
24 All you need is love, love, love is all
      you need.

25 All you need is love (all together now)
26 All you need is love (everybody)
27 All you need is love, love, love is all
      you need.

28 Love is all you need (love is all you need)
29 Love is all you need (love is all you need)
30 Love is all you need (love is all you need)
31 Love is all you need (love is all you need)
32 Love is all you need (wuh) (love is
      all you need)
33 Love is all you need (love is all you need)
34 Love is all you need (love is all you need)
35 Love is all you need (love is all you need)
36 Love is all you need (love is all you need)
37 Love is all you need (love is all you need)
38 Love is all you need (yahoo)
      (eee - hi)
39 Love is all you need (love is all you need)
40 (Love is all you need) Yesterday
      (love is all you need)
41 (Oh) love is all you need
42 Love is all you need (oh yeah)
43 Love is all you need
44 Loves you yeah, yeah, yeah ((love is
      all, love is all))
45 She loves you yeah, yeah, yeah ((love is
      is all, love is all))
46 Love is all you need
47 Love is all you need (wuhoo)
48 Love is all you need (wuhoo)
49 Love is all you need (oh)
50 Love is all you need
51 Love is all you need.

ALL YOU NEED IS LOVE (MMT)
by John Lennon and Paul McCartney

1 Love is all you need
2 (Oh) love is all you need
3 Love is all you need
4 Love is all you need
5 Love is all you need
6 Love is all you need.

AND I LOVE HER
by John Lennon and Paul McCartney

1 I give her all my love
2 That's all I do
3 And if you saw my love
4 You'd love her too
5 I love her.

6 She gives me everything
7 And tenderly
8 The kiss my lover brings
9 She brings to me
10 And I love her.

11 A love like ours
12 Could never die
13 As long as I
14 Have you near me.

15 Bright are the stars that shine
16 Dark is the sky
17 I know this love of mine
18 Will never die
19 And I love her.

20 Bright are the stars that shine
21 Dark is the sky
22 I know this love of mine
23 Will never die
24 And I love her
25 Mmm.

AND YOUR BIRD CAN SING
by John Lennon and Paul McCartney

1 You tell me that you've got everything
   you want
2 And your bird can sing
3 But you don't get me, you don't get me.

4 You say you've seen seven wonders
5 And your bird is green
6 But you can't see me, you can't see me.

7 When your prized possessions start to
   weigh you down
8 Look in my direction
9 I'll be round, I'll be round.

10 When your bird is broken will it bring
   you down?
11 You may be awoken
12 I'll be round, I'll be round.

13 You tell me that you heard every sound
   there is
14 And your bird can swing
15 But you can't hear me, you can't hear me.

ANOTHER GIRL
by John Lennon and Paul McCartney

1 For I have got another girl, another girl.

2 You're making me say that I've got
   nobody but you
3 But as from today well I've got somebody
   that's new
4 I ain't no fool and I don't take what I
   don't want
5 For I have got another girl, another girl.

6 She's sweeter than all the girls and I
   met quite a few
7 Nobody in all the world can do what she
   can do
8 And so I'm telling you this time you'd
   better stop
9 For I have got another girl
10 Another girl who will love me till the end
11 Through thick and thin she will always be
   my friend.

12 I don't wanna say that I've been unhappy
   with you
13 But as from today well I've seen
   somebody that's new
14 I ain't no fool and I don't take what I
   don't want
15 For I have got another girl
16 Another girl who will love me till the end
17 Through thick and thin she will always be
   my friend.

18 I don't wanna say that I've been unhappy
   with you
19 But as from today well I've seen
   somebody that's new
20 I ain't no fool and I don't take what I
   don't want
21 For I have got another girl, another
   girl, another girl.

ANY TIME AT ALL
by John Lennon and Paul McCartney

1 Any time at all, any time at all, any time
   at all
2 All you gotta do is call
3 And I'll be there.

4 If you need somebody to love
5 Just look into my eyes
6 I'll be there to make you feel right
7 If you're feeling sorry and sad,
8 I'd really sympathise
9 Don't you be sad, just call me tonight.

10 Any time at all, any time at all, any time
   at all
11 All you gotta do is call
12 And I'll be there.

13 If the sun has faded away
14 I'll try to make it shine.
15 There is nothing I won't do
16 When you need a shoulder to cry on
17 I hope it will be mine
18 Call me tonight and I'll come to you.

19 Any time at all, any time at all, any time
    at all
20 All ya gotta do is call
21 And I'll be there.

22 Any time at all, any time at all, any time
    at all
23 All you gotta do is call
24 And I'll be there.

25 Any time at all
26 All ya gotta do is call
27 And I'll be there.

ASK ME WHY
by John Lennon and Paul McCartney

1 I love you
2 'cos you tell me things I want to know
3 And it's true
4 That it really only goes to show
5 That I know
6 That I - I - I - I should never
      never, never be blue.

7 Now you're mine
8 My happiness near makes me cry
9 And in time you'll understand the reason why
10 If I cry it's not because I'm sad
11 But you're the only love that I've ever had.

12 I can't believe it's happened to me
13 I can't conceive of any more misery.

14 Ask me why, I'll say I love you
15 And I'm always thinking of you.

16 I love you
17 'cos you tell me things I want to know
18 And it's true
19 That it really only goes to show
20 That I know
21 That I - I - I - I should never
      never, never be blue.

22 Ask me why, I'll say I love you
23 And I'm always thinking of you.

24 I can't believe it's happened to me
25 I can't conceive of any more misery.

26 Ask my why, I'll say I love you
27 And I'm always thinking of you, you, you.

BABY, YOU'RE A RICH MAN
by John Lennon and Paul McCartney

1 How does it feel to be
2 One of the beautiful people?
3 Now that you know who you are
4 What do you want to be?
5 And have you travelled very far?
6 Far as the eye can see.

7 How does it feel to be
8 One of the beautiful people?
9 How often have you been there?
10 Often enough to know.
11 What did you see when you were there?
12 Nothing that doesn't show.

13 Baby, you're a rich man
14 Baby, you're a rich man
15 Baby, you're a rich man too.

16 You keep all your money in a big brown bag,
17 Inside a zoo
18 What a thing to do.

19 Baby, you're a rich man
20 Baby, you're a rich man
21 Baby, you're a rich man too.

22 How does it feel to be
23 One of the beautiful people?
24 Tuned to a natural E
25 Happy to be that way.
26 Now that you've found another key
27 What are you going to play?

28 Baby, you're a rich man
29 Baby, you're a rich man
30 Baby, you're a rich man too.

31 You keep all your money in a big brown bag
32 Inside a zoo
33 What a thing to do (baby).

34 Baby, you're a rich man
35 Baby, you're a rich man
36 Baby, you're a rich man too.

37 Oh, baby you're a rich man
38 Baby, you're a rich (baby) man
39 Baby, you're a rich man too.
40 Wuh-oh, baby, you're a rich (oh) man
41 Baby, you're a rich man
42 Baby, you're a rich man too.
43 Oh, baby, you're a rich man.
44 Baby, you're a rich man.
45 Baby, you're a...

BABY'S IN BLACK
by John Lennon and Paul McCartney

1 Oh dear, what can I do?
2 Baby's in black and I'm feeling blue
3 Tell me, oh what can I do?

4 She thinks of him and so she dresses in
    black
5 And though he'll never come back
6 She's dressed in black.

7 Oh dear, what can I do?
8 Baby's in black and I'm feeling blue
9 Tell me, oh what can I do?

10 I think of her
11 But she thinks only of him
12 And though it's only a whim
13 She thinks of him.

14 Oh how long will it take
15 Till she sees the mistake she has made?

16 Dear what can I do?

17 Baby's in black and I'm feeling blue
18 Tell me oh what can I do?

19 Oh how long will it take
20 Till she sees the mistake she has made?

21 Dear what can I do?
22 Baby's in black and I'm feeling blue
23 Tell me oh what can I do?

24 She thinks of him and so she dresses in
      black
25 And/But though he'll never come back
26 She's dressed in black.

27 Oh dear, what can I do?
28 Baby's in black and I'm feeling blue
29 Tell me oh what can I do?

BACK IN THE USSR
by John Lennon and Paul McCartney

1 Oh - flew in from Miami Beach BOAC
2 Didn't get to bed last night
3 On the way the paper bag was on my knee
4 Man I had a dreadful flight.

5 I'm back in the USSR
6 You don't know how lucky you are boys
7 Back in the USSR (yeah).

8 Been away so long I hardly knew the place
9 Gee, it's good to be back home
10 Leave it till tomorrow to unpack my case
11 Honey disconnect the phone.

12 I'm back in the USSR
13 You don't know how lucky you are boy
14 Back in the US, back in the US, back
      in the USSR.

15 Well, the Ukraine girls really knock me
      out
16 They leave the West behind
17 And Moscow girls make me sing and shout
18 That Georgia's always on my my my my my
      my my my my mind.

19 Oh come on!
20 Wuh - yeah
21 Ooo yeah
22 Ooo yeah
23 Yeah.

24 Hey, I'm back in the USSR.
25 You don't know how lucky you are boys
26 Back in the USSR.

27 Well, the Ukraine girls really knock me
      out
28 They leave the West behind
29 And Moscow girls make me sing and shout
30 That Georgia's always on my my my my my
      my my my my mind.

31 Oh - show me round the snow-peaked
      mountains way down south
32 Take me to your daddy's farm
33 Let me hear your balalaikas ringing out
34 Come and keep your comrade warm.

35 I'm back in the USSR (hey!)

36 You don't know how lucky you are boy
37 Back in the USSR.

38 Oh let me tell you honey
39 Hey, I'm back
40 I'm back in the USSR,
41 Hey, so look at me
42 Yeah - back in the USSR.
43 (I'm back!)

THE BALLAD OF JOHN AND YOKO
by John Lennon and Paul McCartney

1 Standing in the dock at Southampton
2 Trying to get to Holland or France.
3 The man in the mack said you've got to go
      back
4 You know they didn't even give us a chance.

5 Christ! you know it ain't easy
6 You know how hard it can be
7 The way things are going
8 They're gonna crucify me.

9 Finally made the plane into Paris
10 Honeymooning down by the Seine.
11 Peter Brown called to say, you can make
      it OK
12 You can get married in Gibraltar near
      Spain.

13 Christ! you know it ain't easy
14 You know how hard it can be
15 The way things are going
16 They're gonna crucify me.

17 Drove from Paris to the Amsterdam Hilton
18 Talking in our beds for a week.
19 The news-people said, say what're you
      doing in bed?
20 I said we're only trying to get us some
      peace.

21 Christ! you know it ain't easy
22 You know how hard it can be
23 The way things are going
24 They're gonna crucify me.

25 Saving up your money for a rainy day
26 Giving all your clothes to charity.
27 Last night the wife said, oh boy, when
      you're dead
28 You don't take nothing with you but your
      soul - think!

29 Made a lightning trip to Vienna
30 Eating chocolate cake in the bag.
31 The newspapers said, she's gone to his head
32 They look just like two gurus in drag.

33 Christ! you know it ain't easy
34 You know how hard it can be
35 The way things are going
36 They're gonna crucify me.

37 Caught the early plane back to London
38 Fifty acorns tied in a sack.
39 The men from the press said, we wish you
      success
40 It's good to have the both of you back.

41 Christ! you know it ain't easy
42 You know how hard it can be.

43 The way things are going
44 They're gonna crucify me.
45 The way things are going
46 They're gonna crucify me.

BECAUSE
by John Lennon and Paul McCartney

1 Aah!
2 Because the world is round it turns me on
3 Because the world is round.

4 Aah!
5 Because the wind is high it blows my mind
6 Because the wind is high.

7 Aah!
8 Love is old, love is new
9 Love is all, love is you.

10 Because the sky is blue it makes me cry
11 Because the sky is blue.

12 Aah - aah
13 Aah - aah
14 Aah
15 Aah.

BEING FOR THE BENEFIT OF MR. KITE!
by John Lennon and Paul McCartney

1 For the benefit of Mr. Kite
2 There will be a show tonight on trampoline.
3 The Hendersons will all be there
4 Late of Pablo Fanques Fair - what a scene.
5 Over men and horses, hoops and garters
6 Lastly through a hogshead of real fire
7 In this way Mr. K. will challenge the
   world.

8 The celebrated Mr. K.
9 Performs his feat on Saturday at
   Bishopsgate.
10 The Hendersons will dance and sing
11 As Mr. Kite flies through the ring -
   don't be late.
12 Messrs. K. and H. assure the public
13 Their production will be second to none
14 And of course Henry the Horse dances
   the waltz.

15 The band begins at ten to six
16 When Mr. K. performs his tricks -
   without a sound.
17 And Mr. H. will demonstrate
18 Ten somersets he'll undertake on solid
   ground.
19 Having been some days in preparation
20 A splendid time is guaranteed for all
21 And tonight Mr. Kite is topping the bill.

BIRTHDAY
by John Lennon and Paul McCartney

1 You say it's your birthday
2 Well, it's my birthday too - yeah.
3 They say it's your birthday
4 We're gonna have a good time.
5 I'm glad it's your birthday
6 Happy birthday to you.

7 (... Four, five, six, seven, eight!)

8 Yes, we're going to a party, party
9 Yes, we're going to a party, party
10 Yes, we're going to a party, party.

11 I would like you to dance (birthday)
12 Take a cha-cha-cha chance (birthday)
13 I would like you to dance (birthday)
14 Dance! (dance!) (yeah)

15 (Wuh oh)

16 I would like you to dance (birthday)
17 Take a cha-cha-cha chance (birthday)
18 I would like you to dance (birthday) (wuh)
19 Dance! (dance!)

20 You say it's your birthday
21 Well, it's my birthday too - yeah.
22 You say it's your birthday
23 We're gonna have a good time.
24 I'm glad it's your birthday
25 Happy birthday to you.

BLACKBIRD
by John Lennon and Paul McCartney

1 Blackbird singing in the dead of night
2 Take these broken wings and learn to fly.
3 All your life
4 You were only waiting for this moment to
   arise.

5 Blackbird singing in the dead of night
6 Take these sunken eyes and learn to see.
7 All your life
8 You were only waiting for this moment to
   be free.

9 Blackbird fly, blackbird fly
10 Into the light of a dark black night.

11 Blackbird fly, blackbird fly
12 Into the light of a dark black night.

13 Blackbird singing in the dead of night
14 Take these broken wings and learn to fly.
15 All your life
16 You were only waiting for this moment to
   arise
17 You were only waiting for this moment to
   arise
18 You were only waiting for this moment to
   arise.

9 I'll give you all I've got to give
10 If you say you love me too
11 I may not have a lot to give
12 But what I got I'll give to you
13 I don't care too much for money
14 Money can't buy me love.

15 Can't buy me love, oh, everybody tells
   me so
16 Can't buy me love oh - no, no, no - no.

17 Say you don't need no diamond rings
18 And I'll be satisfied
19 Tell me that you want the kind of things
20 That money just can't buy
21 I don't care too much for money
22 Money can't buy me love.

23 (Ow)
24 (Hey)

25 Can't buy me love, oh, everybody tells
   me so
26 Can't buy me love oh - no, no, no - no.

27 Say you don't need no diamond rings
28 And I'll be satisfied
29 Tell me that you want the kind of things
30 That money just can't buy
31 I don't care too much for money
32 Money can't buy me love.

33 Can't buy me love, oh, love, oh
34 Can't buy me love, oh, oh.

BLUE JAY WAY
by George Harrison

1 There's a fog upon LA
2 And my friends have lost their way.
3 We'll be over soon they said
4 Now they've lost themselves instead.

5 Please don't be long
6 Please don't you be very long
7 Please don't be long or I may be asleep.

8 Well it only goes to show (only, only
   goes to show)
9 And I told them where to go.
10 Ask a policeman on the street
11 There's so many there to meet.

12 Please don't be long (don't be long)
13 Please don't you be very long (don't be
   long)
14 Please don't be long or I may be asleep.

15 Now it's past my bed I know (know)
16 And I'd really like to go (go)
17 Soon will be the break of day (day)
18 Sitting here in Blue Jay Way (way).

19 Please don't be long (don't be long)
20 Please don't you be very long (don't be
   long)
21 Please don't be long or I may be asleep.

22 Please don't be long
23 Please don't you be very long
24 Please don't be long.

25 Please don't be long
26 Please don't you be very long
27 Please don't be long (please don't be long).

28 Please don't be long
29 Please don't you be very long
30 Please don't be long.

31 Don't be long - don't be long
32 Don't belong, don't be long

33 Don't belong
34 Don't be long
35 Don't belong.

CARRY THAT WEIGHT
by John Lennon and Paul McCartney

1 Boy, you're gonna carry that weight
2 Carry that weight a long time.
3 Boy, you're gonna carry that weight
4 Carry that weight a long time.

5 I never give you my pillow
6 I only send you my invitations
7 And in the middle of the celebrations
8 I break down.

9 Boy, you're gonna carry that weight
10 Carry that weight a long time.
11 Boy, you're gonna carry that weight
12 Carry that weight a long time.

CAN'T BUY ME LOVE
by John Lennon and Paul McCartney

1 Can't buy me love, oh, love, oh
2 Can't buy me love, oh.

3 I'll buy you a diamond ring my friend
4 If it makes you feel alright
5 I'll get you anything my friend
6 If it makes you feel alright
7 'cos I don't care too much for money
8 Money can't buy me love.

COME TOGETHER
by John Lennon and Paul McCartney

1 Shoot me
2 Shoot me
3 Shoot me
4 Shoot me

5 Here come old flat top
6 He come grooving up slowly
7 He got ju-ju eyeball
8 He one holy roller

9 He got hair down to his knee
10 Got to be a joker he just do what he please

11 Shoot me
12 Shoot me
13 Shoot me
14 Shoot me

15 He wear no shoe-shine
16 He got toe-jam football
17 He got wonky finger
18 He shoot Coca-cola
19 He say I know you, you know me
20 One thing I can tell you is you got to
   be free
21 Come together right now over me

22 Shoot me
23 Shoot me
24 Shoot me

25 He Bag Production
26 He got walrus gumboot
27 He got Ono sideboard
28 He one spinal cracker
29 He got feet down below his knee
30 Hold you in his armchair you can feel his
   disease
31 Come together right now over me

32 Shoot me

33 Right!
34 Ha ha ha ha ha ha ha ha ha ha
   ha ha ha ha ha
35 Come - (oh) - come - come - come

36 He roller-coaster
37 He got early warning
38 He got Muddy Water
39 He one mojo filter
40 He say one and one and one is three
41 Got to be good-looking 'cos he's so hard
   to see
42 Come together right now over me

43 Shoot me
44 Shoot me
45 Shoot me

46 Oh
47 Come together, yeah
48 Come together, yeah
49 Come together, yeah
50 Come together, yeah
51 Come together, yeah
52 Come together, yeah
53 Come together, yeah
54 Oh
55 Come together, yeah
56 Come together, yeah
57 Come together.

THE CONTINUING STORY OF BUNGALOW BILL
by John Lennon and Paul McCartney

1 Hey, Bungalow Bill
2 What did you kill
3 Bungalow Bill?
4 Hey, Bungalow Bill
5 What did you kill
6 Bungalow Bill?

7 He went out tiger hunting with his
   elephant and gun
8 In case of accidents he always took his mom
9 He's the all-American bullet-headed
   Saxon mother's son.

10 All de children sing:
11 Hey, Bungalow Bill
12 What did you kill
13 Bungalow Bill?
14 Hey, Bungalow Bill
15 What did you kill
16 Bungalow Bill?

17 Deep in the jungle where the mighty tiger
   lies
18 Bill and his elephants were taken by
   surprise
19 So Captain Marvel zapped him right
   between the eyes. (Zap!)

20 All de children sing:
21 Hey, Bungalow Bill
22 What did you kill
23 Bungalow Bill?
24 Hey, Bungalow Bill
25 What did you kill
26 Bungalow Bill?

27 The children asked him if to kill was not
   a sin
28 [But when he looked so fierce] his
   mommy butted in
29 If looks could kill it would have been us
   instead of him.

30 All the children sing:
31 Hey, Bungalow Bill
32 What did you kill
33 Bungalow Bill?
34 Hey, Bungalow Bill
35 What did you kill
36 Bungalow Bill?
37 Hey, Bungalow Bill
38 What did you kill
39 Bungalow Bill?
40 Hey, Bungalow Bill
41 What did you kill
42 Bungalow Bill?
43 Hey, Bungalow Bill
44 What did you kill
45 Bungalow Bill?
46 Hey, Bungalow Bill
47 What did you kill
48 Bungalow Bill?
49 Hey, Bungalow Bill
50 What did you kill
51 Bungalow Bill?
52 Hey, Bungalow Bill
53 What did you kill
54 Bungalow Bill?

CRY BABY CRY
by John Lennon and Paul McCartney

1 Cry baby cry
2 Make your mother sigh
3 She's old enough to know better.

4 The King of Marigold was in the kitchen
5 Cooking breakfast for the Queen
6 The Queen was in the parlour
7 Playing piano for the children of the King.

8 Cry baby cry
9 Make your mother sigh
10 She's old enough to know better
11 So cry baby cry.

12 The King was in the garden
13 Picking flowers for a friend who came to
      play
14 The Queen was in the playroom
15 Painting pictures for the childrens' holiday.

16 Cry baby cry
17 Make your mother sigh
18 She's old enough to know better
19 So cry baby cry.

20 The Duchess of Kirkaldy always smiling
21 And arriving late for tea
22 The Duke was having problems
23 With a message at the local bird and bee.

24 Cry baby cry
25 Make your mother sigh
26 She's old enough to know better
27 So cry baby cry.

28 At twelve o'clock a meeting round the table
29 For a seance in the dark
30 With voices out of nowhere
31 Put on specially by the children for a lark.

32 Cry baby cry
33 Make your mother sigh
34 She's old enough to know better
35 So cry baby cry
36 Cry, cry, cry baby
37 Make your mother sigh
38 She's old enough to know better
39 So cry baby cry
40 Cry, cry, cry
41 Make your mother sigh
42 She's old enough to know better
43 So cry baby cry.

44 Can you take me back where I came from
45 Can you take me back?
46 Can you take me back where I came from
47 Brother, can you take me back
48 Can you take me back?
49 Mmm can you take me where I came from
50 Can you take me back?

A DAY IN THE LIFE
by John Lennon and Paul McCartney

1 I read the news today, oh boy
2 About a lucky man who made the grade
3 And though the news was rather sad
4 Well I just had to laugh
5 I saw the photograph

6 He blew his mind out in a car
7 He didn't notice that the lights had changed
8 A crowd of people stood and stared
9 They'd seen his face before
10 Nobody was really sure if he was from the
      House of Lords

11 I saw a film today, oh boy
12 The English Army had just won the war
13 A crowd of people turned away
14 But I just had to look

15 Having read the book

16 I'd love to turn you on

17 (One)
18 Woke up, fell out of bed
19 Dragged a comb across my head
20 Found my way downstairs and drank a cup
21 And looking up I noticed I was late
22 Huh - huh - huh - huh
23 Found my coat and grabbed my hat
24 Made the bus in seconds flat
25 Found my way upstairs and had a smoke
26 And somebody spoke and I went into a dream

27 Aah! aah! aah!

28 I read the news today, oh boy
29 Four thousand holes in Blackburn,
      Lancashire
30 And though the holes were rather small
31 They had to count them all
32 Now they know how many holes it takes
33 To fill the Albert Hall

34 I'd love to turn you on

35 ... Four, five, six, seven, eight,
      nine, ten...

DAY TRIPPER
by John Lennon and Paul McCartney

1 Got a good reason
2 For taking the easy way out
3 Got a good reason
4 For taking the easy way out, now.

5 She was a day tripper
6 One way ticket, yeah
7 It took me so long to find out
8 And I found out.

9 She's a big teaser
10 She took me half the way there
11 She's a big teaser
12 She took me half the way there, now.

13 She was a day tripper
14 One way ticket, yeah
15 It took me so long to find out
16 And I found out.

17 Aah, aah, aah.

18 Tried to please her
19 She only played one night stands
20 Tried to please her
21 And she only played one night stands, now.

22 She was a day tripper
23 Sunday driver, yeah
24 It took me so long to find out
25 And I found out.

26 Day tripper, yeah
27 Day tripper, yeah
28 Day tripper
29 Day tripper, yeah
30 Day tripper
31 Day tripper.

DEAR PRUDENCE
by John Lennon and Paul McCartney

1 Dear Prudence, won't you come out to play?
2 Dear Prudence, greet the brand new day.
3 The sun is up, the sky is blue
4 It's beautiful and so are you.
5 Dear Prudence, won't you come out to play?

6 Dear Prudence, open up your eyes
7 Dear Prudence, see the sunny skies.
8 The wind is low, the birds will sing
9 That you are part of everything.
10 Dear Prudence, won't you open up your eyes?

11 Look around, 'round
12 ('round, 'round, 'round, 'round
     'round, 'round, 'round, 'round)
13 Look around, 'round, 'round
14 ('round, 'round, 'round, 'round
     'round, 'round, 'round)
15 Look around (('round)).

16 Dear Prudence, let me see you smile
17 Dear Prudence, like a little child.
18 The clouds will be a daisy chain
19 So let me see you smile again.
20 Dear Prudence, won't you let me see you
     smile?

21 Dear Prudence, won't you come out to play?
22 Dear Prudence, greet the brand new day.
23 The sun is up, the sky is blue
24 It's beautiful and so are you.
25 Dear Prudence, won't you come out to play?

DIG IT
by John Lennon, Paul McCartney,
George Harrison and Richard Starkey

1 Like a rolling stone
2 Like a rolling stone
3 A - like a rolling stone
4 Like the FBI
5 And the CIA
6 And the BBC
7 BB King
8 And Doris Day
9 Matt Busby.

10 Dig it, dig it, dig it, dig it, dig it
11 ((That was Can You Dig It? by
     Georgie Wood))
12 Dig it, dig it, dig it, dig it, dig
     it, dig it, dig it, dig it...
13 ((And now we'd like to do)) Hark the
     Angels Come...

DO YOU WANT TO KNOW A SECRET?
by John Lennon and Paul McCartney

1 You'll never know how much I really love
     you
2 You'll never know how much I really care.

3 Listen, do you want to know a secret?
4 Do you promise not to tell?
5 Whoa closer
6 Let me whisper in your ear
7 Say the words you long to hear
8 I'm in love with you - ooo.

9 Listen (dodahdo) do you want to know a
     secret? (dodahdo)
10 Do you promise not to tell? (dodahdo)
11 Whoa closer, (dodahdo)
12 Let me whisper in your ear, (dodahdo)
13 Say the words you long to hear
14 I'm in love with you - ooo.

15 I've known a secret for the week or two
16 Nobody knows just we two.

17 Listen (dodahdo) do you want to know a
     secret? (dodahdo)
18 Do you promise not to tell? (dodahdo)
19 Whoa closer, (dodahdo)
20 Let me whisper in your ear, (dodahdo)
21 Say the words you long to hear
22 I'm in love with you - ooo
23 Ooo, ooo.

DR. ROBERT
by John Lennon and Paul McCartney

1 Ring my friend I said you'd call, Dr.
     Robert
2 Day or night he'll be there any time at
     all, Dr. Robert
3 Dr. Robert, you're a new and better man
4 He helps you to understand
5 He does everything he can, Dr. Robert.

6 If you're down he'll pick you up, Dr.
     Robert
7 Take a drink from his special cup, Dr.
     Robert.
8 Dr. Robert, he's a man you must believe
9 Helping anyone in need
10 No-one can succeed like Dr. Robert.

11 Well, well, well, you're feeling fine
12 Well, well, well, he'll make you,
     Dr. Robert.

13 My friend works for the National Health,
     Dr. Robert
14 Don't pay money just to see yourself with
     Dr. Robert.
15 Dr. Robert, you're a new and better man
16 He helps you to understand,
17 He does everything he can, Dr. Robert.

18 Well, well, well, you're feeling fine
19 Well, well, well, he'll make you,
     Dr. Robert.

20 Ring my friend I said you'd call, Dr.
     Robert
21 Ring my friend I said you'd call, Dr.
     Robert

DON'T BOTHER ME
by George Harrison

1 Since she's been gone
2 I want no one to talk to me
3 It's not the same
4 But I'm to blame
5 It's plain to see
6 So go away
7 Leave me alone
8 Don't bother me

9 I can't believe
10 That she would leave me on my own
11 It's just not right
12 When every night I'm all alone

13 I've got no time for you right now
14 Don't bother me

15 I know I'll never be the same
16 If I don't get her back again
17 Because I know she'll always be
18 The only girl for me

19 But till she's here
20 Please don't come near
21 Just stay away

22 I'll let you know
23 When she's come home
24 Until that day
25 Don't come around
26 Leave me alone
27 Don't bother me

28 I've got no time for you right now
29 Don't bother me

30 I know I'll never be the same
31 If I don't get her back again
32 Because I know she'll always be
33 The only girl for me

34 But till she's here
35 Please don't come near
36 Just stay away

37 I'll let you know
38 When she's come home
39 Until that day
40 Don't come around
41 Leave me alone
42 Don't bother me

43 Don't bother me
44 Don't bother me
45 Don't bother me
46 Don't bother me.

DON'T LET ME DOWN
by John Lennon and Paul McCartney

1 Don't let me down
2 Don't let me down
3 Don't let me down
4 Don't let me down.

5 Nobody ever loved me like she does
6 Ooo she does, yes she does
7 And if somebody loved me like she do me
8 Ooo she do me, yes she does.

9 Don't let me down
10 Don't let me down
11 Don't let me down
12 Don't let me down.

13 I'm in love for the first time
14 Don't you know it's gonna last
15 It's a love that lasts forever
16 It's a love that has no past (believe me).

17 Don't let me down
18 Don't let me down (ooo)
19 Don't let me down
20 Don't let me down.

21 And from the first time that she really
    done me
22 Ooo she done me, she done me good
23 I guess nobody ever really done me
24 Ooo she done me, she done me good.

25 Don't let me down (hey)
26 Don't let me down
27 Eee ((don't let me down))
28 Don't let me down.

29 Eee - (yeah) aah
30 Don't let me down
31 Don't let me down, let me down
32 Can you dig it?
33 Don't ((hey)) let me down.

DON'T PASS ME BY
by Richard Starkey

1 All right!

2 I listen for your footsteps
3 Coming up the drive
4 Listen for your footsteps
5 But they don't arrive.
6 Waiting for your knock, dear
7 On my old front door,
8 I don't hear it
9 Does it mean you don't love me any more?

10 I hear the clock a - ticking
11 On the mantelshelf
12 See the hands a - moving
13 But I'm by myself.
14 I wonder where you are tonight
15 And why I'm by myself
16 I don't see you
17 Does it mean you don't love me any more?

18 Don't pass me by, don't make me cry,
    don't make me blue
19 'cos you know, darling, I love only you
20 You'll never know it hurt me so
21 How I hate to see you go
22 Don't pass me by - don't make me cry.

23 I'm sorry that I doubted you

24 I was so unfair
25 You were in a car crash
26 And you lost your hair.
27 You said that you would be late
28 About an hour or two
29 I said that's alright I'm waiting here
30 Just waiting to hear from you.

31 Don't pass me by, don't make me cry,
        don't make me blue
32 'cos you know, darling, I love only you
33 You'll never know it hurt me so
34 How I hate to see you go
35 Don't pass me by - don't make me cry.

36 One, two, three, four, five, six,
        seven, eight.

37 Don't pass me by, don't make me cry,
        don't make me blue
38 'cos you know, darling, I love only you
39 You'll never know it hurt me so
40 How I hate to see you go
41 Don't pass me by - don't make me cry.

DRIVE MY CAR
by John Lennon and Paul McCartney

1 Asked a girl what she wanted to be
2 She said baby can't you see?
3 I wanna be famous, a star of the screen
4 But you can do something in between.

5 Baby you can drive my car
6 Yes I'm gonna be a star.
7 Baby you can drive my car
8 And maybe I'll love you.

9 I told that girl that my prospects were good
10 'n' she said baby it's understood
11 Working for peanuts is all very fine
12 But I can show you a better time.

13 Baby you can drive my car
14 Yes I'm gonna be a star.
15 Baby you can drive my car
16 And maybe I'll love you.

17 Beep beep mmm beep beep yeah.

18 Baby you can drive my car
19 Yes I'm gonna be a star.
20 Baby you can drive my car
21 And maybe I'll love you.

22 I told that girl I could start right away
23 And she said listen babe I've got
        something to say
24 I got no car and it's breaking my heart
25 But I've found a driver and that's a start.

26 Baby you can drive my car
27 Yes I'm gonna be star.
28 Baby you can drive my car
29 And maybe I'll love you.

30 Beep beep mmm beep beep yeah
31 Beep beep mmm beep beep yeah
32 Beep beep mmm beep beep yeah
33 Beep beep mmm beep beep yeah
34 Beep beep mmm beep beep yeah.

EIGHT DAYS A WEEK
by John Lennon and Paul McCartney

1 Ooo I need your love babe
2 Guess you know it's true
3 Hope you need my love babe
4 Just like I need you.

5 Hold me, love me
6 Hold me, love me
7 I ain't got nothing but love babe
8 Eight days a week.

9 Love you every day girl
10 Always on my mind
11 One thing I can say girl
12 Love you all the time.

13 Hold me, love me
14 Hold me, love me
15 I ain't got nothing but love girl
16 Eight days a week.

17 Eight days a week I love you
18 Eight days a week is not enough to show
        I care.

19 Ooo I need your love babe
20 Guess you know it's true
21 Hope you need my love babe
22 Just like I need you, oh - oh.

23 Hold me, love me
24 Hold me, love me
25 I ain't got nothing but love babe
26 Eight days a week.

27 Eight days a week I love you
28 Eight days a week is not enough to show
        I care.

29 Love you every day girl
30 Always on my mind
31 One thing I can say girl
32 Love you all the time.

33 Hold me, love me
34 Hold me, love me
35 I ain't got nothing but love babe
36 Eight days a week
37 Eight days a week
38 Eight days a week.

ELEANOR RIGBY
by John Lennon and Paul McCartney

1 Aah, look at all the lonely people.
2 Aah, look at all the lonely people.

3 Eleanor Rigby picks up the rice in the church
4 Where a wedding has been
5 Lives in a dream.
6 Waits at the window
7 Wearing the face that she keeps in a jar
        by the door
8 Who is it for?

9 All the lonely people, where do they all
   come from?
10 All the lonely people, where do they all
   belong?

11 Father McKenzie writing the words of a sermon
12 That no-one will hear
13 No-one comes near.
14 Look at him working
15 Darning his socks in the night when
   there's nobody there
16 What does he care?

17 All the lonely people, where do they all
   come from?
18 All the lonely people, where do they all
   belong?

19 Aah, look at all the lonely people.
20 Aah, look at all the lonely people.

21 Eleanor Rigby died in the church
22 And was buried along with her name
23 Nobody came.
24 Father McKenzie wiping the dirt from his
   hands
25 As he walks from the grave
26 No-one was saved.

27 All the lonely people, where do they all
   come from?
28 ((Aah, look at all the lonely people.))
29 All the lonely people, where do they all
   belong?
30 ((Aah, look at all the lonely people.))

THE END
by John Lennon and Paul McCartney

1 Oh yeah, alright
2 Are you gonna be in my dreams tonight?

3 Love you, love you, love you, love you,
   love you
4 Love you, love you, love you, love you,
   love you
5 Love you, love you, love you, love you,
   love you
6 Love you, love you, love you, love you,
   love you
7 Love you, love you, love you, love you.

8 And in the end
9 The love you take is equal to the love
   you make.
10 Aah!

EVERY LITTLE THING
by John Lennon and Paul McCartney

1 When I'm walking beside her
2 People tell me I'm lucky
3 Yes I know I'm a lucky guy.
4 I remember the first time

5 I was lonely without her
6 Can't stop thinking about her now.

7 Every little thing she does
8 She does for me, yeah
9 And you know the thing she does
10 She does for me, ooo.

11 When I'm with her I'm happy
12 Just to know that she loves me
13 Yes I know that she loves me now.
14 There is one thing I'm sure of
15 I will love her forever
16 For I know love will never die.

17 Every little thing she does
18 She does for me, yeah
19 And you know the thing she does
20 She does for me, ooo.

21 Every little thing she does
22 She does for me, yeah
23 And you know the thing she does
24 She does for me, ooo.

25 Every little thing
26 Every little thing
27 Every little thing.

EVERYBODY'S GOT SOMETHING TO HIDE
EXCEPT ME AND MY MONKEY
by John Lennon and Paul McCartney

1 Come on, come on - come on, come on
2 Come on is such a joy
3 Come on is such a joy
4 Come on is take it easy
5 Come on is take it easy
6 Take it easy, take it easy
7 Everybody's got something to hide 'cept
   for me and my monkey - wuh.

8 The deeper you go, the higher you fly
9 The higher you fly, the deeper you go
10 So come on (come on) come on
11 Come on is such a joy
12 Come on is such a joy
13 Come on is make it easy,
14 Come on is make it easy - wuh.
15 Take it easy, take it easy - wuh
16 Everybody's got something to hide 'cept
   for me and my monkey (yeah - wuh).

17 Your inside is out when your outside is in
18 Your outside is in when your inside is out
19 So come on (wuh), come on (wuh)
20 Come on is such a joy
21 Come on is such a joy
22 Come on is make it easy
23 Come on is make it easy
24 Make it easy (wuh), make it easy (wuh)
25 Everybody's got something to hide 'cept
   for me and my monkey - hey.

26 (Hey - yeah, wuh, yeah - wuh!)
27 Come on, come on, come on, come on,
   come on, come on, come on,...

FIXING A HOLE
by John Lennon and Paul McCartney

1 I'm fixing a hole where the rain gets in
2 And stops my mind from wandering
3 Where it will go.

4 I'm filling the cracks that ran through
    the door
5 And kept my mind from wandering
6 Where it will go.

7 And it really doesn't matter if I'm
    wrong I'm right
8 Where I belong I'm right where I belong.
9 See the people standing there who
    disagree and never win
10 And wonder why they don't get in my door.

11 I'm painting a room in a colourful way
12 And when my mind is wandering
13 There I will go.

14 Ooo-ooo-aah - hey-hey-hey - hey.

15 And it really doesn't matter if I'm
    wrong I'm right
16 Where I belong I'm right where I belong.
17 Silly people run around they worry me
18 And never ask me why they don't get past
    my door.

19 I'm taking the time for a number of things
20 That weren't important yesterday
21 And I still go.

22 Ooo-ooo-ooo-oh.

23 I'm fixing a hole where the rain gets in
24 Stops my mind from wandering
25 Where it will go, where it will go.

26 I'm fixing a hole where the rain gets in
27 Stops my mind from wandering
28 Where it will go.

FLYING
by John Lennon, Paul McCartney,
George Harrison and Richard Starkey

INSTRUMENTAL

THE FOOL ON THE HILL
by John Lennon and Paul McCartney

1 Day after day, alone on a hill
2 The man with the foolish grin is keeping
    perfectly still
3 But nobody wants to know him
4 They can see that he's just a fool

5 And he never gives an answer.

6 But the fool on the hill sees the sun
    going down
7 And the eyes in his head see the world
    spinning round.

8 Well on the way, head in a cloud
9 The man of a thousand voices talking
    perfectly loud
10 But nobody ever hears him
11 Or the sound he appears to make
12 And he never seems to notice.

13 But the fool on the hill sees the sun
    going down
14 And the eyes in his head see the world
    spinning round.

15 And nobody seems to like him
16 They can tell what he wants to do
17 And he never shows his feelings.

18 But the fool on the hill sees the sun
    going down
19 And the eyes in his head see the world
    spinning round.

20 Oh - oh - oh!
21 Round 'n' round 'n' round 'n' round 'n'
    round.

22 He never listens to them
23 He knows that they're the fool
24 They don't like him.

25 The fool on the hill sees the sun going down
26 And the eyes in his head see the world
    spinning round.

27 Oh, round 'n' round 'n' round 'n' round.

28 Oh!

FOR NO--ONE
by John Lennon and Paul McCartney

1 Your day breaks, your mind aches
2 You find that all her words of kindness
    linger on
3 When she no longer needs you.

4 She wakes up, she makes up
5 She takes her time and doesn't feel she
    has to hurry
6 She no longer needs you.

7 And in her eyes you see nothing
8 No sign of love behind the tears cried
    for no-one
9 A love that should have lasted years.

10 You want her, you need her
11 And yet you don't believe her
12 When she says her love is dead
13 You think she needs you.

14 And in her eyes you see nothing
15 No sign of love behind the tears cried
    for no-one
16 A love that should have lasted years.

17 You stay home, she goes out

18 She says that long ago she knew someone
19 But now he's gone, she doesn't need him.

20 Your day breaks, your mind aches
21 There will be times when all the things
22 She said will fill your head
23 You won't forget her.

24 And in her eyes you see nothing
25 No sign of love behind the tears cried
   for no-one
26 A love that should have lasted years.

FOR YOU BLUE
by George Harrison

1 Queen says no to pot-smoking FBI member.

2 Because you're sweet and lovely girl, I
   love you
3 Because you're sweet and lovely girl,
   it's true
4 I love you more than ever girl, I do.

5 I want you in the morning girl, I love you
6 I want you at the moment I feel blue
7 I'm living every moment girl for you.

8 Bop - bop cat bop
9 Go Johnny go.
10 Them old twelve-bar blues.
11 (Hit it)
12 Elmore James got nothing on this baby - heh.

13 I've loved you from the moment I saw you
14 You looked at me, that's all you had to do
15 I feel it now, I hope you feel it too.

16 Because you're sweet and lovely girl, I
   love you
17 Because you're sweet and lovely girl,
   it's true
18 I love you more than ever girl, I do -
   really love blues.

FROM ME TO YOU
by John Lennon and Paul McCartney

1 Da da da, da da dum dum da
2 Da da da, da da dum dum da.

3 If there's anything that you want
4 If there's anything I can do
5 Just call on me and I'll send it along
6 With love from me to you.

7 I got everything that you want
8 Like a heart that's oh so true
9 Just/So call on me and I'll send it along
10 With love from me to you.

11 I got arms that long to hold you
12 And keep you by my side
13 I got lips that long to kiss you

14 And keep you satisfied - ooo!

15 If there's anything that you want
16 If there's anything I can do
17 Just call on me and I'll send it along
18 With love from me to you.

19 From me - to you.

20 Just call on me and I'll send it along
21 With love from me to you.

22 I got arms that long to hold you
23 And keep you by my side
24 I got lips that long to kiss you
25 And keep you satisfied - ooo!

26 If there's anything that you want
27 If there's anything I can do
28 Just call on me and I'll send it along
29 With love from me to you
30 To you, to you, to you.

GET BACK   (45)
by John Lennon and Paul McCartney

1 Jojo was a man who thought he was a loner
2 But he knew it couldn't last.
3 Jojo left his home in Tucson, Arizona
4 For some California grass.

5 Get back, get back
6 Get back to where you once belonged.
7 Get back, get back
8 Get back to where you once belonged.
9 Get back Jojo.

10 Go home.

11 Get back, get back
12 Back to where you once belonged.
13 Get back, get back
14 Back to where you once belonged.
15 Oh get back Jo.

16 Sweet Loretta Martin thought she was a
   woman
17 But she was another man.
18 All the girls around her say she's got it
   coming
19 But she gets it while she can.

20 Oh get back, get back
21 Get back to where you once belonged.
22 Get back, get back
23 Get back to where you once belonged.
24 Get back Loretta (wuh - wuh).

25 Go home.

26 Oh get back, yeah get back
27 Get back to where you once belonged.
28 Yeah get back, get back
29 Get back to where you once belonged.

30 Ooo - ow, ow!

31 Get back Loretta
32 Your mommy's waiting for you
33 Wearing her high-heel shoes
34 And a low-neck sweater.
35 Get back home Loretta.

36 Get back, get back
37 Get back to where you once belonged.
38 Oh get back, get back yeah, yeah
39 Get back - oh yeah.
40 Jojo, Loretta.

GET BACK   (LP)
by John Lennon and Paul McCartney

1 Rosetta.
2 Sweet Moretta Fart she thought she was
      a cleaner
3 But she was a frying pan ((sweet
      Loretta Martin)).
4 Yeah ((Rosetta)).
5 The picker - the picker, picture the
      fingers going (ooo me).
6 OK one, two, three, four.

7 Jojo was a man who thought he was a loner
8 But he knew it couldn't last
9 Jojo left his home in Tucson, Arizona
10 For some California grass.

11 Get back, get back
12 Get back to where you once belonged
13 Get back, get back
14 Get back to where you once belonged
15 Get back Jojo.

16 Go home.

17 Get back, get back
18 Back to where you once belonged
19 Get back, get back
20 Back to where you once belonged
21 Oh get back Jo.

22 Sweet Loretta Martin thought she was a woman
23 But she was another man
24 All the girls around her say she's got it
      coming
25 But she gets it while she can.

26 Oh get back, get back
27 Get back to where you once belonged
28 Get back, get back
29 Get back to where you once belonged.
30 Get back Loretta (wuh - wuh).

31 Go home.

32 Oh get back, yeah, get back
33 Get back to where you once belonged
34 Yeah, get back, get back
35 Get back to where you once belonged
36 Get back - ooo!

37 Thanks folk.
38 I'd like to say thank you on behalf of
      the group and ourselves
39 And I hope we passed the audition.

GETTING BETTER
by John Lennon and Paul McCartney

1 ... Four, five, six...

2 It's getting better all the time.

3 I used to get mad at my school (now I
      can't complain)
4 The teachers who taught me weren't cool
      (now I can't complain)
5 You're holding me down (aah) turning me
      round (aah)
6 Filling me up with your rules.

7 I've got to admit it's getting better
      (better)
8 A little better all the time (it can't
      get no worse)
9 I have to admit it's getting better (better)
10 It's getting better since you've been mine.

11 Me used to be angry young man
12 Me hiding me head in the sand
13 You gave me the word
14 I finally heard
15 You're doing the best that I can.

16 I've got to admit it's getting better
      (better)
17 A little better all the time (it can't
      get no worse)
18 I have to admit it's getting better (better)
19 It's getting better since you've been mine.

20 Getting so much better all the time.

21 It's getting better all the time
22 Better, better, better
23 It's getting better all the time
24 Better, better, better.

25 I used to be cruel to my woman
26 I beat her and kept her apart from the
      things that she loved
27 Man I was mean but I'm changing my scene
28 And I'm doing the best that I can.

29 I admit it's getting better (better)
30 A little better all the time (it can't
      get no worse)
31 Yes I admit it's getting better (better)
32 It's getting better since you've been mine.

33 Getting so much better all the time.

34 It's getting better all the time
35 Better, better, better
36 It's getting better all the time
37 Better, better, better.

38 Getting so much better all the time.

GIRL
by John Lennon and Paul McCartney

1 Is there anybody going to listen to my story
2 All about the girl who came to stay?
3 She's the kind of girl you want so much
      it makes you sorry
4 Still you don't regret a single day.

5 Ah, girl - (girl) girl.

6 When I think of all the times I tried
   so hard to leave her
7 She will turn to me and start to cry
8 And she promises the earth to me and I
   believe her
9 After all this time I don't know why.

10 Ah, girl - (girl) girl.

11 She's the kind of girl who puts you down
12 ((Tit, tit, tit, tit, tit))
13 When friends are there, you feel a fool.
14 ((Tit, tit, tit, tit, tit, tit,
    tit, tit, tit, tit, tit, tit))
15 When you say she's looking good
16 ((Tit, tit, tit, tit))
17 She acts as if it's understood
18 ((Tit, tit, tit, tit))
19 She's cool - ooo-ooo-ooo.
20 ((Tit, tit, tit, tit, tit, tit,
    tit, tit))

21 Girl - (girl) girl.

22 Was she told when she was young that pain
   would lead to pleasure?
23 Did she understand it when they said
24 That a man must break his back to earn
   his day of leisure?
25 Will she still believe it when he's dead?

26 Ah, girl - (girl) girl.

27 Ah, girl - (girl) girl.

GLASS ONION
by John Lennon and Paul McCartney

1 I told you about Strawberry Fields
2 You know the place where nothing is real
3 Well here's another place you can go
4 Where everything flows
5 Looking through the bent-backed tulips
6 To see how the other half live
7 Looking through a glass onion.

8 I told you about the walrus and me - man
9 You know that we're as close as can be - man
10 Well here's another clue for you all:
11 The walrus was Paul
12 Standing on the cast-iron shore - yeah
13 Lady Madonna trying to make ends meet - yeah
14 Looking through a glass onion.

15 Oh yeah, oh yeah, oh yeah! (yeah)
16 Looking through a glass onion.

17 I told you about the fool on the hill
18 I tell you man he living there still
19 Well here's another place you can be
20 Listen to me
21 Fixing the hole in the ocean
22 Trying to make a dove-tail joint - yeah
23 Looking through a glass onion.

GOLDEN SLUMBERS
by John Lennon and Paul McCartney

1 Once there was a way
2 To get back homeward.
3 Once there was a way
4 To get back home.

5 Sleep pretty darling do not cry
6 And I will sing a lullaby.

7 Golden slumbers fill your eyes
8 Smiles awake you when you rise.

9 Sleep pretty darling do not cry
10 And I will sing a lullaby.

11 Once there was a way
12 To get back homeward.
13 Once there was a way
14 To get back home.

15 Sleep pretty darling do not cry
16 And I will sing a lullaby.

GOOD DAY SUNSHINE
by John Lennon and Paul McCartney

1 Good day sunshine, good day sunshine,
   good day sunshine.

2 I need to laugh and when the sun is out
3 I've got something I can laugh about.
4 I feel good in a special way
5 I'm in love and it's a sunny day.

6 Good day sunshine, good day sunshine,
   good day sunshine.

7 We take a walk, the sun is shining down
8 Burns my feet as they touch the ground.

9 Good day sunshine, good day sunshine,
   good day sunshine.

10 Then we lie beneath a shady tree
11 I love her and she's loving me.
12 She feels good (she feels good), she
    knows she's looking fine
13 I'm so proud to know that she is mine.

14 Good day sunshine, good day sunshine,
   good day sunshine.
15 Good day sunshine, good day sunshine,
   good day sunshine.
16 Good day sunshine (good day sunshine)
   (good day sunshine)
17 (Good day sunshine) (good day...

GOOD MORNING, GOOD MORNING
by John Lennon and Paul McCartney

1 Good morning, good morning, good
   morning, good morning, good morning.

2 Nothing to do to save his life call his
    wife in
3 Nothing to say but what a day how's your
    boy been?
4 Nothing to do it's up to you
5 I've got nothing to say but it's OK.

6 Good morning, good morning, good morning.

7 Go in to work don't want to go feeling
    low down
8 Heading for home you start to roam then
    you're in town.

9 Everbody knows there's nothing doing
10 Everything is closed it's like a ruin
11 Everyone you see is half asleep
12 And you're on your own you're in the street.

13 After a while you start to smile now you
    feel cool
14 Then you decide to take a walk by the old
    school
15 Nothing has changed it's still the same
16 I've got nothing to say but it's OK.

17 Good morning, good morning, good morning.

18 People running round it's five o'clock
19 Everywhere in town is getting dark
20 Everyone you see is full of life
21 It's time for tea and meet the wife.

22 Somebody needs to know the time glad that
    I'm here
23 Watching the skirts you start to flirt
    now you're in gear
24 Go to a show you hope she goes
25 I've got nothing to say but it's OK.

26 Good morning, good morning good
27 Good morning, good morning good
28 Good morning, good morning good
29 Good morning, good morning good
30 Good morning, good morning good
31 Good morning, good morning good
32 Good morning, good morning good
33 Good morning, good morning good.

GOOD NIGHT
by John Lennon and Paul McCartney

1 Now it's time to say good night
2 Good night, sleep tight.
3 Now the sun turns out his light
4 Good night, sleep tight.

5 Dream sweet dreams for me
6 Dream sweet dreams for you.

7 Close your eyes and I'll close mine
8 Good night, sleep tight.
9 Now the moon begins to shine
10 Good night, sleep tight.

11 Dream sweet dreams for me
12 Dream sweet dreams for you.

13 Mmm - mmm - mmm - mmm.

14 Close your eyes and I'll close mine
15 Good night, sleep tight.
16 Now the sun turns out his light

17 Good night, sleep tight.

18 Dream sweet dreams for me
19 Dream sweet dreams for you.

20 Good night
21 Good night everybody
22 Everybody everywhere
23 Good night.

GOT TO GET YOU INTO MY LIFE
by John Lennon and Paul McCartney

1 I was alone, I took a ride
2 I didn't know what I would find there
3 Another road where maybe I
4 Could see another kind of mind there.

5 Ooo then I suddenly see you
6 Ooo did I tell you I need you
7 Every single day of my life?

8 You didn't run, you didn't lie
9 You knew I wanted just to hold you
10 And had you gone, you knew in time
11 We'd meet again for I had told you.

12 Ooo you were meant to be near me
13 Ooo and I want you to hear me
14 Say we'll be together every day.

15 Got to get you into my life.

16 What can I do, what can I be?
17 When I'm with you I want to stay there
18 If I'm true I'll never leave
19 And if I do I know the way there.

20 Ooo then I suddenly see you
21 Ooo did I tell you I need you
22 Every single day of my life?

23 Got to get you into my life.

24 I got to get you into my life.

25 I was alone, I took a ride
26 I didn't know what I would find there
27 Another road where maybe I
28 Could see another kind of mind there.

29 Then suddenly I see you
30 Did I tell you I need you
31 Every single day...

HAPPINESS IS A WARM GUN
by John Lennon and Paul McCartney

1 She's not a girl who misses much
2 Do do do do do do, oh yeah.

3 She's well acquainted with the touch of
    the velvet hand
4 Like a lizard on a window-pane.
5 The man in the crowd with the

multicoloured mirrors on his hobnail
    boots
6 Lying with his eyes while his hands are
    busy working overtime
7 A soap impression of his wife which he ate
8 And donated to the National Trust.

9 I need a fix 'cos I'm going down
10 Down to the bits that I left uptown
11 I need a fix 'cos I'm going down.

12 Mother Superior jump the gun
13 Mother Superior jump the gun
14 Mother Superior jump the gun
15 Mother Superior jump the gun
16 Mother Superior jump the gun
17 Mother Superior jump the gun.

18 Happiness ((happiness)) is a warm gun
19 (Bang, bang, shoot, shoot)
20 Happiness ((happiness)) is a warm gun,
    momma
21 ((Bang, bang, shoot, shoot)),
22 When I hold you in my arms ((oh, yeah))
23 And I feel my finger on your trigger
    ((oh, yeah))
24 I know nobody can do me no harm ((oh,
    yeah))
25 Because - (happiness) is a warm gun, momma
26 ((Bang, bang, shoot, shoot))
27 Happiness ((happiness)) is a warm gun,
    yes it is
28 ((Bang, bang, shoot, shoot))
29 Happiness is a warm, yes it is - gun
30 ((Happiness - bang, bang, shoot,
    shoot))
31 Well, don't you know that happiness
    ((happiness))
32 Is a warm gun, momma ((is a warm gun,
    yeah)).

A HARD DAY'S NIGHT
by John Lennon and Paul McCartney

1 It's been a hard day's night
2 And I been working like a dog
3 It's been a hard day's night
4 I should be sleeping like a log
5 But when I get home to you
6 I find the things that you do
7 Will make me feel alright.

8 You know I work all day
9 To get you money to buy you things
10 And it's worth it just to hear you say
11 You're gonna give me everything
12 So why on earth should I moan
13 'cos when I get you alone
14 You know I feel OK.

15 When I'm home everything seems to be right
16 When I'm home feeling you holding me
    tight, tight, yeah.

17 It's been a hard day's night
18 And I been working like a dog
19 It's been a hard day's night,
20 I should be sleeping like a log
21 But when I get home to you
22 I find the things that you do
23 Will make me feel alright.
24 (Ow)

25 So why on earth should I moan
26 'cos when I get you alone
27 You know I feel OK.

28 When I'm home everything seems to be right
29 When I'm home feeling you holding me
    tight, tight, yeah.

30 Oh, It's been a hard day's night
31 And I been working like a dog
32 It's been a hard day's night
33 I should be sleeping like a log
34 But when I get home to you
35 I find the things that you do
36 Will make me feel alright
37 You know I feel alright
38 You know I feel alright.

HELLO GOODBYE
by John Lennon and Paul McCartney

1 You say yes, I say no
2 You say stop and I say go, go, go.

3 Oh no
4 You say goodbye and I say hello - hello,
    hello.

5 I don't know why you say goodbye, I say
    hello - hello, hello.
6 I don't know why you say goodbye, I say
    hello.

7 I say hi!/high, you say 'lo/low
8 You say why and I say I don't know.

9 Oh no,
10 You say goodbye and I say hello - hello,
    hello.
11 ((Hello, goodbye, hello, goodbye,
    hello, goodbye))

12 I don't know why you say goodbye, I say
    hello - hello, hello
13 ((hello, goodbye, hello, goodbye))
14 I don't know why you say goodbye, I say
    hello
15 ((Hello, goodbye, hello, goodbye)).

16 Why, why, why, why, why, why do you say
17 Goodbye, goodbye, 'bye, 'bye, 'bye?

18 Oh no
19 You say goodbye and I say hello - hello,
    hello.

20 I don't know why you say goodbye, I say
    hello - hello, hello
21 I don't know why you say goodbye, I say
    hello.

22 You say yes, I say no
23 ((I say yes but I may mean no))
24 You say stop but I say go, go, go
25 ((I can stay till it's time to go)).

26 Oh - oh no
27 You say goodbye and I say hello - hello,
    hello.

28 I don't know why you say goodbye, I say

hello - hello, hello
29 I don't know why you say goodbye, I say
   hello - hello, hello
30 I don't know why you say goodbye, I say
   hello - hello.

31 Hela, hello
32 Hela, hello
33 Cha, cha, cha
34 Hela, hello
35 Ooo - hela, hello (hela)
36 Hela, hello
37 Cha, cha, cha
38 Hela, hello
39 Ooo - hela, hello
40 (Uh) cha, cha
41 Hela, hello.
42 Cha, cha
43 Hela, hello.

HELP!
by John Lennon and Paul McCartney

1 Help!
2 I need somebody
3 Help!
4 Not just anybody
5 Help!
6 You know I need someone
7 Help!

8 When ((when)) I was younger ((when I
   was young))
9 So much younger than today
10 I never needed ((never needed))
   anybody's help in any way
11 But now ((but now)) these days are gone
   ((these days are gone))
12 I'm not so self-assured
13 Now I find ((and now I find)) I've
   changed my mind
14 And opened up the doors.

15 Help me if you can, I'm feeling down
16 And I do appreciate you being round
17 Help me get my feet back on the ground
18 Won't you please please help me?

19 And now ((now)) my life has changed
   ((my life has changed))
20 In oh so many ways
21 My independence ((my independence))
   seems to vanish in the haze
22 But ((but)) every now and then ((now
   and then)) I feel so insecure
23 I know that I ((I know that I)) just
   need you like
24 I've never done before.

25 Help me if you can, I'm feeling down
26 And I do appreciate you being round
27 Help me get my feet back on the ground
28 Won't you please please help me?

29 When I was younger, so much younger
   than today
30 I never needed anybody's help in any way
31 But now ((now)) these days are gone
   ((these days are gone))
32 I'm not so self-assured
33 Now I find ((and now I find)) I've
   changed my mind
34 And opened up the doors.

35 Help me if you can, I'm feeling down
36 And I do appreciate you being round
37 Help me get my feet back on the ground
38 Won't you please please help me?

39 Help me, help me - ooo-mmm.

HELTER--SKELTER
by John Lennon and Paul McCartney

1 When I get to the bottom I go back to
   the top of the slide
2 Where I stop and I turn and I go for a
   ride
3 Till I get to the bottom and I see you
   again - yeah, yeah, yeah.

4 A - do you, don't you want me to love you?
5 I'm coming down fast but I'm miles above
   you
6 Tell me, tell me, tell me, come on
   tell me the answer
7 Well, you may be a lover, but you ain't
   no dancer.
8 (Helter-skelter, helter-skelter)

9 Helter-skelter, helter-skelter,
   helter-skelter - yeah.

10 Wuh!

11 A - will you, won't you want me to make you?
12 I'm coming down fast but don't let me
   break you
13 Tell me, tell me, tell me the answer
14 'cos you may be a lover, but you ain't
   no dancer.
15 (Helter-skelter, helter-skelter)

16 Look out helter-skelter, helter-skelter,
   helter-skelter - oh.

17 Look out 'cos here she comes (heh heh heh).

18 When I get to the bottom I go back to
   the top of the slide
19 And I stop and I turn and I go for a ride
20 And I get to the bottom and I see you
   again - yeah, yeah, yeah.

21 Well, do you, don't you want me to make
   you?
22 I'm coming down fast but don't let me
   break you
23 Tell me, tell me, tell me your answer
24 'cos you may be a lover, but you ain't
   no dancer.
25 (Helter-skelter, helter-skelter)

26 Look out helter-skelter, helter-skelter,
   helter-skelter.

27 Well, look out helter-skelter.
28 She's coming down fast
29 Yes she is, yes she is.
30 Coming down fast (oh I hear my baby
   speaking - ooo)...

31 ... Ah (how was that?)
32 I got blisters on my fingers!

HER MAJESTY
by John Lennon and Paul McCartney

1 Her Majesty's a pretty nice girl
2 But she doesn't have a lot to say.

3 Her Majesty's a pretty nice girl
4 But she changes from day to day.

5 I wanna tell her that I love her a lot
6 But I gotta get a bellyfull of wine.

7 Her Majesty's a pretty nice girl
8 Someday I'm gonna make her mine - oh yeah
9 Someday I'm gonna make her mine.

HERE COMES THE SUN
by George Harrison

1 Here comes the sun (do-n-do-do)
2 Here comes the sun
3 'n' I say, it's alright.

4 Little darling, it's been a long, cold
     lonely winter.
5 Little darling, it feels like years
     since it's been here.

6 Here comes the sun (do-n-do-do)
7 Here comes the sun
8 'n' I say, it's alright.

9 Little darling, the smiles returning to
     the faces.
10 Little darling, it seems like years
     since it's been here.

11 Here comes the sun, here comes the sun
12 'n' I say, it's alright.

13 Sun, sun, sun, here it comes
14 Sun, sun, sun, here it comes
15 Sun, sun, sun, here it comes
16 Sun, sun, sun, here it comes
17 Sun, sun, sun, here it comes.

18 Little darling, I feel that ice is
     slowly melting.
19 Little darling, it seems like years
     since it's been clear.

20 Here comes the sun (do-n-do-do)
21 Here comes the sun
22 'n' I say, it's alright.

23 Here comes the sun (do-n-do-do)
24 Here comes the sun
25 It's alright
26 It's alright.

HERE, THERE AND EVERYWHERE
by John Lennon and Paul McCartney

1 To lead a better life, I need my love
     to be here.

2 Here, making each day of the year
3 Changing my life with a wave of her hand
4 Nobody can deny that there's something there.

5 There, running my hands through her hair
6 Both of us thinking how good it can be
7 Someone is speaking but she doesn't know
     he's there.

8 I want her everywhere
9 And if she's beside me I know I need
     never care
10 But to love her is to need her everywhere.

11 Knowing that love is to share
12 Each one believing that love never dies
13 Watching her eyes and hoping I'm always
     there.

14 I want her everywhere
15 And if she's beside me I know I need
     never care
16 But to love her is to need her everywhere.

17 Knowing that love is to share
18 Each one believing that love never dies
19 Watching her eyes and hoping I'm always
     there.

20 I will be there and everywhere,
21 Here, there and everywhere.

HEY BULLDOG
by John Lennon and Paul McCartney

1 Sheep dog standing in the rain
2 Bull-frog doing it again
3 Some kind of happiness is measured out in
     miles
4 What makes you think you're something
     special when you smile?

5 Childlike, no-one understands
6 Jack-knife in your sweaty hands
7 Some kind of innocence is measured out in
     years
8 You don't know what it's like to listen
     to your fears.

9 You can talk to me
10 You can talk to me
11 You can talk to me
12 If you're lonely you can talk to me.

13 Big man (yeah?) walking in the park
14 Wigwam frightened of the dark
15 Some kind of solitude is measured out in you
16 You think you know me but you haven't got
     a clue.

17 You can talk to me
18 You can talk to me
19 You can talk to me
20 If you're lonely you can talk to me - hey!

21 Woof!

22 Hey bulldog (woof), hey bulldog, hey
    bulldog, hey bulldog.

23 Hey man what's that noise? (woof)
24 What do you say?
25 I say woof
26 Do you know any more?
27 Woof - aah! ha ha ha
28 You've got it, that's great, you've
    done it ((ha ha ha ha ha))
29 That's it man (wuh)
30 That's it, you've got it ((ha ha ha ha))
31 Don't look at me man (ha ha ha ha)
32 I only have grandchildren (yahoo ha ha
    ha ha ha ha)
33 Quiet now quiet (OK) quiet
34 Hey bulldog!

HEY JUDE
by John Lennon and Paul McCartney

1 Hey Jude, don't make it bad
2 Take a sad song and make it better
3 Remember to let her into your heart
4 Then you can start to make it better.

5 Hey Jude, don't be afraid
6 You were made to go out and get her
7 The minute you let her under your skin
8 Then you begin to make it better.

9 And any time you feel the pain
10 Hey Jude, refrain
11 Don't carry the world upon your shoulder.
12 For well you know that it's a fool who
    plays it cool
13 By making his world a little colder.

14 Nah nah nah nah nah, nah nah nah nah.

15 Hey Jude, don't let me down
16 You have found her, now go and get her
    (let it out and let it in)
17 Remember (hey Jude) to let her into
    your heart
18 Then you can start to make it better.

19 So let it out and let it in
20 Hey Jude, begin
21 You're waiting for someone to perform with.
22 And don't you know that it's just you
23 Hey Jude, you'll do
24 The movement you need is on your shoulder.

25 Nah nah nah nah nah, nah nah nah nah, yeah.

26 Hey Jude, don't make it bad
27 Take a sad song and make it better
28 Remember to let her under your skin (oh)
29 Then you'll begin ((let it out)) to
    make it better

30 Better, better, better, better ((make
    it Jude)), better.

31 Oh yeah - nah nah nah, nah - nah - nah - nah
32 ((yeah yeah yeah yeah yeah yeah))
33 (Take it Jude) nah - nah - nah - nah,
    hey Jude.
34 Nah nah nah, nah - nah - nah - nah

35 Nah - nah - nah - nah, hey Jude.
36 Nah nah nah, nah - nah - nah - nah (ow)
37 Nah - nah - nah - nah, hey Jude.
38 Nah nah nah, nah - nah - nah - nah
    (take it Jude)
39 Nah - nah - nah - nah, hey Jude
40 Jude, Judy, Judy, Judy, Judy,
    Judy).
41 (Ow - ow) nah nah nah, nah - nah - nah
    - nah,
42 (Ow - ooo nah nah nah) nah - nah - nah
    - nah, hey Jude
43 (Jude, Jude, Jude, Jude, Jude).
44 Nah nah nah, nah - nah - nah - nah
    (yeah, yeah, yeah)
45 Nah - nah - nah - nah, hey Jude.
46 (Well you know you can make it, Jude,
    you've just gotta break it.)
47 Nah nah nah, nah - nah - nah - nah
    ((don't make it bad, Jude))
48 (Take a sad song and make it better)
49 Nah - nah - nah - nah, hey Jude (Jude,
    hey Jude, wah!).
50 Nah nah nah, nah - nah - nah - nah (oh
    Jude)
51 Nah - nah - nah - nah, hey Jude (hey
    hey hey hey hey hey hey).
52 Nah nah nah, nah - nah - nah - nah (hey
    hey hey hey)
53 Nah - nah - nah - nah, hey Jude.
54 (Jude Jude Jude Jude Jude Jude -
    yeah yeah yeah yeah yeah)
55 Nah nah nah, nah - nah - nah - nah
56 Nah - nah - nah - nah, hey Jude.
57 Nah nah nah, nah - nah - nah - nah
58 Nah - nah - nah - nah, hey Jude.
59 (Nah nah nah nah nah nah nah nah...)
60 Nah nah nah, nah - nah - nah - nah
61 Nah - nah - nah - nah, hey Jude (yeah).
62 Nah nah nah, nah - nah - nah - nah
63 Nah - nah - nah - nah, hey Jude.
64 Nah nah nah, nah - nah - nah - nah
    ((hey hey hey hey))
65 (Take it Jude) nah - nah - nah - nah,
    hey Jude.
66 ((Yeah - yeah yeah yeah yeah yeah yeah -
    yeah yeah -
67 yeah yeah yeah - ha ha ha ha ha))
68 Nah nah nah, nah - nah - nah - nah
69 Nah - nah - nah - nah, hey Jude (Jude,
    Jude ma ma ma ma ma ma)
70 Nah nah nah, nah - nah - nah - nah (oh)
71 Nah - nah - nah - nah, hey Jude (ooo).
72 Nah nah nah, nah - nah - nah - nah (oh)
73 Nah - nah - nah - nah, hey Jude (ooo -
    ooo).
74 Well then nah nah nah, nah - nah - nah
    - nah
75 Nah - nah - nah - nah, hey Jude.
76 Nah nah nah, nah - nah - nah - nah.

HOLD ME TIGHT
by John Lennon and Paul McCartney

1 It feels so right now
2 Hold me tight
3 Tell me I'm the only one
4 And then I might
5 Never be the lonely one.

6 So hold (hold) me tight (me tight)
7 Tonight (tonight) tonight (tonight)
8 It's you, you, you, you - ooo-ooo.

9 Hold me tight
10 Let me go on loving you
11 Tonight tonight
12 Making love to only you.

13 So hold (hold) me tight (me tight)
14 Tonight (tonight) tonight (tonight)
15 It's you, you, you, you - ooo-ooo.

16 Don't know what it means to hold you tight
17 Being here alone tonight with you.

18 It feels so right now
19 So hold me tight
20 Tell me I'm the only one
21 And then I might
22 Never be the lonely one.

23 So hold (hold) me tight (me tight)
24 Tonight (tonight) tonight (tonight)
25 It's you, you, you, you - ooo-ooo.

26 Don't know what it means to hold you tight
27 Being here alone tonight with you.

28 It feels so right now
29 So hold me tight
30 Let me go on loving you
31 Tonight tonight
32 Making love to only you.

33 So hold (hold) me tight (me tight)
34 Tonight (tonight) tonight (tonight)
35 It's you, you, you, you - ooo-ooo,
36 You - ooo.

HONEY PIE
by John Lennon and Paul McCartney

1 She was a working girl
2 North of England way
3 Now she's hit the big time
4 In the USA
5 And if she could only hear me
6 This is what I'd say:

7 Honey Pie you are making me crazy
8 I'm in love but I'm lazy
9 So won't you please come home.

10 Oh, Honey Pie my position is tragic
11 Come and show me the magic
12 Of your Hollywood song.

13 You became a legend of the silver screen
14 And now the thought of meeting you
15 Makes me weak in the knee.

16 Oh, Honey Pie you are driving me frantic
17 Sail across the Atlantic
18 To be where you belong.

19 Honey Pie come back to me - ooo.

20 Yeah!

21 I light the light - yeah, ooo - ha.

22 I like this kinda hot kinda music, hot
      kinda music
23 Play it to me
24 Play it to me Hollywood blues.

25 Will the wind that blew her boat
26 Across the sea
27 Kindly send her sailing back to me
28 Tee - tee - tee.

29 Now Honey Pie you are making me crazy
30 I'm in love but I'm lazy
31 So won't you please come home.

32 Come, come back to me Honey Pie
33 Ha-ha-ha - do-do-do - oh-oh
34 Oh-oh-oh - oh - oh
35 Honey Pie, Honey Pie.

I AM THE WALRUS
by John Lennon and Paul McCartney

1 I am he as you are he as you are me and
      we are all together

2 See how they run like pigs from a gun,
      see how they fly
3 I'm crying

4 Sitting on a cornflake, waiting for the
      van to come
5 Corporation T-shirt, stupid bloody Tuesday
6 Man you been a naughty boy, you let your
      face grow long

7 I am the eggman (goo) they are the
      eggmen (goo) I am the walrus
8 Goo goo g'joob

9 Mr. City policeman sitting pretty little
      policemen in a row
10 See how they fly like Lucy in the sky,
      see how they run
11 I'm crying - I'm crying (goo), I'm
      crying, I'm crying

12 Yellow matter custard, dripping from a
      dead dog's eye
13 Crabalocker fishwife, pornographic priestess
14 Boy, you been a naughty girl, you let
      your knickers down

15 I am the eggman (goo) they are the
      eggmen (goo) I am the walrus
16 Goo goo g'joob

17 Sitting in an English garden waiting for
      the sun
18 If the sun don't come you get a tan from
      standing in the English rain

19 I am the eggman, they are the eggmen,
      I am the walrus
20 Goo goo g'joob, g'goo goo g'joob

21 Expert texpert, choking smokers, don't
      you think the joker laughs at you?
22 Ho ho ho, he he he, ha ha ha
23 See how they smile, like pigs in a sty,
'   see how they snied
24 I'm crying

25 Semolina pilchard climbing up the Eiffel
      Tower
26 Elementary penguin singing Hare Krishna
27 Man you should have seen them kicking
      Edgar Allan Poe

28 I am the eggman (goo) they are the
    eggmen (goo) I am the walrus (goo)
29 Goo goo g'joob, g'goo goo g'joob
30 Goo goo g'joob, g'goo goo g'joob g'goo

31 Joob - joob - joob
32 Joob - joob - joob
33 Joob - joob
34 Joob - joob
35 Umpa, umpa, stick it up your jumper
    ((joob - joob))
36 Umpa, umpa, stick it up your jumper.

I CALL YOUR NAME
by John Lennon and Paul McCartney

1 I call your name, but you're not there
2 Was I to blame for being unfair?
3 Oh, I can't sleep at night since you've
    been gone
4 I never weep at night, I can't go on.

5 Don't you know I can't take it?
6 I don't know who can
7 I'm not gonna make it
8 I'm not that kinda man.

9 Oh, I can't sleep at night, but just
    the same
10 I never weep at night, I call your name.

11 Ow!

12 Don't you know I can't take it?
13 I don't know who can
14 I'm not gonna make it
15 I'm not that kinda man.

16 Oh, I can't sleep at night, but just
    the same
17 I never weep at night, I call your name
18 I call your name, I call your name
    (wuh) I call your name.

(I) DIG A PONY
by John Lennon and Paul McCartney

1 Yeah OK.
2 A - one, two, three.
3 Hold it - aah
4 (hold it)
5 A - one, two.

6 I dig a pony
7 Well you can celebrate anything you want
8 Yes you can celebrate anything you want.

9 Oh I do a road hog
10 Well you can penetrate any place you go
11 Yes you can penetrate any place you go
12 I told you so.

13 All I want is you

14 Everything has got to be just like you
    want it to
15 Because.

16 I pick a moon dog
17 Well you can radiate everything you are
18 Yes you can radiate everything you are.

19 Oh now I roll a stony
20 Well you can imitate everyone you know
21 Yes you can imitate everyone you know
22 I told you so.

23 All I want is you
24 Everything has got to be just like you
    want it to
25 Because. (ooo - ow)

26 Oh now I feel the wind blow
27 Well you can indicate everything you see
28 Yes you can indicate anything you see.

29 Oh now I roll a lorry
30 Well you can syndicate any boat you rode/rowed
31 Yeah you can syndicate any boat you rode/rowed
32 I told you so.

33 All I want is you
34 Everything has got to be just like you
    want it to
35 Because.

36 Ooo!

37 Thank you, brothers.
38 Me hand's getting - a too cold to play a
    chord now.

I DON'T WANT TO SPOIL THE PARTY
by John Lennon and Paul McCartney

1 I don't wanna spoil the party so I'll go
2 I would hate my disappointment to show
3 There's nothing for me here so I will
    disappear
4 If she turns up while I'm gone please
    let me know.

5 I've had a drink or two and I don't care
6 There's no fun in what I do when she's
    not there
7 I wonder what went wrong I've waited far
    too long
8 I think I'll take a walk and look for her.

9 Though tonight she's made me sad
10 I still love her.
11 If I find her I'll be glad
12 I still love her.

13 I don't wanna spoil the party so I'll go
14 I would hate my disappointment to show
15 There's nothing for me here so I will
    disappear
16 If she turns up while I'm gone please
    let me know.

17 Hey! - wuh!

18 Though tonight she's made me sad
19 I still love her.
20 If I find her I'll be glad
21 I still love her.

22 Though I've had a drink or two and I
    don't care
23 There's no fun in what I do if she's not
    there
24 I wonder what went wrong I've waited far
    too long
25 But I think I'll take a walk and look
    for her.

I FEEL FINE
by John Lennon and Paul McCartney

1 Baby's good to me, you know
2 She's happy as can be, you know, she
    said so
3 I'm in love with her and I feel fine.

4 Baby says she's mine, you know
5 She tells me all the time, you know,
    she said so
6 I'm in love with her and I feel fine.

7 I'm so glad that she's my little girl
8 She's so glad she's telling all the world
9 That her baby buys her things, you know
10 He buys her diamond rings, you know,
    she said so
11 She's in love with me and I feel fine
    (ooo).

12 Baby said she's mine, you know
13 She tells me all the time, you know,
    she said so
14 I'm in love with her and I feel fine.

15 I'm so glad that she's my little girl
16 She's so glad she's telling all the world
17 That her baby buys her things, you know
18 He buys her diamond rings, you know,
    she said so
19 She's in love with me and I feel fine
20 She's in love with me and I feel fine.

21 Ooo
22 Ooo (wuh - wuh, wuh - wuh, wuh).

I ME MINE
by George Harrison

1 All through the day
2 I me mine, I me mine, I me mine.
3 All through the night
4 I me mine, I me mine, I me mine.

5 Now they're frightened of leaving it
6 Everyone's weaving it
7 Coming off stronger all the time
8 All through the day
9 I me mine.

10 I me me mine
11 I me me mine
12 I me me mine
13 I me me mine.

14 All I can hear
15 I me mine, I me mine, I me mine.
16 Even those tears
17 I me mine, I me mine, I me mine.

18 No-one's frightened of playing it
19 Everyone's saying it
20 Flowing more freely than wine
21 All through the day
22 I me mine.

23 I me me mine
24 I me me mine
25 I me me mine
26 I me me mine.

27 All I can hear
28 I me mine, I me mine, I me mine.
29 Even those tears
30 I me mine, I me mine, I me mine.

31 No-one's frightened of playing it
32 Everyone's saying it
33 Flowing more freely than wine
34 All through your life
35 I me mine.

I NEED YOU
by George Harrison

1 You don't realise how much I need you
2 Love you all the time and never leave you
3 Please come on back to me
4 I'm lonely as can be
5 I need you.

6 Said you had a thing or two to tell me
7 How was I to know you would upset me?
8 I didn't realise
9 As I looked in your eyes
10 You told me
11 Oh yes, you told me
12 You don't want my loving any more
13 That's when it hurt me
14 And feeling like this
15 I just can't go on any more.

16 Please remember how I feel about you
17 I could never really live without you
18 So come on back and see
19 Just what you mean to me
20 I need you.

21 But when you told me
22 You don't want my loving any more
23 That's when it hurt me
24 And feeling like this
25 I just can't go on any more.

26 Please remember how I feel about you
27 I could never really live without you
28 So come on back and see
29 Just what you mean to me
30 I need you
31 I need you
32 I need you.

I SAW HER STANDING THERE
by John Lennon and Paul McCartney

1 One, two, three, four.
2 Well, she was just seventeen
3 You know what I mean
4 And the way she looked was way beyond
    compare.

5 So how could I dance with another
6 Ooh when I saw her standing there.

7 Well she looked at me, and I, I could
    see
8 That before too long I'd fall in love
    with her.

9 She wouldn't dance with another
10 Whoa when I saw her standing there.

11 Well my heart went boom when I crossed
    that room
12 And I held her hand in mine.

13 Well we danced through the night
14 And we held each other tight
15 And before too long I fell in love with her

16 Now I'll never dance with another
17 Whoa since/when I saw her standing there.
    (hey! aah!)

18 Well my heart went boom when I crossed
    that room
19 And I held her hand in mine.

20 Oh (wuh!) we danced through the night
21 And we held each other tight
22 And before too long I fell in love with her.

23 Now I'll never dance with another
24 Oh since I saw her standing there.
25 Whoa since I saw her standing there
26 Yeah, well since I saw her standing there.

I SHOULD HAVE KNOWN BETTER
by John Lennon and Paul McCartney

1 I should have known better with a girl
    like you
2 That I would love everything that you do
3 And I do, hey hey hey, and I do.

4 Whoa, whoa, I never realised what a
    kiss could be
5 This could only happen to me
6 Can't you see, can't you see?
7 That when I tell you that I love you, oh
8 You're gonna say you love me too, oh.

9 And when I ask you to be mine
10 You're gonna say you love me too.

11 So - oh, I should have realised a lot
    of things before

12 If this is love you've got to give me more
13 Give me more, hey hey hey, give me more.

14 Whoa, whoa, I never realised what a
    kiss could be
15 This could only happen to me
16 Can't you see, can't you see?
17 That when I tell you that I love you, oh
18 You're gonna say you love me too, oh.

19 And when I ask you to be mine
20 You're gonna say you love me too.

21 You love me too
22 You love me too
23 You love me too.

I WANNA BE YOUR MAN
by John Lennon and Paul McCartney

1 I wanna be your lover baby
2 I wanna be your man.
3 I wanna be your lover baby
4 I wanna be your man.

5 Love you like no other baby
6 Like no other can.
7 Love you like no other baby
8 Like no other can.

9 I wanna be your man
10 I wanna be your man
11 I wanna be your man
12 I wanna be your man.

13 Tell me that you love me baby
14 Let me understand.
15 Tell me that you love me baby
16 I wanna be your man.

17 I wanna be your lover baby
18 I wanna be your man.
19 I wanna be your lover baby
20 I wanna be your man.

21 I wanna be your man
22 I wanna be your man
23 I wanna be your man
24 I wanna be your man.

25 Wow (ow) - oh
26 Hey!
27 Oh - oh!
28 Ow!
29 Whoa!

30 I wanna be your lover baby
31 I wanna be your man.
32 I wanna be your lover baby
33 I wanna be your man.

34 Love you like no other baby
35 Like no other can (ooo).
36 Love you like no other baby
37 Like no other can.

38 I wanna be your man
39 I wanna be your man
40 I wanna be your man
41 I wanna be your man.

42 Ow! - wuh!

43 I wanna be your man (oh)
44 I wanna be your man (come on!)
45 I wanna be your man (wuh - wuh)
46 I wanna be your man.

I WANT TO HOLD YOUR HAND
by John Lennon and Paul McCartney

1 Oh yeah, I'll tell you something
2 I think you'll understand
3 When I say that something
4 I wanna hold your hand
5 I wanna hold your hand
6 I wanna hold your hand.

7 Oh please say to me
8 And/You'll let me be your man
9 And please say to me
10 You'll let me hold your hand
11 And/You'll let me hold your hand
12 I wanna hold your hand.

13 And when I touch you
14 I feel happy inside
15 It's such a feeling
16 That my love
17 I can't hide
18 I can't hide
19 I can't hide.

20 Yeah, you've got that something
21 I think you'll understand
22 When I say that something
23 I wanna hold your hand
24 I wanna hold your hand
25 I wanna hold your hand.

26 And when I touch you
27 I feel happy inside
28 It's such a feeling
29 That my love
30 I can't hide
31 I can't hide
32 I can't hide.

33 Yeah, you've got that something
34 I think you'll understand
35 When I feel that something
36 I wanna hold your hand
37 I wanna hold your hand
38 I wanna hold your hand
39 I wanna hold your hand.

I WANT TO TELL YOU
by George Harrison

1 I want to tell you
2 My head is filled with things to say
3 When you're here
4 All those words they seem to slip away.

5 When I get near you
6 The games begin to drag me down

7 It's alright
8 I'll make you maybe next time around.

9 But if I seem to act unkind
10 It's only me, it's not my mind
11 That is confusing things.

12 I want to tell you
13 I feel hung up and I don't know why
14 I don't mind, I could wait forever
15 I've got time.

16 Sometimes I wish I knew you well
17 Then I could speak my mind and tell you
18 Maybe you'd understand.

19 I want to tell you
20 I feel hung up and I don't know why
21 I don't mind, I could wait forever
22 I've got time.

23 I've got time.

24 I've got time.

I WANT YOU (SHE'S SO HEAVY)
by John Lennon and Paul McCartney

1 I want you
2 I want you so bad
3 I want you
4 I want you so bad
5 It's driving me mad
6 It's driving me mad

7 I want you
8 I want you so bad, babe
9 I want you
10 I want you so bad
11 It's driving me mad
12 It's driving me

13 I want you
14 I want you so bad, babe
15 I want you
16 I want you so bad
17 It's driving me mad
18 It's driving me mad

19 I want you
20 I want you so bad
21 I want you
22 I want you so bad
23 It's driving me mad
24 It's driving me

25 She's so - heavy (heavy - heavy - heavy)

26 She's so - heavy
27 She's so heavy (heavy - heavy)

28 I want you
29 I want you so bad
30 I want you
31 I want you so bad
32 It's driving me mad
33 It's driving me mad

34 I want you
35 You know I want you so bad, babe
36 I want you
37 You know I want you so bad
38 It's driving me mad

39 It's driving me mad

40 Yeah!

41 She's so -.

I WILL
by John Lennon and Paul McCartney

1 Who knows how long I've loved you?
2 You know I love you still.
3 Will I wait a lonely lifetime?
4 If you want me to, I will.

5 For if I ever saw you
6 I didn't catch your name
7 But it never really mattered
8 I will always feel the same.

9 Love you forever and forever
10 Love you with all my heart
11 Love you whenever we're together
12 Love you when we're apart.

13 And when at last I find you
14 Your song will fill the air
15 Sing it loud so I can hear you
16 Make it easy to be near you
17 For the things you do endear you to me - aah
18 You know I will - I will.

19 Mmm, mmm - da, da, da, da, da, da, da.

IF I FELL
by John Lennon and Paul McCartney

1 If I fell in love with you
2 Would you promise to be true
3 And help me understand?

4 'cos I've been in love before
5 And I found that love was more
6 Than just holding hands.

7 If I give my heart to you
8 I must be sure from the very start
9 That you would love me more than her.

10 If I trust in you
11 Oh please, don't run and hide
12 If I love you too
13 Oh please, don't hurt my pride like her.

14 'cos I couldn't stand the pain
15 And I would be sad
16 If our new love was in vain.

17 So I hope you see
18 That I would love to love you
19 And that she will cry
20 When she learns we are two.

21 'cos I couldn't stand the pain
22 And I would be sad
23 If our new love was in vain.

24 So I hope you see
25 That I would love to love you
26 And that she will cry
27 When she learns we are two.

28 If I fell in love with you.

IF I NEEDED SOMEONE
by George Harrison

1 If I needed someone to love
2 You're the one that I'd be thinking of
3 If I needed someone.

4 If I had some more time to spend
5 Then I guess I'd be with you my friend
6 If I needed someone.

7 Had you come some other day
8 Then it might not have been like this
9 But you see now I'm too much in love.

10 Carve your number on my wall
11 And maybe you will get a call from me
12 If I needed someone.

13 Aah, aah, aah, aah.

14 If I had some more time to spend
15 Then I guess I'd be with you my friend
16 If I needed someone.

17 Had you come some other day
18 Then it might not have been like this
19 But you see now I'm too much in love.

20 Carve your number on my wall
21 And maybe you will get a call from me
22 If I needed someone.

23 Aah, aah.

I'LL BE BACK
by John Lennon and Paul McCartney

1 You know if you break my heart, I'll go
2 But I'll be back again
3 'cos I told you once before goodbye
4 But I came back again.

5 I love you so
6 I'm the one who wants you
7 Yes I'm the one who wants you
8 Oh - ho, oh - ho.

9 You could find better things to do
10 Than to break my heart again
11 This time I will try to show
12 That I'm not trying to pretend.

13 I thought that you would realise
14 That if I ran away from you
15 That you would want me too
16 But I got a big suprise
17 Oh - ho, oh - ho.

18 You could find better things to do
19 Than to break my heart again
20 This time I will try to show
21 That I'm not trying to pretend.

22 I wanna go
23 But I hate to leave you
24 You know I hate to leave you
25 Oh - ho, oh - ho.

26 You if you break my heart, I'll go
27 But I'll be back again.

I'LL CRY INSTEAD
by John Lennon and Paul McCartney

1 I got every reason on earth to be mad
2 'cos I've just lost the only girl I had.
3 If I could get my way
4 I'd get myself locked up today
5 But I can't, so I'll cry instead.

6 I got a chip on my shoulder that's bigger
   than my feet.
7 I can't talk to people that I meet.
8 If I could see you now
9 I'd try to make you sad somehow
10 But I can't, so I'll cry instead.

11 Don't want to cry when there's people there
12 I get shy when they start to stare.
13 I'm gonna hide myself away-hey
14 But I'll come back again some day.

15 And when I do you'd better hide all the
   girls
16 I'm gonna break their hearts all round
   the world
17 Yes, I'm gonna break 'em in two,
18 And show you what your loving man can do
19 Until then I'll cry instead.

20 Don't want to cry when there's people there
21 I get shy when they start to stare.
22 I'm gonna hide myself away-hey
23 But I'll come back again some day.

24 And when I do you'd better hide all the
   girls
25 'cos I'm gonna break their hearts all
   round the world
26 Yes, I'm gonna break 'em in two
27 And show you what your loving man can do
28 Until then I'll cry instead.

I'LL FOLLOW THE SUN
by John Lennon and Paul McCartney

1 One day you'll look to see I've gone
2 For tomorrow may rain so I'll follow the
   sun.

3 Some day you'll know I was the one
4 For tomorrow may rain so I'll follow the
   sun.

5 And now the time has come and so my love
   I must go
6 And though I lose a friend in the end
   you will know, oh.

7 One day you'll find that I have gone
8 For tomorrow may rain so I'll follow the
   sun.

9 Yeah, tomorrow may rain so I'll follow
   the sun.

10 And now the time has come and so my love
   I must go
11 And though I lose a friend in the end
   you will know, oh.

12 One day you'll find that I have gone
13 For tomorrow may rain so I'll follow the
   sun.

I'LL GET YOU
by John Lennon and Paul McCartney

1 Oh yeah, oh yeah, oh yeah, oh yeah.

2 Imagine I'm in love with you
3 It's easy 'cos I know
4 I've imagined I'm in love with you
5 Many, many, many times before.

6 It's not like me to pretend
7 But I'll get you, I'll get you in the end
8 Yes I will I'll get you in the end, oh
   yeah, oh yeah.

9 I think about you night and day
10 I need you and it's true
11 When I think about you, I can say
12 I'm never, never, never, never blue.

13 So I'm telling you, my friend
14 That I'll get you, I'll get you in the end
15 Yes I will, I'll get you in the end,
   oh yeah, oh yeah.

16 Well, there's gonna be a time
17 When I'm gonna change/make your mind
18 So you might as well resign yourself to
   me, oh yeah.

19 Imagine I'm in love with you
20 It's easy 'cos I know
21 I've imagined I'm in love with you
22 Many, many, many times before.

23 It's not like me to pretend
24 But I'll get you, I'll get you in the end
25 Yes I will, I'll get you in the end,
   oh yeah, oh yeah
26 Oh yeah, oh yeah, whoa - yeah.

I'M A LOSER
by John Lennon and Paul McCartney

1 I'm a loser, I'm a loser
2 And I'm not what I appear to be.

3 Of all the love I have won or have lost
4 There is one love I should never have
   crossed.
5 She was a girl in a million, my friend
6 I should have known she would win in the end.

7 I'm a loser and I lost someone who's
   near to me
8 I'm a loser and I'm not what I appear
   to be.

9 Although I laugh and I act like a clown
10 Beneath this mask I am wearing a frown.
11 My tears are falling like rain from the sky
12 Is it for her or myself that I cry?

13 I'm a loser and I lost someone who's
   near to me
14 I'm a loser and I'm not what I appear
   to be.

15 What have I done to deserve such a fate?
16 I realise I have left it too late.
17 And so it's true pride comes before a fall
18 I'm telling you so that you won't lose all.

19 I'm a loser and I lost someone who's
   near to me
20 I'm a loser and I'm not what I appear
   to be.

I'M DOWN
by John Lennon and Paul McCartney

1 You tell lies thinking I can't see
2 You can't cry 'cos you're laughing at me
3 I'm down (I'm really down)
4 I'm down (down on the ground)
5 I'm down (I'm really down).

6 How can you laugh when you know I'm down?
7 (How can you laugh) when you know I'm
   down?

8 Man buys ring, woman throws it away
9 Same old thing happen every day.
10 I'm down (I'm really down)
11 I'm down (down on the ground)
12 I'm down (I'm really down).

13 How can you laugh when you know I'm down?
14 (How can you laugh) when you know I'm
   down?

15 Ow!

16 We're all alone and there's nobody else
17 You still moan keep your hands to yourself
18 I'm down (I'm really down)
19 Oh baby, I'm down (down on the ground)
20 I'm down (I'm really down).

21 How can you laugh when you know I'm down?
22 (How can you laugh) when you know I'm
   down?

23 Wah!
24 Hurry up John
25 Wuh!
26 Can you hear me?
27 Ow - ow - ow - wuh!
28 Baby you know I'm down (I'm really down)
29 Oh yes, I'm down (I'm really down)
30 I'm down on the ground (I'm really down)
31 Ah, down (I'm really down)
32 Oh baby, I'm upside-down
33 Oh yeah, yeah, yeah, yeah, yeah
34 I'm down (I'm really down)
35 Oh baby, I'm down (I'm really down)
36 I'm feeling upside-down (I'm really down)
37 Ooo, I'm down (I'm really down)
38 Baby, I'm down, yeah
39 Oh baby, I'm down, yeah
40 Baby, I'm down (I'm really down)
41 Well baby, I'm down (I'm really down)
42 Upside, upside, upside-down
43 Oh baby, I'm down (I'm really down)
44 I'm down, down, down, down, down,
   down, down, down, down
45 Yeah, aah - ooo I'm down (down on the
   ground)
46 Ooo, you know I'm...

I'M HAPPY JUST TO DANCE WITH YOU
by John Lennon and Paul McCartney

1 Before this dance is through
2 I think I'll love you too
3 I'm so happy when you dance with me.

4 I don't wanna kiss or hold your hand
5 If it's funny try and understand.
6 There is really nothing else I'd rather do
7 'cos I'm happy just to dance with you.

8 I don't need to hug or hold you tight
9 I just wanna dance with you all night
10 In this world there's nothing I would
   rather do
11 'cos I'm happy just to dance with you.

12 Just to dance with you is everything I
   need (oh)
13 Before this dance is through ((aah))
14 I think I'll love you too ((oh))
15 I'm so happy when you dance with me
   ((oh - oh)).

16 If somebody tries to take my place
17 Let's pretend we just can't see his face.
18 In this world there's nothing I would
   rather do
19 'cos I'm happy just to dance with you.

20 Just to dance with you (oh) is
   everything I need (oh)
21 Before this dance is through ((aah))
22 I think I'll love you too ((oh))
23 I'm so happy when you dance with me
   ((oh - oh)).

24 If somebody tries to take my place
25 Let's pretend we just can't see his face.
26 In this world there's nothing I would
   rather do
27 I've discovered I'm in love with you
   (oh - oh).

28 'cos I'm happy just to dance with you

        (oh - oh).
29 Oh - oh, oh.

I'M LOOKING THROUGH YOU
by John Lennon and Paul McCartney

1 I'm looking through you, where did you go?
2 I thought I knew you, what did I know?
3 You don't look different, but you have
    changed
4 I'm looking through you, you're not the
    same.

5 Your lips are moving, I cannot hear,
6 Your voice is soothing but the words
    aren't clear.
7 You don't sound different, I've learned
    the game
8 I'm looking through you, you're not the
    same.

9 Why, tell me why did you not treat me right?
10 Love has a nasty habit of disappearing
    overnight.

11 You're thinking of me the same old way
12 You were above me, but not today.
13 The only difference is you're down there.
14 I'm looking through you and you're nowhere.

15 Why, tell me why did you not treat me right?
16 Love has a nasty habit of disappearing
    overnight.

17 I'm looking through you, where did you go?
18 I thought I knew you, what did I know?
19 You don't look different, but you have
    changed
20 I'm looking through you, you're not the
    same.

21 Yeah, oh baby you've changed.
22 Aah, I'm looking through you.
23 Yeah, I'm looking through you.
24 You've changed.
25 You've changed.
26 You've changed.
27 You've changed.

I'M ONLY SLEEPING
by John Lennon and Paul McCartney

1 When I wake up early in the morning
2 Lift my head, I'm still yawning.
3 When I'm in the middle of a dream
4 Stay in bed, float upstream (float
    upstream).

5 Please don't wake me, no, don't shake me
6 Leave me where I am, I'm only sleeping.

7 Everybody seems to think I'm lazy.
8 I don't mind, I think they're crazy
9 Running everywhere at such a speed
10 Till they find there's no need (there's

    no need).

11 Please don't spoil my day, I'm miles away
12 And after all, I'm only sleeping.

13 Keeping an eye on the world going by my
    window
14 Taking my time.
15 Lying there and staring at the ceiling
16 Waiting for a sleepy feeling.

17 Please don't spoil my day, I'm miles away
18 And after all, I'm only sleeping.

19 Keeping an eye on the world going by my
    window
20 Taking my time.

21 When I wake up early in the morning
22 Lift my head, I'm still yawning.
23 When I'm in the middle of a dream
24 Stay in bed, float upstream (float
    upstream).

25 Please don't wake me, no, don't shake me
26 Leave me where I am, I'm only sleeping.

I'M SO TIRED
by John Lennon and Paul McCartney

1 I'm so tired, I haven't slept a wink
2 I'm so tired, my mind is on the blink
3 I wonder should I get up and fix myself
    a drink
4 No, no, no.

5 I'm so tired, I don't know what to do
6 I'm so tired, my mind is set on you
7 I wonder should I call you
8 But I know what you would do.

9 You'd say I'm putting you on
10 But it's no joke, it's doing me harm
11 You know I can't sleep, I can't stop
    my brain
12 You know it's three weeks, I'm going
    insane
13 You know I'd give you everything I've
    got for a little peace of mind.

14 I'm so tired, I'm feeling so upset
15 Although I'm so tired, I'll have
    another cigarette
16 And curse Sir Walter Raleigh
17 He was such a stupid get.

18 You'd say I'm putting you on
19 But it's no joke, it's doing me harm
20 You know I can't sleep, I can't stop
    my brain
21 You know it's three weeks, I'm going
    insane
22 You know I'd give you everything I've
    got for a little peace of mind.
23 I'd give you everything I've got for a
    little peace of mind
24 I'd give you everything I've got for a
    little peace of mind.

IN MY LIFE
by John Lennon and Paul McCartney

1 There are places I remember
2 All my life, though some have changed.
3 Some forever, not for better
4 Some have gone and some remain.

5 All these places had their moments
6 With lovers and friends I still can recall
7 Some are dead and some are living
8 In my life I've loved them all.

9 But of all these friends and lovers
10 There is no-one compares with you
11 And these memories lose their meaning
12 When I think of love as something new.

13 Though I know I'll never lose affection
14 For people and things that went before
15 I know I'll often stop and think about them
16 In my life I love you more.

17 Though I know I'll never lose affection
18 For people and things that went before
19 I know I'll often stop and think about them
20 In my life I love you more.

21 In my life I love you more.

THE INNER LIGHT
by George Harrison

1 Without going out of my door
2 I can know all things on earth.
3 Without looking out of my window
4 I could know the ways of heaven.

5 The farther one travels
6 The less one knows
7 The less one really knows.

8 Without going out of your door
9 You can know all things on earth.
10 Without looking out of your window
11 You can know the ways of heaven.

12 The farther one travels
13 The less one knows
14 The less one really knows.

15 Arrive without travelling.
16 See all without looking.
17 Do all without doing.

IT WON'T BE LONG
by John Lennon and Paul McCartney

1 It won't be long yeah (yeah) yeah
   (yeah) yeah (yeah)
2 It won't be long yeah (yeah) yeah
   (yeah) yeah (yeah)
3 It won't be long yeah (yeah)
4 Till I belong to you

5 Every night when everybody has fun
6 Here am I sitting all on my own

7 It won't be long yeah (yeah) yeah
   (yeah) yeah (yeah)
8 It won't be long yeah (yeah) yeah
   (yeah) yeah (yeah)
9 It won't be long yeah (yeah)
10 Till I belong to you

11 Since you left me I'm so alone (you
   left me here)
12 Now you're coming, you're coming on home
   (now you're coming on home)
13 I'll be good like I know I should (yes,
   you're coming on home)
14 You're coming home, you're coming home

15 Every night the tears come down from my eye
16 Every day I've done nothing but cry

17 It won't be long yeah (yeah) yeah
   (yeah) yeah (yeah)
18 It won't be long yeah (yeah) yeah
   (yeah) yeah (yeah)
19 It won't be long yeah (yeah)
20 Till I belong to you

21 Well since you left me I'm so alone
   (you left me here)
22 Now you're coming, you're coming on home
   (now you're coming on home)
23 I'll be good like I know I should (yes,
   you're coming on home)
24 You're coming home, you're coming home

25 So every day we'll be happy, I know
26 Now I know that you won't leave me no more

27 It won't be long yeah (yeah) yeah
   (yeah) yeah (yeah)
28 It won't be long (yeah) yeah (yeah)
   yeah (yeah)
29 It won't be long yeah (yeah)
30 Till I belong to you - ooo.

IT'S ALL TOO MUCH
by George Harrison

1 To your mother!

2 It's all too much
3 It's all too much.

4 When I look into your eyes
5 Your love is there for me
6 And the more I go inside
7 The more there is to see.

8 It's all too much for me to take
9 The love that's shining all around you
10 Everywhere it's what you make
11 For us to take, it's all too much.

12 Floating down the stream of time

13 From life to life with me
14 Makes no difference where you are
15 Or where you'd like to be.

16 It's all too much for me to take
17 The love that's shining all around here
18 All the world is birthday cake
19 So take a piece, but not too much.

20 (Wuh!)

21 Sail me on a silver sun
22 Where I know that I'm free
23 Show me that I'm everywhere
24 And get me home for tea.

25 It's all too much for me to see
26 The love that's shining all around here
27 The more I learn, the less I know
28 And what I do is all too much.

29 It's all too much for me to take
30 The love that's shining all around you
31 Everywhere it's what you make
32 For us to take it's all too much.

33 It's too much - aah.
34 It's too much.

35 With your long blonde hair and your eyes
      of blue
36 With your long blonde hair and your eyes
      of blue
37 You're too much - aah.
38 We are dead.

39 Too much, too much, too much, too much,
      too much, too much, too much
40 Too much, too much, too much (wuh!),
      too much, too much, too much
41 Too much, too much, too much, too much,
      too much, too much, too much
42 Too much, too much, too much (come on),
      too much, too much, too much.

43 Too much, too much, too much, too much,
      too much, too much
44 Too much, too much, too much, too much,
      too much, too much
45 Too much, too much, too much, too much,
      too much, too much
46 Too much, too much, too much, too much,
      too much, too much.

IT'S ONLY LOVE
by John Lennon and Paul McCartney

1 I get high when I see you go by, my oh my
2 When you sigh my my inside just flies,
      butterfly.

3 Why am I so shy when I'm beside you?
4 It's only love and that is all
5 Why should I feel the way I do?
6 It's only love and that is all
7 But it's so hard loving you.

8 Is it right that you and I should fight,
      every night
9 Just the sight of you makes night-time
      bright, very bright.

10 Haven't I the right to make it up girl?

11 It's only love and that is all
12 Why should I feel the way I do?
13 It's only love and that is all
14 But it's so hard loving you.

15 Yes, it's so hard loving you, loving
      you - ooo.

I'VE GOT A FEELING
by John Lennon and Paul McCartney

1 I've got a feeling, a feeling deep inside
2 Oh yeah, oh yeah (that's right).
3 I've got a feeling, a feeling I can't hide
4 Oh no, no - oh no, oh no.
5 Yes, yeah, I've got a feeling, yeah.

6 Oh please believe me I'd hate to miss
      the train
7 Oh yeah, (yeah) oh yeah
8 And if you leave me I won't be late again
9 Oh no, oh no, oh no, yeah, yeah!

10 I've got a feeling, yeah, I've got a
      feeling.
11 All these years I've been wandering
      round the world
12 Wondering really how come nobody told me
13 All that I was looking for was somebody
      who looked like you.

14 Ooo I've got a feeling that keeps me on
      my toes
15 Oh yeah, oh yeah ((oh yeah))
16 I've got a feeling I think that
      everybody knows
17 Oh yeah, oh yeah ((oh yeah)), oh yeah
      - yeah, yeah!
18 I've got a feeling yeah - (yeah).

19 Everybody had a hard year
20 Everybody had a good time
21 Everybody had a wet dream
22 Everybody saw the sun shine
23 Oh yeah (oh yeah), oh yeah, oh yeah.

24 (Yeah) everybody had a good year
25 Everybody let their hair down
26 Everybody pulled their socks up (yeah)
27 Everybody put the fool down, oh yeah -
      (yeah)

28 Ooo - hu, everybody had a good year
      ((I've got a feeling))
29 Everybody had a hard time ((a feeling
      deep inside, oh yeah))
30 Everybody had a wet dream (oh yeah)
31 Everybody saw the sun shine.

32 Everybody had a good year ((I've got a
      feeling))
33 Everybody let their hair down ((a
      feeling I can't hide, oh no))
34 Everybody pulled their socks up (oh no,
      no)
35 Everybody put their foot down, oh yeah
      (yeah).

36 I've got a feeling ((oh yeah))
37 I've got a feeling (oh yeah)
38 I've got a feeling, yeah, yeah, yeah,
      yeah.

39 Oh my soul.
40 Oh it's so hard.

I'VE JUST SEEN A FACE
by John Lennon and Paul McCartney

1 I've just seen a face
2 I can't forget the time or place
3 Where we just met
4 She's just the girl for me
5 And I want all the world to see we've met
6 Mmm, mmm, mmm - mmm.

7 Had it been another day
8 I might have looked the other way
9 And I'd have never been aware
10 But as it is I'll dream of her tonight
11 La da da, da n da.

12 Falling, yes I am falling
13 And she keeps calling me back again.

14 I have never known the like of this
15 I've been alone and I have missed things
16 And kept out of sight
17 But other girls were never quite like this
18 La da da, da n da.

19 Falling, yes I am falling
20 And she keeps calling me back again.

21 (Hey)

22 Falling, yes I am falling
23 And she keeps calling me back again.

24 I've just seen a face
25 I can't forget the time or place
26 Where we just met
27 She's just the girl for me
28 And I want all the world to see we've met
29 Mmm mmm mmm la da da.

30 Falling, yes I am falling
31 And she keeps calling me back again.

32 Falling, yes I am falling
33 And she keeps calling me back again.

34 (Oh) falling, yes I am falling
35 And she keeps calling me back again.

JULIA
by John Lennon and Paul McCartney

1 Half of what I say is meaningless
2 But I say it just to reach you, Julia.

3 Julia, Julia oceanchild calls me
4 So I sing the song of love, Julia.

5 Julia seashell eyes windy smile calls me
6 So I sing the song of love, Julia.

7 Her hair of floating sky is shimmering

8 Glimmering in the sun.

9 Julia, Julia morning moon touch me
10 So I sing the song of love, Julia.

11 When I cannot sing my heart
12 I can only speak my mind, Julia.

13 Julia sleeping sand silent cloud touch me
14 So I sing a song of love, Julia.

15 Hmm hmm hmm, calls me
16 So I sing a song of love for Julia
17 Julia, Julia.

LADY MADONNA
by John Lennon and Paul McCartney

1 Lady Madonna, children at your feet
2 Wonder how you manage to make ends meet.

3 Who finds the money when you pay the rent?
4 Did you think that money was heaven sent?

5 Friday night arrives without a suitcase
6 Sunday morning creeping like a nun
7 Monday's child has learned to tie his
      bootlace.
8 See how they run.

9 Lady Madonna, baby at your breast
10 Wonders how you manage to feed the rest.

11 See how they run.

12 Lady Madonna, lying on the bed,
13 Listen to the music playing in your head.

14 Tuesday afternoon is never-ending
15 Wednesday morning papers didn't come
16 Thursday night your stockings needed mending
17 See how they run.

18 Lady Madonna, children at your feet
19 Wonder how you manage to make ends meet.

LET IT BE   (45)
by John Lennon and Paul McCartney

1 When I find myself in times of trouble
2 Mother Mary comes to me
3 Speaking words of wisdom, let it be.

4 And in my hour of darkness
5 She is standing right in front of me
6 Speaking words of wisdom, let it be.

7 Let it be, let it be, let it be, let
   it be.
8 Whisper words of wisdom, let it be.

9 And when the broken-hearted people
10 Living in the world agree
11 There will be an answer, let it be.

12 For though they may be parted
13 There is still a chance that they will see
14 There will be an answer, let it be.

15 Let it be, let it be, let it be, let
    it be.
16 Yeah there will be an answer, let it be.

17 Let it be, let it be, let it be, let
    it be.
18 Whisper words of wisdom, let it be.

19 Let it be, let it be, let it be, yeah
    let it be.
20 Whisper words of wisdom, let it be.

21 And when the night is cloudy
22 There is still a light that shines on me
23 Shine on till tomorrow, let it be.

24 I wake up to the sound of music
25 Mother Mary comes to me
26 Speaking words of wisdom, let it be.

27 Yeah let it be, let it be, let it be,
    yeah let it be.
28 Oh there will be an answer, let it be.

29 Let it be, let it be, let it be, yeah
    let it be.
30 Whisper words of wisdom, let it be.

LET IT BE   (LP)
by John Lennon and Paul McCartney

1 When I find myself in times of trouble
2 Mother Mary comes to me
3 Speaking words of wisdom, let it be.

4 And in my hour of darkness
5 She is standing right in front of me
6 Speaking words of wisdom, let it be.

7 Let it be, let it be, let it be, let
    it be
8 Whisper words of wisdom, let it be.

9 And when the broken-hearted people
10 Living in the world agree
11 There will be an answer, let it be.

12 For though they may be parted
13 There is still a chance that they will see
14 There will be an answer, let it be.

15 Let it be, let it be, let it be, let
    it be
16 Yeah there will be an answer, let it be.

17 Let it be, let it be, let it be, let
    it be
18 Whisper words of wisdom, let it be.

19 Let it be, let it be, let it be, yeah
    let it be
20 Whisper words of wisdom, let it be.

21 And when the night is cloudy
22 There is still a light that shines on me
23 Shine on till tomorrow, let it be.

24 I wake up to the sound of music
25 Mother Mary comes to me

26 Speaking words of wisdom, let it be.

27 Yeah let it be, let it be, let it be,
    yeah let it be
28 Oh there will be an answer, let it be.

29 Let it be, let it be, let it be, yeah
    let it be
30 Oh there will be an answer, let it be.

31 Let it be, let it be, oh let it be,
    yeah let it be
32 Whisper words of wisdom, let it be.

LITTLE CHILD
by John Lennon and Paul McCartney

1 Little child, little child
2 Little child, won't you dance with me?
3 I'm so sad and lonely
4 Baby take a chance with me.

5 Little child, little child
6 Little child, won't you dance with me?
7 I'm so sad and lonely
8 Baby take a chance with me.

9 If you want someone to make you feel so fine
10 Then we'll have some fun when you're mine,
    all mine
11 So come on, come on, come on.

12 Little child, little child
13 Little child, won't you dance with me?
14 I'm so sad and lonely
15 Baby take a chance with me (wuh yeah).

16 When you're by my side, you're the only one
17 Don't you run and hide, just come on
    come on,
18 Yeah come on, come on, come on.

19 Little child, little child
20 Little child, won't you dance with me?
21 I'm so sad and lonely
22 Baby take a chance with me, oh yeah
23 Baby take a chance with me, oh yeah
24 Baby take a chance with me, oh yeah
25 Baby take a chance with me, oh yeah.

THE LONG AND WINDING ROAD
by John Lennon and Paul McCartney

1 The long and winding road that leads to
    your door
2 Will never disappear, I've seen that
    road before.
3 It always leads me here, lead me to your
    door.

4 The wild and windy night that the rain
    washed away
5 Has left a pool of tears crying for the day.
6 Why leave me standing here, let me know
    the way.

7 Many times I've been alone and many
    times I've cried
8 Anyway you'll never know the many ways
    I've tried
9 And still they lead me back to the long,
    winding road.

10 You left me standing here a long, long
    time ago
11 Don't leave me waiting here, lead me to
    your door.

12 But still they lead me back to the long,
    winding road
13 You left me standing here a long, long
    time ago
14 Don't keep me waiting here (don't keep
    me waiting) lead me to your door.

15 Yeah, yeah, yeah, yeah.

LONG, LONG, LONG
by George Harrison

1 It's been a long, long, long time
2 How could I ever have lost you
3 When I loved you?

4 It took a long, long, long time
5 Now I'm so happy I found you
6 How I love you.

7 So many tears I was searching
8 So many tears I was wasting - oh, oh!

9 Now I can see you, be you
10 How can I ever misplace you?
11 How I want you.

12 Oh I love you
13 You know that I need you
14 Oh I love you.

LOVE ME DO
by John Lennon and Paul McCartney

1 Love, love me do
2 You know I love you.
3 I'll always be true
4 So please love me do
5 Whao-ho love me do.

6 Love, love me do
7 You know I love you.
8 I'll always be true
9 So please love me do
10 Whoa-ho love me do.

11 Someone to love, somebody new.
12 Someone to love, someone like you.

13 Love, love me do
14 You know I love you.
15 I'll always be true

16 So please love me do,
17 Whoa-ho love me do (hey hey).

18 Love, love me do
19 You know I love you.
20 I'll always be true
21 So please love me do
22 Whoa-ho love me do.

23 Yes, love me do
24 Whoa-ho love me do
25 Yes, love me do.

LOVE YOU TO/TOO
by George Harrison

1 Each day just goes so fast
2 I turn around, it's past
3 You don't get time to hang a sign on me.

4 Love me while you can
5 Before I'm a dead old man.

6 A lifetime is so short
7 A new one can't be bought
8 But what you've got means such a lot to me.

9 Make love all day long
10 Make love singing songs.

11 Make love all day long
12 Make love singing songs.

13 There's people standing round
14 Who'll screw you in the ground
15 They'll fill you in with all their sins,
    you'll see.

16 I'll make love to you
17 If you want me to.

LOVELY RITA
by John Lennon and Paul McCartney

1 Aah!

2 Lovely Rita meter maid
3 Lovely Rita meter maid (aah)
4 Lovely Rita (oh) meter maid
5 Nothing can come between us
6 When it gets dark I tow your heart away.

7 Standing by a parking meter
8 When I caught a glimpse of Rita
9 Filling in a ticket in her little white book.

10 In a cap she looked much older
11 And the bag across her shoulder
12 Made her look a little like a military man.

13 Lovely Rita meter maid
14 May I inquire discreetly ((lovely Rita))
15 When are you free ((lovely Rita))
16 To take some tea with me? ((maid))

17 Aah!
18 Rita!
19 Ooo - ooo.

20 Took her out and tried to win her
21 Had a laugh and over dinner
22 Told her I would really like to see her
     again.

23 Got the bill and Rita paid it
24 Took her home I nearly made it
25 Sitting on a sofa with a sister or two.

26 Oh, lovely Rita meter maid
27 Where would I be without you?
28 Give us a wink and make me think of you.

29 Lovely Rita ((lovely meter maid))
     meter maid
30 Lovely ((Rita, Rita, Rita)) Rita
     meter maid
31 Lovely Rita ((oh lovely Rita meter,
     meter maid)) meter maid
32 Lovely Rita ((da da da da da da)
     meter maid
33 Da da da da da da da da - da
34 Da da da - da - da - da - wuh - oh
35 Ah - ah - ah (oh) - ah - ah - ah - ah -
     ah - ah - ah
36 Baby!

LUCY IN THE SKY WITH DIAMONDS
by John Lennon and Paul McCartney

1 Picture yourself in a boat on a river
2 With tangerine trees and marmalade skies.
3 Somebody calls you, you answer quite slowly
4 A girl with kaleidoscope eyes.

5 Cellophane flowers of yellow and green
6 Towering over your head.
7 Look for the girl with the sun in her eyes
8 And she's gone.

9 Lucy in the sky with diamonds
10 Lucy in the sky with diamonds
11 Lucy in the sky with diamonds - aah.

12 Follow her down to a bridge by a fountain
13 Where rocking-horse people eat
     marshmallow pies.
14 Everyone smiles as you drift past the flowers
15 That grow so incredibly high (high).

16 Newspaper taxis appear on the shore
17 Waiting to take you away.
18 Climb in the back with your head in the clouds
19 And you're gone.

20 Lucy in the sky with diamonds
21 Lucy in the sky with diamonds
22 Lucy in the sky with diamonds - aah.

23 Picture yourself on a train in a station
24 With plasticine porters with
     looking-glass ties.
25 Suddenly someone is there at the turnstyle
26 The girl with kaleidoscope eyes.

27 Lucy in the sky with diamonds
28 Lucy in the sky with diamonds
29 Lucy in the sky with diamonds - aah.

30 Lucy in the sky with diamonds
31 Lucy in the sky with diamonds
32 Lucy in the sky with diamonds - aah.

33 Lucy in the sky with diamonds
34 Lucy in the sky with diamonds (aah - ooo)
35 Lucy in the sky with diamonds.

MAGICAL MYSTERY TOUR
by John Lennon and Paul McCartney

1 Roll up, roll up for the Mystery Tour
2 Step right this way.

3 Roll up, roll up for the Mystery Tour
4 Roll up, roll up for the Mystery Tour.
5 Roll up (and that's an invitation)
6 Roll up for the Mystery Tour
7 Roll up (to make a reservation)
8 Roll up for the Mystery Tour.
9 The Magical Mystery Tour is waiting to
     take you away
10 (Waiting to take you away).

11 Roll up, roll up for the Mystery Tour
12 Roll up, roll up for the Mystery Tour.
13 Roll up (we've got everything you need)
14 Roll up for the Mystery Tour
15 Roll up (satisfaction guaranteed)
16 Roll up for the Mystery Tour.
17 The Magical Mystery Tour is hoping to
     take you away
18 (Hoping to take you away)

19 The mystery trip.

20 Aah!
21 The Magical Mystery Tour.

22 Roll up, roll up for the Mystery Tour
23 Roll up (and that's an invitation)
24 Roll up for the Mystery Tour
25 Roll up (to make a reservation)
26 Roll up for the Mystery Tour.
27 The Magical Mystery Tour is coming to
     take you away,
28 (Coming/Hoping to take you away)
29 The Magical Mystery Tour is dying to
     take you away
30 (Dying to take you away)
31 Take you today.

MARTHA MY DEAR
by John Lennon and Paul McCartney

1 Martha my dear, though I spend my days
     in conversation
2 Please - remember me, Martha my love
3 Don't forget me, Martha my dear.

4 Hold your head up you silly girl, look
     what you've done
5 When you find yourself in the thick of it

6 Help yourself to a bit of what is all
    around you - silly girl.

7 Take a good look around you
8 Take a good look you're bound to see
9 That you and me were meant to be for each
    other - silly girl.

10 Hold your hand out you silly girl, see
    what you've done
11 When you find yourself in the thick of it
12 Help yourself to a bit of what is all
    around you - silly girl.

13 Martha my dear, you have always been my
    inspiration
14 Please - be good to me, Martha my love
15 Don't forget me, Martha my dear.

MAXWELL'S SILVER HAMMER
by John Lennon and Paul McCartney

1 Joan was quizzical, studied pataphysical
    science in the home
2 Late nights all alone with a test-tube,
    oh oh - oh oh.

3 Maxwell Edison, majoring in medicine,
    calls her on the phone
4 Can I take you out to the pictures, Joan?

5 But as she's getting ready to go, a
    knock comes on the door
6 Bang, bang Maxwell's silver hammer came
    down upon her head
7 Bang, bang Maxwell's silver hammer made
    sure that she was dead.

8 Back in school again, Maxwell plays the
    fool again, teacher gets annoyed
9 Wishing to avoid an unpleasant scene
10 She tells Max to stay when the class has
    gone away
11 So he waits behind, writing fifty times
    I must not be so oh - oh oh.

12 But when she turns her back on the boy,
    he creeps up from behind
13 Bang, bang Maxwell's silver hammer came
    down upon her head
14 (Do do do do do)
15 Bang, bang Maxwell's silver hammer made
    sure that she was dead.
16 (Do do do do do)

17 PC Thirty-One said, we caught a dirty
    one, Maxwell stands alone
18 Painting testimonial pictures oh oh - oh oh.

19 Rose and Valerie screaming from the
    gallery say he must go free
20 (Maxwell must go free)
21 The judge does not agree and he tells
    them so oh - oh oh.

22 But as the words are leaving his lips, a
    noise comes from behind
23 Bang, bang Maxwell's silver hammer came
    down upon his head
24 (Do do do do do)
25 Bang, bang Maxwell's silver hammer made
    sure that he was dead.
26 (Whoa, whoa, whoa)

27 (Do do do do do)

28 Silver hammer man!

MEAN MR. MUSTARD
by John Lennon and Paul McCartney

1 Mean Mr. Mustard sleeps in the park
2 Shaves in the dark
3 Trying to save paper.

4 Sleeps in a hole in the road
5 Saving up to buy some clothes
6 Keeps a ten bob note up his nose
7 Such a mean old man, such a mean old man.

8 His sister Pam works in a shop
9 She never stops
10 She's a go-getter.

11 Takes him out to look at the Queen
12 Only place that he's ever been
13 Always shouts out something obscene
14 Such a dirty old man, dirty old man.

MICHELLE
by John Lennon and Paul McCartney

1 Michelle ma belle
2 These are words that go together well,
    my Michelle.

3 Michelle ma belle
4 Sont des mots qui vont tres bien ensemble,
    tres bien ensemble.

5 I love you, I love you, I love you
6 That's all I want to say
7 Until I find a way
8 I will say the only words I know that
    you'll understand.

9 Michelle ma belle
10 Sont des mots qui vont tres bien ensemble,
    tres bien ensemble.

11 I need to, I need to, I need to
12 I need to make you see
13 Oh, what you mean to me
14 Until I do I'm hoping you will know
    what I mean.

15 I love you.

16 I want you, I want you, I want you
17 I think you know by now
18 I'll get to you somehow
19 Until I do I'm telling you so you'll
    understand.

20 Michelle ma belle
21 Sont des mots qui vont tres bien ensemble,
    tres bien ensemble.

22 And I will say the only words I know

that you'll understand
23 My Michelle.

MISERY
by John Lennon and Paul McCartney

1 The world is treating me bad, misery.

2 I'm the kind of guy, who never used to cry.
3 The world is treating me bad, misery.
4 I've lost her now for sure, I won't see
   her no more
5 It's gonna be a drag, misery.

6 I'll remember all the little things we've
   done
7 Can't she see she'll always be the only
   one, only one.
8 Send her back to me, 'cos everyone can see
9 Without her I will be in misery.

10 I'll remember all the little things we've
   done
11 She'll remember and she'll miss her only
   one, lonely one.
12 Send her back to me, 'cos everyone can see
13 Without her I will be in misery.

14 (Ooho) in misery
15 (Ooo) my misery
16 (La la la la la la) misery.

MOTHER NATURE'S SON
by John Lennon and Paul McCartney

1 Born a poor young country boy - Mother
   Nature's son
2 All day long I'm sitting singing songs
   for everyone.

3 Sit beside a mountain stream - see her
   waters rise
4 Listen to the pretty sound of music as
   she flies.

5 Do do do do do do do do do
6 Do do do do do do do
7 Do do.

8 Find me in my field of grass - Mother
   Nature's son
9 Swaying daisies sing a lazy song beneath
   the sun.

10 Do do do do do do do do do
11 Do do do do do do do
12 Do do do do do - yeah yeah yeah.

13 Mmm mmm mmm
14 Ooo ooo ooo
15 Mmm mmm aah
16 Aah Mother Nature's son.

THE NIGHT BEFORE
by John Lennon and Paul McCartney

1 We said our goodbyes (aah the night before)
2 Love was in your eyes (aah the night before)
3 Now today I find, you have changed your mind
4 Treat me like you did the night before.

5 Were you telling lies? (aah the night
   before)
6 Was I so unwise? (aah the night before)
7 When I held you near, you were so sincere
8 Treat me like you did the night before.

9 Last night is the night I will remember
   you by
10 When I think of things we did it makes
   me wanna cry.

11 We said our goodbyes (aah the night before)
12 Love was in your eyes (aah the night before)
13 Now today I find you have changed your mind
14 Treat me like you did the night before
   (yes).

15 When I held you near, you were so sincere
16 Treat me like you did the night before
   (yeah).

17 Last night is the night I will remember
   you by
18 When I think of things we did it makes
   me wanna cry.

19 Were you telling lies? (aah the night
   before)
20 Was I so unwise? (aah the night before)
21 When I held you near, you were so sincere
22 Treat me like you did the night before.
23 Like the night before.

NO REPLY
by John Lennon and Paul McCartney

1 This happened once before
2 When I came to your door
3 No reply
4 They said it wasn't you
5 But I saw you peep through your window
6 I saw the light, I saw the light.

7 I know that you saw me
8 'cos I looked up to see your face.

9 I tried to telephone
10 They said you were not home
11 That's a lie
12 'cos I know where you've been
13 I saw you walk in your door
14 I nearly died, I nearly died.

15 'cos you walked hand in hand
16 With another man in my place.

17 If I were you I'd realise that I
18 Love you more than any other guy
19 And I'll forgive the lies

20 That I heard before
21 When you gave me no reply.

22 I tried to telephone
23 They said you were not home
24 That's a lie
25 'cos I know where you've been
26 I saw you walk in your door
27 I nearly died, I nearly died.

28 'cos you walked hand in hand
29 With another man in my place.

30 No reply, no reply.

NORWEGIAN WOOD
(THIS BIRD HAS FLOWN)
by John Lennon and Paul McCartney

1 I once had a girl
2 Or should I say
3 She once had me?

4 She showed me her room
5 Isn't it good
6 Norwegian wood?

7 She asked me to stay
8 And she told me to sit anywhere
9 So I looked around
10 And I noticed there wasn't a chair.

11 I sat on a rug
12 Biding my time
13 Drinking her wine.

14 We talked until two
15 And then she said
16 It's time for bed.

17 She told me she worked in the morning
18 And started to laugh
19 I told her I didn't
20 And crawled off to sleep in the bath.

21 And when I awoke
22 I was alone
23 This bird had flown.

24 So I lit a fire
25 Isn't it good
26 Norwegian wood?

NOT A SECOND TIME
by John Lennon and Paul McCartney

1 You know you made me cry
2 I see no use in wondering why
3 I've cried for you.

4 And now you've changed your mind
5 I see no reason to change mine
6 My crying is through, oh.

7 You're giving me the same old line
8 I'm wondering why

9 You hurt me then you're back again
10 No, no, no, not a second time.

11 Wuh!

12 You know you made me cry
13 I see no use in wondering why
14 I've cried for you, yeah.

15 And now you've changed your mind
16 I see no reason to change mine
17 My crying is through, oh.

18 You're giving me the same old line
19 I'm wondering why
20 You hurt me then you're back again
21 No, no, no, not a second time.

22 Not a second time
23 Not a second time
24 No, no, no, not a second time
25 ((No, no, no.))

NOWHERE MAN
by John Lennon and Paul McCartney

1 He's a real Nowhere Man
2 Sitting in his nowhere land
3 Making all his nowhere plans for nobody.

4 Doesn't have a point of view
5 Knows not where he's going to
6 Isn't he a bit like you and me?

7 Nowhere Man please listen
8 You don't know what you're missing
9 Nowhere Man the world is at your command.

10 He's as blind as he can be
11 Just sees what he wants to see
12 Nowhere Man can you see me at all?

13 Nowhere Man don't worry
14 Take your time, don't hurry
15 Leave it all till somebody else lends you
         a hand.

16 Doesn't have a point of view
17 Knows not where he's going to
18 Isn't he a bit like you and me?

19 Nowhere Man please listen
20 You don't know what you're missing
21 Nowhere Man the world is at your command.

22 He's a real Nowhere Man
23 Sitting in his nowhere land
24 Making all his nowhere plans for nobody
25 Making all his nowhere plans for nobody
26 Making all his nowhere plans for nobody.

OB--LA--DI OB--LA--DA
by John Lennon and Paul McCartney

1 Desmond has a barrow in the market-place

2 Molly is the singer in a band
3 Desmond says to Molly, girl I like
 your face
4 And Molly says this as she takes him by
 the hand:

5 Ob-la-di ob-la-da life goes on bra
6 La-la how the life goes on
7 Ob-la-di ob-la-da life goes on bra
8 La-la how the life goes on.

9 Desmond takes a trolly to the jewellery
 store
10 Buys a twenty-carat golden ring (golden
 ring)
11 Takes it back to Molly waiting at the door
12 And as he gives it to her she begins to
 sing (sing):

13 Ob-la-di ob-la-da life goes on bra
14 La-la how the life goes on
15 Ob-la-di ob-la-da life goes on bra
16 La-la how the life goes on - yeah.

17 In a couple of years they have built a
 home sweet home
18 With a couple of kids running in the yard
 of Desmond and Molly Jones.
19 (Ho ho ho ho ho)

20 Happy ever after in the market place
21 Desmond lets the children lend a hand
22 (Ah - yeah)
23 Molly stays at home and does her pretty face
24 And in the evening she still sings it
 with the band, yes.

25 Ob-la-di ob-la-da life goes on bra
26 La-la how the life goes on (he he he)
27 Hey, ob-la-di ob-la-da life goes on bra
28 La-la how the life goes on.

29 In a couple of years they have built a
 home sweet home
30 With a couple of kids running in the yard
 of Desmond and Molly Jones.
31 (Ho ho ho ho ho)

32 Hey, happy ever after in the market place
33 Molly lets the children lend a hand
34 Desmond stays at home and does his pretty face
35 And in the evening she's a singer with
 the band, yeah.

36 Ob-la-di ob-la-da life goes on bra
37 La-la how the life goes on - yeah
38 Ob-la-di ob-la-da life goes on bra
39 La-la how the life goes on (ha ha ha ha
 ha ha).

40 But if you want some fun (ha ha ha)
41 Take ob-la-di 'b-la-da ((ha ha ha))
42 Thank you (ooo) (ha ha ha).

OCTOPUS'S GARDEN
by Richard Starkey

1 I'd like to be under the sea
2 In an octopus's garden in the shade.
3 He'd let us in, knows where we've been
4 In his octopus's garden in the shade.

5 I'd ask my friends to come and see

6 An octopus's garden with me.

7 I'd like to be under the sea
8 In an octopus's garden in the shade.

9 We would be warm below the storm
10 In our little hideaway beneath the waves.
11 Resting our head on the seabed
12 In an octopus's garden near a cave.

13 We would sing and dance around
14 Because we know we can't be found.

15 I'd like to be under the sea
16 In an octopus's garden in the shade.

17 We would shout and swim about
18 The coral that lies beneath the waves
 (lies beneath the ocean waves).
19 Oh, what joy for every girl and boy
20 Knowing they're happy and they're safe
 (happy and they're safe).

21 We would be so happy you and me
22 No-one there to tell us what to do.

23 I'd like to be under the sea
24 In an octopus's garden with you
25 In an octopus's garden with you
26 In an octopus's garden with you.

OH DARLING
by John Lennon and Paul McCartney

1 Oh darling, please believe me, I'll
 never do you no harm.
2 Believe me when I tell you, I'll never
 do you no harm.

3 Oh darling, if you leave me I'll never
 make it alone
4 Believe me when I beg you - ooo - don't
 ever leave me alone.

5 When you told me you didn't need me any more
6 Well you know I nearly broke down and cried.
7 A - when you told me you didn't need me
 any more
8 A - well you know, I nearly broke down
 and died.

9 Oh darling, if you leave me, I'll
 never make it alone.
10 Believe me when I tell you, I'll never
 do you no harm.
11 Believe me, darling.

12 A - when you told me - ooo - you didn't
 need me any more
13 A - well you know I nearly broke down
 and cried.
14 A - when you told me you didn't need me
 any more
15 A - well you know, I nearly broke down
 and died.

16 Oh darling, please believe me, I'll
 never let you down.
17 Oh believe me darling
18 Believe me when I tell you - ooo - I'll
 never do you no harm.

41

OLD BROWN SHOE
by George Harrison

1 I want a love that's right
2 But right is only half of what's wrong
3 I want a short-haired girl
4 Who sometimes wears it twice as long

5 Now I'm stepping out this old brown shoe
6 Baby, I'm in love with you
7 We're so glad you came here
8 It won't be the same now I'm telling you.

9 Though you pick me up
10 From where some try to drag me down
11 When I see your smile
12 Replacing every thoughtless frown.

13 Got me escaping from this zoo
14 Baby, I'm in love with you
15 So glad you came here
16 It won't be the same now that I'm with you.

17 If I grow up I'll be a singer
18 Wearing rings on every finger
19 Not worrying what they or you say
20 I'll live and love and maybe someday
21 Who knows baby, you may comfort me (hey).

22 I may appear to be imperfect
23 My love is something you can't reject.
24 Changing faster than the weather
25 If you and me should get together,
26 Who knows baby, you may comfort me (hey).

27 I want that love of yours
28 To miss that love is something I'd hate.
29 Make an early start
30 Making sure that I'm not late (hey).

31 For your sweet top lip I'm in the queue
32 Baby, I'm in love with you.
33 So glad you came here
34 Won't be the same now that I'm with you.

35 I'm so glad you came here
36 It won't be the same now that I'm with
     you (yeah, yeah, yeah).

37 Do - dow, do - do - do
38 Do - dow, do - do - do
39 Do - dow, do - do - do
40 Do - dow, do - do - do
41 Do - dow, do - do - do
42 Do - dow, do - do - do
43 Do - dow, do - do - do
44 Do - dow, do - do - do
45 Do - dow, do - do - do
46 Do - dow...

ONE AFTER NINE-O-NINE
by John Lennon and Paul McCartney

1 My baby said she's travelling on the one
   after nine-0-nine
2 I said, move over honey, I'm
   travelling on that line
3 I said, move over once, move over twice
4 Come on baby, don't be cold as ice
5 Said you're travelling on the one after
   nine-0-nine.

6 I begged her not to go and I begged her
   on my bended knee, (oh yeah)
7 You're only fooling round, only fooling
   round with me.
8 I said move over once, move over twice
9 Come on baby, don't be cold as ice
10 Said you're travelling on the one after
   nine-0-nine.

11 Pick up my bag, run to the station
12 Railman said, you got the wrong location
13 Pick up my bag, run right home
14 Then I find I've got the number wrong.

15 Well, she said she's travelling on the
   one after nine-0-nine
16 I said a-move over honey, I'm
   travelling on that line
17 Said move over once, move over twice
18 Come on baby, don't be cold as ice
19 Said she's travelling on the one after
   nine-0-nine. (yeah)

20 Oh!

21 Pick up my bag, run to the station
22 Railman said, you got the wrong location
23 Well - pick up my bag, run right home
   (run right home)
24 Then I find I got the number wrong -
   well ((well)).

25 She said she's travelling on the one
   after nine-0-nine
26 Said a - move over honey, I'm
   travelling on that line
27 I said move over once, move over twice
28 Come on baby, don't be cold as ice.

29 Said we're travelling on the one after
   nine-0
30 She said we're travelling on the one
   after nine-0
31 Said we're travelling on the one after
   nine-0-nine
32 (Ooo - ooo).

33 Oh Danny Boy, the odes of Pan are
   calling.

ONLY A NORTHERN SONG
by George Harrison

1 If you're listening to this song
2 You may think the chords are going wrong,
3 But they're not, we just wrote it like that.

4 When you're listening late at night
5 You may think the band are not quite right
6 But they are, they just play it like that.

7 It doesn't really matter what chords I play
8 What words I say or time of day it is
9 As it's only a Northern song.

10 It doesn't really matter what clothes I

wear
11 Or how I fare or if my hair is brown
12 When it's only a Northern song.

13 If you think the harmony
14 Is a little dark and out of key
15 You're correct, there's nobody there.

16 And I told you there's no-one there.

17 ... Make it...

PS I LOVE YOU
by John Lennon and Paul McCartney

1 As I write this letter, send my love to
    you
2 Remember that I'll always be in love
    with you.

3 Treasure ((treasure)) these few words
    ((words))
4 Till we're together ((together))
5 Keep all ((all)) my love forever
    ((ever)).
6 PS I love you, you, you, you.

7 I'll ((I'll)) be coming home ((home))
    again to you love ((you love))
8 And till ((till)) the day I do love
    ((do love))
9 PS I love you, you, you, you.

10 As I write this letter, send my love to
    you
11 Remember that I'll always be in love
    with you.

12 Treasure ((treasure)) these few words
    ((words))
13 Till we're together ((together))
14 Keep all ((all)) my love forever
    ((ever))
15 PS I love you, you, you, you.

16 As I write this letter (oh) send my
    love to you
17 You know I want you to
18 Remember that I'll always, yeah, be in
    love with you.

19 I'll be coming home again to you love
20 And till the day I do love
21 PS I love you, you, you, you
22 You, you, you
23 I love you.

PAPERBACK WRITER
by John Lennon and Paul McCartney

1 Paperback writer ((paperback writer))
    paperback writer.

2 Dear Sir or Madam, will you read my book?
3 It took me years to write, will you take

a look?
4 It's based on a novel by a man named Lear
5 And I need a job
6 So I want to be a paperback writer
7 Paperback writer.

8 It's a dirty story of a dirty man
9 And his clinging wife doesn't understand.
10 His son is working for the Daily Mail
11 It's a steady job
12 But he wants to be a paperback writer
13 Paperback writer.

14 Paperback writer ((paperback writer))
    paperback writer.

15 It's a thousand pages, give or take a
    few, ((paperback))
16 I'll be writing more in a week or two.
    ((writer))
17 I can make it longer if you like the
    style, ((paperback))
18 I can change it round, ((writer))
19 And I want to be a paperback writer
20 Paperback writer.

21 If you really like it you can have the
    rights, ((paperback))
22 It could make a million for you overnight.
    ((writer))
23 If you must return it you can send it
    here, ((paperback))
24 But I need a break, ((writer))
25 And I want to be a paperback writer,
26 Paperback writer.

27 Paperback writer ((paperback writer))
    paperback writer.

28 (Paperback)

29 (Paperback writer) paperback writer.
30 (Paperback writer) paperback writer.
31 (Paperback writer) paperback writer.
32 (Paperback writer) paperback writer.
33 (Paperback...

PENNY LANE
by John Lennon and Paul McCartney

1 Penny Lane: there is a barber showing
    photographs
2 Of every head he's had the pleasure to know
3 And all the people that come and go
4 Stop and say hello.

5 On the corner is a banker with a motorcar
6 The little children laugh at him behind
    his back
7 And the banker never wears a mack
8 In the pouring rain - very strange.

9 Penny Lane is in my ears and in my eyes
10 There beneath the blue suburban skies I sit
11 And meanwhile back

12 In Penny Lane there is a fireman with
    an hour-glass
13 And in his pocket is a portrait of the Queen
14 He likes to keep his fire-engine clean
15 It's a clean machine.

16 Aah, aah, aah, aah - aah!

17 Penny Lane is in my ears and in my eyes
18 A four of fish and finger pies in summer
19 Meanwhile back

20 Behind the shelter in the middle of the
      roundabout
21 The pretty nurse is selling poppies from
      a tray
22 And though she feels as if she's in a play
23 She is anyway.

24 In Penny Lane the barber shaves another
      customer
25 We see the banker sitting waiting for a trim
26 And then the fireman rushes in
27 From the pouring rain - very strange.

28 Penny Lane is in my ears and in my eyes
29 There beneath the blue suburban skies I sit
30 And meanwhile back

31 Penny Lane is in my ears and in my eyes
32 There beneath the blue suburban skies

33 Penny Lane!

7 You don't need me to show the way love
8 Why do I always have to say love
9 Come on (come on), come on (come on)
10 Come on (come on), come on (come on)
11 Please please me, whoa - yeah
12 Like I please you.

13 I don't want to start complaining.
14 But you know there's always rain
15 In my heart (in my heart).
16 I do all the pleasing with you
17 It's so hard to reason with you, whoa - yeah
18 Why do you make me blue?

19 Last night I said these words to my girl
20 I know/why do you never even try girl
21 Come on (come on), come on (come on)
22 Come on (come on), come on (come on)
23 Please please me, whoa - yeah
24 Like I please you.

25 Please me, whoa - yeah
26 Like I please you
27 Please me, whoa - yeah
28 Like I please you.

PIGGIES
by George Harrison

1 Have you seen the little piggies
2 Crawling in the dirt?
3 And for all the little piggies
4 Life is getting worse
5 Always having dirt to play around in.

6 Have you seen the bigger piggies
7 In the starched white shirts?
8 You will find the bigger piggies
9 Stirring up the dirt
10 Always have clean shirts to play around in.

11 In their sties with all their backing
12 They don't care what goes on around.
13 In their lives there's something lacking
14 What they need's a damn good whacking.

15 Everywhere there's lots of piggies
16 Living piggy lives.
17 You can see them out for dinner
18 With their piggy wives
19 Clutching forks and knives to eat the bacon.

20 One more time.

PLEASE PLEASE ME
by John Lennon and Paul McCartney

1 Last night I said these words to my girl
2 I know you never even try girl
3 Come on (come on), come on (come on)
4 Come on (come on), come on (come on)
5 Please please me, whoa - yeah
6 Like I please you.

POLYTHENE PAM
by John Lennon and Paul McCartney

1 Well, you should see Polythene Pam.
2 She's so goodlooking but she looks like a
      man.
3 Well, you should see her in drag
4 Dressed in her polythene bag.
5 Yes, you should see Polythene Pam -
      yeah, yeah, yeah.

6 Get a dose of her in jackboots and kilt
7 She's killer-diller when she's dressed to
      the hilt.
8 She's a kind of a girl that makes the
      News Of The World.
9 Yes, you could say she was attractively
      built - yeah, yeah, yeah.
10 (Yeah)

11 Hey! (great!)
12 ... Four, five...

RAIN
by John Lennon and Paul McCartney

1 If the rain comes they run and hide their
      heads
2 They might as well be dead
3 If the rain comes, if the rain comes.

4 When the sun shines they slip into the
      shade (when the sun shines down)
5 And sip their lemonade (when the sun
      shines down)
6 When the sun shines, when the sun shines
      ((sun shine)).

7 Rain I don't mind
8 Shine the weather's fine.

9 I can show you that when it starts to
   rain (when the rain comes down)
10 Everything's the same (when the rain
   comes down)
11 I can show you, I can show you ((show
   you)).

12 Rain I don't mind
13 Shine the weather's fine.

14 Can you hear me that when it rains and
   shines (when it rains and shines)
15 It's just a state of mind (when it rains
   and shines)
16 Can you hear me, can you hear me?
   ((hear me))

17 Rain.
18 Rain.
19 Rain.

REVOLUTION (45)
by John Lennon and Paul McCartney

1 Aah!

2 You say you wanna revolution
3 Well you know
4 We all wanna change the world.

5 You tell me that it's evolution
6 Well you know
7 We all want to change the world.

8 But when you talk about destruction
9 Don't you know that you can count me out?

10 Don't you know it's gonna be alright,
   alright, alright?
11 (Alright)

12 You say you got a real solution
13 Well you know,
14 We'd all love to see the plan.

15 You ask me for a contribution
16 Well you know,
17 We're all doing what we can.

18 But if you want money for people with
   minds that hate
19 All I can tell you is brother you have
   to wait.

20 Don't you know it's gonna be alright,
   alright ((alright)), alright?
21 Oh!

22 You say you'll change the constitution
23 Well you know
24 We all want to change your head.

25 You tell me it's the institution
26 Well you know
27 You better free your mind instead.

28 But if you go carrying pictures of
   Chairman Mao
29 You ain't gonna make it with anyone anyhow.

30 Don't you know it's gonna be alright,
   alright, alright ((alright))?
31 Alright, alright, alright, alright
32 Alright, alright, alright - alright!

REVOLUTION ONE (LP)
by John Lennon and Paul McCartney

1 Aah
2 Oh yes
3 I say two
4 OK

5 You say you want a revolution
6 Well you know
7 We all wanna change the world.

8 You tell me that it's evolution
9 Well you know
10 We all want to change the world.

11 But when you talk about destruction
12 Don't you know that you can count me out
   (in)?

13 Don't you know it's gonna be ((oh
   shoo-be-do-a))
14 Alright ((oh shoo-be-do-a))?
15 Don't you know it's gonna be ((oh
   shoo-be-do-a))
16 Alright ((oh shoo-be-do-a))?
17 Don't you know it's gonna be ((oh
   shoo-be-do-a))
18 Alright ((oh shoo-be-do-a))?

19 You say you got a real solution
20 Well you know
21 We'd all love to see the plan.
22 (Oh shoo-be-do-a, oh shoo-be-do-a).

23 You ask me for a contribution
24 Well you know
25 We're all doing what we can.
26 (Oh shoo-be-do-a, oh shoo-be-do-a).

27 But if you want money for people with
   minds that hate
28 Well all I can tell you is brother you
   have to wait.

29 Don't you know it's gonna be ((oh
   shoo-be-do-a))
30 Alright ((oh shoo-be-do-a))?
31 Don't you know it's gonna be ((oh
   shoo-be-do-a))
32 Alright ((oh shoo-be-do-a))?
33 Don't you know it's gonna be ((oh
   shoo-be-do-a))
34 Alright ((oh shoo-be-do-a))?

35 You say you'll change the constitution
36 Well you know
37 We'd all love to change our head.
38 (Oh shoo-be-do-a, oh shoo-be-do-a).

39 You tell me it's the institution
40 Well you know
41 You'd better free your mind instead.
42 (Oh shoo-be-do-a, oh shoo-be-do-a).

43 If you go carrying pictures of Chairman
   Mao

44 You ain't gonna make it with anyone anyhow.

45 Don't you know it's gonna be ((oh
      shoo-be-do-a))
46 Alright ((oh shoo-be-do-a))?
47 Don't you know it's gonna be ((oh
      shoo-be-do-a))
48 Alright ((oh shoo-be-do-a))?
49 Don't you know it's gonna be ((oh
      shoo-be-do-a))
50 Alright ((oh shoo-be-do-a))?

51 ((Oh)) (oh shoo-be-do-a)
52 Oh oh
53 Oh oh
54 Oh oh (oh shoo-be-do-a)
55 Oh oh
56 Oh oh (oh shoo-be-do-a)
57 Alright (oh shoo-be-do-a)
58 Alright
59 Alright (oh shoo-be-do-a)
60 Alright
61 Alright (oh shoo-be-do-a)
62 Alright
63 Alright (oh shoo-be-do-a)
64 Alright
65 Alright (oh shoo-be-do-a)
66 Alright
67 Alright (oh shoo-be-do-a)

68 Oh-oh-oh-oh-oh-oh ((oh shoo-be-do-a))
69 (Oh shoo-be-do-a)
70 (Oh shoo-be-do-a)
71 (Oh shoo-be-do-a) alright
72 Alright
73 Alright
74 Alright!

REVOLUTION NINE
by John Lennon and Paul McCartney

EXPERIMENTAL MUSIC
(Tape loops spliced at random)

ROCKY RACCOON
by John Lennon and Paul McCartney

1 Now somewhere in the Black Mountain
      hills of Dakota
2 There lived a young boy name of Rocky
      Raccoon
3 And one day his woman ran off with
      another guy
4 Hit young Rocky in the eye.

5 Rocky didn't like that
6 He said, I'm gonna get that boy
7 So one day he walked into town
8 Booked himself a room in the local saloon.

9 Rocky Raccoon checked into his room
10 Only to find Gideon's Bible
11 Rocky had come equipped with a gun
12 To shoot off the legs of his rival.

13 His rival it seems had broken his dreams
14 By stealing the girl of his fancy
15 Her name was Magill and she called

herself Lil
16 But everyone knew her as Nancy.

17 Now she and her man who called himself Dan
18 Were in the next room at the hoe-down
19 A - Rocky burst in and grinning a grin
20 He said, Danny - Boy this is a showdown.

21 But Daniel was hot, he drew first and shot
22 And Rocky collapsed in the corner - ah.

23 Da da da da da da
24 Da da da da da da
25 Da da da da da da da da da da
26 Do do do do
27 Do - do do do do
28 Do - do do do do do
29 Do - do do do do do do do do
30 Da da da da do do do do do do.

31 Now the doctor came in stinking of gin
32 And proceeded to lie on the table
33 He said, Rocky you met your match
34 And Rocky said, Doc it's only a scratch
35 And I'll be better, I'll be better
      Doc as soon as I am able.

36 A - now Rocky Raccoon, he fell back in
      his room
37 Only to find Gideon's Bible
38 Gideon checked out and he left it no
      doubt ((oh - Rocky - oh))
39 To help with good Rocky's revival - ah.

40 Oh yeah yeah
41 Do do do do do
42 Do - do do do do do
43 Do - do do do do do do do do do
44 Do do do do do
45 Do do do do - come on Rocky - boy
46 Do do do do - come on Rocky - boy
47 Do do do do do do do do
48 The story of Rocky, that's the song.

RUN FOR YOUR LIFE
by John Lennon and Paul McCartney

1 Well I'd rather see you dead, little girl
2 Than to be with another man.
3 You better keep your head, little girl
4 Or I won't know where I am.

5 You better run for your life if you can,
      little girl
6 Hide your head in the sand, little girl.
7 Catch you with another man
8 That's the end'a little girl.

9 Well you know that I'm a wicked guy
10 And I was born with a jealous mind
11 And I can't spend my whole life trying
12 Just to make you toe the line.

13 You better run for your life if you can,
      little girl
14 Hide your head in the sand, little girl.
15 Catch you with another man
16 That's the end'a little girl.

17 Let this be a sermon
18 I mean everything I've said.
19 Baby, I'm determined
20 And I'd rather see you dead.

21 You better run for your life if you can,
     little girl
22 Hide your head in the sand, little girl.
23 Catch you with another man
24 That's the end'a little girl.

25 I'd rather see you dead, little girl
26 Than to be with another man
27 You better keep your head, little girl
28 Or you won't know where I am.

29 You better run for your life if you can,
     little girl
30 Hide your head in the sand, little girl.
31 Catch you with another man
32 That's the end'a little girl.

33 Nah, nah, nah.
34 Nah, nah, nah.
35 Nah, nah, nah.
36 Nah, nah, nah.
37 Nah, nah, nah.

SAVOY TRUFFLE
by George Harrison

1 Creme tangerine, montelimar
2 A ginger sling with a pineapple heart.
3 Coffee dessert - yes you know it's good news
4 But you'll have to have them all pulled out
5 After the Savoy truffle.

6 Cool cherry cream, nice apple tart
7 I feel your taste all the time we're apart
8 Cocoanut fudge really blows down those
     blues (wuh)
9 But you'll have to have them all pulled out
10 After the Savoy truffle.

11 You might not feel it now
12 When the pain cuts through
13 You're gonna know and how.
14 The sweat it's gonna fill your head
15 When it becomes too much
16 You shout aloud.

17 But you'll have to have them all pulled out
18 After the Savoy truffle.

19 You know that what you eat you are
20 But what is sweet now turns so sour.
21 We all know ob-la-di 'b-la-da
22 But can you show me where you are?

23 Creme tangerine and montelimar
24 A ginger sling with a pineapple heart
25 Coffee dessert - yes you know it's good
     news (wuh)
26 But you'll have to have them all pulled out
27 After the Savoy truffle.

28 Yes, you'll have to have them all pulled out
29 After the Savoy truffle.

SGT. PEPPER'S LONELY HEARTS CLUB BAND
by John Lennon and Paul McCartney

1 It was twenty years ago today
2 That Sgt. Pepper taught the band to play
3 They've been going in and out of style
4 But they're guaranteed to raise a smile.

5 So may I introduce to you
6 The act you've known for all these years
7 Sgt. Pepper's Lonely Hearts Club Band.

8 We're Sgt. Pepper's Lonely Hearts
     Club Band
9 We hope you will enjoy the show
10 Sgt. Pepper's Lonely Hearts Club Band
11 Sit back and let the evening go.

12 Sgt. Pepper's Lonely, Sgt. Pepper's
     Lonely
13 Sgt. Pepper's Lonely Hearts Club Band.

14 It's wonderful to be here
15 It's certainly a thrill
16 You're such a lovely audience
17 We'd like to take you home with us
18 We'd love to take you home.

19 I don't really want to stop the show
20 But I thought you might like to know
21 That the singer's gonna sing a song
22 And he wants you all to sing along.

23 So let me introduce to you
24 The one and only Billy Shears
25 And Sgt. Pepper's Lonely Hearts Club
     Band.

26 Billy Shears!

SGT. PEPPER'S LONELY HEARTS CLUB BAND (REPRISE)
by John Lennon and Paul McCartney

1 One, two (ah yeah), three, four.

2 Wuh!

3 We're Sgt. Pepper's Lonely Hearts
     Club Band
4 We hope you have enjoyed the show.
5 Sgt. Pepper's Lonely Hearts Club Band
6 We're sorry but it's time to go.

7 Sgt. Pepper's Lonely
8 Sgt. Pepper's Lonely
9 Sgt. Pepper's Lonely
10 Sgt. Pepper's Lonely.

11 Sgt. Pepper's Lonely Hearts Club Band
12 We'd like to thank you once again.
13 Sgt. Pepper's one and only Lonely
     Hearts Club Band
14 It's getting very near the end.

15 Sgt. Pepper's Lonely
16 Sgt. Pepper's Lonely
17 Sgt. Pepper's Lonely Hearts Club Band.
18 Wuh!

SEXY SADIE
by John Lennon and Paul McCartney

1 Sexy Sadie what have you done?
2 You made a fool of everyone
3 You made a fool of everyone
4 Sexie Sadie - oh what have you done?

5 Sexy Sadie you broke the rules
6 You layed it down for all to see
7 You layed it down for all to see
8 Sexy Sadie - oh you broke the rules

9 One sunny day the world was waiting for
      the lover ((sexy Sadie))
10 She came along to turn on everyone
11 Sexy Sadie (sexy Sadie) the greatest
      of them all ((she's the greatest))

12 Sexy Sadie how did you know
13 The world was waiting just for you?
14 The world was waiting just for you?
15 Sexy Sadie - oh how did you know?

16 Sexy Sadie you'll get yours yet
17 However big you think you are
18 However big you think you are
19 Sexy Sadie - oh you'll get yours yet

20 We gave her everything we owned just to
      sit at her table ((sexy Sadie))
21 Just a smile would lighten everything
22 Sexy Sadie ((sexy Sadie))
23 She's the latest and the greatest (she's
      the greatest) of them all
24 (Sexy Sadie she's the latest and the
      greatest of them all)

25 Ooo

26 She made a fool of everyone
27 (Sexy Sadie)

28 ... However big you think you are.

SHE CAME IN THROUGH THE BATHROOM WINDOW
by John Lennon and Paul McCartney

1 Come on now.
2 Heh heh heh.
3 Oh look out!

4 She came in through the bathroom window
5 Protected by a silver spoon
6 But now she sucks her thumb and wonders
7 By the banks of her own lagoon.

8 Didn't anybody tell her?
9 Didn't anybody see?
10 Sundays on the phone to Monday
11 Tuesdays on the phone to me.

12 She said she'd always been a dancer
13 She worked at fifteen clubs a day
14 And though she thought I knew the answer

15 Well I knew what I could not say.

16 And so I quit the police department
17 And got myself a steady job
18 And though she tried her best to help me
19 She could steal but she could not rob.

20 Didn't anybody tell her?
21 Didn't anybody see?
22 Sundays on the phone to Monday
23 Tuesdays on the phone to me.
24 Oh yeah.

SHE LOVES YOU
by John Lennon and Paul McCartney

1 She loves you yeah, yeah, yeah
2 She loves you yeah, yeah, yeah
3 She loves you yeah, yeah, yeah, yeah.

4 You think you've lost your love
5 Well I saw her yesterday
6 It's you she's thinking of
7 And she told me what to say.

8 She said she loves you
9 And you know that can't be bad
10 Yeah, she loves you
11 And you know you should be glad.

12 She said you hurt her so
13 She almost lost her mind
14 But now she says she knows
15 You're not the hurting kind.

16 She said she loves you
17 And you know that can't be bad
18 Yeah, she loves you
19 And you know you should be glad - ooo!

20 She loves you, yeah, yeah, yeah
21 She loves you, yeah, yeah, yeah
22 With a love like that
23 You know you should be glad.

24 You know it's up to you
25 I think it's only fair
26 Pride can hurt you too
27 Apologize to her.

28 Because she loves you
29 And you know that can't be bad
30 Yeah, she loves you
31 And you know you should be glad - ooo!

32 She loves you, yeah, yeah, yeah
33 She loves you, yeah, yeah, yeah
34 With a love like that
35 You know you should be glad

36 With a love like that
37 You know you should be glad

38 With a love like that
39 You know you should be glad

40 Yeah, yeah, yeah
41 Yeah, yeah, yeah, yeah.

SHE SAID, SHE SAID
by John Lennon and Paul McCartney

1 She said I know what it's like to be dead
2 I know what it is to be sad
3 And she's making me feel like I've never
   been born.

4 I said who put all those things in your head
5 Things that make me feel that I'm mad
6 And you're making me feel like I've
   never been born.

7 She said you don't understand what I said.
8 I said no, no, no you're wrong.
9 When I was a boy everything was right,
   everything was right.

10 I said even though you know what you know
11 I know that I'm ready to leave,
12 'cos you're making me feel like I've
   never been born.

13 She said you don't understand what I said.
14 I said no, no, no you're wrong.
15 When I was a boy everything was right,
   everything was right.

16 I said even though you know what you know
17 I know that I'm ready to leave,
18 'cos you're making me feel like I've
   never been born.

19 She said (she said)
20 I know what it's like to be dead (I
   know what it's like to be dead)
21 I know what it is to be sad (I know
   what it is to be sad).
22 I know what it's like to be dead (I
   know what it's like to be dead).

SHE'S A WOMAN
by John Lennon and Paul McCartney

1 My love don't give me presents
2 I know that she's no peasant
3 Only ever has to give me love forever and
   forever
4 My love don't give me presents

5 Turn me on when I get lonely
6 People tell me that she's only fooling
7 I know she isn't

8 She don't give boys the eye
9 She hates to see me cry
10 She is happy just to hear me say that
11 I will never leave her
12 She don't give boys the eye

13 She will never make me jealous
14 Gives me all her time as well as loving
15 Don't ask me why

16 She's a woman who understands

17 She's a woman who loves her man

18 My love don't give me presents
19 I know that she's no peasant
20 Only ever has to give me love forever and
   forever
21 My love don't give me presents

22 Turn me on when I get lonely
23 People tell me that she's only fooling
24 I know she isn't

25 (Wuh)

26 She's a woman who understands
27 She's a woman who loves her man

28 My love don't give me presents
29 I know that she's no peasant
30 Only ever has to give me love forever and
   forever
31 My love don't give me presents

32 Turn me on when I get lonely
33 People tell me that she's only fooling
34 I know she isn't

35 She's a woman, she's a woman, she's a
   woman.

SHE'S LEAVING HOME
by John Lennon and Paul McCartney

1 Wednesday morning at five o'clock as the
   day begins
2 Silently closing her bedroom door
3 Leaving the note that she hoped would say
   more.

4 She goes downstairs to the kitchen
5 Clutching her handkerchief
6 Quietly turning the backdoor key
7 Stepping outside she is free.

8 She (we gave her most of our lives)
9 Is leaving (sacrificed most of our lives)
10 Home. (we gave her everything money
   could buy)
11 She's leaving home after living alone
12 For so many years. (('bye, 'bye))

13 Father snores as his wife gets into her
   dressing-gown
14 Picks up the letter that's lying there
15 Standing alone at the top of the stairs
16 She breaks down and cries to her husband
17 Daddy, our baby's gone.

18 Why would she treat us so thoughtlessly?
19 How could she do this to me?

20 She (we never thought of ourselves)
21 Is leaving (never a thought for our
   ourselves)
22 Home. (we struggled hard all our lives
   to get by)
23 She's leaving home after living alone
24 For so many years. (('bye, 'bye))

25 Friday morning at nine o'clock she is far away
26 Waiting to keep the appointment she made
27 Meeting a man from the motor trade.

28 She (what did we do that was wrong?)
29 Is having (we didn't know it was wrong)
30 Fun. (fun is the one thing that money
      can't buy)
31 Something inside that was always denied
32 For so many years. (('bye, 'bye))

33 She's leaving home. ('bye, 'bye)

SOMETHING
by George Harrison

1 Something in the way she moves
2 Attracts me like no other lover
3 Something in the way she woos me
4 I don't want to leave her now
5 You know I believe 'n' how.

6 Somewhere in her smile she knows
7 That I don't need no other lover
8 Something in her style that shows me
9 I don't want to leave her now
10 You know I believe 'n' how.

11 You're asking me will my love grow?
12 I don't know, I don't know
13 You stick around now it may show
14 I don't know, I don't know.

15 Something in the way she knows
16 And all I have to do is think of her
17 Something in the things she shows me
18 I don't want to leave her now
19 You know I believe 'n' how.

STRAWBERRY FIELDS FOREVER
by John Lennon and Paul McCartney

1 Let me take you down
2 'cos I'm going to strawberry fields
3 Nothing is real
4 And nothing to get hungabout
5 Strawberry fields forever.

6 Living is easy with eyes closed
7 Misunderstanding all you see
8 It's getting hard to be someone
9 But it all works out
10 It doesn't matter much to me.

11 Let me take you down
12 'cos I'm going to strawberry fields
13 Nothing is real
14 And nothing to get hungabout
15 Strawberry fields forever.

16 No-one, I think, is in my tree
17 I mean, it must be high or low
18 That is you can't, you know, tune in
19 But it's alright
20 That is, I think it's not too bad.

21 Let me take you down
22 'cos I'm going to strawberry fields
23 Nothing is real

24 And nothing to get hungabout
25 Strawberry fields forever.

26 Always, no, sometimes, think it's me
27 But, you know, I know when it's a dream
28 I think I know, I mean, er, yes
29 But it's all wrong
30 That is, I think I disagree.

31 Let me take you down
32 'cos I'm going to strawberry fields
33 Nothing is real
34 And nothing to get hungabout
35 Strawberry fields forever.

36 Strawberry fields forever.
37 Strawberry fields forever.

38 ... Cranberry sauce...

SUN KING
by John Lennon and Paul McCartney

1 Aah - here come the Sun King
2 Here come the Sun King.
3 Everybody's laughing
4 Everybody's happy.
5 Here come the Sun King.

6 Quando paramucho mi amore defeliche carathon
7 Mundo paparatsi mi amore chicka ferde
   parasol
8 Questo obrigado tanta mucho cake and eat
   it carousel.

TAXMAN
by George Harrison

1 One, two, three, four, one, two.
2 (One, two, three, four)

3 Let me tell you how it will be
4 There's one for you, nineteen for me
5 'cos I'm the Taxman
6 Yeah, I'm the Taxman.

7 Should five percent appear too small
8 Be thankful I don't take it all
9 'cos I'm the Taxman
10 Yeah, I'm the Taxman.

11 If you drive a car, I'll tax the street,
      ((car))
12 If you try to sit, I'll tax your seat,
      ((sit))
13 If you get too cold, I'll tax the heat,
      ((cold))
14 If you take a walk, I'll tax your feet.
      ((walk))

15 Taxman.

16 'cos I'm the Taxman
17 Yeah, I'm the Taxman.

18 Don't ask me what I want it for (ha
    ha Mr. Wilson)
19 If you don't want to pay some more (ha
    ha Mr. Heath)
20 'cos I'm the Taxman
21 Yeah, I'm the Taxman.

22 Now my advice for those who die (Taxman)
23 Declare the pennies on your eyes (Taxman)
24 'cos I'm the Taxman
25 Yeah, I'm the Taxman.

26 And you're working for no-one but me
    (Taxman).

TELL ME WHAT YOU SEE
by John Lennon and Paul McCartney

1 If you let me take your heart
2 I will prove to you
3 We will never be apart
4 If I'm part of you

5 Open up your eyes now
6 Tell me what you see
7 It is no surprise now
8 What you see is me

9 Big and black the clouds may be
10 Time will pass away
11 If you put your trust in me
12 I'll make bright your day

13 Look into these eyes now
14 Tell me what you see
15 Don't you realise now
16 What you see is me

17 Tell me what you see

18 Listen to me one more time
19 How can I get through
20 Can't you try to see that I'm
21 Trying to get to you

22 Open up your eyes now
23 Tell me what you see
24 It is no surprise now
25 What you see is me

26 Tell me what you see

27 Listen to me one more time
28 How can I get through
29 Can't you try to see that I'm
30 Trying to get to you

31 Open up your eyes now
32 Tell me what you see
33 It is no surprise now
34 What you see is me

35 Mmm-mmm - mmm-mmm-mmm.

TELL ME WHY
by John Lennon and Paul McCartney

1 Tell me why you cried
2 And why you lied to me
3 Tell me why you cried
4 And why you lied to me.

5 Well I gave you everything I had
6 But you left me sitting on my own
7 Did you have to treat me oh so bad
8 All I do is hang my head and moan.

9 Tell me why you cried
10 And why you lied to me
11 Tell me why you cried
12 And why you lied to me.

13 If it's something that I said or done
14 Tell me what and I'll apologize
15 If you don't I really can't go on
16 Holding back these tears in my eyes.

17 Tell me why you cried
18 And why you lied to me
19 Tell me why you cried
20 And why you lied to me.

21 Well I beg you on my bended knees
22 If you'll only listen to my pleas
23 If there's anything I can do
24 'cos I really can't stand it
25 I'm so in love with you.

26 Tell me why you cried
27 And why you lied to me.
28 Tell me why you cried
29 And why you lied to me.

THANK YOU GIRL
by John Lennon and Paul McCartney

1 Oh, oh - mmm, you've been good to me
2 You made me glad when I was blue
3 And eternally I'll always be in love with you
4 And all I gotta do is thank you girl,
    thank you girl.

5 I could tell the world a thing or two
    about our love
6 I know, little girl, only a fool would
    doubt our love
7 And all I gotta do is thank you girl,
    thank you girl
8 Thank you girl, for loving me the way
    that you do (way that you do).

9 That's the kind of love that is too good
    to be true
10 And all I gotta do is thank you girl,
    thank you girl.

11 Oh, oh - mmm, you've been good to me
12 You made me glad when I was blue
13 And eternally I'll always be in love with you
14 And all I gotta do is thank you girl,
    thank you girl.

15 Oh, oh, oh
16 Oh, oh, oh
17 Oh, oh.

28 Love me all the time girl
29 We'll go on and on.

30 Someday when we're dreaming
31 Deep in love, not a lot to say
32 Then we will remember things we said today.

THERE'S A PLACE
by John Lennon and Paul McCartney

1 There, there's a place where I can go
2 When I feel low, when I feel blue
3 And it's my mind and there's no time
4 When I'm alone.

5 I think of you
6 And things you do go round my head
7 The things you said
8 Like I love only you.

9 In my mind there's no sorrow
10 Don't you know that it's so?
11 There'll be no sad tomorrow
12 Don't you know that it's so?

13 There, there's a place where I can go
14 When I feel low, when I feel blue
15 And it's my mind and there's no time
16 When I'm alone.

17 There's a place, there's a place
18 There's a place, there's a place.

THINGS WE SAID TODAY
by John Lennon and Paul McCartney

1 You say you will love me if I have to go
2 You'll be thinking of me, somehow I
    will know
3 Someday when I'm lonely
4 Wishing you weren't so far away,
5 Then I will remember things we said today.

6 You say you'll be mine girl, till the
    end of time
7 These days such a kind girl seems so hard
    to find
8 Someday when we're dreaming
9 Deep in love, not a lot to say
10 Then we will remember things we said today.

11 Me I'm just the lucky kind
12 Love to hear you say that love is love
13 And though we may be blind
14 Love is here to stay.

15 And that's enough to make you mine girl
16 Be the only one
17 Love me all the time girl
18 We'll go on and on.

19 Someday when we're dreaming
20 Deep in love, not a lot to say
21 Then we will remember things we said today.

22 Me I'm just the lucky kind
23 Love to hear you say that love is love
24 And though we may be blind
25 Love is here to stay.

26 And that's enough to make you mine girl
27 Be the only one

THINK FOR YOURSELF
by George Harrison

1 I've got a word or two
2 To say about the things that you do.
3 You're telling all those lies
4 About the good things
5 That we can have if we close our eyes.

6 Do what you want to do
7 And go where you're going to,
8 Think for yourself
9 'cos I won't be there with you.

10 I left you far behind
11 The ruins of the life that you had in mind
12 And though you still can't see
13 I know your mind's made up
14 You're gonna cause more misery.

15 Do what you want to do
16 And go where you're going to
17 Think for yourself
18 'cos I won't be there with you.

19 Although your mind's opaque
20 Try thinking more if just for your own sake.
21 The future still looks good
22 And you've got time to rectify
23 All the things that you should.

24 Do what you want to do
25 And go where you're going to
26 Think for yourself
27 'cos I won't be there with you.

28 Do what you want to do
29 And go where you're going to
30 Think for yourself
31 'cos I won't be there with you.

32 Think for yourself
33 'cos I won't be there with you.

THIS BOY (RINGO'S THEME)
by John Lennon and Paul McCartney

1 That boy took my love away
2 Though he'll regret it someday
3 But this boy wants you back again.

4 That boy isn't good for you
5 Though he may want you too
6 This boy wants you back again.

7 Oh, and this boy would be happy
8 Just to love you, but oh my!
9 That boy won't be happy

10 Till he's seen you cry.

11 This boy wouldn't mind the pain
12 Would always feel the same
13 If this boy gets you back again.

14 This boy, this boy, this boy.

TICKET TO RIDE
by John Lennon and Paul McCartney

1 One, two, three, four.

2 I think I'm gonna be sad
3 I think it's today, yeah
4 The girl that's driving me mad is going away.

5 She's got a ticket to ride
6 She's got a ticket to ride
7 She's got a ticket to ride
8 But she don't care.

9 She said that living with me
10 Was bringing her down, yeah
11 She would never be free
12 When I was around.

13 She's got a ticket to ride
14 She's got a ticket to ride
15 She's got a ticket to ride
16 But she don't care.

17 I don't know why she's riding so high
18 She ought to think twice
19 She ought to do right by me
20 Before she gets to saying goodbye
21 She ought to think twice
22 She ought to do right by me.

23 I think I'm gonna be sad
24 I think it's today, yeah
25 The girl that's driving me mad is going
    away, yeah.

26 Oh, she's got a ticket to ride
27 She's got a ticket to ride
28 She's got a ticket to ride
29 But she don't care.

30 I don't know why she's riding so high
31 She ought to think twice
32 She ought to do right by me
33 Before she gets to saying goodbye
34 She ought to think twice
35 She ought to do right by me.

36 She said that living with me
37 Was bringing her down, yeah
38 She would never be free
39 When I was around.

40 Ah, she's got a ticket to ride
41 She's got a ticket to ride
42 She's got a ticket to ride
43 But she don't care.

44 My baby don't care
45 My baby don't care
46 My baby don't care
47 My baby don't care
48 My baby don't care
49 My ...

TOMORROW NEVER KNOW
by John Lennon and Paul McCartney

1 Turn off your mind, relax and float
   down-stream
2 It is not dying, it is not dying.

3 Lay down all thought, surrender to the void
4 It is shining, it is shining.

5 That you may see the meaning of within
6 It is being, it is being.

7 That love is all and love is everyone
8 It is knowing, it is knowing.

9 That ignorance and hate may mourn the dead
10 It is believing, it is believing.

11 But listen to the colour of your dreams
12 It is not living, it is not living.

13 Or play the game existence to the end
14 Of the beginning
15 Of the beginning
16 Of the beginning
17 Of the beginning
18 Of the beginning
19 Of the beginning
20 Of the beginning.

TWO OF US
by John Lennon and Paul McCartney

1 I dig a pygmy by Charles Hawtrey and the
   Deaf Aids (ha ha ha)
2 Phase one in which Doris gets her oats.

3 Two of us riding nowhere
4 Spending someone's hard-earned pay.
5 You and me Sunday driving
6 Not arriving on our way back home.
7 We're on our way home
8 We're on our way home
9 We're going home.

10 Two of us sending postcards
11 Writing letters on my wall.
12 You and me burning matches
13 Lifting latches on our way back home.
14 We're on our way home
15 We're on our way home
16 We're going home.

17 You and I have memories
18 Longer than the road that stretches out
    ahead.

19 Two of us wearing raincoats
20 Standing solo in the sun.
21 You and me chasing paper
22 Getting nowhere on our way back home.
23 We're on our way home
24 We're on our way home
25 We're going home.

26 You and I have memories
27 Longer than the road that stretches out
     ahead.

28 Two of us wearing raincoats
29 Standing solo in the sun.
30 You and me chasing paper
31 Getting nowhere on our way back home.
32 We're on our way home
33 We're on our way home
34 We're going home.

35 We're going home.

36 You better believe it.

37 Goodbye.

WAIT
by John Lennon and Paul McCartney

1 It's been a long time, now I'm coming
     back home
2 I've been away now, oh how I've been alone.
3 Wait till I come back to your side
4 We'll forget the tears we've cried.

5 But if your heart breaks, don't wait,
     turn me away
6 And if your heart's strong, hold on, I
     won't delay.
7 Wait till I come back to your side
8 We'll forget the tears we cried.

9 I feel as though you ought to know
10 That I've been good, as good as I can be.
11 And if you do, I'll trust in you
12 And know that you will wait for me.

13 It's been a long time, now I'm coming
     back home
14 I've been away now, oh how I've been alone.
15 Wait till I come back to your side
16 We'll forget the tears we've cried.

17 I feel as though you ought to know
18 That I've been good, as good as I can be.
19 And if you do, I'll trust in you
20 And know that you will wait for me.

21 But if your heart breaks, don't wait,
     turn me away
22 And if your heart's strong, hold on, I
     won't delay.
23 Wait till I come back to your side
24 We'll forget the tears we've cried.

25 It's been a long time, now I'm coming
     back home
26 I've been away now, oh how I've been alone.

WE CAN WORK IT OUT
by John Lennon and Paul McCartney

1 Try to see it my way
2 Do I have to keep on talking till I
     can't go on?
3 While you see it your way
4 Run the risk of knowing that our love may
     soon be gone.
5 We can work it out, we can work it out.

6 Think of what you're saying
7 You can get it wrong and still you think
     that it's alright.
8 Think of what I'm saying
9 We can work it out and get it straight or
     say good night.
10 We can work it out, we can work it out.

11 Life is very short and there's no time
12 For fussing and fighting my friend.
13 I have always thought that it's a crime
14 So I will ask you once again.

15 Try to see it my way
16 Only time will tell if I am right or I
     am wrong.
17 While you see it your way
18 There's a chance that we might fall apart
     before too long.
19 We can work it out, we can work it out.

20 Life is very short and there's no time
21 For fussing and fighting my friend.
22 I have always thought that it's a crime
23 So I will ask you once again.

24 Try to see it my way
25 Only time will tell if I am right or I
     am wrong.
26 While you see it your way
27 There's a chance that we might fall apart
     before too long.
28 We can work it out, we can work it out.

WHAT GOES ON?
by John Lennon, Paul McCartney and Richard Starkey

1 What goes on in your heart? (wuh)
2 What goes on in your mind?
3 You are tearing me apart
4 When you treat me so unkind.
5 What goes on in your mind?

6 The other day I saw you as I walked
     along the road
7 But when I saw him with you I could
     feel my future fold.
8 It's so easy for a girl like you to lie.
9 Tell me why.

10 What goes on in your heart?
11 What goes on in your mind?
12 You are tearing me apart
13 When you treat me so unkind.
14 What goes on in your mind?

15 I met you in the morning waiting for the
     tides of time
16 But now the tide is turning I can see
     that I was blind.
17 It's so easy for a girl like you to lie.
18 Tell me why (tell me why).

19 What goes on in your heart?
20 (Wuh)

21 (What goes on in your mind?)
22 I used to think of no-one else but you
    were just the same
23 You didn't even think of me as someone
    with a name.
24 Did you mean to break my heart and watch
    me die?
25 Tell me why.

26 What goes on in your heart?
27 What goes on in your mind?
28 You are tearing me apart
29 When you treat me so unkind.
30 What goes on in your mind?
31 In your mind.
32 In your mind.

WHAT YOU'RE DOING
by John Lennon and Paul McCartney

1 Look ((look)) what you're doing
2 I'm ((I'm)) feeling blue and lonely
3 Would it be too much to ask of you
4 What you're doing to me?

5 You ((you)) got me running
6 And ((and)) there's no fun in it
7 Why should it be so much to ask of you
8 What you're doing to me?

9 I've been waiting here for you
10 Wondering what you're gonna do
11 'n' should you need a love that's true,
    it's me.

12 Please ((please)) stop your lying
13 You've ((you've)) got me crying, girl
14 Why should it be so much to ask of you
15 What you're doing to me?

16 I've been waiting here for you
17 Wondering what you're gonna do
18 'n' should you need a love that's true
    it's me.

19 Please ((please)) stop your lying
20 You've ((you've)) got me crying, girl
21 Why should it be so much to ask of you
22 What you're doing to me?
23 What you're doing to me?
24 What you're doing to me?

WHEN I GET HOME
by John Lennon and Paul McCartney

1 Whoa-oh-aah, whoa-oh-aah
2 I got a whole lot of things to tell her
3 When I get home.

4 Come on, out my way
5 'cos I'm a - gonna see my baby today
6 I got a whole lot of things I gotta say
    to her.

7 Whoa-oh-aah, whoa-oh-aah
8 I got a whole lot of things to tell her
9 When I get home.

10 Come on if you please
11 I got no time for triviality
12 I got a girl who's waiting home for me
    tonight.

13 Whoa-oh-aah, whoa-oh-aah
14 I got a whole lot of things to tell her
15 When I get home.

16 When I getting home tonight
17 I'm gonna hold her tight
18 I'm gonna love her till the cows come home
19 I bet I'll love her more
20 Till I walk out that door again.

21 Come on, let me through
22 I got so many things I gotta do
23 I got no business being here with you
    this way.

24 Whoa-oh-aah, whoa-oh-aah
25 I got a whole lot of things to tell her
26 When I get home, yeah.

27 I got a whole lot of things to tell her
28 When I get home.

WHEN I'M SIXTY--FOUR
by John Lennon and Paul McCartney

1 When I get older losing my hair
2 Many years from now
3 Will you still be sending me a valentine
4 Birthday greetings, bottle of wine?

5 If I'd been out till quarter to three
6 Would you lock the door?
7 Will you still need me
8 Will you still feed me
9 When I'm sixty-four?

10 You'll be older too
11 And if you say the word
12 I could stay with you.

13 I could be handy mending a fuse
14 When your lights have gone.
15 You can knit a sweater by the fireside
16 Sunday mornings go for a ride.

17 Doing the garden, digging the weeds
18 Who could ask for more?
19 Will you still need me
20 Will you still feed me
21 When I'm sixty-four?

22 Every summer we can rent a cottage
23 In the Isle of Wight
24 If it's not too dear
25 We shall scrimp and save ((we shall
    scrimp and save))
26 Grandchildren on your knee
'27 Vera, Chuck and Dave.

28 Send me a postcard, drop me a line
29 Stating point of view.
30 Indicate precisely what you mean to say
31 Yours sincerely, wasting away.

32 Give me your answer
33 Fill in a form
34 Mine for evermore.

35 A - will you still need me
36 Will you still feed me
37 When I'm sixty-four?
38 Hoo!

WHILE MY GUITAR GENTLY WEEPS
by George Harrison

1 Hey up!

2 I look at you all, see the love there
    that's sleeping
3 While my guitar gently weeps.
4 I look at the floor and I see it needs
    sweeping
5 Still my guitar gently weeps.

6 I don't know why nobody told you how to
    unfold your love
7 I don't know how someone controlled you
8 They bought and sold you.

9 I look at the world and I notice it's
    turning
10 While my guitar gently weeps.
11 With every mistake we must surely be
    learning
12 Still my guitar gently weeps.

13 (Aah - aah)

14 I don't know how you were diverted
15 You were perverted (too/to).
16 I don't know how you were inverted
17 No-one alerted you.

18 I look at you all, see the love there
    that's sleeping
19 While my guitar gently weeps.
20 Look, look at you all
21 Still my guitar gently weeps ((eee)).

22 Oh, oh, oh - oh, oh.
23 Oh - oh, oh - oh, oh - oh, oh ((eee)).
24 Oh - oh, oh - oh, oh - oh ((eee)).
25 Yeah, yeah, yeah, yeah, yeah, yeah
    yeah, yeah, yeah ((eee))
26 Oh - wuh ... ((eee)).

WHY DON'T WE DO IT IN THE ROAD?
by John Lennon and Paul McCartney

1 Why don't we do - do it in the road?
2 Why don't we do it in the road? (ah-ha)
3 Why don't we do it in the road? - mmm
4 Why don't we do it in the road?
5 No-one will be watching us
6 Why don't we do it in the road?

7 Why don't we do it in the road?

8 Why don't we do it in the road?
9 Why don't we do it in the road?
10 Why don't we do it in the road?
11 No-one will be watching us
12 Why don't we do it in the road?

13 Well, why don't we do it in the road?
14 Why don't we do it in the road?
15 Why don't we do - do it, do it in the road?
16 Why don't we do it, yeah, in the road?
17 No-one will be watching us
18 Why don't you do it in the road?

WILD HONEY PIE
by John Lennon and Paul McCartney

1 Honey Pie, Honey Pie.

2 Honey Pie, Honey Pie.

3 Honey Pie, Honey Pie, Honey Pie,
    Honey Pie
4 I love you, yeah, Honey Pie, wuh!

WITH A LITTLE HELP FROM MY FRIENDS
by John Lennon and Paul McCartney

1 What would you think if I sang outta tune
2 Would you stand up and walk out on me?
3 Lend me your ears and I'll sing you a song
4 And I'll try not to sing outta key.

5 Oh I get by with a little help from my
    friends
6 Mmm I get high with a little help from
    my friends
7 Mmm gonna try with a little help from my
    friends.

8 What do I do when my love is away?
9 (Does it worry you to be alone?)
10 How do I feel by the end of the day?
11 (Are you sad because you're on your own?)

12 No I get by with a little help from my
    friends
13 Mmm get high with a little help from my
    friends
14 Mmm gonna try with a little help from my
    friends.

15 (Do you need anybody?)
16 I need somebody to love.
17 (Could it be anybody?)
18 I want somebody to love.

19 (Would you believe in a love at first
    sight?)
20 Yes I'm certain that it happens all the
    time.
21 (What do you see when you turn out the
    light?)
22 I can't tell you but I know it's mine.

23 Oh I get by with a little help from my

friends
24 Mmm get high with a little help from my
    friends
25 Oh I'm gonna try with a little help from
    my friends.

26 (Do you need anybody?)
27 I just need someone to love.
28 (Could it be anybody?)
29 I want somebody to love.

30 Oh I get by with a little help from my
    friends
31 Mmm gonna try with a little help from my
    friends
32 Oh I get high with a little help from my
    friends
33 Yes I get by with a little help from my
    friends
34 With a little help from my friends.

WITHIN YOU, WITHOUT YOU
by George Harrison

1 We were talking
2 About the space between us all
3 And the people
4 Who hide themselves behind a wall of illusion
5 Never glimpse the truth
6 When it's far too late
7 When they pass away.

8 We were talking
9 About the love we all could share
10 When we find it
11 To try our best to hold it there
12 With our love
13 With our love
14 We could save the world
15 If they only knew.

16 Try to realise it's all within yourself
17 No-one else can make you change
18 And to see you're really only very small
19 And life flows on within you and without you.

20 One, two - one, two.

21 We were talking
22 About the love that's gone so cold
23 And the people
24 Who gain the world and lose their soul
25 They don't know
26 They can't see
27 Are you one of them?

28 When you've seen beyond yourself
29 Then you may find
30 Peace of mind is waiting there
31 And the time will come
32 When you see we're all one
33 And life flows on within you and without you.

THE WORD
by John Lennon and Paul McCartney

1 Say the word and you'll be free
2 Say the word and be like me
3 Say the word I'm thinking of
4 Have you heard the word is love?
5 It's so fine, it's sunshine
6 It's the word love.

7 In the beginning I misunderstood
8 But now I've got it the word is good.
9 Spread the word and you'll be free
10 Spread the word and be like me
11 Spread the word I'm thinking of
12 Have you heard the word is love?
13 It's so fine, it's sunshine,
14 It's the word love.

15 Everywhere I go I hear it said
16 In the good and the bad books that I
    have read.
17 Say the word and you'll be free
18 Say the word and be like me
19 Say the word I'm thinking of
20 Have you heard the word is love?
21 It's so fine, it's sunshine
22 It's the word love.

23 Now that I know what I feel must be right
24 I'm here to show everybody the light.
25 Give the word a chance to say
26 That the word is just the way
27 It's the word I'm thinking of
28 And the only word is love.
29 It's so fine, it's sunshine
30 It's the word love.

31 Say the word love
32 Say the word love
33 Say the word love
34 Say the word love.

YELLOW SUBMARINE
by John Lennon and Paul McCartney

1 In the town where I was born
2 Lived a man who sailed to sea
3 And he told us of his life
4 In the land of submarines.

5 So we sailed on to the sun
6 Till we found a sea of green
7 And we lived beneath the waves
8 In our yellow submarine.

9 We all live in a yellow submarine
10 Yellow submarine, yellow submarine.
11 We all live in a yellow submarine
12 Yellow submarine, yellow submarine.

13 And our friends are all aboard
14 Many more of them live next door
15 And the band begins to play.

16 We all live in a yellow submarine
17 Yellow submarine, yellow submarine.
18 We all live in a yellow submarine
19 Yellow submarine, yellow submarine.

20 (Full speed ahead, Mr. Bosun, full
    speed ahead.
21 Full speed ahead it is, Sgt.
22 Cut the cable, drop the cable.
23 Aye, Sir, aye.

24 Captain, Captain.)

25 As we live a life of ease
26 Everyone of us (everyone of us) has all
        we need (has all we need)
27 Sky of blue (sky of blue) and sea of
        green (sea of green)
28 In our yellow (in our yellow) submarine
        (submarine - ah ha!)

29 We all live in a yellow submarine
30 A yellow submarine, a yellow submarine.
31 We all live in a yellow submarine
32 A yellow submarine, yellow submarine.
33 We all live in a yellow submarine
34 Yellow submarine, yellow submarine.
35 We all live in a yellow submarine
36 Yellow submarine, yellow submarine.

YER BLUES
by John Lennon and Paul McCartney

1 Two, three.

2 Yes I'm lonely - wanna die
3 Yes I'm lonely - wanna die
4 If I ain't dead already
5 Ooo - girl you know the reason why.

6 In the morning - wanna die
7 In the evening - wanna die
8 If I ain't dead already
9 Wuh - girl you know the reason why.

10 My mother was of the sky
11 My father was of the earth
12 But I am of the universe
13 And you know what it's worth.

14 I'm lonely - wanna die
15 If I ain't dead already
16 Wuh - girl you know the reason why.

17 The eagle picks my eye
18 The worm he licks my bone,
19 Feel so suicidal
20 Just like Dylan's Mr. Jones.

21 Lonely - wanna die
22 If I ain't dead already
23 Wuh - girl you know the reason why.

24 Black cloud crossed my mind
25 Blue mist round my soul
26 Feels so suicidal
27 Even hate my rock 'n' roll.

28 Wanna die, yeah wanna die
29 If I ain't dead already
30 Wuh girl - you know the reason why.

31 Yes I'm lonely - wanna die
32 Yes I'm lonely - wanna die
33 ... Girl you know the reason why.

34 ... Wanna die
35 In the evening ...

YES IT IS
by John Lennon and Paul McCartney

1 If you wear red tonight
2 Remember what I said tonight
3 For red is the colour that my baby wore
4 And what's more, it's true, yes it is.

5 Scarlet were the clothes she wore
6 Everybody knows I'm sure
7 I would remember all the things we planned
8 Understand it's true
9 Yes it is, it's true, yes it is.

10 I could be happy with you by my side
11 If I could forget her
12 But it's my pride
13 Yes it is, yes it is, oh yes it is, yeah.

14 Please don't wear red tonight
15 This is what I said tonight
16 For red is the colour that will make me blue
17 In spite of you it's true
18 Yes it is, it's true, yes it is.

19 I could be happy with you by my side
20 If I could forget her
21 But it's my pride
22 Yes it is, yes it is, oh yes it is, yeah.

23 Please don't wear red tonight
24 This is what I said tonight
25 For red is the colour that will make me blue
26 In spite of you it's true
27 Yes it is, it's true
28 Yes it is, it's true.

YESTERDAY
by John Lennon and Paul McCartney

1 Yesterday
2 All my troubles seemed so far away
3 Now it looks as though they're here to stay
4 Oh I believe in yesterday.

5 Suddenly
6 I'm not half the man I used to be
7 There's a shadow hanging over me
8 Oh yesterday came suddenly.

9 Why she had to go, I don't know
10 She wouldn't say
11 I said something wrong
12 Now I long for yesterday.

13 Yesterday
14 Love was such an easy game to play
15 Now I need a place to hide away
16 Oh I believe in yesterday.

17 Why she had to go, I don't know
18 She wouldn't say
19 I said something wrong
20 Now I long for yesterday.

21 Yesterday
22 Love was such an easy game to play
23 Now I need a place to hide away
24 Oh I believe in yesterday.

25 Mmm mmm mmm – mmm mmm mmm–mmm.

YOU CAN'T DO THAT
by John Lennon and Paul McCartney

1 I got something to say
2 That might cause you pain
3 If I catch you talking
4 To that boy again.

5 I'm gonna let you down
6 And leave you flat
7 Because I told you before
8 Oh you can't do that.

9 Well, it's the second time
10 I caught you talking to him
11 Do I have to tell you one more time
12 I think it's a sin?

13 I think I'll let you down (let you down)
14 And leave you flat
15 (Gonna let you down and leave you flat)
16 Because I told you before
17 Oh you can't do that.

18 Everybody's green
19 'cos I'm the one who won your love
20 But if they'd seen
21 You talking that way
22 They'd laugh in my face.

23 So please listen to me
24 If you wanna stay mine
25 I can't help my feelings
26 I go outta my mind.

27 I'm gonna let you down (let you down)
28 And leave you flat
29 (Gonna let you down and leave you flat)
30 Because I told you before
31 Oh you can't do that - no!

32 You can't do that
33 You can't do that
34 You can't do that
35 You can't do that
36 You can't do that.

37 Everybody's green
38 'cos I'm the one who won your love
39 But if they'd seen
40 You talking that way
41 They'd laugh in my face.

42 So please listen to me
43 If you wanna stay mine
44 I can't help my feelings
45 I go outta my mind.

46 I'm gonna let you down (let you down)
47 And leave you flat
48 (Gonna let you down and leave you flat)
49 Because I told you before
50 Oh you can't do that.

YOU KNOW MY NAME
(LOOK UP MY NUMBER)
by John Lennon and Paul McCartney

1 You know my name, look up de number
2 You know my name, look up de number.
3 You, you know, you know my name
4 You, you know, you know my name.

5 Good evening and welcome to Slaggers
6 Featuring Dennis O'Fell and Ringo.
7 Good evening (Ringo).
8 Let's hear it for Dennis - ah-hey.

9 Good evening, you know my name, well
       then look up my number
10 You know my name, that's right, look up
       my number (hey)
11 You, you know, you know my name ((you
       know my name))
12 You, you know, you know my name
       (brrrrrr - ha, hey!)
13 You know my name, ba ba ba ba ba ba ba
       ba ((yahoo))
14 Look up the number (heads up boys)
15 You know my name - haa, that's right,
       look up the number
16 (Oh) oh, you know, you know, you
       know my name (come on Dennis)
17 You know, you know, you know my name,
       ha ha ha ha
18 You know my name, ba ba ba bum, look up
       the number
19 You know my name, look up the number
20 You, you know, you know my name, baby
21 You, you know, you know my name
22 You know, you know my name
23 You know, you know my name ((oh, let's
       hear it, come on Dennis))
24 Let's hear it for Dennis O'Fell.

25 My name, you know, you know, ((look
       up the number))
26 You know my name (you know my number).
27 You know, ((you know my name))
28 You know, you know my name. ((you
       know my number))
29 You know my name, look up the number
30 You know my name, look up the number.
31 You know, you know my name, look up the
       number.
32 Yes, you know, ((you know my name))
33 You know my name ((you know)), you
       know me number (too/two)

34 You know my name, you know me number three
35 You know my name, you know me number four
36 You know my name, look up the number
37 You know my name ((you know)), you
       know me number (too/two)

38 (look up my name)
39 You know my name ((you know my name))
40 You know my number, what's up with you? - ha
41 You know my name.

42 That's right (yeah)...
43 ... Heavy, heavy...

44 ... Heavy...

45 ... Heavy, heavy...

46 That's all!
47 How about that?

YOU LIKE ME TOO MUCH
by George Harrison

1 Though you've gone away this morning
2 You'll be back again tonight
3 Telling me there'll be no next time
4 If I just don't treat you right

5 You'll never leave me and you know it's true
6 'cos you like me too much and I like you

7 You've tried before to leave me
8 But you haven't got the nerve
9 To walk out and make me lonely
10 Which is all that I deserve

11 You'll never leave me and you know it's true
12 'cos you like me too much and I like you
13 I really do.

14 And it's nice when you believe me
15 If you leave me I will follow you
16 And bring you back where you belong
17 'cos I couldn't really stand it
18 I'd admit that I was wrong

19 I wouldn't let you leave me 'cos it's true
20 'cos you like me too much and I like you

21 'cos you like me too much and I like you
22 I really do

23 And it's nice when you believe me
24 If you leave me I will follow you
25 And bring you back where you belong
26 'cos I couldn't really stand it
27 I'd admit that I was wrong

28 I wouldn't let you leave me 'cos it's true
29 'cos you like me too much and I like you
30 'cos you like me too much and I like you.

YOU NEVER GIVE ME YOUR MONEY
by John Lennon and Paul McCartney

1 You never give me your money
2 You only give me your funny paper
3 And in the middle of negotiations you
    break down.

4 I never give you my number
5 I only give you my situation
6 And in the middle of investigation I
    break down.

7 Out of college, money spent
8 See no future, pay no rent
9 All the money's gone, nowhere to go.

10 Any jobber got the sack
11 Monday morning turning back
12 Yellow lorry slow, nowhere to go.

13 But oh, that magic feeling, nowhere to go
14 Oh, that magic feeling,

15 Nowhere to go - nowhere to go.

16 Aah - ooo, aah - ooo, aah - ooo.

17 One sweet dream
18 Pick up the bags, get in the limousine.
19 Soon we'll be away from here
20 Step on the gas and wipe that tear away.

21 One sweet dream came true today
22 Came true today, came true today.
23 Yes it did, nah nah nah nah nah nah nah - nah

24 One, two, three, four, five, six,
    seven
25 All good children go to heaven.
26 One, two, three, four, five, six,
    seven
27 All good children go to heaven.
28 One, two, three, four, five, six,
    seven
29 All good children go to heaven.
30 One, two, three, four, five, six,
    seven
31 All good children go to heaven.
32 One, two, three, four, five, six,
    seven
33 All good children go to heaven.
34 One, two, three, four, five, six,
    seven
35 All good children go to heaven.
36 One, two, three, four, five, six,
    seven
37 All good children go to heaven.
38 One, two, three, four, five, six,
    seven
39 All good children go to heaven
40 One, two, three, four, five, six,
    seven
41 All good children...

YOU WON'T SEE ME
by John Lennon and Paul McCartney

1 When I call you up your line's engaged.
2 I have had enough, so act your age.
3 We have lost the time that was so hard to find
4 And I will lose my mind
5 If you won't see me (you won't see me)
6 You won't see me (you won't see me).

7 I don't know why you should want to hide
8 But I can't get through, my hands are tied.
9 I won't want to stay, I don't have much
    to say
10 But I can turn away
11 And you won't see me (you won't see me)
12 You won't see me (you won't see me).

13 Time after time you refuse to even listen
14 I wouldn't mind if I knew what I was
    missing.
15 ((No I wouldn't, no I wouldn't))

16 Though the days are few, they're filled
    with tears
17 And since I lost you it feels like years.
18 Yes it seems so long, girl, since
    you've been gone
19 And I just can't go on
20 If you won't see me (you won't see me)
21 You won't see me (you won't see me)

22 Time after time you refuse to even listen
23 I wouldn't mind if I knew what I was
     missing.
24 ((No I wouldn't, no I wouldn't))

25 Though the days are few they're filled
     with tears
26 And since I lost you it feels like years.
27 Yes it seems so long, girl, since
     you've been gone
28 And I just can't go on
29 If you won't see me (you won't see me)
30 You won't see me (you won't see me).

31 (Yeah) ooo (come on) la la la la
32 (Oh yeah) ooo - la la la la
33 Ooo - la la la la.

YOUR MOTHER SHOULD KNOW
by John Lennon and Paul McCartney

1 Ooo - ooo.
2 Let's all get up and dance to a song
3 That was a hit before your mother was born
4 Though she was born a long, long time ago
5 Your mother should know (your mother
     should)
6 Your mother should know - aah.

7 Sing it again.
8 Let's all get up and dance to a song
9 That was a hit before your mother was born
10 Though she was born a long, long time ago
11 Your mother should know (your mother
     should)
12 Your mother should know - aah.

13 Lift up your hearts and sing me a song
14 That was a hit before your mother was born
15 Though she was born a long, long time ago
16 Your mother should know (your mother
     should)
17 Your mother should know - aah.
18 Your mother should know (your mother
     should)
19 Your mother should know - aah.

20 Sing it again.
21 Da da da-da da da da da da
22 Da da da da da-da-da-da-da.
23 Though she was born a long, long time ago
24 Your mother should know (your mother
     should)
25 Your mother should know - yeah ((ooo)).
26 Your mother should know (your mother
     should)
27 Your mother should know - yeah.
28 Your mother should know (your mother
     should)
29 Your mother should know - yeah.

YOU'RE GOING TO/GONNA LOSE
THAT GIRL
by John Lennon and Paul McCartney

1 You're gonna lose that girl (yes, yes,
     you're gonna lose that girl)
2 You're gonna lose that girl (yes, yes,
     you're gonna lose that girl)

3 If you don't take her out tonight
4 She's gonna change her mind (she's gonna
     change her mind)
5 And I will take her out tonight
6 And I will treat her kind (I'm gonna
     treat her kind)

7 You're gonna lose that girl (yes, yes,
     you're gonna lose that girl)
8 You're gonna lose that girl (yes, yes,
     you're gonna lose that girl)

9 If you don't treat her right my friend
10 You're gonna find her gone (you're gonna
     find her gone)
11 'cos I will treat her right
12 And then you'll be the lonely one
     (you're not the only one)

13 You're gonna lose that girl (yes, yes,
     you're gonna lose that girl)
14 You're gonna lose that girl (yes, yes,
     you're gonna lose that girl)
15 You're gonna lose (yes, yes, you're
     gonna lose that girl)

16 I'll make a point of taking her away from
     you (watch what you do), yeah
17 The way you treat her what else can I do?

18 You're gonna lose that girl
19 You're gonna lose that girl

20 You're gonna lose that girl (yes, yes,
     you're gonna lose that girl)
21 You're gonna lose that girl (yes, yes,
     you're gonna lose that girl)
22 You're gonna lose (yes, yes, you're
     gonna lose that girl)

23 I'll make a point of taking her away from
     you (watch what you do), yeah
24 The way you treat her what else can I do?

25 If you don't take her out tonight
26 She's gonna change her mind (she's gonna
     change her mind)
27 And I will take her out tonight
28 And I will treat her kind (I'm gonna
     treat her kind)

29 You're gonna lose that girl (yes, yes,
     you're gonna lose that girl)
30 You're gonna lose that girl (yes, yes,
     you're gonna lose that girl)
31 You're gonna lose (yes, yes, you're
     gonna lose that girl).

YOU'VE GOT TO HIDE YOUR
LOVE AWAY
by John Lennon and Paul McCartney

1 Here I stand head in hand
2 Turn my face to the wall.
3 If she's gone I can't go on
4 Feeling two-foot small.

5 Everywhere people stare
6 Each and every day.

    7 I can see them laugh at me
    8 And I hear them say.

    9 Hey! you've got to hide your love away.
   10 Hey! you've got to hide your love away.

   11 How can I even try
   12 I can never win
   13 Hearing them, seeing them
   14 In the state I'm in.

   15 How could she say to me
   16 Love will find a way?
   17 Gather round all you clowns
   18 Let me hear you say.

   19 Hey! you've got to hide your love away.
   20 Hey! you've got to hide your love away.

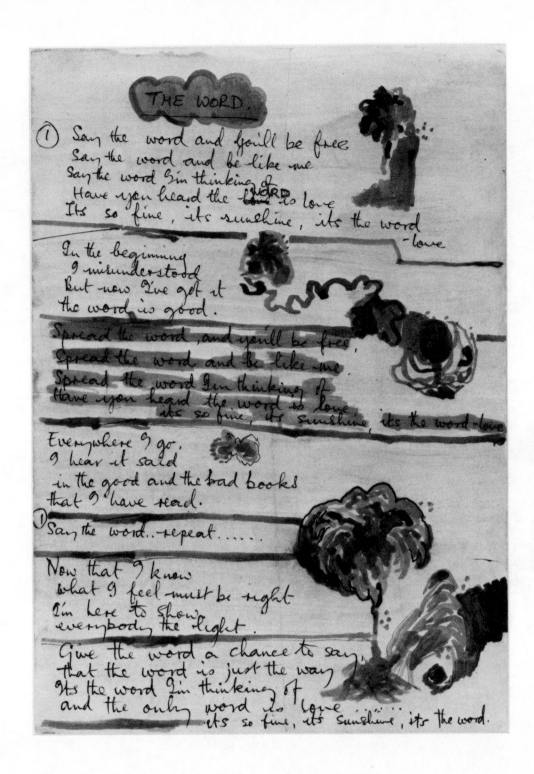

63

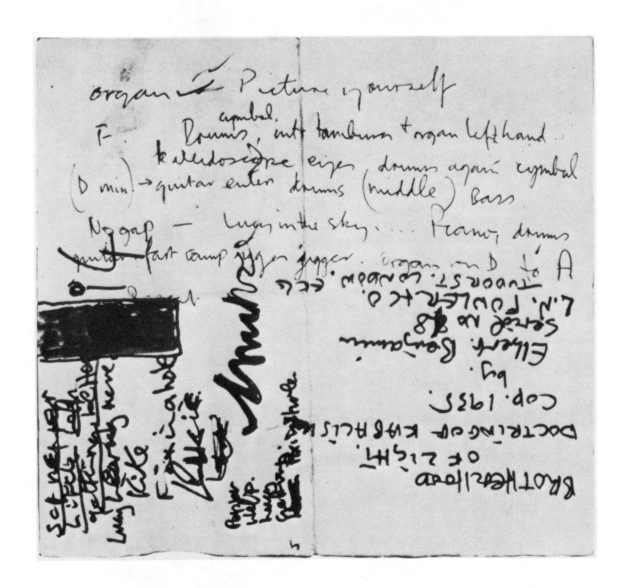

Concordance

NOTE: Articles (a, an, and, 'n', the) are not included as key words. Contractions are listed separately (Appendix One), as are Prefixed Words (Appendix Two), although the latter also appear under the root word in this section.

AAH

Whoa since/when I saw her standing there. (hey! aah!)
--ISAWHERSTA--17
Before this dance is through ((aah)) --IMHAPPYJUS
--13
Before this dance is through ((aah)) --IMHAPPYJUS
--21
Yeah, aah - ooo I'm down (down on the ground)--
IMDOWN--45
We said our goodbyes (aah the night before)--
NIGHTBEFOR--1
Love was in your eyes (aah the night before)--
NIGHTBEFOR--2
Were you telling lies? (aah the night before)--
NIGHTBEFOR--5
Was I so unwise? (aah the night before)--NIGHTBEFOR
--6
We said our goodbyes (aah the night before)--
NIGHTBEFOR--11
Love was in your eyes (aah the night before)--
NIGHTBEFOR--12
Were you telling lies? (aah the night before)--
NIGHTBEFOR--19
Was I so unwise? (aah the night before)--NIGHTBEFOR
--20
Aah, aah, aah.--DAYTRIPPER--17
Aah, aah, aah.--DAYTRIPPER--17
Aah, aah, aah.--DAYTRIPPER--17
Aah, aah, aah, aah.--IFINEEDEDS--13
Aah, aah, aah, aah.--IFINEEDEDS--13
Aah, aah, aah, aah.--IFINEEDEDS--13
Aah, aah, aah, aah.--IFINEEDEDS--13
Aah, aah.--IFINEEDEDS--23
Aah, aah.--IFINEEDEDS--23
Aah, I'm looking through you.--IMLOOKINGT--22
Aah, look at all the lonely people.--ELEANORRIG--1
Aah, look at all the lonely people.--ELEANORRIG--2
Aah, look at all the lonely people.--ELEANORRIG--19
Aah, look at all the lonely people.--ELEANORRIG--20
((Aah, look at all the lonely people.))--ELEANORRIG
--28
((Aah, look at all the lonely people.))--ELEANORRIG
--30
Aah, aah, aah, aah - aah!--PENNYLANE--16
Aah, aah, aah, aah - aah!--PENNYLANE--16
Aah, aah, aah, aah - aah!--PENNYLANE--16
Aah, aah, aah, aah - aah!--PENNYLANE--16
Aah, aah, aah, aah - aah!--PENNYLANE--16
Aah! aah! aah!--DAYINTHELI--27
Aah! aah! aah!--DAYINTHELI--27
Aah! aah! aah!--DAYINTHELI--27
You're holding me down (aah) turning me round
(aah)--GETTINGBET--5
You're holding me down (aah) turning me round
(aah)--GETTINGBET--5
Aah!--LOVELYRITA--1
Lovely Rita meter maid (aah)--LOVELYRITA--3
Aah!--LOVELYRITA--17
Lucy in the sky with diamonds - aah.--LUCYINTHES
--11
Lucy in the sky with diamonds - aah.--LUCYINTHES
--22
Lucy in the sky with diamonds - aah.--LUCYINTHES
--29
Lucy in the sky with diamonds - aah.--LUCYINTHES
--32
Lucy in the sky with diamonds (aah - ooo) --
LUCYINTHES--34
Aah!--MAGICALMYS--20
Your mother should know - aah.--YOURMOTHER--6
Your mother should know - aah.--YOURMOTHER--12
Your mother should know - aah.--YOURMOTHER--17
Your mother should know - aah.--YOURMOTHER--19
Aah!--REVOLUTION--1
For the things you do endear you to me - aah --
IWILL--17
Mmm mmm aah --MOTHERNATU--15
Aah Mother Nature's son.--MOTHERNATU--16
Aah--REVOLUTONE--1
(Aah - aah)--WHILEMYGUI--13
(Aah - aah)--WHILEMYGUI--13
Woof - aah! ha ha ha--HEYBULLDOG--27
It's too much - aah.--ITSALLTOOM--33

You're too much - aah.--ITSALLTOOM--37
Eee - (yeah) aah --DONTLETMED--29
Aah!--BECAUSE--1
Aah!--BECAUSE--4
Aah!--BECAUSE--7
Aah - aah--BECAUSE--12
Aah - aah--BECAUSE--12
Aah - aah--BECAUSE--13
Aah - aah--BECAUSE--13
Aah--BECAUSE--14
Aah.--BECAUSE--15
Aah!--THEEND--10
Aah - here come the Sun King --SUNKING--1
Aah - ooo, aah - ooo, aah - ooo.--YOUNEVERGI--16
Aah - ooo, aah - ooo, aah - ooo.--YOUNEVERGI--16
Aah - ooo, aah - ooo, aah - ooo.--YOUNEVERGI--16
Hold it - aah--IDIGAPONY--3

ABLE

And I'll be better, I'll be better Doc as
soon as I am able.--ROCKYRACCO--35

ABOARD

And our friends are all aboard--YELLOWSUBM--13

ABOUT

I could tell the world a thing or two about our love
--THANKYOUGI--5
I think about you night and day--ILLGETYOU--9
When I think about you, I can say--ILLGETYOU--11
Can't stop thinking about her now.--EVERYLITTL--6
Please remember how I feel about you--INEEDYOU--16
Please remember how I feel about you--INEEDYOU--26
All about the girl who came to stay?--GIRL--2
I know I'll often stop and think about them --
INMYLIFE--15
I know I'll often stop and think about them --
INMYLIFE--19
To say about the things that you do.--THINKFORYO
--2
About the good things--THINKFORYO--4
I've got something I can laugh about.--GOODDAYSUN
--3
About a lucky man who made the grade--DAYINTHELI
--2
About the space between us all--WITHINYOUW--2
About the love we all could share--WITHINYOUW--9
About the love that's gone so cold--WITHINYOUW--22
But when you talk about destruction --REVOLUTION
--8
About an hour or two --DONTPASSME--28
I told you about Strawberry Fields--GLASSONION--1
I told you about the walrus and me - man--
GLASSONION--8
I told you about the fool on the hill--GLASSONION
--17
But when you talk about destruction --REVOLUTONE
--11
We would shout and swim about--OCTOPUSSGA--17
How about that?--YOUKNOWMYN--47

ABOVE

You were above me, but not today.--IMLOOKINGT--12
I'm coming down fast but I'm miles above you --
HELTERSKEL--5

ACCIDENTS

In case of accidents he always took his mom --
CONTINUING--8

ACHES

Your day breaks, your mind aches --FORNOONE--1
Your day breaks, your mind aches --FORNOONE--20

ACORNS

Fifty acorns tied in a sack.--BALLADOFJO--38

ACQUAINTED

She's well acquainted with the touch of the
velvet hand --HAPPINESSI--3

ACROSS

Dragged a comb across my head--DAYINTHELI--19
And the bag across her shoulder--LOVELYRITA--11
Sail across the Atlantic--HONEYPIE--17
Across the sea--HONEYPIE--26
ACROSS THE UNIVERSE.--ACROSSTHEU--Title
They slither wildly as they slip away across the
    universe.--ACROSSTHEU--2
They call me on and on across the universe.--
    ACROSSTHEU--12
They tumble blindly as they make their way across
    the universe.--ACROSSTHEU--14
It calls me on and on across the universe.--
    ACROSSTHEU--24

ACT

Although I laugh and I act like a clown --IMALOSER
    --9
I have had enough, so act your age.--YOUWONTSEE--2
But if I seem to act unkind--IWANTTOTEL--9
The act you've known for all these years--
    SGTPEPPERS--6

ACTS

She acts as if it's understood --GIRL--17

ADMIT

I'd admit that I was wrong--YOULIKEMET--18
I'd admit that I was wrong--YOULIKEMET--27
I've got to admit it's getting better (better)--
    GETTINGBET--7
I have to admit it's getting better (better)--
    GETTINGBET--9
I've got to admit it's getting better (better)--
    GETTINGBET--16
I have to admit it's getting better (better)--
    GETTINGBET--18
I admit it's getting better (better)--GETTINGBET
    --29
Yes I admit it's getting better (better)--
    GETTINGBET--31

ADVICE

Now my advice for those who die (Taxman)--TAXMAN
    --22

AFFECTION

Though I know I'll never lose affection --INMYLIFE
    --13
Though I know I'll never lose affection --INMYLIFE
    --17

AFRAID

Hey Jude, don't be afraid --HEYJUDE--5

AFTER

After all this time I don't know why.--GIRL--9
Time after time you refuse to even listen --
    YOUWONTSEE--13
Time after time you refuse to even listen --
    YOUWONTSEE--22
And after all, I'm only sleeping.--IMONLYSLEE--12
And after all, I'm only sleeping.--IMONLYSLEE--18
After a while you start to smile now you feel cool
    --GOODMORNIN--13
She's leaving home after living alone--SHESLEAVIN
    --11
She's leaving home after living alone--SHESLEAVIN
    --23
Day after day, alone on a hill--FOOLONTHEH--1
Happy ever after in the market place --OBLADIOBLA
    --20
Hey, happy ever after in the market place --
    OBLADIOBLA--32
After the Savoy truffle.--SAVOYTRUFF--5
After the Savoy truffle.--SAVOYTRUFF--10
After the Savoy truffle.--SAVOYTRUFF--18
After the Savoy truffle.--SAVOYTRUFF--27
After the Savoy truffle.--SAVOYTRUFF--29
ONE AFTER NINE-0-NINE.--ONEAFTERNI--Title
My baby said she's travelling on the one after
    nine-0-nine--ONEAFTERNI--1
Said you're travelling on the one after
    nine-0-nine.--ONEAFTERNI--5
Said you're travelling on the one after
    nine-0-nine.--ONEAFTERNI--10
Well, she said she's travelling on the one after

nine-0-nine --ONEAFTERNI--15
Said she's travelling on the one after
    nine-0-nine. (yeah)--ONEAFTERNI--19
She said she's travelling on the one after
    nine-0-nine--ONEAFTERNI--25
Said we're travelling on the one after nine-0 --
    ONEAFTERNI--29
She said we're travelling on the one after nine-0
    --ONEAFTERNI--30
Said we're travelling on the one after nine-0-nine
    --ONEAFTERNI--31

AFTERNOON

Tuesday afternoon is never-ending --LADYMADONN--14

AGAIN

I'll ((I'll)) be coming home ((home)) again
    to you love ((you love)) --PSILOVEYOU--7
I'll be coming home again to you love --PSILOVEYOU
    --19
If I don't get her back again--DONTBOTHER--16
If I don't get her back again--DONTBOTHER--31
You hurt me then you're back again --NOTASECOND--9
You hurt me then you're back again --NOTASECOND--20
But this boy wants you back again.--THISBOY--3
This boy wants you back again.--THISBOY--6
If this boy gets you back again.--THISBOY--13
To that boy again.--YOUCANTDOT--4
But I'll come back again some day.--ILLCRYINST--14
But I'll come back again some day.--ILLCRYINST--23
But I'll be back again --ILLBEBACK--2
But I came back again.--ILLBEBACK--4
Than to break my heart again --ILLBEBACK--10
Than to break my heart again --ILLBEBACK--19
But I'll be back again.--ILLBEBACK--27
Till I walk out that door again.--WHENIGETHO--20
You'll be back again tonight--YOULIKEMET--2
And she keeps calling me back again.--IVEJUSTSEE
    --13
And she keeps calling me back again.--IVEJUSTSEE
    --20
And she keeps calling me back again.--IVEJUSTSEE
    --23
And she keeps calling me back again.--IVEJUSTSEE
    --31
And she keeps calling me back again.--IVEJUSTSEE
    --33
And she keeps calling me back again.--IVEJUSTSEE
    --35
So I will ask you once again.--WECANWORKI--14
So I will ask you once again.--WECANWORKI--23
We'd meet again for I had told you.--GOTTOGETYO--11
Told her I would really like to see her again.--
    LOVELYRITA--22
We'd like to thank you once again.--SGTPEPPREP--12
Sing it again.--YOURMOTHER--7
Sing it again.--YOURMOTHER--20
So let me see you smile again.--DEARPRUDEN--19
Till I get to the bottom and I see you again -
    yeah, yeah, yeah.--HELTERSKEL--3
And I get to the bottom and I see you again -
    yeah, yeah, yeah.--HELTERSKEL--20
Bull-frog doing it again--HEYBULLDOG--2
Back in school again, Maxwell plays the fool
    again, teacher gets annoyed --MAXWELLSIL--8
Back in school again, Maxwell plays the fool
    again, teacher gets annoyed --MAXWELLSIL--8
And if you leave me I won't be late again --
    IVEGOTAFEE--8

AGE

I have had enough, so act your age.--YOUWONTSEE--2

AGO

She says that long ago she knew someone --FORNOONE
    --18
It was twenty years ago today--SGTPEPPERS--1
Though she was born a long, long time ago --
    YOURMOTHER--4
Though she was born a long, long time ago --
    YOURMOTHER--10
Though she was born a long, long time ago --
    YOURMOTHER--15
Though she was born a long, long time ago --
    YOURMOTHER--23
You left me standing here a long, long time ago --
    LONGANDWIN--10
You left me standing here a long, long time ago --
    LONGANDWIN--13

AGREE
     The judge does not agree and he tells them so oh
        - oh oh.--MAXWELLSIL--21
     Living in the world agree --LETITBE/45--10
     Living in the world agree --LETITBE/LP--10

AH
     Ah, she's got a ticket to ride--TICKETTORI--40
     Ah, down (I'm really down)--IMDOWN--31
     Ah, girl - (girl) girl.--GIRL--5
     Ah, girl - (girl) girl.--GIRL--10
     Ah, girl - (girl) girl.--GIRL--26
     Ah, girl - (girl) girl.--GIRL--27
     In our yellow (in our yellow) submarine
        (submarine - ah ha!)--YELLOWSUBM--28
     Ah - ah - ah (oh) - ah - ah - ah - ah - ah
        - ah--LOVELYRITA--35
     Ah - ah - ah (oh) - ah - ah - ah - ah - ah
        - ah--LOVELYRITA--35
     Ah - ah - ah (oh) - ah - ah - ah - ah - ah
        - ah--LOVELYRITA--35
     Ah - ah - ah (oh) - ah - ah - ah - ah - ah
        - ah--LOVELYRITA--35
     Ah - ah - ah (oh) - ah - ah - ah - ah - ah
        - ah--LOVELYRITA--35
     Ah - ah - ah (oh) - ah - ah - ah - ah - ah
        - ah--LOVELYRITA--35
     Ah - ah - ah (oh) - ah - ah - ah - ah - ah
        - ah--LOVELYRITA--35
     Ah - ah - ah (oh) - ah - ah - ah - ah - ah
        - ah--LOVELYRITA--35
     Ah - ah - ah (oh) - ah - ah - ah - ah - ah
        - ah--LOVELYRITA--35
     Ah - ah - ah (oh) - ah - ah - ah - ah - ah
        - ah--LOVELYRITA--35
     One, two (ah yeah), three, four.--SGTPEPPREP--1
     ... Ah (how was that?)--HELTERSKEL--31
     (Ah - yeah)--OBLADIOBLA--22
     And Rocky collapsed in the corner - ah.--ROCKYRACCO
        --22
     To help with good Rocky's revival - ah.--ROCKYRACCO
        --39

AH-HA
     Why don't we do it in the road? (ah-ha)--WHYDONTWED
        --2

AH-HEY
     Let's hear it for Dennis - ah-hey.--YOUKNOWMYN--8

AHEAD
     (Full speed ahead, Mr. Bosun, full speed
        ahead.--YELLOWSUBM--20
     (Full speed ahead, Mr. Bosun, full speed
        ahead.--YELLOWSUBM--20
     Full speed ahead it is, Sgt.--YELLOWSUBM--21
     Longer than the road that stretches out ahead.--
        TWOOFUS--18
     Longer than the road that stretches out ahead.--
        TWOOFUS--27

AIDS
     I dig a pygmy by Charles Hawtrey and the Deaf
        Aids (ha ha ha)--TWOOFUS--1

AIN'T
     I ain't got nothing but love babe --EIGHTDAYSA--7
     I ain't got nothing but love girl --EIGHTDAYSA--15
     I ain't got nothing but love babe --EIGHTDAYSA--25
     I ain't got nothing but love babe --EIGHTDAYSA--35
     I ain't no fool and I don't take what I don't
        want --ANOTHERGIR--4
     I ain't no fool and I don't take what I don't
        want --ANOTHERGIR--14
     I ain't no fool and I don't take what I don't
        want --ANOTHERGIR--20
     You ain't gonna make it with anyone anyhow.--
        REVOLUTION--29
     Well, you may be a lover, but you ain't no
        dancer.--HELTERSKEL--7
     'cos you may be a lover, but you ain't no dancer.
        --HELTERSKEL--14
     'cos you may be a lover, but you ain't no dancer.
        --HELTERSKEL--24
     You ain't gonna make it with anyone anyhow.--
        REVOLUTONE--44
     If I ain't dead already--YERBLUES--4

If I ain't dead already--YERBLUES--8
If I ain't dead already--YERBLUES--15
If I ain't dead already--YERBLUES--22
If I ain't dead already--YERBLUES--29
Christ! you know it ain't easy --BALLADOFJO--5
Christ! you know it ain't easy --BALLADOFJO--13
Christ! you know it ain't easy --BALLADOFJO--21
Christ! you know it ain't easy --BALLADOFJO--33
Christ! you know it ain't easy --BALLADOFJO--41

AIR
     Your song will fill the air --IWILL--14

ALBERT
     To fill the Albert Hall--DAYINTHELI--33

ALERTED
     No-one alerted you.--WHILEMYGUI--17

ALL
     Keep all ((all)) my love forever ((ever)).--
        PSILOVEYOU--5
     Keep all ((all)) my love forever ((ever)).--
        PSILOVEYOU--5
     Keep all ((all)) my love forever ((ever)) --
        PSILOVEYOU--14
     Keep all ((all)) my love forever ((ever)) --
        PSILOVEYOU--14
     ANY TIME AT ALL.--ANYTIMEATA--Title
     Any time at all, any time at all, any time at all--
        ANYTIMEATA--1
     Any time at all, any time at all, any time at all--
        ANYTIMEATA--1
     Any time at all, any time at all, any time at all--
        ANYTIMEATA--1
     All you gotta do is call--ANYTIMEATA--2
     Any time at all, any time at all, any time at all--
        ANYTIMEATA--10
     Any time at all, any time at all, any time at all--
        ANYTIMEATA--10
     Any time at all, any time at all, any time at all--
        ANYTIMEATA--10
     All you gotta do is call--ANYTIMEATA--11
     Any time at all, any time at all, any time at all--
        ANYTIMEATA--19
     Any time at all, any time at all, any time at all--
        ANYTIMEATA--19
     Any time at all, any time at all, any time at all--
        ANYTIMEATA--19
     All ya gotta do is call,----ANYTIMEATA--20
     Any time at all, any time at all, any time at all--
        ANYTIMEATA--22
     Any time at all, any time at all, any time at all--
        ANYTIMEATA--22
     Any time at all, any time at all, any time at all--
        ANYTIMEATA--22
     All you gotta do is call --ANYTIMEATA--23
     Any time at all--ANYTIMEATA--25
     All ya gotta do is call --ANYTIMEATA--26
     I do all the pleasing with you --PLEASEPLEA--16
     I'll remember all the little things we've done --
        MISERY--6
     I'll remember all the little things we've done --
        MISERY--10
     And all I gotta do is thank you girl, thank you
        girl.--THANKYOUGI--4
     And all I gotta do is thank you girl, thank you
        girl--THANKYOUGI--7
     And all I gotta do is thank you girl, thank you
        girl.--THANKYOUGI--10
     And all I gotta do is thank you girl, thank you
        girl.--THANKYOUGI--14
     ALL I'VE GOT TO DO.--ALLIVEGOTT--Title
     All I gotta do --ALLIVEGOTT--2
     Yeah, that's all I gotta do.--ALLIVEGOTT--5
     All I gotta do --ALLIVEGOTT--7
     Whenever you want me at all --ALLIVEGOTT--12
     All I gotta do --ALLIVEGOTT--18
     Yeah, that's all I gotta do.--ALLIVEGOTT--21
     Whenever you want me at all --ALLIVEGOTT--23
     ALL MY LOVING.--ALLMYLOVIN--Title
     And I'll send all my lovin' to you.--ALLMYLOVIN--6
     And I'll send all my lovin' to you.--ALLMYLOVIN--12
     All my lovin', I will send to you --ALLMYLOVIN--13
     All my lovin', darlin', I'll be true.--ALLMYLOVIN
        --14
     And I'll send all my lovin' to you.--ALLMYLOVIN--20
     All my lovin', I will send to you --ALLMYLOVIN--21
     All my lovin', darlin', I'll be true --ALLMYLOVIN
        --22

All my lovin', all my lovin', ooo-ooo --ALLMYLOVIN
  --23
All my lovin', all my lovin', ooo-ooo --ALLMYLOVIN
  --23
All my lovin', I will send to you.--ALLMYLOVIN--24
When every night I'm all alone--DONTBOTHER--12
Here am I sitting all on my own--ITWONTBELO--6
Then we'll have some fun when you're mine, all
  mine --LITTLECHIL--10
I'll give you all I've got to give --CANTBUYMEL--9
I give her all my love --ANDILOVEHE--1
That's all I do --ANDILOVEHE--2
You know I work all day --HARDDAYSNI--8
And when I do you'd better hide all the girls --
  ILLCRYINST--15
I'm gonna break their hearts all round the world
  --ILLCRYINST--16
And when I do you'd better hide all the girls --
  ILLCRYINST--24
'cos I'm gonna break their hearts all round the
  world --ILLCRYINST--25
I just wanna dance with you all night --IMHAPPYJUS
  --9
All I do is hang my head and moan.--TELLMEWHY--8
Love me all the time girl --THINGSWESA--17
Love me all the time girl --THINGSWESA--28
She tells me all the time, you know, she said so
  --IFEELFINE--5
She's so glad she's telling all the world --
  IFEELFINE--8
She tells me all the time, you know, she said so
  --IFEELFINE--13
She's so glad she's telling all the world --
  IFEELFINE--16
Gives me all her time as well as loving--SHESAWOMAN
  --14
Love you all the time.--EIGHTDAYSA--12
Love you all the time.--EIGHTDAYSA--32
Of all the love I have won or have lost --IMALOSER
  --3
I'm telling you so that you won't lose all.--
  IMALOSER--18
I would remember all the things we planned--YESITIS
  --7
Which is all that I deserve--YOULIKEMET--10
We're all alone and there's nobody else --IMDOWN
  --16
She's sweeter than all the girls and I met quite
  a few --ANOTHERGIR--6
Nobody in all the world can do what she can do --
  ANOTHERGIR--7
Love you all the time and never leave you--INEEDYOU
  --2
It's only love and that is all--ITSONLYLOV--4
It's only love and that is all--ITSONLYLOV--6
It's only love and that is all--ITSONLYLOV--11
It's only love and that is all--ITSONLYLOV--13
And I want all the world to see we've met --
  IVEJUSTSEE--5
And I want all the world to see we've met --
  IVEJUSTSEE--28
All my troubles seemed so far away--YESTERDAY--2
Gather round all you clowns--YOUVEGOTTO--17
Working for peanuts is all very fine --DRIVEMYCAR
  --11
All about the girl who came to stay?--GIRL--2
When I think of all the times I tried so hard
  to leave her --GIRL--6
After all this time I don't know why.--GIRL--9
All my life, though some have changed.--INMYLIFE
  --2
All these places had their moments,--INMYLIFE--5
In my life I've loved them all.--INMYLIFE--8
But of all these friends and lovers --INMYLIFE--9
That's all I want to say--MICHELLE--6
Making all his nowhere plans for nobody.--
  NOWHEREMAN--3
Nowhere Man can you see me at all?--NOWHEREMAN--12
Leave it all till somebody else lends you a hand.
  --NOWHEREMAN--15
Making all his nowhere plans for nobody --
  NOWHEREMAN--24
Making all his nowhere plans for nobody --
  NOWHEREMAN--25
Making all his nowhere plans for nobody.--
  NOWHEREMAN--26
You're telling all those lies--THINKFORYO--3
All the things that you should.--THINKFORYO--23
Day or night he'll be there any time at all, Dr.
  Robert --DRROBERT--2
And after all, I'm only sleeping.--IMONLYSLEE--12
And after all, I'm only sleeping.--IMONLYSLEE--18
Aah, look at all the lonely people.--ELEANORRIG--1
Aah, look at all the lonely people.--ELEANORRIG--2

All the lonely people, where do they all come
  from?--ELEANORRIG--9
All the lonely people, where do they all come
  from?--ELEANORRIG--9
All the lonely people, where do they all belong?--
  ELEANORRIG--10
All the lonely people, where do they all belong?--
  ELEANORRIG--10
All the lonely people, where do they all come
  from?--ELEANORRIG--17
All the lonely people, where do they all come
  from?--ELEANORRIG--17
All the lonely people, where do they all belong?--
  ELEANORRIG--18
All the lonely people, where do they all belong?--
  ELEANORRIG--18
Aah, look at all the lonely people.--ELEANORRIG--19
Aah, look at all the lonely people.--ELEANORRIG--20
All the lonely people, where do they all come
  from?--ELEANORRIG--27
All the lonely people, where do they all come
  from?--ELEANORRIG--27
((Aah, look at all the lonely people.))--ELEANORRIG
  --28
All the lonely people, where do they all belong?--
  ELEANORRIG--29
All the lonely people, where do they all belong?--
  ELEANORRIG--29
((Aah, look at all the lonely people.))--ELEANORRIG
  --30
You find that all her words of kindness linger on
  --FORNOONE--2
There will be times when all the things --FORNOONE
  --21
All those words they seem to slip away.--IWANTTOTEL
  --4
Make love all day long--LOVEYOUTWO--9
Make love all day long--LOVEYOUTWO--11
They'll fill you in with all their sins, you'll see.
  --LOVEYOUTWO--15
I said who put all those things in your head?--
  SHESAIDSHE--4
Be thankful I don't take it all --TAXMAN--8
Lay down all thought, surrender to the void--
  TOMORROWNE--3
That love is all and love is everyone--TOMORROWNE
  --7
We all live in a yellow submarine --YELLOWSUBM--9
We all live in a yellow submarine --YELLOWSUBM--11
And our friends are all aboard--YELLOWSUBM--13
We all live in a yellow submarine --YELLOWSUBM--16
We all live in a yellow submarine --YELLOWSUBM--18
Everyone of us (everyone of us) has all we need
  (has all we need) --YELLOWSUBM--26
Everyone of us (everyone of us) has all we need
  (has all we need) --YELLOWSUBM--26
We all live in a yellow submarine --YELLOWSUBM--29
We all live in a yellow submarine --YELLOWSUBM--31
We all live in a yellow submarine --YELLOWSUBM--33
We all live in a yellow submarine --YELLOWSUBM--35
And all the people that come and go--PENNYLANE--3
Misunderstanding all you see--STRAWBERRY--7
But it all works out--STRAWBERRY--9
But it's all wrong--STRAWBERRY--29
The Hendersons will all be there--BEINGFORTH--3
A splendid time is guaranteed for all--BEINGFORTH
  --20
They had to count them all--DAYINTHELI--31
It's getting better all the time.--GETTINGBET--2
A little better all the time (it can't get no
  worse)--GETTINGBET--8
A little better all the time (it can't get no
  worse)--GETTINGBET--17
Getting so much better all the time.--GETTINGBET
  --20
It's getting better all the time--GETTINGBET--21
It's getting better all the time--GETTINGBET--23
A little better all the time (it can't get no
  worse)--GETTINGBET--30
Getting so much better all the time.--GETTINGBET
  --33
It's getting better all the time--GETTINGBET--34
It's getting better all the time--GETTINGBET--36
Getting so much better all the time.--GETTINGBET
  --38
The act you've known for all these years--
  SGTPEPPERS--6
And he wants you all to sing along.--SGTPEPPERS--22
Home. (we struggled hard all our lives to get by)
  --SHESLEAVIN--22
Yes I'm certain that it happens all the time.--
  WITHALITTL--20
About the space between us all--WITHINYOUW--2
About the love we all could share--WITHINYOUW--9

Try to realise it's all within yourself--WITHINYOUW
--16
When you see we're all one--WITHINYOUW--32
ALL YOU NEED IS LOVE.--ALLYOUN/YS--Title
All you need is love, all you need is love --
ALLYOUN/YS--12
All you need is love, all you need is love --
ALLYOUN/YS--12
All you need is love, love, love is all you need.
--ALLYOUN/YS--13
All you need is love, love, love is all you need.
--ALLYOUN/YS--13
All you need is love, (wuh) all you need is
love (hey) --ALLYOUN/YS--17
All you need is love, (wuh) all you need is
love (hey) --ALLYOUN/YS--17
All you need is love, love, love is all you need.
--ALLYOUN/YS--18
All you need is love, love, love is all you need.
--ALLYOUN/YS--18
All you need is love, all you need is love --
ALLYOUN/YS--23
All you need is love, all you need is love --
ALLYOUN/YS--23
All you need is love, love, love is all you need.
--ALLYOUN/YS--24
All you need is love, love, love is all you need.
--ALLYOUN/YS--24
All you need is love (all together now) --
ALLYOUN/YS--25
All you need is love (all together now) --
ALLYOUN/YS--25
All you need is love (everybody) --ALLYOUN/YS--26
All you need is love, love, love is all you need.
--ALLYOUN/YS--27
All you need is love, love, love is all you need.
--ALLYOUN/YS--27
Love is all you need (love is all you need)--
ALLYOUN/YS--28
Love is all you need (love is all you need)--
ALLYOUN/YS--28
Love is all you need (love is all you need)--
ALLYOUN/YS--29
Love is all you need (love is all you need)--
ALLYOUN/YS--29
Love is all you need (love is all you need)--
ALLYOUN/YS--30
Love is all you need (love is all you need)--
ALLYOUN/YS--30
Love is all you need (love is all you need)--
ALLYOUN/YS--31
Love is all you need (love is all you need)--
ALLYOUN/YS--31
Love is all you need (wuh) (love is all you
need)--ALLYOUN/YS--32
Love is all you need (wuh) (love is all you
need)--ALLYOUN/YS--32
Love is all you need (love is all you need)--
ALLYOUN/YS--33
Love is all you need (love is all you need)--
ALLYOUN/YS--33
Love is all you need (love is all you need)--
ALLYOUN/YS--34
Love is all you need (love is all you need)--
ALLYOUN/YS--34
Love is all you need (love is all you need)--
ALLYOUN/YS--35
Love is all you need (love is all you need)--
ALLYOUN/YS--35
Love is all you need (love is all you need)--
ALLYOUN/YS--36
Love is all you need (love is all you need)--
ALLYOUN/YS--36
Love is all you need (love is all you need)--
ALLYOUN/YS--37
Love is all you need (love is all you need)--
ALLYOUN/YS--37
Love is all you need (yahoo) (eee - hi)--
ALLYOUN/YS--38
Love is all you need (love is all you need)--
ALLYOUN/YS--39
Love is all you need (love is all you need)--
ALLYOUN/YS--39
(Love is all you need) Yesterday (love is all
you need)--ALLYOUN/YS--40
(Love is all you need) Yesterday (love is all
you need)--ALLYOUN/YS--40
(Oh) love is all you need--ALLYOUN/YS--41
Love is all you need (oh yeah)--ALLYOUN/YS--42
Love is all you need--ALLYOUN/YS--43
Loves you yeah, yeah, yeah ((love is all, love
is all))--ALLYOUN/YS--44

Loves you yeah, yeah, yeah ((love is all, love
is all))--ALLYOUN/YS--44
She loves you yeah, yeah, yeah ((love is all,
love is all))--ALLYOUN/YS--45
She loves you yeah, yeah, yeah ((love is all,
love is all))--ALLYOUN/YS--45
Love is all you need--ALLYOUN/YS--46
Love is all you need (wuhoo)--ALLYOUN/YS--47
Love is all you need (wuhoo)--ALLYOUN/YS--48
Love is all you need (oh)--ALLYOUN/YS--49
Love is all you need--ALLYOUN/YS--50
Love is all you need.--ALLYOUN/YS--51
You keep all your money in a big brown bag --
BABYYOUREA--16
You keep all your money in a big brown bag --
BABYYOUREA--31
I am he as you are he as you are me and we are
all together--IAMTHEWALR--1
Let's all get up and dance to a song--YOURMOTHER
--2
Let's all get up and dance to a song--YOURMOTHER
--8
I can know all things on earth.--INNERLIGHT--2
You can know all things on earth.--INNERLIGHT--9
See all without looking.--INNERLIGHT--16
Do all without doing.--INNERLIGHT--17
We all wanna change the world.--REVOLUTION--4
We all want to change the world.--REVOLUTION--7
We'd all love to see the plan.--REVOLUTION--14
We're all doing what we can.--REVOLUTION--17
All I can tell you is brother you have to wait.--
REVOLUTION--19
We all want to change your head.--REVOLUTION--24
All your life --BLACKBIRD--3
All your life --BLACKBIRD--7
All your life --BLACKBIRD--15
All de children sing:--CONTINUING--10
All de children sing:--CONTINUING--20
All the children sing:--CONTINUING--30
All right!--DONTPASSME--1
Well here's another clue for you all:--GLASSONION
--10
Love you with all my heart --IWILL--10
Help yourself to a bit of what is all around you
- silly girl.--MARTHAMYDE--6
Help yourself to a bit of what is all around you
- silly girl.--MARTHAMYDE--12
All day long I'm sitting singing songs for
everyone.--MOTHERNATU--2
And for all the little piggies--PIGGIES--3
In their sties with all their backing--PIGGIES--11
We all wanna change the world.--REVOLUTONE--7
We all want to change the world.--REVOLUTONE--10
We'd all love to see the plan.--REVOLUTONE--21
We're all doing what we can.--REVOLUTONE--25
Well all I can tell you is brother you have to
wait.--REVOLUTONE--28
We'd all love to change our head.--REVOLUTONE--37
But you'll have to have them all pulled out--
SAVOYTRUFF--4
I feel your taste all the time we're apart --
SAVOYTRUFF--7
But you'll have to have them all pulled out--
SAVOYTRUFF--9
But you'll have to have them all pulled out--
SAVOYTRUFF--17
We all know ob-la-di 'b-la-da --SAVOYTRUFF--21
But you'll have to have them all pulled out--
SAVOYTRUFF--26
Yes, you'll have to have them all pulled out--
SAVOYTRUFF--28
You layed it down for all to see--SEXYSADIE--6
You layed it down for all to see--SEXYSADIE--7
Sexy Sadie (sexy Sadie) the greatest of them
all ((she's the greatest))--SEXYSADIE--11
She's the latest and the greatest (she's the
greatest) of them all--SEXYSADIE--23
(Sexy Sadie she's the latest and the greatest
of them all)--SEXYSADIE--24
I look at you all, see the love there that's
sleeping --WHILEMYGUI--2
I look at you all, see the love there that's
sleeping--WHILEMYGUI--18
Look, look at you all--WHILEMYGUI--20
ALL TOGETHER NOW.--ALLTOGETHE--Title
All together now (all together now) --ALLTOGETHE
--13
All together now (all together now) --ALLTOGETHE
--13
All together now (all together now) --ALLTOGETHE
--14
All together now (all together now) --ALLTOGETHE
--14
All together now (all together now) --ALLTOGETHE

--15
All together now (all together now) --ALLTOGETHE
--15
All together now (all together now) (all
together now).--ALLTOGETHE--16
All together now (all together now) (all
together now).--ALLTOGETHE--16
All together now (all together now) (all
together now).--ALLTOGETHE--16
All together now (all together now) --ALLTOGETHE
--21
All together now (all together now) --ALLTOGETHE
--21
All together now (all together now) --ALLTOGETHE
--22
All together now (all together now) --ALLTOGETHE
--22
All together now (all together now) --ALLTOGETHE
--23
All together now (all together now) --ALLTOGETHE
--23
All together now (all together now) --ALLTOGETHE
--24
All together now (all together now) --ALLTOGETHE
--24
All together now (all together now) --ALLTOGETHE
--25
All together now (all together now) --ALLTOGETHE
--25
All together now (all together now) --ALLTOGETHE
--26
All together now (all together now) --ALLTOGETHE
--26
All together now (all together now) --ALLTOGETHE
--27
All together now (all together now) --ALLTOGETHE
--27
All together now (all together now) --ALLTOGETHE
--28
All together now (all together now) --ALLTOGETHE
--28
All together now (all together now) --ALLTOGETHE
--33
All together now (all together now) --ALLTOGETHE
--33
All together now (all together now) --ALLTOGETHE
--34
All together now (all together now) --ALLTOGETHE
--34
All together now (all together now) --ALLTOGETHE
--35
All together now (all together now) --ALLTOGETHE
--35
All together now (all together now) --ALLTOGETHE
--36
All together now (all together now) --ALLTOGETHE
--36
All together now (all together now) --ALLTOGETHE
--37
All together now (all together now) --ALLTOGETHE
--37
All together now (all together now) --ALLTOGETHE
--38
All together now (all together now) --ALLTOGETHE
--38
All together now (all together now) --ALLTOGETHE
--39
All together now (all together now) --ALLTOGETHE
--39
All together now (all together now) --ALLTOGETHE
--40
All together now (all together now) --ALLTOGETHE
--40
All together now (all together now) --ALLTOGETHE
--41
All together now (all together now) --ALLTOGETHE
--41
All together now (all together now) --ALLTOGETHE
--42
All together now (all together now) --ALLTOGETHE
--42
All together now (all together now) --ALLTOGETHE
--43
All together now (all together now) --ALLTOGETHE
--43
All together now --ALLTOGETHE--44
All together now! (wuh, yeah, wahoo!)--ALLTOGETHE
--45
ALL YOU NEED·IS LOVE.--ALLYOU/MMT--Title
Love is all you need--ALLYOU/MMT--1
(Oh) love is all you need--ALLYOU/MMT--2
Love is all you need--ALLYOU/MMT--3
Love is all you need--ALLYOU/MMT--4
Love is all you need--ALLYOU/MMT--5

Love is all you need.--ALLYOU/MMT--6
IT'S ALL TOO MUCH.--ITSALLTOOM--Title
It's all too much,--ITSALLTOOM--2
It's all too much.--ITSALLTOOM--3
It's all too much for me to take --ITSALLTOOM--8
The love that's shining all around you --ITSALLTOOM
--9
For us to take, it's all too much.--ITSALLTOOM--11
It's all too much for me to take --ITSALLTOOM--16
The love that's shining all around here --
ITSALLTOOM--17
All the world is birthday cake --ITSALLTOOM--18
It's all too much for me to see --ITSALLTOOM--25
The love that's shining all around here --
ITSALLTOOM--26
And what I do is all too much.--ITSALLTOOM--28
It's all too much for me to take --ITSALLTOOM--29
The love that's shining all around you --ITSALLTOOM
--30
For us to take it's all too much.--ITSALLTOOM--32
All the girls around her say she's got it coming
--GETBACK/45--18
Giving all your clothes to charity.--BALLADOFJO--26
Love is all, love is you.--BECAUSE--9
Late nights all alone with a test-tube, oh oh -
oh oh.--MAXWELLSIL--2
And all I have to do is think of her --SOMETHING
--16
All the money's gone, nowhere to go.--YOUNEVERGI
--9
All good children go to heaven.--YOUNEVERGI--25
All good children go to heaven.--YOUNEVERGI--27
All good children go to heaven.--YOUNEVERGI--29
All good children go to heaven.--YOUNEVERGI--31
All good children go to heaven.--YOUNEVERGI--33
All good children go to heaven.--YOUNEVERGI--35
All good children go to heaven.--YOUNEVERGI--37
All good children go to heaven--YOUNEVERGI--39
All good children...--YOUNEVERGI--41
That's all!--YOUKNOWMYN--46
You looked at me, that's all you had to do --
FORYOUBLUE--14
All the girls around her say she's got it coming--
GETBACK/LP--24
All I want is you--IDIGAPONY--13
All I want is you--IDIGAPONY--23
All I want is you--IDIGAPONY--33
All through the day --IMEMINE--1
All through the night --IMEMINE--3
Coming off stronger all the time --IMEMINE--7
All through the day --IMEMINE--8
All I can hear --IMEMINE--14
All through the day --IMEMINE--21
All I can hear --IMEMINE--27
All through your life --IMEMINE--34
All these years I've been wandering round the
world --IVEGOTAFEE--11
All that I was looking for was somebody who
looked like you.--IVEGOTAFEE--13

ALL-AMERICAN
He's the all-American bullet-headed Saxon
mother's son.--CONTINUING--9

ALLAN
Man you should have seen them kicking Edgar
Allan Poe--IAMTHEWALR--27

ALMOST
She almost lost her mind--SHELOVESYO--13

ALONE
Leave me alone--DONTBOTHER--7
When every night I'm all alone--DONTBOTHER--12
Leave me alone--DONTBOTHER--26
Leave me alone--DONTBOTHER--41
Being here alone tonight with you.--HOLDMETIGH--17
Being here alone tonight with you.--HOLDMETIGH--27
Since you left me I'm so alone (you left me here)
--ITWONTBELO--11
Well since you left me I'm so alone (you left
me here)--ITWONTBELO--21
When I'm alone.--THERESAPLA--4
When I'm alone.--THERESAPLA--16
'cos when I get you alone --HARDDAYSNI--13
'cos when I get you alone --HARDDAYSNI--26
We're all alone and there's nobody else --IMDOWN
--16
I've been alone and I have missed things--
IVEJUSTSEE--15

I was alone--NORWEGIANW--22
I've been away now, oh how I've been alone.--WAIT
    --2
I've been away now, oh how I've been alone.--WAIT
    --14
I've been away now, oh how I've been alone.--WAIT
    --26
I was alone, I took a ride--GOTTOGETYO--1
I was alone, I took a ride--GOTTOGETYO--25
She's leaving home after living alone--SHESLEAVIN
    --11
Standing alone at the top of the stairs--SHESLEAVIN
    --15
She's leaving home after living alone--SHESLEAVIN
    --23
(Does it worry you to be alone?)--WITHALITTL--9
Day after day, alone on a hill--FOOLONTHEH--1
Late nights all alone with a test-tube, oh oh -
    oh oh.--MAXWELLSIL--2
PC Thirty-One said, we caught a dirty one,
    Maxwell stands alone --MAXWELLSIL--17
Oh darling, if you leave me I'll never make it
    alone --OHDARLING--3
Believe me when I beg you - ooo - don't ever
    leave me alone.--OHDARLING--4
Oh darling, if you leave me, I'll never make
    it alone.--OHDARLING--9
Many times I've been alone and many times I've
    cried --LONGANDWIN--7

ALONG
    Just call on me and I'll send it along--FROMMETOYO
        --5
    Just/So call on me and I'll send it along--FROMMETOYO--9
    Just call on me and I'll send it along--FROMMETOYO
        --17
    Just call on me and I'll send it along--FROMMETOYO
        --20
    Just call on me and I'll send it along--FROMMETOYO
        --28
    The other day I saw you as I walked along the
        road --WHATGOESON--6
    And was buried along with her name--ELEANORRIG--22
    And he wants you all to sing along.--SGTPEPPERS--22
    She came along to turn on everyone--SEXYSADIE--10

ALOUD
    You shout aloud.--SAVOYTRUFF--16

ALREADY
    If I ain't dead already--YERBLUES--4
    If I ain't dead already--YERBLUES--8
    If I ain't dead already--YERBLUES--15
    If I ain't dead already--YERBLUES--22
    If I ain't dead already--YERBLUES--29

ALRIGHT
    If it makes you feel alright --CANTBUYMEL--4
    If it makes you feel alright --CANTBUYMEL--6
    Will make me feel alright.--HARDDAYSNI--7
    Will make me feel alright.--HARDDAYSNI--23
    Will make me feel alright --HARDDAYSNI--36
    You know I feel alright --HARDDAYSNI--37
    You know I feel alright.--HARDDAYSNI--38
    You can get it wrong and still you think that
        it's alright.--WECANWORKI--7
    It's alright--IWANTTOTEL--7
    But it's alright--STRAWBERRY--19
    Don't you know it's gonna be alright, alright,
        alright?--REVOLUTION--10
    Don't you know it's gonna be alright, alright,
        alright?--REVOLUTION--10
    Don't you know it's gonna be alright, alright,
        alright?--REVOLUTION--10
    (Alright)--REVOLUTION--11
    Don't you know it's gonna be alright, alright
        ((alright)), alright?--REVOLUTION--20
    Don't you know it's gonna be alright, alright
        ((alright)), alright?--REVOLUTION--20
    Don't you know it's gonna be alright, alright
        ((alright)), alright?--REVOLUTION--20
    Don't you know it's gonna be alright, alright
        ((alright)), alright?--REVOLUTION--20
    Don't you know it's gonna be alright, alright,
        alright ((alright))?--REVOLUTION--30
    Don't you know it's gonna be alright, alright,
        alright ((alright))?--REVOLUTION--30
    Don't you know it's gonna be alright, alright,
        alright ((alright))?--REVOLUTION--30
    Don't you know it's gonna be alright, alright,

alright ((alright))?--REVOLUTION--30
Alright, alright, alright, alright --REVOLUTION--31
Alright, alright, alright, alright --REVOLUTION--31
Alright, alright, alright, alright --REVOLUTION--31
Alright, alright, alright, alright --REVOLUTION--31
Alright, alright, alright - alright!--REVOLUTION
    --32
Alright, alright, alright - alright!--REVOLUTION
    --32
Alright, alright, alright - alright!--REVOLUTION
    --32
Alright, alright, alright - alright!--REVOLUTION
    --32
I said that's alright I'm waiting here --DONTPASSME
    --29
Alright ((oh shoo-be-do-a))?--REVOLUTONE--14
Alright ((oh shoo-be-do-a))?--REVOLUTONE--16
Alright ((oh shoo-be-do-a))?--REVOLUTONE--18
Alright ((oh shoo-be-do-a))?--REVOLUTONE--30
Alright ((oh shoo-be-do-a))?--REVOLUTONE--32
Alright ((oh shoo-be-do-a))?--REVOLUTONE--34
Alright ((oh shoo-be-do-a))?--REVOLUTONE--46
Alright ((oh shoo-be-do-a))?--REVOLUTONE--48
Alright ((oh shoo-be-do-a))?--REVOLUTONE--50
Alright (oh shoo-be-do-a)--REVOLUTONE--57
Alright--REVOLUTONE--58
Alright (oh shoo-be-do-a)--REVOLUTONE--59
Alright--REVOLUTONE--60
Alright (oh shoo-be-do-a)--REVOLUTONE--61
Alright--REVOLUTONE--62
Alright (oh shoo-be-do-a)--REVOLUTONE--63
Alright--REVOLUTONE--64
Alright (oh shoo-be-do-a)--REVOLUTONE--65
Alright--REVOLUTONE--66
Alright (oh shoo-be-do-a)--REVOLUTONE--67
(Oh shoo-be-do-a) alright --REVOLUTONE--71
Alright --REVOLUTONE--72
Alright --REVOLUTONE--73
Alright!--REVOLUTONE--74
Oh yeah, alright --THEEND--1
'n' I say, it's alright.--HERECOMEST--3
'n' I say, it's alright.--HERECOMEST--8
'n' I say, it's alright.--HERECOMEST--12
'n' I say, it's alright.--HERECOMEST--22
It's alright --HERECOMEST--25
It's alright.--HERECOMEST--26

ALTHOUGH
    Although I laugh and I act like a clown --IMALOSER
        --9
    Although your mind's opaque --THINKFORYO--19
    Although I'm so tired, I'll have another
        cigarette--IMSOTIRED--15

ALWAYS
    I'll always be true --LOVEMEDO--3
    I'll always be true --LOVEMEDO--8
    I'll always be true --LOVEMEDO--15
    I'll always be true --LOVEMEDO--20
    Remember that I'll always be in love with you.--
        PSILOVEYOU--2
    Remember that I'll always be in love with you.--
        PSILOVEYOU--11
    Remember that I'll always, yeah, be in love
        with you.--PSILOVEYOU--18
    And I'm always thinking of you.--ASKMEWHY--15
    And I'm always thinking of you.--ASKMEWHY--23
    And I'm always thinking of you, you, you.--ASKMEWHY
        --27
    Why do I always have to say love --PLEASEPLEA--8
    But you know there's always rain--PLEASEPLEA--14
    Can't she see she'll always be the only one,
        only one.--MISERY--7
    And eternally I'll always be in love with you--
        THANKYOUGI--3
    And eternally I'll always be in love with you--
        THANKYOUGI--13
    Remember I'll always be true --ALLMYLOVIN--3
    Remember I'll always be true --ALLMYLOVIN--17
    Because I know she'll always be--DONTBOTHER--17
    Because I know she'll always be--DONTBOTHER
        --32
    Would always feel the same--THISBOY--12
    Always on my mind --EIGHTDAYSA--10
    Always on my mind --EIGHTDAYSA--30
    Through thick and thin she will always be my
        friend.--ANOTHERGIR--11
    Through thick and thin she will always be my
        friend.--ANOTHERGIR--17
    I have always thought that it's a crime--WECANWORKI
        --13
    I have always thought that it's a crime--WECANWORKI

--22
Watching her eyes and hoping I'm always there.--
    HERETHEREA--13
Watching her eyes and hoping I'm always there.--
    HERETHEREA--19
Always, no, sometimes, think it's me--STRAWBERRY
    --26
Something inside that was always denied--SHESLEAVIN
    --31
That Georgia's always on my my my my my my my
    my mind.--BACKINTHEU--18
That Georgia's always on my my my my my my my
    my mind.--BACKINTHEU--30
In case of accidents he always took his mom --
    CONTINUING--8
The Duchess of Kirkaldy always smiling --CRYBABYCRY
    --20
I will always feel the same.--IWILL--8
Martha my dear, you have always been my
    inspiration --MARTHAMYDE--13
Always having dirt to play around in.--PIGGIES--5
Always have clean shirts to play around in.--
    PIGGIES--10
Always shouts out something obscene--MEANMRMUST--13
She said she'd always been a dancer --SHECAMEINT
    --12
It always leads me here, lead me to your door.--
    LONGANDWIN--3

AM
The lips I am missing --ALLMYLOVIN--8
Here am I sitting all on my own--ITWONTBELO--6
Beneath this mask I am wearing a frown.--IMALOSER
    --10
Why am I so shy when I'm beside you?--ITSONLYLOV
    --3
Falling, yes I am falling--IVEJUSTSEE--12
Falling, yes I am falling--IVEJUSTSEE--19
Falling, yes I am falling--IVEJUSTSEE--22
Falling, yes I am falling--IVEJUSTSEE--30
Falling, yes I am falling--IVEJUSTSEE--32
(Oh) falling, yes I am falling--IVEJUSTSEE--34
Only time will tell if I am right or I am wrong.--
    WECANWORKI--16
Only time will tell if I am right or I am wrong.--
    WECANWORKI--16
Only time will tell if I am right or I am wrong.--
    WECANWORKI--25
Only time will tell if I am right or I am wrong.--
    WECANWORKI--25
Or I won't know where I am.--RUNFORYOUR--4
Or you won't know where I am.--RUNFORYOUR--28
Leave me where I am, I'm only sleeping.--IMONLYSLEE
    --6
Leave me where I am, I'm only sleeping.--IMONLYSLEE
    --26
I AM THE WALRUS.--IAMTHEWALR--Title
I am he as you are he as you are me and we are
    all together--IAMTHEWALR--1
I am the eggman (goo) they are the eggmen (goo)
    I am the walrus--IAMTHEWALR--7
I am the eggman (goo) they are the eggmen (goo)
    I am the walrus--IAMTHEWALR--7
I am the eggman (goo) they are the eggmen (goo)
    I am the walrus--IAMTHEWALR--15
I am the eggman (goo) they are the eggmen (goo)
    I am the walrus--IAMTHEWALR--15
I am the eggman, they are the eggmen, I am the
    walrus--IAMTHEWALR--19
I am the eggman, they are the eggmen, I am the
    walrus--IAMTHEWALR--19
I am the eggman (goo) they are the eggmen (goo)
    I am the walrus (goo)--IAMTHEWALR--28
I am the eggman (goo) they are the eggmen (goo)
    I am the walrus (goo)--IAMTHEWALR--28
And I'll be better, I'll be better Doc as
    soon as I am able.--ROCKYRACCO--35
But I am of the universe--YERBLUES--12

AMORE
Quando paramucho mi amore defeliche carathon --
    SUNKING--6
Mundo paparatsi mi amore chicka ferde parasol --
    SUNKING--7

AMSTERDAM
Drove from Paris to the Amsterdam Hilton --
    BALLADOFJO--17

ANGELS
((And now we'd like to do)) Hark the Angels
    Come...--DIGIT--13

ANGRY
Me used to be angry young man--GETTINGBET--11

ANNOYED
Back in school again, Maxwell plays the fool
    again, teacher gets annoyed --MAXWELLSIL--8

ANOTHER
So how could I dance with another --ISAWHERSTA--5
She wouldn't dance with another --ISAWHERSTA--9
Now I'll never dance with another --ISAWHERSTA--16
Now I'll never dance with another --ISAWHERSTA--23
With another man in my place.--NOREPLY--16
With another man in my place.--NOREPLY--29
ANOTHER GIRL.--ANOTHERGIR--Title
For I have got another girl, another girl.--
    ANOTHERGIR--1
For I have got another girl, another girl.--
    ANOTHERGIR--1
For I have got another girl, another girl.--
    ANOTHERGIR--5
For I have got another girl, another girl.--
    ANOTHERGIR--5
For I have got another girl --ANOTHERGIR--9
Another girl who will love me till the end --
    ANOTHERGIR--10
For I have got another girl --ANOTHERGIR--15
Another girl who will love me till the end --
    ANOTHERGIR--16
For I have got another girl, another girl,
    another girl.--ANOTHERGIR--21
For I have got another girl, another girl,
    another girl.--ANOTHERGIR--21
For I have got another girl, another girl,
    another girl.--ANOTHERGIR--21
Had it been another day--IVEJUSTSEE--7
Than to be with another man.--RUNFORYOUR--2
Catch you with another man --RUNFORYOUR--7
Catch you with another man --RUNFORYOUR--15
Catch you with another man --RUNFORYOUR--23
Than to be with another man.--RUNFORYOUR--26
Catch you with another man --RUNFORYOUR--31
Another road where maybe I--GOTTOGETYO--3
Could see another kind of mind there.--GOTTOGETYO
    --4
Another road where maybe I--GOTTOGETYO--27
Could see another kind of mind there.--GOTTOGETYO
    --28
In Penny Lane the barber shaves another customer--
    PENNYLANE--24
Now that you've found another key--BABYYOUREA--26
Well here's another place you can go--GLASSONION
    --3
Well here's another clue for you all:--GLASSONION
    --10
Well here's another place you can be--GLASSONION
    --19
Although I'm so tired, I'll have another
    cigarette--IMSOTIRED--15
And one day his woman ran off with another guy,--
    ' ROCKYRACCO--3
But she was another man.--GETBACK/45--17
But she was another man--GETBACK/LP--23

ANSWER
Somebody calls you, you answer quite slowly--
    LUCYINTHES--3
Give me your answer--WHENIMSIXT--32
And he never gives an answer.--FOOLONTHEH--5
Tell me, tell me, tell me, come on tell me the
    answer --HELTERSKEL--6
Tell me, tell me, tell me the answer --HELTERSKEL
    --13
Tell me, tell me, tell me your answer --HELTERSKEL
    --23
And though she thought I knew the answer --
    SHECAMEINT--14
There will be an answer, let it be.--LETITBE/45--11
There will be an answer, let it be.--LETITBE/45--14
Yeah there will be an answer, let it be.--
    LETITBE/45--16

Oh there will be an answer, let it be.--LETITBE/45
--28
There will be an answer, let it be.--LETITBE/LP--11
There will be an answer, let it be.--LETITBE/LP--14
Yeah there will be an answer, let it be.--
LETITBE/LP--16
Oh there will be an answer, let it be.--LETITBE/LP
--28
Oh there will be an answer, let it be.--LETITBE/LP
--30

ANY
I can't conceive of any more misery.--ASKMEWHY--13
I can't conceive of any more misery.--ASKMEWHY--25
ANY TIME AT ALL.--ANYTIMEATA--Title
Any time at all, any time at all, any time at all--
ANYTIMEATA--1
Any time at all, any time at all, any time at all--
ANYTIMEATA--1
Any time at all, any time at all, any time at all--
ANYTIMEATA--1
Any time at all, any time at all, any time at all--
ANYTIMEATA--10
Any time at all, any time at all, any time at all--
ANYTIMEATA--10
Any time at all, any time at all, any time at all--
ANYTIMEATA--10
Any time at all, any time at all, any time at all--
ANYTIMEATA--19
Any time at all, any time at all, any time at all--
ANYTIMEATA--19
Any time at all, any time at all, any time at all--
ANYTIMEATA--19
Any time at all, any time at all, any time at all--
ANYTIMEATA--22
Any time at all, any time at all, any time at all--
ANYTIMEATA--22
Any time at all, any time at all, any time at all--
ANYTIMEATA--22
Any time at all--ANYTIMEATA--25
Love you more than any other guy--NOREPLY--18
I never needed ((never needed)) anybody's help
in any way--HELP--10
I never needed anybody's help in any way--HELP--30
You don't want my loving any more--INEEDYOU--12
I just can't go on any more.--INEEDYOU--15
You don't want my loving any more--INEEDYOU--22
I just can't go on any more.--INEEDYOU--25
Day or night he'll be there any time at all, Dr.
Robert--DRROBERT--2
And any time you feel the pain--HEYJUDE--9
Does it mean you don't love me any more?--
DONTPASSME--9
Does it mean you don't love me any more?--
DONTPASSME--17
Do you know any more?--HEYBULLDOG--26
When you told me you didn't need me any more --
OHDARLING--5
A - when you told me you didn't need me any more
--OHDARLING--7
A - when you told me - ooo - you didn't need me
any more --OHDARLING--12
A - when you told me you didn't need me any more
--OHDARLING--14
Any jobber got the sack --YOUNEVERGI--10
Well you can penetrate any place you go--IDIGAPONY
--10
Yes you can penetrate any place you go--IDIGAPONY
--11
Well you can syndicate any boat you rode/rowed--
IDIGAPONY--30
Yeah you can syndicate any boat you rode/rowed--
IDIGAPONY--31

ANYBODY
Not just anybody--HELP--4
Is there anybody going to listen to my story--GIRL
--1
(Do you need anybody?)--WITHALITTL--15
(Could it be anybody?)--WITHALITTL--17
(Do you need anybody?)--WITHALITTL--26
(Could it be anybody?)--WITHALITTL--28
Didn't anybody tell her?--SHECAMEINT--8
Didn't anybody see?--SHECAMEINT--9
Didn't anybody tell her?--SHECAMEINT--20
Didn't anybody see?--SHECAMEINT--21

ANYBODY'S
I never needed ((never needed)) anybody's help
in any way--HELP--10
I never needed anybody's help in any way--HELP--30

ANYHOW
You ain't gonna make it with anyone anyhow.--
REVOLUTION--29
You ain't gonna make it with anyone anyhow.--
REVOLUTONE--44

ANYONE
Helping anyone in need --DRROBERT--9
You ain't gonna make it with anyone anyhow.--
REVOLUTION--29
You ain't gonna make it with anyone anyhow.--
REVOLUTONE--44

ANYTHING
If there's anything that you want--FROMMETOYO
--3
If there's anything I can do--FROMMETOYO--4
If there's anything that you want--FROMMETOYO
--15
If there's anything I can do--FROMMETOYO--16
If there's anything that you want--FROMMETOYO
--26
If there's anything I can do--FROMMETOYO--27
I'll get you anything my friend --CANTBUYMEL--5
If there's anything I can do --TELLMEWHY--23
Well you can celebrate anything you want--IDIGAPONY
--7
Yes you can celebrate anything you want.--IDIGAPONY
--8
Yes you can indicate anything you see.--IDIGAPONY
--28

ANYWAY
She is anyway.--PENNYLANE--23
Anyway you'll never know the many ways I've tried
--LONGANDWIN--8

ANYWHERE
And she told me to sit anywhere--NORWEGIANW--8

APART
We will never be apart--TELLMEWHAT--3
There's a chance that we might fall apart before
too long.--WECANWORKI--18
There's a chance that we might fall apart before
too long.--WECANWORKI--27
You are tearing me apart --WHATGOESON--3
You are tearing me apart --WHATGOESON--12
You are tearing me apart --WHATGOESON--28
I beat her and kept her apart from the things
that she loved--GETTINGBET--26
Love you when we're apart.--IWILL--12
I feel your taste all the time we're apart --
SAVOYTRUFF--7

APOLOGIZE
Apologize to her.--SHELOVESYO--27
Tell me what and I'll apologize --TELLMEWHY--14

APPEAR
And I'm not what I appear to be.--IMALOSER--2
I'm a loser and I'm not what I appear to be.--
IMALOSER--8
I'm a loser and I'm not what I appear to be.--
IMALOSER--14
I'm a loser and I'm not what I appear to be.--
IMALOSER--20
Should five percent appear too small --TAXMAN--7
Newspaper taxis appear on the shore--LUCYINTHES
--16
I may appear to be imperfect --OLDBROWNSH--22

APPEARS
Or the sound he appears to make--FOOLONTHEH--11

APPLE
Cool cherry cream, nice apple tart --SAVOYTRUFF
--6

APPOINTMENT
Waiting to keep the appointment she made--
SHESLEAVIN--26

APPRECIATE
    And I do appreciate you being round--HELP--16
    And I do appreciate you being round--HELP--26
    And I do appreciate you being round--HELP--36

ARE
    Bright are the stars that shine --ANDILOVEHE--15
    Bright are the stars that shine --ANDILOVEHE--20
    When she learns we are two.--IFIFELL--20
    When she learns we are two.--IFIFELL--27
    My tears are falling like rain from the sky --
        IMALOSER--11
    But now ((but now)) these days are gone
        ((these days are gone))--HELP--11
    But now ((but now)) these days are gone
        ((these days are gone))--HELP--11
    But now ((now)) these days are gone ((these
        days are gone))--HELP--31
    But now ((now)) these days are gone ((these
        days are gone))--HELP--31
    When friends are there, you feel a fool.--GIRL--13
    Your lips are moving, I cannot hear --IMLOOKINGT
        --5
    There are places I remember --INMYLIFE--1
    Some are dead and some are living --INMYLIFE--7
    Some are dead and some are living --INMYLIFE--7
    These are words that go together well, my
        Michelle.--MICHELLE--2
    You are tearing me apart --WHATGOESON--3
    You are tearing me apart --WHATGOESON--12
    You are tearing me apart --WHATGOESON--28
    But I can't get through, my hands are tied.--
        YOUWONTSEE--8
    Though the days are few, they're filled with tears
        --YOUWONTSEE--16
    Though the days are few they're filled with tears
        --YOUWONTSEE--25
    And our friends are all aboard--YELLOWSUBM--13
    When are you free ((lovely Rita))--LOVELYRITA--15
    (Are you sad because you're on your own?)--
        WITHALITTL--11
    Are you one of them?--WITHINYOUW--27
    Now that you know who you are--BABYYOUREA--3
    What are you going to play?--BABYYOUREA--27
    I am he as you are he as you are me and we are
        all together--IAMTHEWALR--1
    I am he as you are he as you are me and we are
        all together--IAMTHEWALR--1
    I am he as you are he as you are me and we are
        all together--IAMTHEWALR--1
    I am the eggman (goo) they are the eggmen (goo)
        I am the walrus--IAMTHEWALR--7
    I am the eggman (goo) they are the eggmen (goo)
        I am the walrus--IAMTHEWALR--15
    I am the eggman, they are the eggmen, I am the
        walrus--IAMTHEWALR--19
    I am the eggman (goo) they are the eggmen (goo)
        I am the walrus (goo)--IAMTHEWALR--28
    You don't know how lucky you are boys --BACKINTHEU
        --6
    You don't know how lucky you are boy --BACKINTHEU
        --13
    You don't know how lucky you are boys --BACKINTHEU
        --25
    You don't know how lucky you are boy --BACKINTHEU
        --36
    It's beautiful and so are you.--DEARPRUDEN--4
    That you are part of everything.--DEARPRUDEN--9
    It's beautiful and so are you.--DEARPRUDEN--24
    I wonder where you are tonight --DONTPASSME--14
    Lying with his eyes while his hands are busy
        working overtime --HAPPINESSI--6
    Honey Pie you are making me crazy--HONEYPIE--7
    Oh, Honey Pie you are driving me frantic--HONEYPIE
        --16
    Now Honey Pie you are making me crazy--HONEYPIE--29
    You know that what you eat you are --SAVOYTRUFF--19
    But can you show me where you are?--SAVOYTRUFF--22
    However big you think you are--SEXYSADIE--17
    However big you think you are--SEXYSADIE--18
    ... However big you think you are.--SEXYSADIE--28
    Makes no difference where you are--ITSALLTOOM--14
    We are dead.--ITSALLTOOM--38
    You may think the chords are going wrong --
        ONLYANORTH--2
    You may think the band are not quite right --
        ONLYANORTH--5
    But they are, they just play it like that.--
        ONLYANORTH--6
    The way things are going --BALLADOFJO--7
    The way things are going --BALLADOFJO--15
    The way things are going --BALLADOFJO--23
    The way things are going --BALLADOFJO--35

The way things are going --BALLADOFJO--43
The way things are going --BALLADOFJO--45
Are you gonna be in my dreams tonight?--THEEND--2
But as the words are leaving his lips, a noise
    comes from behind --MAXWELLSIL--22
Words are flowing out like endless rain into a
    paper cup --ACROSSTHEU--1
Are drifting through my opened mind--ACROSSTHEU
    --4
Are ringing through my opened ears--ACROSSTHEU
    --21
Well you can radiate everything you are--IDIGAPONY
    --17
Yes you can radiate everything you are.--IDIGAPONY
    --18
Oh Danny Boy, the odes of Pan are calling.--
    ONEAFTERNI--33

AREN'T
    Your voice is soothing but the words aren't clear.
        --IMLOOKINGT--6

ARISE
    You were only waiting for this moment to arise.--
        BLACKBIRD--4
    You were only waiting for this moment to arise --
        BLACKBIRD--16
    You were only waiting for this moment to arise --
        BLACKBIRD--17
    You were only waiting for this moment to arise.--
        BLACKBIRD--18

ARIZONA
    Jojo left his home in Tucson, Arizona--GETBACK/45
        --3
    Jojo left his home in Tucson, Arizona--GETBACK/LP
        --9

ARMCHAIR
    Hold you in his armchair you can feel his disease
        --COMETOGETH--30

ARMS
    I got arms that long to hold you--FROMMETOYO--11
    I got arms that long to hold you--FROMMETOYO--22
    When I hold you in my arms ((oh, yeah)) --
        HAPPINESSI--22

ARMY
    The English Army had just won the war--DAYINTHELI
        --12

AROUND
    Whenever I want you around, yeah --ALLIVEGOTT--1
    Don't come around--DONTBOTHER--25
    Don't come around--DONTBOTHER--40
    When I was around.--TICKETTORI--12
    When I was around.--TICKETTORI--39
    So I looked around--NORWEGIANW--9
    I'll make you maybe next time around.--IWANTTOTEL
        --8
    I turn around, it's past --LOVEYOUTWO--2
    Silly people run around they worry me--FIXINGAHOL
        --17
    Look around, 'round --DEARPRUDEN--11
    Look around, 'round, 'round --DEARPRUDEN--13
    Look around (('round)).--DEARPRUDEN--15
    Help yourself to a bit of what is all around you
        - silly girl.--MARTHAMYDE--6
    Take a good look around you --MARTHAMYDE--7
    Help yourself to a bit of what is all around you
        - silly girl.--MARTHAMYDE--12
    Always having dirt to play around in.--PIGGIES--5
    Always have clean shirts to play around in.--
        PIGGIES--10
    They don't care what goes on around.--PIGGIES--12
    The love that's shining all around you --ITSALLTOOM
        --9
    The love that's shining all around here --
        ITSALLTOOM--17
    The love that's shining all around here --
        ITSALLTOOM--26
    The love that's shining all around you --ITSALLTOOM
        --30
    All the girls around her say she's got it coming
        --GETBACK/45--18
    We would sing and dance around--OCTOPUSSGA--13

You stick around now it may show --SOMETHING--13
Limitless undying love which shines around me
  like a million suns --ACROSSTHEU--23
All the girls around her say she's got it coming--
  GETBACK/LP--24

ARRIVE
  Arrive without travelling.--INNERLIGHT--15
  But they don't arrive.--DONTPASSME--5

ARRIVES
  Friday night arrives without a suitcase --
  LADYMADONN--5

ARRIVING
  And arriving late for tea --CRYBABYCRY--21
  Not arriving on our way back home.--TWOOFUS--6

AS
  As I write this letter, send my love to you --
  PSILOVEYOU--1
  As I write this letter, send my love to you --
  PSILOVEYOU--10
  As I write this letter (oh) send my love to you --
  PSILOVEYOU--16
  So you might as well resign yourself to me, oh
  yeah.--ILLGETYOU--18
  As long as I --ANDILOVEHE--13
  As long as I --ANDILOVEHE--13
  She's happy as can be, you know, she said so --
  IFEELFINE--2
  Gives me all her time as well as loving--SHESAWOMAN
  --14
  Gives me all her time as well as loving--SHESAWOMAN
  --14
  But as from today well I've got somebody that's
  new --ANOTHERGIR--3
  But as from today well I've seen somebody that's
  new --ANOTHERGIR--13
  But as from today well I've seen somebody that's
  new --ANOTHERGIR--19
  I'm lonely as can be--INEEDYOU--4
  As I looked in your eyes--INEEDYOU--9
  But as it is I'll dream of her tonight --IVEJUSTSEE
  --10
  Now it looks as though they're here to stay--
  YESTERDAY--3
  She acts as if it's understood --GIRL--17
  When I think of love as something new.--INMYLIFE
  --12
  He's as blind as he can be --NOWHEREMAN--10
  He's as blind as he can be --NOWHEREMAN--10
  I feel as though you ought to know--WAIT--9
  That I've been good, as good as I can be.--WAIT--10
  That I've been good, as good as I can be.--WAIT--10
  I feel as though you ought to know--WAIT--17
  That I've been good, as good as I can be.--WAIT--18
  That I've been good, as good as I can be.--WAIT--18
  The other day I saw you as I walked along the
  road --WHATGOESON--6
  You didn't even think of me as someone with a name.
  --WHATGOESON--23
  They might as well be dead--RAIN--2
  As he walks from the grave--ELEANORRIG--25
  Burns my feet as they touch the ground.--GOODDAYSUN
  --8
  As we live a life of ease--YELLOWSUBM--25
  And though she feels as if she's in a play--
  PENNYLANE--22
  As Mr. Kite flies through the ring - don't be
  late.--BEINGFORTH--11
  Everyone smiles as you drift past the flowers--
  LUCYINTHES--14
  Wednesday morning at five o'clock as the day begins
  --SHESLEAVIN--1
  Father snores as his wife gets into her
  dressing-gown--SHESLEAVIN--13
  Far as the eye can see.--BABYYOUREA--6
  I am he as you are he as you are me and we are
  all together--IAMTHEWALR--1
  I am he as you are he as you are me and we are
  all together--IAMTHEWALR--1
  You know that we're as close as can be - man--
  GLASSONION--9
  You know that we're as close as can be - man--
  GLASSONION--9
  Listen to the pretty sound of music as she flies.
  --MOTHERNATU--4
  And Molly says this as she takes him by the hand:
  --OBLADIOBLA--4

And as he gives it to her she begins to sing
  (sing):--OBLADIOBLA--12
But everyone knew her as Nancy.--ROCKYRACCO--16
And I'll be better, I'll be better Doc as
  soon as I am able.--ROCKYRACCO--35
And I'll be better, I'll be better Doc as
  soon as I am able.--ROCKYRACCO--35
As it's only a Northern song.--ONLYANORTH--9
Who sometimes wears it twice as long.--OLDBROWNSH
  --4
But as she's getting ready to go, a knock comes
  on the door --MAXWELLSIL--5
But as the words are leaving his lips, a noise
  comes from behind --MAXWELLSIL--22
They slither wildly as they slip away across the
  universe.--ACROSSTHEU--2
They tumble blindly as they make their way across
  the universe.--ACROSSTHEU--14
Come on baby, don't be cold as ice --ONEAFTERNI--4
Come on baby, don't be cold as ice --ONEAFTERNI--9
Come on baby, don't be cold as ice --ONEAFTERNI--18
Come on baby, don't be cold as ice.--ONEAFTERNI--28

ASK
  ASK ME WHY.--ASKMEWHY--Title
  Ask me why, I'll say I love you --ASKMEWHY--14
  Ask me why, I'll say I love you --ASKMEWHY--22
  Ask me why, I'll say I love you --ASKMEWHY--26
  And when I ask you to be mine --ISHOULDHAV--9
  And when I ask you to be mine --ISHOULDHAV--19
  Don't ask me why--SHESAWOMAN--15
  Would it be too much to ask of you --WHATYOURED--3
  Why should it be so much to ask of you --WHATYOURED
  --7
  Why should it be so much to ask of you --WHATYOURED
  --14
  Why should it be so much to ask of you --WHATYOURED
  --21
  So I will ask you once again.--WECANWORKI--14
  So I will ask you once again.--WECANWORKI--23
  Don't ask me what I want it for (ha ha Mr.
  Wilson)--TAXMAN--18
  And never ask me why they don't get past my door.
  --FIXINGAHOL--18
  Who could ask for more?--WHENIMSIXT--18
  Ask a policeman on the street --BLUEJAYWAY--10
  You ask me for a contribution --REVOLUTION--15
  You ask me for a contribution --REVOLUTONE--23
  I'd ask my friends to come and see--OCTOPUSSGA--5

ASKED
  Asked a girl what she wanted to be --DRIVEMYCAR--1
  She asked me to stay--NORWEGIANW--7
  The children asked him if to kill was not a sin --
  CONTINUING--27

ASKING
  You're asking me will my love grow?--SOMETHING--11

ASLEEP
  Everyone you see is half asleep--GOODMORNIN--11
  Please don't be long or I may be asleep.--
  BLUEJAYWAY--7
  Please don't be long or I may be asleep.--
  BLUEJAYWAY--14
  Please don't be long or I may be asleep.--
  BLUEJAYWAY--21

ASSURE
  Messrs. K. and H. assure the public--BEINGFORTH--12

AT
  ANY TIME AT ALL.--ANYTIMEATA--Title.
  Any time at all, any time at all, any time at all--
  ANYTIMEATA--1
  Any time at all, any time at all, any time at all--
  ANYTIMEATA--1
  Any time at all, any time at all, any time at all--
  ANYTIMEATA--1
  Any time at all, any time at all, any time at all--
  ANYTIMEATA--10
  Any time at all, any time at all, any time at all--
  ANYTIMEATA--10
  Any time at all, any time at all, any time at all--
  ANYTIMEATA--10
  Any time at all, any time at all, any time at all--
  ANYTIMEATA--19
  Any time at all, any time at all, any time at all--

ANYTIMEATA--19
Any time at all, any time at all, any time at all--
    ANYTIMEATA--19
Any time at all, any time at all, any time at all--
    ANYTIMEATA--22
Any time at all, any time at all, any time at all--
    ANYTIMEATA--22
Any time at all, any time at all, any time at all--
    ANYTIMEATA--22
Any time at all--ANYTIMEATA--25
Well she looked at me, and I, I could see --
    ISAWHERSTA--7
Whenever you want me at all --ALLIVEGOTT--12
Whenever you want me at all --ALLIVEGOTT--23
Oh, I can't sleep at night since you've been
    gone --ICALLYOURN--3
I never weep at night, I can't go on.--ICALLYOURN
    --4
Oh, I can't sleep at night, but just the same --
    ICALLYOURN--9
I never weep at night, I call your name.--
    ICALLYOURN--10
Oh, I can't sleep at night, but just the same --
    ICALLYOURN--16
I never weep at night, I call your name --
    ICALLYOURN--17
You can't cry 'cos you're laughing at me --IMDOWN
    --2
I can see them laugh at me --YOUVEGOTTO--7
Nowhere Man the world is at your command.--
    NOWHEREMAN--9
Nowhere Man can you see me at all?--NOWHEREMAN--12
Nowhere Man the world is at your command.--
    NOWHEREMAN--21
Day or night he'll be there any time at all, Dr.
    Robert --DRROBERT--2
Running everywhere at such a speed --IMONLYSLEE--9
Lying there and staring at the ceiling --IMONLYSLEE
    --15
Aah, look at all the lonely people.--ELEANORRIG--1
Aah, look at all the lonely people.--ELEANORRIG--2
Waits at the window--ELEANORRIG--6
Look at him working--ELEANORRIG--14
Aah, look at all the lonely people.--ELEANORRIG--19
Aah, look at all the lonely people.--ELEANORRIG--20
((Aah, look at all the lonely people.))--ELEANORRIG
    --28
((Aah, look at all the lonely people.))--ELEANORRIG
    --30
The little children laugh at him behind his back--
    PENNYLANE--6
Performs his feat on Saturday at Bishopsgate.--
    BEINGFORTH--9
The band begins at ten to six--BEINGFORTH--15
I used to get mad at my school (now I can't
    complain)--GETTINGBET--3
Suddenly someone is there at the turnstyle--
    LUCYINTHES--25
Wednesday morning at five o'clock as the day begins
    --SHESLEAVIN--1
Standing alone at the top of the stairs--SHESLEAVIN
    --15
Friday morning at nine o'clock she is far away--
    SHESLEAVIN--25
(Would you believe in a love at first sight?)--
    WITHALITTL--19
Expert texpert, choking smokers, don't you
    think the joker laughs at you?--IAMTHEWALR--21
Lady Madonna, children at your feet --LADYMADONN
    --1
Lady Madonna, baby at your breast --LADYMADONN--9
Lady Madonna, children at your feet --LADYMADONN
    --18
Hey, so look at me --BACKINTHEU--41
With a message at the local bird and bee.--
    CRYBABYCRY--23
At twelve o'clock a meeting round the table --
    CRYBABYCRY--28
And when at last I find you --IWILL--13
Takes it back to Molly waiting at the door--
    OBLADIOBLA--11
Molly stays at home and does her pretty face--
    OBLADIOBLA--23
Desmond stays at home and does his pretty face--
    OBLADIOBLA--34
Were in the next room at the hoe-down --ROCKYRACCO
    --18
We gave her everything we owned just to sit at
    her table ((sexy Sadie))--SEXYSADIE--20
I look at you all, see the love there that's
    sleeping --WHILEMYGUI--2
I look at the floor and I see it needs sweeping --
    WHILEMYGUI--4
I look at the world and I notice it's turning --

WHILEMYGUI--9
I look at you all, see the love there that's
    sleeping --WHILEMYGUI--18
Look, look at you all --WHILEMYGUI--20
Bom-pa bom, look at me.--ALLTOGETHE--12
Bom-pa bom, look at me.--ALLTOGETHE--32
Don't look at me man (ha ha ha ha)--HEYBULLDOG--31
When you're listening late at night --ONLYANORTH
    --4
Standing in the dock at Southampton --BALLADOFJO
    --1
Takes him out to look at the Queen--MEANMRMUST--11
She worked at fifteen clubs a day--SHECAMEINT--13
I want you at the moment I feel blue --FORYOUBLUE
    --6
You looked at me, that's all you had to do --
    FORYOUBLUE--14

ATE
    A soap impression of his wife which he ate --
        HAPPINESSI--7

ATLANTIC
    Sail across the Atlantic--HONEYPIE--17

ATTRACTIVELY
    Yes, you could say she was attractively built -
        yeah, yeah, yeah.--POLYTHENEP--9

ATTRACTS
    Attracts me like no other lover --SOMETHING--2

AUDIENCE
    You're such a lovely audience--SGTPEPPERS--16

AUDITION
    And I hope we passed the audition.--GETBACK/LP--39

AVOID
    Wishing to avoid an unpleasant scene --MAXWELLSIL
        --9

AWAKE
    Smiles awake you when you rise.--GOLDENSLUM--8

AWARE
    And I'd have never been aware--IVEJUSTSEE--9

AWAY
    If the sun has faded away --ANYTIMEATA--13
    And then while I'm away --ALLMYLOVIN--4
    And then while I'm away --ALLMYLOVIN--10
    And then while I'm away --ALLMYLOVIN--18
    So go away--DONTBOTHER--6
    Just stay away--DONTBOTHER--21
    Just stay away--DONTBOTHER--36
    That boy took my love away--THISBOY--1
    That if I ran away from you--ILLBEBACK--14
    Wishing you weren't so far away --THINGSWESA--4
    The girl that's driving me mad is going away.--
        TICKETTORI--4
    The girl that's driving me mad is going away,
        yeah.--TICKETTORI--25
    Time will pass away--TELLMEWHAT--10
    Though you've gone away this morning--YOULIKEMET
        --1
    Man buys ring, woman throws it away --IMDOWN--8
    All my troubles seemed so far away--YESTERDAY--2
    Now I need a place to hide away--YESTERDAY--15
    Now I need a place to hide away--YESTERDAY--16
    I'll make a point of taking her away from you
        (watch what you do), yeah--YOUREGONNA--16
    I'll make a point of taking her away from you
        (watch what you do), yeah--YOUREGONNA--23
    YOU'VE GOT TO HIDE YOUR LOVE AWAY.--YOUVEGOTTO
        --Title
    Hey! you've got to hide your love away.--YOUVEGOTTO--9
    Hey! you've got to hide your love away.--YOUVEGOTTO--10
    Hey! you've got to hide your love away.--YOUVEGOTTO--19
    Hey! you've got to hide your love away.--YOUVEGOTTO
        --20
    I told that girl I could start right away --
        DRIVEMYCAR--22
    I've been away now, oh how I've been alone.--WAIT

--2
But if your heart breaks, don't wait, turn me
   away--WAIT--5
I've been away now, oh how I've been alone.--WAIT
   --14
But if your heart breaks, don't wait, turn me
   away --WAIT--21
I've been away now, oh how I've been alone.--WAIT
   --26
But I can turn away--YOUWONTSEE--10
Please don't spoil my day, I'm miles away --
   IMONLYSLEE--11
Please don't spoil my day, I'm miles away --
   IMONLYSLEE--17
All those words they seem to slip away.--IWANTTOTEL
   --4
A crowd of people turned away--DAYINTHELI--13
When it gets dark I tow your heart away.--
   LOVELYRITA--6
Waiting to take you away.--LUCYINTHES--17
Friday morning at nine o'clock she is far away--
   SHESLEAVIN--25
Yours sincerely, wasting away.--WHENIMSIXT--31
What do I do when my love is away?--WITHALITTL--8
When they pass away.--WITHINYOUW--7
The Magical Mystery Tour is waiting to take
   you away--MAGICALMYS--9
(Waiting to take you away).--MAGICALMYS--10
The Magical Mystery Tour is hoping to take you
   away --MAGICALMYS--17
(Hoping to take you away)--MAGICALMYS--18
The Magical Mystery Tour is coming to take you
   away --MAGICALMYS--27
(Coming/Hoping to take you away)--MAGICALMYS--28
The Magical Mystery Tour is dying to take you
   away --MAGICALMYS--29
(Dying to take you away) --MAGICALMYS--30
Been away so long I hardly knew the place,--
   BACKINTHEU--8
She tells Max to stay when the class has gone
   away --MAXWELLSIL--10
Soon we'll be away from here --YOUNEVERGI--19
Step on the gas and wipe that tear away.--
   YOUNEVERGI--20
They slither wildly as they slip away across the
   universe.--ACROSSTHEU--2
The wild and windy night that the rain washed away
   --LONGANDWIN--4

AWAY-HEY
   I'm gonna hide myself away-hey--ILLCRYINST--13
   I'm gonna hide myself away-hey--ILLCRYINST--22

AWOKE
   And when I awoke--NORWEGIANW--21

AWOKEN
   You may be awoken --ANDYOURBIR--11

AYE
   Aye, Sir, aye.--YELLOWSUBM--23
   Aye, Sir, aye.--YELLOWSUBM--23

B
   A, B, C, D --ALLTOGETHE--5

BA
   You know my name, ba ba ba ba ba ba ba ba
      ((yahoo)) --YOUKNOWMYN--13
   You know my name, ba ba ba ba ba ba ba ba
      ((yahoo)) --YOUKNOWMYN--13
   You know my name, ba ba ba ba ba ba ba ba
      ((yahoo)) --YOUKNOWMYN--13
   You know my name, ba ba ba ba ba ba ba ba
      ((yahoo)) --YOUKNOWMYN--13
   You know my name, ba ba ba ba ba ba ba ba
      ((yahoo)) --YOUKNOWMYN--13
   You know my name, ba ba ba ba ba ba ba ba
      ((yahoo)) --YOUKNOWMYN--13
   You know my name, ba ba ba ba ba ba ba ba
      ((yahoo)) --YOUKNOWMYN--13
   You know my name, ba ba ba ba ba ba ba ba
      ((yahoo)) --YOUKNOWMYN--13
   You know my name, ba ba ba bum, look up the
      number --YOUKNOWMYN--18
   You know my name, ba ba ba bum, look up the
      number --YOUKNOWMYN--18
   You know my name, ba ba ba bum, look up the

   number --YOUKNOWMYN--18

BABE
   Ooo I need your love babe --EIGHTDAYSA--1
   Hope you need my love babe --EIGHTDAYSA--3
   I ain't got nothing but love babe --EIGHTDAYSA--7
   Ooo I need your love babe --EIGHTDAYSA--19
   Hope you need my love babe --EIGHTDAYSA--21
   I ain't got nothing but love babe --EIGHTDAYSA--25
   I ain't got nothing but love babe --EIGHTDAYSA--35
   And she said listen babe I've got something to
      say --DRIVEMYCAR--23
   I want you so bad, babe--IWANTYOUSH--8
   I want you so bad, babe--IWANTYOUSH--14
   You know I want you so bad, babe--IWANTYOUSH--35

BABY
   I wanna be your lover baby --IWANNABEYO--1
   I wanna be your lover baby --IWANNABEYO--3
   Love you like no other baby --IWANNABEYO--5
   Love you like no other baby --IWANNABEYO--7
   Tell me that you love me baby --IWANNABEYO--13
   Tell me that you love me baby --IWANNABEYO--15
   I wanna be your lover baby --IWANNABEYO--17
   I wanna be your lover baby --IWANNABEYO--19
   I wanna be your lover baby --IWANNABEYO--30
   I wanna be your lover baby --IWANNABEYO--32
   Love you like no other baby --IWANNABEYO--34
   Love you like no other baby --IWANNABEYO--36
   Baby take a chance with me.--LITTLECHIL--4
   Baby take a chance with me.--LITTLECHIL--8
   Baby take a chance with me (wuh yeah).--LITTLECHIL
      --15
   Baby take a chance with me, oh yeah --LITTLECHIL
      --22
   Baby take a chance with me, oh yeah --LITTLECHIL
      --23
   Baby take a chance with me, oh yeah --LITTLECHIL
      --24
   Baby take a chance with me, oh yeah.--LITTLECHIL
      --25
   'cos I'm a - gonna see my baby today --WHENIGETHO
      --5
   Baby says she's mine, you know --IFEELFINE--4
   That her baby buys her things, you know --IFEELFINE
      --9
   Baby said she's mine, you know --IFEELFINE--12
   That her baby buys her things, you know --IFEELFINE
      --17
   My baby don't care--TICKETTORI--44
   My baby don't care--TICKETTORI--45
   My baby don't care--TICKETTORI--46
   My baby don't care--TICKETTORI--47
   My baby don't care--TICKETTORI--48
   For red is the colour that my baby wore--YESITIS
      --3
   Oh baby, I'm down (down on the ground)--IMDOWN--19
   Baby you know I'm down (I'm really down)--IMDOWN
      --28
   Oh baby, I'm upside-down--IMDOWN--32
   Oh baby, I'm down (I'm really down)--IMDOWN--35
   Baby, I'm down, yeah--IMDOWN--38
   Oh baby, I'm down, yeah--IMDOWN--39
   Baby, I'm down (I'm really down)--IMDOWN--40
   Well baby, I'm down (I'm really down)--IMDOWN--41
   Oh baby, I'm down (I'm really down)--IMDOWN--43
   'n' she said baby can't you see?--DRIVEMYCAR--2
   Baby you can drive my car --DRIVEMYCAR--5
   Baby you can drive my car --DRIVEMYCAR--7
   She said baby it's understood--DRIVEMYCAR--10
   Baby you can drive my car --DRIVEMYCAR--13
   Baby you can drive my car --DRIVEMYCAR--15
   Baby you can drive my car --DRIVEMYCAR--18
   Baby you can drive my car --DRIVEMYCAR--20
   Baby you can drive my car --DRIVEMYCAR--26
   Baby you can drive my car --DRIVEMYCAR--28
   Yeah, oh baby you've changed.--IMLOOKINGT--21
   Baby, I'm determined --RUNFORYOUR--19
   Baby!--LOVELYRITA--36
   BABY, YOU'RE A RICH MAN.--BABYYOUREA--Title
   Baby, you're a rich man --BABYYOUREA--13
   Baby, you're a rich man --BABYYOUREA--14
   Baby, you're a rich man too.--BABYYOUREA--15
   Baby, you're a rich man --BABYYOUREA--19
   Baby, you're a rich man --BABYYOUREA--20
   Baby, you're a rich man too.--BABYYOUREA--21
   Baby, you're a rich man --BABYYOUREA--28
   Baby, you're a rich man --BABYYOUREA--29
   Baby, you're a rich man too.--BABYYOUREA--30
   What a thing to do (baby).--BABYYOUREA--33
   Baby, you're a rich man --BABYYOUREA--34
   Baby, you're a rich man --BABYYOUREA--35

Baby, you're a rich man too.--BABYYOUREA--36
Oh, baby you're a rich man --BABYYOUREA--37
Baby, you're a rich (baby) man --BABYYOUREA--38
Baby, you're a rich (baby) man --BABYYOUREA--38
Baby, you're a rich man too.--BABYYOUREA--39
Wuh-oh, baby, you're a rich (oh) man --BABYYOUREA
     --40
Baby, you're a rich man --BABYYOUREA--41
Baby, you're a rich man too.--BABYYOUREA--42
Oh, baby, you're a rich man.--BABYYOUREA--43
Baby, you're a rich man.--BABYYOUREA--44
Baby, you're a...--BABYYOUREA--45
Lady Madonna, baby at your breast --LADYMADONN--9
CRY BABY CRY.--CRYBABYCRY--Title
Cry baby cry --CRYBABYCRY--1
Cry baby cry --CRYBABYCRY--8
So cry baby cry.--CRYBABYCRY--11
Cry baby cry --CRYBABYCRY--16
So cry baby cry.--CRYBABYCRY--19
Cry baby cry --CRYBABYCRY--24
So cry baby cry.--CRYBABYCRY--27
Cry baby cry --CRYBABYCRY--32
So cry baby cry --CRYBABYCRY--35
Cry, cry, cry baby --CRYBABYCRY--36
So cry baby cry --CRYBABYCRY--39
So cry baby cry.--CRYBABYCRY--43
Coming down fast (oh I hear my baby speaking -
     ooo)...--HELTERSKEL--30
Baby, I'm in love with you --OLDBROWNSH--6
Baby, I'm in love with you --OLDBROWNSH--14
Who knows baby, you may comfort me (hey).--
     OLDBROWNSH--21
Who knows baby, you may comfort me (hey).--
     OLDBROWNSH--26
Baby, I'm in love with you.--OLDBROWNSH--32
You, you know, you know my name, baby --YOUKNOWMYN
     --20
Elmore James got nothing on this baby - heh.--
     FORYOUBLUE--12
My baby said she's travelling on the one after
     nine-0-nine --ONEAFTERNI--1
Come on baby, don't be cold as ice --ONEAFTERNI--4
Come on baby, don't be cold as ice --ONEAFTERNI--9
Come on baby, don't be cold as ice --ONEAFTERNI--18
Come on baby, don't be cold as ice.--ONEAFTERNI--28

BABY'S
     Baby's good to me, you know --IFEELFINE--1
     BABY'S IN BLACK.--BABYSINBLA--Title
     Baby's in black and I'm feeling blue --BABYSINBLA
          --2
     Baby's in black and I'm feeling blue --BABYSINBLA
          --8
     Baby's in black and I'm feeling blue --BABYSINBLA
          --17
     Baby's in black and I'm feeling blue --BABYSINBLA
          --22
     Baby's in black and I'm feeling blue --BABYSINBLA
          --28
     Daddy, our baby's gone.--SHESLEAVIN--17

BACK
     Send her back to me, 'cos everyone can see--
          MISERY--8
     Send her back to me, 'cos everyone can see--
          MISERY--12
     If I don't get her back again--DONTBOTHER--16
     If I don't get her back again--DONTBOTHER--31
     You hurt me then you're back again --NOTASECOND--9
     You hurt me then you're back again --NOTASECOND--20
     But this boy wants you back again.--THISBOY--3
     This boy wants you back again.--THISBOY--6
     If this boy gets you back again.--THISBOY--13
     But I'll come back again some day.--ILLCRYINST--14
     But I'll come back again some day.--ILLCRYINST--23
     Holding back these tears in my eyes.--TELLMEWHY--16
     I'LL BE BACK.--ILLBEBACK--Title
     But I'll be back again --ILLBEBACK--2
     But I came back again.--ILLBEBACK--4
     But I'll be back again.--ILLBEBACK--27
     And though he'll never come back --BABYSINBLA--5
     And/But though he'll never come back--BABYSINBLA--25
     You'll be back again tonight--YOULIKEMET--2
     And bring you back where you belong--YOULIKEMET--16
     And bring you back where you belong--YOULIKEMET--25
     Help me get my feet back on the ground--HELP--17
     Help me get my feet back on the ground--HELP--27
     Help me get my feet back on the ground--HELP--37
     Please come on back to me--INEEDYOU--3
     So come on back and see--INEEDYOU--18
     So come on back and see--INEEDYOU--28
     And she keeps calling me back again.--IVEJUSTSEE

     --13
And she keeps calling me back again.--IVEJUSTSEE
     --20
And she keeps calling me back again.--IVEJUSTSEE
     --23
And she keeps calling me back again.--IVEJUSTSEE
     --31
And she keeps calling me back again.--IVEJUSTSEE
     --33
And she keeps calling me back again.--IVEJUSTSEE
     --35
That a man must break his back to earn his day of
     leisure?--GIRL--24
It's been a long time, now I'm coming back home --
     WAIT--1
Wait till I come back to your side --WAIT--3
Wait till I come back to your side --WAIT--7
It's been a long time, now I'm coming back home --
     WAIT--13
Wait till I come back to your side --WAIT--15
Wait till I come back to your side --WAIT--23
It's been a long time, now I'm coming back home --
     WAIT--25
The little children laugh at him behind his back--
     PENNYLANE--6
And meanwhile back --PENNYLANE--11
Meanwhile back --PENNYLANE--19
And meanwhile back --PENNYLANE--30
Climb in the back with your head in the clouds--
     LUCYINTHES--18
Sit back and let the evening go.--SGTPEPPERS--11
BACK IN THE USSR.--BACKINTHEU--Title
I'm back in the USSR --BACKINTHEU--5
Back in the USSR (yeah).--BACKINTHEU--7
Gee, it's good to be back home --BACKINTHEU--9
I'm back in the USSR --BACKINTHEU--12
Back in the US, back in the US, back in the
     USSR.--BACKINTHEU--14
Back in the US, back in the US, back in the
     USSR.--BACKINTHEU--14
Back in the US, back in the US, back in the
     USSR.--BACKINTHEU--14
Hey, I'm back in the USSR.--BACKINTHEU--24
Back in the USSR.--BACKINTHEU--26
I'm back in the USSR (hey!) --BACKINTHEU--35
Back in the USSR.--BACKINTHEU--37
Hey, I'm back --BACKINTHEU--39
I'm back in the USSR --BACKINTHEU--40
Yeah - back in the USSR.--BACKINTHEU--42
(I'm back!)--BACKINTHEU--43
Can you take me back where I came from --CRYBABYCRY
     --44
Can you take me back?--CRYBABYCRY--45
Can you take me back where I came from --CRYBABYCRY
     --46
Brother, can you take me back --CRYBABYCRY--47
Can you take me back?--CRYBABYCRY--48
Can you take me back?--CRYBABYCRY--50
When I get to the bottom I go back to the top
     of the slide --HELTERSKEL--1
When I get to the bottom I go back to the top
     of the slide--HELTERSKEL--18
Honey Pie come back to me - ooo.--HONEYPIE--19
Kindly send her sailing back to me--HONEYPIE--27
Come, come back to me Honey Pie--HONEYPIE--32
Takes it back to Molly waiting at the door--
     OBLADIOBLA--11
A - now Rocky Raccoon, he fell back in his room--
     ROCKYRACCO--36
GET BACK.--GETBACK/45--Title
Get back, get back --GETBACK/45--5
Get back, get back --GETBACK/45--5
Get back to where you once belonged.--GETBACK/45
     --6
Get back, get back --GETBACK/45--7
Get back, get back --GETBACK/45--7
Get back to where you once belonged.--GETBACK/45
     --8
Get back Jojo.--GETBACK/45--9
Get back, get back --GETBACK/45--11
Get back, get back --GETBACK/45--11
Back to where you once belonged.--GETBACK/45--12
Get back, get back --GETBACK/45--13
Get back, get back --GETBACK/45--13
Back to where you once belonged.--GETBACK/45--14
Oh get back Jo.--GETBACK/45--15
Oh get back, get back --GETBACK/45--20
Oh get back, get back --GETBACK/45--20
Get back to where you once belonged.--GETBACK/45
     --21
Get back, get back --GETBACK/45--22
Get back, get back --GETBACK/45--22
Get back to where you once belonged.--GETBACK/45
     --23

Get back Loretta (wuh - wuh).--GETBACK/45--24
Oh get back, yeah get back --GETBACK/45--26
Oh get back, yeah get back --GETBACK/45--26
Get back to where you once belonged.--GETBACK/45
    --27
Yeah get back, get back --GETBACK/45--28
Yeah get back, get back --GETBACK/45--28
Get back to where you once belonged.--GETBACK/45
    --29
Get back Loretta --GETBACK/45--31
Get back home Loretta.--GETBACK/45--35
Get back, get back --GETBACK/45--36
Get back, get back --GETBACK/45--36
Get back to where you once belonged.--GETBACK/45
    --37
Oh get back, get back yeah, yeah --GETBACK/45--38
Oh get back, get back yeah, yeah --GETBACK/45--38
Get back - oh yeah.--GETBACK/45--39
The man in the mack said you've got to go back --
    BALLADOFJO--3
Caught the early plane back to London --BALLADOFJO
    --37
It's good to have the both of you back.--BALLADOFJO
    --40
To get back homeward.--GOLDENSLUM--2
To get back home.--GOLDENSLUM--4
To get back homeward.--GOLDENSLUM--12
To get back home.--GOLDENSLUM--14
Back in school again, Maxwell plays the fool
    again, teacher gets annoyed --MAXWELLSIL--8
But when she turns her back on the boy, he
    creeps up from behind --MAXWELLSIL--12
Monday morning turning back --YOUNEVERGI--11
GET BACK.--GETBACK/LP--Title
Get back, get back --GETBACK/LP--11
Get back, get back --GETBACK/LP--11
Get back to where you once belonged--GETBACK/LP--12
Get back, get back --GETBACK/LP--13
Get back, get back --GETBACK/LP--13
Get back to where you once belonged--GETBACK/LP--14
Get back Jojo.--GETBACK/LP--15
Get back, get back --GETBACK/LP--17
Get back, get back --GETBACK/LP--17
Back to where you once belonged--GETBACK/LP--18
Get back, get back --GETBACK/LP--19
Get back, get back --GETBACK/LP--19
Back to where you once belonged--GETBACK/LP--20
Oh get back Jo.--GETBACK/LP--21
Oh get back, get back --GETBACK/LP--26
Oh get back, get back --GETBACK/LP--26
Get back to where you once belonged--GETBACK/LP--27
Get back, get back --GETBACK/LP--28
Get back, get back --GETBACK/LP--28
Get back to where you once belonged.--GETBACK/LP
    --29
Get back Loretta (wuh - wuh).--GETBACK/LP--30
Oh get back, yeah, get back --GETBACK/LP--32
Oh get back, yeah, get back --GETBACK/LP--32
Get back to where you once belonged--GETBACK/LP--33
Yeah, get back, get back --GETBACK/LP--34
Yeah, get back, get back --GETBACK/LP--34
Get back to where you once belonged--GETBACK/LP--35
Get back - ooo!--GETBACK/LP--36
And still they lead me back to the long, winding
    road.--LONGANDWIN--9
But still they lead me back to the long, winding
    road --LONGANDWIN--12
Not arriving on our way back home.--TWOOFUS--6
Lifting latches on our way back home.--TWOOFUS--13
Getting nowhere on our way back home.--TWOOFUS--22
Getting nowhere on our way back home.--TWOOFUS--31

BACKDOOR
    Quietly turning the backdoor key--SHESLEAVIN--6

BACKING
    In their sties with all their backing--PIGGIES--11

BACON
    Clutching forks and knives to eat the bacon.--
    PIGGIES--19

BAD
    The world is treating me bad, misery.--MISERY--1
    The world is treating me bad, misery.--MISERY--3
    And you know that can't be bad--SHELOVESYO--9
    And you know that can't be bad--SHELOVESYO--17
    And you know that can't be bad--SHELOVESYO--29
    Did you have to treat me oh so bad --TELLMEWHY--7
    In the good and the bad books that I have read.--

THEWORD--16
    That is, I think it's not too bad.--STRAWBERRY--20
    Hey Jude, don't make it bad --HEYJUDE--1
    Hey Jude, don't make it bad --HEYJUDE--26
    Nah nah nah, nah - nah - nah - nah ((don't make
        it bad, Jude)) --HEYJUDE--47
    I want you so bad--IWANTYOUSH--2
    I want you so bad--IWANTYOUSH--4
    I want you so bad, babe--IWANTYOUSH--8
    I want you so bad--IWANTYOUSH--10
    I want you so bad, babe--IWANTYOUSH--14
    I want you so bad--IWANTYOUSH--16
    I want you so bad--IWANTYOUSH--20
    I want you so bad--IWANTYOUSH--22
    I want you so bad--IWANTYOUSH--29
    I want you so bad--IWANTYOUSH--31
    You know I want you so bad, babe--IWANTYOUSH--35
    You know I want you so bad--IWANTYOUSH--37

BAG
    And the bag across her shoulder--LOVELYRITA--11
    You keep all your money in a big brown bag --
        BABYYOUREA--16
    You keep all your money in a big brown bag --
        BABYYOUREA--31
    On the way the paper bag was on my knee --
        BACKINTHEU--3
    Eating chocolate cake in the bag.--BALLADOFJO--30
    He Bag Production--COMETOGETH--25
    Dressed in her polythene bag.--POLYTHENEP--4
    Pick up my bag, run to the station --ONEAFTERNI--11
    Pick up my bag, run right home --ONEAFTERNI--13
    Pick up my bag, run to the station --ONEAFTERNI--21
    Well - pick up my bag, run right home (run
        right home) --ONEAFTERNI--23

BAGS
    Pick up the bags, get in the limousine.--YOUNEVERGI
        --18

BALALAIKAS
    Let me hear your balalaikas ringing out --
        BACKINTHEU--33

BALLAD
    THE BALLAD OF JOHN AND YOKO.--BALLADOFJO--Title

BAND
    And the band begins to play.--YELLOWSUBM--15
    The band begins at ten to six--BEINGFORTH--15
    SGT. PEPPER'S LONELY HEARTS CLUB BAND.--SGTPEPPERS
        --Title
    That Sgt. Pepper taught the band to play--
        SGTPEPPERS--2
    Sgt. Pepper's Lonely Hearts Club Band.--SGTPEPPERS
        --7
    We're Sgt. Pepper's Lonely Hearts Club Band--
        SGTPEPPERS--8
    Sgt. Pepper's Lonely Hearts Club Band--SGTPEPPERS
        --10
    Sgt. Pepper's Lonely Hearts Club Band.--SGTPEPPERS
        --13
    And Sgt. Pepper's Lonely Hearts Club Band.--
        SGTPEPPERS--25
    SGT. PEPPER'S LONELY HEARTS CLUB BAND
        (REPRISE).--SGTPEPPREP--Title
    We're Sgt. Pepper's Lonely Hearts Club Band --
        SGTPEPPREP--3
    Sgt. Pepper's Lonely Hearts Club Band --SGTPEPPREP
        --5
    Sgt. Pepper's Lonely Hearts Club Band --SGTPEPPREP
        --11
    Sgt. Pepper's one and only Lonely Hearts Club
        Band --SGTPEPPREP--13
    Sgt. Pepper's Lonely Hearts Club Band.--SGTPEPPREP
        --17
    Molly is the singer in a band --OBLADIOBLA--2
    And in the evening she still sings it with the
        band, yes.--OBLADIOBLA--24
    And in the evening she's a singer with the band,
        yeah.--OBLADIOBLA--35
    You may think the band are not quite right --
        ONLYANORTH--5

BANG
    (Bang, bang, shoot, shoot) --HAPPINESSI--19
    (Bang, bang, shoot, shoot) --HAPPINESSI--19
    ((Bang, bang, shoot, shoot)) --HAPPINESSI--21

((Bang, bang, shoot, shoot)) --HAPPINESSI--21
((Bang, bang, shoot, shoot)) --HAPPINESSI--26
((Bang, bang, shoot, shoot)) --HAPPINESSI--26
((Bang, bang, shoot, shoot)) --HAPPINESSI--28
((Bang, bang, shoot, shoot)) --HAPPINESSI--28
((Happiness - bang, bang, shoot, shoot)) --
    HAPPINESSI--30
((Happiness - bang, bang, shoot, shoot)) --
    HAPPINESSI--30
Bang, bang Maxwell's silver hammer came down
    upon her head --MAXWELLSIL--6
Bang, bang Maxwell's silver hammer came down
    upon her head --MAXWELLSIL--6
Bang, bang Maxwell's silver hammer made sure
    that she was dead.--MAXWELLSIL--7
Bang, bang Maxwell's silver hammer made sure
    that she was dead.--MAXWELLSIL--7
Bang, bang Maxwell's silver hammer came down
    upon her head --MAXWELLSIL--13
Bang, bang Maxwell's silver hammer came down
    upon her head --MAXWELLSIL--13
Bang, bang Maxwell's silver hammer made sure
    that she was dead.--MAXWELLSIL--15
Bang, bang Maxwell's silver hammer made sure
    that she was dead.--MAXWELLSIL--15
Bang, bang Maxwell's silver hammer came down
    upon his head --MAXWELLSIL--23
Bang, bang Maxwell's silver hammer came down
    upon his head --MAXWELLSIL--23
Bang, bang Maxwell's silver hammer made sure
    that he was dead.--MAXWELLSIL--25
Bang, bang Maxwell's silver hammer made sure
    that he was dead.--MAXWELLSIL--25

BANKER
    On the corner is a banker with a motorcar--
        PENNYLANE--5
    And the banker never wears a mack--PENNYLANE--7
    We see the banker sitting waiting for a trim--
        PENNYLANE--25

BANKS
    By the banks of her own lagoon.--SHECAMEINT--7

BARBER
    Penny Lane: there is a barber showing photographs
        --PENNYLANE--1
    In Penny Lane the barber shaves another customer--
        PENNYLANE--24

BARROW
    Desmond has a barrow in the market-place --
        OBLADIOBLA--1

BASED
    It's based on a novel by a man named Lear --
        PAPERBACKW--4

BATH
    And crawled off to sleep in the bath.--NORWEGIANW
        --20

BATHROOM
    SHE CAME IN THROUGH THE BATHROOM WINDOW.--
        SHECAMEINT--Title
    She came in through the bathroom window --
        SHECAMEINT--4

BB
    BB King--DIGIT--7

BBC
    And the BBC--DIGIT--6

BE
    I'll always be true --LOVEMEDO--3
    I'll always be true --LOVEMEDO--8
    I'll always be true --LOVEMEDO--15
    I'll always be true --LOVEMEDO--20
    Remember that I'll always be in love with you.--
        PSILOVEYOU--2
    I'll ((I'll)) be coming home ((home)) again
        to you love ((you love)) --PSILOVEYOU--7
    Remember that I'll always be in love with you.--

PSILOVEYOU--11
Remember that I'll always, yeah, be in love
    with you.--PSILOVEYOU--18
I'll be coming home again to you love --PSILOVEYOU
    --19
And I'll be there.--ANYTIMEATA--3
I'll be there to make you feel right --ANYTIMEATA
    --6
Don't you be sad, just call me tonight.--ANYTIMEATA
    --9
And I'll be there.--ANYTIMEATA--12
I hope it will be mine --ANYTIMEATA--17
And I'll be there.--ANYTIMEATA--21
And I'll be there.--ANYTIMEATA--24
And I'll be there.--ANYTIMEATA--27
That I - I - I - I should never, never,
    never be blue.--ASKMEWHY--6
That I - I - I - I should never, never,
    never be blue.--ASKMEWHY--21
It's gonna be a drag, misery.--MISERY--5
Can't she see she'll always be the only one,
    only one.--MISERY--7
Without her I will be in misery.--MISERY--9
Without her I will be in misery.--MISERY--13
And eternally I'll always be in love with you--
    THANKYOUGI--3
That's the kind of love that is too good to be true
    --THANKYOUGI--9
And eternally I'll always be in love with you--
    THANKYOUGI--13
Well, there's gonna be a time--ILLGETYOU--16
And you know that can't be bad--SHELOVESYO--9
And you know you should be glad.--SHELOVESYO--11
And you know that can't be bad--SHELOVESYO--17
And you know you should be glad - ooo!--SHELOVESYO
    --19
You know you should be glad.--SHELOVESYO--23
And you know that can't be bad--SHELOVESYO--29
And you know you should be glad - ooo!--SHELOVESYO
    --31
You know you should be glad--SHELOVESYO--35
You know you should be glad--SHELOVESYO--37
You know you should be glad--SHELOVESYO--39
And I'll be kissing you.--ALLIVEGOTT--10
I'll be here, yes I will --ALLIVEGOTT--13
I'll be here, yes I will --ALLIVEGOTT--24
Remember I'll always be true --ALLMYLOVIN--3
All my lovin', darlin', I'll be true.--ALLMYLOVIN
    --14
Remember I'll always be true --ALLMYLOVIN--17
All my lovin', darlin', I'll be true --ALLMYLOVIN
    --22
I know I'll never be the same--DONTBOTHER--15
Because I know she'll always be--DONTBOTHER--17
I know I'll never be the same--DONTBOTHER--30
Because I know she'll always be--DONTBOTHER--32
Never be the lonely one.--HOLDMETIGH--5
Never be the lonely one.--HOLDMETIGH--22
I WANNA BE YOUR MAN.--IWANNABEYO--Title
I wanna be your lover baby --IWANNABEYO--1
I wanna be your man.--IWANNABEYO--2
I wanna be your lover baby --IWANNABEYO--3
I wanna be your man.--IWANNABEYO--4
I wanna be your man--IWANNABEYO--9
I wanna be your man.--IWANNABEYO--10
I wanna be your man.--IWANNABEYO--11
I wanna be your man.--IWANNABEYO--12
I wanna be your man.--IWANNABEYO--16
I wanna be your lover baby --IWANNABEYO--17
I wanna be your man.--IWANNABEYO--18
I wanna be your lover baby --IWANNABEYO--19
I wanna be your man.--IWANNABEYO--20
I wanna be your man--IWANNABEYO--21
I wanna be your man.--IWANNABEYO--22
I wanna be your man.--IWANNABEYO--23
I wanna be your man.--IWANNABEYO--24
I wanna be your lover baby --IWANNABEYO--30
I wanna be your man.--IWANNABEYO--31
I wanna be your lover baby --IWANNABEYO--32
I wanna be your man.--IWANNABEYO--33
I wanna be your man--IWANNABEYO--38
I wanna be your man--IWANNABEYO--39
I wanna be your man--IWANNABEYO--40
I wanna be your man.--IWANNABEYO--41
I wanna be your man (oh)--IWANNABEYO--43
I wanna be your man (come on!)--IWANNABEYO--44
I wanna be your man (wuh - wuh)--IWANNABEYO--45
I wanna be your man.--IWANNABEYO--46
IT WON'T BE LONG.--ITWONTBELO--Title
It won't be long yeah (yeah) yeah (yeah) yeah
    (yeah)--ITWONTBELO--1
It won't be long yeah (yeah) yeah (yeah) yeah
    (yeah)--ITWONTBELO--2
It won't be long yeah (yeah)--ITWONTBELO--3

It won't be long yeah (yeah) yeah (yeah) yeah
(yeah)--ITWONTBELO--7
It won't be long yeah (yeah) yeah (yeah) yeah
(yeah)--ITWONTBELO--8
It won't be long yeah (yeah)--ITWONTBELO--9
I'll be good like I know I should (yes,
you're coming on home)--ITWONTBELO--13
It won't be long yeah (yeah) yeah (yeah) yeah
(yeah)--ITWONTBELO--17
It won't be long yeah (yeah) yeah (yeah) yeah
(yeah)--ITWONTBELO--18
It won't be long yeah (yeah)--ITWONTBELO--19
I'll be good like I know I should (yes,
you're coming on home)--ITWONTBELO--23
So every day we'll be happy, I know--ITWONTBELO
--25
It won't be long yeah (yeah) yeah (yeah) yeah
(yeah)--ITWONTBELO--27
It won't be long (yeah) yeah (yeah) yeah
(yeah)--ITWONTBELO--28
It won't be long yeah (yeah)--ITWONTBELO--29
And/You'll let me be your man--IWANTTOHOL--8
Oh, and this boy would be happy--THISBOY--7
That boy won't be happy--THISBOY--9
And I'll be satisfied --CANTBUYMEL--18
And I'll be satisfied --CANTBUYMEL--28
There'll be no sad tomorrow--THERESAPLA--11
I should be sleeping like a log --HARDDAYSNI--4
When I'm home everything seems to be right --
HARDDAYSNI--15
I should be sleeping like a log --HARDDAYSNI--20
When I'm home everything seems to be right --
HARDDAYSNI--28
I should be sleeping like a log --HARDDAYSNI--33
Whoa, whoa, I never realised what a kiss could
be --ISHOULDHAV--4
And when I ask you to be mine --ISHOULDHAV--9
Whoa, whoa, I never realised what a kiss could
be --ISHOULDHAV--14
And when I ask you to be mine --ISHOULDHAV--19
Would you promise to be true --IFIFELL--2
I must be sure from the very start --IFIFELL--8
And I would be sad --IFIFELL--15
And I would be sad --IFIFELL--22
I got every reason on earth to be mad--ILLCRYINST--1
I'LL BE BACK.--ILLBEBACK--Title
But I'll be back again --ILLBEBACK--2
But I'll be back again --ILLBEBACK--27
You'll be thinking of me, somehow I will know --
THINGSWESA--2
You say you'll be mine girl, till the end of time
--THINGSWESA--6
And though we may be blind --THINGSWESA--13
Be the only one --THINGSWESA--16
And though we may be blind --THINGSWESA--24
Be the only one --THINGSWESA--27
She's happy as can be, you know, she said so --
IFEELFINE--2
If I find her I'll be glad --IDONTWANTT--11
If I find her I'll be glad --IDONTWANTT--20
And I'm not what I appear to be.--IMALOSER--2
I'm a loser and I'm not what I appear to be.--
IMALOSER--8
I'm a loser and I'm not what I appear to be.--
IMALOSER--14
I'm a loser and I'm not what I appear to be.--
IMALOSER--20
Would it be too much to ask of you --WHATYOURED--3
Why should it be so much to ask of you --WHATYOURED
--7
Why should it be so much to ask of you --WHATYOURED
--14
Why should it be so much to ask of you --WHATYOURED
--21
I think I'm gonna be sad--TICKETTORI--2
She would never be free--TICKETTORI--11
I think I'm gonna be sad--TICKETTORI--23
She would never be free--TICKETTORI--38
I could be happy with you by my side--YESITIS--10
I could be happy with you by my side--YESITIS--19
We will never be apart--TELLMEWHAT--3
Big and black the clouds may be--TELLMEWHAT--9
You'll be back again tonight--YOULIKEMET--2
Telling me there'll be no next time--YOULIKEMET--3
Through thick and thin she will always be my
friend.--ANOTHERGIR--11
Through thick and thin she will always be my
friend.--ANOTHERGIR--17
I'm lonely as can be--INEEDYOU--4
I'm not half the man I used to be--YESTERDAY--6
And then you'll be the lonely one (you're not
the only one)--YOUREGONNA--12
Run the risk of knowing that our love may soon be
gone.--WECANWORKI--4

Asked a girl what she wanted to be --DRIVEMYCAR--1
I wanna be famous, a star of the screen --
DRIVEMYCAR--3
Yes I'm gonna be a star.--DRIVEMYCAR--6
Yes I'm gonna be a star.--DRIVEMYCAR--14
Yes I'm gonna be a star.--DRIVEMYCAR--19
Yes I'm gonna be star.--DRIVEMYCAR--27
You're the one that I'd be thinking of --IFINEEDS
--2
Then I guess I'd be with you my friend --IFINEEDS
--5
Then I guess I'd be with you my friend --IFINEEDS
--15
He's as blind as he can be --NOWHEREMAN--10
Than to be with another man.--RUNFORYOUR--2
Let this be a sermon --RUNFORYOUR--17
Than to be with another man.--RUNFORYOUR--26
'cos I won't be there with you.--THINKFORYO--9
'cos I won't be there with you.--THINKFORYO--18
'cos I won't be there with you.--THINKFORYO--27
'cos I won't be there with you.--THINKFORYO--31
'cos I won't be there with you.--THINKFORYO--33
That I've been good, as good as I can be.--WAIT--10
That I've been good, as good as I can be.--WAIT--18
Say the word and you'll be free --THEWORD--1
Say the word and be like me --THEWORD--2
Spread the word and you'll be free --THEWORD--9
Spread the word and be like me --THEWORD--10
Say the word and you'll be free --THEWORD--17
Say the word and be like me --THEWORD--18
Now that I know what I feel must be right --THEWORD
--23
So I want to be a paperback writer --PAPERBACKW--6
But he wants to be a paperback writer--PAPERBACKW
--12
I'll be writing more in a week or two. ((writer))
--PAPERBACKW--16
And I want to be a paperback writer --PAPERBACKW
--19
And I want to be a paperback writer --PAPERBACKW
--25
They might as well be dead--RAIN--2
I'll be round, I'll be round.--ANDYOURBIR--9
I'll be round, I'll be round.--ANDYOURBIR--9
You may be awoken --ANDYOURBIR--11
I'll be round, I'll be round.--ANDYOURBIR--12
I'll be round, I'll be round.--ANDYOURBIR--12
Day or night he'll be there any time at all, Dr.
Robert --DRROBERT--2
There will be times when all the things --FORNOONE
--21
Ooo you were meant to be near me--GOTTOGETYO--12
Say we'll be together every day.--GOTTOGETYO--14
What can I do, what can I be?--GOTTOGETYO--16
To lead a better life, I need my love to be here.
--HERETHEREA--1
Both of us thinking how good it can be--HERETHEREA
--6
I will be there and everywhere --HERETHEREA--20
A new one can't be bought--LOVEYOUTWO--7
She said I know what it's like to be dead --
SHESAIDSHE--1
I know what it is to be sad--SHESAIDSHE--2
I know what it's like to be dead (I know what
it's like to be dead) --SHESAIDSHE--20
I know what it's like to be dead (I know what
it's like to be dead) --SHESAIDSHE--20
I know what it is to be sad (I know what it is
to be sad).--SHESAIDSHE--21
I know what it is to be sad (I know what it is
to be sad).--SHESAIDSHE--21
I know what it's like to be dead (I know what
it's like to be dead).--SHESAIDSHE--22
I know what it's like to be dead (I know what
it's like to be dead).--SHESAIDSHE--22
Let me tell you how it will be --TAXMAN--3
Be thankful I don't take it all --TAXMAN--8
It's getting hard to be someone--STRAWBERRY--8
I mean, it must be high or low--STRAWBERRY--17
There will be a show tonight on trampoline.--
BEINGFORTH--2
The Hendersons will all be there--BEINGFORTH--3
As Mr. Kite flies through the ring - don't be
late.--BEINGFORTH--11
Their production will be second to none--BEINGFORTH
--13
Me used to be angry young man--GETTINGBET--11
I used to be cruel to my woman--GETTINGBET--25
Where would I be without you?--LOVELYRITA--27
It's wonderful to be here--SGTPEPPERS--14
Will you still be sending me a valentine--
WHENIMSIXT--3
You'll be older too--WHENIMSIXT--10
I could be handy mending a fuse--WHENIMSIXT--13

(Does it worry you to be alone?)--WITHALITTL--9
(Could it be anybody?)--WITHALITTL--17
(Could it be anybody?)--WITHALITTL--28
There's nothing you can do that can't be done
    ((love))--ALLYOUN/YS--4
Nothing you can sing that can't be sung ((love))--
    ALLYOUN/YS--5
Nothing you can make that can't be made ((love))--
    ALLYOUN/YS--8
No-one you can save that can't be saved ((love))--
    ALLYOUN/YS--9
Nothing you can do but you can learn how to be
    you in time ((love))--ALLYOUN/YS--10
There's nowhere you can be that isn't where
    you're meant to be ((love))--ALLYOUN/YS--21
There's nowhere you can be that isn't where
    you're meant to be ((love))--ALLYOUN/YS--21
How does it feel to be--BABYYOUREA--1
What do you want to be?--BABYYOUREA--4
How does it feel to be--BABYYOUREA--7
How does it feel to be--BABYYOUREA--22
Happy to be that way.--BABYYOUREA--25
We'll be over soon they said --BLUEJAYWAY--3
Please don't be long --BLUEJAYWAY--5
Please don't you be very long --BLUEJAYWAY--6
Please don't be long or I may be asleep.--
    BLUEJAYWAY--7
Please don't be long or I may be asleep.--
    BLUEJAYWAY--7
Please don't be long (don't be long) --BLUEJAYWAY
    --12
Please don't be long (don't be long) --BLUEJAYWAY
    --12
Please don't you be very long (don't be long) --
    BLUEJAYWAY--13
Please don't you be very long (don't be long) --
    BLUEJAYWAY--13
Please don't be long or I may be asleep.--
    BLUEJAYWAY--14
Please don't be long or I may be asleep.--
    BLUEJAYWAY--14
Soon will be the break of day (day) --BLUEJAYWAY
    --17
Please don't be long (don't be long) --BLUEJAYWAY
    --19
Please don't be long (don't be long) --BLUEJAYWAY
    --19
Please don't you be very long (don't be long) --
    BLUEJAYWAY--20
Please don't you be very long (don't be long) --
    BLUEJAYWAY--20
Please don't be long or I may be asleep.--
    BLUEJAYWAY--21
Please don't be long or I may be asleep.--
    BLUEJAYWAY--21
Please don't be long --BLUEJAYWAY--22
Please don't you be very long--BLUEJAYWAY--23
Please don't be long.--BLUEJAYWAY--24
Please don't be long --BLUEJAYWAY--25
Please don't you be very long--BLUEJAYWAY--26
Please don't be long (please don't be long).
    --BLUEJAYWAY--27
Please don't be long (please don't be long).
    --BLUEJAYWAY--27
Please don't be long --BLUEJAYWAY--28
Please don't you be very long --BLUEJAYWAY--29
Please don't be long.--BLUEJAYWAY--30
Don't be long - don't be long --BLUEJAYWAY--31
Don't be long - don't be long --BLUEJAYWAY--31
Don't belong - don't be long--BLUEJAYWAY--32
Don't be long --BLUEJAYWAY--34
Hey Jude, don't be afraid --HEYJUDE--5
Don't you know it's gonna be alright, alright,
    alright?--REVOLUTION--10
Don't you know it's gonna be alright, alright
    ((alright)), alright?--REVOLUTION--20
Don't you know it's gonna be alright, alright,
    alright ((alright))?--REVOLUTION--30
Gee, it's good to be back home --BACKINTHEU
    --9
You were only waiting for this moment to be free.
    --BLACKBIRD--8
The clouds will be a daisy chain--DEARPRUDEN
    --18
You said that you would be late--DONTPASSME
    27
You know that we're as close as can be - man--
    GLASSONIQN--9
Well here's another place you can be--GLASSONION
    --19
Well, you may be a lover, but you ain't no
    dancer.--HELTERSKEL--7
'cos you may be a lover, but you ain't no dancer.
    --HELTERSKEL--14

'cos you may be a lover, but you ain't no dancer.
    --HELTERSKEL--24
To be where you belong.--HONEYPIE--18
Make it easy to be near you --IWILL--16
Now I can see you, be you --LONGLONGLO--9
That you and me were meant to be for each other -
    silly girl.--MARTHAMYDE--9
Please - be good to me, Martha my love --MARTHAMYDE
    --14
Don't you know it's gonna be ((oh shoo-be-do-a))--
    REVOLUTONE--13
Don't you know it's gonna be ((oh shoo-be-do-a))--
    REVOLUTONE--15
Don't you know it's gonna be ((oh shoo-be-do-a))--
    REVOLUTONE--17
Don't you know it's gonna be ((oh shoo-be-do-a))--
    REVOLUTONE--29
Don't you know it's gonna be ((oh shoo-be-do-a))--
    REVOLUTONE--31
Don't you know it's gonna be ((oh shoo-be-do-a))--
    REVOLUTONE--33
Don't you know it's gonna be ((oh shoo-be-do-a))--
    REVOLUTONE--45
Don't you know it's gonna be ((oh shoo-be-do-a))--
    REVOLUTONE--47
Don't you know it's gonna be ((oh shoo-be-do-a))--
    REVOLUTONE--49
And I'll be better, I'll be better Doc as
    soon as I am able.--ROCKYRACCO--35
And I'll be better, I'll be better Doc as
    soon as I am able.--ROCKYRACCO--35
With every mistake we must surely be learning --
    WHILEMYGUI--11
No-one will be watching us --WHYDONTWED--5
No-one will be watching us --WHYDONTWED--11
No-one will be watching us --WHYDONTWED--17
Or where you'd like to be.--ITSALLTOOM--15
You know how hard it can be --BALLADOFJO--6
You know how hard it can be --BALLADOFJO--14
You know how hard it can be --BALLADOFJO--22
You know how hard it can be --BALLADOFJO--34
You know how hard it can be.--BALLADOFJO--42
It won't be the same now I'm telling you.--
    OLDBROWNSH--8
It won't be the same now that I'm with you.--
    OLDBROWNSH--16
If I grow up I'll be a singer --OLDBROWNSH--17
I may appear to be imperfect --OLDBROWNSH--22
Won't be the same now that I'm with you.--
    OLDBROWNSH--34
It won't be the same now that I'm with you
    (yeah, yeah, yeah).--OLDBROWNSH--36
Got to be a joker he just do what he please--
    COMETOGETH--10
One thing I can tell you is you got to be free--
    COMETOGETH--20
Got to be good-looking 'cos he's so hard to see--
    COMETOGETH--41
Are you gonna be in my dreams tonight?--THEEND--2
So he waits behind, writing fifty times I must
    not be so oh - oh oh.--MAXWELLSIL--1
I'd like to be under the sea--OCTOPUSSGA--1
I'd like to be under the sea--OCTOPUSSGA--7
We would be warm below the storm--OCTOPUSSGA--9
Because we know we can't be found.--OCTOPUSSGA--14
I'd like to be under the sea--OCTOPUSSGA--15
We would be so happy you and me--OCTOPUSSGA--21
I'd like to be under the sea--OCTOPUSSGA--23
Soon we'll be away from here --YOUNEVERGI--19
LET IT BE.--LETITBE/45--Title
Speaking words of wisdom, let it be.--LETITBE/45
    --3
Speaking words of wisdom, let it be.--LETITBE/45
    --6
Let it be, let it be, let it be, let it be.--
    LETITBE/45--7
Let it be, let it be, let it be, let it be.--
    LETITBE/45--7
Let it be, let it be, let it be, let it be.--
    LETITBE/45--7
Let it be, let it be, let it be, let it be.--
    LETITBE/45--7
Whisper words of wisdom, let it be.--LETITBE/45--8
There will be an answer, let it be.--LETITBE/45--11
There will be an answer, let it be.--LETITBE/45--11
For though they may be parted,--LETITBE/45--12
There will be an answer, let it be.--LETITBE/45--14
There will be an answer, let it be.--LETITBE/45--14
Let it be, let it be, let it be, let it be.--
    LETITBE/45--15
Let it be, let it be, let it be, let it be.--
    LETITBE/45--15
Let it be, let it be, let it be, let it be.--
    LETITBE/45--15

Let it be, let it be, let it be, let it be.--
  LETITBE/45--15
Yeah there will be an answer, let it be.--
  LETITBE/45--16
Yeah there will be an answer, let it be.--
  LETITBE/45--16
Let it be, let it be, let it be, let it be.--
  LETITBE/45--17
Let it be, let it be, let it be, let it be.--
  LETITBE/45--17
Let it be, let it be, let it be, let it be.--
  LETITBE/45--17
Let it be, let it be, let it be, let it be.--
  LETITBE/45--17
Whisper words of wisdom, let it be.--LETITBE/45--18
Let it be, let it be, let it be, yeah let it
  be.--LETITBE/45--19
Let it be, let it be, let it be, yeah let it
  be.--LETITBE/45--19
Let it be, let it be, let it be, yeah let it
  be.--LETITBE/45--19
Let it be, let it be, let it be, yeah let it
  be.--LETITBE/45--19
Whisper words of wisdom, let it be.--LETITBE/45--20
Shine on till tomorrow, let it be.--LETITBE/45--23
Speaking words of wisdom, let it be.--LETITBE/45
  --26
Yeah let it be, let it be, let it be, yeah let
  it be.--LETITBE/45--27
Yeah let it be, let it be, let it be, yeah let
  it be.--LETITBE/45--27
Yeah let it be, let it be, let it be, yeah let
  it be.--LETITBE/45--27
Yeah let it be, let it be, let it be, yeah let
  it be.--LETITBE/45--27
Oh there will be an answer, let it be.--LETITBE/45
  --28
Oh there will be an answer, let it be.--LETITBE/45
  --28
Let it be, let it be, let it be, yeah let it be.--
  LETITBE/45--29
Let it be, let it be, let it be, yeah let it be.--
  LETITBE/45--29
Let it be, let it be, let it be, yeah let it be.--
  LETITBE/45--29
Let it be, let it be, let it be, yeah let it be.--
  LETITBE/45--29
Whisper words of wisdom, let it be.--LETITBE/45--30
Everything has got to be just like you want it to
  --IDIGAPONY--14
Everything has got to be just like you want it to
  --IDIGAPONY--24
Everything has got to be just like you want it to
  --IDIGAPONY--34
And if you leave me I won't be late again --
  IVEGOTAFEE--8
LET IT BE.--LETITBE/LP--Title
Speaking words of wisdom, let it be.--LETITBE/LP
  --3
Speaking words of wisdom, let it be.--LETITBE/LP
  --6
Let it be, let it be, let it be, let it be --
  LETITBE/LP--7
Let it be, let it be, let it be, let it be --
  LETITBE/LP--7
Let it be, let it be, let it be, let it be --
  LETITBE/LP--7
Let it be, let it be, let it be, let it be --
  LETITBE/LP--7
Whisper words of wisdom, let it be.--LETITBE/LP--8
There will be an answer, let it be.--LETITBE/LP--11
There will be an answer, let it be.--LETITBE/LP--11
For though they may be parted,--LETITBE/LP--12
There will be an answer, let it be.--LETITBE/LP--14
There will be an answer, let it be.--LETITBE/LP--14
Let it be, let it be, let it be, let it be --
  LETITBE/LP--15
Let it be, let it be, let it be, let it be --
  LETITBE/LP--15
Let it be, let it be, let it be, let it be --
  LETITBE/LP--15
Let it be, let it be, let it be, let it be --
  LETITBE/LP--15
Yeah there will be an answer, let it be.--
  LETITBE/LP--16
Yeah there will be an answer, let it be.--
  LETITBE/LP--16
Let it be, let it be, let it be, let it be --
  LETITBE/LP--17
Let it be, let it be, let it be, let it be --
  LETITBE/LP--17
Let it bc, let it be, let it be, let it be --
  LETITBE/LP--17
Let it be, let it be, let it be, let it be --

LETITBE/LP--17
Whisper words of wisdom, let it be.--LETITBE/LP--18
Let it be, let it be, let it be, yeah let it be --
  LETITBE/LP--19
Let it be, let it be, let it be, yeah let it be --
  LETITBE/LP--19
Let it be, let it be, let it be, yeah let it be --
  LETITBE/LP--19
Let it be, let it be, let it be, yeah let it be --
  LETITBE/LP--19
Whisper words of wisdom, let it be.--LETITBE/LP--20
Shine on till tomorrow, let it be.--LETITBE/LP--23
Speaking words of wisdom, let it be.--LETITBE/LP
  --26
Yeah let it be, let it be, let it be, yeah let
  it be --LETITBE/LP--27
Yeah let it be, let it be, let it be, yeah let
  it be --LETITBE/LP--27
Yeah let it be, let it be, let it be, yeah let
  it be --LETITBE/LP--27
Yeah let it be, let it be, let it be, yeah let
  it be --LETITBE/LP--27
Oh there will be an answer, let it be.--LETITBE/LP
  --28
Oh there will be an answer, let it be.--LETITBE/LP
  --28
Let it be, let it be, let it be, yeah let it be --
  LETITBE/LP--29
Let it be, let it be, let it be, yeah let it be --
  LETITBE/LP--29
Let it be, let it be, let it be, yeah let it be --
  LETITBE/LP--29
Let it be, let it be, let it be, yeah let it be --
  LETITBE/LP--29
Oh there will be an answer, let it be.--LETITBE/LP
  --30
Oh there will be an answer, let it be.--LETITBE/LP
  --30
Let it be, let it be, oh let it be, yeah let
  it be --LETITBE/LP--31
Let it be, let it be, oh let it be, yeah let
  it be --LETITBE/LP--31
Let it be, let it be, oh let it be, yeah let
  it be --LETITBE/LP--31
Let it be, let it be, oh let it be, yeah let
  it be --LETITBE/LP--31
Whisper words of wisdom, let it be.--LETITBE/LP--32
Come on baby, don't be cold as ice --ONEAFTERNI--4
Come on baby, don't be cold as ice --ONEAFTERNI--9
Come on baby, don't be cold as ice --ONEAFTERNI--18
Come on baby, don't be cold as ice.--ONEAFTERNI--28

BEACH
  Oh - flew in from Miami Beach BOAC --BACKINTHEU--1

BEAT
  I beat her and kept her apart from the things
    that she loved--GETTINGBET--26

BEAUTIFUL
  One of the beautiful people?--BABYYOUREA--2
  One of the beautiful people?--BABYYOUREA--8
  One of the beautiful people?--BABYYOUREA--23
  It's beautiful and so are you.--DEARPRUDEN--4
  It's beautiful and so are you.--DEARPRUDEN--24

BECAME
  You became a legend of the silver screen--HONEYPIE
    --13

BECAUSE
  If I cry it's not because I'm sad --ASKMEWHY--10
  Because she loves you--SHELOVESYO--28
  Because I know she'll always be--DONTBOTHER--17
  Because I know she'll always be--DONTBOTHER--32
  Because I told you before--YOUCANTDOT--7
  Because I told you before--YOUCANTDOT--16
  Because I told you before--YOUCANTDOT--30
  Because I told you before--YOUCANTDOT--49
  (Are you sad because you're on your own?)--
    WITHALITTL--11
  Because - (happiness) is a warm gun, momma--
    HAPPINESSI--25
  BECAUSE.--BECAUSE--Title
  Because the world is round it turns me on --BECAUSE
    --2
  Because the world is round.--BECAUSE--3
  Because the wind is high it blows my mind --BECAUSE
    --5

BECAUSE

Because the wind is high.--BECAUSE--6
Because the sky is blue it makes me cry --BECAUSE --10
Because the sky is blue.--BECAUSE--11
Because we know we can't be found.--OCTOPUSSGA--14
Because you're sweet and lovely girl, I love you --FORYOUBLUE--2
Because you're sweet and lovely girl, it's true --FORYOUBLUE--3
Because you're sweet and lovely girl, I love you --FORYOUBLUE--16
Because you're sweet and lovely girl, it's true --FORYOUBLUE--17
Because.--IDIGAPONY--15
Because. (ooo - ow)--IDIGAPONY--25
Because.--IDIGAPONY--35

BECOMES

When it becomes too much--SAVOYTRUFF--15

BED

It's time for bed.--NORWEGIANW--16
Stay in bed, float upstream (float upstream).-- IMONLYSLEE--4
Stay in bed, float upstream (float upstream).-- IMONLYSLEE--24
Woke up, fell out of bed--DAYINTHELI--18
Now it's past my bed I know (know) --BLUEJAYWAY--15
Lady Madonna, lying on the bed --LADYMADONN--12
Didn't get to bed last night --BACKINTHEU--2
Can I take my friend to bed?--ALLTOGETHE--18
The news-people said, say what're you doing in bed?--BALLADOFJO--19

BEDROOM

Silently closing her bedroom door--SHESLEAVIN--2

BEDS

Talking in our beds for a week.--BALLADOFJO--18

BEE

With a message at the local bird and bee.-- CRYBABYCRY--23

BEEN

Oh, oh - mmm, you've been good to me--THANKYOUGI --1
Oh, oh - mmm, you've been good to me--THANKYOUGI --11
Since she's been gone--DONTBOTHER--1
Oh, I can't sleep at night since you've been gone --ICALLYOURN--3
It's been a hard day's night --HARDDAYSNI--1
And I been working like a dog --HARDDAYSNI--2
It's been a hard day's night --HARDDAYSNI--3
It's been a hard day's night --HARDDAYSNI--17
And I been working like a dog --HARDDAYSNI--18
It's been a hard day's night --HARDDAYSNI--19
Oh, It's been a hard day's night --HARDDAYSNI--30
And I been working like a dog --HARDDAYSNI--31
It's been a hard day's night --HARDDAYSNI--32
'cos I've been in love before --IFIFELL--4
'cos I know where you've been--NOREPLY--12
'cos I know where you've been--NOREPLY--25
I've been waiting here for you --WHATYOURED--9
I've been waiting here for you --WHATYOURED--16
I don't wanna say that I've been unhappy with you --ANOTHERGIR--12
I don't wanna say that I've been unhappy with you --ANOTHERGIR--18
Had it been another day--IVEJUSTSEE--7
And I'd have never been aware--IVEJUSTSEE--9
I've been alone and I have missed things-- IVEJUSTSEE--15
Then it might not have been like this --IFINEEDEDS --8
Then it might not have been like this --IFINEEDEDS --18
It's been a long time, now I'm coming back home -- WAIT--1
I've been away now, oh how I've been alone.--WAIT --2
I've been away now, oh how I've been alone.--WAIT --2
That I've been good, as good as I can be.--WAIT--10
It's been a long time, now I'm coming back home -- WAIT--13
I've been away now, oh how I've been alone.--WAIT

--14
I've been away now, oh how I've been alone.--WAIT --14
That I've been good, as good as I can be.--WAIT--18
It's been a long time, now I'm coming back home -- WAIT--25
I've been away now, oh how I've been alone.--WAIT --26
I've been away now, oh how I've been alone.--WAIT --26
Yes it seems so long, girl, since you've been gone --YOUWONTSEE--18
Yes it seems so long, girl, since you've been gone --YOUWONTSEE--27
Where a wedding has been--ELEANORRIG--4
And she's making me feel like I've never been born.--SHESAIDSHE--3
And you're making me feel like I've never been born.--SHESAIDSHE--6
'cos you're making me feel like I've never been born.--SHESAIDSHE--12
'cos you're making me feel like I've never been born.--SHESAIDSHE--18
Having been some days in preparation--BEINGFORTH --19
It's getting better since you've been mine.-- GETTINGBET--10
It's getting better since you've been mine.-- GETTINGBET--19
It's getting better since you've been mine.-- GETTINGBET--32
Nothing to say but what a day how's your boy been? --GOODMORNIN--3
They've been going in and out of style--SGTPEPPERS --3
If I'd been out till quarter to three--WHENIMSIXT --5
How often have you been there?--BABYYOUREA--9
Man you been a naughty boy, you let your face grow long--IAMTHEWALR--6
Boy, you been a naughty girl, you let your knickers down--IAMTHEWALR--14
Been away so long I hardly knew the place -- BACKINTHEU--8
If looks could kill it would have been us instead of him.--CONTINUING--29
It's been a long, long, long time --LONGLONGLO--1
Martha my dear, you have always been my inspiration --MARTHAMYDE--13
Little darling, it's been a long, cold lonely winter.--HERECOMEST--4
Little darling, it feels like years since it's been here.--HERECOMEST--5
Little darling, it seems like years since it's been here.--HERECOMEST--10
Little darling, it seems like years since it's been clear.--HERECOMEST--19
Only place that he's ever been--MEANMRMUST--12
He'd let us in, knows where we've been--OCTOPUSSGA --3
She said she'd always been a dancer --SHECAMEINT --12
All these years I've been wandering round the world --IVEGOTAFEE--11
Many times I've been alone and many times I've cried --LONGANDWIN--7

BEEP

Beep beep mmm beep beep yeah.--DRIVEMYCAR--17
Beep beep mmm beep beep yeah.--DRIVEMYCAR--17
Beep beep mmm beep beep yeah.--DRIVEMYCAR--17
Beep beep mmm beep beep yeah.--DRIVEMYCAR--17
Beep beep mmm beep beep yeah --DRIVEMYCAR--30
Beep beep mmm beep beep yeah --DRIVEMYCAR--30
Beep beep mmm beep beep yeah --DRIVEMYCAR--30
Beep beep mmm beep beep yeah --DRIVEMYCAR--31
Beep beep mmm beep beep yeah --DRIVEMYCAR--31
Beep beep mmm beep beep yeah --DRIVEMYCAR--31
Beep beep mmm beep beep yeah --DRIVEMYCAR--31
Beep beep mmm beep beep yeah --DRIVEMYCAR--32
Beep beep mmm beep beep yeah --DRIVEMYCAR--32
Beep beep mmm beep beep yeah --DRIVEMYCAR--32
Beep beep mmm beep beep yeah --DRIVEMYCAR--32
Beep beep mmm beep beep yeah --DRIVEMYCAR--33
Beep beep mmm beep beep yeah --DRIVEMYCAR--33
Beep beep mmm beep beep yeah --DRIVEMYCAR--33
Beep beep mmm beep beep yeah --DRIVEMYCAR--33
Beep beep mmm beep beep yeah.--DRIVEMYCAR--34
Beep beep mmm beep beep yeah.--DRIVEMYCAR--34
Beep beep mmm beep beep yeah.--DRIVEMYCAR--34
Beep beep mmm beep beep yeah.--DRIVEMYCAR--34

BEFORE

That before too long I'd fall in love with her.--
   ISAWHERSTA--8
And before too long I fell in love with her--
   ISAWHERSTA--15
And before too long I fell in love with her.--
   ISAWHERSTA--22
Many, many, many times before.--ILLGETYOU--5
Many, many, many times before.--ILLGETYOU--22
Because I told you before--YOUCANTDOT--7
Because I told you before--YOUCANTDOT--16
Because I told you before--YOUCANTDOT--30
Because I told you before--YOUCANTDOT--49
So - oh, I should have realised a lot of things
   before --ISHOULDHAV--11
'cos I've been in love before --IFIFELL--4
Before this dance is through --IMHAPPYJUS--1
Before this dance is through ((aah)) --IMHAPPYJUS
   --13
Before this dance is through ((aah)) --IMHAPPYJUS
   --21
'cos I told you once before goodbye --ILLBEBACK--3
And so it's true pride comes before a fall --
   IMALOSER--17
This happened once before--NOREPLY--1
That I heard before--NOREPLY--20
Before she gets to saying goodbye--TICKETTORI--20
Before she gets to saying goodbye--TICKETTORI--33
You've tried before to leave me--YOULIKEMET--7
I've never done before.--HELP--24
THE NIGHT BEFORE.--NIGHTBEFOR--Title
We said our goodbyes (aah the night before)--
   NIGHTBEFOR--1
Love was in your eyes (aah the night before)--
   NIGHTBEFOR--2
Treat me like you did the night before.--NIGHTBEFOR
   --4
Were you telling lies? (aah the night before)--
   NIGHTBEFOR--5
Was I so unwise? (aah the night before)--NIGHTBEFOR
   --6
Treat me like you did the night before.--NIGHTBEFOR
   --8
We said our goodbyes (aah the night before)--
   NIGHTBEFOR--11
Love was in your eyes (aah the night before)--
   NIGHTBEFOR--12
Treat me like you did the night before (yes).--
   NIGHTBEFOR--14
Treat me like you did the night before (yeah).--
   NIGHTBEFOR--16
Were you telling lies? (aah the night before)--
   NIGHTBEFOR--19
Was I so unwise? (aah the night before)--NIGHTBEFOR
   --20
Treat me like you did the night before.--NIGHTBEFOR
   --22
Like the night before.--NIGHTBEFOR--23
There's a chance that we might fall apart before
   too long.--WECANWORKI--18
There's a chance that we might fall apart before
   too long.--WECANWORKI--27
For people and things that went before --INMYLIFE
   --14
For people and things that went before --INMYLIFE
   --18
Before I'm a dead old man.--LOVEYOUTWO--5
They'd seen his face before--DAYINTHELI--9
That was a hit before your mother was born --
   YOURMOTHER--3
That was a hit before your mother was born --
   YOURMOTHER--9
That was a hit before your mother was born --
   YOURMOTHER--14
Images of broken light which dance before me like
   a million eyes --ACROSSTHEU--11
Will never disappear, I've seen that road before.
   --LONGANDWIN--2

BEG

Well I beg you on my bended knees --TELLMEWHY--21
Believe me when I beg you - ooo - don't ever
   leave me alone.--OHDARLING--4

BEGGED

I begged her not to go and I begged her on my
   bended knee, (oh yeah)--ONEAFTERNI--6
I begged her not to go and I begged her on my
   bended knee, (oh yeah)--ONEAFTERNI--6

BEGIN

The games begin to drag me down --IWANTTOTEL--6
Then you begin to make it better.--HEYJUDE--8
Hey Jude, begin --HEYJUDE--20
Then you'll begin ((let it out)) to make it
   better --HEYJUDE--29

BEGINNING

In the beginning I misunderstood --THEWORD--7
Of the beginning --TOMORROWNE--14
Of the beginning --TOMORROWNE--15
Of the beginning --TOMORROWNE--16
Of the beginning --TOMORROWNE--17
Of the beginning --TOMORROWNE--18
Of the beginning --TOMORROWNE--19
Of the beginning.--TOMORROWNE--20

BEGINS

And the band begins to play.--YELLOWSUBM--15
The band begins at ten to six--BEINGFORTH--15
Wednesday morning at five o'clock as the day begins
   --SHESLEAVIN--1
Now the moon begins to shine --GOODNIGHT--9
And as he gives it to her she begins to sing
   (sing):--OBLADIOBLA--12

BEHALF

I'd like to say thank you on behalf of the group
   and ourselves--GETBACK/LP--38

BEHIND

I left you far behind--THINKFORYO--10
No sign of love behind the tears cried for no-one
   --FORNOONE--8
No sign of love behind the tears cried for no-one
   --FORNOONE--15
No sign of love behind the tears cried for no-one
   --FORNOONE--25
The little children laugh at him behind his back--
   PENNYLANE--6
Behind the shelter in the middle of the roundabout
   --PENNYLANE--20
Who hide themselves behind a wall of illusion--
   WITHINYOUW--4
They leave the West behind --BACKINTHEU--16
They leave the West behind --BACKINTHEU--28
So he waits behind, writing fifty times I must
   not be so oh - oh oh.--MAXWELLSIL--11
But when she turns her back on the boy, he
   creeps up from behind --MAXWELLSIL--12
But as the words are leaving his lips, a noise
   comes from behind --MAXWELLSIL--22

BEING

Being here alone tonight with you.--HOLDMETIGH--17
Being here alone tonight with you.--HOLDMETIGH--27
Was I to blame for being unfair?--ICALLYOURN--2
I got no business being here with you this way.--
   WHENIGETHO--23
And I do appreciate you being round--HELP--16
And I do appreciate you being round--HELP--26
And I do appreciate you being round--HELP--36
It is being, it is being.--TOMORROWNE--6
It is being, it is being.--TOMORROWNE--6
BEING FOR THE BENEFIT OF MR. KITE!--BEINGFORTH
   --Title

BELIEVE

I can't believe it's happened to me --ASKMEWHY--12
I can't believe it's happened to me --ASKMEWHY--24
I can't believe--DONTBOTHER--9
And it's nice when you believe me--YOULIKEMET--14
And it's nice when you believe me--YOULIKEMET--23
Oh I believe in yesterday.--YESTERDAY--4
Oh I believe in yesterday.--YESTERDAY--16
Oh I believe in yesterday.--YESTERDAY--24
And she promises the earth to me and I believe
   her --GIRL--8
Will she still believe it when he's dead?--GIRL--25
Dr. Robert, he's a man you must believe --DRROBERT
   --8
And yet you don't believe her --FORNOONE--11
(Would you believe in a love at first sight?)--
   WITHALITTL--19
It's a love that has no past (believe me).--
   DONTLETMED--16
Oh darling, please believe me, I'll never do
   you no harm.--OHDARLING--1

BELIEVE

Believe me when I tell you, I'll never do you
no harm.--OHDARLING--2
Believe me when I beg you - ooo - don't ever
leave me alone.--OHDARLING--4
Believe me when I tell you, I'll never do you
no harm.--OHDARLING--10
Believe me, darling.--OHDARLING--11
Oh darling, please believe me, I'll never let
you down.--OHDARLING--16
Oh believe me darling --OHDARLING--17
Believe me when I tell you - ooo - I'll never
do you no harm.--OHDARLING--18
You know I believe 'n' how.--SOMETHING--5
You know I believe 'n' how.--SOMETHING--10
You know I believe 'n' how.--SOMETHING--19
Oh please believe me I'd hate to miss the train --
IVEGOTAFEE--6
You better believe it.--TWOOFUS--36

BELIEVING

Each one believing that love never dies--HERETHEREA
--12
Each one believing that love never dies--HERETHEREA
--18
It is believing, it is believing.--TOMORROWNE--10
It is believing, it is believing.--TOMORROWNE--10

BELLE

Michelle ma belle --MICHELLE--1
Michelle ma belle --MICHELLE--3
Michelle ma belle --MICHELLE--9
Michelle ma belle --MICHELLE--20

BELLYFULL

But I gotta get a bellyfull of wine.--HERMAJESTY
--6

BELONG

Till I belong to you--ITWONTBELO--4
Till I belong to you--ITWONTBELO--10
Till I belong to you--ITWONTBELO--20
Till I belong to you - ooo.--ITWONTBELO--30
And bring you back where you belong--YOULIKEMET--16
And bring you back where you belong--YOULIKEMET--25
All the lonely people, where do they all belong?--
ELEANORRIG--10
All the lonely people, where do they all belong?--
ELEANORRIG--18
All the lonely people, where do they all belong?--
ELEANORRIG--29
Where I belong I'm right where I belong.--
FIXINGAHOL--8
Where I belong I'm right where I belong.--
FIXINGAHOL--8
Where I belong I'm right where I belong.--
FIXINGAHOL--16
Where I belong I'm right where I belong.--
FIXINGAHOL--16
Don't belong, don't be long--BLUEJAYWAY--32
Don't belong--BLUEJAYWAY--33
Don't belong.--BLUEJAYWAY--35
To be where you belong.--HONEYPIE--18

BELONGED

Get back to where you once belonged.--GETBACK/45--6
Get back to where you once belonged.--GETBACK/45--8
Back to where you once belonged.--GETBACK/45--12
Back to where you once belonged.--GETBACK/45--14
Get back to where you once belonged.--GETBACK/45--21
Get back to where you once belonged.--GETBACK/45
--23
Get back to where you once belonged.--GETBACK/45
--27
Get back to where you once belonged.--GETBACK/45
--29
Get back to where you once belonged.--GETBACK/45
--37
Get back to where you once belonged--GETBACK/LP--12
Get back to where you once belonged--GETBACK/LP--14
Back to where you once belonged--GETBACK/LP--18
Back to where you once belonged--GETBACK/LP--20
Get back to where you once belonged--GETBACK/LP--27
Get back to where you once belonged.--GETBACK/LP
--29
Get back to where you once belonged--GETBACK/LP--33
Get back to where you once belonged--GETBACK/LP--35

BELOW

He got feet down below his knee--COMETOGETH--29
We would be warm below the storm--OCTOPUSSGA--9

BENDED

Well I beg you on my bended knees --TELLMEWHY--21
I begged her not to go and I begged her on my
bended knee, (oh yeah)--ONEAFTERNI--6

BENEATH

Beneath this mask I am wearing a frown.--IMALOSER
--10
Then we lie beneath a shady tree --GOODDAYSUN--10
And we lived beneath the waves--YELLOWSUBM--7
There beneath the blue suburban skies I sit--
PENNYLANE--10
There beneath the blue suburban skies I sit--
PENNYLANE--29
There beneath the blue suburban skies --PENNYLANE
--32
Swaying daisies sing a lazy song beneath the sun.
--MOTHERNATU--9
In our little hideaway beneath the waves.--
OCTOPUSSGA--10
The coral that lies beneath the waves (lies
beneath the ocean waves).--OCTOPUSSGA--18
The coral that lies beneath the waves (lies
beneath the ocean waves).--OCTOPUSSGA--18

BENEFIT

BEING FOR THE BENEFIT OF MR. KITE!--BEINGFORTH
--Title
For the benefit of Mr. Kite--BEINGFORTH--1

BENT-BACKED

Looking through the bent-backed tulips--GLASSONION
--5

BESIDE

When I'm walking beside her--EVERYLITTL--1
Why am I so shy when I'm beside you?--ITSONLYLOV
--3
And if she's beside me I know I need never care--
HERETHEREA--9
And if she's beside me I know I need never care--
HERETHEREA--15
Sit beside a mountain stream - see her waters rise
--MOTHERNATU--3

BEST

You're doing the best that I can.--GETTINGBET--15
And I'm doing the best that I can.--GETTINGBET--28
To try our best to hold it there--WITHINYOUW--11
And though she tried her best to help me --
SHECAMEINT--18

BET

I bet I'll love her more --WHENIGETHO--19

BETTER

I SHOULD HAVE KNOWN BETTER.--ISHOULDHAV--Title
I should have known better with a girl like you --
ISHOULDHAV--1
And when I do you'd better hide all the girls --
ILLCRYINST--15
And when I do you'd better hide all the girls --
ILLCRYINST--24
You could find better things to do--ILLBEBACK--9
You could find better things to do--ILLBEBACK--18
And so I'm telling you this time you'd better
stop --ANOTHERGIR--8
But I can show you a better time.--DRIVEMYCAR--12
Some forever, not for better --INMYLIFE--3
You better keep your head, little girl --RUNFORYOUR
--3
You better run for your life if you can, little
girl --RUNFORYOUR--5
You better run for your life if you can, little
girl --RUNFORYOUR--13
You better run for your life if you can, little
girl --RUNFORYOUR--21
You better keep your head, little girl --RUNFORYOUR
--27
You better run for your life if you can, little
girl --RUNFORYOUR--29
Dr. Robert, you're a new and better man --DRROBERT
--3

Dr. Robert, you're a new and better man,--DRROBERT
--15
To lead a better life, I need my love to be here.
--HERETHEREA--1
GETTING BETTER.--GETTINGBET--Title
It's getting better all the time.--GETTINGBET--2
I've got to admit it's getting better (better)--
GETTINGBET--7
I've got to admit it's getting better (better)--
GETTINGBET--7
A little better all the time (it can't get no
worse)--GETTINGBET--8
I have to admit it's getting better (better)--
GETTINGBET--9
I have to admit it's getting better (better)--
GETTINGBET--9
It's getting better since you've been mine.--
GETTINGBET--10
I've got to admit it's getting better (better)--
GETTINGBET--16
I've got to admit it's getting better (better)--
GETTINGBET--16
A little better all the time (it can't get no
worse)--GETTINGBET--17
I have to admit it's getting better (better)--
GETTINGBET--18
I have to admit it's getting better (better)--
GETTINGBET--18
It's getting better since you've been mine.--
GETTINGBET--19
Getting so much better all the time.--GETTINGBET
--20
It's getting better all the time--GETTINGBET--21
Better, better, better--GETTINGBET--22
Better, better, better--GETTINGBET--22
Better, better, better--GETTINGBET--22
It's getting better all the time--GETTINGBET--23
Better, better, better.--GETTINGBET--24
Better, better, better.--GETTINGBET--24
I admit it's getting better (better)--GETTINGBET
--29
I admit it's getting better (better)--GETTINGBET
--29
A little better all the time (it can't get no
worse)--GETTINGBET--30
Yes I admit it's getting better (better)--
GETTINGBET--31
Yes I admit it's getting better (better)--
GETTINGBET--31
It's getting better since you've been mine.--
GETTINGBET--32
Getting so much better all the time.--GETTINGBET
--33
It's getting better all the time--GETTINGBET--34
Better, better, better--GETTINGBET--35
Better, better, better--GETTINGBET--35
Better, better, better--GETTINGBET--35
It's getting better all the time--GETTINGBET--36
Better, better, better.--GETTINGBET--37
Better, better, better.--GETTINGBET--37
Better, better, better.--GETTINGBET--37
Getting so much better all the time.--GETTINGBET
--38
Take a sad song and make it better --HEYJUDE--2
Then you can start to make it better.--HEYJUDE--4
Then you begin to make it better.--HEYJUDE--8
Then you can start to make it better.--HEYJUDE--18
Take a sad song and make it better --HEYJUDE--27
Then you'll begin ((let it out)) to make it
better --HEYJUDE--29
Better, better, better, better ((make it
Jude)), better.--HEYJUDE--30
Better, better, better, better ((make it
Jude)), better.--HEYJUDE--30
Better, better, better, better ((make it
Jude)), better.--HEYJUDE--30
Better, better, better, better ((make it
Jude)), better.--HEYJUDE--30
Better, better, better, better ((make it
Jude)), better.--HEYJUDE--30
(Take a sad song and make it better)--HEYJUDE--48
You better free your mind instead.--REVOLUTION--27
She's old enough to know better.--CRYBABYCRY--3
She's old enough to know better --CRYBABYCRY--10
She's old enough to know better --CRYBABYCRY--18
She's old enough to know better --CRYBABYCRY--26
She's old enough to know better --CRYBABYCRY--34
She's old enough to know better --CRYBABYCRY--38
She's old enoughzto know better --CRYBABYCRY--42
You'd better free your mind instead.--REVOLUTONE
--41
And I'll be better, I'll be better Doc as
soon as I am able.--ROCKYRACCO--35

And I'll be better, I'll be better Doc as
soon as I am able.--ROCKYRACCO--35
You better believe it.--TWOOFUS--36

BETWEEN
But you can do something in between.--DRIVEMYCAR
--4
Nothing can come between us--LOVELYRITA--5
About the space between us all--WITHINYOUW--2
So Captain Marvel zapped him right between the
eyes. (Zap!)--CONTINUING--19

BEYOND
And the way she looked was way beyond compare.--
ISAWHERSTA--4
When you've seen beyond yourself--WITHINYOUW--28

BIBLE
Only to find Gideon's Bible --ROCKYRACCO--10
Only to find Gideon's Bible --ROCKYRACCO--37

BIDING
Biding my time--NORWEGIANW--12

BIEN
Sont des mots qui vont tres bien ensemble, tres
bien ensemble.--MICHELLE--4
Sont des mots qui vont tres bien ensemble, tres
bien ensemble.--MICHELLE--4
Sont des mots qui vont tres bien ensemble, tres
bien ensemble.--MICHELLE--10
Sont des mots qui vont tres bien ensemble, tres
bien ensemble.--MICHELLE--10
Sont des mots qui vont tres bien ensemble, tres
bien ensemble.--MICHELLE--21
Sont des mots qui vont tres bien ensemble, tres
bien ensemble.--MICHELLE--21

BIG
But I got a big surprise--ILLBEBACK--16
Big and black the clouds may be--TELLMEWHAT--9
She's a big teaser --DAYTRIPPER--9
She's a big teaser --DAYTRIPPER--11
You keep all your money in a big brown bag --
BABYYOUREA--16
You keep all your money in a big brown bag --
BABYYOUREA--31
Now she's hit the big time--HONEYPIE--3
However big you think you are--SEXYSADIE--17
However big you think you are--SEXYSADIE--18
... However big you think you are.--SEXYSADIE--28
Big man (yeah?) walking in the park--HEYBULLDOG--13

BIGGER
I got a chip on my shoulder that's bigger than my
feet.--ILLCRYINST--6
Have you seen the bigger piggies--PIGGIES--6
You will find the bigger piggies--PIGGIES--8

BILL
And tonight Mr. Kite is topping the bill.--
BEINGFORTH--21
Got the bill and Rita paid it--LOVELYRITA--23
THE CONTINUING STORY OF BUNGALOW BILL.--CONTINUING
--Title
Hey, Bungalow Bill --CONTINUING--1
Bungalow Bill?--CONTINUING--3
Hey, Bungalow Bill --CONTINUING--4
Bungalow Bill?--CONTINUING--6
Hey, Bungalow Bill --CONTINUING--11
Bungalow Bill?--CONTINUING--13
Hey, Bungalow Bill --CONTINUING--14
Bungalow Bill?--CONTINUING--16
Bill and his elephants were taken by surprise --
CONTINUING--18
Hey, Bungalow Bill --CONTINUING--21
Bungalow Bill?--CONTINUING--23
Hey, Bungalow Bill --CONTINUING--24
Bungalow Bill?--CONTINUING--26
Hey, Bungalow Bill --CONTINUING--31
Bungalow Bill?--CONTINUING--33
Hey, Bungalow Bill --CONTINUING--34
Bungalow Bill?--CONTINUING--36
Hey, Bungalow Bill --CONTINUING--37
Bungalow Bill?--CONTINUING--39
Hey, Bungalow Bill --CONTINUING--40

BILL

Bungalow Bill?--CONTINUING--42
Hey, Bungalow Bill --CONTINUING--43
Bungalow Bill?--CONTINUING--45
Hey, Bungalow Bill --CONTINUING--46
Bungalow Bill?--CONTINUING--48
Hey, Bungalow Bill --CONTINUING--49
Bungalow Bill?--CONTINUING--51
Hey, Bungalow Bill --CONTINUING--52
Bungalow Bill?--CONTINUING--54

BILLY

The one and only Billy Shears--SGTPEPPERS--24
Billy Shears!--SGTPEPPERS--26

BIRD

NORWEGIAN WOOD (THIS BIRD HAS FLOWN).--NORWEGIANW
   --Title
This bird had flown.--NORWEGIANW--23
AND YOUR BIRD CAN SING.--ANDYOURBIR--Title
And your bird can sing --ANDYOURBIR--2
And your bird is green --ANDYOURBIR--5
When your bird is broken will it bring you down?--
   ANDYOURBIR--10
And your bird can swing --ANDYOURBIR--14
With a message at the local bird and bee.--
   CRYBABYCRY--23

BIRDS

The wind is low, the birds will sing --DEARPRUDEN
   --8

BIRTHDAY

Birthday greetings, bottle of wine?--WHENIMSIXT--4
BIRTHDAY.--BIRTHDAY--Title
You say it's your birthday --BIRTHDAY--1
Well, it's my birthday too - yeah.--BIRTHDAY--2
They say it's your birthday --BIRTHDAY--3
I'm glad it's your birthday --BIRTHDAY--5
Happy birthday to you.--BIRTHDAY--6
I would like you to dance (birthday) --BIRTHDAY--11
Take a cha-cha-cha chance (birthday) --BIRTHDAY--12
I would like you to dance (birthday) --BIRTHDAY--13
I would like you to dance (birthday) --BIRTHDAY--16
Take a cha-cha-cha chance (birthday) --BIRTHDAY--17
I would like you to dance (birthday) (wuh)--
   BIRTHDAY--18
You say it's your birthday --BIRTHDAY--20
Well, it's my birthday too - yeah.--BIRTHDAY--21
You say it's your birthday --BIRTHDAY--22
I'm glad it's your birthday --BIRTHDAY--24
Happy birthday to you.--BIRTHDAY--25
All the world is birthday cake --ITSALLTOOM--18

BISHOPSGATE

Performs his feat on Saturday at Bishopsgate.--
   BEINGFORTH--9

BIT

Isn't he a bit like you and me?--NOWHEREMAN--6
Isn't he a bit like you and me?--NOWHEREMAN--18
Help yourself to a bit of what is all around you
   - silly girl.--MARTHAMYDE--6
Help yourself to a bit of what is all around you
   - silly girl.--MARTHAMYDE--12

BITS

Down to the bits that I left uptown --HAPPINESSI
   --10

BLACK

BABY'S IN BLACK.--BABYSINBLA--Title
Baby's in black and I'm feeling blue --BABYSINBLA
   --2
She thinks of him and so she dresses in black --
   BABYSINBLA--4
She's dressed in black.--BABYSINBLA--6
Baby's in black and I'm feeling blue --BABYSINBLA
   --8
Baby's in black and I'm feeling blue --BABYSINBLA
   --17
Baby's in black and I'm feeling blue --BABYSINBLA
   --22
She thinks of him and so she dresses in black --
   BABYSINBLA--24
She's dressed in black.--BABYSINBLA--26
Baby's in black and I'm feeling blue --BABYSINBLA

--28
Big and black the clouds may be--TELLMEWHAT--9
Into the light of a dark black night.--BLACKBIRD
   --10
Into the light of a dark black night.--BLACKBIRD
   --12
Now somewhere in the Black Mountain hills of
   Dakota --ROCKYRACCO--1
Black cloud crossed my mind --YERBLUES--24
Black, white, green, red --ALLTOGETHE--17

BLACKBIRD

BLACKBIRD.--BLACKBIRD--Title
Blackbird singing in the dead of night --BLACKBIRD
   --1
Blackbird singing in the dead of night --BLACKBIRD
   --5
Blackbird fly, blackbird fly--BLACKBIRD--9
Blackbird fly, blackbird fly--BLACKBIRD--9
Blackbird fly, blackbird fly--BLACKBIRD--11
Blackbird fly, blackbird fly--BLACKBIRD--11
Blackbird singing in the dead of night --BLACKBIRD
   --13

BLACKBURN

Four thousand holes in Blackburn, Lancashire--
   DAYINTHELI--29

BLAME

But I'm to blame--DONTBOTHER--4
Was I to blame for being unfair?--ICALLYOURN--2

BLEW

He blew his mind out in a car--DAYINTHELI--6
Will the wind that blew her boat--HONEYPIE--25

BLIND

And though we may be blind --THINGSWESA--13
And though we may be blind --THINGSWESA--24
He's as blind as he can be --NOWHEREMAN--10
But now the tide is turning I can see that I
   was blind.--WHATGOESON--16

BLINDLY

They tumble blindly as they make their way across
   the universe.--ACROSSTHEU--14

BLINK

I'm so tired, my mind is on the blink --IMSOTIRED
   --2

BLISTERS

I got blisters on my fingers!--HELTERSKEL--32

BLONDE

With your long blonde hair and your eyes of blue
   --ITSALLTOOM--35
With your long blonde hair and your eyes of blue
   --ITSALLTOOM--36

BLOODY

Corporation T-shirt, stupid bloody Tuesday--
   IAMTHEWALR--5

BLOW

Oh now I feel the wind blow--IDIGAPONY--26

BLOWS

Cocoanut fudge really blows down those blues
   (wuh) --SAVOYTRUFF--8
Because the wind is high it blows my mind --BECAUSE
   --5

BLUE

That I - I - I - I should never, never,
   never be blue.--ASKMEWHY--6
That I - I - I - I should never, never,
   never be blue.--ASKMEWHY--21
Why do you make me blue?--PLEASEPLEA--18
You made me glad when I was blue--THANKYOUGI--2
You made me glad when I was blue--THANKYOUGI--12

I'm never, never, never, never blue.--ILLGETYOU--12
When I feel low, when I feel blue--THERESAPLA--2
When I feel low, when I feel blue--THERESAPLA--14
Baby's in black and I'm feeling blue --BABYSINBLA
    --2
Baby's in black and I'm feeling blue --BABYSINBLA
    --8
Baby's in black and I'm feeling blue --BABYSINBLA
    --17
Baby's in black and I'm feeling blue --BABYSINBLA
    --22
Baby's in black and I'm feeling blue --BABYSINBLA
    --28
I'm ((I'm)) feeling blue and lonely --WHATYOURED
    --2
For red is the colour that will make me blue--
    YESITIS--16
For red is the colour that will make me blue--
    YESITIS--25
Sky of blue (sky of blue) and sea of green
    (sea of green)--YELLOWSUBM--27
Sky of blue (sky of blue) and sea of green
    (sea of green)--YELLOWSUBM--27
There beneath the blue suburban skies I sit--
    PENNYLANE--10
There beneath the blue suburban skies I sit--
    PENNYLANE--29
There beneath the blue suburban skies --PENNYLANE
    --32
BLUE JAY WAY.--BLUEJAYWAY--Title
Sitting here in Blue Jay Way (way).--BLUEJAYWAY--18
The sun is up, the sky is blue --DEARPRUDEN--3
The sun is up, the sky is blue --DEARPRUDEN--23
Don't pass me by, don't make me cry, don't make
    me blue --DONTPASSME--18
Don't pass me by, don't make me cry, don't make
    me blue --DONTPASSME--31
Don't pass me by, don't make me cry, don't make
    me blue --DONTPASSME--37
Blue mist round my soul --YERBLUES--25
Pink, brown, yellow, orange and blue --ALLTOGETHE
    --19
With your long blonde hair and your eyes of blue
    --ITSALLTOOM--35
With your long blonde hair and your eyes of blue
    --ITSALLTOOM--36
Because the sky is blue it makes me cry --BECAUSE
    --10
Because the sky is blue.--BECAUSE--11
FOR YOU BLUE.--FORYOUBLUE--Title
I want you at the moment I feel blue --FORYOUBLUE
    --6

BLUES
    Play it to me Hollywood blues.--HONEYPIE--24
    Cocoanut fudge really blows down those blues
        (wuh) --SAVOYTRUFF--8
    YER BLUES.--YERBLUES--Title
    Them old twelve-bar blues.--FORYOUBLUE--10
    I love you more than ever girl, I do - really
        love blues.--FORYOUBLUE--18

BOAC
    Oh - flew in from Miami Beach BOAC --BACKINTHEU--1

BOAT
    Picture yourself in a boat on a river--LUCYINTHES
        --1
    Will the wind that blew her boat--HONEYPIE--25
    Well you can syndicate any boat you rode/rowed--
        IDIGAPONY--30
    Yeah you can syndicate any boat you rode/rowed--
        IDIGAPONY--31

BOB
    Keeps a ten bob note up his nose--MEANMRMUST--6

BOM
    Bom bom bom bom-pa bom, sail the ship --ALLTOGETHE
        --9
    Bom bom bom bom-pa bom, sail the ship --ALLTOGETHE
        --9
    Bom bom bom bom-pa bom, sail the ship --ALLTOGETHE
        --9
    Bom bom bom bom-pa bom, sail the ship --ALLTOGETHE
        --9
    Bom-pa bom, chop the tree --ALLTOGETHE--10
    Bom-pa bom, skip the rope --ALLTOGETHE--11
    Bom-pa bom, look at me.--ALLTOGETHE--12

Bom bom bom bom-pa bom, ((Oh! boy)), sail the ship--
    ALLTOGETHE--29
Bom bom bom bom-pa bom, ((Oh! boy)), sail the ship--
    ALLTOGETHE--29
Bom bom bom bom-pa bom, ((Oh! boy)), sail the ship--
    ALLTOGETHE--29
Bom bom bom bom-pa bom, ((Oh! boy)), sail the ship--
    ALLTOGETHE--29
Bom-pa bom, chop the tree --ALLTOGETHE--30
Bom-pa bom, skip the rope --ALLTOGETHE--31
Bom-pa bom, look at me.--ALLTOGETHE--32

BOM-PA
    Bom bom bom bom-pa bom, sail the ship --ALLTOGETHE
        --9
    Bom-pa bom, chop the tree --ALLTOGETHE--10
    Bom-pa bom, skip the rope --ALLTOGETHE--11
    Bom-pa bom, look at me.--ALLTOGETHE--12
    Bom bom bom bom-pa bom, ((Oh! boy)), sail the ship--
        ALLTOGETHE--29
    Bom-pa bom, chop the tree --ALLTOGETHE--30
    Bom-pa bom, skip the rope --ALLTOGETHE--31
    Bom-pa bom, look at me.--ALLTOGETHE--32

BONE
    The worm he licks my bone --YERBLUES--18

BOOK
    Dear Sir or Madam, will you read my book?--
        PAPERBACKW--2
    Having read the book--DAYINTHELI--15
    Filling in a ticket in her little white book.--
        LOVELYRITA--9

BOOKED
    Booked himself a room in the local saloon.--
        ROCKYRACCO--8

BOOKS
    In the good and the bad books that I have read.--
        THEWORD--16

BOOM
    Well my heart went boom when I crossed that room
        --ISAWHERSTA--11
    Well my heart went boom when I crossed that room
        --ISAWHERSTA--18

BOOTLACE
    Monday's child has learned to tie his bootlace.--
        LADYMADONN--7

BOOTS
    The man in the crowd with the multicoloured
        mirrors on his hobnail boots --HAPPINESSI--5

BOP
    Bop - bop cat bop --FORYOUBLUE--8
    Bop - bop cat bop --FORYOUBLUE--8
    Bop - bop cat bop --FORYOUBLUE--8

BORN
    And I was born with a jealous mind,--RUNFORYOUR--10
    And she's making me feel like I've never been
        born.--SHESAIDSHE--3
    And you're making me feel like I've never been
        born.--SHESAIDSHE--6
    'cos you're making me feel like I've never been
        born.--SHESAIDSHE--12
    'cos you're making me feel like I've never been
        born.--SHESAIDSHE--18
    In the town where I was born--YELLOWSUBM--1
    That was a hit before your mother was born --
        YOURMOTHER--3
    Though she was born a long, long time ago --
        YOURMOTHER--4
    That was a hit before your mother was born --
        YOURMOTHER--9
    Though she was born a long, long time ago --
        YOURMOTHER--10
    That was a hit before your mother was born --
        YOURMOTHER--14
    Though she was born a long, long time ago --
        YOURMOTHER--15

Though she was born a long, long time ago --
    YOURMOTHER--23
Born a poor young country boy - Mother Nature's
    son --MOTHERNATU--1

BOSUN
    (Full speed ahead, Mr. Bosun, full speed
        ahead.--YELLOWSUBM--20

BOTH
    Both of us thinking how good it can be--HERETHEREA
        --6
    It's good to have the both of you back.--BALLADOFJO
        --40

BOTHER
    DON'T BOTHER ME.--DONTBOTHER--Title
    Don't bother me--DONTBOTHER--8
    Don't bother me--DONTBOTHER--14
    Don't bother me--DONTBOTHER--27
    Don't bother me--DONTBOTHER--29
    Don't bother me--DONTBOTHER--42
    Don't bother me--DONTBOTHER-43
    Don't bother me--DONTBOTHER-44
    Don't bother me--DONTBOTHER-45
    Don't bother me.--DONTBOTHER--46

BOTTLE
    Birthday greetings, bottle of wine?--WHENIMSIXT--4

BOTTOM
    When I get to the bottom I go back to the top
        of the slide --HELTERSKEL--1
    Till I get to the bottom and I see you again -
        yeah, yeah, yeah.--HELTERSKEL--3
    When I get to the bottom I go back to the top
        of the slide--HELTERSKEL--18
    And I get to the bottom and I see you again -
        yeah, yeah, yeah.--HELTERSKEL--20

BOUGHT
    A new one can't be bought--LOVEYOUTWO--7
    They bought and sold you.--WHILEMYGUI--8

BOUND
    Take a good look you're bound to see --MARTHAMYDE
        --8

BOY
    THIS BOY.--THISBOY--Title
    That boy took my love away--THISBOY--1
    But this boy wants you back again.--THISBOY--3
    That boy isn't good for you--THISBOY--4
    This boy wants you back again.--THISBOY--6
    Oh, and this boy would be happy--THISBOY--7
    That boy won't be happy--THISBOY--9
    This boy wouldn't mind the pain--THISBOY--11
    If this boy gets you back again.--THISBOY--13
    This boy, this boy, this boy.--THISBOY--14
    This boy, this boy, this boy.--THISBOY--14
    This boy, this boy, this boy.--THISBOY--14
    To that boy again.--YOUCANTDOT--4
    When I was a boy everything was right,
        everything was right.--SHESAIDSHE--9
    When I was a boy everything was right,
        everything was right.--SHESAIDSHE--15
    I read the news today, oh boy--DAYINTHELI--1
    I saw a film today, oh boy--DAYINTHELI--11
    I read the news today, oh boy--DAYINTHELI--28
    Nothing to say but what a day how's your boy been?
        --GOODMORNIN--3
    Man you been a naughty boy, you let your face
        grow long--IAMTHEWALR--6
    Boy, you been a naughty girl, you let your
        knickers down--IAMTHEWALR--14
    You don't know how lucky you are boy --BACKINTHEU
        --13
    You don't know how lucky you are boy --BACKINTHEU
        --36
    Born a poor young country boy - Mother Nature's
        son --MOTHERNATU--1
    There lived a young boy name of Rocky Raccoon--
        ROCKYRACCO--2
    He said, I'm gonna get that boy --ROCKYRACCO--6
    He said, Danny - Boy this is a showdown.--
        ROCKYRACCO--20

Do do do do - come on Rocky - boy --ROCKYRACCO--45
Do do do do do - come on Rocky - boy--ROCKYRACCO--46
Bom bom bom bom-pa bom, ((Oh! boy)), sail the ship--
    ALLTOGETHE--29
Last night the wife said, oh boy, when you're
    dead,--BALLADOFJO--27
Boy, you're gonna carry that weight--CARRYTHATW--1
Boy, you're gonna carry that weight--CARRYTHATW--3
Boy, you're gonna carry that weight--CARRYTHATW--9
Boy, you're gonna carry that weight--CARRYTHATW--11
But when she turns her back on the boy, he
    creeps up from behind --MAXWELLSIL--12
Oh, what joy for every girl and boy--OCTOPUSSGA--19
Oh Danny Boy, the odes of Pan are calling.--
    ONEAFTERNI--33

BOYS
    She don't give boys the eye--SHESAWOMAN--8
    She don't give boys the eye--SHESAWOMAN--12
    You don't know how lucky you are boys--BACKINTHEU--6
    You don't know how lucky you are boys --BACKINTHEU
        --25
    Look up the number (heads up boys) --YOUKNOWMYN--14

BRA
    Ob-la-di ob-la-da life goes on bra --OBLADIOBLA--5
    Ob-la-di ob-la-da life goes on bra --OBLADIOBLA--7
    Ob-la-di ob-la-da life goes on bra --OBLADIOBLA--13
    Ob-la-di ob-la-da life goes on bra --OBLADIOBLA--15
    Ob-la-di ob-la-da life goes on bra --OBLADIOBLA--25
    Hey, ob-la-di ob-la-da life goes on bra --
        OBLADIOBLA--27
    Ob-la-di ob-la-da life goes on bra --OBLADIOBLA--36
    Ob-la-di ob-la-da life goes on bra --OBLADIOBLA--38

BRAIN
    You know I can't sleep, I can't stop my brain --
        IMSOTIRED--11
    You know I can't sleep, I can't stop my brain --
        IMSOTIRED--20

BRAND
    Dear Prudence, greet the brand new day.--DEARPRUDEN
        --2
    Dear Prudence, greet the brand new day.--DEARPRUDEN
        --22

BREAK
    I'm gonna break their hearts all round the world
        --ILLCRYINST--16
    Yes, I'm gonna break 'em in two --ILLCRYINST--17
    'cos I'm gonna break their hearts all round the
        world --ILLCRYINST--25
    Yes, I'm gonna break 'em in two --ILLCRYINST--26
    You know if you break my heart, I'll go --ILLBEBACK
        --1
    Than to break my heart again--ILLBEBACK--10
    Than to break my heart again--ILLBEBACK--19
    You if you break my heart, I'll go--ILLBEBACK--26
    That a man must break his back to earn his day of
        leisure?--GIRL--24
    Did you mean to break my heart and watch me die?--
        WHATGOESON--24
    But I need a break, ((writer))--PAPERBACKW--24
    Soon will be the break of day (day) --BLUEJAYWAY
        --17
    (Well you know you can make it, Jude, you've
        just gotta break it.)--HEYJUDE--46
    I'm coming down fast but don't let me break you --
        HELTERSKEL--12
    I'm coming down fast but don't let me break you --
        HELTERSKEL--22
    I break down.--CARRYTHATW--8
    And in the middle of negotiations you break down.
        --YOUNEVERGI--3
    And in the middle of investigation I break down.--
        YOUNEVERGI--6

BREAKFAST
    Cooking breakfast for the Queen --CRYBABYCRY--5

BREAKING
    I got no car and it's breaking my heart --
        DRIVEMYCAR--24

BREAKS

But if your heart breaks, don't wait, turn me
   away --WAIT--5
But if your heart breaks, don't wait, turn me
   away --WAIT--21
Your day breaks, your mind aches --FORNOONE--1
Your day breaks, your mind aches --FORNOONE--20
She breaks down and cries to her husband--
   SHESLEAVIN--16

BREAST
   Lady Madonna, baby at your breast --LADYMADONN--9

BRIDGE
   Follow her down to a bridge by a fountain--
     LUCYINTHES--12

BRIGHT
   Bright are the stars that shine --ANDILOVEHE--15
   Bright are the stars that shine --ANDILOVEHE--20
   I'll make bright your day--TELLMEWHAT--12
   Just the sight of you makes night-time bright,
     very bright.--ITSONLYLOV--9
   Just the sight of you makes night-time bright,
     very bright.--ITSONLYLOV--9

BRING
   And bring you back where you belong--YOULIKEMET--16
   And bring you back where you belong--YOULIKEMET--25
   When your bird is broken will it bring you down?--
     ANDYOURBIR--10
   Can I bring my friend to tea?--ALLTOGETHE--6

BRINGING
   Was bringing her down, yeah--TICKETTORI--10
   Was bringing her down, yeah--TICKETTORI--37

BRINGS
   The kiss my lover brings --ANDILOVEHE--8
   She brings to me --ANDILOVEHE--9

BROKE
   Sexy Sadie you broke the rules--SEXYSADIE--5
   Sexy Sadie - oh you broke the rules--SEXYSADIE--8
   Well you know I nearly broke down and cried.--
     OHDARLING--6
   A - well you know, I nearly broke down and died.--
     OHDARLING--8
   A - well you know I nearly broke down and cried.--
     OHDARLING--13
   A - well you know, I nearly broke down and died.--
     OHDARLING--15

BROKEN
   When your bird is broken will it bring you down?--
     ANDYOURBIR--10
   Take these broken wings and learn to fly.--
     BLACKBIRD--2
   Take these broken wings and learn to fly.--
     BLACKBIRD--14
   His rival it seems had broken his dreams--
     ROCKYRACCO--13
   Images of broken light which dance before me like
     a million eyes,--ACROSSTHEU--11

BROKEN-HEARTED
   And when the broken-hearted people--LETITBE/45--9
   And when the broken-hearted people--LETITBE/LP--9

BROTHER
   All I can tell you is brother you have to wait.--
     REVOLUTION--19
   Brother, can you take me back --CRYBABYCRY--47
   Well all I can tell you is brother you have to
     wait.--REVOLUTONE--28

BROTHERS
   Thank you, brothers.--IDIGAPONY--37

BROWN
   You keep all your money in a big brown bag --
     BABYYOUREA--16
   You keep all your money in a big brown bag --

BABYYOUREA--31
Pink, brown, yellow, orange and blue --ALLTOGETHE
   --19
Or how I fare or if my hair is brown --ONLYANORTH
   --11
Peter Brown called to say, you can make it OK --
   BALLADOFJO--11
OLD BROWN SHOE.--OLDBROWNSH--Title
Now I'm stepping out this old brown shoe --
   OLDBROWNSH--5

BRRRRRR
   You, you know, you know my name (brrrrrr - ha,
     hey!) --YOUKNOWMYN--12

BUILT
   In a couple of years they have built a home sweet
     home --OBLADIOBLA--17
   In a couple of years they have built a home sweet
     home--OBLADIOBLA--29
   Yes, you could say she was attractively built -
     yeah, yeah, yeah.--POLYTHENEP--9

BULL-FROG
   Bull-frog doing it again--HEYBULLDOG--2

BULLDOG
   HEY BULLDOG.--HEYBULLDOG--Title
   Hey bulldog (woof), hey bulldog, hey bulldog,
     hey bulldog.--HEYBULLDOG--22
   Hey bulldog (woof), hey bulldog, hey bulldog,
     hey bulldog.--HEYBULLDOG--22
   Hey bulldog (woof), hey bulldog, hey bulldog,
     hey bulldog.--HEYBULLDOG--22
   Hey bulldog (woof), hey bulldog, hey bulldog,
     hey bulldog.--HEYBULLDOG--22
   Hey bulldog!--HEYBULLDOG--34

BULLET-HEADED
   He's the all-American bullet-headed Saxon
     mother's son.--CONTINUING--9

BUM
   You know my name, ba ba ba bum, look up the
     number --YOUKNOWMYN--18

BUNGALOW
   THE CONTINUING STORY OF BUNGALOW BILL.--CONTINUING
     --Title
   Hey, Bungalow Bill --CONTINUING--1
   Bungalow Bill?--CONTINUING--3
   Hey, Bungalow Bill --CONTINUING--4
   Bungalow Bill?--CONTINUING--6
   Hey, Bungalow Bill --CONTINUING--11
   Bungalow Bill?--CONTINUING--13
   Hey, Bungalow Bill --CONTINUING--14
   Bungalow Bill?--CONTINUING--16
   Hey, Bungalow Bill --CONTINUING--21
   Bungalow Bill?--CONTINUING--23
   Hey, Bungalow Bill --CONTINUING--24
   Bungalow Bill?--CONTINUING--26
   Hey, Bungalow Bill --CONTINUING--31
   Bungalow Bill?--CONTINUING--33
   Hey, Bungalow Bill --CONTINUING--34
   Bungalow Bill?--CONTINUING--36
   Hey, Bungalow Bill --CONTINUING--37
   Bungalow Bill?--CONTINUING--39
   Hey, Bungalow Bill --CONTINUING--40
   Bungalow Bill?--CONTINUING--42
   Hey, Bungalow Bill --CONTINUING--43
   Bungalow Bill?--CONTINUING--45
   Hey, Bungalow Bill --CONTINUING--46
   Bungalow Bill?--CONTINUING--48
   Hey, Bungalow Bill --CONTINUING--49
   Bungalow Bill?--CONTINUING--51
   Hey, Bungalow Bill --CONTINUING--52
   Bungalow Bill?--CONTINUING--54

BURIED
   And was buried along with her name--ELEANORRIG--22

BURNING
   You and me burning matches --TWOOFUS--12

BURNS
    Burns my feet as they touch the ground.--GOODDAYSUN
        --8

BURST
    A - Rocky burst in and grinning a grin--ROCKYRACCO
        --19

BUS
    Made the bus in seconds flat--DAYINTHELI--24

BUSBY
    Matt Busby.--DIGIT--9

BUSINESS
    I got no business being here with you this way.--
        WHENIGETHO--23

BUSY
    Lying with his eyes while his hands are busy
        working overtime --HAPPINESSI--6

BUT
    But you're the only love that I've ever had.--
        ASKMEWHY--11
    But you know there's always rain--PLEASEPLEA--14
    But I'll get you, I'll get you in the end--
        ILLGETYOU--7
    But I'll get you, I'll get you in the end--
        ILLGETYOU--24
    But now she says she knows--SHELOVESYO--14
    But I'm to blame--DONTBOTHER--4
    But till she's here--DONTBOTHER--19
    But till she's here--DONTBOTHER--34
    Every day I've done nothing but cry--ITWONTBELO--16
    But this boy wants you back again.--THISBOY--3
    Just to love you, but oh my!--THISBOY--8
    But what I got I'll give to you --CANTBUYMEL--12
    But if they'd seen--YOUCANTDOT--20
    But if they'd seen--YOUCANTDOT--39
    I call your name, but you're not there --ICALLYOURN
        --1
    Oh, I can't sleep at night, but just the same --
        ICALLYOURN--9
    Oh, I can't sleep at night, but just the same --
        ICALLYOURN--16
    But when I get home to you --HARDDAYSNI--5
    But when I get home to you --HARDDAYSNI--21
    But when I get home to you --HARDDAYSNI--34
    But I can't, so I'll cry instead--ILLCRYINST--5
    But I can't, so I'll cry instead--ILLCRYINST--10
    But I'll come back again some day.--ILLCRYINST--14
    But I'll come back again some day.--ILLCRYINST--23
    But you left me sitting on my own --TELLMEWHY--6
    But I'll be back again --ILLBEBACK--2
    But I came back again.--ILLBEBACK--4
    But I got a big surprise--ILLBEBACK--16
    But I hate to leave you--ILLBEBACK--23
    But I'll be back again.--ILLBEBACK--27
    But she thinks only of him --BABYSINBLA--11
    And/But though he'll never come back--BABYSINBLA--25
    I ain't got nothing but love babe --EIGHTDAYSA--7
    I ain't got nothing but love girl --EIGHTDAYSA--15
    I ain't got nothing but love babe --EIGHTDAYSA--25
    I ain't got nothing but love babe --EIGHTDAYSA--35
    But I think I'll take a walk and look for her.--
        IDONTWANTT--25
    But I saw you peep through your window--NOREPLY--5
    But she don't care.--TICKETTORI--8
    But she don't care.--TICKETTORI--16
    But she don't care.--TICKETTORI--29
    But she don't care.--TICKETTORI--43
    But it's my pride--YESITIS--12
    But it's my pride--YESITIS--21
    But you haven't got the nerve--YOULIKEMET--8
    But now ((but now)) these days are gone
        ((these days are gone))--HELP--11
    But now ((but now)) these days are gone
        ((these days are gone))--HELP--11
    But ((but)) every now and then ((now and then))
        I feel so insecure--HELP--22
    But ((but)) every now and then ((now and then))
        I feel so insecure--HELP--22
    But now ((now)) these days are gone ((these
        days are gone))--HELP--31
    You're making me say that I've got nobody but you
        --ANOTHERGIR--2
    But as from today well I've got somebody that's

new --ANOTHERGIR--3
But as from today well I've seen somebody that's
    new --ANOTHERGIR--13
But as from today well I've seen somebody that's
    new --ANOTHERGIR--19
But when you told me--INEEDYOU--21
But it's so hard loving you.--ITSONLYLOV--7
But it's so hard loving you.--ITSONLYLOV--14
But as it is I'll dream of her tonight --IVEJUSTSEE
    --10
But other girls were never quite like this --
    IVEJUSTSEE--17
But you can do something in between.--DRIVEMYCAR
    --4
But I can show you a better time.--DRIVEMYCAR--12
But I've found a driver and that's a start.--
    DRIVEMYCAR--25
But you see now I'm too much in love.--IFINEEDS
    --9
But you see now I'm too much in love.--IFINEEDS
    --19
You don't look different, but you have changed --
    IMLOOKINGT--3
Your voice is soothing but the words aren't clear.
    --IMLOOKINGT--6
You were above me, but not today.--IMLOOKINGT--12
You don't look different, but you have changed --
    IMLOOKINGT--19
But of all these friends and lovers --INMYLIFE--9
But if your heart breaks, don't wait, turn me
    away --WAIT--5
But if your heart breaks, don't wait, turn me
    away --WAIT--21
But when I saw him with you I could feel my
    future fold.--WHATGOESON--7
But now the tide is turning I can see that I
    was blind.--WHATGOESON--16
I used to think of no-one else but you were just
    the same --WHATGOESON--22
But now I've got it the word is good.--THEWORD--8
But I can't get through, my hands are tied.--
    YOUWONTSEE--8
But I can turn away--YOUWONTSEE--10
But he wants to be a paperback writer--PAPERBACKW
    --12
But I need a break, ((writer))--PAPERBACKW--24
But you don't get me, you don't get me.--ANDYOURBIR
    --3
But you can't see me, you can't see me.--ANDYOURBIR
    --6
But you can't hear me, you can't hear me.--
    ANDYOURBIR--15
But now he's gone, she doesn't need him.--FORNOONE
    --19
Someone is speaking but she doesn't know he's
    there.--HERETHEREA--7
But to love her is to need her everywhere.--
    HERETHEREA--10
But to love her is to need her everywhere.--
    HERETHEREA--16
But if I seem to act unkind--IWANTTOTEL--9
But what you've got means such a lot to me.--
    LOVEYOUTWO--8
And you're working for no-one but me (Taxman).--
    TAXMAN--26
But listen to the colour of your dreams--TOMORROWNE
    --11
But it all works out--STRAWBERRY--9
But it's alright--STRAWBERRY--19
But, you know, I know when it's a dream--STRAWBERRY
    --27
But it's all wrong--STRAWBERRY--29
But I just had to look--DAYINTHELI--14
Man I was mean but I'm changing my scene--
    GETTINGBET--27
Nothing to say but what a day how's your boy been?
    --GOODMORNIN--3
I've got nothing to say but it's OK.--GOODMORNIN
    --5
I've got nothing to say but it's OK.--GOODMORNIN
    --16
I've got nothing to say but it's OK.--GOODMORNIN
    --25
But they're guaranteed to raise a smile.--
    SGTPEPPERS--4
But I thought you might like to know--SGTPEPPERS
    --20
We're sorry but it's time to go.--SGTPEPPREP--6
I can't tell you but I know it's mine.--WITHALITTL
    --22
Nothing you can say but you can learn how to play
    the game ((love))--ALLYOUN/YS--6
Nothing you can do but you can learn how to be
    you in time ((love))--ALLYOUN/YS--10

((I say yes but I may mean no))--HELLOGOODB--23
You say stop but I say go, go, go-HELLOGOODB--24
But nobody wants to know him--FOOLONTHEH--3
But the fool on the hill sees the sun going down--
   FOOLONTHEH--6
But nobody ever hears him--FOOLONTHEH--10
But the fool on the hill sees the sun going down--
   FOOLONTHEH--13
But the fool on the hill sees the sun going down--
   FOOLONTHEH--18
But when you talk about destruction --REVOLUTION
   --8
But if you want money for people with minds that
   hate --REVOLUTION--18
But if you go carrying pictures of Chairman Mao --
   REVOLUTION--28
(But when he looked so fierce) his mommy butted
   in --CONTINUING--28
But they don't arrive.--DONTPASSME--5
But I'm by myself.--DONTPASSME--13
I'm coming down fast but I'm miles above you --
   HELTERSKEL--5
Well, you may be a lover, but you ain't no
   dancer.--HELTERSKEL--7
I'm coming down fast but don't let me break you --
   HELTERSKEL--12
'cos you may be a lover, but you ain't no dancer.
   --HELTERSKEL--14
I'm coming down fast but don't let me break you --
   HELTERSKEL--22
'cos you may be a lover, but you ain't no dancer.
   --HELTERSKEL--24
I'm in love but I'm lazy--HONEYPIE--8
I'm in love but I'm lazy--HONEYPIE--30
But it never really mattered --IWILL--7
But I know what you would do.--IMSOTIRED--8
But it's no joke, it's doing me harm --IMSOTIRED
   --10
But it's no joke, it's doing me harm --IMSOTIRED
   --19
But I say it just to reach you, Julia.--JULIA--2
But if you want some fun (ha ha ha) --OBLADIOBLA
   --40
But when you talk about destruction --REVOLUTONE
   --11
But if you want money for people with minds that
   hate --REVOLUTONE--27
But everyone knew her as Nancy.--ROCKYRACCO--16
But Daniel was hot, he drew first and shot--
   ROCKYRACCO--21
But you'll have to have them all pulled out--
   SAVOYTRUFF--4
But you'll have to have them all pulled out--
   SAVOYTRUFF--9
But you'll have to have them all pulled out--
   SAVOYTRUFF--17
But what is sweet now turns so sour.--SAVOYTRUFF
   --20
But can you show me where you are?--SAVOYTRUFF--22
But you'll have to have them all pulled out--
   SAVOYTRUFF--26
But I am of the universe--YERBLUES--12
You think you know me but you haven't got a clue.
   --HEYBULLDOG--16
So take a piece, but not too much.--ITSALLTOOM
   --19
But they're not, we just wrote it like that.--
   ONLYANORTH--3
But they are, they just play it like that.--
   ONLYANORTH--6
But he knew it couldn't last.--GETBACK/45--2
But she was another man.--GETBACK/45--17
But she gets it while she can.--GETBACK/45--19
You don't take nothing with you but your soul -
   think!--BALLADOFJO--28
But right is only half of what's wrong --OLDBROWNSH
   --2
But she doesn't have a lot to say.--HERMAJESTY--2
But she changes from day to day.--HERMAJESTY--4
But I gotta get a bellyfull of wine.--HERMAJESTY
   --6
But as she's getting ready to go, a knock comes
   on the door --MAXWELLSIL--5
But when she turns her back on the boy, he
   creeps up from behind --MAXWELLSIL--12
But as the words are leaving his lips, a noise
   comes from behind --MAXWELLSIL--22
She's so goodlooking but she looks like a man.--
   POLYTHENEP--2
But now she sucks her thumb and wonders --
   SHECAMEINT--6
She could steal but she could not rob.--SHECAMEINT
   --19
But oh, that magic feeling, nowhere to go --

YOUNEVERGI--13
But she was a frying pan ((sweet Loretta
   Martin)).--GETBACK/LP--3
But he knew it couldn't last--GETBACK/LP--8
But she was another man--GETBACK/LP--23
But she gets it while she can.--GETBACK/LP--25
But still they lead me back to the long, winding
   road --LONGANDWIN--12

BUTTED
   (But when he looked so fierce) his mommy butted
      in --CONTINUING--28

BUTTERFLY
   When you sigh my my inside just flies, butterfly.
      --ITSONLYLOV--2

BUY
   CAN'T BUY ME LOVE.--CANTBUYMEL--Title
   Can't buy me love, oh, love, oh --CANTBUYMEL--1
   Can't buy me love, oh.--CANTBUYMEL--2
   I'll buy you a diamond ring my friend --CANTBUYMEL
      --3
   Money can't buy me love.--CANTBUYMEL--8
   Money can't buy me love.--CANTBUYMEL--14
   Can't buy me love, oh, everybody tells me so --
      CANTBUYMEL--15
   Can't buy me love oh - no, no, no - no.--CANTBUYMEL
      --16
   That money just can't buy --CANTBUYMEL--20
   Money can't buy me love.--CANTBUYMEL--22
   Can't buy me love, oh, everybody tells me so --
      CANTBUYMEL--25
   Can't buy me love oh - no, no, no - no.--CANTBUYMEL
      --26
   That money just can't buy --CANTBUYMEL--30
   Money can't buy me love.--CANTBUYMEL--32
   Can't buy me love, oh, love, oh --CANTBUYMEL--33
   Can't buy me love, oh, oh.--CANTBUYMEL--34
   To get you money to buy you things --HARDDAYSNI--9
   Home. (we gave her everything money could buy)--
      SHESLEAVIN--10
   Fun. (fun is the one thing that money can't buy)--
      SHESLEAVIN--30
   Saving up to buy some clothes--MEANMRMUST--5

BUYS
   That her baby buys her things, you know --IFEELFINE
      --9
   He buys her diamond rings, you know, she said so
      --IFEELFINE--10
   That her baby buys her things, you know --IFEELFINE
      --17
   He buys her diamond rings, you know, she said so
      --IFEELFINE--18
   Man buys ring, woman throws it away --IMDOWN--8
   Buys a twenty-carat golden ring (golden ring) --
      OBLADIOBLA--10

BY
   And keep you by my side--FROMMETOYO--12
   And keep you by my side--FROMMETOYO--23
   When you're by my side, you're the only one --
      LITTLECHIL--16
   She ought to do right by me--TICKETTORI--19
   She ought to do right by me.--TICKETTORI--22
   She ought to do right by me--TICKETTORI--32
   She ought to do right by me.--TICKETTORI--35
   I could be happy with you by my side--YESITIS--10
   I could be happy with you by my side--YESITIS--19
   I get high when I see you go by, my oh my--
      ITSONLYLOV--1
   Last night is the night I will remember you by --
      NIGHTBEFOR--9
   Last night is the night I will remember you by --
      NIGHTBEFOR--17
   I think you know by now--MICHELLE--17
   It's based on a novel by a man named Lear --
      PAPERBACKW--4
   Keeping an eye on the world going by my window --
      IMONLYSLEE--13
   Keeping an eye on the world going by my window --
      IMONLYSLEE--19
   Wearing the face that she keeps in a jar by the door
      --ELEANORRIG--7
   Then you decide to take a walk by the old school--
      GOODMORNIN--14
   Standing by a parking meter--LOVELYRITA--7
   Follow her down to a bridge by a fountain--

LUCYINTHES--12
Home. (we struggled hard all our lives to get by) --SHESLEAVIN--22
You can knit a sweater by the fireside--WHENIMSIXT --15
Oh I get by with a little help from my friends -- WITHALITTL--5
How do I feel by the end of the day?--WITHALITTL --10
No I get by with a little help from my friends -- WITHALITTL--12
Oh I get by with a little help from my friends -- WITHALITTL--23
Oh I get by with a little help from my friends -- WITHALITTL--30
Yes I get by with a little help from my friends -- WITHALITTL--33
By making his world a little colder.--HEYJUDE--13
Bill and his elephants were taken by surprise -- CONTINUING--18
Put on specially by the children for a lark.-- CRYBABYCRY--31
DON'T PASS ME BY.--DONTPASSME--Title
But I'm by myself.--DONTPASSME--13
And why I'm by myself --DONTPASSME--15
Don't pass me by, don't make me cry, don't make me blue --DONTPASSME--18
Don't pass me by - don't make me cry.--DONTPASSME --22
Don't pass me by, don't make me cry, don't make me blue --DONTPASSME--31
Don't pass me by, don't make me cry.--DONTPASSME --35
Don't pass me by, don't make me cry, don't make me blue --DONTPASSME--37
Don't pass me by - don't make me cry.--DONTPASSME --41
And Molly says this as she takes him by the hand: --OBLADIOBLA--4
By stealing the girl of his fancy --ROCKYRACCO--14
Honeymooning down by the Seine.--BALLADOFJO--10
Protected by a silver spoon --SHECAMEINT--5
By the banks of her own lagoon.--SHECAMEINT--7
((That was Can You Dig It? by Georgie Wood))--DIGIT--11
I dig a pygmy by Charles Hawtrey and the Deaf Aids (ha ha ha)--TWOOFUS--1

C

A, B, C, D --ALLTOGETHE--5

CABLE

Cut the cable, drop the cable.--YELLOWSUBM--22
Cut the cable, drop the cable.--YELLOWSUBM--22

CAKE

All the world is birthday cake --ITSALLTOOM--18
Eating chocolate cake in the bag.--BALLADOFJO--30
Questo obrigado tanta mucho cake and eat it carousel.--SUNKING--8

CALIFORNIA

For some California grass.--GETBACK/45--4
For some California grass.--GETBACK/LP--10

CALL

All you gotta do is call --ANYTIMEATA--2
Don't you be sad, just call me tonight.--ANYTIMEATA --9
All you gotta do is call --ANYTIMEATA--11
Call me tonight and I'll come to you.--ANYTIMEATA --18
All ya gotta do is call --ANYTIMEATA--20
All ya gotta do is call --ANYTIMEATA--23
All ya gotta do is call --ANYTIMEATA--26
Just call on me and I'll send it along--FROMMETOYO --5
Just/So call on me and I'll send it along--FROMMETOYO--9
Just call on me and I'll send it along--FROMMETOYO --17
Just call on me and I'll send it along--FROMMETOYO --20
Just call on me and I'll send it along--FROMMETOYO --28
Is call you on the phone --ALLIVEGOTT--3
Whenever you call --ALLIVEGOTT--14
Ya just gotta call on me, yeah --ALLIVEGOTT--15
Ya just gotta call on me.--ALLIVEGOTT--16
Is call you on the phone --ALLIVEGOTT--19

Whenever you call --ALLIVEGOTT--25
Ya just gotta call on me, yeah --ALLIVEGOTT--26
Ya just gotta call on me --ALLIVEGOTT--27
(Ooh) ya just gotta call on me --ALLIVEGOTT--28
I CALL YOUR NAME.--ICALLYOURN--Title
I call your name, but you're not there --ICALLYOURN --1
I never weep at night, I call your name.-- ICALLYOURN--10
I never weep at night, I call your name -- ICALLYOURN--10
I call your name, I call your name, (wuh) I call your name.--ICALLYOURN--18
I call your name, I call your name, (wuh) I call your name.--ICALLYOURN--18
I call your name, I call your name, (wuh) I call your name.--ICALLYOURN--18
And maybe you will get a call from me --IFINEEDEDS --11
And maybe you will get a call from me --IFINEEDEDS --21
When I call you up your line's engaged.--YOUWONTSEE --1
Ring my friend I said you'd call, Dr. Robert -- DRROBERT--1
Ring my friend I said you'd call, Dr. Robert -- DRROBERT--20
Ring my friend I said you'd call, Dr. Robert -- DRROBERT--21
Nothing to do to save his life call his wife in-- GOODMORNIN--2
I wonder should I call you --IMSOTIRED--7
They call me on and on across the universe.-- ACROSSTHEU--12

CALLED

Her name was Magill and she called herself Lil -- ROCKYRACCO--15
Now she and her man who called himself Dan-- ROCKYRACCO--17
Peter Brown called to say, you can make it OK -- BALLADOFJO--11

CALLING

And she keeps calling me back again.--IVEJUSTSEE --13
And she keeps calling me back again.--IVEJUSTSEE --20
And she keeps calling me back again.--IVEJUSTSEE --23
And she keeps calling me back again.--IVEJUSTSEE --31
And she keeps calling me back again.--IVEJUSTSEE --33
And she keeps calling me back again.--IVEJUSTSEE --35
Oh Danny Boy, the odes of Pan are calling.-- ONEAFTERNI--33

CALLS

Somebody calls you, you answer quite slowly-- LUCYINTHES--3
Julia, Julia oceanchild calls me --JULIA--3
Julia seashell eyes windy smile calls me --JULIA --5
Hmm hmm hmm, calls me --JULIA--15
Maxwell Edison, majoring in medicine, calls her on the phone --MAXWELLSIL--3
It calls me on and on across the universe.-- ACROSSTHEU--24

CAME

But I came back again.--ILLBEBACK--4
When I came to your door--NOREPLY--2
Oh yesterday came suddenly.--YESTERDAY--8
All about the girl who came to stay?--GIRL--2
Nobody came.--ELEANORRIG--23
Picking flowers for a friend who came to play -- CRYBABYCRY--13
Can you take me back where I came from --CRYBABYCRY --44
Can you take me back where I came from --CRYBABYCRY --46
Mmm can you take me where I came from --CRYBABYCRY --49
Now the doctor came in stinking of gin--ROCKYRACCO --31
She came along to turn on everyone--SEXYSADIE--10
We're so glad you came here --OLDBROWNSH--7
So glad you came here --OLDBROWNSH--15

So glad you came here --OLDBROWNSH--33
I'm so glad you came here --OLDBROWNSH--35
Bang, bang Maxwell's silver hammer came down
    upon her head --MAXWELLSIL--6
Bang, bang Maxwell's silver hammer came down
    upon her head --MAXWELLSIL--13
Bang, bang Maxwell's silver hammer came down
    upon his head --MAXWELLSIL--23
SHE CAME IN THROUGH THE BATHROOM WINDOW.--
    SHECAMEINT--Title
She came in through the bathroom window --
    SHECAMEINT--4
One sweet dream came true today --YOUNEVERGI--21
Came true today, came true today.--YOUNEVERGI--22
Came true today, came true today.--YOUNEVERGI--22

CAN

Send her back to me, 'cos everyone can see--
    MISERY--8
Send her back to me, 'cos everyone can see--
    MISERY--12
If there's anything I can do--FROMMETOYO--4
If there's anything I can do--FROMMETOYO--16
If there's anything I can do--FROMMETOYO--27
When I think about you, I can say--ILLGETYOU--11
Pride can hurt you too--SHELOVESYO--26
Like no other can.--IWANNABEYO--6
Like no other can.--IWANNABEYO--8
Like no other can (ooo).--IWANNABEYO--35
Like no other can.--IWANNABEYO--37
I don't know who can,--ICALLYOURN--6
I don't know who can,--ICALLYOURN--13
There, there's a place where I can go--THERESAPLA
    --1
There, there's a place where I can go--THERESAPLA
    --13
And show you what your loving man can do --
    ILLCRYINST--18
And show you what your loving man can do --
    ILLCRYINST--27
If there's anything I can do --TELLMEWHY--23
She's happy as can be, you know, she said so --
    IFEELFINE--2
Oh dear, what can I do?--BABYSINBLA--1
Tell me, oh what can I do?--BABYSINBLA--3
Oh dear, what can I do?--BABYSINBLA--7
Tell me, oh what can I do?--BABYSINBLA--9
Dear what can I do?--BABYSINBLA--16
Tell me oh what can I do?--BABYSINBLA--18
Dear what can I do?--BABYSINBLA--21
Tell me oh what can I do?--BABYSINBLA--27
Oh dear, what can I do?--BABYSINBLA--27
Tell me oh what can I do?--BABYSINBLA--29
One thing I can say girl --EIGHTDAYSA--11
One thing I can say girl --EIGHTDAYSA--31
How can I get through--TELLMEWHAT--19
How can I get through--TELLMEWHAT--28
Help me if you can, I'm feeling down--HELP--15
Help me if you can, I'm feeling down--HELP--25
Help me if you can, I'm feeling down--HELP--35
How can you laugh when you know I'm down?--IMDOWN
    --6
(How can you laugh) when you know I'm down?--IMDOWN
    --7
How can you laugh when you know I'm down?--IMDOWN
    --13
(How can you laugh) when you know I'm down?--IMDOWN
    --14
How can you laugh when you know I'm down?--IMDOWN
    --21
(How can you laugh) when you know I'm down?--IMDOWN
    --22
Can you hear me?--IMDOWN--26
Nobody in all the world can do what she can do --
    ANOTHERGIR--7
Nobody in all the world can do what she can do --
    ANOTHERGIR--7
I'm lonely as can be--INEEDYOU--4
The way you treat her what else can I do?--
    YOUREGONNA--17
The way you treat her what else can I do?--
    YOUREGONNA--24
I can see them laugh at me --YOUVEGOTTO--7
How can I even try --YOUVEGOTTO--11
I can never win --YOUVEGOTTO--15
WE CAN WORK IT OUT.--WECANWORKI--Title
We can work it out, we can work it out.--WECANWORKI
    --5
We can work it out, we can work it out.--WECANWORKI
    --5
You can get it wrong and still you think that
    it's alright.--WECANWORKI--7
We can work it out and get it straight or say

good night.--WECANWORKI--9
We can work it out, we can work it out.--WECANWORKI
    --10
We can work it out, we can work it out.--WECANWORKI
    --10
We can work it out, we can work it out.--WECANWORKI
    --19
We can work it out, we can work it out.--WECANWORKI
    --19
We can work it out, we can work it out.--WECANWORKI
    --28
We can work it out, we can work it out.--WECANWORKI
    --28
But you can do something in between.--DRIVEMYCAR
    --4
Baby you can drive my car --DRIVEMYCAR--5
Baby you can drive my car --DRIVEMYCAR--7
But I can show you a better time.--DRIVEMYCAR--12
Baby you can drive my car --DRIVEMYCAR--13
Baby you can drive my car --DRIVEMYCAR--15
Baby you can drive my car --DRIVEMYCAR--18
Baby you can drive my car --DRIVEMYCAR--20
Baby you can drive my car --DRIVEMYCAR--26
Baby you can drive my car --DRIVEMYCAR--28
With lovers and friends I still can recall --
    INMYLIFE--6
He's as blind as he can be --NOWHEREMAN--10
Nowhere Man can you see me at all?--NOWHEREMAN--12
You better run for your life if you can, little
    girl --RUNFORYOUR--5
You better run for your life if you can, little
    girl --RUNFORYOUR--13
You better run for your life if you can, little
    girl --RUNFORYOUR--21
You better run for your life if you can, little
    girl --RUNFORYOUR--29
That we can have if we close our eyes.--THINKFORYO
    --5
That I've been good, as good as I can be.--WAIT--10
That I've been good, as good as I can be.--WAIT--18
But now the tide is turning I can see that I
    was blind.--WHATGOESON--16
But I can turn away--YOUWONTSEE--10
I can make it longer if you like the style,
    ((paperback))--PAPERBACKW--17
I can change it round, ((writer))--PAPERBACKW--18
If you really like it you can have the rights,
    ((paperback))--PAPERBACKW--21
If you must return it you can send it here,
    ((paperback))--PAPERBACKW--23
I can show you that when it starts to rain (when
    the rain comes down)--RAIN--9
I can show you, I can show you ((show you)).--RAIN
    --11
I can show you, I can show you ((show you)).--RAIN
    --11
Can you hear me that when it rains and shines
    (when it rains and shines)--RAIN--14
Can you hear me, can you hear me? ((hear me))--
    RAIN--16
Can you hear me, can you hear me? ((hear me))--
    RAIN--16
AND YOUR BIRD CAN SING.--ANDYOURBIR--Title
And your bird can sing --ANDYOURBIR--2
And your bird can swing --ANDYOURBIR--14
He does everything he can, Dr. Robert.--DRROBERT
    --5
No-one can succeed like Dr. Robert.--DRROBERT--10
He does everything he can, Dr. Robert.--DRROBERT
    --17
I've got something I can laugh about.--GOODDAYSUN
    --3
What can I do, what can I be?--GOTTOGETYO--16
What can I do, what can I be?--GOTTOGETYO--16
Nobody can deny that there's something there.--
    HERETHEREA--4
Both of us thinking how good it can be--HERETHEREA
    --6
Love me while you can--LOVEYOUTWO--4
You're doing the best that I can.--GETTINGBET--15
And I'm doing the best that I can.--GETTINGBET--28
Nothing can come between us--LOVELYRITA--5
You can knit a sweater by the fireside--WHENIMSIXT
    --15
Every summer we can rent a cottage--WHENIMSIXT--22
No-one else can make you change--WITHINYOUW--17
There's nothing you can do that can't be done
    ((love))--ALLYOUN/YS--4
Nothing you can sing that can't be sung ((love))--
    ALLYOUN/YS--5
Nothing you can say but you can learn how to play
    the game ((love))--ALLYOUN/YS--6
Nothing you can say but you can learn how to play
    the game ((love))--ALLYOUN/YS--6

Nothing you can make that can't be made ((love))--
    ALLYOUN/YS--8
No-one you can save that can't be saved ((love))--
    ALLYOUN/YS--9
Nothing you can do but you can learn how to be
    you in time ((love))--ALLYOUN/YS--10
Nothing you can do but you can learn how to be
    you in time ((love))--ALLYOUN/YS--10
There's nothing you can know that isn't known
    ((love))--ALLYOUN/YS--19
Nothing you can see that isn't shown ((love))--
    ALLYOUN/YS--20
There's nowhere you can be that isn't where
    you're meant to be ((love))--ALLYOUN/YS--21
Far as the eye can see.--BABYYOUREA--6
((I can stay till it's time to go)).--HELLOGOODB
    --25
They can see that he's just a fool--FOOLONTHEH--4
They can tell what he wants to do--FOOLONTHEH--16
I can know all things on earth.--INNERLIGHT--2
You can know all things on earth.--INNERLIGHT--9
You can know the ways of heaven.--INNERLIGHT--11
Then you can start to make it better.--HEYJUDE--4
Then you can start to make it better.--HEYJUDE--18
(Well you know you can make it, Jude, you've
    just gotta break it.)--HEYJUDE--46
Don't you know that you can count me out?--
    REVOLUTION--9
We're all doing what we can.--REVOLUTION--17
All I can tell you is brother you have to wait.--
    REVOLUTION--19
Can you take me back where I came from --CRYBABYCRY
    --44
Can you take me back?--CRYBABYCRY--45
Can you take me back where I came from --CRYBABYCRY
    --46
Brother, can you take me back --CRYBABYCRY--47
Can you take me back?--CRYBABYCRY--48
Mmm can you take me where I came from --CRYBABYCRY
    --49
Can you take me back?--CRYBABYCRY--50
Well here's another place you can go--GLASSONION
    --3
You know that we're as close as can be - man--
    GLASSONION--9
Well here's another place you can be--GLASSONION
    --19
I know nobody can do me no harm ((oh, yeah)) --
    HAPPINESSI--24
Sing it loud so I can hear you --IWILL--15
I can only speak my mind, Julia.--JULIA--12
Now I can see you, be you --LONGLONGLO--9
How can I ever misplace you?--LONGLONGLO--10
You can see them out for dinner--PIGGIES--17
Don't you know that you can count me out (in)?--
    REVOLUTONE--12
We're all doing what we can.--REVOLUTONE--25
Well all I can tell you is brother you have to
    wait.--REVOLUTONE--28
But can you show me where you are?--SAVOYTRUFF--22
Can I have a little more?--ALLTOGETHE--2
Can I bring my friend to tea?--ALLTOGETHE--6
Can I take my friend to bed?--ALLTOGETHE--18
You can talk to me--HEYBULLDOG--9
You can talk to me--HEYBULLDOG--10
You can talk to me--HEYBULLDOG--11
If you're lonely you can talk to me.--HEYBULLDOG
    --12
You can talk to me--HEYBULLDOG--17
You can talk to me--HEYBULLDOG--18
You can talk to me--HEYBULLDOG--19
If you're lonely you can talk to me - hey!--
    HEYBULLDOG--20
Can you dig it?--DONTLETMED--32
But she gets it while she can.--GETBACK/45--19
You know how hard it can be --BALLADOFJO--6
Peter Brown called to say, you can make it OK --
    BALLADOFJO--11
You can get married in Gibraltar near Spain.--
    BALLADOFJO--12
You know how hard it can be --BALLADOFJO--14
You know how hard it can be --BALLADOFJO--22
You know how hard it can be--BALLADOFJO--34
You know how hard it can be.--BALLADOFJO--42
One thing I can tell you is you got to be free--
    COMETOGETH--20
Hold you in his armchair you can feel his disease
    --COMETOGETH--30
Can I take you out to the pictures, Joan?--
    MAXWELLSIL--4
((That was Can You Dig It? by Georgie
    Wood))--DIGIT--11
But she gets it while she can.--GETBACK/LP--25
Well you can celebrate anything you want--IDIGAPONY
    --7
Yes you can celebrate anything you want.--IDIGAPONY
    --8
Well you can penetrate any place you go--IDIGAPONY
    --10
Yes you can penetrate any place you go--IDIGAPONY
    --11
Well you can radiate everything you are--IDIGAPONY
    --17
Yes you can radiate everything you are.--IDIGAPONY
    --18
Well you can imitate everyone you know--IDIGAPONY
    --20
Yes you can imitate everyone you know--IDIGAPONY
    --21
Well you can indicate everything you see--IDIGAPONY
    --27
Yes you can indicate anything you see.--IDIGAPONY
    --28
Well you can syndicate any boat you rode/rowed--
    IDIGAPONY--30
Yeah you can syndicate any boat you rode/rowed--
    IDIGAPONY--31
All I can hear --IMEMINE--14
All I can hear --IMEMINE--27

CAN'T

I can't believe it's happened to me --ASKMEWHY--12
I can't conceive of any more misery.--ASKMEWHY--13
I can't believe it's happened to me --ASKMEWHY--24
I can't conceive of any more misery.--ASKMEWHY--25
Can't she see she'll always be the only one,
    only one.--MISERY--7
And you know that can't be bad--SHELOVESYO--9
And you know that can't be bad--SHELOVESYO--17
And you know that can't be bad--SHELOVESYO--29
I can't believe--DONTBOTHER--9
I can't hide--IWANTTOHOL--17
I can't hide--IWANTTOHOL--18
I can't hide.--IWANTTOHOL--19
I can't hide--IWANTTOHOL--30
I can't hide.--IWANTTOHOL--31
I can't hide.--IWANTTOHOL--32
CAN'T BUY ME LOVE.--CANTBUYMEL--Title
Can't buy me love, oh, love, oh --CANTBUYMEL--1
Can't buy me love, oh.--CANTBUYMEL--2
Money can't buy me love.--CANTBUYMEL--8
Money can't buy me love.--CANTBUYMEL--14
Can't buy me love, oh, everybody tells me so --
    CANTBUYMEL--15
Can't buy me love oh - no, no, no - no.--CANTBUYMEL
    --16
That money just can't buy --CANTBUYMEL--20
Money can't buy me love.--CANTBUYMEL--22
Can't buy me love, oh, everybody tells me so --
    CANTBUYMEL--25
Can't buy me love oh - no, no, no - no.--CANTBUYMEL
    --26
That money just can't buy --CANTBUYMEL--30
Money can't buy me love.--CANTBUYMEL--32
Can't buy me love, oh, love, oh --CANTBUYMEL--33
Can't buy me love, oh, oh.--CANTBUYMEL--34
YOU CAN'T DO THAT.--YOUCANTDOT--Title
Oh you can't do that.--YOUCANTDOT--8
Oh you can't do that.--YOUCANTDOT--17
I can't help my feelings--YOUCANTDOT--25
Oh you can't do that - no!--YOUCANTDOT--31
You can't do that--YOUCANTDOT--32
You can't do that--YOUCANTDOT--33
You can't do that--YOUCANTDOT--34
You can't do that--YOUCANTDOT--35
You can't do that--YOUCANTDOT--36
I can't help my feelings--YOUCANTDOT--44
Oh you can't do that.--YOUCANTDOT--50
Oh, I can't sleep at night since you've been
    gone --ICALLYOURN--3
I never weep at night, I can't go on.--ICALLYOURN
    --4
Don't you know I can't take it?--ICALLYOURN--5
Oh, I can't sleep at night, but just the same --
    ICALLYOURN--9
Don't you know I can't take it?--ICALLYOURN--12
Oh, I can't sleep at night, but just the same --
    ICALLYOURN--16
Can't you see, can't you see?--ISHOULDHAV--6
Can't you see, can't you see?--ISHOULDHAV--6
Can't you see, can't you see?--ISHOULDHAV--16
Can't you see, can't you see?--ISHOULDHAV--16
But I can't, so I'll cry instead.--ILLCRYINST--5
I can't talk to people that I meet.--ILLCRYINST--7
But I can't, so I'll cry instead.--ILLCRYINST--10
Let's pretend we just can't see his face.--
    IMHAPPYJUS--17

Let's pretend we just can't see his face.--
    IMHAPPYJUS--25
If you don't I really can't go on --TELLMEWHY--15
'cos I really can't stand it --TELLMEWHY--24
Can't stop thinking about her now.--EVERYLITTL--6
Can't you try to see that I'm-TELLMEWHAT--20
Can't you try to see that I'm-TELLMEWHAT--29
You tell lies thinking I can't see --IMDOWN--1
You can't cry 'cos you're laughing at me --IMDOWN
    --2
I just can't go on any more.--INEEDYOU--15
I just can't go on any more.--INEEDYOU--25
I can't forget the time or place--IVEJUSTSEE--2
I can't forget the time or place--IVEJUSTSEE--25
If she's gone I can't go on --YOUVEGOTTO--3
Do I have to keep on talking till I can't go on?--
    WECANWORKI--2
She said baby can't you see?--DRIVEMYCAR--2
And I can't spend my whole life trying--RUNFORYOUR
    --11
And though you still can't see --THINKFORYO--12
But I can't get through, my hands are tied.--
    YOUWONTSEE--8
And I just can't go on--YOUWONTSEE--19
And I just can't go on--YOUWONTSEE--28
But you can't see me, you can't see me.--ANDYOURBIR
    --6
But you can't see me, you can't see me.--ANDYOURBIR
    --6
But you can't hear me, you can't hear me.--
    ANDYOURBIR--15
But you can't hear me, you can't hear me.--
    ANDYOURBIR--15
A new one can't be bought--LOVEYOUTWO--7
That is you can't, you know, tune in--STRAWBERRY
    --18
I used to get mad at my school (now I can't
    complain)--GETTINGBET--3
The teachers who taught me weren't cool (now I
    can't complain)--GETTINGBET--4
A little better all the time (it can't get no
    worse)--GETTINGBET--8
A little better all the time (it can't get no
    worse)--GETTINGBET--17
A little better all the time (it can't get no
    worse)--GETTINGBET--30
Fun. (fun is the one thing that money can't buy)--
    SHESLEAVIN--30
I can't tell you but I know it's mine.--WITHALITTL
    --22
They can't see--WITHINYOUW--26
There's nothing you can do that can't be done
    ((love))--ALLYOUN/YS--4
Nothing you can sing that can't be sung ((love))--
    ALLYOUN/YS--5
Nothing you can make that can't be made ((love))--
    ALLYOUN/YS--8
No-one you can save that can't be saved ((love))--
    ALLYOUN/YS--9
You know I can't sleep, I can't stop my brain --
    IMSOTIRED--11
You know I can't sleep, I can't stop my brain --
    IMSOTIRED--11
You know I can't sleep, I can't stop my brain --
    IMSOTIRED--20
You know I can't sleep, I can't stop my brain --
    IMSOTIRED--20
My love is something you can't reject.--OLDBROWNSH
    --23
Because we know we can't be found.--OCTOPUSSGA--14
I've got a feeling, a feeling I can't hide --
    IVEGOTAFEE--3
Everybody let their hair down ((a feeling I
    can't hide, oh no)) --IVEGOTAFEE--33

CANNOT
Your lips are moving, I cannot hear --IMLOOKINGT
    --5
When I cannot sing my heart --JULIA--11

CAP
In a cap she looked much older--LOVELYRITA--10

CAPTAIN
Captain, Captain.)--YELLOWSUBM--24
Captain, Captain.)--YELLOWSUBM--24
So Captain Marvel zapped him right between the
    eyes. (Zap!)--CONTINUING--19

CAR

DRIVE MY CAR.--DRIVEMYCAR--Title
Baby you can drive my car --DRIVEMYCAR--5
Baby you can drive my car --DRIVEMYCAR--7
Baby you can drive my car --DRIVEMYCAR--13
Baby you can drive my car --DRIVEMYCAR--15
Baby you can drive my car --DRIVEMYCAR--18
Baby you can drive my car --DRIVEMYCAR--20
I got no car and it's breaking my heart --
    DRIVEMYCAR--24
Baby you can drive my car --DRIVEMYCAR--26
Baby you can drive my car --DRIVEMYCAR--28
If you drive a car, I'll tax the street
    ((car))--TAXMAN--11
If you drive a car, I'll tax the street,
    ((car))--TAXMAN--11
He blew his mind out in a car--DAYINTHELI--6
You were in a car crash --DONTPASSME--25

CARATHON
Quando paramucho mi amore defeliche carathon --
    SUNKING--6

CARE
You'll never know how much I really care.--
    DOYOUWANTT--2
'cos I don't care too much for money --CANTBUYMEL
    --7
I don't care too much for money --CANTBUYMEL--13
I don't care too much for money --CANTBUYMEL--21
I don't care too much for money --CANTBUYMEL--31
Eight days a week is not enough to show I care.--
    EIGHTDAYSA--18
Eight days a week is not enough to show I care.--
    EIGHTDAYSA--28
I've had a drink or two and I don't care --
    IDONTWANTT--5
Though I've had a drink or two and I don't care --
    IDONTWANTT--22
But she don't care.--TICKETTORI--8
But she don't care.--TICKETTORI--16
But she don't care.--TICKETTORI--29
But she don't care.--TICKETTORI--43
My baby don't care--TICKETTORI--44
My baby don't care--TICKETTORI--45
My baby don't care--TICKETTORI--46
My baby don't care--TICKETTORI--47
My baby don't care--TICKETTORI--48
What does he care?--ELEANORRIG--16
And if she's beside me I know I need never care--
    HERETHEREA--9
And if she's beside me I know I need never care--
    HERETHEREA--15
They don't care what goes on around.--PIGGIES--12

CARESSING
Possessing and caressing me.--ACROSSTHEU--5

CAROUSEL
Questo obrigado tanta mucho cake and eat it
    carousel.--SUNKING--8

CARRY
Don't carry the world upon your shoulder.--HEYJUDE
    --11
CARRY THAT WEIGHT.--CARRYTHATW--Title
Boy, you're gonna carry that weight--CARRYTHATW--1
Carry that weight a long time.--CARRYTHATW--2
Boy, you're gonna carry that weight--CARRYTHATW--3
Carry that weight a long time.--CARRYTHATW--4
Boy, you're gonna carry that weight--CARRYTHATW--9
Carry that weight a long time.--CARRYTHATW--10
Boy, you're gonna carry that weight--CARRYTHATW--11
Carry that weight a long time.--CARRYTHATW--12

CARRYING
But if you go carrying pictures of Chairman Mao --
    REVOLUTION--28
If you go carrying pictures of Chairman Mao --
    REVOLUTONE--43

CARVE
Carve your number on my wall --IFINEEDEDS--10
Carve your number on my wall --IFINEEDEDS--20

CASE
Leave it till tomorrow to unpack my case --

BACKINTHEU--10
In case of accidents he always took his mom --
    CONTINUING--8

CAST-IRON
Standing on the cast-iron shore - yeah--GLASSONION
    --12

CAT
Bop - bop cat bop --FORYOUBLUE--8

CATCH
If I catch you talking--YOUCANTDOT--3
Catch you with another man --RUNFORYOUR--7
Catch you with another man --RUNFORYOUR--15
Catch you with another man --RUNFORYOUR--23
Catch you with another man --RUNFORYOUR--31
I didn't catch your name --IWILL--6

CAUGHT
I caught you talking to him--YOUCANTDOT--10
When I caught a glimpse of Rita--LOVELYRITA--8
Caught the early plane back to London --BALLADOFJO
    --37
PC Thirty-One said, we caught a dirty one,
    Maxwell stands alone --MAXWELLSIL--17

CAUSE
That might cause you pain--YOUCANTDOT--2
You're gonna cause more misery.--THINKFORYO--14

CAVE
In an octopus's garden near a cave.--OCTOPUSSGA--12

CEILING
Lying there and staring at the ceiling --IMONLYSLEE
    --15

CELEBRATE
Well you can celebrate anything you want--IDIGAPONY
    --7
Yes you can celebrate anything you want.--IDIGAPONY
    --8

CELEBRATED
The celebrated Mr. K.--BEINGFORTH--8

CELEBRATIONS
And in the middle of the celebrations--CARRYTHATW
    --7

CELLOPHANE
Cellophane flowers of yellow and green--LUCYINTHES
    --5

CERTAIN
Yes I'm certain that it happens all the time.--
    WITHALITTL--20

CERTAINLY
It's certainly a thrill--SGTPEPPERS--15

CHA
Cha, cha, cha --HELLOBOODB--33
Cha, cha, cha --HELLOGOODB--33
Cha, cha, cha --HELLOGOODB--33
Cha, cha, cha --HELLOGOODB--37
Cha, cha, cha --HELLOGOODB--37
Cha, cha, cha --HELLOGOODB--37
(Uh) cha, cha --HELLOGOODB--40
(Uh) cha, cha --HELLOGOODB--40
Cha, cha --HELLOGOODB--42
Cha, cha --HELLOGOODB--42

CHA-CHA-CHA
Take a cha-cha-cha chance (birthday) --BIRTHDAY--12
Take a cha-cha-cha chance (birthday) --BIRTHDAY--17

CHAIN
The clouds will be a daisy chain --DEARPRUDEN--18

CHAIR
And I noticed there wasn't a chair.--NORWEGIANW--10

CHAIRMAN
But if you go carrying pictures of Chairman Mao --
    REVOLUTION--28
If you go carrying pictures of Chairman Mao --
    REVOLUTONE--43

CHALLENGE
In this way Mr. K. will challenge the world.--
    BEINGFORTH--7

CHANCE
Baby take a chance with me.--LITTLECHIL--4
Baby take a chance with me.--LITTLECHIL--8
Baby take a chance with me (wuh yeah).--LITTLECHIL
    --15
Baby take a chance with me, oh yeah --LITTLECHIL
    --22
Baby take a chance with me, oh yeah --LITTLECHIL
    --23
Baby take a chance with me, oh yeah --LITTLECHIL
    --24
Baby take a chance with me, oh yeah.--LITTLECHIL
    --25
There's a chance that we might fall apart before
    too long.--WECANWORKI--18
There's a chance that we might fall apart before
    too long.--WECANWORKI--27
Give the word a chance to say --THEWORD--25
Take a cha-cha-cha chance (birthday) --BIRTHDAY--12
Take a cha-cha-cha chance (birthday) --BIRTHDAY--17
You know they didn't even give us a chance.--
    BALLADOFJO--4
There is still a chance that they will see --
    LETITBE/45--13
There is still a chance that they will see --
    LETITBE/LP--13

CHANGE
When I'm gonna change/make your mind--ILLGETYOU--17
I see no reason to change mine --NOTASECOND--5
I see no reason to change mine --NOTASECOND--16
She's gonna change her mind (she's gonna change
    her mind)--YOUREGONNA--4
She's gonna change her mind (she's gonna change
    her mind)--YOUREGONNA--4
She's gonna change her mind (she's gonna change
    her mind)--YOUREGONNA--26
She's gonna change her mind (she's gonna change
    her mind)--YOUREGONNA--26
I can change it round, ((writer))--PAPERBACKW--18
No-one else can make you change--WITHINYOUW--17
We all wanna change the world.--REVOLUTION--4
We all want to change the world.--REVOLUTION--7
You say you'll change the constitution --REVOLUTION
    --22
We all want to change your head.--REVOLUTION--24
We all wanna change the world.--REVOLUTONE--7
We all want to change the world.--REVOLUTONE--10
You say you'll change the constitution --REVOLUTONE
    --35
We'd all love to change our head.--REVOLUTONE--37
Nothing's gonna change my world --ACROSSTHEU--7
Nothing's gonna change my world --ACROSSTHEU--8
Nothing's gonna change my world --ACROSSTHEU--9
Nothing's gonna change my world.--ACROSSTHEU--10
Nothing's gonna change my world --ACROSSTHEU--16
Nothing's gonna change my world --ACROSSTHEU--17
Nothing's gonna change my world --ACROSSTHEU--18
Nothing's gonna change my world --ACROSSTHEU--19
Nothing's gonna change my world --ACROSSTHEU--26
Nothing's gonna change my world --ACROSSTHEU--27
Nothing's gonna change my world --ACROSSTHEU--28
Nothing's gonna change my world.--ACROSSTHEU--29

CHANGED
And now you've changed your mind--NOTASECOND--4
And now you've changed your mind --NOTASECOND--15
Now I find ((and now I find)) I've changed
    my mind--HELP--13
And now ((now)) my life has changed ((my life
    has changed))--HELP--19
And now ((now)) my life has changed ((my life

has changed))--HELP--19
Now I find ((and now I find)) I've changed
  my mind--HELP--33
Now today I find, you have changed your mind--
  NIGHTBEFOR--3
Now today I find you have changed your mind--
  NIGHTBEFOR--13
You don't look different, but you have changed --
  IMLOOKINGT--3
You don't look different, but you have changed --
  IMLOOKINGT--19
Yeah, oh baby you've changed.--IMLOOKINGT--21
You've changed.--IMLOOKINGT--24
You've changed.--IMLOOKINGT--25
You've changed.--IMLOOKINGT--26
You've changed.--IMLOOKINGT--27
All my life, though some have changed.--INMYLIFE
  --2
He didn't notice that the lights had changed--
  DAYINTHELI--7
Nothing has changed it's still the same--GOODMORNIN
  --15

CHANGES
But she changes from day to day.--HERMAJESTY--4

CHANGING
Changing my life with a wave of her hand--
  HERETHEREA--3
Man I was mean but I'm changing my scene--
  GETTINGBET--27
Changing faster than the weather --OLDBROWNSH--24

CHARITY
Giving all your clothes to charity.--BALLADOFJO--26

CHARLES
I dig a pygmy by Charles Hawtrey and the Deaf
  Aids (ha ha ha)--TWOOFUS--1

CHASING
You and me chasing paper --TWOOFUS--21
You and me chasing paper --TWOOFUS--30

CHECKED
Rocky Raccoon checked into his room --ROCKYRACCO
  --9
Gideon checked out and he left it no doubt ((oh
  - Rocky - oh))--ROCKYRACCO--38

CHERRY
Cool cherry cream, nice apple tart --SAVOYTRUFF--6

CHICKA
Mundo paparatsi mi amore chicka ferde parasol --
  SUNKING--7

CHILD
LITTLE CHILD.--LITTLECHIL--Title
Little child, little child --LITTLECHIL--1
Little child, little child --LITTLECHIL--1
Little child, won't you dance with me?--LITTLECHIL
  --2
Little child, little child --LITTLECHIL--5
Little child, little child --LITTLECHIL--5
Little child, won't you dance with me?--LITTLECHIL
  --6
Little child, little child --LITTLECHIL--12
Little child, little child --LITTLECHIL--12
Little child, won't you dance with me?--LITTLECHIL
  --13
Little child, little child --LITTLECHIL--19
Little child, little child --LITTLECHIL--19
Little child, won't you dance with me?--LITTLECHIL
  --20
Monday's child has learned to tie his bootlace.--
  LADYMADONN--7
Dear Prudence, like a little child.--DEARPRUDEN--17

CHILDLIKE
Childlike, no-one understands--HEYBULLDOG--5

CHILDREN

The little children laugh at him behind his back--
  PENNYLANE--6
Lady Madonna, children at your feet --LADYMADONN
  --1
Lady Madonna, children at your feet --LADYMADONN
  --18
All de children sing:--CONTINUING--10
All de children sing:--CONTINUING--20
The children asked him if to kill was not a sin --
  CONTINUING--27
All the children sing:--CONTINUING--30
Playing piano for the children of the King.--
  CRYBABYCRY--7
Put on specially by the children for a lark.--
  CRYBABYCRY--31
Desmond lets the children lend a hand --OBLADIOBLA
  --21
Molly lets the children lend a hand --OBLADIOBLA
  --33
All good children go to heaven.--YOUNEVERGI--25
All good children go to heaven.--YOUNEVERGI--27
All good children go to heaven.--YOUNEVERGI--29
All good children go to heaven.--YOUNEVERGI--31
All good children go to heaven.--YOUNEVERGI--33
All good children go to heaven.--YOUNEVERGI--35
All good children go to heaven.--YOUNEVERGI--37
All good children go to heaven--YOUNEVERGI--39
All good children...--YOUNEVERGI--41

CHILDRENS'
Painting pictures for the childrens' holiday.--
  CRYBABYCRY--15

CHIP
I got a chip on my shoulder that's bigger than my
  feet.--ILLCRYINST--6

CHOCOLATE
Eating chocolate cake in the bag.--BALLADOFJO--30

CHOKING
Expert texpert, choking smokers, don't you
  think the joker laughs at you?--IAMTHEWALR--21

CHOP
Bom-pa bom, chop the tree --ALLTOGETHE--10
Bom-pa bom, chop the tree --ALLTOGETHE--30

CHORD
Me hand's getting - a too cold to play a chord now.
  --IDIGAPONY--38

CHORDS
You may think the chords are going wrong --
  ONLYANORTH--2
It doesn't really matter what chords I play --
  ONLYANORTH--7

CHRIST
Christ! you know it ain't easy --BALLADOFJO--5
Christ! you know it ain't easy --BALLADOFJO--13
Christ! you know it ain't easy --BALLADOFJO--21
Christ! you know it ain't easy --BALLADOFJO--33
Christ! you know it ain't easy --BALLADOFJO--41

CHUCK
Vera, Chuck and Dave.--WHENIMSIXT--27

CHURCH
Eleanor Rigby picks up the rice in the church--
  ELEANORRIG--3
Eleanor Rigby died in the church--ELEANORRIG--21

CIA
And the CIA--DIGIT--5

CIGARETTE
Although I'm so tired, I'll have another
  cigarette--IMSOTIRED--15

CITY

CITY
Mr. City policeman sitting pretty little
policemen in a row--IAMTHEWALR--9

CLASS
She tells Max to stay when the class has gone
away --MAXWELLSIL--10

CLEAN
He likes to keep his fire-engine clean--PENNYLANE
--14
It's a clean machine.--PENNYLANE--15
Always have clean shirts to play around in.--
PIGGIES--10

CLEANER
Sweet Moretta Fart she thought she was a cleaner--
GETBACK/LP--2

CLEAR
Your voice is soothing but the words aren't clear.
--IMLOOKINGT--6
Little darling, it seems like years since it's
been clear.--HERECOMEST--19

CLIMB
Climb in the back with your head in the clouds--
LUCYINTHES--18

CLIMBING
Semolina pilchard climbing up the Eiffel Tower--
IAMTHEWALR--25

CLINGING
And his clinging wife doesn't understand.--
PAPERBACKW--9

CLOCK
I hear the clock a - ticking --DONTPASSME--10

CLOSE
Close your eyes and I'll kiss you --ALLMYLOVIN--1
Close your eyes and I'll kiss you --ALLMYLOVIN--15
That we can have if we close our eyes.--THINKFORYO
--5
You know that we're as close as can be - man--
GLASSONION--9
Close your eyes and I'll close mine --GOODNIGHT--7
Close your eyes and I'll close mine --GOODNIGHT--7
Close your eyes and I'll close mine --GOODNIGHT--14
Close your eyes and I'll close mine --GOODNIGHT--14

CLOSED
Living is easy with eyes closed--STRAWBERRY--6
Everything is closed it's like a ruin--GOODMORNIN
--10

CLOSER
Whoa closer --DOYOUWANTT--5
Whoa closer, (dodahdo)--DOYOUWANTT--11
Whoa closer, (dodahdo)--DOYOUWANTT--19

CLOSING
Silently closing her bedroom door--SHESLEAVIN--2

CLOTHES
Scarlet were the clothes she wore--YESITIS--5
It doesn't really matter what clothes I wear --
ONLYANORTH--10
Giving all your clothes to charity.--BALLADOFJO--26
Saving up to buy some clothes--MEANMRMUST--5

CLOUD
Well on the way, head in a cloud--FOOLONTHEH--8
Julia sleeping sand silent cloud touch me --JULIA
--13
Black cloud crossed my mind --YERBLUES--24

CLOUDS
Big and black the clouds may be--TELLMEWHAT--9

CLOUDS
Climb in the back with your head in the clouds--
LUCYINTHES--18
The clouds will be a daisy chain --DEARPRUDEN--18

CLOUDY
And when the night is cloudy --LETITBE/45--21
And when the night is cloudy --LETITBE/LP--21

CLOWN
Although I laugh and I act like a clown --IMALOSER
--9

CLOWNS
Gather round all you clowns--YOUVEGOTTO--17

CLUB
SGT. PEPPER'S LONELY HEARTS CLUB BAND.--SGTPEPPERS
--Title
Sgt. Pepper's Lonely Hearts Club Band.--SGTPEPPERS
--7
We're Sgt. Pepper's Lonely Hearts Club Band--
SGTPEPPERS--8
Sgt. Pepper's Lonely Hearts Club Band--SGTPEPPERS
--10
Sgt. Pepper's Lonely Hearts Club Band.--SGTPEPPERS
--13
And Sgt. Pepper's Lonely Hearts Club Band.--
SGTPEPPERS--25
SGT. PEPPER'S LONELY HEARTS CLUB BAND
(REPRISE).--SGTPEPPREP--Title
We're Sgt. Pepper's Lonely Hearts Club Band --
SGTPEPPREP--3
Sgt. Pepper's Lonely Hearts Club Band --SGTPEPPREP
--5
Sgt. Pepper's Lonely Hearts Club Band --SGTPEPPREP
--11
Sgt. Pepper's one and only Lonely Hearts Club
Band --SGTPEPPREP--13
Sgt. Pepper's Lonely Hearts Club Band.--SGTPEPPREP
--17

CLUBS
She worked at fifteen clubs a day--SHECAMEINT--13

CLUE
Well here's another clue for you all:--GLASSONION
--10
You think you know me but you haven't got a clue.
--HEYBULLDOG--16

CLUTCHING
Clutching her handkerchief--SHESLEAVIN--5
Clutching forks and knives to eat the bacon.--
PIGGIES--19

COAT
Found my coat and grabbed my hat--DAYINTHELI--23

COCA-COLA
He shoot Coca-cola--COMETOGETH--18

COCOANUT
Cocoanut fudge really blows down those blues
(wuh) --SAVOYTRUFF--8

COFFEE
Coffee dessert - yes you know it's good news --
SAVOYTRUFF--3
Coffee dessert - yes you know it's good news
(wuh) --SAVOYTRUFF--25

COLD
If you get too cold, I'll tax the heat,
((cold))--TAXMAN--13
If you get too cold, I'll tax the heat,
((cold))--TAXMAN--13
About the love that's gone so cold--WITHINYOUW--22
Little darling, it's been a long, cold lonely
winter.--HERECOMEST--4
Me hand's getting - a too cold to play a chord now.
--IDIGAPONY--38
Come on baby, don't be cold as ice --ONEAFTERNI--4

Come on baby, don't be cold as ice --ONEAFTERNI--9
Come on baby, don't be cold as ice --ONEAFTERNI--18
Come on baby, don't be cold as ice.--ONEAFTERNI--28

COLDER
By making his world a little colder.--HEYJUDE--13

COLLAPSED
And Rocky collapsed in the corner - ah.--ROCKYRACCO
--22

COLLEGE
Out of college, money spent --YOUNEVERGI--7

COLOUR
For red is the colour that my baby wore--YESITIS
--3
For red is the colour that will make me blue--
YESITIS--16
For red is the colour that will make me blue--
YESITIS--25
But listen to the colour of your dreams--TOMORROWNE
--11

COLOURFUL
I'm painting a room in a colourful way--FIXINGAHOL
--11

COMB
Dragged a comb across my head--DAYINTHELI--19

COME
Call me tonight and I'll come to you.--ANYTIMEATA
--18
Come on (come on), come on (come on) --PLEASEPLEA
--3
Come on (come on), come on (come on) --PLEASEPLEA
--3
Come on (come on), come on (come on) --PLEASEPLEA
--3
Come on (come on), come on (come on) --PLEASEPLEA
--3
Come on (come on), come on (come on) --PLEASEPLEA
--4
Come on (come on), come on (come on) --PLEASEPLEA
--4
Come on (come on), come on (come on) --PLEASEPLEA
--4
Come on (come on), come on (come on) --PLEASEPLEA
--4
Come on (come on), come on (come on) --PLEASEPLEA
--9
Come on (come on), come on (come on) --PLEASEPLEA
--9
Come on (come on), come on (come on) --PLEASEPLEA
--9
Come on (come on), come on (come on) --PLEASEPLEA
--10
Come on (come on), come on (come on) --PLEASEPLEA
--10
Come on (come on), come on (come on) --PLEASEPLEA
--10
Come on (come on), come on (come on) --PLEASEPLEA
--10
Come on (come on), come on (come on)--PLEASEPLEA
--21
Come on (come on), come on (come on)--PLEASEPLEA
--21
Come on (come on), come on (come on)--PLEASEPLEA
--21
Come on (come on), come on (come on)--PLEASEPLEA
--21
Come on (come on), come on (come on)--PLEASEPLEA
--22
Come on (come on), come on (come on)--PLEASEPLEA
--22
Come on (come on), come on (come on)--PLEASEPLEA
--22
Come on (come on), come on (come on)--PLEASEPLEA
--22
And you'll come running home --ALLIVEGOTT--4
And you'll come running home --ALLIVEGOTT--20
And hope that my dreams will come true --ALLMYLOVIN
--9
Please don't come near--DONTBOTHER--20

When she's come home--DONTBOTHER--23
Don't come around--DONTBOTHER--25
Please don't come near--DONTBOTHER--35
When she's come home--DONTBOTHER--38
Don't come around--DONTBOTHER--40
I wanna be your man (come on!)--IWANNABEYO--44
Every night the tears come down from my eye--
ITWONTBELO--15
So come on, come on, come on.--LITTLECHIL--11
So come on, come on, come on.--LITTLECHIL--11
So come on, come on, come on.--LITTLECHIL--11
Don't you run and hide, just come on, come on --
LITTLECHIL--17
Don't you run and hide, just come on, come on --
LITTLECHIL--17
Yeah come on, come on, come on.--LITTLECHIL--18
Yeah come on, come on, come on.--LITTLECHIL--18
Yeah come on, come on, come on.--LITTLECHIL--18
But I'll come back again some day.--ILLCRYINST--14
But I'll come back again some day.--ILLCRYINST--23
Come on, out my way --WHENIGETHO--4
Come on if you please --WHENIGETHO--10
I'm gonna love her till the cows come home --
WHENIGETHO--18
Come on, let me through --WHENIGETHO--21
And though he'll never come back --BABYSINBLA--5
And/But though he'll never come back--BABYSINBLA--25
And now the time has come and so my love I must
go --ILLFOLLOWT--5
And now the time has come and so my love I must
go --ILLFOLLOWT--10
Please come on back to me--INEEDYOU--3
So come on back and see--INEEDYOU--18
So come on back and see--INEEDYOU--28
Had you come some other day --IFINEEDEDS--7
Had you come some other day --IFINEEDEDS--17
Wait till I come back to your side --WAIT--3
Wait till I come back to your side --WAIT--7
Wait till I come back to your side --WAIT--15
Wait till I come back to your side --WAIT--23
(Yeah) ooo (come on) la la la--YOUWONTSEE--31
All the lonely people, where do they all come
from?--ELEANORRIG--9
All the lonely people, where do they all come
from?--ELEANORRIG--17
All the lonely people, where do they all come
from?--ELEANORRIG--27
And all the people that come and go--PENNYLANE--3
Nothing can come between us--LOVELYRITA--5
And the time will come--WITHINYOUW--31
Sitting on a cornflake, waiting for the van to come
--IAMTHEWALR--4
If the sun don't come you get a tan from standing
in the English rain--IAMTHEWALR--18
Wednesday morning papers didn't come --LADYMADONN
--15
Oh come on!--BACKINTHEU--19
Come and keep your comrade warm.--BACKINTHEU--34
Dear Prudence, won't you come out to play?--
DEARPRUDEN--1
Dear Prudence, won't you come out to play?--
DEARPRUDEN--5
Dear Prudence, won't you come out to play?--
DEARPRUDEN--21
Dear Prudence, won't you come out to play?--
DEARPRUDEN--25
Come on, come on - come on, come on --EVRBDYMONK
--1
Come on, come on - come on, come on --EVRBDYMONK
--1
Come on, come on - come on, come on --EVRBDYMONK
--1
Come on, come on - come on, come on --EVRBDYMONK
--1
Come on is such a joy --EVRBDYMONK--2
Come on is such a joy --EVRBDYMONK--3
Come on is take it easy --EVRBDYMONK--4
Come on is take it easy --EVRBDYMONK--5
So come on (come on) come on --EVRBDYMONK--10
So come on (come on) come on --EVRBDYMONK--10
So come on (come on) come on --EVRBDYMONK--10
Come on is such a joy --EVRBDYMONK--11
Come on is such a joy --EVRBDYMONK--12
Come on is make it easy --EVRBDYMONK--13
Come on is make it easy - wuh.--EVRBDYMONK--14
So come on (wuh), come on (wuh) --EVRBDYMONK--19
So come on (wuh), come on (wuh) --EVRBDYMONK--19
Come on is such a joy --EVRBDYMONK--20
Come on is such a joy --EVRBDYMONK--21
Come on is make it easy --EVRBDYMONK--22
Come on is make it easy --EVRBDYMONK--23
Come on, come on, come on, come on, come on,
come on, come on,...--EVRBDYMONK--27
Come on, come on, come on, come on, come on,

come on, come on,...--EVRBDYMONK--27
Come on, come on, come on, come on, come on,
    come on, come on,...--EVRBDYMONK--27
Come on, come on, come on, come on, come on,
    come on, come on,...--EVRBDYMONK--27
Come on, come on, come on, come on, come on,
    come on, come on,...--EVRBDYMONK--27
Come on, come on, come on, come on, come on,
    come on, come on,...--EVRBDYMONK--27
Come on, come on, come on, come on, come on,
    come on, come on,...--EVRBDYMONK--27
Tell me, tell me, tell me, come on tell me the
    answer --HELTERSKEL--6
So won't you please come home.--HONEYPIE--9
Come and show me the magic--HONEYPIE--11
Honey Pie come back to me - ooo.--HONEYPIE--19
So won't you please come home.--HONEYPIE--31
Come, come back to me Honey Pie--HONEYPIE--32
Come, come back to me Honey Pie--HONEYPIE--32
Rocky had come equipped with a gun--ROCKYRACCO--11
Do do do do - come on Rocky - boy --ROCKYRACCO--45
Do do do do do - come on Rocky - boy--ROCKYRACCO--46
Too much, too much, too much (come on), too
    much, too much, too much.--ITSALLTOOM--42
COME TOGETHER.--COMETOGETH--Title
Here come old flat top--COMETOGETH--5
He come grooving up slowly--COMETOGETH--6
Come together right now over me--COMETOGETH--21
Come together right now over me--COMETOGETH--31
Come - (oh) - come - come - come--COMETOGETH--35
Come - (oh) - come - come - come--COMETOGETH--35
Come - (oh) - come - come - come--COMETOGETH--35
Come - (oh) - come - come - come--COMETOGETH--35
Come together right now over me--COMETOGETH--42
Come together, yeah--COMETOGETH--47
Come together, yeah--COMETOGETH--48
Come together, yeah--COMETOGETH--49
Come together, yeah--COMETOGETH--50
Come together, yeah--COMETOGETH--51
Come together, yeah--COMETOGETH--52
Come together, yeah--COMETOGETH--53
Come together, yeah--COMETOGETH--55
Come together, yeah--COMETOGETH--56
Come together.--COMETOGETH--57
I'd ask my friends to come and see--OCTOPUSSGA--5
Come on now.--SHECAMEINT--1
Aah - here come the Sun King --SUNKING--1
Here come the Sun King.--SUNKING--2
Here come the Sun King.--SUNKING--5
(Oh) oh, you know, you know, you know my
    name (come on Dennis) --YOUKNOWMYN--16
You know, you know my name ((oh, let's hear it,
    come on Dennis)) --YOUKNOWMYN--23
((And now we'd like to do)) Hark the Angels
    Come...--DIGIT--13
Wondering really how come nobody told me--
    IVEGOTAFEE--12
Come on baby, don't be cold as ice--ONEAFTERNI--4
Come on baby, don't be cold as ice --ONEAFTERNI--9
Come on baby, don't be cold as ice --ONEAFTERNI--18
Come on baby, don't be cold as ice.--ONEAFTERNI--28

COMES
    And so it's true pride comes before a fall --
        IMALOSER--17
    If the rain comes they run and hide their heads--
        RAIN--1
    If the rain comes, if the rain comes.--RAIN--3
    If the rain comes, if the rain comes.--RAIN--3
    I can show you that when it starts to rain (when
        the rain comes down)--RAIN--9
    Everything's the same (when the rain comes down)--
        RAIN--10
    No-one comes near.--ELEANORRIG--13
    Look out 'cos here she comes (heh heh heh).--
        HELTERSKEL--17
    HERE COMES THE SUN.--HERECOMEST--Title
    Here comes the sun (do-n-do-do) --HERECOMEST--1
    Here comes the sun --HERECOMEST--2
    Here comes the sun (do-n-do-do) --HERECOMEST--6
    Here comes the sun --HERECOMEST--7
    Here comes the sun, here comes the sun --HERECOMEST
        --11
    Here comes the sun, here comes the sun --HERECOMEST
        --11
    Sun, sun, sun, here it comes --HERECOMEST--13
    Sun, sun, sun, here it comes --HERECOMEST--14
    Sun, sun, sun, here it comes --HERECOMEST--15
    Sun, sun, sun, here it comes --HERECOMEST--16
    Sun, sun, sun, here it comes --HERECOMEST--17
    Here comes the sun (do-n-do-do) --HERECOMEST--20
    Here comes the sun,--HERECOMEST--21
    Here comes the sun (do-n-do-do) --HERECOMEST--23

Here comes the sun --HERECOMEST--24
But as she's getting ready to go, a knock comes
    on the door --MAXWELLSIL--5
But as the words are leaving his lips, a noise
    comes from behind --MAXWELLSIL--22
Mother Mary comes to me --LETITBE/45--2
Mother Mary comes to me --LETITBE/45--25
Mother Mary comes to me --LETITBE/LP--2
Mother Mary comes to me --LETITBE/LP--25

COMFORT
    Who knows baby, you may comfort me (hey).--
        OLDBROWNSH--21
    Who knows baby, you may comfort me (hey).--
        OLDBROWNSH--26

COMING
    I'll ((I'll)) be coming home ((home)) again
        to you love ((you love)) --PSILOVEYOU--7
    I'll be coming home again to you love --PSILOVEYOU
        --19
    Now you're coming, you're coming on home (now
        you're coming on home)--ITWONTBELO--12
    Now you're coming, you're coming on home (now
        you're coming on home)--ITWONTBELO--12
    Now you're coming, you're coming on home (now
        you're coming on home)--ITWONTBELO--12
    I'll be good like I know I should (yes,
        you're coming on home)--ITWONTBELO--13
    You're coming home, you're coming home--ITWONTBELO
        --14
    You're coming home, you're coming home--ITWONTBELO
        --14
    Now you're coming, you're coming on home (now
        you're coming on home)--ITWONTBELO--22
    Now you're coming, you're coming on home (now
        you're coming on home)--ITWONTBELO--22
    Now you're coming, you're coming on home (now
        you're coming on home)--ITWONTBELO--22
    I'll be good like I know I should (yes,
        you're coming on home)--ITWONTBELO--23
    You're coming home, you're coming home--ITWONTBELO
        --24
    You're coming home, you're coming home--ITWONTBELO
        --24
    It's been a long time, now I'm coming back home --
        WAIT--1
    It's been a long time, now I'm coming back home --
        WAIT--13
    It's been a long time, now I'm coming back home --
        WAIT--25
    The Magical Mystery Tour is coming to take you
        away --MAGICALMYS--27
    (Coming/Hoping to take you away)--MAGICALMYS--28
    Coming up the drive --DONTPASSME--3
    I'm coming down fast but I'm miles above you --
        HELTERSKEL--5
    I'm coming down fast but don't let me break you --
        HELTERSKEL--12
    I'm coming down fast but don't let me break you --
        HELTERSKEL--22
    She's coming down fast --HELTERSKEL--28
    Coming down fast (oh I hear my baby speaking -
        ooo)...--HELTERSKEL--30
    All the girls around her say she's got it coming
        --GETBACK/45--18
    All the girls around her say she's got it coming--
        GETBACK/LP--24
    Coming off stronger all the time --IMEMINE--7

COMMAND
    Nowhere Man the world is at your command.--
        NOWHEREMAN--9
    Nowhere Man the world is at your command.--
        NOWHEREMAN--21

COMPARE
    And the way she looked was way beyond compare.--
        ISAWHERSTA--4

COMPARES
    There is no-one compares with you --INMYLIFE--10

COMPLAIN
    I used to get mad at my school (now I can't
        complain)--GETTINGBET--3
    The teachers who taught me weren't cool (now I
        can't complain)--GETTINGBET--4

COMPLAINING
I don't want to start complaining --PLEASEPLEA--13

COMRADE
Come and keep your comrade warm.--BACKINTHEU--34

CONCEIVE
I can't conceive of any more misery.--ASKMEWHY--13
I can't conceive of any more misery.--ASKMEWHY--25

CONFUSING
That is confusing things.--IWANTTOTEL--11

CONSTITUTION
You say you'll change the constitution --REVOLUTION--22
You say you'll change the constitution --REVOLUTONE--35

CONTINUING
THE CONTINUING STORY OF BUNGALOW BILL.--CONTINUING--Title

CONTRIBUTION
You ask me for a contribution --REVOLUTION--15
You ask me for a contribution --REVOLUTONE--23

CONTROLLED
I don't know how someone controlled you --WHILEMYGUI--7

CONVERSATION
Martha my dear, though I spend my days in conversation --MARTHAMYDE--1

COOKING
Cooking breakfast for the Queen --CRYBABYCRY--5

COOL
She's cool - ooo-ooo-ooo.--GIRL--19
The teachers who taught me weren't cool (now I can't complain)--GETTINGBET--4
After a while you start to smile now you feel cool --GOODMORNIN--13
For well you know that it's a fool who plays it cool --HEYJUDE--12
Cool cherry cream, nice apple tart --SAVOYTRUFF--6

CORAL
The coral that lies beneath the waves (lies beneath the ocean waves).--OCTOPUSSGA--18

CORNER
On the corner is a banker with a motorcar--PENNYLANE--5
And Rocky collapsed in the corner - ah.--ROCKYRACCO--22

CORNFLAKE
Sitting on a cornflake, waiting for the van to come --IAMTHEWALR--4

CORPORATION
Corporation T-shirt, stupid bloody Tuesday--IAMTHEWALR--5

CORRECT
You're correct, there's nobody there.--ONLYANORTH--15

COTTAGE
Every summer we can rent a cottage--WHENIMSIXT--22

COULD
So how could I dance with another --ISAWHERSTA--5
Well she looked at me, and I, I could see --ISAWHERSTA--7

I could tell the world a thing or two about our love --THANKYOUGI--5
Could never die --ANDILOVEHE--12
Whoa, whoa, I never realised what a kiss could be --ISHOULDHAV--4
This could only happen to me --ISHOULDHAV--5
Whoa, whoa, I never realised what a kiss could be --ISHOULDHAV--14
This could only happen to me --ISHOULDHAV--15
If I could get my way --ILLCRYINST--3
If I could see you now --ILLCRYINST--8
You could find better things to do--ILLBEBACK--9
You could find better things to do--ILLBEBACK--18
I could be happy with you by my side--YESITIS--10
If I could forget her--YESITIS--11
I could be happy with you by my side--YESITIS--19
If I could forget her--YESITIS--20
I could never really live without you--INEEDYOU--17
I could never really live without you--INEEDYOU--27
How could she say to me--YOUVEGOTTO--15
I told that girl I could start right away --DRIVEMYCAR--22
But when I saw him with you I could feel my future fold.--WHATGOESON--7
It could make a million for you overnight. ((writer))--PAPERBACKW--22
Could see another kind of mind there.--GOTTOGETYO--4
Could see another kind of mind there.--GOTTOGETYO--28
I don't mind, I could wait forever--IWANTTOTEL--14
Then I could speak my mind and tell you--IWANTTOTEL--17
I don't mind, I could wait forever--IWANTTOTEL--21
Home. (we gave her everything money could buy)--SHESLEAVIN--10
How could she do this to me?--SHESLEAVIN--19
I could stay with you.--WHENIMSIXT--12
I could be handy mending a fuse--WHENIMSIXT--13
Who could ask for more?--WHENIMSIXT--18
(Could it be anybody?)--WITHALITTL--17
(Could it be anybody?)--WITHALITTL--28
About the love we all could share--WITHINYOUW--9
We could save the world--WITHINYOUW--14
I could know the ways of heaven.--INNERLIGHT--4
If looks could kill it would have been us instead of him.--CONTINUING--29
And if she could only hear me--HONEYPIE--5
How could I ever have lost you --LONGLONGLO--2
Yes, you could say she was attractively built - yeah, yeah, yeah.--POLYTHENEP--9
Well I knew what I could not say.--SHECAMEINT--15
She could steal but she could not rob.--SHECAMEINT--19
She could steal but she could not rob.--SHECAMEINT--19

COULDN'T
'cos I couldn't stand the pain --IFIFELL--14
'cos I couldn't stand the pain --IFIFELL--21
'cos I couldn't really stand it--YOULIKEMET--17
'cos I couldn't really stand it--YOULIKEMET--26
But he knew it couldn't last.--GETBACK/45--2
But he knew it couldn't last--GETBACK/LP--8

COUNT
They had to count them all--DAYINTHELI--31
Don't you know that you can count me out?--REVOLUTION--9
Don't you know that you can count me out (in)?--REVOLUTONE--12

COUNTRY
Born a poor young country boy - Mother Nature's son --MOTHERNATU--1

COUPLE
In a couple of years they have built a home sweet home --OBLADIOBLA--17
With a couple of kids running in the yard of Desmond and Molly Jones.--OBLADIOBLA--18
In a couple of years they have built a home sweet home--OBLADIOBLA--29
With a couple of kids running in the yard of Desmond and Molly Jones.--OBLADIOBLA--30

COURSE
And of course Henry the Horse dances the waltz.--BEINGFORTH--14

COWS
I'm gonna love her till the cows come home --
WHENIGETHO--18

CRABALOCKER
Crabalocker fishwife, pornographic priestess--
IAMTHEWALR--13

CRACKER
He one spinal cracker--COMETOGETH--28

CRACKS
I'm filling the cracks that ran through the door--
FIXINGAHOL--4

CRANBERRY
... Cranberry sauce...--STRAWBERRY--38

CRASH
You were in a car crash --DONTPASSME--25

CRAWLED
And crawled off to sleep in the bath.--NORWEGIANW
--20

CRAWLING
Crawling in the dirt?--PIGGIES--2

CRAZY
I don't mind, I think they're crazy --IMONLYSLEE
--8
Honey Pie you are making me crazy--HONEYPIE--7
Now Honey Pie you are making me crazy--HONEYPIE--29

CREAM
Cool cherry cream, nice apple tart --SAVOYTRUFF--6

CREEPING
Sunday morning creeping like a nun --LADYMADONN--6

CREEPS
But when she turns her back on the boy, he
creeps up from behind --MAXWELLSIL--12

CREME
Creme tangerine, montelimar --SAVOYTRUFF--1
Creme tangerine and montelimar --SAVOYTRUFF--23

CRIED
I've cried for you.--NOTASECOND--3
I've cried for you, yeah.--NOTASECOND--14
Tell me why you cried --TELLMEWHY--1
Tell me why you cried --TELLMEWHY--3
Tell me why you cried --TELLMEWHY--9
Tell me why you cried --TELLMEWHY--11
Tell me why you cried --TELLMEWHY--17
Tell me why you cried --TELLMEWHY--19
Tell me why you cried --TELLMEWHY--26
Tell me why you cried --TELLMEWHY--28
We'll forget the tears we've cried.--WAIT--4
We'll forget the tears we cried.--WAIT--8
We'll forget the tears we've cried.--WAIT--16
We'll forget the tears we've cried.--WAIT--24
No sign of love behind the tears cried for no-one
--FORNOONE--8
No sign of love behind the tears cried for no-one
--FORNOONE--15
No sign of love behind the tears cried for no-one
--FORNOONE--25
Well you know I nearly broke down and cried.--
OHDARLING--6
A - well you know I nearly broke down and cried.--
OHDARLING--13
Many times I've been alone and many times I've
cried --LONGANDWIN--7

CRIES
She breaks down and cries to her husband--
SHESLEAVIN--16

CRIME
I have always thought that it's a crime--WECANWORKI
--13
I have always thought that it's a crime--WECANWORKI
--22

CROSSED
Well my heart went boom when I crossed that room
--ISAWHERSTA--11
Well my heart went boom when I crossed that room
--ISAWHERSTA--18
There is one love I should never have crossed.--
IMALOSER--4
Black cloud crossed my mind,--YERBLUES--24

CROWD
A crowd of people stood and stared--DAYINTHELI--8
A crowd of people turned away--DAYINTHELI--13
The man in the crowd with the multicoloured
mirrors on his hobnail boots --HAPPINESSI--5

CRUCIFY
They're gonna crucify me.--BALLADOFJO--8
They're gonna crucify me.--BALLADOFJO--16
They're gonna crucify me.--BALLADOFJO--24
They're gonna crucify me.--BALLADOFJO--36
They're gonna crucify me.--BALLADOFJO--44
They're gonna crucify me.--BALLADOFJO--46

CRUEL
I used to be cruel to my woman--GETTINGBET--25

CRY
When you need a shoulder to cry on --ANYTIMEATA--16
My happiness near makes me cry --ASKMEWHY--8
If I cry it's not because I'm sad --ASKMEWHY--10
I'm the kind of guy, who never used to cry.--MISERY
--2
Every day I've done nothing but cry--ITWONTBELO--16
You know you made me cry --NOTASECOND--1
You know you made me cry --NOTASECOND--12
Till he's seen you cry.--THISBOY--10
And that she will cry --IFIFELL--19
And that she will cry --IFIFELL--26
I'LL CRY INSTEAD.--ILLCRYINST--Title
But I can't, so I'll cry instead.--ILLCRYINST--5
But I can't, so I'll cry instead.--ILLCRYINST--10
Don't want to cry when there's people there --
ILLCRYINST--11
Until then I'll cry instead.--ILLCRYINST--19
Don't want to cry when there's people there --
ILLCRYINST--20
Until then I'll cry instead.--ILLCRYINST--28
She hates to see me cry--SHESAWOMAN--9
Is it for her or myself that I cry?--IMALOSER--12
You can't cry 'cos you're laughing at me --IMDOWN
--2
When I think of things we did it makes me wanna
cry.--NIGHTBEFOR--10
When I think of things we did it makes me wanna
cry.--NIGHTBEFOR--18
She will turn to me and start to cry --GIRL--7
CRY BABY CRY.--CRYBABYCRY--Title
CRY BABY CRY.--CRYBABYCRY--Title
Cry baby cry --CRYBABYCRY--1
Cry baby cry --CRYBABYCRY--1
Cry baby cry --CRYBABYCRY--8
Cry baby cry --CRYBABYCRY--8
So cry baby cry.--CRYBABYCRY--11
So cry baby cry.--CRYBABYCRY--11
Cry baby cry --CRYBABYCRY--16
Cry baby cry --CRYBABYCRY--16
So cry baby cry.--CRYBABYCRY--19
So cry baby cry.--CRYBABYCRY--19
Cry baby cry --CRYBABYCRY--24
Cry baby cry --CRYBABYCRY--24
So cry baby cry.--CRYBABYCRY--27
So cry baby cry.--CRYBABYCRY--27
Cry baby cry --CRYBABYCRY--32
Cry baby cry --CRYBABYCRY--32
So cry baby cry --CRYBABYCRY--35
So cry baby cry --CRYBABYCRY--35
Cry, cry, cry baby --CRYBABYCRY--36
Cry, cry, cry baby --CRYBABYCRY--36
Cry, cry, cry baby --CRYBABYCRY--36
So cry baby cry --CRYBABYCRY--39
So cry baby cry --CRYBABYCRY--39
Cry, cry, cry --CRYBABYCRY--40

Cry, cry, cry --CRYBABYCRY--40
Cry, cry, cry --CRYBABYCRY--40
So cry baby cry.--CRYBABYCRY--43
So cry baby cry.--CRYBABYCRY--43
Don't pass me by, don't make me cry, don't make
    me blue --DONTPASSME--18
Don't pass me by - don't make me cry.--DONTPASSME
    --22
Don't pass me by, don't make me cry, don't make
    me blue --DONTPASSME--31
Don't pass me by - don't make me cry.--DONTPASSME
    --35
Don't pass me by, don't make me cry, don't make
    me blue --DONTPASSME--37
Don't pass me by - don't make me cry.--DONTPASSME
    --41
Because the sky is blue it makes me cry --BECAUSE
    --10
Sleep pretty darling do not cry--GOLDENSLUM--5
Sleep pretty darling do not cry--GOLDENSLUM--9
Sleep pretty darling do not cry--GOLDENSLUM--15

CRYING

My crying is through, oh.--NOTASECOND--6
My crying is through, oh.--NOTASECOND--17
You've ((you've)) got me crying, girl --WHATYOURED
    --13
You've ((you've)) got me crying, girl --WHATYOURED
    --20
I'm crying--IAMTHEWALR--3
I'm crying - I'm crying (goo), I'm crying,
    I'm crying--IAMTHEWALR--11
I'm crying - I'm crying (goo), I'm crying,
    I'm crying--IAMTHEWALR--11
I'm crying - I'm crying (goo), I'm crying,
    I'm crying--IAMTHEWALR--11
I'm crying - I'm crying (goo), I'm crying,
    I'm crying--IAMTHEWALR--11
I'm crying--IAMTHEWALR--24
Has left a pool of tears crying for the day.--
    LONGANDWIN--5

CUP

Take a drink from his special cup, Dr. Robert.--
    DRROBERT--7
Found my way downstairs and drank a cup--DAYINTHELI
    --20
Words are flowing out like endless rain into a
    paper cup --ACROSSTHEU--1

CURSE

And curse Sir Walter Raleigh --IMSOTIRED--16

CUSTARD

Yellow matter custard, dripping from a dead
    dog's eye--IAMTHEWALR--12

CUSTOMER

In Penny Lane the barber shaves another customer--
    PENNYLANE--24

CUT

Cut the cable, drop the cable.--YELLOWSUBM--22

CUTS

When the pain cuts through--SAVOYTRUFF--12

D

A, B, C, D --ALLTOGETHE--5

DA

Da da da, da da dum dum da--FROMMETOYO--1
Da da da, da da dum dum da--FROMMETOYO--1
Da da da, da da dum dum da--FROMMETOYO--1
Da da da, da da dum dum da--FROMMETOYO--1
Da da da, da da dum dum da--FROMMETOYO--1
Da da da, da da dum dum da--FROMMETOYO--1
Da da da, da da dum dum da.--FROMMETOYO--2
Da da da, da da dum dum da.--FROMMETOYO--2
Da da da, da da dum dum da.--FROMMETOYO--2
Da da da, da da dum dum da.--FROMMETOYO--2
Da da da, da da dum dum da.--FROMMETOYO--2
La da da, da n da.--IVEJUSTSEE--11
La da da, da n da.--IVEJUSTSEE--11

La da da, da n da.--IVEJUSTSEE--11
La da da, da n da.--IVEJUSTSEE--11
La da da, da n da.--IVEJUSTSEE--18
La da da, da n da.--IVEJUSTSEE--18
La da da, da n da.--IVEJUSTSEE--18
La da da, da n da.--IVEJUSTSEE--18
Mmm mmm mmm la da da.--IVEJUSTSEE--29
Mmm mmm mmm la da da.--IVEJUSTSEE--29
Lovely Rita ((da da da da da da)) meter maid--
    LOVELYRITA--32
Lovely Rita ((da da da da da da)) meter maid--
    LOVELYRITA--32
Lovely Rita ((da da da da da da)) meter maid--
    LOVELYRITA--32
Lovely Rita ((da da da da da da)) meter maid--
    LOVELYRITA--32
Lovely Rita ((da da da da da da)) meter maid--
    LOVELYRITA--32
Lovely Rita ((da da da da da da)) meter maid--
    LOVELYRITA--32
Da da da da da da da da da - da--LOVELYRITA--33
Da da da da da da da da da - da--LOVELYRITA--33
Da da da da da da da da da - da--LOVELYRITA--33
Da da da da da da da da da - da--LOVELYRITA--33
Da da da da da da da da da - da--LOVELYRITA--33
Da da da da da da da da da - da--LOVELYRITA--33
Da da da da da da da da da - da--LOVELYRITA--33
Da da da da da da da da da - da--LOVELYRITA--33
Da da da - da - da - da - wuh - oh--LOVELYRITA--34
Da da da - da - da - da - wuh - oh--LOVELYRITA--34
Da da da - da - da - da - wuh - oh--LOVELYRITA--34
Da da da - da - da - da - wuh - oh--LOVELYRITA--34
Da da da - da - da - da - wuh - oh--LOVELYRITA--34
Da da da-da da da da da da --YOURMOTHER--21
Da da da-da da da da da da --YOURMOTHER--21
Da da da-da da da da da da --YOURMOTHER--21
Da da da-da da da da da da --YOURMOTHER--21
Da da da-da da da da da da --YOURMOTHER--21
Da da da-da da da da da da --YOURMOTHER--21
Da da da da da-da-da-da-da.--YOURMOTHER--22
Da da da da da-da-da-da-da.--YOURMOTHER--22
Da da da da da-da-da-da-da.--YOURMOTHER--22
Da da da da da-da-da-da-da.--YOURMOTHER--22
Mmm, mmm - da, da, da, da, da, da, da.--IWILL--19
Mmm, mmm - da, da, da, da, da, da, da.--IWILL--19
Mmm, mmm - da, da, da, da, da, da, da.--IWILL--19
Mmm, mmm - da, da, da, da, da, da, da.--IWILL--19
Mmm, mmm - da, da, da, da, da, da, da.--IWILL--19
Mmm, mmm - da, da, da, da, da, da, da.--IWILL--19
Mmm, mmm - da, da, da, da, da, da, da.--IWILL--19
Da da da da da da --ROCKYRACCO--23
Da da da da da da --ROCKYRACCO--23
Da da da da da da --ROCKYRACCO--23
Da da da da da da --ROCKYRACCO--23
Da da da da da da --ROCKYRACCO--23
Da da da da da da --ROCKYRACCO--24
Da da da da da da --ROCKYRACCO--24
Da da da da da da --ROCKYRACCO--24
Da da da da da da --ROCKYRACCO--24
Da da da da da da --ROCKYRACCO--24
Da da da da da da da da da da --ROCKYRACCO--25
Da da da da da da da da da da --ROCKYRACCO--25
Da da da da da da da da da da --ROCKYRACCO--25
Da da da da da da da da da da --ROCKYRACCO--25
Da da da da da da da da da da --ROCKYRACCO--25
Da da da da da da da da da da --ROCKYRACCO--25
Da da da da da da da da da da --ROCKYRACCO--25
Da da da da da da da da da da --ROCKYRACCO--25
Da da da da da da da da da da --ROCKYRACCO--25
Da da da da do do do do do.--ROCKYRACCO--30
Da da da da do do do do do.--ROCKYRACCO--30
Da da da da do do do do do.--ROCKYRACCO--30
Da da da da do do do do do.--ROCKYRACCO--30

DA-DA

Da da da-da da da da da da --YOURMOTHER--21

DA-DA-DA-DA-DA

Da da da da da-da-da-da-da.--YOURMOTHER--22

DADDY

Daddy, our baby's gone.--SHESLEAVIN--17

DADDY'S

Take me to your daddy's farm --BACKINTHEU--32

DAILY
His son is working for the Daily Mail --PAPERBACKW
--10

DAISIES
Swaying daisies sing a lazy song beneath the sun.
--MOTHERNATU--9

DAISY
The clouds will be a daisy chain --DEARPRUDEN--18

DAKOTA
Now somewhere in the Black Mountain hills of
Dakota --ROCKYRACCO--1

DAMN
What they need's a damn good whacking.--PIGGIES--14

DAN
Now she and her man who called himself Dan--
ROCKYRACCO--17

DANCE
So how could I dance with another --ISAWHERSTA--5
She wouldn't dance with another --ISAWHERSTA--9
Now I'll never dance with another --ISAWHERSTA--16
Now I'll never dance with another --ISAWHERSTA--23
Little child, won't you dance with me?--LITTLECHIL
--2
Little child, won't you dance with me?--LITTLECHIL
--6
Little child, won't you dance with me?--LITTLECHIL
--13
Little child, won't you dance with me?--LITTLECHIL
--20
I'M HAPPY JUST TO DANCE WITH YOU.--IMHAPPYJUS
--Title
Before this dance is through --IMHAPPYJUS--1
I'm so happy when you dance with me.--IMHAPPYJUS
--3
'cos I'm happy just to dance with you.--IMHAPPYJUS
--7
I just wanna dance with you all night --IMHAPPYJUS
--9
'cos I'm happy just to dance with you.--IMHAPPYJUS
--11
Just to dance with you is everything I need (oh)
--IMHAPPYJUS--12
Before this dance is through ((aah)) --IMHAPPYJUS
--13
I'm so happy when you dance with me ((oh - oh)).--
IMHAPPYJUS--15
'cos I'm happy just to dance with you.--IMHAPPYJUS
--19
Just to dance with you (oh) is everything I
need (oh),--IMHAPPYJUS--20
Before this dance is through ((aah)) --IMHAPPYJUS
--21
I'm so happy when you dance with me ((oh - oh)).--
IMHAPPYJUS--23
'cos I'm happy just to dance with you (oh - oh).--
IMHAPPYJUS--28
The Hendersons will dance and sing--BEINGFORTH--10
Let's all get up and dance to a song--YOURMOTHER
--2
Let's all get up and dance to a song--YOURMOTHER
--8
I would like you to dance (birthday) --BIRTHDAY--11
I would like you to dance (birthday) --BIRTHDAY--13
Dance! (dance!) (yeah)--BIRTHDAY--14
Dance! (dance!) (yeah)--BIRTHDAY--14
I would like you to dance (birthday) --BIRTHDAY--16
I would like you to dance (birthday) (wuh)--
BIRTHDAY--18
Dance! (dance!)--BIRTHDAY--19
Dance! (dance!)--BIRTHDAY--19
We would sing and dance around--OCTOPUSSGA--13
Images of broken light which dance before me like
a million eyes --ACROSSTHEU--11

DADDCED
Well we danced through the night --ISAWHERSTA--13
Oh (wuh!) we danced through the night --ISAWHERSTA
--20

DANCER
Well, you may be a lover, but you ain't no
dancer.--HELTERSKEL--7
'cos you may be a lover, but you ain't no dancer.
--HELTERSKEL--14
'cos you may be a lover, but you ain't no dancer.
--HELTERSKEL--24
She said she'd always been a dancer --SHECAMEINT
--12

DANCES
And of course Henry the Horse dances the waltz.--
BEINGFORTH--14

DANIEL
But Daniel was hot, he drew first and shot--
ROCKYRACCO--21

DANNY
He said, Danny - Boy this is a showdown.--
ROCKYRACCO--20
Oh Danny Boy, the odes of Pan are calling.--
ONEAFTERNI--33

DARK
Dark is the sky --ANDILOVEHE--16
Dark is the sky --ANDILOVEHE--21
Everywhere in town is getting dark--GOODMORNIN--19
When it gets dark I tow your heart away.--
LOVELYRITA--6
Into the light of a dark black night.--BLACKBIRD
--10
Into the light of a dark black night.--BLACKBIRD
--12
For a seance in the dark --CRYBABYCRY--29
Wigwam frightened of the dark--HEYBULLDOG--14
Is a little dark and out of key --ONLYANORTH--14
Shaves in the dark--MEANMRMUST--2

DARKNESS
And in my hour of darkness--LETITBE/45--4
And in my hour of darkness--LETITBE/LP--4

DARLIN'
All my lovin', darlin', I'll be true.--ALLMYLOVIN
--14
All my lovin', darlin', I'll be true --ALLMYLOVIN
--22

DARLING
'cos you know, darling, I love only you --
DONTPASSME--19
'cos you know, darling, I love only you --
DONTPASSME--32
'cos you know, darling, I love only you --
DONTPASSME--38
Sleep pretty darling do not cry--GOLDENSLUM--5
Sleep pretty darling do not cry--GOLDENSLUM--9
Sleep pretty darling do not cry--GOLDENSLUM--15
Little darling, it's been a long, cold lonely
winter.--HERECOMEST--4
Little darling, it feels like years since it's
been here.--HERECOMEST--5
Little darling, the smiles returning to the faces.
--HERECOMEST--9
Little darling, it seems like years since it's
been here.--HERECOMEST--10
Little darling, I feel that ice is slowly
melting.--HERECOMEST--18
Little darling, it seems like years since it's
been clear.--HERECOMEST--19
OH DARLING.--OHDARLING--Title
Oh darling, please believe me, I'll never do
you no harm.--OHDARLING--1
Oh darling, if you leave me I'll never make it
alone --OHDARLING--3
Oh darling, if you leave me, I'll never make
it alone.--OHDARLING--9
Believe me, darling.--OHDARLING--11
Oh darling, please believe me, I'll never let
you down.--OHDARLING--16
Oh believe me darling --OHDARLING--17

DARNING
Darning his socks in the night when there's

nobody there--ELEANORRIG--15

DAVE
   Vera, Chuck and Dave.--WHENIMSIXT--27

DAY
   And till ((till)) the day I do love ((do love))
     --PSILOVEYOU--8
   And till the day I do love --PSILOVEYOU--20
   I think about you night and day--ILLGETYOU--9
   I'll write home every day --ALLMYLOVIN--5
   I'll write home every day --ALLMYLOVIN--11
   I'll write home every day --ALLMYLOVIN--19
   Until that day--DONTBOTHER--24
   Until that day--DONTBOTHER--39
   Every day I've done nothing but cry--ITWONTBELO--16
   So every day we'll be happy, I know--ITWONTBELO--25
   You know I work all day --HARDDAYSNI--8
   But I'll come back again some day.--ILLCRYINST--14
   But I'll come back again some day.--ILLCRYINST--23
   Love you every day girl --EIGHTDAYSA--9
   Love you every day girl --EIGHTDAYSA--29
   One day you'll look to see I've gone --ILLFOLLOWT
     --1
   Some day you'll know I was the one --ILLFOLLOWT--3
   One day you'll find that I have gone --ILLFOLLOWT
     --7
   One day you'll find that I have gone --ILLFOLLOWT
     --12
   I'll make bright your day--TELLMEWHAT--12
   Same old thing happen every day.--IMDOWN--9
   Had it been another day--IVEJUSTSEE--7
   Each and every day.--YOUVEGOTTO--6
   DAY TRIPPER--DAYTRIPPER--Title
   She was a day tripper --DAYTRIPPER--5
   She was a day tripper --DAYTRIPPER--13
   She was a day tripper --DAYTRIPPER--22
   Day tripper, yeah --DAYTRIPPER--26
   Day tripper, yeah --DAYTRIPPER--27
   Day tripper --DAYTRIPPER--28
   Day tripper, yeah --DAYTRIPPER--29
   Day tripper --DAYTRIPPER--30
   Day tripper.--DAYTRIPPER--31
   Still you don't regret a single day.--GIRL--4
   That a man must break his back to earn his day of
     leisure?--GIRL--24
   Had you come some other day --IFINEEDEDS--7
   Had you come some other day --IFINEEDEDS--17
   The other day I saw you as I walked along the
     road --WHATGOESON--6
   Day or night he'll be there any time at all, Dr.
     Robert --DRROBERT--2
   Please don't spoil my day, I'm miles away --
     IMONLYSLEE--11
   Please don't spoil my day, I'm miles away --
     IMONLYSLEE--17
   Your day breaks, your mind aches --FORNOONE--1
   Your day breaks, your mind aches --FORNOONE--20
   GOOD DAY SUNSHINE.--GOODDAYSUN--Title
   Good day sunshine, good day sunshine, good day
     sunshine.--GOODDAYSUN--1
   Good day sunshine, good day sunshine, good day
     sunshine.--GOODDAYSUN--1
   Good day sunshine, good day sunshine, good day
     sunshine.--GOODDAYSUN--1
   I'm in love and it's a sunny day.--GOODDAYSUN--5
   Good day sunshine, good day sunshine, good day
     sunshine.--GOODDAYSUN--6
   Good day sunshine, good day sunshine, good day
     sunshine.--GOODDAYSUN--6
   Good day sunshine, good day sunshine, good day
     sunshine.--GOODDAYSUN--9
   Good day sunshine, good day sunshine, good day
     sunshine.--GOODDAYSUN--9
   Good day sunshine, good day sunshine, good day
     sunshine.--GOODDAYSUN--9
   Good day sunshine, good day sunshine, good day
     sunshine.--GOODDAYSUN--14
   Good day sunshine, good day sunshine, good day
     sunshine.--GOODDAYSUN--14
   Good day sunshine, good day sunshine, good day
     sunshine.--GOODDAYSUN--14
   Good day sunshine, good day sunshine, good day
     sunshine.--GOODDAYSUN--15
   Good day sunshine, good day sunshine, good day
     sunshine.--GOODDAYSUN--15
   Good day sunshine, good day sunshine, good day
     sunshine.--GOODDAYSUN--15
   Good day sunshine (good day sunshine) (good

day sunshine) --GOODDAYSUN--16
Good day sunshine (good day sunshine) (good
   day sunshine) --GOODDAYSUN--16
Good day sunshine (good day sunshine) (good
   day sunshine) --GOODDAYSUN--16
(Good day sunshine) (good day...--GOODDAYSUN--17
(Good day sunshine) (good day...--GOODDAYSUN--17
Every single day of my life?--GOTTOGETYO--7
Say we'll be together every day.--GOTTOGETYO--14
Every single day of my life?--GOTTOGETYO--22
Every single day...--GOTTOGETYO--31
Here, making each day of the year--HERETHEREA--2
Each day just goes so fast--LOVEYOUTWO--1
Make love all day long--LOVEYOUTWO--9
Make love all day long--LOVEYOUTWO--11
A DAY IN THE LIFE.--DAYINTHELI--Title
Nothing to say but what a day how's your boy been?
   --GOODMORNIN--3
Wednesday morning at five o'clock as the day begins
   --SHESLEAVIN--1
How do I feel by the end of the day?--WITHALITTL
   --10
Soon will be the break of day (day) --BLUEJAYWAY
   --17
Soon will be the break of day (day) --BLUEJAYWAY
   --17
Day after day, alone on a hill--FOOLONTHEH--1
Day after day, alone on a hill--FOOLONTHEH--1
Dear Prudence, greet the brand new day.--DEARPRUDEN
   --2
Dear Prudence, greet the brand new day.--DEARPRUDEN
   --22
All day long I'm sitting singing songs for
   everyone.--MOTHERNATU--2
And one day his woman ran off with another guy --
   ROCKYRACCO--3
So one day he walked into town --ROCKYRACCO--7
One sunny day the world was waiting for the lover
   ((sexy Sadie))--SEXYSADIE--9
What words I say or time of day it is --ONLYANORTH
   --8
Saving up your money for a rainy day --BALLADOFJO
   --25
But she changes from day to day.--HERMAJESTY--4
But she changes from day to day.--HERMAJESTY--4
She worked at fifteen clubs a day--SHECAMEINT--13
And Doris Day--DIGIT--8
All through the day --IMEMINE--1
All through the day --IMEMINE--8
All through the day --IMEMINE--21
Has left a pool of tears crying for the day.--
   LONGANDWIN--5

DAY'S
   A HARD DAY'S NIGHT.--HARDDAYSNI--Title
   It's been a hard day's night --HARDDAYSNI--1
   It's been a hard day's night --HARDDAYSNI--3
   It's been a hard day's night --HARDDAYSNI--17
   It's been a hard day's night --HARDDAYSNI--19
   Oh, It's been a hard day's night --HARDDAYSNI--30
   It's been a hard day's night --HARDDAYSNI--32

DAYS
   These days such a kind girl seems so hard to find
     --THINGSWESA--7
   EIGHT DAYS A WEEK.--EIGHTDAYSA--Title
   Eight days a week.--EIGHTDAYSA--8
   Eight days a week.--EIGHTDAYSA--16
   Eight days a week I love you --EIGHTDAYSA--17
   Eight days a week is not enough to show I care.--
     EIGHTDAYSA--18
   Eight days a week.--EIGHTDAYSA--26
   Eight days a week I love you --EIGHTDAYSA--27
   Eight days a week is not enough to show I care.--
     EIGHTDAYSA--28
   Eight days a week --EIGHTDAYSA--36
   Eight days a week --EIGHTDAYSA--37
   Eight days a week.--EIGHTDAYSA--38
   But now ((but now)) these days are gone
     ((these days are gone))--HELP--11
   But now ((but now)) these days are gone
     ((these days are gone))--HELP--11
   But now ((now)) these days are gone ((these
     days are gone))--HELP--31
   But now ((now)) these days are gone ((these
     days are gone))--HELP--31
   Though the days are few, they're filled with tears
     --YOUWONTSEE--16
   Though the days are few they're filled with tears
     --YOUWONTSEE--25
   Having been some days in preparation--BEINGFORTH
     --19

Martha my dear, though I spend my days in
   conversation --MARTHAMYDE--1

DE
   All de children sing:--CONTINUING--10
   All de children sing:--CONTINUING--20
   You know my name, look up de number --YOUKNOWMYN
      --1
   You know my name, look up de number.--YOUKNOWMYN
      --2

DEAD
   Will she still believe it when he's dead?--GIRL--25
   Some are dead and some are living --INMYLIFE--7
   Well I'd rather see you dead, little girl --
      RUNFORYOUR--1
   And I'd rather see you dead.--RUNFORYOUR--20
   I'd rather see you dead, little girl --RUNFORYOUR
      --25
   They might as well be dead--RAIN--2
   When she says her love is dead --FORNOONE--12
   Before I'm a dead old man.--LOVEYOUTWO--5
   She said I know what it's like to be dead --
      SHESAIDSHE--1
   I know what it's like to be dead (I know what
      it's like to be dead) --SHESAIDSHE--20
   I know what it's like to be dead (I know what
      it's like to be dead) --SHESAIDSHE--20
   I know what it's like to be dead (I know what
      it's like to be dead) --SHESAIDSHE--22
   I know what it's like to be dead (I know what
      it's like to be dead).--SHESAIDSHE--22
   That ignorance and hate may mourn the dead--
      TOMORROWNE--9
   Yellow matter custard, dripping from a dead
      dog's eye--IAMTHEWALR--12
   Blackbird singing in the dead of night --BLACKBIRD
      --1
   Blackbird singing in the dead of night --BLACKBIRD
      --5
   Blackbird singing in the dead of night --BLACKBIRD
      --13
   If I ain't dead already--YERBLUES--4
   If I ain't dead already--YERBLUES--8
   If I ain't dead already--YERBLUES--15
   If I ain't dead already--YERBLUES--22
   If I ain't dead already--YERBLUES--29
   We are dead.--ITSALLTOOM--38
   Last night the wife said, oh boy, when you're
      dead --BALLADOFJO--27
   Bang, bang Maxwell's silver hammer made sure
      that she was dead.--MAXWELLSIL--7
   Bang, bang Maxwell's silver hammer made sure
      that she was dead.--MAXWELLSIL--15
   Bang, bang Maxwell's silver hammer made sure
      that he was dead.--MAXWELLSIL--25

DEAF
   I dig a pygmy by Charles Hawtrey and the Deaf
      Aids (ha ha ha)--TWOOFUS--1

DEAR
   Oh dear, what can I do?--BABYSINBLA--1
   Oh dear, what can I do?--BABYSINBLA--7
   Dear what can I do?--BABYSINBLA--16
   Dear what can I do?--BABYSINBLA--21
   Oh dear, what can I do?--BABYSINBLA--27
   Dear Sir or Madam, will you read my book?--
      PAPERBACKW--2
   If it's not too dear --WHENIMSIXT--24
   DEAR PRUDENCE.--DEARPRUDEN--Title
   Dear Prudence, won't you come out to play?--
      DEARPRUDEN--1
   Dear Prudence, greet the brand new day.--DEARPRUDEN
      --2
   Dear Prudence, won't you come out to play?--
      DEARPRUDEN--5
   Dear Prudence, open up your eyes --DEARPRUDEN--6
   Dear Prudence, see the sunny skies.--DEARPRUDEN--7
   Dear Prudence, won't you open up your eyes?--
      DEARPRUDEN--10
   Dear Prudence, let me see you smile --DEARPRUDEN
      --16
   Dear Prudence, like a little child.--DEARPRUDEN--17
   Dear Prudence, won't you let me see you smile?--
      DEARPRUDEN--20
   Dear Prudence, won't you come out to play?--
      DEARPRUDEN--21
   Dear Prudence, greet the brand new day.--DEARPRUDEN
      --22

Dear Prudence, won't you come out to play?--
   DEARPRUDEN--25
Waiting for your knock, dear --DONTPASSME--6
MARTHA MY DEAR.--MARTHAMYDE--Title
Martha my dear, though I spend my days in
   conversation --MARTHAMYDE--1
Don't forget me, Martha my dear.--MARTHAMYDE--3
Martha my dear, you have always been my
   inspiration --MARTHAMYDE--13
Don't forget me, Martha my dear.--MARTHAMYDE--15

DECIDE
   Then you decide to take a walk by the old school--
      GOODMORNIN--14

DECLARE
   Declare the pennies on your eyes (Taxman)--TAXMAN
      --23

DEEP
   Deep in love, not a lot to say --THINGSWESA--9
   Deep in love, not a lot to say --THINGSWESA--20
   Deep in love, not a lot to say --THINGSWESA--31
   Deep in the jungle where the mighty tiger lies --
      CONTINUING--17
   I've got a feeling, a feeling deep inside --
      IVEGOTAFEE--1
   Everybody had a hard time ((a feeling deep
      inside, oh yeah)) --IVEGOTAFEE--29

DEEPER
   The deeper you go, the higher you fly --EVRBDYMONK
      --8
   The higher you fly, the deeper you go --EVRBDYMONK
      --9

DEFELICHE
   Quando paramucho mi amore defeliche carathon --
      SUNKING--6

DELAY
   And if your heart's strong, hold on, I won't
      delay.--WAIT--6
   And if your heart's strong, hold on, I won't
      delay.--WAIT--22

DEMONSTRATE
   And Mr. H. will demonstrate--BEINGFORTH--17

DENIED
   Something inside that was always denied--SHESLEAVIN
      --31

DENNIS
   Featuring Dennis O'Fell and Ringo.--YOUKNOWMYN--6
   Let's hear it for Dennis - ah-hey.--YOUKNOWMYN--8
   (Oh) oh, you know, you know, you know my
      name (come on Dennis) --YOUKNOWMYN--16
   You know, you know my name ((oh, let's hear it,
      come on Dennis)) --YOUKNOWMYN--23
   ,Let's hear it for Dennis O'Fell.--YOUKNOWMYN--24

DENY
   Nobody can deny that there's something there.--
      HERETHEREA--4

DEPARTMENT
   And so I quit the police department--SHECAMEINT--16

DES
   Sont des mots qui vont tres bien ensemble, tres
      bien ensemble.--MICHELLE--4
   Sont des mots qui vont tres bien ensemble, tres
      bien ensemble.--MICHELLE--10
   Sont des mots qui vont tres bien ensemble, tres
      bien ensemble.--MICHELLE--21

DESERVE
   What have I done to deserve such a fate?--IMALOSER
      --15
   Which is all that I deserve--YOULIKEMET--10

DESMOND

Desmond has a barrow in the market-place --
    OBLADIOBLA--1
Desmond says to Molly, girl I like your face--
    OBLADIOBLA--3
Desmond takes a trolly to the jewellery store --
    OBLADIOBLA--9
With a couple of kids running in the yard of
    Desmond and Molly Jones.--OBLADIOBLA--18
Desmond lets the children lend a hand --OBLADIOBLA
    --21
With a couple of kids running in the yard of
    Desmond and Molly Jones.--OBLADIOBLA--30
Desmond stays at home and does his pretty face--
    OBLADIOBLA--34

DESSERT

Coffee dessert - yes you know it's good news --
    SAVOYTRUFF--3
Coffee dessert - yes you know it's good news
    (wuh) --SAVOYTRUFF--25

DESTRUCTION

But when you talk about destruction --REVOLUTION
    --8
But when you talk about destruction --REVOLUTONE
    --11

DETERMINED

Baby, I'm determined --RUNFORYOUR--19

DEVA

Jai Guru Deva OM.--ACROSSTHEU--6
Jai Guru Deva OM.--ACROSSTHEU--15
Jai Guru Deva OM.--ACROSSTHEU--25
Jai Guru Deva, Jai Guru Deva, Jai Guru
    Deva --ACROSSTHEU--30
Jai Guru Deva, Jai Guru Deva, Jai Guru
    Deva --ACROSSTHEU--30
Jai Guru Deva, Jai Guru Deva, Jai Guru
    Deva --ACROSSTHEU--30
Jai Guru Deva, Jai Guru Deva, Jai Guru
    Deva.--ACROSSTHEU--31
Jai Guru Deva, Jai Guru Deva, Jai Guru
    Deva.--ACROSSTHEU--31
Jai Guru Deva, Jai Guru Deva, Jai Guru
    Deva.--ACROSSTHEU--31

DIAMOND

I'll buy you a diamond ring my friend --CANTBUYMEL
    --3
Say you don't need no diamond rings --CANTBUYMEL
    --17
Say you don't need no diamond rings --CANTBUYMEL
    --27
He buys her diamond rings, you know, she said so
    --IFEELFINE--10
He buys her diamond rings, you know, she said so
    --IFEELFINE--18

DIAMONDS

LUCY IN THE SKY WITH DIAMONDS.--LUCYINTHES--Title
Lucy in the sky with diamonds --LUCYINTHES--9
Lucy in the sky with diamonds --LUCYINTHES--10
Lucy in the sky with diamonds - aah.--LUCYINTHES
    --11
Lucy in the sky with diamonds --LUCYINTHES--20
Lucy in the sky with diamonds --LUCYINTHES--21
Lucy in the sky with diamonds - aah.--LUCYINTHES
    --22
Lucy in the sky with diamonds --LUCYINTHES--27
Lucy in the sky with diamonds --LUCYINTHES--28
Lucy in the sky with diamonds - aah.--LUCYINTHES
    --29
Lucy in the sky with diamonds --LUCYINTHES--30
Lucy in the sky with diamonds --LUCYINTHES--31
Lucy in the sky with diamonds - aah.--LUCYINTHES
    --32
Lucy in the sky with diamonds --LUCYINTHES--33
Lucy in the sky with diamonds (aah - ooo),--
    LUCYINTHES--34
Lucy in the sky with diamonds.--LUCYINTHES--35

DID

Did you have to treat me oh so bad --TELLMEWHY--7
Treat me like you did the night before.--NIGHTBEFOR
    --4
Treat me like you did the night before.--NIGHTBEFOR
    --8
When I think of things we did it makes me wanna
    cry.--NIGHTBEFOR--10
Treat me like you did the night before (yes).--
    NIGHTBEFOR--14
Treat me like you did the night before (yeah).--
    NIGHTBEFOR--16
When I think of things we did it makes me wanna
    cry.--NIGHTBEFOR--18
Treat me like you did the night before.--NIGHTBEFOR
    --22
Did she understand it when they said --GIRL--23
I'm looking through you, where did you go?--
    IMLOOKINGT--1
I thought I knew you, what did I know?--IMLOOKINGT
    --2
Why, tell me why did you not treat me right?--
    IMLOOKINGT--9
Why, tell me why did you not treat me right?--
    IMLOOKINGT--15
I'm looking through you, where did you go?--
    IMLOOKINGT--17
I thought I knew you, what did I know?--IMLOOKINGT
    --18
Did you mean to break my heart and watch me die?--
    WHATGOESON--24
Ooo did I tell you I need you--GOTTOGETYO--6
Ooo did I tell you I need you--GOTTOGETYO--21
Did I tell you I need you--GOTTOGETYO--30
She (what did we do that was wrong?)--SHESLEAVIN
    --28
What did you see when you were there?--BABYYOUREA
    --11
Did you think that money was heaven sent?--
    LADYMADONN--4
What did you kill --CONTINUING--2
What did you kill --CONTINUING--5
What did you kill --CONTINUING--12
What did you kill --CONTINUING--15
What did you kill --CONTINUING--22
What did you kill --CONTINUING--25
What did you kill --CONTINUING--32
What did you kill --CONTINUING--35
What did you kill --CONTINUING--38
What did you kill --CONTINUING--41
What did you kill --CONTINUING--44
What did you kill --CONTINUING--47
What did you kill --CONTINUING--50
What did you kill --CONTINUING--53
Sexy Sadie how did you know--SEXYSADIE--12
Sexy Sadie - oh how did you know?--SEXYSADIE--15
Yes it did, nah nah nah nah nah nah nah - nah--
    YOUNEVERGI--23

DIDN'T

I didn't realise--INEEDYOU--8
I told her I didn't--NORWEGIANW--19
You didn't even think of me as someone with a name.
    --WHATGOESON--23
I didn't know what I would find there--GOTTOGETYO
    --2
You didn't run, you didn't lie--GOTTOGETYO--8
You didn't run, you didn't lie--GOTTOGETYO--8
I didn't know what I would find there--GOTTOGETYO
    --26
He didn't notice that the lights had changed--
    DAYINTHELI--7
Is having (we didn't know it was wrong)--SHESLEAVIN
    --29
Wednesday morning papers didn't come --LADYMADONN
    --15
Didn't get to bed last night --BACKINTHEU--2
I didn't catch your name --IWILL--6
Rocky didn't like that --ROCKYRACCO--5
You know they didn't even give us a chance.--
    BALLADOFJO--4
When you told me you didn't need me any more --
    OHDARLING--5
A - when you told me you didn't need me any more
    --OHDARLING--7
A - when you told me - ooo - you didn't need me
    any more --OHDARLING--12
A - when you told me you didn't need me any more
    --OHDARLING--14
Didn't anybody tell her?--SHECAMEINT--8
Didn't anybody see?--SHECAMEINT--9
Didn't anybody tell her?--SHECAMEINT--20
Didn't anybody see?--SHECAMEINT--21

DIE

Could never die --ANDILOVEHE--12

Will never die --ANDILOVEHE--18
Will never die --ANDILOVEHE--23
For I know love will never die.--EVERYLITTL--16
Did you mean to break my heart and watch me die?--
     WHATGOESON--24
Now my advice for those who die (Taxman)--TAXMAN
     --22
Yes I'm lonely - wanna die --YERBLUES--2
Yes I'm lonely - wanna die --YERBLUES--3
In the morning - wanna die --YERBLUES--6
In the evening - wanna die --YERBLUES--7
I'm lonely - wanna die --YERBLUES--14
Lonely -- wanna die --YERBLUES--21
Wanna die, yeah wanna die --YERBLUES--28
Wanna die, yeah wanna die --YERBLUES--28
Yes I'm lonely - wanna die --YERBLUES--31
Yes I'm lonely - wanna die --YERBLUES--32
... Wanna die --YERBLUES--34

DIED

I nearly died, I nearly died.--NOREPLY--14
I nearly died, I nearly died.--NOREPLY--14
I nearly died, I nearly died.--NOREPLY--27
I nearly died, I nearly died.--NOREPLY--27
Eleanor Rigby died in the church--ELEANORRIG--21
A - well you know, I nearly broke down and died.--
     OHDARLING--8
A - well you know, I nearly broke down and died.--
     OHDARLING--15

DIES

Each one believing that love never dies--HERETHEREA
     --12
Each one believing that love never dies--HERETHEREA
     --18

DIFFERENCE

The only difference is you're down there.--
     IMLOOKINGT--13
Makes no difference where you are--ITSALLTOOM--14

DIFFERENT

You don't look different, but you have changed --
     IMLOOKINGT--3
You don't sound different, I've learned the game
     --IMLOOKINGT--7
You don't look different, but you have changed --
     IMLOOKINGT--19

DIG

Can you dig it?--DONTLETMED--32
DIG IT.--DIGIT--Title
Dig it, dig it, dig it, dig it, dig it --DIGIT--10
Dig it, dig it, dig it, dig it, dig it --DIGIT--10
Dig it, dig it, dig it, dig it, dig it --DIGIT--10
Dig it, dig it, dig it, dig it, dig it --DIGIT--10
Dig it, dig it, dig it, dig it, dig it --DIGIT--10
((That was Can You Dig It? by Georgie
     Wood))--DIGIT--11
Dig it, dig it, dig it, dig it, dig
     it, dig it, dig it....--DIGIT--12
Dig it, dig it, dig it, dig it, dig it, dig
     it, dig it, dig it....--DIGIT--12
Dig it, dig it, dig it, dig it, dig it, dig
     it, dig it, dig it....--DIGIT--12
Dig it, dig it, dig it, dig it, dig it, dig
     it, dig it, dig it....--DIGIT--12
Dig it, dig it, dig it, dig it, dig it, dig
     it, dig it, dig it....--DIGIT--12
Dig it, dig it, dig it, dig it, dig it, dig
     it, dig it, dig it....--DIGIT--12
Dig it, dig it, dig it, dig it, dig it, dig
     it, dig it, dig it....--DIGIT--12
Dig it, dig it, dig it, dig it, dig it, dig
     it, dig it, dig it....--DIGIT--12
(I) DIG A PONY.--IDIGAPONY--Title
I dig a pony--IDIGAPONY--6
I dig a pygmy by Charles Hawtrey and the Deaf
     Aids (ha ha ha)--TWOOFUS--1

DIGGING

Doing the garden, digging the weeds--WHENIMSIXT
     --17

DINNER

Had a laugh and over dinner--LOVELYRITA--21
You can see them out for dinner--PIGGIES--17

DIRECTION

Look in my direction --ANDYOURBIR--8

DIRT

Father McKenzie wiping the dirt from his hands--
     ELEANORRIG--24
Crawling in the dirt?--PIGGIES--2
Always having dirt to play around in.--PIGGIES--5
Stirring up the dirt --PIGGIES--9

DIRTY

It's a dirty story of a dirty man --PAPERBACKW--8
It's a dirty story of a dirty man --PAPERBACKW--8
PC Thirty-One said, we caught a dirty one,
     Maxwell stands alone --MAXWELLSIL--17
Such a dirty old man, dirty old man.--MEANMRMUST
     --14
Such a dirty old man, dirty old man.--MEANMRMUST
     --14

DISAGREE

That is, I think I disagree.--STRAWBERRY--30
See the people standing there who disagree and
     never win--FIXINGAHOL--9

DISAPPEAR

There's nothing for me here so I will disappear --
     IDONTWANTT--3
There's nothing for me here so I will disappear --
     IDONTWANTT--15
Will never disappear, I've seen that road before.
     --LONGANDWIN--2

DISAPPEARING

Love has a nasty habit of disappearing overnight.
     --IMLOOKINGT--10
Love has a nasty habit of disappearing overnight.
     --IMLOOKINGT--16

DISAPPOINTMENT

I would hate my disappointment to show --IDONTWANTT
     --2
I would hate my disappointment to show --IDONTWANTT
     --14

DISCONNECT

Honey disconnect the phone.--BACKINTHEU--11

DISCOVERED

I've discovered I'm in love with you (oh - oh).--
     IMHAPPYJUS--27

DISCREETLY

May I inquire discreetly ((lovely Rita))--
     LOVELYRITA--14

DISEASE

Hold you in his armchair you can feel his disease
     --COMETOGETH--30

DIVERTED

I don't know how you were diverted --WHILEMYGUI--14

DO

LOVE ME DO.--LOVEMEDO--Title
Love, love me do --LOVEMEDO--1
So please love me do --LOVEMEDO--4
Whao-ho love me do.--LOVEMEDO--5
Love, love me do --LOVEMEDO--6
So please love me do --LOVEMEDO--9
Whoa-ho love me do.--LOVEMEDO--10
Love, love me do --LOVEMEDO--13
So please love me do --LOVEMEDO--16
Whoa-ho love me do (hey hey).--LOVEMEDO--17
Love, love me do --LOVEMEDO--18
So please love me do --LOVEMEDO--21
Whoa-ho love me do.--LOVEMEDO--22
Yes, love me do --LOVEMEDO--23
Whoa-ho love me do --LOVEMEDO--24
Yes, love me do.--LOVEMEDO--25
And till ((till)) the day I do love ((do love))

And till ((till)) the day I do love ((do love))
--PSILOVEYOU--8
And till the day I do love --PSILOVEYOU--20
All you gotta do is call --ANYTIMEATA--2
All you gotta do is call --ANYTIMEATA--11
There is nothing I won't do --ANYTIMEATA--15
All ya gotta do is call --ANYTIMEATA--20
All you gotta do is call --ANYTIMEATA--23
All ya gotta do is call --ANYTIMEATA--26
Why do I always have to say love --PLEASEPLEA--8
I do all the pleasing with you --PLEASEPLEA--16
Why do you make me blue?--PLEASEPLEA--18
I know/Why do you never even try girl--PLEASEPLEA--20
DO YOU WANT TO KNOW A SECRET?--DOYOUWANTT--Title
Listen, do you want to know a secret?--DOYOUWANTT
--3
Do you promise not to tell?--DOYOUWANTT--4
Listen (dodahdo) do you want to know a secret?
(dodahdo)--DOYOUWANTT--9
Do you promise not to tell? (dodahdo)--DOYOUWANTT
--10
Listen (dodahdo) do you want to know a secret?
(dodahdo)--DOYOUWANTT--17
Do you promise not to tell? (dodahdo)--DOYOUWANTT
--18
If there's anything I can do--FROMMETOYO--4
If there's anything I can do--FROMMETOYO--16
If there's anything I can do--FROMMETOYO--27
And all I gotta do is thank you girl, thank you
girl.--THANKYOUGI--4
And all I gotta do is thank you girl, thank you
girl--THANKYOUGI--7
Thank you girl, for loving me the way that you
do (way that you do).--THANKYOUGI--8
Thank you girl, for loving me the way that you
do (way that you do).--THANKYOUGI--8
And all I gotta do is thank you girl, thank you
girl.--THANKYOUGI--10
And all I gotta do is thank you girl, thank you
girl.--THANKYOUGI--14
ALL I'VE GOT TO DO.--ALLIVEGOTT--Title
All I gotta do --ALLIVEGOTT--2
Yeah, that's all I gotta do.--ALLIVEGOTT--5
All I gotta do --ALLIVEGOTT--7
All I gotta do --ALLIVEGOTT--18
Yeah, that's all I gotta do.--ALLIVEGOTT--21
YOU CAN'T DO THAT.--YOUCANTDOT--Title
Oh you can't do that.--YOUCANTDOT--8
Do I have to tell you one more time--YOUCANTDOT--11
Oh you can't do that.-YOUCANTDOT--17
Oh you can't do that - no!--YOUCANTDOT--31
You can't do that--YOUCANTDOT--32
You can't do that--YOUCANTDOT--33
You can't do that--YOUCANTDOT--34
You can't do that--YOUCANTDOT--35
You can't do that.--YOUCANTDOT--36
Oh you can't do that.--YOUCANTDOT--50
And things you do go round my head--THERESAPLA--6
That's all I do --ANDILOVEHE--2
I find the things that you do --HARDDAYSNI--6
I find the things that you do --HARDDAYSNI--22
I find the things that you do --HARDDAYSNI--35
That I would love everything that you do --
ISHOULDHAV--2
And I do, hey hey hey, and I do.--ISHOULDHAV--3
And I do, hey hey hey, and I do.--ISHOULDHAV--3
And when I do you'd better hide all the girls --
ILLCRYINST--15
And show you what your loving man can do --
ILLCRYINST--18
And when I do you'd better hide all the girls --
ILLCRYINST--24
And show you what your loving man can do --
ILLCRYINST--27
There is really nothing else I'd rather do --
IMHAPPYJUS--6
In this world there's nothing I would rather do --
IMHAPPYJUS--10
In this world there's nothing I would rather do --
IMHAPPYJUS--18
In this world there's nothing I would rather do --
IMHAPPYJUS--26
All I do is hang my head and moan.--TELLMEWHY--8
If there's anything I can do --TELLMEWHY--23
You could find better things to do--ILLBEBACK--9
You could find better things to do--ILLBEBACK--18
I got so many things I gotta do --WHENIGETHO--22
Oh dear, what can I do?--BABYSINBLA--2
Tell me, oh what can I do?--BABYSINBLA--3
Oh dear, what can I do?--BABYSINBLA--7
Tell me, oh what can I do?--BABYSINBLA--9
Dear what can I do?--BABYSINBLA--16
Tell me oh what can I do?--BABYSINBLA--18

Dear what can I do?--BABYSINBLA--21
Tell me oh what can I do?--BABYSINBLA--23
Oh dear, what can I do?--BABYSINBLA--27
Tell me oh what can I do?--BABYSINBLA--29
There's no fun in what I do when she's not there
--IDONTWANTT--6
There's no fun in what I do if she's not there --
IDONTWANTT--23
Wondering what you're gonna do --WHATYOURED--10
Wondering what you're gonna do --WHATYOURED--17
She ought to do right by me--TICKETTORI--19
She ought to do right by me.--TICKETTORI--22
She ought to do right by me--TICKETTORI--32
She ought to do right by me.--TICKETTORI--35
I really do.--YOULIKEMET--13
I really do--YOULIKEMET--22
And I do appreciate you being round--HELP--16
And I do appreciate you being round--HELP--26
And I do appreciate you being round--HELP--36
Nobody in all the world can do what she can do --
ANOTHERGIR--7
Nobody in all the world can do what she can do --
ANOTHERGIR--7
Why should I feel the way I do?--ITSONLYLOV--5
Why should I feel the way I do?--ITSONLYLOV--12
I'll make a point of taking her away from you
(watch what you do), yeah--YOUREGONNA--16
The way you treat her what else can I do?--
YOUREGONNA--17
I'll make a point of taking her away from you
(watch what you do), yeah--YOUREGONNA--23
The way you treat her what else can I do?--
YOUREGONNA--24
Do I have to keep on talking till I can't go on?--
WECANWORKI--2
But you can do something in between.--DRIVEMYCAR
--4
Until I do I'm hoping you will know what I mean.--
MICHELLE--14
Until I do I'm telling you so you'll understand.--
MICHELLE--19
To say about the things that you do.--THINKFORYO
--2
Do what you want to do --THINKFORYO--6
Do what you want to do --THINKFORYO--6
Do what you want to do --THINKFORYO--15
Do what you want to do --THINKFORYO--15
Do what you want to do --THINKFORYO--24
Do what you want to do --THINKFORYO--24
Do what you want to do --THINKFORYO--28
Do what you want to do --THINKFORYO--28
And if you do, I'll trust in you --WAIT--11
And if you do, I'll trust in you --WAIT--19
All the lonely people, where do they all come
from?--ELEANORRIG--9
All the lonely people, where do they all belong?--
ELEANORRIG--10
All the lonely people, where do they all come
from?--ELEANORRIG--17
All the lonely people, where do they all belong?--
ELEANORRIG--18
All the lonely people, where do they all come
from?--ELEANORRIG--27
All the lonely people, where do they all belong?--
ELEANORRIG--29
What can I do, what can I be?--GOTTOGETYO--16
And if I do I know the way there.--GOTTOGETYO--19
Nothing to do to save his life call his wife in--
GOODMORNIN--2
Nothing to do it's up to you--GOODMORNIN--4
How could she do this to me?--SHESLEAVIN--19
She (what did we do that was wrong?)--SHESLEAVIN
--28
What do I do when my love is away?--WITHALITTL--8
What do I do when my love is away?--WITHALITTL--8
How do I feel by the end of the day?--WITHALITTL
--10
(Do you need anybody?)--WITHALITTL--15
(What do you see when you turn out the light?)--
WITHALITTL--21
(Do you need anybody?)--WITHALITTL--26
There's nothing you can do that can't be done
((love))--ALLYOUN/YS--4
Nothing you can do but you can learn how to be
you in time ((love))--ALLYOUN/YS--10
What do you want to be?--BABYYOUREA--4
What a thing to do.--BABYYOUREA--18
What a thing to do (baby).--BABYYOUREA--33
Why, why, why, why, why, why do you say--HELLOGOODB
--16
They can tell what he wants to do--FOOLONTHEH--16
Do all without doing.--INNERLIGHT--17
Hey Jude, you'll do --HEYJUDE--23
Do do do do do do, oh yeah.--HAPPINESSI--2

Do do do do do do, oh yeah.--HAPPINESSI--2
Do do do do do do, oh yeah.--HAPPINESSI--2
Do do do do do do, oh yeah.--HAPPINESSI--2
Do do do do do do, oh yeah.--HAPPINESSI--2
Do do do do do do, oh yeah.--HAPPINESSI--2
I know nobody can do me no harm ((oh, yeah)) --
    HAPPINESSI--24
A - do you, don't you want me to love you?--
    HELTERSKEL--4
Well, do you, don't you want me to make you?--
    HELTERSKEL--21
For the things you do endear you to me - aah --
    IWILL--17
I'm so tired, I don't know what to do --IMSOTIRED
    --5
But I know what you would do.--IMSOTIRED--8
Do do do do do do do do do --MOTHERNATU--5
Do do do do do do do do do --MOTHERNATU--5
Do do do do do do do do do --MOTHERNATU--5
Do do do do do do do do do --MOTHERNATU--5
Do do do do do do do do do --MOTHERNATU--5
Do do do do do do do do do --MOTHERNATU--5
Do do do do do do do do do --MOTHERNATU--5
Do do do do do do do do do --MOTHERNATU--5
Do do do do do do do --MOTHERNATU--6
Do do do do do do do --MOTHERNATU--6
Do do do do do do do --MOTHERNATU--6
Do do do do do do do --MOTHERNATU--6
Do do do do do do do --MOTHERNATU--6
Do do do do do do do --MOTHERNATU--6
Do do do do do do do --MOTHERNATU--6
Do do.--MOTHERNATU--7
Do do.--MOTHERNATU--7
Do do do do do do do do do do --MOTHERNATU--10
Do do do do do do do do do do --MOTHERNATU--10
Do do do do do do do do do do --MOTHERNATU--10
Do do do do do do do do do do --MOTHERNATU--10
Do do do do do do do do do do --MOTHERNATU--10
Do do do do do do do do do do --MOTHERNATU--10
Do do do do do do do do do do --MOTHERNATU--10
Do do do do do do do do do do --MOTHERNATU--10
Do do do do do do --MOTHERNATU--11
Do do do do do do --MOTHERNATU--11
Do do do do do do --MOTHERNATU--11
Do do do do do do --MOTHERNATU--11
Do do do do do do --MOTHERNATU--11
Do do do do do do --MOTHERNATU--11
Do do do do do - yeah yeah yeah.--MOTHERNATU--12
Do do do do do - yeah yeah yeah.--MOTHERNATU--12
Do do do do do - yeah yeah yeah.--MOTHERNATU--12
Do do do do do - yeah yeah yeah.--MOTHERNATU--12
Do do do do do - yeah yeah yeah.--MOTHERNATU--12
Do do do do --ROCKYRACCO--26
Do do do do --ROCKYRACCO--26
Do do do do --ROCKYRACCO--26
Do do do do --ROCKYRACCO--26
Do - do do do do --ROCKYRACCO--27
Do - do do do do --ROCKYRACCO--27
Do - do do do do --ROCKYRACCO--27
Do - do do do do --ROCKYRACCO--27
Do - do do do do --ROCKYRACCO--27
Do - do do do do do --ROCKYRACCO--28
Do - do do do do do --ROCKYRACCO--28
Do - do do do do do --ROCKYRACCO--28
Do - do do do do do --ROCKYRACCO--28
Do - do do do do do --ROCKYRACCO--28
Do - do do do do do --ROCKYRACCO--28
Do - do do do do do do do --ROCKYRACCO--29
Do - do do do do do do do --ROCKYRACCO--29
Do - do do do do do do do --ROCKYRACCO--29
Do - do do do do do do do --ROCKYRACCO--29
Do - do do do do do do do --ROCKYRACCO--29
Do - do do do do do do do --ROCKYRACCO--29
Do - do do do do do do do --ROCKYRACCO--29
Da da da da do do do do do.--ROCKYRACCO--30
Da da da da do do do do do.--ROCKYRACCO--30
Da da da da do do do do do.--ROCKYRACCO--30
Da da da da do do do do do.--ROCKYRACCO--30
Da da da da do do do do do.--ROCKYRACCO--30
Do do do do do --ROCKYRACCO--41
Do do do do do --ROCKYRACCO--41
Do do do do do --ROCKYRACCO--41
Do do do do do --ROCKYRACCO--41
Do do do do do --ROCKYRACCO--41
Do - do do do do do --ROCKYRACCO--42
Do - do do do do do --ROCKYRACCO--42
Do - do do do do do --ROCKYRACCO--42
Do - do do do do do --ROCKYRACCO--42
Do - do do do do do --ROCKYRACCO--42
Do - do do do do do --ROCKYRACCO--42

Do - do do do do do do do do do --ROCKYRACCO--43
Do - do do do do do do do do do --ROCKYRACCO--43
Do - do do do do do do do do do --ROCKYRACCO--43
Do - do do do do do do do do do --ROCKYRACCO--43
Do - do do do do do do do do do --ROCKYRACCO--43
Do - do do do do do do do do do --ROCKYRACCO--43
Do - do do do do do do do do do --ROCKYRACCO--43
Do - do do do do do do do do do --ROCKYRACCO--43
Do - do do do do do do do do do --ROCKYRACCO--43
Do - do do do do do do do do do --ROCKYRACCO--43
Do do do do do --ROCKYRACCO--44
Do do do do do --ROCKYRACCO--44
Do do do do do --ROCKYRACCO--44
Do do do do do --ROCKYRACCO--44
Do do do do do --ROCKYRACCO--44
Do do do do - come on Rocky - boy --ROCKYRACCO--45
Do do do do - come on Rocky - boy --ROCKYRACCO--45
Do do do do - come on Rocky - boy --ROCKYRACCO--45
Do do do do - come on Rocky - boy --ROCKYRACCO--45
Do do do do - come on Rocky - boy --ROCKYRACCO
    --46
Do do do do - come on Rocky - boy --ROCKYRACCO
    --46
Do do do do - come on Rocky - boy --ROCKYRACCO
    --46
Do do do do - come on Rocky - boy --ROCKYRACCO
    --46
Do do do do - come on Rocky - boy --ROCKYRACCO
    --46
Do do do do do do do do --ROCKYRACCO--47
Do do do do do do do do --ROCKYRACCO--47
Do do do do do do do do --ROCKYRACCO--47
Do do do do do do do do --ROCKYRACCO--47
Do do do do do do do do --ROCKYRACCO--47
Do do do do do do do do --ROCKYRACCO--47
Do do do do do do do do --ROCKYRACCO--47
WHY DON'T WE DO IT IN THE ROAD?--WHYDONTWED--Title
Why don't we do - do it in the road?--WHYDONTWED
    --1
Why don't we do - do it in the road?--WHYDONTWED
    --1
Why don't we do it in the road? (ah-ha)--WHYDONTWED
    --2
Why don't we do it in the road? - mmm--WHYDONTWED
    --3
Why don't we do it in the road?--WHYDONTWED--4
Why don't we do it in the road?--WHYDONTWED--6
Why don't we do it in the road?--WHYDONTWED--7
Why don't we do it in the road?--WHYDONTWED--8
Why don't we do it in the road?--WHYDONTWED--9
Why don't we do it in the road?--WHYDONTWED--10
Why don't we do it in the road?--WHYDONTWED--12
Well, why don't we do it in the road?--WHYDONTWED
    --13
Why don't we do it in the road?--WHYDONTWED--14
Why don't we do - do it, do it in the road?--
    WHYDONTWED--15
Why don't we do - do it, do it in the road?--
    WHYDONTWED--15
Why don't we do - do it, do it in the road?--
    WHYDONTWED--15
Why don't we do it, yeah, in the road?--WHYDONTWED
    --16
Why don't you do it in the road?--WHYDONTWED--18
What do you say?--HEYBULLDOG--24
Do you know any more?--HEYBULLDOG--26
And what I do is all too much.--ITSALLTOOM--28
And if somebody loved me like she do me --
    DONTLETMED--7
Ooo she do me, yes she does.--DONTLETMED--8
Do - dow, do - do - do --OLDBROWNSH--37
Do - dow, do - do - do --OLDBROWNSH--37
Do - dow, do - do - do --OLDBROWNSH--37
Do - dow, do - do - do --OLDBROWNSH--37
Do - dow, do - do - do --OLDBROWNSH--38
Do - dow, do - do - do --OLDBROWNSH--38
Do - dow, do - do - do --OLDBROWNSH--38
Do - dow, do - do - do --OLDBROWNSH--38
Do - dow, do - do - do --OLDBROWNSH--39
Do - dow, do - do - do --OLDBROWNSH--39
Do - dow, do - do - do --OLDBROWNSH--39
Do - dow, do - do - do --OLDBROWNSH--39
Do - dow, do - do - do --OLDBROWNSH--40
Do - dow, do - do - do --OLDBROWNSH--40
Do - dow, do - do - do --OLDBROWNSH--40
Do - dow, do - do - do --OLDBROWNSH--41
Do - dow, do - do - do --OLDBROWNSH--41
Do - dow, do - do - do --OLDBROWNSH--41
Do - dow, do - do - do --OLDBROWNSH--41
Do - dow, do - do - do --OLDBROWNSH--42
Do - dow, do - do - do --OLDBROWNSH--42
Do - dow, do - do - do --OLDBROWNSH--42

Do - dow, do - do - do --OLDBROWNSH--42
Do - dow, do - do - do --OLDBROWNSH--43
Do - dow, do - do - do --OLDBROWNSH--43
Do - dow, do - do - do --OLDBROWNSH--43
Do - dow, do - do - do --OLDBROWNSH--44
Do - dow, do - do - do --OLDBROWNSH--44
Do - dow, do - do - do --OLDBROWNSH--44
Do - dow, do - do - do --OLDBROWNSH--44
Do - dow, do - do - do --OLDBROWNSH--45
Do - dow, do - do - do --OLDBROWNSH--45
Do - dow, do - do - do --OLDBROWNSH--45
Do - dow, do - do - do --OLDBROWNSH--45
Do - dow....--OLDBROWNSH--46
Got to be a joker he just do what he please--
    COMETOGETH--10
Sleep pretty darling do not cry--GOLDENSLUM--5
Sleep pretty darling do not cry--GOLDENSLUM--9
Sleep pretty darling do not cry--GOLDENSLUM--15
(Do do do do do)--MAXWELLSIL--14
(Do do do do do)--MAXWELLSIL--14
(Do do do do do)--MAXWELLSIL--14
(Do do do do do)--MAXWELLSIL--14
(Do do do do do)--MAXWELLSIL--14
(Do do do do do)--MAXWELLSIL--16
(Do do do do do)--MAXWELLSIL--16
(Do do do do do)--MAXWELLSIL--16
(Do do do do do)--MAXWELLSIL--16
(Do do do do do)--MAXWELLSIL--24
(Do do do do do)--MAXWELLSIL--24
(Do do do do do)--MAXWELLSIL--24
(Do do do do do)--MAXWELLSIL--24
(Do do do do do)--MAXWELLSIL--27
(Do do do do do)--MAXWELLSIL--27
(Do do do do do)--MAXWELLSIL--27
(Do do do do do)--MAXWELLSIL--27
(Do do do do do)--MAXWELLSIL--27
No-one there to tell us what to do.--OCTOPUSSGA--22
Oh darling, please believe me, I'll never do
    you no harm.--OHDARLING--1
Believe me when I tell you, I'll never do you
    no harm.--OHDARLING--2
Believe me when I tell you, I'll never do you
    no harm.--OHDARLING--10
Believe me when I tell you - ooo - I'll never
    do you no harm.--OHDARLING--18
And all I have to do is think of her --SOMETHING
    --16
((And now we'd like to do)) Hark the Angels
    Come...--DIGIT--13
I love you more than ever girl, I do.--FORYOUBLUE
    --4
You looked at me, that's all you had to do --
    FORYOUBLUE--14
I love you more than ever girl, I do - really
    love blues.--FORYOUBLUE--18
Oh I do a road hog--IDIGAPONY--9

DO-DO-DO
    Ha-ha-ha - do-do-do - oh-oh--HONEYPIE--33

DO-N-DO-DO
    Here comes the sun (do-n-do-do) --HERECOMEST--1
    Here comes the sun (do-n-do-do) --HERECOMEST--6
    Here comes the sun (do-n-do-do) --HERECOMEST--20
    Here comes the sun (do-n-do-do) --HERECOMEST--23

DOC
    And Rocky said, Doc it's only a scratch--ROCKYRACCO
        --34
    And I'll be better, I'll be better Doc as
        soon as I am able.--ROCKYRACCO--35

DOCK
    Standing in the dock at Southampton --BALLADOFJO
        --1

DOCTOR
    Now the doctor came in stinking of gin--ROCKYRACCO
        --31

DODAHDO
    Listen (dodahdo) do you want to know a secret?
        (dodahdo)--DOYOUWANTT--9
    Listen (dodahdo) do you want to know a secret?
        (dodahdo)--DOYOUWANTT--9
    Do you promise not to tell? (dodahdo)--DOYOUWANTT
        --10
    Whoa closer, (dodahdo)--DOYOUWANTT--11
    Let me whisper in your ear, (dodahdo)--DOYOUWANTT
        --12
    Listen (dodahdo) do you want to know a secret?
        (dodahdo)--DOYOUWANTT--17
    Listen (dodahdo) do you want to know a secret?
        (dodahdo)--DOYOUWANTT--17
    Do you promise not to tell? (dodahdo)--DOYOUWANTT
        --18
    Whoa closer, (dodahdo)--DOYOUWANTT--19
    Let me whisper in your ear, (dodahdo)--DOYOUWANTT
        --20

DOES
    Every little thing she does--EVERYLITTL--7
    She does for me, yeah--EVERYLITTL--8
    And you know the thing she does--EVERYLITTL--9
    She does for me, ooo.--EVERYLITTL--10
    Every little thing she does--EVERYLITTL--17
    She does for me, yeah--EVERYLITTL--18
    And you know the thing she does--EVERYLITTL--19
    She does for me, ooo.--EVERYLITTL--20
    Every little thing she does--EVERYLITTL--21
    She does for me, yeah--EVERYLITTL--22
    And you know the thing she does--EVERYLITTL--23
    She does for me, ooo.--EVERYLITTL--24
    He does everything he can, Dr. Robert.--DRROBERT
        --5
    He does everything he can, Dr. Robert.--DRROBERT
        --17
    What does he care?--ELEANORRIG--16
    (Does it worry you to be alone?)--WITHALITTL--9
    How does it feel to be--BABYYOUREA--1
    How does it feel to be--BABYYOUREA--7
    How does it feel to be--BABYYOUREA--22
    Does it mean you don't love me any more?--
        DONTPASSME--9
    Does it mean you don't love me any more?--
        DONTPASSME--17
    Molly stays at home and does her pretty face--
        OBLADIOBLA--23
    Desmond stays at home and does his pretty face--
        OBLADIOBLA--34
    Nobody ever loved me like she does --DONTLETMED--5
    Ooo she does, yes she does --DONTLETMED--6
    Ooo she does, yes she does --DONTLETMED--6
    Ooo she do me, yes she does.--DONTLETMED--8
    The judge does not agree and he tells them so oh
        - oh oh.--MAXWELLSIL--21

DOESN'T
    Doesn't have a point of view --NOWHEREMAN--4
    Doesn't have a point of view --NOWHEREMAN--16
    And his clinging wife doesn't understand.--
        PAPERBACKW--9
    She takes her time and doesn't feel she has to
        hurry --FORNOONE--5
    But now he's gone, she doesn't need him.--FORNOONE
        --19
    Someone is speaking but she doesn't know he's
        there.--HERETHEREA--7
    It doesn't matter much to me.--STRAWBERRY--10
    And it really doesn't matter if I'm wrong I'm
        right--FIXINGAHOL--8
    And it really doesn't matter if I'm wrong I'm
        right--FIXINGAHOL--15
    Nothing that doesn't show.--BABYYOUREA--12
    It doesn't really matter what chords I play --
        ONLYANORTH--7
    It doesn't really matter what clothes I wear --
        ONLYANORTH--10
    But she doesn't have a lot to say.--HERMAJESTY--2

DOG
    And I been working like a dog --HARDDAYSNI--2
    And I been working like a dog --HARDDAYSNI--18
    And I been working like a dog --HARDDAYSNI--31
    Sheep dog standing in the rain--HEYBULLDOG--1
    I pick a moon dog--IDIGAPONY--16

DOG'S
    Yellow matter custard, dripping from a dead
        dog's eye--IAMTHEWALR--12

DOING

WHAT YOU'RE DOING.--WHATYOURED--Title
Look ((look)) what you're doing --WHATYOURED--1
What you're doing to me?--WHATYOURED--4
What you're doing to me?--WHATYOURED--8
What you're doing to me?--WHATYOURED--15
What you're doing to me?--WHATYOURED--22
What you're doing to me?--WHATYOURED--23
What you're doing to me?--WHATYOURED--24
You're doing the best that I can.--GETTINGBET--15
And I'm doing the best that I can.--GETTINGBET--28
Everbody knows there's nothing doing--GOODMORNIN
    --9
Doing the garden, digging the weeds--WHENIMSIXT--17
Do all without doing.--INNERLIGHT--17
We're all doing what we can.--REVOLUTION--17
But it's no joke, it's doing me harm --IMSOTIRED
    --10
But it's no joke, it's doing me harm --IMSOTIRED
    --19
We're all doing what we can.--REVOLUTONE--25
Bull-frog doing it again--HEYBULLDOG--2
The news-people said, say what're you doing in
    bed?--BALLADOFJO--19

DON'T

Don't you be sad, just call me tonight.--ANYTIMEATA
    --9
You don't need me to show the way love --PLEASEPLEA
    --7
I don't want to start complaining --PLEASEPLEA--13
DON'T BOTHER ME.--DONTBOTHER--Title
Don't bother me--DONTBOTHER--8
Don't bother me--DONTBOTHER--14
If I don't get her back again--DONTBOTHER--16
Please don't come near--DONTBOTHER--20
Don't come around--DONTBOTHER--25
Don't bother me--DONTBOTHER--27
Don't bother me--DONTBOTHER--29
If I don't get her back again--DONTBOTHER--31
Please don't come near--DONTBOTHER--35
Don't come around--DONTBOTHER--40
Don't bother me--DONTBOTHER--42
Don't bother me--DONTBOTHER--43
Don't bother me--DONTBOTHER--44
Don't bother me--DONTBOTHER--45
Don't bother me.--DONTBOTHER--46
Don't know what it means to hold you tight --
    HOLDMETIGH--16
Don't know what it means to hold you tight --
    HOLDMETIGH--26
Don't you run and hide, just come on, come on --
    LITTLECHIL--17
'cos I don't care too much for money --CANTBUYMEL
    --7
I don't care too much for money --CANTBUYMEL--13
Say you don't need no diamond rings --CANTBUYMEL
    --17
I don't care too much for money --CANTBUYMEL--21
Say you don't need no diamond rings --CANTBUYMEL
    --27
I don't care too much for money --CANTBUYMEL--31
Don't you know I can't take it?--ICALLYOURN--5
I don't know who can --ICALLYOURN--6
Don't you know I can't take it?--ICALLYOURN--12
I don't know who can --ICALLYOURN--13
Don't you know that it's so?--THERESAPLA--10
Don't you know that it's so?--THERESAPLA--12
Oh please, don't run and hide --IFIFELL--11
Oh please, don't hurt my pride like her.--IFIFELL
    --13
Don't want to cry when there's people there --
    ILLCRYINST--11
Don't want to cry when there's people there --
    ILLCRYINST--20
I don't wanna kiss or hold your hand --IMHAPPYJUS
    --4
I don't need to hug or hold you tight --IMHAPPYJUS
    --8
If you don't I really can't go on --TELLMEWHY--15
My love don't give me presents--SHESAWOMAN--1
My love don't give me presents--SHESAWOMAN--4
She don't give boys the eye--SHESAWOMAN--8
She don't give boys the eye--SHESAWOMAN--12
Don't ask me why--SHESAWOMAN--15
My love don't give me presents--SHESAWOMAN--18
My love don't give me presents--SHESAWOMAN--21
My love don't give me presents--SHESAWOMAN--28
My love don't give me presents--SHESAWOMAN--31
I DON'T WANT TO SPOIL THE PARTY.--IDONTWANTT--Title
I don't wanna spoil the party so I'll go --
    IDONTWANTT--1
I've had a drink or two and I don't care --
    IDONTWANTT--5
I don't wanna spoil the party so I'll go --
    IDONTWANTT--13
Though I've had a drink or two and I don't care --
    IDONTWANTT--22
But she don't care.--TICKETTORI--8
But she don't care.--TICKETTORI--16
I don't know why she's riding so high--TICKETTORI
    --17
But she don't care.--TICKETTORI--29
I don't know why she's riding so high--TICKETTORI
    --30
But she don't care.--TICKETTORI--43
My baby don't care--TICKETTORI--44
My baby don't care--TICKETTORI--45
My baby don't care--TICKETTORI--46
My baby don't care--TICKETTORI--47
My baby don't care--TICKETTORI--48
Please don't wear red tonight--YESITIS--14
Please don't wear red tonight--YESITIS--23
Don't you realise now--TELLMEWHAT--15
If I just don't treat you right--YOULIKEMET--4
I ain't no fool and I don't take what I don't
    want --ANOTHERGIR--4
I ain't no fool and I don't take what I don't
    want --ANOTHERGIR--4
I don't wanna say that I've been unhappy with you
    --ANOTHERGIR--12
I ain't no fool and I don't take what I don't
    want --ANOTHERGIR--14
I ain't no fool and I don't take what I don't
    want --ANOTHERGIR--14
I don't wanna say that I've been unhappy with you
    --ANOTHERGIR--18
I ain't no fool and I don't take what I don't
    want --ANOTHERGIR--20
I ain't no fool and I don't take what I don't
    want --ANOTHERGIR--20
You don't realise how much I need you--INEEDYOU--1
You don't want my loving any more--INEEDYOU--12
You don't want my loving any more--INEEDYOU--22
Why she had to go, I don't know--YESTERDAY--9
Why she had to go, I don't know--YESTERDAY--17
If you don't take her out tonight--YOUREGONNA--3
If you don't treat her right my friend--YOUREGONNA
    --9
If you don't take her out tonight--YOUREGONNA--25
Still you don't regret a single day.--GIRL--4
After all this time I don't know why--GIRL--9
You don't look different, but you have changed --
    IMLOOKINGT--3
You don't sound different, I've learned the game
    --IMLOOKINGT--7
You don't look different, but you have changed --
    IMLOOKINGT--19
You don't know what you're missing --NOWHEREMAN--8
Nowhere Man don't worry --NOWHEREMAN--13
Take your time, don't hurry --NOWHEREMAN--14
You don't know what you're missing --NOWHEREMAN--20
But if your heart breaks, don't wait, turn me
    away --WAIT--5
But if your heart breaks, don't wait, turn me
    away --WAIT--21
I don't know why you should want to hide --
    YOUWONTSEE--7
I won't want to stay, I don't have much to say --
    YOUWONTSEE--9
Rain I don't mind--RAIN--7
Rain I don't mind--RAIN--7
But you don't get me, you don't get me.--ANDYOURBIR
    --3
But you don't get me, you don't get me.--ANDYOURBIR
    --3
Don't pay money just to see yourself with Dr.
    Robert.--DRROBERT--14
Please don't wake me, no, don't shake me --
    IMONLYSLEE--5
Please don't wake me, no, don't shake me --
    IMONLYSLEE--5
I don't mind, I think they're crazy --IMONLYSLEE
    --8
Please don't spoil my day, I'm miles away --
    IMONLYSLEE--11
Please don't spoil my day, I'm miles away --
    IMONLYSLEE--17
Please don't wake me, no, don't shake me --
    IMONLYSLEE--25
Please don't wake me, no, don't shake me --
    IMONLYSLEE--25
And yet you don't believe her --FORNOONE--11
I feel hung up and I don't know why --IWANTTOTEL
    --13
I don't mind, I could wait forever--IWANTTOTEL--14
I feel hung up and I don't know why --IWANTTOTEL

--20
I don't mind, I could wait forever--IWANTTOTEL--21
You don't get time to hang a sign on me.--
   LOVEYOUTWO--3
She said you don't understand what I said.--
   SHESAIDSHE--7
She said you don't understand what I said.--
   SHESAIDSHE--13
Be thankful I don't take it all --TAXMAN--8
Don't ask me what I want it for (ha ha Mr.
   Wilson)--TAXMAN--18
If you don't want to pay some more (ha ha Mr.
   Heath)--TAXMAN--19
As Mr. Kite flies through the ring - don't be
   late.--BEINGFORTH--11
And wonder why they don't get in my door.--
   FIXINGAHOL--10
And never ask me why they don't get past my door.
   --FIXINGAHOL--18
Go in to work don't want to go feeling low down--
   GOODMORNIN--7
I don't really want to stop the show--SGTPEPPERS
   --19
They don't know--WITHINYOUW--25
I don't know why you say goodbye, I say hello -
   hello, hello.--HELLOGOODB--5
I don't know why you say goodbye, I say hello.--
   HELLOGOODB--6
You say why and I say I don't know.--HELLOGOODB--8
I don't know why you say goodbye, I say hello -
   hello, hello.--HELLOGOODB--12
I don't know why you say goodbye, I say hello--
   HELLOGOODB--14
I don't know why you say goodbye, I say hello -
   hello, hello--HELLOGOODB--20
I don't know why you say goodbye, I say hello.--
   HELLOGOODB--21
I don't know why you say goodbye, I say hello -
   hello, hello--HELLOGOODB--28
I don't know why you say goodbye, I say hello -
   hello, hello--HELLOGOODB--29
I don't know why you say goodbye, I say hello -
   hello.--HELLOGOODB--30
If the sun don't come you get a tan from standing
   in the English rain--IAMTHEWALR--18
Expert texpert, choking smokers, don't you
   think the joker laughs at you?--IAMTHEWALR--21
Please don't be long --BLUEJAYWAY--5
Please don't you be very long --BLUEJAYWAY--6
Please don't be long or I may be asleep.--
   BLUEJAYWAY--7
Please don't be long (don't be long) --BLUEJAYWAY
   --12
Please don't be long (don't be long) --BLUEJAYWAY
   --12
Please don't you be very long (don't be long) --
   BLUEJAYWAY--13
Please don't you be very long (don't be long) --
   BLUEJAYWAY--13
Please don't be long or I may be asleep.--
   BLUEJAYWAY--14
Please don't be long (don't be long) --BLUEJAYWAY
   --19
Please don't be long (don't be long) --BLUEJAYWAY
   --19
Please don't you be very long (don't be long) --
   BLUEJAYWAY--20
Please don't you be very long (don't be long) --
   BLUEJAYWAY--20
Please don't be long or I may be asleep.--
   BLUEJAYWAY--21
Please don't be long --BLUEJAYWAY--22
Please don't you be very long--BLUEJAYWAY--23
Please don't be long.--BLUEJAYWAY--24
Please don't be long --BLUEJAYWAY--25
Please don't you be very long--BLUEJAYWAY--26
Please don't be long (please don't be long).--
   BLUEJAYWAY--27
Please don't be long (please don't be long).--
   BLUEJAYWAY--27
Please don't be long --BLUEJAYWAY--28
Please don't you be very long --BLUEJAYWAY--29
Please don't be long.--BLUEJAYWAY--30
Don't be long - don't be long --BLUEJAYWAY--31
Don't be long - don't be long --BLUEJAYWAY--31
Don't belong - don't be long--BLUEJAYWAY--32
Don't belong - don't be long--BLUEJAYWAY--32
Don't belong--BLUEJAYWAY--33
Don't belong--BLUEJAYWAY--34
Don't be long.--BLUEJAYWAY--35
They don't like him.--FOOLONTHEH--24
Hey Jude, don't make it bad --HEYJUDE--1
Hey Jude, don't be afraid --HEYJUDE--5
Don't carry the world upon your shoulder.--HEYJUDE

--11
Hey Jude, don't let me down --HEYJUDE--15
And don't you know that it's just you --HEYJUDE--22
Hey Jude, don't make it bad --HEYJUDE--26
Nah nah nah, nah - nah - nah - nah ((don't make
   it bad, Jude)) --HEYJUDE--47
Don't you know that you can count me out?--
   REVOLUTION--9
Don't you know it's gonna be alright, alright,
   alright?--REVOLUTION--10
Don't you know it's gonna be alright, alright
   ((alright)), alright?--REVOLUTION--20
Don't you know it's gonna be alright, alright,
   alright ((alright))?--REVOLUTION--30
You don't know how lucky you are boys --BACKINTHEU
   --6
You don't know how lucky you are boy --BACKINTHEU
   --13
You don't know how lucky you are boys --BACKINTHEU
   --25
You don't know how lucky you are boy --BACKINTHEU
   --36
DON'T PASS ME BY.--DONTPASSME--Title
But they don't arrive.--DONTPASSME--5
I don't hear it --DONTPASSME--8
Does it mean you don't love me any more?--
   DONTPASSME--9
I don't see you --DONTPASSME--16
Does it mean you don't love me any more?--
   DONTPASSME--17
Don't pass me by, don't make me cry, don't make
   me blue --DONTPASSME--18
Don't pass me by, don't make me cry, don't make
   me blue --DONTPASSME--18
Don't pass me by, don't make me cry, don't make
   me blue --DONTPASSME--18
Don't pass me by - don't make me cry.--DONTPASSME
   --22
Don't pass me by - don't make me cry.--DONTPASSME
   --22
Don't pass me by, don't make me cry, don't make
   me blue --DONTPASSME--31
Don't pass me by, don't make me cry, don't make
   me blue --DONTPASSME--31
Don't pass me by, don't make me cry, don't make
   me blue --DONTPASSME--31
Don't pass me by - don't make me cry.--DONTPASSME
   --35
Don't pass me by - don't make me cry.--DONTPASSME
   --35
Don't pass me by, don't make me cry, don't make
   me blue --DONTPASSME--37
Don't pass me by, don't make me cry, don't make
   me blue --DONTPASSME--37
Don't pass me by, don't make me cry, don't make
   me blue --DONTPASSME--37
Don't pass me by - don't make me cry.--DONTPASSME
   --41
Don't pass me by - don't make me cry.--DONTPASSME
   --41
Well, don't you know that happiness ((happiness))
   --HAPPINESSI--31
A - do you, don't you want me to love you?--
   HELTERSKEL--4
I'm coming down fast but don't let me break you --
   HELTERSKEL--12
Well, do you, don't you want me to make you?--
   HELTERSKEL--21
I'm coming down fast but don't let me break you --
   HELTERSKEL--22
I'm so tired, I don't know what to do,--IMSOTIRED
   --5
Don't forget me, Martha my dear.--MARTHAMYDE--3
Don't forget me, Martha my dear.--MARTHAMYDE--15
They don't care what goes on around.--PIGGIES--12
Don't you know that you can count me out (in)?--
   REVOLUTONE--12
Don't you know it's gonna be ((oh shoo-be-do-a))--
   REVOLUTONE--13
Don't you know it's gonna be ((oh shoo-be-do-a))--
   REVOLUTONE--15
Don't you know it's gonna be ((oh shoo-be-do-a))--
   REVOLUTONE--17
Don't you know it's gonna be ((oh shoo-be-do-a))--
   REVOLUTONE--29
Don't you know it's gonna be ((oh shoo-be-do-a))-
   --REVOLUTONE--31
Don't you know it's gonna be ((oh shoo-be-do-a))--
   REVOLUTONE--33
Don't you know it's gonna be ((oh shoo-be-do-a))--
   REVOLUTONE--45
Don't you know it's gonna be ((oh shoo-be-do-a))--
   REVOLUTONE--47
Don't you know it's gonna be ((oh shoo-be-do-a))--

REVOLUTONE--49
I don't know why nobody told you how to unfold
  your love --WHILEMYGUI--6
I don't know how someone controlled you --
  WHILEMYGUI--7
I don't know how you were diverted --WHILEMYGUI--14
I don't know how you were inverted --WHILEMYGUI--16
WHY DON'T WE DO IT IN THE ROAD?--WHYDONTWED--Title
Why don't we do - do it in the road?--WHYDONTWED
  --1
Why don't we do it in the road? (ah-ha)--WHYDONTWED
  --2
Why don't we do it in the road? - mmm--WHYDONTWED
  --3
Why don't we do it in the road?--WHYDONTWED--4
Why don't we do it in the road?--WHYDONTWED--6
Why don't we do it in the road?--WHYDONTWED--7
Why don't we do it in the road?--WHYDONTWED--8
Why don't we do it in the road?--WHYDONTWED--9
Why don't we do it in the road?--WHYDONTWED--10
Why don't we do it in the road?--WHYDONTWED--12
Well, why don't we do it in the road?--WHYDONTWED
  --13
Why don't we do it in the road?--WHYDONTWED--14
Why don't we do - do it, do it in the road?--
  WHYDONTWED--15
Why don't we do it, yeah, in the road?--WHYDONTWED
  --16
Why don't you do it in the road?--WHYDONTWED--18
You don't know what it's like to listen to your
  fears.--HEYBULLDOG--8
Don't look at me man (ha ha ha ha)--HEYBULLDOG--31
DON'T LET ME DOWN.--DONTLETMED--Title
Don't let me down --DONTLETMED--1
Don't let me down --DONTLETMED--2
Don't let me down --DONTLETMED--3
Don't let me down.--DONTLETMED--4
Don't let me down --DONTLETMED--9
Don't let me down --DONTLETMED--10
Don't let me down --DONTLETMED--11
Don't let me down --DONTLETMED--12
Don't you know it's gonna last,--DONTLETMED--14
Don't let me down --DONTLETMED--17
Don't let me down (ooo) --DONTLETMED--18
Don't let me down.--DONTLETMED--19
Don't let me down.--DONTLETMED--20
Don't let me down (hey) --DONTLETMED--25
Don't let me down --DONTLETMED--26
Eee ((don't let me down)) --DONTLETMED--27
Don't let me down.--DONTLETMED--28
Don't let me down.--DONTLETMED--30
Don't let me down, let me down --DONTLETMED--31
Don't ((hey)) let me down.--DONTLETMED--33
You don't take nothing with you but your soul -
  think!--BALLADOFJO--28
Believe me when I beg you - ooo - don't ever
  leave me alone.--OHDARLING--4
I don't want to leave her now --SOMETHING--4
That I don't need no other lover --SOMETHING--7
I don't want to leave her now,--SOMETHING--9
I don't know, I don't know --SOMETHING--12
I don't know, I don't know --SOMETHING--12
I don't know, I don't know.--SOMETHING--14
I don't know, I don't know.--SOMETHING--14
I don't want to leave her now --SOMETHING--18
Don't leave me waiting here, lead me to your door.
  --LONGANDWIN--11
Don't keep me waiting here (don't keep me
  waiting) lead me to your door.--LONGANDWIN--14
Don't keep me waiting here (don't keep me
  waiting) lead me to your door.--LONGANDWIN--14
Come on baby, don't be cold as ice --ONEAFTERNI--4
Come on baby, don't be cold as ice --ONEAFTERNI--9
Come on baby, don't be cold as ice --ONEAFTERNI--18
Come on baby, don't be cold as ice.--ONEAFTERNI--28

DONATED
  And donated to the National Trust.--HAPPINESSI--8

DONE
  I'll remember all the little things we've done --
    MISERY--6
  I'll remember all the little things we've done --
    MISERY--10
  Every day I've done nothing but cry--ITWONTBELO--16
  If it's something that I said or done --TELLMEWHY
    --13
  What have I done to deserve such a fate?--IMALOSER
    --15
  I've never done before.--HELP--24
  There's nothing you can do that can't be done
    ((love))--ALLYOUN/YS--4

Hold your head up you silly girl, look what
  you've done --MARTHAMYDE--4
Hold your hand out you silly girl, see what
  you've done --MARTHAMYDE--10
Sexy Sadie what have you done?--SEXYSADIE--1
Sexie Sadie - oh what have you done?--SEXYSADIE--4
You've got it, that's great, you've done it
  ((ha ha ha ha ha))--HEYBULLDOG--28
And from the first time that she really done me --
  DONTLETMED--21
Ooo she done me, she done me good --DONTLETMED--22
Ooo she done me, she done me good --DONTLETMED--22
I guess nobody ever really done me --DONTLETMED--23
Ooo she done me, she done me good.--DONTLETMED--24
Ooo she done me, she done me good.--DONTLETMED--24

DOOR
  Till I walk out that door again.--WHENIGETHO--20
  When I came to your door--NOREPLY--2
  I saw you walk in your door--NOREPLY--13
  I saw you walk in your door--NOREPLY--26
  Wearing the face that she keeps in a jar by the door
    --ELEANORRIG--7
  Many more of them live next door--YELLOWSUBM--14
  I'm filling the cracks that ran through the door--
    FIXINGAHOL--4
  And wonder why they don't get in my door.--
    FIXINGAHOL--10
  And never ask me why they don't get past my door.
    --FIXINGAHOL--18
  Silently closing her bedroom door--SHESLEAVIN--2
  Would you lock the door?--WHENIMSIXT--6
  Without going out of my door --INNERLIGHT--1
  Without going out of your door --INNERLIGHT--8
  On my old front door --DONTPASSME--7
  Takes it back to Molly waiting at the door--
    OBLADIOBLA--11
  But as she's getting ready to go, a knock comes
    on the door --MAXWELLSIL--5
  The long and winding road that leads to your door
    --LONGANDWIN--1
  It always leads me here, lead me to your door.--
    LONGANDWIN--3
  Don't leave me waiting here, lead me to your door.
    --LONGANDWIN--11
  Don't keep me waiting here (don't keep me
    waiting) lead me to your door.--LONGANDWIN--14

DOORS
  And opened up the doors.--HELP--14
  And opened up the doors.--HELP--34

DORIS
  And Doris Day--DIGIT--8
  Phase one in which Doris gets her oats.--TWOOFUS
    --2

DOSE
  Get a dose of her in jackboots and kilt --
    POLYTHENEP--6

DOUBT
  I know, little girl, only a fool would doubt
    our love--THANKYOUGI--6
  Gideon checked out and he left it no doubt ((oh
    - Rocky - oh))--ROCKYRACCO--38

DOUBTED
  I'm sorry that I doubted you --DONTPASSME--23

DOVE-TAIL
  Trying to make a dove-tail joint - yeah--GLASSONION
    --22

DOW
  Do - dow, do - do - do --OLDBROWNSH--37
  Do - dow, do - do - do --OLDBROWNSH--38
  Do - dow, do - do - do --OLDBROWNSH--39
  Do - dow, do - do - do --OLDBROWNSH--40
  Do - dow, do - do - do --OLDBROWNSH--41
  Do - dow, do - do - do --OLDBROWNSH--42
  Do - dow, do - do - do --OLDBROWNSH--43
  Do - dow, do - do - do --OLDBROWNSH--44
  Do - dow, do - do - do --OLDBROWNSH--45
  Do - dow...--OLDBROWNSH--46

DOWN
    Every night the tears come down from my eye--
        ITWONTBELO--15
    I'm gonna let you down--YOUCANTDOT--5
    I think I'll let you down (let you down)--
        YOUCANTDOT--13
    I think I'll let you down (let you down)--
        YOUCANTDOT--13
    (Gonna let you down and leave you flat)--YOUCANTDOT
        --15
    I'm gonna let you down (let you down)--YOUCANTDOT
        --27
    I'm gonna let you down (let you down)--YOUCANTDOT
        --27
    (Gonna let you down and leave you flat)--YOUCANTDOT
        --29
    I'm gonna let you down (let you down)--YOUCANTDOT
        --46
    I'm gonna let you down (let you down)--YOUCANTDOT
        --46
    (Gonna let you down and leave you flat)--YOUCANTDOT
        --48
    Was bringing her down, yeah--TICKETTORI--10
    Was bringing her down, yeah--TICKETTORI--37
    Help me if you can, I'm feeling down--HELP--15
    Help me if you can, I'm feeling down--HELP--25
    Help me if you can, I'm feeling down--HELP--35
    I'M DOWN.--IMDOWN--Title
    I'm down (I'm really down)--IMDOWN--3
    I'm down (I'm really down)--IMDOWN--3
    I'm down (down on the ground)--IMDOWN--4
    I'm down (down on the ground)--IMDOWN--4
    I'm down (I'm really down).--IMDOWN--5
    I'm down (I'm really down).--IMDOWN--5
    How can you laugh when you know I'm down?--IMDOWN
        --6
    (How can you laugh) when you know I'm down?--IMDOWN
        --7
    I'm down (I'm really down)--IMDOWN--10
    I'm down (I'm really down)--IMDOWN--10
    I'm down (down on the ground)--IMDOWN--11
    I'm down (down on the ground)--IMDOWN--11
    I'm down (I'm really down).--IMDOWN--12
    I'm down (I'm really down).--IMDOWN--12
    How can you laugh when you know I'm down?--IMDOWN
        --13
    (How can you laugh) when you know I'm down?--IMDOWN
        --14
    I'm down (I'm really down)--IMDOWN--18
    I'm down (I'm really down)--IMDOWN--18
    Oh baby, I'm down (down on the ground)--IMDOWN--19
    Oh baby, I'm down (down on the ground)--IMDOWN--19
    I'm down (I'm really down).--IMDOWN--20
    I'm down (I'm really down).--IMDOWN--20
    How can you laugh when you know I'm down?--IMDOWN
        --21
    (How can you laugh) when you know I'm down?--IMDOWN
        --22
    Baby you know I'm down (I'm really down)--IMDOWN
        --28
    Baby you know I'm down (I'm really down)--IMDOWN
        --28
    Oh yes, I'm down (I'm really down)--IMDOWN--29
    Oh yes, I'm down (I'm really down)--IMDOWN--29
    I'm down on the ground (I'm really down)--IMDOWN
        --30
    I'm down on the ground (I'm really down)--IMDOWN
        --30
    Ah, down (I'm really down)--IMDOWN--31
    Ah, down (I'm really down)--IMDOWN--31
    I'm down (I'm really down)--IMDOWN--34
    I'm down (I'm really down)--IMDOWN--34
    Oh baby, I'm down (I'm really down)--IMDOWN--35
    Oh baby, I'm down (I'm really down)--IMDOWN--35
    I'm feeling upside-down (I'm really down)--IMDOWN
        --36
    Ooo, I'm down (I'm really down)--IMDOWN--37
    Ooo, I'm down (I'm really down)--IMDOWN--37
    Baby, I'm down, yeah--IMDOWN--38
    Oh baby, I'm down, yeah--IMDOWN--39
    Baby, I'm down (I'm really down)--IMDOWN--40
    Baby, I'm down (I'm really down)--IMDOWN--40
    Well baby, I'm down (I'm really down)--IMDOWN--41
    Well baby, I'm down (I'm really down)--IMDOWN--41
    Oh baby, I'm down (I'm really down)--IMDOWN--43
    Oh baby, I'm down (I'm really down)--IMDOWN--43
    I'm down, down, down, down, down,
        down, down, down--IMDOWN--44
    I'm down, down, down, down, down, down,
        down, down, down--IMDOWN--44
    I'm down, down, down, down, down, down,
        down, down, down--IMDOWN--44
    I'm down, down, down, down, down, down,

    down, down, down--IMDOWN--44
    I'm down, down, down, down, down, down,
        down, down, down--IMDOWN--44
    I'm down, down, down, down, down, down,
        down, down, down--IMDOWN--44
    I'm down, down, down, down, down, down,
        down, down, down--IMDOWN--44
    I'm down, down, down, down, down, down,
        down, down, down--IMDOWN--44
    I'm down, down, down, down, down, down,
        down, down, down--IMDOWN--44
    Yeah, aah - ooo I'm down (down on the ground)--
        IMDOWN--45
    Yeah, aah - ooo I'm down (down on the ground)--
        IMDOWN--45
    She's the kind of girl who puts you down--GIRL--11
    The only difference is you're down there.--
        IMLOOKINGT--13
    When the sun shines they slip into the shade
        (when the sun shines down)--RAIN--4
    And sip their lemonade (when the sun shines down)
        --RAIN--5
    I can show you that when it starts to rain (when
        the rain comes down)--RAIN--9
    Everything's the same (when the rain comes down)--
        RAIN--10
    When your prized possessions start to weigh you
        down --ANDYOURBIR--7
    When your bird is broken will it bring you down?--
        ANDYOURBIR--10
    If you're down he'll pick you up, Dr. Robert --
        DRROBERT--6
    We take a walk, the sun is shining down --
        GOODDAYSUN--7
    The games begin to drag me down,--IWANTTOTEL--6
    Lay down all thought, surrender to the void--
        TOMORROWNE--3
    Let me take you down--STRAWBERRY--1
    Let me take you down--STRAWBERRY--11
    Let me take you down--STRAWBERRY--21
    Let me take you down--STRAWBERRY--31
    You're holding me down (aah) turning me round
        (aah)--GETTINGBET--5
    Go in to work don't want to go feeling low down--
        GOODMORNIN--7
    Follow her down to a bridge by a fountain--
        LUCYINTHES--12
    She breaks down and cries to her husband--
        SHESLEAVIN--16
    Boy, you been a naughty girl, you let your
        knickers down--IAMTHEWALR--14
    But the fool on the hill sees the sun going down--
        FOOLONTHEH--6
    But the fool on the hill sees the sun going down--
        FOOLONTHEH--13
    But the fool on the hill sees the sun going down--
        FOOLONTHEH--18
    The fool on the hill sees the sun going down--
        FOOLONTHEH--25
    Hey Jude, don't let me down --HEYJUDE--15
    Oh - show me round the snow-peaked mountains way
        down south --BACKINTHEU--31
    I need a fix 'cos I'm going down --HAPPINESSI--9
    Down to the bits that I left uptown --HAPPINESSI
        --10
    I need a fix 'cos I'm going down.--HAPPINESSI--11
    I'm coming down fast but I'm miles above you --
        HELTERSKEL--5
    I'm coming down fast but don't let me break you --
        HELTERSKEL--12
    I'm coming down fast but don't let me break you --
        HELTERSKEL--22
    She's coming down fast --HELTERSKEL--28
    Coming down fast (oh I hear my baby speaking -
        ooo)...--HELTERSKEL--30
    Cocoanut fudge really blows down those blues
        (wuh) --SAVOYTRUFF--8
    You layed it down for all to see--SEXYSADIE--6
    You layed it down for all to see--SEXYSADIE--7
    Floating down the stream of time--ITSALLTOOM--12
    DON'T LET ME DOWN.--DONTLETMED--Title
    Don't let me down --DONTLETMED--1
    Don't let me down --DONTLETMED--2
    Don't let me down --DONTLETMED--3
    Don't let me down.--DONTLETMED--4
    Don't let me down --DONTLETMED--9
    Don't let me down --DONTLETMED--10
    Don't let me down --DONTLETMED--11
    Don't let me down --DONTLETMED--12
    Don't let me down --DONTLETMED--17
    Don't let me down (ooo) --DONTLETMED--18
    Don't let me down.--DONTLETMED--19
    Don't let me down.--DONTLETMED--20
    Don't let me down (hey) --DONTLETMED--25

Don't let me down --DONTLETMED--26
Eee ((don't let me down)) --DONTLETMED--27
Don't let me down.--DONTLETMED--28
Don't let me down --DONTLETMED--30
Don't let me down, let me down --DONTLETMED--31
Don't let me down, let me down --DONTLETMED--31
Don't ((hey)) let me down.--DONTLETMED--33
Honeymooning down by the Seine.--BALLADOFJO--10
From where some try to drag me down --OLDBROWNSH
    --10
I break down.--CARRYTHATW--8
He got hair down to his knee--COMETOGETH--9
He got feet down below his knee--COMETOGETH--29
Bang, bang Maxwell's silver hammer came down
    upon her head --MAXWELLSIL--6
Bang, bang Maxwell's silver hammer came down
    upon her head --MAXWELLSIL--13
Bang, bang Maxwell's silver hammer came down
    upon his head --MAXWELLSIL--23
Well you know I nearly broke down and cried.--
    OHDARLING--6
A - well you know, I nearly broke down and died.--
    OHDARLING--8
A - well you know I nearly broke down and cried.--
    OHDARLING--13
A - well you know, I nearly broke down and died.--
    OHDARLING--15
Oh darling, please believe me, I'll never let
    you down.--OHDARLING--16
And in the middle of negotiations you break down.
    --YOUNEVERGI--3
And in the middle of investigation I break down.--
    YOUNEVERGI--6
Everybody let their hair down --IVEGOTAFEE--25
Everybody put the fool down, oh yeah - (yeah).--
    IVEGOTAFEE--27
Everybody let their hair down ((a feeling I
    can't hide, oh no)) --IVEGOTAFEE--33
Everybody put their foot down, oh yeah (yeah).--
    IVEGOTAFEE--35

DOWN-STREAM

Turn off your mind, relax and float down-stream--
    TOMORROWNE--1

DOWNSTAIRS

Found my way downstairs and drank a cup--DAYINTHELI
    --20
She goes downstairs to the kitchen--SHESLEAVIN--4

DR

DR. ROBERT.--DRROBERT--Title
Ring my friend I said you'd call, Dr. Robert --
    DRROBERT--1
Day or night he'll be there any time at all, Dr.
    Robert --DRROBERT--2
Dr. Robert, you're a new and better man --DRROBERT
    --3
He does everything he can, Dr. Robert.--DRROBERT
    --5
If you're down he'll pick you up, Dr. Robert --
    DRROBERT--6
Take a drink from his special cup, Dr. Robert.--
    DRROBERT--7
Dr. Robert, he's a man you must believe --DRROBERT
    --8
No-one can succeed like Dr. Robert.--DRROBERT--10
Well, well, well, he'll make you, Dr. Robert.--
    DRROBERT--12
My friend works for the National Health, Dr.
    Robert --DRROBERT--13
Don't pay money just to see yourself with Dr.
    Robert.--DRROBERT--14
Dr. Robert, you're a new and better man --DRROBERT
    --15
He does everything he can, Dr. Robert.--DRROBERT
    --17
Well, well, well, he'll make you, Dr. Robert.--
    DRROBERT--19
Ring my friend I said you'd call, Dr. Robert --
    DRROBERT--20
Ring my friend I said you'd call, Dr. Robert --
    DRROBERT--21
Dr. Robert!--DRROBERT--22

DRAG

It's gonna be a drag, misery.--MISERY--5
The games begin to drag me down --IWANTTOTEL--6
They look just like two gurus in drag.--BALLADOFJO
    --32

From where some try to drag me down --OLDBROWNSH
    --10
Well, you should see her in drag --POLYTHENEP--3

DRAGGED

Dragged a comb across my head--DAYINTHELI--19

DRANK

Found my way downstairs and drank a cup--DAYINTHELI
    --20

DREADFUL

Man I had a dreadful flight.--BACKINTHEU--4

DREAM

But as it is I'll dream of her tonight --IVEJUSTSEE
    --10
When I'm in the middle of a dream --IMONLYSLEE--3
When I'm in the middle of a dream --IMONLYSLEE--23
Lives in a dream.--ELEANORRIG--5
But, you know, I know when it's a dream--STRAWBERRY
    --27
And somebody spoke and I went into a dream--
    DAYINTHELI--26
Dream sweet dreams for me --GOODNIGHT--5
Dream sweet dreams for you.--GOODNIGHT--6
Dream sweet dreams for me --GOODNIGHT--11
Dream sweet dreams for you.--GOODNIGHT--12
Dream sweet dreams for me --GOODNIGHT--18
Dream sweet dreams for you.--GOODNIGHT--19
One sweet dream,--YOUNEVERGI--17
One sweet dream came true today --YOUNEVERGI--21
Everybody had a wet dream --IVEGOTAFEE--21
Everybody had a wet dream (oh yeah) --IVEGOTAFEE
    --30

DREAMING

Someday when we're dreaming --THINGSWESA--8
Someday when we're dreaming --THINGSWESA--19
Someday when we're dreaming --THINGSWESA--30

DREAMS

And hope that my dreams will come true --ALLMYLOVIN
    --9
But listen to the colour of your dreams--TOMORROWNE
    --11
Dream sweet dreams for me --GOODNIGHT--5
Dream sweet dreams for you.--GOODNIGHT--6
Dream sweet dreams for me --GOODNIGHT--11
Dream sweet dreams for you.--GOODNIGHT--12
Dream sweet dreams for me --GOODNIGHT--18
Dream sweet dreams for you.--GOODNIGHT--19
His rival it seems had broken his dreams--
    ROCKYRACCO--13
Are you gonna be in my dreams tonight?--THEEND--2

DRESSED

She's dressed in black.--BABYSINBLA--6
She's dressed in black.--BABYSINBLA--26
Dressed in her polythene bag.--POLYTHENEP--4
She's killer-diller when she's dressed to the hilt.
    --POLYTHENEP--7

DRESSES

She thinks of him and so she dresses in black --
    BABYSINBLA--4
She thinks of him and so she dresses in black --
    BABYSINBLA--24

DRESSING-GOWN

Father snores as his wife gets into her
    dressing-gown--SHESLEAVIN--13

DREW

But Daniel was hot, he drew first and shot--
    ROCKYRACCO--21

DRIFT

Everyone smiles as you drift past the flowers--
    LUCYINTHES--14

DRIFTING

Are drifting through my opened mind--ACROSSTHEU
--4

DRINK
I've had a drink or two and I don't care --
IDONTWANTT--5
Though I've had a drink or two and I don't care --
IDONTWANTT--22
Take a drink from his special cup, Dr. Robert.--
DRROBERT--7
I wonder should I get up and fix myself a drink --
IMSOTIRED--3

DRINKING
Drinking her wine.--NORWEGIANW--13

DRIPPING
Yellow matter custard, dripping from a dead
dog's eye--IAMTHEWALR--12

DRIVE
DRIVE MY CAR.--DRIVEMYCAR--Title
Baby you can drive my car --DRIVEMYCAR--5
Baby you can drive my car --DRIVEMYCAR--7
Baby you can drive my car --DRIVEMYCAR--13
Baby you can drive my car --DRIVEMYCAR--15
Baby you can drive my car --DRIVEMYCAR--18
Baby you can drive my car --DRIVEMYCAR--20
Baby you can drive my car --DRIVEMYCAR--26
Baby you can drive my car --DRIVEMYCAR--28
If you drive a car, I'll tax the street,
((car))--TAXMAN--11
Coming up the drive --DONTPASSME--3

DRIVER
Sunday driver, yeah --DAYTRIPPER--23
But I've found a driver and that's a start.--
DRIVEMYCAR--25

DRIVING
The girl that's driving me mad is going away.--
TICKETTORI--4
The girl that's driving me mad is going away,
yeah.--TICKETTORI--25
Oh, Honey Pie you are driving me frantic--HONEYPIE
--16
It's driving me mad--IWANTYOUSH--5
It's driving me mad--IWANTYOUSH--6
It's driving me mad--IWANTYOUSH--11
It's driving me--IWANTYOUSH--12
It's driving me mad--IWANTYOUSH--17
It's driving me mad--IWANTYOUSH--18
It's driving me mad--IWANTYOUSH--23
It's driving me--IWANTYOUSH--24
It's driving me mad--IWANTYOUSH--32
It's driving me mad--IWANTYOUSH--33
It's driving me mad--IWANTYOUSH--38
It's driving me mad--IWANTYOUSH--39
You and me Sunday driving --TWOOFUS--5

DROP
Cut the cable, drop the cable.--YELLOWSUBM--22
Send me a postcard, drop me a line--WHENIMSIXT--28

DROVE
Drove from Paris to the Amsterdam Hilton --
BALLADOFJO--17

DUCHESS
The Duchess of Kirkaldy always smiling --CRYBABYCRY
--20

DUKE
The Duke was having problems --CRYBABYCRY--22

DUM
Da da da, da da dum dum da--FROMMETOYO--1
Da da da, da da dum dum da--FROMMETOYO--1
Da da da, da da dum dum da.--FROMMETOYO--2
Da da da, da da dum dum da.--FROMMETOYO--2

DYING

It is not dying, it is not dying.--TOMORROWNE--2
It is not dying, it is not dying.--TOMORROWNE--2
The Magical Mystery Tour is dying to take you
away--MAGICALMYS--29
(Dying to take you away)--MAGICALMYS--30

DYLAN'S
Just like Dylan's Mr. Jones.--YERBLUES--20

E
Tuned to a natural E --BABYYOUREA--24
E, F, G, H, I, J --ALLTOGETHE--7

EACH
And we held each other tight --ISAWHERSTA--14
And we held each other tight --ISAWHERSTA--21
Each and every day.--YOUVEGOTTO--6
Here, making each day of the year--HERETHEREA--2
Each one believing that love never dies--HERETHEREA
--12
Each one believing that love never dies--HERETHEREA
--18
Each day just goes so fast--LOVEYOUTWO--1
That you and me were meant to be for each other -
silly girl.--MARTHAMYDE--9

EAGLE
The eagle picks my eye --YERBLUES--17

EAR
Let me whisper in your ear --DOYOUWANTT--6
Let me whisper in your ear, (dodahdo)--DOYOUWANTT
--12
Let me whisper in your ear, (dodahdo)--DOYOUWANTT
--20
Is whisper in your ear --ALLIVEGOTT--8

EARLY
When I wake up early in the morning --IMONLYSLEE
--1
When I wake up early in the morning --IMONLYSLEE
--21
Caught the early plane back to London --BALLADOFJO
--37
Make an early start --OLDBROWNSH--29
He got early warning--COMETOGETH--37

EARN
That a man must break his back to earn his day of
leisure?--GIRL--24

EARS
Penny Lane is in my ears and in my eyes--PENNYLANE
--9
Penny Lane is in my ears and in my eyes--PENNYLANE
--17
Penny Lane is in my ears and in my eyes--PENNYLANE
--28
Penny Lane is in my ears and in my eyes--PENNYLANE
--31
Lend me your ears and I'll sing you a song--
WITHALITTL--3
Are ringing through my opened ears--ACROSSTHEU
--21

EARTH
So why on earth should I moan --HARDDAYSNI--12
So why on earth should I moan --HARDDAYSNI--25
I got every reason on earth to be mad --ILLCRYINST
--1
And she promises the earth to me and I believe
her --GIRL--8
I can know all things on earth.--INNERLIGHT--2
You can know all things on earth.--INNERLIGHT--9
My father was of the earth --YERBLUES--11

EASE
As we live a life of ease--YELLOWSUBM--25

EASY
It's easy 'cos I know--ILLGETYOU--3
It's easy 'cos I know--ILLGETYOU--20
Love was such an easy game to play--YESTERDAY--14

Love was such an easy game to play--YESTERDAY--22
For taking the easy way out --DAYTRIPPER--2
For taking the easy way out, now.--DAYTRIPPER--4
It's so easy for a girl like you to lie.--
    WHATGOESON--8
It's so easy for a girl like you to lie.--
    WHATGOESON--17
Living is easy with eyes closed--STRAWBERRY--6
It's easy.--ALLYOUN/YS--7
It's easy.--ALLYOUN/YS--11
It's easy.--ALLYOUN/YS--22
Come on is take it easy --EVRBDYMONK--4
Come on is take it easy --EVRBDYMONK--5
Take it easy, take it easy --EVRBDYMONK--6
Take it easy, take it easy --EVRBDYMONK--6
Come on is make it easy --EVRBDYMONK--13
Come on is make it easy - wuh.--EVRBDYMONK--14
Take it easy, take it easy - wuh --EVRBDYMONK--15
Take it easy, take it easy - wuh --EVRBDYMONK--15
Come on is make it easy --EVRBDYMONK--22
Come on is make it easy --EVRBDYMONK--23
Make it easy (wuh), make it easy (wuh) --EVRBDYMONK
    --24
Make it easy (wuh), make it easy (wuh) --EVRBDYMONK
    --24
Make it easy to be near you --IWILL--16
Christ! you know it ain't easy --BALLADOFJO--5
Christ! you know it ain't easy --BALLADOFJO--13
Christ! you know it ain't easy --BALLADOFJO--21
Christ! you know it ain't easy --BALLADOFJO--33
Christ! you know it ain't easy --BALLADOFJO--41

EAT
Where rocking-horse people eat marshmallow pies.--
    LUCYINTHES--13
Clutching forks and knives to eat the bacon.--
    PIGGIES--3
You know that what you eat you are --SAVOYTRUFF--19
Questo obrigado tanta mucho cake and eat it
    carousel.--SUNKING--8

EATING
Eating chocolate cake in the bag.--BALLADOFJO--30

EDGAR
Man you should have seen them kicking Edgar
    Allan Poe--IAMTHEWALR--27

EDISON
Maxwell Edison, majoring in medicine, calls
    her on the phone --MAXWELLSIL--3

EEE
Love is all you need (yahoo) (eee - hi)--
    ALLYOUN/YS--38
Still my guitar gently weeps ((eee)).--WHILEMYGUI--21
Oh - oh, oh - oh, oh - oh, oh ((eee)).--WHILEMYGUI--23
Oh - oh, oh - oh, oh - oh ((eee)).--WHILEMYGUI--24
Yeah, yeah, yeah, yeah, yeah, yeah, yeah,
    yeah, yeah ((eee))--WHILEMYGUI--25
Oh - wuh... ((eee))--WHILEMYGUI--26
Eee ((don't let me down)) --DONTLETMED--27
Eee - (yeah) aah --DONTLETMED--29

EGGMAN
I am the eggman (goo) they are the eggmen (goo)
    I am the walrus--IAMTHEWALR--7
I am the eggman (goo) they are the eggmen (goo)
    I am the walrus--IAMTHEWALR--15
I am the eggman, they are the eggmen, I am the
    walrus--IAMTHEWALR--19
I am the eggman (goo) they are the eggmen (goo)
    I am the walrus (goo)--IAMTHEWALR--28

EGGMEN
I am the eggman (goo) they are the eggmen (goo)
    I am the walrus--IAMTHEWALR--7
I am the eggman (goo) they are the eggmen (goo)
    I am the walrus--IAMTHEWALR--15
I am the eggman, they are the eggmen, I am the
    walrus--IAMTHEWALR--19
I am the eggman (goo) they are the eggmen (goo)
    I am the walrus (goo)--IAMTHEWALR--28

EIFFEL
Semolina pilchard climbing up the Eiffel Tower--

IAMTHEWALR--25

EIGHT
EIGHT DAYS A WEEK.--EIGHTDAYSA--Title
Eight days a week.--EIGHTDAYSA--8
Eight days a week.--EIGHTDAYSA--16
Eight days a week I love you,--EIGHTDAYSA--17
Eight days a week is not enough to show I care.--
    EIGHTDAYSA--18
Eight days a week.--EIGHTDAYSA--26
Eight days a week I love you --EIGHTDAYSA--27
Eight days a week is not enough to show I care.--
    EIGHTDAYSA--28
Eight days a week --EIGHTDAYSA--36
Eight days a week.--EIGHTDAYSA--37
Eight days a week.--EIGHTDAYSA--38
... Four, five, six, seven, eight, nine,
    ten ...--DAYINTHELI--35
(... Four, five, six, seven, eight!)--BIRTHDAY--7
One, two, three, four, five, six, seven,
    eight.--DONTPASSME--36
Five, six, seven, eight, nine, ten --ALLTOGETHE--3

ELEANOR
ELEANOR RIGBY.--ELEANORRIG--Title
Eleanor Rigby picks up the rice in the church--
    ELEANORRIG--3
Eleanor Rigby died in the church--ELEANORRIG--21

ELEMENTARY
Elementary penguin singing Hare Krishna--IAMTHEWALR
    --26

ELEPHANT
He went out tiger hunting with his elephant and
    gun --CONTINUING--7

ELEPHANTS
Bill and his elephants were taken by surprise --
    CONTINUING--18

ELMORE
Elmore James got nothing on this baby - heh.--
    FORYOUBLUE--12

ELSE
There is really nothing else I'd rather do --
    IMHAPPYJUS--6
We're all alone and there's nobody else --IMDOWN
    --16
The way you treat her what else can I do?--
    YOUREGONNA--17
The way you treat her what else can I do?--
    YOUREGONNA--24
Leave it all till somebody else lends you a hand.
    --NOWHEREMAN--15
I used to think of no-one else but you were just
    the same --WHATGOESON--22
No-one else can make you change--WITHINYOUW--17

END
But I'll get you, I'll get you in the end--
    ILLGETYOU--7
Yes I will I'll get you in the end, oh yeah,
    oh yeah.--ILLGETYOU--8
That I'll get you, I'll get you in the end--
    ILLGETYOU--14
Yes I will, I'll get you in the end, oh yeah,
    oh yeah.--ILLGETYOU--15
But I'll get you, I'll get you in the end--
    ILLGETYOU--24
Yes I will, I'll get you in the end, oh yeah,
    oh yeah--ILLGETYOU--25
You say you'll be mine girl, till the end of time
    --THINGSWESA--6
And though I lose a friend in the end you will
    know, oh.--ILLFOLLOWT--6
And though I lose a friend in the end you will
    know, oh.--ILLFOLLOWT--11
I should have known she would win in the end.--
    IMALOSER--6
Another girl who will love me till the end --
    ANOTHERGIR--10
Another girl who will love me till the end --
    ANOTHERGIR--16
Or play the game existence to the end--TOMORROWNE

--13
It's getting very near the end.--SGTPEPPREP--14
How do I feel by the end of the day?--WITHALITTL--10
THE END.--THEEND--Title
And in the end --THEEND--8

END'A
That's the end'a little girl.--RUNFORYOUR--8
That's the end'a little girl.--RUNFORYOUR--16
That's the end'a little girl.--RUNFORYOUR--24
That's the end'a little girl.--RUNFORYOUR--32

ENDEAR
For the things you do endear you to me - aah --
    IWILL--17

ENDLESS
Words are flowing out like endless rain into a
    paper cup --ACROSSTHEU--1

ENDS
Wonder how you manage to make ends meet.--
    LADYMADONN--2
Wonder how you manage to make ends meet.--
    LADYMADONN--19
Lady Madonna trying to make ends meet - yeah--
    GLASSONION--13

ENGAGED
When I call you up your line's engaged.--YOUWONTSEE--1

ENGLAND
North of England way--HONEYPIE--2

ENGLISH
The English Army had just won the war--DAYINTHELI--12
Sitting in an English garden waiting for the sun--
    IAMTHEWALR--17
If the sun don't come you get a tan from standing
    in the English rain--IAMTHEWALR--18

ENJOY
We hope you will enjoy the show--SGTPEPPERS--9

ENJOYED
We hope you have enjoyed the show.--SGTPEPPREP--4

ENOUGH
And that's enough to make you mine girl --
    THINGSWESA--15
And that's enough to make you mine girl --
    THINGSWESA--26
Eight days a week is not enough to show I care.--
    EIGHTDAYSA--18
Eight days a week is not enough to show I care.--
    EIGHTDAYSA--28
I have had enough, so act your age.--YOUWONTSEE--2
Often enough to know.--BABYYOUREA--10
She's old enough to know better.--CRYBABYCRY--3
She's old enough to know better --CRYBABYCRY--10
She's old enough to know better --CRYBABYCRY--18
She's old enough to know better --CRYBABYCRY--26
She's old enough to know better --CRYBABYCRY--34
She's old enough to know better --CRYBABYCRY--38
She's old enough to know better --CRYBABYCRY--42

ENSEMBLE
Sont des mots qui vont tres bien ensemble, tres
    bien ensemble.--MICHELLE--4
Sont des mots qui vont tres bien ensemble, tres
    bien ensemble.--MICHELLE--4
Sont des mots qui vont tres bien ensemble, tres
    bien ensemble.--MICHELLE--10
Sont des mots qui vont tres bien ensemble, tres
    bien ensemble.--MICHELLE--10
Sont des mots qui vont tres bien ensemble, tres
    bien ensemble.--MICHELLE--21
Sont des mots qui vont tres bien ensemble, tres
    bien ensemble.--MICHELLE--21

EQUAL
The love you take is equal to the love you make.--

THEEND--9

EQUIPPED
Rocky had come equipped with a gun--ROCKYRACCO--11

ER
I think I know, I mean, er, yes--STRAWBERRY--28

ESCAPING
Got me escaping from this zoo --OLDBROWNSH--13

ETERNALLY
And eternally I'll always be in love with you--
    THANKYOUGI--3
And eternally I'll always be in love with you--
    THANKYOUGI--13

EVEN
I know you never even try girl --PLEASEPLEA--2
I know/Why do you never even try girl--PLEASEPLEA--20
How can I even try --YOUVEGOTTO--11
You didn't even think of me as someone with a name.
    --WHATGOESON--23
Time after time you refuse to even listen --
    YOUWONTSEE--13
Time after time you refuse to even listen --
    YOUWONTSEE--22
I said even though you know what you know --
    SHESAIDSHE--10
I said even though you know what you know --
    SHESAIDSHE--16
Even hate my rock 'n' roll.--YERBLUES--27
You know they didn't even give us a chance.--
    BALLADOFJO--4
Even those tears --IMEMINE--16
Even those tears --IMEMINE--29

EVENING
Sit back and let the evening go.--SGTPEPPERS--11
And in the evening she still sings it with the
    band, yes.--OBLADIOBLA--24
And in the evening she's a singer with the band,
    yeah.--OBLADIOBLA--35
In the evening - wanna die --YERBLUES--7
In the evening...--YERBLUES--35
Good evening and welcome to Slaggers --YOUKNOWMYN
    --5
Good evening (Ringo).--YOUKNOWMYN--7
Good evening, you know my name, well then look
    up my number --YOUKNOWMYN--9

EVER
Keep all ((all)) my love forever ((ever)).--
    PSILOVEYOU--5
Keep all ((all)) my love forever ((ever)) --
    PSILOVEYOU--14
But you're the only love that I've ever had.--
    ASKMEWHY--11
Only ever has to give me love forever and forever
    --SHESAWOMAN--3
Only ever has to give me love forever and forever
    --SHESAWOMAN--20
Only ever has to give me love forever and forever
    --SHESAWOMAN--30
But nobody ever hears him--FOOLONTHEH--10
For if I ever saw you --IWILL--5
How could I ever have lost you --LONGLONGLO--2
How can I ever misplace you?--LONGLONGLO--4
Happy ever after in the market place --OBLADIOBLA
    --20
Hey, happy ever after in the market place --
    OBLADIOBLA--32
Nobody ever loved me like she does --DONTLETMED--5
I guess nobody ever really done me --DONTLETMED--23
Only place that he's ever been--MEANMRMUST--12
Believe me when I beg you - ooo - don't ever
    leave me alone.--OHDARLING--4
I love you more than ever girl, I do.--FORYOUBLUE
    --4
I love you more than ever girl, I do - really
    love blues.--FORYOUBLUE--18

EVERBODY
Everbody knows there's nothing doing--GOODMORNIN
    --9

EVERMORE
    Mine for evermore.--WHENIMSIXT--34

EVERY
    I'll write home every day --ALLMYLOVIN--5
    I'll write home every day --ALLMYLOVIN--11
    I'll write home every day --ALLMYLOVIN--19
    When every night I'm all alone--DONTBOTHER--12
    Every night when everybody has fun--ITWONTBELO--5
    Every night the tears come down from my eye--
        ITWONTBELO--15
    Every day I've done nothing but cry-ITWONTBELO--16
    So every day we'll be happy, I know--ITWONTBELO--25
    I got every reason on earth to be mad --ILLCRYINST
        --1
    Love you every day girl --EIGHTDAYSA--9
    Love you every day girl --EIGHTDAYSA--29
    EVERY LITTLE THING.--EVERYLITTL--Title
    Every little thing she does--EVERYLITTL--7
    Every little thing she does--EVERYLITTL--17
    Every little thing she does--EVERYLITTL--21
    Every little thing--EVERYLITTL--25
    Every little thing.--EVERYLITTL--26
    Every little thing.--EVERYLITTL--27
    But ((but)) every now and then ((now and then))
        I feel so insecure--HELP--22
    Same old thing happen every day.--IMDOWN--9
    Is it right that you and I should fight, every
        night--ITSONLYLOV--8
    Each and every day.--YOUVEGOTTO--6
    You tell me that you heard every sound there is --
        ANDYOURBIR--13
    Every single day of my life?--GOTTOGETYO--7
    Say we'll be together every day.--GOTTOGETYO--14
    Every single day of my life?--GOTTOGETYO--22
    Every single day...--GOTTOGETYO--31
    Of every head he's had the pleasure to know--
        PENNYLANE--2
    Every summer we can rent a cottage--WHENIMSIXT--22
    With every mistake we must surely be learning --
        WHILEMYGUI--11
    Replacing every thoughtless frown.--OLDBROWNSH--12
    Wearing rings on every finger --OLDBROWNSH--18
    Oh, what joy for every girl and boy--OCTOPUSSGA--19
    I'm living every moment girl for you.--FORYOUBLUE
        --7

EVERYBODY
    Every night when everybody has fun--ITWONTBELO--5
    Can't buy me love, oh, everybody tells me so --
        CANTBUYMEL--15
    Can't buy me love, oh, everybody tells me so --
        CANTBUYMEL--25
    Everybody knows I'm sure--YESITIS--6
    I'm here to show everybody the light.--THEWORD--24
    Everybody seems to think I'm lazy.--IMONLYSLEE--7
    All you need is love (everybody) --ALLYOUN/YS--26
    Good night everybody --GOODNIGHT--21
    Everybody everywhere --GOODNIGHT--22
    I've got a feeling I think that everybody knows --
        IVEGOTAFEE--16
    Everybody had a hard year --IVEGOTAFEE--19
    Everybody had a good time --IVEGOTAFEE--20
    Everybody had a wet dream --IVEGOTAFEE--21
    Everybody saw the sun shine --IVEGOTAFEE--22
    (Yeah) everybody had a good year --IVEGOTAFEE--24
    Everybody let their hair down --IVEGOTAFEE--25
    Everybody pulled their socks up (yeah) --IVEGOTAFEE
        --26
    Everybody put the fool down, oh yeah - (yeah).--
        IVEGOTAFEE--27
    Ooo - hu, everybody had a good year ((I've got
        a feeling)) --IVEGOTAFEE--28
    Everybody had a hard time ((a feeling deep
        inside, oh yeah)) --IVEGOTAFEE--29
    Everybody had a wet dream (oh yeah) --IVEGOTAFEE
        --30
    Everybody saw the sun shine.--IVEGOTAFEE--31
    Everybody had a good year ((I've got a feeling))
        --IVEGOTAFEE--32
    Everybody let their hair down ((a feeling I
        can't hide, oh no)) --IVEGOTAFEE--33
    Everybody pulled their socks up (oh no, no) --
        IVEGOTAFEE--34
    Everybody put their foot down, oh yeah (yeah).--
        IVEGOTAFEE--35

EVERYBODY'S
    Everybody's green--YOUCANTDOT--18
    Everybody's green--YOUCANTDOT--37

EVERYBODY'S GOT SOMETHING TO HIDE EXCEPT ME
    AND MY MONKEY.--EVRBDYMONK--Title
    Everybody's got something to hide 'cept for me
        and my monkey - wuh.--EVRBDYMONK--7
    Everybody's got something to hide 'cept for me
        and my monkey (yeah - wuh).--EVRBDYMONK--16
    Everybody's got something to hide 'cept for me
        and my monkey - hey.--EVRBDYMONK--25
    Everybody's laughing --SUNKING--3
    Everybody's happy.--SUNKING--4

EVERYONE
    Send her back to me, 'cos everyone can see--
        MISERY--8
    Send her back to me, 'cos everyone can see--
        MISERY--12
    That love is all and love is everyone--TOMORROWNE
        --7
    Everyone of us (everyone of us) has all we need
        (has all we need) --YELLOWSUBM--26
    Everyone of us (everyone of us) has all we need
        (has all we need) --YELLOWSUBM--26
    Everyone you see is half asleep--GOODMORNIN--11
    Everyone you see is full of life--GOODMORNIN--20
    Everyone smiles as you drift past the flowers--
        LUCYINTHES--14
    All day long I'm sitting singing songs for
        everyone.--MOTHERNATU--2
    But everyone knew her as Nancy.--ROCKYRACCO--16
    You made a fool of everyone--SEXYSADIE--2
    You made a fool of everyone--SEXYSADIE--3
    She came along to turn on everyone--SEXYSADIE--10
    She made a fool of everyone--SEXYSADIE--26
    Well you can imitate everyone you know--IDIGAPONY
        --20
    Yes you can imitate everyone you know--IDIGAPONY
        --21

EVERYONE'S
    Everyone's weaving it --IMEMINE--6
    Everyone's saying it --IMEMINE--19
    Everyone's saying it --IMEMINE--32

EVERYTHING
    I got everything that you want--FROMMETOYO--7
    She gives me everything --ANDILOVEHE--6
    You're gonna give me everything --HARDDAYSNI--11
    When I'm home everything seems to be right --
        HARDDAYSNI--15
    When I'm home everything seems to be right --
        HARDDAYSNI--28
    That I would love everything that you do --
        ISHOULDHAV--2
    Just to dance with you is everything I need (oh)
        --IMHAPPYJUS--12
    Just to dance with you (oh) is everything I
        need (oh) --IMHAPPYJUS--20
    Well I gave you everything I had --TELLMEWHY--5
    I mean everything I've said.--RUNFORYOUR--18
    You tell me that you've got everything you want --
        ANDYOURBIR--1
    He does everything he can, Dr. Robert.--DRROBERT
        --5
    He does everything he can, Dr. Robert.--DRROBERT
        --17
    When I was a boy everything was right,
        everything was right.--SHESAIDSHE--9
    When I was a boy everything was right,
        everything was right.--SHESAIDSHE--9
    When I was a boy everything was right,
        everything was right.--SHESAIDSHE--15
    When I was a boy everything was right,
        everything was right.--SHESAIDSHE--15
    Everything is closed it's like a ruin--GOODMORNIN
        --10
    Home. (we gave her everything money could buy)--
        SHESLEAVIN--10
    Roll up (we've got everything you need)--MAGICALMYS
        --13
    That you are part of everything.--DEARPRUDEN--9
    Where everything flows--GLASSONION--4
    You know I'd give you everything I've got for a
        little peace of mind.--IMSOTIRED--13
    You know I'd give you everything I've got for a
        little peace of mind.--IMSOTIRED--22
    I'd give you everything I've got for a little
        peace of mind,--IMSOTIRED--23
    I'd give you everything I've got for a little
        peace of mind.--IMSOTIRED--24
    We gave her everything we owned just to sit at
        her table ((sexy Sadie))--SEXYSADIE--20

Just a smile would lighten everything--SEXYSADIE
--21
Everything has got to be just like you want it to
--IDIGAPONY--14
Well you can radiate everything you are--IDIGAPONY
--17
Yes you can radiate everything you are.--IDIGAPONY
--18
Everything has got to be just like you want it to
--IDIGAPONY--24
Well you can indicate everything you see--IDIGAPONY
--27
Everything has got to be just like you want it to
--IDIGAPONY--34

EVERYTHING'S
Everything's the same (when the rain comes down)--
RAIN--10

EVERYWHERE
Everywhere people stare --YOUVEGOTTO--5
Everywhere I go I hear it said --THEWORD--15
Running everywhere at such a speed --IMONLYSLEE--9
HERE, THERE AND EVERYWHERE.--HERETHEREA--Title
I want her everywhere--HERETHEREA--8
But to love her is to need her everywhere.--
HERETHEREA--10
I want her everywhere--HERETHEREA--14
But to love her is to need her everywhere.--
HERETHEREA--16
I will be there and everywhere --HERETHEREA--20
Here, there and everywhere.--HERETHEREA--21
Everywhere in town is getting dark--GOODMORNIN--19
Everybody everywhere --GOODNIGHT--22
Everywhere there's lots of piggies--PIGGIES--15
Everywhere it's what you make --ITSALLTOOM--10
Show me that I'm everywhere --ITSALLTOOM--23
Everywhere it's what you make --ITSALLTOOM--31

EVOLUTION
You tell me that it's evolution --REVOLUTION--5
You tell me that it's evolution --REVOLUTONE--8

EXCEPT
EVERYBODY'S GOT SOMETHING TO HIDE EXCEPT ME
AND MY MONKEY.--EVRBDYMONK--Title

EXISTENCE
Or play the game existence to the end--TOMORROWNE
--13

EXPERT
Expert texpert, choking smokers, don't you
think the joker laughs at you?--IAMTHEWALR--21

EYE
Every night the tears come down from my eye--
ITWONTBELO--15
She don't give boys the eye--SHESAWOMAN--8
She don't give boys the eye--SHESAWOMAN--12
Keeping an eye on the world going by my window --
IMONLYSLEE--13
Keeping an eye on the world going by my window --
IMONLYSLEE--19
Far as the eye can see.--BABYYOUREA--6
Yellow matter custard, dripping from a dead
dog's eye--IAMTHEWALR--12
Hit young Rocky in the eye.--ROCKYRACCO--4
The eagle picks my eye --YERBLUES--17

EYEBALL
He got ju-ju eyeball--COMETOGETH--7

EYES
Just look into my eyes --ANYTIMEATA--5
Close your eyes and I'll kiss you --ALLMYLOVIN--1
Close your eyes and I'll kiss you --ALLMYLOVIN--15
Holding back these tears in my eyes.--TELLMEWHY--16
Open up your eyes now--TELLMEWHAT--5
Look into these eyes now--TELLMEWHAT--13
Open up your eyes now--TELLMEWHAT--22
Open up your eyes now--TELLMEWHAT--31
As I looked in your eyes--INEEDYOU--9
Love was in your eyes (aah the night before)--
NIGHTBEFOR--2

Love was in your eyes (aah the night before)--
NIGHTBEFOR--12
That we can have if we close our eyes.--THINKFORYO
--5
And in her eyes you see nothing --FORNOONE--7
And in her eyes you see nothing --FORNOONE--14
And in her eyes you see nothing --FORNOONE--24
Watching her eyes and hoping I'm always there.--
HERETHEREA--13
Watching her eyes and hoping I'm always there.--
HERETHEREA--19
Declare the pennies on your eyes (Taxman)--TAXMAN
--23
Penny Lane is in my ears and in my eyes--PENNYLANE
--9
Penny Lane is in my ears and in my eyes--PENNYLANE
--17
Penny Lane is in my ears and in my eyes--PENNYLANE
--28
Penny Lane is in my ears and in my eyes--PENNYLANE
--31
Living is easy with eyes closed--STRAWBERRY--6
A girl with kaleidoscope eyes.--LUCYINTHES--4
Look for the girl with the sun in her eyes--
LUCYINTHES--7
The girl with kaleidoscope eyes.--LUCYINTHES--26
And the eyes in his head see the world spinning
round.--FOOLONTHEH--7
And the eyes in his head see the world spinning
round.--FOOLONTHEH--14
And the eyes in his head see the world spinning
round.--FOOLONTHEH--19
And the eyes in his head see the world spinning
round.--FOOLONTHEH--26
Take these sunken eyes and learn to see.--BLACKBIRD
--6
So Captain Marvel zapped him right between the
eyes. (Zap!)--CONTINUING--19
Dear Prudence, open up your eyes --DEARPRUDEN--6
Dear Prudence, won't you open up your eyes?--
DEARPRUDEN--10
Close your eyes and I'll close mine --GOODNIGHT--7
Close your eyes and I'll close mine --GOODNIGHT--14
Lying with his eyes while his hands are busy
working overtime,--HAPPINESSI--6
Julia seashell eyes windy smile calls me --JULIA
--5
When I look into your eyes --ITSALLTOOM--4
With your long blonde hair and your eyes of blue
--ITSALLTOOM--35
With your long blonde hair and your eyes of blue
--ITSALLTOOM--36
Golden slumbers fill your eyes--GOLDENSLUM--7
Images of broken light which dance before me like
a million eyes --ACROSSTHEU--11

F
E, F, G, H, I, J --ALLTOGETHE--7

FACE
They'd laugh in my face.--YOUCANTDOT--22
They'd laugh in my face.--YOUCANTDOT--41
Let's pretend we just can't see his face.--
IMHAPPYJUS--17
Let's pretend we just can't see his face.--
IMHAPPYJUS--25
'cos I looked up to see your face.--NOREPLY--8
I'VE JUST SEEN A FACE.--IVEJUSTSEE--Title
I've just seen a face--IVEJUSTSEE--19
I've just seen a face--IVEJUSTSEE--24
Turn my face to the wall.--YOUVEGOTTO--2
Wearing the face that she keeps in a jar by the door
--ELEANORRIG--7
They'd seen his face before--DAYINTHELI--9
Man you been a naughty boy, you let your face
grow long--IAMTHEWALR--6
Desmond says to Molly, girl I like your face--
OBLADIOBLA--3
Molly stays at home and does her pretty face--
OBLADIOBLA--23
Desmond stays at home and does his pretty face--
OBLADIOBLA--34

FACES
Little darling, the smiles returning to the faces.
--HERECOMEST--9

FADED
If the sun has faded away --ANYTIMEATA--13

FAIR
    I think it's only fair--SHELOVESYO--25
    Late of Pablo Fanques Fair - what a scene.--
        BEINGFORTH--4

FALL
    That before too long I'd fall in love with her.--
        ISAWHERSTA--8
    And so it's true pride comes before a fall --
        IMALOSER--17
    There's a chance that we might fall apart before
        too long.--WECANWORKI--18
    There's a chance that we might fall apart before
        too long.--WECANWORKI--27

FALLING
    My tears are falling like rain from the sky --
        IMALOSER--11
    Falling, yes I am falling--IVEJUSTSEE--12
    Falling, yes I am falling--IVEJUSTSEE--12
    Falling, yes I am falling--IVEJUSTSEE--19
    Falling, yes I am falling--IVEJUSTSEE--19
    Falling, yes I am falling--IVEJUSTSEE--22
    Falling, yes I am falling--IVEJUSTSEE--22
    Falling, yes I am falling--IVEJUSTSEE--30
    Falling, yes I am falling--IVEJUSTSEE--30
    Falling, yes I am falling--IVEJUSTSEE--32
    Falling, yes I am falling--IVEJUSTSEE--32
    (Oh) falling, yes I am falling--IVEJUSTSEE--34
    (Oh) falling, yes I am falling--IVEJUSTSEE--34

FAMOUS
    I wanna be famous, a star of the screen --
        DRIVEMYCAR--3

FANCY
    By stealing the girl of his fancy --ROCKYRACCO--14

FANQUES
    Late of Pablo Fanques Fair - what a scene.--
        BEINGFORTH--4

FAR
    Wishing you weren't so far away --THINGSWESA--4
    I wonder what went wrong I've waited far too long
        --IDONTWANTT--7
    I wonder what went wrong I've waited far too long
        --IDONTWANTT--24
    All my troubles seemed so far away--YESTERDAY--2
    I left you far behind--THINKFORYO--10
    Friday morning at nine o'clock she is far away--
        SHESLEAVIN--25
    When it's far too late--WITHINYOUW--6
    And have you travelled very far?--BABYYOUREA--5
    Far as the eye can see.--BABYYOUREA--6

FARE
    Or how I fare or if my hair is brown --ONLYANORTH
        --11

FARM
    Take me to your daddy's farm --BACKINTHEU--32

FART
    Sweet Moretta Fart she thought she was a cleaner--
        GETBACK/LP--2

FARTHER
    The farther one travels --INNERLIGHT--5
    The farther one travels --INNERLIGHT--12

FAST
    Each day just goes so fast--LOVEYOUTWO--1
    I'm coming down fast but I'm miles above you --
        HELTERSKEL--5
    I'm coming down fast but don't let me break you --
        HELTERSKEL--12
    I'm coming down fast but don't let me break you --
        HELTERSKEL--22
    She's coming down fast --HELTERSKEL--28
    Coming down fast (oh I hear my baby speaking -
        ooo)...--HELTERSKEL--30

FASTER
    Changing faster than the weather --OLDBROWNSH--24

FATE
    What have I done to deserve such a fate?--IMALOSER
        --15

FATHER
    Father McKenzie writing the words of a sermon--
        ELEANORRIG--11
    Father McKenzie wiping the dirt from his hands--
        ELEANORRIG--24
    Father snores as his wife gets into her
        dressing-gown--SHESLEAVIN--13
    My father was of the earth --YERBLUES--11

FBI
    Like the FBI--DIGIT--4
    Queen says no to pot-smoking FBI member.--
        FORYOUBLUE--1

FEARS
    You don't know what it's like to listen to your
        fears.--HEYBULLDOG--8

FEAT
    Performs his feat on Saturday at Bishopsgate.--
        BEINGFORTH--9

FEATURING
    Featuring Dennis O'Fell and Ringo.--YOUKNOWMYN--6

FEED
    Will you still feed me --WHENIMSIXT--8
    Will you still feed me --WHENIMSIXT--20
    Will you still feed me --WHENIMSIXT--36
    Wonders how you manage to feed the rest.--
        LADYMADONN--10

FEEL
    I'll be there to make you feel right --ANYTIMEATA
        --6
    If you want someone to make you feel so fine--
        LITTLECHIL--9
    I feel happy inside--IWANTTOHOL--14
    I feel happy inside--IWANTTOHOL--27
    When I feel that something--IWANTTOHOL--35
    Would always feel the same--THISBOY--12
    If it makes you feel alright --CANTBUYMEL--4
    If it makes you feel alright --CANTBUYMEL--6
    When I feel low, when I feel blue--THERESAPLA--2
    When I feel low, when I feel blue--THERESAPLA--2
    When I feel low, when I feel blue--THERESAPLA--14
    When I feel low, when I feel blue--THERESAPLA--14
    Will make me feel alright.--HARDDAYSNI--7
    You know I feel OK.--HARDDAYSNI--14
    Will make me feel alright.--HARDDAYSNI--23
    You know I feel OK.--HARDDAYSNI--27
    Will make me feel alright --HARDDAYSNI--36
    You know I feel alright --HARDDAYSNI--37
    You know I feel alright.--HARDDAYSNI--38
    I FEEL FINE.--IFEELFINE--Title
    I'm in love with her and I feel fine.--IFEELFINE
        --3
    I'm in love with her and I feel fine.--IFEELFINE
        --6
    She's in love with me and I feel fine (ooo).--
        IFEELFINE--11
    I'm in love with her and I feel fine.--IFEELFINE
        --14
    She's in love with me and I feel fine --IFEELFINE
        --19
    She's in love with me and I feel fine.--IFEELFINE
        --20
    But ((but)) every now and then ((now and then))
        I feel so insecure--HELP--22
    Please remember how I feel about you--INEEDYOU--16
    Please remember how I feel about you--INEEDYOU--26
    Why should I feel the way I do?--ITSONLYLOV--5
    Why should I feel the way I do?--ITSONLYLOV--12
    When friends are there, you feel a fool.--GIRL--13
    I feel as though you ought to know--WAIT--9
    I feel as though you ought to know--WAIT--17
    But when I saw him with you I could feel my

FEEL

Now that I know what I feel must be right --THEWORD
--23
She takes her time and doesn't feel she has to
hurry --FORNOONE--5
I feel good in a special way --GOODDAYSUN--4
I feel hung up and I don't know why --IWANTTOTEL
--13
I feel hung up and I don't know why --IWANTTOTEL
--20
And she's making me feel like I've never been
born.--SHESAIDSHE--3
Things that make me feel that I'm mad--SHESAIDSHE
--5
And you're making me feel like I've never been
born.--SHESAIDSHE--6
'cos you're making me feel like I've never been
born.--SHESAIDSHE--12
'cos you're making me feel like I've never been
born.--SHESAIDSHE--18
After a while you start to smile now you feel cool
--GOODMORNIN--13
How do I feel by the end of the day?--WITHALITTL
--10
How does it feel to be--BABYYOUREA--1
How does it feel to be--BABYYOUREA--7
How does it feel to be--BABYYOUREA--22
And any time you feel the pain--HEYJULE--9
And I feel my finger on your trigger ((oh,
yeah)) --HAPPINESSI--23
I will always feel the same.--IWILL--8
I feel your taste all the time we're apart --
SAVOYTRUFF--7
You might not feel it now --SAVOYTRUFF--11
Feel so suicidal --YERBLUES--19
Hold you in his armchair you can feel his disease
--COMETOGETH--30
Little darling, I feel that ice is slowly
melting.--HERECOMEST--18
I want you at the moment I feel blue --FORYOUBLUE
--6
I feel it now, I hope you feel it too.--FORYOUBLUE
--15
I feel it now, I hope you feel it too.--FORYOUBLUE
--15
Oh now I feel the wind blow--IDIGAPONY--26

FEELING

If you're feeling sorry and sad --ANYTIMEATA--7
It's such a feeling--IWANTTOHOL--15
It's such a feeling--IWANTTOHOL--28
When I'm home feeling you holding me tight,
tight, yeah.--HARDDAYSNI--16
When I'm home feeling you holding me tight,
tight, yeah.--HARDDAYSNI--29
Baby's in black and I'm feeling blue --BABYSINBLA
--2
Baby's in black and I'm feeling blue --BABYSINBLA
--8
Baby's in black and I'm feeling blue --BABYSINBLA
--17
Baby's in black and I'm feeling blue --BABYSINBLA
--22
Baby's in black and I'm feeling blue --BABYSINBLA
--28
I'm ((I'm)) feeling blue and lonely --WHATYOURED
--2
Help me if you can, I'm feeling down--HELP--15
Help me if you can, I'm feeling down--HELP--25
Help me if you can, I'm feeling down--HELP--35
I'm feeling upside-down (I'm really down)--IMDOWN
--36
And feeling like this--INEEDYOU--14
And feeling like this--INEEDYOU--24
Feeling two-foot small.--YOUVEGOTTO--4
Well, well, well, you're feeling fine --DRROBERT
--11
Well, well, well, you're feeling fine --DRROBERT
--18
Waiting for a sleepy feeling.--IMONLYSLEE--16
Go in to work don't want to go feeling low down--
GOODMORNIN--7
I'm so tired, I'm feeling so upset --IMSOTIRED--14
But oh, that magic feeling, nowhere to go --
YOUNEVERGI--13
Oh, that magic feeling --YOUNEVERGI--14
I'VE GOT A FEELING.--IVEGOTAFEE--Title
I've got a feeling, a feeling deep inside --
IVEGOTAFEE--1
I've got a feeling, a feeling deep inside --
IVEGOTAFEE--1
I've got a feeling, a feeling I can't hide --
IVEGOTAFEE--3
I've got a feeling, a feeling I can't hide --

IVEGOTAFEE--3
Yes, yeah, I've got a feeling, yeah.--IVEGOTAFEE
--5
I've got a feeling, yeah, I've got a feeling.--
IVEGOTAFEE--10
I've got a feeling, yeah, I've got a feeling.--
IVEGOTAFEE--10
Ooo I've got a feeling that keeps me on my toes --
IVEGOTAFEE--14
I've got a feeling I think that everybody knows --
IVEGOTAFEE--16
I've got a feeling yeah - (yeah).--IVEGOTAFEE--18
Ooo - hu, everybody had a good year ((I've got
a feeling)) --IVEGOTAFEE--28
Everybody had a hard time ((a feeling deep
inside, oh yeah)) --IVEGOTAFEE--29
Everybody had a good year ((I've got a feeling))
--IVEGOTAFEE--32
Everybody let their hair down ((a feeling I
can't hide, oh no)) --IVEGOTAFEE--33
I've got a feeling ((oh yeah)) --IVEGOTAFEE--36
I've got a feeling (oh yeah) --IVEGOTAFEE--37
I've got a feeling, yeah, yeah, yeah, yeah.--
IVEGOTAFEE--38

FEELINGS

I can't help my feelings--YOUCANTDOT--25
I can't help my feelings--YOUCANTDOT--44
And he never shows his feelings.--FOOLONTHEH--17

FEELS

It feels so right now --HOLDMETIGH--1
It feels so right now --HOLDMETIGH--18
It feels so right now --HOLDMETIGH--28
And since I lost you it feels like years.--
YOUWONTSEE--17
And since I lost you it feels like years.--
YOUWONTSEE--26
She feels good (she feels good), she knows
she's looking fine --GOODDAYSUN--12
She feels good (she feels good), she knows
she's looking fine --GOODDAYSUN--12
And though she feels as if she's in a play--
PENNYLANE--22
Feels so suicidal--YERBLUES--26
Little darling, it feels like years since it's
been here.--HERECOMEST--5

FEET

I got a chip on my shoulder that's bigger than my
feet.--ILLCRYINST--6
Help me get my feet back on the ground--HELP--17
Help me get my feet back on the ground--HELP--27
Help me get my feet back on the ground--HELP--37
Burns my feet as they touch the ground.--GOODDAYSUN
--8
If you take a walk, I'll tax your feet.
((walk))--TAXMAN--14
Lady Madonna, children at your feet --LADYMADONN
--1
Lady Madonna, children at your feet --LADYMADONN
--18
He got feet down below his knee--COMETOGETH--29

FELL

And before too long I fell in love with her--
ISAWHERSTA--15
And before too long I fell in love with her.--
ISAWHERSTA--22
IF I FELL.--IFIFELL--Title
If I fell in love with you --IFIFELL--1
If I fell in love with you.--IFIFELL--28
Woke up, fell out of bed--DAYINTHELI--18
A - now Rocky Raccoon, he fell back in his room--
ROCKYRACCO--36

FERDE

Mundo paparatsi mi amore chicka ferde parasol --
SUNKING--7

FEW

Treasure ((treasure)) these few words ((words))
--PSILOVEYOU--3
Treasure ((treasure)) these few words ((words))
--PSILOVEYOU--12
She's sweeter than all the girls and I met quite
a few --ANOTHERGIR--6
Though the days are few, they're filled with tears

FEW

--YOUWONTSEE--16
Though the days are few they're filled with tears
    --YOUWONTSEE--25
It's a thousand pages, give or take a few,
    ((paperback))--PAPERBACKW--15

FIELD

Find me in my field of grass - Mother Nature's
    son --MOTHERNATU--8

FIELDS

STRAWBERRY FIELDS FOREVER.--STRAWBERRY--Title
'cos I'm going to strawberry fields--STRAWBERRY--2
Strawberry fields forever.--STRAWBERRY--5
'cos I'm going to strawberry fields--STRAWBERRY--12
Strawberry fields forever.--STRAWBERRY--15
'cos I'm going to strawberry fields--STRAWBERRY--22
Strawberry fields forever.--STRAWBERRY--25
'cos I'm going to strawberry fields--STRAWBERRY--32
Strawberry fields forever.--STRAWBERRY--35
Strawberry fields forever.--STRAWBERRY--36
Strawberry fields forever.--STRAWBERRY--37
I told you about Strawberry Fields--GLASSONION--1

FIERCE

(But when he looked so fierce) his mommy butted
    in --CONTINUING--28

FIFTEEN

She worked at fifteen clubs a day--SHECAMEINT--13

FIFTY

Fifty acorns tied in a sack.--BALLADOFJO--38
So he waits behind, writing fifty times I must
    not be so oh - oh oh.--MAXWELLSIL--11

FIGHT

Is it right that you and I should fight, every
    night--ITSONLYLOV--8

FIGHTING

For fussing and fighting my friend.--WECANWORKI--12
For fussing and fighting my friend.--WECANWORKI--21

FILL

She said will fill your head --FORNOONE--22
They'll fill you in with all their sins, you'll see.
    --LOVEYOUTWO--15
To fill the Albert Hall--DAYINTHELI--33
Fill in a form--WHENIMSIXT--33
Your song will fill the air --IWILL--14
The sweat it's gonna fill your head --SAVOYTRUFF
    --14
Golden slumbers fill your eyes--GOLDENSLUM--7

FILLED

Though the days are few, they're filled with tears
    --YOUWONTSEE--16
Though the days are few they're filled with tears
    --YOUWONTSEE--25
My head is filled with things to say --IWANTTOTEL
    --2

FILLING

I'm filling the cracks that ran through the door--
    FIXINGAHOL--4
Filling me up with your rules.--GETTINGBET--6
Filling in a ticket in her little white book.--
    LOVELYRITA--9

FILM

I saw a film today, oh boy--DAYINTHELI--11

FILTER

He one mojo filter--COMETOGETH--39

FINALLY

I finally heard--GETTINGBET--14
Finally made the plane into Paris --BALLADOFJO--9

FIND

I find the things that you do --HARDDAYSNI--6
I find the things that you do --HARDDAYSNI--22
I find the things that you do --HARDDAYSNI--35
You could find better things to do--ILLBEBACK--9
You could find better things to do--ILLBEBACK--18
These days such a kind girl seems so hard to find
    --THINGSWESA--7
If I find her I'll be glad --IDONTWANTT--11
If I find her I'll be glad --IDONTWANTT--20
One day you'll find that I have gone --ILLFOLLOWT
    --7
One day you'll find that I have gone --ILLFOLLOWT
    --12
Now I find ((and now I find)) I've changed
    my mind--HELP--13
Now I find ((and now I find)) I've changed
    my mind--HELP--13
Now I find ((and now I find)) I've changed
    my mind--HELP--33
Now I find ((and now I find)) I've changed
    my mind--HELP--33
Now today I find, you have changed your mind--
    NIGHTBEFOR--3
Now today I find you have changed your mind--
    NIGHTBEFOR--13
You're gonna find her gone (you're gonna find
    her gone)--YOUREGONNA--10
You're gonna find her gone (you're gonna find
    her gone)--YOUREGONNA--10
Love will find a way?--YOUVEGOTTO--16
It took me so long to find out --DAYTRIPPER--7
It took me so long to find out --DAYTRIPPER--15
It took me so long to find out --DAYTRIPPER--24
Until I find a way--MICHELLE--7
We have lost the time that was so hard to find--
    YOUWONTSEE--3
Till they find there's no need (there's no need).
    --IMONLYSLEE--10
You find that all her words of kindness linger on
    --FORNOONE--2
I didn't know what I would find there--GOTTOGETYO
    --2
I didn't know what I would find there--GOTTOGETYO
    --26
When we find it--WITHINYOUW--10
Then you may find--WITHINYOUW--29
And when at last I find you,--IWILL--13
When you find yourself in the thick of it --
    MARTHAMYDE--5
When you find yourself in the thick of it --
    MARTHAMYDE--11
Find me in my field of grass - Mother Nature's
    son --MOTHERNATU--8
You will find the bigger piggies--PIGGIES--8
Only to find Gideon's Bible --ROCKYRACCO--10
Only to find Gideon's Bible --ROCKYRACCO--37
When I find myself in times of trouble --LETITBE/45
    --1
When I find myself in times of trouble --LETITBE/LP
    --1
Then I find I've got the number wrong.--ONEAFTERNI
    --14
Then I find I got the number wrong - well ((well)).
    --ONEAFTERNI--24

FINDS

Who finds the money when you pay the rent?--
    LADYMADONN--3

FINE

If you want someone to make you feel so fine--
    LITTLECHIL--9
I FEEL FINE.--IFEELFINE--Title
I'm in love with her and I feel fine.--IFEELFINE
    --3
I'm in love with her and I feel fine.--IFEELFINE
    --6
She's in love with me and I feel fine (ooo).--
    IFEELFINE--11
I'm in love with her and I feel fine.--IFEELFINE
    --14
She's in love with me and I feel fine --IFEELFINE
    --19
She's in love with me and I feel fine.--IFEELFINE
    --20
Working for peanuts is all very fine --DRIVEMYCAR
    --11
It's so fine, it's sunshine --THEWORD--5
It's so fine, it's sunshine --THEWORD--13
It's so fine, it's sunshine --THEWORD--21
It's so fine, it's sunshine --THEWORD--29

Shine the weather's fine.--RAIN--8
Shine the weather's fine.--RAIN--13
Well, well, well, you're feeling fine --DRROBERT
    --11
Well, well, well, you're feeling fine --DRROBERT
    --18
She feels good (she feels good), she knows
    she's looking fine --GOODDAYSUN--12

FINGER
    A four of fish and finger pies in summer--PENNYLANE
        --18
    And I feel my finger on your trigger ((oh,
        yeah)) --HAPPINESSI--23
    Wearing rings on every finger --OLDBROWNSH--18
    He got wonky finger--COMETOGETH--17

FINGERS
    I got blisters on my fingers!--HELTERSKEL--32
    The picker - the picker, picture the fingers
        going (ooo me).--GETBACK/LP--5

FIRE
    So I lit a fire--NORWEGIANW--24
    Lastly through a hogshead of real fire--BEINGFORTH
        --6

FIRE-ENGINE
    He likes to keep his fire-engine clean--PENNYLANE
        --14

FIREMAN
    In Penny Lane there is a fireman with an
        hour-glass--PENNYLANE--12
    And then the fireman rushes in--PENNYLANE--26

FIRESIDE
    You can knit a sweater by the fireside--WHENIMSIXT
        --15

FIRST
    I remember the first time--EVERYLITTL--4
    (Would you believe in a love at first sight?)--
        WITHALITTL--19
    But Daniel was hot, he drew first and shot--
        ROCKYRACCO--21
    I'm in love for the first time --DONTLETMED--13
    And from the first time that she really done me --
        DONTLETMED--21

FISH
    A four of fish and finger pies in summer--PENNYLANE
        --18

FISHWIFE
    Crabalocker fishwife, pornographic priestess--
        IAMTHEWALR--13

FIVE
    Should five percent appear too small,--TAXMAN--7
    ... Four, five, six, seven, eight, nine,
        ten ....--DAYINTHELI--35
    ... Four, five, six...--GETTINGBET--1
    People running round it's five o'clock--GOODMORNIN
        --18
    Wednesday morning at five o'clock as the day begins
        --SHESLEAVIN--1
    (... Four, five, six, seven, eight!)--BIRTHDAY--7
    One, two, three, four, five, six, seven,
        eight.--DONTPASSME--36
    Five, six, seven, eight, nine, ten --ALLTOGETHE--3
    ... Four, five...--POLYTHENEP--12
    One, two, three, four, five, six, seven --
        YOUNEVERGI--24
    One, two, three, four, five, six, seven --
        YOUNEVERGI--26
    One, two, three, four, five, six, seven --
        YOUNEVERGI--28
    One, two, three, four, five, six, seven --
        YOUNEVERGI--30
    One, two, three, four, five, six, seven --
        YOUNEVERGI--32
    One, two, three, four, five, six, seven --
        YOUNEVERGI--34

One, two, three, four, five, six, seven --
    YOUNEVERGI--36
One, two, three, four, five, six, seven --
    YOUNEVERGI--38
One, two, three, four, five, six, seven --
    YOUNEVERGI--40

FIX
    I need a fix 'cos I'm going down --HAPPINESSI--9
    I need a fix 'cos I'm going down.--HAPPINESSI--11
    I wonder should I get up and fix myself a drink --
        IMSOTIRED--3

FIXING
    FIXING A HOLE.--FIXINGAHOL--Title
    I'm fixing a hole where the rain gets in--
        FIXINGAHOL--1
    I'm fixing a hole where the rain gets in--
        FIXINGAHOL--23
    I'm fixing a hole where the rain gets in--
        FIXINGAHOL--26
    Fixing the hole in the ocean--GLASSONION--21

FLAT
    And leave you flat--YOUCANTDOT--6
    And leave you flat--YOUCANTDOT--14
    (Gonna let you down and leave you flat)--YOUCANTDOT
        --15
    And leave you flat--YOUCANTDOT--28
    (Gonna let you down and leave you flat)--YOUCANTDOT
        --29
    And leave you flat--YOUCANTDOT--47
    (Gonna let you down and leave you flat)--YOUCANTDOT
        --48
    Made the bus in seconds flat--DAYINTHELI--24
    Here come old flat top--COMETOGETH--5

FLEW
    Oh - flew in from Miami Beach BOAC --BACKINTHEU--1

FLIES
    When you sigh my my inside just flies, butterfly.
        --ITSONLYLOV--2
    As Mr. Kite flies through the ring - don't be
        late.--BEINGFORTH--11
    Listen to the pretty sound of music as she flies.
        --MOTHERNATU--4

FLIGHT
    Man I had a dreadful flight.--BACKINTHEU--4

FLIRT
    Watching the skirts you start to flirt now you're
        in gear--GOODMORNIN--23

FLOAT
    Stay in bed, float upstream (float upstream).--
        IMONLYSLEE--4
    Stay in bed, float upstream (float upstream).--
        IMONLYSLEE--4
    Stay in bed, float upstream (float upstream).--
        IMONLYSLEE--24
    Stay in bed, float upstream (float upstream).--
        IMONLYSLEE--24
    Turn off your mind, relax and float down-stream--
        TOMORROWNE--1

FLOATING
    Her hair of floating sky is shimmering --JULIA--7
    Floating down the stream of time--ITSALLTOOM--12

FLOOR
    I look at the floor and I see it needs sweeping --
        WHILEMYGUI--4

FLOWERS
    Cellophane flowers of yellow and green--LUCYINTHES
        --5
    Everyone smiles as you drift past the flowers--
        LUCYINTHES--14
    Picking flowers for a friend who came to play --
        CRYBABYCRY--13

FLOWING
Words are flowing out like endless rain into a
paper cup --ACROSSTHEU--1
Flowing more freely than wine --IMEMINE--20
Flowing more freely than wine --IMEMINE--33

FLOWN
NORWEGIAN WOOD (THIS BIRD HAS FLOWN).--NORWEGIANW
--Title
This bird had flown.--NORWEGIANW--23

FLOWS
And life flows on within you and without you.--
WITHINYOUW--19
And life flows on within you and without you.--
WITHINYOUW--33
Where everything flows--GLASSONION--4

FLY
See how they run like pigs from a gun, see how
they fly--IAMTHEWALR--2
See how they fly like Lucy in the sky, see how
they run--IAMTHEWALR--10
Take these broken wings and learn to fly.--
BLACKBIRD--2
Blackbird fly, blackbird fly--BLACKBIRD--9
Blackbird fly, blackbird fly--BLACKBIRD--9
Blackbird fly, blackbird fly--BLACKBIRD--11
Blackbird fly, blackbird fly--BLACKBIRD--11
Take these broken wings and learn to fly.--
BLACKBIRD--14
The deeper you go, the higher you fly --EVRBDYMONK
--8
The higher you fly, the deeper you go --EVRBDYMONK
--9

FLYING
FLYING.--FLYING--Title

FOG
There's a fog upon LA --BLUEJAYWAY--1

FOLD
But when I saw him with you I could feel my
future fold.--WHATGOESON--7

FOLK
Thanks folk.--GETBACK/LP--37

FOLLOW
I'LL FOLLOW THE SUN.--ILLFOLLOWT--Title
For tomorrow may rain so I'll follow the sun.--
ILLFOLLOWT--2
For tomorrow may rain so I'll follow the sun.--
ILLFOLLOWT--4
For tomorrow may rain so I'll follow the sun.--
ILLFOLLOWT--8
Yeah, tomorrow may rain so I'll follow the sun.--
ILLFOLLOWT--9
For tomorrow may rain so I'll follow the sun.--
ILLFOLLOWT--13
If you leave me I will follow you--YOULIKEMET--15
If you leave me I will follow you--YOULIKEMET--24
Follow her down to a bridge by a fountain--
LUCYINTHES--12

FOOL
I know, little girl, only a fool would doubt
our love--THANKYOUGI--6
I ain't no fool and I don't take what I don't
want --ANOTHERGIR--4
I ain't no fool and I don't take what I don't
want --ANOTHERGIR--14
I ain't no fool and I don't take what I don't
want --ANOTHERGIR--20
When friends are there, you feel a fool.--GIRL--13
THE FOOL ON THE HILL.--FOOLONTHEH--Title
They can see that he's just a fool--FOOLONTHEH--4
But the fool on the hill sees the sun going down--
FOOLONTHEH--6
But the fool on the hill sees the sun going down--
FOOLONTHEH--13
But the fool on the hill sees the sun going down--
FOOLONTHEH--18

He knows that they're the fool--FOOLONTHEH--23
The fool on the hill sees the sun going down--
FOOLONTHEH--25
For well you know that it's a fool who plays it
cool --HEYJUDE--12
I told you about the fool on the hill--GLASSONION
--17
You made a fool of everyone--SEXYSADIE--2
You made a fool of everyone--SEXYSADIE--3
She made a fool of everyone--SEXYSADIE--26
Back in school again, Maxwell plays the fool
again, teacher gets annoyed --MAXWELLSIL--8
Everybody put the fool down, oh yeah - (yeah).--
IVEGOTAFEE--27

FOOLING
People tell me that she's only fooling--SHESAWOMAN
--6
People tell me that she's only fooling--SHESAWOMAN
--23
People tell me that she's only fooling--SHESAWOMAN
--33
You're only fooling round, only fooling round
with me.--ONEAFTERNI--7
You're only fooling round, only fooling round
with me.--ONEAFTERNI--7

FOOLISH
The man with the foolish grin is keeping
perfectly still--FOOLONTHEH--2

FOOT
Everybody put their foot down, oh yeah (yeah).--
IVEGOTAFEE--35

FOOTBALL
He got toe-jam football--COMETOGETH--16

FOOTSTEPS
I listen for your footsteps --DONTPASSME--2
Listen for your footsteps --DONTPASSME--4

FOR
I've known a secret for the week or two --
DOYOUWANTT--15
I've lost her now for sure, I won't see her no
more --MISERY--4
Thank you girl, for loving me the way that you
do (way that you do).--THANKYOUGI--8
And the same goes for me --ALLIVEGOTT--11
And the same goes for me --ALLIVEGOTT--22
I've got no time for you right now--DONTBOTHER--13
The only girl for me--DONTBOTHER--18
I've got no time for you right now--DONTBOTHER--28
The only girl for me--DONTBOTHER--33
I've cried for you.--NOTASECOND--3
I've cried for you, yeah.--NOTASECOND--14
That boy isn't good for you--THISBOY--4
'cos I don't care too much for money --CANTBUYMEL
--7
I don't care too much for money --CANTBUYMEL--13
I don't care too much for money --CANTBUYMEL--21
I don't care too much for money --CANTBUYMEL--31
'Was I to blame for being unfair?--ICALLYOURN--2
I got no time for triviality --WHENIGETHO--11
I got a girl who's waiting home for me tonight.--
WHENIGETHO--12
She does for me, yeah--EVERYLITTL--8
She does for me, ooo.--EVERYLITTL--10
For I know love will never die.--EVERYLITTL--16
She does for me, yeah--EVERYLITTL--18
She does for me, ooo.--EVERYLITTL--20
She does for me, yeah--EVERYLITTL--22
She does for me, ooo.--EVERYLITTL--24
There's nothing for me here so I will disappear --
IDONTWANTT--3
I think I'll take a walk and look for her.--
IDONTWANTT--8
There's nothing for me here so I will disappear --
IDONTWANTT--15
But I think I'll take a walk and look for her.--
IDONTWANTT--25
For tomorrow may rain so I'll follow the sun.--
ILLFOLLOWT--2
For tomorrow may rain so I'll follow the sun.--
ILLFOLLOWT--4
For tomorrow may rain so I'll follow the sun.--
ILLFOLLOWT--8

For tomorrow may rain so I'll follow the sun.--
    ILLFOLLOWT--13
Is it for her or myself that I cry?--IMALOSER--12
I've been waiting here for you --WHATYOURED--9
I've been waiting here for you --WHATYOURED--16
For red is the colour that my baby wore--YESITIS
    --3
For red is the colour that will make me blue--
    YESITIS--16
For red is the colour that will make me blue--
    YESITIS--25
For I have got another girl, another girl.--
    ANOTHERGIR--1
For I have got another girl, another girl.--
    ANOTHERGIR--5
For I have got another girl --ANOTHERGIR--9
For I have got another girl --ANOTHERGIR--15
For I have got another girl, another girl,
    another girl.--ANOTHERGIR--21
She's just the girl for me--IVEJUSTSEE--4
She's just the girl for me--IVEJUSTSEE--27
Now I long for yesterday.--YESTERDAY--12
Now I long for yesterday.--YESTERDAY--20
For taking the easy way out --DAYTRIPPER--2
For taking the easy way out, now.--DAYTRIPPER--4
For fussing and fighting my friend.--WECANWORKI--12
For fussing and fighting my friend.--WECANWORKI--21
Working for peanuts is all very fine --DRIVEMYCAR
    --11
Some forever, not for better --INMYLIFE--3
For people and things that went before --INMYLIFE
    --14
For people and things that went before --INMYLIFE
    --18
It's time for bed.--NORWEGIANW--16
Making all his nowhere plans for nobody.--
    NOWHEREMAN--3
Making all his nowhere plans for nobody --
    NOWHEREMAN--24
Making all his nowhere plans for nobody --
    NOWHEREMAN--25
Making all his nowhere plans for nobody.--
    NOWHEREMAN--26
RUN FOR YOUR LIFE.--RUNFORYOUR--Title
You better run for your life if you can, little
    girl --RUNFORYOUR--5
You better run for your life if you can, little
    girl --RUNFORYOUR--13
You better run for your life if you can, little
    girl --RUNFORYOUR--21
You better run for your life if you can, little
    girl --RUNFORYOUR--29
THINK FOR YOURSELF.--THINKFORYO--Title
Think for yourself --THINKFORYO--8
Think for yourself --THINKFORYO--17
Try thinking more if just for your own sake.--
    THINKFORYO--20
Think for yourself --THINKFORYO--26
Think for yourself --THINKFORYO--30
Think for yourself --THINKFORYO--32
And know that you will wait for me.--WAIT--12
And know that you will wait for me.--WAIT--20
It's so easy for a girl like you to lie.--
    WHATGOESON--8
I met you in the morning waiting for the tides of
    time --WHATGOESON--15
It's so easy for a girl like you to lie.--
    WHATGOESON--17
His son is working for the Daily Mail --PAPERBACKW
    --10
It could make a million for you overnight.
    ((writer))--PAPERBACKW--22
My friend works for the National Health, Dr.
    Robert --DRROBERT--13
Waiting for a sleepy feeling.--IMONLYSLEE--16
Who is it for?--ELEANORRIG--8
FOR NO-ONE.--FORNOONE--Title
No sign of love behind the tears cried for no-one
    --FORNOONE--8
No sign of love behind the tears cried for no-one
    --FORNOONE--15
No sign of love behind the tears cried for no-one
    --FORNOONE--25
We'd meet again for I had told you.--GOTTOGETYO--11
There's one for you, nineteen for me --TAXMAN--4
There's one for you, nineteen for me --TAXMAN--4
Don't ask me what I want it for (ha ha Mr.
    Wilson)--TAXMAN--18
Now my advice for those who die (Taxman)--TAXMAN
    --22
And you're working for no-one but me (Taxman).--
    TAXMAN--26
We see the banker sitting waiting for a trim--
    PENNYLANE--25

BEING FOR THE BENEFIT OF MR. KITE!--BEINGFORTH
    --Title
For the benefit of Mr. Kite--BEINGFORTH--1
A splendid time is guaranteed for all--BEINGFORTH
    --20
I'm taking the time for a number of things--
    FIXINGAHOL--19
Heading for home you start to roam then you're in
    town.--GOODMORNIN--8
It's time for tea and meet the wife.--GOODMORNIN
    --21
Look for the girl with the sun in her eyes--
    LUCYINTHES--7
The act you've known for all these years--
    SGTPEPPERS--6
For so many years. (('bye, 'bye))--SHESLEAVIN--12
Is leaving (never a thought for our ourselves)--
    SHESLEAVIN--21
For so many years. (('bye, 'bye))--SHESLEAVIN--24
For so many years. (('bye, 'bye))--SHESLEAVIN--32
Sunday mornings go for a ride.--WHENIMSIXT--16
Who could ask for more?--WHENIMSIXT--18
Mine for evermore.--WHENIMSIXT--34
Sitting on a cornflake, waiting for the van to come
    --IAMTHEWALR--4
Sitting in an English garden waiting for the sun--
    IAMTHEWALR--17
Roll up, roll up for the Mystery Tour --MAGICALMYS
    --1
Roll up, roll up for the Mystery Tour --MAGICALMYS
    --3
Roll up, roll up for the Mystery Tour.--MAGICALMYS
    --4
Roll up for the Mystery Tour --MAGICALMYS--6
Roll up for the Mystery Tour.--MAGICALMYS--8
Roll up, roll up for the Mystery Tour.--MAGICALMYS
    --11
Roll up, roll up for the Mystery Tour.--MAGICALMYS
    --12
Roll up for the Mystery Tour --MAGICALMYS--14
Roll up for the Mystery Tour.--MAGICALMYS--16
Roll up, roll up for the Mystery Tour--MAGICALMYS
    --22
Roll up for the Mystery Tour--MAGICALMYS--24
Roll up for the Mystery Tour--MAGICALMYS--26
For well you know that it's a fool who plays it
    cool --HEYJUDE--12
You're waiting for someone to perform with.--
    HEYJUDE--21
You ask me for a contribution --REVOLUTION--15
But if you want money for people with minds that
    hate,--REVOLUTION--18
You were only waiting for this moment to arise.--
    BLACKBIRD--4
You were only waiting for this moment to be free.
    --BLACKBIRD--8
You were only waiting for this moment to arise --
    BLACKBIRD--16
You were only waiting for this moment to arise --
    BLACKBIRD--17
You were only waiting for this moment to arise.--
    BLACKBIRD--18
Cooking breakfast for the Queen --CRYBABYCRY--5
Playing piano for the children of the King.--
    CRYBABYCRY--7
Picking flowers for a friend who came to play --
    CRYBABYCRY--13
Painting pictures for the childrens' holiday.--
    CRYBABYCRY--15
And arriving late for tea --CRYBABYCRY--21
For a seance in the dark --CRYBABYCRY--29
Put on specially by the children for a lark.--
    CRYBABYCRY--31
I listen for your footsteps --DONTPASSME--2
Listen for your footsteps --DONTPASSME--4
Waiting for your knock, dear --DONTPASSME--6
Everybody's got something to hide 'cept for me
    and my monkey - wuh.--EVRBDYMONK--7
Everybody's got something to hide 'cept for me
    and my monkey (yeah - wuh).--EVRBDYMONK--16
Everybody's got something to hide 'cept for me
    and my monkey - hey.--EVRBDYMONK--25
Well here's another clue for you all:--GLASSONION
    --10
Dream sweet dreams for me --GOODNIGHT--5
Dream sweet dreams for you.--GOODNIGHT--6
Dream sweet dreams for me --GOODNIGHT--11
Dream sweet dreams for you.--GOODNIGHT--12
Dream sweet dreams for me --GOODNIGHT--18
Dream sweet dreams for you.--GOODNIGHT--19
Where I stop and I turn and I go for a ride --
    HELTERSKEL--2
And I stop and I turn and I go for a ride--
    HELTERSKEL--19

For if I ever saw you --IWILL--5
For the things you do endear you to me - aah --
     IWILL--17
You know I'd give you everything I've got for a
     little peace of mind.--IMSOTIRED--13
You know I'd give you everything I've got for a
     little peace of mind.--IMSOTIRED--22
I'd give you everything I've got for a little
     peace of mind --IMSOTIRED--23
I'd give you everything I've got for a little
     peace of mind.--IMSOTIRED--24
So I sing a song of love for Julia --JULIA--16
That you and me were meant to be for each other -
     silly girl.--MARTHAMYDE--9
All day long I'm sitting singing songs for
     everyone.--MOTHERNATU--2
And for all the little piggies--PIGGIES--3
You can see them out for dinner--PIGGIES--17
You ask me for a contribution --REVOLUTONE--23
But if you want money for people with minds that
     hate --REVOLUTONE--27
You layed it down for all to see--SEXYSADIE--6
You layed it down for all to see--SEXYSADIE--7
One sunny day the world was waiting for the lover
     ((sexy Sadie))--SEXYSADIE--9
The world was waiting just for you?--SEXYSADIE--13
The world was waiting just for you?--SEXYSADIE--14
Your love is there for me--ITSALLTOOM--5
It's all too much for me to take --ITSALLTOOM--8
For us to take, it's all too much.--ITSALLTOOM--11
It's all too much for me to take --ITSALLTOOM--16
And get me home for tea.--ITSALLTOOM--24
It's all too much for me to see --ITSALLTOOM--25
It's all too much for me to take --ITSALLTOOM--29
For us to take it's all too much.--ITSALLTOOM--32
I'm in love for the first time --DONTLETMED--13
For some California grass.--GETBACK/45--4
Your mommy's waiting for you --GETBACK/45--32
Talking in our beds for a week.--BALLADOFJO--18
Saving up your money for a rainy day --BALLADOFJO
     --25
For your sweet top lip I'm in the queue --
     OLDBROWNSH--31
Oh, what joy for every girl and boy--OCTOPUSSGA--19
For though they may be parted --LETITBE/45--12
Let's hear it for Dennis - ah-hey.--YOUKNOWMYN--8
Let's hear it for Dennis O'Fell.--YOUKNOWMYN--24
FOR YOU BLUE.--FORYOUBLUE--Title
I'm living every moment girl for you.--FORYOUBLUE
     --7
For some California grass.--GETBACK/LP--10
All that I was looking for was somebody who
     looked like you.--IVEGOTAFEE--13
For though they may be parted --LETITBE/LP--12
Has left a pool of tears crying for the day.--
     LONGANDWIN--5

FOREVER
     Keep all ((all)) my love forever ((ever)).--
          PSILOVEYOU--5
     Keep all ((all)) my love forever ((ever)) --
          PSILOVEYOU--14
     Only ever has to give me love forever and forever
          --SHESAWOMAN--3
     Only ever has to give me love forever and forever
          --SHESAWOMAN--3
     Only ever has to give me love forever and forever
          --SHESAWOMAN--20
     Only ever has to give me love forever and forever
          --SHESAWOMAN--20
     Only ever has to give me love forever and forever
          --SHESAWOMAN--30
     Only ever has to give me love forever and forever
          --SHESAWOMAN--30
     I will love her forever--EVERYLITTL--15
     Some forever, not for better --INMYLIFE--3
     I don't mind, I could wait forever--IWANTTOTEL--14
     I don't mind, I could wait forever--IWANTTOTEL--21
     STRAWBERRY FIELDS FOREVER.--STRAWBERRY--Title
     Strawberry fields forever.--STRAWBERRY--5
     Strawberry fields forever.--STRAWBERRY--15
     Strawberry fields forever.--STRAWBERRY--25
     Strawberry fields forever.--STRAWBERRY--35
     Strawberry fields forever.--STRAWBERRY--36
     Strawberry fields forever.--STRAWBERRY--37
     Love you forever and forever --IWILL--9
     Love you forever and forever --IWILL--9
     It's a love that lasts forever --DONTLETMED--15

FORGET
     If I could forget her--YESITIS--11
     If I could forget her--YESITIS--20

I can't forget the time or place--IVEJUSTSEE--2
I can't forget the time or place--IVEJUSTSEE--25
We'll forget the tears we've cried.--WAIT--4
We'll forget the tears we cried.--WAIT--8
We'll forget the tears we've cried.--WAIT--16
We'll forget the tears we've cried.--WAIT--24
You won't forget her.--FORNOONE--23
Don't forget me, Martha my dear.--MARTHAMYDE--3
Don't forget me, Martha my dear.--MARTHAMYDE--15

FORGIVE
     And I'll forgive the lies--NOREPLY--19

FORKS
     Clutching forks and knives to eat the bacon.--
          PIGGIES--19

FORM
     Fill in a form--WHENIMSIXT--33

FOUND
     And I found that love was more --IFIFELL--5
     And I found out.--DAYTRIPPER--8
     And I found out.--DAYTRIPPER--16
     And I found out.--DAYTRIPPER--25
     But I've found a driver and that's a start.--
          DRIVEMYCAR--25
     Till we found a sea of green--YELLOWSUBM--6
     Found my way downstairs and drank a cup--DAYINTHELI
          --20
     Found my coat and grabbed my hat--DAYINTHELI--23
     Found my way upstairs and had a smoke--DAYINTHELI
          --25
     Now that you've found another key--BABYYOUREA--26
     You have found her, now go and get her (let it
          out and let it in) --HEYJUDE--16
     Now I'm so happy I found you --LONGLONGLO--5
     Because we know we can't be found.--OCTOPUSSGA--14

FOUNTAIN
     Follow her down to a bridge by a fountain--
          LUCYINTHES--12

FOUR
     One, two, three, four.--ISAWHERSTA--1
     One, two, three, four.--TICKETTORI--1
     One, two, three, four, one, two.--TAXMAN--1
     (One, two, three, four)--TAXMAN--2
     A four of fish and finger pies in summer--PENNYLANE
          --18
     Four thousand holes in Blackburn, Lancashire--
          DAYINTHELI--29
     ... Four, five, six, seven, eight, nine,
          ten ...--DAYINTHELI--35
     ... Four, five, six...--GETTINGBET--1
     One, two (ah yeah), three, four.--SGTPEPPREP--1
     (... Four, five, six, seven, eight!)--BIRTHDAY--7
     One, two, three, four, five, six, seven,
          eight.--DONTPASSME--36
     One, two, three, four --ALLTOGETHE--1
     ... Four, five...--POLYTHENEP--12
     One, two, three, four, five, six, seven --
          YOUNEVERGI--24
     One, two, three, four, five, six, seven --
          YOUNEVERGI--26
     One, two, three, four, five, six, seven --
          YOUNEVERGI--28
     One, two, three, four, five, six, seven --
          YOUNEVERGI--30
     One, two, three, four, five, six, seven --
          YOUNEVERGI--32
     One, two, three, four. five, six, seven --
          YOUNEVERGI--34
     One, two, three, four, five, six, seven --
          YOUNEVERGI--36
     One, two, three, four, five, six, seven --
          YOUNEVERGI--38
     One, two, three, four, five, six, seven --
          YOUNEVERGI--40
     You know my name, you know me number four --
          YOUKNOWMYN--35
     OK one, two, three, four.--GETBACK/LP--6

FRANCE
     Trying to get to Holland or France.--BALLADOFJO--2

FRANTIC
    Oh, Honey Pie you are driving me frantic--HONEYPIE
      --16

FREE
    She would never be free--TICKETTORI--11
    She would never be free--TICKETTORI--38
    Say the word and you'll be free --THEWORD--1
    Spread the word and you'll be free --THEWORD--9
    Say the word and you'll be free --THEWORD--17
    When are you free ((lovely Rita))--LOVELYRITA--15
    Stepping outside she is free.--SHESLEAVIN--7
    You better free your mind instead.--REVOLUTION--27
    You were only waiting for this moment to be free.
      --BLACKBIRD--8
    You'd better free your mind instead.--REVOLUTONE
      --41
    Where I know that I'm free --ITSALLTOOM--22
    One thing I can tell you is you got to be free--
      COMETOGETH--20
    Rose and Valerie screaming from the gallery say
      he must go free --MAXWELLSIL--19
    (Maxwell must go free)--MAXWELLSIL--20

FREELY
    Flowing more freely than wine --IMEMINE--20
    Flowing more freely than wine --IMEMINE--33

FRIDAY
    Friday morning at nine o'clock she is far away--
      SHESLEAVIN--25
    Friday night arrives without a suitcase --
      LADYMADONN--5

FRIEND
    So I'm telling you, my friend--ILLGETYOU--13
    I'll buy you a diamond ring my friend --CANTBUYMEL
      --3
    I'll get you anything my friend --CANTBUYMEL--5
    And though I lose a friend in the end you will
      know, oh.--ILLFOLLOWT--6
    And though I lose a friend in the end you will
      know, oh.--ILLFOLLOWT--11
    She was a girl in a million, my friend --IMALOSER
      --5
    Through thick and thin she will always be my
      friend.--ANOTHERGIR--11
    Through thick and thin she will always be my
      friend.--ANOTHERGIR--17
    If you don't treat her right my friend--YOUREGONNA
      --9
    For fussing and fighting my friend.--WECANWORKI--12
    For fussing and fighting my friend.--WECANWORKI--21
    Then I guess I'd be with you my friend --IFINEEDEDS
      --5
    Then I guess I'd be with you my friend --IFINEEDEDS
      --15
    Ring my friend I said you'd call, Dr. Robert --
      DRROBERT--1
    My friend works for the National Health, Dr.
      Robert --DRROBERT--13
    Ring my friend I said you'd call, Dr. Robert --
      DRROBERT--20
    Ring my friend I said you'd call, Dr. Robert --
      DRROBERT--21
    Picking flowers for a friend who came to play --
      CRYBABYCRY--13
    Can I bring my friend to tea?--ALLTOGETHE--6
    Can I take my friend to bed?--ALLTOGETHE--18

FRIENDS
    When friends are there, you feel a fool.--GIRL--13
    With lovers and friends I still can recall --
      INMYLIFE--6
    But of all these friends and lovers --INMYLIFE--9
    And our friends are all aboard--YELLOWSUBM--13
    WITH A LITTLE HELP FROM MY FRIENDS.--WITHALITTL
      --Title
    Oh I get by with a little help from my friends --
      WITHALITTL--5
    Mmm I get high with a little help from my friends
      --WITHALITTL--6
    Mmm gonna try with a little help from my friends.
      --WITHALITTL--7
    No I get by with a little help from my friends --
      WITHALITTL--12
    Mmm get high with a little help from my friends --
      WITHALITTL--13
    Mmm gonna try with a little help from my friends.

      --WITHALITTL--14
    Oh I get by with a little help from my friends --
      WITHALITTL--23
    Mmm get high with a little help from my friends --
      WITHALITTL--24
    Oh I'm gonna try with a little help from my
      friends.--WITHALITTL--25
    Oh I get by with a little help from my friends --
      WITHALITTL--30
    Mmm gonna try with a litcle help from my friends
      --WITHALITTL--31
    Oh I get high with a little help from my friends
      --WITHALITTL--32
    Yes I get by with a little help from my friends --
      WITHALITTL--33
    With a little help from my friends.--WITHALITTL--34
    And my friends have lost their way.--BLUEJAYWAY--2
    I'd ask my friends to come and see--OCTOPUSSGA--5

FRIGHTENED
    Wigwam frightened of the dark--HEYBULLDOG--14
    Now they're frightened of leaving it --IMEMINE--5
    No-one's frightened of playing it --IMEMINE--18
    No-one's frightened of playing it --IMEMINE--31

FROM
    FROM ME TO YOU.--FROMMETOYO--Title
    With love from me to you.--FROMMETOYO--6
    With love from me to you.--FROMMETOYO--10
    With love from me to you.--FROMMETOYO--18
    From me - to you.--FROMMETOYO--19
    With love from me to you.--FROMMETOYO--21
    With love from me to you--FROMMETOYO--29
    Every night the tears come down from my eye--
      ITWONTBELO--15
    I must be sure from the very start --IFIFELL--8
    That if I ran away from you--ILLBEBACK--14
    My tears are falling like rain from the sky --
      IMALOSER--11
    But as from today well I've got somebody that's
      new --ANOTHERGIR--3
    But as from today well I've seen somebody that's
      new --ANOTHERGIR--13
    But as from today well I've seen somebody that's
      new --ANOTHERGIR--19
    I'll make a point of taking her away from you
      (watch what you do), yeah--YOUREGONNA--16
    I'll make a point of taking her away from you
      (watch what you do), yeah--YOUREGONNA--23
    And maybe you will get a call from me --IFINEEDEDS
      --11
    And maybe you will get a call from me --IFINEEDEDS
      --21
    Take a drink from his special cup, Dr. Robert.--
      DRROBERT--7
    All the lonely people, where do they all come
      from?--ELEANORRIG--9
    All the lonely people, where do they all come
      from?--ELEANORRIG--17
    Father McKenzie wiping the dirt from his hands--
      ELEANORRIG--24
    As he walks from the grave--ELEANORRIG--25
    All the lonely people, where do they all come
      from?--ELEANORRIG--27
    The pretty nurse is selling poppies from a tray--
      PENNYLANE--21
    From the pouring rain - very strange.--PENNYLANE
      --27
    Nobody was really sure if he was from the House
      of Lords--DAYINTHELI--10
    And stops my mind from wandering--FIXINGAHOL--2
    And kept my mind from wandering--FIXINGAHOL--5
    Stops my mind from wandering--FIXINGAHOL--24
    Stops my mind from wandering--FIXINGAHOL--27
    I beat her and kept her apart from the things
      that she loved--GETTINGBET--26
    Meeting a man from the motor trade.--SHESLEAVIN--27
    Many years from now --WHENIMSIXT--2
    WITH A LITTLE HELP FROM MY FRIENDS.--WITHALITTL
      --Title
    Oh I get by with a little help from my friends --
      WITHALITTL--5
    Mmm I get high with a little help from my friends
      --WITHALITTL--6
    Mmm gonna try with a little help from my friends.
      --WITHALITTL--7
    No I get by with a little help from my friends --
      WITHALITTL--12
    Mmm get high with a little help from my friends --
      WITHALITTL--13
    Mmm gonna try with a little help from my friends.
      --WITHALITTL--14

Oh I get by with a little help from my friends --
WITHALITTL--23
Mmm get high with a little help from my friends --
WITHALITTL--24
Oh I'm gonna try with a little help from my
friends.--WITHALITTL--25
Oh I get by with a little help from my friends --
WITHALITTL--30
Mmm gonna try with a little help from my friends
--WITHALITTL--31
Oh I get high with a little help from my friends
--WITHALITTL--32
Yes I get by with a little help from my friends --
WITHALITTL--33
With a little help from my friends.--WITHALITTL--34
See how they run like pigs from a gun, see how
they fly--IAMTHEWALR--2
Yellow matter custard, dripping from a dead
dog's eye--IAMTHEWALR--12
If the sun don't come you get a tan from standing
in the English rain--IAMTHEWALR--18
Oh - flew in from Miami Beach BOAC --BACKINTHEU--1
Can you take me back where I came from --CRYBABYCRY
--44
Can you take me back where I came from --CRYBABYCRY
--46
Mmm can you take me where I came from --CRYBABYCRY
--49
Just waiting to hear from you.--DONTPASSME--30
From life to life with me --ITSALLTOOM--13
And from the first time that she really done me --
DONTLETMED--21
Drove from Paris to the Amsterdam Hilton --
BALLADOFJO--17
The men from the press said, we wish you success
--BALLADOFJO--39
From where some try to drag me down --OLDBROWNSH
--10
Got me escaping from this zoo --OLDBROWNSH--13
But she changes from day to day.--HERMAJESTY--4
But when she turns her back on the boy, he
creeps up from behind --MAXWELLSIL--12
Rose and Valerie screaming from the gallery say
he must go free --MAXWELLSIL--19
But as the words are leaving his lips, a noise
comes from behind --MAXWELLSIL--22
Soon we'll be away from here --YOUNEVERGI--19
I've loved you from the moment I saw you --
FORYOUBLUE--13

FRONT
On my old front door --DONTPASSME--7
She is standing right in front of me --LETITBE/45
--5
She is standing right in front of me --LETITBE/LP
--5

FROWN
Beneath this mask I am wearing a frown.--IMALOSER
--10
Replacing every thoughtless frown.--OLDBROWNSH--12

FRYING
But she was a frying pan ((sweet Loretta
Martin)).--GETBACK/LP--3

FUDGE
Cocoanut fudge really blows down those blues
(wuh) --SAVOYTRUFF--8

FULL
(Full speed ahead, Mr. Bosun, full speed
ahead.--YELLOWSUBM--20
(Full speed ahead, Mr. Bosun, full speed
ahead.--YELLOWSUBM--20
Full speed ahead it is, Sgt.--YELLOWSUBM--21
Everyone you see is full of life--GOODMORNIN--20

FUN
Every night when everybody has fun--ITWONTBELO--5
Then we'll have some fun when you're mine, all
mine --LITTLECHIL--10
There's no fun in what I do when she's not there
--IDONTWANTT--6
There's no fun in what I do if she's not there --
IDONTWANTT--23
And ((and)) there's no fun in it --WHATYOURED--6
Fun. (fun is the one thing that money can't buy)--

SHESLEAVIN--30
Fun. (fun is the one thing that money can't buy)--
SHESLEAVIN--30
But if you want some fun (ha ha ha) --OBLADIOBLA
--40

FUNNY
If it's funny try and understand.--IMHAPPYJUS--5
You only give me your funny paper--YOUNEVERGI--2

FUSE
I could be handy mending a fuse--WHENIMSIXT--13

FUSSING
For fussing and fighting my friend.--WECANWORKI--12
For fussing and fighting my friend.--WECANWORKI--21

FUTURE
The future still looks good --THINKFORYO--21
But when I saw him with you I could feel my
future fold.--WHATGOESON--7
See no future, pay no rent --YOUNEVERGI--8

G
E, F, G, H, I, J --ALLTOGETHE--7

G'GOO
Goo goo g'joob, g'goo goo g'joob--IAMTHEWALR--20
Goo goo g'joob, g'goo goo g'joob--IAMTHEWALR--29
Goo goo g'joob, g'goo goo g'joob g'goo--IAMTHEWALR
--30
Goo goo g'joob, g'goo goo g'joob g'goo--IAMTHEWALR
--30

G'JOOB
Goo goo g'joob--IAMTHEWALR--8
Goo goo g'joob--IAMTHEWALR--16
Goo goo g'joob, g'goo goo g'joob--IAMTHEWALR--20
Goo goo g'joob, g'goo goo g'joob--IAMTHEWALR--20
Goo goo g'joob, g'goo goo g'joob--IAMTHEWALR--29
Goo goo g'joob, g'goo goo g'joob--IAMTHEWALR--29
Goo goo g'joob, g'goo goo g'joob g'goo--IAMTHEWALR
--30
Goo goo g'joob, g'goo goo g'joob g'goo--IAMTHEWALR
--30

GAIN
Who gain the world and lose their soul--WITHINYOUW
--24

GALLERY
Rose and Valerie screaming from the gallery say
he must go free --MAXWELLSIL--19

GAME
Love was such an easy game to play--YESTERDAY--14
Love was such an easy game to play--YESTERDAY--22
You don't sound different, I've learned the game
--IMLOOKINGT--7
Or play the game existence to the end--TOMORROWNE
--13
Nothing you can say but you can learn how to play
the game ((love))--ALLYOUN/YS--6

GAMES
The games begin to drag me down --IWANTTOTEL--6

GARDEN
Doing the garden, digging the weeds--WHENIMSIXT--17
Sitting in an English garden waiting for the sun--
IAMTHEWALR--17
The King was in the garden --CRYBABYCRY--12
OCTOPUS'S GARDEN.--OCTOPUSSGA--Title
In an octopus's garden in the shade.--OCTOPUSSGA
--2
In his octopus's garden in the shade.--OCTOPUSSGA
--4
An octopus's garden with me.--OCTOPUSSGA--6
In an octopus's garden in the shade.--OCTOPUSSGA
--8
In an octopus's garden near a cave.--OCTOPUSSGA--12
In an octopus's garden in the shade.--OCTOPUSSGA

--16
In an octopus's garden with you --OCTOPUSSGA--24
In an octopus's garden with you --OCTOPUSSGA--25
In an octopus's garden with you.--OCTOPUSSGA--26

GARTERS
Over men and horses, hoops and garters--BEINGFORTH
--5

GAS
Step on the gas and wipe that tear away.--
YOUNEVERGI--20

GATHER
Gather round all you clowns--YOUVEGOTTO--17

GAVE
Well I gave you everything I had --TELLMEWHY--5
When you gave me no reply.--NOREPLY--21
You gave me the word--GETTINGBET--13
She (we gave her most of our lives)--SHESLEAVIN--8
Home. (we gave her everything money could buy)--
SHESLEAVIN--10
We gave her everything we owned just to sit at
her table ((sexy Sadie))--SEXYSADIE--20

GEAR
Watching the skirts you start to flirt now you're
in gear--GOODMORNIN--23

GEE
Gee, it's good to be back home --BACKINTHEU--9

GENTLY
WHILE MY GUITAR GENTLY WEEPS.--WHILEMYGUI--Title
While my guitar gently weeps.--WHILEMYGUI--3
Still my guitar gently weeps.--WHILEMYGUI--5
While my guitar gently weeps.--WHILEMYGUI--10
Still my guitar gently weeps.--WHILEMYGUI--12
While my guitar gently weeps.--WHILEMYGUI--19
Still my guitar gently weeps ((eee)).--WHILEMYGUI--21

GEORGIA'S
That Georgia's always on my my my my my my my
my mind.--BACKINTHEU--18
That Georgia's always on my my my my my my my my
my mind.--BACKINTHEU--30

GEORGIE
((That was Can You Dig It? by Georgie
Wood))--DIGIT--11

GET
I'LL GET YOU.--ILLGETYOU--Title
But I'll get you, I'll get you in the end--
ILLGETYOU--7
But I'll get you, I'll get you in the end--
ILLGETYOU--7
Yes I will I'll get you in the end, oh yeah,
oh yeah.--ILLGETYOU--8
That I'll get you, I'll get you in the end--
ILLGETYOU--14
That I'll get you, I'll get you in the end--
ILLGETYOU--14
Yes I will, I'll get you in the end, oh yeah,
oh yeah.--ILLGETYOU--15
But I'll get you, I'll get you in the end--
ILLGETYOU--24
But I'll get you, I'll get you in the end--
ILLGETYOU--24
Yes I will, I'll get you in the end, oh yeah,
oh yeah--ILLGETYOU--25
If I don't get her back again--DONTBOTHER--16
If I don't get her back again--DONTBOTHER--31
I'll get you anything my friend --CANTBUYMEL--5
But when I get home to you,--HARDDAYSNI--5
To get you money to buy you things,--HARDDAYSNI--9
'cos when I get you alone --HARDDAYSNI--13
But when I get home to you --HARDDAYSNI--21
'cos when I get you alone --HARDDAYSNI--26
But when I get home to you --HARDDAYSNI--34
If I could get my way --ILLCRYINST--3
I'd get myself locked up today --ILLCRYINST--4
I get shy when they start to stare.--ILLCRYINST--12

I get shy when they start to stare.--ILLCRYINST--21
WHEN I GET HOME.--WHENIGETHO--Title
When I get home.--WHENIGETHO--3
When I get home.--WHENIGETHO--9
When I get home.--WHENIGETHO--15
When I get home, yeah.--WHENIGETHO--26
When I get home.--WHENIGETHO--28
Turn me on when I get lonely--SHESAWOMAN--5
Turn me on when I get lonely--SHESAWOMAN--22
Turn me on when I get lonely--SHESAWOMAN--32
How can I get through--TELLMEWHAT--19
Trying to get to you--TELLMEWHAT--21
How can I get through--TELLMEWHAT--28
Trying to get to you--TELLMEWHAT--30
Help me get my feet back on the ground--HELP--17
Help me get my feet back on the ground--HELP--27
Help me get my feet back on the ground--HELP--37
I get high when I see you go by, my oh my--
ITSONLYLOV--1
You can get it wrong and still you think that
it's alright.--WECANWORKI--7
We can work it out and get it straight or say
good night.--WECANWORKI--9
And maybe you will get a call from me --IFINEEDEDS
--11
And maybe you will get a call from me --IFINEEDEDS
--21
I'll get to you somehow--MICHELLE--18
But I can't get through, my hands are tied.--
YOUWONTSEE--8
But you don't get me, you don't get me.--ANDYOURBIR
--3
But you don't get me, you don't get me.--ANDYOURBIR
--3
GOT TO GET YOU INTO MY LIFE.--GOTTOGETYO--Title
Got to get you into my life.--GOTTOGETYO--15
Got to get you into my life.--GOTTOGETYO--23
I got to get you into my life.--GOTTOGETYO--24
When I get near you--IWANTTOTEL--5
You don't get time to hang a sign on me.--
LOVEYOUTWO--3
If you get too cold, I'll tax the heat,
((cold))--TAXMAN--13
And nothing to get hungabout--STRAWBERRY--4
And nothing to get hungabout--STRAWBERRY--14
And nothing to get hungabout--STRAWBERRY--24
And nothing to get hungabout--STRAWBERRY--34
And wonder why they don't get in my door.--
FIXINGAHOL--10
And never ask me why they don't get past my door.
--FIXINGAHOL--18
I used to get mad at my school (now I can't
complain)--GETTINGBET--3
A little better all the time (it can't get no
worse)--GETTINGBET--8
A little better all the time (it can't get no
worse)--GETTINGBET--17
A little better all the time (it can't get no
worse)--GETTINGBET--30
Home. (we struggled hard all our lives to get by)
--SHESLEAVIN--22
When I get older losing my hair--WHENIMSIXT--1
Oh I get by with a little help from my friends --
WITHALITTL--5
Mmm I get high with a little help from my friends
--WITHALITTL--6
No I get by with a little help from my friends --
WITHALITTL--12
Mmm get high with a little help from my friends --
WITHALITTL--13
Oh I get by with a little help from my friends --
WITHALITTL--23
Mmm get high with a little help from my friends --
WITHALITTL--24
Oh I get by with a little help from my friends --
WITHALITTL--30
Oh I get high with a little help from my friends
--WITHALITTL--32
Yes I get by with a little help from my friends --
WITHALITTL--33
If the sun don't come you get a tan from standing
in the English rain--IAMTHEWALR--18
Let's all get up and dance to a song--YOURMOTHER
--2
Let's all get up and dance to a song--YOURMOTHER
--8
You were made to go out and get her --HEYJUDE--6
You have found her, now go and get her (let it
out and let it in) --HEYJUDE--16
Didn't get to bed last night --BACKINTHEU--2
When I get to the bottom I go back to the top
of the slide --HELTERSKEL--1
Till I get to the bottom and I see you again -
yeah, yeah, yeah.--HELTERSKEL--3

When I get to the bottom I go back to the top
    of the slide--HELTERSKEL--18
And I get to the bottom and I see you again -
    yeah, yeah, yeah.--HELTERSKEL--20
I wonder should I get up and fix myself a drink --
    IMSOTIRED--3
He was such a stupid get.--IMSOTIRED--17
He said, I'm gonna get that boy --ROCKYRACCO--6
Sexy Sadie you'll get yours yet--SEXYSADIE--16
Sexy Sadie - oh you'll get yours yet--SEXYSADIE--19
And get me home for tea.--ITSALLTOOM--24
GET BACK.--GETBACK/45--Title
Get back, get back --GETBACK/45--5
Get back, get back --GETBACK/45--5
Get back to where you once belonged.--GETBACK/45
    --6
Get back, get back --GETBACK/45--7
Get back, get back --GETBACK/45--7
Get back to where you once belonged.--GETBACK/45
    --8
Get back Jojo.--GETBACK/45--9
Get back, get back --GETBACK/45--11
Get back, get back --GETBACK/45--11
Get back, get back --GETBACK/45--13
Get back, get back --GETBACK/45--13
Oh get back Jo.--GETBACK/45--15
Oh get back, get back --GETBACK/45--20
Oh get back, get back --GETBACK/45--20
Get back to where you once belonged.--GETBACK/45
    --21
Get back, get back --GETBACK/45--22
Get back, get back --GETBACK/45--22
Get back to where you once belonged.--GETBACK/45
    --23
Get back Loretta (wuh - wuh).--GETBACK/45--24
Oh get back, yeah get back --GETBACK/45--26
Oh get back, yeah get back --GETBACK/45--26
Get back to where you once belonged.--GETBACK/45
    --27
Yeah get back, get back --GETBACK/45--28
Yeah get back, get back --GETBACK/45--28
Get back to where you once belonged.--GETBACK/45
    --29
Get back Loretta --GETBACK/45--31
Get back home Loretta.--GETBACK/45--35
Get back, get back --GETBACK/45--36
Get back, get back --GETBACK/45--36
Get back to where you once belonged.--GETBACK/45
    --37
Oh get back, get back yeah, yeah --GETBACK/45--38
Oh get back, get back yeah, yeah --GETBACK/45--38
Get back - oh yeah.--GETBACK/45--39
Trying to get to Holland or France.--BALLADOFJO--2
You can get married in Gibraltar near Spain.--
    BALLADOFJO--12
I said we're only trying to get us some peace.--
    BALLADOFJO--20
If you and me should get together --OLDBROWNSH--25
To get back homeward.--GOLDENSLUM--2
To get back home.--GOLDENSLUM--4
To get back homeward.--GOLDENSLUM--12
To get back home.--GOLDENSLUM--14
But I gotta get a bellyfull of wine.--HERMAJESTY
    --6
Get a dose of her in jackboots and kilt --
    POLYTHENEP--6
Pick up the bags, get in the limousine.--YOUNEVERGI
    --18
GET BACK.--GETBACK/LP--Title
Get back, get back --GETBACK/LP--11
Get back, get back --GETBACK/LP--11
Get back to where you once belonged--GETBACK/LP--12
Get back, get back --GETBACK/LP--13
Get back, get back --GETBACK/LP--13
Get back to where you once belonged--GETBACK/LP--14
Get back Jojo.--GETBACK/LP--15
Get back, get back --GETBACK/LP--17
Get back, get back --GETBACK/LP--17
Get back, get back --GETBACK/LP--19
Get back, get back --GETBACK/LP--19
Oh get back Jo.--GETBACK/LP--21
Oh get back, get back --GETBACK/LP--26
Oh get back, get back --GETBACK/LP--26
Get back to where you once belonged--GETBACK/LP--27
Get back, get back --GETBACK/LP--28
Get back, get back --GETBACK/LP--28
Get back to where you once belonged.--GETBACK/LP
    --29
Get back Loretta (wuh - wuh).--GETBACK/LP--30
Oh get back, yeah, get back --GETBACK/LP--32
Oh get back, yeah, get back --GETBACK/LP--32
Get back to where you once belonged--GETBACK/LP--33
Yeah, get back, get back --GETBACK/LP--34
Yeah, get back, get back --GETBACK/LP--34

Get back to where you once belonged--GETBACK/LP--35
Get back - ooo!--GETBACK/LP--36

GETS
If this boy gets you back again.--THISBOY--13
Before she gets to saying goodbye--TICKETTORI--20
Before she gets to saying goodbye--TICKETTORI--33
I'm fixing a hole where the rain gets in--
    FIXINGAHOL--1
I'm fixing a hole where the rain gets in--
    FIXINGAHOL--23
I'm fixing a hole where the rain gets in--
    FIXINGAHOL--26
When it gets dark I tow your heart away.--
    LOVELYRITA--6
Father snores as his wife gets into her
    dressing-gown--SHESLEAVIN--13
But she gets it while she can.--GETBACK/45--19
Back in school again, Maxwell plays the fool
    again, teacher gets annoyed --MAXWELLSIL--8
But she gets it while she can.--GETBACK/LP--25
Phase one in which Doris gets her oats.--TWOOFUS
    --2

GETTING
When I getting home tonight --WHENIGETHO--16
It's getting hard to be someone--STRAWBERRY--8
GETTING BETTER.--GETTINGBET--Title
It's getting better all the time.--GETTINGBET--2
I've got to admit it's getting better (better)--
    GETTINGBET--7
I have to admit it's getting better (better)--
    GETTINGBET--9
It's getting better since you've been mine.--
    GETTINGBET--10
I've got to admit it's getting better (better)--
    GETTINGBET--16
I have to admit it's getting better (better)--
    GETTINGBET--18
It's getting better since you've been mine.--
    GETTINGBET--19
Getting so much better all the time.--GETTINGBET--20
It's getting better all the time--GETTINGBET--21
It's getting better all the time.--GETTINGBET--23
I admit it's getting better (better)--GETTINGBET--29
Yes I admit it's getting better (better)--
    GETTINGBET--31
It's getting better since you've been mine.--
    GETTINGBET--32
Getting so much better all the time.--GETTINGBET--33
It's getting better all the time--GETTINGBET--34
It's getting better all the time--GETTINGBET--36
Getting so much better all the time.--GETTINGBET
    --38
Everywhere in town is getting dark--GOODMORNIN--19
It's getting very near the end.--SGTPEPPREP--14
Life is getting worse --PIGGIES--4
But as she's getting ready to go, a knock comes
    on the door --MAXWELLSIL--5
Getting nowhere on our way back home.--TWOOFUS--22
Getting nowhere on our way back home.--TWOOFUS--31

GETTING-A
Me hand's getting-a too cold to play a chord now.
    --IDIGAPONY--38

GIBRALTAR
You can get married in Gibraltar near Spain.--
    BALLADOFJO--12

GIDEON
Gideon checked out and he left it no doubt ((oh
    - Rocky - oh))--ROCKYRACCO--38

GIDEON'S
Only to find Gideon's Bible --ROCKYRACCO--10
Only to find Gideon's Bible --ROCKYRACCO--37

GIN
Now the doctor came in stinking of gin--ROCKYRACCO
    --31

GINGER
A ginger sling with a pineapple heart --SAVOYTRUFF
    --2
A ginger sling with a pineapple heart --SAVOYTRUFF

--24

GIRL
    Last night I said these words to my girl --
        PLEASEPLEA--1
    I know you never even try girl --PLEASEPLEA--2
    Last night I said these words to my girl --
        PLEASEPLEA--19
    I know/Why do you never even try girl--PLEASEPLEA--20
    THANK YOU GIRL.--THANKYOUGI--Title
    And all I gotta do is thank you girl, thank you
        girl.--THANKYOUGI--4
    And all I gotta do is thank you girl, thank you
        girl.--THANKYOUGI--4
    I know, little girl, only a fool would doubt
        our love--THANKYOUGI--6
    And all I gotta do is thank you girl, thank you
        girl--THANKYOUGI--7
    And all I gotta do is thank you girl, thank you
        girl--THANKYOUGI--7
    Thank you girl, for loving me the way that you
        do (way that you do).--THANKYOUGI--8
    And all I gotta do is thank you girl, thank you
        girl.--THANKYOUGI--10
    And all I gotta do is thank you girl, thank you
        girl.--THANKYOUGI--10
    And all I gotta do is thank you girl, thank you
        girl.--THANKYOUGI--14
    And all I gotta do is thank you girl, thank you
        girl.--THANKYOUGI--14
    The only girl for me--DONTBOTHER--18
    The only girl for me--DONTBOTHER--33
    I should have known better with a girl like you --
        ISHOULDHAV--1
    'cos I've just lost the only girl I had.--
        ILLCRYINST--2
    You say you'll be mine girl, till the end of time
        --THINGSWESA--6
    These days such a kind girl seems so hard to find
        --THINGSWESA--7
    And that's enough to make you mine girl --
        THINGSWESA--15
    Love me all the time girl --THINGSWESA--17
    And that's enough to make you mine girl --
        THINGSWESA--26
    Love me all the time girl --THINGSWESA--28
    I got a girl who's waiting home for me tonight.--
        WHENIGETHO--12
    I'm so glad that she's my little girl --IFEELFINE
        --7
    I'm so glad that she's my little girl --IFEELFINE
        --15
    Love you every day girl --EIGHTDAYSA--9
    One thing I can say girl --EIGHTDAYSA--11
    I ain't got nothing but love girl --EIGHTDAYSA--15
    Love you every day girl --EIGHTDAYSA--29
    One thing I can say girl --EIGHTDAYSA--31
    She was a girl in a million, my friend --IMALOSER
        --5
    You've ((you've)) got me crying, girl --WHATYOURED
        --13
    You've ((you've)) got me crying, girl --WHATYOURED
        --20
    The girl that's driving me mad is going away.--
        TICKETTORI--4
    The girl that's driving me mad is going away,
        yeah.--TICKETTORI--25
    ANOTHER GIRL.--ANOTHERGIR--Title
    For I have got another girl, another girl.--
        ANOTHERGIR--1
    For I have got another girl, another girl.--
        ANOTHERGIR--1
    For I have got another girl, another girl.--
        ANOTHERGIR--5
    For I have got another girl, another girl.--
        ANOTHERGIR--5
    For I have got another girl --ANOTHERGIR--9
    Another girl who will love me till the end --
        ANOTHERGIR--10
    For I have got another girl --ANOTHERGIR--15
    Another girl who will love me till the end --
        ANOTHERGIR--16
    For I have got another girl, another girl,
        another girl.--ANOTHERGIR--21
    For I have got another girl, another girl,
        another girl.--ANOTHERGIR--21
    For I have got another girl, another girl,
        another girl.--ANOTHERGIR--21
    Haven't I the right to make it up girl?--ITSONLYLOV
        --10
    She's just the girl for me--IVEJUSTSEE--4
    She's just the girl for me--IVEJUSTSEE--27
    YOU'RE GOING TO/GONNA LOSE THAT GIRL.--YOUREGONNA--Title

You're gonna lose that girl (yes, yes, you're
    gonna lose that girl)--YOUREGONNA--1
You're gonna lose that girl (yes, yes, you're
    gonna lose that girl)--YOUREGONNA--1
You're gonna lose that girl (yes, yes, you're
    gonna lose that girl)--YOUREGONNA--2
You're gonna lose that girl (yes, yes, you're
    gonna lose that girl)--YOUREGONNA--2
You're gonna lose that girl (yes, yes, you're
    gonna lose that girl)--YOUREGONNA--7
You're gonna lose that girl (yes, yes, you're
    gonna lose that girl)--YOUREGONNA--7
You're gonna lose that girl (yes, yes, you're
    gonna lose that girl)--YOUREGONNA--8
You're gonna lose that girl (yes, yes, you're
    gonna lose that girl)--YOUREGONNA--8
You're gonna lose that girl (yes, yes, you're
    gonna lose that girl)--YOUREGONNA--13
You're gonna lose that girl (yes, yes, you're
    gonna lose that girl)--YOUREGONNA--13
You're gonna lose that girl (yes, yes, you're
    gonna lose that girl)--YOUREGONNA--14
You're gonna lose that girl (yes, yes, you're
    gonna lose that girl)--YOUREGONNA--14
You're gonna lose (yes, yes, you're gonna lose
    that girl)--YOUREGONNA--15
You're gonna lose that girl--YOUREGONNA--18
You're gonna lose that girl--YOUREGONNA--19
You're gonna lose that girl (yes, yes, you're
    gonna lose that girl)--YOUREGONNA--20
You're gonna lose that girl (yes, yes, you're
    gonna lose that girl)--YOUREGONNA--20
You're gonna lose that girl (yes, yes, you're
    gonna lose that girl)--YOUREGONNA--21
You're gonna lose that girl (yes, yes, you're
    gonna lose that girl)--YOUREGONNA--21
You're gonna lose (yes, yes, you're gonna lose
    that girl)--YOUREGONNA--22
You're gonna lose that girl (yes, yes, you're
    gonna lose that girl)--YOUREGONNA--29
You're gonna lose that girl (yes, yes, you're
    gonna lose that girl)--YOUREGONNA--29
You're gonna lose that girl (yes, yes, you're
    gonna lose that girl)--YOUREGONNA--30
You're gonna lose that girl (yes, yes, you're
    gonna lose that girl)--YOUREGONNA--30
You're gonna lose (yes, yes, you're gonna lose
    that girl).--YOUREGONNA--31
Asked a girl what she wanted to be --DRIVEMYCAR--1
I told that girl that my prospects were good --
    DRIVEMYCAR--9
I told that girl I could start right away --
    DRIVEMYCAR--22
GIRL.--GIRL--Title
All about the girl who came to stay?--GIRL--2
She's the kind of girl you want so much it makes
    you sorry --GIRL--3
Ah, girl - (girl) girl.--GIRL--5
Ah, girl - (girl) girl.--GIRL--5
Ah, girl - (girl) girl.--GIRL--5
Ah, girl - (girl) girl.--GIRL--10
Ah, girl - (girl) girl.--GIRL--10
Ah, girl - (girl) girl.--GIRL--10
She's the kind of girl who puts you down--GIRL--11
Girl - (girl) girl.--GIRL--21
Girl - (girl) girl.--GIRL--21
Girl - (girl) girl.--GIRL--21
Ah, girl - (girl) girl.--GIRL--26
Ah, girl - (girl) girl.--GIRL--26
Ah, girl - (girl) girl.--GIRL--26
Ah, girl - (girl) girl.--GIRL--27
Ah, girl - (girl) girl.--GIRL--27
Ah, girl - (girl) girl.--GIRL--27
I once had a girl--NORWEGIANW--1
Well I'd rather see you dead, little girl --
    RUNFORYOUR--1
You better keep your head, little girl,--RUNFORYOUR
    --3
You better run for your life if you can, little
    girl --RUNFORYOUR--5
Hide your head in the sand, little girl.--
    RUNFORYOUR--6
That's the end'a little girl.--RUNFORYOU--8
You better run for your life if you can, little
    girl --RUNFORYOUR--13
Hide your head in the sand, little girl.--
    RUNFORYOUR--14
That's the end'a little girl.--RUNFORYOUR--16
You better run for your life if you can, little
    girl --RUNFORYOUR--21
Hide your head in the sand, little girl.--
    RUNFORYOUR--22
That's the end'a little girl.--RUNFORYOUR--24
I'd rather see you dead, little girl --RUNFORYOUR

--25

You better keep your head, little girl --RUNFORYOUR
--27
You better run for your life if you can, little
girl --RUNFORYOUR--29
Hide your head in the sand, little girl.--
RUNFORYOUR--30
That's the end'a little girl.--RUNFORYOUR--32
It's so easy for a girl like you to lie.--
WHATGOESON--8
It's so easy for a girl like you to lie.--
WHATGOESON--17
Yes it seems so long, girl, since you've been gone
--YOUWONTSEE--18
Yes it seems so long, girl, since you've been gone
--YOUWONTSEE--27
A girl with kaleidoscope eyes.--LUCYINTHES--4
Look for the girl with the sun in her eyes--
LUCYINTHES--7
The girl with kaleidoscope eyes.--LUCYINTHES--26
Boy, you been a naughty girl, you let your
knickers down--IAMTHEWALR--14
She's not a girl who misses much --HAPPINESSI--1
She was a working girl--HONEYPIE--1
Hold your head up you silly girl, look what
you've done --MARTHAMYDE--4
Help yourself to a bit of what is all around you
- silly girl.--MARTHAMYDE--6
That you and me were meant to be for each other -
silly girl.--MARTHAMYDE--9
Hold your hand out you silly girl, see what
you've done --MARTHAMYDE--10
Help yourself to a bit of what is all around you
- silly girl.--MARTHAMYDE--12
Desmond says to Molly, girl I like your face--
OBLADIOBLA--3
By stealing the girl of his fancy --ROCKYRACCO--14
Ooo - girl you know the reason why.--YERBLUES--5
Wuh - girl you know the reason why.--YERBLUES--9
Wuh - girl you know the reason why.--YERBLUES--16
Wuh - girl you know the reason why.--YERBLUES--23
Wuh girl - you know the reason why.--YERBLUES--30
... Girl you know the reason why.--YERBLUES--33
I want a short-haired girl --OLDBROWNSH--3
Her Majesty's a pretty nice girl--HERMAJESTY--1
Her Majesty's a pretty nice girl--HERMAJESTY--3
Her Majesty's a pretty nice girl--HERMAJESTY--7
Oh, what joy for every girl and boy--OCTOPUSSGA--19
She's a kind of a girl that makes the News Of
The World.--POLYTHENEP--8
Because you're sweet and lovely girl I love you,
--FORYOUBLUE--2
Because you're sweet and lovely girl, it's true --
FORYOUBLUE--3
I love you more than ever girl, I do.--FORYOUBLUE
--4
I want you in the morning girl, I love you --
FORYOUBLUE--5
I'm living every moment girl for you.--FORYOUBLUE
--7
Because you're sweet and lovely girl, I love you
--FORYOUBLUE--16
Because you're sweet and lovely girl, it's true --
FORYOUBLUE--17
I love you more than ever girl, I do - really
love blues.--FORYOUBLUE--18

GIRLS
And when I do you'd better hide all the girls --
ILLCRYINST--15
And when I do you'd better hide all the girls --
ILLCRYINST--24
She's sweeter than all the girls and I met quite
a few,--ANOTHERGIR--6
But other girls were never quite like this --
IVEJUSTSEE--17
Well, the Ukraine girls really knock me out --
BACKINTHEU--15
And Moscow girls make me sing and shout --
BACKINTHEU--17
Well, the Ukraine girls really knock me out --
BACKINTHEU--27
And Moscow girls make me sing and shout --
BACKINTHEU--29
All the girls around her say she's got it coming
--GETBACK/45--18
All the girls around her say she's got it coming--
GETBACK/LP--24

GIVE
I'll give you all I've got to give --CANTBUYMEL--9
I'll give you all I've got to give --CANTBUYMEL--9

I may not have a lot to give --CANTBUYMEL--11
But what I got I'll give to you --CANTBUYMEL--12
I give her all my love --ANDILOVEHE--1
You're gonna give me everything --HARDDAYSNI--11
If this is love you've got to give me more --
ISHOULDHAV--12
Give me more, hey hey hey, give me more.--
ISHOULDHAV--13
Give me more, hey hey hey, give me more.--
ISHOULDHAV--13
If I give my heart to you --IFIFELL--7
My love don't give me presents--SHESAWOMAN--1
Only ever has to give me love forever and forever
--SHESAWOMAN--3
My love don't give me presents--SHESAWOMAN--4
She don't give boys the eye--SHESAWOMAN--8
She don't give boys the eye--SHESAWOMAN--12
My love don't give me presents--SHESAWOMAN--18
Only ever has to give me love forever and forever
--SHESAWOMAN--20
My love don't give me presents--SHESAWOMAN--21
My love don't give me presents--SHESAWOMAN--28
Only ever has to give me love forever and forever
--SHESAWOMAN--30
My love don't give me presents--SHESAWOMAN--31
Give the word a chance to say --THEWORD--25
It's a thousand pages, give or take a few,
((paperback))--PAPERBACKW--15
Give us a wink and make me think of you.--
LOVELYRITA--28
Give me your answer--WHENIMSIXT--32
You know I'd give you everything I've got for a
little peace of mind.--IMSOTIRED--13
You know I'd give you everything I've got for a
little peace of mind.--IMSOTIRED--22
I'd give you everything I've got for a little
peace of mind --IMSOTIRED--23
I'd give you everything I've got for a little
peace of mind.--IMSOTIRED--24
You know they didn't even give us a chance.--
BALLADOFJO--4
I never give you my pillow--CARRYTHATW--5
YOU NEVER GIVE ME YOUR MONEY.--YOUNEVERGI--Title
You never give me your money --YOUNEVERGI--1
You only give me your funny paper--YOUNEVERGI--2
I never give you my number --YOUNEVERGI--4
I only give you my situation--YOUNEVERGI--5

GIVES
She gives me everything --ANDILOVEHE--6
Gives me all her time as well as loving--SHESAWOMAN
--14
And he never gives an answer.--FOOLONTHEH--5
And as he gives it to her she begins to sing
(sing):--OBLADIOBLA--12

GIVING
You're giving me the same old line --NOTASECOND--7
You're giving me the same old line --NOTASECOND--18
Giving all your clothes to charity.--BALLADOFJO--26

GLAD
You made me glad when I was blue--THANKYOUGI--2
You made me glad when I was blue--THANKYOUGI--12
And you know you should be glad.--SHELOVESYO--11
And you know you should be glad - ooo!--SHELOVESYO
--19
You know you should be glad.--SHELOVESYO--23
And you know you should be glad - ooo!--SHELOVESYO
--31
You know you should be glad--SHELOVESYO--35
You know you should be glad--SHELOVESYO--37
You know you should be glad--SHELOVESYO--39
I'm so glad that she's my little girl --IFEELFINE
--7
She's so glad she's telling all the world --
IFEELFINE--8
I'm so glad that she's my little girl --IFEELFINE
--15
She's so glad she's telling all the world --
IFEELFINE--16
If I find her I'll be glad --IDONTWANTT--11
If I find her I'll be glad --IDONTWANTT--20
Somebody needs to know the time glad that I'm here
--GOODMORNIN--22
I'm glad it's your birthday --BIRTHDAY--5
I'm glad it's your birthday --BIRTHDAY--24
We're so glad you came here --OLDBROWNSH--7
So glad you came here --OLDBROWNSH--15
So glad you came here --OLDBROWNSH--33
I'm so glad you came here --OLDBROWNSH--35

GLASS
    GLASS ONION.--GLASSONION--Title
    Looking through a glass onion.--GLASSONION--7
    Looking through a glass onion.--GLASSONION--14
    Looking through a glass onion.--GLASSONION--16
    Looking through a glass onion.--GLASSONION--23

GLIMMERING
    Glimmering in the sun.--JULIA--8

GLIMPSE
    When I caught a glimpse of Rita--LOVELYRITA--8
    Never glimpse the truth--WITHINYOUW--5

GO
    So go away--DONTBOTHER--6
    Let me go on loving you --HOLDMETIGH--10
    Let me go on loving you --HOLDMETIGH--30
    I go outta my mind.--YOUCANTDOT--26
    I go outta my mind.--YOUCANTDOT--45
    I never weep at night, I can't go on.--ICALLYOURN
        --4
    There, there's a place where I can go--THERESAPLA
        --1
    And things you do go round my head--THERESAPLA--6
    There, there's a place where I can go--THERESAPLA
        --13
    If you don't I really can't go on --TELLMEWHY--15
    You know if you break my heart, I'll go --ILLBEBACK
        --1
    You if you break my heart, I'll go--ILLBEBACK
        --26
    You say you will love me if I have to go --
        THINGSWESA--1
    We'll go on and on.--THINGSWESA--18
    We'll go on and on.--THINGSWESA--29
    I don't wanna spoil the party so I'll go --
        IDONTWANTT--1
    I don't wanna spoil the party so I'll go --
        IDONTWANTT--13
    And now the time has come and so my love I must
        go --ILLFOLLOWT--5
    And now the time has come and so my love I must
        go --ILLFOLLOWT--10
    I just can't go on any more.--INEEDYOU--15
    I just can't go on any more.--INEEDYOU--25
    I get high when I see you go by, my oh my--
        ITSONLYLOV--1
    Why she had to go, I don't know--YESTERDAY--9
    Why she had to go, I don't know--YESTERDAY--17
    If she's gone I can't go on --YOUVEGOTTO--3
    Do I have to keep on talking till I can't go on?--
        WECANWORKI--2
    I'm looking through you, where did you go?--
        IMLOOKINGT--1
    I'm looking through you, where did you go?--
        IMLOOKINGT--17
    These are words that go together well, my
        Michelle.--MICHELLE--2
    And go where you're going to --THINKFORYO--7
    And go where you're going to --THINKFORYO--16
    And go where you're going to --THINKFORYO--25
    And go where you're going to --THINKFORYO--29
    Everywhere I go I hear it said --THEWORD--15
    And I just can't go on--YOUWONTSEE--19
    And I just can't go on--YOUWONTSEE--28
    And all the people that come and go--PENNYLANE--3
    Where it will go.--FIXINGAHOL--3
    Where it will go.--FIXINGAHOL--6
    There I will go.--FIXINGAHOL--13
    And I still go.--FIXINGAHOL--21
    Where it will go, where it will go.--FIXINGAHOL--25
    Where it will go, where it will go.--FIXINGAHOL--25
    Where it will go.--FIXINGAHOL--28
    Go in to work don't want to go feeling low down--
        GOODMORNIN--7
    Go in to work don't want to go feeling low down--
        GOODMORNIN--7
    Go to a show you hope she goes--GOODMORNIN--24
    Sit back and let the evening go.--SGTPEPPERS--11
    We're sorry but it's time to go.--SGTPEPPREP--6
    Sunday mornings go for a ride.--WHENIMSIXT--16
    You say stop and I say go, go, go.--HELLOGOODB--2
    You say stop and I say go, go, go.--HELLOGOODB--2
    You say stop and I say go, go, go.--HELLOGOODB--2
    You say stop but I say go, go, go--HELLOGOODB--24
    You say stop but I say go, go, go--HELLOGOODB--24
    You say stop but I say go, go, go--HELLOGOODB--24
    ((I can stay till it's time to go)).--HELLOGOODB
        --25
    And I told them where to go.--BLUEJAYWAY--9

    And I'd really like to go (go) --BLUEJAYWAY--16
    And I'd really like to go (go) --BLUEJAYWAY--16
    You were made to go out and get her --HEYJUDE--6
    You have found her, now go and get her (let it
        out and let it in) --HEYJUDE--16
    But if you go carrying pictures of Chairman Mao --
        REVOLUTION--28
    How I hate to see you go --DONTPASSME--21
    How I hate to see you go --DONTPASSME--34
    How I hate to see you go --DONTPASSME--40
    The deeper you go, the higher you fly --EVRBDYMONK
        --8
    The higher you fly, the deeper you go --EVRBDYMONK
        --9
    Well here's another place you can go--GLASSONION
        --3
    When I get to the bottom I go back to the top
        of the slide --HELTERSKEL--1
    Where I stop and I turn and I go for a ride --
        HELTERSKEL--2
    When I get to the bottom I go back to the top
        of the slide--HELTERSKEL--18
    And I stop and I turn and I go for a ride--
        HELTERSKEL--19
    If you go carrying pictures of Chairman Mao --
        REVOLUTONE--43
    And the more I go inside --ITSALLTOOM--6
    Go home.--GETBACK/45--10
    Go home.--GETBACK/45--25
    The man in the mack said you've got to go back --
        BALLADOFJO--3
    But as she's getting ready to go, a knock comes
        on the door --MAXWELLSIL--5
    Rose and Valerie screaming from the gallery say
        he must go free --MAXWELLSIL--19
    (Maxwell must go free)--MAXWELLSIL--20
    All the money's gone, nowhere to go.--YOUNEVERGI
        --9
    Yellow lorry slow, nowhere to go.--YOUNEVERGI--12
    But oh, that magic feeling, nowhere to go --
        YOUNEVERGI--13
    Nowhere to go - nowhere to go.--YOUNEVERGI--15
    Nowhere to go - nowhere to go.--YOUNEVERGI--15
    All good children go to heaven.--YOUNEVERGI--25
    All good children go to heaven.--YOUNEVERGI--27
    All good children go to heaven.--YOUNEVERGI--29
    All good children go to heaven.--YOUNEVERGI--31
    All good children go to heaven.--YOUNEVERGI--33
    All good children go to heaven.--YOUNEVERGI--35
    All good children go to heaven.--YOUNEVERGI--37
    All good children go to heaven--YOUNEVERGI--39
    Go Johnny go.--FORYOUBLUE--9
    Go Johnny go.--FORYOUBLUE--9
    Go home.--GETBACK/LP--16
    Go home.--GETBACK/LP--31
    Well you can penetrate any place you go--IDIGAPONY
        --10
    Yes you can penetrate any place you go--IDIGAPONY
        --11
    I begged her not to go and I begged her on my
        bended knee, (oh yeah)--ONEAFTERNI--6

GO-GETTER
    She's a go-getter.--MEANMRMUST--10

GOES
    That it really only goes to show --ASKMEWHY--4
    That it really only goes to show --ASKMEWHY--19
    And the same goes for me --ALLIVEGOTT--11
    And the same goes for me --ALLIVEGOTT--22
    WHAT GOES ON?--WHATGOESON--Title
    What goes on in your heart? (wuh)--WHATGOESON--1
    What goes on in your mind?--WHATGOESON--2
    What goes on in your mind?--WHATGOESON--5
    What goes on in your heart?--WHATGOESON--10
    What goes on in your mind?--WHATGOESON--11
    What goes on in your mind?--WHATGOESON--14
    What goes on in your heart?--WHATGOESON--19
    (What goes on in your mind?)--WHATGOESON--21
    What goes on in your heart?--WHATGOESON--26
    What goes on in your mind?--WHATGOESON--27
    What goes on in your mind?--WHATGOESON--30
    You stay home, she goes out --FORNOONE--17
    Each day just goes so fast--LOVEYOUTWO--1
    Go to a show you hope she goes--GOODMORNIN--24
    She goes downstairs to the kitchen--SHESLEAVIN--4
    Well it only goes to show (only, only goes to
        show) --BLUEJAYWAY--8
    Well it only goes to show (only, only goes to
        show) --BLUEJAYWAY--8
    Ob-la-di ob-la-da life goes on bra --OBLADIOBLA--5
    La-la how the life goes on --OBLADIOBLA--6

Ob-la-di ob-la-da life goes on bra --OBLADIOBLA--7
La-la how the life goes on.--OBLADIOBLA--8
Ob-la-di ob-la-da life goes on bra --OBLADIOBLA--13
La-la how the life goes on --OBLADIOBLA--14
Ob-la-di ob-la-da life goes on bra --OBLADIOBLA--15
La-la how the life goes on - yeah.--OBLADIOBLA--16
Ob-la-di ob-la-da life goes on bra --OBLADIOBLA--25
La-la how the life goes on (he he he) --OBLADIOBLA
   --26
Hey, ob-la-di ob-la-da life goes on bra --
   OBLADIOBLA--27
La-la how the life goes on.--OBLADIOBLA--28
Ob-la-di ob-la-da life goes on bra --OBLADIOBLA--36
La-la how the life goes on - yeah --OBLADIOBLA--37
Ob-la-di ob-la-da life goes on bra --OBLADIOBLA--38
La-la how the life goes on (ha ha ha ha ha ha).--
   OBLADIOBLA--39
They don't care what goes on around.--PIGGIES--12

GOING
The girl that's driving me mad is going away.--
   TICKETTORI--4
The girl that's driving me mad is going away,
   yeah.--TICKETTORI--25
YOU'RE GOING TO/GONNA LOSE THAT GIRL.--YOUREGONNA--Title
Is there anybody going to listen to my story--GIRL
   --1
Knows not where he's going to --NOWHEREMAN--5
Knows not where he's going to --NOWHEREMAN--17
And go where you're going to --THINKFORYO--7
And go where you're going to --THINKFORYO--16
And go where you're going to --THINKFORYO--25
And go where you're going to --THINKFORYO--29
Keeping an eye on the world going by my window --
   IMONLYSLEE--13
Keeping an eye on the world going by my window --
   IMONLYSLEE--19
'cos I'm going to strawberry fields--STRAWBERRY--2
'cos I'm going to strawberry fields--STRAWBERRY--12
'cos I'm going to strawberry fields--STRAWBERRY--22
'cos I'm going to strawberry fields--STRAWBERRY--32
They've been going in and out of style--SGTPEPPERS
   --3
What are you going to play?--BABYYOUREA--27
But the fool on the hill sees the sun going down--
   FOOLONTHEH--6
But the fool on the hill sees the sun going down--
   FOOLONTHEH--13
But the fool on the hill sees the sun going down--
   FOOLONTHEH--18
The fool on the hill sees the sun going down--
   FOOLONTHEH--25
Without going out of my door --INNERLIGHT--1
Without going out of your door --INNERLIGHT--8
Yes, we're going to a party, party --BIRTHDAY--8
Yes, we're going to a party, party --BIRTHDAY--9
Yes, we're going to a party, party.--BIRTHDAY--10
I need a fix 'cos I'm going down --HAPPINESSI--9
I need a fix 'cos I'm going down.--HAPPINESSI--11
You know it's three weeks, I'm going insane --
   IMSOTIRED--12
You know it's three weeks, I'm going insane --
   IMSOTIRED--21
You may think the chords are going wrong --
   ONLYANORTH--2
The way things are going --BALLADOFJO--7
The way things are going --BALLADOFJO--15
The way things are going --BALLADOFJO--23
The way things are going --BALLADOFJO--35
The way things are going --BALLADOFJO--43
The way things are going --BALLADOFJO--45
The picker - the picker, picture the fingers
   going (ooo me).--GETBACK/LP--5
We're going home.--TWOOFUS--9
We're going home.--TWOOFUS--16
We're going home.--TWOOFUS--25
We're going home.--TWOOFUS--34
We're going home.--TWOOFUS--35

GOLDEN
Buys a twenty-carat golden ring (golden ring) --
   OBLADIOBLA--10
Buys a twenty-carat golden ring (golden ring) --
   OBLADIOBLA--10
GOLDEN SLUMBERS.--GOLDENSLUM--Title
Golden slumbers fill your eyes--GOLDENSLUM--7

GONE
Since she's been gone--DONTBOTHER--1
Oh, I can't sleep at night since you've been
   gone --ICALLYOURN--3

If she turns up while I'm gone please let me know.
   --IDONTWANTT--4
If she turns up while I'm gone please let me know.
   --IDONTWANTT--16
One day you'll look to see I've gone --ILLFOLLOWT
   --1
One day you'll find that I have gone --ILLFOLLOWT
   --7
One day you'll find that I have gone --ILLFOLLOWT
   --12
Though you've gone away this morning--YOULIKEMET
   --1
But now ((but now)) these days are gone
   ((these days are gone))--HELP--11
But now ((but now)) these days are gone
   ((these days are gone))--HELP--11
But now ((now)) these days are gone ((these
   days are gone))--HELP--31
But now ((now)) these days are gone ((these
   days are gone))--HELP--31
You're gonna find her gone (you're gonna find
   her gone)--YOUREGONNA--10
You're gonna find her gone (you're gonna find
   her gone)--YOUREGONNA--10
If she's gone I can't go on --YOUVEGOTTO--3
Run the risk of knowing that our love may soon be
   gone.--WECANWORKI--4
Some have gone and some remain.--INMYLIFE--4
Yes it seems so long, girl, since you've been gone
   --YOUWONTSEE--18
Yes it seems so long, girl, since you've been gone
   --YOUWONTSEE--27
But now he's gone, she doesn't need him.--FORNOONE
   --19
And had you gone, you knew in time--GOTTOGETYO--10
And she's gone.--LUCYINTHES--8
And you're gone.--LUCYINTHES--19
Daddy, our baby's gone.--SHESLEAVIN--17
When your lights have gone.--WHENIMSIXT--14
About the love that's gone so cold--WITHINYOUW--22
The newspapers said, she's gone to his head --
   BALLADOFJO--31
She tells Max to stay when the class has gone
   away --MAXWELLSIL--10
All the money's gone, nowhere to go.--YOUNEVERGI
   --9

GONNA
It's gonna be a drag, misery.--MISERY--5
Well, there's gonna be a time--ILLGETYOU--16
When I'm gonna change/make your mind--ILLGETYOU
   --17
I'm gonna let you down--YOUCANTDOT--5
(Gonna let you down and leave you flat)--YOUCANTDOT
   --15
I'm gonna let you down (let you down)--YOUCANTDOT
   --27
(Gonna let you down and leave you flat)--YOUCANTDOT
   --29
I'm gonna let you down (let you down)--YOUCANTDOT
   --46
(Gonna let you down and leave you flat)--YOUCANTDOT
   --48
I'm not gonna make it --ICALLYOURN--7
I'm not gonna make it --ICALLYOURN--14
You're gonna give me everything --HARDDAYSNI--11
You're gonna say you love me too, oh.--ISHOULDHAV--8
You're gonna say you love me too.--ISHOULDHAV--10
You're gonna say you love me too, oh.--ISHOULDHAV
   --18
You're gonna say you love me too.--ISHOULDHAV--20
I'm gonna hide myself away-hey--ILLCRYINST--13
I'm gonna break their hearts all round the world
   --ILLCRYINST--16
Yes, I'm gonna break 'em in two --ILLCRYINST--17
I'm gonna hide myself away-hey--ILLCRYINST--22
'cos I'm gonna break their hearts all round the
   world --ILLCRYINST--25
Yes, I'm gonna break 'em in two --ILLCRYINST--26
'cos I'm a - gonna see my baby today --WHENIGETHO
   --5
I'm gonna hold her tight,--WHENIGETHO--17
I'm gonna love her till the cows come home --
   WHENIGETHO--18
Wondering what you're gonna do --WHATYOURED--10
Wondering what you're gonna do --WHATYOURED--17
I think I'm gonna be sad--TICKETTORI--2
I think I'm gonna be sad--TICKETTORI--23
YOU'RE GOING TO/GONNA LOSE THAT GIRL.--YOUREGONNA
   --Title
You're gonna lose that girl (yes, yes, you're
   gonna lose that girl)--YOUREGONNA--1
You're gonna lose that girl (yes, yes, you're
   gonna lose that girl)--YOUREGONNA--1

You're gonna lose that girl (yes, yes, you're
    gonna lose that girl)--YOUREGONNA--2
You're gonna lose that girl (yes, yes, you're
    gonna lose that girl)--YOUREGONNA--2
She's gonna change her mind (she's gonna change
    her mind)--YOUREGONNA--4
She's gonna change her mind (she's gonna change
    her mind)--YOUREGONNA--4
And I will treat her kind (I'm gonna treat her
    kind)--YOUREGONNA--6
You're gonna lose that girl (yes, yes, you're
    gonna lose that girl)--YOUREGONNA--7
You're gonna lose that girl (yes, yes, you're
    gonna lose that girl)--YOUREGONNA--7
You're gonna lose that girl (yes, yes, you're
    gonna lose that girl)--YOUREGONNA--8
You're gonna lose that girl (yes, yes, you're
    gonna lose that girl)--YOUREGONNA--8
You're gonna find her gone (you're gonna find
    her gone)--YOUREGONNA--10
You're gonna find her gone (you're gonna find
    her gone)--YOUREGONNA--10
You're gonna lose that girl (yes, yes, you're
    gonna lose that girl)--YOUREGONNA--13
You're gonna lose that girl (yes, yes, you're
    gonna lose that girl)--YOUREGONNA--13
You're gonna lose that girl (yes, yes, you're
    gonna lose that girl)--YOUREGONNA--14
You're gonna lose that girl (yes, yes, you're
    gonna lose that girl)--YOUREGONNA--14
You're gonna lose (yes, yes, you're gonna lose
    that girl)--YOUREGONNA--15
You're gonna lose (yes, yes, you're gonna lose
    that girl)--YOUREGONNA--15
You're gonna lose that girl--YOUREGONNA--18
You're gonna lose that girl--YOUREGONNA--19
You're gonna lose that girl (yes, yes, you're
    gonna lose that girl)--YOUREGONNA--20
You're gonna lose that girl (yes, yes, you're
    gonna lose that girl)--YOUREGONNA--20
You're gonna lose that girl (yes, yes, you're
    gonna lose that girl)--YOUREGONNA--21
You're gonna lose that girl (yes, yes, you're
    gonna lose that girl)--YOUREGONNA--21
You're gonna lose (yes, yes, you're gonna lose
    that girl)--YOUREGONNA--22
You're gonna lose (yes, yes, you're gonna lose
    that girl)--YOUREGONNA--22
She's gonna change her mind (she's gonna change
    her mind)--YOUREGONNA--26
She's gonna change her mind (she's gonna change
    her mind)--YOUREGONNA--26
And I will treat her kind (I'm gonna treat her
    kind)--YOUREGONNA--28
You're gonna lose that girl (yes, yes, you're
    gonna lose that girl)--YOUREGONNA--29
You're gonna lose that girl (yes, yes, you're
    gonna lose that girl)--YOUREGONNA--29
You're gonna lose that girl (yes, yes, you're
    gonna lose that girl)--YOUREGONNA--30
You're gonna lose that girl (yes, yes, you're
    gonna lose that girl)--YOUREGONNA--30
You're gonna lose (yes, yes, you're gonna lose
    that girl).--YOUREGONNA--31
You're gonna lose (yes, yes, you're gonna lose
    that girl).--YOUREGONNA--31
Yes I'm gonna be a star.--DRIVEMYCAR--6
Yes I'm gonna be a star.--DRIVEMYCAR--14
Yes I'm gonna be a star.--DRIVEMYCAR--19
Yes I'm gonna be star.--DRIVEMYCAR--27
You're gonna cause more misery.--THINKFORYO--14
That the singer's gonna sing a song--SGTPEPPERS--21
Mmm gonna try with a little help from my friends.
    --WITHALITTL--7
Mmm gonna try with a little help from my friends.
    --WITHALITTL--14
Oh I'm gonna try with a little help from my
    friends.--WITHALITTL--25
Mmm gonna try with a little help from my friends
    --WITHALITTL--31
Don't you know it's gonna be alright, alright,
    alright?--REVOLUTION--10
Don't you know it's gonna be alright, alright
    ((alright)), alright?--REVOLUTION--20
You ain't gonna make it with anyone anyhow.--
    REVOLUTION--29
Don't you know it's gonna be alright, alright,
    alright ((alright))?--REVOLUTION--30
We're gonna have a good time.--BIRTHDAY--4
We're gonna have a good time.--BIRTHDAY--23
Don't you know it's gonna be ((oh shoo-be-do-a))--
    REVOLUTONE--13
Don't you know it's gonna be ((oh shoo-be-do-a))--
    REVOLUTONE--15

Don't you know it's gonna be ((oh shoo-be-do-a))--
    REVOLUTONE--17
Don't you know it's gonna be ((oh shoo-be-do-a))--
    REVOLUTONE--29
Don't you know it's gonna be ((oh shoo-be-do-a))--
    REVOLUTONE--31
Don't you know it's gonna be ((oh shoo-be-do-a))--
    REVOLUTONE--33
You ain't gonna make it with anyone anyhow.--
    REVOLUTONE--44
Don't you know it's gonna be ((oh shoo-be-do-a))--
    REVOLUTONE--45
Don't you know it's gonna be ((oh shoo-be-do-a))--
    REVOLUTONE--47
Don't you know it's gonna be ((oh shoo-be-do-a))--
    REVOLUTONE--49
He said, I'm gonna get that boy --ROCKYRACCO--6
You're gonna know and how.--SAVOYTRUFF--13
The sweat it's gonna fill your head --SAVOYTRUFF
    --14
Don't you know it's gonna last --DONTLETMED--14
They're gonna crucify me.--BALLADOFJO--8
They're gonna crucify me.--BALLADOFJO--16
They're gonna crucify me.--BALLADOFJO--24
They're gonna crucify me.--BALLADOFJO--36
They're gonna crucify me.--BALLADOFJO--44
They're gonna crucify me.--BALLADOFJO--46
Boy, you're gonna carry that weight--CARRYTHATW--1
Boy, you're gonna carry that weight--CARRYTHATW--3
Boy, you're gonna carry that weight--CARRYTHATW--9
Boy, you're gonna carry that weight--CARRYTHATW--11
Are you gonna be in my dreams tonight?--THEEND--2
Someday I'm gonna make her mine - oh yeah --
    HERMAJESTY--8
Someday I'm gonna make her mine.--HERMAJESTY--9
Nothing's gonna change my world --ACROSSTHEU--7
Nothing's gonna change my world --ACROSSTHEU--8
Nothing's gonna change my world --ACROSSTHEU--9
Nothing's gonna change my world.--ACROSSTHEU--10
Nothing's gonna change my world --ACROSSTHEU--16
Nothing's gonna change my world --ACROSSTHEU--17
Nothing's gonna change my world --ACROSSTHEU--18
Nothing's gonna change my world.--ACROSSTHEU--19
Nothing's gonna change my world --ACROSSTHEU--26
Nothing's gonna change my world --ACROSSTHEU--27
Nothing's gonna change my world --ACROSSTHEU--28
Nothing's gonna change my world.--ACROSSTHEU--29

GOO

I am the eggman (goo) they are the eggmen (goo)
    I am the walrus--IAMTHEWALR--7
I am the eggman (goo) they are the eggmen (goo)
    I am the walrus--IAMTHEWALR--7
Goo goo g'joob--IAMTHEWALR--8
Goo goo g'joob--IAMTHEWALR--8
I'm crying - I'm crying (goo), I'm crying,
    I'm crying--IAMTHEWALR--11
I am the eggman (goo) they are the eggmen (goo)
    I am the walrus--IAMTHEWALR--15
I am the eggman (goo) they are the eggmen (goo)
    I am the walrus--IAMTHEWALR--15
Goo goo g'joob--IAMTHEWALR--16
Goo goo g'joob--IAMTHEWALR--16
Goo goo g'joob, g'goo goo g'joob--IAMTHEWALR--20
Goo goo g'joob, g'goo goo g'joob--IAMTHEWALR--20
Goo goo g'joob, g'goo goo g'joob--IAMTHEWALR--20
I am the eggman (goo) they are the eggmen (goo)
    I am the walrus (goo)--IAMTHEWALR--28
I am the eggman (goo) they are the eggmen (goo)
    I am the walrus (goo)--IAMTHEWALR--28
I am the eggman (goo) they are the eggmen (goo)
    I am the walrus (goo)--IAMTHEWALR--28
Goo goo g'joob, g'goo goo g'joob--IAMTHEWALR--29
Goo goo g'joob, g'goo goo g'joob--IAMTHEWALR--29
Goo goo g'joob, g'goo goo g'joob--IAMTHEWALR--29
Goo goo g'joob, g'goo goo g'joob g'goo--IAMTHEWALR
    --30
Goo goo g'joob, g'goo goo g'joob g'goo--IAMTHEWALR
    --30
Goo goo g'joob, g'goo goo g'joob g'goo--IAMTHEWALR
    --30

GOOD

Oh, oh - mmm, you've been good to me--THANKYOUGI
    --1
That's the kind of love that is too good to be true
    --THANKYOUGI--9
Oh, oh - mmm, you've been good to me--THANKYOUGI
    --11
I'll be good like I know I should (yes,
    you're coming on home)--ITWONTBELO--13
I'll be good like I know I should (yes,

you're coming on home)--ITWONTBELO--23
That boy isn't good for you--THISBOY--4
Baby's good to me, you know --IFEELFINE--1
Got a good reason --DAYTRIPPER--1
Got a good reason --DAYTRIPPER--3
We can work it out and get it straight or say
    good night.--WECANWORKI--9
I told that girl that my prospects were good --
    DRIVEMYCAR--9
When you say she's looking good --GIRL--15
Isn't it good --NORWEGIANW--5
Isn't it good --NORWEGIANW--25
About the good things--THINKFORYO--4
The future still looks good --THINKFORYO--21
That I've been good, as good as I can be.--WAIT--10
That I've been good, as good as I can be.--WAIT--10
That I've been good, as good as I can be.--WAIT--18
That I've been good, as good as I can be.--WAIT--18
But now I've got it the word is good.--THEWORD--8
In the good and the bad books that I have read.--
    THEWORD--16
GOOD DAY SUNSHINE.--GOODDAYSUN--Title
Good day sunshine, good day sunshine, good day
    sunshine.--GOODDAYSUN--1
Good day sunshine, good day sunshine, good day
    sunshine.--GOODDAYSUN--1
Good day sunshine, good day sunshine, good day
    sunshine.--GOODDAYSUN--1
I feel good in a special way --GOODDAYSUN--4
Good day sunshine, good day sunshine, good day
    sunshine.--GOODDAYSUN--6
Good day sunshine, good day sunshine, good day
    sunshine.--GOODDAYSUN--6
Good day sunshine, good day sunshine, good day
    sunshine.--GOODDAYSUN--6
Good day sunshine, good day sunshine, good day
    sunshine.--GOODDAYSUN--9
Good day sunshine, good day sunshine, good day
    sunshine.--GOODDAYSUN--9
Good day sunshine, good day sunshine, good day
    sunshine.--GOODDAYSUN--9
She feels good (she feels good), she knows
    she's looking fine --GOODDAYSUN--12
She feels good (she feels good), she knows
    she's looking fine --GOODDAYSUN--12
Good day sunshine, good day sunshine, good day
    sunshine.--GOODDAYSUN--14
Good day sunshine, good day sunshine, good day
    sunshine.--GOODDAYSUN--14
Good day sunshine, good day sunshine, good day
    sunshine.--GOODDAYSUN--14
Good day sunshine, good day sunshine, good day
    sunshine.--GOODDAYSUN--15
Good day sunshine, good day sunshine, good day
    sunshine.--GOODDAYSUN--15
Good day sunshine, good day sunshine, good day
    sunshine.--GOODDAYSUN--15
Good day sunshine (good day sunshine) (good
    day sunshine) --GOODDAYSUN--16
Good day sunshine (good day sunshine) (good
    day sunshine) --GOODDAYSUN--16
Good day sunshine (good day sunshine) (good
    day sunshine) --GOODDAYSUN--16
(Good day sunshine) (good day....--GOODDAYSUN--17
(Good day sunshine) (good day....--GOODDAYSUN--17
Both of us thinking how good it can be--HERETHEREA
    --6
GOOD MORNING, GOOD MORNING.--GOODMORNIN--Title
GOOD MORNING, GOOD MORNING.--GOODMORNIN--Title
Good morning, good morning, good morning, good
    morning, good morning.--GOODMORNIN--1
Good morning, good morning, good morning, good
    morning, good morning.--GOODMORNIN--1
Good morning, good morning, good morning, good
    morning, good morning.--GOODMORNIN--1
Good morning, good morning, good morning, good
    morning, good morning.--GOODMORNIN--1
Good morning, good morning, good morning, good
    morning, good morning.--GOODMORNIN--1
Good morning, good morning, good morning.--
    GOODMORNIN--6
Good morning, good morning, good morning.--
    GOODMORNIN--6
Good morning, good morning, good morning.--
    GOODMORNIN--6
Good morning, good morning, good morning.--
    GOODMORNIN--17
Good morning, good morning, good morning.--
    GOODMORNIN--17
Good morning, good morning, good morning.--
    GOODMORNIN--17
Good morning, good morning good--GOODMORNIN--26
Good morning, good morning good--GOODMORNIN--26
Good morning, good morning good--GOODMORNIN--26

Good morning, good morning good--GOODMORNIN--27
Good morning, good morning good--GOODMORNIN--27
Good morning, good morning good--GOODMORNIN--27
Good morning, good morning good--GOODMORNIN--28
Good morning, good morning good--GOODMORNIN--28
Good morning, good morning good--GOODMORNIN--28
Good morning, good morning good--GOODMORNIN--29
Good morning, good morning good--GOODMORNIN--29
Good morning, good morning good--GOODMORNIN--29
Good morning, good morning good--GOODMORNIN--30
Good morning, good morning good--GOODMORNIN--30
Good morning, good morning good--GOODMORNIN--30
Good morning, good morning good--GOODMORNIN--31
Good morning, good morning good--GOODMORNIN--31
Good morning, good morning good--GOODMORNIN--31
Good morning, good morning good--GOODMORNIN--32
Good morning, good morning good--GOODMORNIN--32
Good morning, good morning good--GOODMORNIN--32
Good morning, good morning good.--GOODMORNIN--33
Good morning, good morning good.--GOODMORNIN--33
Good morning, good morning good.--GOODMORNIN--33
Gee, it's good to be back home --BACKINTHEU--9
We're gonna have a good time.--BIRTHDAY--4
We're gonna have a good time.--BIRTHDAY--23
GOOD NIGHT.--GOODNIGHT--Title
Now it's time to say good night,--GOODNIGHT--1
Good night, sleep tight.--GOODNIGHT--2
Good night, sleep tight.--GOODNIGHT--4
Good night, sleep tight.--GOODNIGHT--8
Good night, sleep tight.--GOODNIGHT--10
Good night, sleep tight.--GOODNIGHT--15
Good night, sleep tight.--GOODNIGHT--17
Good night --GOODNIGHT--20
Good night everybody --GOODNIGHT--21
Good night.--GOODNIGHT--23
Take a good look around you --MARTHAMYDE--7
Take a good look you're bound to see --MARTHAMYDE
    --8
Please - be good to me, Martha my love --MARTHAMYDE
    --14
What they need's a damn good whacking.--PIGGIES--14
To help with good Rocky's revival - ah.--ROCKYRACCO
    --39
Coffee dessert - yes you know it's good news --
    SAVOYTRUFF--3
Coffee dessert - yes you know it's good news
    (wuh) --SAVOYTRUFF--25
Ooo she done me, she done me good --DONTLETMED--22
Ooo she done me, she done me good.--DONTLETMED--24
It's good to have the both of you back.--BALLADOFJO
    --40
All good children go to heaven.--YOUNEVERGI--25
All good children go to heaven.--YOUNEVERGI--27
All good children go to heaven.--YOUNEVERGI--29
All good children go to heaven.--YOUNEVERGI--31
All good children go to heaven.--YOUNEVERGI--33
All good children go to heaven.--YOUNEVERGI--35
All good children go to heaven.--YOUNEVERGI--37
All good children go to heaven--YOUNEVERGI--39
All good children.--YOUNEVERGI--41
Good evening and welcome to Slaggers --YOUKNOWMYN
    --5
Good evening (Ringo).--YOUKNOWMYN--7
Good evening, you know my name, well then look
    up my number --YOUKNOWMYN--9
Everybody had a good time --IVEGOTAFEE--20
(Yeah) everybody had a good year --IVEGOTAFEE--24
Ooo - hu, everybody had a good year ((I've got
    a feeling)) --IVEGOTAFEE--28
Everybody had a good year ((I've got a feeling))
    --IVEGOTAFEE--32

GOOD-LOOKING
    Got to be good-looking 'cos he's so hard to see--
        COMETOGETH--41

GOODBYE
    'cos I told you once before goodbye --ILLBEBACK--3
    Before she gets to saying goodbye--TICKETTORI--20
    Before she gets to saying goodbye--TICKETTORI--33
    HELLO GOODBYE.--HELLOGOODB--Title
    You say goodbye and I say hello - hello, hello.--
        HELLOGOODB--4
    I don't know why you say goodbye, I say hello -
        hello, hello.--HELLOGOODB--5
    I don't know why you say goodbye, I say hello.--
        HELLOGOODB--6
    You say goodbye and I say hello - hello, hello.--
        HELLOGOODB--10
    ((Hello, goodbye, hello, goodbye, hello,
        goodbye))--HELLOGOODB--11
    ((Hello, goodbye, hello, goodbye, hello,

```
                                      goodbye))--HELLOGOODB--11
((hello, goodbye, hello, goodbye, hello,
     goodbye))--HELLOGOODB--11
I don't know why you say goodbye, I say hello -
     hello, hello--HELLOGOODB--12
((hello, goodbye, hello, goodbye)) --HELLOGOODB--13
((hello, goodbye, hello, goodbye)) --HELLOGOODB--13
I don't know why you say goodbye, I say hello--
     HELLOGOODB--14
((Hello, goodbye, hello, goodbye)).--HELLOGOODB--15
((Hello, goodbye, hello, goodbye)).--HELLOGOODB--15
Goodbye, goodbye, 'bye, 'bye, 'bye?--HELLOGOODB--17
Goodbye, goodbye, 'bye, 'bye, 'bye?--HELLOGOODB--17
You say goodbye and I say hello - hello, hello.--
     HELLOGOODB--19
I don't know why you say goodbye, I say hello -
     hello, hello--HELLOGOODB--20
I don't know why you say goodbye, I say hello.--
     HELLOGOODB--21
You say goodbye and I say hello - hello, hello.--
     HELLOGOODB--27
I don't know why you say goodbye, I say hello -
     hello, hello--HELLOGOODB--28
I don't know why you say goodbye, I say hello -
     hello, hello--HELLOGOODB--29
I don't know why you say goodbye, I say hello -
     hello.--HELLOGOODB--30
Goodbye.--TWOOFUS--37
```

GOODBYES
```
We said our goodbyes (aah the night before)--
     NIGHTBEFOR--1
We said our goodbyes (aah the night before)--
     NIGHTBEFOR--11
```

GOODLOOKING
```
She's so goodlooking but she looks like a man.--
     POLYTHENEP--2
```

GOT
```
I got everything that you want--FROMMETOYO--7
I got arms that long to hold you--FROMMETOYO--11
I got lips that long to kiss you--FROMMETOYO--13
I got arms that long to hold you--FROMMETOYO--22
I got lips that long to kiss you--FROMMETOYO--24
ALL I'VE GOT TO DO.--ALLIVEGOTT--Title
I've got no time for you right now--DONTBOTHER--13
I've got no time for you right now--DONTBOTHER--28
Yeah, you've got that something--IWANTTOHOL--20
Yeah, you've got that something--IWANTTOHOL--33
I'll give you all I've got to give --CANTBUYMEL--9
But what I got I'll give to you --CANTBUYMEL--12
I got something to say--YOUCANTDOT--1
If this is love you've got to give me more --
     ISHOULDHAV--12
I got every reason on earth to be mad --ILLCRYINST
     --1
I got a chip on my shoulder that's bigger than my
     feet.--ILLCRYINST--6
But I got a big surprise--ILLBEBACK--16
I got a whole lot of things to tell her --
     WHENIGETHO--2
I got a whole lot of things I gotta say to her.--
     WHENIGETHO--6
I got a whole lot of things to tell her,--
     WHENIGETHO--8
I got no time for triviality,--WHENIGETHO--11
I got a girl who's waiting home for me tonight.--
     WHENIGETHO--12
I got a whole lot of things to tell her --
     WHENIGETHO--14
I got so many things I gotta do --WHENIGETHO--22
I got no business being here with you this way.--
     WHENIGETHO--23
I got a whole lot of things to tell her --
     WHENIGETHO--25
I got a whole lot of things to tell her --
     WHENIGETHO--27
I ain't got nothing but love babe --EIGHTDAYSA--7
I ain't got nothing but love girl --EIGHTDAYSA--15
I ain't got nothing but love babe --EIGHTDAYSA--25
I ain't got nothing but love babe --EIGHTDAYSA--35
You ((you)) got me running--WHATYOURED--5
You've ((you've)) got me crying, girl --WHATYOURED
     --13
You've ((you've)) got me crying, girl --WHATYOURED
     --20
She's got a ticket to ride--TICKETTORI--5
She's got a ticket to ride--TICKETTORI--6
She's got a ticket to ride--TICKETTORI--7
She's got a ticket to ride--TICKETTORI--13
```

```
She's got a ticket to ride--TICKETTORI--14
She's got a ticket to ride--TICKETTORI--15
Oh, she's got a ticket to ride--TICKETTORI--26
She's got a ticket to ride--TICKETTORI--27
She's got a ticket to ride--TICKETTORI--28
Ah, she's got a ticket to ride--TICKETTORI--40
She's got a ticket to ride--TICKETTORI--41
She's got a ticket to ride--TICKETTORI--42
But you haven't got the nerve--YOULIKEMET--8
For I have got another girl, another girl.--
     ANOTHERGIR--1
You're making me say that I've got nobody but you
     --ANOTHERGIR--2
But as from today well I've got somebody that's
     new --ANOTHERGIR--3
For I have got another girl, another girl.--
     ANOTHERGIR--5
For I have got another girl --ANOTHERGIR--9
For I have got another girl --ANOTHERGIR--15
For I have got another girl  another girl,
     another girl.--ANOTHERGIR--21
YOU'VE GOT TO HIDE YOUR LOVE AWAY.--YOUVEGOTTO
     --Title
Hey! you've got to hide your love away.--YOUVEGOTTO
     --9
Hey! you've got to hide your love away.--YOUVEGOTTO
     --10
Hey! you've got to hide your love away.--YOUVEGOTTO
     --19
Hey! you've got to hide your love away.--YOUVEGOTTO
     --20
Got a good reason --DAYTRIPPER--1
Got a good reason --DAYTRIPPER--3
And she said listen babe I've got something to
     say --DRIVEMYCAR--23
I got no car and it's breaking my heart --
     DRIVEMYCAR--24
I've got a word or two--THINKFORYO--1
And you've got time to rectify--THINKFORYO--22
But now I've got it the word is good.--THEWORD--8
You tell me that you've got everything you want --
     ANDYOURBIR--1
I've got something I can laugh about.--GOODDAYSUN
     --3
GOT TO GET YOU INTO MY LIFE.--GOTTOGETYO--Title
Got to get you into my life.--GOTTOGETYO--15
Got to get you into my life.--GOTTOGETYO--23
I got to get you into my life.--GOTTOGETYO--24
I've got time.--IWANTTOTEL--15
I've got time.--IWANTTOTEL--22
I've got time.--IWANTTOTEL--23
I've got time.--IWANTTOTEL--24
But what you've got means such a lot to me.--
     LOVEYOUTWO--8
I've got to admit it's getting better (better)--
     GETTINGBET--7
I've got to admit it's getting better (better)--
     GETTINGBET--16
I've got nothing to say but it's OK.--GOODMORNIN
     --5
I've got nothing to say but it's OK.--GOODMORNIN
     --16
I've got nothing to say but it's OK.--GOODMORNIN
     --25
Got the bill and Rita paid it--LOVELYRITA--23
Roll up (we've got everything you need)--MAGICALMYS
     --13
You say you got a real solution --REVOLUTION--12
EVERYBODY'S GOT SOMETHING TO HIDE EXCEPT ME
     AND MY MONKEY.--EVRBDYMONK--Title
Everybody's got something to hide 'cept for me
     and my monkey - wuh.--EVRBDYMONK--7
Everybody's got something to hide 'cept for me
     and my monkey (yeah - wuh).--EVRBDYMONK--16
Everybody's got something to hide 'cept for me
     and my monkey - hey.--EVRBDYMONK--25
I got blisters on my fingers!--HELTERSKEL--32
You know I'd give you everything I've got for a
     little peace of mind.--IMSOTIRED--13
You know I'd give you everything I've got for a
     little peace of mind.--IMSOTIRED--22
I'd give you everything I've got for a little
     peace of mind --IMSOTIRED--23
I'd give you everything I've got for a little
     peace of mind.--IMSOTIRED--24
You say you got a real solution --REVOLUTONE--19
You think you know me but you haven't got a clue.
     --HEYBULLDOG--16
You've got it, that's great, you've done it
     ((ha ha ha ha ha))--HEYBULLDOG--28
That's it, you've got it ((ha ha ha ha))--
     HEYBULLDOG--30
All the girls around her say she's got it coming
     --GETBACK/45--18
```

The man in the mack said you've got to go back --
    BALLADOFJO--3
Got me escaping from this zoo --OLDBROWNSH--13
He got ju-ju eyeball --COMETOGETH--7
He got hair down to his knee--COMETOGETH--9
Got to be a joker he just do what he please--
    COMETOGETH--10
He got toe-jam football--COMETOGETH--16
He got wonky finger--COMETOGETH--17
One thing I can tell you is you got to be free--
    COMETOGETH--20
He got walrus gumboot--COMETOGETH--26
He got Ono sideboard--COMETOGETH--27
He got feet down below his knee--COMETOGETH--29
He got early warning--COMETOGETH--37
He got Muddy Water--COMETOGETH--38
Got to be good-looking 'cos he's so hard to see--
    COMETOGETH--41
And got myself a steady job--SHECAMEINT--17
Any jobber got the sack --YOUNEVERGI--10
Elmore James got nothing on this baby - heh.--
    FORYOUBLUE--12
All the girls around her say she's got it coming--
    GETBACK/LP--24
Everything has got to be just like you want it to
    --IDIGAPONY--14
Everything has got to be just like you want it to
    --IDIGAPONY--24
Everything has got to be just like you want it to
    --IDIGAPONY--34
I'VE GOT A FEELING.--IVEGOTAFEE--Title
I've got a feeling, a feeling deep inside --
    IVEGOTAFEE--1
I've got a feeling, a feeling I can't hide --
    IVEGOTAFEE--3
Yes, yeah, I've got a feeling, yeah.--IVEGOTAFEE
    --5
I've got a feeling, yeah, I've got a feeling.--
    IVEGOTAFEE--10
I've got a feeling, yeah, I've got a feeling.--
    IVEGOTAFEE--10
Ooo I've got a feeling that keeps me on my toes --
    IVEGOTAFEE--14
I've got a feeling I think that everybody knows --
    IVEGOTAFEE--16
I've got a feeling yeah - (yeah).--IVEGOTAFEE--18
Ooo - hu, everybody had a good year ((I've got
    a feeling)) --IVEGOTAFEE--28
Everybody had a good year ((I've got a feeling))
    --IVEGOTAFEE--32
I've got a feeling ((oh yeah)) --IVEGOTAFEE--36
I've got a feeling (oh yeah) --IVEGOTAFEE--37
I've got a feeling, yeah, yeah, yeah, yeah.--
    IVEGOTAFEE--38
Railman said, you got the wrong location --
    ONEAFTERNI--12
Then I find I've got the number wrong.--ONEAFTERNI
    --14
Railman said, you got the wrong location --
    ONEAFTERNI--22
Then I find I got the number wrong - well ((well)).
    --ONEAFTERNI--24

GOTTA
    All you gotta do is call --ANYTIMEATA--2
    All you gotta do is call --ANYTIMEATA--11
    All ya gotta do is call --ANYTIMEATA--20
    All you gotta do is call --ANYTIMEATA--23
    All ya gotta do is call --ANYTIMEATA--26
    And all I gotta do is thank you girl, thank you
        girl.--THANKYOUGI--4
    And all I gotta do is thank you girl, thank you
        girl--THANKYOUGI--7
    And all I gotta do is thank you girl, thank you
        girl.--THANKYOUGI--10
    And all I gotta do is thank you girl, thank you
        girl.--THANKYOUGI--14
    All I gotta do --ALLIVEGOTT--2
    Yeah, that's all I gotta do.--ALLIVEGOTT--5
    All I gotta do --ALLIVEGOTT--7
    Ya just gotta call on me, yeah --ALLIVEGOTT--15
    Ya just gotta call on me.--ALLIVEGOTT--16
    All I gotta do --ALLIVEGOTT--18
    Yeah, that's all I gotta do.--ALLIVEGOTT--21
    Ya just gotta call on me, yeah --ALLIVEGOTT--26
    Ya just gotta call on me --ALLIVEGOTT--27
    (Ooh) ya just gotta call on me --ALLIVEGOTT--28
    I got a whole lot of things I gotta say to her.--
        WHENIGETHO--6
    I got so many things I gotta do --WHENIGETHO--22
    (Well you know you can make it, Jude, you've
        just gotta break it.)--HEYJUDE--46
    But I gotta get a bellyfull of wine.--HERMAJESTY

    --6

GRABBED
    Found my coat and grabbed my hat--DAYINTHELI--23

GRADE
    About a lucky man who made the grade--DAYINTHELI
        --2

GRANDCHILDREN
    Grandchildren on your knee --WHENIMSIXT--26
    I only have grandchildren (yahoo ha ha ha ha ha
        ha ha)--HEYBULLDOG--32

GRASS
    Find me in my field of grass - Mother Nature's
        son --MOTHERNATU--8
    For some California grass.--GETBACK/45--4
    For some California grass.--GETBACK/LP--10

GRAVE
    As he walks from the grave--ELEANORRIG--25

GREAT
    You've got it, that's great, you've done it
        ((ha ha ha ha ha))--HEYBULLDOG--28
    Hey! (great!)--POLYTHENEP--11

GREATEST
    Sexy Sadie (sexy Sadie) the greatest of them
        all ((she's the greatest))--SEXYSADIE--11
    Sexy Sadie (sexy Sadie) the greatest of them
        all ((she's the greatest))--SEXYSADIE--11
    She's the latest and the greatest (she's the
        greatest) of them all--SEXYSADIE--23
    She's the latest and the greatest (she's the
        greatest) of them all--SEXYSADIE--23
    (Sexy Sadie she's the latest and the greatest
        of them all)--SEXYSADIE--24

GREEN
    Everybody's green--YOUCANTDOT--18
    Everybody's green--YOUCANTDOT--37
    And your bird is green --ANDYOURBIR--5
    Till we found a sea of green--YELLOWSUBM--6
    Sky of blue (sky of blue) and sea of green
        (sea of green)--YELLOWSUBM--27
    Sky of blue (sky of blue) and sea of green
        (sea of green)--YELLOWSUBM--27
    Cellophane flowers of yellow and green--LUCYINTHES
        --5
    Black, white, green, red --ALLTOGETHE--17

GREET
    Dear Prudence, greet the brand new day.--DEARPRUDEN
        --2
    Dear Prudence, greet the brand new day.--DEARPRUDEN
        --22

GREETINGS
    Birthday greetings, bottle of wine?--WHENIMSIXT--4

GRIN
    The man with the foolish grin is keeping
        perfectly still--FOOLONTHEH--2
    A - Rocky burst in and grinning a grin--ROCKYRACCO
        --19

GRINNING
    A - Rocky burst in and grinning a grin--ROCKYRACCO
        --19

GROOVING
    He come grooving up slowly--COMETOGETH--6

GROUND
    Help me get my feet back on the ground--HELP--17
    Help me get my feet back on the ground--HELP--27
    Help me get my feet back on the ground--HELP--37
    I'm down (down on the ground)--IMDOWN--4

I'm down (down on the ground)--IMDOWN--11
Oh baby, I'm down (down on the ground)--IMDOWN--19
I'm down on the ground (I'm really down)--IMDOWN
    --30
Yeah, aah - ooo I'm down (down on the ground)--
    IMDOWN--45
Burns my feet as they touch the ground.--GOODDAYSUN
    --8
Who'll screw you in the ground--LOVEYOUTWO--14
Ten somersets he'll undertake on solid ground.--
    BEINGFORTH--18

GROUP
I'd like to say thank you on behalf of the group
    and ourselves--GETBACK/LP--38

GROW
That grow so incredibly high (high).--LUCYINTHES
    --15
Man you been a naughty boy, you let your face
    grow long--IAMTHEWALR--6
If I grow up I'll be a singer --OLDBROWNSH--17
You're asking me will my love grow?--SOMETHING--11

GUARANTEED
A splendid time is guaranteed for all--BEINGFORTH
    --20
But they're guaranteed to raise a smile.--
    SGTPEPPERS--4
Roll up (satisfaction guaranteed)--MAGICALMYS--15

GUESS
Guess you know it's true --EIGHTDAYSA--2
Guess you know it's true --EIGHTDAYSA--20
Then I guess I'd be with you my friend --IFINEEDEDS
    --5
Then I guess I'd be with you my friend --IFINEEDEDS
    --15
I guess nobody ever really done me --DONTLETMED--23

GUITAR
WHILE MY GUITAR GENTLY WEEPS.--WHILEMYGUI--Title
While my guitar gently weeps.--WHILEMYGUI--3
Still my guitar gently weeps.--WHILEMYGUI--5
While my guitar gently weeps.--WHILEMYGUI--10
Still my guitar gently weeps.--WHILEMYGUI--12
While my guitar gently weeps.--WHILEMYGUI--19
Still my guitar gently weeps ((eee)).--WHILEMYGUI--21

GUMBOOT
He got walrus gumboot--COMETOGETH--26

GUN
See how they run like pigs from a gun, see how
    they fly--IAMTHEWALR--2
He went out tiger hunting with his elephant and
    gun --CONTINUING--7
HAPPINESS IS A WARM GUN.--HAPPINESSI--Title
Mother Superior jump the gun --HAPPINESSI--12
Mother Superior jump the gun --HAPPINESSI--13
Mother Superior jump the gun --HAPPINESSI--14
Mother Superior jump the gun --HAPPINESSI--15
Mother Superior jump the gun --HAPPINESSI--16
Mother Superior jump the gun.--HAPPINESSI--17
Happiness ((happiness)) is a warm gun--HAPPINESSI
    --18
Happiness ((happiness)) is a warm gun, momma--
    HAPPINESSI--20
Because - (happiness) is a warm gun, momma--
    HAPPINESSI--25
Happiness ((happiness)) is a warm gun, yes it is--
    HAPPINESSI--27
Happiness is a warm, yes it is - gun--HAPPINESSI
    --29
Is a warm gun, momma ((is a warm gun, yeah)).--
    HAPPINESSI--32
Is a warm gun, momma ((is a warm gun, yeah)).--
    HAPPINESSI--32
Rocky had come equipped with a gun--ROCKYRACCO--11

GURU
Jai Guru Deva OM.--ACROSSTHEU--6
Jai Guru Deva OM.--ACROSSTHEU--15
Jai Guru Deva OM.--ACROSSTHEU--25
Jai Guru Deva, Jai Guru Deva, Jai Guru
    Deva --ACROSSTHEU--30

Jai Guru Deva, Jai Guru Deva, Jai Guru
    Deva --ACROSSTHEU--30
Jai Guru Deva, Jai Guru Deva, Jai Guru
    Deva --ACROSSTHEU--30
Jai Guru Deva, Jai Guru Deva, Jai Guru
    Deva.--ACROSSTHEU--31
Jai Guru Deva, Jai Guru Deva, Jai Guru
    Deva.--ACROSSTHEU--31
Jai Guru Deva, Jai Guru Deva, Jai Guru
    Deva.--ACROSSTHEU--31

GURUS
They look just like two gurus in drag.--BALLADOFJO
    --32

GUY
I'm the kind of guy, who never used to cry.--MISERY
    --2
Yes I know I'm a lucky guy.--EVERYLITTL--3
Love you more than any other guy--NOREPLY--18
Well you know that I'm a wicked guy--RUNFORYOUR--9
And one day his woman ran off with another guy --
    ROCKYRACCO--3

H
Messrs. K. and H. assure the public--BEINGFORTH--12
And Mr. H. will demonstrate--BEINGFORTH--17
E, F, G, H, I, J --ALLTOGETHE--7

HA
Don't ask me what I want it for (ha ha Mr.
    Wilson)--TAXMAN--18
Don't ask me what I want it for (ha ha Mr.
    Wilson)--TAXMAN--18
If you don't want to pay some more (ha ha Mr.
    Heath)--TAXMAN--19
If you don't want to pay some more (ha ha Mr.
    Heath)--TAXMAN--19
In our yellow (in our yellow) submarine
    (submarine - ah ha!)--YELLOWSUBM--28
Ho ho ho, he he he, ha ha ha--IAMTHEWALR--22
Ho ho ho, he he he, ha ha ha--IAMTHEWALR--22
Ho ho ho, he he he, ha ha ha--IAMTHEWALR--22
yeah yeah yeah - ha ha ha ha ha))--HEYJUDE--67
yeah yeah yeah - ha ha ha ha ha))--HEYJUDE--67
yeah yeah yeah - ha ha ha ha ha))--HEYJUDE--67
yeah yeah yeah - ha ha ha ha ha))--HEYJUDE--67
yeah yeah yeah - ha ha ha ha ha))--HEYJUDE--67
I light the light - yeah, ooo - ha.--HONEYPIE--21
La-la how the life goes on (ha ha ha ha ha ha).--
    OBLADIOBLA--39
La-la how the life goes on (ha ha ha ha ha ha).--
    OBLADIOBLA--39
La-la how the life goes on (ha ha ha ha ha ha).--
    OBLADIOBLA--39
La-la how the life goes on (ha ha ha ha ha ha).--
    OBLADIOBLA--39
La-la how the life goes on (ha ha ha ha ha ha).--
    OBLADIOBLA--39
La-la how the life goes on (ha ha ha ha ha ha).--
    OBLADIOBLA--39
But if you want some fun (ha ha ha) --OBLADIOBLA
    --40
But if you want some fun (ha ha ha) --OBLADIOBLA
    --40
But if you want some fun (ha ha ha) --OBLADIOBLA
    --40
Take ob-la-di 'b-la-da ((ha ha ha)) --OBLADIOBLA
    --41
Take ob-la-di 'b-la-da ((ha ha ha)) --OBLADIOBLA
    --41
Take ob-la-di 'b-la-da ((ha ha ha)) --OBLADIOBLA
    --41
Thank you (ooo) (ha ha ha).--OBLADIOBLA--42
Thank you (ooo) (ha ha ha).--OBLADIOBLA--42
Thank you (ooo) (ha ha ha).--OBLADIOBLA--42
Woof - aah! ha ha ha--HEYBULLDOG--27
Woof - aah! ha ha ha--HEYBULLDOG--27
Woof - aah! ha ha ha--HEYBULLDOG--27
You've got it, that's great, you've done it
    ((ha ha ha ha ha))--HEYBULLDOG--28
You've got it, that's great, you've done it
    ((ha ha ha ha ha))--HEYBULLDOG--28
You've got it, that's great, you've done it
    ((ha ha ha ha ha))--HEYBULLDOG--28

You've got it, that's great, you've done it
   ((ha ha ha ha ha))--HEYBULLDOG--28
You've got it, that's great, you've done it
   ((ha ha ha ha ha))--HEYBULLDOG--28
That's it, you've got it ((ha ha ha ha))--
   HEYBULLDOG--30
That's it, you've got it ((ha ha ha ha))--
   HEYBULLDOG--30
That's it, you've got it ((ha ha ha ha))--
   HEYBULLDOG--30
That's it, you've got it ((ha ha ha ha))--
   HEYBULLDOG--30
Don't look at me man (ha ha ha ha)--HEYBULLDOG--31
Don't look at me man (ha ha ha ha)--HEYBULLDOG--31
Don't look at me man (ha ha ha ha)--HEYBULLDOG--31
Don't look at me man (ha ha ha ha)--HEYBULLDOG--31
I only have grandchildren (yahoo ha ha ha ha ha
   ha)--HEYBULLDOG--32
I only have grandchildren (yahoo ha ha ha ha ha
   ha)--HEYBULLDOG--32
I only have grandchildren (yahoo ha ha ha ha ha
   ha)--HEYBULLDOG--32
I only have grandchildren (yahoo ha ha ha ha ha
   ha)--HEYBULLDOG--32
I only have grandchildren (yahoo ha ha ha ha ha
   ha)--HEYBULLDOG--32
I only have grandchildren (yahoo ha ha ha ha ha
   ha)--HEYBULLDOG--32
I only have grandchildren (yahoo ha ha ha ha ha
   ha)--HEYBULLDOG--32
Ha ha ha ha ha ha ha ha ha ha ha ha
   ha ha ha--COMETOGETH--34
Ha ha ha ha ha ha ha ha ha ha ha ha
   ha ha ha--COMETOGETH--34
Ha ha ha ha ha ha ha ha ha ha ha ha
   ha ha ha--COMETOGETH--34
Ha ha ha ha ha ha ha ha ha ha ha ha
   ha ha ha--COMETOGETH--34
Ha ha ha ha ha ha ha ha ha ha ha ha
   ha ha ha--COMETOGETH--34
Ha ha ha ha ha ha ha ha ha ha ha ha
   ha ha ha--COMETOGETH--34
Ha ha ha ha ha ha ha ha ha ha ha ha
   ha ha ha--COMETOGETH--34
Ha ha ha ha ha ha ha ha ha ha ha ha
   ha ha ha--COMETOGETH--34
Ha ha ha ha ha ha ha ha ha ha ha ha
   ha ha ha--COMETOGETH--34
Ha ha ha ha ha ha ha ha ha ha ha ha
   ha ha ha--COMETOGETH--34
Ha ha ha ha ha ha ha ha ha ha ha ha
   ha ha ha--COMETOGETH--34
Ha ha ha ha ha ha ha ha ha ha ha ha
   ha ha ha--COMETOGETH--34
Ha ha ha ha ha ha ha ha ha ha ha ha
   ha ha ha--COMETOGETH--34
You, you know, you know my name (brrrrrr - ha,
   hey!) --YOUKNOWMYN--12
You know, you know, you know my name, ha ha ha
   ha --YOUKNOWMYN--17
You know, you know, you know my name, ha ha ha
   ha --YOUKNOWMYN--17
You know, you know, you know my name, ha ha ha
   ha --YOUKNOWMYN--17
You know, you know, you know my name, ha ha ha
   ha --YOUKNOWMYN--17
You know my number, what's up with you? - ha--
   YOUKNOWMYN--40
I dig a pygmy by Charles Hawtrey and the Deaf
   Aids (ha ha ha)--TWOOFUS--1
I dig a pygmy by Charles Hawtrey and the Deaf
   Aids (ha ha ha)--TWOOFUS--1
I dig a pygmy by Charles Hawtrey and the Deaf
   Aids (ha ha ha)--TWOOFUS--1

HA-HA-HA
   Ha-ha-ha - do-do-do - oh-oh--HONEYPIE--33

HAA
   You know my name - haa, that's right, look up
      the number --YOUKNOWMYN--15

HABIT
   Love has a nasty habit of disappearing overnight.
      --IMLOOKINGT--10
   Love has a nasty habit of disappearing overnight.
      --IMLOOKINGT--16

HAD
   But you're the only love that I've ever had.--
      ASKMEWHY--11
   'cos I've just lost the only girl I had.--
      ILLCRYINST--2
   Well I gave you everything I had --TELLMEWHY--5
   I've had a drink or two and I don't care --
      IDONTWANTT--5
   Though I've had a drink or two and I don't care --
      IDONTWANTT--22
   Said you had a thing or two to tell me--INEEDYOU
      --6
   Had it been another day--IVEJUSTSEE--7
   Why she had to go, I don't know--YESTERDAY--9
   Why she had to go, I don't know--YESTERDAY--17
   If I had some more time to spend --IFINEEDEDS--4
   Had you come some other day --IFINEEDEDS--7
   If I had some more time to spend --IFINEEDEDS--14
   Had you come some other day --IFINEEDEDS--17
   All these places had their moments --INMYLIFE--5
   I once had a girl--NORWEGIANW--1
   She once had me?--NORWEGIANW--3
   This bird had flown.--NORWEGIANW--23
   The ruins of the life that you had in mind --
      THINKFORYO--11
   I have had enough, so act your age.--YOUWONTSEE--2
   And had you gone, you knew in time--GOTTOGETYO--10
   We'd meet again for I had told you.--GOTTOGETYO--11
   Of every head he's had the pleasure to know--
      PENNYLANE--2
   Well I just had to laugh--DAYINTHELI--4
   He didn't notice that the lights had changed--
      DAYINTHELI--7
   The English Army had just won the war--DAYINTHELI
      --12
   But I just had to look--DAYINTHELI--14
   Found my way upstairs and had a smoke--DAYINTHELI
      --25
   They had to count them all--DAYINTHELI--31
   Had a laugh and over dinner--LOVELYRITA--21
   Man I had a dreadful flight.--BACKINTHEU--4
   Rocky had come equipped with a gun--ROCKYRACCO--11
   His rival it seems had broken his dreams--
      ROCKYRACCO--13
   You looked at me, that's all you had to do --
      FORYOUBLUE--14
   Everybody had a hard year --IVEGOTAFEE--19
   Everybody had a good time --IVEGOTAFEE--20
   Everybody had a wet dream --IVEGOTAFEE--21
   (Yeah) everybody had a good year --IVEGOTAFEE--24
   Ooo - hu, everybody had a good year ((I've got
      a feeling)) --IVEGOTAFEE--28
   Everybody had a hard time ((a feeling deep
      inside, oh yeah)) --IVEGOTAFEE--29
   Everybody had a wet dream (oh yeah) --IVEGOTAFEE
      --30
   Everybody had a good year ((I've got a feeling))
      --IVEGOTAFEE--32

HAIR
   There, running my hands through her hair--
      HERETHEREA--5
   When I get older losing my hair--WHENIMSIXT--1
   And you lost your hair.--DONTPASSME--26
   Her hair of floating sky is shimmering --JULIA--7
   With your long blonde hair and your eyes of blue
      --ITSALLTOOM--35
   With your long blonde hair and your eyes of blue
      --ITSALLTOOM--36
   Or how I fare or if my hair is brown --ONLYANORTH
      --11
   He got hair down to his knee--COMETOGETH--9
   Everybody let their hair down --IVEGOTAFEE--25
   Everybody let their hair down ((a feeling I
      can't hide, oh no)) --IVEGOTAFEE--33

HALF
   I'm not half the man I used to be--YESTERDAY--6
   She took me half the way there --DAYTRIPPER--10
   She took me half the way there, now.--DAYTRIPPER
      --12
   Everyone you see is half asleep--GOODMORNIN--11
   To see how the other half live--GLASSONION--6
   Half of what I say is meaningless --JULIA--1
   But right is only half of what's wrong --OLDBROWNSH
      --2

HALL
   To fill the Albert Hall--DAYINTHELI--33

HAMMER
    MAXWELL'S SILVER HAMMER.--MAXWELLSIL--Title
    Bang, bang Maxwell's silver hammer came down
        upon her head --MAXWELLSIL--6
    Bang, bang Maxwell's silver hammer made sure
        that she was dead.--MAXWELLSIL--7
    Bang, bang Maxwell's silver hammer came down
        upon her head --MAXWELLSIL--13
    Bang, bang Maxwell's silver hammer made sure
        that she was dead.--MAXWELLSIL--15
    Bang, bang Maxwell's silver hammer came down
        upon his head --MAXWELLSIL--23
    Bang, bang Maxwell's silver hammer made sure
        that he was dead.--MAXWELLSIL--25
    Silver hammer man!--MAXWELLSIL--28

HAND
    And I held her hand in mine.--ISAWHERSTA--12
    And I held her hand in mine.--ISAWHERSTA--20
    I WANT TO HOLD YOUR HAND.--IWANTTOHOL--Title
    I wanna hold your hand--IWANTTOHOL--4
    I wanna hold your hand--IWANTTOHOL--5
    I wanna hold your hand--IWANTTOHOL--6
    You'll let me hold your hand--IWANTTOHOL--10
    And/You'll let me hold your hand--IWANTTOHOL--11
    I wanna hold your hand.--IWANTTOHOL--12
    I wanna hold your hand.--IWANTTOHOL--23
    I wanna hold your hand.--IWANTTOHOL--24
    I wanna hold your hand.--IWANTTOHOL--25
    I wanna hold your hand.--IWANTTOHOL--36
    I wanna hold your hand.--IWANTTOHOL--37
    I wanna hold your hand.--IWANTTOHOL--38
    I wanna hold your hand.--IWANTTOHOL--39
    I don't wanna kiss or hold your hand --IMHAPPYJUS
        --4
    'cos you walked hand in hand--NOREPLY--15
    'cos you walked hand in hand--NOREPLY--15
    'cos you walked hand in hand--NOREPLY--28
    'cos you walked hand in hand--NOREPLY--28
    Here I stand head in hand--YOUVEGOTTO--1
    Leave it all till somebody else lends you a hand.
        --NOWHEREMAN--15
    Changing my life with a wave of her hand--
        HERETHEREA--3
    She's well acquainted with the touch of the
        velvet hand --HAPPINESSI--3
    Hold your hand out you silly girl, see what
        you've done --MARTHAMYDE--10
    And Molly says this as she takes him by the hand:
        --OBLADIOBLA--4
    Desmond lets the children lend a hand --OBLADIOBLA
        --21
    Molly lets the children lend a hand --OBLADIOBLA
        --33

HAND'S
    Me hand's getting - a too cold to play a chord now.
        --IDIGAPONY--38

HANDKERCHIEF
    Clutching her handkerchief--SHESLEAVIN--5

HANDS
    Than just holding hands.--IFIFELL--6
    You still moan keep your hands to yourself --IMDOWN
        --17
    But I can't get through, my hands are tied.--
        YOUWONTSEE--8
    Father McKenzie wiping the dirt from his hands--
        ELEANORRIG--24
    There, running my hands through her hair--
        HERETHEREA--5
    See the hands a - moving --DONTPASSME--12
    Lying with his eyes while his hands are busy
        working overtime --HAPPINESSI--6
    Jack-knife in your sweaty hands--HEYBULLDOG--6

HANDY
    I could be handy mending a fuse--WHENIMSIXT--13

HANG
    All I do is hang my head and moan.--TELLMEWHY--8
    You don't get time to hang a sign on me.--
        LOVEYOUTWO--3

HANGING
    There's a shadow hanging over me--YESTERDAY--7

HAPPEN
    This could only happen to me --ISHOULDHAV--5
    This could only happen to me --ISHOULDHAV--15
    Same old thing happen every day.--IMDOWN--9

HAPPENED
    I can't believe it's happened to me --ASKMEWHY--12
    I can't believe it's happened to me --ASKMEWHY--24
    This happened once before--NOREPLY--1

HAPPENS
    Yes I'm certain that it happens all the time.--
        WITHALITTL--20

HAPPINESS
    My happiness near makes me cry --ASKMEWHY--8
    HAPPINESS IS A WARM GUN.--HAPPINESSI--Title
    Happiness ((happiness)) is a warm gun--HAPPINESSI
        --18
    Happiness ((happiness)) is a warm gun--HAPPINESSI
        --18
    Happiness ((happiness)) is a warm gun, momma--
        HAPPINESSI--20
    Happiness ((happiness)) is a warm gun, momma--
        HAPPINESSI--20
    Because - (happiness) is a warm gun, momma--
        HAPPINESSI--25
    Happiness ((happiness)) is a warm gun, yes it is--
        HAPPINESSI--27
    Happiness ((happiness)) is a warm gun, yes it is--
        HAPPINESSI--27
    Happiness is a warm, yes it is - gun--HAPPINESSI
        --29
    ((Happiness - bang, bang, shoot, shoot)) --
        HAPPINESSI--30
    Well, don't you know that happiness ((happiness))
        --HAPPINESSI--31
    Well, don't you know that happiness ((happiness))
        --HAPPINESSI--31
    Some kind of happiness is measured out in miles--
        HEYBULLDOG--3

HAPPY
    So every day we'll be happy, I know--ITWONTBELO--25
    I feel happy inside--IWANTTOHOL--14
    I feel happy inside--IWANTTOHOL--27
    Oh, and this boy would be happy--THISBOY--7
    That boy won't be happy--THISBOY--9
    I'M HAPPY JUST TO DANCE WITH YOU.--IMHAPPYJUS
        --Title
    I'm so happy when you dance with me.--IMHAPPYJUS
        --3
    'cos I'm happy just to dance with you.--IMHAPPYJUS
        --7
    'cos I'm happy just to dance with you.--IMHAPPYJUS
        --11
    I'm so happy when you dance with me ((oh - oh)).--
        IMHAPPYJUS--15
    'cos I'm happy just to dance with you.--IMHAPPYJUS
        --19
    I'm so happy when you dance with me ((oh - oh)).--
        IMHAPPYJUS--23
    'cos I'm happy just to dance with you (oh - oh).--
        IMHAPPYJUS--28
    She's happy as can be, you know, she said so --
        IFEELFINE--2
    She is happy just to hear me say that--SHESAWOMAN
        --10
    When I'm with her I'm happy--EVERYLITTL--11
    I could be happy with you by my side--YESITIS--10
    I could be happy with you by my side--YESITIS--19
    Happy to be that way.--BABYYOUREA--25
    Happy birthday to you.--BIRTHDAY--6
    Happy birthday to you.--BIRTHDAY--25
    Now I'm so happy I found you --LONGLONGLO--5
    Happy ever after in the market place --OBLADIOBLA
        --20
    Hey, happy ever after in the market place --
        OBLADIOBLA--32
    Knowing they're happy and they're safe (happy
        and they're safe).--OCTOPUSSGA--20
    Knowing they're happy and they're safe (happy
        and they're safe).--OCTOPUSSGA--20
    We would be so happy you and me--OCTOPUSSGA--21
    Everybody's happy.--SUNKING--4

HARD

It's so hard to reason with you, whoa - yeah--
   PLEASEPLEA--17
A HARD DAY'S NIGHT.--HARDDAYSNI--Title
It's been a hard day's night --HARDDAYSNI--1
It's been a hard day's night --HARDDAYSNI--3
It's been a hard day's night --HARDDAYSNI--17
It's been a hard day's night --HARDDAYSNI--19
Oh, It's been a hard day's night --HARDDAYSNI--30
It's been a hard day's night --HARDDAYSNI--32
These days such a kind girl seems so hard to find
   --THINGSWESA--7
But it's so hard loving you.--ITSONLYLOV--7
But it's so hard loving you.--ITSONLYLOV--14
Yes, it's so hard loving you, loving you - ooo.--
   ITSONLYLOV--15
When I think of all the times I tried so hard
   to leave her --GIRL--6
We have lost the time that was so hard to find--
   YOUWONTSEE--3
It's getting hard to be someone--STRAWBERRY--8
Home. (we struggled hard all our lives to get by)
   --SHESLEAVIN--22
You know how hard it can be --BALLADOFJO--6
You know how hard it can be --BALLADOFJO--14
You know how hard it can be --BALLADOFJO--22
You know how hard it can be --BALLADOFJO--34
You know how hard it can be.--BALLADOFJO--42
Got to be good-looking 'cos he's so hard to see--
   COMETOGETH--41
Everybody had a hard year --IVEGOTAFEE--19
Everybody had a hard time ((a feeling deep
   inside, oh yeah)) --IVEGOTAFEE--29
Oh it's so hard.--IVEGOTAFEE--40

HARD-EARNED
   Spending someone's hard-earned pay.--TWOOFUS--4

HARDLY
   Been away so long I hardly knew the place --
      BACKINTHEU--8

HARE
   Elementary penguin singing Hare Krishna--IAMTHEWALR
      --26

HARK
   ((And now we'd like to do)) Hark the Angels
      Come...--DIGIT--13

HARM
   I know nobody can do me no harm ((oh, yeah)) --
      HAPPINESSI--24
   But it's no joke, it's doing me harm --IMSOTIRED
      --10
   But it's no joke, it's doing me harm --IMSOTIRED
      --19
   Oh darling, please believe me, I'll never do
      you no harm.--OHDARLING--1
   Believe me when I tell you, I'll never do you
      no harm.--OHDARLING--2
   Believe me when I tell you, I'll never do you
      no harm.--OHDARLING--10
   Believe me when I tell you - ooo - I'll never
      do you no harm.--OHDARLING--18

HARMONY
   If you think the harmony--ONLYANORTH--13

HAS
   If the sun has faded away --ANYTIMEATA--13
   Every night when everybody has fun--ITWONTBELO--5
   Only ever has to give me love forever and forever
      --SHESAWOMAN--3
   Only ever has to give me love forever and forever
      --SHESAWOMAN--20
   Only ever has to give me love forever and forever
      --SHESAWOMAN--30
   Till she sees the mistake she has made?--BABYSINBLA
      --15
   Till she sees the mistake she has made?--BABYSINBLA
      --20
   And now the time has come and so my love I must
      go --ILLFOLLOWT--5
   And now the time has come and so my love I must
      go --ILLFOLLOWT--10
   And now ((now)) my life has changed ((my life
      has changed))--HELP--19

And now ((now)) my life has changed ((my life
   has changed))--HELP--19
Love has a nasty habit of disappearing overnight.
   --IMLOOKINGT--10
Love has a nasty habit of disappearing overnight.
   --IMLOOKINGT--16
NORWEGIAN WOOD (3THIS BIRD HAS FLOWN).--NORWEGIANW
   --Title
Where a wedding has been--ELEANORRIG--4
She takes her time and doesn't feel she has to
   hurry --FORNOONE--5
Everyone of us (everyone of us) has all we need
   (has all we need) --YELLOWSUBM--26
Everyone of us (everyone of us) has all we need
   (has all we need) --YELLOWSUBM--26
Nothing has changed it's still the same--GOODMORNIN
   --15
Monday's child has learned to tie his bootlace.--
   LADYMADONN--7
Desmond has a barrow in the market-place --
   OBLADIOBLA--1
It's a love that has no past (believe me).--
   DONTLETMED--16
She tells Max to stay when the class has gone
   away --MAXWELLSIL--10
Everything has got to be just like you want it to
   --IDIGAPONY--14
Everything has got to be just like you want it to
   --IDIGAPONY--24
Everything has got to be just like you want it to
   --IDIGAPONY--34
Has left a pool of tears crying for the day.--
   LONGANDWIN--5

HAT
   Found my coat and grabbed my hat--DAYINTHELI--23

HATE
   But I hate to leave you--ILLBEBACK--21
   You know I hate to leave you--ILLBEBACK--24
   I would hate my disappointment to show --IDONTWANTT
      --2
   I would hate my disappointment to show --IDONTWANTT
      --14
   That ignorance and hate may mourn the dead--
      TOMORROWNE--9
   But if you want money for people with minds that
      hate --REVOLUTION--18
   How I hate to see you go --DONTPASSME--21
   How I hate to see you go --DONTPASSME--34
   How I hate to see you go --DONTPASSME--40
   But if you want money for people with minds that
      hate --REVOLUTONE--27
   Even hate my rock 'n' roll.--YERBLUES--27
   To miss that love is something I'd hate.--
      OLDBROWNSH--28
   Oh please believe me I'd hate to miss the train --
      IVEGOTAFEE--6

HATES
   She hates to see me cry--SHESAWOMAN--9

HAVE
   Why do I always have to say love --PLEASEPLEA--8
   Then we'll have some fun when you're mine, all
      mine --LITTLECHIL--10
   I may not have a lot to give --CANTBUYMEL--11
   Do I have to tell you one more time--YOUCANTDOT--11
   Have you near me.--ANDILOVEHE--14
   I SHOULD HAVE KNOWN BETTER.--ISHOULDHAV--Title
   I should have known better with a girl like you --
      ISHOULDHAV--1
   So - oh, I should have realised a lot of things
      before --ISHOULDHAV--11
   Did you have to treat me oh so bad --TELLMEWHY--7
   You say you will love me if I have to go --
      THINGSWESA--1
   One day you'll find that I have gone --ILLFOLLOWT
      --7
   One day you'll find that I have gone --ILLFOLLOWT
      --12
   Of all the love I have won or have lost --IMALOSER
      --3
   Of all the love I have won or have lost --IMALOSER
      --3
   There is one love I should never have crossed.--
      IMALOSER--4
   I should have known she would win in the end.--
      IMALOSER--6
   What have I done to deserve such a fate?--IMALOSER

--15
I realise I have left it too late.--IMALOSER--16
For I have got another girl, another girl.--
  ANOTHERGIR--1
For I have got another girl, another girl.--
  ANOTHERGIR--5
For I have got another girl --ANOTHERGIR--9
For I have got another girl --ANOTHERGIR--15
For I have got another girl, another girl,
  another girl.--ANOTHERGIR--21
I might have looked the other way--IVEJUSTSEE--8
And I'd have never been aware--IVEJUSTSEE--9
I have never known the like of this--IVEJUSTSEE--14
I've been alone and I have missed things--
  IVEJUSTSEE--15
Now today I find, you have changed your mind--
  NIGHTBEFOR--3
Now today I find you have changed your mind--
  NIGHTBEFOR--13
Do I have to keep on talking till I can't go on?--
  WECANWORKI--2
I have always thought that it's a crime--WECANWORKI
  --13
I have always thought that it's a crime--WECANWORKI
  --22
Then it might not have been like this --IFINEEDEDS
  --8
Then it might not have been like this --IFINEEDEDS
  --18
You don't look different, but you have changed --
  IMLOOKINGT--3
You don't look different, but you have changed --
  IMLOOKINGT--19
All my life, though some have changed.--INMYLIFE
  --2
Some have gone and some remain.--INMYLIFE--4
Doesn't have a point of view --NOWHEREMAN--4
Doesn't have a point of view --NOWHEREMAN--16
That we can have if we close our eyes.--THINKFORYO
  --5
Have you heard the word is love?--THEWORD--4
Have you heard the word is love?--THEWORD--12
In the good and the bad books that I have read.--
  THEWORD--16
Have you heard the word is love?--THEWORD--20
I have had enough, so act your age.--YOUWONTSEE--2
We have lost the time that was so hard to find--
  YOUWONTSEE--3
I won't want to stay, I don't have much to say --
  YOUWONTSEE--9
If you really like it you can have the rights,
  ((paperback))--PAPERBACKW--21
A love that should have lasted years.--FORNOONE--9
A love that should have lasted years.--FORNOONE--16
A love that should have lasted years.--FORNOONE--26
I have to admit it's getting better (better)--
  GETTINGBET--9
I have to admit it's getting better (better)--
  GETTINGBET--18
We hope you have enjoyed the show.--SGTPEPPREP--4
When your lights have gone.--WHENIMSIXT--14
And have you travelled very far?--BABYYOUREA--5
How often have you been there?--BABYYOUREA--9
Man you should have seen them kicking Edgar
  Allan Poe--IAMTHEWALR--27
And my friends have lost their way.--BLUEJAYWAY--2
You have found her, now go and get her (let it
  out and let it in) --HEYJUDE--16
All I can tell you is brother you have to wait.--
  REVOLUTION--19
We're gonna have a good time.--BIRTHDAY--4
We're gonna have a good time.--BIRTHDAY--23
If looks could kill it would have been us instead
  of him.--CONTINUING--29
Although I'm so tired, I'll have another
  cigarette--IMSOTIRED--15
How could I ever have lost you --LONGLONGLO--2
Martha my dear, you have always been my
  inspiration --MARTHAMYDE--13
In a couple of years they have built a home sweet
  home --OBLADIOBLA--17
In a couple of years they have built a home sweet
  home--OBLADIOBLA--29
Have you seen the little piggies--PIGGIES--1
Have you seen the bigger piggies--PIGGIES--6
Always have clean shirts to play around in.--
  PIGGIES--10
Well all I can tell you is brother you have to
  wait.--REVOLUTONE--28
But you'll have to have them all pulled out--
  SAVOYTRUFF--4
But you'll have to have them all pulled out--
  SAVOYTRUFF--4
But you'll have to have them all pulled out--

SAVOYTRUFF--9
But you'll have to have them all pulled out--
  SAVOYTRUFF--9
But you'll have to have them all pulled out--
  SAVOYTRUFF--17
But you'll have to have them all pulled out--
  SAVOYTRUFF--17
But you'll have to have them all pulled out--
  SAVOYTRUFF--26
But you'll have to have them all pulled out--
  SAVOYTRUFF--26
Yes, you'll have to have them all pulled out--
  SAVOYTRUFF--28
Yes, you'll have to have them all pulled out--
  SAVOYTRUFF--28
Sexy Sadie what have you done?--SEXYSADIE--1
Sexie Sadie - oh what have you done?--SEXYSADIE--4
Can I have a little more?--ALLTOGETHE--1
I only have grandchildren (yahoo ha ha ha ha ha
  ha ha)--HEYBULLDOG--32
It's good to have the both of you back.--BALLADOFJO
  --40
But she doesn't have a lot to say.--HERMAJESTY--2
And all I have to do is think of her --SOMETHING
  --16
You and I have memories --TWOOFUS--17
You and I have memories --TWOOFUS--26

HAVEN'T
  But you haven't got the nerve--YOULIKEMET--8
  Haven't I the right to make it up girl?--ITSONLYLOV
    --10
  I'm so tired, I haven't slept a wink --IMSOTIRED
    --1
  You think you know me but you haven't got a clue.
    --HEYBULLDOG--16

HAVING
  Having been some days in preparation--BEINGFORTH
    --19
  Having read the book--DAYINTHELI--15
  Is having (we didn't know it was wrong)--SHESLEAVIN
    --29
  The Duke was having problems --CRYBABYCRY--22
  Always having dirt to play around in.--PIGGIES--5

HAWTREY
  I dig a pygmy by Charles Hawtrey and the Deaf
    Aids (ha ha ha)--TWOOFUS--1

HAZE
  My independence ((my independence)) seems to
    vanish in the haze--HELP--21

HE
  Though he may want you too--THISBOY--5
  He buys her diamond rings, you know, she said so
    --IFEELFINE--10
  He buys her diamond rings, you know, she said so
    --IFEELFINE--18
  Isn't he a bit like you and me?--NOWHEREMAN--6
  He's as blind as he can be --NOWHEREMAN--10
  Just sees what he wants to see --NOWHEREMAN--11
  Isn't he a bit like you and me?--NOWHEREMAN--18
  But he wants to be a paperback writer--PAPERBACKW
    --12
  He helps you to understand --DRROBERT--4
  He does everything he can, Dr. Robert.--DRROBERT
    --5
  He does everything he can, Dr. Robert.--DRROBERT
    --5
  He helps you to understand --DRROBERT--16
  He does everything he can, Dr. Robert.--DRROBERT
    --17
  He does everything he can, Dr. Robert.--DRROBERT
    --17
  What does he care?--ELEANORRIG--16
  As he walks from the grave--ELEANORRIG--25
  And he told us of his life--YELLOWSUBM--3
  He likes to keep his fire-engine clean--PENNYLANE
    --14
  He blew his mind out in a car--DAYINTHELI--6
  He didn't notice that the lights had changed--
    DAYINTHELI--7
  Nobody was really sure if he was from the House
    of Lords--DAYINTHELI--10
  And he wants you all to sing along.--SGTPEPPERS--22
  I am he as you are he as you are me and we are
    all together--IAMTHEWALR--1

I am he as you are he as you are me and we are
   all together--IAMTHEWALR--1
Ho ho ho, he he he, ha ha ha--IAMTHEWALR--22
Ho ho ho, he he he, ha ha ha--IAMTHEWALR--22
Ho ho ho, he he he, ha ha ha--IAMTHEWALR--22
And he never gives an answer.--FOOLONTHEH--5
Or the sound he appears to make--FOOLONTHEH--11
And he never seems to notice.--FOOLONTHEH--12
They can tell what he wants to do--FOOLONTHEH--16
And he never shows his feelings.--FOOLONTHEH--17
He never listens to them--FOOLONTHEH--22
He knows that they're the fool--FOOLONTHEH--23
He went out tiger hunting with his elephant and
   gun --CONTINUING--7
In case of accidents he always took his mom --
   CONTINUING--8
(But when he looked so fierce) his mommy butted
   in --CONTINUING--28
I tell you man he living there still--GLASSONION
   --18
A soap impression of his wife which he ate --
   HAPPINESSI--7
He was such a stupid get.--IMSOTIRED--17
And as he gives it to her she begins to sing
   (sing):--OBLADIOBLA--12
La-la how the life goes on (he he he) --OBLADIOBLA
   --26
La-la how the life goes on (he he he) --OBLADIOBLA
   --26
La-la how the life goes on (he he he) --OBLADIOBLA
   --26
He said, I'm gonna get that boy --ROCKYRACCO--6
So one day he walked into town --ROCKYRACCO--7
He said, Danny - Boy this is a showdown.--
   ROCKYRACCO--20
But Daniel was hot, he drew first and shot--
   ROCKYRACCO--21
He said, Rocky you met your match--ROCKYRACCO--33
A - now Rocky Raccoon, he fell back in his room--
   ROCKYRACCO--36
Gideon checked out and he left it no doubt ((oh
   - Rocky - oh))--ROCKYRACCO--38
The worm he licks my bone --YERBLUES--18
Jojo was a man who thought he was a loner --
   GETBACK/45--1
But he knew it couldn't last.--GETBACK/45--2
He come grooving up slowly--COMETOGETH--6
He got ju-ju eyeball--COMETOGETH--7
He one holy roller--COMETOGETH--8
He got hair down to his knee--COMETOGETH--9
Got to be a joker he just do what he please--
   COMETOGETH--10
Got to be a joker he just do what he please--
   COMETOGETH--10
He wear no shoe-shine--COMETOGETH--15
He got toe-jam football--COMETOGETH--16
He got wonky finger--COMETOGETH--17
He shoot Coca-cola--COMETOGETH--18
He say I know you, you know me--COMETOGETH--19
He Bag Production--COMETOGETH--25
He got walrus gumboot--COMETOGETH--26
He got Ono sideboard--COMETOGETH--27
He one spinal cracker--COMETOGETH--28
He got feet down below his knee--COMETOGETH--29
He roller-coaster--COMETOGETH--36
He got early warning--COMETOGETH--37
He got Muddy Water--COMETOGETH--38
He one mojo filter--COMETOGETH--39
He say one and one and one is three--COMETOGETH--40
So he waits behind, writing fifty times I must
   not be so oh - oh oh.--MAXWELLSIL--11
But when she turns her back on the boy, he
   creeps up from behind --MAXWELLSIL--12
Rose and Valerie screaming from the gallery say
   he must go free --MAXWELLSIL--19
The judge does not agree and he tells them so oh
   - oh oh.--MAXWELLSIL--21
Bang, bang Maxwell's silver hammer made sure
   that he was dead.--MAXWELLSIL--25
Jojo was a man who thought he was a loner--
   GETBACK/LP--7
But he knew it couldn't last--GETBACK/LP--8

HE'D
   He'd let us in, knows where we've been--OCTOPUSSGA
      --3

HE'LL
   Though he'll regret it someday--THISBOY--2
   And though he'll never come back --BABYSINBLA--5
   And/But though he'll never come back--BABYSINBLA--25
   Day or night he'll be there any time at all, Dr.

Robert --DRROBERT--2
If you're down he'll pick you up, Dr. Robert --
   DRROBERT--6
Well, well, well, he'll make you, Dr. Robert.--
   DRROBERT--12
Well, well, well, he'll make you, Dr. Robert.--
   DRROBERT--19
Ten somersets he'll undertake on solid ground.--
   BEINGFORTH--18

HE'S
   Till he's seen you cry.--THISBOY--10
   Will she still believe it when he's dead?--GIRL--25
   He's a real Nowhere Man --NOWHEREMAN--1
   Knows not where he's going to --NOWHEREMAN--5
   He's as blind as he can be --NOWHEREMAN--10
   Knows not where he's going to --NOWHEREMAN--17
   He's a real Nowhere Man --NOWHEREMAN--22
   Dr. Robert, he's a man you must believe --DRROBERT
      --8
   But now he's gone, she doesn't need him.--FORNOONE
      --19
   Someone is speaking but she doesn't know he's
      there.--HERETHEREA--7
   Of every head he's had the pleasure to know--
      PENNYLANE--2
   They can see that he's just a fool--FOOLONTHEH--4
   He's the all-American bullet-headed Saxon
      mother's son.--CONTINUING--9
   Got to be good-looking 'cos he's so hard to see--
      COMETOGETH--41
   Only place that he's ever been--MEANMRMUST--12

HEAD
   And things you do go round my head--THERESAPLA--6
   All I do is hang my head and moan.--TELLMEWHY--8
   Here I stand head in hand--YOUVEGOTTO--1
   You better keep your head, little girl --RUNFORYOUR
      --3
   Hide your head in the sand, little girl.--
      RUNFORYOUR--6
   Hide your head in the sand, little girl.--
      RUNFORYOUR--14
   Hide your head in the sand, little girl.--
      RUNFORYOUR--22
   You better keep your head, little girl --RUNFORYOUR
      --27
   Hide your head in the sand, little girl.--
      RUNFORYOUR--30
   Lift my head, I'm still yawning.--IMONLYSLEE--2
   Lift my head, I'm still yawning.--IMONLYSLEE--22
   She said will fill your head --FORNOONE--22
   My head is filled with things to say --IWANTTOTEL
      --2
   I said who put all those things in your head?--
      SHESAIDSHE--4
   Of every head he's had the pleasure to know--
      PENNYLANE--2
   Dragged a comb across my head--DAYINTHELI--19
   Me hiding me head in the sand--GETTINGBET--12
   Towering over your head.--LUCYINTHES--6
   Climb in the back with your head in the clouds--
      LUCYINTHES--18
   And the eyes in his head see the world spinning
      round.--FOOLONTHEH--7
   Well on the way, head in a cloud--FOOLONTHEH--8
   And the eyes in his head see the world spinning
      round.--FOOLONTHEH--14
   And the eyes in his head see the world spinning
      round.--FOOLONTHEH--19
   And the eyes in his head see the world spinning
      round.--FOOLONTHEH--26
   Listen to the music playing in your head.--
      LADYMADONN--13
   We all want to change your head.--REVOLUTION--24
   Hold your head up you silly girl, look what
      you've done --MARTHAMYDE--4
   We'd all love to change our head.--REVOLUTONE--37
   The sweat it's gonna fill your head --SAVOYTRUFF
      --14
   The newspapers said, she's gone to his head --
      BALLADOFJO--31
   Bang, bang Maxwell's silver hammer came down
      upon her head --MAXWELLSIL--6
   Bang, bang Maxwell's silver hammer came down
      upon her head --MAXWELLSIL--13
   Bang, bang Maxwell's silver hammer came down
      upon his head --MAXWELLSIL--23
   Resting our head on the seabed--OCTOPUSSGA--11

HEADING

HEADING

Heading for home you start to roam then you're in town.--GOODMORNIN--8

HEADS

If the rain comes they run and hide their heads--RAIN--1
Look up the number (heads up boys) --YOUKNOWMYN--14

HEALTH

My friend works for the National Health, Dr. Robert --DRROBERT--13

HEAR

Say the words you long to hear --DOYOUWANTT--7
Say the words you long to hear --DOYOUWANTT--13
Say the words you long to hear --DOYOUWANTT--21
The words you long to hear --ALLIVEGOTT--9
And it's worth it just to hear you say --HARDDAYSNI--10
Love to hear you say that love is love--THINGSWESA--12
Love to hear you say that love is love--THINGSWESA--23
She is happy just to hear me say that--SHESAWOMAN--10
Can you hear me?--IMDOWN--26
And I hear them say.--YOUVEGOTTO--8
Let me hear you say.--YOUVEGOTTO--18
Your lips are moving, I cannot hear--IMLOOKINGT--5
Everywhere I go I hear it said --THEWORD--15
Can you hear me that when it rains and shines
    (when it rains and shines)--RAIN--14
Can you hear me, can you hear me? ((hear me))--RAIN--16
Can you hear me, can you hear me? ((hear me))--RAIN--16
Can you hear me, can you hear me? ((hear me))--RAIN--16
But you can't hear me, you can't hear me.--ANDYOURBIR--15
But you can't hear me, you can't hear me.--ANDYOURBIR--15
That no-one will hear--ELEANORRIG--12
Ooo and I want you to hear me--GOTTOGETYO--13
Let me hear your balalaikas ringing out --BACKINTHEU--33
I don't hear it --DONTPASSME--8
I hear the clock a - ticking --DONTPASSME--10
Just waiting to hear from you.--DONTPASSME--30
Coming down fast (oh I hear my baby speaking - ooo)...--HELTERSKEL--30
And if she could only hear me--HONEYPIE--5
Sing it loud so I can hear you --IWILL--15
Let's hear it for Dennis - ah-hey.--YOUKNOWMYN--8
You know, you know my name ((oh, let's hear it, come on Dennis))--YOUKNOWMYN--23
Let's hear it for Dennis O'Fell.--YOUKNOWMYN--24
All I can hear --IMEMINE--14
All I can hear --IMEMINE--27

HEARD

That I heard before--NOREPLY--20
Have you heard the word is love?--THEWORD--4
Have you heard the word is love?--THEWORD--12
Have you heard the word is love?--THEWORD--20
You tell me that you heard every sound there is --ANDYOURBIR--13
I finally heard--GETTINGBET--14

HEARING

Hearing them, seeing them--YOUVEGOTTO--13

HEARS

But nobody ever hears him--FOOLONTHEH--10

HEART

In my heart (in my heart).--PLEASEPLEA--15
In my heart (in my heart).--PLEASEPLEA--15
Well my heart went boom when I crossed that room --ISAWHERSTA--11
Well my heart went boom when I crossed that room --ISAWHERSTA--18
Like a heart that's oh so true--FROMMETOYO--8
If I give my heart to you --IFIFELL--7
You know if you break my heart, I'll go --ILLBEBACK--1
Than to break my heart again--ILLBEBACK--10

Than to break my heart again--ILLBEBACK--19
You if you break my heart, I'll go--ILLBEBACK--26
If you let me take your heart--TELLMEWHAT--1
I got no car and it's breaking my heart --DRIVEMYCAR--24
But if your heart breaks, don't wait, turn me away --WAIT--5
But if your heart breaks, don't wait, turn me away --WAIT--21
What goes on in your heart? (wuh)--WHATGOESON--1
What goes on in your heart?--WHATGOESON--10
What goes on in your heart?--WHATGOESON--19
Did you mean to break my heart and watch me die?--WHATGOESON--24
What goes on in your heart?--WHATGOESON--26
When it gets dark I tow your heart away.--LOVELYRITA--6
Remember to let her into your heart --HEYJUDE--3
Remember (hey Jude) to let her into your heart --HEYJUDE--17
Love you with all my heart --IWILL--10
When I cannot sing my heart --JULIA--11
A ginger sling with a pineapple heart --SAVOYTRUFF--2
A ginger sling with a pineapple heart --SAVOYTRUFF--24

HEART'S

And if your heart's strong, hold on, I won't delay.--WAIT--6
And if your heart's strong, hold on, I won't delay.--WAIT--22

HEARTS

I'm gonna break their hearts all round the world --ILLCRYINST--16
'cos I'm gonna break their hearts all round the world,--ILLCRYINST--25
SGT. PEPPER'S LONELY HEARTS CLUB BAND.--SGTPEPPERS--Title
Sgt. Pepper's Lonely Hearts Club Band.--SGTPEPPERS--7
We're Sgt. Pepper's Lonely Hearts Club Band--SGTPEPPERS--8
Sgt. Pepper's Lonely Hearts Club Band--SGTPEPPERS--10
Sgt. Pepper's Lonely Hearts Club Band.--SGTPEPPERS--13
And Sgt. Pepper's Lonely Hearts Club Band.--SGTPEPPERS--25
SGT. PEPPER'S LONELY HEARTS CLUB BAND (REPRISE).--SGTPEPPREP--Title
We're Sgt. Pepper's Lonely Hearts Club Band --SGTPEPPREP--3
Sgt. Pepper's Lonely Hearts Club Band --SGTPEPPREP--5
Sgt. Pepper's Lonely Hearts Club Band --SGTPEPPREP--11
Sgt. Pepper's one and only Lonely Hearts Club Band--SGTPEPPREP--13
Sgt. Pepper's Lonely Hearts Club Band.--SGTPEPPREP--17
Lift up your hearts and sing me a song--YOURMOTHER--13

HEAT

If you get too cold, I'll tax the heat, ((cold))--TAXMAN--13

HEATH

If you don't want to pay some more (ha ha Mr. Heath)--TAXMAN--19

HEAVEN

I could know the ways of heaven.--INNERLIGHT--4
You can know the ways of heaven.--INNERLIGHT--11
Did you think that money was heaven sent?--LADYMADONN--4
All good children go to heaven.--YOUNEVERGI--25
All good children go to heaven.--YOUNEVERGI--27
All good children go to heaven.--YOUNEVERGI--29
All good children go to heaven.--YOUNEVERGI--31
All good children go to heaven.--YOUNEVERGI--33
All good children go to heaven.--YOUNEVERGI--35
All good children go to heaven.--YOUNEVERGI--37
All good children go to heaven--YOUNEVERGI--39

HEAVY

I WANT YOU (SHE'S SO HEAVY).--IWANTYOUSH--Title
She's so - heavy (heavy - heavy - heavy)--
    IWANTYOUSH--25
She's so - heavy (heavy - heavy - heavy)--
    IWANTYOUSH--25
She's so - heavy (heavy - heavy - heavy)--
    IWANTYOUSH--25
She's so - heavy (heavy - heavy - heavy)--
    IWANTYOUSH--25
She's so - heavy--IWANTYOUSH--26
She's so heavy (heavy - heavy)--IWANTYOUSH--27
She's so heavy (heavy - heavy)--IWANTYOUSH--27
... Heavy, heavy...--YOUKNOWMYN--43
... Heavy, heavy...--YOUKNOWMYN--43
... Heavy...--YOUKNOWMYN--44
... Heavy, heavy...--YOUKNOWMYN--45
... Heavy, heavy...--YOUKNOWMYN--45

HEH
    Look out 'cos here she comes (heh heh heh).--
        HELTERSKEL--17
    Look out 'cos here she comes (heh heh heh).--
        HELTERSKEL--17
    Look out 'cos here she comes (heh heh heh).--
        HELTERSKEL--17
    Heh heh heh.--SHECAMEINT--2
    Heh heh heh.--SHECAMEINT--2
    Heh heh heh.--SHECAMEINT--2
    Elmore James got nothing on this baby - heh.--
        FORYOUBLUE--12

HELA
    Hela, hello --HELLOGOODB--31
    Hela, hello --HELLOGOODB--32
    Hela, hello --HELLOGOODB--34
    Ooo - hela, hello (hela)--HELLOGOODB--35
    Hela, hello --HELLOGOODB--36
    Hela, hello --HELLOGOODB--38
    Ooo - hela, hello --HELLOGOODB--39
    Hela, hello.--HELLOGOODB--41
    Hela, hello.--HELLOGOODB--43

HELD
    And I held her hand in mine.--ISAWHERSTA--12
    And we held each other tight --ISAWHERSTA--14
    And I held her hand in mine.--ISAWHERSTA--19
    And we held each other tight --ISAWHERSTA--21
    When I held you near, you were so sincere--
        NIGHTBEFOR--7
    When I held you near, you were so sincere --
        NIGHTBEFOR--15
    When I held you near, you were so sincere --
        NIGHTBEFOR--21

HELLO
    Stop and say hello.--PENNYLANE--4
    HELLO GOODBYE.--HELLOGOODB--Title
    You say goodbye and I say hello - hello, hello.--
        HELLOGOODB--4
    You say goodbye and I say hello - hello, hello.--
        HELLOGOODB--4
    You say goodbye and I say hello - hello, hello.--
        HELLOGOODB--4
    I don't know why you say goodbye, I say hello -
        hello, hello.--HELLOGOODB--5
    I don't know why you say goodbye, I say hello -
        hello, hello.--HELLOGOODB--5
    I don't know why you say goodbye, I say hello -
        hello, hello.--HELLOGOODB--5
    I don't know why you say goodbye, I say hello.--
        HELLOGOODB--6
    You say goodbye and I say hello - hello, hello.--
        HELLOGOODB--10
    You say goodbye and I say hello - hello, hello.--
        HELLOGOODB--10
    You say goodbye and I say hello - hello, hello.--
        HELLOGOODB--10
    ((Hello, goodbye, hello, goodbye, hello,
        goodbye))--HELLOGOODB--11
    ((Hello, goodbye, hello, goodbye, hello,
        goodbye))--HELLOGOODB--11
    ((Hello, goodbye, hello, goodbye, hello,
        goodbye'))--HELLOGOODB--11
    I don't know why you say goodbye, I say hello -
        hello, hello--HELLOGOODB--12
    I don't know why you say goodbye, I say hello -
        hello, hello--HELLOGOODB--12
    I don't know why you say goodbye, I say hello -

hello, hello--HELLOGOODB--12
((hello, goodbye, hello, goodbye)) --HELLOGOODB--13
((hello, goodbye, hello, goodbye)) --HELLOGOODB--13
I don't know why you say goodbye, I say hello--
    HELLOGOODB--14
((Hello, goodbye, hello, goodbye)).--HELLOGOODB--15
((Hello, goodbye, hello, goodbye)).--HELLOGOODB--15
You say goodbye and I say hello - hello, hello.--
    HELLOGOODB--19
You say goodbye and I say hello - hello, hello.--
    HELLOGOODB--19
You say goodbye and I say hello - hello, hello.--
    HELLOGOODB--19
I don't know why you say goodbye, I say hello -
    hello, hello --HELLOGOODB--20
I don't know why you say goodbye, I say hello -
    hello, hello --HELLOGOODB--20
I don't know why you say goodbye, I say hello -
    hello, hello --HELLOGOODB--20
I don't know why you say goodbye, I say hello.--
    HELLOGOODB--21
You say goodbye and I say hello - hello, hello.--
    HELLOGOODB--27
You say goodbye and I say hello - hello, hello.--
    HELLOGOODB--27
You say goodbye and I say hello - hello, hello.--
    HELLOGOODB--27
I don't know why you say goodbye, I say hello -
    hello, hello --HELLOGOODB--28
I don't know why you say goodbye, I say hello -
    hello, hello --HELLOGOODB--28
I don't know why you say goodbye, I say hello -
    hello, hello --HELLOGOODB--28
I don't know why you say goodbye, I say hello -
    hello, hello --HELLOGOODB--29
I don't know why you say goodbye, I say hello -
    hello, hello --HELLOGOODB--29
I don't know why you say goodbye, I say hello -
    hello, hello --HELLOGOODB--29
I don't know why you say goodbye, I say hello -
    hello.--HELLOGOODB--30
I don't know why you say goodbye, I say hello -
    hello.--HELLOGOODB--30
Hela, hello --HELLOGOODB--31
Hela, hello --HELLOGOODB--32
Hela, hello --HELLOGOODB--34
Ooo - hela, hello (hela)--HELLOGOODB--35
Hela, hello --HELLOGOODB--36
Hela, hello--HELLOGOODB--38
Ooo - hela, hello --HELLOGOODB--39
Hela, hello.--HELLOGOODB--41
Hela, hello.--HELLOGOODB--43

HELP
    I can't help my feelings--YOUCANTDOT--25
    I can't help my feelings--YOUCANTDOT--44
    And help me understand?--IFIFELL--3
    HELP!--HELP--Title
    Help!--HELP--1
    Help!--HELP--3
    Help!--HELP--5
    Help!--HELP--7
    I never needed ((never needed)) anybody's help
        in any way--HELP--10
    Help me if you can, I'm feeling down--HELP--15
    Help me get my feet back on the ground--HELP--17
    Won't you please please help me?--HELP--18
    Help me if you can, I'm feeling down--HELP--25
    Help me get my feet back on the ground--HELP--27
    Won't you please please help me?--HELP--28
    I never needed anybody's help in any way--HELP--30
    Help me if you can, I'm feeling down--HELP--35
    Help me get my feet back on the ground--HELP--37
    Won't you please please help me?--HELP--38
    Help me, help me - ooo-mmm.--HELP--39
    Help me, help me - ooo-mmm.--HELP--39
    WITH A LITTLE HELP FROM MY FRIENDS.--WITHALITTL
        --Title
    Oh I get by with a little help from my friends --
        WITHALITTL--5
    Mmm I get high with a little help from my friends
        --WITHALITTL--6
    Mmm gonna try with a little help from my friends.
        --WITHALITTL--7
    No I get by with a little help from my friends --
        WITHALITTL--12
    Mmm get high with a little help from my friends --
        WITHALITTL--13
    Mmm gonna try with a little help from my friends.
        --WITHALITTL--14
    Oh I get by with a little help from my friends --
        WITHALITTL--23
    Mmm get high with a little help from my friends --

WITHALITTL--24
Oh I'm gonna try with a little help from my
friends.--WITHALITTL--25
Oh I get by with a little help from my friends --
WITHALITTL--30
Mmm gonna try with a little help from my friends
--WITHALITTL--31
Oh I get high with a little help from my friends
--WITHALITTL--32
Yes I get by with a little help from my friends --
WITHALITTL--33
With a little help from my friends.--WITHALITTL--34
Help yourself to a bit of what is all around you
- silly girl.--MARTHAMYDE--6
Help yourself to a bit of what is all around you
- silly girl.--MARTHAMYDE--12
To help with good Rocky's revival - ah.--ROCKYRACCO
--39
And though she tried her best to help me --
SHECAMEINT--18

HELPING
Helping anyone in need.--DRROBERT--9

HELPS
He helps you to understand --DRROBERT--4
He helps you to understand --DRROBERT--16

HELTER-SKELTER
HELTER-SKELTER.--HELTERSKEL--Title
(Helter-skelter, helter-skelter)--HELTERSKEL--8
(Helter-skelter, helter-skelter)--HELTERSKEL--8
Helter-skelter, helter-skelter, helter-skelter
- yeah.--HELTERSKEL--9
Helter-skelter, helter-skelter, helter-skelter
- yeah.--HELTERSKEL--9
Helter-skelter, helter-skelter, helter-skelter
- yeah.--HELTERSKEL--9
(Helter-skelter, helter-skelter)--HELTERSKEL--15
(Helter-skelter, helter-skelter)--HELTERSKEL--15
Look out helter-skelter, helter-skelter,
helter-skelter - oh.--HELTERSKEL--16
Look out helter-skelter, helter-skelter,
helter-skelter - oh.--HELTERSKEL--16
Look out helter-skelter, helter-skelter,
helter-skelter - oh.--HELTERSKEL--16
(Helter-skelter, helter-skelter)--HELTERSKEL--25
(Helter-skelter, helter-skelter)--HELTERSKEL--25
Look out helter-skelter, helter-skelter,
helter-skelter.--HELTERSKEL--26
Look out helter-skelter, helter-skelter,
helter-skelter.--HELTERSKEL--26
Look out helter-skelter, helter-skelter,
helter-skelter.--HELTERSKEL--26
Well, look out helter-skelter.--HELTERSKEL--27

HENDERSONS
The Hendersons will all be there--BEINGFORTH--3
The Hendersons will dance and sing--BEINGFORTH--10

HENRY
And of course Henry the Horse dances the waltz.--
BEINGFORTH--14

HER
I SAW HER STANDING THERE.--ISAWHERSTA--Title
Ooh when I saw her standing there.--ISAWHERSTA--6
That before too long I'd fall in love with her.--
ISAWHERSTA--8
Whoa when I saw her standing there.--ISAWHERSTA--10
And I held her hand in mine.--ISAWHERSTA--12
And before too long I fell in love with her--
ISAWHERSTA--15
Whoa since/when I saw her standing there. (hey! aah!)
--ISAWHERSTA--17
And I held her hand in mine.--ISAWHERSTA--19
And before too long I fell in love with her.--
ISAWHERSTA--22
Oh since I saw her standing there.--ISAWHERSTA--24
Whoa since I saw her standing there--ISAWHERSTA--25
Yeah, well since I saw her standing there.--
ISAWHERSTA--26
I've lost her now for sure, I won't see her no
more --MISERY--4
I've lost her now for sure, I won't see her no
more --MISERY--4
Send her back to me, 'cos everyone can see--
MISERY--8

Without her I will be in misery.--MISERY--9
She'll remember and she'll miss her only one,
lonely one.--MISERY--11
Send her back to me, 'cos everyone can see--
MISERY--12
Without her I will be in misery.--MISERY--13
Well I saw her yesterday--SHELOVESYO--5
She said you hurt her so--SHELOVESYO--12
She almost lost her mind--SHELOVESYO--13
Apologize to her.--SHELOVESYO--27
If I don't get her back again--DONTBOTHER--16
If I don't get her back again--DONTBOTHER--31
AND I LOVE HER.--ANDILOVEHE--Title
I give her all my love --ANDILOVEHE--1
You'd love her too --ANDILOVEHE--4
I love her.--ANDILOVEHE--5
And I love her.--ANDILOVEHE--10
And I love her.--ANDILOVEHE--19
And I love her --ANDILOVEHE--24
That you would love me more than her.--IFIFELL--9
Oh please, don't hurt my pride like her.--IFIFELL
--13
I got a whole lot of things to tell her --
WHENIGETHO--2
I got a whole lot of things I gotta say to her.--
WHENIGETHO--6
I got a whole lot of things to tell her --
WHENIGETHO--8
I got a whole lot of things to tell her --
WHENIGETHO--14
I'm gonna hold her tight --WHENIGETHO--17
I'm gonna love her till the cows come home --
WHENIGETHO--18
I bet I'll love her more --WHENIGETHO--19
I got a whole lot of things to tell her --
WHENIGETHO--25
I got a whole lot of things to tell her --
WHENIGETHO--27
I'm in love with her and I feel fine.--IFEELFINE
--3
I'm in love with her and I feel fine.--IFEELFINE
--6
That her baby buys her things, you know --IFEELFINE
--9
That her baby buys her things, you know --IFEELFINE
--9
He buys her diamond rings, you know, she said so
--IFEELFINE--10
I'm in love with her and I feel fine.--IFEELFINE
--14
That her baby buys her things, you know --IFEELFINE
--17
That her baby buys her things, you know --IFEELFINE
--17
He buys her diamond rings, you know, she said so
--IFEELFINE--18
I will never leave her--SHESAWOMAN--11
Gives me all her time as well as loving--SHESAWOMAN
--14
She's a woman who loves her man--SHESAWOMAN--17
She's a woman who loves her man--SHESAWOMAN--27
I think of her --BABYSINBLA--10
When I'm walking beside her--EVERYLITTL--1
I was lonely without her--EVERYLITTL--5
Can't stop thinking about her now.--EVERYLITTL--6
When I'm with her I'm happy--EVERYLITTL--11
I will love her forever--EVERYLITTL--15
I think I'll take a walk and look for her.--
IDONTWANTT--8
I still love her.--IDONTWANTT--10
If I find her I'll be glad --IDONTWANTT--11
I still love her.--IDONTWANTT--12
I still love her.--IDONTWANTT--19
If I find her I'll be glad --IDONTWANTT--20
I still love her.--IDONTWANTT--21
But I think I'll take a walk and look for her.--
IDONTWANTT--25
Is it for her or myself that I cry?--IMALOSER--12
Was bringing her down, yeah--TICKETTORI--10
Was bringing her down, yeah--TICKETTORI--37
If I could forget her--YESITIS--11
If I could forget her--YESITIS--20
But as it is I'll dream of her tonight --IVEJUSTSEE
--10
If you don't take her out tonight--YOUREGONNA--3
She's gonna change her mind (she's gonna change
her mind)--YOUREGONNA--4
She's gonna change her mind (she's gonna change
her mind)--YOUREGONNA--4
And I will take her out tonight--YOUREGONNA--5
And I will treat her kind (I'm gonna treat her
kind)--YOUREGONNA--6
And I will treat her kind (I'm gonna treat her
kind)--YOUREGONNA--6

If you don't treat her right my friend--YOUREGONNA
--9
You're gonna find her gone (you're gonna find
her gone)--YOUREGONNA--10
You're gonna find her gone (you're gonna find
her gone)--YOUREGONNA--10
'cos I will treat her right--YOUREGONNA--11
I'll make a point of taking her away from you
(watch what you do), yeah--YOUREGONNA--16
The way you treat her what else can I do?--
YOUREGONNA--17
I'll make a point of taking her away from you
(watch what you do), yeah--YOUREGONNA--23
The way you treat her what else can I do?--
YOUREGONNA--24
If you don't take her out tonight--YOUREGONNA--25
She's gonna change her mind (she's gonna change
her mind)--YOUREGONNA--26
She's gonna change her mind (she's gonna change
her mind)--YOUREGONNA--26
And I will take her out tonight--YOUREGONNA--27
And I will treat her kind (I'm gonna treat her
kind)--YOUREGONNA--28
And I will treat her kind (I'm gonna treat her
kind)--YOUREGONNA--28
Tried to please her --DAYTRIPPER--18
Tried to please her --DAYTRIPPER--20
When I think of all the times I tried so hard
to leave her --GIRL--6
And she promises the earth to me and I believe
her --GIRL--8
She showed me her room--NORWEGIANW--4
Drinking her wine.--NORWEGIANW--13
I told her I didn't--NORWEGIANW--19
And was buried along with her name--ELEANORRIG--22
You find that all her words of kindness linger on
--FORNOONE--2
She takes her time and doesn't feel she has to
hurry --FORNOONE--5
And in her eyes you see nothing --FORNOONE--7
You want her, you need her --FORNOONE--10
You want her, you need her --FORNOONE--10
And yet you don't believe her --FORNOONE--11
When she says her love is dead --FORNOONE--12
And in her eyes you see nothing --FORNOONE--14
You won't forget her.--FORNOONE--24
And in her eyes you see nothing --FORNOONE--24
I love her and she's loving me.--GOODDAYSUN--11
Changing my life with a wave of her hand--
HERETHEREA--3
There, running my hands through her hair--
HERETHEREA--5
I want her everywhere--HERETHEREA--8
But to love her is to need her everywhere.--
HERETHEREA--10
But to love her is to need her everywhere.--
HERETHEREA--10
Watching her eyes and hoping I'm always there.--
HERETHEREA--13
I want her everywhere--HERETHEREA--14
But to love her is to need her everywhere.--
HERETHEREA--16
But to love her is to need her everywhere.--
HERETHEREA--16
Watching her eyes and hoping I'm always there.--
HERETHEREA--19
I beat her and kept her apart from the things
that she loved--GETTINGBET--26
I beat her and kept her apart from the things
that she loved--GETTINGBET--26
Filling in a ticket in her little white book.--
LOVELYRITA--9
And the bag across her shoulder--LOVELYRITA--11
Made her look a little like a military man.--
LOVELYRITA--12
Took her out and tried to win her--LOVELYRITA--20
Took her out and tried to win her--LOVELYRITA--20
Told her I would really like to see her again.--
LOVELYRITA--22
Told her I would really like to see her again.--
LOVELYRITA--22
Took her home I nearly made it--LOVELYRITA--24
Look for the girl with the sun in her eyes--
LUCYINTHES--7
Follow her down to a bridge by a fountain--
LUCYINTHES--12
Silently closing her bedroom door--SHESLEAVIN--2
Clutching her handkerchief--SHESLEAVIN--5
She (we gave her most of our lives)--SHESLEAVIN--8
Home. (we gave her everything money could buy)--
SHESLEAVIN--10
Father snores as his wife gets into her
dressing-gown--SHESLEAVIN--13
She breaks down and cries to her husband--

SHESLEAVIN--16
Remember to let her into your heart --HEYJUDE--3
You were made to go out and get her --HEYJUDE--6
The minute you let her under your skin --HEYJUDE
--7
You have found her, now go and get her (let it
out and let it in) --HEYJUDE--16
You have found her, now go and get her (let it
out and let it in) --HEYJUDE--16
Remember (hey Jude) to let her into your heart --
HEYJUDE--28
Remember to let her under your skin (oh) --HEYJUDE
--28
Will the wind that blew her boat--HONEYPIE--25
Kindly send her sailing back to me--HONEYPIE--27
Her hair of floating sky is shimmering --JULIA--7
Sit beside a mountain stream - see her waters rise
--MOTHERNATU--3
And as he gives it to her she begins to sing
(sing):--OBLADIOBLA--12
Molly stays at home and does her pretty face--
OBLADIOBLA--23
Her name was Magill and she called herself Lil --
ROCKYRACCO--15
But everyone knew her as Nancy.--ROCKYRACCO--16
Now she and her man who called himself Dan--
ROCKYRACCO--17
We gave her everything we owned just to sit at
her table ((sexy Sadie))--SEXYSADIE--20
We gave her everything we owned just to sit at
her table ((sexy Sadie))--SEXYSADIE--20
All the girls around her say she's got it coming
--GETBACK/45--18
Wearing her high-heel shoes --GETBACK/45--33
HER MAJESTY, --HERMAJESTY--Title
Her Majesty's a pretty nice girl--HERMAJESTY--1
Her Majesty's a pretty nice girl--HERMAJESTY--3
I wanna tell her that I love her a lot--HERMAJESTY
--5
I wanna tell her that I love her a lot--HERMAJESTY
--5
Her Majesty's a pretty nice girl--HERMAJESTY--7
Someday I'm gonna make her mine - oh yeah --
HERMAJESTY--8
Someday I'm gonna make her mine.--HERMAJESTY--9
Maxwell Edison, majoring in medicine, calls
her on the phone --MAXWELLSIL--3
Bang, bang Maxwell's silver hammer came down
upon her head --MAXWELLSIL--6
But when she turns her back on the boy, he
creeps up from behind --MAXWELLSIL--12
Bang, bang Maxwell's silver hammer came down
upon her head --MAXWELLSIL--13
Well, you should see her in drag --POLYTHENEP--3
Dressed in her polythene bag.--POLYTHENEP--4
Get a dose of her in jackboots and kilt --
POLYTHENEP--6
But now she sucks her thumb and wonders --
SHECAMEINT--7
By the banks of her own lagoon.--SHECAMEINT--7
Didn't anybody tell her?--SHECAMEINT--8
And though she tried her best to help me --
SHECAMEINT--18
Didn't anybody tell her?--SHECAMEINT--20
I don't want to leave her now --SOMETHING--4
Somewhere in her smile she knows--SOMETHING--6
Something in her style that shows me --SOMETHING
--8
I don't want to leave her now --SOMETHING--9
And all I have to do is think of her --SOMETHING
--16
I don't want to leave her now --SOMETHING--18
All the girls around her say she's got it coming--
GETBACK/LP--24
I begged her not to go and I begged her on my
bended knee, (oh yeah)--ONEAFTERNI--6
I begged her not to go and I begged her on my
bended knee, (oh yeah)--ONEAFTERNI--6
Phase one in which Doris gets her oats.--TWOOFUS
--2

HERE
I'll be here, yes I will --ALLIVEGOTT--13
I'll be here, yes I will --ALLIVEGOTT--24
But till she's here--DONTBOTHER--19
But till she's here--DONTBOTHER--34
Being here alone tonight with you.--HOLDMETIGH--17
Being here alone tonight with you.--HOLDMETIGH--27
Here am I sitting all on my own--ITWONTBELO--6
Since you left me I'm so alone (you left me here)
--ITWONTBELO--11
Well since you left me I'm so alone (you left
me here)--ITWONTBELO--21

Love is here to stay.--THINGSWESA--14
Love is here to stay.--THINGSWESA--25
I got no business being here with you this way.--
   WHENIGETHO--23
There's nothing for me here so I will disappear --
   IDONTWANTT--3
There's nothing for me here so I will disappear --
   IDONTWANTT--15
I've been waiting here for you --WHATYOURED--9
I've been waiting here for you --WHATYOURED--16
Now it looks as though they're here to stay--
   YESTERDAY--3
Here I stand head in hand--YOUVEGOTTO--1
I'm here to show everybody the light.--THEWORD--24
If you must return it you can send it here,
   ((paperback))--PAPERBACKW--23
HERE, THERE AND EVERYWHERE.--HERETHEREA--Title
To lead a better life, I need my love to be here.
   --HERETHEREA--1
Here, making each day of the year--HERETHEREA--2
Here, there and everywhere.--HERETHEREA--21
When you're here--IWANTTOTEL--3
Somebody needs to know the time glad that I'm here
   --GOODMORNIN--22
It's wonderful to be here--SGTPEPPERS--14
Sitting here in Blue Jay Way (way).--BLUEJAYWAY--18
I said that's alright I'm waiting here --DONTPASSME
   --29
Look out 'cos here she comes (heh heh heh).--
   HELTERSKEL--17
The love that's shining all around here --
   ITSALLTOOM--17
The love that's shining all around here --
   ITSALLTOOM--26
We're so glad you came here --OLDBROWNSH--7
So glad you came here --OLDBROWNSH--15
So glad you came here --OLDBROWNSH--33
I'm so glad you came here,--OLDBROWNSH--35
Here come old flat top--COMETOGETH--5
HERE COMES THE SUN.--HERECOMEST--Title
Here comes the sun (do-n-do-do) --HERECOMEST--1
Here comes the sun --HERECOMEST--2
Little darling, it feels like years since it's
   been here.--HERECOMEST--5
Here comes the sun (do-n-do-do) --HERECOMEST--6
Here comes the sun --HERECOMEST--7
Little darling, it seems like years since it's
   been here.--HERECOMEST--10
Here comes the sun, here comes the sun --HERECOMEST
   --11
Here comes the sun, here comes the sun --HERECOMEST
   --11
Sun, sun, sun, here it comes --HERECOMEST--13
Sun, sun, sun, here it comes --HERECOMEST--14
Sun, sun, sun, here it comes --HERECOMEST--15
Sun, sun, sun, here it comes --HERECOMEST--16
Sun, sun, sun, here it comes.--HERECOMEST--17
Here comes the sun (do-n-do-do) --HERECOMEST--20
Here comes the sun --HERECOMEST--21
Here comes the sun (do-n-do-do) --HERECOMEST--23
Here comes the sun --HERECOMEST--24
Aah - here come the Sun King --SUNKING--1
Here come the Sun King.--SUNKING--2
Here come the Sun King.--SUNKING--5
Soon we'll be away from here --YOUNEVERGI--19
It always leads me here, lead me to your door.--
   LONGANDWIN--3
Why leave me standing here, let me know the way.--
   LONGANDWIN--6
You left me standing here a long, long time ago --
   LONGANDWIN--10
Don't leave me waiting here, lead me to your door.
   --LONGANDWIN--11
You left me standing here a long, long time ago --
   LONGANDWIN--13
Don't keep me waiting here (don't keep me
   waiting) lead me to your door.--LONGANDWIN
   --14

HERE'S
   Well here's another place you can go--GLASSONION
      --3
   Well here's another clue for you all:--GLASSONION
      --10
   Well here's another place you can be--GLASSONION
      --19

HERSELF
   Her name was Magill and she called herself Lil --
      ROCKYRACCO--15

HEY
Whoa-ho love me do (hey hey).--LOVEMEDO--17
Whoa-ho love me do (hey hey).--LOVEMEDO--17
Whoa since/when I saw her standing there. (hey! aah!)
   --ISAWHERSTA--17
Hey!--IWANNABEYO--26
(Hey)--CANTBUYMEL--24
And I do, hey hey hey, and I do.--ISHOULDHAV--3
And I do, hey hey hey, and I do.--ISHOULDHAV--3
And I do, hey hey hey, and I do.--ISHOULDHAV--3
Give me more, hey hey hey, give me more.--
   ISHOULDHAV--13
Give me more, hey hey hey, give me more.--
   ISHOULDHAV--13
Give me more, hey hey hey, give me more.--
   ISHOULDHAV--13
Hey! - wuh!--IDONTWANTT--17
(Hey)--IVEJUSTSEE--21
Hey! you've got to hide your love away.--YOUVEGOTTO
   --9
Hey! you've got to hide your love away.--YOUVEGOTTO
   --10
Hey! you've got to hide your love away.--YOUVEGOTTO
   --19
Hey! you've got to hide your love away.--YOUVEGOTTO
   --20
Ooo-ooo-aah - hey-hey-hey - hey.--FIXINGAHOL--14
All you need is love, (wuh) all you need is
   love (hey),--ALLYOUN/YS--17
HEY JUDE.--HEYJUDE--Title
Hey Jude, don't make it bad --HEYJUDE--1
Hey Jude, don't be afraid --HEYJUDE--5
Hey Jude, refrain --HEYJUDE--10
Hey Jude, don't let me down --HEYJUDE--15
Remember (hey Jude) to let her into your heart --
   HEYJUDE--17
Hey Jude, begin --HEYJUDE--20
Hey Jude, you'll do --HEYJUDE--23
Hey Jude, don't make it bad --HEYJUDE--26
(Take it Jude) nah - nah - nah - nah, hey
   Jude.--HEYJUDE--33
Nah - nah - nah - nah, hey Jude.--HEYJUDE--35
Nah - nah - nah - nah, hey Jude.--HEYJUDE--37
Nah - nah - nah - nah, hey Jude.--HEYJUDE--39
(Ow - ooo nah nah nah) nah - nah - nah - nah,
   hey Jude--HEYJUDE--42
Nah - nah - nah - nah, hey Jude.--HEYJUDE--45
Nah - nah - nah - nah, hey Jude (Jude, hey
   Jude, wah!).--HEYJUDE--49
Nah - nah - nah - nah, hey Jude (Jude, hey
   Jude, wah!).--HEYJUDE--49
Nah - nah - nah - nah, hey Jude (hey hey hey
   hey hey hey hey).--HEYJUDE--51
Nah - nah - nah - nah, hey Jude (hey hey hey
   hey hey hey hey).--HEYJUDE--51
Nah - nah - nah - nah, hey Jude (hey hey hey
   hey hey hey hey).--HEYJUDE--51
Nah - nah - nah - nah, hey Jude (hey hey hey
   hey hey hey hey).--HEYJUDE--51
Nah - nah - nah - nah, hey Jude (hey hey hey
   hey hey hey hey).--HEYJUDE--51
Nah - nah - nah - nah, hey Jude (hey hey hey
   hey hey hey hey).--HEYJUDE--51
Nah - nah - nah - nah, hey Jude (hey hey hey
   hey hey hey hey).--HEYJUDE--51
Nah nah nah, nah - nah - nah (hey hey hey
   hey) --HEYJUDE--52
Nah nah nah, nah - nah - nah (hey hey hey
   hey) --HEYJUDE--52
Nah nah nah, nah - nah - nah (hey hey hey
   hey) --HEYJUDE--52
Nah nah nah, nah - nah - nah (hey hey hey
   hey) --HEYJUDE--52
Nah - nah - nah - nah, hey Jude.--HEYJUDE--53
Nah - nah - nah - nah, hey Jude.--HEYJUDE--56
Nah - nah - nah - nah, hey Jude.--HEYJUDE--58
Nah - nah - nah - nah, hey Jude (yeah).--HEYJUDE
   --61
Nah - nah - nah - nah, hey Jude.--HEYJUDE--63
Nah nah nah, nah - nah - nah ((hey hey
   hey hey)) --HEYJUDE--64
Nah nah nah, nah - nah - nah ((hey hey
   hey hey)) --HEYJUDE--64
Nah nah nah, nah - nah - nah ((hey hey
   hey hey)) --HEYJUDE--64
Nah nah nah, nah - nah - nah ((hey hey
   hey hey)) --HEYJUDE--64
(Take it Jude) nah - nah - nah - nah, hey
   Jude.--HEYJUDE--65
Nah - nah - nah - nah, hey Jude (Jude, Jude
   ma ma ma ma ma ma)--HEYJUDE--69
Nah - nah - nah - nah, hey Jude (ooo).--HEYJUDE--71

Nah - nah - nah - nah, hey Jude (ooo - ooo).--
    HEYJUDE--73
Nah - nah - nah - nah, hey Jude.--HEYJUDE--75
Hey, I'm back in the USSR.--BACKINTHEU--24
I'm back in the USSR (hey!)--BACKINTHEU
    --35
Hey, I'm back --BACKINTHEU--39
Hey, so look at me --BACKINTHEU--41
Hey, Bungalow Bill --CONTINUING--1
Hey, Bungalow Bill --CONTINUING--4
Hey, Bungalow Bill --CONTINUING--11
Hey, Bungalow Bill --CONTINUING--14
Hey, Bungalow Bill --CONTINUING--21
Hey, Bungalow Bill --CONTINUING--24
Hey, Bungalow Bill --CONTINUING--31
Hey, Bungalow Bill --CONTINUING--34
Hey, Bungalow Bill --CONTINUING--37
Hey, Bungalow Bill --CONTINUING--40
Hey, Bungalow Bill --CONTINUING--43
Hey, Bungalow Bill --CONTINUING--46
Hey, Bungalow Bill --CONTINUING--49
Hey, Bungalow Bill --CONTINUING--52
Everybody's got something to hide 'cept for me
    and my monkey - hey.--EVRBDYMONK--25
(Hey - yeah, wuh, yeah - wuh!)--EVRBDYMONK--26
Hey, ob-la-di ob-la-da life goes on bra --
    OBLADIOBLA--27
Hey, happy ever after in the market place --
    OBLADIOBLA--32
Hey up!--WHILEMYGUI--1
HEY BULLDOG.--HEYBULLDOG--Title
If you're lonely you can talk to me - hey!--
    HEYBULLDOG--20
Hey bulldog (woof), hey bulldog, hey bulldog,
    hey bulldog.--HEYBULLDOG--22
Hey bulldog (woof), hey bulldog, hey bulldog,
    hey bulldog.--HEYBULLDOG--22
Hey bulldog (woof), hey bulldog, hey bulldog,
    hey bulldog.--HEYBULLDOG--22
Hey bulldog (woof), hey bulldog, hey bulldog,
    hey bulldog.--HEYBULLDOG--22
Hey man what's that noise? (woof)--HEYBULLDOG--23
Hey bulldog!--HEYBULLDOG--34
Don't let me down (hey) --DONTLETMED--25
Don't ((hey)) let me down.--DONTLETMED--33
Who knows baby, you may comfort me. (hey)--
    OLDBROWNSH--21
Who knows baby, you may comfort me (hey).--
    OLDBROWNSH--26
Making sure that I'm not late (hey).--OLDBROWNSH
    --30
Hey! (great!)--POLYTHENEP--11
You know my name, that's right, look up my
    number (hey) --YOUKNOWMYN--10
You, you know, you know my name (brrrrrr - ha,
    hey!) --YOUKNOWMYN--12

HEY-HEY-HEY
    Ooo-ooo-aah - hey-hey-hey - hey.--FIXINGAHOL--14

HI
    Love is all you need (yahoo) (eee - hi)--
        ALLYOUN/YS--38
    I say hi!/high, you say 'lo/low--HELLOGOODB--7

HIDE
    Don't you run and hide, just come on, come on --
        LITTLECHIL--17
    I can't hide--IWANTTOHOL--17
    I can't hide--IWANTTOHOL--18
    I can't hide.--IWANTTOHOL--19
    I can't hide--IWANTTOHOL--30
    I can't hide--IWANTTOHOL--31
    I can't .hide.--IWANTTOHOL--32
    Oh please, don't run and hide --IFIFELL--11
    I'm gonna hide myself away-hey--ILLCRYINST--13
    And when I do you'd better hide all the girls --
        ILLCRYINST--15
    I'm gonna hide myself away-hey--ILLCRYINST--22
    And when I do you'd better hide all the girls --
        ILLCRYINST--24
    Now I need a place to hide away--YESTERDAY--15
    Now I need a place to hide away--YESTERDAY--23
    YOU'VE GOT TO HIDE YOUR LOVE AWAY.--YOUVEGOTTO
        --Title
    Hey! you've got to hide your love away.--YOUVEGOTTO
        --9
    Hey! you've got to hide your love away.--YOUVEGOTTO
        --10
    Hey! you've got to hide your love away.--YOUVEGOTTO
        --19

Hey! you've got to hide your love away.--YOUVEGOTTO
    --20
Hide your head in the sand, little girl.--
    RUNFORYOUR--6
Hide your head in the sand, little girl.--
    RUNFORYOUR--14
Hide your head in the sand, little girl.--
    RUNFORYOUR--22
Hide your head in the sand, little girl.--
    RUNFORYOUR--30
I don't know why you should want to hide --
    YOUWONTSEE--7
If the rain comes they run and hide their heads--
    RAIN--1
Who hide themselves behind a wall of illusion--
    WITHINYOUW--4
EVERYBODY'S GOT SOMETHING TO HIDE EXCEPT ME
    AND MY MONKEY.--EVRBDYMONK--Title
Everybody's got something to hide 'cept for me
    and my monkey - wuh.--EVRBDYMONK--7
Everybody's got something to hide 'cept for me
    and my monkey (yeah - wuh).--EVRBDYMONK--16
Everybody's got something to hide 'cept for me
    and my monkey - hey.--EVRBDYMONK--25
I've got a feeling, a feeling I can't hide --
    IVEGOTAFEE--3
Everybody let their hair down ((a feeling I
    can't hide, oh no)) --IVEGOTAFEE--33

HIDEAWAY
    In our little hideaway beneath the waves.--
        OCTOPUSSGA--10

HIDING
    Me hiding me head in the sand--GETTINGBET--12

HIGH
    I don't know why she's riding so high--TICKETTORI
        --17
    I don't know why she's riding so high--TICKETTORI
        --30
    I get high when I see you go by, my oh my--
        ITSONLYLOV--1
    I mean, it must be high or low--STRAWBERRY--17
    That grow so incredibly high (high).--LUCYINTHES
        --15
    That grow so incredibly high (high).--LUCYINTHES
        --15
    Mmm I get high with a little help from my friends
        --WITHALITTL--6
    Mmm get high with a little help from my friends --
        WITHALITTL--13
    Mmm get high with a little help from my friends --
        WITHALITTL--24
    Oh I get high with a little help from my friends
        --WITHALITTL--32
    I say hi!/high, you say 'lo/low--HELLOGOODB--7
    Because the wind is high it blows my mind --BECAUSE
        --5
    Because the wind is high.--BECAUSE--6

HIGH-HEEL
    Wearing her high-heel shoes --GETBACK/45--33

HIGHER
    The deeper you go, the higher you fly --EVRBDYMONK
        --8
    The higher you fly, the deeper you go --EVRBDYMONK
        --9

HILL
    THE FOOL ON THE HILL.--FOOLONTHEH--Title
    Day after day, alone on a hill--FOOLONTHEH--1
    But the fool on the hill sees the sun going down--
        FOOLONTHEH--6
    But the fool on the hill sees the sun going down--
        FOOLONTHEH--13
    But the fool on the hill sees the sun going down--
        FOOLONTHEH--18
    The fool on the hill sees the sun going down--
        FOOLONTHEH--25
    I told you about the fool on the hill--GLASSONION
        --17

HILLS
    Now somewhere in the Black Mountain hills of
        Dakota --ROCKYRACCO--1

HILT
   She's killer-diller when she's dressed to the hilt.
   --POLYTHENEP--7

HILTON
   Drove from Paris to the Amsterdam Hilton --
   BALLADOFJO--17

HIM
   I caught you talking to him--YOUCANTDOT--10
   She thinks of him and so she dresses in black --
   BABYSINBLA--4
   But she thinks only of him --BABYSINBLA--11
   She thinks of him.--BABYSINBLA--13
   She thinks of him and so she dresses in black --
   BABYSINBLA--24
   But when I saw him with you I could feel my
   future fold.--WHATGOESON--7
   Look at him working--ELEANORRIG--14
   But now he's gone, she doesn't need him.--FORNOONE
   --19
   The little children laugh at him behind his back--
   PENNYLANE--6
   But nobody wants to know him--FOOLONTHEH--3
   But nobody ever hears him--FOOLONTHEH--10
   And nobody seems to like him--FOOLONTHEH--15
   They don't like him.--FOOLONTHEH--24
   So Captain Marvel zapped him right between the
   eyes. (Zap!)--CONTINUING--19
   The children asked him if to kill was not a sin --
   CONTINUING--27
   If looks could kill it would have been us instead
   of him.--CONTINUING--29
   And Molly says this as she takes him by the hand:
   --OBLADIOBLA--4
   Takes him out to look at the Queen--MEANMRMUST--11

HIMSELF
   Booked himself a room in the local saloon.--
   ROCKYRACCO--8
   Now she and her man who called himself Dan--
   ROCKYRACCO--17

HIS
   Let's pretend we just can't see his face.--
   IMHAPPYJUS--17
   Let's pretend we just can't see his face.--
   IMHAPPYJUS--25
   That a man must break his back to earn his day of
   leisure?--GIRL--24
   That a man must break his back to earn his day of
   leisure?--GIRL--24
   Sitting in his nowhere land --NOWHEREMAN--2
   Making all his nowhere plans for nobody.--
   NOWHEREMAN--3
   Sitting in his nowhere land --NOWHEREMAN--23
   Making all his nowhere plans for nobody --
   NOWHEREMAN--24
   Making all his nowhere plans for nobody --
   NOWHEREMAN--25
   Making all his nowhere plans for nobody.--
   NOWHEREMAN--26
   And his clinging wife doesn't understand.--
   PAPERBACKW--9
   His son is working for the Daily Mail --PAPERBACKW
   --10
   Take a drink from his special cup, Dr. Robert.--
   DRROBERT--7
   Darning his socks in the night when there's
   nobody there--ELEANORRIG--15
   Father McKenzie wiping the dirt from his hands--
   ELEANORRIG--24
   And he told us of his life--YELLOWSUBM--3
   The little children laugh at him behind his back--
   PENNYLANE--6
   And in his pocket is a portrait of the Queen--
   PENNYLANE--13
   He likes to keep his fire-engine clean--PENNYLANE
   --14
   Performs his feat on Saturday at Bishopsgate.--
   BEINGFORTH--9
   When Mr. K. performs his tricks - without a
   sound.--BEINGFORTH--16
   He blew his mind out in a car--DAYINTHELI--6
   They'd seen his face before--DAYINTHELI--9
   Nothing to do to save his life call his wife in--
   GOODMORNIN--2
   Nothing to do to save his life call his wife in--
   GOODMORNIN--2
   Father snores as his wife gets into her

dressing-gown--SHESLEAVIN--13
And the eyes in his head see the world spinning
   round.--FOOLONTHEH--7
And the eyes in his head see the world spinning
   round.--FOOLONTHEH--14
And he never shows his feelings.--FOOLONTHEH--17
And the eyes in his head see the world spinning
   round.--FOOLONTHEH--19
And the eyes in his head see the world spinning
   round.--FOOLONTHEH--26
Monday's child has learned to tie his bootlace.--
   LADYMADONN--7
By making his world a little colder.--HEYJUDE--13
He went out tiger hunting with his elephant and
   gun --CONTINUING--7
In case of accidents he always took his mom --
   CONTINUING--8
Bill and his elephants were taken by surprise --
   CONTINUING--18
(But when he looked so fierce) his mommy butted
   in --CONTINUING--28
Now the sun turns out his light --GOODNIGHT--3
Now the sun turns out his light --GOODNIGHT--16
The man in the crowd with the multicoloured
   mirrors on his hobnail boots --HAPPINESSI--5
Lying with his eyes while his hands are busy
   working overtime --HAPPINESSI--6
Lying with his eyes while his hands are busy
   working overtime --HAPPINESSI--6
A soap impression of his wife which he ate --
   HAPPINESSI--7
Desmond stays at home and does his pretty face--
   OBLADIOBLA--34
And one day his woman ran off with another guy --
   ROCKYRACCO--3
Rocky Raccoon checked into his room --ROCKYRACCO
   --9
To shoot off the legs of his rival.--ROCKYRACCO--12
His rival it seems had broken his dreams--
   ROCKYRACCO--13
His rival it seems had broken his dreams--
   ROCKYRACCO--13
By stealing the girl of his fancy --ROCKYRACCO--14
A - now Rocky Raccoon, he fell back in his room--
   ROCKYRACCO--36
Jojo left his home in Tucson, Arizona--GETBACK/45
   --3
The newspapers said, she's gone to his head --
   BALLADOFJO--31
He got hair down to his knee--COMETOGETH--9
He got feet down below his knee--COMETOGETH--29
Hold you in his armchair you can feel his disease
   --COMETOGETH--30
Hold you in his armchair you can feel his disease
   --COMETOGETH--30
But as the words are leaving his lips, a noise
   comes from behind --MAXWELLSIL--22
Bang, bang Maxwell's silver hammer came down
   upon his head --MAXWELLSIL--23
Keeps a ten bob note up his nose--MEANMRMUST--6
His sister Pam works in a shop--MEANMRMUST--8
In his octopus's garden in the shade.--OCTOPUSSGA
   --4
Jojo left his home in Tucson, Arizona--GETBACK/LP
   --9

HIT
   That was a hit before your mother was born --
   YOURMOTHER--3
   That was a hit before your mother was born --
   YOURMOTHER--9
   That was a hit before your mother was born --
   YOURMOTHER--14
   Now she's hit the big time--HONEYPIE--3
   Hit young Rocky in the eye.--ROCKYRACCO--4
   (Hit it)--FORYOUBLUE--11

HMM
   Hmm hmm hmm, calls me --JULIA--15
   Hmm hmm hmm, calls me --JULIA--15
   Hmm hmm hmm, calls me --JULIA--15

HO
   Oh - ho, oh - ho.--ILLBEBACK--8
   Oh - ho, oh - ho.--ILLBEBACK--8
   Oh - ho, oh - ho.--ILLBEBACK--17
   Oh - ho, oh - ho.--ILLBEBACK--17
   Oh - ho, oh - ho.--ILLBEBACK--25
   Oh - ho, oh - ho.--ILLBEBACK--25
   Ho ho ho, he he he, ha ha ha--IAMTHEWALR--22
   Ho ho ho, he he he, ha ha ha--IAMTHEWALR--22

Ho ho ho, he he he, ha ha ha--IAMTHEWALR--22
(Ho ho ho ho ho)--OBLADIOBLA--19
(Ho ho ho ho ho)--OBLADIOBLA--19
(Ho ho ho ho ho)--OBLADIOBLA--19
(Ho ho ho ho ho)--OBLADIOBLA--19
(Ho ho ho ho ho)--OBLADIOBLA--31
(Ho ho ho ho ho)--OBLADIOBLA--31
(Ho ho ho ho ho)--OBLADIOBLA--31
(Ho ho ho ho ho)--OBLADIOBLA--31
(Ho ho ho ho ho)--OBLADIOBLA--31

HOBNAIL
    The man in the crowd with the multicoloured
        mirrors on his hobnail boots --HAPPINESSI--5

HOE-DOWN
    Were in the next room at the hoe-down --ROCKYRACCO
        --18

HOG
    Oh I do a road hog--IDIGAPONY--9

HOGSHEAD
    Lastly through a hogshead of real fire--BEINGFORTH
        --6

HOLD
    I got arms that long to hold you--FROMMETOYO--11
    I got arms that long to hold you--FROMMETOYO--22
    HOLD ME TIGHT.--HOLDMETIGH--Title
    Hold me tight --HOLDMETIGH--2
    So hold (hold) me tight (me tight) --HOLDMETIGH--6
    So hold (hold) me tight (me tight) --HOLDMETIGH--6
    Hold me tight,--HOLDMETIGH--9
    So hold (hold) me tight (me tight) --HOLDMETIGH--13
    So hold (hold) me tight (me tight) --HOLDMETIGH--13
    Don't know what it means to hold you tight --
        HOLDMETIGH--16
    So hold me tight --HOLDMETIGH--19
    So hold (hold) me tight (me tight) --HOLDMETIGH--23
    So hold (hold) me tight (me tight) --HOLDMETIGH--23
    Don't know what it means to hold you tight --
        HOLDMETIGH--26
    So hold me tight --HOLDMETIGH--29
    So hold (hold) me tight (me tight) --HOLDMETIGH--33
    So hold (hold) me tight (me tight) --HOLDMETIGH--33
    I WANT TO HOLD YOUR HAND.--IWANTTOHOL--Title
    I wanna hold your hand--IWANTTOHOL--4
    I wanna hold your hand--IWANTTOHOL--5
    I wanna hold your hand.--IWANTTOHOL--6
    You'll let me hold your hand--IWANTTOHOL--10
    And/You'll let me hold your hand--IWANTTOHOL--11
    I wanna hold your hand.--IWANTTOHOL--12
    I wanna hold your hand--IWANTTOHOL--23
    I wanna hold your hand--IWANTTOHOL--24
    I wanna hold your hand--IWANTTOHOL--25
    I wanna hold your hand--IWANTTOHOL--36
    I wanna hold your hand--IWANTTOHOL--37
    I wanna hold your hand--IWANTTOHOL--38
    I wanna hold your hand.--IWANTTOHOL--39
    I don't wanna kiss or hold your hand --IMHAPPYJUS
        --4
    I don't need to hug or hold you tight --IMHAPPYJUS
        --8
    I'm gonna hold her tight --WHENIGETHO--17
    Hold me, love me --EIGHTDAYSA--5
    Hold me, love me --EIGHTDAYSA--6
    Hold me, love me --EIGHTDAYSA--13
    Hold me, love me --EIGHTDAYSA--14
    Hold me, love me --EIGHTDAYSA--23
    Hold me, love me --EIGHTDAYSA--24
    Hold me, love me --EIGHTDAYSA--33
    Hold me, love me --EIGHTDAYSA--34
    And if your heart's strong, hold on, I won't
        delay.--WAIT--6
    And if your heart's strong, hold on, I won't
        delay.--WAIT--22
    You knew I wanted just to hold you--GOTTOGETYO--9
    To try our best to hold it there--WITHINYOUW--11
    When I hold you in my arms ((oh, yeah)) --
        HAPPINESSI--22
    Hold your head up you silly girl, look what
        you've done --MARTHAMYDE--4
    Hold your hand out you silly girl, see what
        you've done --MARTHAMYDE--10
    Hold you in his armchair you can feel his disease
        --COMETOGETH--30
    Hold it - aah--IDIGAPONY--3

(hold it)--IDIGAPONY--4

HOLDING
    When I'm home feeling you holding me tight,
        tight, yeah.--HARDDAYSNI--16
    When I'm home feeling you holding me tight,
        tight, yeah.--HARDDAYSNI--29
    Than just holding hands.--IFIFELL--6
    Holding back these tears in my eyes.--TELLMEWHY--16
    You're holding me down (aah) turning me round
        (aah)--GETTINGBET--5

HOLE
    FIXING A HOLE.--FIXINGAHOL--Title
    I'm fixing a hole where the rain gets in--
        FIXINGAHOL--1
    I'm fixing a hole where the rain gets in--
        FIXINGAHOL--23
    I'm fixing a hole where the rain gets in--
        FIXINGAHOL--26
    Fixing the hole in the ocean--GLASSONION--21
    Sleeps in a hole in the road--MEANMRMUST--4

HOLES
    Four thousand holes in Blackburn, Lancashire--
        DAYINTHELI--29
    And though the holes were rather small--DAYINTHELI
        --30
    Now they know how many holes it takes--DAYINTHELI
        --32

HOLIDAY
    Painting pictures for the childrens' holiday.--
        CRYBABYCRY--15

HOLLAND
    Trying to get to Holland or France.--BALLADOFJO--2

HOLLYWOOD
    Of your Hollywood song.--HONEYPIE--12
    Play it to me Hollywood blues.--HONEYPIE--24

HOLY
    He one holy roller--COMETOGETH--8

HOME
    I'll ((I'll)) be coming home ((home)) again
        to you love ((you love)) --PSILOVEYOU--7
    I'll ((I'll)) be coming home ((home)) again
        to you love ((you love)) --PSILOVEYOU--7
    I'll be coming home again to you love --PSILOVEYOU
        --19
    And you'll come running home --ALLIVEGOTT--4
    And you'll come running home --ALLIVEGOTT--20
    I'll write home every day --ALLMYLOVIN--5
    I'll write home every day --ALLMYLOVIN--11
    I'll write home every day --ALLMYLOVIN--19
    When she's come home--DONTBOTHER--23
    When she's come home--DONTBOTHER--38
    Now you're coming, you're coming on home (now
        you're coming on home)--ITWONTBELO--12
    Now you're coming, you're coming on home (now
        you're coming on home)--ITWONTBELO--12
    I'll be good like I know I should (yes,
        you're coming on home)--ITWONTBELO--13
    You're coming home, you're coming home--ITWONTBELO
        --14
    You're coming home, you're coming home--ITWONTBELO
        --14
    Now you're coming, you're coming on home (now
        you're coming on home)--ITWONTBELO--22
    Now you're coming, you're coming on home (now
        you're coming on home)--ITWONTBELO--22
    I'll be good like I know I should (yes,
        you're coming on home)--ITWONTBELO--23
    You're coming home, you're coming home--ITWONTBELO
        --24
    You're coming home, you're coming home--ITWONTBELO
        --24
    But when I get home to you --HARDDAYSNI--5
    When I'm home everything seems to be right --
        HARDDAYSNI--15
    When I'm home feeling you holding me tight,
        tight, yeah.--HARDDAYSNI--16
    But when I get home to you --HARDDAYSNI--21
    When I'm home everything seems to be right --

HARDDAYSNI--28
When I'm home feeling you holding me tight,
    tight, yeah.--HARDDAYSNI--29
But when I get home to you,--HARDDAYSNI--34
WHEN I GET HOME.--WHENIGETHO--Title
When I get home.--WHENIGETHO--3
When I get home.--WHENIGETHO--9
I got a girl who's waiting home for me tonight.--
    WHENIGETHO--12
When I get home.--WHENIGETHO--15
When I getting home tonight --WHENIGETHO--16
I'm gonna love her till the cows come home --
    WHENIGETHO--18
When I get home, yeah.--WHENIGETHO--26
When I get home.--WHENIGETHO--28
They said you were not home--NOREPLY--10
They said you were not home--NOREPLY--23
It's been a long time, now I'm coming back home --
    WAIT--1
It's been a long time, now I'm coming back home --
    WAIT--13
It's been a long time, now I'm coming back home --
    WAIT--25
You stay home, she goes out --FORNOONE--17
Heading for home you start to roam then you're in
    town.--GOODMORNIN--8
Took her home I nearly made it--LOVELYRITA--24
We'd like to take you home with us--SGTPEPPERS--17
We'd love to take you home.--SGTPEPPERS--18
SHE'S LEAVING HOME.--SHESLEAVIN--Title
Home. (we gave her everything money could buy)--
    SHESLEAVIN--10
She's leaving home after living alone--SHESLEAVIN
    --11
Home. (we struggled hard all our lives to get by)
    --SHESLEAVIN--22
She's leaving home after living alone--SHESLEAVIN
    --23
She's leaving home. ('bye, 'bye)--SHESLEAVIN--33
Gee, it's good to be back home --BACKINTHEU--9
So won't you please come home.--HONEYPIE--9
So won't you please come home.--HONEYPIE--31
In a couple of years they have built a home sweet
    home --OBLADIOBLA--17
In a couple of years they have built a home sweet
    home --OBLADIOBLA--17
Molly stays at home and does her pretty face--
    OBLADIOBLA--23
In a couple of years they have built a home sweet
    home--OBLADIOBLA--29
In a couple of years they have built a home sweet
    home--OBLADIOBLA--29
Desmond stays at home and does his pretty face--
    OBLADIOBLA--34
And get me home for tea.--ITSALLTOOM--24
Jojo left his home in Tucson, Arizona--GETBACK/45
    --3
Go home.--GETBACK/45--10
Go home.--GETBACK/45--25
Get back home Loretta.--GETBACK/45--35
To get back home.--GOLDENSLUM--4
To get back home.--GOLDENSLUM--14
Joan was quizzical, studied pataphysical science
    in the home --MAXWELLSIL--1
Jojo left his home in Tucson, Arizona--GETBACK/LP
    --9
Go home.--GETBACK/LP--16
Go home.--GETBACK/LP--31
Pick up my bag, run right home --ONEAFTERNI--13
Well - pick up my bag, run right home (run
    right home) --ONEAFTERNI--23
Well - pick up my bag, run right home (run
    right home) --ONEAFTERNI--23
Not arriving on our way back home.--TWOOFUS--6
We're on our way home --TWOOFUS--7
We're on our way home --TWOOFUS--8
We're going home.--TWOOFUS--9
Lifting latches on our way back home.--TWOOFUS--13
We're on our way home --TWOOFUS--14
We're on our way home --TWOOFUS--15
We're going home.--TWOOFUS--16
Getting nowhere on our way back home.--TWOOFUS--22
We're on our way home --TWOOFUS--23
We're on our way home --TWOOFUS--24
We're going home.--TWOOFUS--25
Getting nowhere on our way back home.--TWOOFUS--31
We're on our way home --TWOOFUS--32
We're on our way home --TWOOFUS--33
We're going home.--TWOOFUS--34
We're going home.--TWOOFUS--35

HOMEWARD
    To get back homeward.--GOLDENSLUM--2

To get back homeward.--GOLDENSLUM--12

HONEY
    Honey disconnect the phone.--BACKINTHEU--11
    Oh let me tell you honey --BACKINTHEU--38
    HONEY PIE.--HONEYPIE--Title
    Honey Pie you are making me crazy--HONEYPIE--7
    Oh, Honey Pie my position is tragic--HONEYPIE--10
    Oh, Honey Pie you are driving me frantic--HONEYPIE
        --16
    Honey Pie come back to me - ooo.--HONEYPIE--19
    Now Honey Pie you are making me crazy--HONEYPIE--29
    Come, come back to me Honey Pie--HONEYPIE--32
    Honey Pie, Honey Pie.--HONEYPIE--35
    Honey Pie, Honey Pie.--HONEYPIE--35
    WILD HONEY PIE.--WILDHONEYP--Title
    Honey Pie, Honey Pie.--WILDHONEYP--1
    Honey Pie, Honey Pie.--WILDHONEYP--1
    Honey Pie, Honey Pie.--WILDHONEYP--2
    Honey Pie, Honey Pie.--WILDHONEYP--2
    Honey Pie, Honey Pie, Honey Pie, Honey
        Pie --WILDHONEYP--3
    Honey Pie, Honey Pie, Honey Pie, Honey
        Pie --WILDHONEYP--3
    Honey Pie, Honey Pie, Honey Pie, Honey
        Pie --WILDHONEYP--3
    Honey Pie, Honey Pie, Honey Pie, Honey
        Pie --WILDHONEYP--3
    I love you, yeah, Honey Pie, wuh!--WILDHONEYP--4
    I said, move over honey, I'm travelling on
        that line --ONEAFTERNI--2
    I said a-move over honey, I'm travelling on
        that line --ONEAFTERNI--16
    Said a - move over honey, I'm travelling on
        that line --ONEAFTERNI--26

HONEYMOONING
    Honeymooning down by the Seine.--BALLADOFJO--10

HOO
    Hoo!--WHENIMSIXT--38

HOOPS
    Over men and horses, hoops and garters--BEINGFORTH
        --5

HOPE
    I hope it will be mine --ANYTIMEATA--17
    And hope that my dreams will come true --ALLMYLOVIN
        --9
    So I hope you see --IFIFELL--17
    So I hope you see --IFIFELL--24
    Hope you need my love babe --EIGHTDAYSA--3
    Hope you need my love babe --EIGHTDAYSA--21
    Go to a show you hope she goes--GOODMORNIN--24
    We hope you will enjoy the show--SGTPEPPERS--9
    We hope you have enjoyed the show.--SGTPEPPREP--4
    I feel it now, I hope you feel it too.--FORYOUBLUE
        --15
    And I hope we passed the audition.--GETBACK/LP--39

HOPED
    Leaving the note that she hoped would say more.--
        SHESLEAVIN--3

HOPING
    Until I do I'm hoping you will know what I mean.--
        MICHELLE--14
    Watching her eyes and hoping I'm always there.--
        HERETHEREA--13
    Watching her eyes and hoping I'm always there.--
        HERETHEREA--19
    The Magical Mystery Tour is hoping to take you
        away --MAGICALMYS--17
    (Hoping to take you away)--MAGICALMYS--18
    (Coming/Hoping to take you away)--MAGICALMYS--28

HORSE
    And of course Henry the Horse dances the waltz.--
        BEINGFORTH--14

HORSES
    Over men and horses, hoops and garters--BEINGFORTH
        --5

HOT

    I like this kinda hot kinda music, hot kinda music
      --HONEYPIE--22
    I like this kinda hot kinda music, hot kinda music
      --HONEYPIE--22
    But Daniel was hot, he drew first and shot--
      ROCKYRACCO--21

HOUR

    About an hour or two --DONTPASSME--28
    And in my hour of darkness--LETITBE/45--4
    And in my hour of darkness--LETITBE/LP--4

HOUR-GLASS

    In Penny Lane there is a fireman with an
      hour-glass--PENNYLANE--12

HOUSE

    Nobody was really sure if he was from the House
      of Lords--DAYINTHELI--10

HOW

    You'll never know how much I really love you --
      DOYOUWANTT--1
    You'll never know how much I really care.--
      DOYOUWANTT--2
    So how could I dance with another --ISAWHERSTA--5
    Oh how long will it take --BABYSINBLA--14
    Oh how long will it take --BABYSINBLA--19
    How can I get through--TELLMEWHAT--19
    How can I get through--TELLMEWHAT--28
    How can you laugh when you know I'm down?--IMDOWN
      --6
    (How can you laugh) when you know I'm down?--IMDOWN
      --7
    How can you laugh when you know I'm down?--IMDOWN
      --13
    (How can you laugh) when you know I'm down?--IMDOWN
      --14
    How can you laugh when you know I'm down?--IMDOWN
      --21
    (How can you laugh) when you know I'm down?--IMDOWN
      --22
    You don't realise how much I need you--INEEDYOU--1
    How was I to know you would upset me?--INEEDYOU--7
    Please remember how I feel about you--INEEDYOU--16
    Please remember how I feel about you--INEEDYOU--26
    How can I even try --YOUVEGOTTO--11
    How could she say to me--YOUVEGOTTO--15
    I've been away now, oh how I've been alone.--WAIT
      --2
    I've been away now, oh how I've been alone.--WAIT
      --14
    I've been away now, oh how I've been alone.--WAIT
      --26
    Both of us thinking how good it can be--HERETHEREA
      --6
    Let me tell you how it will be --TAXMAN--3
    Now they know how many holes it takes--DAYINTHELI
      --32
    How could she do this to me?--SHESLEAVIN--19
    How do I feel by the end of the day?--WITHALITTL
      --10
    Nothing you can say but you can learn how to play
      the game ((love))--ALLYOUN/YS--6
    Nothing you can do but you can learn how to be
      you in time ((love))--ALLYOUN/YS--10
    How does it feel to be--BABYYOUREA--1
    How does it feel to be--BABYYOUREA--7
    How often have you been there?--BABYYOUREA--9
    How does it feel to be--BABYYOUREA--22
    See how they run like pigs from a gun, see how
      they fly--IAMTHEWALR--2
    See how they run like pigs from a gun, see how
      they fly--IAMTHEWALR--2
    See how they fly like Lucy in the sky, see how
      they run--IAMTHEWALR--10
    See how they fly like Lucy in the sky, see how
      they run--IAMTHEWALR--10
    See how they smile, like pigs in a sty, see how
      they snied--IAMTHEWALR--23
    See how they smile, like pigs in a sty, see how
      they snied--IAMTHEWALR--23
    Wonder how you manage to make ends meet.--
      LADYMADONN--2
    See how they run.--LADYMADONN--8
    Wonders how you manage to feed the rest.--
      LADYMADONN--10
    See how they run.--LADYMADONN--11

    See how they run.--LADYMADONN--17
    Wonder how you manage to make ends meet.--
      LADYMADONN--19
    You don't know how lucky you are boys --BACKINTHEU
      --6
    You don't know how lucky you are boy --BACKINTHEU
      --13
    You don't know how lucky you are boys --BACKINTHEU
      --25
    You don't know how lucky you are boy--BACKINTHEU--36
    How I hate to see you go --DONTPASSME--21
    How I hate to see you go --DONTPASSME--34
    How I hate to see you go --DONTPASSME--40
    To see how the other half live--GLASSONION--6
    ... Ah (how was that?)--HELTERSKEL--31
    Who knows how long I've loved you?--IWILL--1
    How could I ever have lost you,--LONGLONGLO--2
    How I love you.--LONGLONGLO--6
    How can I ever misplace you?--LONGLONGLO--10
    How I want you.--LONGLONGLO--11
    La-la how the life goes on --OBLADIOBLA--6
    La-la how the life goes on.--OBLADIOBLA--8
    La-la how the life goes on --OBLADIOBLA--14
    La-la how the life goes on - yeah.--OBLADIOBLA--16
    La-la how the life goes on (he he he)--OBLADIOBLA--26
    La-la how the life goes on.--OBLADIOBLA--28
    La-la how the life goes on - yeah --OBLADIOBLA--37
    La-la how the life goes on (ha ha ha ha ha ha).--
      OBLADIOBLA--39
    You're gonna know and how.--SAVOYTRUFF--13
    Sexy Sadie how did you know--SEXYSADIE--12
    Sexy Sadie - oh how did you know?--SEXYSADIE--15
    I don't know why nobody told you how to unfold
      your love --WHILEMYGUI--6
    I don't know how someone controlled you --
      WHILEMYGUI--7
    I don't know how you were diverted --WHILEMYGUI--14
    I don't know how you were inverted--WHILEMYGUI--16
    Or how I fare or if my hair is brown--ONLYANORTH--11
    You know how hard it can be --BALLADOFJO--6
    You know how hard it can be --BALLADOFJO--14
    You know how hard it can be --BALLADOFJO--22
    You know how hard it can be --BALLADOFJO--34
    You know how hard it can be.--BALLADOFJO--42
    You know I believe 'n' how.--SOMETHING--5
    You know I believe 'n' how.--SOMETHING--10
    You know I believe 'n' how.--SOMETHING--19
    How about that?--YOUKNOWMYN--47
    Wondering really how come nobody told me--
      IVEGOTAFEE--12

HOW'S

    Nothing to say but what a day how's your boy been?
      --GOODMORNIN--3

HOWEVER

    However big you think you are--SEXYSADIE--17
    However big you think you are--SEXYSADIE--18
    ... However big you think you are.--SEXYSADIE--28

HU

    Ooo - hu, everybody had a good year ((I've got
      a feeling)) --IVEGOTAFEE--28

HUG

    I don't need to hug or hold you tight--IMHAPPYJUS--8

HUH

    Huh - huh - huh - huh--DAYINTHELI--22
    Huh - huh - huh - huh--DAYINTHELI--22
    Huh - huh - huh - huh--DAYINTHELI--22
    Huh - huh - huh - huh--DAYINTHELI--22

HUNG

    I feel hung up and I don't know why--IWANTTOTEL--13
    I feel hung up and I don't know why--IWANTTOTEL--20

HUNGABOUT

    And nothing to get hungabout--STRAWBERRY--4
    And nothing to get hungabout--STRAWBERRY--14
    And nothing to get hungabout--STRAWBERRY--24
    And nothing to get hungabout--STRAWBERRY--34

HUNTING

    He went out tiger hunting with his elephant and
      gun --CONTINUING--7

HURRY

Hurry up John--IMDOWN--24
Take your time, don't hurry --NOWHEREMAN--14
She takes her time and doesn't feel she has to
hurry --FORNOONE--5

HURT

She said you hurt her so--SHELOVESYO--12
Pride can hurt you too--SHELOVESYO--26
You hurt me then you're back again --NOTASECOND--9
You hurt me then you're back again --NOTASECOND--20
Oh please, don't hurt my pride like her.--IFIFELL
--13
That's when it hurt me--INEEDYOU--13
That's when it hurt me--INEEDYOU--23
You'll never know it hurt me so --DONTPASSME--20
You'll never know it hurt me so --DONTPASSME--33
You'll never know it hurt me so --DONTPASSME--39

HURTING

You're not the hurting kind.--SHELOVESYO--15

HUSBAND

She breaks down and cries to her husband--
SHESLEAVIN--16

I

You know I love you.--LOVEMEDO--2
You know I love you.--LOVEMEDO--7
You know I love you.--LOVEMEDO--14
You know I love you.--LOVEMEDO--19
PS I LOVE YOU.--PSILOVEYOU--Title
As I write this letter, send my love to you --
PSILOVEYOU--1
PS I love you, you, you, you.--PSILOVEYOU--6
And till ((till)) the day I do love ((do love))
--PSILOVEYOU--8
PS I love you, you, you, you.--PSILOVEYOU--9
As I write this letter, send my love to you --
PSILOVEYOU--10
PS I love you, you, you, you.--PSILOVEYOU--15
As I write this letter (oh) send my love to you --
PSILOVEYOU--16
You know I want you to --PSILOVEYOU--17
And till the day I do love --PSILOVEYOU--20
PS I love you, you, you, you --PSILOVEYOU--21
I love you.--PSILOVEYOU--23
There is nothing I won't do --ANYTIMEATA--15
I hope it will be mine --ANYTIMEATA--17
I love you --ASKMEWHY--1
'cos you tell me things I want to know --ASKMEWHY
--2
That I know,--ASKMEWHY--5
That I - I - I - I should never, never,
never be blue.--ASKMEWHY--6
That I - I - I - I should never, never,
never be blue.--ASKMEWHY--6
That I - I - I - I should never, never,
never be blue.--ASKMEWHY--6
That I - I - I - I should never, never,
never be blue.--ASKMEWHY--6
If I cry it's not because I'm sad --ASKMEWHY--10
I can't believe it's happened to me --ASKMEWHY--12
I can't conceive of any more misery.--ASKMEWHY--13
Ask me why, I'll say I love you --ASKMEWHY--14
I love you --ASKMEWHY--16
'cos you tell me things I want to know --ASKMEWHY
--17
That I know --ASKMEWHY--20
That I - I - I - I should never, never,
never be blue.--ASKMEWHY--21
That I - I - I - I should never, never,
never be blue.--ASKMEWHY--21
That I - I - I - I should never, never,
never be blue.--ASKMEWHY--21
That I - I - I - I should never, never,
never be blue.--ASKMEWHY--21
Ask me why, I'll say I love you --ASKMEWHY--22
I can't believe it's happened to me --ASKMEWHY--24
I can't conceive of any more misery.--ASKMEWHY--25
Ask me why, I'll say I love you--ASKMEWHY--26
Last night I said these words to my girl --
PLEASEPLEA--1
I know you never even try girl --PLEASEPLEA--2
Like I please you.--PLEASEPLEA--6
Why do I always have to say love --PLEASEPLEA--8
Like I please you.--PLEASEPLEA--12
I don't want to start complaining --PLEASEPLEA--13
I do all the pleasing with you --PLEASEPLEA--16
Last night I said these words to my girl --

PLEASEPLEA--19
I know/Why do you never even try girl--PLEASEPLEA--20
Like I please you.--PLEASEPLEA--24
Like I please you--PLEASEPLEA--26
Like I please you.--PLEASEPLEA--28
You'll never know how much I really love you --
DOYOUWANTT--1
You'll never know how much I really care.--
DOYOUWANTT--2
I SAW HER STANDING THERE.--ISAWHERSTA--Title
You know what I mean --ISAWHERSTA--3
So how could I dance with another --ISAWHERSTA--5
Ooh when I saw her standing there.--ISAWHERSTA--6
Well she looked at me, and I, I could see --
ISAWHERSTA--7
Well she looked at me, and I, I could see --
ISAWHERSTA--7
Whoa when I saw her standing there.--ISAWHERSTA--10
Well my heart went boom when I crossed that room
--ISAWHERSTA--11
And I held her hand in mine.--ISAWHERSTA--12
And before too long I fell in love with her--
ISAWHERSTA--15
Whoa since/when I saw her standing there. (hey! aah!)
--ISAWHERSTA--17
Well my heart went boom when I crossed that room
--ISAWHERSTA--18
And I held her hand in mine.--ISAWHERSTA--19
And before too long I fell in love with her.--
ISAWHERSTA--22
Oh since I saw her standing there.--ISAWHERSTA--24
Whoa since I saw her standing there--ISAWHERSTA--25
Yeah, well since I saw her standing there.--
ISAWHERSTA--26
I've lost her now for sure, I won't see her no
more --MISERY--4
Without her I will be in misery.--MISERY--9
Without her I will be in misery.--MISERY--13
If there's anything I can do--FROMMETOYO--4
I got everything that you want--FROMMETOYO--7
I got arms that long to hold you--FROMMETOYO--11
I got lips that long to kiss you--FROMMETOYO--13
If there's anything I can do--FROMMETOYO--16
I got arms that long to hold you--FROMMETOYO--22
I got lips that long to kiss you--FROMMETOYO--24
If there's anything I can do--FROMMETOYO--27
You made me glad when I was blue--THANKYOUGI--2
And all I gotta do is thank you girl, thank you
girl.--THANKYOUGI--4
I could tell the world a thing or two about our love
--THANKYOUGI--5
I know, little girl, only a fool would doubt
our love--THANKYOUGI--6
And all I gotta do is thank you girl, thank you
girl--THANKYOUGI--7
And all I gotta do is thank you girl, thank you
girl.--THANKYOUGI--10
You made me glad when I was blue--THANKYOUGI--12
And all I gotta do is thank you girl, thank you
girl.--THANKYOUGI--14
It's easy 'cos I know--ILLGETYOU--3
Yes I will I'll get you in the end, oh yeah,
oh yeah.--ILLGETYOU--8
I think about you night and day--ILLGETYOU--9
I need you and it's true--ILLGETYOU--10
When I think about you, I can say--ILLGETYOU--11
When I think about you, I can say--ILLGETYOU--11
Yes I will, I'll get you in the end, oh yeah,
oh yeah.--ILLGETYOU--15
It's easy 'cos I know--ILLGETYOU--20
Yes I will, I'll get you in the end, oh yeah,
oh yeah--ILLGETYOU--25
Well I saw her yesterday--SHELOVESYO--5
I think it's only fair--SHELOVESYO--25
Whenever I want you around, yeah --ALLIVEGOTT--1
All I gotta do --ALLIVEGOTT--2
Yeah, that's all I gotta do.--ALLIVEGOTT--5
And when I, I wanna kiss you, yeah --ALLIVEGOTT--6
And when I, I wanna kiss you, yeah --ALLIVEGOTT--6
All I gotta do --ALLIVEGOTT--7
I'll be here, yes I will --ALLIVEGOTT--13
And when I, I wanna kiss you, yeah --ALLIVEGOTT--17
And when I, I wanna kiss you, yeah --ALLIVEGOTT--17
All I gotta do --ALLIVEGOTT--18
Yeah, that's all I gotta do.--ALLIVEGOTT--21
I'll be here, yes I will --ALLIVEGOTT--24
The lips I am missing --ALLMYLOVIN--8
All my lovin', I will send to you --ALLMYLOVIN--13
All my lovin', I will send to you --ALLMYLOVIN--21
All my lovin', I will send to you --ALLMYLOVIN--24
I want no one to talk to me--DONTBOTHER--2
I can't believe--DONTBOTHER--9
I know I'll never be the same--DONTBOTHER--15
If I don't get her back again--DONTBOTHER--16

Because I know she'll always be--DONTBOTHER--17
I know I'll never be the same--DONTBOTHER--30
If I don't get her back again--DONTBOTHER--31
Because I know she'll always be--DONTBOTHER--32
And then I might --HOLDMETIGH--4
And then I might --HOLDMETIGH--21
I WANNA BE YOUR MAN.--IWANNABEYO--Title
I wanna be your lover baby --IWANNABEYO--1
I wanna be your man.--IWANNABEYO--2
I wanna be your lover baby --IWANNABEYO--3
I wanna be your man.--IWANNABEYO--4
I wanna be your man--IWANNABEYO--9
I wanna be your man--IWANNABEYO--10
I wanna be your man--IWANNABEYO--11
I wanna be your man.--IWANNABEYO--12
I wanna be your man.--IWANNABEYO--16
I wanna be your lover baby --IWANNABEYO--17
I wanna be your man.--IWANNABEYO--18
I wanna be your lover baby --IWANNABEYO--19
I wanna be your man.--IWANNABEYO--20
I wanna be your man--IWANNABEYO--21
I wanna be your man--IWANNABEYO--22
I wanna be your man.--IWANNABEYO--23
I wanna be your man.--IWANNABEYO--24
I wanna be your lover baby,--IWANNABEYO--30
I wanna be your man.--IWANNABEYO--31
I wanna be your lover baby --IWANNABEYO--32
I wanna be your man.--IWANNABEYO--33
I wanna be your man--IWANNABEYO--38
I wanna be your man--IWANNABEYO--39
I wanna be your man--IWANNABEYO--40
I wanna be your man--IWANNABEYO--41
I wanna be your man (oh)--IWANNABEYO--43
I wanna be your man (come on!)--IWANNABEYO--44
I wanna be your man (wuh - wuh)--IWANNABEYO--45
I wanna be your man.--IWANNABEYO--46
Till I belong to you--ITWONTBELO--4
Here am I sitting all on my own--ITWONTBELO--6
Till I belong to you--ITWONTBELO--10
I'll be good like I know I should (yes,
   you're coming on home)--ITWONTBELO--13
I'll be good like I know I should (yes,
   you're coming on home)--ITWONTBELO--13
Till I belong to you--ITWONTBELO--20
I'll be good like I know I should (yes,
   you're coming on home)--ITWONTBELO--23
I'll be good like I know I should (yes,
   you're coming on home)--ITWONTBELO--23
So every day we'll be happy, I know--ITWONTBELO--25
Now I know that you won't leave me no more--
   ITWONTBELO--26
Till I belong to you - ooo.--ITWONTBELO--30
I see no use in wondering why --NOTASECOND--2
I see no reason to change mine --NOTASECOND--5
I see no use in wondering why --NOTASECOND--13
I see no reason to change mine --NOTASECOND--16
I WANT TO HOLD YOUR HAND.--IWANTTOHOL--Title
I think you'll understand--IWANTTOHOL--2
When I say that something--IWANTTOHOL--3
I wanna hold your hand--IWANTTOHOL--4
I wanna hold your hand--IWANTTOHOL--5
I wanna hold your hand.--IWANTTOHOL--6
I wanna hold your hand.--IWANTTOHOL--12
And when I touch you--IWANTTOHOL--13
I feel happy inside--IWANTTOHOL--14
I can't hide--IWANTTOHOL--17
I can't hide--IWANTTOHOL--18
I can't hide.--IWANTTOHOL--19
I think you'll understand--IWANTTOHOL--21
When I say that something--IWANTTOHOL--22
I wanna hold your hand--IWANTTOHOL--23
I wanna hold your hand--IWANTTOHOL--24
I wanna hold your hand--IWANTTOHOL--25
And when I touch you--IWANTTOHOL--26
I feel happy inside--IWANTTOHOL--27
I can't hide--IWANTTOHOL--30
I can't hide--IWANTTOHOL--31
I can't hide.--IWANTTOHOL--32
I think you'll understand--IWANTTOHOL--34
When I feel that something--IWANTTOHOL--35
I wanna hold your hand--IWANTTOHOL--36
I wanna hold your hand--IWANTTOHOL--37
I wanna hold your hand--IWANTTOHOL--38
I wanna hold your hand.--IWANTTOHOL--39
'cos I don't care too much for money --CANTBUYMEL
   --7
I may not have a lot to give --CANTBUYMEL--11
But what I got I'll give to you --CANTBUYMEL--12
I don't care too much for money --CANTBUYMEL--13
I don't care too much for money --CANTBUYMEL--21
I don't care too much for money --CANTBUYMEL--31
I got something to say--YOUCANTDOT--1
If I catch you talking--YOUCANTDOT--3
Because I told you before--YOUCANTDOT--7

I caught you talking to him--YOUCANTDOT--10
Do I have to tell you one more time--YOUCANTDOT--11
I think it's a sin?--YOUCANTDOT--12
I think I'll let you down (let you down)--
   YOUCANTDOT--13
Because I told you before--YOUCANTDOT--16
I can't help my feelings--YOUCANTDOT--25
I go outta my mind.--YOUCANTDOT--26
Because I told you before--YOUCANTDOT--30
I can't help my feelings--YOUCANTDOT--44
I go outta my mind.--YOUCANTDOT--45
Because I told you before--YOUCANTDOT--49
I CALL YOUR NAME.--ICALLYOURN--Title
I call your name, but you're not there --ICALLYOURN
   --1
Was I to blame for being unfair?--ICALLYOURN--2
Oh, I can't sleep at night since you've been
   gone --ICALLYOURN--3
I never weep at night, I can't go on.--ICALLYOURN
   --4
I never weep at night, I can't go on.--ICALLYOURN
   --4
Don't you know I can't take it?--ICALLYOURN--5
I don't know who can --ICALLYOURN--6
Oh, I can't sleep at night, but just the same --
   ICALLYOURN--9
I never weep at night, I call your name.--
   ICALLYOURN--10
I never weep at night, I call your name.--
   ICALLYOURN--10
Don't you know I can't take it?--ICALLYOURN--12
I don't know who can --ICALLYOURN--13
Oh, I can't sleep at night, but just the same --
   ICALLYOURN--16
I never weep at night, I call your name --
   ICALLYOURN--17
I never weep at night, I call your name --
   ICALLYOURN--17
I call your name, I call your name, (wuh) I
   call your name.--ICALLYOURN--18
I call your name, I call your name, (wuh) I
   call your name.--ICALLYOURN--18
I call your name, I call your name, (wuh) I
   call your name.--ICALLYOURN--18
There, there's a place where I can go--THERESAPLA
   --1
When I feel low, when I feel blue--THERESAPLA--2
When I feel low, when I feel blue--THERESAPLA--2
I think of you--THERESAPLA--5
Like I love only you.--THERESAPLA--8
There, there's a place where I can go--THERESAPLA
   --13
When I feel low, when I feel blue--THERESAPLA--14
When I feel low, when I feel blue--THERESAPLA--14
AND I LOVE HER.--ANDILOVEHE--Title
I give her all my love --ANDILOVEHE--1
That's all I do --ANDILOVEHE--2
I love her.--ANDILOVEHE--5
And I love her.--ANDILOVEHE--10
As long as I --ANDILOVEHE--13
I know this love of mine --ANDILOVEHE--17
And I love her.--ANDILOVEHE--19
I know this love of mine --ANDILOVEHE--22
And I love her --ANDILOVEHE--24
And I been working like a dog --HARDDAYSNI--2
I should be sleeping like a log --HARDDAYSNI--4
But when I get home to you --HARDDAYSNI--5
I find the things that you do --HARDDAYSNI--6
You know I work all day --HARDDAYSNI--8
So why on earth should I moan --HARDDAYSNI--12
'cos when I get you alone --HARDDAYSNI--13
You know I feel OK.--HARDDAYSNI--14
And I been working like a dog --HARDDAYSNI--18
I should be sleeping like a log --HARDDAYSNI--20
But when I get home to you --HARDDAYSNI--21
I find the things that you do --HARDDAYSNI--22
So why on earth should I moan --HARDDAYSNI--25
'cos when I get you alone --HARDDAYSNI--26
You know I feel OK.--HARDDAYSNI--27
And I been working like a dog --HARDDAYSNI--31
I should be sleeping like a log --HARDDAYSNI--33
But when I get home to you --HARDDAYSNI--34
I find the things that you do --HARDDAYSNI--35
You know I feel alright --HARDDAYSNI--37
You know I feel alright.--HARDDAYSNI--38
I SHOULD HAVE KNOWN BETTER.--ISHOULDHAV--Title
I should have known better with a girl like you --
   ISHOULDHAV--1
That I would love everything that you do --
   ISHOULDHAV--2
And I do, hey hey hey, and I do.--ISHOULDHAV--3
And I do, hey hey hey, and I do.--ISHOULDHAV--3
Whoa, whoa, I never realised what a kiss could
   be --ISHOULDHAV--4

That when I tell you that I love you, oh --
   ISHOULDHAV--7
That when I tell you that I love you, oh --
   ISHOULDHAV--7
And when I ask you to be mine --ISHOULDHAV--9
So - oh, I should have realised a lot of things
   before --ISHOULDHAV--11
Whoa, whoa, I never realised what a kiss could
   be --ISHOULDHAV--14
That when I tell you that I love you, oh --
   ISHOULDHAV--17
That when I tell you that I love you, oh --
   ISHOULDHAV--17
And when I ask you to be mine --ISHOULDHAV--19
IF I FELL.--IFIFELL--Title
If I fell in love with you --IFIFELL--1
And I found that love was more --IFIFELL--5
If I give my heart to you,--IFIFELL--7
I must be sure from the very start --IFIFELL--8
If I trust in you --IFIFELL--10
If I love you too --IFIFELL--12
'cos I couldn't stand the pain --IFIFELL--14
And I would be sad --IFIFELL--15
So I hope you see --IFIFELL--17
That I would love to love you --IFIFELL--18
'cos I couldn't stand the pain --IFIFELL--21
And I would be sad --IFIFELL--22
So I hope you see --IFIFELL--24
That I would love to love you --IFIFELL--25
If I fell in love with you.--IFIFELL--28
I got every reason on earth to be mad --ILLCRYINST
   --1
'cos I've just lost the only girl I had.--
   ILLCRYINST--2
If I could get my way --ILLCRYINST--3
But I can't, so I'll cry instead.--ILLCRYINST--5
I got a chip on my shoulder that's bigger than my
   feet.--ILLCRYINST--6
I can't talk to people that I meet.--ILLCRYINST--7
I can't talk to people that I meet.--ILLCRYINST--7
If I could see you now --ILLCRYINST--8
But I can't, so I'll cry instead.--ILLCRYINST--10
I get shy when they start to stare.--ILLCRYINST--12
And when I do you'd better hide all the girls --
   ILLCRYINST--15
I get shy when they start to stare.--ILLCRYINST--21
And when I do you'd better hide all the girls --
   ILLCRYINST--24
I think I'll love you too --IMHAPPYJUS--2
I don't wanna kiss or hold your hand --IMHAPPYJUS
   --4
I don't need to hug or hold you tight --IMHAPPYJUS
   --8
I just wanna dance with you all night --IMHAPPYJUS
   --9
In this world there's nothing I would rather do --
   IMHAPPYJUS--10
Just to dance with you is everything I need (oh)
   --IMHAPPYJUS--12
I think I'll love you too ((oh)) --IMHAPPYJUS--14
In this world there's nothing I would rather do --
   IMHAPPYJUS--18
Just to dance with you (oh) is everything I
   need (oh) --IMHAPPYJUS--20
I think I'll love you too ((oh)) --IMHAPPYJUS--22
In this world there's nothing I would rather do --
   IMHAPPYJUS--26
Well I gave you everything I had --TELLMEWHY--5
Well I gave you everything I had --TELLMEWHY--5
All I do is hang my head and moan.--TELLMEWHY--8
If it's something that I said or done --TELLMEWHY
   --13
If you don't I really can't go on --TELLMEWHY--15
Well I beg you on my bended knees --TELLMEWHY--21
If there's anything I can do --TELLMEWHY--23
'cos I really can't stand it --TELLMEWHY--24
'cos I told you once before goodbye--ILLBEBACK
   --3
But I Came back again.--ILLBEBACK--4
I love you so--ILLBEBACK--5
This time I will try to show--ILLBEBACK--11
I thought that you would realise--ILLBEBACK--13
That if I ran away from you--ILLBEBACK--14
But I got a big surprise--ILLBEBACK--16
This time I will try to show--ILLBEBACK--20
I wanna go--ILLBEBACK--22
But I hate to leave you--ILLBEBACK--23
You know I hate to leave you--ILLBEBACK--24
You say you will love me if I have to go --
   THINGSWESA--1
You'll be thinking of me, somehow I will know --
   THINGSWESA--2
Then I will remember things we said today.--
   THINGSWESA--5

WHEN I GET HOME.--WHENIGETHO--Title
I got a whole lot of things to tell her --
   WHENIGETHO--2
When I get home.--WHENIGETHO--3
I got a whole lot of things I gotta say to her.--
   WHENIGETHO--6
I got a whole lot of things I gotta say to her.--
   WHENIGETHO--6
I got a whole lot of things to tell her --
   WHENIGETHO--8
When I get home.--WHENIGETHO--9
I got no time for triviality --WHENIGETHO--11
I got a girl who's waiting home for me tonight.--
   WHENIGETHO--12
I got a whole lot of things to tell her --
   WHENIGETHO--14
When I get home.--WHENIGETHO--15
When I getting home tonight --WHENIGETHO--16
I bet I'll love her more --WHENIGETHO--19
Till I walk out that door again.--WHENIGETHO--20
I got so many things I gotta do --WHENIGETHO--22
I got so many things I gotta do --WHENIGETHO--22
I got no business being here with you this way.--
   WHENIGETHO--23
I got a whole lot of things to tell her --
   WHENIGETHO--25
When I get home, yeah.--WHENIGETHO--26
I got a whole lot of things to tell her --
   WHENIGETHO--27
When I get home.--WHENIGETHO--28
I FEEL FINE.--IFEELFINE--Title
I'm in love with her and I feel fine.--IFEELFINE
   --3
I'm in love with her and I feel fine.--IFEELFINE
   --6
She's in love with me and I feel fine (ooo).--
   IFEELFINE--11
I'm in love with her and I feel fine.--IFEELFINE
   --14
She's in love with me and I feel fine --IFEELFINE
   --19
She's in love with me and I feel fine.--IFEELFINE
   --20
I know that she's no peasant--SHESAWOMAN--2
Turn me on when I get lonely--SHESAWOMAN--5
I know she isn't--SHESAWOMAN--7
I will never leave her--SHESAWOMAN--11
I know that she's no peasant--SHESAWOMAN--19
Turn me on when I get lonely--SHESAWOMAN--22
I know she isn't--SHESAWOMAN--24
I know that she's no peasant--SHESAWOMAN--29
Turn me on when I get lonely--SHESAWOMAN--32
I know she isn't--SHESAWOMAN--34
Oh dear, what can I do?--BABYSINBLA--1
Tell me, oh what can I do?--BABYSINBLA--3
Oh dear, what can I do?--BABYSINBLA--7
Tell me, oh what can I do?--BABYSINBLA--9
I think of her --BABYSINBLA--10
Dear what can I do?--BABYSINBLA--16
Tell me oh what can I do?--BABYSINBLA--18
Dear what can I do?--BABYSINBLA--21
Tell me oh what can I do?--BABYSINBLA--23
Oh dear, what can I do?--BABYSINBLA--28
Tell me oh what can I do?--BABYSINBLA--29
Ooo I need your love babe --EIGHTDAYSA--1
Just like I need you.--EIGHTDAYSA--4
I ain't got nothing but love babe --EIGHTDAYSA--7
One thing I can say girl --EIGHTDAYSA--11
I ain't got nothing but love girl --EIGHTDAYSA--15
Eight days a week I love you --EIGHTDAYSA--17
Eight days a week is not enough to show I care.--
   EIGHTDAYSA--18
Ooo I need your love babe --EIGHTDAYSA--19
Just like I need you, oh - oh.--EIGHTDAYSA--22
I ain't got nothing but love babe --EIGHTDAYSA--25
Eight days a week I love you --EIGHTDAYSA--27
Eight days a week is not enough to show I care.--
   EIGHTDAYSA--28
One thing I can say girl --EIGHTDAYSA--31
I ain't got nothing but love babe --EIGHTDAYSA--35
Yes I know I'm a lucky guy.--EVERYLITTL--3
I remember the first time--EVERYLITTL--4
I was lonely without her--EVERYLITTL--9
Yes I know that she loves me now.--EVERYLITTL--13
I will love her forever--EVERYLITTL--15
For I know love will never die.--EVERYLITTL--16
I DON'T WANT TO SPOIL THE PARTY.--IDONTWANTT--Title
I don't wanna spoil the party so I'll go --
   IDONTWANTT--1
I would hate my disappointment to show --IDONTWANTT
   --2
There's nothing for me here so I will disappear --
   IDONTWANTT--3
I've had a drink or two and I don't care --

IDONTWANTT--5
There's no fun in what I do when she's not there
--IDONTWANTT--6
I wonder what went wrong I've waited far too long
--IDONTWANTT--7
I think I'll take a walk and look for her.--
IDONTWANTT--8
I still love her.--IDONTWANTT--10
If I find her I'll be glad --IDONTWANTT--11
I still love her.--IDONTWANTT--12
I don't wanna spoil the party so I'll go --
IDONTWANTT--13
I would hate my disappointment to show --IDONTWANTT
--14
There's nothing for me here so I will disappear --
IDONTWANTT--15
I still love her.--IDONTWANTT--19
If I find her I'll be glad --IDONTWANTT--20
I still love her.--IDONTWANTT--21
Though I've had a drink or two and I don't care --
IDONTWANTT--22
There's no fun in what I do if she's not there --
IDONTWANTT--23
I wonder what went wrong I've waited far too long
--IDONTWANTT--24
But I think I'll take a walk and look for her.--
IDONTWANTT--25
Some day you'll know I was the one --ILLFOLLOWT--3
And now the time has come and so my love I must
go --ILLFOLLOWT--5
And though I lose a friend in the end you will
know, oh.--ILLFOLLOWT--6
One day you'll find that I have gone --ILLFOLLOWT
--7
And now the time has come and so my love I must
go --ILLFOLLOWT--10
And though I lose a friend in the end you will
know, oh.--ILLFOLLOWT--11
One day you'll find that I have gone --ILLFOLLOWT
--12
And I'm not what I appear to be.--IMALOSER--2
Of all the love I have won or have lost --IMALOSER
--3
There is one love I should never have crossed.--
IMALOSER--4
I should have known she would win in the end.--
IMALOSER--6
I'm a loser and I lost someone who's near to me --
IMALOSER--7
I'm a loser and I'm not what I appear to be.--
IMALOSER--8
Although I laugh and I act like a clown --IMALOSER
--9
Although I laugh and I act like a clown --IMALOSER
--9
Beneath this mask I am wearing a frown.--IMALOSER
--10
Is it for her or myself that I cry?--IMALOSER--12
I'm a loser and I lost someone who's near to me --
IMALOSER--13
I'm a loser and I'm not what I appear to be.--
IMALOSER--14
What have I done to deserve such a fate?--IMALOSER
--15
I realise I have left it too late.--IMALOSER--16
I realise I have left it too late.--IMALOSER--16
I'm a loser and I lost someone who's near to me --
IMALOSER--19
I'm a loser and I'm not what I appear to be.--
IMALOSER--20
When I came to your door--NOREPLY--2
But I saw you peep through your window--NOREPLY--5
I saw the light, I saw the light.--NOREPLY--6
I saw the light, I saw the light.--NOREPLY--6
I know that you saw me--NOREPLY--7
'cos I looked up to see your face.--NOREPLY--8
I tried to telephone--NOREPLY--9
'cos I know where you've been--NOREPLY--12
I saw you walk in your door--NOREPLY--13
I nearly died, I nearly died.--NOREPLY--14
I nearly died, I nearly died.--NOREPLY--14
If I were you I'd realise that I--NOREPLY--17
If I were you I'd realise that I--NOREPLY--17
That I heard before--NOREPLY--20
I tried to telephone--NOREPLY--22
'cos I know where you've been--NOREPLY--25
I saw you walk in your door--NOREPLY--26
I nearly died, I nearly died.--NOREPLY--27
I nearly died, I nearly died.--NOREPLY--27
I think I'm gonna be sad--TICKETTORI--2
I think it's today, yeah--TICKETTORI--3
When I was around.--TICKETTORI--12
I don't know why she's riding so high--TICKETTORI
--17

I think I'm gonna be sad--TICKETTORI--23
I think it's today, yeah--TICKETTORI--24
I don't know why she's riding so high--TICKETTORI
--30
When I was around.--TICKETTORI--39
Remember what I said tonight--YESITIS--2
I would remember all the things we planned--YESITIS
--7
I could be happy with you by my side--YESITIS--10
If I could forget her--YESITIS--11
This is what I said tonight--YESITIS--15
I could be happy with you by my side--YESITIS--19
If I could forget her--YESITIS--20
This is what I said tonight--YESITIS--24
I will prove to you--TELLMEWHAT--2
How can I get through--TELLMEWHAT--19
How can I get through--TELLMEWHAT--28
If I just don't treat you right--YOULIKEMET--4
'cos you like me too much and I like you--
YOULIKEMET--6
Which is all that I deserve--YOULIKEMET--10
'cos you like me too much and I like you--
YOULIKEMET--12
I really do.--YOULIKEMET--13
If you leave me I will follow you--YOULIKEMET--15
'cos I couldn't really stand it--YOULIKEMET--17
I'd admit that I was wrong--YOULIKEMET--18
I wouldn't let you leave me 'cos it's true--
YOULIKEMET--19
'cos you like me too much and I like you--
YOULIKEMET--20
'cos you like me too much and I like you--
YOULIKEMET--21
I really do--YOULIKEMET--22
If you leave me I will follow you--YOULIKEMET--24
'cos I couldn't really stand it--YOULIKEMET--26
I'd admit that I was wrong--YOULIKEMET--27
I wouldn't let you leave me 'cos it's true--
YOULIKEMET--28
'cos you like me too much and I like you--
YOULIKEMET--29
'cos you like me too much and I like you.--
YOULIKEMET--30
I need somebody--HELP--2
You know I need someone--HELP--6
When ((when)) I was younger ((when I was
young))--HELP--8
When ((when)) I was younger ((when I was
young))--HELP--8
I never needed ((never needed)) anybody's help
in any way--HELP--10
Now I find ((and now I find)) I've changed
my mind--HELP--13
Now I find ((and now I find)) I've changed
my mind--HELP--13
And I do appreciate you being round--HELP--16
But ((but)) every now and then ((now and then))
I feel so insecure--HELP--22
I know that I ((I know that I)) just need
you like--HELP--23
I know that I ((I know that I)) just need
you like--HELP--23
I know that I ((I know that I)) just need
you like--HELP--23
I know that I ((I know that I)) just need
you like--HELP--23
And I do appreciate you being round--HELP--26
When I was younger, so much younger than today--
HELP--29
I never needed anybody's help in any way--HELP--30
Now I find ((and now I find)) I've changed
my mind--HELP--33
Now I find ((and now I find)) I've changed
my mind--HELP--33
And I do appreciate you being round--HELP--36
You tell lies thinking I can't see --IMDOWN--1
For I have got another girl, another girl.--
ANOTHERGIR--1
I ain't no fool and I don't take what I don't
want --ANOTHERGIR--4
I ain't no fool and I don't take what I don't
want --ANOTHERGIR--4
I ain't no fool and I don't take what I don't
want --ANOTHERGIR--4
For I have got another girl, another girl.--
ANOTHERGIR--5
She's sweeter than all the girls and I met quite
a few --ANOTHERGIR--6
For I have got another girl,--ANOTHERGIR--9
I don't wanna say that I've been unhappy with you
--ANOTHERGIR--12
I ain't no fool and I don't take what I don't
want --ANOTHERGIR--14
I ain't no fool and I don't take what I don't

want --ANOTHERGIR--14
I ain't no fool and I don't take what I don't
    want --ANOTHERGIR--14
For I have got another girl --ANOTHERGIR--15
I don't wanna say that I've been unhappy with you
    --ANOTHERGIR--18
I ain't no fool and I don't take what I don't
    want --ANOTHERGIR--20
I ain't no fool and I don't take what I don't
    want --ANOTHERGIR--20
I ain't no fool and I don't take what I don't
    want --ANOTHERGIR--20
For I have got another girl, another girl,
    another girl.--ANOTHERGIR--21
I NEED YOU.--INEEDYOU--Title
You don't realise how much I need you--INEEDYOU--1
I need you.--INEEDYOU--5
How was I to know you would upset me?--INEEDYOU--7
I didn't realise--INEEDYOU--8
As I looked in your eyes--INEEDYOU--9
I just can't go on any more.--INEEDYOU--15
Please remember how I feel about you--INEEDYOU--16
I could never really live without you--INEEDYOU--17
I need you.--INEEDYOU--20
I just can't go on any more.--INEEDYOU--25
Please remember how I feel about you.--INEEDYOU--26
I could never really live without you--INEEDYOU--27
I need you--INEEDYOU--30
I need you--INEEDYOU--31
I need you.--INEEDYOU--32
I get high when I see you go by, my oh my--
    ITSONLYLOV--1
I get high when I see you go by, my oh my--
    ITSONLYLOV--1
Why am I so shy when I'm beside you?--ITSONLYLOV
    --3
Why should I feel the way I do?--ITSONLYLOV--5
Why should I feel the way I do?--ITSONLYLOV--5
Is it right that you and I should fight, every
    night--ITSONLYLOV--8
Haven't I the right to make it up girl?--ITSONLYLOV
    --10
Why should I feel the way I do?--ITSONLYLOV--12
Why should I feel the way I do?--ITSONLYLOV--12
I can't forget the time or place--IVEJUSTSEE--2
And I want all the world to see we've met --
    IVEJUSTSEE--5
I might have looked the other way--IVEJUSTSEE--8
Falling, yes I am falling--IVEJUSTSEE--11
I have never known the like of this--IVEJUSTSEE--14
I've been alone and I have missed things--
    IVEJUSTSEE--15
Falling, yes I am falling--IVEJUSTSEE--19
Falling, yes I am falling--IVEJUSTSEE--22
I can't forget the time or place--IVEJUSTSEE--25
And I want all the world to see we've met --
    IVEJUSTSEE--28
Falling, yes I am falling--IVEJUSTSEE--30
Falling, yes I am falling--IVEJUSTSEE--32
(Oh) falling, yes I am falling--IVEJUSTSEE--34
Now today I find, you have changed your mind--
    NIGHTBEFOR--3
Was I so unwise? (aah the night before)--NIGHTBEFOR
    --6
When I held you near, you were so sincere--
    NIGHTBEFOR--7
Last night is the night I will remember you by --
    NIGHTBEFOR--9
When I think of things we did it makes me wanna
    cry.--NIGHTBEFOR--10
Now today I find you have changed your mind--
    NIGHTBEFOR--13
When I held you near, you were so sincere --
    NIGHTBEFOR--15
Last night is the night I will remember you by --
    NIGHTBEFOR--17
When I think of things we did it makes me wanna
    cry.--NIGHTBEFOR--18
Was I so unwise? (aah the night before)--NIGHTBEFOR
    --20
When I held you near, you were so sincere --
    NIGHTBEFOR--21
Oh I believe in yesterday.--YESTERDAY--4
I'm not half the man I used to be--YESTERDAY--6
Why she had to go, I don't know--YESTERDAY--9
I said something wrong--YESTERDAY--11
Now I long for yesterday.--YESTERDAY--12
Now I need a place to hide away--YESTERDAY--15
Oh I believe in yesterday.--YESTERDAY--16
Why she had to go, I don't know--YESTERDAY--17
I said something wrong--YESTERDAY--19
Now I long for yesterday.--YESTERDAY--20
Now I need a place to hide away--YESTERDAY--23
Oh I believe in yesterday.--YESTERDAY--24

And I will take her out tonight--YOUREGONNA--5
And I will treat her kind (I'm gonna treat her
    kind)--YOUREGONNA--6
'cos I will treat her right--YOUREGONNA--11
The way you treat her what else can I do?--
    YOUREGONNA--17
The way you treat her what else can I do?--
    YOUREGONNA--24
And I will take her out tonight--YOUREGONNA--27
And I will treat her kind (I'm gonna treat her
    kind)--YOUREGONNA--28
Here I stand head in hand--YOUVEGOTTO--1
If she's gone I can't go on --YOUVEGOTTO--3
I can see them laugh at me --YOUVEGOTTO--7
And I hear them say.--YOUVEGOTTO--8
How can I even try --YOUVEGOTTO--11
I can never win --YOUVEGOTTO--12
And I found out.--DAYTRIPPER--8
And I found out.--DAYTRIPPER--16
And I found out.--DAYTRIPPER--25
Do I have to keep on talking till I can't go on?--
    WECANWORKI--2
Do I have to keep on talking till I can't go on?--
    WECANWORKI--2
I have always thought that it's a crime--WECANWORKI
    --13
So I will ask you once again.--WECANWORKI--14
Only time will tell if I am right or I am wrong.--
    WECANWORKI--16
Only time will tell if I am right or I am wrong.--
    WECANWORKI--16
I have always thought that it's a crime--WECANWORKI
    --22
So I will ask you once again.--WECANWORKI--23
Only time will tell if I am right or I am wrong.--
    WECANWORKI--25
Only time will tell if I am right or I am wrong.--
    WECANWORKI--25
I wanna be famous, a star of the screen --
    DRIVEMYCAR--3
I told that girl that my prospects were good --
    DRIVEMYCAR--9
But I can show you a better time.--DRIVEMYCAR--12
I told that girl I could start right away --
    DRIVEMYCAR--22
I told that girl I could start right away --
    DRIVEMYCAR--22
I got no car and it's breaking my heart --
    DRIVEMYCAR--24
When I think of all the times I tried so hard
    to leave her --GIRL--6
When I think of all the times I tried so hard
    to leave her --GIRL--6
And she promises the earth to me and I believe
    her --GIRL--8
After all this time I don't know why.--GIRL--9
IF I NEEDED SOMEONE.--IFINEEDS--Title
If I needed someone to love --IFINEEDS--1
If I needed someone.--IFINEEDS--3
If I had some more time to spend --IFINEEDS--4
Then I guess I'd be with you my friend --IFINEEDS
    --5
If I needed someone.--IFINEEDS--6
If I needed someone.--IFINEEDS--12
If I had some more time to spend --IFINEEDS--14
Then I guess I'd be with you my friend --IFINEEDS
    --15
If I needed someone.--IFINEEDS--16
If I needed someone.--IFINEEDS--22
I thought I knew you, what did I know?--IMLOOKINGT
    --2
I thought I knew you, what did I know?--IMLOOKINGT
    --2
I thought I knew you, what did I know?--IMLOOKINGT
    --2
Your lips are moving, I cannot hear --IMLOOKINGT
    --5
I thought I knew you, what did I know?--IMLOOKINGT
    --18
I thought I knew you, what did I know?--IMLOOKINGT
    --18
I thought I knew you, what did I know?--IMLOOKINGT
    --18
There are places I remember --INMYLIFE--1
With lovers and friends I still can recall --
    INMYLIFE--6
When I think of love as something new.--INMYLIFE
    --12
Though I know I'll never lose affection --INMYLIFE
    --13
I know I'll often stop and think about them --
    INMYLIFE--15
In my life I love you more.--INMYLIFE--16
Though I know I'll never lose affection --INMYLIFE

--17
I know I'll often stop and think about them --
    INMYLIFE--19
In my life I love you more.--INMYLIFE--20
In my life I love you more.--INMYLIFE--21
I love you, I love you, I love you--MICHELLE--5
I love you, I love you, I love you--MICHELLE--5
I love you, I love you, I love you--MICHELLE--5
That's all I want to say--MICHELLE--6
Until I find a way--MICHELLE--7
I will say the only words I know that you'll
    understand.--MICHELLE--8
I will say the only words I know that you'll
    understand.--MICHELLE--8
I need to, I need to, I need to--MICHELLE--11
I need to, I need to, I need to--MICHELLE--11
I need to, I need to, I need to--MICHELLE--11
I need to make you see--MICHELLE--12
Until I do I'm hoping you will know what I mean.--
    MICHELLE--14
Until I do I'm hoping you will know what I mean.--
    MICHELLE--14
I love you.--MICHELLE--15
I want you, I want you, I want you--MICHELLE--16
I want you, I want you, I want you--MICHELLE--16
I want you, I want you, I want you--MICHELLE--16
I think you know by now--MICHELLE--17
Until I do I'm telling you so you'll understand.--
    MICHELLE--19
And I will say the only words I know that
    you'll understand --MICHELLE--22
And I will say the only words I know that
    you'll understand --MICHELLE--22
I once had a girl--NORWEGIANW--1
Or should I say--NORWEGIANW--2
So I looked around--NORWEGIANW--9
And I noticed there wasn't a chair.--NORWEGIANW--10
I sat on a rug--NORWEGIANW--11
I told her I didn't--NORWEGIANW--19
I told her I didn't--NORWEGIANW--19
And when I awoke--NORWEGIANW--21
I was alone--NORWEGIANW--22
So I lit a fire--NORWEGIANW--24
Or I won't know where I am.--RUNFORYOUR--4
Or I won't know where I am.--RUNFORYOUR--4
And I was born with a jealous mind--RUNFORYOUR--10
And I can't spend my whole life trying--RUNFORYOUR
    --11
I mean everything I've said.--RUNFORYOUR--18
Or you won't know where I am.--RUNFORYOUR--28
'cos I won't be there with you.--THINKFORYO--9
I left you far behind--THINKFORYO--10
I know your mind's made up,--THINKFORYO--13
'cos I won't be there with you.--THINKFORYO--18
'cos I won't be there with you.--THINKFORYO--27
'cos I won't be there with you.--THINKFORYO--31
'cos I won't be there with you.--THINKFORYO--33
Wait till I come back to your side --WAIT--3
And if your heart's strong, hold on, I won't
    delay.--WAIT--5
Wait till I come back to your side --WAIT--7
I feel as though you ought to know--WAIT--9
That I've been good, as good as I can be.--WAIT--10
Wait till I come back to your side --WAIT--15
I feel as though you ought to know--WAIT--17
That I've been good, as good as I can be.--WAIT--18
And if your heart's strong, hold on, I won't
    delay.--WAIT--22
Wait till I come back to your side --WAIT--23
The other day I saw you as I walked along the
    road --WHATGOESON--6
The other day I saw you as I walked along the
    road --WHATGOESON--6
But when I saw him with you I could feel my
    future fold.--WHATGOESON--7
But when I saw him with you I could feel my
    future fold.--WHATGOESON--7
I met you in the morning waiting for the tides of
    time --WHATGOESON--15
But now the tide is turning I can see that I
    was blind.--WHATGOESON--16
But now the tide is turning I can see that I
    was blind.--WHATGOESON--16
I used to think of no-one else but you were just
    the same --WHATGOESON--22
In the beginning I misunderstood --THEWORD--7
Everywhere I go I hear it said --THEWORD--15
Everywhere I go I hear it said --THEWORD--15
In the good and the bad books that I have read.--
    THEWORD--16
Now that I know what I feel must be right --THEWORD
    --23
Now that I know what I feel must be right --THEWORD
    --23

When I call you up your line's engaged.--YOUWONTSEE
    --1
I have had enough, so act your age.--YOUWONTSEE--2
And I will lose my mind--YOUWONTSEE--4
I don't know why you should want to hide --
    YOUWONTSEE--7
But I can't get through, my hands are tied.--
    YOUWONTSEE--8
I won't want to stay, I don't have much to say --
    YOUWONTSEE--9
I won't want to stay, I don't have much to say --
    YOUWONTSEE--9
But I can turn away--YOUWONTSEE--10
I wouldn't mind if I knew what I was missing.--
    YOUWONTSEE--14
I wouldn't mind if I knew what I was missing.--
    YOUWONTSEE--14
I wouldn't mind if I knew what I was missing.--
    YOUWONTSEE--14
((No I wouldn't, no I wouldn't))--YOUWONTSEE--15
((No I wouldn't, no I wouldn't))--YOUWONTSEE--15
And since I lost you it feels like years.--
    YOUWONTSEE--17
And I just can't go on--YOUWONTSEE--19
I wouldn't mind if I knew what I was missing.--
    YOUWONTSEE--23
I wouldn't mind if I knew what I was missing.--
    YOUWONTSEE--23
I wouldn't mind if I knew what I was missing.--
    YOUWONTSEE--23
((No I wouldn't, no I wouldn't))--YOUWONTSEE--24
((No I wouldn't, no I wouldn't))--YOUWONTSEE--24
And since I lost you it feels like years.--
    YOUWONTSEE--26
And I just can't go on--YOUWONTSEE--28
And I need a job --PAPERBACKW--5
So I want to be a paperback writer --PAPERBACKW--6
I can make it longer if you like the style,
    ((paperback))--PAPERBACKW--17
I can change it round, ((writer))--PAPERBACKW--18
And I want to be a paperback writer --PAPERBACKW
    --19
But I need a break, ((writer))--PAPERBACKW--24
And I want to be a paperback writer --PAPERBACKW
    --25
Rain I don't mind--RAIN--7
I can show you that when it starts to rain (when
    the rain comes down)--RAIN--9
I can show you, I can show you ((show you)).--RAIN
    --11
I can show you, I can show you ((show you)).--RAIN
    --11
Rain I don't mind--RAIN--12
Ring my friend I said you'd call, Dr. Robert --
    DRROBERT--1
Ring my friend I said you'd call, Dr. Robert --
    DRROBERT--20
Ring my friend I said you'd call, Dr. Robert --
    DRROBERT--21
When I wake up early in the morning --IMONLYSLEE
    --1
Leave me where I am, I'm only sleeping.--IMONLYSLEE
    --6
I don't mind, I think they're crazy --IMONLYSLEE
    --8
I don't mind, I think they're crazy --IMONLYSLEE
    --8
When I wake up early in the morning --IMONLYSLEE
    --21
Leave me where I am, I'm only sleeping.--IMONLYSLEE
    --26
I need to laugh and when the sun is out --
    GOODDAYSUN--2
I've got something I can laugh about.--GOODDAYSUN
    --3
I feel good in a special way --GOODDAYSUN--4
I love her and she's loving me.--GOODDAYSUN--11
I was alone, I took a ride--GOTTOGETYO--1
I was alone, I took a ride--GOTTOGETYO--1
I didn't know what I would find there--GOTTOGETYO
    --2
I didn't know what I would find there--GOTTOGETYO
    --2
Another road where maybe I--GOTTOGETYO--3
Ooo then I suddenly see you--GOTTOGETYO--5
Ooo did I tell you I need you--GOTTOGETYO--6
Ooo did I tell you I need you--GOTTOGETYO--6
You knew I wanted just to hold you--GOTTOGETYO--9
We'd meet again for I had told you.--GOTTOGETYO--11
Ooo and I want you to hear me--GOTTOGETYO--13
What can I do, what can I be?--GOTTOGETYO--16
What can I do, what can I be?--GOTTOGETYO--16
When I'm with you I want to stay there--GOTTOGETYO
    --17

And if I do I know the way there.--GOTTOGETYO--19
And if I do I know the way there.--GOTTOGETYO--19
Ooo then I suddenly see you--GOTTOGETYO--20
Ooo did I tell you I need you--GOTTOGETYO--21
Ooo did I tell you I need you--GOTTOGETYO--21
I got to get you into my life.--GOTTOGETYO--24
I was alone, I took a ride--GOTTOGETYO--25
I was alone, I took a ride--GOTTOGETYO--25
I didn't know what I would find there--GOTTOGETYO
--26
I didn't know what I would find there--GOTTOGETYO
--26
Another road where maybe I--GOTTOGETYO--27
Then suddenly I see you--GOTTOGETYO--29
Did I tell you I need you--GOTTOGETYO--30
Did I tell you I need you--GOTTOGETYO--30
To lead a better life, I need my love to be here.
--HERETHEREA--1
I want her everywhere--HERETHEREA--8
And if she's beside me I know I need never care--
HERETHEREA--9
And if she's beside me I know I need never care--
HERETHEREA--9
I want her everywhere--HERETHEREA--14
And if she's beside me I know I need never care--
HERETHEREA--15
And if she's beside me I know I need never care--
HERETHEREA--15
I will be there and everywhere --HERETHEREA--20
I WANT TO TELL YOU.--IWANTTOTEL--Title
I want to tell you--IWANTTOTEL--1
When I get near you--IWANTTOTEL--5
But if I seem to act unkind--IWANTTOTEL--9
I want to tell you--IWANTTOTEL--12
I feel hung up and I don't know why --IWANTTOTEL
--13
I feel hung up and I don't know why --IWANTTOTEL
--13
I don't mind, I could wait forever--IWANTTOTEL--14
I don't mind, I could wait forever--IWANTTOTEL--14
Sometimes I wish I knew you well--IWANTTOTEL--16
Sometimes I wish I knew you well--IWANTTOTEL--16
Then I could speak my mind and tell you--IWANTTOTEL
--17
I want to tell you--IWANTTOTEL--19
I feel hung up and I don't know why --IWANTTOTEL
--20
I feel hung up and I don't know why --IWANTTOTEL
--20
I don't mind, I could wait forever--IWANTTOTEL--21
I don't mind, I could wait forever--IWANTTOTEL--21
I turn around, it's past--ILOVEYOUTWO--2
She said I know what it's like to be dead --
SHESAIDSHE--1
I know what it is to be sad--SHESAIDSHE--2
I said who put all those things in your head?--
SHESAIDSHE--4
She said you don't understand what I said.--
SHESAIDSHE--7
I said no, no, no you're wrong.--SHESAIDSHE--8
When I was a boy everything was right,
everything was right.--SHESAIDSHE--9
I said even though you know what you know --
SHESAIDSHE--10
I know that I'm ready to leave --SHESAIDSHE--11
She said you don't understand what I said.--
SHESAIDSHE--13
I said no, no, no you're wrong.--SHESAIDSHE--14
When I was a boy everything was right,
everything was right.--SHESAIDSHE--15
I said even though you know what you know --
SHESAIDSHE--16
I know that I'm ready to leave --SHESAIDSHE--17
I know what it's like to be dead (I know what
it's like to be dead) --SHESAIDSHE--20
I know what it's like to be dead (I know what
it's like to be dead) --SHESAIDSHE--20
I know what it is to be sad (I know what it is
to be sad).--SHESAIDSHE--21
I know what it is to be sad (I know what it is
to be sad).--SHESAIDSHE--21
I know what it's like to be dead (I know what
it's like to be dead).--SHESAIDSHE--22
I know what it's like to be dead (I know what
it's like to be dead).--SHESAIDSHE--22
Be thankful I don't take it all --TAXMAN--8
Don't ask me what I want it for (ha ha Mr.
Wilson)--TAXMAN--18
In the town where I was born--YELLOWSUBM--1
There beneath the blue suburban skies I sit--
PENNYLANE--10
There beneath the blue suburban skies I sit--
PENNYLANE--29
No-one, I think, is in my tree--STRAWBERRY--16

I mean, it must be high or low--STRAWBERRY--17
That is, I think it's not too bad.--STRAWBERRY--20
But, you know, I know when it's a dream--STRAWBERRY
--27
I think I know, I mean, er, yes--STRAWBERRY--28
I think I know, I mean, er, yes--STRAWBERRY--28
I think I know, I mean, er, yes--STRAWBERRY--28
That is, I think I disagree.--STRAWBERRY--30
That is, I think I disagree.--STRAWBERRY--30
I read the news today, oh boy--DAYINTHELI--1
Well I just had to laugh--DAYINTHELI--4
I saw the photograph--DAYINTHELI--5
I saw a film today, oh boy--DAYINTHELI--11
But I just had to look--DAYINTHELI--14
And looking up I noticed I was late--DAYINTHELI--21
And looking up I noticed I was late--DAYINTHELI--21
And somebody spoke and I went into a dream--
DAYINTHELI--26
I read the news today, oh boy--DAYINTHELI--28
Where I belong I'm right where I belong.--
FIXINGAHOL--8
Where I belong I'm right where I belong.--
FIXINGAHOL--8
There I will go.--FIXINGAHOL--13
Where I belong I'm right where I belong.--
FIXINGAHOL--16
Where I belong I'm right where I belong.--
FIXINGAHOL--16
And I still go.--FIXINGAHOL--21
I used to get mad at my school (now I can't
complain)--GETTINGBET--3
I used to get mad at my school (now I can't
complain)--GETTINGBET--3
The teachers who taught me weren't cool (now I
can't complain)--GETTINGBET--4
I have to admit it's getting better (better)--
GETTINGBET--9
I finally heard--GETTINGBET--14
You're doing the best that I can.--GETTINGBET--15
I have to admit it's getting better (better)--
GETTINGBET--18
I used to be cruel to my woman--GETTINGBET--25
I beat her and kept her apart from the things
that she loved--GETTINGBET--26
Man I was mean but I'm changing my scene--
GETTINGBET--27
And I'm doing the best that I can.--GETTINGBET--28
I admit it's getting better (better)--GETTINGBET
--29
Yes I admit it's getting better (better)--
GETTINGBET--31
When it gets dark I tow your heart away.--
LOVELYRITA--6
When I caught a glimpse of Rita--LOVELYRITA--8
May I inquire discreetly ((lovely Rita))--
LOVELYRITA--14
Told her I would really like to see her again.--
LOVELYRITA--22
Took her home I nearly made it--LOVELYRITA--24
Where would I be without you?--LOVELYRITA--27
So may I introduce to you--SGTPEPPERS--5
I don't really want to stop the show--SGTPEPPERS
--19
But I thought you might like to know--SGTPEPPERS
--20
When I get older losing my hair--WHENIMSIXT--1
I could stay with you.--WHENIMSIXT--12
I could be handy mending a fuse--WHENIMSIXT--13
What would you think if I sang outta tune --
WITHALITTL--1
Oh I get by with a little help from my friends --
WITHALITTL--5
Mmm I get high with a little help from my friends
--WITHALITTL--6
What do I do when my love is away?--WITHALITTL--8
How do I feel by the end of the day?--WITHALITTL
--10
No I get by with a little help from my friends --
WITHALITTL--12
I need somebody to love.--WITHALITTL--16
I want somebody to love.--WITHALITTL--18
I can't tell you but I know it's mine.--WITHALITTL
--22
I can't tell you but I know it's mine.--WITHALITTL
--22
Oh I get by with a little help from my friends --
WITHALITTL--23
I just need someone to love.--WITHALITTL--27
I want somebody to love.--WITHALITTL--29
Oh I get by with a little help from my friends --
WITHALITTL--30
Oh I get high with a little help from my friends
--WITHALITTL--32
Yes I get by with a little help from my friends --

WITHALITTL--33
You say yes, I say no --HELLOGOODB--1
You say stop and I say go, go, go.--HELLOGOODB--2
You say goodbye and I say hello - hello, hello.--
    HELLOGOODB--4
I don't know why you say goodbye, I say hello -
    hello, hello.--HELLOGOODB--5
I don't know why you say goodbye, I say hello -
    hello, hello.--HELLOGOODB--5
I don't know why you say goodbye, I say hello.--
    HELLOGOODB--6
I don't know why you say goodbye, I say hello.--
    HELLOGOODB--6
I say hi!/high, you say 'lo/low--HELLOGOODB--7
You say why and I say I don't know.--HELLOGOODB--8
You say why and I say I don't know.--HELLOGOODB--8
You say goodbye and I say hello - hello, hello.--
    HELLOGOODB--10
I don't know why you say goodbye, I say hello -
    hello, hello--HELLOGOODB--12
I don't know why you say goodbye, I say hello -
    hello, hello--HELLOGOODB--12
I don't know why you say goodbye, I say hello--
    HELLOGOODB--14
I don't know why you say goodbye, I say hello --
    HELLOGOODB--14
You say goodbye and I say hello - hello, hello.--
    HELLOGOODB--19
I don't know why you say goodbye, I say hello -
    hello, hello--HELLOGOODB--20
I don't know why you say goodbye, I say hello -
    hello, hello--HELLOGOODB--20
I don't know why you say goodbye, I say hello.--
    HELLOGOODB--21
I don't know why you say goodbye, I say hello.--
    HELLOGOODB--21
You say yes, I say no--HELLOGOODB--22
((I say yes but I may mean no)) --HELLOGOODB--23
((I say yes but I may mean no)) --HELLOGOODB--23
You say stop but I say go, go, go--HELLOGOODB--24
((I can stay till it's time to go)).--HELLOGOODB
    --25
You say goodbye and I say hello - hello, hello.--
    HELLOGOODB--27
I don't know why you say goodbye, I say hello -
    hello, hello--HELLOGOODB--28
I don't know why you say goodbye, I say hello -
    hello, hello--HELLOGOODB--28
I don't know why you say goodbye, I say hello -
    hello, hello--HELLOGOODB--29
I don't know why you say goodbye, I say hello -
    hello, hello--HELLOGOODB--29
I don't know why you say goodbye, I say hello -
    hello.--HELLOGOODB--30
I don't know why you say goodbye, I say hello -
    hello.--HELLOGOODB--30
I AM THE WALRUS.--IAMTHEWALR--Title
I am he as you are he as you are me and we are
    all together--IAMTHEWALR--1
I am the eggman (goo) they are the eggmen (goo)
    I am the walrus--IAMTHEWALR--7
I am the eggman (goo) they are the eggmen (goo)
    I am the walrus--IAMTHEWALR--7
I am the eggman (goo) they are the eggmen (goo)
    I am the walrus--IAMTHEWALR--15
I am the eggman (goo) they are the eggmen (goo)
    I am the walrus--IAMTHEWALR--15
I am the eggman, they are the eggmen, I am the
    walrus--IAMTHEWALR--19
I am the eggman, they are the eggmen, I am the
    walrus--IAMTHEWALR--19
I am the eggman (goo) they are the eggmen (goo)
    I am the walrus (goo)--IAMTHEWALR--28
I am the eggman (goo) they are the eggmen (goo)
    I am the walrus (goo)--IAMTHEWALR--28
Please don't be long or I may be asleep.--
    BLUEJAYWAY--7
And I told them where to go.--BLUEJAYWAY--9
Please don't be long or I may be asleep.--
    BLUEJAYWAY--14
Now it's past my bed I know (know),--BLUEJAYWAY--15
Please don't be long or I may be asleep.--
    BLUEJAYWAY--21
I can know all things on earth.--INNERLIGHT--2
I could know the ways of heaven.--INNERLIGHT--4
All I can tell you is brother you have to wait.--
    REVOLUTION--19
Man I had a dreadful flight.--BACKINTHEU--4
Been away so long I hardly knew the place --
    BACKINTHEU--8
I would like you to dance (birthday) --BIRTHDAY--11
I would like you to dance (birthday) --BIRTHDAY--13
I would like you to dance (birthday) --BIRTHDAY--16
I would like you to dance (birthday) (wuh)--

BIRTHDAY--18
Can you take me back where I came from --CRYBABYCRY
    --44
Can you take me back where I came from --CRYBABYCRY
    --46
Mmm can you take me where I came from --CRYBABYCRY
    --49
I listen for your footsteps --DONTPASSME--2
I don't hear it --DONTPASSME--8
I hear the clock a - ticking --DONTPASSME--10
I wonder where you are tonight --DONTPASSME--14
I don't see you --DONTPASSME--16
'cos you know, darling, I love only you --
    DONTPASSME--19
How I hate to see you go --DONTPASSME--21
I'm sorry that I doubted you --DONTPASSME--23
I was so unfair --DONTPASSME--24
I said that's alright I'm waiting here --DONTPASSME
    --29
'cos you know, darling, I love only you --
    DONTPASSME--32
How I hate to see you go --DONTPASSME--34
'cos you know, darling, I love only you --
    DONTPASSME--38
How I hate to see you go --DONTPASSME--40
I told you about Strawberry Fields--GLASSONION--1
I told you about the walrus and me - man--
    GLASSONION--8
I told you about the fool on the hill--GLASSONION
    --17
I tell you man he living there still--GLASSONION
    --18
I need a fix 'cos I'm going down --HAPPINESSI--9
Down to the bits that I left uptown --HAPPINESSI
    --10
I need a fix 'cos I'm going down.--HAPPINESSI--11
When I hold you in my arms ((oh, yeah)) --
    HAPPINESSI--22
And I feel my finger on your trigger ((oh,
    yeah)).--HAPPINESSI--23
I know nobody can do me no harm ((oh, yeah)) --
    HAPPINESSI--24
When I get to the bottom I go back to the top
    of the slide --HELTERSKEL--1
When I get to the bottom I go back to the top
    of the slide --HELTERSKEL--1
Where I stop and I turn and I go for a ride --
    HELTERSKEL--2
Where I stop and I turn and I go for a ride --
    HELTERSKEL--2
Where I stop and I turn and I go for a ride --
    HELTERSKEL--2
Till I get to the bottom and I see you again -
    yeah, yeah, yeah.--HELTERSKEL--3
Till I get to the bottom and I see you again -
    yeah, yeah, yeah.--HELTERSKEL--3
When I get to the bottom I go back to the top
    of the slide--HELTERSKEL--18
When I get to the bottom I go back to the top
    of the slide--HELTERSKEL--18
And I stop and I turn and I go for a ride--
    HELTERSKEL--19
And I stop and I turn and I go for a ride--
    HELTERSKEL--19
And I stop and I turn and I go for a ride--
    HELTERSKEL--19
And I get to the bottom and I see you again -
    yeah, yeah, yeah.--HELTERSKEL--20
And I get to the bottom and I see you again -
    yeah, yeah, yeah.--HELTERSKEL--20
Coming down fast (oh I hear my baby speaking -
    ooo)....--HELTERSKEL--30
I got blisters on my fingers!--HELTERSKEL--32
I light the light - yeah, ooo - ha.--HONEYPIE--21
I like this kinda hot kinda music, hot kinda music
    --HONEYPIE--22
I WILL.--IWILL--Title
You know I love you still.--IWILL--2
Will I wait a lonely lifetime?--IWILL--3
If you want me to, I will.--IWILL--4
For if I ever saw you --IWILL--5
I didn't catch your name --IWILL--6
I will always feel the same.--IWILL--8
And when at last I find you --IWILL--13
Sing it loud so I can hear you --IWILL--15
You know I will - I will.--IWILL--18
You know I will - I will.--IWILL--18
I'm so tired, I haven't slept a wink --IMSOTIRED
    --1
I wonder should I get up and fix myself a drink --
    IMSOTIRED--3
I wonder should I get up and fix myself a drink --
    IMSOTIRED--3
I'm so tired, I don't know what to do --IMSOTIRED

--5
I wonder should I call you --IMSOTIRED--7
I wonder should I call you --IMSOTIRED--7
But I know what you would do.--IMSOTIRED--8
You know I can't sleep, I can't stop my brain --
    IMSOTIRED--11
You know I can't sleep, I can't stop my brain --
    IMSOTIRED--11
You know I can't sleep, I can't stop my brain --
    IMSOTIRED--20
You know I can't sleep, I can't stop my brain --
    IMSOTIRED--20
Half of what I say is meaningless --JULIA--1
But I say it just to reach you, Julia.--JULIA--2
So I sing the song of love, Julia.--JULIA--4
So I sing the song of love, Julia.--JULIA--6
So I sing the song of love, Julia.--JULIA--10
When I cannot sing my heart --JULIA--11
I can only speak my mind, Julia.--JULIA--12
So I sing a song of love, Julia.--JULIA--14
So I sing a song of love for Julia --JULIA--16
How could I ever have lost you --LONGLONGLO--2
When I loved you?--LONGLONGLO--3
Now I'm so happy I found you --LONGLONGLO--5
How I love you.--LONGLONGLO--6
So many tears I was searching --LONGLONGLO--7
So many tears I was wasting - oh, oh!--LONGLONGLO
    --8
Now I can see you, be you --LONGLONGLO--9
How can I ever misplace you?--LONGLONGLO--10
How I want you.--LONGLONGLO--11
Oh I love you --LONGLONGLO--12
You know that I need you,--LONGLONGLO--13
Oh I love you.--LONGLONGLO--14
Martha my dear, though I spend my days in
    conversation --MARTHAMYDE--1
Desmond says to Molly, girl I like your face--
    OBLADIOBLA--3
I say two--REVOLUTONE--3
Well all I can tell you is brother you have to
    wait.--REVOLUTONE--28
And I'll be better, I'll be better Doc as
    soon as I am able.--ROCKYRACCO--35
I feel your taste all the time we're apart --
    SAVOYTRUFF--7
I look at you all, see the love there that's
    sleeping --WHILEMYGUI--2
I look at the floor and I see it needs sweeping --
    WHILEMYGUI--4
I look at the floor and I see it needs sweeping --
    WHILEMYGUI--4
I don't know why nobody told you how to unfold
    your love --WHILEMYGUI--6
I don't know how someone controlled you --
    WHILEMYGUI--7
I look at the world and I notice it's turning --
    WHILEMYGUI--9
I look at the world and I notice it's turning --
    WHILEMYGUI--9
I don't know how you were diverted --WHILEMYGUI--14
I don't know how you were inverted--WHILEMYGUI--16
I look at you all, see the love there that's
    sleeping--WHILEMYGUI--18
I love you, yeah, Honey Pie, wuh!--WILDHONEYP--4
If I ain't dead already--YERBLUES--4
If I ain't dead already--YERBLUES--8
But I am of the universe--YERBLUES--12
If I ain't dead already--YERBLUES--15
If I ain't dead already--YERBLUES--22
If I ain't dead already--YERBLUES--29
Can I have a little more?--ALLTOGETHE--2
I love you.--ALLTOGETHE--4
Can I bring my friend to tea?--ALLTOGETHE--6
E, F, G, H, I, J --ALLTOGETHE--7
I love you.--ALLTOGETHE--8
Can I take my friend to bed?--ALLTOGETHE--18
I love you.--ALLTOGETHE--20
I say woof--HEYBULLDOG--25
I only have grandchildren (yahoo ha ha ha ha ha
    ha ha)--HEYBULLDOG--32
When I look into your eyes --ITSALLTOOM--4
And the more I go inside --ITSALLTOOM--6
Where I know that I'm free --ITSALLTOOM--22
The more I learn, the less I know --ITSALLTOOM--27
The more I learn, the less I know --ITSALLTOOM--27
And what I do is all too much.--ITSALLTOOM--28
It doesn't really matter what chords I play --
    ONLYANORTH--7
What words I say or time of day it is --ONLYANORTH
    --8
It doesn't really matter what clothes I wear --
    ONLYANORTH--10
Or how I fare or if my hair is brown --ONLYANORTH
    --11

And I told you there's no-one there.--ONLYANORTH
    --16
I guess nobody ever really done me --DONTLETMED--23
I said we're only trying to get us some peace.--
    BALLADOFJO--20
I want a love that's right --OLDBROWNSH--1
I want a short-haired girl --OLDBROWNSH--3
When I see your smile --OLDBROWNSH--11
If I grow up I'll be a singer --OLDBROWNSH--17
I may appear to be imperfect --OLDBROWNSH--22
I want that love of yours --OLDBROWNSH--27
I never give you my pillow--CARRYTHATW--5
I only send you my invitations--CARRYTHATW--6
I break down.--CARRYTHATW--8
He say I know you, you know me--COMETOGETH--19
One thing I can tell you is you got to be free--
    COMETOGETH--20
And I will sing a lullaby.--GOLDENSLUM--6
And I will sing a lullaby.--GOLDENSLUM--10
And I will sing a lullaby.--GOLDENSLUM--16
I wanna tell her that I love her a lot--HERMAJESTY
    --5
I wanna tell her that I love her a lot--HERMAJESTY
    --5
But I gotta get a bellyfull of wine.--HERMAJESTY
    --6
'n' I say, it's alright.--HERECOMEST--3
'n' I say, it's alright.--HERECOMEST--8
'n' I say, it's alright.--HERECOMEST--12
Little darling, I feel that ice is slowly
    melting.--HERECOMEST--18
'n' I say, it's alright.--HERECOMEST--22
I WANT YOU (SHE'S SO HEAVY).--IWANTYOUSH--Title
I want you--IWANTYOUSH--1
I want you so bad--IWANTYOUSH--2
I want you so bad--IWANTYOUSH--3
I want you so bad--IWANTYOUSH--4
I want you--IWANTYOUSH--7
I want you so bad, babe--IWANTYOUSH--8
I want you--IWANTYOUSH--9
I want you so bad--IWANTYOUSH--10
I want you--IWANTYOUSH--13
I want you so bad, babe--IWANTYOUSH--14
I want you--IWANTYOUSH--15
I want you so bad--IWANTYOUSH--16
I want you so bad--IWANTYOUSH--19
I want you--IWANTYOUSH--20
I want you--IWANTYOUSH--21
I want you so bad--IWANTYOUSH--22
I want you so bad--IWANTYOUSH--28
I want you so bad--IWANTYOUSH--29
I want you--IWANTYOUSH--30
I want you so bad--IWANTYOUSH--31
I want you--IWANTYOUSH--34
You know I want you so bad, babe--IWANTYOUSH--35
I want you--IWANTYOUSH--36
You know I want you so bad--IWANTYOUSH--37
Can I take you out to the pictures, Joan?--
    MAXWELLSIL--4
So he waits behind, writing fifty times I must
    not be so oh - oh oh.--MAXWELLSIL--11
Believe me when I tell you, I'll never do you
    no harm.--OHDARLING--2
Believe me when I beg you - ooo - don't ever
    leave me alone.--OHDARLING--4
Well you know I nearly broke down and cried.--
    OHDARLING--6
A - well you know, I nearly broke down and died.--
    OHDARLING--8
Believe me when I tell you, I'll never do you.
    no harm.--OHDARLING--10
A - well you know I nearly broke down and cried.--
    OHDARLING--13
A - well you know, I nearly broke down and died.--
    OHDARLING--15
Believe me when I tell you - ooo - I'll never
    do you no harm.--OHDARLING--18
And though she thought I knew the answer --
    SHECAMEINT--14
Well I knew what I could not say.--SHECAMEINT--15
Well I knew what I could not say.--SHECAMEINT--15
And so I quit the police department--SHECAMEINT--16
I don't want to leave her now --SOMETHING--4
You know I believe 'n' how.--SOMETHING--5
That I don't need no other lover --SOMETHING--7
I don't want to leave her now --SOMETHING--9
You know I believe 'n' how.--SOMETHING--10
I don't know, I don't know --SOMETHING--12
I don't know, I don't know --SOMETHING--12
I don't know, I don't know.--SOMETHING--14
I don't know, I don't know.--SOMETHING--14
And all I have to do is think of her --SOMETHING
    --16
I don't want to leave her now --SOMETHING--18

You know I believe 'n' how.--SOMETHING--19
I never give you my number --YOUNEVERGI--4
I only give you my situation--YOUNEVERGI--5
And in the middle of investigation I break down.--
    YOUNEVERGI--6
When I find myself in times of trouble --LETITBE/45
    --1
I wake up to the sound of music --LETITBE/45--24
Because you're sweet and lovely girl, I love you
    --FORYOUBLUE--2
I love you more than ever girl, I do.--FORYOUBLUE
    --4
I love you more than ever girl, I do.--FORYOUBLUE
    --4
I want you in the morning girl, I love you --
    FORYOUBLUE--5
I want you in the morning girl, I love you --
    FORYOUBLUE--5
I want you at the moment I feel blue --FORYOUBLUE
    --6
I want you at the moment I feel blue --FORYOUBLUE
    --6
I've loved you from the moment I saw you --
    FORYOUBLUE--13
I feel it now, I hope you feel it too.--FORYOUBLUE
    --15
I feel it now, I hope you feel it too.--FORYOUBLUE
    --15
Because you're sweet and lovely girl, I love you
    --FORYOUBLUE--16
I love you more than ever girl, I do - really
    love blues.--FORYOUBLUE--18
I love you more than ever girl, I do - really
    love blues.--FORYOUBLUE--18
And I hope we passed the audition.--GETBACK/LP--39
(I) DIG A PONY.--IDIGAPONY--Title
I dig a pony--IDIGAPONY--6
Oh I do a road hog--IDIGAPONY--9
I told you so.--IDIGAPONY--12
All I want is you--IDIGAPONY--13
I pick a moon dog--IDIGAPONY--16
Oh now I roll a stony--IDIGAPONY--19
I told you so.--IDIGAPONY--22
All I want is you--IDIGAPONY--23
Oh now I feel the wind blow--IDIGAPONY--26
Oh now I roll a lorry--IDIGAPONY--29
I told you so.--IDIGAPONY--32
All I want is you--IDIGAPONY--33
I ME MINE.--IMEMINE--Title
I me mine, I me mine, I me mine.--IMEMINE--2
I me mine, I me mine, I me mine.--IMEMINE--2
I me mine, I me mine, I me mine.--IMEMINE--2
I me mine, I me mine, I me mine.--IMEMINE--4
I me mine, I me mine, I me mine.--IMEMINE--4
I me mine, I me mine, I me mine.--IMEMINE--4
I me mine.--IMEMINE--9
I me me mine --IMEMINE--10
I me me mine --IMEMINE--11
I me me mine --IMEMINE--12
I me me mine.--IMEMINE--13
All I can hear,--IMEMINE--14
I me mine, I me mine, I me mine.--IMEMINE--15
I me mine, I me mine, I me mine.--IMEMINE--15
I me mine, I me mine, I me mine.--IMEMINE--15
I me mine, I me mine, I me mine.--IMEMINE--17
I me mine, I me mine, I me mine.--IMEMINE--17
I me mine, I me mine, I me mine.--IMEMINE--17
I me mine.--IMEMINE--22
I me me mine --IMEMINE--23
I me me mine --IMEMINE--24
I me me mine --IMEMINE--25
I me me mine.--IMEMINE--26
All I can hear --IMEMINE--27
I me mine, I me mine, I me mine.--IMEMINE--28
I me mine, I me mine, I me mine.--IMEMINE--28
I me mine, I me mine, I me mine.--IMEMINE--28
I me mine, I me mine, I me mine.--IMEMINE--30
I me mine, I me mine, I me mine.--IMEMINE--30
I me mine, I me mine, I me mine.--IMEMINE--30
I me mine.--IMEMINE--35
I've got a feeling, a feeling I can't hide --
    IVEGOTAFEE--3
And if you leave me I won't be late again --
    IVEGOTAFEE--8
All that I was looking for was somebody who
    looked like you.--IVEGOTAFEE--13
I've got a feeling I think that everybody knows --
    IVEGOTAFEE--16
Everybody let their hair down ((a feeling I
    can't hide, oh no)) --IVEGOTAFEE--33
When I find myself in times of trouble --LETITBE/LP
    --1
I wake up to the sound of music --LETITBE/LP--24
I said, move over honey, I'm travelling on

that line --ONEAFTERNI--2
I said, move over once, move over twice --
    ONEAFTERNI--3
I begged her not to go and I begged her on my
    bended knee, (oh yeah)--ONEAFTERNI--6
I begged her not to go and I begged her on my
    bended knee, (oh yeah)--ONEAFTERNI--6
I said move over once, move over twice --ONEAFTERNI
    --8
Then I find I've got the number wrong.--ONEAFTERNI
    --14
I said a-move over honey, I'm travelling on
    that line --ONEAFTERNI--16
Then I find I got the number wrong - well ((well)).
    --ONEAFTERNI--24
Then I find I got the number wrong - well ((well)).
    --ONEAFTERNI--24
I said move over once, move over twice --ONEAFTERNI
    --27
I dig a pygmy by Charles Hawtrey and the Deaf
    Aids (ha ha ha)--TWOOFUS--1
You and I have memories --TWOOFUS--17
You and I have memories --TWOOFUS--26

I'D
    I'd really sympathise --ANYTIMEATA--8
    That before too long I'd fall in love with her.--
        ISAWHERSTA--8
    I'd get myself locked up today --ILLCRYINST--4
    I'd try to make you sad somehow --ILLCRYINST--9
    There is really nothing else I'd rather do --
        IMHAPPYJUS--6
    If I were you I'd realise that I--NOREPLY--17
    I'd admit that I was wrong--YOULIKEMET--18
    I'd admit that I was wrong--YOULIKEMET--27
    And I'd have never been aware--IVEJUSTSEE--9
    You're the one that I'd be thinking of --IFINEEDEDS
        --2
    Then I guess I'd be with you my friend --IFINEEDEDS
        --5
    Then I guess I'd be with you my friend --IFINEEDEDS
        --15
    Well I'd rather see you dead, little girl --
        RUNFORYOUR--1
    And I'd rather see you dead.--RUNFORYOUR--20
    I'd rather see you dead, little girl --RUNFORYOUR
        --25
    I'd love to turn you on--DAYINTHELI--16
    I'd love to turn you on--DAYINTHELI--34
    If I'd been out till quarter to three--WHENIMSIXT
        --5
    And I'd really like to go (go) --BLUEJAYWAY--16
    This is what I'd say:--HONEYPIE--6
    You know I'd give you everything I've got for a
        little peace of mind.--IMSOTIRED--13
    You know I'd give you everything I've got for a
        little peace of mind.--IMSOTIRED--22
    I'd give you everything I've got for a little
        peace of mind --IMSOTIRED--23
    I'd give you everything I've got for a little
        peace of mind.--IMSOTIRED--24
    To miss that love is something I'd hate.--
        OLDBROWNSH--28
    I'd like to be under the sea--OCTOPUSSGA--1
    I'd ask my friends to come and see--OCTOPUSSGA--5
    I'd like to be under the sea--OCTOPUSSGA--7
    I'd like to be under the sea--OCTOPUSSGA--15
    I'd like to be under the sea--OCTOPUSSGA--23
    I'd like to say thank you on behalf of the group
        and ourselves--GETBACK/LP--38
    Oh please believe me I'd hate to miss the train --
        IVEGOTAFEE--6

I'LL
    I'll always be true --LOVEMEDO--3
    I'll always be true --LOVEMEDO--8
    I'll always be true --LOVEMEDO--15
    I'll always be true --LOVEMEDO--20
    Remember that I'll always be in love with you.--
        PSILOVEYOU--2
    I'll ((I'll)) be coming home ((home)) again
        to you love ((you love)) --PSILOVEYOU--7
    I'll ((I'll)) be coming home ((home)) again
        to you love ((you love)) --PSILOVEYOU--7
    Remember that I'll always be in love with you.--
        PSILOVEYOU--11
    Remember that I'll always, yeah, be in love
        with you.--PSILOVEYOU--18
    I'll be coming home again to you love --PSILOVEYOU
        --19
    And I'll be there.--ANYTIMEATA--3
    I'll be there to make you feel right --ANYTIMEATA

--6
And I'll be there.--ANYTIMEATA--12
I'll try to make it shine.--ANYTIMEATA--14
Call me tonight and I'll come to you.--ANYTIMEATA
  --18
And I'll be there.--ANYTIMEATA--21
And I'll be there.--ANYTIMEATA--24
And I'll be there.--ANYTIMEATA--27
Ask me why, I'll say I love you --ASKMEWHY--14
Ask me why, I'll say I love you --ASKMEWHY--22
Ask me why, I say I'll love you --ASKMEWHY--26
Now I'll never dance with another --ISAWHERSTA--16
Now I'll never dance with another--ISAWHERSTA--23
I'll remember all the little things we've done --
  MISERY--6
I'll remember all the little things we've done --
  MISERY--10
Just call on me and I'll send it along--FROMMETOYO
  --5
Just/So call on me and I'll send it along--FROMMETOYO--9
Just call on me and I'll send it along--FROMMETOYO
  --17
Just call on me and I'll send it along--FROMMETOYO
  --20
Just call on me and I'll send it along--FROMMETOYO
  --28
And eternally I'll always be in love with you--
  THANKYOUGI--3
And eternally I'll always be in love with you--
  THANKYOUGI--13
I'LL GET YOU.--ILLGETYOU--Title
But I'll get you, I'll get you in the end--
  ILLGETYOU--7
But I'll get you, I'll get you in the end--
  ILLGETYOU--7
Yes I will I'll get you in the end, oh yeah,
  oh yeah.--ILLGETYOU--8
That I'll get you, I'll get you in the end--
  ILLGETYOU--14
That I'll get you, I'll get you in the end--
  ILLGETYOU--14
Yes I will, I'll get you in the end, oh yeah,
  oh yeah.--ILLGETYOU--15
But I'll get you, I'll get you in the end--
  ILLGETYOU--24
But I'll get you, I'll get you in the end--
  ILLGETYOU--24
Yes I will, I'll get you in the end, oh yeah,
  oh yeah--ILLGETYOU--25
And I'll be kissing you.--ALLIVEGOTT--10
I'll be here, yes I will --ALLIVEGOTT--13
I'll be here, yes I will --ALLIVEGOTT--24
Close your eyes and I'll kiss you --ALLMYLOVIN--1
Tomorrow I'll miss you --ALLMYLOVIN--2
Remember I'll always be true --ALLMYLOVIN--3
I'll write home every day --ALLMYLOVIN--5
And I'll send all my lovin' to you.--ALLMYLOVIN--6
I'll pretend that I'm kissing --ALLMYLOVIN--7
I'll write home every day --ALLMYLOVIN--11
And I'll send all my lovin' to you.--ALLMYLOVIN--12
All my lovin', darlin', I'll be true.--ALLMYLOVIN
  --14
Close your eyes and I'll kiss you --ALLMYLOVIN--15
Tomorrow I'll miss you --ALLMYLOVIN--16
Remember I'll always be true --ALLMYLOVIN--17
I'll write home every day --ALLMYLOVIN--19
And I'll send all my lovin' to you.--ALLMYLOVIN--20
All my lovin', darlin', I'll be true --ALLMYLOVIN
  --22
I know I'll never be the same--DONTBOTHER--15
I'll let you know--DONTBOTHER--22
I know I'll never be the same--DONTBOTHER--30
I'll let you know--DONTBOTHER--37
I'll be good like I know I should (yes,
  you're coming on home)--ITWONTBELO--13
I'll be good like I know I should (yes,
  you're coming on home)--ITWONTBELO--23
Oh yeah, I'll tell you something--IWANTTOHOL--1
I'll buy you a diamond ring my friend --CANTBUYMEL
  --3
I'll get you anything my friend --CANTBUYMEL--5
I'll give you all I've got to give --CANTBUYMEL--9
But what I got I'll give to you,--CANTBUYMEL--12
And I'll be satisfied --CANTBUYMEL--18
And I'll be satisfied --CANTBUYMEL--28
I think I'll let you down (let you down)--
  YOUCANTDOT--13
I'LL CRY INSTEAD.--ILLCRYINST--Title
But I can't, so I'll cry instead.--ILLCRYINST--5
But I can't, so I'll cry instead.--ILLCRYINST--10
But I'll come back again some day.--ILLCRYINST--14
Until then I'll cry instead.--ILLCRYINST--19
But I'll come back again some day.--ILLCRYINST--23
Until then I'll cry instead.--ILLCRYINST--28

I think I'll love you too --IMHAPPYJUS--2
I think I'll love you too ((oh)) --IMHAPPYJUS--14
I think I'll love you too ((oh)) --IMHAPPYJUS--22
Tell me what and I'll apologize --TELLMEWHY--14
I'LL BE BACK.--ILLBEBACK--Title
You know if you break my heart, I'll go --ILLBEBACK
  --1
But I'll be back again --ILLBEBACK--2
You if you break my heart, I'll go--ILLBEBACK--26
But I'll be back again.--ILLBEBACK--27
I bet I'll love her more --WHENIGETHO--19
I don't wanna spoil the party so I'll go --
  IDONTWANTT--1
I think I'll take a walk and look for her.--
  IDONTWANTT--8
If I find her I'll be glad --IDONTWANTT--11
I don't wanna spoil the party so I'll go --
  IDONTWANTT--13
If I find her I'll be glad --IDONTWANTT--20
But I think I'll take a walk and look for her.--
  IDONTWANTT--25
I'LL FOLLOW THE SUN.--ILLFOLLOWT--Title
For tomorrow may rain so I'll follow the sun.--
  ILLFOLLOWT--2
For tomorrow may rain so I'll follow the sun.--
  ILLFOLLOWT--4
For tomorrow may rain so I'll follow the sun.--
  ILLFOLLOWT--8
Yeah, tomorrow may rain so I'll follow the sun.--
  ILLFOLLOWT--9
For tomorrow may rain so I'll follow the sun.--
  ILLFOLLOWT--13
And I'll forgive the lies--NOREPLY--19
I'll make bright your day--TELLMEWHAT--12
But as it is I'll dream of her tonight --IVEJUSTSEE
  --10
I'll make a point of taking her away from you
  (watch what you do), yeah--YOUREGONNA--16
I'll make a point of taking her away from you
  (watch what you do), yeah--YOUREGONNA--23
And maybe I'll love you.--DRIVEMYCAR--8
And maybe I'll love you.--DRIVEMYCAR--16
And maybe I'll love you.--DRIVEMYCAR--21
And maybe I'll love you.--DRIVEMYCAR--29
Though I know I'll never lose affection --INMYLIFE
  --13
I know I'll often stop and think about them --
  INMYLIFE--15
Though I know I'll never lose affection --INMYLIFE
  --17
I know I'll often stop and think about them --
  INMYLIFE--19
I'll get to you somehow--MICHELLE--18
And if you do, I'll trust in you --WAIT--11
And if you do, I'll trust in you --WAIT--19
I'll be writing more in a week or two. ((writer))
  --PAPERBACKW--16
I'll be round, I'll be round.--ANDYOURBIR--9
I'll be round, I'll be round.--ANDYOURBIR--9
I'll be round, I'll be round.--ANDYOURBIR--12
I'll be round, I'll be round.--ANDYOURBIR--12
If I'm true I'll never leave--GOTTOGETYO--18
I'll make you maybe next time around.--IWANTTOTEL
  --8
I'll make love to you --LOVEYOUTWO--16
If you drive a car, I'll tax the street,
  ((car))--TAXMAN--11
If you try to sit, I'll tax your seat, ((sit))--
  TAXMAN--12
If you get too cold, I'll tax the heat,
  ((cold))--TAXMAN--13
If you take a walk, I'll tax your feet.
  ((walk))--TAXMAN--14
Lend me your ears and I'll sing you a song--
  WITHALITTL--3
And I'll try not to sing outta key.--WITHALITTL--4
Close your eyes and I'll close mine --GOODNIGHT--7
Close your eyes and I'll close mine --GOODNIGHT--14
Although I'm so tired, I'll have another
  cigarette--IMSOTIRED--15
And I'll be better, I'll be better Doc as
  soon as I am able.--ROCKYRACCO--35
And I'll be better, I'll be better Doc as
  soon as I am able.--ROCKYRACCO--35
If I grow up I'll be a singer --OLDBROWNSH--17
I'll live and love and maybe someday --OLDBROWNSH
  --20
Oh darling, please believe me, I'll never do
  you no harm.--OHDARLING--1
Believe me when I tell you, I'll never do you
  no harm.--OHDARLING--2
Oh darling, if you leave me I'll never make it
  alone --OHDARLING--3
Oh darling, if you leave me, I'll never make

it alone.--OHDARLING--9
Believe me when I tell you, I'll never do you
   no harm.--OHDARLING--10
Oh darling, please believe me, I'll never let
   you down.--OHDARLING--16
Believe me when I tell you - ooo - I'll never
   do you no harm.--OHDARLING--18

I'M

If I cry it's not because I'm sad --ASKMEWHY--10
And I'm always thinking of you.--ASKMEWHY--15
And I'm always thinking of you.--ASKMEWHY--23
And I'm always thinking of you you, you.--ASKMEWHY
   --27
I'm in love with you - ooo.--DOYOUWANTT--8
I'm in love with you - ooo.--DOYOUWANTT--14
I'm in love with you - ooo --DOYOUWANTT--22
I'm the kind of guy, who never used to cry.--MISERY
   --2
Imagine I'm in love with you--ILLGETYOU--2
I've imagined I'm in love with you--ILLGETYOU--4
I'm never, never, never, never blue.--ILLGETYOU--12
So I'm telling you, my friend--ILLGETYOU--13
When I'm gonna change/make your mind--ILLGETYOU--17
Imagine I'm in love with you--ILLGETYOU--19
I've imagined I'm in love with you--ILLGETYOU--21
And then while I'm away --ALLMYLOVIN--4
I'll pretend that I'm kissing,--ALLMYLOVIN--7
And then while I'm away --ALLMYLOVIN--10
And then while I'm away --ALLMYLOVIN--18
But I'm to blame--DONTBOTHER--4
When every night I'm all alone--DONTBOTHER--12
Tell me I'm the only one --HOLDMETIGH--3
Tell me I'm the only one --HOLDMETIGH--20
Since you left me I'm so alone (you left me here)
   --ITWONTBELO--11
Well since you left me I'm so alone (you left
   me here)--ITWONTBELO--21
I'm so sad and lonely --LITTLECHIL--3
I'm so sad and lonely --LITTLECHIL--7
I'm so sad and lonely --LITTLECHIL--14
I'm so sad and lonely --LITTLECHIL--21
I'm wondering why --NOTASECOND--8
I'm wondering why --NOTASECOND--19
I'm gonna let you down--YOUCANTDOT--5
'cos I'm the one who won your love--YOUCANTDOT--19
I'm gonna let you down (let you down)--YOUCANTDOT
   --27
'cos I'm the one who won your love--YOUCANTDOT--38
I'm gonna let you down (let you down)--YOUCANTDOT
   --46
I'm not gonna make it --ICALLYOURN--7
I'm not that kinda man.--ICALLYOURN--8
I'm not gonna make it --ICALLYOURN--14
I'm not that kinda man.--ICALLYOURN--15
When I'm alone.--THERESAPLA--4
When I'm alone.--THERESAPLA--16
When I'm home everything seems to be right --
   HARDDAYSNI--15
When I'm home feeling you holding me tight,
   tight, yeah.--HARDDAYSNI--16
When I'm home everything seems to be right --
   HARDDAYSNI--28
When I'm home feeling you holding me tight,
   tight, yeah.--HARDDAYSNI--29
I'm gonna hide myself away-hey--ILLCRYINST--13
I'm gonna break their hearts all round the world
   --ILLCRYINST--16
Yes, I'm gonna break 'em in two --ILLCRYINST--17
I'm gonna hide myself away-hey--ILLCRYINST--22
'cos I'm gonna break their hearts all round the
   world --ILLCRYINST--25
Yes, I'm gonna break 'em in two --ILLCRYINST--26
I'M HAPPY JUST TO DANCE WITH YOU.--IMHAPPYJUS
   --Title
I'm so happy when you dance with me.--IMHAPPYJUS
   --3
'cos I'm happy just to dance with you.--IMHAPPYJUS
   --7
'cos I'm happy just to dance with you.--IMHAPPYJUS
   --11
I'm so happy when you dance with me ((oh - oh)).--
   IMHAPPYJUS--15
'cos I'm happy just to dance with you.--IMHAPPYJUS
   --19
I'm so happy when you dance with me ((oh - oh)).--
   IMHAPPYJUS--23
I've discovered I'm in love with you (oh - oh).--
   IMHAPPYJUS--27
'cos I'm happy just to dance with you (oh - oh).--
   IMHAPPYJUS--28
I'm so in love with you.--TELLMEWHY--25
I'm the one who wants you--ILLBEBACK--6

Yes I'm the one who wants you --ILLBEBACK--7
That I'm not trying to pretend.--ILLBEBACK--12
That I'm not trying to pretend.--ILLBEBACK--21
Someday when I'm lonely --THINGSWESA--3
Me I'm just the lucky kind --THINGSWESA--11
Me I'm just the lucky kind --THINGSWESA--22
'cos I'm a - gonna see my baby today --WHENIGETHO
   --5
I'm gonna hold her tight --WHENIGETHO--17
I'm gonna love her till the cows come home --
   WHENIGETHO--18
I'm in love with her and I feel fine.--IFEELFINE
   --3
I'm in love with her and I feel fine.--IFEELFINE
   --6
I'm so glad that she's my little girl --IFEELFINE
   --7
I'm in love with her and I feel fine.--IFEELFINE
   --14
I'm so glad that she's my little girl --IFEELFINE
   --15
Baby's in black and I'm feeling blue --BABYSINBLA
   --2
Baby's in black and I'm feeling blue --BABYSINBLA
   --8
Baby's in black and I'm feeling blue --BABYSINBLA
   --17
Baby's in black and I'm feeling blue --BABYSINBLA
   --22
Baby's in black and I'm feeling blue --BABYSINBLA
   --28
When I'm walking beside her--EVERYLITTL--1
People tell me I'm lucky--EVERYLITTL--2
Yes I know I'm a lucky guy.--EVERYLITTL--3
When I'm with her I'm happy--EVERYLITTL--11
When I'm with her I'm happy--EVERYLITTL--11
There is one thing I'm sure of--EVERYLITTL
   --14
If she turns up while I'm gone please let me know.
   --IDONTWANTT--4
If she turns up while I'm gone please let me know.
   --IDONTWANTT--16
I'M A LOSER.--IMALOSER--Title
I'm a loser, I'm a loser --IMALOSER--1
I'm a loser, I'm a loser --IMALOSER--1
And I'm not what I appear to be.--IMALOSER--2
I'm a loser and I lost someone who's near to me --
   IMALOSER--7
I'm a loser and I'm not what I appear to be.--
   IMALOSER--8
I'm a loser and I'm not what I appear to be.--
   IMALOSER--8
I'm a loser and I lost someone who's near to me --
   IMALOSER--13
I'm a loser and I'm not what I appear to be.--
   IMALOSER--14
I'm a loser and I'm not what I appear to be.--
   IMALOSER--14
I'm telling you so that you won't lose all.--
   IMALOSER--18
I'm a loser and I lost someone who's near to me --
   IMALOSER--19
I'm a loser and I'm not what I appear to be.--
   IMALOSER--20
I'm a loser and I'm not what I appear to be.--
   IMALOSER--20
I'm ((I'm)) feeling blue and lonely --WHATYOURED
   --2
I'm ((I'm)) feeling blue and lonely --WHATYOURED
   --2
I think I'm gonna be sad--TICKETTORI--2
I think I'm gonna be sad--TICKETTORI--23
Everybody knows I'm sure--YESITIS--6
If I'm part of you--TELLMEWHAT--4
Can't you try to see that I'm--TELLMEWHAT--20
Can't you try to see that I'm--TELLMEWHAT--29
I'm not so self-assured--HELP--12
Help me if you can, I'm feeling down--HELP--15
Help me if you can, I'm feeling down--HELP--25
I'm not so self-assured--HELP--32
Help me if you can, I'm feeling down--HELP--35
I'M DOWN.--IMDOWN--Title
I'm down (I'm really down)--IMDOWN--3
I'm down (I'm really down)--IMDOWN--3
I'm down (down on the ground)--IMDOWN--4
I'm down (I'm really down).--IMDOWN--5
I'm down (I'm really down)--IMDOWN--5
How can you laugh when you know I'm down?--IMDOWN
   --6
(How can you laugh) when you know I'm down?--IMDOWN
   --7
I'm down (I'm really down)--IMDOWN--10
I'm down (I'm really down)--IMDOWN--10
I'm down (down on the ground)--IMDOWN--11

I'm down (I'm really down).--IMDOWN--12
I'm down (I'm really down).--IMDOWN--12
How can you laugh when you know I'm down?--IMDOWN
   --13
(How can you laugh) when you know I'm down?--IMDOWN
   --14
I'm down (I'm really down)--IMDOWN--18
I'm down (I'm really down)--IMDOWN--18
Oh baby, I'm down (down on the ground)--IMDOWN--19
I'm down (I'm really down).--IMDOWN--20
I'm down (I'm really down).--IMDOWN--20
How can you laugh when you know I'm down?--IMDOWN
   --21
(How can you laugh) when you know I'm down?--IMDOWN
   --22
Baby you know I'm down (I'm really down)--IMDOWN
   --28
Baby you know I'm down (I'm really down)--IMDOWN
   --28
Oh yes, I'm down (I'm really down)--IMDOWN--29
Oh yes, I'm down (I'm really down)--IMDOWN--29
I'm down on the ground (I'm really down)--IMDOWN
   --30
I'm down on the ground (I'm really down)--IMDOWN
   --30
Ah, down (I'm really down)--IMDOWN--31
Oh baby, I'm upside-down--IMDOWN--32
I'm down (I'm really down)--IMDOWN--34
I'm down (I'm really down)--IMDOWN--34
Oh baby, I'm down (I'm really down)--IMDOWN--35
Oh baby, I'm down (I'm really down)--IMDOWN--35
I'm feeling upside-down (I'm really down)--IMDOWN
   --36
I'm feeling upside-down (I'm really down)--IMDOWN
   --36
Ooo, I'm down (I'm really down)--IMDOWN--37
Ooo, I'm down (I'm really down)--IMDOWN--37
Baby, I'm down, yeah--IMDOWN--38
Oh baby, I'm down, yeah--IMDOWN--39
Baby, I'm down (I'm really down)--IMDOWN--40
Baby, I'm down (I'm really down)--IMDOWN--40
Well baby, I'm down (I'm really down)--IMDOWN--41
Well baby, I'm down (I'm really down)--IMDOWN--41
Oh baby, I'm down (I'm really down)--IMDOWN--43
Oh baby, I'm down (I'm really down)--IMDOWN--43
I'm down, down, down, down, down, down,
   down, down, down--IMDOWN--44
Yeah, aah - ooo I'm down (down on the ground)--
   IMDOWN--45
Ooo, you know I'm...--IMDOWN--46
And so I'm telling you this time you'd better
   stop --ANOTHERGIR--8
I'm lonely as can be--INEEDYOU--4
Why am I so shy when I'm beside you?--ITSONLYLOV
   --3
I'm not half the man I used to be--YESTERDAY--6
And I will treat her kind (I'm gonna treat her
   kind)--YOUREGONNA--6
And I will treat her kind (I'm gonna treat her
   kind)--YOUREGONNA--28
In the state I'm in.--YOUVEGOTTO--14
Think of what I'm saying --WECANWORKI--8
Yes I'm gonna be a star.--DRIVEMYCAR--6
Yes I'm gonna be a star.--DRIVEMYCAR--14
Yes I'm gonna be a star.--DRIVEMYCAR--19
Yes I'm gonna be star.--DRIVEMYCAR--27
But you see now I'm too much in love.--IFINEEDEDS
   --9
But you see now I'm too much in love.--IFINEEDEDS
   --19
I'M LOOKING THROUGH YOU.--IMLOOKINGT--Title
I'm looking through you, where did you go?--
   IMLOOKINGT--1
I'm looking through you, you're not the same.--
   IMLOOKINGT--4
I'm looking through you, you're not the same.--
   IMLOOKINGT--8
I'm looking through you and you're nowhere.--
   IMLOOKINGT--14
I'm looking through you, where did you go?--
   IMLOOKINGT--17
I'm looking through you, you're not the same.--
   IMLOOKINGT--20
Aah, I'm looking through you.--IMLOOKINGT--22
Yeah, I'm looking through you.--IMLOOKINGT--23
Until I do I'm hoping you will know what I mean.--
   MICHELLE--14
Until I do I'm telling you so you'll understand.--
   MICHELLE--19
Well you know that I'm a wicked guy--RUNFORYOUR--9
Baby, I'm determined --RUNFORYOUR--19
It's been a long time, now I'm coming back home --
   WAIT--1
It's been a long time, now I'm coming back home --

WAIT--13
It's been a long time, now I'm coming back home --
   WAIT--25
Say the word I'm thinking of --THEWORD--3
Spread the word I'm thinking of --THEWORD--11
Say the word I'm thinking of --THEWORD--19
I'm here to show everybody the light.--THEWORD--24
It's the word I'm thinking of --THEWORD--27
I'M ONLY SLEEPING.--IMONLYSLEE--Title
Lift my head, I'm still yawning.--IMONLYSLEE--2
When I'm in the middle of a dream --IMONLYSLEE--3
Leave me where I am, I'm only sleeping.--IMONLYSLEE
   --6
Everybody seems to think I'm lazy.--IMONLYSLEE--7
Please don't spoil my day, I'm miles away --
   IMONLYSLEE--11
And after all, I'm only sleeping.--IMONLYSLEE--12
Please don't spoil my day, I'm miles away --
   IMONLYSLEE--17
And after all, I'm only sleeping.--IMONLYSLEE--18
Lift my head, I'm still yawning.--IMONLYSLEE--22
When I'm in the middle of a dream --IMONLYSLEE--23
Leave me where I am, I'm only sleeping.--IMONLYSLEE
   --26
I'm in love and it's a sunny day.--GOODDAYSUN--5
I'm so proud to know that she is mine.--GOODDAYSUN
   --13
When I'm with you I want to stay there--GOTTOGETYO
   --17
If I'm true I'll never leave--GOTTOGETYO--18
Watching her eyes and hoping I'm always there.--
   HERETHEREA--13
Watching her eyes and hoping I'm always there.--
   HERETHEREA--19
Before I'm a dead old man.--LOVEYOUTWO--5
Things that make me feel that I'm mad--SHESAIDSHE
   --5
I know that I'm ready to leave --SHESAIDSHE--11
I know that I'm ready to leave --SHESAIDSHE--17
'cos I'm the Taxman --TAXMAN--5
Yeah, I'm the Taxman.--TAXMAN--6
'cos I'm the Taxman --TAXMAN--9
Yeah, I'm the Taxman.--TAXMAN--10
'cos I'm the Taxman --TAXMAN--16
Yeah, I'm the Taxman.--TAXMAN--17
'cos I'm the Taxman --TAXMAN--20
Yeah, I'm the Taxman.--TAXMAN--21
'cos I'm the Taxman --TAXMAN--24
Yeah, I'm the Taxman.--TAXMAN--25
'cos I'm going to strawberry fields--STRAWBERRY--2
'cos I'm going to strawberry fields--STRAWBERRY--12
'cos I'm going to strawberry fields--STRAWBERRY--22
'cos I'm going to strawberry fields--STRAWBERRY--32
I'm fixing a hole where the rain gets in--
   FIXINGAHOL--1
I'm filling the cracks that ran through the door--
   FIXINGAHOL--4
And it really doesn't matter if I'm wrong I'm
   right--FIXINGAHOL--7
And it really doesn't matter if I'm wrong I'm
   right--FIXINGAHOL--7
Where I belong I'm right where I belong.--
   FIXINGAHOL--8
I'm painting a room in a colourful way--FIXINGAHOL
   --11
And it really doesn't matter if I'm wrong I'm
   right--FIXINGAHOL--15
And it really doesn't matter if I'm wrong I'm
   right--FIXINGAHOL--15
Where I belong I'm right where I belong.--
   FIXINGAHOL--16
I'm taking the time for a number of things--
   FIXINGAHOL--19
I'm fixing a hole where the rain gets in--
   FIXINGAHOL--23
I'm fixing a hole where the rain gets in--
   FIXINGAHOL--26
Man I was mean but I'm changing my scene--
   GETTINGBET--27
And I'm doing the best that I can.--GETTINGBET--28
Somebody needs to know the time glad that I'm here
   --GOODMORNIN--22
WHEN I'M SIXTY-FOUR.--WHENIMSIXT--Title
When I'm sixty-four?--WHENIMSIXT--9
When I'm sixty-four?--WHENIMSIXT--21
When I'm sixty-four?--WHENIMSIXT--37
Yes I'm certain that it happens all the time.--
   WITHALITTL--20
Oh I'm gonna try with a little help from my
   friends.--WITHALITTL--25
I'm crying--IAMTHEWALR--3
I'm crying - I'm crying (goo), I'm crying,
   I'm crying--IAMTHEWALR--11
I'm crying - I'm crying (goo), I'm crying,

I'm crying--IAMTHEWALR--11
I'm crying - I'm crying (goo), I'm crying,
　I'm crying--IAMTHEWALR--11
I'm crying - I'm crying (goo), I'm crying,
　I'm crying--IAMTHEWALR--11
I'm crying--IAMTHEWALR--24
I'm back in the USSR --BACKINTHEU--5
I'm back in the USSR --BACKINTHEU--12
Hey, I'm back in the USSR.--BACKINTHEU--24
I'm back in the USSR (hey!) --BACKINTHEU--35
Hey, I'm back --BACKINTHEU--39
I'm back in the USSR --BACKINTHEU--40
(I'm back!)--BACKINTHEU--43
I'm glad it's your birthday --BIRTHDAY--5
I'm glad it's your birthday --BIRTHDAY--24
But I'm by myself.--DONTPASSME--13
And why I'm by myself --DONTPASSME--15
I'm sorry that I doubted you --DONTPASSME--23
I said that's alright I'm waiting here --DONTPASSME
　--29
I need a fix 'cos I'm going down --HAPPINESSI--9
I need a fix 'cos I'm going down.--HAPPINESSI--11
I'm coming down fast but I'm miles above you --
　HELTERSKEL--5
I'm coming down fast but I'm miles above you --
　HELTERSKEL--5
I'm coming down fast but don't let me break you --
　HELTERSKEL--12
I'm coming down fast but don't let me break you --
　HELTERSKEL--22
I'm in love but I'm lazy--HONEYPIE--8
I'm in love but I'm lazy--HONEYPIE--8
I'm in love but I'm lazy--HONEYPIE--30
I'm in love but I'm lazy--HONEYPIE--30
I'M SO TIRED.--IMSOTIRED--Title
I'm so tired, I haven't slept a wink --IMSOTIRED
　--1
I'm so tired, my mind is on the blink --IMSOTIRED
　--2
I'm so tired, I don't know what to do.--IMSOTIRED
　--5
I'm so tired, my mind is set on you --IMSOTIRED--6
You'd say I'm putting you on --IMSOTIRED--9
You know it's three weeks, I'm going insane --
　IMSOTIRED--12
I'm so tired, I'm feeling so upset --IMSOTIRED--14
I'm so tired, I'm feeling so upset --IMSOTIRED--14
Although I'm so tired, I'll have another
　cigarette--IMSOTIRED--15
You'd say I'm putting you on --IMSOTIRED--18
You know it's three weeks, I'm going insane --
　IMSOTIRED--21
Now I'm so happy I found you --LONGLONGLO--5
All day long I'm sitting singing songs for
　everyone.--MOTHERNATU--2
He said, I'm gonna get that boy --ROCKYRACCO--6
Yes I'm lonely - wanna die --YERBLUES--2
Yes I'm lonely - wanna die --YERBLUES--3
I'm lonely - wanna die --YERBLUES--14
Yes I'm lonely - wanna die --YERBLUES--31
Yes I'm lonely - wanna die --YERBLUES--32
Where I know that I'm free --ITSALLTOOM--22
Show me that I'm everywhere --ITSALLTOOM--23
I'm in love for the first time --DONTLETMED--13
Now I'm stepping out this old brown shoe --
　OLDBROWNSH--5
Baby, I'm in love with you --OLDBROWNSH--6
It won't be the same now I'm telling you.--
　OLDBROWNSH--8
Baby, I'm in love with you --OLDBROWNSH--14
It won't be the same now that I'm with you.--
　OLDBROWNSH--16
Making sure that I'm not late (hey).--OLDBROWNSH
　--30
For your sweet top lip I'm in the queue --
　OLDBROWNSH--31
Baby, I'm in love with you.--OLDBROWNSH--32
Won't be the same now that I'm with you.--
　OLDBROWNSH--34
I'm so glad you came here --OLDBROWNSH--35
It won't be the same now that I'm with you
　(yeah, yeah, yeah)--OLDBROWNSH--36
Someday I'm gonna make her mine - oh yeah --
　HERMAJESTY--8
Someday I'm gonna make her mine.--HERMAJESTY--9
I'm living every moment girl for you.--FORYOUBLUE
　--7
I said, move over honey, I'm travelling on
　that line --ONEAFTERNI--2
I said a-move over honey, I'm travelling on
　that line --ONEAFTERNI--16
Said a - move over honey, I'm travelling on
　that line --ONEAFTERNI--26

I'VE

But you're the only love that I've ever had.--
　ASKMEWHY--11
I've known a secret for the week or two --
　DOYOUWANTT--15
I've lost her now for sure, I won't see her no
　more --MISERY--4
I've imagined I'm in love with you--ILLGETYOU--4
I've imagined I'm in love with you--ILLGETYOU--21
ALL I'VE GOT TO DO.--ALLIVEGOTT--Title
I've got no time for you right now--DONTBOTHER--13
I've got no time for you right now--DONTBOTHER--28
Every day I've done nothing but cry--ITWONTBELO--16
I've cried for you.--NOTASECOND--3
I've cried for you, yeah.--NOTASECOND--14
I'll give you all I've got to give --CANTBUYMEL--9
'cos I've been in love before --IFIFELL--4
'cos I've just lost the only girl I had.--
　ILLCRYINST--2
I've discovered I'm in love with you (oh - oh).--
　IMHAPPYJUS--27
I've had a drink or two and I don't care --
　IDONTWANTT--5
I wonder what went wrong I've waited far too long
　--IDONTWANTT--7
Though I've had a drink or two and I don't care --
　IDONTWANTT--22
I wonder what went wrong I've waited far too long
　--IDONTWANTT--24
One day you'll look to see I've gone --ILLFOLLOWT
　--1
I've been waiting here for you --WHATYOURED--9
I've been waiting here for you --WHATYOURED--16
Now I find ((and now I find)) I've changed
　my mind--HELP--13
I've never done before.--HELP--24
Now I find ((and now I find)) I've changed
　my mind--HELP--33
You're making me say that I've got nobody but you
　--ANOTHERGIR--2
But as from today well I've got somebody that's
　new --ANOTHERGIR--3
I don't wanna say that I've been unhappy with you
　--ANOTHERGIR--12
But as from today well I've seen somebody that's
　new --ANOTHERGIR--13
I don't wanna say that I've been unhappy with you
　--ANOTHERGIR--18
But as from today well I've seen somebody that's
　new --ANOTHERGIR--19
I'VE JUST SEEN A FACE.--IVEJUSTSEE--Title
I've just seen a face--IVEJUSTSEE--1
I've been alone and I have missed things--
　IVEJUSTSEE--15
I've just seen a face--IVEJUSTSEE--24
And she said listen babe I've got something to
　say --DRIVEMYCAR--23
But I've found a driver and that's a start.--
　DRIVEMYCAR--25
You don't sound different, I've learned the game
　--IMLOOKINGT--7
In my life I've loved them all.--INMYLIFE--8
I mean everything I've said.--RUNFORYOUR--18
I've got a word or two--THINKFORYO--1
I've been away now, oh how I've been alone.--WAIT
　--2
I've been away now, oh how I've been alone.--WAIT
　--2
That I've been good, as good as I can be.--WAIT--10
I've been away now, oh how I've been alone.--WAIT
　--14
I've been away now, oh how I've been alone.--WAIT
　--14
That I've been good, as good as I can be.--WAIT--18
I've been away now, oh how I've been alone.--WAIT
　--26
I've been away now, oh how I've been alone.--WAIT
　--26
But now I've got it the word is good.--THEWORD--8
I've got something I can laugh about.--GOODDAYSUN
　--3
I've got time.--IWANTTOTEL--15
I've got time.--IWANTTOTEL--22
I've got time.--IWANTTOTEL--23
I've got time.--IWANTTOTEL--24
And she's making me feel like I've never been
　born.--SHESAIDSHE--3
And you're making me feel like I've never been
　born.--SHESAIDSHE--6
'cos you're making me feel like I've never been
　born.--SHESAIDSHE--12
'cos you're making me feel like I've never been
　born.--SHESAIDSHE--18

I've got to admit it's getting better (better)--
  GETTINGBET--7
I've got to admit it's getting better (better)--
  GETTINGBET--16
I've got nothing to say but it's OK.--GOODMORNIN
  --5
I've got nothing to say but it's OK.--GOODMORNIN
  --16
I've got nothing to say but it's OK.--GOODMORNIN
  --25
Who knows how long I've loved you?--IWILL--1
You know I'd give you everything I've got for a
  little peace of mind.--IMSOTIRED--13
You know I'd give you everything I've got for a
  little peace of mind.--IMSOTIRED--22
I'd give you everything I've got for a little
  peace of mind --IMSOTIRED--23
I'd give you everything I've got for a little
  peace of mind.--IMSOTIRED--24
I've loved you from the moment I saw you --
  FORYOUBLUE--13
I'VE GOT A FEELING.--IVEGOTAFEE--Title
I've got a feeling, a feeling deep inside --
  IVEGOTAFEE--1
I've got a feeling, a feeling I can't hide --
  IVEGOTAFEE--3
Yes, yeah, I've got a feeling, yeah.--IVEGOTAFEE
  --5
I've got a feeling, yeah, I've got a feeling.--
  IVEGOTAFEE--10
I've got a feeling, yeah, I've got a feeling.--
  IVEGOTAFEE--10
All these years I've been wandering round the
  world --IVEGOTAFEE--11
Ooo I've got a feeling that keeps me on my toes --
  IVEGOTAFEE--14
I've got a feeling I think that everybody knows --
  IVEGOTAFEE--16
I've got a feeling yeah - (yeah).--IVEGOTAFEE--18
Ooo - hu, everybody had a good year ((I've got
  a feeling)) --IVEGOTAFEE--28
Everybody had a good year ((I've got a feeling))
  --IVEGOTAFEE--32
I've got a feeling ((oh yeah)) --IVEGOTAFEE--36
I've got a feeling (oh yeah) --IVEGOTAFEE--37
I've got a feeling, yeah, yeah, yeah, yeah.--
  IVEGOTAFEE--38
Will never disappear, I've seen that road before.
  --LONGANDWIN--2
Many times I've been alone and many times I've
  cried --LONGANDWIN--7
Many times I've been alone and many times I've
  cried --LONGANDWIN--7
Anyway you'll never know the many ways I've tried
  --LONGANDWIN--8
Then I find I've got the number wrong.--ONEAFTERNI
  --14

ICE

Little darling, I feel that ice is slowly
  melting.--HERECOMEST--18
Come on baby, don't be cold as ice --ONEAFTERNI--4
Come on baby, don't be cold as ice --ONEAFTERNI--9
Come on baby, don't be cold as ice --ONEAFTERNI--18
Come on baby, don't be cold as ice.--ONEAFTERNI--28

IF

If you need somebody to love --ANYTIMEATA--4
If you're feeling sorry and sad --ANYTIMEATA--7
If the sun has faded away --ANYTIMEATA--13
If I cry it's not because I'm sad --ASKMEWHY--10
If there's anything that you want--FROMMETOYO--3
If there's anything I can do--FROMMETOYO--4
If there's anything that you want--FROMMETOYO--15
If there's anything I can do--FROMMETOYO--16
If there's anything that you want--FROMMETOYO--26
If there's anything I can do--FROMMETOYO--27
If I don't get her back again--DONTBOTHER--16
If I don't get her back again--DONTBOTHER--31
If you want someone to make you feel so fine--
  LITTLECHIL--9
If this boy gets you back again.--THISBOY--13
If it makes you feel alright --CANTBUYMEL--4
If it makes you feel alright --CANTBUYMEL--6
If you say you love me too --CANTBUYMEL--10
If I catch you talking--YOUCANTDOT--3
But if they'd seen--YOUCANTDOT--20
If you wanna stay mine--YOUCANTDOT--24
But if they'd seen--YOUCANTDOT--39
If you wanna stay mine--YOUCANTDOT--43
And if you saw my love --ANDILOVEHE--3
If this is love you've got to give me more --

ISHOULDHAV--12
IF I FELL.--IFIFELL--Title
If I fell in love with you --IFIFELL--1
If I give my heart to you --IFIFELL--7
If I trust in you --IFIFELL--10
If I love you too --IFIFELL--12
If our new love was in vain.--IFIFELL--16
If our new love was in vain.--IFIFELL--23
If I fell in love with you.--IFIFELL--28
If I could get my way --ILLCRYINST--3
If I could see you now --ILLCRYINST--8
If it's funny try and understand.--IMHAPPYJUS--5
If somebody tries to take my place --IMHAPPYJUS--16
If somebody tries to take my place --IMHAPPYJUS--24
If it's something that I said or done --TELLMEWHY
  --13
If you don't I really can't go on --TELLMEWHY--15
If you'll only listen to my pleas --TELLMEWHY--22
If there's anything I can do --TELLMEWHY--23
You know if you break my heart, I'll go --ILLBEBACK
  --1
That if I ran away from you --ILLBEBACK--14
You if you break my heart, I'll go --ILLBEBACK--26
You say you will love me if I have to go --
  THINGSWESA--1
Come on if you please --WHENIGETHO--10
If she turns up while I'm gone please let me know.
  --IDONTWANTT--4
If I find her I'll be glad --IDONTWANTT--11
If she turns up while I'm gone please let me know.
  --IDONTWANTT--16
If I find her I'll be glad --IDONTWANTT--20
There's no fun in what I do if she's not there.--
  IDONTWANTT--23
If I were you I'd realise that I--NOREPLY--17
If you wear red tonight--YESITIS--1
If I could forget her--YESITIS--11
If I could forget her--YESITIS--20
If you let me take your heart--TELLMEWHAT--1
If I'm part of you--TELLMEWHAT--4
If you put your trust in me--TELLMEWHAT--11
If I just don't treat you right--YOULIKEMET--4
If you leave me I will follow you--YOULIKEMET--15
If you leave me I will follow you--YOULIKEMET--24
Help me if you can, I'm feeling down--HELP--15
Help me if you can, I'm feeling down--HELP--25
Help me if you can, I'm feeling down--HELP--35
If you don't take her out tonight--YOUREGONNA--3
If you don't treat her right my friend--YOUREGONNA
  --9
If you don't take her out tonight--YOUREGONNA--25
If she's gone I can't go on --YOUVEGOTTO--3
Only time will tell if I am right or I am wrong.--
  WECANWORKI--16
Only time will tell if I am right or I am wrong.--
  WECANWORKI--25
She acts as if it's understood --GIRL--17
IF I NEEDED SOMEONE.--IFINEEDS--Title
If I needed someone to love --IFINEEDS--1
If I needed someone.--IFINEEDS--3
If I had some more time to spend --IFINEEDS--4
If I needed someone.--IFINEEDS--6
If I needed someone.--IFINEEDS--12
If I had some more time to spend --IFINEEDS--14
If I needed someone.--IFINEEDS--16
If I needed someone.--IFINEEDS--22
You better run for your life if you can, little
  girl --RUNFORYOUR--5
You better run for your life if you can, little
  girl --RUNFORYOUR--13
You better run for your life if you can, little
  girl --RUNFORYOUR--21
You better run for your life if you can, little
  girl --RUNFORYOUR--21
That we can have if we close our eyes.--THINKFORYO
  --5
Try thinking more if just for your own sake.--
  THINKFORYO--20
But if your heart breaks, don't wait, turn me
  away --WAIT--5
And if your heart's strong, hold on, I won't
  delay.--WAIT--6
And if you do, I'll trust in you --WAIT--11
And if you do, I'll trust in you --WAIT--19
But if your heart breaks, don't wait, turn me
  away --WAIT--21
And if your heart's strong, hold on, I won't
  delay.--WAIT--22
If you won't see me (you won't see me) --YOUWONTSEE
  --5
I wouldn't mind if I knew what I was missing.--
  YOUWONTSEE--14
If you won't see me (you won't see me) --YOUWONTSEE
  --20

I wouldn't mind if I knew what I was missing.--
  YOUWONTSEE--23
If you won't see me (you won't see me) --YOUWONTSEE
  --29
I can make it longer if you like the style,
  ((paperback))--PAPERBACKW--17
If you really like it you can have the rights,
  ((paperback))--PAPERBACKW--21
If you must return it you can send it here,
  ((paperback))--PAPERBACKW--23
If the rain comes they run and hide their heads--
  RAIN--1
If the rain comes, if the rain comes.--RAIN--3
If the rain comes, if the rain comes.--RAIN--3
If you're down he'll pick you up, Dr. Robert --
  DRROBERT--6
If I'm true I'll never leave--GOTTOGETYO--18
And if I do I know the way there.--GOTTOGETYO--19
And if she's beside me I know I need never care--
  HERETHEREA--9
And if she's beside me I know I need never care--
  HERETHEREA--15
But if I seem to act unkind--IWANTTOTEL--9
If you want me to.--LOVEYOUTWO--17
If you drive a car, I'll tax the street,
  ((car))--TAXMAN--11
If you try to sit, I'll tax your seat, ((sit))--
  TAXMAN--12
If you get too cold, I'll tax the heat,
  ((cold))--TAXMAN--13
If you take a walk, I'll tax your feet.
  ((walk))--TAXMAN--14
If you don't want to pay some more (ha ha Mr.
  Heath)--TAXMAN--19
And though she feels as if she's in a play--
  PENNYLANE--22
Nobody was really sure if he was from the House
  of Lords--DAYINTHELI--10
And it really doesn't matter if I'm wrong I'm
  right--FIXINGAHOL--7
And it really doesn't matter if I'm wrong I'm
  right--FIXINGAHOL--15
If I'd been out till quarter to three--WHENIMSIXT
  --5
And if you say the word--WHENIMSIXT--11
If it's not too dear --WHENIMSIXT--24
What would you think if I sang outta tune --
  WITHALITTL--1
If they only knew.--WITHINYOUW--15
If the sun don't come you get a tan from standing
  in the English rain--IAMTHEWALR--18
But if you want money for people with minds that
  hate --REVOLUTION--18
But if you go carrying pictures of Chairman Mao --
  REVOLUTION--28
The children asked him if to kill was not a sin --
  CONTINUING--27
If looks could kill it would have been us instead
  of him.--CONTINUING--29
And if she could only hear me--HONEYPIE--5
If you want me to, I will.--IWILL--4
For if I ever saw you --IWILL--5
But if you want some fun (ha ha ha) --OBLADIOBLA
  --40
But if you want money for people with minds that
  hate --REVOLUTONE--27
If you go carrying pictures of Chairman Mao --
  REVOLUTONE--43
If I ain't dead already--YERBLUES--4
If I ain't dead already--YERBLUES--8
If I ain't dead already--YERBLUES--15
If I ain't dead already--YERBLUES--22
If I ain't dead already--YERBLUES--29
If you're lonely you can talk to me.--HEYBULLDOG
  --12
If you're lonely you can talk to me - hey!--
  HEYBULLDOG--20
If you're listening to this song --ONLYANORTH--1
Or how I fare or if my hair is brown --ONLYANORTH
  --11
If you think the harmony--ONLYANORTH--13
And if somebody loved me like she do me --
  DONTLETMED--7
If I grow up I'll be a singer --OLDBROWNSH--17
If you and me should get together --OLDBROWNSH--25
Oh darling, if you leave me I'll never make it
  alone --OHDARLING--3
Oh darling, if you leave me, I'll never make
  it alone.--OHDARLING--9
And if you leave me I won't be late again --
  IVEGOTAFEE--8

IGNORANCE

That ignorance and hate may mourn the dead--
  TOMORROWNE--9

ILLUSION
  Who hide themselves behind a wall of illusion---
    WITHINYOUW--4

IMAGES
  Images of broken light which dance before me like
    a million eyes --ACROSSTHEU--11

IMAGINE
  Imagine I'm in love with you--ILLGETYOU--2
  Imagine I'm in love with you--ILLGETYOU--19

IMAGINED
  I've imagined I'm in love with you--ILLGETYOU--4
  I've imagined I'm in love with you--ILLGETYOU--21

IMITATE
  Well you can imitate everyone you know--IDIGAPONY
    --20
  Yes you can imitate everyone you know--IDIGAPONY
    --21

IMPERFECT
  I may appear to be imperfect --OLDBROWNSH--22

IMPORTANT
  That weren't important yesterday--FIXINGAHOL--20

IMPRESSION
  A soap impression of his wife which he ate --
    HAPPINESSI--7

IN
  Remember that I'll always be in love with you.--
    PSILOVEYOU--2
  Remember that I'll always be in love with you.--
    PSILOVEYOU--11
  Remember that I'll always, yeah, be in love
    with you.--PSILOVEYOU--18
  And in time you'll understand the reason why --
    ASKMEWHY--9
  In my heart (in my heart).--PLEASEPLEA--15
  In my heart (in my heart).--PLEASEPLEA--15
  Let me whisper in your ear --DOYOUWANTT--6
  I'm in love with you - ooo--DOYOUWANTT--8
  Let me whisper in your ear, (dodahdo)--DOYOUWANTT
    --12
  I'm in love with you - ooo.--DOYOUWANTT--14
  Let me whisper in your ear, (dodahdo)--DOYOUWANTT
    --20
  I'm in love with you - ooo --DOYOUWANTT--22
  That before too long I'd fall in love with her.--
    ISAWHERSTA--8
  And I held her hand in mine.--ISAWHERSTA--12
  And before too long I fell in love with her--
    ISAWHERSTA--15
  And I held her hand in mine.--ISAWHERSTA--19
  And before too long I fell in love with her.--
    ISAWHERSTA--22
  Without her I will be in misery.--MISERY--9
  Without her I will be in misery.--MISERY--13
  (Ooho) in misery--MISERY--14
  And eternally I'll always be in love with you--
    THANKYOUGI--3
  And eternally I'll always be in love with you--
    THANKYOUGI--13
  Imagine I'm in love with you--ILLGETYOU--2
  I've imagined I'm in love with you--ILLGETYOU--4
  But I'll get you, I'll get you in the end--
    ILLGETYOU--7
  Yes I will I'll get you in the end, oh yeah,
    oh yeah.--ILLGETYOU--8
  That I'll get you, I'll get you in the end--
    ILLGETYOU--14
  Yes I will, I'll get you in the end, oh yeah,
    oh yeah.--ILLGETYOU--15
  Imagine I'm in love with you--ILLGETYOU--19
  I've imagined I'm in love with you--ILLGETYOU--21
  But I'll get you, I'll get you in the end--
    ILLGETYOU--24
  Yes I will, I'll get you in the end, oh yeah,
    oh yeah--ILLGETYOU--25

Is whisper in your ear --ALLIVEGOTT--8
I see no use in wondering why --NOTASECOND--2
I see no use in wondering why --NOTASECOND--13
They'd laugh in my face.--YOUCANTDOT--22
They'd laugh in my face.--YOUCANTDOT--41
In my mind there's no sorrow--THERESAPLA--9
If I fell in love with you --IFIFELL--1
'cos I've been in love before --IFIFELL--4
If I trust in you --IFIFELL--10
If our new love was in vain.--IFIFELL--16
If our new love was in vain.--IFIFELL--23
If I fell in love with you.--IFIFELL--28
Yes, I'm gonna break 'em in two --ILLCRYINST--17
Yes, I'm gonna break 'em in two --ILLCRYINST--26
In this world there's nothing I would rather do --
    IMHAPPYJUS--10
In this world there's nothing I would rather do --
    IMHAPPYJUS--18
In this world there's nothing I would rather do --
    IMHAPPYJUS--26
I've discovered I'm in love with you (oh - oh).--
    IMHAPPYJUS--27
Holding back these tears in my eyes.--TELLMEWHY--16
I'm so in love with you.--TELLMEWHY--25
Deep in love, not a lot to say --THINGSWESA--9
Deep in love, not a lot to say --THINGSWESA--20
Deep in love, not a lot to say --THINGSWESA--31
I'm in love with her and I feel fine.--IFEELFINE
    --3
I'm in love with her and I feel fine.--IFEELFINE
    --6
She's in love with me and I feel fine (ooo).--
    IFEELFINE--11
I'm in love with her and I feel fine.--IFEELFINE
    --14
She's in love with me and I feel fine.--IFEELFINE
    --19
She's in love with me and I feel fine.--IFEELFINE
    --20
BABY'S IN BLACK.--BABYSINBLA--Title
Baby's in black and I'm feeling blue --BABYSINBLA
    --2
She thinks of him and so she dresses in black --
    BABYSINBLA--4
She's dressed in black.--BABYSINBLA--6
Baby's in black and I'm feeling blue --BABYSINBLA
    --8
Baby's in black and I'm feeling blue --BABYSINBLA
    --17
Baby's in black and I'm feeling blue --BABYSINBLA
    --22
She thinks of him and so she dresses in black --
    BABYSINBLA--24
She's dressed in black.--BABYSINBLA--26
Baby's in black and I'm feeling blue --BABYSINBLA
    --28
There's no fun in what I do when she's not there
    --IDONTWANTT--6
There's no fun in what I do if she's not there --
    IDONTWANTT--23
And though I lose a friend in the end you will
    know, oh.--ILLFOLLOWT--6
And though I lose a friend in the end you will
    know, oh.--ILLFOLLOWT--11
She was a girl in a million, my friend --IMALOSER
    --5
I should have known she would win in the end.--
    IMALOSER--6
I saw you walk in your door--NOREPLY--13
'cos you walked hand in hand--NOREPLY--15
With another man in my place.--NOREPLY--16
I saw you walk in your door--NOREPLY--26
'cos you walked hand in hand--NOREPLY--28
With another man in my place.--NOREPLY--29
And ((and)) there's no fun in it --WHATYOURED--6
In spite of you it's true--YESITIS--17
In spite of you it's true--YESITIS--26
If you put your trust in me--TELLMEWHAT--11
I never needed ((never needed)) anybody's help
    in any way--HELP--10
In oh so many ways--HELP--20
My independence ((my independence)) seems to
    vanish in the haze--HELP--21
I never needed anybody's help in any way--HELP--30
Nobody in all the world can do what she can do --
    ANOTHERGIR--7
As I looked in your eyes--INEEDYOU--9
Love was in your eyes (aah the night before)--
    NIGHTBEFOR--2
Love was in your eyes (aah the night before)--
    NIGHTBEFOR--12
Oh I believe in yesterday.--YESTERDAY--4
Oh I believe in yesterday.--YESTERDAY--16
Oh I believe in yesterday.--YESTERDAY--24

Here I stand head in hand--YOUVEGOTTO--1
In the state I'm in.--YOUVEGOTTO--14
In the state I'm in.--YOUVEGOTTO--14
But you can do something in between.--DRIVEMYCAR
    --4
But you see now I'm too much in love.--IFINEEDS
    --9
But you see now I'm too much in love.--IFINEEDS
    --19
IN MY LIFE.--INMYLIFE--Title
In my life I've loved them all.--INMYLIFE--8
In my life I love you more.--INMYLIFE--16
In my life I love you more.--INMYLIFE--20
In my life I love you more.--INMYLIFE--21
She told me she worked in the morning--NORWEGIANW
    --17
And crawled off to sleep in the bath.--NORWEGIANW
    --20
Sitting in his nowhere land --NOWHEREMAN--2
Sitting in his nowhere land --NOWHEREMAN--23
Hide your head in the sand, little girl.--
    RUNFORYOUR--6
Hide your head in the sand, little girl.--
    RUNFORYOUR--14
Hide your head in the sand, little girl.--
    RUNFORYOUR--22
Hide your head in the sand, little girl.--
    RUNFORYOUR--30
The ruins of the life that you had in mind --
    THINKFORYO--11
And if you do, I'll trust in you --WAIT--11
And if you do, I'll trust in you --WAIT--19
What goes on in your heart? (wuh)--WHATGOESON--1
What goes on in your mind?--WHATGOESON--2
What goes on in your mind?--WHATGOESON--5
What goes on in your heart?--WHATGOESON--10
What goes on in your mind?--WHATGOESON--11
What goes on in your mind?--WHATGOESON--14
I met you in the morning waiting for the tides of
    time --WHATGOESON--15
What goes on in your heart?--WHATGOESON--19
(What goes on in your mind?)--WHATGOESON--21
What goes on in your heart?--WHATGOESON--26
What goes on in your mind?--WHATGOESON--27
What goes on in your mind?--WHATGOESON--30
In your mind.--WHATGOESON--31
In your mind.--WHATGOESON--32
In the beginning I misunderstood --THEWORD--7
In the good and the bad books that I have read.--
    THEWORD--16
I'll be writing more in a week or two. ((writer))
    --PAPERBACKW--16
Look in my direction --ANDYOURBIR--8
Helping anyone in need --DRROBERT--9
When I wake up early in the morning --IMONLYSLEE
    --1
When I'm in the middle of a dream --IMONLYSLEE--3
Stay in bed, float upstream (float upstream).--
    IMONLYSLEE--4
When I wake up early in the morning --IMONLYSLEE
    --21
When I'm in the middle of a dream --IMONLYSLEE--23
Stay in bed, float upstream (float upstream).--
    IMONLYSLEE--24
Eleanor Rigby picks up the rice in the church--
    ELEANORRIG--3
Lives in a dream.--ELEANORRIG--5
Wearing the face that she keeps in a jar by the door
    --ELEANORRIG--7
Darning his socks in the night when there's
    nobody there--ELEANORRIG--15
Eleanor Rigby died in the church--ELEANORRIG--21
And in her eyes you see nothing --FORNOONE--7
And in her eyes you see nothing --FORNOONE--14
And in her eyes you see nothing --FORNOONE--24
I feel good in a special way --GOODDAYSUN--4
I'm in love and it's a sunny day.--GOODDAYSUN--5
And had you gone, you knew in time--GOTTOGETYO--10
Who'll screw you in the ground--LOVEYOUTWO--14
They'll fill you in with all their sins, you'll see.
    --LOVEYOUTWO--15
I said who put all those things in your head?--
    SHESAIDSHE--4
In the town where I was born--YELLOWSUBM--1
In the land of submarines.--YELLOWSUBM--4
In our yellow submarine.--YELLOWSUBM--8
We all live in a yellow submarine --YELLOWSUBM--9
We all live in a yellow submarine --YELLOWSUBM--11
We all live in a yellow submarine --YELLOWSUBM--16
We all live in a yellow submarine --YELLOWSUBM--18
In our yellow (in our yellow) submarine
    (submarine - ah ha!)--YELLOWSUBM--28
In our yellow (in our yellow) submarine
    (submarine - ah ha!)--YELLOWSUBM--28

We all live in a yellow submarine --YELLOWSUBM--29
We all live in a yellow submarine --YELLOWSUBM--31
We all live in a yellow submarine --YELLOWSUBM--33
We all live in a yellow submarine --YELLOWSUBM--35
In the pouring rain - very strange.--PENNYLANE--8
Penny Lane is in my ears and in my eyes--PENNYLANE
  --9
Penny Lane is in my ears and in my eyes--PENNYLANE
  --9
In Penny Lane there is a fireman with an
  hour-glass--PENNYLANE--12
And in his pocket is a portrait of the Queen--
  PENNYLANE--13
Penny Lane is in my ears and in my eyes--PENNYLANE
  --17
Penny Lane is in my ears and in my eyes--PENNYLANE
  --17
A four of fish and finger pies in summer--PENNYLANE
  --18
Behind the shelter in the middle of the roundabout
  --PENNYLANE--20
And though she feels as if she's in a play--
  PENNYLANE--22
In Penny Lane the barber shaves another customer--
  PENNYLANE--24
And then the fireman rushes in--PENNYLANE--26
Penny Lane is in my ears and in my eyes--PENNYLANE
  --28
Penny Lane is in my ears and in my eyes--PENNYLANE
  --28
Penny Lane is in my ears and in my eyes--PENNYLANE
  --31
Penny Lane is in my ears and in my eyes--PENNYLANE
  --31
No-one, I think, is in my tree--STRAWBERRY--16
That is you can't, you know, tune in--STRAWBERRY
  --18
In this way Mr. K. will challenge the world.--
  BEINGFORTH--7
Having been some days in preparation--BEINGFORTH
  --19
A DAY IN THE LIFE.--DAYINTHELI--Title
He blew his mind out in a car--DAYINTHELI--6
Made the bus in seconds flat--DAYINTHELI--24
Four thousand holes in Blackburn, Lancashire--
  DAYINTHELI--29
I'm fixing a hole where the rain gets in--
  FIXINGAHOL--1
And wonder why they don't get in my door.--
  FIXINGAHOL--10
I'm painting a room in a colourful way--FIXINGAHOL
  --11
I'm fixing a hole where the rain gets in--
  FIXINGAHOL--23
I'm fixing a hole where the rain gets in--
  FIXINGAHOL--26
Me hiding me head in the sand--GETTINGBET--12
Nothing to do to save his life call his wife in--
  GOODMORNIN--2
Go in to work don't want to go feeling low down--
  GOODMORNIN--7
Heading for home you start to roam then you're in
  town.--GOODMORNIN--8
And you're on your own you're in the street.--
  GOODMORNIN--12
Everywhere in town is getting dark--GOODMORNIN--19
Watching the skirts you start to flirt now you're
  in gear--GOODMORNIN--23
Filling in a ticket in her little white book.--
  LOVELYRITA--9
Filling in a ticket in her little white book.--
  LOVELYRITA--9
In a cap she looked much older--LOVELYRITA--10
LUCY IN THE SKY WITH DIAMONDS.--LUCYINTHES--Title
Picture yourself in a boat on a river--LUCYINTHES
  --1
Look for the girl with the sun in her eyes--
  LUCYINTHES--7
Lucy in the sky with diamonds --LUCYINTHES--9
Lucy in the sky with diamonds --LUCYINTHES--10
Lucy in the sky with diamonds - aah.--LUCYINTHES
  --11
Climb in the back with your head in the clouds--
  LUCYINTHES--18
Climb in the back with your head in the clouds--
  LUCYINTHES--18
Lucy in the sky with diamonds --LUCYINTHES--20
Lucy in the sky with diamonds --LUCYINTHES--21
Lucy in the sky with diamonds - aah.--LUCYINTHES
  --22
Picture yourself on a train in a station--
  LUCYINTHES--23
Lucy in the sky with diamonds --LUCYINTHES--27
Lucy in the sky with diamonds --LUCYINTHES--28

Lucy in the sky with diamonds - aah.--LUCYINTHES
  --29
Lucy in the sky with diamonds --LUCYINTHES--30
Lucy in the sky with diamonds --LUCYINTHES--31
Lucy in the sky with diamonds - aah.--LUCYINTHES
  --32
Lucy in the sky with diamonds --LUCYINTHES--33
Lucy in the sky with diamonds (aah - ooo) --
  LUCYINTHES--34
Lucy in the sky with diamonds.--LUCYINTHES--35
They've been going in and out of style--SGTPEPPERS
  --3
In the Isle of Wight --WHENIMSIXT--23
Fill in a form--WHENIMSIXT--33
(Would you believe in a love at first sight?)--
  WITHALITTL--19
Nothing you can do but you can learn how to be
  you in time ((love))--ALLYOUN/YS--10
You keep all your money in a big brown bag --
  BABYYOUREA--16
You keep all your money in a big brown bag --
  BABYYOUREA--31
Mr. City policeman sitting pretty little
  policemen in a row--IAMTHEWALR--9
See how they fly like Lucy in the sky, see how
  they run--IAMTHEWALR--10
Sitting in an English garden waiting for the sun--
  IAMTHEWALR--17
If the sun don't come you get a tan from standing
  in the English rain--IAMTHEWALR--18
See how they smile, like pigs in a sty, see how
  they snied--IAMTHEWALR--23
Sitting here in Blue Jay Way (way).--BLUEJAYWAY--18
And the eyes in his head see the world spinning
  round.--FOOLONTHEH--7
Well on the way, head in a cloud--FOOLONTHEH--8
And the eyes in his head see the world spinning
  round.--FOOLONTHEH--14
And the eyes in his head see the world spinning
  round.--FOOLONTHEH--19
And the eyes in his head see the world spinning
  round.--FOOLONTHEH--26
Listen to the music playing in your head.--
  LADYMADONN--13
You have found her, now go and get her (let it
  out and let it in) --HEYJUDE--16
So let it out and let it in --HEYJUDE--19
BACK IN THE USSR.--BACKINTHEU--Title
Oh - flew in from Miami Beach BOAC --BACKINTHEU--1
I'm back in the USSR --BACKINTHEU--5
Back in the USSR (yeah).--BACKINTHEU--7
I'm back in the USSR --BACKINTHEU--12
Back in the US, back in the US, back in the
  USSR.--BACKINTHEU--14
Back in the US, back in the US, back in the
  USSR.--BACKINTHEU--14
Back in the US, back in the US, back in the
  USSR.--BACKINTHEU--14
Hey, I'm back in the USSR.--BACKINTHEU--24
Back in the USSR.--BACKINTHEU--26
I'm back in the USSR (hey!) --BACKINTHEU--35
Back in the USSR.--BACKINTHEU--37
I'm back in the USSR --BACKINTHEU--40
Yeah - back in the USSR.--BACKINTHEU--42
Blackbird singing in the dead of night --BLACKBIRD
  --1
Blackbird singing in the dead of night --BLACKBIRD
  --5
Blackbird singing in the dead of night --BLACKBIRD
  --13
In case of accidents he always took his mom --
  CONTINUING--8
Deep in the jungle where the mighty tiger lies --
  CONTINUING--17
(But when he looked so fierce) his mommy butted
  in --CONTINUING--28
The King of Marigold was in the kitchen --
  CRYBABYCRY--4
The Queen was in the parlour --CRYBABYCRY--6
The King was in the garden --CRYBABYCRY--12
The Queen was in the playroom --CRYBABYCRY--14
For a seance in the dark --CRYBABYCRY--29
You were in a car crash --DONTPASSME--25
Your inside is out when your outside is in --
  EVRBDYMONK--17
Your outside is in when your inside is out --
  EVRBDYMONK--18
Fixing the hole in the ocean--GLASSONION--21
The man in the crowd with the multicoloured
  mirrors on his hobnail boots --HAPPINESSI--5
When I hold you in my arms ((oh, yeah)) --
  HAPPINESSI--22
In the USA--HONEYPIE--4
I'm in love but I'm lazy--HONEYPIE--8

Makes me weak in the knee.--HONEYPIE--15
I'm in love but I'm lazy--HONEYPIE--30
Glimmering in the sun.--JULIA--8
Martha my dear, though I spend my days in
    conversation --MARTHAMYDE--1
When you find yourself in the thick of it --
    MARTHAMYDE--5
When you find yourself in the thick of it --
    MARTHAMYDE--11
Find me in my field of grass - Mother Nature's
    son --MOTHERNATU--8
Desmond has a barrow in the market-place --
    OBLADIOBLA--1
Molly is the singer in a band --OBLADIOBLA--2
In a couple of years they have built a home sweet
    home --OBLADIOBLA--17
With a couple of kids running in the yard of
    Desmond and Molly Jones.--OBLADIOBLA--18
Happy ever after in the market place --OBLADIOBLA
    --20
And in the evening she still sings it with the
    band, yes.--OBLADIOBLA--24
In a couple of years they have built a home sweet
    home--OBLADIOBLA--29
With a couple of kids running in the yard of
    Desmond and Molly Jones.--OBLADIOBLA--30
Hey, happy ever after in the market place --
    OBLADIOBLA--32
And in the evening she's a singer with the band,
    yeah.--OBLADIOBLA--35
Crawling in the dirt?--PIGGIES--2
Always having dirt to play around in.--PIGGIES--5
In the starched white shirts?--PIGGIES--7
Always have clean shirts to play around in.--
    PIGGIES--10
In their sties with all their backing--PIGGIES--11
In their lives there's something lacking--PIGGIES
    --13
Don't you know that you can count me out (in)?--
    REVOLUTONE--12
Now somewhere in the Black Mountain hills of
    Dakota --ROCKYRACCO--1
Hit young Rocky in the eye.--ROCKYRACCO--4
Booked himself a room in the local saloon.--
    ROCKYRACCO--8
Were in the next room at the hoe-down --ROCKYRACCO
    --18
A - Rocky burst in and grinning a grin--ROCKYRACCO
    --19
And Rocky collapsed in the corner - ah.--ROCKYRACCO
    --22
Now the doctor came in stinking of gin--ROCKYRACCO
    --31
A - now Rocky Raccoon, he fell back in his room--
    ROCKYRACCO--36
WHY DON'T WE DO IT IN THE ROAD?--WHYDONTWED--Title
Why don't we do - do it in the road?--WHYDONTWED
    --1
Why don't we do it in the road? (ah-ha)--WHYDONTWED
    --2
Why don't we do it in the road? - mmm--WHYDONTWED
    --3
Why don't we do it in the road?--WHYDONTWED--4
Why don't we do it in the road?--WHYDONTWED--6
Why don't we do it in the road?--WHYDONTWED--7
Why don't we do it in the road?--WHYDONTWED--8
Why don't we do it in the road?--WHYDONTWED--9
Why don't we do it in the road?--WHYDONTWED--10
Why don't we do it in the road?--WHYDONTWED--12
Well, why don't we do it in the road?--WHYDONTWED
    --13
Why don't we do it in the road?--WHYDONTWED--14
Why don't we do - do it, do it in the road?--
    WHYDONTWED--15
Why don't we do it, yeah, in the road?--WHYDONTWED
    --16
Why don't you do it in the road?--WHYDONTWED--18
In the morning - wanna die --YERBLUES--6
In the evening - wanna die --YERBLUES--7
In the evening...--YERBLUES--35
Sheep dog standing in the rain--HEYBULLDOG--1
Some kind of happiness is measured out in miles--
    HEYBULLDOG--3
Jack-knife in your sweaty hands--HEYBULLDOG--6
Some kind of innocence is measured out in years--
    HEYBULLDOG--7
Big man (yeah?) walking in the park--HEYBULLDOG--13
Some kind of solitude is measured out in you--
    HEYBULLDOG--15
I'm in love for the first time --DONTLETMED--13
Jojo left his home in Tucson, Arizona--GETBACK/45
    --3
Standing in the dock at Southampton --BALLADOFJO
    --1

The man in the mack said you've got to go back --
    BALLADOFJO--3
You can get married in Gibraltar near Spain.--
    BALLADOFJO--12
Talking in our beds for a week.--BALLADOFJO--18
    --18
The news-people said, say what're you doing in
    bed?--BALLADOFJO--19
Eating chocolate cake in the bag.--BALLADOFJO
    --30
They look just like two gurus in drag.--BALLADOFJO
    --32
Fifty acorns tied in a sack.--BALLADOFJO--38
Baby, I'm in love with you --OLDBROWNSH--6
Baby, I'm in love with you --OLDBROWNSH--14
For your sweet top lip I'm in the queue --
    OLDBROWNSH--31
Baby, I'm in love with you.--OLDBROWNSH--32
And in the middle of the celebrations--CARRYTHATW
    --7
Hold you in his armchair you can feel his disease
    --COMETOGETH--30
Are you gonna come in my dreams tonight?--THEEND
    --2
And in the end --THEEND--8
Joan was quizzical, studied pataphysical science
    in the home --MAXWELLSIL--1
Maxwell Edison, majoring in medicine, calls
    her on the phone --MAXWELLSIL--3
Back in school again Maxwell plays the fool
    again, teacher gets annoyed --MAXWELLSIL--8
Mean Mr. Mustard sleeps in the park--MEANMRMUST--1
Shaves in the dark--MEANMRMUST--2
Sleeps in a hole in the road--MEANMRMUST--4
Sleeps in a hole in the road--MEANMRMUST--8
His sister Pam works in a shop--MEANMRMUST--8
In an octopus's garden in the shade.--OCTOPUSSGA
    --2
In an octopus's garden in the shade.--OCTOPUSSGA
    --2
He'd let us in, knows where we've been--OCTOPUSSGA
    --3
In his octopus's garden in the shade.--OCTOPUSSGA
    --4
In his octopus's garden in the shade.--OCTOPUSSGA
    --4
In an octopus's garden in the shade.--OCTOPUSSGA
    --8
In an octopus's garden in the shade.--OCTOPUSSGA
    --8
In our little hideaway beneath the waves.--
    OCTOPUSSGA--10
In an octopus's garden near a cave.--OCTOPUSSGA--12
In an octopus's garden in the shade.--OCTOPUSSGA
    --16
In an octopus's garden in the shade.--OCTOPUSSGA
    --16
In an octopus's garden with you --OCTOPUSSGA--24
In an octopus's garden with you --OCTOPUSSGA--25
In an octopus's garden with you.--OCTOPUSSGA--26
Well, you should see her in drag --POLYTHENEP--3
Dressed in her polythene bag.--POLYTHENEP--4
Get a dose of her in jackboots and kilt --
    POLYTHENEP--6
SHE CAME IN THROUGH THE BATHROOM WINDOW.--
    SHECAMEINT--Title
She came in through the bathroom window --
    SHECAMEINT--4
Something in the way she moves--SOMETHING--1
Something in the way she woos me --SOMETHING--3
Somewhere in her smile she knows--SOMETHING--6
Something in her style that shows me --SOMETHING
    --8
Something in the way she knows--SOMETHING--15
Something in the things she shows me --SOMETHING
    --17
And in the middle of negotiations you break down.
    --YOUNEVERGI--3
And in the middle of investigation I break down.--
    YOUNEVERGI--6
Pick up the bags, get in the limousine.--YOUNEVERGI
    --18
When I find myself in times of trouble --LETITBE/45
    --1
And in my hour of darkness--LETITBE/45--4
She is standing right in front of me --LETITBE/45
    --5
Living in the world agree --LETITBE/45--10
I want you in the morning girl, I love you --
    FORYOUBLUE--5
Jojo left his home in Tucson, Arizona--GETBACK/LP
    --9
When I find myself in times of trouble --LETITBE/LP
    --1

And in my hour of darkness--LETITBE/LP--4
She is standing right in front of me --LETITBE/LP
--5
Living in the world agree --LETITBE/LP--10
Phase one in which Doris gets her oats.--TWOOFUS
--2
Standing solo in the sun.--TWOOFUS--20
Standing solo in the sun.--TWOOFUS--29

INCITING
Inciting and inviting me.--ACROSSTHEU--22

INCREDIBLY
That grow so incredibly high (high).--LUCYINTHES
--15

INDEPENDENCE
My independence ((my independence)) seems to
vanish in the haze--HELP--21
My independence ((my independence)) seems to
vanish in the haze--HELP--21

INDICATE
Indicate precisely what you mean to say--WHENIMSIXT
--30
Well you can indicate everything you see--IDIGAPONY
--27
Yes you can indicate anything you see.--IDIGAPONY
--28

INNER
THE INNER LIGHT.--INNERLIGHT--Title

INNOCENCE
Some kind of innocence is measured out in years--
HEYBULLDOG--7

INQUIRE
May I inquire discreetly ((lovely Rita))--
LOVELYRITA--14

INSANE
You know it's three weeks, I'm going insane --
IMSOTIRED--12
You know it's three weeks, I'm going insane --
IMSOTIRED--21

INSECURE
But ((but)) every now and then ((now and then))
I feel so insecure--HELP--22

INSIDE
I feel happy inside--IWANTTOHOL--14
I feel happy inside--IWANTTOHOL--17
When you sigh my my inside just flies, butterfly.
--ITSONLYLOV--2
Something inside that was always denied--SHESLEAVIN
--31
Inside a zoo --BABYYOUREA--17
Inside a zoo --BABYYOUREA--32
Your inside is out when your outside is in --
EVRBDYMONK--17
Your outside is in when your inside is out --
EVRBDYMONK--18
And the more I go inside --ITSALLTOOM--6
Thoughts meander like a restless wind inside a
letter-box --ACROSSTHEU--13
I've got a feeling, a feeling deep inside --
IVEGOTAFEE--1
Everybody had a hard time ((a feeling deep
inside, oh yeah)) --IVEGOTAFEE--29

INSPIRATION
Martha my dear, you have always been my
inspiration --MARTHAMYDE--13

INSTEAD
I'LL CRY INSTEAD.--ILLCRYINST--Title
But I can't, so I'll cry instead.--ILLCRYINST--5
But I can't, so I'll cry instead.--ILLCRYINST--10
Until then I'll cry instead.--ILLCRYINST--19
Until then I'll cry instead.--ILLCRYINST--28

Now they've lost themselves instead.--BLUEJAYWAY
--4
You better free your mind instead.--REVOLUTION--27
If looks could kill it would have been us instead
of him.--CONTINUING--29
You'd better free your mind instead.--REVOLUTONE
--41

INSTITUTION
You tell me it's the institution --REVOLUTION--25
You tell me it's the institution --REVOLUTONE--39

INTO
Just look into my eyes --ANYTIMEATA--5
Look into these eyes now--TELLMEWHAT--13
When the sun shines they slip into the shade
(when the sun shines down)--RAIN--4
GOT TO GET YOU INTO MY LIFE.--GOTTOGETYO--Title
Got to get you into my life.--GOTTOGETYO--15
Got to get you into my life.--GOTTOGETYO--23
I got to get you into my life.--GOTTOGETYO--24
And somebody spoke and I went into a dream--
DAYINTHELI--26
Father snores as his wife gets into her
dressing-gown--SHESLEAVIN--13
Remember to let her into your heart --HEYJUDE--3
Remember (hey jude) to let her into your heart --
HEYJUDE--17
Into the light of a dark black night.--BLACKBIRD
--10
Into the light of a dark black night.--BLACKBIRD
--12
So one day he walked into town --ROCKYRACCO--7
Rocky Raccoon checked into his room --ROCKYRACCO
--9
When I look into your eyes --ITSALLTOOM--4
Finally made the plane into Paris --BALLADOFJO--9
Words are flowing out like endless rain into a
paper cup --ACROSSTHEU--1

INTRODUCE
So may I introduce to you--SGTPEPPERS--5
So let me introduce to you--SGTPEPPERS--23

INVERTED
I don't know how you were inverted--WHILEMYGUI--16

INVESTIGATION
And in the middle of investigation I break down.--
YOUNEVERGI--6

INVITATION
Roll up (and that's an invitation)--MAGICALMYS--5
Roll up (and that's an invitation)--MAGICALMYS--23

INVITATIONS
I only send you my invitations--CARRYTHATW--6

INVITING
Inciting and inviting me.--ACROSSTHEU--22

IS
All you gotta do is call --ANYTIMEATA--2
All you gotta do is call --ANYTIMEATA--11
There is nothing I won't do --ANYTIMEATA--15
All ya gotta do is call --ANYTIMEATA--20
All you gotta do is call --ANYTIMEATA--23
All ya gotta do is call --ANYTIMEATA--26
The world is treating me bad, misery.--MISERY--1
The world is treating me bad, misery.--MISERY--3
And all I gotta do is thank you girl, thank you
girl.--THANKYOUGI--4
And all I gotta do is thank you girl, thank you
girl--THANKYOUGI--7
That's the kind of love that is too good to be true
--THANKYOUGI--9
And all I gotta do is thank you girl, thank you
girl.--THANKYOUGI--10
And all I gotta do is thank you girl, thank you
girl.--THANKYOUGI--14
Is call you on the phone --ALLIVEGOTT--3
Is whisper in your ear --ALLIVEGOTT--8
Is call you on the phone --ALLIVEGOTT--19
My crying is through, oh.--NOTASECOND--6
My crying is through, oh.--NOTASECOND--17

Dark is the sky --ANDILOVEHE--16
Dark is the sky --ANDILOVEHE--21
If this is love you've got to give me more --
   ISHOULDHAV--12
Before this dance is through --IMHAPPYJUS--1
There is really nothing else I'd rather do --
   IMHAPPYJUS--6
Just to dance with you is everything I need (oh)
   --IMHAPPYJUS--12
Before this dance is through ((aah)) --IMHAPPYJUS
   --13
Just to dance with you (oh) is everything I
   need (oh) --IMHAPPYJUS--20
Before this dance is through ((aah)) --IMHAPPYJUS
   --21
All I do is hang my head and moan.--TELLMEWHY--8
Love to hear you say that love is love--THINGSWESA
   --12
Love is here to stay.--THINGSWESA--14
Love to hear you say that love is love--THINGSWESA
   --23
Love is here to stay.--THINGSWESA--25
She is happy just to hear me say that--SHESAWOMAN
   --10
Eight days a week is not enough to show I care.--
   EIGHTDAYSA--18
Eight days a week is not enough to show I care.--
   EIGHTDAYSA--28
There is one thing I'm sure of--EVERYLITTL--14
There is one love I should never have crossed.--
   IMALOSER--4
Is it for her or myself that I cry?--IMALOSER--12
The girl that's driving me mad is going away.--
   TICKETTORI--4
The girl that's driving me mad is going away,
   yeah.--TICKETTORI--25
YES IT IS.--YESITIS--Title
For red is the colour that my baby wore--YESITIS
   --3
And what's more, it's true, yes it is.--YESITIS--4
Yes it is, it's true, yes it is.--YESITIS--9
Yes it is, it's true, yes it is.--YESITIS--9
Yes it is, yes it is, oh yes it is, yeah.--YESITIS
   --13
Yes it is, yes it is, oh yes it is, yeah.--YESITIS
   --13
Yes it is, yes it is, oh yes it is, yeah.--YESITIS
   --13
This is what I said tonight--YESITIS--15
For red is the colour that will make me blue--
   YESITIS--16
Yes it is, it's true, yes it is.--YESITIS--18
Yes it is, it's true, yes it is.--YESITIS--18
Yes it is, yes it is, oh yes it is, yeah.--YESITIS
   --22
Yes it is, yes it is, oh yes it is, yeah.--YESITIS
   --22
Yes it is, yes it is, oh yes it is, yeah.--YESITIS
   --22
This is what I said tonight--YESITIS--24
For red is the colour that will make me blue--
   YESITIS--25
Yes it is, it's true--YESITIS--27
Yes it is, it's true.--YESITIS--28
It is no surprise now--TELLMEWHAT--7
What you see is me--TELLMEWHAT--8
What you see is me--TELLMEWHAT--16
It is no surprise now--TELLMEWHAT--24
What you see is me--TELLMEWHAT--25
It is no surprise now--TELLMEWHAT--33
What you see is me--TELLMEWHAT--34
Which is all that I deserve--YOULIKEMET--10
It's only love and that is all--ITSONLYLOV--4
It's only love and that is all--ITSONLYLOV--6
Is it right that you and I should fight, every
   night--ITSONLYLOV--8
It's only love and that is all--ITSONLYLOV--11
It's only love and that is all--ITSONLYLOV--13
But as it is I'll dream of her tonight --IVEJUSTSEE
   --10
Last night is the night I will remember you by --
   NIGHTBEFOR--9
Last night is the night I will remember you by --
   NIGHTBEFOR--17
Life is very short and there's no time--WECANWORKI
   --11
Life is very short and there's no time--WECANWORKI
   --20
Working for peanuts is all very fine --DRIVEMYCAR
   --11
Is there anybody going to listen to my story--GIRL
   --1
Your voice is soothing but the words aren't clear.
   --IMLOOKINGT--6

The only difference is you're down there.--
   IMLOOKINGT--13
There is no-one compares with you --INMYLIFE--10
Nowhere Man the world is at your command.--
   NOWHEREMAN--9
Nowhere Man the world is at your command.--
   NOWHEREMAN--21
But now the tide is turning I can see that I
   was blind.--WHATGOESON--16
Have you heard the word is love?--THEWORD--4
But now I've got it the word is good.--THEWORD--8
Have you heard the word is love?--THEWORD--12
Have you heard the word is love?--THEWORD--20
That the word is just the way --THEWORD--26
And the only word is love.--THEWORD--28
His son is working for the Daily Mail --PAPERBACKW
   --10
And your bird is green --ANDYOURBIR--5
When your bird is broken will it bring you down?--
   ANDYOURBIR--10
You tell me that you heard every sound there is --
   ANDYOURBIR--13
Who is it for?--ELEANORRIG--8
When she says her love is dead --FORNOONE--12
I need to laugh and when the sun is out --
   GOODDAYSUN--2
We take a walk, the sun is shining down --
   GOODDAYSUN--7
I'm so proud to know that she is mine.--GOODDAYSUN
   --13
Someone is speaking but she doesn't know he's
   there.--HERETHEREA--7
But to love her is to need her everywhere.--
   HERETHEREA--10
Knowing that love is to share--HERETHEREA--11
But to love her is to need her everywhere.--
   HERETHEREA--16
Knowing that love is to share--HERETHEREA--17
My head is filled with things to say --IWANTTOTEL
   --2
That is confusing things.--IWANTTOTEL--11
A lifetime is so short--LOVEYOUTWO--6
I know what it is to be sad--SHESAIDSHE--2
I know what it is to be sad (I know what it is
   to be sad).--SHESAIDSHE--21
I know what it is to be sad (I know what it is
   to be sad).--SHESAIDSHE--21
It is not dying, it is not dying.--TOMORROWNE--2
It is not dying, it is not dying.--TOMORROWNE--2
It is shining, it is shining.--TOMORROWNE--4
It is shining, it is shining.--TOMORROWNE--4
It is being, it is being.--TOMORROWNE--6
It is being, it is being.--TOMORROWNE--6
That love is all and love is everyone--TOMORROWNE
   --7
That love is all and love is everyone--TOMORROWNE
   --7
It is knowing, it is knowing.--TOMORROWNE--8
It is knowing, it is knowing.--TOMORROWNE--8
It is believing, it is believing.--TOMORROWNE--10
It is believing, it is believing.--TOMORROWNE--10
It is not living, it is not living.--TOMORROWNE--12
It is not living, it is not living.--TOMORROWNE--12
Full speed ahead it is, Sgt.--YELLOWSUBM--21
Penny Lane: there is a barber showing photographs
   --PENNYLANE--1
On the corner is a banker with a motorcar--
   PENNYLANE--5
Penny Lane is in my ears and in my eyes--PENNYLANE
   --9
In Penny Lane there is a fireman with an
   hour-glass--PENNYLANE--12
And in his pocket is a portrait of the Queen--
   PENNYLANE--13
Penny Lane is in my ears and in my eyes--PENNYLANE
   --17
The pretty nurse is selling poppies from a tray--
   PENNYLANE--21
She is anyway.--PENNYLANE--23
Penny Lane is in my ears and in my eyes--PENNYLANE
   --28
Penny Lane is in my ears and in my eyes--PENNYLANE
   --31
Nothing is real--STRAWBERRY--3
Living is easy with eyes closed--STRAWBERRY--6
Nothing is real--STRAWBERRY--13
No-one, I think, is in my tree--STRAWBERRY--16
That is you can't, you know, tune in--STRAWBERRY
   --18
That is, I think it's not too bad.--STRAWBERRY--20
Nothing is real--STRAWBERRY--23
That is, I think I disagree.--STRAWBERRY--30
Nothing is real--STRAWBERRY--33
A splendid time is guaranteed for all--BEINGFORTH

--20
And tonight Mr. Kite is topping the bill.--
   BEINGFORTH--21
And when my mind is wandering--FIXINGAHOL--12
Everything is closed it's like a ruin--GOODMORNIN
   --10
Everyone you see is half asleep--GOODMORNIN--11
Everywhere in town is getting dark--GOODMORNIN--19
Everyone you see is full of life--GOODMORNIN--20
Suddenly someone is there at the turnstyle--
   LUCYINTHES--25
Stepping outside she is free.--SHESLEAVIN--7
Is leaving (sacrificed most of our lives)--
   SHESLEAVIN--9
Is leaving (never a thought for our ourselves)--
   SHESLEAVIN--21
Friday morning at nine o'clock she is far away--
   SHESLEAVIN--25
Is having (we didn't know it was wrong)--SHESLEAVIN
   --29
Fun. (fun is the one thing that money can't buy)--
   SHESLEAVIN--30
What do I do when my love is away?--WITHALITTL--8
Peace of mind is waiting there--WITHINYOUW--30
ALL YOU NEED IS LOVE.--ALLYOUN/YS--Title
All you need is love, all you need is love --
   ALLYOUN/YS--12
All you need is love, all you need is love --
   ALLYOUN/YS--12
All you need is love, love, love is all you need.
   --ALLYOUN/YS--13
All you need is love, love, love is all you need.
   --ALLYOUN/YS--13
All you need is love, (wuh) all you need is
   love (hey) --ALLYOUN/YS--17
All you need is love, (wuh) all you need is
   love (hey) --ALLYOUN/YS--17
All you need is love, love, love is all you need.
   --ALLYOUN/YS--18
All you need is love, love, love is all you need.
   --ALLYOUN/YS--18
All you need is love, all you need is love --
   ALLYOUN/YS--23
All you need is love, all you need is love --
   ALLYOUN/YS--23
All you need is love, love, love is all you need.
   --ALLYOUN/YS--24
All you need is love, love, love is all you need.
   --ALLYOUN/YS--24
All you need is love (all together now) --
   ALLYOUN/YS--25
All you need is love (everybody),--ALLYOUN/YS--26
All you need is love, love, love is all you need.
   --ALLYOUN/YS--27
All you need is love, love, love is all you need.
   --ALLYOUN/YS--27
Love is all you need (love is all you need)--
   ALLYOUN/YS--28
Love is all you need (love is all you need)--
   ALLYOUN/YS--28
Love is all you need (love is all you need)--
   ALLYOUN/YS--29
Love is all you need (love is all you need)--
   ALLYOUN/YS--29
Love is all you need (love is all you need)--
   ALLYOUN/YS--30
Love is all you need (love is all you need)--
   ALLYOUN/YS--30
Love is all you need (love is all you need)--
   ALLYOUN/YS--31
Love is all you need (love is all you need)--
   ALLYOUN/YS--31
Love is all you need (wuh) (love is all you
   need)--ALLYOUN/YS--32
Love is all you need (wuh) (love is all you
   need)--ALLYOUN/YS--32
Love is all you need (love is all you need)--
   ALLYOUN/YS--33
Love is all you need (love is all you need)--
   ALLYOUN/YS--33
Love is all you need (love is all you need)--
   ALLYOUN/YS--34
Love is all you need (love is all you need)--
   ALLYOUN/YS--34
Love is all you need (love is all you need)--
   ALLYOUN/YS--35
Love is all you need (love is all you need)--
   ALLYOUN/YS--35
Love is all you need (love is all you need)--
   ALLYOUN/YS--36
Love is all you need (love is all you need)--
   ALLYOUN/YS--36
Love is all you need (love is all you need)--
   ALLYOUN/YS--37

Love is all you need (love is all you need)--
   ALLYOUN/YS--37
Love is all you need (yahoo) (eee - hi)--
   ALLYOUN/YS--38
Love is all you need (love is all you need)--
   ALLYOUN/YS--39
Love is all you need (love is all you need)--
   ALLYOUN/YS--39
(Love is all you need) Yesterday (love is all
   you need)--ALLYOUN/YS--40
(Love is all you need) Yesterday (love is all
   you need)--ALLYOUN/YS--40
(Oh) love is all you need--ALLYOUN/YS--41
Love is all you need (oh yeah)--ALLYOUN/YS
   --42
Love is all you need--ALLYOUN/YS--43
Loves you yeah, yeah, yeah ((love is all, love
   is all))--ALLYOUN/YS--44
Loves you yeah, yeah, yeah ((love is all, love
   is all))--ALLYOUN/YS--44
She loves you yeah, yeah, yeah ((love is all,
   love is all))--ALLYOUN/YS--45
She loves you yeah, yeah, yeah ((love is all,
   love is all))--ALLYOUN/YS--45
Love is all you need--ALLYOUN/YS--46
Love is all you need (wuhoo)--ALLYOUN/YS--47
Love is all you need (wuhoo)--ALLYOUN/YS--48
Love is all you need (oh)--ALLYOUN/YS--49
Love is all you need--ALLYOUN/YS--50
Love is all you need.--ALLYOUN/YS--51
The man with the foolish grin is keeping
   perfectly still--FOOLONTHEH--2
The Magical Mystery Tour is waiting to take
   you away--MAGICALMYS--9
The Magical Mystery Tour is hoping to take you
   away --MAGICALMYS--17
The Magical Mystery Tour is coming to take you
   away --MAGICALMYS--27
The Magical Mystery Tour is dying to take you
   away--MAGICALMYS--29
Tuesday afternoon is never-ending--LADYMADONN
   --14
The movement you need is on your shoulder.--HEYJUDE
   --24
All I can tell you is brother you have to wait.--
   REVOLUTION--19
The sun is up, the sky is blue --DEARPRUDEN--3
The sun is up, the sky is blue --DEARPRUDEN--3
The wind is low, the birds will sing --DEARPRUDEN
   --8
The sun is up, the sky is blue --DEARPRUDEN--23
The sun is up, the sky is blue --DEARPRUDEN--23
Come on is such a joy --EVRBDYMONK--2
Come on is such a joy --EVRBDYMONK--3
Come on is take it easy --EVRBDYMONK--4
Come on is take it easy --EVRBDYMONK--5
Come on is such a joy --EVRBDYMONK--11
Come on is such a joy --EVRBDYMONK--12
Come on is make it easy --EVRBDYMONK--13
Come on is make it easy - wuh.--EVRBDYMONK--14
Your inside is out when your outside is in --
   EVRBDYMONK--17
Your inside is out when your outside is in --
   EVRBDYMONK--17
Your outside is in when your inside is out --
   EVRBDYMONK--18
Your outside is in when your inside is out --
   EVRBDYMONK--18
Come on is such a joy --EVRBDYMONK--20
Come on is such a joy --EVRBDYMONK--21
Come on is make it easy --EVRBDYMONK--22
Come on is make it easy --EVRBDYMONK--23
You know the place where nothing is real--
   GLASSONION--2
HAPPINESS IS A WARM GUN.--HAPPINESSI--Title
Happiness ((happiness)) is a warm gun--HAPPINESSI
   --18
Happiness ((happiness)) is a warm gun, momma--
   HAPPINESSI--20
Because - (happiness) is a warm gun, momma--
   HAPPINESSI--25
Happiness ((happiness)) is a warm gun, yes it is--
   HAPPINESSI--27
Happiness ((happiness)) is a warm gun, yes it is--
   HAPPINESSI--27
Happiness is a warm, yes it is - gun--HAPPINESSI
   --29
Happiness is a warm, yes it is - gun--HAPPINESSI
   --29
Is a warm gun, momma ((is a warm gun, yeah)).--
   HAPPINESSI--32
Is a warm gun, momma ((is a warm gun, yeah)).--
   HAPPINESSI--32
Yes she is, yes she is.--HELTERSKEL--29

Yes she is, yes she is.--HELTERSKEL--29
This is what I'd say:--HONEYPIE--6
Oh, Honey Pie my position is tragic--HONEYPIE--10
I'm so tired, my mind is on the blink --IMSOTIRED
     --2
I'm so tired, my mind is set on you --IMSOTIRED--6
Half of what I say is meaningless --JULIA--1
Her hair of floating sky is shimmering --JULIA--7
Help yourself to a bit of what is all around you
     - silly girl.--MARTHAMYDE--6
Help yourself to a bit of what is all around you
     - silly girl.--MARTHAMYDE--12
Molly is the singer in a band --OBLADIOBLA--2
Life is getting worse --PIGGIES--4
Well all I can tell you is brother you have to
     wait.--REVOLUTONE--28
He said, Danny - Boy this is a showdown.--
     ROCKYRACCO--20
But what is sweet now turns so sour.--SAVOYTRUFF
     --20
ALL YOU NEED IS LOVE.--ALLYOU/MMT--Title
Love is all you need--ALLYOU/MMT--1
(Oh) love is all you need--ALLYOU/MMT--2
Love is all you need--ALLYOU/MMT--3
Love is all you need--ALLYOU/MMT--4
Love is all you need--ALLYOU/MMT--5
Love is all you need.--ALLYOU/MMT--6
Some kind of happiness is measured out in miles--
     HEYBULLDOG--3
Some kind of innocence is measured out in years--
     HEYBULLDOG--7
Some kind of solitude is measured out in you--
     HEYBULLDOG--15
Your love is there for me--ITSALLTOOM--5
The more there is to see.--ITSALLTOOM--7
All the world is birthday cake --ITSALLTOOM--18
And what I do is all too much.--ITSALLTOOM--28
What words I say or time of day it is --ONLYANORTH
     --8
Or how I fare or if my hair is brown --ONLYANORTH
     --11
Is a little dark and out of key --ONLYANORTH--14
But right is only half of what's wrong --OLDBROWNSH
     --2
My love is something you can't reject.--OLDBROWNSH
     --23
To miss that love is something I'd hate.--
     OLDBROWNSH--28
Because the world is round it turns me on --BECAUSE
     --2
Because the world is round.--BECAUSE--3
Because the wind is high it blows my mind --BECAUSE
     --5
Because the wind is high.--BECAUSE--6
Love is old, love is new --BECAUSE--8
Love is old, love is new --BECAUSE--8
Love is all, love is you.--BECAUSE--9
Love is all, love is you.--BECAUSE--9
Because the sky is blue it makes me cry --BECAUSE
     --10
Because the sky is blue.--BECAUSE--11
One thing I can tell you is you got to be free--
     COMETOGETH--20
He say one and one and one is three--COMETOGETH--40
The love you take is equal to the love you make.--
     THEEND--9
Little darling, I feel that ice is slowly
     melting.--HERECOMEST--18
And all I have to do is think of her --SOMETHING
     --16
She is standing right in front of me --LETITBE/45
     --5
There is still a chance that they will see --
     LETITBE/45--13
And when the night is cloudy --LETITBE/45--21
There is still a light that shines on me --
     LETITBE/45--22
All I want is you--IDIGAPONY--13
All I want is you--IDIGAPONY--23
All I want is you--IDIGAPONY--33
She is standing right in front of me --LETITBE/LP
     --5
There is still a chance that they will see --
     LETITBE/LP--13
And when the night is cloudy --LETITBE/LP--21
There is still a light that shines on me --
     LETITBE/LP--22

ISLE

In the Isle of Wight --WHENIMSIXT--23

ISN'T

That boy isn't good for you--THISBOY--4
I know she isn't--SHESAWOMAN--7
I know she isn't--SHESAWOMAN--24
I know she isn't--SHESAWOMAN--34
Isn't it good --NORWEGIANW--5
Isn't it good --NORWEGIANW--25
Isn't he a bit like you and me?--NOWHEREMAN--6
Isn't he a bit like you and me?--NOWHEREMAN--18
There's nothing you can know that isn't known
     ((love))--ALLYOUN/YS--19
Nothing you can see that isn't shown ((love))--
     ALLYOUN/YS--20
There's nowhere you can be that isn't where
     you're meant to be ((love))--ALLYOUN/YS--21

IT

I'll try to make it shine.--ANYTIMEATA--14
I hope it will be mine --ANYTIMEATA--17
That it really only goes to show --ASKMEWHY--4
That it really only goes to show --ASKMEWHY--19
Just call on me and I'll send it along--FROMMETOYO
     --5
Just/So call on me and I'll send it along--FROMMETOYO--9
Just call on me and I'll send it along--FROMMETOYO
     --17
Just call on me and I'll send it along--FROMMETOYO
     --20
Just call on me and I'll send it along--FROMMETOYO
     --28
It feels so right now --HOLDMETIGH--1
Don't know what it means to hold you tight --
     HOLDMETIGH--16
It feels so right now --HOLDMETIGH--18
Don't know what it means to hold you tight --
     HOLDMETIGH--26
It feels so right now --HOLDMETIGH--28
IT WON'T BE LONG.--ITWONTBELO--Title
It won't be long yeah (yeah) yeah (yeah) yeah
     (yeah)--ITWONTBELO--1
It won't be long yeah (yeah) yeah (yeah) yeah
     (yeah)--ITWONTBELO--2
It won't be long yeah (yeah)--ITWONTBELO--3
It won't be long yeah (yeah) yeah (yeah) yeah
     (yeah)--ITWONTBELO--7
It won't be long yeah (yeah) yeah (yeah) yeah
     (yeah)--ITWONTBELO--8
It won't be long yeah (yeah)--ITWONTBELO--9
It won't be long yeah (yeah) yeah (yeah) yeah
     (yeah)--ITWONTBELO--17
It won't be long yeah (yeah) yeah (yeah) yeah
     (yeah)--ITWONTBELO--18
It won't be long yeah (yeah)--ITWONTBELO--19
It won't be long yeah (yeah) yeah (yeah) yeah
     (yeah)--ITWONTBELO--28
It won't be long (yeah) yeah (yeah) yeah
     (yeah)--ITWONTBELO--28
It won't be long (yeah) yeah (yeah) yeah
     (yeah)--ITWONTBELO--29
Though he'll regret it someday--THISBOY--24
If it makes you feel alright --CANTBUYMEL--4
If it makes you feel alright --CANTBUYMEL--6
Don't you know I can't take it?--ICALLYOURN--5
I'm not gonna make it --ICALLYOURN--7
Don't you know I can't take it?--ICALLYOURN--12
I'm not gonna make it --ICALLYOURN--14
And it's worth it just to hear you say --HARDDAYSNI
     --10
'cos I really can't stand it --TELLMEWHY--24
Oh how long will it take --BABYSINBLA--14
Oh how long will it take --BABYSINBLA--19
Is it for her or myself that I cry?--IMALOSER--12
I realise I have left it too late.--IMALOSER--16
They said it wasn't you--NOREPLY--4
Would it be too much to ask of you --WHATYOURED--3
And ((and)) there's no fun in it --WHATYOURED--6
Why should it be so much to ask of you --WHATYOURED
     --7
Why should it be so much to ask of you --WHATYOURED
     --14
Why should it be so much to ask of you --WHATYOURED
     --21
YES IT IS.--YESITIS--Title
And what's more, it's true, yes it is.--YESITIS--4
Yes it is, it's true, yes it is.--YESITIS--9
Yes it is, it's true, yes it is.--YESITIS--9
Yes it is, yes it is, oh yes it is, yeah.--YESITIS
     --13
Yes it is, yes it is, oh yes it is, yeah.--YESITIS
     --13
Yes it is, yes it is, oh yes it is, yeah.--YESITIS
     --13
Yes it is, it's true, yes it is.--YESITIS--18
Yes it is, it's true, yes it is.--YESITIS--18
Yes it is, yes it is, oh yes it is, yeah.--YESITIS

--22
Yes it is, yes it is, oh yes it is, yeah.--YESITIS
  --22
Yes it is, yes it is, oh yes it is, yeah.--YESITIS
  --22
Yes it is, it's true--YESITIS--27
Yes it is, it's true.--YESITIS--28
It is no surprise now--TELLMEWHAT--7
It is no surprise now--TELLMEWHAT--24
It is no surprise now--TELLMEWHAT--33
'cos I couldn't really stand it--YOULIKEMET--17
'cos I couldn't really stand it--YOULIKEMET--26
Man buys ring, woman throws it away --IMDOWN--8
That's when it hurt me--INEEDYOU--13
That's when it hurt me--INEEDYOU--23
Is it right that you and I should fight, every
  night--ITSONLYLOV--8
Haven't I the right to make it up girl?--ITSONLYLOV
  --10
Had it been another day--IVEJUSTSEE--7
But as it is I'll dream of her tonight --IVEJUSTSEE
  --10
When I think of things we did it makes me wanna
  cry.--NIGHTBEFOR--10
When I think of things we did it makes me wanna
  cry.--NIGHTBEFOR--18
Now it looks as though they're here to stay--
  YESTERDAY--3
It took me so long to find out --DAYTRIPPER--7
It took me so long to find out --DAYTRIPPER--15
It took me so long to find out --DAYTRIPPER--24
WE CAN WORK IT OUT.--WECANWORKI--Title
Try to see it my way --WECANWORK1--1
While you see it your way--WECANWORKI--3
We can work it out, we can work it out.--WECANWORKI
  --5
We can work it out, we can work it out.--WECANWORKI
  --5
You can get it wrong and still you think that
  it's alright.--WECANWORKI--7
We can work it out and get it straight or say
  good night.--WECANWORKI--9
We can work it out and get it straight or say
  good night.--WECANWORKI--9
We can work it out, we can work it out.--WECANWORKI
  --10
We can work it out, we can work it out.--WECANWORKI
  --10
Try to see it my way --WECANWORKI--15
While you see it your way --WECANWORKI--17
We can work it out, we can work it out.--WECANWORKI
  --19
We can work it out, we can work it out.--WECANWORKI
  --19
Try to see it my way --WECANWORKI--24
While you see it your way --WECANWORKI--26
We can work it out, we can work it out.--WECANWORKI
  --28
We can work it out, we can work it out.--WECANWORKI
  --28
She's the kind of girl you want so much it makes
  you sorry --GIRL--3
Did she understand it when they said --GIRL--23
Will she still believe it when he's dead?--GIRL--25
Then it might not have been like this --IFINEEDEDS
  --8
Then it might not have been like this --IFINEEDEDS
  --18
Isn't it good --NORWEGIANW--5
Isn't it good --NORWEGIANW--25
Leave it all till somebody else lends you a hand.
  --NOWHEREMAN--15
But now I've got it the word is good.--THEWORD--8
Everywhere I go I hear it said --THEWORD--15
And since I lost you it feels like years.--
  YOUWONTSEE--17
Yes it seems so long, girl, since you've been gone
  --YOUWONTSEE--18
And since I lost you it feels like years.--
  YOUWONTSEE--26
Yes it seems so long, girl, since you've been gone
  --YOUWONTSEE--27
It took me years to write, will you take a look?--
  PAPERBACKW--3
I can make it longer if you like the style,
  ((paperback))--PAPERBACKW--17
I can change it round, ((writer))--PAPERBACKW--18
If you really like it you can have the rights,
  ((paperback))--PAPERBACKW--21
It could make a million for you overnight.
  ((writer))--PAPERBACKW--22
If you must return it you can send it here,
  ((paperback))--PAPERBACKW--23
If you must return it you can send it here,

((paperback))--PAPERBACKW--23
I can show you that when it starts to rain (when
  the rain comes down)--RAIN--9
Can you hear me that when it rains and shines
  (when it rains and shines)--RAIN--14
Can you hear me that when it rains and shines
  (when it rains and shines)--RAIN--14
It's just a state of mind (when it rains and
  shines)--RAIN--15
When your bird is broken will it bring you down?--
  ANDYOURBIR--10
Who is it for?--ELEANORRIG--8
Both of us thinking how good it can be--HERETHEREA
  --6
I know what it is to be sad--SHESAIDSHE--2
I know what it is to be sad (I know what it is
  to be sad).--SHESAIDSHE--21
I know what it is to be sad (I know what it is
  to be sad).--SHESAIDSHE--21
Let me tell you how it will be --TAXMAN--3
Be thankful I don't take it all --TAXMAN--8
Don't ask me what I want it for (ha ha Mr.
  Wilson)--TAXMAN--18
It is not dying, it is not dying.--TOMORROWNE--2
It is not dying, it is not dying.--TOMORROWNE--2
It is shining, it is shining.--TOMORROWNE--4
It is shining, it is shining.--TOMORROWNE--4
It is being, it is being.--TOMORROWNE--6
It is being, it is being.--TOMORROWNE--6
It is knowing, it is knowing.--TOMORROWNE--8
It is knowing, it is knowing.--TOMORROWNE--8
It is believing, it is believing.--TOMORROWNE--10
It is believing, it is believing.--TOMORROWNE--10
It is not living, it is not living.--TOMORROWNE--12
It is not living, it is not living.--TOMORROWNE--12
Full speed ahead it is, Sgt.--YELLOWSUBM--21
But it all works out--STRAWBERRY--9
It doesn't matter much to me.--STRAWBERRY--10
I mean, it must be high or low--STRAWBERRY--17
Now they know how many holes it takes--DAYINTHELI
  --32
Where it will go.--FIXINGAHOL--3
Where it will go.--FIXINGAHOL--6
And it really doesn't matter if I'm wrong I'm
  right--FIXINGAHOL--7
And it really doesn't matter if I'm wrong I'm
  right--FIXINGAHOL--15
Where it will go, where it will go.--FIXINGAHOL--25
Where it will go, where it will go.--FIXINGAHOL--25
Where it will go.--FIXINGAHOL--28
A little better all the time (it can't get no
  worse)--GETTINGBET--8
A little better all the time (it can't get no
  worse)--GETTINGBET--17
A little better all the time (it can't get no
  worse)--GETTINGBET--30
When it gets dark I tow your heart away.--
  LOVELYRITA--6
Got the bill and Rita paid it--LOVELYRITA--23
Took her home I nearly made it--LOVELYRITA--24
It was twenty years ago today--SGTPEPPERS--1
Is having (we didn't know it was wrong)--SHESLEAVIN
  --29
(Does it worry you to be alone?)--WITHALITTL--9
(Could it be anybody?)--WITHALITTL--17
Yes I'm certain that it happens all the time.--
  WITHALITTL--20
(Could it be anybody?)--WITHALITTL--28
When we find it--WITHINYOUW--10
To try our best to hold it there--WITHINYOUW--11
How does it feel to be--BABYYOUREA--1
How does it feel to be--BABYYOUREA--7
How does it feel to be--BABYYOUREA--22
Umpa, umpa, stick it up your jumper ((joob -
  joob))--IAMTHEWALR--35
Umpa, umpa, stick it up your jumper.--IAMTHEWALR
  --36
Well it only goes to show (only, only goes to
  show) --BLUEJAYWAY--8
Sing it again.--YOURMOTHER--7
Sing it again.--YOURMOTHER--20
Hey Jude, don't make it bad --HEYJUDE--1
Take a sad song and make it better --HEYJUDE--2
Then you can start to make it better.--HEYJUDE--4
Then you begin to make it better.--HEYJUDE--8
For well you know that it's a fool who plays it
  cool --HEYJUDE--12
You have found her, now go and get her (let it
  out and let it in) --HEYJUDE--16
You have found her, now go and get her (let it
  out and let it in) --HEYJUDE--16
Then you can start to make it better.--HEYJUDE--18
So let it out and let it in --HEYJUDE--19
So let it out and let it in --HEYJUDE--19

Hey Jude, don't make it bad --HEYJUDE--26
Take a sad song and make it better --HEYJUDE--27
Then you'll begin ((let it out)) to make it
   better --HEYJUDE--29
Then you'll begin ((let it out)) to make it
   better --HEYJUDE--29
Better, better, better, better ((make it
   Jude)) better.--HEYJUDE--30
(Take it Jude) nah - nah - nah - nah, hey
   Jude.--HEYJUDE--33
Nah nah nah, nah - nah - nah - nah (take it
   Jude) --HEYJUDE--38
(Well you know you can make it, Jude, you've
   just gotta break it.)--HEYJUDE--46
(Well you know you can make it, Jude, you've
   just gotta break it.)--HEYJUDE--46
Nah nah nah, nah - nah - nah - nah ((don't make
   it bad, Jude)) --HEYJUDE--47
(Take a sad song and make it better)--HEYJUDE--48
(Take it Jude) nah - nah - nah - nah, hey
   Jude.--HEYJUDE--65
You ain't gonna make it with anyone anyhow.--
   REVOLUTION--29
Leave it till tomorrow to unpack my case --
   BACKINTHEU--10
If looks could kill it would have been us instead
   of him.--CONTINUING--29
I don't hear it --DONTPASSME--8
Does it mean you don't love me any more?--
   DONTPASSME--9
Does it mean you don't love me any more?--
   DONTPASSME--17
You'll never know it hurt me so --DONTPASSME--20
You'll never know it hurt me so --DONTPASSME--33
You'll never know it hurt me so --DONTPASSME--39
Come on is take it easy --EVRBDYMONK--4
Come on is take it easy --EVRBDYMONK--5
Take it easy, take it easy --EVRBDYMONK--6
Take it easy, take it easy,--EVRBDYMONK--6
Come on is make it easy --EVRBDYMONK--13
Come on is make it easy - wuh.--EVRBDYMONK--14
Take it easy, take it easy - wuh --EVRBDYMONK--15
Take it easy, take it easy - wuh --EVRBDYMONK--15
Come on is make it easy --EVRBDYMONK--22
Come on is make it easy --EVRBDYMONK--23
Make it easy (wuh), make it easy (wuh) --EVRBDYMONK
   --24
Make it easy (wuh), make it easy (wuh) --EVRBDYMONK
   --24
Happiness ((happiness)) is a warm gun, yes it is--
   HAPPINESSI--27
Happiness is a warm, yes it is - gun--HAPPINESSI
   --29
Play it to me--HONEYPIE--23
Play it to me Hollywood blues.--HONEYPIE--24
But it never really mattered --IWILL--7
Sing it loud so I can hear you --IWILL--15
Make it easy to be near you --IWILL--16
But I say it just to reach you, Julia.--JULIA--2
It took a long, long, long time --LONGLONGLO--4
When you find yourself in the thick of it --
   MARTHAMYDE--5
When you find yourself in the thick of it --
   MARTHAMYDE--11
Takes it back to Molly waiting at the door--
   OBLADIOBLA--11
And as he gives it to her she begins to sing
   (sing):--OBLADIOBLA--12
And in the evening she still sings it with the
   band, yes.--OBLADIOBLA--24
You ain't gonna make it with anyone anyhow.--
   REVOLUTONE--44
His rival it seems had broken his dreams--
   ROCKYRACCO--13
Gideon checked out and he left it no doubt ((oh
   - Rocky - oh))--ROCKYRACCO--38
You might not feel it now --SAVOYTRUFF--11
When it becomes too much--SAVOYTRUFF--15
You layed it down for all to see--SEXYSADIE--6
You layed it down for all to see--SEXYSADIE--7
I look at the floor and I see it needs sweeping --
   WHILEMYGUI--4
WHY DON'T WE DO IT IN THE ROAD?--WHYDONTWED--Title
Why don't we do - do it in the road?--WHYDONTWED
   --1
Why don't we do it in the road? (ah-ha)--WHYDONTWED
   --2
Why don't we do it in the road? - mmm--WHYDONTWED
   --3
Why don't we do it in the road?--WHYDONTWED--4
Why don't we do it in the road?--WHYDONTWED--6
Why don't we do it in the road?--WHYDONTWED--7
Why don't we do it in the road?--WHYDONTWED--8
Why don't we do it in the road?--WHYDONTWED--9

Why don't we do it in the road?--WHYDONTWED--10
Why don't we do it in the road?--WHYDONTWED--12
Well, why don't we do it in the road?--WHYDONTWED
   --13
Why don't we do it in the road?--WHYDONTWED--14
Why don't we do - do it, do it in the road?--
   WHYDONTWED--15
Why don't we do - do it, do it in the road?--
   WHYDONTWED--15
Why don't we do it, yeah, in the road?--WHYDONTWED
   --16
Why don't you do it in the road?--WHYDONTWED--18
Bull-frog doing it again--HEYBULLDOG--2
You've got it, that's great, you've done it
   ((ha ha ha ha ha))--HEYBULLDOG--28
You've got it, that's great, you've done it
   ((ha ha ha ha ha))--HEYBULLDOG--28
That's it man (wuh)--HEYBULLDOG--29
That's it, you've got it ((ha ha ha ha))--
   HEYBULLDOG--30
That's it, you've got it ((ha ha ha ha))--
   HEYBULLDOG--30
But they're not, we just wrote it like that.--
   ONLYANORTH--3
But they are, they just play it like that.--
   ONLYANORTH--6
It doesn't really matter what chords I play --
   ONLYANORTH--7
What words I say or time of day it is --ONLYANORTH
   --8
It doesn't really matter what clothes I wear --
   ONLYANORTH--10
... Make it...--ONLYANORTH--17
Can you dig it?--DONTLETMED--32
But he knew it couldn't last.--GETBACK/45--2
All the girls around her say she's got it coming
   --GETBACK/45--18
But she gets it while she can.--GETBACK/45--19
Christ! you know it ain't easy --BALLADOFJO--5
You know how hard it can be --BALLADOFJO--6
Peter Brown called to say, you can make it OK,--
   BALLADOFJO--11
Christ! you know it ain't easy --BALLADOFJO--13
You know how hard it can be --BALLADOFJO--14
Christ! you know it ain't easy --BALLADOFJO--21
You know how hard it can be --BALLADOFJO--22
Christ! you know it ain't easy --BALLADOFJO--33
You know how hard it can be --BALLADOFJO--34
Christ! you know it ain't easy --BALLADOFJO--41
You know how hard it can be.--BALLADOFJO--42
Who sometimes wears it twice as long.--OLDBROWNSH
   --4
It won't be the same now I'm telling you.--
   OLDBROWNSH--8
It won't be the same now that I'm with you.--
   OLDBROWNSH--16
It won't be the same now that I'm with you
   (yeah, yeah, yeah)--OLDBROWNSH--36
Because the world is round it turns me on --BECAUSE
   --2
Because the wind is high it blows my mind --BECAUSE
   --5
Because the sky is blue it makes me cry --BECAUSE
   --10
Little darling, it feels like years since it's
   been here.--HERECOMEST--5
Little darling, it seems like years since it's
   been here.--HERECOMEST--10
Sun, sun, sun, here it comes --HERECOMEST--13
Sun, sun, sun, here it comes --HERECOMEST--14
Sun, sun, sun, here it comes --HERECOMEST--15
Sun, sun, sun, here it comes --HERECOMEST--16
Sun, sun, sun, here it comes.--HERECOMEST--17
Little darling, it seems like years since it's
   been clear.--HERECOMEST--19
Oh darling, if you leave me I'll never make it
   alone --OHDARLING--3
Oh darling, if you leave me, I'll never make
   it alone.--OHDARLING--9
You stick around now it may show --SOMETHING--13
Questo obrigado tanta mucho cake and eat it
   carousel.--SUNKING--8
Yes it did, nah nah nah nah nah nah nah - nah--
   YOUNEVERGI--23
LET IT BE.--LETITBE/45--Title
Speaking words of wisdom, let it be.--LETITBE/45
   --3
Speaking words of wisdom, let it be.--LETITBE/45
   --6
Let it be, let it be, let it be, let it be.--
   LETITBE/45--7
Let it be, let it be, let it be, let it be.--
   LETITBE/45--7
Let it be, let it be, let it be, let it be.--

LETITBE/45--7
Let it be, let it be, let it be, let it be.--
    LETITBE/45--7
Whisper words of wisdom, let it be.--LETITBE/45--8
There will be an answer, let it be.--LETITBE/45--11
There will be an answer, let it be.--LETITBE/45--14
Let it be, let it be, let it be, let it be.--
    LETITBE/45--15
Let it be, let it be, let it be, let it be.--
    LETITBE/45--15
Let it be, let it be, let it be, let it be.--
    LETITBE/45--15
Let it be, let it be, let it be, let it be.--
    LETITBE/45--15
Yeah there will be an answer, let it be.--
    LETITBE/45--16
Let it be, let it be, let it be, let it be.--
    LETITBE/45--17
Let it be, let it be, let it be, let it be.--
    LETITBE/45--17
Let it be, let it be, let it be, let it be.--
    LETITBE/45--17
Let it be, let it be, let it be, let it be.--
    LETITBE/45--17
Whisper words of wisdom, let it be.--LETITBE/45--18
Let it be, let it be, let it be, yeah let it
    be.--LETITBE/45--19
Let it be, let it be, let it be, yeah let it
    be.--LETITBE/45--19
Let it be, let it be, let it be, yeah let it
    be.--LETITBE/45--19
Let it be, let it be, let it be, yeah let it
    be.--LETITBE/45--19
Whisper words of wisdom, let it be.--LETITBE/45--20
Shine on till tomorrow, let it be.--LETITBE/45--23
Speaking words of wisdom, let it be.--LETITBE/45
    --26
Yeah let it be, let it be, let it be, yeah let
    it be.--LETITBE/45--27
Yeah let it be, let it be, let it be, yeah let
    it be.--LETITBE/45--27
Yeah let it be, let it be, let it be, yeah let
    it be.--LETITBE/45--27
Yeah let it be, let it be, let it be, yeah let
    it be.--LETITBE/45--27
Oh there will be an answer, let it be.--LETITBE/45
    --28
Let it be, let it be, let it be, yeah let it be.--
    LETITBE/45--29
Let it be, let it be, let it be, yeah let it be.--
    LETITBE/45--29
Let it be, let it be, let it be, yeah let it be.--
    LETITBE/45--29
Let it be, let it be, let it be, yeah let it be.--
    LETITBE/45--29
Whisper words of wisdom, let it be.--LETITBE/45--30
Let's hear it for Dennis - ah-hey.--YOUKNOWMYN--8
You know, you know my name ((oh, let's hear it,
    come on Dennis)) --YOUKNOWMYN--23
Let's hear it for Dennis O'Fell.--YOUKNOWMYN--24
It calls me on and on across the universe.--
    ACROSSTHEU--24
DIG IT.--DIGIT--Title
Dig it, dig it, dig it, dig it, dig it --DIGIT--10
Dig it, dig it, dig it, dig it, dig it --DIGIT--10
Dig it, dig it, dig it, dig it, dig it --DIGIT--10
Dig it, dig it, dig it, dig it, dig it --DIGIT--10
Dig it, dig it, dig it, dig it, dig it --DIGIT--10
((That was Can You Dig It? by Georgie
    Wood))--DIGIT--11
Dig it, dig it, dig it, dig it, dig it, dig
    it, dig it, dig it....--DIGIT--12
Dig it, dig it, dig it, dig it, dig it, dig
    it, dig it, dig it....--DIGIT--12
Dig it, dig it, dig it, dig it, dig it, dig
    it, dig it, dig it....--DIGIT--12
Dig it, dig it, dig it, dig it, dig it, dig
    it, dig it, dig it....--DIGIT--12
Dig it, dig it, dig it, dig it, dig it, dig
    it, dig it, dig it....--DIGIT--12
Dig it, dig it, dig it, dig it, dig it, dig
    it, dig it, dig it....--DIGIT--12
Dig it, dig it, dig it, dig it, dig it, dig
    it, dig it, dig it....--DIGIT--12
Dig it, dig it, dig it, dig it, dig it, dig
    it, dig it, dig it....--DIGIT--12
(Hit it)--FORYOUBLUE--11
I feel it now, I hope you feel it too.--FORYOUBLUE
    --15
I feel it now, I hope you feel it too.--FORYOUBLUE
    --15
But he knew it couldn't last--GETBACK/LP--8
All the girls around her say she's got it coming--
    GETBACK/LP--24

But she gets it while she can.--GETBACK/LP--25
Hold it - aah--IDIGAPONY--3
(hold it)--IDIGAPONY--4
Everything has got to be just like you want it to
    --IDIGAPONY--14
Everything has got to be just like you want it to
    --IDIGAPONY--24
Everything has got to be just like you want it to
    --IDIGAPONY--34
Now they're frightened of leaving it --IMEMINE--5
Everyone's weaving it --IMEMINE--6
No-one's frightened of playing it --IMEMINE--18
Everyone's saying it --IMEMINE--19
No-one's frightened of playing it --IMEMINE--31
Everyone's saying it --IMEMINE--32
LET IT BE.--LETITBE/LP--Title
Speaking words of wisdom, let it be.--LETITBE/LP
    --3
Speaking words of wisdom, let it be.--LETITBE/LP
    --6
Let it be, let it be, let it be, let it be --
    LETITBE/LP--7
Let it be, let it be, let it be, let it be --
    LETITBE/LP--7
Let it be, let it be, let it be, let it be --
    LETITBE/LP--7
Let it be, let it be, let it be, let it be --
    LETITBE/LP--7
Whisper words of wisdom, let it be.--LETITBE/LP--8
There will be an answer, let it be.--LETITBE/LP--11
There will be an answer, let it be.--LETITBE/LP--14
Let it be, let it be, let it be, let it be --
    LETITBE/LP--15
Let it be, let it be, let it be, let it be --
    LETITBE/LP--15
Let it be, let it be, let it be, let it be --
    LETITBE/LP--15
Let it be, let it be, let it be, let it be --
    LETITBE/LP--15
Yeah there will be an answer, let it be.--
    LETITBE/LP--16
Let it be, let it be, let it be, let it be --
    LETITBE/LP--17
Let it be, let it be, let it be, let it be --
    LETITBE/LP--17
Let it be, let it be, let it be, let it be --
    LETITBE/LP--17
Let it be, let it be, let it be, let it be --
    LETITBE/LP--17
Whisper words of wisdom, let it be.--LETITBE/LP--18
Let it be, let it be, let it be, yeah let it be --
    LETITBE/LP--19
Let it be, let it be, let it be, yeah let it be --
    LETITBE/LP--19
Let it be, let it be, let it be, yeah let it be --
    LETITBE/LP--19
Let it be, let it be, let it be, yeah let it be --
    LETITBE/LP--19
Whisper words of wisdom, let it be.--LETITBE/LP--20
Shine on till tomorrow, let it be.--LETITBE/LP--23
Speaking words of wisdom, let it be.--LETITBE/LP
    --26
Yeah let it be, let it be, let it be, yeah let
    it be --LETITBE/LP--27
Yeah let it be, let it be, let it be, yeah let
    it be --LETITBE/LP--27
Yeah let it be, let it be, let it be, yeah let
    it be --LETITBE/LP--27
Yeah let it be, let it be, let it be, yeah let
,   it be --LETITBE/LP--27
Oh there will be an answer, let it be.--LETITBE/LP
    --28
Let it be, let it be, let it be, yeah let it be --
    LETITBE/LP--29
Let it be, let it be, let it be, yeah let it be --
    LETITBE/LP--29
Let it be, let it be, let it be, yeah let it be --
    LETITBE/LP--29
Let it be, let it be, let it be, yeah let it be --
    LETITBE/LP--29
Oh there will be an answer, let it be.--LETITBE/LP
    --30
Let it be, let it be, oh let it be, yeah let
    it be --LETITBE/LP--31
Let it be, let it be, oh let it be, yeah let
    it be --LETITBE/LP--31
Let it be, let it be, oh let it be, yeah let
    it be --LETITBE/LP--31
Let it be, let it be, oh let it be, yeah let
    it be --LETITBE/LP--31
Whisper words of wisdom, let it be.--LETITBE/LP--32
It always leads me here, lead me to your door.--
    LONGANDWIN--3
You better believe it.--TWOOFUS--36

IT'S

And it's true --ASKMEWHY--3
If I cry it's not because I'm sad --ASKMEWHY--10
I can't believe it's happened to me --ASKMEWHY--12
And it's true --ASKMEWHY--18
I can't believe it's happened to me --ASKMEWHY--24
It's so hard to reason with you, whoa - yeah--
    PLEASEPLEA--17
It's gonna be a drag, misery.--MISERY--5
It's easy 'cos I know--ILLGETYOU--8
It's not like me to pretend--ILLGETYOU--6
I need you and it's true--ILLGETYOU--10
It's easy 'cos I know--ILLGETYOU--20
It's not like me to pretend--ILLGETYOU--23
It's you she's thinking of--SHELOVESYO--6
You know it's up to you--SHELOVESYO--24
I think it's only fair--SHELOVESYO--25
It's not the same--DONTBOTHER--3
It's plain to see--DONTBOTHER--5
It's just not right--DONTBOTHER--11
It's you, you, you, you - ooo-ooo.--HOLDMETIGH--8
It's you, you, you, you - ooo-ooo.--HOLDMETIGH--15
It's you, you, you, you - ooo-ooo.--HOLDMETIGH--25
It's you, you, you, you - ooo-ooo --HOLDMETIGH--35
It's such a feeling--IWANTTOHOL--15
It's such a feeling--IWANTTOHOL--28
Well, it's the second time--YOUCANTDOT--9
I think it's a sin?--YOUCANTDOT--12
And it's my mind and there's no time--THERESAPLA
    --3
Don't you know that it's so?--THERESAPLA--10
Don't you know that it's so?--THERESAPLA--12
And it's my mind and there's no time--THERESAPLA
    --15
It's been a hard day's night --HARDDAYSNI--1
It's been a hard day's night --HARDDAYSNI--3
And it's worth it just to hear you say --HARDDAYSNI
    --10
It's been a hard day's night --HARDDAYSNI--17
It's been a hard day's night --HARDDAYSNI--19
Oh, It's been a hard day's night --HARDDAYSNI--30
It's been a hard day's night --HARDDAYSNI--32
If it's funny try and understand.--IMHAPPYJUS--5
If it's something that I said or done --TELLMEWHY
    --13
And though it's only a whim --BABYSINBLA--12
Guess you know it's true --EIGHTDAYSA--2
Guess you know it's true --EIGHTDAYSA--20
And so it's true pride comes before a fall --
    IMALOSER--17
'n' should you need a love that's true, it's me.--
    WHATYOURED--11
'n' should you need a love that's true, it's me.--
    WHATYOURED--18
I think it's today, yeah--TICKETTORI--3
I think it's today, yeah--TICKETTORI--24
And what's more, it's true, yes it is.--YESITIS--4
Understand it's true--YESITIS--8
Yes it is, it's true, yes it is.--YESITIS--9
But it's my pride--YESITIS--12
In spite of you it's true--YESITIS--17
Yes it is, it's true, yes it is.--YESITIS--18
But it's my pride--YESITIS--21
In spite of you it's true--YESITIS--26
Yes it is, it's true--YESITIS--27
Yes it is, it's true.--YESITIS--28
You'll never leave me and you know it's true--
    YOULIKEMET--5
You'll never leave me and you know it's true--
    YOULIKEMET--11
And it's nice when you believe me--YOULIKEMET--14
I wouldn't let you leave me 'cos it's true--
    YOULIKEMET--19
And it's nice when you believe me--YOULIKEMET--23
I wouldn't let you leave me 'cos it's true--
    YOULIKEMET--28
IT'S ONLY LOVE.--ITSONLYLOV--Title
It's only love and that is all--ITSONLYLOV--4
It's only love and that is all--ITSONLYLOV--6
But it's so hard loving you.--ITSONLYLOV--7
It's only love and that is all--ITSONLYLOV--11
It's only love and that is all--ITSONLYLOV--13
But it's so hard loving you.--ITSONLYLOV--14
Yes, it's so hard loving you, loving you - ooo.--
    ITSONLYLOV--15
You can get it wrong and still you think that
    it's alright.--WECANWORKI--7
I have always thought that it's a crime--WECANWORKI
    --13
I have always thought that it's a crime--WECANWORKI
    --22
'n' she said baby it's understood --DRIVEMYCAR--10
I got no car and it's breaking my heart --
    DRIVEMYCAR--24

She acts as if it's understood --GIRL--17
It's time for bed.--NORWEGIANW--16
It's been a long time, now I'm coming back home --
    WAIT--1
It's been a long time, now I'm coming back home --
    WAIT--13
It's been a long time, now I'm coming back home --
    WAIT--25
It's so easy for a girl like you to lie.--
    WHATGOESON--1
It's so easy for a girl like you to lie.--
    WHATGOESON--17
It's so fine, it's sunshine --THEWORD--5
It's so fine, it's sunshine --THEWORD--5
It's the word love.--THEWORD--6
It's so fine, it's sunshine --THEWORD--13
It's so fine, it's sunshine --THEWORD--13
It's the word love.--THEWORD--14
It's so fine, it's sunshine --THEWORD--21
It's so fine, it's sunshine --THEWORD--21
It's the word love.--THEWORD--22
It's the word I'm thinking of --THEWORD--27
It's so fine, it's sunshine --THEWORD--29
It's so fine, it's sunshine --THEWORD--29
It's the word love.--THEWORD--30
It's based on a novel by a man named Lear --
    PAPERBACKW--4
It's a dirty story of a dirty man --PAPERBACKW--8
It's a steady job --PAPERBACKW--11
It's a thousand pages, give or take a few,
    ((paperback))--PAPERBACKW--15
It's just a state of mind (when it rains and
    shines)--RAIN--15
I'm in love and it's a sunny day.--GOODDAYSUN--5
It's alright--IWANTTOTEL--7
It's only me, it's not my mind--IWANTTOTEL--10
It's only me, it's not my mind--IWANTTOTEL--10
I turn around, it's past--LOVEYOUTWO--2
She said I know what it's like to be dead --
    SHESAIDSHE--1
I know what it's like to be dead (I know what
    it's like to be dead) --SHESAIDSHE--20
I know what it's like to be dead (I know what
    it's like to be dead) --SHESAIDSHE--20
I know what it's like to be dead (I know what
    it's like to be dead).--SHESAIDSHE--22
I know what it's like to be dead (I know what
    it's like to be dead).--SHESAIDSHE--22
It's a clean machine.--PENNYLANE--15
It's getting hard to be someone--STRAWBERRY--8
But it's alright--STRAWBERRY--19
That is, I think it's not too bad.--STRAWBERRY--20
Always, no, sometimes, think it's me--STRAWBERRY
    --26
But, you know, I know when it's a dream--STRAWBERRY
    --27
But it's all wrong--STRAWBERRY--29
It's getting better all the time.--GETTINGBET--2
I've got to admit it's getting better (better)--
    GETTINGBET--7
I have to admit it's getting better (better)--
    GETTINGBET--9
It's getting better since you've been mine.--
    GETTINGBET--10
I've got to admit it's getting better (better)--
    GETTINGBET--16
I have to admit it's getting better (better)--
    GETTINGBET--18
It's getting better since you've been mine.--
    GETTINGBET--19
It's getting better all the time--GETTINGBET--21
It's getting better all the time--GETTINGBET--23
I admit it's getting better (better)--GETTINGBET
    --29
Yes I admit it's getting better (better)--
    GETTINGBET--31
It's getting better since you've been mine.--
    GETTINGBET--32
It's getting better all the time--GETTINGBET--34
It's getting better all the time--GETTINGBET--36
Nothing to do it's up to you--GOODMORNIN--4
I've got nothing to say but it's OK.--GOODMORNIN
    --5
Everything is closed it's like a ruin--GOODMORNIN
    --10
Nothing has changed it's still the same--GOODMORNIN
    --15
I've got nothing to say but it's OK.--GOODMORNIN
    --16
People running round it's five o'clock--GOODMORNIN
    --18
It's time for tea and meet the wife.--GOODMORNIN
    --21
I've got nothing to say but it's OK.--GOODMORNIN

--25
It's wonderful to be here--SGTPEPPERS--14
It's certainly a thrill--SGTPEPPERS--15
We're sorry but it's time to go.--SGTPEPPREP--6
It's getting very near the end.--SGTPEPPREP--14
If it's not too dear --WHENIMSIXT--24
I can't tell you but I know it's mine.--WITHALITTL
   --22
When it's far too late--WITHINYOUW--6
Try to realise it's all within yourself--WITHINYOUW
   --16
It's easy.--ALLYOUN/YS--7
It's easy.--ALLYOUN/YS--11
It's easy.--ALLYOUN/YS--22
((I can stay till it's time to go)).--HELLOGOODB
   --25
Now it's past my bed I know (know) --BLUEJAYWAY--15
For well you know that it's a fool who plays it
   cool --HEYJUDE--12
And don't you know that it's just you --HEYJUDE--22
You tell me that it's evolution --REVOLUTION--5
Don't you know it's gonna be alright, alright,
   alright?--REVOLUTION--10
Don't you know it's gonna be alright, alright
   ((alright)), alright?--REVOLUTION--20
You tell me it's the institution --REVOLUTION--25
Don't you know it's gonna be alright, alright,
   alright ((alright))?--REVOLUTION--30
Gee, it's good to be back home --BACKINTHEU--9
You say it's your birthday --BIRTHDAY--1
Well, it's my birthday too - yeah.--BIRTHDAY--2
They say it's your birthday --BIRTHDAY--3
I'm glad it's your birthday --BIRTHDAY--5
You say it's your birthday --BIRTHDAY--20
Well, it's my birthday too - yeah.--BIRTHDAY--21
You say it's your birthday --BIRTHDAY--22
I'm glad it's your birthday --BIRTHDAY--24
It's beautiful and so are you.--DEARPRUDEN--4
It's beautiful and so are you.--DEARPRUDEN--24
Now it's time to say good night --GOODNIGHT--1
But it's no joke, it's doing me harm --IMSOTIRED
   --10
But it's no joke, it's doing me harm --IMSOTIRED
   --10
You know it's three weeks, I'm going insane --
   IMSOTIRED--12
But it's no joke, it's doing me harm --IMSOTIRED
   --19
But it's no joke, it's doing me harm --IMSOTIRED
   --19
You know it's three weeks, I'm going insane --
   IMSOTIRED--21
lt's been a long, long, long time --LONGLONGLO--1
You tell me that it's evolution --REVOLUTONE--8
Don't you know it's gonna be ((oh shoo-be-do-a))--
   REVOLUTONE--13
Don't you know it's gonna be ((oh shoo-be-do-a))--
   REVOLUTONE--15
Don't you know it's gonna be ((oh shoo-be-do-a))--
   REVOLUTONE--17
Don't you know it's gonna be ((oh shoo-be-do-a))--
   REVOLUTONE--29
Don't you know it's gonna be ((oh shoo-be-do-a))--
   REVOLUTONE--31
Don't you know it's gonna be ((oh shoo-be-do-a))--
   REVOLUTONE--33
You tell me it's the institution --REVOLUTONE--39
Don't you know it's gonna be ((oh shoo-be-do-a))--
   REVOLUTONE--45
Don't you know it's gonna be ((oh shoo-be-do-a))--
   REVOLUTONE--47
Don't you know it's gonna be ((oh shoo-be-do-a))--
   REVOLUTONE--49
And Rocky said, Doc it's only a scratch--ROCKYRACCO
   --34
Coffee dessert - yes you know it's good news --
   SAVOYTRUFF--3
The sweat it's gonna fill your head --SAVOYTRUFF
   --14
Coffee dessert - yes you know it's good news
   (wuh) --SAVOYTRUFF--25
I look at the world and I notice it's turning --
   WHILEMYGUI--9
And you know what it's worth.--YERBLUES--13
You don't know what it's like to listen to your
   fears.--HEYBULLDOG--8
IT'S ALL TOO MUCH.--ITSALLTOOM--Title
It's all too much --ITSALLTOOM--2
It's all too much --ITSALLTOOM--3
It's all too much for me to take --ITSALLTOOM--8
Everywhere it's what you make --ITSALLTOOM--10
For us to take, it's all too much.--ITSALLTOOM--11
It's all too much for me to take --ITSALLTOOM--16
It's all too much for me to see --ITSALLTOOM--25

It's all too much for me to take --ITSALLTOOM--29
Everywhere it's what you make --ITSALLTOOM--31
For us to take it's all too much.--ITSALLTOOM--32
It's too much - aah.--ITSALLTOOM--33
It's too much.--ITSALLTOOM--34
As it's only a Northern song.--ONLYANORTH--9
When it's only a Northern song.--ONLYANORTH--12
Don't you know it's gonna last --DONTLETMED--14
It's a love that lasts forever --DONTLETMED--15
It's a love that has no past (believe me).--
   DONTLETMED--16
It's good to have the both of you back.--BALLADOFJO
   --40
'n' I say, it's alright.--HERECOMEST--3
Little darling, it's been a long, cold lonely
   winter.--HERECOMEST--4
Little darling, it feels like years since it's
   been here.--HERECOMEST--5
'n' I say, it's alright.--HERECOMEST--8
Little darling, it seems like years since it's
   been here.--HERECOMEST--10
'n' I say, it's alright.--HERECOMEST--12
Little darling, it seems like years since it's
   been clear.--HERECOMEST--19
'n' I say, it's alright.--HERECOMEST--22
It's alright --HERECOMEST--25
It's alright --HERECOMEST--26
It's driving me mad--IWANTYOUSH--5
It's driving me mad--IWANTYOUSH--6
It's driving me mad--IWANTYOUSH--11
It's driving me--IWANTYOUSH--12
It's driving me mad--IWANTYOUSH--17
It's driving me mad--IWANTYOUSH--18
It's driving me mad--IWANTYOUSH--23
It's driving me--IWANTYOUSH--24
It's driving me mad--IWANTYOUSH--32
It's driving me mad--IWANTYOUSH--33
It's driving me mad--IWANTYOUSH--38
It's driving me mad--IWANTYOUSH--39
Because you're sweet and lovely girl, it's true --
   FORYOUBLUE--3
Because you're sweet and lovely girl, it's true --
   FORYOUBLUE--17
Oh it's so hard.--IVEGOTAFEE--40

J
   E, F, G, H, I, J --ALLTOGETHE--7

JACK-KNIFE
   Jack-knife in your sweaty hands--HEYBULLDOG--6

JACKBOOTS
   Get a dose of her in jackboots and kilt --
      POLYTHENEP--6

JAI
   Jai Guru Deva OM.--ACROSSTHEU--6
   Jai Guru Deva OM.--ACROSSTHEU--15
   Jai Guru Deva OM.--ACROSSTHEU--25
   Jai Guru Deva, Jai Guru Deva, Jai Guru
      Deva --ACROSSTHEU--30
   Jai Guru Deva, Jai Guru Deva, Jai Guru
      Deva --ACROSSTHEU--30
   Jai Guru Deva, Jai Guru Deva, Jai Guru
      Deva --ACROSSTHEU--30
   Jai Guru Deva, Jai Guru Deva, Jai Guru
      Deva.--ACROSSTHEU--31
   Jai Guru Deva, Jai Guru Deva, Jai Guru
      Deva.--ACROSSTHEU--31
   Jai Guru Deva, Jai Guru Deva, Jai Guru
      Deva.--ACROSSTHEU--31

JAMES
   Elmore James got nothing on this baby - heh.--
      FORYOUBLUE--12

JAR
   Wearing the face that she keeps in a jar by the door
      --ELEANORRIG--7

JAY
   BLUE JAY WAY.--BLUEJAYWAY--Title
   Sitting here in Blue Jay Way (way).--BLUEJAYWAY--18

JEALOUS
   She will never make me jealous--SHESAWOMAN--13

And I was born with a jealous mind --RUNFORYOUR--10

JEWELLERY
    Desmond takes a trolly to the jewellery store --
        OBLADIOBLA--9

JO
    Oh get back Jo.--GETBACK/45--15
    Oh get back Jo.--GETBACK/LP--21

JOAN
    Joan was quizzical, studied pataphysical science
        in the home --MAXWELLSIL--1
    Can I take you out to the pictures, Joan?--
        MAXWELLSIL--4

JOB
    And I need a job --PAPERBACKW--5
    It's a steady job --PAPERBACKW--11
    And got myself a steady job--SHECAMEINT--17

JOBBER
    Any jobber got the sack --YOUNEVERGI--10

JOHN
    Hurry up John--IMDOWN--24
    THE BALLAD OF JOHN AND YOKO.--BALLADOFJO--Title

JOHNNY
    Go Johnny go.--FORYOUBLUE--9

JOINT
    Trying to make a dove-tail joint - yeah--GLASSONION
        --22

JOJO
    Jojo was a man who thought he was a loner --
        GETBACK/45--1
    Jojo left his home in Tucson, Arizona--GETBACK/45
        --3
    Get back Jojo.--GETBACK/45--9
    Jojo, Loretta.--GETBACK/45--40
    Jojo was a man who thought he was a loner--
        GETBACK/LP--7
    Jojo left his home in Tucson, Arizona--GETBACK/LP
        --9
    Get back Jojo.--GETBACK/LP--15

JOKE
    But it's no joke, it's doing me harm --IMSOTIRED
        --10
    But it's no joke, it's doing me harm --IMSOTIRED
        --19

JOKER
    Expert texpert, choking smokers, don't you
        think the joker laughs at you?--IAMTHEWALR--21
    Got to be a joker he just do what he please--
        COMETOGETH--10

JONES
    With a couple of kids running in the yard of
        Desmond and Molly Jones.--OBLADIOBLA--18
    With a couple of kids running in the yard of
        Desmond and Molly Jones.--OBLADIOBLA--30
    Just like Dylan's Mr. Jones.--YERBLUES--20

JOOB
    Joob - joob - joob--IAMTHEWALR--31
    Joob - joob - joob--IAMTHEWALR--31
    Joob - joob - joob--IAMTHEWALR--31
    Joob - joob - joob--IAMTHEWALR--32
    Joob - joob - joob--IAMTHEWALR--32
    Joob - joob - joob--IAMTHEWALR--32
    Joob - joob--IAMTHEWALR--33
    Joob - joob--IAMTHEWALR--33
    Joob - joob--IAMTHEWALR--34
    Joob - joob--IAMTHEWALR--34
    Umpa, umpa, stick it up your jumper ((joob -
        joob))--IAMTHEWALR--35
    Umpa, umpa, stick it up your jumper ((joob -

joob))--IAMTHEWALR--35

JOY
    Come on is such a joy --EVRBDYMONK--2
    Come on is such a joy --EVRBDYMONK--3
    Come on is such a joy --EVRBDYMONK--11
    Come on is such a joy --EVRBDYMONK--12
    Come on is such a joy --EVRBDYMONK--20
    Come on is such a joy --EVRBDYMONK--21
    Oh, what joy for every girl and boy--OCTOPUSSGA--19
    Pools of sorrow, waves of joy--ACROSSTHEU
        --3

JU-JU
    He got ju-ju eyeball--COMETOGETH--7

JUDE
    HEY JUDE.--HEYJUDE--Title
    Hey Jude, don't make it bad --HEYJUDE--1
    Hey Jude, don't be afraid --HEYJUDE--5
    Hey Jude, refrain --HEYJUDE--10
    Hey Jude, don't let me down --HEYJUDE--15
    Remember (hey Jude) to let her into your heart --
        HEYJUDE--17
    Hey Jude, begin --HEYJUDE--20
    Hey Jude, you'll do --HEYJUDE--23
    Hey Jude, don't make it bad --HEYJUDE--26
    Better, better, better, better ((make it
        Jude)), better.--HEYJUDE--30
    (Take it Jude) nah - nah - nah - nah, hey
        Jude.--HEYJUDE--33
    (Take it Jude) nah - nah - nah - nah, hey
        Jude.--HEYJUDE--33
    Nah - nah - nah - nah, hey Jude.--HEYJUDE--35
    Nah - nah - nah - nah, hey Jude.--HEYJUDE--37
    Nah nah nah, nah - nah - nah - nah (take it
        Jude) --HEYJUDE--38
    Nah - nah - nah - nah, hey Jude--HEYJUDE--39
    Jude, Judy, Judy, Judy, Judy, Judy).--HEYJUDE--40
    (Ow - ooo nah nah nah) nah - nah - nah - nah,
        hey Jude--HEYJUDE--42
    (Jude, Jude, Jude, Jude, Jude).--HEYJUDE--43
    (Jude, Jude, Jude, Jude, Jude).--HEYJUDE--43
    (Jude, Jude, Jude, Jude, Jude).--HEYJUDE--43
    (Jude, Jude, Jude, Jude, Jude).--HEYJUDE--43
    (Jude, Jude, Jude, Jude, Jude).--HEYJUDE--43
    Nah - nah - nah - nah, hey Jude.--HEYJUDE--45
    (Well you know you can make it, Jude, you've
        just gotta break it.)--HEYJUDE--46
    Nah nah nah, nah - nah - nah - nah ((don't make
        it bad, Jude)) --HEYJUDE--47
    Nah - nah - nah - nah, hey Jude (Jude, hey
        Jude, wah!).--HEYJUDE--49
    Nah - nah - nah - nah, hey Jude (Jude, hey
        Jude, wah!).--HEYJUDE--49
    Nah - nah - nah - nah, hey Jude (Jude, hey
        Jude, wah!).--HEYJUDE--49
    Nah nah nah, nah - nah - nah - nah (oh Jude) --
        HEYJUDE--50
    Nah - nah - nah - nah, hey Jude (hey hey hey
        hey hey hey).--HEYJUDE--51
    Nah - nah - nah - nah, hey Jude.--HEYJUDE--53
    (Jude Jude Jude Jude Jude Jude - yeah yeah
        yeah yeah yeah)--HEYJUDE--54
    (Jude Jude Jude Jude Jude Jude - yeah yeah
        yeah yeah yeah)--HEYJUDE--54
    (Jude Jude Jude Jude Jude Jude - yeah yeah
        yeah yeah yeah)--HEYJUDE--54
    (Jude Jude Jude Jude Jude Jude - yeah yeah
        yeah yeah yeah)--HEYJUDE--54
    (Jude Jude Jude Jude Jude Jude - yeah yeah
        yeah yeah yeah)--HEYJUDE--54
    (Jude Jude Jude Jude Jude Jude - yeah yeah
        yeah yeah yeah)--HEYJUDE--54
    Nah - nah - nah - nah, hey Jude.--HEYJUDE--56
    Nah - nah - nah - nah, hey Jude.--HEYJUDE--58
    Nah - nah - nah - nah, hey Jude (yeah).--HEYJUDE
        --61
    Nah - nah - nah - nah, hey Jude.--HEYJUDE--63
    (Take it Jude) nah - nah - nah - nah, hey
        Jude.--HEYJUDE--65
    (Take it Jude) nah - nah - nah - nah, hey
        Jude.--HEYJUDE--65
    Nah - nah - nah - nah, hey Jude (Jude, Jude
        ma ma ma ma ma ma)--HEYJUDE--69
    Nah - nah - nah - nah, hey Jude (Jude, Jude
        ma ma ma ma ma ma)--HEYJUDE--69
    Nah - nah - nah - nah, hey Jude (Jude, Jude
        ma ma ma ma ma ma)--HEYJUDE--69
    Nah - nah - nah - nah, hey Jude (ooo).--HEYJUDE--71
    Nah - nah - nah - nah, hey Jude (ooo - ooo).--

JUDE

HEYJUDE--73
Nah - nah - nah - nah, hey Jude.--HEYJUDE--75

JUDGE

The judge does not agree and he tells them so oh
- oh oh.--MAXWELLSIL--21

JUDY

Jude, Judy, Judy, Judy, Judy, Judy).--HEYJUDE--40
Jude, Judy, Judy, Judy, Judy, Judy).--HEYJUDE--40
Jude, Judy, Judy, Judy, Judy, Judy).--HEYJUDE--40
Jude, Judy, Judy, Judy, Judy, Judy).--HEYJUDE--40
Jude, Judy, Judy, Judy, Judy, Judy).--HEYJUDE--40

JULIA

JULIA.--JULIA--Title
But I say it just to reach you, Julia.--JULIA--2
Julia, Julia oceanchild calls me --JULIA--3
Julia, Julia oceanchild calls me --JULIA--3
So I sing the song of love, Julia.--JULIA--4
Julia seashell eyes windy smile calls me --JULIA
--5
So I sing the song of love, Julia.--JULIA--6
Julia, Julia morning moon touch me --JULIA--9
Julia, Julia morning moon touch me --JULIA--9
So I sing the song of love, Julia.--JULIA--10
I can only speak my mind, Julia.--JULIA--12
Julia sleeping sand silent cloud touch me --JULIA
--13
So I sing a song of love, Julia.--JULIA--14
So I sing a song of love for Julia.--JULIA--16
Julia, Julia.--JULIA--17
Julia, Julia.--JULIA--17

JUMP

Mother Superior jump the gun --HAPPINESSI--12
Mother Superior jump the gun --HAPPINESSI--13
Mother Superior jump the gun --HAPPINESSI--14
Mother Superior jump the gun --HAPPINESSI--15
Mother Superior jump the gun --HAPPINESSI--16
Mother Superior jump the gun.--HAPPINESSI--17

JUMPER

Umpa, umpa, stick it up your jumper ((joob -
joob))--IAMTHEWALR--35
Umpa, umpa, stick it up your jumper.--IAMTHEWALR
--36

JUNGLE

Deep in the jungle where the mighty tiger lies --
CONTINUING--17

JUST

Just look into my eyes --ANYTIMEATA--5
Don't you be sad, just call me tonight.--ANYTIMEATA
--9
Nobody knows just we two.--DOYOUWANTT--16
Well, she was just seventeen --ISAWHERSTA--2
Just call on me and I'll send it along--FROMMETOYO
--5
Just/So call on me and I'll send it along--FROMMETOYO--9
Just call on me and I'll send it along--FROMMETOYO
--17
Just call on me and I'll send it along--FROMMETOYO
--20
Just call on me and I'll send it along--FROMMETOYO
--28
Ya just gotta call on me, yeah --ALLIVEGOTT--15
Ya just gotta call on me, yeah --ALLIVEGOTT--16
Ya just gotta call on me, yeah --ALLIVEGOTT--26
Ya just gotta call on me --ALLIVEGOTT--27
(Ooh) ya just gotta call on me --ALLIVEGOTT--28
It's just not right--DONTBOTHER--11
Just stay away--DONTBOTHER--21
Just stay away--DONTBOTHER--36
Don't you run and hide, just come on, come on --
LITTLECHIL--17
Just to love you, but oh my!--THISBOY--8
That money just can't buy --CANTBUYMEL--20
That money just can't buy --CANTBUYMEL--30
Oh, I can't sleep at night, but just the same --
ICALLYOURN--9
Oh, I can't sleep at night, but just the same --
ICALLYOURN--16
And it's worth it just to hear you say --HARDDAYSNI
--10
Than just holding hands.--IFIFELL--6

'cos I've just lost the only girl I had.--
ILLCRYINST--2
I'M HAPPY JUST TO DANCE WITH YOU.--IMHAPPYJUS
--Title
'cos I'm happy just to dance with you.--IMHAPPYJUS
--7
I just wanna dance with you all night --IMHAPPYJUS
--9
'cos I'm happy just to dance with you.--IMHAPPYJUS
--11
Just to dance with you is everything I need (oh)
--IMHAPPYJUS--12
Let's pretend we just can't see his face.--
IMHAPPYJUS--17
'cos I'm happy just to dance with you.--IMHAPPYJUS
--19
Just to dance with you (oh) is everything I
need (oh) --IMHAPPYJUS--20
Let's pretend we just can't see his face.--
IMHAPPYJUS--25
'cos I'm happy just to dance with you (oh - oh).--
IMHAPPYJUS--28
Me I'm just the lucky kind --THINGSWESA--11
Me I'm just the lucky kind --THINGSWESA--11
She is happy just to hear me say that--SHESAWOMAN
--10
Just like I need you.--EIGHTDAYSA--4
Just like I need you, oh - oh.--EIGHTDAYSA--22
Just to know that she loves me--EVERYLITTL--12
If I just don't treat you right--YOULIKEMET--4
Not just anybody--HELP--4
I know that I ((I know that I)) just need
you like--HELP--23
I just can't go on any more.--INEEDYOU--15
Just what you mean to me--INEEDYOU--19
I just can't go on any more.--INEEDYOU--25
Just what you mean to me--INEEDYOU--29
When you sigh my my inside just flies, butterfly.
--ITSONLYLOV--2
Just the sight of you makes night-time bright,
very bright.--ITSONLYLOV--9
I'VE JUST SEEN A FACE.--IVEJUSTSEE--Title
I've just seen a face--IVEJUSTSEE--1
Where we just met--IVEJUSTSEE--3
She's just the girl for me--IVEJUSTSEE--4
I've just seen a face--IVEJUSTSEE--24
Where we just met--IVEJUSTSEE--26
She's just the girl for me--IVEJUSTSEE--27
Just sees what he wants to see --NOWHEREMAN--11
Just to make you toe the line.--RUNFORYOUR--12
Try thinking more if just for your own sake.--
THINKFORYO--20
I used to think of no-one else but you were just
the same --WHATGOESON--22
That the word is just the way --THEWORD--26
And I just can't go on--YOUWONTSEE--19
And I just can't go on--YOUWONTSEE--28
It's just a state of mind (when it rains and
shines)--RAIN--15
Don't pay money just to see yourself with Dr.
Robert.--DRROBERT--14
You knew I wanted just to hold you--GOTTOGETYO--9
Each day just goes so fast--LOVEYOUTWO--1
Well I just had to laugh--DAYINTHELI--4
The English Army had just won the war--DAYINTHELI
--12
But I just had to look--DAYINTHELI--14
I just need someone to love.--WITHALITTL--27
They can see that he's just a fool--FOOLONTHEH--4
And don't you know that it's just you --HEYJUDE--22
(Well you know you can make it, Jude, you've
just gotta break it.)--HEYJUDE--46
Just waiting to hear from you.--DONTPASSME--30
But I say it just to reach you, Julia.--JULIA--2
The world was waiting just for you?--SEXYSADIE--13
The world was waiting just for you?--SEXYSADIE--14
We gave her everything we owned just to sit at
her table ((sexy Sadie))--SEXYSADIE--20
Just a smile would lighten everything--SEXYSADIE
--21
Just like Dylan's Mr. Jones.--YERBLUES--20
But they're not, we just wrote it like that.--
ONLYANORTH--3
But they are, they just play it like that.--
ONLYANORTH--6
They look just like two gurus in drag.--BALLADOFJO
--32
Got to be a joker he just do what he please--
COMETOGETH--10
Everything has got to be just like you want it to
--IDIGAPONY--14
Everything has got to be just like you want it to
--IDIGAPONY--24
Everything has got to be just like you want it to

--IDIGAPONY--34

Allan Poe--IAMTHEWALR--27

K

In this way Mr. K. will challenge the world.--
BEINGFORTH--7
The celebrated Mr. K.--BEINGFORTH--8
Messrs. K. and H. assure the public--BEINGFORTH--12
When Mr. K. performs his tricks - without a
sound.--BEINGFORTH--16

KALEIDOSCOPE

A girl with kaleidoscope eyes.--LUCYINTHES--4
The girl with kaleidoscope eyes.--LUCYINTHES--26

KEEP

Keep all ((all)) my love forever ((ever)).--
PSILOVEYOU--5
Keep all ((all)) my love forever ((ever)) --
PSILOVEYOU--14
And keep you by my side--FROMMETOYO--12
And keep you satisfied - ooo!--FROMMETOYO--14
And keep you by my side--FROMMETOYO--23
And keep you satisfied - ooo!--FROMMETOYO--25
You still moan keep your hands to yourself --IMDOWN
--17
Do I have to keep on talking till I can't go on?--
WECANWORKI--2
You better keep your head, little girl --RUNFORYOUR
--3
You better keep your head, little girl --RUNFORYOUR
--27
He likes to keep his fire-engine clean--PENNYLANE
--14
Waiting to keep the appointment she made--
SHESLEAVIN--26
You keep all your money in a big brown bag --
BABYYOUREA--16
You keep all your money in a big brown bag --
BABYYOUREA--31
Come and keep your comrade warm.--BACKINTHEU--34
Don't keep me waiting here (don't keep me
waiting) lead me to your door.--LONGANDWIN--14
Don't keep me waiting here (don't keep me
waiting) lead me to your door.--LONGANDWIN--14

KEEPING

Keeping an eye on the world going by my window --
IMONLYSLEE--13
Keeping an eye on the world going by my window --
IMONLYSLEE--19
The man with the foolish grin is keeping
perfectly still--FOOLONTHEH--2

KEEPS

And she keeps calling me back again.--IVEJUSTSEE
--13
And she keeps calling me back again.--IVEJUSTSEE
--20
And she keeps calling me back again.--IVEJUSTSEE
--23
And she keeps calling me back again.--IVEJUSTSEE
--31
And she keeps calling me back again.--IVEJUSTSEE
--33
And she keeps calling me back again.--IVEJUSTSEE
--35
Wearing the face that she keeps in a jar by the door
--ELEANORRIG--7
Keeps a ten bob note up his nose--MEANMRMUST--6
Ooo I've got a feeling that keeps me on my toes --
IVEGOTAFEE--14

KEPT

And kept out of sight--IVEJUSTSEE--16
And kept my mind from wandering--FIXINGAHOL--5
I beat her and kept her apart from the things
that she loved--GETTINGBET--26

KEY

Quietly turning the backdoor key--SHESLEAVIN--6
And I'll try not to sing outta key.--WITHALITTL--4
Now that you've found another key--BABYYOUREA--26
Is a little dark and out of key --ONLYANORTH--14

KICKING

Man you should have seen them kicking Edgar

KIDS

With a couple of kids running in the yard of
Desmond and Molly Jones.--OBLADIOBLA--18
With a couple of kids running in the yard of
Desmond and Molly Jones.--OBLADIOBLA--30

KILL

What did you kill --CONTINUING--2
What did you kill --CONTINUING--5
What did you kill --CONTINUING--12
What did you kill --CONTINUING--15
What did you kill --CONTINUING--22
What did you kill --CONTINUING--25
The children asked him if to kill was not a sin,--
CONTINUING--27
If looks could kill it would have been us instead
of him.--CONTINUING--29
What did you kill --CONTINUING--32
What did you kill --CONTINUING--35
What did you kill --CONTINUING--38
What did you kill --CONTINUING--41
What did you kill --CONTINUING--44
What did you kill --CONTINUING--47
What did you kill --CONTINUING--50
What did you kill --CONTINUING--53

KILLER-DILLER

She's killer-diller when she's dressed to the hilt.
--POLYTHENEP--7

KILT

Get a dose of her in jackboots and kilt --
POLYTHENEP--6

KIND

I'm the kind of guy, who never used to cry.--MISERY
--2
That's the kind of love that is too good to be true
--THANKYOUGI--9
You're not the hurting kind.--SHELOVESYO--15
Tell me that you want the kind of things --
CANTBUYMEL--19
Tell me that you want the kind of things --
CANTBUYMEL--29
These days such a kind girl seems so hard to find
--THINGSWESA--7
Me I'm just the lucky kind --THINGSWESA--11
Me I'm just the lucky kind --THINGSWESA--22
And I will treat her kind (I'm gonna treat her
kind)--YOUREGONNA--6
And I will treat her kind (I'm gonna treat her
kind)--YOUREGONNA--6
And I will treat her kind (I'm gonna treat her
kind)--YOUREGONNA--28
And I will treat her kind (I'm gonna treat her
kind)--YOUREGONNA--28
She's the kind of girl you want so much it makes
you sorry --GIRL--3
She's the kind of girl who puts you down--GIRL--11
Could see another kind of mind there.--GOTTOGETYO
--4
Could see another kind of mind there.--GOTTOGETYO
--28
Some kind of happiness is measured out in miles--
HEYBULLDOG--3
Some kind of innocence is measured out in years--
HEYBULLDOG--7
Some kind of solitude is measured out in you--
HEYBULLDOG--15
She's a kind of a girl that makes the News Of
The World.--POLYTHENEP--8

KINDA

I'm not that kinda man.--ICALLYOURN--8
I'm not that kinda man.--ICALLYOURN--15
I like this kinda hot kinda music, hot kinda music
--HONEYPIE--22
I like this kinda hot kinda music, hot kinda music
--HONEYPIE--22
I like this kinda hot kinda music, hot kinda music
--HONEYPIE--22

KINDLY

Kindly send her sailing back to me--HONEYPIE--27

KINDNESS
You find that all her words of kindness linger on
--FORNOONE--2

KING
The King of Marigold was in the kitchen --
CRYBABYCRY--4
Playing piano for the children of the King.--
CRYBABYCRY--7
The King was in the garden --CRYBABYCRY--12
SUN KING.--SUNKING--Title
Aah - here come the Sun King --SUNKING--1
Here come the Sun King.--SUNKING--2
Here come the Sun King.--SUNKING--5
BB King--DIGIT--7

KIRKALDY
The Duchess of Kirkaldy always smiling --CRYBABYCRY
--20

KISS
I got lips that long to kiss you--FROMMETOYO--13
I got lips that long to kiss you--FROMMETOYO--24
And when I, I wanna kiss you, yeah --ALLIVEGOTT--6
And when I, I wanna kiss you, yeah --ALLIVEGOTT--17
Close your eyes and I'll kiss you --ALLMYLOVIN--1
Close your eyes and I'll kiss you --ALLMYLOVIN--15
The kiss my lover brings --ANDILOVEHE--8
Whoa, whoa, I never realised what a kiss could
be --ISHOULDHAV--4
Whoa, whoa, I never realised what a kiss could
be --ISHOULDHAV--14
I don't wanna kiss or hold your hand --IMHAPPYJUS
--4

KISSING
And I'll be kissing you.--ALLIVEGOTT--10
I'll pretend that I'm kissing --ALLMYLOVIN--7

KITCHEN
She goes downstairs to the kitchen--SHESLEAVIN--4
The King of Marigold was in the kitchen --
CRYBABYCRY--4

KITE
BEING FOR THE BENEFIT OF MR. KITE!--BEINGFORTH
--Title
For the benefit of Mr. Kite--BEINGFORTH--1
As Mr. Kite flies through the ring - don't be
late.--BEINGFORTH--11
And tonight Mr. Kite is topping the bill.--
BEINGFORTH--21

KNEE
Grandchildren on your knee --WHENIMSIXT--26
On the way the paper bag was on my knee --
BACKINTHEU--3
Makes me weak in the knee.--HONEYPIE--15
He got hair down to his knee--COMETOGETH--9
He got feet down below his knee--COMETOGETH--29
I begged her not to go and I begged her on my
bended knee, (oh yeah)--ONEAFTERNI--6

KNEES
Well I beg you on my bended knees --TELLMEWHY--21

KNEW
I thought I knew you, what did I know?--IMLOOKINGT
--2
I thought I knew you, what did I know?--IMLOOKINGT
--18
I wouldn't mind if I knew what I was missing.--
YOUWONTSEE--14
I wouldn't mind if I knew what I was missing.--
YOUWONTSEE--23
She says that long ago she knew someone --FORNOONE
--18
You knew I wanted just to hold you--GOTTOGETYO--9
And had you gone, you knew in time--GOTTOGETYO--10
Sometimes I wish I knew you well--IWANTTOTEL--16
If they only knew.--WITHINYOUW--15
Been away so long I hardly knew the place --
BACKINTHEU--8
But everyone knew her as Nancy.--ROCKYRACCO--16

KNOW
But he knew it couldn't last.--GETBACK/45--2
And though she thought I knew the answer --
SHECAMEINT--14
Well I knew what I could not say.--SHECAMEINT--15
But he knew it couldn't last--GETBACK/LP--8

KNICKERS
Boy, you been a naughty girl, you let your
knickers down--IAMTHEWALR--14

KNIT
You can knit a sweater by the fireside--WHENIMSIXT
--15

KNIVES
Clutching forks and knives to eat the bacon.--
PIGGIES--19

KNOCK
Well, the Ukraine girls really knock me out --
BACKINTHEU--15
Well, the Ukraine girls really knock me out --
BACKINTHEU--27
Waiting for your knock, dear --DONTPASSME--6
But as she's getting ready to go, a knock comes
on the door --MAXWELLSIL--5

KNOW
You know I love you.--LOVEMEDO--2
You know I love you.--LOVEMEDO--7
You know I love you.--LOVEMEDO--14
You know I love you.--LOVEMEDO--19
You know I want you to --PSILOVEYOU--17
'cos you tell me things I want to know --ASKMEWHY
--2
That I know --ASKMEWHY--5
'cos you tell me things I want to know --ASKMEWHY
--17
That I know --ASKMEWHY--20
I know you never even try girl --PLEASEPLEA--2
But you know there's always rain--PLEASEPLEA--14
I know/Why do you never even try girl--PLEASEPLEA--20
DO YOU WANT TO KNOW A SECRET?--DOYOUWANTT--Title
You'll never know how much I really love you --
DOYOUWANTT--1
You'll never know how much I really care.--
DOYOUWANTT--2
Listen, do you want to know a secret?--DOYOUWANTT
--3
Listen (dodahdo) do you want to know a secret?
(dodahdo)--DOYOUWANTT--9
Listen (dodahdo) do you want to know a secret?
(dodahdo)--DOYOUWANTT--17
You know what I mean --ISAWHERSTA--3
I know, little girl, only a fool would doubt
our love--THANKYOUGI--6
It's easy 'cos I know--ILLGETYOU--3
It's easy 'cos I know--ILLGETYOU--20
And you know that can't be bad--SHELOVESYO--9
And you know you should be glad.--SHELOVESYO--11
And you know that can't be bad--SHELOVESYO--17
And you know you should be glad - ooo!--SHELOVESYO
--19
You know you should be glad.--SHELOVESYO--23
You know it's up to you--SHELOVESYO--24
And you know that can't be bad--SHELOVESYO--29
And you know you should be glad - ooo!--SHELOVESYO
--31
You know you should be glad--SHELOVESYO--35
You know you should be glad--SHELOVESYO--37
You know you should be glad--SHELOVESYO--39
I know I'll never be the same--DONTBOTHER--15
Because I know she'll always be--DONTBOTHER--17
I'll let you know--DONTBOTHER--22
I know I'll never be the same--DONTBOTHER--30
Because I know she'll always be--DONTBOTHER--32
I'll let you know--DONTBOTHER--37
Don't know what it means to hold you tight --
HOLDMETIGH--16
Don't know what it means to hold you tight --
HOLDMETIGH--26
I'll be good like I know I should (yes,
you're coming on home)--ITWONTBELO--13
I'll be good like I know I should (yes,
you're coming on home)--ITWONTBELO--23
So every day we'll be happy, I know--ITWONTBELO--25
Now I know that you won't leave me no more--
ITWONTBELO--26
You know you made me cry --NOTASECOND--1

You know you made me cry --NOTASECOND--12
Don't you know I can't take it?--ICALLYOURN--5
I don't know who can --ICALLYOURN--6
Don't you know I can't take it?--ICALLYOURN--12
I don't know who can --ICALLYOURN--13
Don't you know that it's so?--THERESAPLA--10
Don't you know that it's so?--THERESAPLA--12
I know this love of mine --ANDILOVEHE--17
I know this love of mine --ANDILOVEHE--22
You know I work all day --HARDDAYSNI--8
You know I feel OK.--HARDDAYSNI--14
You know I feel OK.--HARDDAYSNI--27
You know I feel alright --HARDDAYSNI--37
You know I feel alright.--HARDDAYSNI--38
You know if you break my heart, I'll go --ILLBEBACK
    --1
You know I hate to leave you--ILLBEBACK--24
You'll be thinking of me, somehow I will know --
    THINGSWESA--2
Baby's good to me, you know --IFEELFINE--1
She's happy as can be, you know, she said so --
    IFEELFINE--2
Baby says she's mine, you know --IFEELFINE--4
She tells me all the time, you know, she said so
    --IFEELFINE--5
That her baby buys her things, you know --IFEELFINE
    --9
He buys her diamond rings, you know, she said so
    --IFEELFINE--10
Baby said she's mine, you know --IFEELFINE--12
She tells me all the time, you know, she said so
    --IFEELFINE--13
That her baby buys her things, you know --IFEELFINE
    --17
He buys her diamond rings, you know, she said so
    --IFEELFINE--18
I know that she's no peasant--SHESAWOMAN--2
I know she isn't--SHESAWOMAN--7
I know that she's no peasant--SHESAWOMAN--19
I know she isn't--SHESAWOMAN--24
I know that she's no peasant--SHESAWOMAN--29
I know she isn't--SHESAWOMAN--34
Guess you know it's true --EIGHTDAYSA--2
Guess you know it's true --EIGHTDAYSA--20
Yes I know I'm a lucky guy.--EVERYLITTL--3
And you know the thing she does--EVERYLITTL--9
Just to know that she loves me--EVERYLITTL--12
Yes I know that she loves me now.--EVERYLITTL--13
For I know love will never die.--EVERYLITTL--16
And you know the thing she does--EVERYLITTL--19
And you know the thing she does--EVERYLITTL--23
If she turns up while I'm gone please let me know.
    --IDONTWANTT--4
If she turns up while I'm gone please let me know.
    --IDONTWANTT--16
Some day you'll know I was the one --ILLFOLLOWT--3
And though I lose a friend in the end you will
    know, oh.--ILLFOLLOWT--6
And though I lose a friend in the end you will
    know, oh.--ILLFOLLOWT--11
I know that you saw me--NOREPLY--7
'cos I know where you've been--NOREPLY--12
'cos I know where you've been--NOREPLY--25
I don't know why she's riding so high--TICKETTORI
    --17
I don't know why she's riding so high--TICKETTORI
    --30
You'll never leave me and you know it's true--
    YOULIKEMET--5
You'll never leave me and you know it's true--
    YOULIKEMET--11
You know I need someone--HELP--6
I know that I ((I know that I)) just need
    you like--HELP--23
I know that I ((I know that I)) just need
    you like--HELP--23
How can you laugh when you know I'm down?--IMDOWN
    --6
(How can you laugh) when you know I'm down?--IMDOWN
    --7
How can you laugh when you know I'm down?--IMDOWN
    --13
(How can you laugh) when you know I'm down?--IMDOWN
    --14
How can you laugh when you know I'm down?--IMDOWN
    --21
(How can you laugh) when you know I'm down?--IMDOWN
    --22
Baby you know I'm down (I'm really down)--IMDOWN
    --28
Ooo, you know I'm...--IMDOWN--46
How was I to know you would upset me?--INEEDYOU--7
Why she had to go, I don't know--YESTERDAY--9
Why she had to go, I don't know--YESTERDAY--17

After all this time I don't know why.--GIRL--9
I thought I knew you, what did I know?--IMLOOKINGT
    --2
I thought I knew you, what did I know?--IMLOOKINGT
    --18
Though I know I'll never lose affection --INMYLIFE
    --13
I know I'll often stop and think about them --
    INMYLIFE--15
Though I know I'll never lose affection --INMYLIFE
    --17
I know I'll often stop and think about them --
    INMYLIFE--19
I will say the only words I know that you'll
    understand.--MICHELLE--8
Until I do I'm hoping you will know what I mean.--
    MICHELLE--14
I think you know by now--MICHELLE--17
And I will say the only words I know that
    you'll understand --MICHELLE--22
You don't know what you're missing --NOWHEREMAN--8
You don't know what you're missing --NOWHEREMAN--20
Or I won't know where I am.--RUNFORYOUR--4
Well you know that I'm a wicked guy--RUNFORYOUR--9
Or you won't know where I am.--RUNFORYOUR--28
I know your mind's made up --THINKFORYO--13
I feel as though you ought to know--WAIT--9
And know that you will wait for me.--WAIT--12
I feel as though you ought to know--WAIT--17
And know that you will wait for me.--WAIT--20
Now that I know what I feel must be right --THEWORD
    --23
I don't know why you should want to hide --
    YOUWONTSEE--7
I'm so proud to know that she is mine.--GOODDAYSUN
    --13
I didn't know what I would find there--GOTTOGETYO
    --2
And if I do I know the way there.--GOTTOGETYO--19
I didn't know what I would find there--GOTTOGETYO
    --26
Someone is speaking but she doesn't know he's
    there.--HERETHEREA--7
And if she's beside me I know I need never care--
    HERETHEREA--9
And if she's beside me I know I need never care--
    HERETHEREA--15
I feel hung up and I don't know why --IWANTTOTEL
    --13
I feel hung up and I don't know why --IWANTTOTEL
    --20
She said I know what it's like to be dead --
    SHESAIDSHE--1
I know what it is to be sad--SHESAIDSHE--2
I said even though you know what you know --
    SHESAIDSHE--10
I said even though you know what you know --
    SHESAIDSHE--10
I know that I'm ready to leave --SHESAIDSHE--11
I said even though you know what you know --
    SHESAIDSHE--16
I said even though you know what you know --
    SHESAIDSHE--16
I know that I'm ready to leave --SHESAIDSHE--17
I know what it's like to be dead (I know what
    it's like to be dead) --SHESAIDSHE--20
I know what it's like to be dead (I know what
    it's like to be dead) --SHESAIDSHE--20
I know what it is to be sad (I know what it is
    to be sad).--SHESAIDSHE--21
I know what it is to be sad (I know what it is
    to be sad).--SHESAIDSHE--21
I know what it's like to be dead (I know what
    it's like to be dead).--SHESAIDSHE--22
I know what it's like to be dead (I know what
    it's like to be dead).--SHESAIDSHE--22
Of every head he's had the pleasure to know--
    PENNYLANE--2
That is you can't, you know, tune in--STRAWBERRY
    --18
But, you know, I know when it's a dream--STRAWBERRY
    --27
But, you know, I know when it's a dream--STRAWBERRY
    --27
I think I know, I mean, er, yes--STRAWBERRY--28
Now they know how many holes it takes--DAYINTHELI
    --32
Somebody needs to know the time glad that I'm here
    --GOODMORNIN--22
But I thought you might like to know--SGTPEPPERS
    --20
Is having (we didn't know it was wrong)--SHESLEAVIN
    --29
I can't tell you but I know it's mine.--WITHALITTL

--22
They don't know--WITHINYOUW--25
There's nothing you can know that isn't known
((love))--ALLYOUN/YS--19
Now that you know who you are--BABYYOUREA--3
Often enough to know.--BABYYOUREA--10
I don't know why you say goodbye, I say hello -
hello, hello.--HELLOGOODB--5
I don't know why you say goodbye, I say hello.--
HELLOGOODB--6
You say why and I say I don't know.--HELLOGOODB--8
I don't know why you say goodbye, I say hello -
hello, hello--HELLOGOODB--12
I don't know why you say goodbye, I say hello--
HELLOGOODB--14
I don't know why you say goodbye, I say hello -
hello, hello--HELLOGOODB--20
I don't know why you say goodbye, I say hello.--
HELLOGOODB--21
I don't know why you say goodbye, I say hello -
hello, hello--HELLOGOODB--28
I don't know why you say goodbye, I say hello -
hello, hello--HELLOGOODB--29
I don't know why you say goodbye, I say hello -
hello.--HELLOGOODB--30
Now it's past my bed I know (know) --BLUEJAYWAY--15
Now it's past my bed I know (know) --BLUEJAYWAY--15
But nobody wants to know him--FOOLONTHEH--3
YOUR MOTHER SHOULD KNOW.--YOURMOTHER--Title
Your mother should know (your mother should) --
YOURMOTHER--5
Your mother should know - aah.--YOURMOTHER--6
Your mother should know (your mother should) --
YOURMOTHER--11
Your mother should know - aah.--YOURMOTHER--12
Your mother should know (your mother should) --
YOURMOTHER--16
Your mother should know - aah.--YOURMOTHER--17
Your mother should know (your mother should) --
YOURMOTHER--18
Your mother should know - aah.--YOURMOTHER--19
Your mother should know (your mother should) --
YOURMOTHER--24
Your mother should know - yeah ((ooo)).--YOURMOTHER
--25
Your mother should know (your mother should) --
YOURMOTHER--26
Your mother should know - yeah.--YOURMOTHER--27
Your mother should know (your mother should) --
YOURMOTHER--28
Your mother should know - yeah.--YOURMOTHER--29
I can know all things on earth.--INNERLIGHT--2
I could know the ways of heaven.--INNERLIGHT--4
You can know all things on earth.--INNERLIGHT--9
You can know the ways of heaven.--INNERLIGHT--11
For well you know that it's a fool who plays it
cool --HEYJUDE--12
And don't you know that it's just you --HEYJUDE--22
(Well you know you can make it, Jude, you've
just gotta break it.)--HEYJUDE--46
Well you know --REVOLUTION--3
Well you know --REVOLUTION--6
Don't you know that you can count me out?--
REVOLUTION--9
Don't you know it's gonna be alright, alright,
alright?--REVOLUTION--10
Well you know --REVOLUTION--13
Well you know --REVOLUTION--16
Don't you know it's gonna be alright, alright
((alright)), alright?--REVOLUTION--20
Well you know --REVOLUTION--23
Well you know --REVOLUTION--26
Don't you know it's gonna be alright, alright,
alright ((alright))?--REVOLUTION--30
You don't know how lucky you are boys --BACKINTHEU
--6
You don't know how lucky you are boy --BACKINTHEU
--13
You don't know how lucky you are boys --BACKINTHEU
--25
You don't know how lucky you are boy --BACKINTHEU
--36
She's old enough to know better.--CRYBABYCRY--3
She's old enough to know better --CRYBABYCRY--10
She's old enough to know better --CRYBABYCRY--18
She's old enough to know better --CRYBABYCRY--26
She's old enough to know better --CRYBABYCRY--34
She's old enough to know better --CRYBABYCRY--38
She's old enough to know better --CRYBABYCRY--42
'cos you know, darling, I love only you --
DONTPASSME--19
You'll never know it hurt me so --DONTPASSME--20
'cos you know, darling, I love only you --
DONTPASSME--32

You'll never know it hurt me so --DONTPASSME--33
'cos you know, darling, I love only you --
DONTPASSME--38
You'll never know it hurt me so --DONTPASSME--39
You know the place where nothing is real--
GLASSONION--2
You know that we're as close as can be - man--
GLASSONION--9
I know nobody can do me no harm ((oh, yeah)) --
HAPPINESSI--24
Well, don't you know that happiness ((happiness))
--HAPPINESSI--31
You know I love you still.--IWILL--2
You know I will - I will.--IWILL--18
I'm so tired, I don't know what to do --IMSOTIRED
--5
But I know what you would do.--IMSOTIRED--8
You know I can't sleep, I can't stop my brain --
IMSOTIRED--11
You know it's three weeks, I'm going insane --
IMSOTIRED--12
You know I'd give you everything I've got for a
little peace of mind.--IMSOTIRED--13
You know I can't sleep, I can't stop my brain --
IMSOTIRED--20
You know it's three weeks, I'm going insane --
IMSOTIRED--21
You know I'd give you everything I've got for a
little peace of mind.--IMSOTIRED--22
You know that I need you --LONGLONGLO--13
Well you know --REVOLUTONE--6
Well you know --REVOLUTONE--9
Don't you know that you can count me out (in)?--
REVOLUTONE--12
Don't you know it's gonna be ((oh shoo-be-do-a))--
REVOLUTONE--13
Don't you know it's gonna be ((oh shoo-be-do-a))--
REVOLUTONE--15
Don't you know it's gonna be ((oh shoo-be-do-a))--
REVOLUTONE--17
Well you know --REVOLUTONE--20
Well you know --REVOLUTONE--24
Don't you know it's gonna be ((oh shoo-be-do-a))--
REVOLUTONE--29
Don't you know it's gonna be ((oh shoo-be-do-a))--
REVOLUTONE--31
Don't you know it's gonna be ((oh shoo-be-do-a))--
REVOLUTONE--33
Well you know --REVOLUTONE--36
Well you know --REVOLUTONE--40
Don't you know it's gonna be ((oh shoo-be-do-a))--
REVOLUTONE--45
Don't you know it's gonna be ((oh shoo-be-do-a))--
REVOLUTONE--47
Don't you know it's gonna be ((oh shoo-be-do-a))--
REVOLUTONE--49
Coffee dessert - yes you know it's good news --
SAVOYTRUFF--3
You're gonna know and how.--SAVOYTRUFF--13
You know that what you eat you are --SAVOYTRUFF--19
We all know ob-la-di 'b-la-da --SAVOYTRUFF--21
Coffee dessert - yes you know it's good news
(wuh) --SAVOYTRUFF--25
Sexy Sadie how did you know--SEXYSADIE--12
Sexy Sadie - oh how did you know?--SEXYSADIE--15
I don't know why nobody told you how to unfold
your love --WHILEMYGUI--6
I don't know how someone controlled you --
WHILEMYGUI--7
I' don't know how you were diverted --WHILEMYGUI--14
I don't know how you were inverted --WHILEMYGUI--16
Ooo - girl you know the reason why.--YERBLUES--5
Wuh - girl you know the reason why.--YERBLUES--9
And you know what it's worth.--YERBLUES--13
Wuh - girl you know the reason why.--YERBLUES--16
Wuh - girl you know the reason why.--YERBLUES--23
Wuh girl - you know the reason why.--YERBLUES--30
... Girl you know the reason why.--YERBLUES--33
You don't know what it's like to listen to your
fears.--HEYBULLDOG--8
You think you know me but you haven't got a clue.
--HEYBULLDOG--16
Do you know any more?--HEYBULLDOG--26
Where I know that I'm free --ITSALLTOOM--22
The more I learn, the less I know --ITSALLTOOM--27
Don't you know it's gonna last --DONTLETMED--14
You know they didn't even give us a chance.--
BALLADOFJO--4
Christ! you know it ain't easy --BALLADOFJO--5
You know how hard it can be --BALLADOFJO--6
Christ! you know it ain't easy --BALLADOFJO--13
You know how hard it can be --BALLADOFJO--14
Christ! you know it ain't easy --BALLADOFJO--21
You know how hard it can be --BALLADOFJO--22

Christ! you know it ain't easy --BALLADOFJO--33
You know how hard it can be --BALLADOFJO--34
Christ! you know it ain't easy --BALLADOFJO--41
You know how hard it can be.--BALLADOFJO--42
He say I know you, you know me--COMETOGETH--19
He say I know you, you know me--COMETOGETH--19
You know I want you so bad, babe--IWANTYOUSH--35
You know I want you so bad--IWANTYOUSH--37
Because we know we can't be found.--OCTOPUSSGA--14
Well you know I nearly broke down and cried.--
    OHDARLING--6
A - well you know, I nearly broke down and died.--
    OHDARLING--8
A - well you know I nearly broke down and cried.--
    OHDARLING--13
A - well you know, I nearly broke down and died.--
    OHDARLING--15
You know I believe 'n' how.--SOMETHING--5
You know I believe 'n' how.--SOMETHING--10
I don't know, I don't know --SOMETHING--12
I don't know, I don't know --SOMETHING--12
I don't know, I don't know.--SOMETHING--14
I don't know, I don't know.--SOMETHING--14
You know I believe 'n' how.--SOMETHING--19
YOU KNOW MY NAME (LOOK UP MY NUMBER).--YOUKNOWMYN
    --Title
You know my name, look up de number,--YOUKNOWMYN
    --1
You know my name, look up de number.--YOUKNOWMYN
    --2
You, you know, you know my name --YOUKNOWMYN--3
You, you know, you know my name --YOUKNOWMYN--3
You, you know, you know my name.--YOUKNOWMYN--4
You, you know, you know my name.--YOUKNOWMYN--4
Good evening, you know my name, well then look
    up my number --YOUKNOWMYN--9
You know my name, that's right, look up my
    number (hey) --YOUKNOWMYN--10
You, you know, you know my name ((you know my
    name)) --YOUKNOWMYN--11
You, you know, you know my name ((you know my
    name)) --YOUKNOWMYN--11
You, you know, you know my name ((you know my
    name)) --YOUKNOWMYN--11
You, you know, you know my name (brrrrr - ha,
    hey!) --YOUKNOWMYN--12
You, you know, you know my name (brrrrr - ha,
    hey!) --YOUKNOWMYN--12
You know my name, ba ba ba ba ba ba ba ba
    ((yahoo)) --YOUKNOWMYN--13
You know my name - haa, that's right, look up
    the number --YOUKNOWMYN--15
(Oh) oh, you know, you know, you know my
    name (come on Dennis) --YOUKNOWMYN--16
(Oh) oh, you know, you know, you know my
    name (come on Dennis) --YOUKNOWMYN--16
(Oh) oh, you know, you know, you know my
    name (come on Dennis) --YOUKNOWMYN--16
You know, you know, you know my name, ha ha ha
    ha --YOUKNOWMYN--17
You know, you know, you know my name, ha ha ha
    ha --YOUKNOWMYN--17
You know, you know, you know my name, ha ha ha
    ha --YOUKNOWMYN--17
You know my name, ba ba ba bum, look up the
    number --YOUKNOWMYN--18
You know my name, look up the number --YOUKNOWMYN
    --19
You, you know, you know my name, baby --YOUKNOWMYN
    --20
You, you know, you know my name, baby --YOUKNOWMYN
    --20
You, you know, you know my name --YOUKNOWMYN--21
You, you know, you know my name --YOUKNOWMYN--21
You know, you know my name --YOUKNOWMYN--22
You know, you know my name --YOUKNOWMYN--22
You know, you know my name ((oh, let's hear it,
    come on Dennis)) --YOUKNOWMYN--23
You know, you know my name ((oh, let's hear it,
    come on Dennis)) --YOUKNOWMYN--23
My name, you know, you know, ((look up the
    number))--YOUKNOWMYN--25
My name, you know, you know, ((look up the
    number))--YOUKNOWMYN--25
You know my name (you know my number).--YOUKNOWMYN
    --26
You know my name (you know my number).--YOUKNOWMYN
    --26
You know, ((you know my name))--YOUKNOWMYN--27
You know, ((you know my name))--YOUKNOWMYN--27
You, you know my name. ((you know my
    number))--YOUKNOWMYN--28
You, you know my name. ((you know my
    number))--YOUKNOWMYN--28

You know, you know my name. ((you know my
    number))--YOUKNOWMYN--28
You know my name, look up the number --YOUKNOWMYN
    --29
You know my name, look up the number.--YOUKNOWMYN
    --30
You know, you know my name, look up the number.--
    YOUKNOWMYN--31
You know, you know my name, look up the number.--
    YOUKNOWMYN--31
Yes, you know, ((you know my name))--YOUKNOWMYN--32
Yes, you know, ((you know my name))--YOUKNOWMYN--32
You know my name ((you know)), you know me
    number (too/two)--YOUKNOWMYN--33
You know my name ((you know)), you know me
    number (too/two)--YOUKNOWMYN--33
You know my name ((you know)), you know me
    number (too/two)--YOUKNOWMYN--33
You know my name, you know me number three --
    YOUKNOWMYN--34
You know my name, you know me number three --
    YOUKNOWMYN--34
You know my name, you know me number four --
    YOUKNOWMYN--35
You know my name, you know me number four --
    YOUKNOWMYN--35
You know my name, look up the number --YOUKNOWMYN
    --36
You know my name ((you know)), you know me
    number (too/two)--YOUKNOWMYN--37
You know my name ((you know)), you know me
    number (too/two)--YOUKNOWMYN--37
You know my name ((you know)), you know me
    number (too/two)--YOUKNOWMYN--37
You know my name ((you know my name)) --YOUKNOWMYN
    --39
You know my name ((you know my name)) --YOUKNOWMYN
    --39
You know my number, what's up with you? - ha--
    YOUKNOWMYN--40
You know my name.--YOUKNOWMYN--41
Well you can imitate everyone you know--IDIGAPONY
    --20
Yes you can imitate everyone you know--IDIGAPONY
    --21
Why leave me standing here, let me know the way.--
    LONGANDWIN--6
Anyway you'll never know the many ways I've tried
    --LONGANDWIN--8

KNOWING
    Run the risk of knowing that our love may soon be
        gone.--WECANWORKI--4
    Knowing that love is to share--HERETHEREA--11
    Knowing that love is to share--HERETHEREA--17
    It is knowing, it is knowing.--TOMORROWNE--8
    It is knowing, it is knowing.--TOMORROWNE--8
    Knowing they're happy and they're safe (happy
        and they're safe).--OCTOPUSSGA--20

KNOWN
    I've known a secret for the week or two --
        DOYOUWANTT--15
    I SHOULD HAVE KNOWN BETTER.--ISHOULDHAV--Title
    I should have known better with a girl like you --
        ISHOULDHAV--1
    I should have known she would win in the end.--
        IMALOSER--6
    I have never known the like of this--IVEJUSTSEE--14
    The act you've known for all these years--
        SGTPEPPERS--6
    There's nothing you can know that isn't known
        ((love))--ALLYOUN/YS--19

KNOWS
    Nobody knows just we two.--DOYOUWANTT--16
    But now she says she knows--SHELOVESYO--14
    Everybody knows I'm sure--YESITIS--6
    Knows not where he's going to --NOWHEREMAN--5
    Knows not where he's going to --NOWHEREMAN--17
    She feels good (she feels good), she knows
        she's looking fine --GOODDAYSUN--12
    TOMORROW NEVER KNOWS.--TOMORROWNE--Title
    Everbody knows there's nothing doing--GOODMORNIN
        --9
    He knows that they're the fool--FOOLONTHEH--23
    The less one knows --INNERLIGHT--6
    The less one really knows.--INNERLIGHT--7
    The less one knows --INNERLIGHT--13
    The less one really knows.--INNERLIGHT--14
    Who knows how long I've loved you?--IWILL--1

Who knows baby, you may comfort me (hey).--
   OLDBROWNSH--21
Who knows baby, you may comfort me (hey).--
   OLDBROWNSH--26
He'd let us in, knows where we've been--OCTOPUSSGA
   --3
Somewhere in her smile she knows--SOMETHING--6
Something in the way she knows--SOMETHING--15
I've got a feeling I think that everybody knows --
   IVEGOTAFEE--16

KRISHNA
   Elementary penguin singing Hare Krishna--IAMTHEWALR
      --26

LA
   (La la la la la la) misery.--MISERY--16
   (La la la la la la) misery.--MISERY--16
   (La la la la la la) misery.--MISERY--16
   (La la la la la la) misery.--MISERY--16
   (La la la la la la) misery.--MISERY--16
   (La la la la la la) misery.--MISERY--16
   La da da, da n da.--IVEJUSTSEE--11
   La da da, da n da.--IVEJUSTSEE--11
   Mmm mmm mmm la da da.--IVEJUSTSEE--29
   (Yeah) ooo (come on) la la la--YOUWONTSEE--31
   (Yeah) ooo (come on) la la la--YOUWONTSEE--31
   (Yeah) ooo (come on) la la la--YOUWONTSEE--31
   (Oh yeah) ooo - la la la--YOUWONTSEE--32
   (Oh yeah) ooo - la la la--YOUWONTSEE--32
   (Oh yeah) ooo - la la la--YOUWONTSEE--32
   Ooo - la la la.--YOUWONTSEE--33
   Ooo - la la la.--YOUWONTSEE--33
   Ooo - la la la.--YOUWONTSEE--33
   There's a fog upon LA --BLUEJAYWAY--1

LA-LA
   La-la how the life goes on --OBLADIOBLA--6
   La-la how the life goes on.--OBLADIOBLA--8
   La-la how the life goes on --OBLADIOBLA--14
   La-la how the life goes on - yeah.--OBLADIOBLA--16
   La-la how the life goes on (he he he) --OBLADIOBLA
      --26
   La-la how the life goes on.--OBLADIOBLA--28
   La-la how the life goes on - yeah --OBLADIOBLA--37
   La-la how the life goes on (ha ha ha ha ha ha).--
      OBLADIOBLA--39

LACKING
   In their lives there's something lacking--PIGGIES
      --13

LADY
   LADY MADONNA.--LADYMADONN--Title
   Lady Madonna, children at your feet --LADYMADONN
      --1
   Lady Madonna, baby at your breast --LADYMADONN--9
   Lady Madonna, lying on the bed --LADYMADONN--12
   Lady Madonna, children at your feet --LADYMADONN
      --18
   Lady Madonna trying to make ends meet - yeah--
      GLASSONION--13

LAGOON
   By the banks of her own lagoon.--SHECAMEINT--7

LANCASHIRE
   Four thousand holes in Blackburn, Lancashire--
      DAYINTHELI--29

LAND
   Sitting in his nowhere land --NOWHEREMAN--2
   Sitting in his nowhere land --NOWHEREMAN--23
   In the land of submarines.--YELLOWSUBM--4

LANE
   PENNY LANE.--PENNYLANE--Title
   Penny Lane: there is a barber showing photographs
      --PENNYLANE--1
   Penny Lane is in my ears and in my eyes--PENNYLANE
      --9
   In Penny Lane there is a fireman with an
      hour-glass--PENNYLANE--12
   Penny Lane is in my ears and in my eyes--PENNYLANE
      --17

In Penny Lane the barber shaves another customer--
   PENNYLANE--24
Penny Lane is in my ears and in my eyes--PENNYLANE
   --28
Penny Lane is in my ears and in my eyes--PENNYLANE
   --31
Penny Lane!--PENNYLANE--33

LARK
   Put on specially by the children for a lark.--
      CRYBABYCRY--31

LAST
   Last night I said these words to my girl --
      PLEASEPLEA--1
   Last night I said these words to my girl --
      PLEASEPLEA--19
   Last night is the night I will remember you by --
      NIGHTBEFOR--9
   Last night is the night I will remember you by --
      NIGHTBEFOR--17
   Didn't get to bed last night --BACKINTHEU--2
   And when at last I find you --IWILL--13
   Don't you know it's gonna last --DONTLETMED--14
   But he knew it couldn't last.--GETBACK/45--2
   Last night the wife said, oh boy, when you're
      dead --BALLADOFJO--27
   But he knew it couldn't last--GETBACK/LP--8

LASTED
   A love that should have lasted years.--FORNOONE--9
   A love that should have lasted years.--FORNOONE--16
   A love that should have lasted years.--FORNOONE--26

LASTLY
   Lastly through a hogshead of real fire--BEINGFORTH
      --6

LASTS
   It's a love that lasts forever --DONTLETMED--15

LATCHES
   Lifting latches on our way back home.--TWOOFUS--13

LATE
   I realise I have left it too late.--IMALOSER--16
   Late of Pablo Fanques Fair - what a scene.--
      BEINGFORTH--4
   As Mr. Kite flies through the ring - don't be
      late.--BEINGFORTH--11
   And looking up I noticed I was late--DAYINTHELI--21
   When it's far too late--WITHINYOUW--6
   And arriving late for tea --CRYBABYCRY--21
   You said that you would be late --DONTPASSME--27
   When you're listening late at night --ONLYANORTH
      --4
   Making sure that I'm not late (hey).--OLDBROWNSH
      --30
   Late nights all alone with a test-tube, oh oh -
      oh oh.--MAXWELLSIL--2
   And if you leave me I won't be late again --
      IVEGOTAFEE--8

LATEST
   She's the latest and the greatest (she's the
      greatest) of them all--SEXYSADIE--23
   (Sexy Sadie she's the latest and the greatest
      of them all)--SEXYSADIE--24

LAUGH
   They'd laugh in my face.--YOUCANTDOT--22
   They'd laugh in my face.--YOUCANTDOT--41
   Although I laugh and I act like a clown --IMALOSER
      --9
   How can you laugh when you know I'm down?--IMDOWN
      --6
   (How can you laugh) when you know I'm down?--IMDOWN
      --7
   How can you laugh when you know I'm down?--IMDOWN
      --13
   (How can you laugh) when you know I'm down?--IMDOWN
      --14
   How can you laugh when you know I'm down?--IMDOWN
      --21
   (How can you laugh) when you know I'm down?--IMDOWN

--22
I can see them laugh at me --YOUVEGOTTO--7
And started to laugh--NORWEGIANW--18
I need to laugh and when the sun is out --
    GOODDAYSUN--2
I've got something I can laugh about.--GOODDAYSUN
    --3
The little children laugh at him behind his back--
    PENNYLANE--6
Well I just had to laugh--DAYINTHELI--4
Had a laugh and over dinner--LOVELYRITA--21

LAUGHING
    You can't cry 'cos you're laughing at me --IMDOWN
        --2
    Everybody's laughing --SUNKING--3

LAUGHS
    Expert texpert, choking smokers, don't you
        think the joker laughs at you?--IAMTHEWALR--21

LAUGHTER
    Sounds of laughter, shades of life--ACROSSTHEU--20

LAY
    Lay down all thought, surrender to the void--
        TOMORROWNE--3

LAYED
    You layed it down for all to see--SEXYSADIE--6
    You layed it down for all to see--SEXYSADIE--7

LAZY
    Everybody seems to think I'm lazy.--IMONLYSLEE--7
    I'm in love but I'm lazy--HONEYPIE--8
    I'm in love but I'm lazy--HONEYPIE--30
    Swaying daisies sing a lazy song beneath the sun.
        --MOTHERNATU--9

LEAD
    Was she told when she was young that pain would
        lead to pleasure?--GIRL--22
    To lead a better life, I need my love to be here.
        --HERETHEREA--1
    It always leads me here, lead me to your door.--
        LONGANDWIN--3
    And still they lead me back to the long, winding
        road.--LONGANDWIN--9
    Don't leave me waiting here, lead me to your door.
        --LONGANDWIN--11
    But still they lead me back to the long, winding
        road --LONGANDWIN--12
    Don't keep me waiting here (don't keep me
        waiting) lead me to your door.--LONGANDWIN--14

LEADS
    The long and winding road that leads to your door
        --LONGANDWIN--1
    It always leads me here, lead me to your door.--
        LONGANDWIN--3

LEAR
    It's based on a novel by a man named Lear --
        PAPERBACKW--4

LEARN
    Nothing you can say but you can learn how to play
        the game ((love))--ALLYOUN/YS--6
    Nothing you can do but you can learn how to be
        you in time ((love))--ALLYOUN/YS--10
    Take these broken wings and learn to fly.--
        BLACKBIRD--2
    Take these sunken eyes and learn to see.--BLACKBIRD
        --6
    Take these broken wings and learn to fly.--
        BLACKBIRD--14
    The more I learn, the less I know --ITSALLTOOM--27

LEARNED
    You don't sound different, I've learned the game
        --IMLOOKINGT--7
    Monday's child has learned to tie his bootlace.--
        LADYMADONN--7

LEARNING
    With every mistake we must surely be learning,--
        WHILEMYGUI--11

LEARNS
    When she learns we are two.--IFIFELL--20
    When she learns we are two.--IFIFELL--27

LEAVE
    Leave me alone--DONTBOTHER--7
    That she would leave me on my own--DONTBOTHER--10
    Leave me alone--DONTBOTHER--26
    Leave me alone--DONTBOTHER--41
    Now I know that you won't leave me no more--
        ITWONTBELO--26
    And leave you flat--YOUCANTDOT--6
    And leave you flat--YOUCANTDOT--14
    (Gonna let you down and leave you flat)--YOUCANTDOT
        --15
    And leave you flat--YOUCANTDOT--28
    (Gonna let you down and leave you flat)--YOUCANTDOT
        --29
    And leave you flat--YOUCANTDOT--47
    (Gonna let you down and leave you flat)--YOUCANTDOT
        --48
    But I hate to leave you--ILLBEBACK--23
    You know I hate to leave you--ILLBEBACK--24
    I will never leave her--SHESAWOMAN--11
    You'll never leave me and you know it's true--
        YOULIKEMET--5
    You've tried before to leave me--YOULIKEMET--7
    You'll never leave me and you know it's true--
        YOULIKEMET--11
    If you leave me I will follow you--YOULIKEMET--15
    I wouldn't let you leave me 'cos it's true--
        YOULIKEMET--19
    If you leave me I will follow you--YOULIKEMET--24
    I wouldn't let you leave me 'cos it's true--
        YOULIKEMET--28
    Love you all the time and never leave you--INEEDYOU
        --2
    When I think of all the times I tried so hard
        to leave her --GIRL--6
    Leave it all till somebody else lends you a hand.
        --NOWHEREMAN--15
    Leave me where I am, I'm only sleeping.--IMONLYSLEE
        --6
    Leave me where I am, I'm only sleeping.--IMONLYSLEE
        --26
    If I'm true I'll never leave--GOTTOGETYO--18
    I know that I'm ready to leave --SHESAIDSHE--11
    I know that I'm ready to leave --SHESAIDSHE--17
    Leave it till tomorrow to unpack my case --
        BACKINTHEU--10
    They leave the West behind --BACKINTHEU--16
    They leave the West behind --BACKINTHEU--28
    Oh darling, if you leave me I'll never make it
        alone --OHDARLING--3
    Believe me when I beg you - ooo - don't ever
        leave me alone.--OHDARLING--4
    Oh darling, if you leave me, I'll never make
        it alone.--OHDARLING--9
    I don't want to leave her now --SOMETHING--4
    I don't want to leave her now --SOMETHING--9
    I don't want to leave her now --SOMETHING--18
    And if you leave me I won't be late again --
        IVEGOTAFEE--8
    Why leave me standing here, let me know the way.--
        LONGANDWIN--6
    Don't leave me waiting here, lead me to your door.
        --LONGANDWIN--11

LEAVING
    SHE'S LEAVING HOME.--SHESLEAVIN--Title
    Leaving the note that she hoped would say more.--
        SHESLEAVIN--3
    Is leaving (sacrificed most of our lives)--
        SHESLEAVIN--9
    She's leaving home after living alone--SHESLEAVIN
        --11
    Is leaving (never a thought for our ourselves)--
        SHESLEAVIN--21
    She's leaving home after living alone--SHESLEAVIN
        --23
    She's leaving home. ('bye, 'bye)--SHESLEAVIN--33
    But as the words are leaving his lips, a noise
        comes from behind --MAXWELLSIL--22
    Now they're frightened of leaving it --IMEMINE--5

LEFT
  Since you left me I'm so alone (you left me here)
    --ITWONTBELO--11
  Since you left me I'm so alone (you left me here)
    --ITWONTBELO--11
  Well since you left me I'm so alone (you left
    me here)--ITWONTBELO--21
  Well since you left me I'm so alone (you left
    me here)--ITWONTBELO--21
  But you left me sitting on my own --TELLMEWHY--6
  I realise I have left it too late.--IMALOSER--16
  I left you far behind--THINKFORYO--10
  Down to the bits that I left uptown --HAPPINESSI
    --10
  Gideon checked out and he left it no doubt ((oh
    - Rocky - oh))--ROCKYRACCO--38
  Jojo left his home in Tucson, Arizona--GETBACK/45
    --3
  Jojo left his home in Tucson, Arizona--GETBACK/LP
    --9
  Has left a pool of tears crying for the day.--
    LONGANDWIN--5
  You left me standing here a long, long time ago --
    LONGANDWIN--10
  You left me standing here a long, long time ago --
    LONGANDWIN--13

LEGEND
  You became a legend of the silver screen--HONEYPIE
    --13

LEGS
  To shoot off the legs of his rival.--ROCKYRACCO--12

LEISURE
  That a man must break his back to earn his day of
    leisure?--GIRL--24

LEMONADE
  And sip their lemonade (when the sun shines down)
    --RAIN--5

LEND
  Lend me your ears and I'll sing you a song--
    WITHALITTL--3
  Desmond lets the children lend a hand --OBLADIOBLA
    --21
  Molly lets the children lend a hand --OBLADIOBLA
    --33

LENDS
  Leave it all till somebody else lends you a hand.
    --NOWHEREMAN--15

LESS
  The less one knows --INNERLIGHT--6
  The less one really knows.--INNERLIGHT--7
  The less one knows --INNERLIGHT--13
  The less one really knows.--INNERLIGHT--14
  The more I learn, the less I know --ITSALLTOOM--27

LET
  Let me whisper in your ear --DOYOUWANTT--6
  Let me whisper in your ear, (dodahdo)--DONYOUWANTT
    --12
  Let me whisper in your ear, (dodahdo)--DOYOUWANTT
    --20
  I'll let you know--DONTBOTHER--22
  I'll let you know--DONTBOTHER--37
  Let me go on loving you --HOLDMETIGH--10
  Let me go on loving you --HOLDMETIGH--30
  Let me understand.--IWANNABEYO--14
  And/You'll let me be your man--IWANTTOHOL--8
  You'll let me hold your hand--IWANTTOHOL--10
  And/You'll let me hold your hand--IWANTTOHOL--11
  I'm gonna let you down--YOUCANTDOT--5
  I think I'll let you down (let you down)--
    YOUCANTDOT--13
  I think I'll let you down (let you down)--
    YOUCANTDOT--13
  (Gonna let you down and leave you flat)--YOUCANTDOT
    --15
  I'm gonna let you down (let you down)--YOUCANTDOT
    --27
  I'm gonna let you down (let you down)--YOUCANTDOT

  --27
  (Gonna let you down and leave you flat)--YOUCANTDOT
    --29
  I'm gonna let you down (let you down)--YOUCANTDOT
    --46
  I'm gonna let you down (let you down)--YOUCANTDOT
    --46
  (Gonna let you down and leave you flat)--YOUCANTDOT
    --48
  Come on, let me through --WHENIGETHO--21
  If she turns up while I'm gone please let me know.
    --IDONTWANTT--4
  If she turns up while I'm gone please let me know.
    --IDONTWANTT--16
  If you let me take your heart--TELLMEWHAT--1
  I wouldn't let you leave me 'cos it's true--
    YOULIKEMET--19
  I wouldn't let you leave me 'cos it's true--
    YOULIKEMET--28
  Let me hear you say.--YOUVEGOTTO--18
  Let this be a sermon --RUNFORYOUR--17
  Let me tell you how it will be,--TAXMAN--3
  Let me take you down--STRAWBERRY--1
  Let me take you down--STRAWBERRY--11
  Let me take you down--STRAWBERRY--21
  Let me take you down--STRAWBERRY--31
  Sit back and let the evening go.--SGTPEPPERS--11
  So let me introduce to you--SGTPEPPERS--23
  Man you been a naughty boy, you let your face
    grow long--IAMTHEWALR--6
  Boy, you been a naughty girl, you let your
    knickers down--IAMTHEWALR--14
  Remember to let her into your heart --HEYJUDE--3
  The minute you let her under your skin --HEYJUDE
    --7
  Hey Jude, don't let me down --HEYJUDE--15
  You have found her, now go and get her (let it
    out and let it in) --HEYJUDE--16
  You have found her, now go and get her (let it
    out and let it in) --HEYJUDE--16
  Remember (hey Jude) to let her into your heart,--
    HEYJUDE--17
  So let it out and let it in --HEYJUDE--19
  So let it out and let it in --HEYJUDE--19
  Remember to let her under your skin (oh) --HEYJUDE
    --28
  Then you'll begin ((let it out)) to make it
    better --HEYJUDE--29
  Let me hear your balalaikas ringing out --
    BACKINTHEU--33
  Oh let me tell you honey --BACKINTHEU--38
  Dear Prudence, let me see you smile --DEARPRUDEN
    --16
  So let me see you smile again.--DEARPRUDEN--19
  Dear Prudence, won't you let me see you smile?--
    DEARPRUDEN--20
  I'm coming down fast but don't let me break you --
    HELTERSKEL--12
  I'm coming down fast but don't let me break you --
    HELTERSKEL--22
  DON'T LET ME DOWN.--DONTLETMED--Title
  Don't let me down --DONTLETMED--1
  Don't let me down --DONTLETMED--2
  Don't let me down --DONTLETMED--3
  Don't let me down.--DONTLETMED--4
  Don't let me down --DONTLETMED--9
  Don't let me down --DONTLETMED--10
  Don't let me down --DONTLETMED--11
  Don't let me down --DONTLETMED--12
  Don't let me down --DONTLETMED--17
  Don't let me down (ooo) --DONTLETMED--18
  Don't let me down --DONTLETMED--19
  Don't let me down --DONTLETMED--20
  Don't let me down (hey) --DONTLETMED--25
  Don't let me down --DONTLETMED--26
  Eee ((don't let me down)) --DONTLETMED--27
  Don't let me down.--DONTLETMED--28
  Don't let me down --DONTLETMED--30
  Don't let me down, let me down --DONTLETMED--31
  Don't let me down, let me down --DONTLETMED--31
  Don't ((hey)) let me down.--DONTLETMED--33
  He'd let us in, knows where we've been--OCTOPUSSGA
    --3
  Oh darling, please believe me, I'll never let
    you down.--OHDARLING--16
  LET IT BE.--LETITBE/45--Title
  Speaking words of wisdom, let it be.--LETITBE/45
    --3
  Speaking words of wisdom, let it be.--LETITBE/45
    --6
  Let it be, let it be, let it be, let it be.--
    LETITBE/45--7
  Let it be, let it be, let it be, let it be.--
    LETITBE/45--7

Let it be, let it be, let it be, let it be.--
    LETITBE/45--7
Let it be, let it be, let it be, let it be.--
    LETITBE/45--7
Whisper words of wisdom, let it be.--LETITBE/45--8
There will be an answer, let it be.--LETITBE/45--11
There will be an answer, let it be.--LETITBE/45--14
Let it be, let it be, let it be, let it be.--
    LETITBE/45--15
Let it be, let it be, let it be, let it be.--
    LETITBE/45--15
Let it be, let it be, let it be, let it be.--
    LETITBE/45--15
Let it be, let it be, let it be, let it be.--
    LETITBE/45--15
Yeah there will be an answer, let it be.--
    LETITBE/45--16
Let it be, let it be, let it be, let it be.--
    LETITBE/45--17
Let it be, let it be, let it be, let it be.--
    LETITBE/45--17
Let it be, let it be, let it be, let it be.--
    LETITBE/45--17
Let it be, let it be, let it be, let it be.--
    LETITBE/45--17
Whisper words of wisdom, let it be.--LETITBE/45--18
Let it be, let it be, let it be, yeah let it
    be.--LETITBE/45--19
Let it be, let it be, let it be, yeah let it
    be.--LETITBE/45--19
Let it be, let it be, let it be, yeah let it
    be.--LETITBE/45--19
Let it be, let it be, let it be, yeah let it
    be.--LETITBE/45--19
Whisper words of wisdom, let it be.--LETITBE/45--20
Shine on till tomorrow, let it be.--LETITBE/45--23
Speaking words of wisdom, let it be.--LETITBE/45
    --26
Yeah let it be, let it be, let it be, yeah let
    it be.--LETITBE/45--27
Yeah let it be, let it be, let it be, yeah let
    it be.--LETITBE/45--27
Yeah let it be, let it be, let it be, yeah let
    it be.--LETITBE/45--27
Yeah let it be, let it be, let it be, yeah let
    it be.--LETITBE/45--27
Oh there will be an answer, let it be.--LETITBE/45
    --28
Let it be, let it be, let it be, yeah let it be.--
    LETITBE/45--29
Let it be, let it be, let it be, yeah let it be.--
    LETITBE/45--29
Let it be, let it be, let it be, yeah let it be.--
    LETITBE/45--29
Let it be, let it be, let it be, yeah let it be.--
    LETITBE/45--29
Whisper words of wisdom, let it be.--LETITBE/45--30
Everybody let their hair down --IVEGOTAFEE--25
Everybody let their hair down ((a feeling I
    can't hide, oh no)) --IVEGOTAFEE--33
LET IT BE.--LETITBE/LP--Title
Speaking words of wisdom, let it be.--LETITBE/LP
    --3
Speaking words of wisdom, let it be.--LETITBE/LP
    --6
Let it be, let it be, let it be, let it be --
    LETITBE/LP--7
Let it be, let it be, let it be, let it be --
    LETITBE/LP--7
Let it be, let it be, let it be, let it be --
    LETITBE/LP--7
Let it be, let it be, let it be, let it be --
    LETITBE/LP--7
Whisper words of wisdom, let it be.--LETITBE/LP--8
There will be an answer, let it be.--LETITBE/LP--11
There will be an answer, let it be.--LETITBE/LP--14
Let it be, let it be, let it be, let it be --
    LETITBE/LP--15
Let it be, let it be, let it be, let it be --
    LETITBE/LP--15
Let it be, let it be, let it be, let it be --
    LETITBE/LP--15
Let it be, let it be, let it be, let it be --
    LETITBE/LP--15
Yeah there will be an answer, let it be.--
    LETITBE/LP--16
Let it be, let it be, let it be, let it be --
    LETITBE/LP--17
Let it be, let it be, let it be, let it be --
    LETITBE/LP--17
Let it be, let it be, let it be, let it be --
    LETITBE/LP--17
Let it be, let it be, let it be, let it be --
    LETITBE/LP--17

Whisper words of wisdom, let it be.--LETITBE/LP--18
Let it be, let it be, let it be, yeah let it be --
    LETITBE/LP--19
Let it be, let it be, let it be, yeah let it be --
    LETITBE/LP--19
Let it be, let it be, let it be, yeah let it be --
    LETITBE/LP--19
Let it be, let it be, let it be, yeah let it be --
    LETITBE/LP--19
Whisper words of wisdom, let it be.--LETITBE/LP--20
Shine on till tomorrow, let it be.--LETITBE/LP--23
Speaking words of wisdom, let it be.--LETITBE/LP
    --26
Yeah let it be, let it be, let it be, yeah let
    it be --LETITBE/LP--27
Yeah let it be, let it be, let it be, yeah let
    it be --LETITBE/LP--27
Yeah let it be, let it be, let it be, yeah let
    it be --LETITBE/LP--27
Yeah let it be, let it be, let it be, yeah let
    it be --LETITBE/LP--27
Oh there will be an answer, let it be.--LETITBE/LP
    --28
Let it be, let it be, let it be, yeah let it be --
    LETITBE/LP--29
Let it be, let it be, let it be, yeah let it be --
    LETITBE/LP--29
Let it be, let it be, let it be, yeah let it be --
    LETITBE/LP--29
Let it be, let it be, let it be, yeah let it be --
    LETITBE/LP--29
Oh there will be an answer, let it be.--LETITBE/LP
    --30
Let it be, let it be, oh let it be, yeah let
    it be --LETITBE/LP--31
Let it be, let it be, oh let it be, yeah let
    it be --LETITBE/LP--31
Let it be, let it be, oh let it be, yeah let
    it be --LETITBE/LP--31
Let it be, let it be, oh let it be, yeah let
    it be --LETITBE/LP--31
Whisper words of wisdom, let it be.--LETITBE/LP--32
Why leave me standing here, let me know the way.--
    LONGANDWIN--6

LET'S
    Let's pretend we just can't see his face.--
        IMHAPPYJUS--17
    Let's pretend we just can't see his face.--
        IMHAPPYJUS--25
    Let's all get up and dance to a song--YOURMOTHER
        --2
    Let's all get up and dance to a song--YOURMOTHER
        --8
    Let's hear it for Dennis - ah-hey.--YOUKNOWMYN--8
    You know, you know my name ((oh, let's hear it,
        come on Dennis)) --YOUKNOWMYN--23
    Let's hear it for Dennis O'Fell.--YOUKNOWMYN--24

LETS
    Desmond lets the children lend a hand --OBLADIOBLA
        --21
    Molly lets the children lend a hand --OBLADIOBLA
        --33

LETTER
    As I write this letter, send my love to you --
        PSILOVEYOU--1
    As I write this letter, send my love to you --
        PSILOVEYOU--10
    As I write this letter (oh) send my love to you --
        PSILOVEYOU--16
    Picks up the letter that's lying there--SHESLEAVIN
        --14

LETTER-BOX
    Thoughts meander like a restless wind inside a
        letter-box --ACROSSTHEU--13

LETTERS
    Writing letters on my wall.--TWOOFUS--11

LICKS
    The worm he licks my bone --YERBLUES--18

LIE
    That's a lie--NOREPLY--11

That's a lie--NOREPLY--24
It's so easy for a girl like you to lie.--
   WHATGOESON--8
It's so easy for a girl like you to lie.--
   WHATGOESON--17
Then we lie beneath a shady tree --GOODDAYSUN--10
You didn't run, you didn't lie--GOTTOGETYO--8
And proceeded to lie on the table --ROCKYRACCO--32

LIED
And why you lied to me --TELLMEWHY--2
And why you lied to me.--TELLMEWHY--4
And why you lied to me --TELLMEWHY--10
And why you lied to me --TELLMEWHY--12
And why you lied to me --TELLMEWHY--18
And why you lied to me.--TELLMEWHY--20
And why you lied to me.--TELLMEWHY--27
And why you lied to me.--TELLMEWHY--29

LIES
And I'll forgive the lies--NOREPLY--19
You tell lies thinking I can't see --IMDOWN--1
Were you telling lies? (aah the night before)--
   NIGHTBEFOR--5
Were you telling lies? (aah the night before)--
   NIGHTBEFOR--19
You're telling all those lies--THINKFORYO--3
Deep in the jungle where the mighty tiger lies --
   CONTINUING--17
The coral that lies beneath the waves (lies
   beneath the ocean waves).--OCTOPUSSGA--18
The coral that lies beneath the waves (lies
   beneath the ocean waves).--OCTOPUSSGA--18

LIFE
And now ((now)) my life has changed ((my life
   has changed))--HELP--19
And now ((now)) my life has changed ((my life
   has changed))--HELP--19
Life is very short and there's no time--WECANWORKI
   --11
Life is very short and there's no time--WECANWORKI
   --20
IN MY LIFE.--INMYLIFE--Title
All my life, though some have changed.--INMYLIFE
   --2
In my life I've loved them all.--INMYLIFE--8
In my life I love you more.--INMYLIFE--16
In my life I love you more.--INMYLIFE--20
In my life I love you more.--INMYLIFE--21
RUN FOR YOUR LIFE.--RUNFORYOUR--Title
You better run for your life if you can, little
   girl --RUNFORYOUR--5
And I can't spend my whole life trying--RUNFORYOUR
   --11
You better run for your life if you can, little
   girl --RUNFORYOUR--13
You better run for your life if you can, little
   girl --RUNFORYOUR--21
You better run for your life if you can, little
   girl --RUNFORYOUR--29
The ruins of the life that you had in mind --
   THINKFORYO--11
GOT TO GET YOU INTO MY LIFE.--GOTTOGETYO--Title
Every single day of my life?--GOTTOGETYO--7
Got to get you into my life.--GOTTOGETYO--15
Every single day of my life?--GOTTOGETYO--22
Got to get you into my life.--GOTTOGETYO--23
I got to get you into my life.--GOTTOGETYO--24
To lead a better life, I need my love to be here.
   --HERETHEREA--1
Changing my life with a wave of her hand--
   HERETHEREA--3
And he told us of his life--YELLOWSUBM--3
As we live a life of ease--YELLOWSUBM--25
A DAY IN THE LIFE.--DAYINTHELI--Title
Nothing to do to save his life call his wife in--
   GOODMORNIN--2
Everyone you see is full of life--GOODMORNIN--20
And life flows on within you and without you.--
   WITHINYOUW--19
And life flows on within you and without you.--
   WITHINYOUW--33
All your life --BLACKBIRD--3
All your life --BLACKBIRD--7
All your life --BLACKBIRD--15
Ob-la-di ob-la-da life goes on bra --OBLADIOBLA--5
La-la how the life goes on --OBLADIOBLA--6
Ob-la-di ob-la-da life goes on bra --OBLADIOBLA--7
La-la how the life goes on.--OBLADIOBLA--8
Ob-la-di ob-la-da life goes on bra --OBLADIOBLA--13

La-la how the life goes on --OBLADIOBLA--14
Ob-la-di ob-la-da life goes on bra --OBLADIOBLA--15
La-la how the life goes on - yeah.--OBLADIOBLA--16
Ob-la-di ob-la-da life goes on bra --OBLADIOBLA--25
La-la how the life goes on (he he he) --OBLADIOBLA
   --26
Hey, ob-la-di ob-la-da life goes on bra --
   OBLADIOBLA--27
La-la how the life goes on.--OBLADIOBLA--28
Ob-la-di ob-la-da life goes on bra --OBLADIOBLA--36
La-la how the life goes on - yeah --OBLADIOBLA--37
Ob-la-di ob-la-da life goes on bra --OBLADIOBLA--38
La-la how the life goes on (ha ha ha ha ha ha).--
   OBLADIOBLA--39
Life is getting worse --PIGGIES--4
From life to life with me --ITSALLTOOM--13
From life to life with me --ITSALLTOOM--13
Sounds of laughter, shades of life--ACROSSTHEU
   --20
All through your life --IMEMINE--34

LIFETIME
A lifetime is so short--LOVEYOUTWO--6
Will I wait a lonely lifetime?--IWILL--3

LIFT
Lift my head, I'm still yawning.--IMONLYSLEE--2
Lift my head, I'm still yawning.--IMONLYSLEE--22
Lift up your hearts and sing me a song--YOURMOTHER
   --13

LIFTING
Lifting latches on our way back home.--TWOOFUS--13

LIGHT
I saw the light, I saw the light.--NOREPLY--6
I saw the light, I saw the light.--NOREPLY--6
I'm here to show everybody the light.--THEWORD--24
(What do you see when you turn out the light?)--
   WITHALITTL--21
THE INNER LIGHT.--INNERLIGHT--Title
Into the light of a dark black night.--BLACKBIRD
   --10
Into the light of a dark black night.--BLACKBIRD
   --12
Now the sun turns out his light --GOODNIGHT--3
Now the sun turns out his light --GOODNIGHT--16
I light the light - yeah, ooo - ha.--HONEYPIE--21
I light the light - yeah, ooo - ha.--HONEYPIE--21
There is still a light that shines on me --
   LETITBE/45--22
Images of broken light which dance before me like
   a million eyes --ACROSSTHEU--11
There is still a light that shines on me --
   LETITBE/LP--22

LIGHTEN
Just a smile would lighten everything--SEXYSADIE
   --21

LIGHTNING
Made a lightning trip to Vienna --BALLADOFJO--29

LIGHTS
He didn't notice that the lights had changed--
   DAYINTHELI--7
When your lights have gone.--WHENIMSIXT--14

LIKE
Someone to love, someone like you.--LOVEMEDO--12
Like I please you.--PLEASEPLEA--6
Like I please you.--PLEASEPLEA--12
Like I please you.--PLEASEPLEA--24
Like I please you--PLEASEPLEA--26
Like I please you.--PLEASEPLEA--28
Like a heart that's oh so true--FROMMETOYO--8
It's not like me to pretend--ILLGETYOU--6
It's not like me to pretend--ILLGETYOU--23
With a love like that--SHELOVESYO--22
With a love like that--SHELOVESYO--34
With a love like that--SHELOVESYO--36
With a love like that--SHELOVESYO--38
Love you like no other baby --IWANNABEYO--5
Like no other can.--IWANNABEYO--6
Love you like no other baby --IWANNABEYO--7
Like no other can.--IWANNABEYO--8

Love you like no other baby --IWANNABEYO--34
Like no other can (ooo).--IWANNABEYO--35
Love you like no other baby --IWANNABEYO--36
Like no other can.--IWANNABEYO--37
I'll be good like I know I should (yes,
    you're coming on home)--ITWONTBELO--13
I'll be good like I know I should (yes,
    you're coming on home)--ITWONTBELO--23
Like I love only you.--THERESAPLA--8
A love like ours --ANDILOVEHE--11
And I been working like a dog --HARDDAYSNI--2
I should be sleeping like a log --HARDDAYSNI--4
And I been working like a dog --HARDDAYSNI--18
I should be sleeping like a log --HARDDAYSNI--20
And I been working like a dog --HARDDAYSNI--31
I should be sleeping like a log --HARDDAYSNI--33
I should have known better with a girl like you --
    ISHOULDHAV--1
Oh please, don't hurt my pride like her.--IFIFELL
    --13
Just like I need you.--EIGHTDAYSA--4
Just like I need you, oh - oh.--EIGHTDAYSA--22
Although I laugh and I act like a clown --IMALOSER
    --9
My tears are falling like rain from the sky --
    IMALOSER--11
YOU LIKE ME TOO MUCH.--YOULIKEMET--Title
'cos you like me too much and I like you--
    YOULIKEMET--6
'cos you like me too much and I like you--
    YOULIKEMET--6
'cos you like me too much and I like you--
    YOULIKEMET--12
'cos you like me too much and I like you--
    YOULIKEMET--12
'cos you like me too much and I like you--
    YOULIKEMET--20
'cos you like me too much and I like you--
    YOULIKEMET--20
'cos you like me too much and I like you--
    YOULIKEMET--21
'cos you like me too much and I like you--
    YOULIKEMET--21
'cos you like me too much and I like you--
    YOULIKEMET--29
'cos you like me too much and I like you--
    YOULIKEMET--29
'cos you like me too much and I like you.--
    YOULIKEMET--30
'cos you like me too much and I like you.--
    YOULIKEMET--30
I know that I ((I know that I)) just need
    you like--HELP--23
And feeling like this--INEEDYOU--14
And feeling like this--INEEDYOU--14
I have never known the like of this--IVEJUSTSEE--14
But other girls were never quite like this --
    IVEJUSTSEE--17
Treat me like you did the night before.--NIGHTBEFOR
    --4
Treat me like you did the night before.--NIGHTBEFOR
    --8
Treat me like you did the night before (yes).--
    NIGHTBEFOR--14
Treat me like you did the night before (yeah).--
    NIGHTBEFOR--16
Treat me like you did the night before.--NIGHTBEFOR
    --22
Like the night before.--NIGHTBEFOR--23
Then it might not have been like this --IFINEEDEDS
    --8
Then it might not have been like this --IFINEEDEDS
    --18
Isn't he a bit like you and me?--NOWHEREMAN--6
Isn't he a bit like you and me?--NOWHEREMAN--18
It's so easy for a girl like you to lie.--
    WHATGOESON--8
It's so easy for a girl like you to lie.--
    WHATGOESON--17
Say the word and be like me --THEWORD--2
Spread the word and be like me --THEWORD--10
Say the word and be like me --THEWORD--18
And since I lost you it feels like years.--
    YOUWONTSEE--17
And since I lost you it feels like years.--
    YOUWONTSEE--26
I can make it longer if you like the style
    ((paperback))--PAPERBACKW--17
If you really like it you can have the rights
    ((paperback))--PAPERBACKW--21
No-one can succeed like Dr. Robert.--DRROBERT--10
She said I know what it's like to be dead --
    SHESAIDSHE--1
And she's making me feel like I've never been

born.--SHESAIDSHE--3
And you're making me feel like I've never been
    born.--SHESAIDSHE--6
'cos you're making me feel like I've never been
    born.--SHESAIDSHE--12
'cos you're making me feel like I've never been
    born.--SHESAIDSHE--18
I know what it's like to be dead (I know what
    it's like to be dead) --SHESAIDSHE--20
I know what it's like to be dead (I know what
    it's like to be dead) --SHESAIDSHE--20
I know what it's like to be dead (I know what
    it's like to be dead).--SHESAIDSHE--22
I know what it's like to be dead (I know what
    it's like to be dead).--SHESAIDSHE--22
Everything is closed it's like a ruin--GOODMORNIN
    --10
Made her look a little like a military man.--
    LOVELYRITA--12
Told her I would really like to see her again.--
    LOVELYRITA--22
We'd like to take you home with us--SGTPEPPERS--17
But I thought you might like to know--SGTPEPPERS
    --20
We'd like to thank you once again.--SGTPEPPREP--12
See how they run like pigs from a gun, see how
    they fly--IAMTHEWALR--2
See how they fly like Lucy in the sky, see how
    they run--IAMTHEWALR--10
See how they smile, like pigs in a sty, see how
    they snied--IAMTHEWALR--23
And I'd really like to go (go) --BLUEJAYWAY--16
And nobody seems to like him--FOOLONTHEH--15
They don't like him.--FOOLONTHEH--24
Sunday morning creeping like a nun --LADYMADONN--6
I would like you to dance (birthday) --BIRTHDAY--11
I would like you to dance (birthday) --BIRTHDAY--13
I would like you to dance (birthday) --BIRTHDAY--16
I would like you to dance (birthday) (wuh)--
    BIRTHDAY--18
Dear Prudence, like a little child.--DEARPRUDEN--17
Like a lizard on a window-pane.--HAPPINESSI--4
I like this kinda hot kinda music, hot kinda music
    --HONEYPIE--22
Desmond says to Molly, girl I like your face--
    OBLADIOBLA--3
Rocky didn't like that --ROCKYRACCO--5
Just like Dylan's Mr. Jones.--YERBLUES--20
You don't know what it's like to listen to your
    fears.--HEYBULLDOG--8
Or where you'd like to be.--ITSALLTOOM--15
But they're not, we just wrote it like that.--
    ONLYANORTH--3
But they are, they just play it like that.--
    ONLYANORTH--6
Nobody ever loved me like she does --DONTLETMED--5
And if somebody loved me like she do me --
    DONTLETMED--7
They look just like two gurus in drag.--BALLADOFJO
    --32
Little darling, it feels like years since it's
    been here.--HERECOMEST--5
Little darling, it feels like years since it's
    been here.--HERECOMEST--10
Little darling, it seems like years since it's
    been clear.--HERECOMEST--19
I'd like to be under the sea--OCTOPUSSGA--1
I'd like to be under the sea--OCTOPUSSGA--7
I'd like to be under the sea--OCTOPUSSGA--15
I'd like to be under the sea--OCTOPUSSGA--23
She's so goodlooking but she looks like a man.--
    POLYTHENEP--2
Attracts me like no other lover --SOMETHING--2
Words are flowing out like endless rain into a
    paper cup --ACROSSTHEU--1
Images of broken light which dance before me like
    a million eyes --ACROSSTHEU--11
Thoughts meander like a restless wind inside a
    letter-box --ACROSSTHEU--13
Limitless undying love which shines around me
    like a million suns --ACROSSTHEU--23
Like a rolling stone--DIGIT--1
Like a rolling stone--DIGIT--2
A - like a rolling stone--DIGIT--3
Like the FBI--DIGIT--4
((And now we'd like to do)) Hark the Angels
    Come...--DIGIT--13
I'd like to say thank you on behalf of the group
    and ourselves--GETBACK/LP--38
Everything has got to be just like you want it to
    --IDIGAPONY--14
Everything has got to be just like you want it to
    --IDIGAPONY--24
Everything has got to be just like you want it to

--IDIGAPONY--34
All that I was looking for was somebody who
looked like you.--IVEGOTAFEE--13

LIKES
He likes to keep his fire-engine clean--PENNYLANE
--14

LIL
Her name was Magill and she called herself Lil --
ROCKYRACCO--15

LIMITLESS
Limitless undying love which shines around me
like a million suns --ACROSSTHEU--23

LIMOUSINE
Pick up the bags, get in the limousine.--YOUNEVERGI
--18

LINE
You're giving me the same old line --NOTASECOND--7
You're giving me the same old line --NOTASECOND--18
Just to make you toe the line.--RUNFORYOUR--12
Send me a postcard, drop me a line--WHENIMSIXT--28
I said, move over honey, I'm travelling on
that line --ONEAFTERNI--2
I said a-move over honey, I'm travelling on
that line --ONEAFTERNI--16
Said a - move over honey, I'm travelling on
that line --ONEAFTERNI--26

LINE'S
When I call you up your line's engaged.--YOUWONTSEE
--1

LINGER
You find that all her words of kindness linger on
--FORNOONE--2

LIP
For your sweet top lip I'm in the queue --
OLDBROWNSH--31

LIPS
I got lips that long to kiss you--FROMMETOYO--13
I got lips that long to kiss you--FROMMETOYO--24
The lips I am missing --ALLMYLOVIN--8
Your lips are moving, I cannot hear --IMLOOKINGT
--5
But as the words are leaving his lips, a noise
comes from behind --MAXWELLSIL--22

LISTEN
Listen, do you want to know a secret?--DOYOUWANTT
--3
Listen (dodahdo) do you want to know a secret?
(dodahdo)--DOYOUWANTT--9
Listen (dodahdo) do you want to know a secret?
(dodahdo)--DOYOUWANTT--17
So please listen to me--YOUCANTDOT--23
So please listen to me--YOUCANTDOT--42
If you'll only listen to my pleas --TELLMEWHY--22
Listen to me one more time--TELLMEWHAT--18
Listen to me one more time--TELLMEWHAT--27
And she said listen babe I've got something to
say --DRIVEMYCAR--23
Is there anybody going to listen to my story--GIRL
--1
Nowhere Man please listen --NOWHEREMAN--7
Nowhere Man please listen --NOWHEREMAN--19
Time after time you refuse to even listen --
YOUWONTSEE--13
Time after time you refuse to even listen --
YOUWONTSEE--22
But listen to the colour of your dreams--TOMORROWNE
--11
Listen to the music playing in your head.--
LADYMADONN--13
I listen for your footsteps --DONTPASSME--2
Listen for your footsteps --DONTPASSME--4
Listen to me--GLASSONION--20
Listen to the pretty sound of music as she flies.
--MOTHERNATU--4

You don't know what it's like to listen to your
fears.--HEYBULLDOG--8

LISTENING
If you're listening to this song --ONLYANORTH--1
When you're listening late at night --ONLYANORTH
--4

LISTENS
He never listens to them--FOOLONTHEH--22

LIT
So I lit a fire--NORWEGIANW--24

LITTLE
I'll remember all the little things we've done --
MISERY--6
I'll remember all the little things we've done --
MISERY--10
I know, little girl, only a fool would doubt
our love--THANKYOUGI--6
LITTLE CHILD.--LITTLECHIL--Title
Little child, little child --LITTLECHIL--1
Little child, little child --LITTLECHIL--1
Little child, won't you dance with me?--LITTLECHIL
--2
Little child, little child --LITTLECHIL--5
Little child, little child --LITTLECHIL--5
Little child, won't you dance with me?--LITTLECHIL
--6
Little child, little child --LITTLECHIL--12
Little child, little child --LITTLECHIL--12
Little child, won't you dance with me?--LITTLECHIL
--13
Little child, little child --LITTLECHIL--19
Little child, little child --LITTLECHIL--19
Little child, won't you dance with me?--LITTLECHIL
--20
I'm so glad that she's my little girl --IFEELFINE
--7
I'm so glad that she's my little girl --IFEELFINE
--15
EVERY LITTLE THING.--EVERYLITTL--Title
Every little thing she does--EVERYLITTL--7
Every little thing she does--EVERYLITTL--17
Every little thing she does--EVERYLITTL--21
Every little thing-EVERYLITTL--25
Every little thing--EVERYLITTL--26
Every little thing.--EVERYLITTL--27
Well I'd rather see you dead, little girl --
RUNFORYOUR--1
You better keep your head, little girl --RUNFORYOUR
--3
You better run for your life if you can, little
girl --RUNFORYOUR--5
Hide your head in the sand, little girl.--
RUNFORYOUR--6
That's the end'a little girl.--RUNFORYOUR--8
You better run for your life if you can, little
girl --RUNFORYOUR--13
Hide your head in the sand, little girl.--
RUNFORYOUR--14
That's the end'a little girl.--RUNFORYOUR--16
You better run for your life if you can, little
girl --RUNFORYOUR--21
'Hide your head in the sand, little girl.--
RUNFORYOUR--22
That's the end'a little girl.--RUNFORYOUR--24
I'd rather see you dead, little girl --RUNFORYOUR
--25
You better keep your head, little girl --RUNFORYOUR
--27
You better run for your life if you can, little
girl --RUNFORYOUR--29
Hide your head in the sand, little girl.--
RUNFORYOUR--30
That's the end'a little girl.--RUNFORYOUR--32
The little children laugh at him behind his back--
PENNYLANE--6
A little better all the time (it can't get no
worse)--GETTINGBET--8
A little better all the time (it can't get no
worse)--GETTINGBET--17
A little better all the time (it can't get no
worse)--GETTINGBET--30
Filling in a ticket in her little white book.--
LOVELYRITA--9
Made her look a little like a military man.--
LOVELYRITA--12
WITH A LITTLE HELP FROM MY FRIENDS.--WITHALITTL

--Title
Oh I get by with a little help from my friends --
    WITHALITTL--5
Mmm I get high with a little help from my friends
    --WITHALITTL--6
Mmm gonna try with a little help from my friends.
    --WITHALITTL--7
No I get by with a little help from my friends --
    WITHALITTL--12
Mmm get high with a little help from my friends --
    WITHALITTL--13
Mmm gonna try with a little help from my friends.
    --WITHALITTL--14
Oh I get by with a little help from my friends --
    WITHALITTL--23
Mmm get high with a little help from my friends --
    WITHALITTL--24
Oh I'm gonna try with a little help from my
    friends.--WITHALITTL--25
Oh I get by with a little help from my friends --
    WITHALITTL--30
Mmm gonna try with a little help from my friends
    --WITHALITTL--31
Oh I get high with a little help from my friends
    --WITHALITTL--32
Yes I get by with a little help from my friends --
    WITHALITTL--33
With a little help from my friends.--WITHALITTL--34
Mr. City policeman sitting pretty little
    policemen in a row--IAMTHEWALR--9
By making his world a little colder.--HEYJUDE--13
Dear Prudence, like a little child.--DEARPRUDEN--17
You know I'd give you everything I've got for a
    little peace of mind.--IMSOTIRED--13
You know I'd give you everything I've got for a
    little peace of mind.--IMSOTIRED--22
I'd give you everything I've got for a little
    peace of mind --IMSOTIRED--23
I'd give you everything I've got for a little
    peace of mind.--IMSOTIRED--24
Have you seen the little piggies--PIGGIES--1
And for all the little piggies--PIGGIES--3
Can I have a little more?--ALLTOGETHE--2
Is a little dark and out of key,--ONLYANORTH--14
Little darling, it's been a long, cold lonely
    winter.--HERECOMEST--4
Little darling, it feels like years since it's
    been here.--HERECOMEST--5
Little darling, the smiles returning to the faces.
    --HERECOMEST--9
Little darling, it seems like years since it's
    been here.--HERECOMEST--10
Little darling, I feel that ice is slowly
    melting.--HERECOMEST--18
Little darling, it seems like years since it's
    been clear.--HERECOMEST--19
In our little hideaway beneath the waves.--
    OCTOPUSSGA--10

LIVE
I could never really live without you--INEEDYOU--17
I could never really live without you--INEEDYOU--27
We all live in a yellow submarine --YELLOWSUBM--9
We all live in a yellow submarine --YELLOWSUBM--11
Many more of them live next door--YELLOWSUBM--14
We all live in a yellow submarine --YELLOWSUBM--16
We all live in a yellow submarine --YELLOWSUBM--18
As we live a life of ease--YELLOWSUBM--25
We all live in a yellow submarine --YELLOWSUBM--29
We all live in a yellow submarine --YELLOWSUBM--31
We all live in a yellow submarine --YELLOWSUBM--33
We all live in a yellow submarine --YELLOWSUBM--35
To see how the other half live--GLASSONION--6
I'll live and love and maybe someday --OLDBROWNSH
    --20

LIVED
Lived a man who sailed to sea--YELLOWSUBM--2
And we lived beneath the waves--YELLOWSUBM--7
There lived a young boy name of Rocky Raccoon--
    ROCKYRACCO--2

LIVES
Lives in a dream.--ELEANORRIG--5
She (we gave her most of our lives)--SHESLEAVIN--8
Is leaving (sacrificed most of our lives)--
    SHESLEAVIN--9
Home. (we struggled hard all our lives to get by)
    --SHESLEAVIN--22
In their lives there's something lacking--PIGGIES
    --13

Living piggy lives.--PIGGIES--16

LIVING
She said that living with me--TICKETTORI--9
She said that living with me--TICKETTORI--36
Some are dead and some are living --INMYLIFE--7
It is not living, it is not living.--TOMORROWNE--12
It is not living, it is not living.--TOMORROWNE--12
Living is easy with eyes closed--STRAWBERRY--6
She's leaving home after living alone--SHESLEAVIN
    --11
She's leaving home after living alone--SHESLEAVIN
    --23
I tell you man he living there still--GLASSONION
    --18
Living piggy lives.--PIGGIES--16
Living in the world agree --LETITBE/45--10
I'm living every moment girl for you.--FORYOUBLUE
    --7
Living in the world agree --LETITBE/LP--10

LIZARD
Like a lizard on a window-pane.--HAPPINESSI--4

LOCAL
With a message at the local bird and bee.--
    CRYBABYCRY--23
Booked himself a room in the local saloon.--
    ROCKYRACCO--8

LOCATION
Railman said, you got the wrong location --
    ONEAFTERNI--12
Railman said, you got the wrong location --
    ONEAFTERNI--22

LOCK
Would you lock the door?--WHENIMSIXT--6

LOCKED
I'd get myself locked up today --ILLCRYINST--4

LOG
I should be sleeping like a log --HARDDAYSNI--4
I should be sleeping like a log --HARDDAYSNI--20
I should be sleeping like a log --HARDDAYSNI--33

LONDON
Caught the early plane back to London --BALLADOFJO
    --37

LONELY
She'll remember and she'll miss her only one,
    lonely one.--MISERY--11
Never be the lonely one.--HOLDMETIGH--5
Never be the lonely one.--HOLDMETIGH--22
I'm so sad and lonely --LITTLECHIL--3
I'm so sad and lonely --LITTLECHIL--7
I'm so sad and lonely --LITTLECHIL--14
I'm so sad and lonely --LITTLECHIL--21
Someday when I'm lonely --THINGSWESA--3
Turn me on when I get lonely--SHESAWOMAN--5
Turn me on when I get lonely--SHESAWOMAN--22
Turn me on when I get lonely--SHESAWOMAN--32
I was lonely without her--EVERYLITTL--5
I'm ((I'm)) feeling blue and lonely --WHATYOURED
    --2
To walk out and make me lonely--YOULIKEMET--9
I'm lonely as can be--INEEDYOU--4
And then you'll be the lonely one (you're not
    the only one)--YOUREGONNA--12
Aah, look at all the lonely people.--ELEANORRIG--1
Aah, look at all the lonely people.--ELEANORRIG--2
All the lonely people, where do they all come
    from?--ELEANORRIG--9
All the lonely people, where do they all belong?--
    ELEANORRIG--10
All the lonely people, where do they all come
    from?--ELEANORRIG--17
All the lonely people, where do they all belong?--
    ELEANORRIG--18
Aah, look at all the lonely people.--ELEANORRIG--19
Aah, look at all the lonely people.--ELEANORRIG--20
All the lonely people, where do they all come
    from?--ELEANORRIG--27

((Aah, look at all the lonely people.))--ELEANORRIG
--28
All the lonely people, where do they all belong?--
ELEANORRIG--29
((Aah, look at all the lonely people.))--ELEANORRIG
--30
SGT. PEPPER'S LONELY HEARTS CLUB BAND.--SGTPEPPERS
--Title
Sgt. Pepper's Lonely Hearts Club Band.--SGTPEPPERS
--7
We're Sgt. Pepper's Lonely Hearts Club Band--
SGTPEPPERS--8
Sgt. Pepper's Lonely Hearts Club Band--SGTPEPPERS
--10
Sgt. Pepper's Lonely, Sgt. Pepper's Lonely--
SGTPEPPERS--12
Sgt. Pepper's Lonely, Sgt. Pepper's Lonely--
SGTPEPPERS--12
Sgt. Pepper's Lonely Hearts Club Band.--SGTPEPPERS
--13
And Sgt. Pepper's Lonely Hearts Club Band.--
WAIT--25
SGT. PEPPER'S LONELY HEARTS CLUB BAND
(REPRISE).--SGTPEPPREP--Title
We're Sgt. Pepper's Lonely Hearts Club Band --
SGTPEPPREP--3
Sgt. Pepper's Lonely Hearts Club Band --SGTPEPPREP
--5
Sgt. Pepper's Lonely --SGTPEPPREP--7
Sgt. Pepper's Lonely --SGTPEPPREP--8
Sgt. Pepper's Lonely --SGTPEPPREP--9
Sgt. Pepper's Lonely.--SGTPEPPREP--10
Sgt. Pepper's Lonely Hearts Club Band --SGTPEPPREP
--11
Sgt. Pepper's one and only Lonely Hearts Club
Band --SGTPEPPREP--13
Sgt. Pepper's Lonely --SGTPEPPREP--15
Sgt. Pepper's Lonely --SGTPEPPREP--16
Sgt. Pepper's Lonely Hearts Club Band.--SGTPEPPREP
--17
Will I wait a lonely lifetime?--IWILL--3
Yes I'm lonely - wanna die --YERBLUES--2
Yes I'm lonely - wanna die --YERBLUES--3
I'm lonely - wanna die --YERBLUES--14
Lonely - wanna die --YERBLUES--21
Yes I'm lonely - wanna die --YERBLUES--31
Yes I'm lonely - wanna die --YERBLUES--32
If you're lonely you can talk to me.--HEYBULLDOG
--12
If you're lonely you can talk to me - hey!--
HEYBULLDOG--20
Little darling, it's been a long, cold lonely
winter.--HERECOMEST--4

LONER
Jojo was a man who thought he was a loner --
GETBACK/45--1
Jojo was a man who thought he was a loner--
GETBACK/LP--7

LONG
Say the words you long to hear --DOYOUWANTT--7
Say the words you long to hear --DOYOUWANTT--13
Say the words you long to hear --DOYOUWANTT--21
That before too long I'd fall in love with her.--
ISAWHERSTA--8
And before too long I fell in love with her--
ISAWHERSTA--15
And before too long I fell in love with her.--
ISAWHERSTA--22
I got arms that long to hold you--FROMMETOYO--11
I got lips that long to kiss you--FROMMETOYO--13
I got arms that long to hold you--FROMMETOYO--22
I got lips that long to kiss you--FROMMETOYO--24
The words you long to hear --ALLIVEGOTT--9
IT WON'T BE LONG.--ITWONTBELO--Title
It won't be long yeah (yeah) yeah (yeah) yeah
(yeah)--ITWONTBELO--1
It won't be long yeah (yeah) yeah (yeah) yeah
(yeah)--ITWONTBELO--2
It won't be long yeah (yeah)--ITWONTBELO--3
It won't be long yeah (yeah) yeah (yeah) yeah
(yeah)--ITWONTBELO--7
It won't be long yeah (yeah) yeah (yeah) yeah
(yeah)--ITWONTBELO--8
It won't be long yeah (yeah)--ITWONTBELO--9
It won't be long yeah (yeah) yeah (yeah) yeah
(yeah)--ITWONTBELO--17
It won't be long yeah (yeah) yeah (yeah) yeah
(yeah)--ITWONTBELO--18
It won't be long yeah (yeah)--ITWONTBELO--19
It won't be long yeah (yeah) yeah (yeah) yeah

(yeah)--ITWONTBELO--27
It won't be long (yeah) yeah (yeah) yeah
(yeah)--ITWONTBELO--28
It won't be long yeah (yeah)--ITWONTBELO--29
As long as I --ANDILOVEHE--13
Oh how long will it take --BABYSINBLA--14
Oh how long will it take --BABYSINBLA--19
I wonder what went wrong I've waited far too long
--IDONTWANTT--13
I wonder what went wrong I've waited far too long
--IDONTWANTT--24
Now I long for yesterday.--YESTERDAY--12
Now I long for yesterday.--YESTERDAY--20
It took me so long to find out --DAYTRIPPER--7
It took me so long to find out --DAYTRIPPER--15
It took me so long to find out --DAYTRIPPER--24
There's a chance that we might fall apart before
too long.--WECANWORKI--18
There's a chance that we might fall apart before
too long.--WECANWORKI--27
It's been a long time, now I'm coming back home --
WAIT--1
It's been a long time, now I'm coming back home --
WAIT--13
It's been a long time, now I'm coming back home --
WAIT--25
Yes it seems so long, girl, since you've been gone
--YOUWONTSEE--18
Yes it seems so long, girl, since you've been gone
--YOUWONTSEE--27
She says that long ago she knew someone --FORNOONE
--18
Make love all day long --LOVEYOUTWO--9
Make love all day long --LOVEYOUTWO--11
Man you been a naughty boy, you let your face
grow long--IAMTHEWALR--6
Please don't be long --BLUEJAYWAY--5
Please don't you be very long --BLUEJAYWAY--6
Please don't be long or I may be asleep.--
BLUEJAYWAY--7
Please don't be long (don't be long) --BLUEJAYWAY
--12
Please don't be long (don't be long) --BLUEJAYWAY
--12
Please don't you be very long (don't be long) --
BLUEJAYWAY--13
Please don't you be very long (don't be long) --
BLUEJAYWAY--13
Please don't be long or I may be asleep.--
BLUEJAYWAY--14
Please don't be long (don't be long) --BLUEJAYWAY
--19
Please don't be long (don't be long) --BLUEJAYWAY
--19
Please don't you be very long (don't be long) --
BLUEJAYWAY--20
Please don't you be very long (don't be long) --
BLUEJAYWAY--20
Please don't be long or I may be asleep.--
BLUEJAYWAY--21
Please don't be long --BLUEJAYWAY--22
Please don't you be very long--BLUEJAYWAY--23
Please don't be long.--BLUEJAYWAY--24
Please don't be long --BLUEJAYWAY--25
Please don't you be very long--BLUEJAYWAY--26
Please don't be long (please don't be long).--
BLUEJAYWAY--27
Please don't be long (please don't be long).--
BLUEJAYWAY--27
Please don't be long--BLUEJAYWAY--28
Please don't you be very long --BLUEJAYWAY--29
Please don't be long.--BLUEJAYWAY--30
Don't be long - don't be long --BLUEJAYWAY--31
Don't be long - don't be long --BLUEJAYWAY--31
Don't belong - don't be long--BLUEJAYWAY
--32
Don't be long--BLUEJAYWAY--34
Though she was born a long, long time ago --
YOURMOTHER--4
Though she was born a long, long time ago --
YOURMOTHER--4
Though she was born a long, long time ago --
YOURMOTHER--10
Though she was born a long, long time ago --
YOURMOTHER--10
Though she was born a long, long time ago --
YOURMOTHER--15
Though she was born a long, long time ago --
YOURMOTHER--15
Though she was born a long, long time ago --
YOURMOTHER--23
Though she was born a long, long time ago --
YOURMOTHER--23
Been away so long I hardly knew the place --

BACKINTHEU--8
Who knows how long I've loved you?--IWILL--1
LONG, LONG, LONG.--LONGLONGLO--Title
LONG, LONG, LONG.--LONGLONGLO--Title
LONG, LONG, LONG.--LONGLONGLO--Title
It's been a long, long, long time --LONGLONGLO--1
It's been a long, long, long time --LONGLONGLO--1
It's been a long, long, long time --LONGLONGLO--1
It took a long, long, long time --LONGLONGLO--4
It took a long, long, long time --LONGLONGLO--4
It took a long, long, long time --LONGLONGLO--4
All day long I'm sitting singing songs for
  everyone.--MOTHERNATU--2
With your long blonde hair and your eyes of blue
  --ITSALLTOOM--35
With your long blonde hair and your eyes of blue
  --ITSALLTOOM--36
Who sometimes wears it twice as long.--OLDBROWNSH
  --4
Carry that weight a long time.--CARRYTHATW--2
Carry that weight a long time.--CARRYTHATW--4
Carry that weight a long time.--CARRYTHATW--10
Carry that weight a long time.--CARRYTHATW--12
Little darling, it's been a long, cold lonely
  winter.--HERECOMEST--4
THE LONG AND WINDING ROAD.--LONGANDWIN--Title
The long and winding road that leads to your door
  --LONGANDWIN--1
And still they lead me back to the long, winding
  road.--LONGANDWIN--9
You left me standing here a long, long time ago --
  LONGANDWIN--10
You left me standing here a long, long time ago --
  LONGANDWIN--10
But still they lead me back to the long, winding
  road --LONGANDWIN--12
You left me standing here a long, long time ago --
  LONGANDWIN--13
You left me standing here a long, long time ago --
  LONGANDWIN--13

LONGER
I can make it longer if you like the style,
  ((paperback))--PAPERBACKW--17
When she no longer needs you.--FORNOONE--3
She no longer needs you.--FORNOONE--6
Longer than the road that stretches out ahead.--
  TWOOFUS--18
Longer than the road that stretches out ahead.--
  TWOOFUS--27

LOOK
Just look into my eyes --ANYTIMEATA--5
I think I'll take a walk and look for her.--
  IDONTWANTT--8
But I think I'll take a walk and look for her.--
  IDONTWANTT--25
One day you'll look to see I've gone --ILLFOLLOWT
  --1
Look ((look)) what you're doing --WHATYOURED--1
Look ((look)) what you're doing --WHATYOURED--1
Look into these eyes now--TELLMEWHAT--13
You don't look different, but you have changed --
  IMLOOKINGT--3
You don't look different, but you have changed --
  IMLOOKINGT--19
It took me years to write, will you take a look?--
  PAPERBACKW--3
Look in my direction --ANDYOURBIR--8
Aah, look at all the lonely people.--ELEANORRIG--1
Aah, look at all the lonely people.--ELEANORRIG--2
Look at him working--ELEANORRIG--14
Aah, look at all the lonely people.--ELEANORRIG--19
Aah, look at all the lonely people.--ELEANORRIG--20
((Aah, look at all the lonely people.))--ELEANORRIG
  --28
((Aah, look at all the lonely people.))--ELEANORRIG
  --30
But I just had to look--DAYINTHELI--14
Made her look a little like a military man.--
  LOVELYRITA--12
Look for the girl with the sun in her eyes--
  LUCYINTHES--7
Hey, so look at me --BACKINTHEU--41
Look around, 'round --DEARPRUDEN--11
Look around, 'round, 'round --DEARPRUDEN--13
Look around (('round)).--DEARPRUDEN--15
Look out helter-skelter, helter-skelter,
  helter-skelter - oh.--HELTERSKEL--16
Look out 'cos here she comes (heh heh heh).--
  HELTERSKEL--17
Look out helter-skelter, helter-skelter,

helter-skelter.--HELTERSKEL--26
Well, look out helter-skelter.--HELTERSKEL--27
Hold your head up you silly girl, look what
  you've done --MARTHAMYDE--4
Take a good look around you --MARTHAMYDE--7
Take a good look you're bound to see --MARTHAMYDE
  --8
I look at you all, see the love there that's
  sleeping --WHILEMYGUI--2
I look at the floor and I see it needs sweeping --
  WHILEMYGUI--4
I look at the world and I notice it's turning --
  WHILEMYGUI--9
I look at you all, see the love there that's
  sleeping --WHILEMYGUI--18
Look, look at you all --WHILEMYGUI--20
Look, look at you all --WHILEMYGUI--20
Bom-pa bom, look at me.--ALLTOGETHE--12
Bom-pa bom, look at me.--ALLTOGETHE--32
Don't look at me man (ha ha ha ha)--HEYBULLDOG--31
When I look into your eyes --ITSALLTOOM--31
They look just like two gurus in drag.--BALLADOFJO
  --32
Takes him out to look at the Queen--MEANMRMUST--11
Oh look out!--SHECAMEINT--3
YOU KNOW MY NAME (LOOK UP MY NUMBER).--YOUKNOWMYN
  --Title
You know my name, look up de number --YOUKNOWMYN
  --1
You know my name, look up de number.--YOUKNOWMYN
  --2
Good evening, you know my name, well then look
  up my number --YOUKNOWMYN--9
You know my name, that's right, look up my
  number (hey) --YOUKNOWMYN--10
Look up the number (heads up boys) --YOUKNOWMYN--14
You know my name - haa, that's right, look up
  the number --YOUKNOWMYN--15
You know my name, ba ba ba bum, look up the
  number --YOUKNOWMYN--18
You know my name, look up the number --YOUKNOWMYN
  --19
My name, you know, you know, ((look up the
  number))--YOUKNOWMYN--25
You know my name, look up the number --YOUKNOWMYN
  --29
You know my name, look up the number.--YOUKNOWMYN
  --30
You know, you know my name, look up the number.--
  YOUKNOWMYN--31
You know my name, look up the number --YOUKNOWMYN
  --36
(look up my name)--YOUKNOWMYN--38

LOOKED
And the way she looked was way beyond compare.--
  ISAWHERSTA--4
Well she looked at me, and I, I could see --
  ISAWHERSTA--7
'cos I looked up to see your face.--NOREPLY--8
As I looked in your eyes --INEEDYOU--8
I might have looked the other way--IVEJUSTSEE--8
So I looked around--NORWEGIANW--9
In a cap she looked much older--LOVELYRITA--10
(But when he looked so fierce) his mommy butted
  in --CONTINUING--28
You looked at me, that's all you had to do --
  FORYOUBLUE--14
All that I was looking for was somebody who
  looked like you.--IVEGOTAFEE--13

LOOKING
When you say she's looking good --GIRL--15
I'M LOOKING THROUGH YOU.--IMLOOKINGT--Title
I'm looking through you, where did you go?--
  IMLOOKINGT--1
I'm looking through you, you're not the same.--
  IMLOOKINGT--4
I'm looking through you, you're not the same.--
  IMLOOKINGT--8
I'm looking through you and you're nowhere.--
  IMLOOKINGT--14
I'm looking through you, where did you go?--
  IMLOOKINGT--17
I'm looking through you, you're not the same.--
  IMLOOKINGT--20
Aah, I'm looking through you.--IMLOOKINGT--22
Yeah, I'm looking through you.--IMLOOKINGT--23
She feels good (she feels good), she knows
  she's looking fine --GOODDAYSUN--12
And looking up I noticed I was late--DAYINTHELI--21
Without looking out of my window --INNERLIGHT--3

Without looking out of your window --INNERLIGHT--10
See all without looking.--INNERLIGHT--16
Looking through the bent-backed tulips--GLASSONION
--5
Looking through a glass onion.--GLASSONION--7
Looking through a glass onion.--GLASSONION--14
Looking through a glass onion.--GLASSONION--16
Looking through a glass onion.--GLASSONION--23
All that I was looking for was somebody who
looked like you.--IVEGOTAFEE--13

LOOKING-GLASS
With plasticine porters with looking-glass ties.--
LUCYINTHES--24

LOOKS
Now it looks as though they're here to stay--
YESTERDAY--3
The future still looks good --THINKFORYO--21
If looks could kill it would have been us instead
of him.--CONTINUING--29
She's so goodlooking but she looks like a man.--
POLYTHENEP--2

LORDS
Nobody was really sure if he was from the House
of Lords--DAYINTHELI--10

LORETTA
Sweet Loretta Martin thought she was a woman --
GETBACK/45--16
Get back Loretta (wuh - wuh).--GETBACK/45--24
Get back Loretta --GETBACK/45--31
Get back home Loretta.--GETBACK/45--35
Jojo, Loretta.--GETBACK/45--40
But she was a frying pan ((sweet Loretta
Martin)).--GETBACK/LP--3
Sweet Loretta Martin thought she was a woman--
GETBACK/LP--22
Get back Loretta (wuh - wuh).--GETBACK/LP--30

LORRY
Yellow lorry slow, nowhere to go.--YOUNEVERGI--12
Oh now I roll a lorry--IDIGAPONY--29

LOSE
And though I lose a friend in the end you will
know, oh.--ILLFOLLOWT--6
And though I lose a friend in the end you will
know, oh.--ILLFOLLOWT--11
I'm telling you so that you won't lose all.--
IMALOSER--18
YOU'RE GOING TO/GONNA LOSE THAT GIRL.--YOUREGONNA--Title
You're gonna lose that girl (yes, yes, you're
gonna lose that girl)--YOUREGONNA--1
You're gonna lose that girl (yes, yes, you're
gonna lose that girl)--YOUREGONNA--1
You're gonna lose that girl (yes, yes, you're
gonna lose that girl)--YOUREGONNA--2
You're gonna lose that girl (yes, yes, you're
gonna lose that girl)--YOUREGONNA--2
You're gonna lose that girl (yes, yes, you're
gonna lose that girl)--YOUREGONNA--7
You're gonna lose that girl (yes, yes, you're
gonna lose that girl)--YOUREGONNA--7
You're gonna lose that girl (yes, yes, you're
gonna lose that girl)--YOUREGONNA--8
You're gonna lose that girl (yes, yes, you're
gonna lose that girl)--YOUREGONNA--8
You're gonna lose that girl (yes, yes, you're
gonna lose that girl)--YOUREGONNA--13
You're gonna lose that girl (yes, yes, you're
gonna lose that girl)--YOUREGONNA--13
You're gonna lose that girl (yes, yes, you're
gonna lose that girl)--YOUREGONNA--14
You're gonna lose that girl (yes, yes, you're
gonna lose that girl)--YOUREGONNA--14
You're gonna lose (yes, yes, you're gonna lose
that girl)--YOUREGONNA--15
You're gonna lose (yes, yes, you're gonna lose
that girl)--YOUREGONNA--15
You're gonna lose that girl--YOUREGONNA--18
You're gonna lose that girl--YOUREGONNA--19
You're gonna lose that girl (yes, yes, you're
gonna lose that girl)--YOUREGONNA--20
You're gonna lose that girl (yes, yes, you're
gonna lose that girl)--YOUREGONNA--20
You're gonna lose that girl (yes, yes, you're

gonna lose that girl)--YOUREGONNA--21
You're gonna lose that girl (yes, yes, you're
gonna lose that girl)--YOUREGONNA--21
You're gonna lose (yes, yes, you're gonna lose
that girl)--YOUREGONNA--22
You're gonna lose (yes, yes, you're gonna lose
that girl)--YOUREGONNA--22
You're gonna lose that girl (yes, yes, you're
gonna lose that girl)--YOUREGONNA--29
You're gonna lose that girl (yes, yes, you're
gonna lose that girl)--YOUREGONNA--29
You're gonna lose that girl (yes, yes, you're
gonna lose that girl)--YOUREGONNA--30
You're gonna lose that girl (yes, yes, you're
gonna lose that girl)--YOUREGONNA--30
You're gonna lose (yes, yes, you're gonna lose
that girl).--YOUREGONNA--32
You're gonna lose (yes, yes, you're gonna lose
that girl).--YOUREGONNA--32
And these memories lose their meaning--INMYLIFE--11
Though I know I'll never lose affection --INMYLIFE
--13
Though I know I'll never lose affection --INMYLIFE
--17
And I will lose my mind--YOUWONTSEE--4
Who gain the world and lose their soul--WITHINYOUW
--24

LOSER
I'M A LOSER.--IMALOSER--Title
I'm a loser, I'm a loser --IMALOSER--1
I'm a loser, I'm a loser --IMALOSER--1
I'm a loser and I lost someone who's near to me --
IMALOSER--7
I'm a loser and I'm not what I appear to be.--
IMALOSER--8
I'm a loser and I lost someone who's near to me --
IMALOSER--13
I'm a loser and I'm not what I appear to be.--
IMALOSER--14
I'm a loser and I lost someone who's near to me --
IMALOSER--19
I'm a loser and I'm not what I appear to be.--
IMALOSER--20

LOSING
When I get older losing my hair--WHENIMSIXT--1

LOST
I've lost her now for sure, I won't see her no
more --MISERY--4
You think you've lost your love--SHELOVESYO--4
She almost lost her mind--SHELOVESYO--13
'cos I've just lost the only girl I had.--
ILLCRYINST--2
Of all the love I have won or have lost --IMALOSER
--3
I'm a loser and I lost someone who's near to me --
IMALOSER--7
I'm a loser and I lost someone who's near to me --
IMALOSER--13
I'm a loser and I lost someone who's near to me --
IMALOSER--19
We have lost the time that was so hard to find--
YOUWONTSEE--3
And since I lost you it feels like years.--
YOUWONTSEE--17
And since I lost you it feels like years.--
YOUWONTSEE--26
And my friends have lost their way.--BLUEJAYWAY--2
Now they've lost themselves instead.--BLUEJAYWAY
--4
And you lost your hair.--DONTPASSME--26
How could I ever have lost you --LONGLONGLO--2

LOT
I may not have a lot to give --CANTBUYMEL--11
So - oh, I should have realised a lot of things
before --ISHOULDHAV--11
Deep in love, not a lot to say --THINGSWESA--9
Deep in love, not a lot to say --THINGSWESA--20
Deep in love, not a lot to say --THINGSWESA--31
I got a whole lot of things to tell her --
WHENIGETHO--2
I got a whole lot of things I gotta say to her.--
WHENIGETHO--6
I got a whole lot of things to tell her --
WHENIGETHO--8
I got a whole lot of things to tell her --
WHENIGETHO--14

I got a whole lot of things to tell her --
   WHENIGETHO--25
I got a whole lot of things to tell her --
   WHENIGETHO--27
But what you've got means such a lot to me.--
   LOVEYOUTWO--8
But she doesn't have a lot to say.--HERMAJESTY--2
I wanna tell her that I love her a lot--HERMAJESTY
   --5

LOTS
Everywhere there's lots of piggies--PIGGIES--15

LOUD
The man of a thousand voices talking perfectly loud
   --FOOLONTHEH--9
Sing it loud so I can hear you --IWILL--15

LOVE
LOVE ME DO.--LOVEMEDO--Title
Love, love me do --LOVEMEDO--1
Love, love me do --LOVEMEDO--1
You know I love you.--LOVEMEDO--2
So please love me do --LOVEMEDO--4
Whao-ho love me do.--LOVEMEDO--5
Love, love me do --LOVEMEDO--6
Love, love me do --LOVEMEDO--6
You know I love you.--LOVEMEDO--7
So please love me do --LOVEMEDO--9
Whoa-ho love me do.--LOVEMEDO--10
Someone to love, somebody new.--LOVEMEDO--11
Someone to love, someone like you.--LOVEMEDO--12
Love, love me do --LOVEMEDO--13
Love, love me do --LOVEMEDO--13
You know I love you.--LOVEMEDO--14
So please love me do --LOVEMEDO--16
Whoa-ho love me do (hey hey).--LOVEMEDO--17
Love, love me do --LOVEMEDO--18
Love, love me do --LOVEMEDO--18
You know I love you.--LOVEMEDO--19
So please love me do --LOVEMEDO--21
Whoa-ho love me do.--LOVEMEDO--22
Yes, love me do --LOVEMEDO--23
Whoa-ho love me do.--LOVEMEDO--24
Yes, love me do.--LOVEMEDO--25
PS I LOVE YOU.--PSILOVEYOU--Title
As I write this letter, send my love to you --
   PSILOVEYOU--1
Remember that I'll always be in love with you.--
   PSILOVEYOU--2
Keep all ((all)) my love forever ((ever)).--
   PSILOVEYOU--5
PS I love you, you, you, you.--PSILOVEYOU--6
I'll ((I'll)) be coming home ((home)) again
   to you love ((you love)) --PSILOVEYOU--7
I'll ((I'll)) be coming home ((home)) again
   to you love ((you love)) --PSILOVEYOU--7
And till ((till)) the day I do love ((do love))
   --PSILOVEYOU--8
And till ((till)) the day I do love ((do love))
   --PSILOVEYOU--8
PS I love you, you, you, you.--PSILOVEYOU--9
As I write this letter, send my love to you,--
   PSILOVEYOU--10
Remember that I'll always be in love with you.--
   PSILOVEYOU--11
Keep all ((all)) my love forever ((ever)) --
   PSILOVEYOU--14
PS I love you, you, you, you.--PSILOVEYOU--15
As I write this letter (oh) send my love to you --
   PSILOVEYOU--16
Remember that I'll always, yeah, be in love
   with you.--PSILOVEYOU--18
I'll be coming home again to you love --PSILOVEYOU
   --19
And till the day I do love --PSILOVEYOU--20
PS I love you, you, you, you --PSILOVEYOU--21
I love you.--PSILOVEYOU--23
If you need somebody to love --ANYTIMEATA--4
I love you --ASKMEWHY--1
But you're the only love that I've ever had.--
   ASKMEWHY--11
Ask me why, I'll say I love you --ASKMEWHY--14
I love you --ASKMEWHY--16
Ask me why, I'll say I love you --ASKMEWHY--22
Ask me why, I'll say I love you--ASKMEWHY--26
You don't need me to show the way love --PLEASEPLEA
   --7
Why do I always have to say love --PLEASEPLEA--8
You'll never know how much I really love you --
   DOYOUWANTT--1

I'm in love with you - ooo.--DOYOUWANTT--8
I'm in love with you --DOYOUWANTT--14
I'm in love with you - ooo --DOYOUWANTT--22
That before too long I'd fall in love with her.--
   ISAWHERSTA--8
And before too long I fell in love with her--
   ISAWHERSTA--15
And before too long I fell in love with her.--
   ISAWHERSTA--22
With love from me to you.--FROMMETOYO--6
With love from me to you.--FROMMETOYO--10
With love from me to you.--FROMMETOYO--18
With love from me to you.--FROMMETOYO--21
With love from me to you--FROMMETOYO--29
And eternally I'll always be in love with you--
   THANKYOUGI--3
I could tell the world a thing or two about our love
   --THANKYOUGI--5
I know, little girl, only a fool would doubt
   our love--THANKYOUGI--6
That's the kind of love that is too good to be true
   --THANKYOUGI--9
And eternally I'll always be in love with you--
   THANKYOUGI--13
Imagine I'm in love with you--ILLGETYOU--2
I've imagined I'm in love with you--ILLGETYOU--4
Imagine I'm in love with you--ILLGETYOU--19
I've imagined I'm in love with you--ILLGETYOU--21
You think you've lost your love--SHELOVESYO--4
With a love like that--SHELOVESYO--22
With a love like that--SHELOVESYO--34
With a love like that--SHELOVESYO--36
With a love like that--SHELOVESYO--38
Making love to only you.--HOLDMETIGH--12
Making love to only you.--HOLDMETIGH--32
Love you like no other baby --IWANNABEYO--5
Love you like no other baby --IWANNABEYO--7
Tell me that you love me baby --IWANNABEYO--13
Tell me that you love me baby --IWANNABEYO--15
Love you like no other baby --IWANNABEYO--34
Love you like no other baby --IWANNABEYO--36
That my love--IWANTTOHOL--16
That my love--IWANTTOHOL--29
That boy took my love away--THISBOY--1
Just to love you, but oh my!--THISBOY--8
CAN'T BUY ME LOVE.--CANTBUYMEL--Title
Can't buy me love, oh, love, oh --CANTBUYMEL--1
Can't buy me love, oh, love, oh --CANTBUYMEL--1
Can't buy me love, oh.--CANTBUYMEL--2
Money can't buy me love --CANTBUYMEL--8
If you say you love me too --CANTBUYMEL--10
Money can't buy me love.--CANTBUYMEL--14
Can't buy me love, oh, everybody tells me so --
   CANTBUYMEL--15
Can't buy me love oh - no, no, no - no.--CANTBUYMEL
   --16
Money can't buy me love.--CANTBUYMEL--22
Can't buy me love, oh, everybody tells me so --
   CANTBUYMEL--25
Can't buy me love oh - no, no, no - no.--CANTBUYMEL
   --26
Money can't buy me love.--CANTBUYMEL--32
Can't buy me love, oh, love, oh --CANTBUYMEL--33
Can't buy me love, oh, love, oh --CANTBUYMEL--33
Can't buy me love, oh, oh.--CANTBUYMEL--34
'cos I'm the one who won your love--YOUCANTDOT--19
'cos I'm the one who won your love--YOUCANTDOT--38
Like I love only you.--THERESAPLA--8
AND I LOVE HER.--ANDILOVEHE--Title
I give her all my love --ANDILOVEHE--1
And if you saw my love --ANDILOVEHE--3
You'd love her too --ANDILOVEHE--4
I love her.--ANDILOVEHE--5
And I love her.--ANDILOVEHE--10
A love like ours --ANDILOVEHE--11
I know this love of mine --ANDILOVEHE--17
And I love her.--ANDILOVEHE--19
I know this love of mine --ANDILOVEHE--22
And I love her --ANDILOVEHE--24
That I would love everything that you do --
   ISHOULDHAV--2
That when I tell you that I love you, oh --
   ISHOULDHAV--7
You're gonna say you love me too, oh.--ISHOULDHAV
   --8
You're gonna say you love me too.--ISHOULDHAV--10
If this is love you've got to give me more --
   ISHOULDHAV--12
That when I tell you that I love you, oh --
   ISHOULDHAV--17
You're gonna say you love me too, oh.--ISHOULDHAV
   --18
You're gonna say you love me too.--ISHOULDHAV--20
You love me too --ISHOULDHAV--21

You love me too --ISHOULDHAV--22
You love me too.--ISHOULDHAV--23
If I fell in love with you --IFIFELL--1
'cos I've been in love before --IFIFELL--4
And I found that love was more --IFIFELL--5
That you would love me more than her.--IFIFELL--9
If I love you too --IFIFELL--12
If our new love was in vain.--IFIFELL--16
That I would love to love you --IFIFELL--18
That I would love to love you --IFIFELL--18
If our new love was in vain.--IFIFELL--23
That I would love to love you --IFIFELL--25
That I would love to love you --IFIFELL--25
If I fell in love with you.--IFIFELL--28
I think I'll love you too --IMHAPPYJUS--2
I think I'll love you too ((oh)) --IMHAPPYJUS--14
I think I'll love you too ((oh)) --IMHAPPYJUS--22
I've discovered I'm in love with you (oh - oh).--
    IMHAPPYJUS--27
I'm so in love with you.--TELLMEWHY--25
I love you so--ILLBEBACK--5
You say you will love me if I have to go--
    THINGSWESA--1
Deep in love, not a lot to say --THINGSWESA--9
Love to hear you say that love is love--THINGSWESA
    --12
Love to hear you say that love is love--THINGSWESA
    --12
Love to hear you say that love is love--THINGSWESA
    --12
Love is here to stay.--THINGSWESA--14
Love me all the time girl --THINGSWESA--17
Deep in love, not a lot to say --THINGSWESA--20
Love to hear you say that love is love--THINGSWESA
    --23
Love to hear you say that love is love--THINGSWESA
    --23
Love to hear you say that love is love--THINGSWESA
    --23
Love is here to stay.--THINGSWESA--25
Love me all the time girl --THINGSWESA--28
Deep in love, not a lot to say --THINGSWESA--31
I'm gonna love her till the cows come home --
    WHENIGETHO--18
I bet I'll love her more --WHENIGETHO--19
I'm in love with her and I feel fine.--IFEELFINE
    --3
I'm in love with her and I feel fine.--IFEELFINE
    --6
She's in love with me and I feel fine (ooo).--
    IFEELFINE--11
I'm in love with her and I feel fine.--IFEELFINE
    --14
She's in love with me and I feel fine.--IFEELFINE
    --19
She's in love with me and I feel fine.--IFEELFINE
    --20
My love don't give me presents--SHESAWOMAN--1
Only ever has to give me love forever and forever
    --SHESAWOMAN--3
My love don't give me presents--SHESAWOMAN--4
My love don't give me presents--SHESAWOMAN--18
Only ever has to give me love forever and forever
    --SHESAWOMAN--20
My love don't give me presents--SHESAWOMAN--21
My love don't give me presents--SHESAWOMAN--28
Only ever has to give me love forever and forever
    --SHESAWOMAN--30
My love don't give me presents--SHESAWOMAN--31
Ooo I need your love babe --EIGHTDAYSA--1
Hope you need my love babe --EIGHTDAYSA--3
Hold me, love me --EIGHTDAYSA--5
Hold me, love me --EIGHTDAYSA--6
I ain't got nothing but love babe --EIGHTDAYSA--7
Love you every day girl --EIGHTDAYSA--9
Love you all the time.--EIGHTDAYSA--12
Hold me, love me --EIGHTDAYSA--13
Hold me, love me --EIGHTDAYSA--14
I ain't got nothing but love girl --EIGHTDAYSA--15
Eight days a week I love you --EIGHTDAYSA--17
Ooo I need your love babe --EIGHTDAYSA--19
Hope you need my love babe --EIGHTDAYSA--21
Hold me, love me --EIGHTDAYSA--23
Hold me, love me --EIGHTDAYSA--24
I ain't got nothing but love babe --EIGHTDAYSA--25
Eight days a week I love you --EIGHTDAYSA--27
Love you every day girl --EIGHTDAYSA--29
Love you all the time.--EIGHTDAYSA--32
Hold me, love me --EIGHTDAYSA--33
Hold me, love me --EIGHTDAYSA--34
I ain't got nothing but love babe --EIGHTDAYSA--35
I will love her forever--EVERYLITTL--15
For I know love will never die.--EVERYLITTL--16

I still love her.--IDONTWANTT--10
I still love her.--IDONTWANTT--12
I still love her.--IDONTWANTT--19
I still love her.--IDONTWANTT--21
And now the time has come and so my love I must
    go --ILLFOLLOWT--5
And now the time has come and so my love I must
    go --ILLFOLLOWT--10
Of all the love I have won or have lost --IMALOSER
    --3
There is one love I should never have crossed.--
    IMALOSER--4
Love you more than any other guy--NOREPLY--18
'n' should you need a love that's true, it's me.--
    WHATYOURED--11
'n' should you need a love that's true, it's me.--
    WHATYOURED--18
Another girl who will love me till the end --
    ANOTHERGIR--10
Another girl who will love me till the end --
    ANOTHERGIR--16
Love you all the time and never leave you--INEEDYOU
    --2
IT'S ONLY LOVE.--ITSONLYLOV--Title
It's only love and that is all--ITSONLYLOV--4
It's only love and that is all--ITSONLYLOV--6
It's only love and that is all--ITSONLYLOV--11
It's only love and that is all--ITSONLYLOV--13
Love was in your eyes (aah the night before)--
    NIGHTBEFOR--2
Love was in your eyes (aah the night before)--
    NIGHTBEFOR--12
Love was such an easy game to play--YESTERDAY--14
Love was such an easy game to play--YESTERDAY--22
YOU'VE GOT TO HIDE YOUR LOVE AWAY.--YOUVEGOTTO
    --Title
Hey! you've got to hide your love away.--YOUVEGOTTO
    --9
Hey! you've got to hide your love away.--YOUVEGOTTO
    --10
Love will find a way?--YOUVEGOTTO--16
Hey! you've got to hide your love away.--YOUVEGOTTO
    --19
Hey! you've got to hide your love away.--YOUVEGOTTO
    --20
Run the risk of knowing that our love may soon be
    gone.--WECANWORKI--4
And maybe I'll love you.--DRIVEMYCAR--8
And maybe I'll love you.--DRIVEMYCAR--16
And maybe I'll love you.--DRIVEMYCAR--21
And maybe I'll love you.--DRIVEMYCAR--29
If I needed someone to love --IFINEEDS--1
But you see now I'm too much in love.--IFINEEDS
    --9
But you see now I'm too much in love.--IFINEEDS
    --19
Love has a nasty habit of disappearing overnight.
    --IMLOOKINGT--10
Love has a nasty habit of disappearing overnight.
    --IMLOOKINGT--16
When I think of love as something new.--INMYLIFE
    --12
In my life I love you more.--INMYLIFE--16
In my life I love you more.--INMYLIFE--20
In my life I love you more.--INMYLIFE--21
I love you, I love you, I love you--MICHELLE--5
I love you, I love you, I love you--MICHELLE--5
I love you, I love you, I love you--MICHELLE--5
I love you.--MICHELLE--15
Have you heard the word is love?--THEWORD--4
It's the word love.--THEWORD--6
Have you heard the word is love?--THEWORD--12
It's the word love.--THEWORD--14
Have you heard the word is love?--THEWORD--20
It's the word love.--THEWORD--22
And the only word is love.--THEWORD--28
It's the word love.--THEWORD--30
Say the word love --THEWORD--31
Say the word love --THEWORD--32
Say the word love --THEWORD--33
Say the word love.--THEWORD--34
No sign of love behind the tears cried for no-one
    --FORNOONE--8
A love that should have lasted years.--FORNOONE--9
When she says her love is dead --FORNOONE--12
No sign of love behind the tears cried for no-one
    --FORNOONE--15
A love that should have lasted years.--FORNOONE--16
No sign of love behind the tears cried for no-one
    --FORNOONE--25
A love that should have lasted years.--FORNOONE--26
I'm in love and it's a sunny day.--GOODDAYSUN--5
I love her and she's loving me.--GOODDAYSUN--11
To lead a better life, I need my love to be here.

--HERETHEREA--1
But to love her is to need her everywhere.--
    HERETHEREA--10
Knowing that love is to share--HERETHEREA--11
Each one believing that love never dies--HERETHEREA
    --12
But to love her is to need her everywhere.--
    HERETHEREA--16
Knowing that love is to share--HERETHEREA--17
Each one believing that love never dies--HERETHEREA
    --18
LOVE YOU TO/TOO.--LOVEYOUTWO--Title
Love me while you can --LOVEYOUTWO--4
Make love all day long --LOVEYOUTWO--9
Make love singing songs.--LOVEYOUTWO--10
Make love all day long --LOVEYOUTWO--11
Make love singing songs.--LOVEYOUTWO--12
I'll make love to you --LOVEYOUTWO--16
That love is all and love is everyone--TOMORROWNE
    --7
That love is all and love is everyone--TOMORROWNE
    --7
I'd love to turn you on--DAYINTHELI--16
I'd love to turn you on--DAYINTHELI--34
We'd love to take you home.--SGTPEPPERS--18
What do I do when my love is away?--WITHALITTL--8
I need somebody to love.--WITHALITTL--16
I want somebody to love.--WITHALITTL--18
(Would you believe in a love at first sight?)--
    WITHALITTL--19
I just need someone to love.--WITHALITTL--27
I want somebody to love.--WITHALITTL--29
About the love we all could share--WITHINYOUW--9
With our love--WITHINYOUW--12
With our love--WITHINYOUW--13
About the love that's gone so cold--WITHINYOUW--22
ALL YOU NEED IS LOVE.--ALLYOUN/YS--Title
Love, love, love --ALLYOUN/YS--1
Love, love, love --ALLYOUN/YS--1
Love, love, love --ALLYOUN/YS--1
Love, love, love --ALLYOUN/YS--2
Love, love, love --ALLYOUN/YS--2
Love, love, love.--ALLYOUN/YS--3
Love, love, love.--ALLYOUN/YS--3
Love, love, love.--ALLYOUN/YS--3
There's nothing you can do that can't be done
    ((love))--ALLYOUN/YS--4
Nothing you can sing that can't be sung ((love))--
    ALLYOUN/YS--5
Nothing you can say but you can learn how to play
    the game ((love))--ALLYOUN/YS--6
Nothing you can make that can't be made ((love))--
    ALLYOUN/YS--8
No-one you can save that can't be saved ((love))--
    ALLYOUN/YS--9
Nothing you can do but you can learn how to be
    you in time ((love))--ALLYOUN/YS--10
All you need is love, all you need is love --
    ALLYOUN/YS--12
All you need is love, all you need is love --
    ALLYOUN/YS--12
All you need is love, love, love is all you need.
    --ALLYOUN/YS--13
All you need is love, love, love is all you need.
    --ALLYOUN/YS--13
All you need is love, love, love is all you need.
    --ALLYOUN/YS--13
Love, love, love --ALLYOUN/YS--14
Love, love, love --ALLYOUN/YS--14
Love, love, love --ALLYOUN/YS--14
Love, love, love --ALLYOUN/YS--15
Love, love, love --ALLYOUN/YS--15
Love, love, love --ALLYOUN/YS--15
Love, love, love.--ALLYOUN/YS--16
Love, love, love.--ALLYOUN/YS--16
Love, love, love.--ALLYOUN/YS--16
All you need is love, (wuh) all you need is
    love (hey) --ALLYOUN/YS--17
All you need is love, (wuh) all you need is
    love (hey) --ALLYOUN/YS--17
All you need is love, love, love is all you need.
    --ALLYOUN/YS--18
All you need is love, love, love is all you need.
    --ALLYOUN/YS--18
All you need is love, love, love is all you need.
    --ALLYOUN/YS--18
There's nothing you can know that isn't known
    ((love))--ALLYOUN/YS--19
Nothing you can see that isn't shown ((love))--
    ALLYOUN/YS--20
There's nowhere you can be that isn't where
    you're meant to be ((love))--ALLYOUN/YS--21
All you need is love, all you need is love --

ALLYOUN/YS--23
All you need is love, all you need is love --
    ALLYOUN/YS--23
All you need is love, love, love is all you need.
    --ALLYOUN/YS--24
All you need is love, love, love is all you need.
    --ALLYOUN/YS--24
All you need is love, love, love is all you need.
    --ALLYOUN/YS--24
All you need is love (all together now) --
    ALLYOUN/YS--25
All you need is love (everybody) --ALLYOUN/YS--26
All you need is love, love, love is all you need.
    --ALLYOUN/YS--27
All you need is love, love, love is all you need.
    --ALLYOUN/YS--27
All you need is love, love, love is all you need.
    --ALLYOUN/YS--27
Love is all you need (love is all you need)--
    ALLYOUN/YS--28
Love is all you need (love is all you need)--
    ALLYOUN/YS--28
Love is all you need (love is all you need)--
    ALLYOUN/YS--29
Love is all you need (love is all you need)--
    ALLYOUN/YS--29
Love is all you need (love is all you need)--
    ALLYOUN/YS--30
Love is all you need (love is all you need)--
    ALLYOUN/YS--30
Love is all you need (love is all you need)--
    ALLYOUN/YS--31
Love is all you need (love is all you need)--
    ALLYOUN/YS--31
Love is all you need (wuh) (love is all you
    need)--ALLYOUN/YS--32
Love is all you need (wuh) (love is all you
    need)--ALLYOUN/YS--32
Love is all you need (love is all you need)--
    ALLYOUN/YS--33
Love is all you need (love is all you need)--
    ALLYOUN/YS--33
Love is all you need (love is all you need)--
    ALLYOUN/YS--34
Love is all you need (love is all you need)--
    ALLYOUN/YS--34
Love is all you need (love is all you need)--
    ALLYOUN/YS--35
Love is all you need (love is all you need)--
    ALLYOUN/YS--35
Love is all you need (love is all you need)--
    ALLYOUN/YS--36
Love is all you need (love is all you need)--
    ALLYOUN/YS--36
Love is all you need (love is all you need)--
    ALLYOUN/YS--37
Love is all you need (love is all you need)--
    ALLYOUN/YS--37
Love is all you need (yahoo) (eee - hi)--
    ALLYOUN/YS--38
Love is all you need (love is all you need)--
    ALLYOUN/YS--39
Love is all you need (love is all you need)--
    ALLYOUN/YS--39
(Love is all you need) Yesterday (love is all
    you need)--ALLYOUN/YS--40
(Love is all you need) Yesterday (love is all
    you need)--ALLYOUN/YS--40
(Oh) love is all you need--ALLYOUN/YS--41
Love is all you need (oh yeah)--ALLYOUN/YS
    --42
Love is all you need--ALLYOUN/YS--43
Loves you yeah, yeah, yeah ((love is all, love
    is all))--ALLYOUN/YS--44
Loves you yeah, yeah, yeah ((love is all, love
    is all))--ALLYOUN/YS--44
She loves you yeah, yeah, yeah ((love is all,
    love is all))--ALLYOUN/YS--45
She loves you yeah, yeah, yeah ((love is all,
    love is all))--ALLYOUN/YS--45
Love is all you need--ALLYOUN/YS--46
Love is all you need (wuhoo)--ALLYOUN/YS--47
Love is all you need (wuhoo)--ALLYOUN/YS--48
Love is all you need (oh)--ALLYOUN/YS--49
Love is all you need--ALLYOUN/YS--50
Love is all you need.--ALLYOUN/YS--51
We'd all love to see the plan.--REVOLUTION
    --14
Does it mean you don't love me any more?--
    DONTPASSME--9
Does it mean you don't love me any more?--
    DONTPASSME--17
'cos you know, darling, I love only you --
    DONTPASSME--19

'cos you know, darling, I love only you --
   DONTPASSME--32
'cos you know, darling, I love only you --
   DONTPASSME--38
A - do you, don't you want me to love you?--
   HELTERSKEL--4
I'm in love but I'm lazy--HONEYPIE--8
I'm in love but I'm lazy--HONEYPIE--30
You know I love you still.--IWILL--2
Love you forever and forever --IWILL--9
Love you with all my heart --IWILL--10
Love you whenever we're together --IWILL--11
Love you when we're apart.--IWILL--12
So I sing the song of love, Julia.--JULIA--4
So I sing the song of love, Julia.--JULIA--6
So I sing the song of love, Julia.--JULIA--10
So I sing a song of love, Julia.--JULIA--14
So I sing a song of love for Julia --JULIA--16
How I love you.--LONGLONGLO--6
Oh I love you --LONGLONGLO--12
Oh I love you.--LONGLONGLO--14
Please - remember me, Martha my love --MARTHAMYDE
   --2
Please - be good to me, Martha my love --MARTHAMYDE
   --14
We'd all love to see the plan.--REVOLUTONE--21
We'd all love to change our head.--REVOLUTONE--37
I look at you all, see the love there that's
   sleeping --WHILEMYGUI--2
I don't know why nobody told you how to unfold
   your love --WHILEMYGUI--6
I look at you all, see the love there that's
   sleeping--WHILEMYGUI--18
I love you, yeah, Honey Pie, wuh!--WILDHONEYP--4
I love you.--ALLTOGETHE--4
I love you.--ALLTOGETHE--8
I love you.--ALLTOGETHE--20
ALL YOU NEED IS LOVE.--ALLYOU/MMT--Title
Love is all you need--ALLYOU/MMT--1
(Oh) love is all you need--ALLYOU/MMT--2
Love is all you need--ALLYOU/MMT--3
Love is all you need--ALLYOU/MMT--4
Love is all you need--ALLYOU/MMT--5
Love is all you need.--ALLYOU/MMT--6
Your love is there for me--ITSALLTOOM--5
The love that's shining all around you --ITSALLTOOM
   --9
The love that's shining all around here --
   ITSALLTOOM--17
The love that's shining all around here --
   ITSALLTOOM--26
The love that's shining all around you --ITSALLTOOM
   --30
I'm in love for the first time --DONTLETMED--13
It's a love that lasts forever --DONTLETMED--15
It's a love that has no past (believe me).--
   DONTLETMED--16
I want a love that's right --OLDBROWNSH--1
Baby, I'm in love with you --OLDBROWNSH--6
Baby, I'm in love with you --OLDBROWNSH--14
I'll live and love and maybe someday --OLDBROWNSH
   --20
My love is something you can't reject.--OLDBROWNSH
   --23
I want that love of yours --OLDBROWNSH--27
To miss that love is something I'd hate.--
   OLDBROWNSH--28
Baby, I'm in love with you.--OLDBROWNSH--32
Love is old, love is new --BECAUSE--8
Love is old, love is new --BECAUSE--8
Love is all, love is you.--BECAUSE--9
Love is all, love is you.--BECAUSE--9
Love you, love you, love you, love you, love
   you --THEEND--3
Love you, love you, love you, love you, love
   you --THEEND--3
Love you, love you, love you, love you, love
   you --THEEND--3
Love you, love you, love you, love you, love
   you --THEEND--3
Love you, love you, love you, love you, love
   you --THEEND--3
Love you, love you, love you, love you, love
   you --THEEND--4
Love you, love you, love you, love you, love
   you --THEEND--4
Love you, love you, love you, love you, love
   you --THEEND--4
Love you, love you, love you, love you, love
   you --THEEND--4
Love you, love you, love you, love you, love
   you --THEEND--4
Love you, love you, love you, love you, love
   you --THEEND--5

Love you, love you, love you, love you, love
   you --THEEND--5
Love you, love you, love you, love you, love
   you --THEEND--5
Love you, love you, love you, love you, love
   you --THEEND--5
Love you, love you, love you, love you, love
   you --THEEND--5
Love you, love you, love you, love you, love
   you --THEEND--6
Love you, love you, love you, love you, love
   you --THEEND--6
Love you, love you, love you, love you, love
   you --THEEND--6
Love you, love you, love you, love you, love
   you --THEEND--6
Love you, love you, love you, love you, love
   you --THEEND--6
Love you, love you, love you, love you.--THEEND--7
Love you, love you, love you, love you.--THEEND--7
Love you, love you, love you, love you.--THEEND--7
Love you, love you, love you, love you.--THEEND--7
The love you take is equal to the love you make.--
   THEEND--9
The love you take is equal to the love you make.--
   THEEND--9
I wanna tell her that I love her a lot--HERMAJESTY
   --5
You're asking me will my love grow?--SOMETHING--11
Limitless undying love which shines around me
   like a million suns --ACROSSTHEU--23
Because you're sweet and lovely girl, I love you
   --FORYOUBLUE--2
I love you more than ever girl, I do.--FORYOUBLUE
   --4
I want you in the morning girl, I love you --
   FORYOUBLUE--5
Because you're sweet and lovely girl, I love you
   --FORYOUBLUE--16
I love you more than ever girl, I do - really
   love blues.--FORYOUBLUE--18
I love you more than ever girl, I do - really
   love blues.--FORYOUBLUE--18

LOVED
   In my life I've loved them all.--INMYLIFE--8
   I beat her and kept her apart from the things
      that she loved--GETTINGBET--26
   Who knows how long I've loved you?--IWILL--1
   When I loved you?--LONGLONGLO--3
   Nobody ever loved me like she does --DONTLETMED--5
   And if somebody loved me like she do me --
      DONTLETMED--7
   I've loved you from the moment I saw you --
      FORYOUBLUE--13

LOVELY
   LOVELY RITA.--LOVELYRITA--Title
   Lovely Rita meter maid--LOVELYRITA--2
   Lovely Rita meter maid (aah)--LOVELYRITA--3
   Lovely Rita (oh) meter maid--LOVELYRITA--4
   Lovely Rita meter maid--LOVELYRITA--13
   May I inquire discreetly ((lovely Rita))--
      LOVELYRITA--14
   When are you free ((lovely Rita))--LOVELYRITA--15
   Oh, lovely Rita meter maid--LOVELYRITA--26
   Lovely Rita ((lovely meter maid)) meter maid--
      LOVELYRITA--29
   Lovely Rita ((lovely meter maid)) meter maid--
      LOVELYRITA--29
   Lovely ((Rita, Rita, Rita)) Rita meter maid--
      LOVELYRITA--30
   Lovely Rita ((oh lovely Rita meter, meter
      maid)) meter maid--LOVELYRITA--31
   Lovely Rita ((oh lovely Rita meter, meter
      maid)) meter maid--LOVELYRITA--31
   Lovely Rita ((da da da da da da)) meter maid--
      LOVELYRITA--32
   You're such a lovely audience--SGTPEPPERS--16
   Because you're sweet and lovely girl, I love you
      --FORYOUBLUE--2
   Because you're sweet and lovely girl, it's true --
      FORYOUBLUE--3
   Because you're sweet and lovely girl, I love you
      --FORYOUBLUE--16
   Because you're sweet and lovely girl, it's true --
      FORYOUBLUE--17

LOVER
   I wanna be your lover baby --IWANNABEYO--1
   I wanna be your lover baby --IWANNABEYO--3

I wanna be your lover baby --IWANNABEYO--17
I wanna be your lover baby --IWANNABEYO--19
I wanna be your lover baby --IWANNABEYO--30
I wanna be your lover baby --IWANNABEYO--32
The kiss my lover brings --ANDILOVEHE--8
Well, you may be a lover, but you ain't no
   dancer.--HELTERSKEL--7
'cos you may be a lover, but you ain't no dancer.
   --HELTERSKEL--14
'cos you may be a lover, but you ain't no dancer.
   --HELTERSKEL--24
One sunny day the world was waiting for the lover
   ((sexy Sadie))--SEXYSADIE--9
Attracts me like no other lover --SOMETHING--2
That I don't need no other lover --SOMETHING--7

LOVERS
   With lovers and friends I still can recall --
      INMYLIFE--6
   But of all these friends and lovers --INMYLIFE--9

LOVES
   SHE LOVES YOU.--SHELOVESYO--Title
   She loves you yeah, yeah, yeah--SHELOVESYO--1
   She loves you yeah, yeah, yeah--SHELOVESYO--3
   She loves you yeah, yeah, yeah, yeah.--SHELOVESYO
      --3
   She said she loves you--SHELOVESYO--8
   Yeah, she loves you--SHELOVESYO--10
   She said she loves you--SHELOVESYO--16
   Yeah, she loves you--SHELOVESYO--18
   She loves you, yeah, yeah, yeah--SHELOVESYO--20
   She loves you, yeah, yeah, yeah--SHELOVESYO--21
   Because she loves you--SHELOVESYO--28
   Yeah, she loves you--SHELOVESYO--30
   She loves you, yeah, yeah, yeah--SHELOVESYO--32
   She loves you, yeah, yeah, yeah--SHELOVESYO--33
   She's a woman who loves her man--SHESAWOMAN--17
   She's a woman who loves her man--SHESAWOMAN--27
   Just to know that she loves me--EVERYLITTL--12
   Yes I know that she loves me now.--EVERYLITTL--13
   Loves you yeah, yeah, yeah ((love is all, love
      is all))--ALLYOUN/YS--44
   She loves you yeah, yeah, yeah ((love is all,
      love is all))--ALLYOUN/YS--45

LOVIN'
   And I'll send all my lovin' to you.--ALLMYLOVIN--6
   And I'll send all my lovin' to you.--ALLMYLOVIN--12
   All my lovin', I will send to you --ALLMYLOVIN--13
   All my lovin', darlin', I'll be true.--ALLMYLOVIN
      --14
   And I'll send all my lovin' to you.--ALLMYLOVIN--20
   All my lovin', I will send to you --ALLMYLOVIN--21
   All my lovin', darlin', I'll be true --ALLMYLOVIN
      --22
   All my lovin', all my lovin', ooo-ooo --ALLMYLOVIN
      --23
   All my lovin', all my lovin', ooo-ooo --ALLMYLOVIN
      --23
   All my lovin', I will send to you.--ALLMYLOVIN--24

LOVING
   Thank you girl, for loving me the way that you
      do (way that you do).--THANKYOUGI--8
   ALL MY LOVING.--ALLMYLOVIN--Title
   Let me go on loving you --HOLDMETIGH--10
   Let me go on loving you --HOLDMETIGH--30
   And show you what your loving man can do --
      ILLCRYINST--18
   And show you what your loving man can do --
      ILLCRYINST--27
   Gives me all her time as well as loving--SHESAWOMAN
      --14
   You don't want my loving any more--INEEDYOU--12
   You don't want my loving any more--INEEDYOU--22
   But it's so hard loving you.--ITSONLYLOV--7
   But it's so hard loving you.--ITSONLYLOV--14
   Yes, it's so hard loving you, loving you - ooo.--
      ITSONLYLOV--15
   Yes, it's so hard loving you, loving you - ooo.--
      ITSONLYLOV--15
   I love her and she's loving me.--GOODDAYSUN--11

LOW
   When I feel low, when I feel blue--THERESAPLA--2
   When I feel low, when I feel blue--THERESAPLA--14
   I mean, it must be high or low--STRAWBERRY--17
   Go in to work don't want to go feeling low down--

GOODMORNIN--7
I say hi!/high, you say 'lo/low--HELLOGOODB--7
The wind is low, the birds will sing --DEARPRUDEN
   --8

LOW-NECK
   And a low-neck sweater.--GETBACK/45--34

LUCKY
   Me I'm just the lucky kind --THINGSWESA--11
   Me I'm just the lucky kind --THINGSWESA--22
   People tell me I'm lucky--EVERYLITTL--2
   Yes I know I'm a lucky guy.--EVERYLITTL--3
   About a lucky man who made the grade--DAYINTHELI
      --2
   You don't know how lucky you are boys --BACKINTHEU
      --6
   You don't know how lucky you are boy --BACKINTHEU
      --13
   You don't know how lucky you are boys --BACKINTHEU
      --25
   You don't know how lucky you are boy --BACKINTHEU
      --36

LUCY
   LUCY IN THE SKY WITH DIAMONDS.--LUCYINTHES--Title
   Lucy in the sky with diamonds --LUCYINTHES--9
   Lucy in the sky with diamonds --LUCYINTHES--10
   Lucy in the sky with diamonds - aah.--LUCYINTHES
      --11
   Lucy in the sky with diamonds --LUCYINTHES--20
   Lucy in the sky with diamonds --LUCYINTHES--21
   Lucy in the sky with diamonds - aah.--LUCYINTHES
      --22
   Lucy in the sky with diamonds --LUCYINTHES--27
   Lucy in the sky with diamonds --LUCYINTHES--28
   Lucy in the sky with diamonds - aah.--LUCYINTHES
      --29
   Lucy in the sky with diamonds --LUCYINTHES--30
   Lucy in the sky with diamonds --LUCYINTHES--31
   Lucy in the sky with diamonds - aah.--LUCYINTHES
      --32
   Lucy in the sky with diamonds --LUCYINTHES--33
   Lucy in the sky with diamonds (aah - ooo) --
      LUCYINTHES--34
   Lucy in the sky with diamonds.--LUCYINTHES--35
   See how they fly like Lucy in the sky, see how
      they run--IAMTHEWALR--10

LULLABY
   And I will sing a lullaby.--GOLDENSLUM--6
   And I will sing a lullaby.--GOLDENSLUM--10
   And I will sing a lullaby.--GOLDENSLUM--16

LYING
   Please ((please)) stop your lying --WHATYOURED--12
   Please ((please)) stop your lying --WHATYOURED--19
   Lying there and staring at the ceiling --IMONLYSLEE
      --15
   Picks up the letter that's lying there--SHESLEAVIN
      --14
   Lady Madonna, lying on the bed --LADYMADONN--12
   Lying with his eyes while his hands are busy
      working overtime --HAPPINESSI--6

MA
   Michelle ma belle --MICHELLE--1
   Michelle ma belle --MICHELLE--3
   Michelle ma belle --MICHELLE--9
   Michelle ma belle --MICHELLE--20
   Nah - nah - nah - nah, hey Jude (Jude, Jude
      ma ma ma ma ma ma)--HEYJUDE--69
   Nah - nah - nah - nah, hey Jude (Jude, Jude
      ma ma ma ma ma ma)--HEYJUDE--69
   Nah - nah - nah - nah, hey Jude (Jude, Jude
      ma ma ma ma ma ma)--HEYJUDE--69
   Nah - nah - nah - nah, hey Jude (Jude, Jude
      ma ma ma ma ma ma)--HEYJUDE--69
   Nah - nah - nah - nah, hey Jude (Jude, Jude
      ma ma ma ma ma ma)--HEYJUDE--69
   Nah - nah - nah - nah, hey Jude (Jude, Jude
      ma ma ma ma ma ma)--HEYJUDE--69

MACHINE
   It's a clean machine.--PENNYLANE--15

MACK

    And the banker never wears a mack--PENNYLANE--7
    The man in the mack said you've got to go back --
        BALLADOFJO--3

MAD

    I got every reason on earth to be mad --ILLCRYINST
        --1
    The girl that's driving me mad is going away.--
        TICKETTORI--4
    The girl that's driving me mad is going away,
        yeah.--TICKETTORI--25
    Things that make me feel that I'm mad--SHESAIDSHE
        --5
    I used to get mad at my school (now I can't
        complain)--GETTINGBET--3
    It's driving me mad--IWANTYOUSH--5
    It's driving me mad--IWANTYOUSH--6
    It's driving me mad--IWANTYOUSH--11
    It's driving me mad--IWANTYOUSH--17
    It's driving me mad--IWANTYOUSH--18
    It's driving me mad--IWANTYOUSH--23
    It's driving me mad--IWANTYOUSH--32
    It's driving me mad--IWANTYOUSH--33
    It's driving me mad--IWANTYOUSH--38
    It's driving me mad--IWANTYOUSH--39

MADAM

    Dear Sir or Madam, will you read my book?--
        PAPERBACKW--2

MADE

    You made me glad when I was blue--THANKYOUGI--2
    You made me glad when I was blue--THANKYOUGI--12
    You know you made me cry --NOTASECOND--1
    You know you made me cry --NOTASECOND--12
    Till she sees the mistake she has made?--BABYSINBLA
        --15
    Till she sees the mistake she has made?--BABYSINBLA
        --20
    Though tonight she's made me sad --IDONTWANTT--9
    Though tonight she's made me sad --IDONTWANTT--18
    I know your mind's made up --THINKFORYO--13
    About a lucky man who made the grade--DAYINTHELI
        --2
    Made the bus in seconds flat--DAYINTHELI--24
    Made her look a little like a military man.--
        LOVELYRITA--12
    Took her home I nearly made it--LOVELYRITA--24
    Waiting to keep the appointment she made--
        SHESLEAVIN--26
    Nothing you can make that can't be made ((love))--
        ALLYOUN/YS--8
    You were made to go out and get her --HEYJUDE--6
    You made a fool of everyone--SEXYSADIE--2
    You made a fool of everyone--SEXYSADIE--3
    She made a fool of everyone--SEXYSADIE--26
    Finally made the plane into Paris --BALLADOFJO--9
    Made a lightning trip to Vienna --BALLADOFJO--29
    Bang, bang Maxwell's silver hammer made sure
        that she was dead.--MAXWELLSIL--7
    Bang, bang Maxwell's silver hammer made sure
        that she was dead.--MAXWELLSIL--15
    Bang, bang Maxwell's silver hammer made sure
        that he was dead.--MAXWELLSIL--25

MADONNA

    LADY MADONNA.--LADYMADONN--Title
    Lady Madonna, children at your feet --LADYMADONN
        --1
    Lady Madonna, baby at your breast --LADYMADONN--9
    Lady Madonna, lying on the bed --LADYMADONN--12
    Lady Madonna, children at your feet --LADYMADONN
        --18
    Lady Madonna trying to make ends meet - yeah--
        GLASSONION--13

MAGIC

    Come and show me the magic--HONEYPIE--11
    But oh, that magic feeling, nowhere to go --
        YOUNEVERGI--13
    Oh, that magic feeling --YOUNEVERGI--14

MAGICAL

    MAGICAL MYSTERY TOUR.--MAGICALMYS--Title
    The Magical Mystery Tour is waiting to take
        you away--MAGICALMYS--9
    The Magical Mystery Tour is hoping to take you

away --MAGICALMYS--17
The Magical Mystery Tour.--MAGICALMYS--21
The Magical Mystery Tour is coming to take you
    away --MAGICALMYS--27
The Magical Mystery Tour is dying to take you
    away--MAGICALMYS--29

MAGILL

    Her name was Magill and she called herself Lil --
        ROCKYRACCO--15

MAID

    Lovely Rita meter maid--LOVELYRITA--2
    Lovely Rita meter maid (aah)--LOVELYRITA--3
    Lovely Rita (oh) meter maid--LOVELYRITA--4
    Lovely Rita meter maid--LOVELYRITA--13
    To take some tea with me? ((maid))--LOVELYRITA--16
    Oh, lovely Rita meter maid--LOVELYRITA--26
    Lovely Rita ((lovely meter maid)) meter maid--
        LOVELYRITA--29
    Lovely Rita ((lovely meter maid)) meter maid--
        LOVELYRITA--29
    Lovely ((Rita, Rita, Rita)) Rita meter maid--
        LOVELYRITA--30
    Lovely Rita ((oh lovely Rita meter, meter
        maid)) meter maid--LOVELYRITA--31
    Lovely Rita ((oh lovely Rita meter, meter
        maid)) meter maid--LOVELYRITA--31
    Lovely Rita ((da da da da da da)) meter maid--
        LOVELYRITA--32

MAIL

    His son is working for the Daily Mail --PAPERBACKW
        --10

MAJESTY

    HER MAJESTY.--HERMAJESTY--Title

MAJESTY'S

    Her Majesty's a pretty nice girl--HERMAJESTY--1
    Her Majesty's a pretty nice girl--HERMAJESTY--3
    Her Majesty's a pretty nice girl--HERMAJESTY--7

MAJORING

    Maxwell Edison, majoring in medicine, calls
        her on the phone --MAXWELLSIL--3

MAKE

    I'm gonna change/make your mind--ILLGETYOU--17
    I'll be there to make you feel right--ANYTIMEATA--6
    I'll try to make it shine.--ANYTIMEATA--14
    Why do you make me blue?--PLEASEPLEA--18
    If you want someone to make you feel so fine--
        LITTLECHIL--3
    I'm not gonna make it --ICALLYOURN--7
    I'm not gonna make it --ICALLYOURN--14
    Will make me feel alright.--HARDDAYSNI--7
    Will make me feel alright --HARDDAYSNI--23
    Will make me feel alright --HARDDAYSNI--36
    I'd try to make you sad somehow --ILLCRYINST--9
    And that's enough to make you mine girl --
        THINGSWESA--15
    And that's enough to make you mine girl --
        THINGSWESA--26
    She will never make me jealous--SHESAWOMAN--13
    For red is the colour that will make me blue--
        YESITIS--16
    For red is the colour that will make me blue--
        YESITIS--25
    I'll make bright your day--TELLMEWHAT--12
    To walk out and make me lonely--YOULIKEMET--9
    Haven't I the right to make it up girl?--ITSONLYLOV
        --10
    I'll make a point of taking her away from you
        (watch what you do), yeah--YOUREGONNA--16
    I'll make a point of taking her away from you
        (watch what you do), yeah--YOUREGONNA--23
    I need to make you see--MICHELLE--12
    Just to make you toe the line.--RUNFORYOUR--12
    I can make it longer if you like the style,
        ((paperback))--PAPERBACKW--17
    It could make a million for you overnight.
        ((writer))--PAPERBACKW--22
    Well, well, well, he'll make you, Dr. Robert.--
        DRROBERT--12
    Well, well, well, he'll make you, Dr. Robert.--
        DRROBERT--19

I'll make you maybe next time around.--IWANTTOTEL
--8
Make love all day long --LOVEYOUTWO--9
Make love singing songs.--LOVEYOUTWO--10
Make love all day long --LOVEYOUTWO--11
Make love singing songs.--LOVEYOUTWO--12
I'll make love to you --LOVEYOUTWO--16
Things that make me feel that I'm mad--SHESAIDSHE
--5
Give us a wink and make me think of you.--
LOVELYRITA--28
No-one else can make you change--WITHINYOUW--17
Nothing you can make that can't be made ((love))--
ALLYOUN/YS--8
Or the sound he appears to make--FOOLONTHEH--11
Roll up (to make a reservation)--MAGICALMYS--7
Roll up (to make a reservation)--MAGICALMYS--25
Wonder how you manage to make ends meet.--
LADYMADONN--2
Wonder how you manage to make ends meet.--
LADYMADONN--19
Hey Jude, don't make it bad --HEYJUDE--1
Take a sad song and make it better --HEYJUDE--2
Then you can start to make it better.--HEYJUDE--4
Then you begin to make it better.--HEYJUDE--8
Then you can start to make it better.--HEYJUDE--18
Hey Jude, don't make it bad --HEYJUDE--26
Take a sad song and make it better --HEYJUDE--27
Then you'll begin ((let it out)) to make it
better --HEYJUDE--29
Better, better, better, better ((make it
Jude)), better.--HEYJUDE--30
(Well you know you can make it, Jude, you've
just gotta break it.)--HEYJUDE--46
Nah nah nah, nah - nah - nah - nah ((don't make
it bad, Jude)) --HEYJUDE--47
(Take a sad song and make it better)--HEYJUDE--48
You ain't gonna make it with anyone anyhow.--
REVOLUTION--29
And Moscow girls make me sing and shout --
BACKINTHEU--17
And Moscow girls make me sing and shout --
BACKINTHEU--29
Make your mother sigh --CRYBABYCRY--2
Make your mother sigh --CRYBABYCRY--9
Make your mother sigh --CRYBABYCRY--17
Make your mother sigh --CRYBABYCRY--25
Make your mother sigh --CRYBABYCRY--33
Make your mother sigh --CRYBABYCRY--37
Make your mother sigh --CRYBABYCRY--41
Don't pass me by, don't make me cry, don't make
me blue --DONTPASSME--18
Don't pass me by, don't make me cry, don't make
me blue --DONTPASSME--18
Don't pass me by - don't make me cry.--DONTPASSME
--22
Don't pass me by, don't make me cry, don't make
me blue --DONTPASSME--31
Don't pass me by, don't make me cry, don't make
me blue --DONTPASSME--31
Don't pass me by - don't make me cry.--DONTPASSME
--35
Don't pass me by, don't make me cry, don't make
me blue --DONTPASSME--37
Don't pass me by, don't make me cry, don't make
me blue --DONTPASSME--37
Don't pass me by - don't make me cry.--DONTPASSME
--41
Come on is make it easy --EVRBDYMONK--13
Come on is make it easy - wuh.--EVRBDYMONK--14
Come on is make it easy --EVRBDYMONK--22
Come on is make it easy --EVRBDYMONK--23
Make it easy (wuh), make it easy (wuh) --EVRBDYMONK
--24
Make it easy (wuh), make it easy (wuh) --EVRBDYMONK
--24
Lady Madonna trying to make ends meet - yeah--
GLASSONION--13
Trying to make a dove-tail joint - yeah--GLASSONION
--22
A - will you, won't you want me to make you?--
HELTERSKEL--11
Well, do you, don't you want me to make you?--
HELTERSKEL--21
Make it easy to be near you --IWILL--16
You ain't gonna make it with anyone anyhow.--
REVOLUTONE--44
Everywhere it's what you make --ITSALLTOOM--10
Everywhere it's what you make --ITSALLTOOM--31
... Make it...--ONLYANORTH--17
Peter Brown called to say, you can make it OK --
BALLADOFJO--11
Make an early start --OLDBROWNSH--29
The love you take is equal to the love you make.--

THEEND--9
Someday I'm gonna make her mine - oh yeah --
HERMAJESTY--8
Someday I'm gonna make her mine.--HERMAJESTY--9
Oh darling, if you leave me I'll never make it
alone --OHDARLING--3
Oh darling, if you leave me, I'll never make
it alone.--OHDARLING--9
They tumble blindly as they make their way across
the universe.--ACROSSTHEU--14

MAKES
My happiness near makes me cry --ASKMEWHY--8
If it makes you feel alright --CANTBUYMEL--4
If it makes you feel alright --CANTBUYMEL--6
Just the sight of you makes night-time bright,
very bright.--ITSONLYLOV--9
When I think of things we did it makes me wanna
cry.--NIGHTBEFOR--10
When I think of things we did it makes me wanna
cry.--NIGHTBEFOR--18
She's the kind of girl you want so much it makes
you sorry --GIRL--3
She wakes up, she makes up --FORNOONE--4
Makes me weak in the knee.--HONEYPIE--15
What makes you think you're something special
when you smile?--HEYBULLDOG--4
Makes no difference where you are--ITSALLTOOM--14
Because the sky is blue it makes me cry --BECAUSE
--10
She's a kind of a girl that makes the News Of
The World.--POLYTHENEP--8

MAKING
Making love to only you.--HOLDMETIGH--12
Making love to only you.--HOLDMETIGH--32
You're making me say that I've got nobody but you
--ANOTHERGIR--2
Making all his nowhere plans for nobody.--
NOWHEREMAN--3
Making all his nowhere plans for nobody --
NOWHEREMAN--24
Making all his nowhere plans for nobody --
NOWHEREMAN--25
Making all his nowhere plans for nobody.--
NOWHEREMAN--26
Here, making each day of the year--HERETHEREA--2
And she's making me feel like I've never been
born.--SHESAIDSHE--3
And you're making me feel like I've never been
born.--SHESAIDSHE--6
'cos you're making me feel like I've never been
born.--SHESAIDSHE--12
'cos you're making me feel like I've never been
born.--SHESAIDSHE--18
By making his world a little colder.--HEYJUDE--13
Honey Pie you are making me crazy--HONEYPIE--7
Now Honey Pie you are making me crazy--HONEYPIE--29
Making sure that I'm not late (hey).--OLDBROWNSH
--30

MAN
I WANNA BE YOUR MAN.--IWANNABEYO--Title
I wanna be your man.--IWANNABEYO--2
I wanna be your man.--IWANNABEYO--4
I wanna be your man--IWANNABEYO--9
I wanna be your man.--IWANNABEYO--10
I wanna be your man.--IWANNABEYO--11
I wanna be your man.--IWANNABEYO--12
I wanna be your man.--IWANNABEYO--16
I wanna be your man.--IWANNABEYO--18
I wanna be your man.--IWANNABEYO--20
I wanna be your man.--IWANNABEYO--21
I wanna be your man.--IWANNABEYO--22
I wanna be your man.--IWANNABEYO--23
I wanna be your man.--IWANNABEYO--24
I wanna be your man.--IWANNABEYO--31
I wanna be your man.--IWANNABEYO--33
I wanna be your man.--IWANNABEYO--38
I wanna be your man.--IWANNABEYO--39
I wanna be your man.--IWANNABEYO--40
I wanna be your man.--IWANNABEYO--41
I wanna be your man (oh)--IWANNABEYO--43
I wanna be your man (come on!)--IWANNABEYO--44
I wanna be your man (wuh - wuh)--IWANNABEYO--45
I wanna be your man--IWANNABEYO--46
And/You'll let me be your man--IWANTTOHOL--8
I'm not that kinda man.--ICALLYOURN--8
I'm not that kinda man.--ICALLYOURN--15
And show you what your loving man can do --
ILLCRYINST--18

And show you what your loving man can do --
    ILLCRYINST--27
She's a woman who loves her man--SHESAWOMAN--17
She's a woman who loves her man--SHESAWOMAN--27
With another man in my place.--NOREPLY--16
With another man in my place.--NOREPLY--29
Man buys ring, woman throws it away --IMDOWN--8
I'm not half the man I used to be--YESTERDAY--6
That a man must break his back to earn his day of
    leisure?--GIRL--24
NOWHERE MAN.--NOWHEREMAN--Title
He's a real Nowhere Man --NOWHEREMAN--1
Nowhere Man please listen --NOWHEREMAN--7
Nowhere Man the world is at your command.--
    NOWHEREMAN--9
Nowhere Man can you see me at all?--NOWHEREMAN--12
Nowhere Man don't worry --NOWHEREMAN--13
Nowhere Man please listen --NOWHEREMAN--19
Nowhere Man the world is at your command.--
    NOWHEREMAN--21
He's a real Nowhere Man --NOWHEREMAN--22
Than to be with another man.--RUNFORYOUR--2
Catch you with another man --RUNFORYOUR--7
Catch you with another man --RUNFORYOUR--15
Catch you with another man --RUNFORYOUR--23
Than to be with another man.--RUNFORYOUR--26
Catch you with another man --RUNFORYOUR--31
It's based on a novel by a man named Lear --
    PAPERBACKW--4
It's a dirty story of a dirty man --PAPERBACKW--8
Dr. Robert, you're a new and better man --DRROBERT
    --3
Dr. Robert, he's a man you must believe --DRROBERT
    --8
Dr. Robert, you're a new and better man --DRROBERT
    --15
Before I'm a dead old man.--LOVEYOUTWO--5
Lived a man who sailed to sea--YELLOWSUBM--2
About a lucky man who made the grade--DAYINTHELI
    --2
Me used to be angry young man--GETTINGBET--11
Man I was mean but I'm changing my scene--
    GETTINGBET--27
Made her look a little like a military man.--
    LOVELYRITA--12
Meeting a man from the motor trade.--SHESLEAVIN--27
BABY, YOU'RE A RICH MAN.--BABYYOUREA--Title
Baby, you're a rich man --BABYYOUREA--13
Baby, you're a rich man --BABYYOUREA--14
Baby, you're a rich man too.--BABYYOUREA--15
Baby, you're a rich man --BABYYOUREA--19
Baby, you're a rich man --BABYYOUREA--20
Baby, you're a rich man too.--BABYYOUREA--21
Baby, you're a rich man --BABYYOUREA--28
Baby, you're a rich man --BABYYOUREA--29
Baby, you're a rich man too.--BABYYOUREA--30
Baby, you're a rich man --BABYYOUREA--34
Baby, you're a rich man --BABYYOUREA--35
Baby, you're a rich man too.--BABYYOUREA--36
Oh, baby you're a rich man --BABYYOUREA--37
Baby, you're a rich (baby) man --BABYYOUREA--38
Baby, you're a rich man too.--BABYYOUREA--39
Wuh-oh, baby, you're a rich (oh) man --BABYYOUREA
    --40
Baby, you're a rich man --BABYYOUREA--41
Baby, you're a rich man too.--BABYYOUREA--42
Oh, baby, you're a rich man.--BABYYOUREA--43
Baby, you're a rich man.--BABYYOUREA--44
Man you been a naughty boy, you let your face
    grow long--IAMTHEWALR--6
Man you should have seen them kicking Edgar
    Allan Poe--IAMTHEWALR--27
The man with the foolish grin is keeping
    perfectly still--FOOLONTHEH--2
The man of a thousand voices talking perfectly loud
    --FOOLONTHEH--9
Man I had a dreadful flight.--BACKINTHEU--4
I told you about the walrus and me - man--
    GLASSONION--8
You know that we're as close as can be - man--
    GLASSONION--9
I tell you man he living there still--GLASSONION
    --18
The man in the crowd with the multicoloured
    mirrors on his hobnail boots --HAPPINESSI--5
Now she and her man who called himself Dan--
    ROCKYRACCO--17
Big man (yeah?) walking in the park--HEYBULLDOG--13
Hey man what's that noise? (woof)--HEYBULLDOG--23
That's it man (wuh)--HEYBULLDOG--29
Don't look at me man (ha ha ha ha)--HEYBULLDOG--31
Jojo was a man who thought he was a loner --
    GETBACK/45--1
But she was another man.--GETBACK/45--17

The man in the mack said you've got to go back --
    BALLADOFJO--3
Silver hammer man!--MAXWELLSIL--28
Such a mean old man, such a mean old man.--
    MEANMRMUST--7
Such a mean old man, such a mean old man.--
    MEANMRMUST--7
Such a dirty old man, dirty old man.--MEANMRMUST
    --14
Such a dirty old man, dirty old man.--MEANMRMUST
    --14
She's so goodlooking but she looks like a man.--
    POLYTHENEP--2
Jojo was a man who thought he was a loner--
    GETBACK/LP--7
But she was another man--GETBACK/LP--23

MANAGE

Wonder how you manage to make ends meet.--
    LADYMADONN--2
Wonders how you manage to feed the rest.--
    LADYMADONN--10
Wonder how you manage to make ends meet.--
    LADYMADONN--19

MANTELSHELF

On the mantelshelf --DONTPASSME--11

MANY

Many, many, many times before.--ILLGETYOU--5
Many, many, many times before.--ILLGETYOU--5
Many, many, many times before.--ILLGETYOU--5
Many, many, many times before.--ILLGETYOU--22
Many, many, many times before.--ILLGETYOU--22
Many, many, many times before.--ILLGETYOU--22
I got so many things I gotta do --WHENIGETHO--22
In oh so many ways--HELP--20
Many more of them live next door--YELLOWSUBM--14
Now they know how many holes it takes--DAYINTHELI
    --32
For so many years. (('bye, 'bye))--SHESLEAVIN--12
For so many years. (('bye, 'bye))--SHESLEAVIN--24
For so many years. (('bye, 'bye))--SHESLEAVIN--32
Many years from now --WHENIMSIXT--2
There's so many there to meet.--BLUEJAYWAY--11
So many tears I was searching --LONGLONGLO--7
So many tears I was wasting - oh, oh!--LONGLONGLO
    --8
Many times I've been alone and many times I've
    cried --LONGANDWIN--7
Many times I've been alone and many times I've
    cried --LONGANDWIN--7
Anyway you'll never know the many ways I've tried
    --LONGANDWIN--8

MAO

But if you go carrying pictures of Chairman Mao --
    REVOLUTION--28
If you go carrying pictures of Chairman Mao --
    REVOLUTONE--43

MARIGOLD

The King of Marigold was in the kitchen --
    CRYBABYCRY--4

MARKET

Happy ever after in the market place --OBLADIOBLA
    --20
Hey, happy ever after in the market place --
    OBLADIOBLA--32

MARKET-PLACE

Desmond has a barrow in the market-place --
    OBLADIOBLA--1

MARMALADE

With tangerine trees and marmalade skies.--
    LUCYINTHES--2

MARRIED

You can get married in Gibraltar near Spain.--
    BALLADOFJO--12

MARSHMALLOW

Where rocking-horse people eat marshmallow pies --
LUCYINTHES--13

MARTHA
MARTHA MY DEAR.--MARTHAMYDE--Title
Martha my dear, though I spend my days in
conversation --MARTHAMYDE--1
Please - remember me, Martha my love --MARTHAMYDE
--2
Don't forget me, Martha my dear.--MARTHAMYDE--3
Martha my dear, you have always been my
inspiration --MARTHAMYDE--13
Please - be good to me, Martha my love --MARTHAMYDE
--14
Don't forget me, Martha my dear.--MARTHAMYDE--15

MARTIN
Sweet Loretta Martin thought she was a woman --
GETBACK/45--16
But she was a frying pan ((sweet Loretta
Martin)).--GETBACK/LP--3
Sweet Loretta Martin thought she was a woman--
GETBACK/LP--22

MARVEL
So Captain Marvel zapped him right between the
eyes. (Zap!)--CONTINUING--19

MARY
Mother Mary comes to me --LETITBE/45--2
Mother Mary comes to me --LETITBE/45--25
Mother Mary comes to me --LETITBE/LP--2
Mother Mary comes to me --LETITBE/LP--25

MASK
Beneath this mask I am wearing a frown.--IMALOSER
--10

MATCH
He said, Rocky you met your match--ROCKYRACCO--33

MATCHES
You and me burning matches --TWOOFUS--12

MATT
Matt Busby.--DIGIT--9

MATTER
It doesn't matter much to me.--STRAWBERRY--10
And it really doesn't matter if I'm wrong I'm
right--FIXINGAHOL--7
And it really doesn't matter if I'm wrong I'm
right--FIXINGAHOL--15
Yellow matter custard, dripping from a dead
dog's eye--IAMTHEWALR--12
It doesn't really matter what chords I play --
ONLYANORTH--7
It doesn't really matter what clothes I wear --
ONLYANORTH--10

MATTERED
But it never really mattered --IWILL--7

MAX
She tells Max to stay when the class has gone
away --MAXWELLSIL--10

MAXWELL
Maxwell Edison, majoring in medicine, calls
her on the phone --MAXWELLSIL--3
Back in school again, Maxwell plays the fool
again, teacher gets annoyed --MAXWELLSIL--8
PC Thirty-One said, we caught a dirty one,
Maxwell stands alone --MAXWELLSIL--17
(Maxwell must go free)--MAXWELLSIL--20

MAXWELL'S
MAXWELL'S SILVER HAMMER.--MAXWELLSIL--Title
Bang, bang Maxwell's silver hammer came down
upon her head --MAXWELLSIL--6
Bang, bang Maxwell's silver hammer made sure

that she was dead.--MAXWELLSIL--7
Bang, bang Maxwell's silver hammer came down
upon her head --MAXWELLSIL--13
Bang, bang Maxwell's silver hammer made sure
that she was dead.--MAXWELLSIL--15
Bang, bang Maxwell's silver hammer came down
upon his head --MAXWELLSIL--23
Bang, bang Maxwell's silver hammer made sure
that he was dead.--MAXWELLSIL--25

MAY
Though he may want you too--THISBOY--5
I may not have a lot to give --CANTBUYMEL--11
And though we may be blind --THINGSWESA--13
And though we may be blind --THINGSWESA--24
For tomorrow may rain so I'll follow the sun.--
ILLFOLLOWT--2
For tomorrow may rain so I'll follow the sun.--
ILLFOLLOWT--4
For tomorrow may rain so I'll follow the sun.--
ILLFOLLOWT--8
Yeah, tomorrow may rain so I'll follow the sun.--
ILLFOLLOWT--9
For tomorrow may rain so I'll follow the sun.--
ILLFOLLOWT--13
Big and black the clouds may be--TELLMEWHAT--9
Run the risk of knowing that our love may soon be
gone.--WECANWORKI--4
You may be awoken --ANDYOURBIR--11
That you may see the meaning of within--TOMORROWNE
--5
That ignorance and hate may mourn the dead--
TOMORROWNE--9
May I inquire discreetly ((lovely Rita))--
LOVELYRITA--14
So may I introduce to you--SGTPEPPERS--5
Then you may find--WITHINYOUW--29
((I say yes but I may mean no))--HELLOGOODB--23
Please don't be long or I may be asleep.--
BLUEJAYWAY--7
Please don't be long or I may be asleep.--
BLUEJAYWAY--14
Please don't be long or I may be asleep.--
BLUEJAYWAY--21
Well, you may be a lover, but you ain't no
dancer.--HELTERSKEL--7
'cos you may be a lover, but you ain't no dancer.
--HELTERSKEL--14
'cos you may be a lover, but you ain't no dancer.
--HELTERSKEL--24
You may think the chords are going wrong --
ONLYANORTH--2
You may think the band are not quite right --
ONLYANORTH--5
Who knows baby, you may comfort me (hey).--
OLDBROWNSH--21
I may appear to be imperfect --OLDBROWNSH--22
Who knows baby, you may comfort me. (hey)--
OLDBROWNSH--26
You stick around now it may show --SOMETHING--13
For though they may be parted --LETITBE/45--12
For though they may be parted --LETITBE/LP--12

MAYBE
And maybe I'll love you.--DRIVEMYCAR--8
And maybe I'll love you.--DRIVEMYCAR--16
And maybe I'll love you.--DRIVEMYCAR--21
And maybe I'll love you.--DRIVEMYCAR--29
And maybe you will get a call from me --IFINEEDS
--11
And maybe you will get a call from me --IFINEEDS
--21
Another road where maybe I--GOTTOGETYO--3
Another road where maybe I--GOTTOGETYO--27
I'll make you maybe next time around.--IWANTTOTEL
--8
Maybe you'd understand.--IWANTTOTEL--18
I'll live and love and maybe someday --OLDBROWNSH
--20

MCKENZIE
Father McKenzie writing the words of a sermon--
ELEANORRIG--11
Father McKenzie wiping the dirt from his hands--
ELEANORRIG--24

ME
LOVE ME DO.--LOVEMEDO--Title
Love, love me do --LOVEMEDO--1
So please love me do --LOVEMEDO--4

Whao-ho love me do.--LOVEMEDO--5
Love, love me do --LOVEMEDO--6
So please love me do --LOVEMEDO--9
Whoa-ho love me do.--LOVEMEDO--10
Love, love me do --LOVEMEDO--13
So please love me do --LOVEMEDO--16
Whoa-ho love me do (hey hey).--LOVEMEDO--17
Love, love me do --LOVEMEDO--18
So please love me do --LOVEMEDO--21
Whoa-ho love me do.--LOVEMEDO--22
Yes, love me do --LOVEMEDO--23
Whoa-ho love me do --LOVEMEDO--24
Yes, love me do.--LOVEMEDO--25
Don't you be sad, just call me tonight.--ANYTIMEATA
    --9
Call me tonight and I'll come to you.--ANYTIMEATA
    --18
ASK ME WHY.--ASKMEWHY--Title
'cos you tell me things I want to know --ASKMEWHY
    --2
My happiness near makes me cry --ASKMEWHY--8
I can't believe it's happened to me --ASKMEWHY--12
Ask me why, I'll say I love you --ASKMEWHY--14
'cos you tell me things I want to know --ASKMEWHY
    --17
Ask me why, I'll say I love you --ASKMEWHY--22
I can't believe it's happened to me --ASKMEWHY--24
Ask me why, I'll say I love you --ASKMEWHY--26
PLEASE PLEASE ME.--PLEASEPLEA--Title
Please please me, whoa - yeah--PLEASEPLEA--5
You don't need me to show the way love --PLEASEPLEA
    --7
Please please me, whoa - yeah--PLEASEPLEA--11
Why do you make me blue?--PLEASEPLEA--18
Please please me, whoa - yeah--PLEASEPLEA--23
Please me, whoa - yeah--PLEASEPLEA--25
Please me, whoa - yeah--PLEASEPLEA--27
Let me whisper in your ear --DOYOUWANTT--6
Let me whisper in your ear, (dodahdo)--DOYOUWANTT
    --12
Let me whisper in your ear, (dodahdo)--DOYOUWANTT
    --20
Well she looked at me, and I, I could see --
    ISAWHERSTA--7
The world is treating me bad, misery.--MISERY--1
The world is treating me bad, misery.--MISERY--3
Send her back to me, 'cos everyone can see--
    MISERY--8
Send her back to me, 'cos everyone can see--
    MISERY--12
FROM ME TO YOU.--FROMMETOYO--Title
Just call on me and I'll send it along--FROMMETOYO
    --5
With love from me to you.--FROMMETOYO--6
Just/So call on me and I'll send it along--FROMMETOYO--9
With love from me to you.--FROMMETOYO--10
Just call on me and I'll send it along--FROMMETOYO
    --17
With love from me to you.--FROMMETOYO--18
From me - to you.--FROMMETOYO--19
Just call on me and I'll send it along--FROMMETOYO
    --20
With love from me to you.--FROMMETOYO--21
Just call on me and I'll send it along--FROMMETOYO
    --28
With love from me to you--FROMMETOYO--29
Oh, oh - mmm, you've been good to me--THANKYOUGI
    --1
You made me glad when I was blue--THANKYOUGI--2
Thank you girl, for loving me the way that you
    do (way that you do).--THANKYOUGI--8
Oh, oh - mmm, you've been good to me--THANKYOUGI
    --11
You made me glad when I was blue--THANKYOUGI--12
It's not like me to pretend--ILLGETYOU--6
So you might as well resign yourself to me, oh
    yeah.--ILLGETYOU--18
It's not like me to pretend--ILLGETYOU--23
And she told me what to say.--SHELOVESYO--7
And the same goes for me --ALLIVEGOTT--11
Whenever you want me at all --ALLIVEGOTT--12
Ya just gotta call on me, yeah --ALLIVEGOTT--15
Ya just gotta call on me.--ALLIVEGOTT--16
And the same goes for me --ALLIVEGOTT--22
Whenever you want me at all --ALLIVEGOTT--23
Ya just gotta call on me, yeah --ALLIVEGOTT--26
Ya just gotta call on me --ALLIVEGOTT--27
(Ooh) ya just gotta call on me --ALLIVEGOTT--28
DON'T BOTHER ME.--DONTBOTHER--Title
I want no one to talk to me--DONTBOTHER--2
Leave me alone--DONTBOTHER--7
Don't bother me--DONTBOTHER--8
That she would leave me on my own--DONTBOTHER--10
Don't bother me--DONTBOTHER--14

The only girl for me--DONTBOTHER--18
Leave me alone--DONTBOTHER--26
Don't bother me--DONTBOTHER--27
Don't bother me--DONTBOTHER--29
The only girl for me--DONTBOTHER--33
Leave me alone--DONTBOTHER--41
Don't bother me--DONTBOTHER--42
Don't bother me--DONTBOTHER--43
Don't bother me--DONTBOTHER--44
Don't bother me--DONTBOTHER--45
Don't bother me.--DONTBOTHER--46
HOLD ME TIGHT.--HOLDMETIGH--Title
Hold me tight --HOLDMETIGH--2
Tell me I'm the only one --HOLDMETIGH--3
So hold (hold) me tight (me tight) --HOLDMETIGH--6
So hold (hold) me tight (me tight) --HOLDMETIGH--6
Hold me tight --HOLDMETIGH--9
Let me go on loving you,--HOLDMETIGH--10
So hold (hold) me tight (me tight) --HOLDMETIGH--13
So hold (hold) me tight (me tight) --HOLDMETIGH--13
So hold me tight --HOLDMETIGH--19
Tell me I'm the only one --HOLDMETIGH--20
So hold (hold) me tight (me tight) --HOLDMETIGH--23
So hold (hold) me tight (me tight) --HOLDMETIGH--23
So hold me tight --HOLDMETIGH--29
Let me go on loving you --HOLDMETIGH--30
So hold (hold) me tight (me tight) --HOLDMETIGH--33
So hold (hold) me tight (me tight) --HOLDMETIGH--33
Tell me that you love me baby --IWANNABEYO--13
Tell me that you love me baby --IWANNABEYO--13
Let me understand.--IWANNABEYO--14
Tell me that you love me baby --IWANNABEYO--15
Tell me that you love me baby --IWANNABEYO--15
Since you left me I'm so alone (you left me here)
    --ITWONTBELO--11
Since you left me I'm so alone (you left me here)
    --ITWONTBELO--11
Well since you left me I'm so alone (you left
    me here)--ITWONTBELO--21
Well since you left me I'm so alone (you left
    me here)--ITWONTBELO--21
Now I know that you won't leave me no more--
    ITWONTBELO--26
Little child, won't you dance with me?--LITTLECHIL
    --2
Baby take a chance with me.--LITTLECHIL--4
Little child, won't you dance with me?--LITTLECHIL
    --6
Baby take a chance with me.--LITTLECHIL--8
Little child, won't you dance with me?--LITTLECHIL
    --13
Baby take a chance with me (wuh yeah).--LITTLECHIL
    --15
Little child, won't you dance with me?--LITTLECHIL
    --20
Baby take a chance with me, oh yeah --LITTLECHIL
    --22
Baby take a chance with me, oh yeah --LITTLECHIL
    --23
Baby take a chance with me, oh yeah --LITTLECHIL
    --24
Baby take a chance with me, oh yeah.--LITTLECHIL
    --25
You know you made me cry --NOTASECOND--1
You're giving me the same old line --NOTASECOND--7
You hurt me then you're back again --NOTASECOND--9
You know you made me cry --NOTASECOND--12
You're giving me the same old line --NOTASECOND--18
You hurt me then you're back again --NOTASECOND--20
Oh please say to me--IWANTTOHOL--7
You'll let me be your man--IWANTTOHOL--8
And please say to me--IWANTTOHOL--9
You'll let me hold your hand--IWANTTOHOL--10
And/You'll let me hold your hand--IWANTTOHOL--11
CAN'T BUY ME LOVE.--CANTBUYMEL--Title
Can't buy me love, love --CANTBUYMEL--1
Can't buy me love, oh.--CANTBUYMEL--2
Money can't buy me love.--CANTBUYMEL--8
If you say you love me too --CANTBUYMEL--10
Money can't buy me love.--CANTBUYMEL--14
Can't buy me love, oh, everybody tells me so --
    CANTBUYMEL--15
Can't buy me love, oh, everybody tells me so --
    CANTBUYMEL--15
Can't buy me love oh - no, no, no - no.--CANTBUYMEL
    --16
Tell me that you want the kind of things --
    CANTBUYMEL--19
Money can't buy me love.--CANTBUYMEL--22
Can't buy me love, oh, everybody tells me so --
    CANTBUYMEL--25
Can't buy me love, oh, everybody tells me so --
    CANTBUYMEL--25
Can't buy me love oh - no, no, no - no.--CANTBUYMEL

--26
Tell me that you want the kind of things --
    CANTBUYMEL--29
Money can't buy me love.--CANTBUYMEL--32
Can't buy me love, oh, love, oh --CANTBUYMEL--33
Can't buy me love, oh, oh.--CANTBUYMEL--34
So please listen to me--YOUCANTDOT--23
So please listen to me--YOUCANTDOT--42
She gives me everything --ANDILOVEHE--6
She brings to me --ANDILOVEHE--9
Have you near me.--ANDILOVEHE--14
Will make me feel alright.--HARDDAYSNI--7
You're gonna give me everything --HARDDAYSNI--11
When I'm home feeling you holding me tight,
    tight, yeah.--HARDDAYSNI--16
Will make me feel alright.--HARDDAYSNI--23
When I'm home feeling you holding me tight,
    tight, yeah.--HARDDAYSNI--29
Will make me feel alright --HARDDAYSNI--36
This could only happen to me --ISHOULDHAV--5
You're gonna say you love me too, oh.--ISHOULDHAV
    --8
You're gonna say you love me too.--ISHOULDHAV--10
If this is love you've got to give me more --
    ISHOULDHAV--12
Give me more, hey hey hey, give me more.--
    ISHOULDHAV--13
Give me more, hey hey hey, give me more.--
    ISHOULDHAV--13
This could only happen to me --ISHOULDHAV--15
You're gonna say you love me too, oh.--ISHOULDHAV
    --18
You're gonna say you love me too.--ISHOULDHAV--20
You love me too --ISHOULDHAV--21
You love me too --ISHOULDHAV--22
You love me too.--ISHOULDHAV--23
And help me understand?--IFIFELL--3
That you would love me more than her.--IFIFELL--9
I'm so happy when you dance with me.--IMHAPPYJUS
    --3
I'm so happy when you dance with me ((oh - oh)).--
    IMHAPPYJUS--15
I'm so happy when you dance with me ((oh - oh)).--
    IMHAPPYJUS--23
TELL ME WHY.--TELLMEWHY--Title
Tell me why you cried --TELLMEWHY--1
And why you lied to me --TELLMEWHY--2
Tell me why you cried --TELLMEWHY--3
And why you lied to me.--TELLMEWHY--4
But you left me sitting on my own --TELLMEWHY--6
Did you have to treat me oh so bad --TELLMEWHY--7
Tell me why you cried --TELLMEWHY--9
And why you lied to me --TELLMEWHY--10
Tell me why you cried --TELLMEWHY--11
And why you lied to me.--TELLMEWHY--12
Tell me what and I'll apologize --TELLMEWHY--14
Tell me why you cried --TELLMEWHY--17
And why you lied to me --TELLMEWHY--18
Tell me why you cried --TELLMEWHY--19
And why you lied to me.--TELLMEWHY--20
Tell me why you cried --TELLMEWHY--26
And why you lied to me.--TELLMEWHY--27
Tell me why you cried --TELLMEWHY--28
And why you lied to me.--TELLMEWHY--29
That you would want me too--ILLBEBACK--15
You say you will love me if I have to go --
    THINGSWESA--1
You'll be thinking of me, somehow I will know --
    THINGSWESA--2
Me I'm just the lucky kind --THINGSWESA--11
Love me all the time girl --THINGSWESA--17
Me I'm just the lucky kind --THINGSWESA--22
Love me all the time girl --THINGSWESA--28
I got a girl who's waiting home for me tonight.--
    WHENIGETHO--12
Come on, let me through --WHENIGETHO--21
Baby's good to me, you know --IFEELFINE--1
She tells me all the time, you know, she said so
    --IFEELFINE--5
She's in love with me and I feel fine (ooo).--
    IFEELFINE--11
She tells me all the time, you know, she said so
    --IFEELFINE--13
She's in love with me and I feel fine --IFEELFINE
    --19
She's in love with me and I feel fine.--IFEELFINE
    --20
My love don't give me presents--SHESAWOMAN--1
Only ever has to give me love forever and forever
    --SHESAWOMAN--3
My love don't give me presents--SHESAWOMAN--4
Turn me on when I get lonely--SHESAWOMAN--5
People tell me that she's only fooling--SHESAWOMAN
    --6

She hates to see me cry--SHESAWOMAN--9
She is happy just to hear me say that--SHESAWOMAN
    --10
She will never make me jealous--SHESAWOMAN--13
Gives me all her time as well as loving--SHESAWOMAN
    --14
Don't ask me why--SHESAWOMAN--15
My love don't give me presents--SHESAWOMAN--18
Only ever has to give me love forever and forever
    --SHESAWOMAN--20
My love don't give me presents--SHESAWOMAN--21
Turn me on when I get lonely--SHESAWOMAN--22
People tell me that she's only fooling--SHESAWOMAN
    --23
My love don't give me presents--SHESAWOMAN--28
Only ever has to give me love forever and forever
    --SHESAWOMAN--30
My love don't give me presents--SHESAWOMAN--31
Turn me on when I get lonely--SHESAWOMAN--32
People tell me that she's only fooling--SHESAWOMAN
    --33
Tell me, oh what can I do?--BABYSINBLA--3
Tell me, oh what can I do?--BABYSINBLA--9
Tell me oh what can I do?--BABYSINBLA--18
Tell me oh what can I do?--BABYSINBLA--23
Tell me oh what can I do?--BABYSINBLA--29
Hold me, love me --EIGHTDAYSA--5
Hold me, love me --EIGHTDAYSA--5
Hold me, love me --EIGHTDAYSA--6
Hold me, love me --EIGHTDAYSA--6
Hold me, love me --EIGHTDAYSA--13
Hold me, love me --EIGHTDAYSA--13
Hold me, love me --EIGHTDAYSA--14
Hold me, love me --EIGHTDAYSA--14
Hold me, love me --EIGHTDAYSA--23
Hold me, love me --EIGHTDAYSA--23
Hold me, love me --EIGHTDAYSA--24
Hold me, love me --EIGHTDAYSA--24
Hold me, love me --EIGHTDAYSA--33
Hold me, love me --EIGHTDAYSA--33
Hold me, love me --EIGHTDAYSA--34
Hold me, love me --EIGHTDAYSA--34
People tell me I'm lucky--EVERYLITTL--2
She does for me, yeah--EVERYLITTL--8
She does for me, ooo.--EVERYLITTL--10
Just to know that she loves me--EVERYLITTL--12
Yes I know that she loves me now.--EVERYLITTL--13
She does for me, yeah--EVERYLITTL--18
She does for me, ooo.--EVERYLITTL--20
She does for me, yeah--EVERYLITTL--22
She does for me, ooo.--EVERYLITTL--24
There's nothing for me here so I will disappear --
    IDONTWANTT--3
If she turns up while I'm gone please let me know.
    --IDONTWANTT--4
Though tonight she's made me sad --IDONTWANTT--9
There's nothing for me here so I will disappear --
    IDONTWANTT--15
If she turns up while I'm gone please let me know.
    --IDONTWANTT--16
Though tonight she's made me sad --IDONTWANTT--18
I'm a loser and I lost someone who's near to me --
    IMALOSER--7
I'm a loser and I lost someone who's near to me --
    IMALOSER--13
I'm a loser and I lost someone who's near to me --
    IMALOSER--19
I know that you saw me--NOREPLY--7
When you gave me no reply.--NOREPLY--21
What you're doing to me?--WHATYOURED--4
You ((you)) got me running--WHATYOURED--5
What you're doing to me?--WHATYOURED--8
'n' should you need a love that's true, it's me.--
    WHATYOURED--11
You've ((you've)) got me crying, girl --WHATYOURED
    --13
What you're doing to me?--WHATYOURED--15
'n' should you need a love that's true, it's me.--
    WHATYOURED--18
You've ((you've)) got me crying, girl --WHATYOURED
    --20
What you're doing to me?--WHATYOURED--22
What you're doing to me?--WHATYOURED--23
What you're doing to me?--WHATYOURED--24
The girl that's driving me mad is going away.--
    TICKETTORI--4
She said that living with me--TICKETTORI--9
She ought to do right by me--TICKETTORI--19
She ought to do right by me--TICKETTORI--22
The girl that's driving me mad is going away,
    yeah.--TICKETTORI--25
She ought to do right by me--TICKETTORI--32
She ought to do right by me--TICKETTORI--35
She said that living with me--TICKETTORI--36

For red is the colour that will make me blue--
    YESITIS--16
For red is the colour that will make me blue--
    YESITIS--25
TELL ME WHAT YOU SEE.--TELLMEWHAT--Title
If you let me take your heart--TELLMEWHAT--1
Tell me what you see--TELLMEWHAT--6
What you see is me--TELLMEWHAT--8
If you put your trust in me--TELLMEWHAT--11
Tell me what you see--TELLMEWHAT--14
What you see is me--TELLMEWHAT--16
Tell me what you see--TELLMEWHAT--17
Listen to me one more time--TELLMEWHAT--18
Tell me what you see--TELLMEWHAT--23
What you see is me--TELLMEWHAT--25
Tell me what you see--TELLMEWHAT--26
Listen to me one more time--TELLMEWHAT--27
Tell me what you see--TELLMEWHAT--32
What you see is me--TELLMEWHAT--34
YOU LIKE ME TOO MUCH.--YOULIKEMET--Title
Telling me there'll be no next time--YOULIKEMET--3
You'll never leave me and you know it's true--
    YOULIKEMET--5
'cos you like me too much and I like you--
    YOULIKEMET--6
You've tried before to leave me--YOULIKEMET--7
To walk out and make me lonely--YOULIKEMET--9
You'll never leave me and you know it's true--
    YOULIKEMET--11
'cos you like me too much and I like you--
    YOULIKEMET--12
And it's nice when you believe me--YOULIKEMET--14
If you leave me I will follow you--YOULIKEMET--15
I wouldn't let you leave me 'cos it's true--
    YOULIKEMET--19
'cos you like me too much and I like you--
    YOULIKEMET--20
'cos you like me too much and I like you--
    YOULIKEMET--21
And it's nice when you believe me--YOULIKEMET--23
If you leave me I will follow you--YOULIKEMET--24
I wouldn't let you leave me 'cos it's true--
    YOULIKEMET--28
'cos you like me too much and I like you--
    YOULIKEMET--29
'cos you like me too much and I like you.--
    YOULIKEMET--30
Help me if you can, I'm feeling down--HELP--15
Help me get my feet back on the ground--HELP--17
Won't you please please help me?--HELP--18
Help me if you can, I'm feeling down--HELP--25
Help me get my feet back on the ground--HELP--27
Won't you please please help me?--HELP--28
Help me if you can, I'm feeling down--HELP--35
Help me get my feet back on the ground--HELP--37
Won't you please please help me?--HELP--38
Help me, help me - ooo-mmm.--HELP--39
Help me, help me - ooo-mmm.--HELP--39
You can't cry 'cos you're laughing at me --IMDOWN
    --2
Can you hear me?--IMDOWN--26
You're making me say that I've got nobody but you
    --ANOTHERGIR--2
Another girl who will love me till the end --
    ANOTHERGIR--10
Another girl who will love me till the end --
    ANOTHERGIR--16
Please come on back to me--INEEDYOU--3
Said you had a thing or two to tell me--INEEDYOU
    --6
How was I to know you would upset me?--INEEDYOU--7
You told me--INEEDYOU--10
Oh yes, you told me--INEEDYOU--11
That's when it hurt me--INEEDYOU--13
Just what you mean to me--INEEDYOU--19
But when you told me--INEEDYOU--21
That's when it hurt me--INEEDYOU--23
Just what you mean to me--INEEDYOU--29
She's just the girl for me--IVEJUSTSEE--4
And she keeps calling me back again.--IVEJUSTSEE
    --13
And she keeps calling me back again.--IVEJUSTSEE
    --20
And she keeps calling me back again.--IVEJUSTSEE
    --23
She's just the girl for me--IVEJUSTSEE--27
And she keeps calling me back again.--IVEJUSTSEE
    --31
And she keeps calling me back again.--IVEJUSTSEE
    --33
And she keeps calling me back again.--IVEJUSTSEE
    --35
Treat me like you did the night before.--NIGHTBEFOR
    --4

Treat me like you did the night before.--NIGHTBEFOR
    --8
When I think of things we did it makes me wanna
    cry.--NIGHTBEFOR--10
Treat me like you did the night before (yes).--
    NIGHTBEFOR--14
Treat me like you did the night before (yeah).--
    NIGHTBEFOR--16
When I think of things we did it makes me wanna
    cry.--NIGHTBEFOR--18
Treat me like you did the night before.--NIGHTBEFOR
    --22
There's a shadow hanging over me--YESTERDAY--7
I can see them laugh at me --YOUVEGOTTO--7
How could she say to me--YOUVEGOTTO--15
Let me hear you say.--YOUVEGOTTO--18
It took me so long to find out --DAYTRIPPER--7
She took me half the way there --DAYTRIPPER--10
She took me half the way there, now.--DAYTRIPPER
    --12
It took me so long to find out --DAYTRIPPER--15
It took me so long to find out --DAYTRIPPER--24
She will turn to me and start to cry --GIRL--7
And she promises the earth to me and I believe
    her --GIRL--8
And maybe you will get a call from me --IFINEEDEDS
    --11
And maybe you will get a call from me --IFINEEDEDS
    --21
Why, tell me why did you not treat me right?--
    IMLOOKINGT--9
Why, tell me why did you not treat me right?--
    IMLOOKINGT--9
You're thinking of me the same old way --IMLOOKINGT
    --11
You were above me, but not today.--IMLOOKINGT--12
Why, tell me why did you not treat me right?--
    IMLOOKINGT--15
Why, tell me why did you not treat me right?--
    IMLOOKINGT--15
Oh, what you mean to me--MICHELLE--13
She once had me?--NORWEGIANW--3
She showed me her room--NORWEGIANW--4
She asked me to stay--NORWEGIANW--7
And she told me to sit anywhere--NORWEGIANW--8
She told me she worked in the morning--NORWEGIANW
    --17
Isn't he a bit like you and me?--NOWHEREMAN--6
Nowhere Man can you see me at all?--NOWHEREMAN--12
Isn't he a bit like you and me?--NOWHEREMAN--18
But if your heart breaks, don't wait, turn me
    away --WAIT--5
And know that you will wait for me.--WAIT--12
And know that you will wait for me.--WAIT--20
But if your heart breaks, don't wait, turn me
    away --WAIT--21
You are tearing me apart --WHATGOESON--3
When you treat me so unkind.--WHATGOESON--4
Tell me why.--WHATGOESON--9
You are tearing me apart --WHATGOESON--12
When you treat me so unkind.--WHATGOESON--13
Tell me why (tell me why).--WHATGOESON--18
Tell me why (tell me why).--WHATGOESON--18
You didn't even think of me as someone with a name.
    --WHATGOESON--23
Did you mean to break my heart and watch me die?--
    WHATGOESON--24
Tell me why.--WHATGOESON--25
You are tearing me apart --WHATGOESON--28
When you treat me so unkind.--WHATGOESON--29
Say the word and be like me --THEWORD--2
Spread the word and be like me --THEWORD--10
Say the word and be like me --THEWORD--18
YOU WON'T SEE ME.--YOUWONTSEE--Title
If you won't see me (you won't see me) --YOUWONTSEE
    --5
If you won't see me (you won't see me) --YOUWONTSEE
    --5
You won't see me (you won't see me).--YOUWONTSEE
    --6
You won't see me (you won't see me).--YOUWONTSEE
    --6
And you won't see me (you won't see me) --
    YOUWONTSEE--11
And you won't see me (you won't see me) --
    YOUWONTSEE--11
You won't see me (you won't see me).--YOUWONTSEE
    --12
You won't see me (you won't see me).--YOUWONTSEE
    --12
If you won't see me (you won't see me) --YOUWONTSEE
    --20
If you won't see me (you won't see me) --YOUWONTSEE
    --20

You won't see me (you won't see me)--YOUWONTSEE--21
You won't see me (you won't see me)--YOUWONTSEE--21
If you won't see me (you won't see me) --YOUWONTSEE
   --29
If you won't see me (you won't see me) --YOUWONTSEE
   --29
You won't see me (you won't see me).--YOUWONTSEE
   --30
You won't see me (you won't see me).--YOUWONTSEE
   --30
It took me years to write, will you take a look?--
   PAPERBACKW--3
Can you hear me that when it rains and shines
   (when it rains and shines)--RAIN--14
Can you hear me, can you hear me? ((hear me))--
   RAIN--16
Can you hear me, can you hear me? ((hear me))--
   RAIN--16
Can you hear me, can you hear me? ((hear me))--
   RAIN--16
You tell me that you've got everything you want --
   ANDYOURBIR--1
But you don't get me, you don't get me.--ANDYOURBIR
   --3
But you don't get me, you don't get me.--ANDYOURBIR
   --3
But you can't see me, you can't see me.--ANDYOURBIR
   --6
But you can't see me, you can't see me.--ANDYOURBIR
   --6
You tell me that you heard every sound there is --
   ANDYOURBIR--13
But you can't hear me, you can't hear me.--
   ANDYOURBIR--15
But you can't hear me, you can't hear me.--
   ANDYOURBIR--15
Please don't wake me, no, don't shake me --
   IMONLYSLEE--5
Please don't wake me, no, don't shake me --
   IMONLYSLEE--5
Leave me where I am, I'm only sleeping.--IMONLYSLEE
   --6
Please don't wake me, no, don't shake me --
   IMONLYSLEE--25
Please don't wake me, no, don't shake me --
   IMONLYSLEE--25
Leave me where I am, I'm only sleeping.--IMONLYSLEE
   --26
I love her and she's loving me.--GOODDAYSUN--11
Ooo you were meant to be near me--GOTTOGETYO--12
Ooo and I want you to hear me--GOTTOGETYO--13
And if she's beside me I know I need never care--
   HERETHEREA--9
And if she's beside me I know I need never care--
   HERETHEREA--15
The games begin to drag me down --IWANTTOTEL--6
It's only me, it's not my mind--IWANTTOTEL--10
You don't get time to hang a sign on me.--
   LOVEYOUTWO--3
Love me while you can--LOVEYOUTO--4
But what you've got means such a lot to me.--
   LOVEYOUTWO--8
If you want me to.--LOVEYOUTWO--17
And she's making me feel like I've never been
   born.--SHESAIDSHE--3
Things that make me feel that I'm mad--SHESAIDSHE
   --5
And you're making me feel like I've never been
   born.--SHESAIDSHE--6
'cos you're making me feel like I've never been
   born.--SHESAIDSHE--12
'cos you're making me feel like I've never been
   born.--SHESAIDSHE--18
Let me tell you how it will be --TAXMAN--3
There's one for you, nineteen for me --TAXMAN--4
Don't ask me what I want it for (ha ha Mr.
   Wilson)--TAXMAN--18
And you're working for no-one but me (Taxman).--
   TAXMAN--26
Let me take you down--STRAWBERRY--1
It doesn't matter much to me.--STRAWBERRY--10
Let me take you down--STRAWBERRY--11
Let me take you down--STRAWBERRY--21
Always, no, sometimes, think it's me--STRAWBERRY
   --26
Let me take you down--STRAWBERRY--31
Silly people run around they worry me--FIXINGAHOL
   --17
And never ask me why they don't get past my door.
   --FIXINGAHOL--18
The teachers who taught me weren't cool (now I
   can't complain)--GETTINGBET--4
You're holding me down (aah) turning me round
   (aah)--GETTINGBET--5

You're holding me down (aah) turning me round
   (aah)--GETTINGBET--5
Filling me up with your rules.--GETTINGBET--6
Me used to be angry young man--GETTINGBET--11
Me hiding me head in the sand--GETTINGBET--12
Me hiding me head in the sand--GETTINGBET--12
You gave me the word--GETTINGBET--13
To take some tea with me? ((maid))--LOVELYRITA--16
Give us a wink and make me think of you.--
   LOVELYRITA--28
So let me introduce to you--SGTPEPPERS--23
How could she do this to me?--SHESLEAVIN--19
Will you still be sending me a valentine--
   WHENIMSIXT--3
Will you still need me --WHENIMSIXT--7
Will you still feed me --WHENIMSIXT--8
Will you still need me --WHENIMSIXT--19
Will you still feed me --WHENIMSIXT--20
Send me a postcard, drop me a line--WHENIMSIXT--28
Send me a postcard, drop me a line--WHENIMSIXT--28
Give me your answer--WHENIMSIXT--32
A - will you still need me --WHENIMSIXT--35
Will you still feed me --WHENIMSIXT--36
Would you stand up and walk out on me?--WITHALITTL
   --2
Lend me your ears and I'll sing you a song--
   WITHALITTL--3
I am he as you are he as you are me and we are
   all together--IAMTHEWALR--1
Lift up your hearts and sing me a song--YOURMOTHER
   --13
Hey Jude, don't let me down --HEYJUDE--15
You tell me that it's evolution --REVOLUTION--5
Don't you know that you can count me out?--
   REVOLUTION--9
You ask me for a contribution --REVOLUTION--15
You tell me it's the institution --REVOLUTION--25
Well, the Ukraine girls really knock me out --
   BACKINTHEU--15
And Moscow girls make me sing and shout --
   BACKINTHEU--17
Well, the Ukraine girls really knock me out --
   BACKINTHEU--27
And Moscow girls make me sing and shout --
   BACKINTHEU--29
Oh - show me round the snow-peaked mountains way
   down south --BACKINTHEU--31
Take me to your daddy's farm --BACKINTHEU--32
Let me hear your balalaikas ringing out --
   BACKINTHEU--33
Oh let me tell you honey --BACKINTHEU--38
Hey, so look at me --BACKINTHEU--41
Can you take me back where I came from,--CRYBABYCRY
   --44
Can you take me back?--CRYBABYCRY--45
Can you take me back where I came from --CRYBABYCRY
   --46
Brother, can you take me back --CRYBABYCRY--47
Can you take me back?--CRYBABYCRY--48
Mmm can you take me where I came from --CRYBABYCRY
   --49
Can you take me back?--CRYBABYCRY--50
Dear Prudence, let me see you smile --DEARPRUDEN
   --16
So let me see you smile again.--DEARPRUDEN--19
Dear Prudence, won't you let me see you smile?--
   DEARPRUDEN--20
DON'T PASS ME BY.--DONTPASSME--Title
Does it mean you don't love me any more?--
   DONTPASSME--9
Does it mean you don't love me any more?--
   DONTPASSME--17
Don't pass me by, don't make me cry, don't make
   me blue --DONTPASSME--18
Don't pass me by, don't make me cry, don't make
   me blue --DONTPASSME--18
Don't pass me by, don't make me cry, don't make
   me blue --DONTPASSME--18
You'll never know it hurt me so --DONTPASSME--20
Don't pass me by - don't make me cry.--DONTPASSME
   --22
Don't pass me by - don't make me cry.--DONTPASSME
   --22
Don't pass me by, don't make me cry, don't make
   me blue --DONTPASSME--31
Don't pass me by, don't make me cry, don't make
   me blue --DONTPASSME--31
Don't pass me by, don't make me cry, don't make
   me blue --DONTPASSME--31
You'll never know it hurt me so --DONTPASSME--33
Don't pass me by - don't make me cry.--DONTPASSME
   --35
Don't pass me by - don't make me cry.--DONTPASSME
   --35

Don't pass me by, don't make me cry, don't make
    me blue --DONTPASSME--37
Don't pass me by, don't make me cry, don't make
    me blue --DONTPASSME--37
Don't pass me by, don't make me cry, don't make
    me blue --DONTPASSME--37
You'll never know it hurt me so --DONTPASSME--39
Don't pass me by - don't make me cry.--DONTPASSME
    --41
Don't pass me by - don't make me cry.--DONTPASSME
    --41
EVERYBODY'S GOT SOMETHING TO HIDE EXCEPT ME
    AND MY MONKEY.--EVRBDYMONK--Title
Everybody's got something to hide 'cept for me
    and my monkey - wuh.--EVRBDYMONK--7
Everybody's got something to hide 'cept for me
    and my monkey (yeah - wuh).--EVRBDYMONK--16
Everybody's got something to hide 'cept for me
    and my monkey - hey.--EVRBDYMONK--25
I told you about the walrus and me - man--
    GLASSONION--8
Listen to me--GLASSONION--20
Dream sweet dreams for me --GOODNIGHT--5
Dream sweet dreams for me --GOODNIGHT--11
Dream sweet dreams for me --GOODNIGHT--18
I know nobody can do me no harm ((oh, yeah)) --
    HAPPINESSI--24
A - do you, don't you want me to love you?--
    HELTERSKEL--4
Tell me, tell me, tell me, come on tell me the
    answer --HELTERSKEL--6
Tell me, tell me, tell me, come on tell me the
    answer --HELTERSKEL--6
Tell me, tell me, tell me, come on tell me the
    answer --HELTERSKEL--6
Tell me, tell me, tell me, come on tell me the
    answer --HELTERSKEL--6
A - will you, won't you want me to make you?--
    HELTERSKEL--11
I'm coming down fast but don't let me break you --
    HELTERSKEL--12
Tell me, tell me, tell me the answer --HELTERSKEL
    --13
Tell me, tell me, tell me the answer --HELTERSKEL
    --13
Tell me, tell me, tell me the answer --HELTERSKEL
    --13
Well, do you, don't you want me to make you?--
    HELTERSKEL--21
I'm coming down fast but don't let me break you --
    HELTERSKEL--22
Tell me, tell me, tell me your answer --HELTERSKEL
    --23
Tell me, tell me, tell me your answer --HELTERSKEL
    --23
Tell me, tell me, tell me your answer --HELTERSKEL
    --23
And if she could only hear me--HONEYPIE--5
Honey Pie you are making me crazy--HONEYPIE--7
Come and show me the magic--HONEYPIE--11
Makes me weak in the knee.--HONEYPIE--15
Oh, Honey Pie you are driving me frantic--HONEYPIE
    --16
Honey Pie come back to me - ooo.--HONEYPIE--19
Play it to me--HONEYPIE--23
Play it to me Hollywood blues.--HONEYPIE--24
Kindly send her sailing back to me--HONEYPIE--27
Now Honey Pie you are making me crazy--HONEYPIE--29
Come, come back to me Honey Pie--HONEYPIE--32
If you want me to, I will.--IWILL--4
For the things you do endear you to me - aah --
    IWILL--17
But it's no joke, it's doing me harm --IMSOTIRED
    --10
But it's no joke, it's doing me harm --IMSOTIRED
    --19
Julia, Julia oceanchild calls me --JULIA--3
Julia seashell eyes windy smile calls me --JULIA
    --5
Julia, Julia morning moon touch me --JULIA--9
Julia sleeping sand silent cloud touch me --JULIA
    --13
Hmm hmm hmm, calls me --JULIA--15
Please - remember me, Martha my love --MARTHAMYDE
    --2
Don't forget me, Martha my dear.--MARTHAMYDE--3
That you and me were meant to be for each other -
    silly girl.--MARTHAMYDE--9
Please - be good to me, Martha my love --MARTHAMYDE
    --14
Don't forget me, Martha my dear.--MARTHAMYDE--15
Find me in my field of grass - Mother Nature's
    son --MOTHERNATU--8
You tell me that it's evolution --REVOLUTONE--8

Don't you know that you can count me out (in)?--
    REVOLUTONE--12
You ask me for a contribution --REVOLUTONE--23
You tell me it's the institution --REVOLUTONE--39
But can you show me where you are?--SAVOYTRUFF--22
Bom-pa bom, look at me.--ALLTOGETHE--12
Bom-pa bom, look at me.--ALLTOGETHE--32
You can talk to me--HEYBULLDOG--9
You can talk to me--HEYBULLDOG--10
You can talk to me--HEYBULLDOG--11
If you're lonely you can talk to me.--HEYBULLDOG
    --12
You think you know me but you haven't got a clue.
    --HEYBULLDOG--16
You can talk to me--HEYBULLDOG--17
You can talk to me--HEYBULLDOG--18
You can talk to me--HEYBULLDOG--19
If you're lonely you can talk to me - hey!--
    HEYBULLDOG--20
Don't look at me man (ha ha ha ha)--HEYBULLDOG--31
Your love is there for me--ITSALLTOOM--5
It's all too much for me to take --ITSALLTOOM--8
From life to life with me --ITSALLTOOM--13
It's all too much for me to take --ITSALLTOOM--16
Sail me on a silver sun --ITSALLTOOM--21
Show me that I'm everywhere --ITSALLTOOM--23
And get me home for tea.--ITSALLTOOM--24
It's all too much for me to see --ITSALLTOOM--25
It's all too much for me to take --ITSALLTOOM--29
DON'T LET ME DOWN.--DONTLETMED--Title
Don't let me down --DONTLETMED--1
Don't let me down --DONTLETMED--2
Don't let me down --DONTLETMED--3
Don't let me down.--DONTLETMED--4
Nobody ever loved me like she does --DONTLETMED--5
And if somebody loved me like she do me --
    DONTLETMED--7
And if somebody loved me like she do me --
    DONTLETMED--7
Ooo she do me, yes she does.--DONTLETMED--8
Don't let me down --DONTLETMED--9
Don't let me down --DONTLETMED--10
Don't let me down --DONTLETMED--11
Don't let me down --DONTLETMED--12
It's a love that has no past (believe me).--
    DONTLETMED--16
Don't let me down --DONTLETMED--17
Don't let me down (ooo) --DONTLETMED--18
Don't let me down --DONTLETMED--19
Don't let me down.--DONTLETMED--20
And from the first time that she really done me --
    DONTLETMED--21
Ooo she done me, she done me good --DONTLETMED--22
Ooo she done me, she done me good --DONTLETMED--22
I guess nobody ever really done me --DONTLETMED--23
Ooo she done me, she done me good.--DONTLETMED--24
Ooo she done me, she done me good.--DONTLETMED--24
Don't let me down (hey) --DONTLETMED--25
Don't let me down --DONTLETMED--26
Eee ((don't let me down)) --DONTLETMED--27
Don't let me down.--DONTLETMED--28
Don't let me down --DONTLETMED--30
Don't let me down, let me down --DONTLETMED--31
Don't let me down, let me down --DONTLETMED--31
Don't ((hey)) let me down.--DONTLETMED--33
They're gonna crucify me.--BALLADOFJO--8
They're gonna crucify me.--BALLADOFJO--16
They're gonna crucify me.--BALLADOFJO--24
They're gonna crucify me.--BALLADOFJO--36
They're gonna crucify me.--BALLADOFJO--44
They're gonna crucify me.--BALLADOFJO--46
Though you pick me up --OLDBROWNSH--9
From where some try to drag me down --OLDBROWNSH
    --10
Got me escaping from this zoo --OLDBROWNSH--13
Who knows baby, you may comfort me (hey).--
    OLDBROWNSH--21
If you and me should get together --OLDBROWNSH--25
Who knows baby, you may comfort me (hey).--
    OLDBROWNSH--26
Because the world is round it turns me on --BECAUSE
    --2
Because the sky is blue it makes me cry --BECAUSE
    --10
Shoot me--COMETOGETH--1
Shoot me--COMETOGETH--2
Shoot me--COMETOGETH--3
Shoot me--COMETOGETH--4
Shoot me--COMETOGETH--11
Shoot me--COMETOGETH--12
Shoot me--COMETOGETH--13
Shoot me--COMETOGETH--14
He say I know you, you know me--COMETOGETH--19
Come together right now over me--COMETOGETH--21

Shoot me--COMETOGETH--22
Shoot me--COMETOGETH--23
Shoot me--COMETOGETH--24
Come together right now over me--COMETOGETH--31
Shoot me--COMETOGETH--32
Come together right now over me--COMETOGETH--42
Shoot me--COMETOGETH--43
Shoot me--COMETOGETH--44
Shoot me--COMETOGETH--45
It's driving me mad--IWANTYOUSH--5
It's driving me mad--IWANTYOUSH--6
It's driving me mad--IWANTYOUSH--11
It's driving me--IWANTYOUSH--12
It's driving me mad--IWANTYOUSH--17
It's driving me mad--IWANTYOUSH--18
It's driving me mad--IWANTYOUSH--23
It's driving me--IWANTYOUSH--24
It's driving me mad--IWANTYOUSH--32
It's driving me mad--IWANTYOUSH--33
It's driving me mad--IWANTYOUSH--38
It's driving me mad--IWANTYOUSH--39
An octopus's garden with me.--OCTOPUSSGA--6
We would be so happy you and me--OCTOPUSSGA--21
Oh darling, please believe me, I'll never do
    you no harm.--OHDARLING--1
Believe me when I tell you, I'll never do you
    no harm.--OHDARLING--2
Oh darling, if you leave me I'll never make it
    alone --OHDARLING--3
Believe me when I beg you - ooo - don't ever
    leave me alone.--OHDARLING--4
Believe me when I beg you - ooo - don't ever
    leave me alone.--OHDARLING--4
When you told me you didn't need me any more --
    OHDARLING--5
When you told me you didn't need me any more --
    OHDARLING--5
A - when you told me you didn't need me any more
    --OHDARLING--7
A - when you told me you didn't need me any more
    --OHDARLING--7
Oh darling, if you leave me, I'll never make
    it alone.--OHDARLING--9
Believe me when I tell you, I'll never do you
    no harm.--OHDARLING--10
Believe me, darling.--OHDARLING--11
A - when you told me - ooo - you didn't need me
    any more --OHDARLING--12
A - when you told me - ooo - you didn't need me
    any more --OHDARLING--12
A - when you told me you didn't need me any more
    --OHDARLING--14
A - when you told me you didn't need me any more
    --OHDARLING--14
Oh darling, please believe me, I'll never let
    you down.--OHDARLING--16
Oh believe me darling --OHDARLING--17
Believe me when I tell you - ooo - I'll never
    do you no harm.--OHDARLING--18
Tuesdays on the phone to me.--SHECAMEINT--11
And though she tried her best to help me --
    SHECAMEINT--18
Tuesdays on the phone to me.--SHECAMEINT--23
Attracts me like no other lover --SOMETHING--2
Something in the way she woos me --SOMETHING--3
Something in her style that shows me --SOMETHING
    --8
You're asking me will my love grow?--SOMETHING--11
Something in the things she shows me --SOMETHING
    --17
YOU NEVER GIVE ME YOUR MONEY.--YOUNEVERGI--Title
You never give me your money --YOUNEVERGI--1
You only give me your funny paper--YOUNEVERGI--2
Mother Mary comes to me --LETITBE/45--2
She is standing right in front of me --LETITBE/45
    --5
There is still a light that shines on me --
    LETITBE/45--22
Mother Mary comes to me --LETITBE/45--25
You know my name ((you know)), you know me
    number (too/two)--YOUKNWOMYN--33
You know my name, you know me number three --
    YOUKNOWMYN--34
You know my name, you know me number four --
    YOUKNOWMYN--35
You know my name ((you know)), you know me
    number (too/two)--YOUKNOWMYN--37
Possessing and caressing me.--ACROSSTHEU--5
Images of broken light which dance before me like
    a million eyes --ACROSSTHEU--11
They call me on and on across the universe.--
    ACROSSTHEU--12
Inciting and inviting me.--ACROSSTHEU--22
Limitless undying love which shines around me

like a million suns --ACROSSTHEU--23
It calls me on and on across the universe.--
    ACROSSTHEU--24
You looked at me, that's all you had to do --
    FORYOUBLUE--14
The picker - the picker, picture the fingers
    going (ooo me).--GETBACK/LP--5
Me hand's getting - a too cold to play a chord now.
    --IDIGAPONY--38
I ME MINE.--IMEMINE--Title
I me mine, I me mine, I me mine.--IMEMINE--2
I me mine, I me mine, I me mine.--IMEMINE--2
I me mine, I me mine, I me mine.--IMEMINE--2
I me mine, I me mine, I me mine.--IMEMINE--4
I me mine, I me mine, I me mine.--IMEMINE--4
I me mine, I me mine, I me mine.--IMEMINE--4
I me mine.--IMEMINE--9
I me me mine --IMEMINE--10
I me me mine --IMEMINE--10
I me me mine --IMEMINE--11
I me me mine --IMEMINE--11
I me me mine --IMEMINE--12
I me me mine --IMEMINE--12
I me me mine --IMEMINE--13
I me me mine --IMEMINE--13
I me mine, I me mine, I me mine.--IMEMINE--15
I me mine, I me mine, I me mine.--IMEMINE--15
I me mine, I me mine, I me mine.--IMEMINE--15
I me mine, I me mine, I me mine.--IMEMINE--17
I me mine, I me mine, I me mine.--IMEMINE--17
I me mine, I me mine, I me mine.--IMEMINE--17
I me mine.--IMEMINE--22
I me me mine --IMEMINE--23
I me me mine --IMEMINE--23
I me me mine --IMEMINE--24
I me me mine --IMEMINE--24
I me me mine --IMEMINE--25
I me me mine --IMEMINE--25
I me mine.--IMEMINE--26
I me mine.--IMEMINE--26
I me mine, I me mine, I me mine.--IMEMINE--28
I me mine, I me mine, I me mine.--IMEMINE--28
I me mine, I me mine, I me mine.--IMEMINE--28
I me mine, I me mine, I me mine.--IMEMINE--30
I me mine, I me mine, I me mine.--IMEMINE--30
I me mine, I me mine, I me mine.--IMEMINE--30
I me mine.--IMEMINE--35
Oh please believe me I'd hate to miss the train --
    IVEGOTAFEE--6
And if you leave me I won't be late again --
    IVEGOTAFEE--8
Wondering really how come nobody told me--
    IVEGOTAFEE--12
Ooo I've got a feeling that keeps me on my toes --
    IVEGOTAFEE--14
Mother Mary comes to me --LETITBE/LP--2
She is standing right in front of me--LETITBE/LP--5
There is still a light that shines on me --
    LETITBE/LP--22
Mother Mary comes to me --LETITBE/LP--25
It always leads me here, lead me to your door.--
    LONGANDWIN--3
It always leads me here, lead me to your door.--
    LONGANDWIN--3
Why leave me standing here, let me know the way.--
    LONGANDWIN--6
Why leave me standing here, let me know the way.--
    LONGANDWIN--6
And still they lead me back to the long, winding
    road.--LONGANDWIN--9
You left me standing here a long, long time ago --
    LONGANDWIN--10
Don't leave me waiting here, lead me to your door.
    --LONGANDWIN--11
Don't leave me waiting here, lead me to your door.
    --LONGANDWIN--11
But still they lead me back to the long, winding
    road --LONGANDWIN--12
You left me standing here a long, long time ago --
    LONGANDWIN--13
Don't keep me waiting here (don't keep me
    waiting) lead me to your door.--LONGANDWIN--14
Don't keep me waiting here (don't keep me
    waiting) lead me to your door.--LONGANDWIN--14
Don't keep me waiting here (don't keep me
    waiting) lead me to your door.--LONGANDWIN--14
You're only fooling round, only fooling round
    with me.--ONEAFTERNI--7
You and me Sunday driving --TWOOFUS--5
You and me burning matches --TWOOFUS--12
You and me chasing paper --TWOOFUS--21
You and me chasing paper --TWOOFUS--30

MEAN

You know what I mean --ISAWHERSTA--3
Just what you mean to me--INEEDYOU--19
Just what you mean to me--INEEDYOU--29
Oh, what you mean to me--MICHELLE--13
Until I do I'm hoping you will know what I mean.--
    MICHELLE--14
I mean everything I've said.--RUNFORYOUR--18
Did you mean to break my heart and watch me die?--
    WHATGOESON--24
I mean, it must be high or low--STRAWBERRY--17
I think I know, I mean, er, yes--STRAWBERRY--28
Man I was mean but I'm changing my scene--
    GETTINGBET--27
Indicate precisely what you mean to say--WHENIMSIXT
    --30
((I say yes but I may mean no))--HELLOGOODB--23
Does it mean you don't love me any more?--
    DONTPASSME--9
Does it mean you don't love me any more?--
    DONTPASSME--17
MEAN MR. MUSTARD.--MEANMRMUST--Title
Mean Mr. Mustard sleeps in the park--MEANMRMUST--1
Such a mean old man, such a mean old man.--
    MEANMRMUST--7
Such a mean old man, such a mean old man.--
    MEANMRMUST--7

MEANDER

Thoughts meander like a restless wind inside a
    letter-box --ACROSSTHEU--13

MEANING

And these memories lose their meaning--INMYLIFE--11
That you may see the meaning of within--TOMORROWNE
    --5

MEANINGLESS

Half of what I say is meaningless --JULIA--1

MEANS

Don't know what it means to hold you tight --
    HOLDMETIGH--16
Don't know what it means to hold you tight --
    HOLDMETIGH--26
But what you've got means such a lot to me.--
    LOVEYOUTWO--8

MEANT

Ooo you were meant to be near me--GOTTOGETYO--12
There's nowhere you can be that isn't where
    you're meant to be ((love))--ALLYOUN/YS--21
That you and me were meant to be for each other -
    silly girl.--MARTHAMYDE--9

MEANWHILE

And meanwhile back --PENNYLANE--11
Meanwhile back --PENNYLANE--19
And meanwhile back --PENNYLANE--30

MEASURED

Some kind of happiness is measured out in miles--
    HEYBULLDOG--3
Some kind of innocence is measured out in years--
    HEYBULLDOG--7
Some kind of solitude is measured out in you--
    HEYBULLDOG--15

MEDICINE

Maxwell Edison, majoring in medicine, calls
    her on the phone --MAXWELLSIL--3

MEET

I can't talk to people that I meet.--ILLCRYINST--7
We'd meet again for I had told you.--GOTTOGETYO--11
It's time for tea and meet the wife.--GOODMORNIN
    --21
There's so many there to meet.--BLUEJAYWAY--11
Wonder how you manage to make ends meet.--
    LADYMADONN--2
Wonder how you manage to make ends meet.--
    LADYMADONN--19
Lady Madonna trying to make ends meet - yeah--
    GLASSONION--13

MEETING

Meeting a man from the motor trade.--SHESLEAVIN--27
At twelve o'clock a meeting round the table --
    CRYBABYCRY--28
And now the thought of meeting you--HONEYPIE--14

MELTING

Little darling, I feel that ice is slowly
    melting.--HERECOMEST--18

MEMBER

Queen says no to pot-smoking FBI member.--
    FORYOUBLUE--1

MEMORIES

And these memories lose their meaning--INMYLIFE--11
You and I have memories --TWOOFUS--17
You and I have memories --TWOOFUS--26

MEN

Over men and horses, hoops and garters--BEINGFORTH
    --5
The men from the press said, we wish you success
    --BALLADOFJO--39

MENDING

I could be handy mending a fuse--WHENIMSIXT--13
Thursday night your stockings needed mending.--
    LADYMADONN--16

MESSAGE

With a message at the local bird and bee.--
    CRYBABYCRY--23

MESSRS

Messrs. K. and H. assure the public--BEINGFORTH--12

MET

She's sweeter than all the girls and I met quite
    a few --ANOTHERGIR--6
Where we just met--IVEJUSTSEE--3
And I want all the world to see we've met --
    IVEJUSTSEE--5
Where we just met--IVEJUSTSEE--26
And I want all the world to see we've met --
    IVEJUSTSEE--28
I met you in the morning waiting for the tides of
    time --WHATGOESON--15
He said, Rocky you met your match--ROCKYRACCO--33

METER

Lovely Rita meter maid--LOVELYRITA--2
Lovely Rita meter maid (aah)--LOVELYRITA--3
Lovely Rita (oh) meter maid--LOVELYRITA--4
Standing by a parking meter--LOVELYRITA--7
Lovely Rita meter maid--LOVELYRITA--13
Oh, lovely Rita meter maid--LOVELYRITA--26
Lovely Rita ((lovely meter maid)) meter maid--
    LOVELYRITA--29
Lovely Rita ((lovely meter maid)) meter maid--
    LOVELYRITA--29
Lovely ((Rita, Rita, Rita)) Rita meter maid--
    LOVELYRITA--30
Lovely Rita ((oh lovely Rita meter, meter
    maid)) meter maid--LOVELYRITA--31
Lovely Rita ((oh lovely Rita meter, meter
    maid)) meter maid--LOVELYRITA--31
Lovely Rita ((oh lovely Rita meter, meter
    maid)) meter maid--LOVELYRITA--31
Lovely Rita ((da da da da da da)) meter maid--
    LOVELYRITA--32

MI

Quando paramucho mi amore defeliche carathon --
    SUNKING--6
Mundo paparatsi mi amore chicka ferde parasol --
    SUNKING--7

MIAMI

Oh - flew in from Miami Beach BOAC --BACKINTHEU--1

MICHELLE
    MICHELLE.--MICHELLE--Title
    Michelle ma belle --MICHELLE--1
    These are words that go together well, my
        Michelle.--MICHELLE--2
    Michelle ma belle --MICHELLE--3
    Michelle ma belle --MICHELLE--9
    Michelle ma belle --MICHELLE--20
    My Michelle.--MICHELLE--23

MIDDLE
    When I'm in the middle of a dream --IMONLYSLEE--3
    When I'm in the middle of a dream --IMONLYSLEE--23
    Behind the shelter in the middle of the roundabout
        --PENNYLANE--20
    And in the middle of the celebrations--CARRYTHATW
        --7
    And in the middle of negotiations you break down.
        --YOUNEVERGI--3
    And in the middle of investigation I break down.--
        YOUNEVERGI--6

MIGHT
    So you might as well resign yourself to me, oh
        yeah.--ILLGETYOU--18
    And then I might --HOLDMETIGH--4
    And then I might --HOLDMETIGH--21
    That might cause you pain--YOUCANTDOT--2
    I might have looked the other way--IVEJUSTSEE--8
    There's a chance that we might fall apart before
        too long.--WECANWORKI--18
    There's a chance that we might fall apart before
        too long.--WECANWORKI--27
    Then it might not have been like this --IFINEEDEDS
        --8
    Then it might not have been like this --IFINEEDEDS
        --18
    They might as well be dead--RAIN--2
    But I thought you might like to know--SGTPEPPERS
        --20
    You might not feel it now --SAVOYTRUFF--11

MIGHTY
    Deep in the jungle where the mighty tiger lies --
        CONTINUING--17

MILES
    Please don't spoil my day, I'm miles away --
        IMONLYSLEE--11
    Please don't spoil my day, I'm miles away --
        IMONLYSLEE--17
    I'm coming down fast but I'm miles above you --
        HELTERSKEL--5
    Some kind of happiness is measured out in miles--
        HEYBULLDOG--3

MILITARY
    Made her look a little like a military man.--
        LOVELYRITA--12

MILLION
    She was a girl in a million, my friend --IMALOSER
        --5
    It could make a million for you overnight.
        ((writer))--PAPERBACKW--22
    Images of broken light which dance before me like
        a million eyes --ACROSSTHEU--11
    Limitless undying love which shines around me
        like a million suns --ACROSSTHEU--23

MIND
    When I'm gonna change/make your mind--ILLGETYOU--17
    She almost lost her mind--SHELOVESYO--13
    And now you've changed your mind--NOTASECOND--4
    And now you've changed your mind --NOTASECOND--15
    This boy wouldn't mind the pain--THISBOY--11
    I go outta my mind.--YOUCANTDOT--26
    I go outta my mind.--YOUCANTDOT--45
    And it's my mind and there's no time--THERESAPLA
        --3
    In my mind there's no sorrow--THERESAPLA--9
    And it's my mind and there's no time--THERESAPLA
        --15
    Always on my mind --EIGHTDAYSA--10
    Always on my mind --EIGHTDAYSA--30
    Now I find ((and now I find)) I've changed
        my mind--HELP--13

Now I find ((and now I find)) I've changed
    my mind--HELP--33
Now today I find, you have changed your mind--
    NIGHTBEFOR--3
Now today I find you have changed your mind--
    NIGHTBEFOR--13
She's gonna change her mind (she's gonna change
    her mind)--YOUREGONNA--4
She's gonna change her mind (she's gonna change
    her mind)--YOUREGONNA--4
She's gonna change her mind (she's gonna change
    her mind)--YOUREGONNA--26
She's gonna change her mind (she's gonna change
    her mind)--YOUREGONNA--26
And I was born with a jealous mind --RUNFORYOUR--10
The ruins of the life that you had in mind --
    THINKFORYO--11
What goes on in your mind?--WHATGOESON--2
What goes on in your mind?--WHATGOESON--5
What goes on in your mind?--WHATGOESON--11
What goes on in your mind?--WHATGOESON--14
(What goes on in your mind?)--WHATGOESON--21
What goes on in your mind?--WHATGOESON--27
What goes on in your mind?--WHATGOESON--30
In your mind.--WHATGOESON--31
In your mind.--WHATGOESON--32
And I will lose my mind--YOUWONTSEE--4
I wouldn't mind if I knew what I was missing.--
    YOUWONTSEE--14
I wouldn't mind if I knew what I was missing.--
    YOUWONTSEE--23
Rain I don't mind--RAIN--7
Rain I don't mind--RAIN--12
It's just a state of mind (when it rains and
    shines)--RAIN--15
I don't mind, I think they're crazy --IMONLYSLEE
    --8
Your day breaks, your mind aches --FORNOONE--1
Your day breaks, your mind aches --FORNOONE--20
Could see another kind of mind there.--GOTTOGETYO
    --4
Could see another kind of mind there.--GOTTOGETYO
    --28
It's only me, it's not my mind--IWANTTOTEL--10
I don't mind, I could wait forever--IWANTTOTEL--14
Then I could speak my mind and tell you--IWANTTOTEL
    --17
I don't mind, I could wait forever--IWANTTOTEL--21
Turn off your mind, relax and float down-stream--
    TOMORROWNE--1
He blew his mind out in a car--DAYINTHELI--6
And stops my mind from wandering--FIXINGAHOL--2
And kept my mind from wandering--FIXINGAHOL--5
And when my mind is wandering--FIXINGAHOL--12
Stops my mind from wandering--FIXINGAHOL--24
Stops my mind from wandering--FIXINGAHOL--27
Peace of mind is waiting there--WITHINYOUW--30
You better free your mind instead.--REVOLUTION--27
That Georgia's always on my my my my my my my my
    my mind.--BACKINTHEU--18
That Georgia's always on my my my my my my my my
    my mind.--BACKINTHEU--30
I'm so tired, my mind is on the blink --IMSOTIRED
    --2
I'm so tired, my mind is set on you --IMSOTIRED--6
You know I'd give you everything I've got for a
    little peace of mind.--IMSOTIRED--13
You know I'd give you everything I've got for a
    little peace of mind.--IMSOTIRED--22
I'd give you everything I've got for a little
    peace of mind --IMSOTIRED--23
I'd give you everything I've got for a little
    peace of mind.--IMSOTIRED--24
I can only speak my mind, Julia.--JULIA--12
You'd better free your mind instead.--REVOLUTONE
    --41
Black cloud crossed my mind --YERBLUES--24
Because the wind is high it blows my mind --BECAUSE
    --5
Are drifting through my opened mind--ACROSSTHEU
    --4

MIND'S
    I know your mind's made up --THINKFORYO--13
    Although your mind's opaque --THINKFORYO--19

MINDS
    But if you want money for people with minds that
        hate --REVOLUTION--18
    But if you want money for people with minds that
        hate --REVOLUTONE--27

MINE
    I hope it will be mine --ANYTIMEATA--17
    Now you're mine --ASKMEWHY--7
    And I held her hand in mine.--ISAWHERSTA--12
    And I held her hand in mine.--ISAWHERSTA--19
    Then we'll have some fun when you're mine, all
       mine --LITTLECHIL--10
    Then we'll have some fun when you're mine, all
       mine --LITTLECHIL--10
    I see no reason to change mine --NOTASECOND--5
    I see no reason to change mine --NOTASECOND--16
    If you wanna stay mine--YOUCANTDOT--24
    If you wanna stay mine--YOUCANTDOT--43
    I know this love of mine --ANDILOVEHE--17
    I know this love of mine --ANDILOVEHE--22
    And when I ask you to be mine --ISHOULDHAV--9
    And when I ask you to be mine --ISHOULDHAV--19
    You say you'll be mine girl, till the end of time
       --THINGSWESA--6
    And that's enough to make you mine girl --
       THINGSWESA--15
    And that's enough to make you mine girl --
       THINGSWESA--26
    Baby says she's mine, you know --IFEELFINE--4
    Baby said she's mine, you know --IFEELFINE--12
    I'm so proud to know that she is mine.--GOODDAYSUN
       --13
    It's getting better since you've been mine.--
       GETTINGBET--10
    It's getting better since you've been mine.--
       GETTINGBET--19
    It's getting better since you've been mine.--
       GETTINGBET--32
    Mine for evermore.--WHENIMSIXT--34
    I can't tell you but I know it's mine.--WITHALITTL
       --22
    Close your eyes and I'll close mine --GOODNIGHT--7
    Close your eyes and I'll close mine --GOODNIGHT--14
    Someday I'm gonna make her mine - oh yeah --
       HERMAJESTY--8
    Someday I'm gonna make her mine.--HERMAJESTY--9
    I ME MINE.--IMEMINE--Title
    I me mine, I me mine, I me mine.--IMEMINE--2
    I me mine, I me mine, I me mine.--IMEMINE--2
    I me mine, I me mine, I me mine.--IMEMINE--2
    I me mine, I me mine, I me mine.--IMEMINE--4
    I me mine, I me mine, I me mine.--IMEMINE--4
    I me mine, I me mine, I me mine.--IMEMINE--4
    I me mine.--IMEMINE--9
    I me me mine --IMEMINE--10
    I me me mine --IMEMINE--11
    I me me mine --IMEMINE--12
    I me me mine.--IMEMINE--13
    I me mine, I me mine, I me mine.--IMEMINE--15
    I me mine, I me mine, I me mine.--IMEMINE--15
    I me mine, I me mine, I me mine.--IMEMINE--15
    I me mine, I me mine, I me mine.--IMEMINE--17
    I me mine, I me mine, I me mine.--IMEMINE--17
    I me mine, I me mine, I me mine.--IMEMINE--17
    I me mine.--IMEMINE--22
    I me me mine --IMEMINE--23
    I me me mine --IMEMINE--24
    I me me mine --IMEMINE--25
    I me me mine.--IMEMINE--26
    I me mine, I me mine, I me mine.--IMEMINE--28
    I me mine, I me mine, I me mine.--IMEMINE--28
    I me mine, I me mine, I me mine.--IMEMINE--28
    I me mine, I me mine, I me mine.--IMEMINE--30
    I me mine, I me mine, I me mine.--IMEMINE--30
    I me mine, I me mine, I me mine.--IMEMINE--30
    I me mine.--IMEMINE--35

MINUTE
    The minute you let her under your skin --HEYJUDE
       --7

MIRRORS
    The man in the crowd with the multicoloured
       mirrors on his hobnail boots --HAPPINESSI--5

MISERY
    I can't conceive of any more misery.--ASKMEWHY--13
    I can't conceive of any more misery.--ASKMEWHY--25
    MISERY.--MISERY--Title
    The world is treating me bad, misery.--MISERY--1
    The world is treating me bad, misery.--MISERY--3
    It's gonna be a drag, misery.--MISERY--5
    Without her I will be in misery.--MISERY--9
    Without her I will be in misery.--MISERY--13
    (Ooho) in misery--MISERY--14

    (Ooo) my misery--MISERY--15
    (La la la la la la la) misery.--MISERY--16
    You're gonna cause more misery.--THINKFORYO--14

MISPLACE
    How can I ever misplace you?--LONGLONGLO--10

MISS
    She'll remember and she'll miss her only one,
       lonely one.--MISERY--11
    Tomorrow I'll miss you --ALLMYLOVIN--2
    Tomorrow I'll miss you --ALLMYLOVIN--16
    To miss that love is something I'd hate.--
       OLDBROWNSH--28
    Oh please believe me I'd hate to miss the train --
       IVEGOTAFEE--6

MISSED
    I've been alone and I have missed things--
       IVEJUSTSEE--15

MISSES
    She's not a girl who misses much --HAPPINESSI--1

MISSING
    The lips I am missing --ALLMYLOVIN--8
    You don't know what you're missing --NOWHEREMAN--8
    You don't know what you're missing --NOWHEREMAN--20
    I wouldn't mind if I knew what I was missing.--
       YOUWONTSEE--14
    I wouldn't mind if I knew what I was missing.--
       YOUWONTSEE--23

MIST
    Blue mist round my soul --YERBLUES--25

MISTAKE
    Till she sees the mistake she has made?--BABYSINBLA
       --15
    Till she sees the mistake she has made?--BABYSINBLA
       --20
    With every mistake we must surely be learning --
       WHILEMYGUI--11

MISUNDERSTANDING
    Misunderstanding all you see--STRAWBERRY--7

MISUNDERSTOOD
    In the beginning I misunderstood --THEWORD--7

MMM
    Oh, oh - mmm, you've been good to me--THANKYOUGI
       --1
    Oh, oh - mmm, you've been good to me--THANKYOUGI
       --11
    Mmm mmm mmm.--ALLIVEGOTT--29
    Mmm mmm mmm.--ALLIVEGOTT--29
    Mmm mmm mmm.--ALLIVEGOTT--29
    Mmm.--ANDILOVEHE--25
    Mmm, mmm, mmm - mmm.--IVEJUSTSEE--6
    Mmm, mmm, mmm - mmm.--IVEJUSTSEE--6
    Mmm, mmm, mmm - mmm.--IVEJUSTSEE--6
    Mmm, mmm, mmm - mmm.--IVEJUSTSEE--6
    Mmm mmm mmm la da da.--IVEJUSTSEE--29
    Mmm mmm mmm la da da.--IVEJUSTSEE--29
    Mmm mmm mmm la da da.--IVEJUSTSEE--29
    Mmm mmm mmm - mmm mmm mmm-mmm.--YESTERDAY--25
    Mmm mmm mmm - mmm mmm mmm-mmm.--YESTERDAY--25
    Mmm mmm mmm - mmm mmm mmm-mmm.--YESTERDAY--25
    Mmm mmm mmm - mmm mmm mmm-mmm.--YESTERDAY--25
    Mmm mmm mmm - mmm mmm mmm-mmm.--YESTERDAY--25
    Beep beep mmm beep beep yeah.--DRIVEMYCAR--17
    Beep beep mmm beep beep yeah.--DRIVEMYCAR--30
    Beep beep mmm beep beep yeah --DRIVEMYCAR--31
    Beep beep mmm beep beep yeah.--DRIVEMYCAR--32
    Beep beep mmm beep beep yeah.--DRIVEMYCAR--33
    Beep beep mmm beep beep yeah.--DRIVEMYCAR--34
    Mmm I get high with a little help from my friends
       --WITHALITTL--6
    Mmm gonna try with a little help from my friends.
       --WITHALITTL--7
    Mmm get high with a little help from my friends --
       WITHALITTL--13
    Mmm gonna try with a little help from my friends.

--WITHALITTL--14
Mmm get high with a little help from my friends --
   WITHALITTL--24
Mmm gonna try with a little help from my friends
   --WITHALITTL--31
Mmm can you take me where I came from --CRYBABYCRY
   --49
Mmm - mmm - mmm - mmm.--GOODNIGHT--13
Mmm - mmm - mmm - mmm.--GOODNIGHT--13
Mmm - mmm - mmm - mmm.--GOODNIGHT--13
Mmm - mmm - mmm - mmm.--GOODNIGHT--13
Mmm, mmm - da, da, da, da, da, da, da.--IWILL--19
Mmm, mmm - da, da, da, da, da, da, da.--IWILL--19
Mmm mmm mmm --MOTHERNATU--13
Mmm mmm mmm --MOTHERNATU--13
Mmm mmm mmm --MOTHERNATU--13
Mmm mmm aah --MOTHERNATU--15
Mmm mmm aah --MOTHERNATU--15
Why don't we do it in the road? - mmm--WHYDONTWED
   --3

MMM-MMM

Mmm-mmm - mmm-mmm-mmm.--TELLMEWHAT--35
Mmm mmm mmm - mmm mmm mmm-mmm.--YESTERDAY--25

MMM-MMM-MMM

Mmm-mmm - mmm-mmm-mmm.--TELLMEWHAT--35

MOAN

So why on earth should I moan --HARDDAYSNI--12
So why on earth should I moan --HARDDAYSNI--25
All I do is hang my head and moan.--TELLMEWHY--8
You still moan keep your hands to yourself --IMDOWN
   --17

MOJO

He one mojo filter--COMETOGETH--39

MOLLY

Molly is the singer in a band --OBLADIOBLA--2
Desmond says to Molly, girl I like your face--
   OBLADIOBLA--3
And Molly says this as she takes him by the hand:
   --OBLADIOBLA--4
Takes it back to Molly waiting at the door--
   OBLADIOBLA--11
With a couple of kids running in the yard of
   Desmond and Molly Jones.--OBLADIOBLA--18
Molly stays at home and does her pretty face--
   OBLADIOBLA--23
With a couple of kids running in the yard of
   Desmond and Molly Jones.--OBLADIOBLA--30
Molly lets the children lend a hand --OBLADIOBLA
   --33

MOM

In case of accidents he always took his mom --
   CONTINUING--8

MOMENT

You were only waiting for this moment to arise.--
   BLACKBIRD--4
You were only waiting for this moment to be free.
   --BLACKBIRD--8
You were only waiting for this moment to arise --
   BLACKBIRD--16
You were only waiting for this moment to arise --
   BLACKBIRD--17
You were only waiting for this moment to arise.--
   BLACKBIRD--18
I want you at the moment I feel blue --FORYOUBLUE
   --6
I'm living every moment girl for you.--FORYOUBLUE
   --7
I've loved you from the moment I saw you --
   FORYOUBLUE--13

MOMENTS

All these places had their moments --INMYLIFE--5

MOMMA

Happiness ((happiness)) is a warm gun, momma--
   HAPPINESSI--20
Because - (happiness) is a warm gun, momma--
   HAPPINESSI--25

Is a warm gun, momma ((is a warm gun, yeah)).--
   HAPPINESSI--32

MOMMY

(But when he looked so fierce) his mommy butted
   in --CONTINUING--28

MOMMY'S

Your mommy's waiting for you --GETBACK/45--32

MONDAY

Sundays on the phone to Monday --SHECAMEINT--10
Sundays on the phone to Monday --SHECAMEINT--22
Monday morning turning back --YOUNEVERGI--11

MONDAY'S

Monday's child has learned to tie his bootlace.--
   LADYMADONN--7

MONEY

'cos I don't care too much for money --CANTBUYMEL
   --7
Money can't buy me love.--CANTBUYMEL--8
I don't care too much for money --CANTBUYMEL--13
Money can't buy me love.--CANTBUYMEL--14
That money just can't buy --CANTBUYMEL--20
I don't care too much for money --CANTBUYMEL--21
Money can't buy me love.--CANTBUYMEL--22
That money just can't buy --CANTBUYMEL--30
I don't care too much for money --CANTBUYMEL--31
Money can't buy me love.--CANTBUYMEL--32
To get you money to buy you things --HARDDAYSNI--9
Don't pay money just to see yourself with Dr.
   Robert.--DRROBERT--14
Home. (we gave her everything money could buy)--
   SHESLEAVIN--10
Fun. (fun is the one thing that money can't buy)--
   SHESLEAVIN--30
You keep all your money in a big brown bag --
   BABYYOUREA--16
You keep all your money in a big brown bag --
   BABYYOUREA--31
Who finds the money when you pay the rent?--
   LADYMADONN--3
Did you think that money was heaven sent?--
   LADYMADONN--4
But if you want money for people with minds that
   hate --REVOLUTION--18
But if you want money for people with minds that
   hate --REVOLUTONE--27
Saving up your money for a rainy day --BALLADOFJO
   --25
YOU NEVER GIVE ME YOUR MONEY.--YOUNEVERGI--Title
You never give me your money --YOUNEVERGI--1
Out of college, money spent --YOUNEVERGI--7

MONEY'S

All the money's gone, nowhere to go.--YOUNEVERGI
   --9

MONKEY

EVERYBODY'S GOT SOMETHING TO HIDE EXCEPT ME
   AND MY MONKEY.--EVRBDYMONK--Title
Everybody's got something to hide 'cept for me
   and my monkey - wuh.--EVRBDYMONK--7
Everybody's got something to hide 'cept for me
   and my monkey (yeah - wuh).--EVRBDYMONK--16
Everybody's got something to hide 'cept for me
   and my monkey - hey.--EVRBDYMONK--25

MONTELIMAR

Creme tangerine, montelimar --SAVOYTRUFF--1
Creme tangerine and montelimar --SAVOYTRUFF--23

MOON

Now the moon begins to shine --GOODNIGHT--9
Julia, Julia morning moon touch me --JULIA--9
I pick a moon dog--IDIGAPONY--16

MORE

I can't conceive of any more misery.--ASKMEWHY--13
I can't conceive of any more misery.--ASKMEWHY--25
I've lost her now for sure, I won't see her no
   more --MISERY--4

Now I know that you won't leave me no more--
ITWONTBELO--26
Do I have to tell you one more time--YOUCANTDOT--11
If this is love you've got to give me more --
ISHOULDHAV--12
Give me more, hey hey hey, give me more.--
ISHOULDHAV--13
Give me more, hey hey hey, give me more.--
ISHOULDHAV--13
And I found that love was more --IFIFELL--5
That you would love me more than her.--IFIFELL--9
I bet I'll love her more --WHENIGETHO--19
Love you more than any other guy--NOREPLY--18
And what's more, it's true, yes it is.--YESITIS--4
Listen to me one more time--TELLMEWHAT--18
Listen to me one more time--TELLMEWHAT--27
You don't want my loving any more--INEEDYOU--12
I just can't go on any more.--INEEDYOU--15
You don't want my loving any more--INEEDYOU--22
I just can't go on any more.--INEEDYOU--25
If I had some more time to spend --IFINEEDEDS--4
If I had some more time to spend --IFINEEDEDS--14
In my life I love you more.--INMYLIFE--16
In my life I love you more.--INMYLIFE--20
In my life I love you more.--INMYLIFE--21
You're gonna cause misery.--THINKFORYO--14
Try thinking more if just for your own sake.--
THINKFORYO--20
I'll be writing more in a week or two. ((writer))
--PAPERBACKW--16
If you don't want to pay some more (ha ha Mr.
Heath)--TAXMAN--19
Many more of them live next door--YELLOWSUBM--14
Leaving the note that she hoped would say more.--
SHESLEAVIN--3
Who could ask for more?--WHENIMSIXT--18
Does it mean you don't love me any more?--
DONTPASSME--9
Does it mean you don't love me any more?--
DONTPASSME--17
One more time.--PIGGIES--20
Can I have a little more?--ALLTOGETHE--2
Do you know any more?--HEYBULLDOG--26
And the more I go inside --ITSALLTOOM--6
The more there is to see.--ITSALLTOOM--7
The more I learn, the less I know --ITSALLTOOM--27
When you told me you didn't need me any more --
OHDARLING--5
A - when you told me you didn't need me any more
--OHDARLING--7
A - when you told me - ooo - you didn't need me
any more --OHDARLING--12
A - when you told me you didn't need me any more
--OHDARLING--14
I love you more than ever girl, I do.--FORYOUBLUE
--4
I love you more than ever girl, I do - really
love blues.--FORYOUBLUE--18
Flowing more freely than wine --IMEMINE--20
Flowing more freely than wine --IMEMINE--33

MORETTA
Sweet Moretta Fart she thought she was a cleaner--
GETBACK/LP--2

MORNING
Though you've gone away this morning--YOULIKEMET
--1
She told me she worked in the morning--NORWEGIANW
--17
I met you in the morning waiting for the tides of
time --WHATGOESON--15
When I wake up early in the morning --IMONLYSLEE
--1
When I wake up early in the morning --IMONLYSLEE
--21
GOOD MORNING, GOOD MORNING.--GOODMORNIN--Title
GOOD MORNING, GOOD MORNING.--GOODMORNIN--Title
Good morning, good morning, good morning, good
morning, good morning.--GOODMORNIN--1
Good morning, good morning, good morning, good
morning, good morning.--GOODMORNIN--1
Good morning, good morning, good morning, good
morning, good morning.--GOODMORNIN--1
Good morning, good morning, good morning, good
morning, good morning.--GOODMORNIN--1
Good morning, good morning, good morning, good
morning, good morning.--GOODMORNIN--1
Good morning, good morning, good morning.--
GOODMORNIN--6
Good morning, good morning, good morning.--
GOODMORNIN--6

Good morning, good morning, good morning.--
GOODMORNIN--6
Good morning, good morning, good morning.--
GOODMORNIN--17
Good morning, good morning, good morning.--
GOODMORNIN--17
Good morning, good morning, good morning.--
GOODMORNIN--17
Good morning, good morning good--GOODMORNIN--26
Good morning, good morning good--GOODMORNIN--26
Good morning, good morning good--GOODMORNIN--27
Good morning, good morning good--GOODMORNIN--27
Good morning, good morning good--GOODMORNIN--28
Good morning, good morning good--GOODMORNIN--28
Good morning, good morning good--GOODMORNIN--29
Good morning, good morning good--GOODMORNIN--29
Good morning, good morning good--GOODMORNIN--30
Good morning, good morning good--GOODMORNIN--30
Good morning, good morning good--GOODMORNIN--31
Good morning, good morning good--GOODMORNIN--31
Good morning, good morning good--GOODMORNIN--32
Good morning, good morning good--GOODMORNIN--32
Good morning, good morning good.--GOODMORNIN--33
Good morning, good morning good.--GOODMORNIN--33
Wednesday morning at five o'clock as the day begins
--SHESLEAVIN--1
Friday morning at nine o'clock she is far away--
SHESLEAVIN--25
Sunday morning creeping like a nun --LADYMADONN--6
Wednesday morning papers didn't come --LADYMADONN
--15
Julia, Julia morning moon touch me --JULIA--9
In the morning - wanna die --YERBLUES--6
Monday morning turning back --YOUNEVERGI--11
I want you in the morning girl, I love you --
FORYOUBLUE--5

MORNINGS
Sunday mornings go for a ride.--WHENIMSIXT--16

MOSCOW
And Moscow girls make me sing and shout --
BACKINTHEU--17
And Moscow girls make me sing and shout --
BACKINTHEU--29

MOST
She (we gave her most of our lives)--SHESLEAVIN--8
Is leaving (sacrificed most of our lives)--
SHESLEAVIN--9

MOTHER
YOUR MOTHER SHOULD KNOW.--YOURMOTHER--Title
That was a hit before your mother was born --
YOURMOTHER--3
Your mother should know (your mother should) --
YOURMOTHER--5
Your mother should know (your mother should) --
YOURMOTHER--5
Your mother should know - aah.--YOURMOTHER--6
That was a hit before your mother was born --
YOURMOTHER--9
Your mother should know (your mother should) --
YOURMOTHER--11
Your mother should know (your mother should) --
YOURMOTHER--11
Your mother should know - aah.--YOURMOTHER--12
That was a hit before your mother was born --
YOURMOTHER--14
Your mother should know (your mother should) --
YOURMOTHER--16
Your mother should know (your mother should) --
YOURMOTHER--16
Your mother should know - aah.--YOURMOTHER--17
Your mother should know (your mother should) --
YOURMOTHER--18
Your mother should know (your mother should) --
YOURMOTHER--18
Your mother should know - aah.--YOURMOTHER--19
Your mother should know (your mother should) --
YOURMOTHER--24
Your mother should know (your mother should) --
YOURMOTHER--24
Your mother should know - yeah ((ooo)).--YOURMOTHER
--25
Your mother should know (your mother should) --
YOURMOTHER--26
Your mother should know (your mother should) --
YOURMOTHER--26
Your mother should know - yeah.--YOURMOTHER--27

Your mother should know (your mother should) --
    YOURMOTHER--28
Your mother should know (your mother should) --
    YOURMOTHER--28
Your mother should know - yeah.--YOURMOTHER--29
Make your mother sigh --CRYBABYCRY--2
Make your mother sigh --CRYBABYCRY--9
Make your mother sigh --CRYBABYCRY--17
Make your mother sigh --CRYBABYCRY--25
Make your mother sigh --CRYBABYCRY--33
Make your mother sigh --CRYBABYCRY--37
Make your mother sigh --CRYBABYCRY--41
Mother Superior jump the gun --HAPPINESSI--12
Mother Superior jump the gun --HAPPINESSI--13
Mother Superior jump the gun --HAPPINESSI--14
Mother Superior jump the gun --HAPPINESSI--15
Mother Superior jump the gun --HAPPINESSI--16
Mother Superior jump the gun.--HAPPINESSI--17
MOTHER NATURE'S SON.--MOTHERNATU--Title
Born a poor young country boy - Mother Nature's
    son --MOTHERNATU--1
Find me in my field of grass - Mother Nature's
    son --MOTHERNATU--8
Aah Mother Nature's son.--MOTHERNATU--16
My mother was of the sky --YERBLUES--10
To your mother!--ITSALLTOOM--1
Mother Mary comes to me --LETITBE/45--2
Mother Mary comes to me --LETITBE/45--25
Mother Mary comes to me --LETITBE/LP--2
Mother Mary comes to me --LETITBE/LP--25

MOTHER'S
He's the all-American bullet-headed Saxon
    mother's son.--CONTINUING--9

MOTOR
Meeting a man from the motor trade.--SHESLEAVIN--27

MOTORCAR
On the corner is a banker with a motorcar--
    PENNYLANE--5

MOTS
Sont des mots qui vont tres bien ensemble, tres
    bien ensemble.--MICHELLE--4
Sont des mots qui vont tres bien ensemble, tres
    bien ensemble.--MICHELLE--10
Sont des mots qui vont tres bien ensemble, tres
    bien ensemble.--MICHELLE--21

MOUNTAIN
Sit beside a mountain stream - see her waters rise
    --MOTHERNATU--3
Now somewhere in the Black Mountain hills of
    Dakota --ROCKYRACCO--1

MOUNTAINS
Oh - show me round the snow-peaked mountains way
    down south --BACKINTHEU--31

MOURN
That ignorance and hate may mourn the dead--
    TOMORROWNE--9

MOVE
I said, move over honey, I'm travelling on
    that line --ONEAFTERNI--2
I said, move over once, move over twice --
    ONEAFTERNI--3
I said, move over once, move over twice --
    ONEAFTERNI--3
I said move over once, move over twice --ONEAFTERNI
    --8
I said move over once, move over twice --ONEAFTERNI
    --8
Said move over once, move over twice --ONEAFTERNI
    --17
Said move over once, move over twice --ONEAFTERNI
    --17
Said a - move over honey, I'm travelling on
    that line --ONEAFTERNI--26
I said, move over once, move over twice --ONEAFTERNI
    --27
I said, move over once, move over twice --ONEAFTERNI
    --27

MOVEMENT
The movement you need is on your shoulder.--HEYJUDE
    --24

MOVES
Something in the way she moves--SOMETHING--1

MOVING
Your lips are moving, I cannot hear --IMLOOKINGT
    --5
See the hands a - moving --DONTPASSME--12

MR
Don't ask me what I want it for (ha ha Mr.
    Wilson)--TAXMAN--18
If you don't want to pay some more (ha ha Mr.
    Heath)--TAXMAN--19
(Full speed ahead, Mr. Bosun, full speed
    ahead.--YELLOWSUBM--20
BEING FOR THE BENEFIT OF MR. KITE!--BEINGFORTH
    --Title
For the benefit of Mr. Kite--BEINGFORTH--1
In this way Mr. K. will challenge the world.--
    BEINGFORTH--7
The celebrated Mr. K.--BEINGFORTH--8
As Mr. Kite flies through the ring - don't be
    late.--BEINGFORTH--11
When Mr. K. performs his tricks - without a
    sound.--BEINGFORTH--16
And Mr. H. will demonstrate--BEINGFORTH--17
And tonight Mr. Kite is topping the bill.--
    BEINGFORTH--21
Mr. City policeman sitting pretty little
    policemen in a row--IAMTHEWALR--9
Just like Dylan's Mr. Jones.--YERBLUES--20
MEAN MR. MUSTARD.--MEANMRMUST--Title
Mean Mr. Mustard sleeps in the park--MEANMRMUST--1

MUCH
You'll never know how much I really love you --
    DOYOUWANTT--1
You'll never know how much I really care.--
    DOYOUWANTT--2
'cos I don't care too much for money --CANTBUYMEL
    --7
I don't care too much for money --CANTBUYMEL--13
I don't care too much for money --CANTBUYMEL--21
I don't care too much for money --CANTBUYMEL--31
Would it be too much to ask of you --WHATYOURED--3
Why should it be so much to ask of you --WHATYOURED
    --7
Why should it be so much to ask of you --WHATYOURED
    --14
Why should it be so much to ask of you --WHATYOURED
    --21
YOU LIKE ME TOO MUCH.--YOULIKEMET--Title
'cos you like me too much and I like you--
    YOULIKEMET--6
'cos you like me too much and I like you--
    YOULIKEMET--12
'cos you like me too much and I like you--
    YOULIKEMET--20
'cos you like me too much and I like you--
    YOULIKEMET--21
'cos you like me too much and I like you--
    YOULIKEMET--29
'cos you like me too much and I like you.--
    YOULIKEMET--30
So much younger than today--HELP--9
When I was younger, so much younger than today--
    HELP--29
You don't realise how much I need you--INEEDYOU--1
She's the kind of girl you want so much it makes
    you sorry --GIRL--3
But you see now I'm too much in love.--IFINEEDSDS
    --9
But you see now I'm too much in love.--IFINEEDSDS
    --19
I won't want to stay, I don't have much to say --
    YOUWONTSEE--9
It doesn't matter much to me.--STRAWBERRY--10
Getting so much better all the time.--GETTINGBET
    --20
Getting so much better all the time.--GETTINGBET
    --33
Getting so much better all the time.--GETTINGBET
    --38
In a cap she looked much older--LOVELYRITA--10
She's not a girl who misses much --HAPPINESSI--1

When it becomes too much--SAVOYTRUFF--15
IT'S ALL TOO MUCH.--ITSALLTOOM--Title
It's all too much --ITSALLTOOM--2
It's all too much.--ITSALLTOOM--3
It's all too much for me to take --ITSALLTOOM--8
For us to take, it's all too much.--ITSALLTOOM--11
It's all too much for me to take --ITSALLTOOM--16
So take a piece, but not too much.--ITSALLTOOM
  --19
It's all too much for me to see --ITSALLTOOM--25
And what I do is all too much.--ITSALLTOOM--28
It's all too much for me to take --ITSALLTOOM--29
For us to take it's all too much.--ITSALLTOOM--32
It's too much - aah.--ITSALLTOOM--33
It's too much.--ITSALLTOOM--34
You're too much - aah.--ITSALLTOOM--37
Too much, too much, too much, too much, too
  much, too much, too much --ITSALLTOOM--39
Too much, too much, too much, too much, too
  much, too much, too much --ITSALLTOOM--39
Too much, too much, too much, too much, too
  much, too much, too much --ITSALLTOOM--39
Too much, too much, too much, too much, too
  much, too much, too much --ITSALLTOOM--39
Too much, too much, too much, too much, too
  much, too much, too much --ITSALLTOOM--39
Too much, too much, too much, too much, too
  much, too much, too much --ITSALLTOOM--39
Too much, too much, too much, too much, too
  much, too much, too much --ITSALLTOOM--39
Too much, too much, too much (wuh!), too
  much, too much, too much --ITSALLTOOM--40
Too much, too much, too much (wuh!), too
  much, too much, too much --ITSALLTOOM--40
Too much, too much, too much (wuh!), too
  much, too much, too much --ITSALLTOOM--40
Too much, too much, too much (wuh!), too
  much, too much, too much --ITSALLTOOM--40
Too much, too much, too much (wuh!), too
  much, too much, too much --ITSALLTOOM--40
Too much, too much, too much (wuh!), too
  much, too much, too much --ITSALLTOOM--40
Too much, too much, too much, too much, too
  much, too much, too much --ITSALLTOOM--41
Too much, too much, too much, too much, too
  much, too much, too much --ITSALLTOOM--41
Too much, too much, too much, too much, too
  much, too much, too much --ITSALLTOOM--41
Too much, too much, too much, too much, too
  much, too much, too much --ITSALLTOOM--41
Too much, too much, too much, too much, too
  much, too much, too much --ITSALLTOOM--41
Too much, too much, too much, too much, too
  much, too much, too much --ITSALLTOOM--41
Too much, too much, too much, too much, too
  much, too much, too much --ITSALLTOOM--41
Too much, too much, too much (come on), too
  much, too much, too much.--ITSALLTOOM--42
Too much, too much, too much (come on), too
  much, too much, too much.--ITSALLTOOM--42
Too much, too much, too much (come on), too
  much, too much, too much.--ITSALLTOOM--42
Too much, too much, too much (come on), too
  much, too much, too much.--ITSALLTOOM--42
Too much, too much, too much (come on), too
  much, too much, too much.--ITSALLTOOM--42
Too much, too much, too much (come on), too
  much, too much, too much.--ITSALLTOOM--42
Too much, too much, too much, too much, too
  much, too much --ITSALLTOOM--43
Too much, too much, too much, too much, too
  much, too much --ITSALLTOOM--43
Too much, too much, too much, too much, too
  much, too much --ITSALLTOOM--43
Too much, too much, too much, too much, too
  much, too much --ITSALLTOOM--43
Too much, too much, too much, too much, too
  much, too much --ITSALLTOOM--43
Too much, too much, too much, too much, too
  much, too much --ITSALLTOOM--43
Too much, too much, too much, too much, too
  much, too much --ITSALLTOOM--44
Too much, too much, too much, too much, too
  much, too much --ITSALLTOOM--44
Too much, too much, too much, too much, too
  much, too much --ITSALLTOOM--44
Too much, too much, too much, too much, too
  much, too much --ITSALLTOOM--44
Too much, too much, too much, too much, too
  much, too much --ITSALLTOOM--44
Too much, too much, too much, too much, too
  much, too much --ITSALLTOOM--44
Too much, too much, too much, too much, too
  much, too much --ITSALLTOOM--45

Too much, too much, too much, too much, too
  much, too much --ITSALLTOOM--45
Too much, too much, too much, too much, too
  much, too much --ITSALLTOOM--45
Too much, too much, too much, too much, too
  much, too much --ITSALLTOOM--45
Too much, too much, too much, too much, too
  much, too much --ITSALLTOOM--45
Too much, too much, too much, too much, too
  much, too much --ITSALLTOOM--45
Too much, too much, too much, too much, too
  much, too much.--ITSALLTOOM--46
Too much, too much, too much, too much, too
  much, too much.--ITSALLTOOM--46
Too much, too much, too much, too much, too
  much, too much.--ITSALLTOOM--46
Too much, too much, too much, too much, too
  much, too much.--ITSALLTOOM--46
Too much, too much, too much, too much, too
  much, too much.--ITSALLTOOM--46
Too much, too much, too much, too much, too
  much, too much.--ITSALLTOOM--46

MUCHO
  Questo obrigado tanta mucho cake and eat it
    carousel.--SUNKING--8

MUDDY
  He got Muddy Water--COMETOGETH--38

MULTICOLOURED
  The man in the crowd with the multicoloured
    mirrors on his hobnail boots --HAPPINESSI--5

MUNDO
  Mundo paparatsi mi amore chicka ferde parasol --
    SUNKING--7

MUSIC
  Listen to the music playing in your head.--
    LADYMADONN--13
  I like this kinda hot kinda music, hot kinda music
    --HONEYPIE--22
  I like this kinda hot kinda music, hot kinda music
    --HONEYPIE--22
  Listen to the pretty sound of music as she flies.
    --MOTHERNATU--4
  I wake up to the sound of music --LETITBE/45--24
  I wake up to the sound of music --LETITBE/LP--24

MUST
  I must be sure from the very start --IFIFELL--8
  And now the time has come and so my love I must
    go --ILLFOLLOWT--5
  And now the time has come and so my love I must
    go --ILLFOLLOWT--10
  That a man must break his back to earn his day of
    leisure?--GIRL--24
  Now that I know what I feel must be right --THEWORD
    --23
  If you must return it you can send it here,
    ((paperback))--PAPERBACKW--23
  Dr. Robert, he's a man you must believe --DRROBERT
    --8
  I mean, it must be high or low--STRAWBERRY--17
  With every mistake we must surely be learning --
    WHILEMYGUI--11
  So he waits behind, writing fifty times I must
    not be so oh - oh oh.--MAXWELLSIL--11
  Rose and Valerie screaming from the gallery say
    he must go free --MAXWELLSIL--19
  (Maxwell must go free)--MAXWELLSIL--20

MUSTARD
  MEAN MR. MUSTARD.--MEANMRMUST--Title
  Mean Mr. Mustard sleeps in the park--MEANMRMUST--1

MY
  As I write this letter, send my love to you --
    PSILOVEYOU--1
  Keep all ((all)) my love forever ((ever)).--
    PSILOVEYOU--5
  As I write this letter, send my love to you --
    PSILOVEYOU--10
  Keep all ((all)) my love forever ((ever)) --
    PSILOVEYOU--14

As I write this letter (oh) send my love to you --
    PSILOVEYOU--16
Just look into my eyes --ANYTIMEATA--5
My happiness near makes me cry --ASKMEWHY--8
Last night I said these words to my girl --
    PLEASEPLEA--1
In my heart (in my heart).--PLEASEPLEA--15
In my heart (in my heart).--PLEASEPLEA--15
Last night I said these words to my girl --
    PLEASEPLEA--19
Well my heart went boom when I crossed that room
    --ISAWHERSTA--11
Well my heart went boom when I crossed that room
    --ISAWHERSTA--18
(Ooo) my misery--MISERY--15
And keep you by my side--FROMMETOYO--12
And keep you by my side--FROMMETOYO--23
So I'm telling you, my friend --ILLGETYOU--13
ALL MY LOVING.--ALLMYLOVIN--Title
And I'll send all my lovin' to you.--ALLMYLOVIN--6
And hope that my dreams will come true --ALLMYLOVIN
    --9
And I'll send all my lovin' to you.--ALLMYLOVIN--12
All my lovin', I will send to you --ALLMYLOVIN--13
All my lovin', darlin', I'll be true.--ALLMYLOVIN
    --14
And I'll send all my lovin' to you.--ALLMYLOVIN--20
All my lovin', I will send to you --ALLMYLOVIN--21
All my lovin', darlin', I'll be true --ALLMYLOVIN
    --22
All my lovin', all my lovin', ooo-ooo --ALLMYLOVIN
    --23
All my lovin', all my lovin', ooo-ooo --ALLMYLOVIN
    --23
All my lovin', I will send to you.--ALLMYLOVIN--24
That she would leave me on my own--DONTBOTHER--10
Here am I sitting all on my own--ITWONTBELO--6
Every night the tears come down from my eye--
    ITWONTBELO--15
When you're by my side, you're the only one --
    LITTLECHIL--16
My crying is through, oh.--NOTASECOND--6
My crying is through, oh.--NOTASECOND--17
That my love--IWANTTOHOL--16
That my love--IWANTTOHOL--29
That boy took my love away--THISBOY--1
Just to love you, but oh my!--THISBOY--8
I'll buy you a diamond ring my friend --CANTBUYMEL
    --3
I'll get you anything my friend --CANTBUYMEL--5
They'd laugh in my face.--YOUCANTDOT--22
I can't help my feelings--YOUCANTDOT--25
I go outta my mind.--YOUCANTDOT--26
They'd laugh in my face.--YOUCANTDOT--41
I can't help my feelings--YOUCANTDOT--44
I go outta my mind.--YOUCANTDOT--45
And it's my mind and there's no time--THERESAPLA
    --3
And things you do go round my head--THERESAPLA--6
In my mind there's no sorrow--THERESAPLA--9
And it's my mind and there's no time--THERESAPLA
    --15
I give her all my love --ANDILOVEHE--1
And if you saw my love --ANDILOVEHE--3
The kiss my lover brings --ANDILOVEHE--8
If I give my heart to you --IFIFELL--7
Oh please, don't hurt my pride like her.--IFIFELL
    --13
If I could get my way --ILLCRYINST--3
I got a chip on my shoulder that's bigger than my
    feet.--ILLCRYINST--6
I got a chip on my shoulder that's bigger than my
    feet.--ILLCRYINST--6
If somebody tries to take my place --IMHAPPYJUS--16
If somebody tries to take my place --IMHAPPYJUS--24
But you left me sitting on my own --TELLMEWHY--6
All I do is hang my head and moan.--TELLMEWHY--8
Holding back these tears in my eyes.--TELLMEWHY--16
Well I beg you on my bended knees --TELLMEWHY--21
If you'll only listen to my pleas --TELLMEWHY--22
You know if you break my heart, I'll go --ILLBEBACK
    --1
Than to break my heart again --ILLBEBACK--10
Than to break my heart again --ILLBEBACK--19
You if you break my heart, I'll go --ILLBEBACK--26
Come on, out my way --WHENIGETHO--4
'cos I'm a - gonna see my baby today --WHENIGETHO
    --5
I'm so glad that she's my little girl --IFEELFINE
    --7
I'm so glad that she's my little girl --IFEELFINE
    --15
My love don't give me presents--SHESAWOMAN--1
My love don't give me presents--SHESAWOMAN--4

My love don't give me presents--SHESAWOMAN--18
My love don't give me presents--SHESAWOMAN--21
My love don't give me presents--SHESAWOMAN--28
My love don't give me presents--SHESAWOMAN--31
Hope you need my love babe --EIGHTDAYSA--3
Always on my mind --EIGHTDAYSA--10
Hope you need my love babe --EIGHTDAYSA--21
Always on my mind --EIGHTDAYSA--30
I would hate my disappointment to show --IDONTWANTT
    --2
I would hate my disappointment to show --IDONTWANTT
    --14
And now the time has come and so my love I must
    go --ILLFOLLOWT--5
And now the time has come and so my love I must
    go --ILLFOLLOWT--10
She was a girl in a million, my friend --IMALOSER
    --5
My tears are falling like rain from the sky --
    IMALOSER--11
With another man in my place.--NOREPLY--16
With another man in my place.--NOREPLY--29
My baby don't care--TICKETTORI--44
My baby don't care--TICKETTORI--45
My baby don't care--TICKETTORI--46
My baby don't care--TICKETTORI--47
My baby don't care--TICKETTORI--48
My...--TICKETTORI--49
For red is the colour that my baby wore--YESITIS
    --3
I could be happy with you by my side--YESITIS--10
But it's my pride--YESITIS--12
I could be happy with you by my side--YESITIS--19
But it's my pride--YESITIS--21
Now I find ((and now I find)) I've changed
    my mind--HELP--13
Help me get my feet back on the ground--HELP--17
And now ((now)) my life has changed ((my life
    has changed))--HELP--19
And now ((now)) my life has changed ((my life
    has changed))--HELP--19
My independence ((my independence)) seems to
    vanish in the haze--HELP--21
My independence ((my independence)) seems to
    vanish in the haze--HELP--21
Help me get my feet back on the ground--HELP--27
Now I find ((and now I find)) I've changed
    my mind--HELP--33
Help me get my feet back on the ground--HELP--37
Through thick and thin she will always be my
    friend.--ANOTHERGIR--11
Through thick and thin she will always be my
    friend.--ANOTHERGIR--17
You don't want my loving any more--INEEDYOU--12
You don't want my loving any more--INEEDYOU--22
I get high when I see you go by, my oh my--
    ITSONLYLOV--1
I get high when I see you go by, my oh my--
    ITSONLYLOV--1
When you sigh my my inside just flies, butterfly.
    --ITSONLYLOV--2
When you sigh my my inside just flies, butterfly.
    --ITSONLYLOV--2
All my troubles seemed so far away--YESTERDAY--2
If you don't treat her right my friend--YOUREGONNA
    --9
Turn my face to the wall.--YOUVEGOTTO--2
Try to see it my way --WECANWORKI--1
For fussing and fighting my friend.--WECANWORKI--12
Try to see it my way --WECANWORKI--15
For fussing and fighting my friend.--WECANWORKI--21
Try to see it my way --WECANWORKI--24
DRIVE MY CAR.--DRIVEMYCAR--Title
Baby you can drive my car --DRIVEMYCAR--5
Baby you can drive my car --DRIVEMYCAR--7
I told that girl that my prospects were good --
    DRIVEMYCAR--9
Baby you can drive my car --DRIVEMYCAR--13
Baby you can drive my car --DRIVEMYCAR--15
Baby you can drive my car --DRIVEMYCAR--18
Baby you can drive my car --DRIVEMYCAR--20
I got no car and it's breaking my heart --
    DRIVEMYCAR--24
Baby you can drive my car --DRIVEMYCAR--26
Baby you can drive my car --DRIVEMYCAR--28
Is there anybody going to listen to my story--GIRL
    --1
Then I guess I'd be with you my friend --IFINEEDEDS
    --5
Carve your number on my wall --IFINEEDEDS--10
Then I guess I'd be with you my friend,--IFINEEDEDS
    --15
Carve your number on my wall --IFINEEDEDS--20
IN MY LIFE.--INMYLIFE--Title

All my life, though some have changed.--INMYLIFE
--2
In my life I've loved them all.--INMYLIFE--8
In my life I love you more.--INMYLIFE--16
In my life I love you more.--INMYLIFE--20
In my life I love you more.--INMYLIFE--21
These are words that go together well, my
Michelle.--MICHELLE--2
My Michelle.--MICHELLE--23
Biding my time--NORWEGIANW--12
And I can't spend my whole life trying--RUNFORYOUR
--11
But when I saw him with you I could feel my
future fold.--WHATGOESON--7
Did you mean to break my heart and watch me die?--
WHATGOESON--24
And I will lose my mind--YOUWONTSEE--4
But I can't get through, my hands are tied.--
YOUWONTSEE--8
Dear Sir or Madam, will you read my book?--
PAPERBACKW--2
Look in my direction --ANDYOURBIR--8
Ring my friend I said you'd call, Dr. Robert --
DRROBERT--1
My friend works for the National Health, Dr.
Robert --DRROBERT--13
Ring my friend I said you'd call, Dr. Robert --
DRROBERT--20
Ring my friend I said you'd call, Dr. Robert --
DRROBERT--21
Lift my head, I'm still yawning.--IMONLYSLEE--2
Please don't spoil my day, I'm miles away --
IMONLYSLEE--11
Keeping an eye on the world going by my window --
IMONLYSLEE--13
Taking my time.--IMONLYSLEE--14
Please don't spoil my day, I'm miles away --
IMONLYSLEE--17
Keeping an eye on the world going by my window --
IMONLYSLEE--19
Taking my time.--IMONLYSLEE--20
Lift my head, I'm still yawning.--IMONLYSLEE--22
Burns my feet as they touch the ground.--GOODDAYSUN
--8
GOT TO GET YOU INTO MY LIFE.--GOTTOGETYO--Title
Every single day of my life?--GOTTOGETYO--7
Got to get you into my life.--GOTTOGETYO--15
Every single day of my life?--GOTTOGETYO--22
Got to get you into my life.--GOTTOGETYO--23
I got to get you into my life.--GOTTOGETYO--24
To lead a better life, I need my love to be here.
--HERETHEREA--1
Changing my life with a wave of her hand--
HERETHEREA--3
There, running my hands through her hair--
HERETHEREA--5
My head is filled with things to say --IWANTTOTEL
--2
It's only me, it's not my mind--IWANTTOTEL--10
Then I could speak my mind and tell you--IWANTTOTEL
--17
Now my advice for those who die (Taxman)--TAXMAN
--22
Penny Lane is in my ears and in my eyes--PENNYLANE
--9
Penny Lane is in my ears and in my eyes--PENNYLANE
--9
Penny Lane is in my ears and in my eyes--PENNYLANE
--17
Penny Lane is in my ears and in my eyes--PENNYLANE
--17
Penny Lane is in my ears and in my eyes--PENNYLANE
--28
Penny Lane is in my ears and in my eyes--PENNYLANE
--28
Penny Lane is in my ears and in my eyes--PENNYLANE
--31
Penny Lane is in my ears and in my eyes--PENNYLANE
--31
No-one, I think, is in my tree--STRAWBERRY--16
Dragged a comb across my head--DAYINTHELI--19
Found my way downstairs and drank a cup--DAYINTHELI
--20
Found my coat and grabbed my hat--DAYINTHELI--23
Found my coat and grabbed my hat--DAYINTHELI--23
Found my way upstairs and had a smoke--DAYINTHELI
--25
And stops my mind from wandering--FIXINGAHOL--2
And kept my mind from wandering--FIXINGAHOL--5
And wonder why they don't get in my door.--
FIXINGAHOL--10
And when my mind is wandering--FIXINGAHOL--12
And never ask me why they don't get past my door.
--FIXINGAHOL--18

Stops my mind from wandering--FIXINGAHOL--24
Stops my mind from wandering--FIXINGAHOL--27
I used to get mad at my school (now I can't
complain)--GETTINGBET--3
I used to be cruel to my woman--GETTINGBET--25
Man I was mean but I'm changing my scene--
GETTINGBET--27
When I get older losing my hair--WHENIMSIXT--1
WITH A LITTLE HELP FROM MY FRIENDS.--WITHALITTL
--Title
Oh I get by with a little help from my friends --
WITHALITTL--5
Mmm I get high with a little help from my friends
--WITHALITTL--6
Mmm gonna try with a little help from my friends.
--WITHALITTL--7
What do I do when my love is away?--WITHALITTL--8
No I get by with a little help from my friends --
WITHALITTL--12
Mmm get high with a little help from my friends --
WITHALITTL--13
Mmm gonna try with a little help from my friends.
--WITHALITTL--14
Oh I get by with a little help from my friends --
WITHALITTL--23
Mmm get high with a little help from my friends --
WITHALITTL--24
Oh I'm gonna try with a little help from my
friends.--WITHALITTL--25
Oh I get by with a little help from my friends --
WITHALITTL--30
Mmm gonna try with a little help from my friends
--WITHALITTL--31
Oh I get high with a little help from my friends
--WITHALITTL--32
Yes I get by with a little help from my friends --
WITHALITTL--33
With a little help from my friends.--WITHALITTL--34
And my friends have lost their way.--BLUEJAYWAY--2
Now it's past my bed I know (know) --BLUEJAYWAY--15
Without going out of my door --INNERLIGHT--1
Without looking out of my window --INNERLIGHT--3
On the way the paper bag was on my knee --
BACKINTHEU--3
Leave it till tomorrow to unpack my case --
BACKINTHEU--10
That Georgia's always on my my my my my my my my
my mind.--BACKINTHEU--18
That Georgia's always on my my my my my my my my
my mind.--BACKINTHEU--18
That Georgia's always on my my my my my my my my
my mind.--BACKINTHEU--18
That Georgia's always on my my my my my my my my
my mind.--BACKINTHEU--18
That Georgia's always on my my my my my my my my
my mind.--BACKINTHEU--18
That Georgia's always on my my my my my my my my
my mind.--BACKINTHEU--18
That Georgia's always on my my my my my my my my
my mind.--BACKINTHEU--18
That Georgia's always on my my my my my my my my
my mind.--BACKINTHEU--18
That Georgia's always on my my my my my my my my
my mind.--BACKINTHEU--18
That Georgia's always on my my my my my my my my
my mind.--BACKINTHEU--30
That Georgia's always on my my my my my my my my
my mind.--BACKINTHEU--30
That Georgia's always on my my my my my my my my
my mind.--BACKINTHEU--30
That Georgia's always on my my my my my my my my
my mind.--BACKINTHEU--30
That Georgia's always on my my my my my my my my
my mind.--BACKINTHEU--30
That Georgia's always on my my my my my my my my
my mind.--BACKINTHEU--30
That Georgia's always on my my my my my my my my
my mind.--BACKINTHEU--30
That Georgia's always on my my my my my my my my
my mind.--BACKINTHEU--30
Well, it's my birthday too - yeah.--BIRTHDAY--2
Well, it's my birthday too - yeah.--BIRTHDAY--21
On my old front door --DONTPASSME--7
EVERYBODY'S GOT SOMETHING TO HIDE EXCEPT ME
AND MY MONKEY.--EVRBDYMONK--Title
Everybody's got something to hide 'cept for me
and my monkey - wuh.--EVRBDYMONK--7
Everybody's got something to hide 'cept for me
and my monkey (yeah - wuh).--EVRBDYMONK--16
Everybody's got something to hide 'cept for me
and my monkey - hey.--EVRBDYMONK--25
When I hold you in my arms ((oh, yeah)) --

HAPPINESSI--22
And I feel my finger on your trigger ((oh, yeah)) --HAPPINESSI--23
Coming down fast (oh I hear my baby speaking - ooo)...--HELTERSKEL--30
I got blisters on my fingers!--HELTERSKEL--32
Oh, Honey Pie my position is tragic--HONEYPIE--10
Love you with all my heart --IWILL--10
I'm so tired, my mind is on the blink --IMSOTIRED --2
I'm so tired, my mind is set on you --IMSOTIRED--6
You know I can't sleep, I can't stop my brain -- IMSOTIRED--11
You know I can't sleep, I can't stop my brain -- IMSOTIRED--20
When I cannot sing my heart --JULIA--11
I can only speak my mind, Julia.--JULIA--12
MARTHA MY DEAR.--MARTHAMYDE--Title
Martha my dear, though I spend my days in conversation --MARTHAMYDE--1
Martha my dear, though I spend my days in conversation --MARTHAMYDE--1
Please - remember me, Martha my love --MARTHAMYDE --2
Don't forget me, Martha my dear.--MARTHAMYDE--3
Martha my dear, you have always been my inspiration --MARTHAMYDE--13
Martha my dear, you have always been my inspiration --MARTHAMYDE--13
Please - be good to me, Martha my love --MARTHAMYDE --14
Don't forget me, Martha my dear.--MARTHAMYDE--15
Find me in my field of grass - Mother Nature's son --MOTHERNATU--8
WHILE MY GUITAR GENTLY WEEPS.--WHILEMYGUI--Title
While my guitar gently weeps.--WHILEMYGUI--3
Still my guitar gently weeps.--WHILEMYGUI--5
While my guitar gently weeps.--WHILEMYGUI--10
Still my guitar gently weeps.--WHILEMYGUI--12
While my guitar gently weeps.--WHILEMYGUI--19
Still my guitar gently weeps ((eee)).--WHILEMYGUI--21
My mother was of the sky --YERBLUES--10
My father was of the earth --YERBLUES--11
The eagle picks my eye --YERBLUES--17
The worm he licks my bone --YERBLUES--18
Black cloud crossed my mind --YERBLUES--24
Blue mist round my soul --YERBLUES--25
Even hate my rock 'n' roll.--YERBLUES--27
Can I bring my friend to tea?--ALLTOGETHE--6
Can I take my friend to bed?--ALLTOGETHE--18
Or how I fare or if my hair is brown --ONLYANORTH --11
My love is something you can't reject.--OLDBROWNSH --23
Because the wind is high it blows my mind --BECAUSE --5
I never give you my pillow--CARRYTHATW--5
I only send you my invitations--CARRYTHATW--6
Are you gonna be in my dreams tonight?--THEEND--2
I'd ask my friends to come and see--OCTOPUSSGA--5
You're asking me will my love grow?--SOMETHING--11
I never give you my number --YOUNEVERGI--4
I only give you my situation --YOUNEVERGI--5
And in my hour of darkness--LETITBE/45--4
YOU KNOW MY NAME (LOOK UP MY NUMBER).--YOUKNOWMYN --Title
YOU KNOW MY NAME (LOOK UP MY NUMBER).--YOUKNOWMYN --Title
You know my name, look up de number --YOUKNOWMYN --1
You know my name, look up de number.--YOUKNOWMYN --2
You, you know, you know my name --YOUKNOWMYN--3
You, you know, you know my name.--YOUKNOWMYN--4
Good evening, you know my name, well then look up my number --YOUKNOWMYN--9
Good evening, you know my name, well then look up my number --YOUKNOWMYN--9
You know my name, that's right, look up my number (hey) --YOUKNOWMYN--10
You know my name, that's right, look up my number (hey) --YOUKNOWMYN--10
You, you know, you know my name ((you know my name)) --YOUKNOWMYN--11
You, you know, you know my name ((you know my name)) --YOUKNOWMYN--11
You, you know, you know my name (brrrrrr - ha, hey!) --YOUKNOWMYN--12
You know my name, ba ba ba ba ba ba ba ba ((yahoo)) --YOUKNOWMYN--13
You know my name - haa, that's right, look up the number --YOUKNOWMYN--15
(Oh) oh, you know, you know, you know my name (come on Dennis) --YOUKNOWMYN--16

You know, you know, you know my name, ha ha ha ha --YOUKNOWMYN--17
You know my name, ba ba ba bum, look up the number --YOUKNOWMYN--18
You know my name, look up the number --YOUKNOWMYN --19
You, you know, you know my name, baby --YOUKNOWMYN --20
You know my name, you know my name --YOUKNOWMYN--21
You know, you know my name --YOUKNOWMYN--22
You know, you know my name ((oh, let's hear it, come on Dennis)) --YOUKNOWMYN--23
My name, you know, you know, ((look up the number))--YOUKNOWMYN--25
You know my name (you know my number).--YOUKNOWMYN --26
You know my name (you know my number).--YOUKNOWMYN --26
You know, ((you know my name))--YOUKNOWMYN--27
You know, you know my name. ((you know my number))--YOUKNOWMYN--28
You know, you know my name. ((you know my number))--YOUKNOWMYN--28
You know my name, look up the number --YOUKNOWMYN --29
You know my name, look up the number.--YOUKNOWMYN --30
You know, you know my name, look up the number.-- YOUKNOWMYN--31
Yes, you know, ((you know my name))--YOUKNOWMYN--32
You know my name ((you know)), you know me number (too/two)--YOUKNOWMYN--33
You know my name, you know me number three -- YOUKNOWMYN--34
You know my name, you know me number four -- YOUKNOWMYN--35
You know my name, look up the number --YOUKNOWMYN --36
You know my name ((you know)), you know me number (too/two) --YOUKNOWMYN--37
(look up my name)--YOUKNOWMYN--38
You know my name ((you know my name)) --YOUKNOWMYN --39
You know my name ((you know my name)) --YOUKNOWMYN --39
You know my number, what's up with you? - ha-- YOUKNOWMYN--40
You know my name.--YOUKNWOMYN--41
Are drifting through my opened mind--ACROSSTHEU --4
Nothing's gonna change my world --ACROSSTHEU--7
Nothing's gonna change my world --ACROSSTHEU--8
Nothing's gonna change my world --ACROSSTHEU--9
Nothing's gonna change my world.--ACROSSTHEU--10
Nothing's gonna change my world --ACROSSTHEU--16
Nothing's gonna change my world --ACROSSTHEU--17
Nothing's gonna change my world --ACROSSTHEU--18
Nothing's gonna change my world.--ACROSSTHEU--19
Are ringing through my opened ears--ACROSSTHEU --21
Nothing's gonna change my world --ACROSSTHEU--26
Nothing's gonna change my world --ACROSSTHEU--27
Nothing's gonna change my world --ACROSSTHEU--28
Nothing's gonna change my world.--ACROSSTHEU--29
Ooo I've got a feeling that keeps me on my toes -- IVEGOTAFEE--14
Oh my soul.--IVEGOTAFEE--39
And in my hour of darkness--LETITBE/LP--4
My baby said she's travelling on the one after nine-0-nine --ONEAFTERNI--1
I begged her not to go and I begged her on my bended knee, (oh yeah)--ONEAFTERNI--6
Pick up my bag, run to the station --ONEAFTERNI--11
Pick up my bag, run right home --ONEAFTERNI--13
Pick up my bag, run to the station --ONEAFTERNI--21
Well - pick up my bag, run right home (run right home) --ONEAFTERNI--23
Writing letters on my wall.--TWOOFUS--11

MYSELF
I'd get myself locked up today --ILLCRYINST--4
I'm gonna hide myself away-hey--ILLCRYINST--13
I'm gonna hide myself away-hey--ILLCRYINST--22
Is it for her or myself that I cry?--IMALOSER--12
But I'm by myself.--DONTPASSME--13
And why I'm by myself --DONTPASSME--15
I wonder should I get up and fix myself a drink -- IMSOTIRED--3
And got myself a steady job--SHECAMEINT--17
When I find myself in times of trouble --LETITBE/45 --1
When I find myself in times of trouble --LETITBE/LP --1

MYSTERY
    MAGICAL MYSTERY TOUR.--MAGICALMYS--Title
    Roll up, roll up for the Mystery Tour --MAGICALMYS
      --1
    Roll up, roll up for the Mystery Tour --MAGICALMYS
      --3
    Roll up, roll up for the Mystery Tour.--MAGICALMYS
      --4
    Roll up for the Mystery Tour --MAGICALMYS--6
    Roll up for the Mystery Tour.--MAGICALMYS--8
    The Magical Mystery Tour is waiting to take
      you away--MAGICALMYS--9
    Roll up, roll up for the Mystery Tour --MAGICALMYS
      --11
    Roll up, roll up for the Mystery Tour.--MAGICALMYS
      --12
    Roll up for the Mystery Tour --MAGICALMYS--14
    Roll up for the Mystery Tour.--MAGICALMYS--16
    The Magical Mystery Tour is hoping to take you
      away --MAGICALMYS--17
    The mystery trip.--MAGICALMYS--19
    The Magical Mystery Tour.--MAGICALMYS--21
    Roll up, roll up for the Mystery Tour--MAGICALMYS
      --22
    Roll up for the Mystery Tour--MAGICALMYS--24
    Roll up for the Mystery Tour.--MAGICALMYS--26
    The Magical Mystery Tour is coming to take you
      away --MAGICALMYS--27
    The Magical Mystery Tour is dying to take you
      away--MAGICALMYS--29

N
    La da da, da n da.--IVEJUSTSEE--11
    La da da, da n da.--IVEJUSTSEE--18

NAH
    Nah, nah, nah.--RUNFORYOUR--33
    Nah, nah, nah.--RUNFORYOUR--33
    Nah, nah, nah.--RUNFORYOUR--33
    Nah, nah, nah.--RUNFORYOUR--34
    Nah, nah, nah.--RUNFORYOUR--34
    Nah, nah, nah.--RUNFORYOUR--34
    Nah, nah, nah.--RUNFORYOUR--35
    Nah, nah, nah.--RUNFORYOUR--35
    Nah, nah, nah.--RUNFORYOUR--35
    Nah, nah, nah.--RUNFORYOUR--36
    Nah, nah, nah.--RUNFORYOUR--36
    Nah, nah, nah.--RUNFORYOUR--36
    Nah, nah, nah.--RUNFORYOUR--37
    Nah, nah, nah.--RUNFORYOUR--37
    Nah, nah, nah.--RUNFORYOUR--37
    Nah nah nah nah nah, nah nah nah nah.--HEYJUDE--14
    Nah nah nah nah nah, nah nah nah nah.--HEYJUDE--14
    Nah nah nah nah nah, nah nah nah nah.--HEYJUDE--14
    Nah nah nah nah nah, nah nah nah nah.--HEYJUDE--14
    Nah nah nah nah nah, nah nah nah nah.--HEYJUDE--14
    Nah nah nah nah nah, nah nah nah nah.--HEYJUDE--14
    Nah nah nah nah nah, nah nah nah nah.--HEYJUDE--14
    Nah nah nah nah nah, nah nah nah nah.--HEYJUDE--14
    Nah nah nah nah nah, nah nah nah nah.--HEYJUDE--14
    Nah nah nah nah nah, nah nah nah nah, yeah.--
      HEYJUDE--25
    Nah nah nah nah nah, nah nah nah nah, yeah.--
      HEYJUDE--25
    Nah nah nah nah nah, nah nah nah nah, yeah.--
      HEYJUDE--25
    Nah nah nah nah nah, nah nah nah nah, yeah.--
      HEYJUDE--25
    Nah nah nah nah nah, nah nah nah nah, yeah.--
      HEYJUDE--25
    Nah nah nah nah nah, nah nah nah nah, yeah.--
      HEYJUDE--25
    Nah nah nah nah nah, nah nah nah nah, yeah.--
      HEYJUDE--25
    Nah nah nah nah nah, nah nah nah nah, yeah.--
      HEYJUDE--25
    Oh yeah - nah nah nah, nah - nah - nah - nah--
      HEYJUDE--31
    Oh yeah - nah nah nah, nah - nah - nah - nah--
      HEYJUDE--31
    Oh yeah - nah nah nah, nah - nah - nah - nah--
      HEYJUDE--31
    Oh yeah - nah nah nah, nah - nah - nah - nah--
      HEYJUDE--31
    Oh yeah - nah nah nah, nah - nah - nah - nah--
      HEYJUDE--31
    Oh yeah - nah nah nah, nah - nah - nah - nah--
      HEYJUDE--31
    Oh yeah - nah nah nah, nah - nah - nah - nah--
      HEYJUDE--31

(Take it Jude) nah - nah - nah - nah, hey
    Jude.--HEYJUDE--33
(Take it Jude) nah - nah - nah - nah, hey
    Jude.--HEYJUDE--33
(Take it Jude) nah - nah - nah - nah, hey
    Jude.--HEYJUDE--33
(Take it Jude) nah - nah - nah - nah, hey
    Jude.--HEYJUDE--33
Nah nah nah, nah - nah - nah - nah --HEYJUDE--34
Nah nah nah, nah - nah - nah - nah --HEYJUDE--34
Nah nah nah, nah - nah - nah - nah --HEYJUDE--34
Nah nah nah, nah - nah - nah - nah --HEYJUDE--34
Nah nah nah, nah - nah - nah - nah --HEYJUDE--34
Nah nah nah, nah - nah - nah - nah --HEYJUDE--34
Nah nah nah, nah - nah - nah - nah --HEYJUDE--34
Nah - nah - nah - nah, hey Jude.--HEYJUDE--35
Nah - nah - nah - nah, hey Jude.--HEYJUDE--35
Nah - nah - nah - nah, hey Jude.--HEYJUDE--35
Nah - nah - nah - nah, hey Jude.--HEYJUDE--35
Nah nah nah, nah - nah - nah - nah (ow) --HEYJUDE
    --36
Nah nah nah, nah - nah - nah - nah (ow) --HEYJUDE
    --36
Nah nah nah, nah - nah - nah - nah (ow) --HEYJUDE
    --36
Nah nah nah, nah - nah - nah - nah (ow) --HEYJUDE
    --36
Nah nah nah, nah - nah - nah - nah (ow) --HEYJUDE
    --36
Nah nah nah, nah - nah - nah - nah (ow) --HEYJUDE
    --36
Nah nah nah, nah - nah - nah - nah (ow) --HEYJUDE
    --36
Nah - nah - nah - nah, hey Jude.--HEYJUDE--37
Nah - nah - nah - nah, hey Jude.--HEYJUDE--37
Nah - nah - nah - nah, hey Jude.--HEYJUDE--37
Nah - nah - nah - nah, hey Jude.--HEYJUDE--37
Nah nah nah, nah - nah - nah - nah (take it
    Jude) --HEYJUDE--38
Nah nah nah, nah - nah - nah - nah (take it
    Jude) --HEYJUDE--38
Nah nah nah, nah - nah - nah - nah (take it
    Jude) --HEYJUDE--38
Nah nah nah, nah - nah - nah - nah (take it
    Jude) --HEYJUDE--38
Nah nah nah, nah - nah - nah - nah (take it
    Jude) --HEYJUDE--38
Nah - nah - nah - nah, hey Jude--HEYJUDE--39
Nah - nah - nah - nah, hey Jude--HEYJUDE--39
Nah - nah - nah - nah, hey Jude--HEYJUDE--39
Nah - nah - nah - nah, hey Jude--HEYJUDE--39
(Ow - ow) nah nah nah, nah - nah - nah - nah --
    HEYJUDE--41
(Ow - ow) nah nah nah, nah - nah - nah - nah --
    HEYJUDE--41
(Ow - ow) nah nah nah, nah - nah - nah - nah --
    HEYJUDE--41
(Ow - ow) nah nah nah, nah - nah - nah - nah --
    HEYJUDE--41
(Ow - ow) nah nah nah, nah - nah - nah - nah --
    HEYJUDE--41
(Ow - ow) nah nah nah, nah - nah - nah - nah --
    HEYJUDE--41
(Ow - ow) nah nah nah, nah - nah - nah - nah --
    HEYJUDE--41
(Ow - ooo nah nah nah) nah - nah - nah - nah,
    hey Jude--HEYJUDE--42
(Ow - ooo nah nah nah) nah - nah - nah - nah,
    hey Jude--HEYJUDE--42
(Ow - ooo nah nah nah) nah - nah - nah - nah,
    hey Jude--HEYJUDE--42
(Ow - ooo nah nah nah) nah - nah - nah - nah,
    hey Jude--HEYJUDE--42
(Ow - ooo nah nah nah) nah - nah - nah - nah,
    hey Jude--HEYJUDE--42
(Ow - ooo nah nah nah) nah - nah - nah - nah,
    hey Jude--HEYJUDE--42
(Ow - ooo nah nah nah) nah - nah - nah - nah,
    hey Jude--HEYJUDE--42
Nah nah nah, nah - nah - nah - nah (yeah, yeah,
    yeah) --HEYJUDE--44
Nah nah nah, nah - nah - nah - nah (yeah, yeah,
    yeah) --HEYJUDE--44
Nah nah nah, nah - nah - nah - nah (yeah, yeah,
    yeah) --HEYJUDE--44
Nah nah nah, nah - nah - nah - nah (yeah, yeah,
    yeah) --HEYJUDE--44
Nah nah nah, nah - nah - nah - nah (yeah, yeah,
    yeah) --HEYJUDE--44
Nah nah nah, nah - nah - nah - nah (yeah, yeah,

```
             yeah) --HEYJUDE--44
Nah nah nah, nah - nah - nah - nah (yeah, yeah,
   yeah) --HEYJUDE--44
Nah - nah - nah - nah, hey Jude.--HEYJUDE--45
Nah - nah - nah - nah, hey Jude.--HEYJUDE--45
Nah - nah - nah - nah, hey Jude.--HEYJUDE--45
Nah - nah - nah - nah, hey Jude.--HEYJUDE--45
Nah nah nah, nah - nah - nah - nah ((don't make
   it bad, Jude)) --HEYJUDE--47
Nah nah nah, nah - nah - nah - nah ((don't make
   it bad, Jude)) --HEYJUDE--47
Nah nah nah, nah - nah - nah - nah ((don't make
   it bad, Jude)) --HEYJUDE--47
Nah nah nah, nah - nah - nah - nah ((don't make
   it bad, Jude)) --HEYJUDE--47
Nah nah nah, nah - nah - nah - nah ((don't make
   it bad, Jude)) --HEYJUDE--47
Nah nah nah, nah - nah - nah - nah ((don't make
   it bad, Jude)) --HEYJUDE--47
Nah - nah - nah - nah, hey Jude (Jude, hey
   Jude, wah!).--HEYJUDE--49
Nah - nah - nah - nah, hey Jude (Jude, hey
   Jude, wah!).--HEYJUDE--49
Nah - nah - nah - nah, hey Jude (Jude, hey
   Jude, wah!).--HEYJUDE--49
Nah - nah - nah - nah, hey Jude (Jude, hey
   Jude, wah!).--HEYJUDE--49
Nah nah nah, nah - nah - nah - nah (oh Jude) --
   HEYJUDE--50
Nah nah nah, nah - nah - nah - nah (oh Jude) --
   HEYJUDE--50
Nah nah nah, nah - nah - nah - nah (oh Jude) --
   HEYJUDE--50
Nah nah nah, nah - nah - nah - nah (oh Jude) --
   HEYJUDE--50
Nah nah nah, nah - nah - nah - nah (oh Jude) --
   HEYJUDE--50
Nah nah nah, nah - nah - nah - nah (oh Jude) --
   HEYJUDE--50
Nah - nah - nah - nah, hey Jude (hey hey hey
   hey hey hey hey).--HEYJUDE--51
Nah - nah - nah - nah, hey Jude (hey hey hey
   hey hey hey hey).--HEYJUDE--51
Nah - nah - nah - nah, hey Jude (hey hey hey
   hey hey hey hey).--HEYJUDE--51
Nah - nah - nah - nah, hey Jude (hey hey hey
   hey hey hey hey).--HEYJUDE--51
Nah nah nah, nah - nah - nah - nah (hey hey hey
   hey) --HEYJUDE--52
Nah nah nah, nah - nah - nah - nah (hey hey hey
   hey) --HEYJUDE--52
Nah nah nah, nah - nah - nah - nah (hey hey hey
   hey) --HEYJUDE--52
Nah nah nah, nah - nah - nah - nah (hey hey hey
   hey) --HEYJUDE--52
Nah nah nah, nah - nah - nah - nah (hey hey hey
   hey) --HEYJUDE--52
Nah nah nah, nah - nah - nah - nah (hey hey hey
   hey) --HEYJUDE--52
Nah - nah - nah - nah, hey Jude.--HEYJUDE--53
Nah - nah - nah - nah, hey Jude.--HEYJUDE--53
Nah - nah - nah - nah, hey Jude.--HEYJUDE--53
Nah - nah - nah - nah, hey Jude.--HEYJUDE--53
Nah nah nah, nah - nah - nah - nah --HEYJUDE--55
Nah nah nah, nah - nah - nah - nah --HEYJUDE--55
Nah nah nah, nah - nah - nah - nah --HEYJUDE--55
Nah nah nah, nah - nah - nah - nah --HEYJUDE--55
Nah nah nah, nah - nah - nah - nah --HEYJUDE--55
Nah nah nah, nah - nah - nah - nah --HEYJUDE--55
Nah - nah - nah - nah, hey Jude.--HEYJUDE--56
Nah - nah - nah - nah, hey Jude.--HEYJUDE--56
Nah - nah - nah - nah, hey Jude.--HEYJUDE--56
Nah - nah - nah - nah, hey Jude.--HEYJUDE--56
Nah nah nah, nah - nah - nah - nah --HEYJUDE--57
Nah nah nah, nah - nah - nah - nah --HEYJUDE--57
Nah nah nah, nah - nah - nah - nah --HEYJUDE--57
Nah nah nah, nah - nah - nah - nah --HEYJUDE--57
Nah nah nah, nah - nah - nah - nah --HEYJUDE--57
Nah nah nah, nah - nah - nah - nah --HEYJUDE--57
Nah - nah - nah - nah, hey Jude.--HEYJUDE--58
Nah - nah - nah - nah, hey Jude.--HEYJUDE--58
Nah - nah - nah - nah, hey Jude.--HEYJUDE--58
Nah - nah - nah - nah, hey Jude.--HEYJUDE--58
(Nah nah nah nah nah nah nah nah...)--HEYJUDE--59
(Nah nah nah nah nah nah nah nah...)--HEYJUDE--59
(Nah nah nah nah nah nah nah nah...)--HEYJUDE--59
```

```
(Nah nah nah nah nah nah nah nah...)--HEYJUDE--59
(Nah nah nah nah nah nah nah nah...)--HEYJUDE--59
(Nah nah nah nah nah nah nah nah...)--HEYJUDE--59
(Nah nah nah nah nah nah nah nah...)--HEYJUDE--59
(Nah nah nah nah nah nah nah nah...)--HEYJUDE--59
Nah nah nah, nah - nah - nah - nah --HEYJUDE--60
Nah nah nah, nah - nah - nah - nah --HEYJUDE--60
Nah nah nah, nah - nah - nah - nah --HEYJUDE--60
Nah nah nah, nah - nah - nah - nah --HEYJUDE--60
Nah nah nah, nah - nah - nah - nah --HEYJUDE--60
Nah nah nah, nah - nah - nah - nah --HEYJUDE--60
Nah nah nah, nah - nah - nah - nah --HEYJUDE--60
Nah - nah - nah - nah, hey Jude (yeah).--HEYJUDE
   --61
Nah - nah - nah - nah, hey Jude (yeah).--HEYJUDE
   --61
Nah - nah - nah - nah, hey Jude (yeah).--HEYJUDE
   --61
Nah - nah - nah - nah, hey Jude (yeah).--HEYJUDE
   --61
Nah nah nah, nah - nah - nah - nah --HEYJUDE--62
Nah nah nah, nah - nah - nah - nah --HEYJUDE--62
Nah nah nah, nah - nah - nah - nah --HEYJUDE--62
Nah nah nah, nah - nah - nah - nah --HEYJUDE--62
Nah nah nah, nah - nah - nah - nah --HEYJUDE--62
Nah nah nah, nah - nah - nah - nah --HEYJUDE--62
Nah - nah - nah - nah, hey Jude.--HEYJUDE--63
Nah - nah - nah - nah, hey Jude.--HEYJUDE--63
Nah - nah - nah - nah, hey Jude.--HEYJUDE--63
Nah - nah - nah - nah, hey Jude.--HEYJUDE--63
Nah nah nah, nah - nah - nah - nah ((hey hey
   hey hey)) --HEYJUDE--64
Nah nah nah, nah - nah - nah - nah ((hey hey
   hey hey)) --HEYJUDE--64
Nah nah nah, nah - nah - nah - nah ((hey hey
   hey hey)) --HEYJUDE--64
Nah nah nah, nah - nah - nah - nah ((hey hey
   hey hey)) --HEYJUDE--64
Nah nah nah, nah - nah - nah - nah ((hey hey
   hey hey)) --HEYJUDE--64
Nah nah nah, nah - nah - nah - nah ((hey hey
   hey hey)) --HEYJUDE--64
(Take it Jude) nah - nah - nah - nah, hey
   Jude.--HEYJUDE--65
(Take it Jude) nah - nah - nah - nah, hey
   Jude.--HEYJUDE--65
(Take it Jude) nah - nah - nah - nah, hey
   Jude.--HEYJUDE--65
(Take it Jude) nah - nah - nah - nah, hey
   Jude.--HEYJUDE--65
Nah nah nah, nah - nah - nah - nah --HEYJUDE--68
Nah nah nah, nah - nah - nah - nah --HEYJUDE--68
Nah nah nah, nah - nah - nah - nah --HEYJUDE--68
Nah nah nah, nah - nah - nah - nah --HEYJUDE--68
Nah nah nah, nah - nah - nah - nah --HEYJUDE--68
Nah nah nah, nah - nah - nah - nah --HEYJUDE--68
Nah nah nah, nah - nah - nah - nah --HEYJUDE--68
Nah - nah - nah - nah, hey Jude (Jude, Jude
   ma ma ma ma ma ma)--HEYJUDE--69
Nah - nah - nah - nah, hey Jude (Jude, Jude
   ma ma ma ma ma ma)--HEYJUDE--69
Nah - nah - nah - nah, hey Jude (Jude, Jude
   ma ma ma ma ma ma)--HEYJUDE--69
Nah - nah - nah - nah, hey Jude (Jude, Jude
   ma ma ma ma ma ma)--HEYJUDE--69
Nah nah nah, nah - nah - nah - nah (oh) --HEYJUDE
   --70
Nah nah nah, nah - nah - nah - nah (oh) --HEYJUDE
   --70
Nah nah nah, nah - nah - nah - nah (oh) --HEYJUDE
   --70
Nah nah nah, nah - nah - nah - nah (oh) --HEYJUDE
   --70
Nah nah nah, nah - nah - nah - nah (oh) --HEYJUDE
   --70
Nah nah nah, nah - nah - nah - nah (oh) --HEYJUDE
   --70
Nah - nah - nah - nah, hey Jude (ooo).--HEYJUDE--71
Nah - nah - nah - nah, hey Jude (ooo).--HEYJUDE--71
Nah - nah - nah - nah, hey Jude (ooo).--HEYJUDE--71
Nah - nah - nah - nah, hey Jude (ooo).--HEYJUDE--71
Nah nah nah, nah - nah - nah - nah (oh) --HEYJUDE
   --72
Nah nah nah, nah - nah - nah - nah (oh) --HEYJUDE
   --72
Nah nah nah, nah - nah - nah - nah (oh) --HEYJUDE
   --72
Nah nah nah, nah - nah - nah - nah (oh) --HEYJUDE
   --72
```

Nah nah nah, nah - nah - nah - nah (oh) --HEYJUDE
--72
Nah nah nah, nah - nah - nah - nah (oh) --HEYJUDE
--72
Nah nah nah, nah - nah - nah - nah (oh) --HEYJUDE
--72
Nah - nah - nah - nah, hey Jude (ooo - ooo).--
HEYJUDE--73
Nah - nah - nah - nah, hey Jude (ooo - ooo).--
HEYJUDE--73
Nah - nah - nah - nah, hey Jude (ooo - ooo).--
HEYJUDE--73
Nah - nah - nah - nah, hey Jude (ooo - ooo).--
HEYJUDE--73
Well then nah nah nah, nah - nah - nah - nah
--HEY JUDE--74
Well then nah nah nah, nah - nah - nah - nah
--HEY JUDE--74
Well then nah nah nah, nah - nah - nah - nah
--HEY JUDE--74
Well then nah nah nah, nah - nah - nah - nah
--HEY JUDE--74
Well then nah nah nah, nah - nah - nah - nah
--HEY JUDE--74
Well then nah nah nah, nah - nah - nah - nah
--HEY JUDE--74
Well then nah nah nah, nah - nah - nah - nah
--HEY JUDE--74
Nah - nah - nah - nah, hey Jude--HEY JUDE
--75
Nah - nah - nah - nah, hey Jude--HEY JUDE
--75
Nah - nah - nah - nah, hey Jude--HEY JUDE
--75
Nah - nah - nah - nah, hey Jude--HEY JUDE
--75
Nah nah nah, nah - nah - nah - nah.--HEYJUDE--76
Nah nah nah, nah - nah - nah - nah.--HEYJUDE--76
Nah nah nah, nah - nah - nah - nah.--HEYJUDE--76
Nah nah nah, nah - nah - nah - nah.--HEYJUDE--76
Nah nah nah, nah - nah - nah - nah.--HEYJUDE--76
Nah nah nah, nah - nah - nah - nah.--HEYJUDE--76
Nah nah nah, nah - nah - nah - nah.--HEYJUDE--76
Yes it did, nah nah nah nah nah nah nah - nah--
YOUNEVERGI--23
Yes it did, nah nah nah nah nah nah nah - nah--
YOUNEVERGI--23
Yes it did, nah nah nah nah nah nah nah - nah--
YOUNEVERGI--23
Yes it did, nah nah nah nah nah nah nah - nah--
YOUNEVERGI--23
Yes it did, nah nah nah nah nah nah nah - nah--
YOUNEVERGI--23
Yes it did, nah nah nah nah nah nah nah - nah--
YOUNEVERGI--23
Yes it did, nah nah nah nah nah nah nah - nah--
YOUNEVERGI--23

NAME

I CALL YOUR NAME.--ICALLYOURN--Title
I call your name, but you're not there --ICALLYOURN
--1
I never weep at night, I call your name.--
ICALLYOURN--10
I never weep at night, I call your name --
ICALLYOURN--17
I call your name, I call your name, (wuh) I
call your name.--ICALLYOURN--18
I call your name, I call your name, (wuh) I
call your name.--ICALLYOURN--18
I call your name, I call your name, (wuh) I
call your name.--ICALLYOURN--18
You didn't even think of me as someone with a name.
--WHATGOESON--23
And was buried along with her name--ELEANORRIG--22
I didn't catch your name --IWILL--6
There lived a young boy name of Rocky Raccoon--
ROCKYRACCO--2
Her name was Magill and she called herself Lil --
ROCKYRACCO--15
YOU KNOW MY NAME (LOOK UP MY NUMBER).--YOUKNOWMYN
--Title
You know my name, look up de number --YOUKNOWMYN
--1
You know my name, look up de number.--YOUKNOWMYN
--2
You, you know, you know my name --YOUKNOWMYN--3
You, you know, you know my name.--YOUKNOWMYN--4
Good evening, you know my name, well then look
up my number --YOUKNOWMYN--9
You know my name, that's right, look up my

number (hey) --YOUKNOWMYN--10
You, you know, you know my name ((you know my
name)) --YOUKNOWMYN--11
You, you know, you know my name ((you know my
name)) --YOUKNOWMYN--11
You, you know, you know my name (brrrrrr - ha,
hey!) --YOUKNOWMYN--12
You know my name, ba ba ba ba ba ba ba ba
((yahoo)) --YOUKNOWMYN--13
You know my name - haa, that's right, look up
the number --YOUKNOWMYN--15
(Oh) oh, you know, you know, you know my
name (come on Dennis) --YOUKNOWMYN--16
You know, you know, you know my name, ha ha ha
ha --YOUKNOWMYN--17
You know my name, ba ba ba bum, look up the
number --YOUKNOWMYN--18
You know my name, look up the number --YOUKNOWMYN
--19
You, you know, you know my name, baby --YOUKNOWMYN
--20
You, you know, you know my name --YOUKNOWMYN--21
You know, you know my name --YOUKNOWMYN--22
You know, you know my name ((oh, let's hear it,
come on Dennis)) --YOUKNOWMYN--23
My name, you know, you know, ((look up the
number))--YOUKNOWMYN--25
You know my name (you know my number).--YOUKNOWMYN
--26
You know, ((you know my name))--YOUKNOWMYN--27
You know, you know my name. ((you know my
number))--YOUKNOWMYN--28
You know my name, look up the number --YOUKNOWMYN
--29
You know my name, look up the number.--YOUKNOWMYN
--30
You know, you know my name, look up the number.--
YOUKNOWMYN--31
Yes, you know, ((you know my name))--YOUKNOWMYN--32
You know my name ((you know)), you know me
number (too/two)--YOUKNOWMYN--33
You know my name, you know me number three --
YOUKNOWMYN--34
You know my name, you know me number four --
YOUKNOWMYN--35
You know my name, look up the number --YOUKNOWMYN
--36
You know my name ((you know)), you know me
number (too/two)--YOUKNOWMYN--37
(look up my name)--YOUKNOWMYN--38
You know my name ((you know my name)) --YOUKNOWMYN
--39
You know my name ((you know my name)) --YOUKNOWMYN
--39
You know my name.--YOUKNOWMYN--41

NAMED

It's based on a novel by a man named Lear --
PAPERBACKW--4

NANCY

But everyone knew her as Nancy.--ROCKYRACCO--16

NASTY

Love has a nasty habit of disappearing overnight.
--IMLOOKINGT--10
Love has a nasty habit of disappearing overnight.
--IMLOOKINGT--16

NATIONAL

My friend works for the National Health, Dr.
Robert --DRROBERT--13
And donated to the National Trust.--HAPPINESSI--8

NATURAL

Tuned to a natural E --BABYYOUREA--24

NATURE'S

MOTHER NATURE'S SON.--MOTHERNATU--Title
Born a poor young country boy - Mother Nature's
son --MOTHERNATU--1
Find me in my field of grass - Mother Nature's
son --MOTHERNATU--8
Aah Mother Nature's son.--MOTHERNATU--16

NAUGHTY

Man you been a naughty boy, you let your face

grow long--IAMTHEWALR--6
Boy, you been a naughty girl, you let your
    knickers down--IAMTHEWALR--14

NEAR
My happiness near makes me cry --ASKMEWHY--8
Please don't come near--DONTBOTHER--20
Please don't come near--DONTBOTHER--35
Have you near me.--ANDILOVEHE--14
I'm a loser and I lost someone who's near to me --
    IMALOSER--7
I'm a loser and I lost someone who's near to me --
    IMALOSER--13
I'm a loser and I lost someone who's near to me --
    IMALOSER--19
When I held you near, you were so sincere--
    NIGHTBEFOR--7
When I held you near, you were so sincere --
    NIGHTBEFOR--15
When I held you near, you were so sincere --
    NIGHTBEFOR--21
No-one comes near.--ELEANORRIG--13
Ooo you were meant to be near me--GOTTOGETYO--12
When I get near you--IWANTTOTEL--5
It's getting very near the end.--SGTPEPPREP--14
Make it easy to be near you --IWILL--16
You can get married in Gibraltar near Spain.--
    BALLADOFJO--12
In an octopus's garden near a cave.--OCTOPUSSGA--12

NEARLY
I nearly died, I nearly died.--NOREPLY--14
I nearly died, I nearly died.--NOREPLY--14
I nearly died, I nearly died.--NOREPLY--27
I nearly died, I nearly died.--NOREPLY--27
Took her home I nearly made it--LOVELYRITA--24
Well you know I nearly broke down and cried.--
    OHDARLING--6
A - well you know, I nearly broke down and died.--
    OHDARLING--8
A - well you know I nearly broke down and cried.--
    OHDARLING--13
A - well you know, I nearly broke down and died.--
    OHDARLING--15

NEED
If you need somebody to love --ANYTIMEATA--4
When you need a shoulder to cry on --ANYTIMEATA--16
You don't need me to show the way love --PLEASEPLEA
    --7
I need you and it's true--ILLGETYOU--10
Say you don't need no diamond rings --CANTBUYMEL
    --17
Say you don't need no diamond rings --CANTBUYMEL
    --27
I don't need to hug or hold you tight --IMHAPPYJUS
    --8
Just to dance with you is everything I need (oh),
    --IMHAPPYJUS--12
Just to dance with you (oh) is everything I
    need (oh) --IMHAPPYJUS--20
Ooo I need your love babe --EIGHTDAYSA--1
Hope you need my love babe --EIGHTDAYSA--3
Just like I need you.--EIGHTDAYSA--4
Ooo I need your love babe --EIGHTDAYSA--19
Hope you need my love babe --EIGHTDAYSA--21
Just like I need you, oh - oh.--EIGHTDAYSA--22
'n' should you need a love that's true, it's me.--
    WHATYOURED--11
'n' should you need a love that's true, it's me.--
    WHATYOURED--18
I need somebody--HELP--2
You know I need someone--HELP--6
I know that I ((I know that I)) just need
    you like--HELP--23
I NEED YOU.--INEEDYOU--Title
You don't realise how much I need you--INEEDYOU--1
I need you.--INEEDYOU--5
I need you.--INEEDYOU--20
I need you.--INEEDYOU--30
I need you.--INEEDYOU--31
I need you.--INEEDYOU--32
Now I need a place to hide away--YESTERDAY--15
Now I need a place to hide away--YESTERDAY--23
I need to, I need to, I need to--MICHELLE--11
I need to, I need to, I need to--MICHELLE--11
I need to, I need to, I need to--MICHELLE--11
I need to make you see--MICHELLE--12
And I need a job --PAPERBACKW--5
But I need a break, ((writer))--PAPERBACKW--24
Helping anyone in need --DRROBERT--9

Till they find there's no need (there's no need).
    --IMONLYSLEE--10
Till they find there's no need (there's no need).
    --IMONLYSLEE--10
You want her, you need her --FORNOONE--10
But now he's gone, she doesn't need him.--FORNOONE
    --19
I need to laugh and when the sun is out --
    GOODDAYSUN--2
Ooo did I tell you I need you--GOTTOGETYO--6
Ooo did I tell you I need you--GOTTOGETYO--21
Did I tell you I need you--GOTTOGETYO--30
To lead a better life, I need my love to be here.
    --HERETHEREA--1
And if she's beside me I know I need never care--
    HERETHEREA--9
But to love her is to need her everywhere.--
    HERETHEREA--10
And if she's beside me I know I need never care--
    HERETHEREA--15
But to love her is to need her everywhere.--
    HERETHEREA--16
Everyone of us (everyone of us) has all we need
    (has all we need) --YELLOWSUBM--26
Everyone of us (everyone of us) has all we need
    (has all we need) --YELLOWSUBM--26
Will you still need me --WHENIMSIXT--7
Will you still need me --WHENIMSIXT--19
A - will you still need me --WHENIMSIXT--35
(Do you need anybody?)--WITHALITTL--15
I need somebody to love.--WITHALITTL--16
(Do you need anybody?)--WITHALITTL--26
I just need someone to love.--WITHALITTL--27
ALL YOU NEED IS LOVE.--ALLYOUN/YS--Title
All you need is love, all you need is love --
    ALLYOUN/YS--12
All you need is love, all you need is love --
    ALLYOUN/YS--12
All you need is love, love, love is all you need.
    --ALLYOUN/YS--13
All you need is love, love, love is all you need.
    --ALLYOUN/YS--13
All you need is love, (wuh) all you need is
    love (hey) --ALLYOUN/YS--17
All you need is love, (wuh) all you need is
    love (hey) --ALLYOUN/YS--17
All you need is love, love, love is all you need.
    --ALLYOUN/YS--18
All you need is love, love, love is all you need.
    --ALLYOUN/YS--18
All you need is love, all you need is love --
    ALLYOUN/YS--23
All you need is love, all you need is love --
    ALLYOUN/YS--23
All you need is love, love, love is all you need.
    --ALLYOUN/YS--24
All you need is love, love, love is all you need.
    --ALLYOUN/YS--24
All you need is love (all together now) --
    ALLYOUN/YS--25
All you need is love (everybody) --ALLYOUN/YS--26
All you need is love, love, love is all you need.
    --ALLYOUN/YS--27
All you need is love, love, love is all you need.
    --ALLYOUN/YS--27
Love is all you need (love is all you need)--
    ALLYOUN/YS--28
Love is all you need (love is all you need)--
    ALLYOUN/YS--28
Love is all you need (love is all you need)--
    ALLYOUN/YS--29
Love is all you need (love is all you need)--
    ALLYOUN/YS--29
Love is all you need (love is all you need)--
    ALLYOUN/YS--30
Love is all you need (love is all you need)--
    ALLYOUN/YS--30
Love is all you need (love is all you need)--
    ALLYOUN/YS--31
Love is all you need (love is all you need)--
    ALLYOUN/YS--31
Love is all you need (wuh) (love is all you
    need)--ALLYOUN/YS--32
Love is all you need (wuh) (love is all you
    need)--ALLYOUN/YS--32
Love is all you need (love is all you need)--
    ALLYOUN/YS--33
Love is all you need (love is all you need)--
    ALLYOUN/YS--33
Love is all you need (love is all you need)--
    ALLYOUN/YS--34
Love is all you need (love is all you need)--
    ALLYOUN/YS--34
Love is all you need (love is all you need)--

ALLYOUN/YS--35
Love is all you need (love is all you need)--
ALLYOUN/YS--35
Love is all you need (love is all you need)--
ALLYOUN/YS--36
Love is all you need (love is all you need)--
ALLYOUN/YS--36
Love is all you need (love is all you need)--
ALLYOUN/YS--37
Love is all you need (love is all you need)--
ALLYOUN/YS--37
Love is all you need (yahoo) (eee - hi)--
ALLYOUN/YS--38
Love is all you need (love is all you need)--
ALLYOUN/YS--39
Love is all you need (love is all you need)--
ALLYOUN/YS--39
(Love is all you need) Yesterday (love is all
you need)--ALLYOUN/YS--40
(Love is all you need) Yesterday (love is all
you need)--ALLYOUN/YS--40
(Oh) love is all you need--ALLYOUN/YS--41
Love is all you need (oh yeah)--ALLYOUN/YS
--42
Love is all you need--ALLYOUN/YS--43
Love is all you need--ALLYOUN/YS--46
Love is all you need (wuhoo)--ALLYOUN/YS--47
Love is all you need (wuhoo)--ALLYOUN/YS--48
Love is all you need (oh)--ALLYOUN/YS--49
Love is all you need--ALLYOUN/YS--50
Love is all you need.--ALLYOUN/YS--51
Roll up (we've got everything you need)--MAGICALMYS
--13
The movement you need is on your shoulder.--HEYJUDE
--24
I need a fix 'cos I'm going down --HAPPINESSI--9
I need a fix 'cos I'm going down.--HAPPINESSI--11
You know that I need you,--LONGLONGLO--13
ALL YOU NEED IS LOVE.--ALLYOU/MMT--Title
Love is all you need--ALLYOU/MMT--1
(Oh) love is all you need--ALLYOU/MMT--2
Love is all you need--ALLYOU/MMT--3
Love is all you need--ALLYOU/MMT--4
Love is all you need--ALLYOU/MMT--5
Love is all you need.--ALLYOU/MMT--6
When you told me you didn't need me any more --
OHDARLING--5
A - when you told me you didn't need me any more
--OHDARLING--7
A - when you told me - ooo - you didn't need me
any more --OHDARLING--12
A - when you told me you didn't need me any more
--OHDARLING--14
That I don't need no other lover --SOMETHING--7

NEED'S
What they need's a damn good whacking.--PIGGIES
--14

NEEDED
I never needed ((never needed)) anybody's help
in any way--HELP--10
I never needed ((never needed)) anybody's help
in any way--HELP--10
I never needed anybody's help in any way--HELP--30
IF I NEEDED SOMEONE.--IFINEEDS--Title
If I needed someone to love --IFINEEDS--1
If I needed someone.--IFINEEDS--3
If I needed someone.--IFINEEDS--6
If I needed someone.--IFINEEDS--12
If I needed someone.--IFINEEDS--16
If I needed someone.--IFINEEDS--22
Thursday night your stockings needed mending.--
LADYMADONN--16

NEEDS
When she no longer needs you.--FORNOONE--3
She no longer needs you.--FORNOONE--6
You think she needs you.--FORNOONE--13
Somebody needs to know the time glad that I'm here
--GOODMORNIN--22
I look at the floor and I see it needs sweeping --
WHILEMYGUI--4

NEGOTIATIONS
And in the middle of negotiations you break down.
--YOUNEVERGI--3

NERVE

But you haven't got the nerve--YOULIKEMET--8

NEVER
That I - I - I - I should never, never,
never be blue.--ASKMEWHY--6
That I - I - I - I should never, never,
never be blue.--ASKMEWHY--6
That I - I - I - I should never, never,
never be blue.--ASKMEWHY--6
That I - I - I - I should never, never,
never be blue.--ASKMEWHY--21
That I - I - I - I should never, never,
never be blue.--ASKMEWHY--21
That I - I - I - I should never, never,
never be blue.--ASKMEWHY--21
I know you never even try girl --PLEASEPLEA--2
I know/Why do you never even try girl--PLEASEPLEA--20
You'll never know how much I really love you --
DOYOUWANTT--1
You'll never know how much I really care.--
DOYOUWANTT--2
Now I'll never dance with another --ISAWHERSTA--16
Now I'll never dance with another--ISAWHERSTA--23
I'm the kind of guy, who never used to cry.--MISERY
--2
I'm never, never, never, never blue.--ILLGETYOU--12
I'm never, never, never, never blue.--ILLGETYOU--12
I'm never, never, never, never blue.--ILLGETYOU--12
I'm never, never, never, never blue.--ILLGETYOU--12
I know I'll never be the same--DONTBOTHER--15
I know I'll never be the same--DONTBOTHER--30
Never be the lonely one.--HOLDMETIGH--5
Never be the lonely one.--HOLDMETIGH--22
I never weep at night, I can't go on.--ICALLYOURN
--4
I never weep at night, I call your name.--
ICALLYOURN--10
I never weep at night, I call your name --
ICALLYOURN--17
Could never die --ANDILOVEHE--12
Will never die --ANDILOVEHE--18
Will never die --ANDILOVEHE--23
Whoa, whoa, I never realised what a kiss could
be --ISHOULDHAV--4
Whoa, whoa, I never realised what a kiss could
be --ISHOULDHAV--14
I will never leave her--SHESAWOMAN--11
She will never make me jealous--SHESAWOMAN--13
And though he'll never come back --BABYSINBLA--5
And/But though he'll never come back--BABYSINBLA--25
For I know love will never die.--EVERYLITTL--16
There is one love I should never have crossed.--
IMALOSER--4
She would never be free--TICKETTORI--11
She would never be free--TICKETTORI--38
We will never be apart--TELLMEWHAT--3
You'll never leave me and you know it's true--
YOULIKEMET--5
You'll never leave me and you know it's true--
YOULIKEMET--11
I never needed ((never needed)) anybody's help
in any way--HELP--10
I never needed ((never needed)) anybody's help
in any way--HELP--10
I've never done before.--HELP--24
I never needed anybody's help in any way--HELP--30
Love you all the time and never leave you--INEEDYOU
--2
I could never really live without you--INEEDYOU--17
I could never really live without you--INEEDYOU--27
And I'd have never been aware--IVEJUSTSEE--9
I have never known the like of this--IVEJUSTSEE--14
But other girls were never quite like this --
IVEJUSTSEE--17
I can never win --YOUVEGOTTO--12
Though I know I'll never lose affection --INMYLIFE
--13
Though I know I'll never lose affection --INMYLIFE
--17
If I'm true I'll never leave--GOTTOGETYO--18
And if she's beside me I know I need never care--
HERETHEREA--9
Each one believing that love never dies--HERETHEREA
--12
And if she's beside me I know I need never care--
HERETHEREA--15
Each one believing that love never dies--HERETHEREA
--18
And she's making me feel like I've never been
born.--SHESAIDSHE--3
And you're making me feel like I've never been
born.--SHESAIDSHE--6
'cos you're making me feel like I've never been

born.--SHESAIDSHE--12
'cos you're making me feel like I've never been
   born.--SHESAIDSHE--18
TOMORROW NEVER KNOWS.--TOMORROWNE--Title
And the banker never wears a mack--PENNYLANE--7
See the people standing there who disagree and
   never win--FIXINGAHOL--9
And never ask me why they don't get past my door.
   --FIXINGAHOL--18
She (we never thought of ourselves)--SHESLEAVIN--20
Is leaving (never a thought for our ourselves)--
   SHESLEAVIN--21
Never glimpse the truth--WITHINYOUW--5
And he never gives an answer.--FOOLONTHEH--5
And he never seems to notice.--FOOLONTHEH--12
And he never shows his feelings.--FOOLONTHEH--17
He never listens to them--FOOLONTHEH--22
You'll never know it hurt me so --DONTPASSME--20
You'll never know it hurt me so --DONTPASSME--33
You'll never know it hurt me so --DONTPASSME--39
But it never really mattered --IWILL--7
I never give you my pillow--CARRYTHATW--5
She never stops--MEANMRMUST--9
Oh darling, please believe me, I'll never do
   you no harm.--OHDARLING--1
Believe me when I tell you, I'll never do you
   no harm.--OHDARLING--2
Oh darling, if you leave me I'll never make it
   alone --OHDARLING--3
Oh darling, if you leave me, I'll never make
   it alone.--OHDARLING--9
Believe me when I tell you, I'll never do you
   no harm.--OHDARLING--10
Oh darling, please believe me, I'll never let
   you down.--OHDARLING--16
Believe me when I tell you - ooo - I'll never
   do you no harm.--OHDARLING--18
YOU NEVER GIVE ME YOUR MONEY.--YOUNEVERGI--Title
You never give me your money --YOUNEVERGI--1
I never give you my number --YOUNEVERGI--4
Will never disappear, I've seen that road before.
   --LONGANDWIN--2
Anyway you'll never know the many ways I've tried
   --LONGANDWIN--8

NEVER-ENDING
Tuesday afternoon is never-ending --LADYMADONN--14

NEW
Someone to love, somebody new.--LOVEMEDO--11
If our new love was in vain.--IFIFELL--16
If our new love was in vain.--IFIFELL--23
But as from today well I've got somebody that's
   new --ANOTHERGIR--3
But as from today well I've seen somebody that's
   new --ANOTHERGIR--13
But as from today well I've seen somebody that's
   new --ANOTHERGIR--19
When I think of love as something new.--INMYLIFE
   --12
Dr. Robert, you're a new and better man --DRROBERT
   --3
Dr. Robert, you're a new and better man --DRROBERT
   --15
A new one can't be bought--LOVEYOUTWO--7
Dear Prudence, greet the brand new day.--DEARPRUDEN
   --2
Dear Prudence, greet the brand new day.--DEARPRUDEN
   --22
Love is old, love is new --BECAUSE--8

NEWS
I read the news today, oh boy--DAYINTHELI--1
And though the news was rather sad--DAYINTHELI--3
I read the news today, oh boy--DAYINTHELI--28
Coffee dessert - yes you know it's good news --
   SAVOYTRUFF--3
Coffee dessert - yes you know it's good news
   (wuh) --SAVOYTRUFF--25
She's a kind of a girl that makes the News Of
   The World.--POLYTHENEP--8

NEWS-PEOPLE
The news-people said, say what're you doing in
   bed?--BALLADOFJO--19

NEWSPAPER
Newspaper taxis appear on the shore--LUCYINTHES--16

NEWSPAPERS
The newspapers said, she's gone to his head --
   BALLADOFJO--31

NEXT
Telling me there'll be no next time--YOULIKEMET--3
I'll make you maybe next time around.--IWANTTOTEL
   --8
Many more of them live next door--YELLOWSUBM--14
Were in the next room at the hoe-down --ROCKYRACCO
   --18

NICE
And it's nice when you believe me--YOULIKEMET--14
And it's nice when you believe me--YOULIKEMET--23
Cool cherry cream, nice apple tart --SAVOYTRUFF--6
Her Majesty's a pretty nice girl--HERMAJESTY--1
Her Majesty's a pretty nice girl--HERMAJESTY--3
Her Majesty's a pretty nice girl--HERMAJESTY--7

NIGHT
Last night I said these words to my girl --
   PLEASEPLEA--1
Last night I said these words to my girl --
   PLEASEPLEA--19
Well we danced through the night --ISAWHERSTA--13
Oh (wuh!) we danced through the night --ISAWHERSTA
   --20
I think about you night and day--ILLGETYOU--9
When every night I'm all alone--DONTBOTHER--12
Every night when everybody has fun--ITWONTBELO--5
Every night the tears come down from my eye--
   ITWONTBELO--15
Oh, I can't sleep at night since you've been
   gone --ICALLYOURN--3
I never weep at night, I can't go on.--ICALLYOURN
   --4
Oh, I can't sleep at night, but just the same --
   ICALLYOURN--9
I never weep at night, I call your name.--
   ICALLYOURN--10
Oh, I can't sleep at night, but just the same --
   ICALLYOURN--16
I never weep at night, I call your name --
   ICALLYOURN--17
A HARD DAY'S NIGHT.--HARDDAYSNI--Title
It's been a hard day's night --HARDDAYSNI--1
It's been a hard day's night --HARDDAYSNI--3
It's been a hard day's night --HARDDAYSNI--17
It's been a hard day's night --HARDDAYSNI--19
Oh, It's been a hard day's night --HARDDAYSNI--30
It's been a hard day's night --HARDDAYSNI--32
I just wanna dance with you all night --IMHAPPYJUS
   --9
Is it right that you and I should fight, every
   night--ITSONLYLOV--8
THE NIGHT BEFORE.--NIGHTBEFOR--Title
We said our goodbyes (aah the night before)--
   NIGHTBEFOR--1
Love was in your eyes (aah the night before)--
   NIGHTBEFOR--2
Treat me like you did the night before.--NIGHTBEFOR
   --4
Were you telling lies? (aah the night before)--
   NIGHTBEFOR--5
Was I so unwise? (aah the night before)--NIGHTBEFOR
   --6
Treat me like you did the night before.--NIGHTBEFOR
   --8
Last night is the night I will remember you by --
   NIGHTBEFOR--9
Last night is the night I will remember you by --
   NIGHTBEFOR--9
We said our goodbyes (aah the night before)--
   NIGHTBEFOR--11
Love was in your eyes (aah the night before)--
   NIGHTBEFOR--12
Treat me like you did the night before (yes).--
   NIGHTBEFOR--14
Treat me like you did the night before (yeah).--
   NIGHTBEFOR--16
Last night is the night I will remember you by --
   NIGHTBEFOR--17
Last night is the night I will remember you by --
   NIGHTBEFOR--17
Were you telling lies? (aah the night before)--
   NIGHTBEFOR--19
Was I so unwise? (aah the night before)--NIGHTBEFOR
   --20
Treat me like you did the night before.--NIGHTBEFOR

--22
Like the night before.--NIGHTBEFOR--23
She only played one night stands --DAYTRIPPER--19
And she only played one night stands, now.--
   DAYTRIPPER--21
We can work it out and get it straight or say
   good night.--WECANWORKI--9
Day or night he'll be there any time at all, Dr.
   Robert --DRROBERT--2
Darning his socks in the night when there's
   nobody there--ELEANORRIG--15
Friday night arrives without a suitcase --
   LADYMADONN--5
Thursday night your stockings needed mending.--
   LADYMADONN--16
Didn't get to bed last night --BACKINTHEU--2
Blackbird singing in the dead of night --BLACKBIRD
   --1
Blackbird singing in the dead of night --BLACKBIRD
   --5
Into the light of a dark black night.--BLACKBIRD
   --10
Into the light of a dark black night.--BLACKBIRD
   --12
Blackbird singing in the dead of night --BLACKBIRD
   --13
GOOD NIGHT.--GOODNIGHT--Title
Now it's time to say good night,--GOODNIGHT--1
Good night, sleep tight.--GOODNIGHT--2
Good night, sleep tight.--GOODNIGHT--4
Good night, sleep tight.--GOODNIGHT--8
Good night, sleep tight.--GOODNIGHT--10
Good night, sleep tight.--GOODNIGHT--15
Good night, sleep tight.--GOODNIGHT--17
Good night,--GOODNIGHT--20
Good night everybody,--GOODNIGHT--21
Good night.--GOODNIGHT--23
When you're listening late at night --ONLYANORTH
   --4
Last night the wife said, oh boy, when you're
   dead --BALLADOFJO--27
And when the night is cloudy,--LETITBE/45--21
All through the night --IMEMINE--3
And when the night is cloudy --LETITBE/LP--21
The wild and windy night that the rain washed away
   --LONGANDWIN--4

NIGHT-TIME
   Just the sight of you makes night-time bright,
     very bright.--ITSONLYLOV--9

NIGHTS
   Late nights all alone with a test-tube, oh oh -
     oh oh.--MAXWELLSIL--2

NINE
   ... Four, five, six, seven, eight, nine,
     ten...--DAYINTHELI--35
   Friday morning at nine o'clock she is far away--
     SHESLEAVIN--25
   REVOLUTION NINE.--REVOLUNINE--Title
   Five, six, seven, eight, nine, ten --ALLTOGETHE--3

NINE-0
   Said we're travelling on the one after nine-0 --
     ONEAFTERNI--29
   She said we're travelling on the one after nine-0
     --ONEAFTERNI--30

NINE-0-NINE
   ONE AFTER NINE-0-NINE.--ONEAFTERNI--Title
   My baby said she's travelling on the one after
     nine-0-nine --ONEAFTERNI--1
   Said you're travelling on the one after
     nine-0-nine --ONEAFTERNI--5
   Said you're travelling on the one after
     nine-0-nine --ONEAFTERNI--10
   Well, she said she's travelling on the one after
     nine-0-nine --ONEAFTERNI--15
   Said she's travelling on the one after
     nine-o-nine. (yeah)--ONEAFTERNI--19
   She said she's travelling on the one after
     nine-0-nine --ONEAFTERNI--25
   Said we're travelling on the one after nine-0-nine
     --ONEAFTERNI--31

NINETEEN
   There's one for you, nineteen for me --TAXMAN--4

I've lost her now for sure, I won't see her no
   more --MISERY--4
I want no one to talk to me--DONTBOTHER--2
I've got no time for you right now--DONTBOTHER--13
I've got no time for you right now--DONTBOTHER--28
Love you like no other baby --IWANNABEYO--5
Like no other can.--IWANNABEYO--6
Love you like no other baby --IWANNABEYO--7
Like no other can.--IWANNABEYO--8
Love you like no other baby --IWANNABEYO--34
Like no other can (ooo).--IWANNABEYO--35
Love you like no other baby --IWANNABEYO--36
Like no other can.--IWANNABEYO--37
Now I know that you won't leave me no more--
   ITWONTBELO--26
I see no use in wondering why --NOTASECOND--2
I see no reason to change mine --NOTASECOND--5
No, no, no, not a second time.--NOTASECOND--10
No, no, no, not a second time.--NOTASECOND--10
No, no, no, not a second time.--NOTASECOND--10
I see no use in wondering why --NOTASECOND--13
I see no reason to change mine --NOTASECOND--16
No, no, no, not a second time.--NOTASECOND--21
No, no, no, not a second time.--NOTASECOND--21
No, no, no, not a second time.--NOTASECOND--21
No, no, no, not a second time--NOTASECOND--24
No, no, no, not a second time--NOTASECOND--24
No, no, no, not a second time--NOTASECOND--24
((No, no, no.))--NOTASECOND--25
((No, no, no.))--NOTASECOND--25
((No, no, no.))--NOTASECOND--25
Can't buy me love oh - no, no, no - no.--CANTBUYMEL
   --16
Can't buy me love oh - no, no, no - no.--CANTBUYMEL
   --16
Can't buy me love oh - no, no, no - no.--CNATBUYMEL
   --16
Can't buy me love oh - no, no, no - no.--CANTBUYMEL
   --16
Say you don't need no diamond rings --CANTBUYMEL
   --17
Can't buy me love oh - no, no, no - no.--CANTBUYMEL
   --26
Can't buy me love oh - no, no, no - no.--CANTBUYMEL
   --26
Can't buy me love oh - no, no, no - no.--CANTBUYMEL
   --26
Can't buy me love oh - no, no, no - no.--CANTBUYMEL
   --26
Say you don't need no diamond rings --CANTBUYMEL
   --27
Oh you can't do that - no!--YOUCANTDOT--31
And it's my mind and there's no time--THERESAPLA
   --3
In my mind there's no sorrow--THERESAPLA--9
There'll be no sad tomorrow--THERESAPLA--11
And it's my mind and there's no time--THERESAPLA
   --15
I got no time for triviality --WHENIGETHO--11
I got no business being here with you this way.--
   WHENIGETHO--23
I know that she's no peasant--SHESAWOMAN--2
I know that she's no peasant--SHESAWOMAN--19
I know that she's no peasant--SHESAWOMAN--29
There's no fun in what I do when she's not there
   --IDONTWANTT--6
There's no fun in what I do if she's not there --
   IDONTWANTT--23
NO REPLY.--NOREPLY--Title
No reply--NOREPLY--3
When you gave me no reply.--NOREPLY--21
No reply, no reply.--NOREPLY--30
No reply, no reply.--NOREPLY--30
And ((and)) there's no fun in it --WHATYOURED--6
It is no surprise now--TELLMEWHAT--7
It is no surprise now--TELLMEWHAT--24
It is no surprise now--TELLMEWHAT--33
Telling me there'll be no next time--YOULIKEMET--3
I ain't no fool and I don't take what I don't
   want --ANOTHERGIR--4
I ain't no fool and I don't take what I don't
   want --ANOTHERGIR--14
I ain't no fool and I don't take what I don't
   want --ANOTHERGIR--20
Life is very short and there's no time--WECANWORKI
   --11
Life is very short and there's no time--WECANWORKI
   --20
I got no car and it's breaking my heart --
   DRIVEMYCAR--24
((No I wouldn't, no I wouldn't))--YOUWONTSEE--15

((No I wouldn't, no I wouldn't))--YOUWONTSEE--15
((No I wouldn't, no I wouldn't))--YOUWONTSEE--24
((No I wouldn't, no I wouldn't))--YOUWONTSEE--24
Please don't wake me, no, don't shake me --
    IMONLYSLEE--5
Till they find there's no need (there's no need).
    --IMONLYSLEE--10
Till they find there's no need (there's no need).
    --IMONLYSLEE--10
Please don't wake me, no, don't shake me --
    IMONLYSLEE--25
When she no longer needs you.--FORNOONE--3
She no longer needs you.--FORNOONE--6
No sign of love behind the tears cried for no-one
    --FORNOONE--8
No sign of love behind the tears cried for no-one
    --FORNOONE--15
No sign of love behind the tears cried for no-one
    --FORNOONE--25
I said no, no, no you're wrong.--SHESAIDSHE--8
I said no, no, no you're wrong.--SHESAIDSHE--8
I said no, no, no you're wrong.--SHESAIDSHE--8
I said no, no, no you're wrong.--SHESAIDSHE--14
I said no, no, no you're wrong.--SHESAIDSHE--14
I said no, no, no you're wrong.--SHESAIDSHE--14
Always, no, sometimes, think it's me--STRAWBERRY
    --26
A little better all the time (it can't get no
    worse)--GETTINGBET--8
A little better all the time (it can't get no
    worse)--GETTINGBET--17
A little better all the time (it can't get no
    worse)--GETTINGBET--30
No I get by with a little help from my friends --
    WITHALITTL--12
You say yes, I say no --HELLOGOODB--1
Oh no --HELLOGOODB--3
Oh no --HELLOGOODB--9
Oh no --HELLOGOODB--18
You say yes, I say no--HELLOGOODB--22
((I say yes but I may mean no))--HELLOGOODB--23
Oh - oh no --HELLOGOODB--26
I know nobody can do me no harm ((oh, yeah)) --
    HAPPINESSI--24
Well, you may be a lover, but you ain't no
    dancer.--HELTERSKEL--7
'cos you may be a lover, but you ain't no dancer.
    --HELTERSKEL--14
'cos you may be a lover, but you ain't no dancer.
    --HELTERSKEL--24
No, no, no.--IMSOTIRED--4
No, no, no.--IMSOTIRED--4
No, no, no.--IMSOTIRED--4
But it's no joke, it's doing me harm --IMSOTIRED
    --10
But it's no joke, it's doing me harm,--IMSOTIRED
    --19
Gideon checked out and he left it no doubt ((oh
    - Rocky - oh))--ROCKYRACCO--38
Makes no difference where you are--ITSALLTOOM--14
It's a love that has no past (believe me).--
    DONTLETMED--16
He wear no shoe-shine--COMETOGETH--15
Oh darling, please believe me, I'll never do
    you no harm.--OHDARLING--1
Believe me when I tell you, I'll never do you
    no harm.--OHDARLING--2
Believe me when I tell you, I'll never do you
    no harm.--OHDARLING--10
Believe me when I tell you - ooo - I'll never
    do you no harm.--OHDARLING--18
Attracts me like no other lover --SOMETHING--2
That I don't need no other lover --SOMETHING--7
See no future, pay no rent --YOUNEVERGI--8
See no future, pay no rent --YOUNEVERGI--8
Queen says no to pot-smoking FBI member.--
    FORYOUBLUE--1
Oh no, no - oh no, oh no.--IVEGOTAFEE--4
Oh no, no - oh no, oh no.--IVEGOTAFEE--4
Oh no, no - oh no, oh no.--IVEGOTAFEE--4
Oh no, no - oh no, oh no.--IVEGOTAFEE--4
Oh no, oh no, oh no, yeah, yeah!--IVEGOTAFEE--9
Oh no, oh no, oh no, yeah, yeah!--IVEGOTAFEE--9
Oh no, oh no, oh no, yeah, yeah!--IVEGOTAFEE--9
Everybody let their hair down ((a feeling I
    can't hide, oh no)) --IVEGOTAFEE--33
Everybody pulled their socks up (oh no, no) --
    IVEGOTAFEE--34
Everybody pulled their socks up (oh no, no) --
    IVEGOTAFEE--34

NO-ONE
    There is no-one compares with you --INMYLIFE--10

I used to think of no-one else but you were just
    the same --WHATGOESON--22
No-one can succeed like Dr. Robert.--DRROBERT--10
That no-one will hear--ELEANORRIG--12
No-one comes near.--ELEANORRIG--13
No-one was saved.--ELEANORRIG--26
FOR NO-ONE.--FORNOONE--Title
No sign of love behind the tears cried for no-one
    --FORNOONE--8
No sign of love behind the tears cried for no-one
    --FORNOONE--15
No sign of love behind the tears cried for no-one
    --FORNOONE--25
And you're working for no-one but me (Taxman).--
    TAXMAN--26
No-one, I think, is in my tree--STRAWBERRY--16
No-one else can make you change--WITHINYOUW--17
No-one you can save that can't be saved ((love))--
    ALLYOUN/YS--9
No-one alerted you.--WHILEMYGUI--17
No-one will be watching us --WHYDONTWED--5
No-one will be watching us --WHYDONTWED--11
No-one will be watching us --WHYDONTWED--11
Childlike, no-one understands--HEYBULLDOG--5
And I told you there's no-one there.--ONLYANORTH
    --16
No-one there to tell us what to do.--OCTOPUSSGA--22

NO-ONE'S
    No-one's frightened of playing it --IMEMINE--18
    No-one's frightened of playing it --IMEMINE--31

NOBODY
    Nobody knows just we two.--DOYOUWANTT--16
    We're all alone and there's nobody else--IMDOWN--16
    You're making me say that I've got nobody but you
        --ANOTHERGIR--2
    Nobody in all the world can do what she can do --
        ANOTHERGIR--7
    Making all his nowhere plans for nobody.--
        NOWHEREMAN--3
    Making all his nowhere plans for nobody --
        NOWHEREMAN--24
    Making all his nowhere plans for nobody --
        NOWHEREMAN--25
    Making all his nowhere plans for nobody.--
        NOWHEREMAN--26
    Darning his socks in the night when there's
        nobody there--ELEANORRIG--15
    Nobody came.--ELEANORRIG--23
    Nobody can deny that there's something there.--
        HERETHEREA--4
    Nobody was really sure if he was from the House
        of Lords--DAYINTHELI--10
    But nobody wants to know him--FOOLONTHEH--3
    But nobody ever hears him--FOOLONTHEH--10
    And nobody seems to like him--FOOLONTHEH--15
    I know nobody can do me no harm ((oh, yeah)) --
        HAPPINESSI--24
    I don't know why nobody told you how to unfold
        your love --WHILEMYGUI--6
    You're correct, there's nobody there.--ONLYANORTH
        --15
    Nobody ever loved me like she does --DONTLETMED--5
    I guess nobody ever really done me --DONTLETMED--23
    Wondering really how come nobody told me--IVEGOTAFEE
        --12

NOISE
    Hey man what's that noise? (woof)--HEYBULLDOG--23
    But as the words are leaving his lips, a noise
        comes from behind --MAXWELLSIL--22

NONE
    Their production will be second to none--BEINGFORTH
        --13

NORTH
    North of England way--HONEYPIE--2

NORTHERN
    ONLY A NORTHERN SONG.--ONLYANORTH--Title
    As it's only a Northern song.--ONLYANORTH--9
    When it's only a Northern song.--ONLYANORTH--12

NORWEGIAN
    NORWEGIAN WOOD (THIS BIRD HAS FLOWN).--NORWEGIANW

--Title
Norwegian wood?--NORWEGIANW--6
Norwegian wood?--NORWEGIANW--26

NOSE
Keeps a ten bob note up his nose--MEANMRMUST--6

NOT
If I cry it's not because I'm sad --ASKMEWHY--10
Do you promise not to tell?--DOYOUWANTT--4
Do you promise not to tell? (dodahdo)--DOYOUWANTT--10
Do you promise not to tell? (dodahdo)--DOYOUWANTT--18
It's not like me to pretend--ILLGETYOU--6
It's not like me to pretend--ILLGETYOU--23
You're not the hurting kind.--SHELOVESYO--15
It's not the same--DONTBOTHER--3
It's just not right--DONTBOTHER--11
NOT A SECOND TIME.--NOTASECOND--Title
No, no, no, not a second time.--NOTASECOND--10
No, no, no, not a second time.--NOTASECOND--21
Not a second time--NOTASECOND--22
Not a second time--NOTASECOND--23
No, no, no, not a second time.--NOTASECOND--24
I may not have a lot to give --CANTBUYMEL--11
I call your name, but you're not there --ICALLYOURN--1
I'm not gonna make it --ICALLYOURN--7
I'm not that kinda man.--ICALLYOURN--8
I'm not gonna make it --ICALLYOURN--14
I'm not that kinda man.--ICALLYOURN--15
That I'm not trying to pretend.--ILLBEBACK--12
That I'm not trying to pretend.--ILLBEBACK--21
Deep in love, not a lot to say --THINGSWESA--9
Deep in love, not a lot to say --THINGSWESA--20
Deep in love, not a lot to say --THINGSWESA--31
Eight days a week is not enough to show I care.--EIGHTDAYSA--18
Eight days a week is not enough to show I care.--EIGHTDAYSA--28
There's no fun in what I do when she's not there --IDONTWANTT--6
There's no fun in what I do if she's not there --IDONTWANTT--23
And I'm not what I appear to be.--IMALOSER--2
I'm a loser and I'm not what I appear to be.--IMALOSER--8
I'm a loser and I'm not what I appear to be.--IMALOSER--14
I'm a loser and I'm not what I appear to be.--IMALOSER--20
They said you were not home--NOREPLY--10
They said you were not home--NOREPLY--23
Not just anybody--HELP--4
I'm not so self-assured--HELP--12
I'm not so self-assured--HELP--32
I'm not half the man I used to be--YESTERDAY--6
And then you'll be the lonely one (you're not the only one)--YOUREGONNA--12
Then it might not have been like this --IFINEEDEDS--8
Then it might not have been like this --IFINEEDEDS--18
I'm looking through you, you're not the same.--IMLOOKINGT--4
I'm looking through you, you're not the same.--IMLOOKINGT--8
Why, tell me why did you not treat me right?--IMLOOKINGT--9
You were above me, but not today.--IMLOOKINGT--12
Why, tell me why did you not treat me right?--IMLOOKINGT--15
I'm looking through you, you're not the same.--IMLOOKINGT--20
Some forever, not for better --INMYLIFE--3
Knows not where he's going to --NOWHEREMAN--5
Knows not where he's going to --NOWHEREMAN--17
It's only me, it's not my mind--IWANTTOTEL--10
It is not dying, it is not dying.--TOMORROWNE--2
It is not dying, it is not dying.--TOMORROWNE--2
It is not living, it is not living.--TOMORROWNE--12
It is not living, it is not living.--TOMORROWNE--12
That is, I think it's not too bad.--STRAWBERRY--20
If it's not too dear --WHENIMSIXT--24
And I'll try not to sing outta key.--WITHALITTL--4
The children asked him if to kill was not a sin --CONTINUING--27
She's not a girl who misses much --HAPPINESSI--1
You might not feel it now --SAVOYTRUFF--11
So take a piece, but not too much.--ITSALLTOOM--19

But they're not, we just wrote it like that.--ONLYANORTH--3
You may think the band are not quite right --ONLYANORTH--5
Not worrying what they or you say --OLDBROWNSH--19
Making sure that I'm not late (hey).--OLDBROWNSH--30
Sleep pretty darling do not cry--GOLDENSLUM--5
Sleep pretty darling do not cry--GOLDENSLUM--9
Sleep pretty darling do not cry--GOLDENSLUM--15
So he waits behind, writing fifty times I must not be so oh - oh oh.--MAXWELLSIL--11
The judge does not agree and he tells them so oh - oh oh.--MAXWELLSIL--21
Well I knew what I could not say.--SHECAMEINT--15
She could steal but she could not rob.--SHECAMEINT--19
I begged her not to go and I begged her on my bended knee, (oh yeah)--ONEAFTERNI--6
Not arriving on our way back home.--TWOOFUS--6

NOTE
Leaving the note that she hoped would say more.--SHESLEAVIN--3
Keeps a ten bob note up his nose--MEANMRMUST--6

NOTHING
There is nothing I won't do --ANYTIMEATA--15
Every day I've done nothing but cry--ITWONTBELO--16
There is really nothing else I'd rather do --IMHAPPYJUS--6
In this world there's nothing I would rather do --IMHAPPYJUS--10
In this world there's nothing I would rather do --IMHAPPYJUS--18
In this world there's nothing I would rather do --IMHAPPYJUS--26
I ain't got nothing but love babe --EIGHTDAYSA--7
I ain't got nothing but love girl --EIGHTDAYSA--15
I ain't got nothing but love babe --EIGHTDAYSA--25
I ain't got nothing but love babe --EIGHTDAYSA--35
There's nothing for me here so I will disappear --IDONTWANTT--3
There's nothing for me here so I will disappear --IDONTWANTT--15
And in her eyes you see nothing --FORNOONE--7
And in her eyes you see nothing --FORNOONE--14
And in her eyes you see nothing --FORNOONE--24
Nothing is real--STRAWBERRY--3
And nothing to get hungabout--STRAWBERRY--4
Nothing is real--STRAWBERRY--13
And nothing to get hungabout--STRAWBERRY--14
Nothing is real--STRAWBERRY--23
And nothing to get hungabout--STRAWBERRY--24
Nothing is real--STRAWBERRY--33
And nothing to get hungabout--STRAWBERRY--34
Nothing to do to save his life call his wife in--GOODMORNIN--2
Nothing to say but what a day how's your boy been?--GOODMORNIN--3
Nothing to do it's up to you--GOODMORNIN--4
I've got nothing to say but it's OK.--GOODMORNIN--5
Everbody knows there's nothing doing--GOODMORNIN--9
Nothing has changed it's still the same--GOODMORNIN--15
I've got nothing to say but it's OK.--GOODMORNIN--16
I've got nothing to say but it's OK.--GOODMORNIN--25
Nothing can come between us--LOVELYRITA--5
There's nothing you can do that can't be done ((love))--ALLYOUN/YS--4
Nothing you can sing that can't be sung ((love))--ALLYOUN/YS--5
Nothing you can say but you can learn how to play the game ((love))--ALLYOUN/YS--6
Nothing you can make that can't be made ((love))--ALLYOUN/YS--8
Nothing you can do but you can learn how to be you in time ((love))--ALLYOUN/YS--10
There's nothing you can know that isn't known ((love))--ALLYOUN/YS--19
Nothing you can see that isn't shown ((love))--ALLYOUN/YS--20
Nothing that doesn't show.--BABYYOUREA--12
You know the place where nothing is real--GLASSONION--2
You don't take nothing with you but your soul - think!--BALLADOFJO--28
Elmore James got nothing on this baby - heh.--

FORYOUBLUE--12

NOTHING'S

Nothing's gonna change my world --ACROSSTHEU--7
Nothing's gonna change my world --ACROSSTHEU--8
Nothing's gonna change my world --ACROSSTHEU--9
Nothing's gonna change my world.--ACROSSTHEU--10
Nothing's gonna change my world --ACROSSTHEU--16
Nothing's gonna change my world --ACROSSTHEU--17
Nothing's gonna change my world --ACROSSTHEU--18
Nothing's gonna change my world.--ACROSSTHEU--19
Nothing's gonna change my world --ACROSSTHEU--26
Nothing's gonna change my world --ACROSSTHEU--27
Nothing's gonna change my world --ACROSSTHEU--28
Nothing's gonna change my world.--ACROSSTHEU--29

NOTICE

He didn't notice that the lights had changed--
DAYINTHELI--7
And he never seems to notice.--FOOLONTHEH--12
I look at the world and I notice it's turning --
WHILEMYGUI--9

NOTICED

And I noticed there wasn't a chair.--NORWEGIANW--10
And looking up I noticed I was late--DAYINTHELI--21

NOVEL

It's based on a novel by a man named Lear --
PAPERBACKW--4

NOW

Now you're mine --ASKMEWHY--7
Now I'll never dance with another --ISAWHERSTA--16
Now I'll never dance with another --ISAWHERSTA--23
I've lost her now for sure, I won't see her no
more --MISERY--4
But now she says she knows--SHELOVESYO--14
I've got no time for you right now--DONTBOTHER--13
I've got no time for you right now--DONTBOTHER--28
It feels so right now --HOLDMETIGH--1
It feels so right now --HOLDMETIGH--18
It feels so right now --HOLDMETIGH--28
Now you're coming, you're coming on home (now
you're coming on home)--ITWONTBELO--12
Now you're coming, you're coming on home (now
you're coming on home)--ITWONTBELO--12
Now you're coming, you're coming on home (now
you're coming on home)--ITWONTBELO--22
Now you're coming, you're coming on home (now
you're coming on home)--ITWONTBELO--22
Now I know that you won't leave me no more--
ITWONTBELO--26
And now you've changed your mind--NOTASECOND--4
And now you've changed your mind --NOTASECOND--15
If I could see you now --ILLCRYINST--8
Can't stop thinking about her now.--EVERYLITTL--6
Yes I know that she loves me now--EVERYLITTL--13
And now the time has come and so my love I must
go --ILLFOLLOWT--5
And now the time has come and so my love I must
go --ILLFOLLOWT--10
Open up your eyes now--TELLMEWHAT--5
It is no surprise now--TELLMEWHAT--7
Look into these eyes now--TELLMEWHAT--13
Don't you realise now--TELLMEWHAT--15
Open up your eyes now--TELLMEWHAT--22
It is no surprise now--TELLMEWHAT--24
Open up your eyes now--TELLMEWHAT--31
It is no surprise now--TELLMEWHAT--33
But now ((but now)) these days are gone
((these days are gone))--HELP--11
But now ((but now)) these days are gone
((these days are gone))--HELP--11
Now I find ((and now I find)) I've changed
my mind--HELP--13
Now I find ((and now I find)) I've changed
my mind--HELP--13
And now ((now)) my life has changed ((my life
has changed))--HELP--19
And now ((now)) my life has changed ((my life
has changed))--HELP--19
But ((but)) every now and then ((now and then))
I feel so insecure--HELP--22
But ((but)) every now and then ((now and then))
I feel so insecure--HELP--22
But now ((now)) these days are gone ((these
days are gone))--HELP--31
But now ((now)) these days are gone ((these

days are gone))--HELP--31
Now I find ((and now I find)) I've changed
my mind--HELP--33
Now I find ((and now I find)) I've changed
my mind--HELP--33
Now today I find, you have changed your mind--
NIGHTBEFOR--3
Now today I find you have changed your mind--
NIGHTBEFOR--13
Now it looks as though they're here to stay--
YESTERDAY--3
Now I long for yesterday.--YESTERDAY--12
Now I need a place to hide away--YESTERDAY--15
Now I long for yesterday.--YESTERDAY--20
Now I need a place to hide away--YESTERDAY--23
For taking the easy way out, now.--DAYTRIPPER--4
She took me half the way there, now.--DAYTRIPPER
--12
And she only played one night stands, now.--
DAYTRIPPER--21
But you see now I'm too much in love.--IFINEEDEDS
--9
But you see now I'm too much in love.--IFINEEDEDS
--19
I think you know by now--MICHELLE--17
It's been a long time, now I'm coming back home --
WAIT--1
I've been away now, oh how I've been alone.--WAIT
--2
It's been a long time, now I'm coming back home --
WAIT--13
I've been away now, oh how I've been alone.--WAIT
--14
It's been a long time, now I'm coming back home --
WAIT--25
I've been away now, oh how I've been alone.--WAIT
--26
But now the tide is turning I can see that I
was blind.--WHATGOESON--16
But now I've got it the word is good.--THEWORD--8
Now that I know what I feel must be right --THEWORD
--23
But now he's gone, she doesn't need him.--FORNOONE
--19
Now my advice for those who die (Taxman)--TAXMAN
--22
Now they know how many holes it takes--DAYINTHELI
--32
I used to get mad at my school (now I can't
complain)--GETTINGBET--3
The teachers who taught me weren't cool (now I
can't complain)--GETTINGBET--4
After a while you start to smile now you feel cool
--GOODMORNIN--13
Watching the skirts you start to flirt now you're
in gear--GOODMORNIN--23
Many years from now --WHENIMSIXT--2
All you need is love (all together now) --
ALLYOUN/YS--25
Now that you know who you are--BABYYOUREA--3
Now that you've found another key--BABYYOUREA--26
Now they've lost themselves instead.--BLUEJAYWAY
--4
Now it's past my bed I know (know) --BLUEJAYWAY--15
You have found her, now go and get her (let it
out and let it in) --HEYJUDE--16
Now it's time to say good night --GOODNIGHT--1
Now the sun turns out his light --GOODNIGHT--3
Now the moon begins to shine --GOODNIGHT--9
Now the sun turns out his light --GOODNIGHT--16
Now she's hit the big time--HONEYPIE--3
And now the thought of meeting you--HONEYPIE--14
Now Honey Pie you are making me crazy--HONEYPIE--29
Now I'm so happy I found you --LONGLONGLO--5
Now I can see you, be you --LONGLONGLO--9
Now somewhere in the Black Mountain hills of
Dakota --ROCKYRACCO--1
Now she and her man who called himself Dan--
ROCKYRACCO--17
Now the doctor came in stinking of gin--ROCKYRACCO
--31
A - now Rocky Raccoon, he fell back in his room--
ROCKYRACCO--36
You might not feel it now --SAVOYTRUFF--11
But what is sweet now turns so sour.--SAVOYTRUFF
--20
ALL TOGETHER NOW.--ALLTOGETHE--Title
All together now (all together now) --ALLTOGETHE
--13
All together now (all together now) --ALLTOGETHE
--13
All together now (all together now) --ALLTOGETHE
--14
All together now (all together now) --ALLTOGETHE

All together now (all together now) --ALLTOGETHE
--14
All together now (all together now) --ALLTOGETHE
--15
All together now (all together now) --ALLTOGETHE
--15
All together now (all together now) (all
together now).--ALLTOGETHE--16
All together now (all together now) (all
together now).--ALLTOGETHE--16
All together now (all together now) (all
together now).--ALLTOGETHE--16
All together now (all together now) --ALLTOGETHE
--21
All together now (all together now) --ALLTOGETHE
--21
All together now (all together now) --ALLTOGETHE
--22
All together now (all together now) --ALLTOGETHE
--22
All together now (all together now) --ALLTOGETHE
--23
All together now (all together now) --ALLTOGETHE
--23
All together now (all together now) --ALLTOGETHE
--24
All together now (all together now) --ALLTOGETHE
--24
All together now (all together now) --ALLTOGETHE
--25
All together now (all together now) --ALLTOGETHE
--25
All together now (all together now) --ALLTOGETHE
--26
All together now (all together now) --ALLTOGETHE
--26
All together now (all together now) --ALLTOGETHE
--27
All together now (all together now) --ALLTOGETHE
--27
All together now (all together now).--ALLTOGETHE
--28
All together now (all together now).--ALLTOGETHE
--28
All together now (all together now) --ALLTOGETHE
--33
All together now (all together now) --ALLTOGETHE
--33
All together now (all together now) --ALLTOGETHE
--34
All together now (all together now) --ALLTOGETHE
--34
All together now (all together now) --ALLTOGETHE
--35
All together now (all together now) --ALLTOGETHE
--35
All together now (all together now) --ALLTOGETHE
--36
All together now (all together now) --ALLTOGETHE
--36
All together now (all together now) --ALLTOGETHE
--37
All together now (all together now) --ALLTOGETHE
--37
All together now (all together now) --ALLTOGETHE
--38
All together now (all together now) --ALLTOGETHE
--38
All together now (all together now) --ALLTOGETHE
--39
All together now (all together now) --ALLTOGETHE
--39
All together now (all together now) --ALLTOGETHE
--40
All together now (all together now) --ALLTOGETHE
--40
All together now (all together now) --ALLTOGETHE
--41
All together now (all together now) --ALLTOGETHE
--41
All together now (all together now) --ALLTOGETHE
--42
All together now (all together now) --ALLTOGETHE
--42
All together now (all together now) --ALLTOGETHE
--43
All together now - (all together now) --ALLTOGETHE
--43
All together now --ALLTOGETHE--44
All together now! (wuh, yeah, wahoo!)--ALLTOGETHE
--45
Quiet now quiet (OK) quiet--HEYBULLDOG--33
Now I'm stepping out this old brown shoe --
OLDBROWNSH--5
It won't be the same now I'm telling you.--

OLDBROWNSH--8
It won't be the same now that I'm with you.--
OLDBROWNSH--16
Won't be the same now that I'm with you.--
OLDBROWNSH--34
It won't be the same now that I'm with you
(yeah, yeah, yeah)--OLDBROWNSH--36
Come together right now over me--COMETOGETH--21
Come together right now over me--COMETOGETH--31
Come together right now over me--COMETOGETH--42
Come on now.--SHECAMEINT--1
But now she sucks her thumb and wonders --
SHECAMEINT--6
I don't want to leave her now --SOMETHING--4
I don't want to leave her now --SOMETHING--9
You stick around now it may show --SOMETHING--13
I don't want to leave her now --SOMETHING--18
((And now we'd like to do)) Hark the Angels
Come...--DIGIT--13
I feel it now, I hope you feel it too.--FORYOUBLUE
--15
Oh now I roll a stony--IDIGAPONY--19
Oh now I feel the wind blow--IDIGAPONY--26
Oh now I roll a lorry--IDIGAPONY--29
Me hand's getting - a too cold to play a chord now.
--IDIGAPONY--38
Now they're frightened of leaving it --IMEMINE--5

NOWHERE
I'm looking through you and you're nowhere.--
IMLOOKINGT--14
NOWHERE MAN.--NOWHEREMAN--Title
He's a real Nowhere Man --NOWHEREMAN--1
Sitting in his nowhere land --NOWHEREMAN--2
Making all his nowhere plans for nobody.--
NOWHEREMAN--3
Nowhere Man please listen --NOWHEREMAN--7
Nowhere Man the world is at your command.--
NOWHEREMAN--9
Nowhere Man can you see me at all?--NOWHEREMAN--12
Nowhere Man don't worry --NOWHEREMAN--13
Nowhere Man please listen --NOWHEREMAN--19
Nowhere Man the world is at your command.--
NOWHEREMAN--21
He's a real Nowhere Man --NOWHEREMAN--22
Sitting in his nowhere land --NOWHEREMAN--23
Making all his nowhere plans for nobody --
NOWHEREMAN--24
Making all his nowhere plans for nobody --
NOWHEREMAN--25
Making all his nowhere plans for nobody.--
NOWHEREMAN--26
There's nowhere you can be that isn't where
you're meant to be ((love))--ALLYOUN/YS--21
With voices out of nowhere --CRYBABYCRY--30
All the money's gone, nowhere to go.--YOUNEVERGI
--9
Yellow lorry slow, nowhere to go.--YOUNEVERGI--12
But oh, that magic feeling, nowhere to go --
YOUNEVERGI--13
Nowhere to go - nowhere to go.--YOUNEVERGI--15
Nowhere to go - nowhere to go.--YOUNEVERGI--15
Two of us riding nowhere --TWOOFUS--3
Getting nowhere on our way back home.--TWOOFUS--22
Getting nowhere on our way back home.--TWOOFUS--31

,
NUMBER
Carve your number on my wall --IFINEEDEDS--10
Carve your number on my wall --IFINEEDEDS--20
I'm taking the time for a number of things--
FIXINGAHOL--19
I never give you my number --YOUNEVERGI--4
YOU KNOW MY NAME (LOOK UP MY NUMBER).--YOUKNOWMYN
--Title
You know my name, look up de number --YOUKNOWMYN
--1
You know my name, look up de number.--YOUKNOWMYN
--2
Good evening, you know my name, well then look
up my number --YOUKNOWMYN--9
You know my name, that's right, look up my
number (hey) --YOUKNOWMYN--10
Look up the number (heads up boys) --YOUKNOWMYN--14
You know my name - haa, that's right, look up
the number --YOUKNOWMYN--15
You know my name, ba ba ba bum, look up the
number --YOUKNOWMYN--18
You know my name, look up the number --YOUKNOWMYN
--19
My name, you know, you know, ((look up the

number))--YOUKNOWMYN--25
You know my name (you know my number).--YOUKNOWMYN
--26
You know, you know my name. ((you know my
number))--YOUKNOWMYN--28
You know my name, look up the number --YOUKNOWMYN
--29
You know my name, look up the number.--YOUKNOWMYN
--30
You know, you know my name, look up the number.--
YOUKNOWMYN--31
You know my name ((you know)), you know me
number (too/two)--YOUKNOWMYN--33
You know my name, you know me number three --
YOUKNOWMYN--34
You know my name, you know me number four --
YOUKNOWMYN--35
You know my name, look up the number --YOUKNOWMYN
--36
You know my name ((you know)), you know me
number (too/two)--YOUKNOWMYN--37
You know my number, what's up with you? - ha--
YOUKNOWMYN--40
Then I find I've got the number wrong.--ONEAFTERNI
--14
Then I find I got the number wrong - well ((well)).
--ONEAFTERNI--24

NUN
Sunday morning creeping like a nun --LADYMADONN--6

NURSE
The pretty nurse is selling poppies from a tray--
PENNYLANE--21

O'CLOCK
People running round it's five o'clock--GOODMORNIN
--18
Wednesday morning at five o'clock as the day begins
--SHESLEAVIN--1
Friday morning at nine o'clock she is far away--
SHESLEAVIN--25
At twelve o'clock a meeting round the table --
CRYBABYCRY--28

O'FELL
Featuring Dennis O'Fell and Ringo.--YOUKNOWMYN--6
Let's hear it for Dennis O'Fell.--YOUKNOWMYN--24

OATS
Phase one in which Doris gets her oats.--TWOOFUS
--2

OB-LA-DA
OB-LA-DI OB-LA-DA.--OBLADIOBLA--Title
Ob-la-di ob-la-da life goes on bra --OBLADIOBLA--5
Ob-la-di ob-la-da life goes on bra --OBLADIOBLA--7
Ob-la-di ob-la-da life goes on bra --OBLADIOBLA--13
Ob-la-di ob-la-da life goes on bra --OBLADIOBLA--15
Ob-la-di ob-la-da life goes on bra --OBLADIOBLA--25
Hey, ob-la-di ob-la-da life goes on bra --
OBLADIOBLA--27
Ob-la-di ob-la-da life goes on bra --OBLADIOBLA--36
Ob-la-di ob-la-da life goes on bra --OBLADIOBLA--38

OB-LA-DI
OB-LA-DI OB-LA-DA.--OBLADIOBLA--Title
Ob-la-di ob-la-da life goes on bra --OBLADIOBLA--5
Ob-la-di ob-la-da life goes on bra --OBLADIOBLA--7
Ob-la-di ob-la-da life goes on bra --OBLADIOBLA--13
Ob-la-di ob-la-da life goes on bra --OBLADIOBLA--15
Ob-la-di ob-la-da life goes on bra --OBLADIOBLA--25
Hey, ob-la-di ob-la-da life goes on bra --
OBLADIOBLA--27
Ob-la-di ob-la-da life goes on bra --OBLADIOBLA--36
Ob-la-di ob-la-da life goes on bra --OBLADIOBLA--38
Take ob-la-di 'b-la-da ((ha ha ha)) --OBLADIOBLA
--41
We all know ob-la-di 'b-la-da --SAVOYTRUFF--21

OBRIGADO
Questo obrigado tanta mucho cake and eat it
carousel.--SUNKING--8

OBSCENE

Always shouts out something obscene--MEANMRMUST--13

OCEAN
Fixing the hole in the ocean--GLASSONION--21
The coral that lies beneath the waves (lies
beneath the ocean waves).--OCTOPUSSGA--18

OCEANCHILD
Julia, Julia oceanchild calls me --JULIA--3

OCTOPUS'S
OCTOPUS'S GARDEN.--OCTOPUSSGA--Title
In an octopus's garden in the shade.--OCTOPUSSGA
--2
In his octopus's garden in the shade.--OCTOPUSSGA
--4
An octopus's garden with me.--OCTOPUSSGA--6
In an octopus's garden in the shade.--OCTOPUSSGA
--8
In an octopus's garden near a cave.--OCTOPUSSGA--12
In an octopus's garden in the shade.--OCTOPUSSGA
--16
In an octopus's garden with you --OCTOPUSSGA--24
In an octopus's garden with you --OCTOPUSSGA--25
In an octopus's garden with you.--OCTOPUSSGA--26

ODES
Oh Danny Boy, the odes of Pan are calling.--
ONEAFTERNI--33

OF
I can't conceive of any more misery.--ASKMEWHY
--13
And I'm always thinking of you.--ASKMEWHY--15
And I'm always thinking of you.--ASKMEWHY--23
I can't conceive of any more misery.--ASKMEWHY--25
And I'm always thinking of you, you, you.--ASKMEWHY
--27
I'm the kind of guy, who never used to cry.--MISERY
--2
That's the kind of love that is too good to be true
--THANKYOUGI--9
It's you she's thinking of--SHELOVESYO--6
Tell me that you want the kind of things --
CANTBUYMEL--19
Tell me that you want the kind of things --
CANTBUYMEL--29
I think of you--THERESAPLA--5
I know this love of mine --ANDILOVEHE--17
I know this love of mine --ANDILOVEHE--22
So - oh, I should have realised a lot of things
before --ISHOULDHAV--11
You'll be thinking of me, somehow I will know --
THINGSWESA--2
You say you'll be mine girl, till the end of time
--THINGSWESA--4
I got a whole lot of things to tell her --
WHENIGETHO--2
I got a whole lot of things I gotta say to her.--
WHENIGETHO--6
I got a whole lot of things to tell her --
WHENIGETHO--8
I got a whole lot of things to tell her --
WHENIGETHO--14
I got a whole lot of things to tell her --
WHENIGETHO--25
I got a whole lot of things to tell her --
WHENIGETHO--27
She thinks of him and so she dresses in black --
BABYSINBLA--4
I think of her --BABYSINBLA--10
But she thinks only of him --BABYSINBLA--11
She thinks of him.--BABYSINBLA--13
She thinks of him and so she dresses in black --
BABYSINBLA--24
There is one thing I'm sure of--EVERYLITTL--14
Of all the love I have won or have lost --IMALOSER
--3
Would it be too much to ask of you --WHATYOURED--3
Why should it be so much to ask of you --WHATYOURED
--7
Why should it be so much to ask of you --WHATYOURED
--14
Why should it be so much to ask of you --WHATYOURED
--21
In spite of you it's true--YESITIS--17
In spite of you it's true--YESITIS--26
If I'm part of you--TELLMEWHAT--4
Just the sight of you makes night-time bright,

very bright.--ITSONLYLOV--9

But as it is I'll dream of her tonight --IVEJUSTSEE
--10

I have never known the like of this--IVEJUSTSEE
--14

And kept out of sight--IVEJUSTSEE--16

When I think of things we did it makes me wanna
cry.--NIGHTBEFOR--10

When I think of things we did it makes me wanna
cry.--NIGHTBEFOR--18

I'll make a point of taking her away from you
(watch what you do), yeah--YOUREGONNA--16

I'll make a point of taking her away from you
(watch what you do), yeah--YOUREGONNA--23

Run the risk of knowing that our love may soon be
gone.--WECANWORKI--4

Think of what you're saying --WECANWORKI--6

Think of what I'm saying --WECANWORKI--8

I wanna be famous, a star of the screen --
DRIVEMYCAR--3

She's the kind of girl you want so much it makes
you sorry --GIRL--3

When I think of all the times I tried so hard
to leave her --GIRL--6

She's the kind of girl who puts you down--GIRL
--11

That a man must break his back to earn his day of
leisure?--GIRL--24

You're the one that I'd be thinking of --IFINEEDEDS
--2

Love has a nasty habit of disappearing overnight.
--IMLOOKINGT--10

You're thinking of me the same old way --IMLOOKINGT
--11

Love has a nasty habit of disappearing overnight.
--IMLOOKINGT--16

But of all these friends and lovers --INMYLIFE--9

When I think of love as something new.--INMYLIFE
--12

Doesn't have a point of view --NOWHEREMAN--4

Doesn't have a point of view --NOWHEREMAN--16

The ruins of the life that you had in mind --
THINKFORYO--11

I met you in the morning waiting for the tides of
time --WHATGOESON--5

I used to think of no-one else but you were just
the same --WHATGOESON--22

You didn't even think of me as someone with a name.
--WHATGOESON--23

Say the word I'm thinking of --THEWORD--3

Spread the word I'm thinking of --THEWORD--11

Say the word I'm thinking of --THEWORD--19

It's the word I'm thinking of --THEWORD--27

It's a dirty story of a dirty man --PAPERBACKW--8

It's just a state of mind (when it rains and
shines)--RAIN--15

When I'm in the middle of a dream--IMONLYSLEE
--3

When I'm in the middle of a dream--IMONLYSLEE
--23

Father McKenzie writing the words of a sermon--
ELEANORRIG--11

You find that all her words of kindness linger on
--FORNOONE--2

No sign of love behind the tears cried for no-one
--FORNOONE--8

No sign of love behind the tears cried for no-one
--FORNOONE--15

No sign of love behind the tears cried for no-one
--FORNOONE--25

Could see another kind of mind there.--GOTTOGETYO
--4

Every single day of my life?--GOTTOGETYO--7

Every single day of my life?--GOTTOGETYO--22

Could see another kind of mind there.--GOTTOGETYO
--28

Here, making each day of the year--HERETHEREA--2

Changing my life with a wave of her hand--
HERETHEREA--3

Both of us thinking how good it can be--HERETHEREA
--6

That you may see the meaning of within--TOMORROWNE
--5

But listen to the colour of your dreams--TOMORROWNE
--11

Of the beginning --TOMORROWNE--14

Of the beginning --TOMORROWNE--15

Of the beginning --TOMORROWNE--16

Of the beginning --TOMORROWNE--17

Of the beginning --TOMORROWNE--18

Of the beginning --TOMORROWNE--19

Of the beginning --TOMORROWNE--20

And he told us of his life--YELLOWSUBM--3

In the land of submarines.--YELLOWSUBM--4

Till we found a sea of green--YELLOWSUBM--6

Many more of them live next door--YELLOWSUBM--14

As we live a life of ease--YELLOWSUBM--25

Everyone of us (everyone of us) has all we need
(has all we need) --YELLOWSUBM--26

Everyone of us (everyone of us) has all we need
(has all we need) --YELLOWSUBM--26

Sky of blue (sky of blue) and sea of green
(sea of green)--YELLOWSUBM--27

Sky of blue (sky of blue) and sea of green
(sea of green)--YELLOWSUBM--27

Sky of blue (sky of blue) and sea of green
(sea of green)--YELLOWSUBM--27

Sky of blue (sky of blue) and sea of green
(sea of green)--YELLOWSUBM--27

Of every head he's had the pleasure to know--
PENNYLANE--2

And in his pocket is a portrait of the Queen--
PENNYLANE--13

A four of fish and finger pies in summer--PENNYLANE
--18

Behind the shelter in the middle of the roundabout
--PENNYLANE--20

BEING FOR THE BENEFIT OF MR. KITE!--BEINGFORTH
--Title

For the benefit of Mr. Kite--BEINGFORTH--1

Late of Pablo Fanques Fair - what a scene.--
BEINGFORTH--4

Lastly through a hogshead of real fire--BEINGFORTH
--6

And of course Henry the Horse dances the waltz.--
BEINGFORTH--14

A crowd of people stood and stared--DAYINTHELI--8

Nobody was really sure if he was from the House
of Lords--DAYINTHELI--10

A crowd of people turned away--DAYINTHELI--13

Woke up, fell out of bed--DAYINTHELI--15

I'm taking the time for a number of things--
FIXINGAHOL--19

Everyone you see is full of life--GOODMORNIN--20

When I caught a glimpse of Rita--LOVELYRITA--8

Give us a wink and make me think of you.--
LOVELYRITA--28

Cellophane flowers of yellow and green--LUCYINTHES
--5

They've been going in and out of style--SGTPEPPERS
--3

She (we gave her most of our lives)--SHESLEAVIN--8

Is leaving (sacrificed most of our lives)--
SHESLEAVIN--9

Standing alone at the top of the stairs--SHESLEAVIN
--15

She (we never thought of ourselves)--SHESLEAVIN--20

Birthday greetings, bottle of wine?--WHENIMSIXT--4

In the Isle of Wight --WHENIMSIXT--23

Stating point of view.--WHENIMSIXT--29

How do I feel by the end of the day?--WITHALITTL
--10

Who hide themselves behind a wall of illusion--
WITHINYOUW--4

Are you one of them?--WITHINYOUW--27

Peace of mind is waiting there--WITHINYOUW--30

One of the beautiful people?--BABYYOUREA--2

One of the beautiful people?--BABYYOUREA--8

One of the beautiful people?--BABYYOUREA--23

Soon will be the break of day (day) --BLUEJAYWAY
--17

The man of a thousand voices talking perfectly loud
--FOOLONTHEH--9

Without going out of my door --INNERLIGHT--1

Without looking out of my window --INNERLIGHT--3

I could know the ways of heaven.--INNERLIGHT--4

Without going out of your door --INNERLIGHT--8

Without looking out of your window --INNERLIGHT--10

You can know the ways of heaven.--INNERLIGHT--11

But if you go carrying pictures of Chairman Mao --
REVOLUTION--28

Blackbird singing in the dead of night --BLACKBIRD
--1

Blackbird singing in the dead of night --BLACKBIRD
--5

Into the light of a dark black night.--BLACKBIRD
--10

Into the light of a dark black night.--BLACKBIRD
--12

Blackbird singing in the dead of night --BLACKBIRD
--13

THE CONTINUING STORY OF BUNGALOW BILL.--CONTINUING
--Title

In case of accidents he always took his mom --
CONTINUING--8

If looks could kill it would have been us instead
of him.--CONTINUING--29

The King of Marigold was in the kitchen --

CRYBABYCRY--4
Playing piano for the children of the King.--
    CRYBABYCRY--7
The Duchess of Kirkaldy always smiling --CRYBABYCRY
    --20
With voices out of nowhere --CRYBABYCRY--30
That you are part of everything.--DEARPRUDEN--9
She's well acquainted with the touch of the
    velvet hand --HAPPINESSI--3
A soap impression of his wife which he ate --
    HAPPINESSI--7
When I get to the bottom I go back to the top
    of the slide --HELTERSKEL--1
When I get to the bottom I go back to the top
    of the slide--HELTERSKEL--18
North of England way--HONEYPIE--2
Of your Hollywood song.--HONEYPIE--12
You became a legend of the silver screen--HONEYPIE
    --13
And now the thought of meeting you--HONEYPIE--14
You know I'd give you everything I've got for a
    little peace of mind.--IMSOTIRED--13
You know I'd give you everything I've got for a
    little peace of mind.--IMSOTIRED--22
I'd give you everything I've got for a little
    peace of mind --IMSOTIRED--23
I'd give you everything I've got for a little
    peace of mind.--IMSOTIRED--24
Half of what I say is meaningless --JULIA--1
So I sing the song of love, Julia.--JULIA--4
So I sing the song of love, Julia.--JULIA--6
Her hair of floating sky is shimmering --JULIA--7
So I sing the song of love, Julia.--JULIA--10
So I sing a song of love, Julia.--JULIA--14
So I sing a song of love for Julia --JULIA--16
When you find yourself in the thick of it --
    MARTHAMYDE--5
Help yourself to a bit of what is all around you
    - silly girl.--MARTHAMYDE--6
When you find yourself in the thick of it --
    MARTHAMYDE--11
Help yourself to a bit of what is all around you
    - silly girl.--MARTHAMYDE--12
Listen to the pretty sound of music as she flies.
    --MOTHERNATU--4
Find me in my field of grass - Mother Nature's
    son --MOTHERNATU--8
In a couple of years they have built a home sweet
    home --OBLADIOBLA--17
With a couple of kids running in the yard of
    Desmond and Molly Jones.--OBLADIOBLA--18
With a couple of kids running in the yard of
    Desmond and Molly Jones.--OBLADIOBLA--18
In a couple of years they have built a home sweet
    home--OBLADIOBLA--29
With a couple of kids running in the yard of
    Desmond and Molly Jones.--OBLADIOBLA--30
With a couple of kids running in the yard of
    Desmond and Molly Jones.--OBLADIOBLA--30
Everywhere there's lots of piggies--PIGGIES--15
If you go carrying pictures of Chairman Mao --
    REVOLUTONE--43
Now somewhere in the Black Mountain hills of
    Dakota --ROCKYRACCO--1
There lived a young boy name of Rocky Raccoon--
    ROCKYRACCO--2
To shoot off the legs of his rival.--ROCKYRACCO--12
By stealing the girl of his fancy --ROCKYRACCO--14
Now the doctor came in stinking of gin--ROCKYRACCO
    --31
The story of Rocky, that's the song.--ROCKYRACCO
    --48
You made a fool of everyone--SEXYSADIE--2
You made a fool of everyone--SEXYSADIE--3
Sexy Sadie (sexy Sadie) the greatest of them
    all ((she's the greatest))--SEXYSADIE--11
She's the latest and the greatest (she's the
    greatest) of them all--SEXYSADIE--23
(Sexy Sadie she's the latest and the greatest
    of them all)--SEXYSADIE--24
She made a fool of everyone--SEXYSADIE--26
My mother was of the sky --YERBLUES--10
My father was of the earth --YERBLUES--11
But I am of the universe --YERBLUES--12
Some kind of happiness is measured out in miles--
    HEYBULLDOG--3
Some kind of innocence is measured out in years--
    HEYBULLDOG--7
Wigwam frightened of the dark--HEYBULLDOG--14
Some kind of solitude is measured out in you--
    HEYBULLDOG--15
Floating down the stream of time--ITSALLTOOM--12
With your long blonde hair and your eyes of blue
    --ITSALLTOOM--35

With your long blonde hair and your eyes of blue
    --ITSALLTOOM--36
What words I say or time of day it is --ONLYANORTH
    --8
Is a little dark and out of key --ONLYANORTH--14
THE BALLAD OF JOHN AND YOKO.--BALLADOFJO--Title
It's good to have the both of you back.--BALLADOFJO
    --40
But right is only half of what's wrong --OLDBROWNSH
    --2
I want that love of yours --OLDBROWNSH--27
And in the middle of the celebrations--CARRYTHATW
    --7
But I gotta get a bellyfull of wine.--HERMAJESTY
    --6
Get a dose of her in jackboots and kilt --
    POLYTHENEP--6
She's a kind of a girl that makes the News Of
    The World.--POLYTHENEP--8
She's a kind of a girl that makes the News Of
    The World.--POLYTHENEP--8
By the banks of her own lagoon.--SHECAMEINT--7
And all I have to do is think of her --SOMETHING
    --16
And in the middle of negotiations you break down.
    --YOUNEVERGI--3
And in the middle of investigation I break down.--
    YOUNEVERGI--6
Out of college, money spent --YOUNEVERGI--7
When I find myself in times of trouble --LETITBE/45
    --1
Speaking words of wisdom, let it be.--LETITBE/45
    --3
And in my hour of darkness--LETITBE/45--4
She is standing right in front of me --LETITBE/45
    --5
Speaking words of wisdom, let it be.--LETITBE/45
    --6
Whisper words of wisdom, let it be.--LETITBE/45--8
Whisper words of wisdom, let it be.--LETITBE/45--18
Whisper words of wisdom, let it be.--LETITBE/45--20
I wake up to the sound of music --LETITBE/45--24
Speaking words of wisdom, let it be.--LETITBE/45
    --26
Whisper words of wisdom, let it be.--LETITBE/45--30
Pools of sorrow, waves of joy--ACROSSTHEU--3
Pools of sorrow, waves of joy--ACROSSTHEU--3
Images of broken light which dance before me like
    a million eyes--ACROSSTHEU--11
Sounds of laughter, shades of life--ACROSSTHEU
    --20
Sounds of laughter, shades of life--ACROSSTHEU-
    --20
I'd like to say thank you on behalf of the group
    and ourselves--GETBACK/LP--38
Now they're frightened of leaving it --IMEMINE--5
No-one's frightened of playing it --IMEMINE--18
No-one's frightened of playing it --IMEMINE--31
When I find myself in times of trouble --LETITBE/LP
    --1
Speaking words of wisdom, let it be.--LETITBE/LP
    --3
And in my hour of darkness--LETITBE/LP--4
She is standing right in front of me --LETITBE/LP
    --5
Speaking words of wisdom, let it be.--LETITBE/LP
    --6
Whisper words of wisdom, let it be.--LETITBE/LP--8
Whisper words of wisdom, let it be.--LETITBE/LP--18
Whisper words of wisdom, let it be.--LETITBE/LP--20
I wake up to the sound of music --LETITBE/LP--24
Speaking words of wisdom, let it be.--LETITBE/LP
    --26
Whisper words of wisdom, let it be.--LETITBE/LP--32
Has left a pool of tears crying for the day.--
    LONGANDWIN--5
Oh Danny Boy, the odes of Pan are calling.--
    ONEAFTERNI--33
TWO OF US.--TWOOFUS--Title
Two of us riding nowhere --TWOOFUS--3
Two of us sending postcards --TWOOFUS--10
Two of us wearing raincoats --TWOOFUS--19
Two of us wearing raincoats --TWOOFUS--28

OFF
    And crawled off to sleep in the bath.--NORWEGIANW
        --20
    Turn off your mind, relax and float down-stream--
        TOMORROWNE--1
    And one day his woman ran off with another guy --
        ROCKYRACCO--3
    To shoot off the legs of his rival.--ROCKYRACCO--12
    Coming off stronger all the time --IMEMINE--7

OFTEN

I know I'll often stop and think about them --
     INMYLIFE--15
I know I'll often stop and think about them --
     INMYLIFE--19
How often have you been there?--BABYYOUREA--9
Often enough to know.--BABYYOUREA--10

OH

As I write this letter (oh) send my love to you --
     PSILOVEYOU--16
Oh (wuh!) we danced through the night --ISAWHERSTA
     --20
Oh since I saw her standing there--ISAWHERSTA--24
Like a heart that's oh so true--FROMMETOYO--8
Oh, oh - mmm, you've been good to me--THANKYOUGI
     --1
Oh, oh - mmm, you've been good to me--THANKYOUGI
     --1
Oh, oh - mmm, you've been good to me--THANKYOUGI
     --11
Oh, oh - mmm, you've been good to me--THANKYOUGI
     --11
Oh, oh, oh --THANKYOUGI--15
Oh, oh, oh --THANKYOUGI--15
Oh, oh, oh --THANKYOUGI--15
Oh, oh, oh --THANKYOUGI--16
Oh, oh, oh --THANKYOUGI--16
Oh, oh, oh --THANKYOUGI--16
Oh, oh.--THANKYOUGI--17
Oh, oh.--THANKYOUGI--17
Oh yeah, oh yeah, oh yeah, oh yeah.--ILLGETYOU--1
Oh yeah, oh yeah, oh yeah, oh yeah.--ILLGETYOU--1
Oh yeah, oh yeah, oh yeah, oh yeah.--ILLGETYOU--1
Oh yeah, oh yeah, oh yeah, oh yeah.--ILLGETYOU--1
Yes I will I'll get you in the end, oh yeah,
     oh yeah.--ILLGETYOU--8
Yes I will I'll get you in the end, oh yeah,
     oh yeah.--ILLGETYOU--8
Yes I will, I'll get you in the end, oh yeah,
     oh yeah.--ILLGETYOU--15
Yes I will, I'll get you in the end, oh yeah,
     oh yeah.--ILLGETYOU--15
So you might as well resign yourself to me, oh
     yeah.--ILLGETYOU--18
Yes I will, I'll get you in the end, oh yeah,
     oh yeah--ILLGETYOU--25
Yes I will, I'll get you in the end, oh yeah,
     oh yeah--ILLGETYOU--25
Oh yeah, oh yeah, whoa - yeah.--ILLGETYOU--26
Oh yeah, oh yeah, whoa - yeah.--ILLGETYOU--26
Wow (ow) - oh--IWANNABEYO--25
Oh - oh!--IWANNABEYO--27
Oh - oh!--IWANNABEYO--27
I wanna be your man (oh)--IWANNABEYO--43
Baby take a chance with me, oh yeah --LITTLECHIL
     --22
Baby take a chance with me, oh yeah --LITTLECHIL
     --23
Baby take a chance with me, oh yeah --LITTLECHIL
     --24
Baby take a chance with me, oh yeah.--LITTLECHIL
     --25
My crying is through, oh.--NOTASECOND--6
My crying is through, oh.--NOTASECOND--17
Oh yeah, I'll tell you something--IWANTTOHOL--1
Oh please say to me--IWANTTOHOL--7
Oh, and this boy would be happy--THISBOY--7
Just to love you, but oh my!--THISBOY--8
Can't buy me love, oh, love, oh --CANTBUYMEL--1
Can't buy me love, oh, love, oh --CANTBUYMEL--1
Can't buy me love, oh.--CANTBUYMEL--2
Can't buy me love, oh, everybody tells me so --
     CANTBUYMEL--15
Can't buy me love oh - no, no - no.--CANTBUYMEL--
     --16
Can't buy me love, oh, everybody tells me so --
     CANTBUYMEL--25
Can't buy me love oh - no, no, no - no.--CANTBUYMEL
     --26
Can't buy me love, oh, love, oh --CANTBUYMEL--33
Can't buy me love, oh, love, oh --CANTBUYMEL--33
Can't buy me love, oh, oh.--CANTBUYMEL--34
Can't buy me love, oh, oh.--CANTBUYMEL--34
Oh you can't do that.--YOUCANTDOT--8
Oh you can't do that.--YOUCANTDOT--17
Oh you can't do that - no!--YOUCANTDOT--31
Oh you can't do that.--YOUCANTDOT--50
Oh, I can't sleep at night since you've been
     gone --ICALLYOURN--3
Oh, I can't sleep at night, but just the same --
     ICALLYOURN--9
Oh, I can't sleep at night, but just the same --

ICALLYOURN--16
Oh, It's been a hard day's night --HARDDAYSNI--30
That when I tell you that I love you, oh --
     ISHOULDHAV--7
You're gonna say you love me too, oh.--ISHOULDHAV
     --8
So - oh, I should have realised a lot of things
     before --ISHOULDHAV--11
That when I tell you that I love you, oh --
     ISHOULDHAV--17
You're gonna say you love me too, oh.--ISHOULDHAV
     --18
Oh please, don't run and hide --IFIFELL--11
Oh please, don't hurt my pride like her.--IFIFELL
     --13
Just to dance with you is everything I need (oh)
     --IMHAPPYJUS--12
I think I'll love you too ((oh)) --IMHAPPYJUS--14
I'm so happy when you dance with me ((oh - oh)).--
     IMHAPPYJUS--15
I'm so happy when you dance with me ((oh - oh)).--
     IMHAPPYJUS--15
Just to dance with you (oh) is everything I
     need (oh) --IMHAPPYJUS--20
Just to dance with you (oh) is everything I
     need (oh) --IMHAPPYJUS--20
I think I'll love you too ((oh)) --IMHAPPYJUS--22
I'm so happy when you dance with me ((oh - oh)).--
     IMHAPPYJUS--23
I'm so happy when you dance with me ((oh - oh)).--
     IMHAPPYJUS--23
I've discovered I'm in love with you (oh - oh).--
     IMHAPPYJUS--27
I've discovered I'm in love with you (oh - oh).--
     IMHAPPYJUS--27
'cos I'm happy just to dance with you (oh - oh).--
     IMHAPPYJUS--28
'cos I'm happy just to dance with you (oh - oh).--
     IMHAPPYJUS--28
Oh - oh, oh.--IMHAPPYJUS--29
Oh - oh, oh.--IMHAPPYJUS--29
Oh - oh, oh.--IMHAPPYJUS--29
Did you have to treat me oh so bad,--TELLMEWHY--7
Oh - ho, oh - ho.--ILLBEBACK--8
Oh - ho, oh - ho.--ILLBEBACK--8
Oh - ho, oh - ho.--ILLBEBACK--17
Oh - ho, oh - ho.--ILLBEBACK--17
Oh - ho, oh - ho.--ILLBEBACK--25
Oh - ho, oh - ho.--ILLBEBACK--25
Oh dear, what can I do?--BABYSINBLA--1
Tell me, oh what can I do?--BABYSINBLA--3
Oh dear, what can I do?--BABYSINBLA--7
Tell me, oh what can I do?--BABYSINBLA--9
Oh how long will it take --BABYSINBLA--14
Tell me oh what can I do?--BABYSINBLA--18
Oh how long will it take --BABYSINBLA--19
Tell me oh what can I do?--BABYSINBLA--23
Oh dear, what can I do?--BABYSINBLA--27
Tell me oh what can I do?--BABYSINBLA--29
Just like I need you, oh - oh.--EIGHTDAYSA--22
Just like I need you, oh - oh.--EIGHTDAYSA--22
And though I lose a friend in the end you will
     know, oh.--ILLFOLLOWT--6
And though I lose a friend in the end you will
     know, oh.--ILLFOLLOWT--11
Oh, she's got a ticket to ride--TICKETTORI--26
Yes it is, yes it is, oh yes it is, yeah.--YESITIS
     --13
Yes it is, yes it is, oh yes it is, yeah.--YESITIS
     '--22
In oh so many ways--HELP--20
Oh baby, I'm down (down on the ground)--IMDOWN--19
Oh yes, I'm down (I'm really down)--IMDOWN--29
Oh baby, I'm upside-down--IMDOWN--32
Oh yeah, yeah, yeah, yeah, yeah--IMDOWN--33
Oh baby, I'm down (I'm really down)--IMDOWN--35
Oh baby, I'm down, yeah--IMDOWN--39
Oh baby, I'm down (I'm really down)--IMDOWN--43
Oh yes, you told me--INEEDYOU--11
I get high when I see you go by, my oh my--
     ITSONLYLOV--1
Oh I believe in yesterday.--YESTERDAY--4
Oh yesterday came suddenly.--YESTERDAY--8
Oh I believe in yesterday.--YESTERDAY--16
Oh I believe in yesterday.--YESTERDAY--24
Yeah, oh baby you've changed.--IMLOOKINGT--21
Oh, what you mean to me--MICHELLE--13
I've been away now, oh how I've been alone.--WAIT
     --2
I've been away now, oh how I've been alone.--WAIT
     --14
I've been away now, oh how I've been alone.--WAIT
     --26
(Oh yeah) ooo - la la la la--YOUWONTSEE--32

I read the news today, oh boy--DAYINTHELI--1
I saw a film today, oh boy--DAYINTHELI--11
I read the news today, oh boy--DAYINTHELI--28
Lovely Rita (oh) meter maid--LOVELYRITA--4
Oh, lovely Rita meter maid--LOVELYRITA--26
Lovely Rita ((oh lovely Rita meter, meter
   maid)) meter maid--LOVELYRITA--31
Da da da - da - da - da - wuh - oh--LOVELYRITA--34
Ah - ah - ah (oh) - ah - ah - ah - ah - ah - ah
   - ah--LOVELYRITA--35
Oh I get by with a little help from my friends --
   WITHALITTL--5
Oh I get by with a little help from my friends --
   WITHALITTL--23
Oh I'm gonna try with a little help from my
   friends.--WITHALITTL--25
Oh I get by with a little help from my friends --
   WITHALITTL--30
Oh I get high with a little help from my friends,
   --WITHALITTL--32
(Oh) love is all you need--ALLYOUN/YS--41
Love is all you need (oh yeah)--ALLYOUN/YS--42
Love is all you need (oh)--ALLYOUN/YS--49
Oh, baby you're a rich man --BABYYOUREA--37
Wuh-oh, baby, you're a rich (oh) man--BABYYOUREA--40
Oh, baby, you're a rich man.--BABYYOUREA--43
Oh no --HELLOGOODB--3
Oh no --HELLOGOODB--9
Oh no --HELLOGOODB--18
Oh - oh no --HELLOGOODB--26
Oh - oh no --HELLOGOODB--26
Oh - oh - oh!--FOOLONTHEH--20
Oh - oh - oh!--FOOLONTHEH--20
Oh - oh - oh!--FOOLONTHEH--20
Oh, round 'n' round 'n' round 'n' round.--
   FOOLONTHEH--27
Oh!--FOOLONTHEH--28
Remember to let her under your skin (oh) --HEYJUDE
   --28
Oh yeah - nah nah nah, nah - nah - nah - nah--
   HEYJUDE--31
Nah nah nah, nah - nah - nah - nah (oh Jude) --
   HEYJUDE--50
Nah nah nah, nah - nah - nah - nah (oh) --HEYJUDE
   --70
Nah nah nah, nah - nah - nah - nah (oh) --HEYJUDE
   --72
Oh!--REVOLUTION--21
Oh - flew in from Miami Beach BOAC --BACKINTHEU--1
Oh come on!--BACKINTHEU--19
Oh - show me round the snow-peaked mountains way
   down south --BACKINTHEU--31
Oh let me tell you honey --BACKINTHEU--38
(Wuh oh)--BIRTHDAY--15
Oh yeah, oh yeah, oh yeah! (yeah)--GLASSONION--15
Oh yeah, oh yeah, oh yeah! (yeah)--GLASSONION--15
Oh yeah, oh yeah, oh yeah! (yeah)--GLASSONION--15
Do do do do do do, oh yeah.--HAPPINESSI--2
When I hold you in my arms ((oh, yeah)) --
   HAPPINESSI--22
And I feel my finger on your trigger ((oh,
   yeah)) --HAPPINESSI--23
I know nobody can do me no harm ((oh, yeah)) --
   HAPPINESSI--24
Look out helter-skelter, helter-skelter,
   helter-skelter - oh.--HELTERSKEL--16
Coming down fast (oh I hear my baby speaking -
   ooo)...--HELTERSKEL--30
Oh, Honey Pie my position is tragic--HONEYPIE--10
Oh, Honey Pie you are driving me frantic--HONEYPIE
   --16
Oh-oh-oh - oh - oh--HONEYPIE--34
Oh-oh-oh - oh - oh--HONEYPIE--34
So many tears I was wasting - oh, oh!--LONGLONGLO
   --8
So many tears I was wasting - oh, oh!--LONGLONGLO
   --8
Oh I love you --LONGLONGLO--12
Oh I love you.--LONGLONGLO--14
Oh yes--REVOLUTONE--2
Don't you know it's gonna be ((oh shoo-be-do-a))--
   REVOLUTONE--13
Alright ((oh shoo-be-do-a))?--REVOLUTONE--14
Don't you know it's gonna be ((oh shoo-be-do-a))--
   REVOLUTONE--15
Alright ((oh shoo-be-do-a))?--REVOLUTONE--16
Don't you know it's gonna be ((oh shoo-be-do-a))--
   REVOLUTONE--17
Alright ((oh shoo-be-do-a))?--REVOLUTONE--18
(Oh shoo-be-do-a, oh shoo-be-do-a).--REVOLUTONE--22
(Oh shoo-be-do-a, oh shoo-be-do-a).--REVOLUTONE--22
(Oh shoo-be-do-a, oh shoo-be-do-a).--REVOLUTONE--26
(Oh shoo-be-do-a, oh shoo-be-do-a).--REVOLUTIONE--26
Don't you know it's gonna be ((oh shoo-be-do-a))--

REVOLUTONE--29
Alright ((oh shoo-be-do-a))?--REVOLUTONE--30
Don't you know it's gonna be ((oh shoo-be-do-a))--
   REVOLUTONE--31
Alright ((oh shoo-be-do-a))?--REVOLUTONE--32
Don't you know it's gonna be ((oh shoo-be-do-a))--
   REVOLUTONE--33
Alright ((oh shoo-be-do-a))?--REVOLUTONE--34
(Oh shoo-be-do-a, oh shoo-be-do-a).--REVOLUTONE--38
(Oh shoo-be-do-a, oh shoo-be-do-a).--REVOLUTONE--38
(Oh shoo-be-do-a, oh shoo-be-do-a).--REVOLUTONE--42
(Oh shoo-be-do-a, oh shoo-be-do-a).--REVOLUTONE--42
Don't you know it's gonna be ((oh shoo-be-do-a))--
   REVOLUTONE--45
Alright ((oh shoo-be-do-a))?--REVOLUTONE--46
Don't you know it's gonna be ((oh shoo-be-do-a))--
   REVOLUTONE--47
Alright ((oh shoo-be-do-a))?--REVOLUTONE--48
Don't you know it's gonna be ((oh shoo-be-do-a))--
   REVOLUTONE--49
Alright ((oh shoo-be-do-a))?--REVOLUTONE--50
((Oh)) (oh shoo-be-do-a)--REVOLUTONE--51
((Oh)) (oh shoo-be-do-a)--REVOLUTONE--51
Oh oh--REVOLUTONE--52
Oh oh--REVOLUTONE--52
Oh oh--REVOLUTONE--53
Oh oh--REVOLUTONE--53
Oh oh (oh shoo-be-do-a)--REVOLUTONE--54
Oh oh (oh shoo-be-do-a)--REVOLUTONE--54
Oh oh (oh shoo-be-do-a)--REVOLUTONE--54
Oh oh--REVOLUTONE--55
Oh oh--REVOLUTONE--55
Oh oh (oh shoo-be-do-a)--REVOLUTONE--56
Oh oh (oh shoo-be-do-a)--REVOLUTONE--56
Oh oh (oh shoo-be-do-a)--REVOLUTONE--56
Alright (oh shoo-be-do-a)--REVOLUTONE--57
Alright (oh shoo-be-do-a)--REVOLUTONE--59
Alright (oh shoo-be-do-a)--REVOLUTONE--61
Alright (oh shoo-be-do-a)--REVOLUTONE--63
Alright (oh shoo-be-do-a)--REVOLUTONE--65
Alright (oh shoo-be-do-a)--REVOLUTONE--67
Oh-oh-oh-oh-oh-oh ((oh shoo-be-do-a))--REVOLUTIONE--68
(Oh shoo-be-do-a)--REVOLUTONE--69
(Oh shoo-be-do-a)--REVOLUTONE--70
(Oh shoo-be-do-a) alright --REVOLUTONE--71
Gideon checked out and he left it no doubt ((oh
   - Rocky - oh))--ROCKYRACCO--38
Gideon checked out and he left it no doubt ((oh
   - Rocky - oh))--ROCKYRACCO--38
Oh yeah yeah --ROCKYRACCO--40
Sexie Sadie - oh what have you done?--SEXYSADIE--4
Sexy Sadie - oh you broke the rules--SEXYSADIE--8
Sexy Sadie - oh how did you know?--SEXYSADIE--15
Sexy Sadie - oh you'll get yours yet--SEXYSADIE--19
Oh, oh, oh - oh, oh.--WHILEMYGUI--22
Oh, oh, oh - oh, oh.--WHILEMYGUI--22
Oh, oh, oh - oh, oh.--WHILEMYGUI--22
Oh, oh, oh - oh, oh.--WHILEMYGUI--22
Oh, oh, oh - oh, oh.--WHILEMYGUI--22
Oh - oh, oh - oh, oh - oh, oh ((eee)).--WHILEMYGUI
   --23
Oh - oh, oh - oh, oh - oh, oh ((eee)).--WHILEMYGUI
   --23
Oh - oh, oh - oh, oh - oh, oh ((eee)).--WHILEMYGUI
   --23
Oh - oh, oh - oh, oh - oh, oh ((eee)).--WHILEMYGUI
   --23
Oh - oh, oh - oh, oh - oh, oh ((eee)).--WHILEMYGUI
   --23
Oh - oh, oh - oh, oh - oh, oh ((eee)).--WHILEMYGUI
   --23
Oh - oh, oh - oh, oh - oh, oh ((eee)).--WHILEMYGUI
   --23
Oh - oh, oh - oh, oh - oh ((eee)).--WHILEMYGUI--24
Oh - oh, oh - oh, oh - oh ((eee)).--WHILEMYGUI--24
Oh - oh, oh - oh, oh - oh ((eee)).--WHILEMYGUI--24
Oh - oh, oh - oh, oh - oh ((eee)).--WHILEMYGUI--24
Oh - oh, oh - oh, oh - oh ((eee)).--WHILEMYGUI--24
Oh - oh, oh - oh, oh - oh ((eee)).--WHILEMYGUI--24
Oh - wuh... ((eee))--WHILEMYGUI--26
Bom bom bom bom-pa bom, ((Oh boy)), sail the ship
   --ALLTOGETHE--29
(Oh) love is all you need--ALLYOU/MMT--2
Oh get back Jo.--GETBACK/45--15
Oh get back, get back --GETBACK/45--20
Oh get back, yeah get back --GETBACK/45--26
Oh get back, get back yeah, yeah --GETBACK/45--38
Get back - oh yeah.--GETBACK/45--39
Last night the wife said, oh boy, when you're
   dead --BALLADOFJO--27
Come - (oh) - come - come - come--COMETOGETH--35
Oh--COMETOGETH--46
Oh--COMETOGETH--54
Oh yeah, alright --THEEND--1

Someday I'm gonna make her mine - oh yeah --
  HERMAJESTY--8
Late nights all alone with a test-tube, oh oh -
  oh oh.--MAXWELLSIL--2
Late nights all alone with a test-tube, oh oh -
  oh oh.--MAXWELLSIL--2
Late nights all alone with a test-tube, oh oh -
  oh oh.--MAXWELLSIL--2
Late nights all alone with a test-tube, oh oh -
  oh oh.--MAXWELLSIL--2
So he waits behind, writing fifty times I must
  not be so oh - oh oh.--MAXWELLSIL--11
So he waits behind, writing fifty times I must
  not be so oh - oh oh.--MAXWELLSIL--11
So he waits behind, writing fifty times I must
  not be so oh - oh oh.--MAXWELLSIL--11
Painting testimonial pictures oh oh - oh oh.--
  MAXWELLSIL--18
Painting testimonial pictures oh oh - oh oh.--
  MAXWELLSIL--18
Painting testimonial pictures oh oh - oh oh.--
  MAXWELLSIL--18
Painting testimonial pictures oh oh - oh oh.--
  MAXWELLSIL--18
The judge does not agree and he tells them so oh
  - oh oh.--MAXWELLSIL--21
The judge does not agree and he tells them so oh
  - oh oh.--MAXWELLSIL--21
The judge does not agree and he tells them so oh
  - oh oh.--MAXWELLSIL--21
Oh, what joy for every girl and boy--OCTOPUSSGA--19
OH DARLING.--OHDARLING--Title
Oh darling, please believe me, I'll never do
  you no harm.--OHDARLING--1
Oh darling, if you leave me I'll never make it
  alone --OHDARLING--3
Oh darling, if you leave me, I'll never make
  it alone.--OHDARLING--9
Oh darling, please believe me, I'll never let
  you down.--OHDARLING--16
Oh believe me darling --OHDARLING--17
Oh look out!--SHECAMEINT--3
Oh yeah.--SHECAMEINT--24
But oh, that magic feeling, nowhere to go --
  YOUNEVERGI--13
Oh, that magic feeling --YOUNEVERGI--14
Oh there will be an answer, let it be.--LETITBE/45
  --28
(Oh) oh, you know, you know, you know my
  name (come on Dennis) --YOUKNOWMYN--16
(Oh) oh, you know, you know, you know my
  name (come on Dennis) --YOUKNOWMYN--16
You know, you know my name ((oh, let's hear it,
  come on Dennis)) --YOUKNOWMYN--23
Oh get back Jo.--GETBACK/LP--21
Oh get back, get back --GETBACK/LP--26
Oh get back, yeah, get back --GETBACK/LP--32
Oh I do a road hog--IDIGAPONY--9
Oh now I roll a stony--IDIGAPONY--19
Oh now I feel the wind blow--IDIGAPONY--26
Oh now I roll a lorry--IDIGAPONY--29
Oh yeah, oh yeah (that's right).--IVEGOTAFEE--2
Oh yeah, oh yeah (that's right).--IVEGOTAFEE--2
Oh no, no - oh no, oh no.--IVEGOTAFEE--4
Oh no, no - oh no, oh no.--IVEGOTAFEE--4
Oh no, no - oh no, oh no.--IVEGOTAFEE--4
Oh please believe me I'd hate to miss the train --
  IVEGOTAFEE--6
Oh yeah, (yeah) oh yeah --IVEGOTAFEE--7
Oh yeah, (yeah) oh yeah --IVEGOTAFEE--7
Oh no, oh no, oh no, yeah, yeah!--IVEGOTAFEE--9
Oh no, oh no, oh no, yeah, yeah!--IVEGOTAFEE--9
Oh no, oh no, oh no, yeah, yeah!--IVEGOTAFEE--9
Oh yeah, oh yeah ((oh yeah)) --IVEGOTAFEE--15
Oh yeah, oh yeah ((oh yeah)) --IVEGOTAFEE--15
Oh yeah, oh yeah ((oh yeah)) --IVEGOTAFEE--15
Oh yeah, oh yeah ((oh yeah)), oh yeah - yeah,
  yeah!--IVEGOTAFEE--17
Oh yeah, oh yeah ((oh yeah)), oh yeah - yeah,
  yeah!--IVEGOTAFEE--17
Oh yeah, oh yeah ((oh yeah)), oh yeah - yeah,
  yeah!--IVEGOTAFEE--17
Oh yeah, oh yeah ((oh yeah)), oh yeah - yeah,
  yeah!--IVEGOTAFEE--17
Oh yeah (oh yeah), oh yeah, oh yeah.--IVEGOTAFEE
  --23
Oh yeah (oh yeah), oh yeah, oh yeah.--IVEGOTAFEE
  --23
Oh yeah (oh yeah), oh yeah, oh yeah.--IVEGOTAFEE
  --23
Oh yeah (oh yeah), oh yeah, oh yeah.--IVEGOTAFEE
  --23
Everybody put the fool down, oh yeah - (yeah).--
  IVEGOTAFEE--27

Everybody had a hard time ((a feeling deep
  inside, oh yeah)) --IVEGOTAFEE--29
Everybody had a wet dream (oh yeah) --IVEGOTAFEE
  --30
Everybody let their hair down ((a feeling I
  can't hide, oh no)) --IVEGOTAFEE--33
Everybody pulled their socks up (oh no, no) --
  IVEGOTAFEE--34
Everybody put their foot down, oh yeah (yeah).--
  IVEGOTAFEE--35
I've got a feeling ((oh yeah)) --IVEGOTAFEE--36
I've got a feeling (oh yeah) --IVEGOTAFEE--37
Oh my soul.--IVEGOTAFEE--39
Oh it's so hard.--IVEGOTAFEE--40
Oh there will be an answer, let it be.--LETITBE/LP
  --28
Oh there will be an answer, let it be.--LETITBE/LP
  --30
Let it be, let it be, oh let it be, yeah let
  it be --LETITBE/LP--31
I begged her not to go and I begged her on my
  bended knee, (oh yeah)--ONEAFTERNI--6
Oh!--ONEAFTERNI--20
Oh Danny Boy, the odes of Pan are calling.--
  ONEAFTERNI--33

OH-OH
  Ha-ha-ha - do-do-do - oh-oh--HONEYPIE--33

OH-OH-OH
  Oh-oh-oh - oh - oh--HONEYPIE--34

OH-OH-OH-OH-OH-OH
  Oh-oh-oh-oh-oh-oh ((oh shoo-be-do-a))--REVOLUTONE
    --68

OK
  You know I feel OK.--HARDDAYSNI--14
  You know I feel OK.--HARDDAYSNI--27
  I've got nothing to say but it's OK.--GOODMORNIN
    --5
  I've got nothing to say but it's OK.--GOODMORNIN
    --16
  I've got nothing to say but it's OK.--GOODMORNIN
    --25
  OK--REVOLUTONE--4
  Quiet now quiet (OK) quiet--HEYBULLDOG--33
  Peter Brown called to say, you can make it OK --
    BALLADOFJO--11
  OK one, two, three, four.--GETBACK/LP--6
  Yeah OK.--IDIGAPONY--3

OLD
  You're giving me the same old line --NOTASECOND--7
  You're giving me the same old line --NOTASECOND--18
  Same old thing happen every day.--IMDOWN--9
  You're thinking of me the same old way --IMLOOKINGT
    --11
  Before I'm a dead old man.--LOVEYOUTWO--5
  Then you decide to take a walk by the old school--
    GOODMORNIN--14
  She's old enough to know better.--CRYBABYCRY--3
  She's old enough to know better --CRYBABYCRY--10
  She's old enough to know better --CRYBABYCRY--18
  She's old enough to know better --CRYBABYCRY--26
  She's old enough to know better --CRYBABYCRY--34
  She's old enough to know better --CRYBABYCRY--38
  She's old enough to know better --CRYBABYCRY--42
  On my old front door --DONTPASSME--7
  OLD BROWN SHOE.--OLDBROWNSH--Title
  Now I'm stepping out this old brown shoe --
    OLDBROWNSH--5
  Love is old, love is new --BECAUSE--8
  Here come old flat top--COMETOGETH--5
  Such a mean old man, such a mean old man.--
    MEANMRMUST--7
  Such a mean old man, such a mean old man.--
    MEANMRMUST--7
  Such a dirty old man, dirty old man.--MEANMRMUST
    --14
  Such a dirty old man, dirty old man.--MEANMRMUST
    --14
  Them old twelve-bar blues.--FORYOUBLUE--10

OLDER
  In a cap she looked much older--LOVELYRITA--10
  When I get older losing my hair--WHENIMSIXT--1
  You'll be older too--WHENIMSIXT--10

OM

    Jai Guru Deva OM.--ACROSSTHEU--6
    Jai Guru Deva OM.--ACROSSTHEU--15
    Jai Guru Deva OM.--ACROSSTHEU--25

ON

    When you need a shoulder to cry on --ANYTIMEATA--16
    Come on (come on), come on (come on) --PLEASEPLEA
      --3
    Come on (come on), come on (come on) --PLEASEPLEA
      --3
    Come on (come on), come on (come on) --PLEASEPLEA
      --3
    Come on (come on), come on (come on) --PLEASEPLEA
      --4
    Come on (come on), come on (come on) --PLEASEPLEA
      --4
    Come on (come on), come on (come on) --PLEASEPLEA
      --4
    Come on (come on), come on (come on) --PLEASEPLEA
      --4
    Come on (come on), come on (come on) --PLEASEPLEA
      --9
    Come on (come on), come on (come on) --PLEASEPLEA
      --9
    Come on (come on), come on (come on) --PLEASEPLEA
      --9
    Come on (come on), come on (come on) --PLEASEPLEA
      --9
    Come on (come on), come on (come on) --PLEASEPLEA
      --10
    Come on (come on), come on (come on) --PLEASEPLEA
      --10
    Come on (come on), come on (come on) --PLEASEPLEA
      --10
    Come on (come on), come on (come on) --PLEASEPLEA
      --10
    Come on (come on), come on (come on)--PLEASEPLEA
      --21
    Come on (come on), come on (come on)--PLEASEPLEA
      --21
    Come on (come on), come on (come on)--PLEASEPLEA
      --21
    Come on (come on), come on (come on)--PLEASEPLEA
      --21
    Come on (come on), come on (come on)--PLEASEPLEA
      --22
    Come on (come on), come on (come on)--PLEASEPLEA
      --22
    Come on (come on), come on (come on)--PLEASEPLEA
      --22
    Come on (come on), come on (come on)--PLEASEPLEA
      --22
    Just call on me and I'll send it along--FROMMETOYO
      --5
    Just/So call on me and I'll send it along--FROMMETOYO--9
    Just call on me and I'll send it along--FROMMETOYO
      --17
    Just call on me and I'll send it along--FROMMETOYO
      --20
    Just call on me and I'll send it along--FROMMETOYO
      --28
    Is call you on the phone --ALLIVEGOTT--3
    Ya just gotta call on me yeah,--ALLIVEGOTT--15
    Ya just gotta call on me.--ALLIVEGOTT--16
    Is call you on the phone --ALLIVEGOTT--19
    Ya just gotta call on me, yeah --ALLIVEGOTT--26
    Ya just gotta call on me --ALLIVEGOTT--27
    (Ooh) ya just gotta call on me --ALLIVEGOTT--28
    That she would leave me on my own--DONTBOTHER--10
    Let me go on loving you --HOLDMETIGH--10
    Let me go on loving you --HOLDMETIGH--30
    I wanna be your man (come on!)--IWANNABEYO--44
    Here am I sitting all on my own--ITWONTBELO--6
    Now you're coming, you're coming on home (now
      you're coming on home)--ITWONTBELO--12
    Now you're coming, you're coming on home (now
      you're coming on home)--ITWONTBELO--12
    I'll be good like I know I should (yes,
      you're coming on home)--ITWONTBELO--13
    Now you're coming, you're coming on home (now
      you're coming on home)--ITWONTBELO--22
    Now you're coming, you're coming on home (now
      you're coming on home)--ITWONTBELO--22
    I'll be good like I know I should (yes,
      you're coming on home)--ITWONTBELO--23
    So come on, come on, come on.--LITTLECHIL--11
    So come on, come on, come on.--LITTLECHIL--11
    So come on, come on, come on.--LITTLECHIL--11
    Don't you run and hide, just come on, come on --
      LITTLECHIL--17

    Don't you run and hide, just come on, come on --
      LITTLECHIL--17
    Yeah come on, come on, come on.--LITTLECHIL--18
    Yeah come on, come on, come on.--LITTLECHIL--18
    Yeah come on, come on, come on.--LITTLECHIL--18
    I never weep at night, I can't go on.--ICALLYOURN
      --4
    So why on earth should I moan --HARDDAYSNI--12
    So why on earth should I moan --HARDDAYSNI--25
    I got every reason on earth to be mad --ILLCRYINST
      --1
    I got a chip on my shoulder that's bigger than my
      feet.--ILLCRYINST--6
    But you left me sitting on my own.--TELLMEWHY--6
    If you don't I really can't go on.--TELLMEWHY--15
    Well I beg you on my bended knees --TELLMEWHY--21
    We'll go on and on.--THINGSWESA--18
    We'll go on and on.--THINGSWESA--18
    We'll go on and on.--THINGSWESA--29
    We'll go on and on.--THINGSWESA--29
    Come on, out my way --WHENIGETHO--4
    Come on if you please --WHENIGETHO--10
    Come on, let me through --WHENIGETHO--21
    Turn me on when I get lonely--SHESAWOMAN--5
    Turn me on when I get lonely--SHESAWOMAN--22
    Turn me on when I get lonely--SHESAWOMAN--32
    Always on my mind --EIGHTDAYSA--10
    Always on my mind --EIGHTDAYSA--30
    Help me get my feet back on the ground--HELP--17
    Help me get my feet back on the ground--HELP--27
    Help me get my feet back on the ground--HELP--37
    I'm down (down on the ground)--IMDOWN--4
    I'm down (down on the ground)--IMDOWN--11
    Oh baby, I'm down (down on the ground)--IMDOWN--19
    I'm down on the ground (I'm really down)--IMDOWN
      --30
    Yeah, aah - ooo I'm down (down on the ground)--
      IMDOWN--45
    Please come on back to me--INEEDYOU--3
    I just can't go on any more.--INEEDYOU--15
    So come on back and see--INEEDYOU--18
    I just can't go on any more.--INEEDYOU--25
    So come on back and see--INEEDYOU--28
    If she's gone I can't go on --YOUVEGOTTO--3
    Do I have to keep on talking till I can't go on?--
      WECANWORKI--2
    Do I have to keep on talking till I can't go on?--
      WECANWORKI--2
    Carve your number on my wall --IFINEEDEDS--10
    Carve your number on my wall --IFINEEDEDS--20
    I sat on a rug--NORWEGIANW--11
    And if your heart's strong, hold on, I won't
      delay.--WAIT--6
    And if your heart's strong, hold on, I won't
      delay.--WAIT--22
    WHAT GOES ON?--WHATGOESON--Title
    What goes on in your heart? (wuh)--WHATGOESON--1
    What goes on in your mind?--WHATGOESON--2
    What goes on in your mind?--WHATGOESON--5
    What goes on in your heart?--WHATGOESON--10
    What goes on in your mind?--WHATGOESON--11
    What goes on in your mind?--WHATGOESON--14
    What goes on in your heart?--WHATGOESON--19
    (What goes on in your mind?)--WHATGOESON--21
    What goes on in your heart?--WHATGOESON--26
    What goes on in your mind?--WHATGOESON--27
    What goes on in your mind?--WHATGOESON--30
    And I just can't go on--YOUWONTSEE--19
    And I just can't go on--YOUWONTSEE--28
    (Yeah) ooo (come on) la la la--YOUWONTSEE--31
    It's based on a novel by a man named Lear --
      PAPERBACKW--4
    Keeping an eye on the world going by my window --
      IMONLYSLEE--13
    Keeping an eye on the world going by my window --
      IMONLYSLEE--19
    You find that all her words of kindness linger on
      --FORNOONE--2
    You don't get time to hang a sign on me.--
      LOVEYOUTWO--3
    Declare the pennies on your eyes (Taxman)--TAXMAN
      --23
    So we sailed on to the sun--YELLOWSUBM--5
    On the corner is a banker with a motorcar--
      PENNYLANE--5
    There will be a show tonight on trampoline.--
      BEINGFORTH--2
    Performs his feat on Saturday at Bishopsgate.--
      BEINGFORTH--9
    Ten somersets he'll undertake on solid ground.--
      BEINGFORTH--18
    I'd love to turn you on--DAYINTHELI--16
    I'd love to turn you on--DAYINTHELI--34
    And you're on your own you're in the street.--

GOODMORNIN--12
Sitting on a sofa with a sister or two.--LOVELYRITA
--25
Picture yourself in a boat on a river--LUCYINTHES
--1
Newspaper taxis appear on the shore.--LUCYINTHES--16
Picture yourself on a train in a station--
LUCYINTHES--23
Grandchildren on your knee --WHENIMSIXT--26
Would you stand up and walk out on me?--WITHALITTL
--2
(Are you sad because you're on your own?)--
WITHALITTL--11
And life flows on within you and without you.--
WITHINYOUW--19
And life flows on within you and without you.--
WITHINYOUW--33
Sitting on a cornflake, waiting for the van to come
--IAMTHEWALR--4
Ask a policeman on the street --BLUEJAYWAY--10
THE FOOL ON THE HILL.--FOOLONTHEH--Title
Day after day, alone on a hill--FOOLONTHEH--1
But the fool on the hill sees the sun going down--
FOOLONTHEH--6
Well on the way, head in a cloud--FOOLONTHEH--8
But the fool on the hill sees the sun going down--
FOOLONTHEH--13
But the fool on the hill sees the sun going down--
FOOLONTHEH--18
The fool on the hill sees the sun going down--
FOOLONTHEH--25
I can know all things on earth.--INNERLIGHT--2
You can know all things on earth.--INNERLIGHT--9
Lady Madonna, lying on the bed --LADYMADONN--12
The movement you need is on your shoulder.--HEYJUDE
--24
On the way the paper bag was on my knee --
BACKINTHEU--3
On the way the paper bag was on my knee --
BACKINTHEU--3
That Georgia's always on my my my my my my my my
my mind.--BACKINTHEU--18
Oh come on!--BACKINTHEU--19
That Georgia's always on my my my my my my my my
my mind.--BACKINTHEU--30
Put on specially by the children for a lark.--
CRYBABYCRY--31
On my old front door --DONTPASSME--7
On the mantelshelf --DONTPASSME--11
Come on, come on - come on, come on --EVRBDYMONK
--1
Come on, come on - come on, come on --EVRBDYMONK
--1
Come on, come on - come on, come on --EVRBDYMONK
--1
Come on, come on - come on, come on --EVRBDYMONK
--1
Come on is such a joy --EVRBDYMONK--2
Come on is such a joy --EVRBDYMONK--3
Come on is take it easy --EVRBDYMONK--4
Come on is take it easy --EVRBDYMONK--5
So come on (come on) come on --EVRBDYMONK--10
So come on (come on) come on --EVRBDYMONK--10
So come on (come on) come on --EVRBDYMONK--10
Come on is such a joy --EVRBDYMONK--11
Come on is such a joy --EVRBDYMONK--12
Come on is make it easy --EVRBDYMONK--13
Come on is make it easy - wuh.--EVRBDYMONK--14
So come on (wuh), come on (wuh) --EVRBDYMONK--19
So come on (wuh), come on (wuh) --EVRBDYMONK--19
Come on is such a joy --EVRBDYMONK--20
Come on is such a joy --EVRBDYMONK--21
Come on is make it easy --EVRBDYMONK--22
Come on is make it easy --EVRBDYMONK--23
Come on, come on, come on, come on, come on,
come on, come on,...--EVRBDYMONK--27
Come on, come on, come on, come on, come on,
come on, come on,...--EVRBDYMONK--27
Come on, come on, come on, come on, come on,
come on, come on,...--EVRBDYMONK--27
Come on, come on, come on, come on, come on,
come on, come on,...--EVRBDYMONK--27
Come on, come on, come on, come on, come on,
come on, come on,...--EVRBDYMONK--27
Come on, come on, come on, come on, come on,
come on, come on,...--EVRBDYMONK--27
Come on, come on, come on, come on, come on,
come on, come on,...--EVRBDYMONK--27
Standing on the cast-iron shore - yeah--GLASSONION
--12
I told you about the fool on the hill--GLASSONION
--17
Like a lizard on a window-pane.--HAPPINESSI--4
The man in the crowd with the multicoloured

mirrors on his hobnail boots --HAPPINESSI--5
And I feel my finger on your trigger ((oh,
yeah)) --HAPPINESSI--23
Tell me, tell me, tell me, come on tell me the
answer --HELTERSKEL--6
I got blisters on my fingers!--HELTERSKEL--32
I'm so tired, my mind is on the blink --IMSOTIRED
--2
I'm so tired, my mind is set on you --IMSOTIRED--6
You'd say I'm putting you on --IMSOTIRED--9
You'd say I'm putting you on --IMSOTIRED--18
Ob-la-di ob-la-da life goes on bra --OBLADIOBLA--5
La-la how the life goes on --OBLADIOBLA--6
Ob-la-di ob-la-da life goes on bra --OBLADIOBLA--7
La-la how the life goes on.--OBLADIOBLA--8
Ob-la-di ob-la-da life goes on bra --OBLADIOBLA--13
La-la how the life goes on --OBLADIOBLA--14
Ob-la-di ob-la-da life goes on bra --OBLADIOBLA--15
La-la how the life goes on - yeah.--OBLADIOBLA--16
Ob-la-di ob-la-da life goes on bra --OBLADIOBLA--25
La-la how the life goes on (he he he) --OBLADIOBLA
--26
Hey, ob-la-di ob-la-da life goes on bra --
OBLADIOBLA--27
La-la how the life goes on.--OBLADIOBLA--28
Ob-la-di ob-la-da life goes on bra --OBLADIOBLA--36
La-la how the life goes on - yeah --OBLADIOBLA--37
Ob-la-di ob-la-da life goes on bra --OBLADIOBLA--38
La-la how the life goes on (ha ha ha ha ha ha).--
OBLADIOBLA--39
They don't care what goes on around.--PIGGIES--12
And proceeded to lie on the table --ROCKYRACCO--32
Do do do do - come on Rocky - boy --ROCKYRACCO--45
Do do do do do - come on Rocky - boy --ROCKYRACCO
--46
She came along to turn on everyone--SEXYSADIE--10
Sail me on a silver sun --ITSALLTOOM--21
Too much, too much, too much (come on), too
much, too much, too much.--ITSALLTOOM--42
Wearing rings on every finger --OLDBROWNSH--18
Because the world is round it turns me on --BECAUSE
--2
Maxwell Edison, majoring in medicine, calls
her on the phone --MAXWELLSIL--3
But as she's getting ready to go, a knock comes
on the door --MAXWELLSIL--5
But when she turns her back on the boy, he
creeps up from behind --MAXWELLSIL--12
Resting our head on the seabed--OCTOPUSSGA--11
Come on now.--SHECAMEINT--1
Sundays on the phone to Monday --SHECAMEINT--10
Tuesdays on the phone to me.--SHECAMEINT--11
Sundays on the phone to Monday --SHECAMEINT--22
Tuesdays on the phone to me.--SHECAMEINT--23
Step on the gas and wipe that tear away.--
YOUNEVERGI--20
There is still a light that shines on me --
LETITBE/45--22
Shine on till tomorrow, let it be.--LETITBE/45--23
(Oh) oh, you know, you know, you know my
name (come on Dennis) --YOUKNOWMYN--16
You know, you know my name ((oh, let's hear it,
come on Dennis)) --YOUKNOWMYN--23
They call me on and on across the universe.--
ACROSSTHEU--12
They call me on and on across the universe.--
ACROSSTHEU--12
It calls me on and on across the universe.--
ACROSSTHEU--24
It calls me on and on across the universe.--
ACROSSTHEU--24
Elmore James got nothing on this baby - heh.--
FORYOUBLUE--12
I'd like to say thank you on behalf of the group
and ourselves--GETBACK/LP--38
Ooo I've got a feeling that keeps me on my toes --
IVEGOTAFEE--14
There is still a light that shines on me --
LETITBE/LP--22
Shine on till tomorrow, let it be.--LETITBE/LP--23
My baby said she's travelling on the one after
nine-0-nine --ONEAFTERNI--1
I said, move over honey, I'm travelling on
that line --ONEAFTERNI--2
Come on baby, don't be cold as ice --ONEAFTERNI--4
Said you're travelling on the one after
nine-0-nine.--ONEAFTERNI--5
I begged her not to go and I begged her on my
bended knee, (oh yeah)--ONEAFTERNI--6
Come on baby, don't be cold as ice --ONEAFTERNI--9
Said you're travelling on the one after
nine-0-nine.--ONEAFTERNI--10
Well, she said she's travelling on the one after
nine-0-nine --ONEAFTERNI--15

I said a-move over honey, I'm travelling on
    that line --ONEAFTERNI--16
Come on baby, don't be cold as ice--ONEAFTERNI
    --18
Said she's travelling on the one after
    nine-0-nine. (yeah)--ONEAFTERNI--19
She said she's travelling on the one after
    nine-0-nine --ONEAFTERNI--25
Said a - move over honey, I'm travelling on
    that line --ONEAFTERNI--26
Come on baby, don't be cold as ice.--ONEAFTERNI
    --28
Said we're travelling on the one after nine-0 --
    ONEAFTERNI--29
She said we're travelling on the one after nine-0
    --ONEAFTERNI--30
Said we're travelling on the one after nine-0-nine
    --ONEAFTERNI--31
Not arriving on our way back home.--TWOOFUS--6
We're on our way home --TWOOFUS--7
We're on our way home --TWOOFUS--8
Writing letters on my wall.--TWOOFUS--11
Lifting latches on our way back home.--TWOOFUS--13
We're on our way home --TWOOFUS--14
We're on our way home --TWOOFUS--15
Getting nowhere on our way back home.--TWOOFUS--22
We're on our way home --TWOOFUS--23
We're on our way home --TWOOFUS--24
Getting nowhere on our way back home.--TWOOFUS--31
We're on our way home --TWOOFUS--32
We're on our way home --TWOOFUS--33

ONCE

'cos I told you once before goodbye --ILLBEBACK--3
This happened once before--NOREPLY--1
So I will ask you once again.--WECANWORKI--14
So I will ask you once again.--WECANWORKI--23
I once had a girl--NORWEGIANW--1
She once had me?--NORWEGIANW--3
We'd like to thank you once again.--SGTPEPPREP--12
Get back to where you once belonged.--GETBACK/45
    --6
Get back to where you once belonged.--GETBACK/45
    --8
Back to where you once belonged.--GETBACK/45--12
Back to where you once belonged.--GETBACK/45--14
Get back to where you once belonged.--GETBACK/45
    --21
Get back to where you once belonged.--GETBACK/45
    --23
Get back to where you once belonged.--GETBACK/45
    --27
Get back to where you once belonged.--GETBACK/45
    --29
Get back to where you once belonged.--GETBACK/45
    --37
Once there was a way--GOLDENSLUM--1
Once there was a way--GOLDENSLUM--3
Once there was a way--GOLDENSLUM--11
Once there was a way--GOLDENSLUM--13
Get back to where you once belonged--GETBACK/LP--12
Get back to where you once belonged--GETBACK/LP--14
Back to where you once belonged--GETBACK/LP--18
Back to where you once belonged--GETBACK/LP--20
Get back to where you once belonged--GETBACK/LP--27
Get back to where you once belonged.--GETBACK/LP
    --29
Get back to where you once belonged--GETBACK/LP--33
Get back to where you once belonged--GETBACK/LP--35
I said, move over once, move over twice --
    ONEAFTERNI--3
I said move over once, move over twice --ONEAFTERNI
    --8
Said move over once, move over twice --ONEAFTERNI
    --17
I said move over once, move over twice --ONEAFTERNI
    --27

ONE

One, two, three, four.--ISAWHERSTA--1
Can't she see she'll always be the only one,
    only one.--MISERY--7
Can't she see she'll always be the only one,
    only one.--MISERY--7
She'll remember and she'll miss her only one,
    lonely one.--MISERY--11
She'll remember and she'll miss her only one,
    lonely one.--MISERY--11
I want no one to talk to me--DONTBOTHER--2
Tell me I'm the only one --HOLDMETIGH--3
Never be the lonely one.--HOLDMETIGH--5
Tell me I'm the only one --HOLDMETIGH--20

Never be the lonely one.--HOLDMETIGH--22
When you're by my side, you're the only one --
    LITTLECHIL--16
Do I have to tell you one more time--YOUCANTDOT--11
'cos I'm the one who won your love--YOUCANTDOT--19
'cos I'm the one who won your love--YOUCANTDOT--38
I'm the one who wants you--ILLBEBACK
    --5
Yes I'm the one who wants you --ILLBEBACK--7
Be the only one --THINGSWESA--16
Be the only one --THINGSWESA--27
One thing I can say girl --EIGHTDAYSA--11
One thing I can say girl --EIGHTDAYSA--31
There is one thing I'm sure of--EVERYLITTL--14
One day you'll look to see I've gone --ILLFOLLOWT
    --1
Some day you'll know I was the one --ILLFOLLOWT--3
One day you'll find that I have gone --ILLFOLLOWT
    --7
One day you'll find that I have gone --ILLFOLLOWT
    --12
There is one love I should never have crossed.--
    IMALOSER--4
One, two, three, four.--TICKETTORI--1
Listen to me one more time--TELLMEWHAT--18
Listen to me one more time--TELLMEWHAT--27
And then you'll be the lonely one (you're not
    the only one)--YOUREGONNA--12
And then you'll be the lonely one (you're not
    the only one)--YOUREGONNA--12
One way ticket, yeah --DAYTRIPPER--6
One way ticket, yeah --DAYTRIPPER--14
She only played one night stands --DAYTRIPPER--19
And she only played one night stands, now.--
    DAYTRIPPER--21
You're the one that I'd be thinking of --IFINEEDS
    --2
Each one believing that love never dies--HERETHEREA
    --12
Each one believing that love never dies--HERETHEREA
    --18
A new one can't be bought--LOVEYOUTWO--7
One, two, three, four, one, two.--TAXMAN--1
One, two, three, four, one, two.--TAXMAN--1
(One, two, three, four)--TAXMAN--2
There's one for you, nineteen for me --TAXMAN--4
(One)--DAYINTHELI--17
The one and only Billy Shears--SGTPEPPERS--24
One, two (ah yeah), three, four.--SGTPEPPREP--1
Sgt. Pepper's one and only Lonely Hearts Club
    Band --SGTPEPPREP--13
Fun. (fun is the one thing that money can't buy)--
    SHESLEAVIN--30
One, two - one, two.--WITHINYOUW--20
One, two - one, two.--WITHINYOUW--20
Are you one of them?--WITHINYOUW--27
When you see we're all one--WITHINYOUW--32
One of the beautiful people?--BABYYOUREA--2
One of the beautiful people?--BABYYOUREA--8
One of the beautiful people?--BABYYOUREA--23
The farther one travels --INNERLIGHT--5
The less one knows --INNERLIGHT--6
The less one really knows.--INNERLIGHT--7
The farther one travels --INNERLIGHT--12
The less one knows --INNERLIGHT--13
The less one really knows.--INNERLIGHT--14
One, two, three, four, five, six, seven,
    eight.--DONTPASSME--36
One more time.--PIGGIES--20
REVOLUTION ONE.--REVOLUTONE--Title
And one day his woman ran off with another guy --
    ROCKYRACCO--3
So one day he walked into town --ROCKYRACCO--7
One sunny day the world was waiting for the lover
    ((sexy Sadie))--SEXYSADIE--9
One, two, three, four --ALLTOGETHE--1
He one holy roller--COMETOGETH--8
One thing I can tell you is you got to be free--
    COMETOGETH--20
He one spinal cracker--COMETOGETH--28
He one mojo filter--COMETOGETH--39
He say one and one and one is three--COMETOGETH--40
He say one and one and one is three--COMETOGETH--40
He say one and one and one is three--COMETOGETH--40
PC Thirty-One said, we caught a dirty one,
    Maxwell stands alone --MAXWELLSIL--17
One sweet dream --YOUNEVERGI--17
One sweet dream came true today --YOUNEVERGI--21
One, two, three, four, five, six, seven --
    YOUNEVERGI--24
One, two, three, four, five, six, seven --
    YOUNEVERGI--26
One, two, three, four, five, six, seven --
    YOUNEVERGI--28

One, two, three, four, five, six, seven --
    YOUNEVERGI--30
One, two, three, four, five, six, seven --
    YOUNEVERGI--32
One, two, three, four, five, six, seven --
    YOUNEVERGI--34
One, two, three, four, five, six, seven --
    YOUNEVERGI--36
One, two, three, four, five, six, seven --
    YOUNEVERGI--38
One, two, three, four, five, six, seven --
    YOUNEVERGI--40
OK one, two, three, four.--GETBACK/LP--6
A - one, two, three.--IDIGAPONY--2
A - one, two.--IDIGAPONY--5
ONE AFTER NINE-0-NINE.--ONEAFTERNI--Title
My baby said she's travelling on the one after
    nine-0-nine --ONEAFTERNI--1
Said you're travelling on the one after
    nine-0-nine.--ONEAFTERNI--5
Said you're travelling on the one after
    nine-0-nine.--ONEAFTERNI--10
Well, she said she's travelling on the one after
    nine-0-nine --ONEAFTERNI--15
Said she's travelling on the one after
    nine-0-nine. (yeah)--ONEAFTERNI--19
She said she's travelling on the one after
    nine-0-nine --ONEAFTERNI--25
Said we're travelling on the one after nine-0 --
    ONEAFTERNI--29
She said we're travelling on the one after nine-0
    --ONEAFTERNI--30
Said we're travelling on the one after nine-0-nine
    --ONEAFTERNI--31
Phase one in which Doris gets her oats.--TWOOFUS
    --2

ONION
    GLASS ONION.--GLASSONION--Title
    Looking through a glass onion.--GLASSONION--7
    Looking through a glass onion.--GLASSONION--14
    Looking through a glass onion.--GLASSONION--16
    Looking through a glass onion.--GLASSONION--23

ONLY
    That it really only goes to show --ASKMEWHY--4
    But you're the only love that I've ever had.--
        ASKMEWHY--11
    That it really only goes to show --ASKMEWHY--19
    Can't she see she'll always be the only one,
        only one.--MISERY--7
    Can't she see she'll always be the only one,
        only one.--MISERY--9
    She'll remember and she'll miss her only one,
        lonely one.--MISERY--11
    I know, little girl, only a fool would doubt
        our love--THANKYOUGI--6
    I think it's only fair--SHELOVESYO--25
    The only girl for me--DONTBOTHER--18
    The only girl for me--DONTBOTHER--33
    Tell me I'm the only one --HOLDMETIGH--3
    Making love to only you.--HOLDMETIGH--12
    Tell me I'm the only one --HOLDMETIGH--20
    Making love to only you.--HOLDMETIGH--32
    When you're by my side, you're the only one --
        LITTLECHIL--16
    Like I love only you.--THERESAPLA--8
    This could only happen to me --ISHOULDHAV--5
    This could only happen to me --ISHOULDHAV--15
    'cos I've just lost the only girl I had.--
        ILLCRYINST--2
    If you'll only listen to my pleas --TELLMEWHY--22
    Be the only one --THINGSWESA--16
    Be the only one --THINGSWESA--27
    Only ever has to give me love forever and forever
        --SHESAWOMAN--3
    People tell me that she's only fooling--SHESAWOMAN
        --6
    Only ever has to give me love forever and forever
        --SHESAWOMAN--20
    People tell me that she's only fooling--SHESAWOMAN
        --23
    Only ever has to give me love forever and forever
        --SHESAWOMAN--30
    People tell me that she's only fooling--SHESAWOMAN
        --33
    But she thinks only of him --BABYSINBLA--11
    And though it's only a whim --BABYSINBLA--12
    IT'S ONLY LOVE.--ITSONLYLOV--Title
    It's only love and that is all--ITSONLYLOV--4
    It's only love and that is all--ITSONLYLOV--6
    It's only love and that is all--ITSONLYLOV--11

It's only love and that is all--ITSONLYLOV--13
And then you'll be the lonely one (you're not
    the only one)--YOUREGONNA--12
She only played one night stands--DAYTRIPPER
    --19
And she only played one night stands, now.--
    DAYTRIPPER--21
Only time will tell if I am right or I am wrong.--
    WECANWORKI--16
Only time will tell if I am right or I am wrong.--
    WECANWORKI--25
The only difference is you're down there.--
    IMLOOKINGT--13
I will say the only words I know that you'll
    understand.--MICHELLE--8
And I will say the only words I know that
    you'll understand --MICHELLE--22
And the only word is love.--THEWORD--28
I'M ONLY SLEEPING.--IMONLYSLEE--Title
Leave me where I am, I'm only sleeping.--IMONLYSLEE
    --6
And after all, I'm only sleeping.--IMONLYSLEE
    --12
And after all, I'm only sleeping.--IMONLYSLEE
    --18
Leave me where I am, I'm only sleeping.--IMONLYSLEE
    --26
It's only me, it's not my mind--IWANTTOTEL--10
The one and only Billy Shears--SGTPEPPERS--24
Sgt. Pepper's one and only Lonely Hearts Club
    Band --SGTPEPPREP--13
If they only knew.--WITHINYOUW--15
And to see you're really only very small--
    WITHINYOUW--18
Well it only goes to show (only, only goes to
    show) --BLUEJAYWAY--8
Well it only goes to show (only, only goes to
    show) --BLUEJAYWAY--8
Well it only goes to show (only, only goes to
    show) --BLUEJAYWAY--8
You were only waiting for this moment to arise.--
    BLACKBIRD--4
You were only waiting for this moment to be free.
    --BLACKBIRD--8
You were only waiting for this moment to arise --
    BLACKBIRD--16
You were only waiting for this moment to arise --
    BLACKBIRD--17
You were only waiting for this moment to arise.--
    BLACKBIRD--18
'cos you know, darling, I love only you --
    DONTPASSME--19
'cos you know, darling, I love only you --
    DONTPASSME--32
'cos you know, darling, I love only you --
    DONTPASSME--38
And if she could only hear me--HONEYPIE--5
I can only speak my mind, Julia.--JULIA--12
Only to find Gideon's Bible --ROCKYRACCO--10
And Rocky said, Doc it's only a scratch--ROCKYRACCO
    --34
Only to find Gideon's Bible --ROCKYRACCO--37
I only have grandchildren (yahoo ha ha ha ha ha
    ha ha)--HEYBULLDOG--32
ONLY A NORTHERN SONG.--ONLYANORTH--Title
As it's only a Northern song.--ONLYANORTH--9
When it's only a Northern song.--ONLYANORTH--12
I said we're only trying to get us some peace.--
    BALLADOFJO--20
But right is only half of what's wrong --OLDBROWNSH
    --2
I only send you my invitations--CARRYTHATW--6
Only place that he's ever been--MEANMRMUST--12
You only give me your funny paper--YOUNEVERGI--2
I only give you my situation--YOUNEVERGI--5
You're only fooling round, only fooling round
    with me.--ONEAFTERNI--7
You're only fooling round, only fooling round
    with me.--ONEAFTERNI--7

ONO
    He got Ono sideboard--COMETOGETH--27

OOH
    Ooh when I saw her standing there.--ISAWHERSTA--6
    (Ooh) ya just gotta call on me --ALLIVEGOTT--28

OOHO
    (Ooho) in misery--MISERY--14

OOO

I'm in love with you - ooo.--DOYOUWANTT--8
I'm in love with you - ooo --DOYOUWANTT--14
I'm in love with you - ooo --DOYOUWANTT--22
Ooo, ooo.--DOYOUWANTT--23
Ooo, ooo.--DOYOUWANTT--23
(Ooo) my misery--MISERY--15
And keep you satisfied - ooo!--FROMMETOYO--14
And keep you satisfied - ooo!--FROMMETOYO--25
And you know you should be glad - ooo!--SHELOVESYO
     --19
And you know you should be glad - ooo!--SHELOVESYO
     --31
You - ooo.--HOLDMETIGH--36
Like no other can (ooo).--IWANNABEYO--35
Till I belong to you - ooo.--ITWONTBELO--30
She's in love with me and I feel fine (ooo).--
     IFEELFINE--11
Ooo,--IFEELFINE--21
Ooo (wuh - wuh, wuh - wuh, wuh).--IFEELFINE--22
Ooo I need your love babe --EIGHTDAYSA--1
Ooo I need your love babe --EIGHTDAYSA--19
She does for me, ooo.--EVERYLITTL--10
She does for me, ooo.--EVERYLITTL--20
She does for me, ooo.--EVERYLITTL--24
Ooo, I'm down (I'm really down)--IMDOWN--37
Yeah, aah - ooo I'm down (down on the ground)--
     IMDOWN--45
Ooo, you know I'm...--IMDOWN--46
Yes, it's so hard loving you, loving you - ooo.--
     ITSONLYLOV--15
(Yeah) ooo (come on) la la la--YOUWONTSEE--31
(Oh yeah) ooo - la la la--YOUWONTSEE--32
Ooo - la la la.--YOUWONTSEE--33
Ooo then I suddenly see you--GOTTOGETYO--5
Ooo did I tell you I need you--GOTTOGETYO--6
Ooo you were meant to be near me--GOTTOGETYO--12
Ooo and I want you to hear me--GOTTOGETYO--13
Ooo then I suddenly see you--GOTTOGETYO--20
Ooo did I tell you I need you--GOTTOGETYO--21
Ooo - ooo.--LOVELYRITA--19
Ooo - ooo.--LOVELYRITA--19
Lucy in the sky with diamonds (aah - ooo) --
     LUCYINTHES--34
Ooo - hela, hello (hela)--HELLOGOODB--35
Ooo - hela, hello--HELLOGOODB--39
Ooo - ooo.--YOURMOTHER--1
Ooo - ooo.--YOURMOTHER--1
Your mother should know - yeah ((ooo)).--YOURMOTHER
     --25
(Ow - ooo nah nah nah) nah - nah - nah - nah,
     hey Jude--HEYJUDE--42
Nah - nah - nah - nah, hey Jude (ooo).--HEYJUDE--71
Nah - nah - nah - nah, hey Jude (ooo - ooo).--
     HEYJUDE--73
Nah - nah - nah - nah, hey Jude (ooo - ooo).--
     HEYJUDE--73
Ooo yeah --BACKINTHEU--21
Ooo yeah --BACKINTHEU--22
Coming down fast (oh I hear my baby speaking -
     ooo)...--HELTERSKEL--30
Honey Pie come back to me - ooo.--HONEYPIE--19
I light the light - yeah, ooo - ha.--HONEYPIE--21
Ooo ooo ooo --MOTHERNATU--14
Ooo ooo ooo --MOTHERNATU--14
Ooo ooo ooo --MOTHERNATU--14
Thank you (ooo) (ha ha ha).--OBLADIOBLA--42
Ooo--SEXYSADIE--25
Ooo - girl you know the reason why.--YERBLUES--5
Ooo she does, yes she does --DONTLETMED--6
Ooo she do me, yes she does.--DONTLETMED--8
Don't let me down (ooo) --DONTLETMED--18
Ooo she done me, she done me good --DONTLETMED--22
Ooo she done me, she done me good --DONTLETMED--24
Ooo - ow, ow!--GETBACK/45--30
Believe me when I beg you - ooo - don't ever
     leave me alone.--OHDARLING--4
A - when you told me - ooo - you didn't need me
     any more --OHDARLING--12
Believe me when I tell you - ooo - I'll never
     do you no harm.--OHDARLING--18
Aah - ooo, aah - ooo, aah - ooo.--YOUNEVERGI--16
Aah - ooo, aah - ooo, aah - ooo.--YOUNEVERGI--16
Aah - ooo, aah - ooo, aah - ooo.--YOUNEVERGI--16
The picker - the picker, picture the fingers
     going (ooo me).--GETBACK/LP--5
Get back - ooo!--GETBACK/LP--36
Because. (ooo - ow)--IDIGAPONY--25
Ooo!--IDIGAPONY--36
Ooo I've got a feeling that keeps me on my toes --
     IVEGOTAFEE--14
Ooo - hu, everybody had a good year ((I've got
     a feeling)) --IVEGOTAFEE--28
(Ooo - ooo).--ONEAFTERNI--32

(Ooo - ooo).--ONEAFTERNI--32

OOO-MMM

Help me, help me - ooo-mmm.--HELP--39

OOO-OOO

All my lovin', all my lovin', ooo-ooo --ALLMYLOVIN
     --23
It's you, you, you, you - ooo-ooo.--HOLDMETIGH--8
It's you, you, you, you - ooo-ooo.--HOLDMETIGH--15
It's you, you, you, you - ooo-ooo.--HOLDMETIGH--25
It's you, you, you, you - ooo-ooo --HOLDMETIGH--35

OOO-OOO-AAH

Ooo-ooo-aah - hey-hey-hey - hey.--FIXINGAHOL--14

OOO-OOO-OOO

She's cool - ooo-ooo-ooo.--GIRL--19

OOO-OOO-OOO-OH

Ooo-ooo-ooo-oh.--FIXINGAHOL--22

OPAQUE

Although your mind's opaque --THINKFORYO--19

OPEN

Open up your eyes now--TELLMEWHAT--5
Open up your eyes now--TELLMEWHAT--22
Open up your eyes now--TELLMEWHAT--31
Dear Prudence, open up your eyes --DEARPRUDEN--6
Dear Prudence, won't you open up your eyes?--
     DEARPRUDEN--10

OPENED

And opened up the doors.--HELP--14
And opened up the doors.--HELP--34
Are drifting through my opened mind
     --ACROSSTHEU--4
Are ringing through my opened ears
     --ACROSSTHEU--21

OR

I've known a secret for the week or two --
     DOYOUWANTT--15
I could tell the world a thing or two about our love
     --THANKYOUGI--5
I don't wanna kiss or hold your hand --IMHAPPYJUS
     --4
I don't need to hug or hold you tight --IMHAPPYJUS
     --8
If it's something that I said or done --TELLMEWHY
     --13
I've had a drink or two and I don't care --
     IDONTWANTT--5
Though I've had a drink or two and I don't care --
     IDONTWANTT--22
Of all the love I have won or have lost --IMALOSER
     --3
Is it for her or myself that I cry?--IMALOSER--12.
Said you had a thing or two to tell me--INEEDYOU
     --6
I can't forget the time or place--IVEJUSTSEE--2
I can't forget the time or place--IVEJUSTSEE--25
We can work it out and get it straight or say
     good night.--WECANWORKI--9
Only time will tell if I am right or I am wrong.--
     WECANWORKI--16
Only time will tell if I am right or I am wrong.--
     WECANWORKI--25
Or should I say--NORWEGIANW--2
Or I won't know where I am.--RUNFORYOUR--4
Or you won't know where I am.--RUNFORYOUR--28
I've got a word or two--THINKFORYO--1
Dear Sir or Madam, will you read my book?--
     PAPERBACKW--2
It's a thousand pages, give or take a few,
     ((paperback))--PAPERBACKW--15
I'll be writing more in a week or two. ((writer))
     --PAPERBACKW--16
Day or night he'll be there any time at all, Dr.
     Robert --DRROBERT--2
Or play the game existence to the end--TOMORROWNE
     --13
I mean, it must be high or low--STRAWBERRY--17
Sitting on a sofa with a sister or two.--LOVELYRITA

--25
Please don't be long or I may be asleep.--
  BLUEJAYWAY--7
Please don't be long or I may be asleep.--
  BLUEJAYWAY--14
Please don't be long or I may be asleep.--
  BLUEJAYWAY--21
Or the sound he appears to make--FOOLONTHEH--11
About an hour or two --DONTPASSME--28
Or where you'd like to be.--ITSALLTOOM--15
What words I say or time of day it is --ONLYANORTH
  --8
Or how I fare or if my hair is brown --ONLYANORTH
  --11
Or how I fare or if my hair is brown --ONLYANORTH
  --11
Trying to get to Holland or France.--BALLADOFJO--2
Not worrying what they or you say --OLDBROWNSH--19

ORANGE
    Pink, brown, yellow, orange and blue --ALLTOGETHE
      --19

OTHER
    And we held each other tight --ISAWHERSTA--14
    And we held each other tight --ISAWHERSTA--21
    Love you like no other baby --IWANNABEYO--5
    Like no other can.--IWANNABEYO--6
    Love you like no other baby --IWANNABEYO--7
    Like no other can.--IWANNABEYO--8
    Love you like no other baby --IWANNABEYO--34
    Like no other can (ooo).--IWANNABEYO--35
    Love you like no other baby --IWANNABEYO--36
    Like no other can.--IWANNABEYO--37
    Love you more than any other guy--NOREPLY--18
    I might have looked the other way--IVEJUSTSEE--8
    But other girls were never quite like this --
      IVEJUSTSEE--17
    Had you come some other day --IFINEEDEDS--7
    Had you come some other day --IFINEEDEDS--17
    The other day I saw you as I walked along the
      road --WHATGOESON--6
    To see how the other half live--GLASSONION--6
    That you and me were meant to be for each other -
      silly girl.--MARTHAMYDE--9
    Attracts me like no other lover --SOMETHING--2
    That I don't need no other lover --SOMETHING--7

OUGHT
    She ought to think twice--TICKETTORI--18
    She ought to do right by me--TICKETTORI--19
    She ought to think twice--TICKETTORI--21
    She ought to do right by me.--TICKETTORI--22
    She ought to think twice--TICKETTORI--31
    She ought to do right by me--TICKETTORI--32
    She ought to think twice--TICKETTORI--34
    She ought to do right by me.--TICKETTORI--35
    I feel as though you ought to know--WAIT--9
    I feel as though you ought to know--WAIT--17

OUR
    I could tell the world a thing or two about our love
      --THANKYOUGI--5
    I know, little girl, only a fool would doubt
      our love--THANKYOUGI--6
    If our new love was in vain.--IFIFELL--16
    If our new love was in vain.--IFIFELL--23
    We said our goodbyes (aah the night before)--
      NIGHTBEFOR--1
    We said our goodbyes (aah the night before)--
      NIGHTBEFOR--11
    Run the risk of knowing that our love may soon be
      gone.--WECANWORKI--4
    That we can have if we close our eyes.--THINKFORYO
      --5
    In our yellow submarine.--YELLOWSUBM--8
    And our friends are all aboard--YELLOWSUBM--13
    In our yellow (in our yellow) submarine
      (submarine - ah ha!)--YELLOWSUBM--28
    In our yellow (in our yellow) submarine
      (submarine - ah ha!)--YELLOWSUBM--28
    She (we gave her most of our lives)--SHESLEAVIN--8
    Is leaving (sacrificed most of our lives)--
      SHESLEAVIN--9
    Daddy, our baby's gone.--SHESLEAVIN--17
    Is leaving (never a thought for our ourselves)--
      SHESLEAVIN--21
    Home. (we struggled hard all our lives to get by)
      --SHESLEAVIN--22
    To try our best to hold it there--WITHINYOUW--11

With our love--WITHINYOUW--12
With our love--WITHINYOUW--13
We'd all love to change our head.--REVOLUTONE--37
Talking in our beds for a week.--BALLADOFJO--18
In our little hideaway beneath the waves.--
  OCTOPUSSGA--10
Resting our head on the seabed--OCTOPUSSGA--11
Not arriving on our way back home.--TWOOFUS--6
We're on our way home --TWOOFUS--7
We're on our way home --TWOOFUS--8
Lifting latches on our way back home.--TWOOFUS--13
We're on our way home --TWOOFUS--14
We're on our way home --TWOOFUS--15
Getting nowhere on our way back home.--TWOOFUS--22
We're on our way home --TWOOFUS--23
We're on our way home --TWOOFUS--24
Getting nowhere on our way back home.--TWOOFUS--31
We're on our way home --TWOOFUS--32
We're on our way home --TWOOFUS--33

OURS
    A love like ours --ANDILOVEHE--11

OURSELVES
    She (we never thought of ourselves)--SHESLEAVIN--20
    Is leaving (never a thought for our ourselves)--
      SHESLEAVIN--21
    I'd like to say thank you on behalf of the group
      and ourselves--GETBACK/LP--38

OUT
    Come on, out my way --WHENIGETHO--4
    Till I walk out that door again.--WHENIGETHO--20
    To walk out and make me lonely--YOULIKEMET--9
    And kept out of sight--IVEJUSTSEE--16
    If you don't take her out tonight--YOUREGONNA--3
    And I will take her out tonight--YOUREGONNA--5
    If you don't take her out tonight--YOUREGONNA--25
    And I will take her out tonight--YOUREGONNA--27
    For taking the easy way out --DAYTRIPPER--2
    For taking the easy way out, now.--DAYTRIPPER--4
    It took me so long to find out --DAYTRIPPER--7
    And I found out.--DAYTRIPPER--8
    It took me so long to find out --DAYTRIPPER--15
    And I found out.--DAYTRIPPER--16
    It took me so long to find out --DAYTRIPPER--24
    And I found out.--DAYTRIPPER--25
    WE CAN WORK IT OUT.--WECANWORKI--Title
    We can work it out, we can work it out.--WECANWORKI
      --5
    We can work it out, we can work it out.--WECANWORKI
      --5
    We can work it out and get it straight or say
      good night.--WECANWORKI--9
    We can work it out, we can work it out.--WECANWORKI
      --10
    We can work it out, we can work it out.--WECANWORKI
      --10
    We can work it out, we can work it out.--WECANWORKI
      --19
    We can work it out, we can work it out.--WECANWORKI
      --19
    We can work it out, we can work it out.--WECANWORKI
      --28
    We can work it out, we can work it out.--WECANWORKI
      --28
    You stay home, she goes out --FORNOONE--17
    I need to laugh and when the sun is out --
      GOODDAYSUN--2
    But it all works out--STRAWBERRY--9
    He blew his mind out in a car--DAYINTHELI--6
    Woke up, fell out of bed--DAYINTHELI--18
    Took her out and tried to win her--LOVELYRITA--20
    They've been going in and out of style--SGTPEPPERS
      --3
    If I'd been out till quarter to three--WHENIMSIXT
      --5
    Would you stand up and walk out on me?--WITHALITTL
      --2
    (What do you see when you turn out the light?)--
      WITHALITTL--21
    Without going out of my door --INNERLIGHT--1
    Without looking out of my window --INNERLIGHT--3
    Without going out of your door --INNERLIGHT--8
    Without looking out of your window --INNERLIGHT--10
    You were made to go out and get her --HEYJUDE--6
    You have found her, now go and get her (let it
      out and let it in) --HEYJUDE--16
    So let it out and let it in --HEYJUDE--19
    Then you'll begin ((let it out)) to make it
      better --HEYJUDE--29

Don't you know that you can count me out?--
   REVOLUTION--9
Well, the Ukraine girls really knock me out --
   BACKINTHEU--15
Well, the Ukraine girls really knock me out --
   BACKINTHEU--27
Let me hear your balalaikas ringing out --
   BACKINTHEU--33
He went out tiger hunting with his elephant and
   gun --CONTINUING--8
With voices out of nowhere --CRYBABYCRY--30
Dear Prudence, won't you come out to play?--
   DEARPRUDEN--1
Dear Prudence, won't you come out to play?--
   DEARPRUDEN--5
Dear Prudence, won't you come out to play?--
   DEARPRUDEN--21
Dear Prudence, won't you come out to play?--
   DEARPRUDEN--25
Your inside is out when your outside is in --
   EVRBDYMONK--17
Your outside is in when your inside is out --
   EVRBDYMONK--18
Now the sun turns out his light --GOODNIGHT--3
Now the sun turns out his light --GOODNIGHT--16
Look out helter-skelter, helter-skelter,
   helter-skelter - oh.--HELTERSKEL--16
Look out 'cos here she comes (heh heh heh).--
   HELTERSKEL--17
Look out helter-skelter, helter-skelter,
   helter-skelter.--HELTERSKEL--26
Well, look out helter-skelter.--HELTERSKEL--27
Hold your hand out you silly girl, see what
   you've done --MARTHAMYDE--10
You can see them out for dinner--PIGGIES--17
Don't you know that you can count me out (in)?--
   REVOLUTONE--12
Gideon checked out and he left it no doubt ((oh
   - Rocky - oh))--ROCKYRACCO--38
But you'll have to have them all pulled out--
   SAVOYTRUFF--4
But you'll have to have them all pulled out--
   SAVOYTRUFF--9
But you'll have to have them all pulled out--
   SAVOYTRUFF--17
But you'll have to have them all pulled out--
   SAVOYTRUFF--26
Yes, you'll have to have them all pulled out--
   SAVOYTRUFF--28
Some kind of happiness is measured out in miles--
   HEYBULLDOG--3
Some kind of innocence is measured out in years--
   HEYBULLDOG--7
Some kind of solitude is measured out in you--
   HEYBULLDOG--15
Is a little dark and out of key --ONLYANORTH--14
Now I'm stepping out this old brown shoe --
   OLDBROWNSH--5
Can I take you out to the pictures, Joan?--
   MAXWELLSIL--4
Takes him out to look at the Queen--MEANMRMUST--11
Always shouts out something obscene--MEANMRMUST--13
Oh look out!--SHECAMEINT--3
Out of college, money spent --YOUNEVERGI--7
Words are flowing out like endless rain into a
   paper cup --ACROSSTHEU--1
Longer than the road that stretches out ahead.--
   TWOOFUS--18
Longer than the road that stretches out ahead.--
   TWOOFUS--27

OUTSIDE
Stepping outside she is free.--SHESLEAVIN--7
Your inside is out when your outside is in --
   EVRBDYMONK--17
Your outside is in when your inside is out --
   EVRBDYMONK--18

OUTTA
I go outta my mind.--YOUCANTDOT--26
I go outta my mind.--YOUCANTDOT--45
What would you think if I sang outta tune --
   WITHALITTL--1
And I'll try not to sing outta key.--WITHALITTL--4

OVER
There's a shadow hanging over me--YESTERDAY--7
Over men and horses, hoops and garters--BEINGFORTH
   --5
Had a laugh and over dinner--LOVELYRITA--21
Towering over your head.--LUCYINTHES--6

We'll be over soon they said --BLUEJAYWAY--3
Come together right now over me--COMETOGETH--21
Come together right now over me--COMETOGETH--31
Come together right now over me--COMETOGETH--42
I said, move over honey, I'm travelling on
   that line --ONEAFTERNI--2
I said, move over once, move over twice --
   ONEAFTERNI--3
I said, move over once, move over twice --
   ONEAFTERNI--3
I said move over once, move over twice --ONEAFTERNI
   --8
I said move over once, move over twice --ONEAFTERNI
   --8
I said a-move over honey, I'm travelling on
   that line --ONEAFTERNI--16
Said move over once, move over twice --ONEAFTERNI
   --17
Said move over once, move over twice --ONEAFTERNI
   --17
Said a - move over honey, I'm travelling on
   that line --ONEAFTERNI--26
I said move over once, move over twice --ONEAFTERNI
   --27
I said move over once, move over twice --ONEAFTERNI
   --27

OVERNIGHT
Love has a nasty habit of disappearing overnight.
   --IMLOOKINGT--10
Love has a nasty habit of disappearing overnight.
   --IMLOOKINGT--16
It could make a million for you overnight.
   ((writer))--PAPERBACKW--22

OVERTIME
Lying with his eyes while his hands are busy
   working overtime --HAPPINESSI--6

OW
Wow (ow) - oh--IWANNABEYO--25
Ow!--IWANNABEYO--28
Ow! - wuh!--IWANNABEYO--42
(Ow)--CANTBUYMEL--23
Ow!--ICALLYOURN--11
(Ow)--HARDDAYSNI--24
Ow!--IMDOWN--15
Ow - ow - ow - wuh!--IMDOWN--27
Ow - ow - ow - wuh!--IMDOWN--27
Ow - ow - ow - wuh!--IMDOWN--27
Nah nah nah, nah - nah - nah - nah (ow) --HEYJUDE
   --36
(Ow - ow) nah nah nah, nah - nah - nah - nah --
   HEYJUDE--41
(Ow - ow) nah nah nah, nah - nah - nah - nah --
   HEYJUDE--41
(Ow - ooo nah nah nah) nah - nah - nah - nah,
   hey Jude--HEYJUDE--42
Ooo - ow, ow!--GETBACK/45--30
Ooo - ow, ow!--GETBACK/45--30
Because. (ooo - ow)--IDIGAPONY--25

OWN
That she would leave me on my own--DONTBOTHER--10
Here am I sitting all on my own--ITWONTBELO--6
But you left me sitting on my own --TELLMEWHY--6
Try thinking more if just for your own sake.--
   THINKFORYO--20
And you're on your own you're in the street.--
   GOODMORNIN--12
(Are you sad because you're on your own?)--
   WITHALITTL--11
By the banks of her own lagoon.--SHECAMEINT--7

OWNED
We gave her everything we owned just to sit at
   her table ((sexy Sadie))--SEXYSADIE--20

PABLO
Late of Pablo Fanques Fair - what a scene.--
   BEINGFORTH--4

PAGES
It's a thousand pages, give or take a few,
   ((paperback))--PAPERBACKW--15

PAID
>   Got the bill and Rita paid it--LOVELYRITA--23

PAIN
>   This boy wouldn't mind the pain--THISBOY--11
>   That might cause you pain--YOUCANTDOT--2
>   'cos I couldn't stand the pain --IFIFELL--14
>   'cos I couldn't stand the pain --IFIFELL--21
>   Was she told when she was young that pain would
>   lead to pleasure?--GIRL--22
>   And any time you feel the pain--HEYJUDE--9
>   When the pain cuts through--SAVOYTRUFF--12

PAINTING
>   I'm painting a room in a colourful way--FIXINGAHOL
>   --11
>   Painting pictures for the childrens' holiday.--
>   CRYBABYCRY--15
>   Painting testimonial pictures oh oh - oh oh.--
>   MAXWELLSIL--18

PAM
>   His sister Pam works in a shop--MEANMRMUST--8
>   POLYTHENE PAM.--POLYTHENEP--Title
>   Well, you should see Polythene Pam.--POLYTHENEP--1
>   Yes, you should see Polythene Pam - yeah,
>   yeah, yeah.--POLYTHENEP--5

PAN
>   But she was a frying pan ((sweet Loretta
>   Martin)).--GETBACK/LP--3
>   Oh Danny Boy, the odes of Pan are calling.--
>   ONEAFTERNI--33

PAPARATSI
>   Mundo paparatsi mi amore chicka ferde parasol --
>   SUNKING--7

PAPER
>   On the way the paper bag was on my knee --
>   BACKINTHEU--3
>   Trying to save paper.--MEANMRMUST--3
>   You only give me your funny paper--YOUNEVERGI--2
>   Words are flowing out like endless rain into a
>   paper cup --ACROSSTHEU--1
>   You and me chasing paper --TWOOFUS--21
>   You and me chasing paper --TWOOFUS--30

PAPERBACK
>   PAPERBACK WRITER.--PAPERBACKW--Title
>   Paperback writer ((paperback writer)) paperback
>   writer.--PAPERBACKW--1
>   Paperback writer ((paperback writer)) paperback
>   writer.--PAPERBACKW--1
>   Paperback writer ((paperback writer)) paperback
>   writer.--PAPERBACKW--1
>   So I want to be a paperback writer --PAPERBACKW--6
>   Paperback writer.--PAPERBACKW--7
>   But he wants to be a paperback writer--PAPERBACKW
>   --12
>   Paperback writer.--PAPERBACKW--13
>   Paperback writer ((paperback writer)) paperback
>   writer.--PAPERBACKW--14
>   Paperback writer ((paperback writer)) paperback
>   writer.--PAPERBACKW--14
>   Paperback writer ((paperback writer)) paperback
>   writer.--PAPERBACKW--14
>   It's a thousand pages, give or take a few,
>   ((paperback))--PAPERBACKW--15
>   I can make it longer if you like the style,
>   ((papérback))--PAPERBACKW--17
>   And I want to be a paperback writer --PAPERBACKW
>   --19
>   Paperback writer.--PAPERBACKW--20
>   If you really like it you can have the rights,
>   ((paperback))--PAPERBACKW--21
>   If you must return it you can send it here,
>   ((paperback))--PAPERBACKW--23
>   And I want to be a paperback writer --PAPERBACKW
>   --25
>   Paperback writer.--PAPERBACKW--26
>   Paperback writer ((paperback writer)) paperback
>   writer.--PAPERBACKW--27
>   Paperback writer ((paperback writer)) paperback
>   writer.--PAPERBACKW--27
>   Paperback writer ((paperback writer)) paperback
>   writer.--PAPERBACKW--27

(Paperback)--PAPERBACKW--28
(Paperback writer) paperback writer.--PAPERBACKW
    --29
(Paperback writer) paperback writer.--PAPERBACKW
    --29
(Paperback writer) paperback writer.--PAPERBACKW
    --30
(Paperback writer) paperback writer.--PAPERBACKW
    --30
(Paperback writer) paperback writer.--PAPERBACKW
    --31
(Paperback writer) paperback writer.--PAPERBACKW
    --31
(Paperback writer) paperback writer.--PAPERBACKW
    --32
(Paperback writer) paperback writer.--PAPERBACKW
    --32
(Paperback...--PAPERBACKW--33

PAPERS
>   Wednesday morning papers didn't come --LADYMADONN
>   --15

PARAMUCHO
>   Quando paramucho mi amore defeliche carathon --
>   SUNKING--6

PARASOL
>   Mundo paparatsi mi amore chicka ferde parasol --
>   SUNKING--7

PARIS
>   Finally made the plane into Paris --BALLADOFJO--9
>   Drove from Paris to the Amsterdam Hilton --
>   BALLADOFJO--17

PARK
>   Big man (yeah?) walking in the park--HEYBULLDOG--13
>   Mean Mr. Mustard sleeps in the park--MEANMRMUST--1

PARKING
>   Standing by a parking meter--LOVELYRITA--7

PARLOUR
>   The Queen was in the parlour --CRYBABYCRY--6

PART
>   If I'm part of you--TELLMEWHAT--4
>   That you are part of everything.--DEARPRUDEN--9

PARTED
>   For though they may be parted --LETITBE/45--12
>   For though they may be parted --LETITBE/LP--12

PARTY
>   I DON'T WANT TO SPOIL THE PARTY.--IDONTWANTT--Title
>   I don't wanna spoil the party so I'll go --
>   IDONTWANTT--1
>   I don't wanna spoil the party so I'll go --
>   IDONTWANTT--13
>   Yes, we're going to a party, party --BIRTHDAY--8
>   Yes, we're going to a party, party --BIRTHDAY--8
>   Yes, we're going to a party, party --BIRTHDAY--9
>   Yes, we're going to a party, party --BIRTHDAY--9
>   Yes, we're going to a party, party.--BIRTHDAY--10
>   Yes, we're going to a party, party.--BIRTHDAY--10

PASS
>   Time will pass away--TELLMEWHAT--10
>   When they pass away.--WITHINYOUW--7
>   DON'T PASS ME BY.--DONTPASSME--Title
>   Don't pass me by, don't make me cry, don't make
>   me blue --DONTPASSME--18
>   Don't pass me by - don't make me cry.--DONTPASSME
>   --22
>   Don't pass me by, don't make me cry, don't make
>   me blue --DONTPASSME--31
>   Don't pass me by - don't make me cry.--DONTPASSME
>   --35
>   Don't pass me by, don't make me cry, don't make
>   me blue --DONTPASSME--37
>   Don't pass me by - don't make me cry.--DONTPASSME
>   --41

PASSED
And I hope we passed the audition.--GETBACK/LP--39

PAST
I turn around, it's past--LOVEYOUTWO--2
And never ask me why they don't get past my door.
--FIXINGAHOL--18
Everyone smiles as you drift past the flowers--
LUCYINTHES--14
Now it's past my bed I know (know) --BLUEJAYWAY--15
It's a love that has no past (believe me).--
DONTLETMED--16

PATAPHYSICAL
Joan was quizzical, studied pataphysical science
in the home --MAXWELLSIL--1

PAUL
The walrus was Paul--GLASSONION--11

PAY
Don't pay money just to see yourself with Dr.
Robert.--DRROBERT--14
If you don't want to pay some more (ha ha Mr.
Heath)--TAXMAN--19
Who finds the money when you pay the rent?--
LADYMADONN--3
See no future, pay no rent --YOUNEVERGI--8
Spending someone's hard-earned pay.--TWOOFUS--4

PC
PC Thirty-One said, we caught a dirty one,
Maxwell stands alone --MAXWELLSIL--17

PEACE
Peace of mind is waiting there--WITHINYOUW--30
You know I'd give you everything I've got for a
little peace of mind.--IMSOTIRED--13
You know I'd give you everything I've got for a
little peace of mind.--IMSOTIRED--22
I'd give you everything I've got for a little
peace of mind --IMSOTIRED--23
I'd give you everything I've got for a little
peace of mind.--IMSOTIRED--24
I said we're only trying to get us some peace.--
BALLADOFJO--20

PEANUTS
Working for peanuts is all very fine --DRIVEMYCAR
--11

PEASANT
I know that she's no peasant--SHESAWOMAN--2
I know that she's no peasant--SHESAWOMAN--19
I know that she's no peasant--SHESAWOMAN--29

PEEP
But I saw you peep through your window--NOREPLY--5

PENETRATE
Well you can penetrate any place you go--IDIGAPONY
--10
Yes you can penetrate any place you go--IDIGAPONY
--11

PENGUIN
Elementary penguin singing Hare Krishna--IAMTHEWALR
--26

PENNIES
Declare the pennies on your eyes (Taxman)--TAXMAN
--23

PENNY
PENNY LANE.--PENNYLANE--Title
Penny Lane: there is a barber showing photographs
--PENNYLANE--1
Penny Lane is in my ears and in my eyes--PENNYLANE
--9
In Penny Lane there is a fireman with an
hour-glass--PENNYLANE--12

Penny Lane is in my ears and in my eyes--PENNYLANE
--17
In Penny Lane the barber shaves another customer--
PENNYLANE--24
Penny Lane is in my ears and in my eyes--PENNYLANE
--28
Penny Lane is in my ears and in my eyes--PENNYLANE
--31
Penny Lane!--PENNYLANE--33

PEOPLE
I can't talk to people that I meet.--ILLCRYINST--7
Don't want to cry when there's people there --
ILLCRYINST--11
Don't want to cry when there's people there --
ILLCRYINST--20
People tell me that she's only fooling--SHESAWOMAN
--6
People tell me that she's only fooling--SHESAWOMAN
--23
People tell me that she's only fooling--SHESAWOMAN
--33
People tell me I'm lucky--EVERYLITTL--2
Everywhere people stare --YOUVEGOTTO--5
For people and things that went before --INMYLIFE
--14
For people and things that went before --INMYLIFE
--18
Aah, look at all the lonely people.--ELEANORRIG--1
Aah, look at all the lonely people.--ELEANORRIG--2
All the lonely people, where do they all come
from?--ELEANORRIG--9
All the lonely people, where do they all belong?--
ELEANORRIG--10
All the lonely people, where do they all come
from?--ELEANORRIG--17
All the lonely people, where do they all belong?--
ELEANORRIG--18
Aah, look at all the lonely people.--ELEANORRIG--19
Aah, look at all the lonely people.--ELEANORRIG--20
All the lonely people, where do they all come
from?--ELEANORRIG--27
((Aah, look at all the lonely people.))--ELEANORRIG
--28
All the lonely people, where do they all belong?--
ELEANORRIG--29
((Aah, look at all the lonely people.))--ELEANORRIG
--30
There's people standing round--LOVEYOUTWO--13
And all the people that come and go--PENNYLANE--3
A crowd of people stood and stared--DAYINTHELI--8
A crowd of people turned away--DAYINTHELI--13
See the people standing there who disagree and
never win--FIXINGAHOL--9
Silly people run around they worry me--FIXINGAHOL
--17
People running round it's five o'clock--GOODMORNIN
--18
Where rocking-horse people eat marshmallow pies.--
LUCYINTHES--13
And the people--WITHINYOUW--3
And the people--WITHINYOUW--23
One of the beautiful people?--BABYYOUREA--2
One of the beautiful people?--BABYYOUREA--8
One of the beautiful people?--BABYYOUREA--23
But if you want money for people with minds that
hate --REVOLUTION--18
But if you want money for people with minds that
hate --REVOLUTONE--27
And when the broken-hearted people--LETITBE/45--9
And when the broken-hearted people--LETITBE/LP--9

PEPPER
That Sgt. Pepper taught the band to play--
SGTPEPPERS--2

PEPPER'S
SGT. PEPPER'S LONELY HEARTS CLUB BAND.--SGTPEPPERS
--Title
Sgt. Pepper's Lonely Hearts Club Band.--SGTPEPPERS
--7
We're Sgt. Pepper's Lonely Hearts Club Band--
SGTPEPPERS--8
Sgt. Pepper's Lonely Hearts Club Band--SGTPEPPERS
--10
Sgt. Pepper's Lonely, Sgt. Pepper's Lonely--
SGTPEPPERS--12
Sgt. Pepper's Lonely, Sgt. Pepper's Lonely--
SGTPEPPERS--12
Sgt. Pepper's Lonely Hearts Club Band.--SGTPEPPERS
--13

And Sgt. Pepper's Lonely Hearts Club Band.--
    SGTPEPPERS--25
SGT. PEPPER'S LONELY HEARTS CLUB BAND
    (REPRISE).--SGTPEPPREP--Title
We're Sgt. Pepper's Lonely Hearts Club Band --
    SGTPEPPREP--3
Sgt. Pepper's Lonely Hearts Club Band --SGTPEPPREP
    --5
Sgt. Pepper's Lonely --SGTPEPPREP--7
Sgt. Pepper's Lonely --SGTPEPPREP--8
Sgt. Pepper's Lonely --SGTPEPPREP--9
Sgt. Pepper's Lonely.--SGTPEPPREP--10
Sgt. Pepper's Lonely Hearts Club Band --SGTPEPPREP
    --11
Sgt. Pepper's one and only Lonely Hearts Club
    Band --SGTPEPPREP--13
Sgt. Pepper's Lonely --SGTPEPPREP--15
Sgt. Pepper's Lonely --SGTPEPPREP--16
Sgt. Pepper's Lonely Hearts Club Band.--SGTPEPPREP
    --17

PERCENT
    Should five percent appear too small --TAXMAN--7

PERFECTLY
    The man with the foolish grin is keeping
        perfectly still--FOOLONTHEH--2
    The man of a thousand voices talking perfectly loud
        --FOOLONTHEH--9

PERFORM
    You're waiting for someone to perform with.--
        HEYJUDE--21

PERFORMS
    Performs his feat on Saturday at Bishopsgate.--
        BEINGFORTH--9
    When Mr. K. performs his tricks - without a
        sound.--BEINGFORTH--16

PERVERTED
    You were perverted (too/to)--WHILEMYGUI--15

PETER
    Peter Brown called to say, you can make it OK --
        BALLADOFJO--11

PHASE
    Phase one in which Doris gets her oats.--TWOOFUS
        --2

PHONE
    Is call you on the phone --ALLIVEGOTT--3
    Is call you on the phone --ALLIVEGOTT--19
    Honey disconnect the phone.--BACKINTHEU--11
    Maxwell Edison, majoring in medicine, calls
        her on the phone --MAXWELLSIL--3
    Sundays on the phone to Monday --SHECAMEINT--10
    Tuesdays on the phone to me.--SHECAMEINT--11
    Sundays on the phone to Monday --SHECAMEINT--22
    Tuesdays on the phone to me.--SHECAMEINT--23

PHOTOGRAPH
    I saw the photograph--DAYINTHELI--5

PHOTOGRAPHS
    Penny Lane: there is a barber showing photographs
        --PENNYLANE--1

PIANO
    Playing piano for the children of the King.--
        CRYBABYCRY--7

PICK
    If you're down he'll pick you up, Dr. Robert --
        DRROBERT--6
    Though you pick me up --OLDBROWNSH--9
    Pick up the bags, get in the limousine.--YOUNEVERGI
        --18
    I pick a moon dog--IDIGAPONY--16
    Pick up my bag, run to the station --ONEAFTERNI--11
    Pick up my bag, run right home --ONEAFTERNI--13

Pick up my bag, run to the station --ONEAFTERNI--21
Well - pick up my bag, run right home (run
    right home) --ONEAFTERNI--23

PICKER
    The picker - the picker, picture the fingers
        going (ooo me).--GETBACK/LP--5
    The picker - the picker, picture the fingers
        going (ooo me).--GETBACK/LP--5

PICKING
    Picking flowers for a friend who came to play --
        CRYBABYCRY--13

PICKS
    Eleanor Rigby picks up the rice in the church--
        ELEANORRIG--3
    Picks up the letter that's lying there--SHESLEAVIN
        --14
    The eagle picks my eye --YERBLUES--17

PICTURE
    Picture yourself in a boat on a river--LUCYINTHES
        --1
    Picture yourself on a train in a station--
        LUCYINTHES--23
    The picker - the picker, picture the fingers
        going (ooo me).--GETBACK/LP--5

PICTURES
    But if you go carrying pictures of Chairman Mao --
        REVOLUTION--28
    Painting pictures for the childrens' holiday.--
        CRYBABYCRY--15
    If you go carrying pictures of Chairman Mao --
        REVOLUTONE--43
    Can I take you out to the pictures, Joan?--
        MAXWELLSIL--4
    Painting testimonial pictures oh oh - oh oh.--
        MAXWELLSIL--18

PIE
    HONEY PIE.--HONEYPIE--Title
    Honey Pie you are making me crazy--HONEYPIE--7
    Oh, Honey Pie my position is tragic--HONEYPIE--10
    Oh, Honey Pie you are driving me frantic--HONEYPIE
        --16
    Honey Pie come back to me - ooo.--HONEYPIE--19
    Now Honey Pie you are making me crazy--HONEYPIE--29
    Come, come back to me Honey Pie--HONEYPIE--32
    Honey Pie, Honey Pie.--HONEYPIE--35
    Honey Pie, Honey Pie.--HONEYPIE--35
    WILD HONEY PIE.--WILDHONEYP--Title
    Honey Pie, Honey Pie.--WILDHONEYP--1
    Honey Pie, Honey Pie.--WILDHONEYP--1
    Honey Pie, Honey Pie.--WILDHONEYP--2
    Honey Pie, Honey Pie.--WILDHONEYP--2
    Honey Pie, Honey Pie, Honey Pie, Honey
        Pie --WILDHONEYP--3
    Honey Pie, Honey Pie, Honey Pie, Honey
        Pie,--WILDHONEYP--3
    Honey Pie, Honey Pie, Honey Pie, Honey
        ' Pie --WILDHONEYP--3
    Honey Pie, Honey Pie, Honey Pie, Honey
        Pie --WILDHONEYP--3
    I love you, yeah, Honey Pie, wuh!--WILDHONEYP--4

PIECE
    So take a piece, but not too much.--ITSALLTOOM
        --19

PIES
    A four of fish and finger pies in summer--PENNYLANE
        --18
    Where rocking-horse people eat marshmallow pies.--
        LUCYINTHES--13

PIGGIES
    PIGGIES.--PIGGIES--Title
    Have you seen the little piggies--PIGGIES--1
    And for all the little piggies--PIGGIES--3
    Have you seen the bigger piggies--PIGGIES--6
    You will find the bigger piggies--PIGGIES--8
    Everywhere there's lots of piggies--PIGGIES--15

PIGGY
　　Living piggy lives.--PIGGIES--16
　　With their piggy wives --PIGGIES--18

PIGS
　　See how they run like pigs from a gun, see how
　　　they fly--IAMTHEWALR--2
　　See how they smile, like pigs in a sty, see how
　　　they snied--IAMTHEWALR--23

PILCHARD
　　Semolina pilchard climbing up the Eiffel Tower--
　　　IAMTHEWALR--25

PILLOW
　　I never give you my pillow--CARRYTHATW--5

PINEAPPLE
　　A ginger sling with a pineapple heart --SAVOYTRUFF
　　　--2
　　A ginger sling with a pineapple heart --SAVOYTRUFF
　　　--24

PINK
　　Pink, brown, yellow, orange and blue --ALLTOGETHE
　　　--19

PLACE
　　THERE'S A PLACE.--THERESAPLA--Title
　　There, there's a place where I can go--THERESAPLA
　　　--1
　　There, there's a place where I can go--THERESAPLA
　　　--13
　　There's a place, there's a place--THERESAPLA--17
　　There's a place, there's a place--THERESAPLA--17
　　There's a place, there's a place.--THERESAPLA--18
　　There's a place, there's a place.--THERESAPLA--18
　　If somebody tries to take my place --IMHAPPYJUS--16
　　If somebody tries to take my place --IMHAPPYJUS--24
　　With another man in my place.--NOREPLY--16
　　With another man in my place.--NOREPLY--29
　　I can't forget the time or place--IVEJUSTSEE--2
　　I can't forget the time or place--IVEJUSTSEE--25
　　Now I need a place to hide away--YESTERDAY--15
　　Now I need a place to hide away--YESTERDAY--23
　　Been away so long I hardly knew the place --
　　　BACKINTHEU--8
　　You know the place where nothing is real--
　　　GLASSONION--2
　　Well here's another place you can go--GLASSONION
　　　--3
　　Well here's another place you can be--GLASSONION
　　　--19
　　Happy ever after in the market place --OBLADIOBLA
　　　--20
　　Hey, happy ever after in the market place --
　　　OBLADIOBLA--32
　　Only place that he's ever been--MEANMRMUST--12
　　Well you can penetrate any place you go--IDIGAPONY
　　　--10
　　Yes you can penetrate any place you go--IDIGAPONY
　　　--11

PLACES
　　There are places I remember --INMYLIFE--1
　　All these places had their moments --INMYLIFE--5

PLAIN
　　It's plain to see--DONTBOTHER--5

PLAN
　　We'd all love to see the plan.--REVOLUTION--14
　　We'd all love to see the plan.--REVOLUTONE--21

PLANE
　　Finally made the plane into Paris --BALLADOFJO--9
　　Caught the early plane back to London --BALLADOFJO
　　　--37

PLANNED
　　I would remember all the things we planned--YESITIS
　　　--7

PLANS
　　Making all his nowhere plans for nobody.--
　　　NOWHEREMAN--3
　　Making all his nowhere plans for nobody --
　　　NOWHEREMAN--24
　　Making all his nowhere plans for nobody --
　　　NOWHEREMAN--25
　　Making all his nowhere plans for nobody.--
　　　NOWHEREMAN--26

PLASTICINE
　　With plasticine porters with looking-glass ties.--
　　　LUCYINTHES--24

PLAY
　　Love was such an easy game to play--YESTERDAY--14
　　Love was such an easy game to play--YESTERDAY--22
　　Or play the game existence to the end--TOMORROWNE
　　　--13
　　And the band begins to play.--YELLOWSUBM--15
　　And though she feels as if she's in a play--
　　　PENNYLANE--22
　　That Sgt. Pepper taught the band to play--
　　　SGTPEPPERS--2
　　Nothing you can say but you can learn how to play
　　　the game ((love))--ALLYOUN/YS--6
　　What are you going to play?--BABYYOUREA--27
　　Picking flowers for a friend who came to play --
　　　CRYBABYCRY--13
　　Dear Prudence, won't you come out to play?--
　　　DEARPRUDEN--1
　　Dear Prudence, won't you come out to play?--
　　　DEARPRUDEN--5
　　Dear Prudence, won't you come out to play?--
　　　DEARPRUDEN--21
　　Dear Prudence, won't you come out to play?--
　　　DEARPRUDEN--25
　　Play it to me--HONEYPIE--23
　　Play it to me Hollywood blues.--HONEYPIE--24
　　Always having dirt to play around in.--PIGGIES--5
　　Always have clean shirts to play around in.--
　　　PIGGIES--10
　　But they are, they just play it like that.--
　　　ONLYANORTH--6
　　It doesn't really matter what chords I play --
　　　ONLYANORTH--7
　　Me hand's getting - a too cold to play a chord now.
　　　--IDIGAPONY--38

PLAYED
　　She only played one night stands --DAYTRIPPER--19
　　And she only played one night stands, now.--
　　　DAYTRIPPER--21

PLAYING
　　Listen to the music playing in your head.--
　　　LADYMADONN--13
　　Playing piano for the children of the King.--
　　　CRYBABYCRY--7
　　No-one's frightened of playing it --IMEMINE--18
　　No-one's frightened of playing it --IMEMINE--31

PLAYROOM
　　The Queen was in the playroom --CRYBABYCRY--14

PLAYS
　　For well you know that it's a fool who plays it
　　　cool --HEYJUDE--12
　　Back in school again, Maxwell plays the fool
　　　again, teacher gets annoyed --MAXWELLSIL--8

PLEAS
　　If you'll only listen to my pleas --TELLMEWHY--22

PLEASE
　　So please love me do --LOVEMEDO--4
　　So please love me do --LOVEMEDO--9
　　So please love me do --LOVEMEDO--16
　　So please love me do --LOVEMEDO--21
　　PLEASE PLEASE ME.--PLEASEPLEA--Title
　　PLEASE PLEASE ME.--PLEASEPLEA--Title
　　Please please me, whoa - yeah--PLEASEPLEA--5
　　Please please me, whoa - yeah--PLEASEPLEA--5
　　Like I please you.--PLEASEPLEA--6

Please please me, whoa - yeah--PLEASEPLEA--11
Please please me, whoa - yeah--PLEASEPLEA--11
Like I please you.--PLEASEPLEA--12
Please please me, whoa - yeah--PLEASEPLEA--23
Please please me, whoa - yeah--PLEASEPLEA--23
Like I please you.--PLEASEPLEA--24
Please me, whoa - yeah--PLEASEPLEA--25
Like I please you--PLEASEPLEA--26
Please me, whoa - yeah--PLEASEPLEA--27
Like I please you.--PLEASEPLEA--28
Please don't come near--DONTBOTHER--20
Please don't come near--DONTBOTHER--35
Oh please say to me--IWANTTOHOL--7
And please say to me--IWANTTOHOL--9
So please listen to me--YOUCANTDOT--23
So please listen to me--YOUCANTDOT--42
Oh please, don't run and hide --IFIFELL--11
Oh please, don't hurt my pride like her.--IFIFELL
    --13
Come on if you please --WHENIGETHO--10
If she turns up while I'm gone please let me know.
    --IDONTWANTT--4
If she turns up while I'm gone please let me know.
    --IDONTWANTT--16
Please ((please)) stop your lying --WHATYOURED--12
Please ((please)) stop your lying --WHATYOURED--12
Please ((please)) stop your lying --WHATYOURED--19
Please ((please)) stop your lying --WHATYOURED--19
Please don't wear red tonight--YESITIS--14
Please don't wear red tonight--YESITIS--23
Won't you please please help me?--HELP--18
Won't you please please help me?--HELP--18
Won't you please please help me?--HELP--28
Won't you please please help me?--HELP--28
Won't you please please help me?--HELP--38
Won't you please please help me?--HELP--38
Please come on back to me--INEEDYOU--3
Please remember how I feel about you--INEEDYOU--16
Please remember how I feel about you--INEEDYOU--26
Tried to please her --DAYTRIPPER--18
Tried to please her --DAYTRIPPER--20
Nowhere Man please listen --NOWHEREMAN--7
Nowhere Man please listen --NOWHEREMAN--19
Please don't wake me, no, don't shake me --
    IMONLYSLEE--5
Please don't spoil my day, I'm miles away --
    IMONLYSLEE--11
Please don't spoil my day, I'm miles away --
    IMONLYSLEE--17
Please don't wake me, no, don't shake me --
    IMONLYSLEE--25
Please don't be long --BLUEJAYWAY--5
Please don't you be very long --BLUEJAYWAY--6
Please don't be long or I may be asleep.--
    BLUEJAYWAY--7
Please don't be long (don't be long) --BLUEJAYWAY
    --12
Please don't you be very long (don't be long) --
    BLUEJAYWAY--13
Please don't be long or I may be asleep.--
    BLUEJAYWAY--14
Please don't be long (don't be long) --BLUEJAYWAY
    --19
Please don't you be very long (don't be long) --
    BLUEJAYWAY--20
Please don't be long or I may be asleep.--
    BLUEJAYWAY--21
Please don't be long --BLUEJAYWAY--22
Please don't you be very long--BLUEJAYWAY--23
Please don't be long.--BLUEJAYWAY--24
Please don't be long --BLUEJAYWAY--25
Please don't you be very long--BLUEJAYWAY--26
Please don't be long (please don't be long).
    --BLUEJAYWAY--27
Please don't be long (please don't be long).
    --BLUEJAYWAY--27
Please don't be long --BLUEJAYWAY--28
Please don't you be very long --BLUEJAYWAY--29
Please don't be long.--BLUEJAYWAY--30
So won't you please come home.--HONEYPIE--9
So won't you please come home.--HONEYPIE--31
Please - remember me, Martha my love --MARTHAMYDE
    --2
Please - be good to me, Martha my love --MARTHAMYDE
    --14
Got to be a joker he just do what he please--
    COMETOGETH--10
Oh darling, please believe me, I'll never do
    you no harm.--OHDARLING--1
Oh darling, please believe me, I'll never let
    you down.--OHDARLING--16
Oh please believe me I'd hate to miss the train --
    IVEGOTAFEE--6

PLEASING
    I do all the pleasing with you --PLEASEPLEA--16

PLEASURE
    Was she told when she was young that pain would
        lead to pleasure?--GIRL--22
    Of every head he's had the pleasure to know--
        PENNYLANE--2

POCKET
    And in his pocket is a portrait of the Queen--
        PENNYLANE--13

POE
    Man you should have seen them kicking Edgar
        Allan Poe--IAMTHEWALR--27

POINT
    I'll make a point of taking her away from you
        (watch what you do), yeah--YOUREGONNA--16
    I'll make a point of taking her away from you
        (watch what you do), yeah--YOUREGONNA--23
    Doesn't have a point of view --NOWHEREMAN--4
    Doesn't have a point of view --NOWHEREMAN--16
    Stating point of view.--WHENIMSIXT--29

POLICE
    And so I quit the police department--SHECAMEINT--16

POLICEMAN
    Mr. City policeman sitting pretty little
        policemen in a row--IAMTHEWALR--9
    Ask a policeman on the street --BLUEJAYWAY--10

POLICEMEN
    Mr. City policeman sitting pretty little
        policemen in a row--IAMTHEWALR--9

POLYTHENE
    POLYTHENE PAM.--POLYTHENEP--Title
    Well, you should see Polythene Pam.--POLYTHENEP--1
    Dressed in her polythene bag.--POLYTHENEP--4
    Yes, you should see Polythene Pam - yeah,
        yeah, yeah.--POLYTHENEP--5

PONY
    (I) DIG A PONY.--IDIGAPONY--Title
    I dig a pony--IDIGAPONY--6

POOL
    Has left a pool of tears crying for the day.--
        LONGANDWIN--5

POOLS
    Pools of sorrow, waves of joy--ACROSSTHEU--3

POOR
    Born a poor young country boy - Mother Nature's
        son --MOTHERNATU--1

POPPIES
    The pretty nurse is selling poppies from a tray--
        PENNYLANE--21

PORNOGRAPHIC
    Crabalocker fishwife, pornographic priestess--
        IAMTHEWALR--13

PORTERS
    With plasticine porters with looking-glass ties.--
        LUCYINTHES--24

PORTRAIT
    And in his pocket is a portrait of the Queen--
        PENNYLANE--13

POSITION
Oh, Honey Pie my position is tragic--HONEYPIE--10

POSSESSING
Possessing and caressing me.--ACROSSTHEU--5

POSSESSIONS
When your prized possessions start to weigh you
down --ANDYOURBIR--7

POSTCARD
Send me a postcard, drop me a line--WHENIMSIXT--28

POSTCARDS
Two of us sending postcards --TWOOFUS--10

POT-SMOKING
Queen says no to pot-smoking FBI member.--
FORYOUBLUE--1

POURING
In the pouring rain - very strange.--PENNYLANE--8
From the pouring rain - very strange.--PENNYLANE
--27

PRECISELY
Indicate precisely what you mean to say--WHENIMSIXT
--30

PREPARATION
Having been some days in preparation--BEINGFORTH
--19

PRESENTS
My love don't give me presents--SHESAWOMAN--1
My love don't give me presents--SHESAWOMAN--4
My love don't give me presents--SHESAWOMAN--18
My love don't give me presents--SHESAWOMAN--21
My love don't give me presents--SHESAWOMAN--28
My love don't give me presents--SHESAWOMAN--31

PRESS
The men from the press said, we wish you success
--BALLADOFJO--39

PRETEND
It's not like me to pretend--ILLGETYOU--6
It's not like me to pretend--ILLGETYOU--23
I'll pretend that I'm kissing --ALLMYLOVIN--7
Let's pretend we just can't see his face.--
IMHAPPYJUS--17
Let's pretend we just can't see his face.--
IMHAPPYJUS--25
That I'm not trying to pretend.--ILLBEBACK--12
That I'm not trying to pretend.--ILLBEBACK--21

PRETTY
The pretty nurse is selling poppies from a tray--
PENNYLANE--21
Mr. City policeman sitting pretty little
policemen in a row--IAMTHEWALR--9
Listen to the pretty sound of music as she flies.
--MOTHERNATU--4
Molly stays at home and does her pretty face--
OBLADIOBLA--23
Desmond stays at home and does his pretty face--
OBLADIOBLA--34
Sleep pretty darling do not cry--GOLDENSLUM--5
Sleep pretty darling do not cry--GOLDENSLUM--9
Sleep pretty darling do not cry--GOLDENSLUM--15
Her Majesty's a pretty nice girl--HERMAJESTY--1
Her Majesty's a pretty nice girl--HERMAJESTY--3
Her Majesty's a pretty nice girl--HERMAJESTY--7

PRIDE
Pride can hurt you too--SHELOVESYO--26
Oh please, don't hurt my pride like her.--IFIFELL
--13
And so it's true pride comes before a fall --
IMALOSER--17
But it's my pride--YESITIS--12

But it's my pride--YESITIS--21

PRIESTESS
Crabalocker fishwife, pornographic priestess--
IAMTHEWALR--13

PRIZED
When your prized possessions start to weigh you
down --ANDYOURBIR--7

PROBLEMS
The Duke was having problems --CRYBABYCRY--22

PROCEEDED
And proceeded to lie on the table --ROCKYRACCO--32

PRODUCTION
Their production will be second to none--BEINGFORTH
--13
He Bag Production--COMETOGETH--25

PROMISE
Do you promise not to tell?--DOYOUWANTT--4
Do you promise not to tell? (dodahdo)--DOYOUWANTT
--10
Do you promise not to tell? (dodahdo)--DOYOUWANTT
--18
Would you promise to be true --IFIFELL--2

PROMISES
And she promises the earth to me and I believe
her --GIRL--8

PROSPECTS
I told that girl that my prospects were good --
DRIVEMYCAR--9

PROTECTED
Protected by a silver spoon --SHECAMEINT--5

PROUD
I'm so proud to know that she is mine.--GOODDAYSUN
--13

PROVE
I will prove to you--TELLMEWHAT--2

PRUDENCE
DEAR PRUDENCE.--DEARPRUDEN--Title
Dear Prudence, won't you come out to play?--
DEARPRUDEN--1
Dear Prudence, greet the brand new day.--DEARPRUDEN
--2
Dear Prudence, won't you come out to play?--
DEARPRUDEN--5
Dear Prudence, open up your eyes --DEARPRUDEN--6
Dear Prudence, see the sunny skies.--DEARPRUDEN--7
Dear Prudence, won't you open up your eyes?--
DEARPRUDEN--10
Dear Prudence, let me see you smile --DEARPRUDEN
--16
Dear Prudence, like a little child.--DEARPRUDEN--17
Dear Prudence, won't you let me see you smile?--
DEARPRUDEN--20
Dear Prudence, won't you come out to play?--
DEARPRUDEN--21
Dear Prudence, greet the brand new day.--DEARPRUDEN
--22
Dear Prudence, won't you come out to play?--
DEARPRUDEN--25

PS
PS I LOVE YOU.--PSILOVEYOU--Title
PS I love you, you, you, you.--PSILOVEYOU--6
PS I love you, you, you, you.--PSILOVEYOU--9
PS I love you, you, you, you.--PSILOVEYOU--15
PS I love you, you, you, you --PSILOVEYOU--21

PUBLIC
Messrs. K. and H. assure the public--BEINGFORTH--12

PULLED
 But you'll have to have them all pulled out--
    SAVOYTRUFF--4
 But you'll have to have them all pulled out--
    SAVOYTRUFF--9
 But you'll have to have them all pulled out--
    SAVOYTRUFF--17
 But you'll have to have them all pulled out--
    SAVOYTRUFF--26
 Yes, you'll have to have them all pulled out--
    SAVOYTRUFF--28
 Everybody pulled their socks up (yeah) --IVEGOTAFEE
    --26
 Everybody pulled their socks up (oh no, no) --
    IVEGOTAFEE--34

PUT
 If you put your trust in me--TELLMEWHAT--11
 I said who put all those things in your head?--
    SHESAIDSHE--4
 Put on specially by the children for a lark.--
    CRYBABYCRY--31
 Everybody put the fool down, oh yeah - (yeah).--
    IVEGOTAFEE--27
 Everybody put their foot down, oh yeah (yeah).--
    IVEGOTAFEE--35

PUTS
 She's the kind of girl who puts you down--GIRL--11

PUTTING
 You'd say I'm putting you on --IMSOTIRED--9
 You'd say I'm putting you on --IMSOTIRED--18

PYGMY
 I dig a pygmy by Charles Hawtrey and the Deaf
    Aids (ha ha ha)--TWOOFUS--1

QUANDO
 Quando paramucho mi amore defeliche carathon --
    SUNKING--6

QUARTER
 If I'd been out till quarter to three--WHENIMSIXT
    --5

QUEEN
 And in his pocket is a portrait of the Queen--
    PENNYLANE--13
 Cooking breakfast for the Queen --CRYBABYCRY--5
 The Queen was in the parlour --CRYBABYCRY--6
 The Queen was in the playroom --CRYBABYCRY--14
 Takes him out to look at the Queen--MEANMRMUST--11
 Queen says no to pot-smoking FBI member.--
    FORYOUBLUE--1

QUESTO
 Questo obrigado tanta mucho cake and eat it
    carousel.--SUNKING--8

QUEUE
 For your sweet top lip I'm in the queue --
    OLDBROWNSH--31

QUI
 Sont des mots qui vont tres bien ensemble, tres
    bien ensemble.--MICHELLE--4
 Sont des mots qui vont tres bien ensemble, tres
    bien ensemble.--MICHELLE--10
 Sont des mots qui vont tres bien ensemble, tres
    bien ensemble.--MICHELLE--21

QUIET
 Quiet now quiet (OK) quiet--HEYBULLDOG--33
 Quiet now quiet (OK) quiet--HEYBULLDOG--33
 Quiet now quiet (OK) quiet--HEYBULLDOG--33

QUIETLY
 Quietly turning the backdoor key--SHESLEAVIN--6

QUIT

And so I quit the police department--SHECAMEINT--16

QUITE
 She's sweeter than all the girls and I met quite
    a few --ANOTHERGIR--6
 But other girls were never quite like this --
    IVEJUSTSEE--17
 Somebody calls you, you answer quite slowly--
    LUCYINTHES--3
 You may think the band are not quite right --
    ONLYANORTH--5

QUIZZICAL
 Joan was quizzical, studied pataphysical science
    in the home --MAXWELLSIL--1

RACCOON
 ROCKY RACCOON.--ROCKYRACCO--Title
 There lived a young boy name of Rocky Raccoon--
    ROCKYRACCO--2
 Rocky Raccoon checked into his room --ROCKYRACCO
    --9
 A - now Rocky Raccoon, he fell back in his room--
    ROCKYRACCO--36

RADIATE
 Well you can radiate everything you are--IDIGAPONY
    --17
 Yes you can radiate everything you are.--IDIGAPONY
    --18

RAILMAN
 Railman said, you got the wrong location --
    ONEAFTERNI--12
 Railman said, you got the wrong location --
    ONEAFTERNI--22

RAIN
 But you know there's always rain--PLEASEPLEA--14
 For tomorrow may rain so I'll follow the sun.--
    ILLFOLLOWT--2
 For tomorrow may rain so I'll follow the sun.--
    ILLFOLLOWT--4
 For tomorrow may rain so I'll follow the sun.--
    ILLFOLLOWT--8
 Yeah, tomorrow may rain so I'll follow the sun.--
    ILLFOLLOWT--9
 For tomorrow may rain so I'll follow the sun.--
    ILLFOLLOWT--13
 My tears are falling like rain from the sky --
    IMALOSER--11
 RAIN.--RAIN--Title
 If the rain comes they run and hide their heads--
    RAIN--1
 If the rain comes, if the rain comes.--RAIN--3
 If the rain comes, if the rain comes.--RAIN--3
 Rain I don't mind--RAIN--7
 I can show you that when it starts to rain (when
    the rain comes down)--RAIN--9
 I can show you that when it starts to rain (when
    the rain comes down)--RAIN--9
 Everything's the same (when the rain comes down)--
    , RAIN--10
 Rain I don't mind--RAIN--12
 Rain.--RAIN--17
 Rain.--RAIN--18
 Rain.--RAIN--19
 In the pouring rain - very strange.--PENNYLANE--8
 From the pouring rain - very strange.--PENNYLANE
    --27
 I'm fixing a hole where the rain gets in--
    FIXINGAHOL--1
 I'm fixing a hole where the rain gets in--
    FIXINGAHOL--23
 I'm fixing a hole where the rain gets in--
    FIXINGAHOL--26
 If the sun don't come you get a tan from standing
    in the English rain--IAMTHEWALR--18
 Sheep dog standing in the rain--HEYBULLDOG--1
 Words are flowing out like endless rain into a
    paper cup --ACROSSTHEU--1
 The wild and windy night that the rain washed away
    --LONGANDWIN--4

RAINCOATS
 Two of us wearing raincoats --TWOOFUS--19
 Two of us wearing raincoats --TWOOFUS--28

RAINS
    Can you hear me that when it rains and shines
      (when it rains and shines)--RAIN--14
    Can you hear me that when it rains and shines
      (when it rains and shines)--RAIN--14
    It's just a state of mind (when it rains and
      shines)--RAIN--15

RAINY
    Saving up your money for a rainy day --BALLADOFJO
    --25

RAISE
    But they're guaranteed to raise a smile.--
    SGTPEPPERS--4

RALEIGH
    And curse Sir Walter Raleigh --IMSOTIRED--16

RAN
    That if I ran away from you--ILLBEBACK--14
    I'm filling the cracks that ran through the door--
    FIXINGAHOL--4
    And one day his woman ran off with another guy --
    ROCKYRACCO--3

RATHER
    There is really nothing else I'd rather do --
    IMHAPPYJUS--6
    In this world there's nothing I would rather do --
    IMHAPPYJUS--10
    In this world there's nothing I would rather do --
    IMHAPPYJUS--18
    In this world there's nothing I would rather do --
    IMHAPPYJUS--26
    Well I'd rather see you dead, little girl --
    RUNFORYOUR--1
    And I'd rather see you dead.--RUNFORYOUR--20
    I'd rather see you dead, little girl --RUNFORYOUR
    --25
    And though the news was rather sad--DAYINTHELI--3
    And though the holes were rather small--DAYINTHELI
    --30

REACH
    But I say it just to reach you, Julia.--JULIA--2

READ
    In the good and the bad books that I have read.--
    THEWORD--16
    Dear Sir or Madam, will you read my book?--
    PAPERBACKW--2
    I read the news today, oh boy--DAYINTHELI--1
    Having read the book--DAYINTHELI--15
    I read the news today, oh boy--DAYINTHELI--28

READY
    I know that I'm ready to leave --SHESAIDSHE--11
    I know that I'm ready to leave --SHESAIDSHE--17
    But as she's getting ready to go, a knock comes
    on the door --MAXWELLSIL--5

REAL
    He's a real Nowhere Man --NOWHEREMAN--1
    He's a real Nowhere Man --NOWHEREMAN--22
    Nothing is real--STRAWBERRY--3
    Nothing is real--STRAWBERRY--13
    Nothing is real--STRAWBERRY--23
    Nothing is real--STRAWBERRY--33
    Lastly through a hogshead of real fire--BEINGFORTH
    --6
    You say you got a real solution --REVOLUTION--12
    You know the place where nothing is real--
    GLASSONION--2
    You say you got a real solution --REVOLUTONE--19

REALISE
    I thought that you would realise--ILLBEBACK--13
    I realise I have left it too late.--IMALOSER--16
    If I were you I'd realise that I--NOREPLY--17
    Don't you realise now--TELLMEWHAT--15
    You don't realise how much I need you--INEEDYOU--1
    I didn't realise--INEEDYOU--8
    Try to realise it's all within yourself--WITHINYOUW

    --16

REALISED
    Whoa, whoa, I never realised what a kiss could
    be --ISHOULDHAV--4
    So - oh, I should have realised a lot of things
    before --ISHOULDHAV--11
    Whoa, whoa, I never realised what a kiss could
    be --ISHOULDHAV--14

REALLY
    I'd really sympathise --ANYTIMEATA--8
    That it really only goes to show --ASKMEWHY--4
    That it really only goes to show --ASKMEWHY--19
    You'll never know how much I really love you --
    DOYOUWANTT--1
    You'll never know how much I really care.--
    DOYOUWANTT--2
    There is really nothing else I'd rather do --
    IMHAPPYJUS--6
    If you don't I really can't go on --TELLMEWHY--15
    'cos I really can't stand it --TELLMEWHY--24
    I really do.--YOULIKEMET--13
    'cos I couldn't really stand it--YOULIKEMET--17
    I really do--YOULIKEMET--22
    'cos I couldn't really stand it--YOULIKEMET--26
    I'm down (I'm really down)--IMDOWN--3
    I'm down (I'm really down).--IMDOWN--5
    I'm down (I'm really down).--IMDOWN--10
    I'm down (I'm really down).--IMDOWN--12
    I'm down (I'm really down).--IMDOWN--18
    I'm down (I'm really down).--IMDOWN--20
    Baby you know I'm down (I'm really down)--IMDOWN
    --28
    Oh yes, I'm down (I'm really down)--IMDOWN--29
    I'm down on the ground (I'm really down)--IMDOWN
    --30
    Ah, down (I'm really down)--IMDOWN--31
    I'm down (I'm really down)--IMDOWN--34
    Oh baby, I'm down (I'm really down)--IMDOWN--35
    I'm feeling upside-down (I'm really down)--IMDOWN--36
    Ooo, I'm down (I'm really down)--IMDOWN--37
    Baby, I'm down (I'm really down)--IMDOWN--40
    Well baby, I'm down (I'm really down)--IMDOWN--41
    Oh baby, I'm down (I'm really down)--IMDOWN--43
    I could never really live without you--INEEDYOU--17
    I could never really live without you--INEEDYOU--27
    If you really like it you can have the rights,
    ((paperback))--PAPERBACKW--21
    Nobody was really sure if he was from the House
    of Lords--DAYINTHELI--10
    And it really doesn't matter if I'm wrong I'm
    right--FIXINGAHOL--7
    And it really doesn't matter if I'm wrong I'm
    right--FIXINGAHOL--15
    Told her I would really like to see her again.--
    LOVELYRITA--22
    I don't really want to stop the show--SGTPEPPERS--19
    And to see you're really only very small--
    WITHINYOUW--18
    And I'd really like to go (go) --BLUEJAYWAY--16
    The less one really knows.--INNERLIGHT--7
    The less one really knows.--INNERLIGHT--14
    Well, the Ukraine girls really knock me out --
    BACKINTHEU--15
    Well, the Ukraine girls really knock me out --
    BACKINTHEU--27
    But it never really mattered --IWILL--7
    Cocoanut fudge really blows down those blues
    (wuh) --SAVOYTRUFF--8
    It doesn't really matter what chords I play --
    ONLYANORTH--7
    It doesn't really matter what clothes I wear --
    ONLYANORTH--10
    And from the first time that she really done me --
    DONTLETMED--21
    I guess nobody ever really done me --DONTLETMED--23
    I love you more than ever girl, I do - really
    love blues.--FORYOUBLUE--18
    Wondering really how come nobody told me--
    IVEGOTAFEE--12

REASON
    And in time you'll understand the reason why --
    ASKMEWHY--9
    It's so hard to reason with you, whoa - yeah--
    PLEASEPLEA--17
    I see no reason to change mine --NOTASECOND--5
    I see no reason to change mine --NOTASECOND--16
    I got every reason on earth to be mad --ILLCRYINST
    --1

Got a good reason --DAYTRIPPER--1
Got a good reason --DAYTRIPPER--3
Ooo - girl you know the reason why.--YERBLUES--5
Wuh - girl you know the reason why.--YERBLUES--9
Wuh - girl you know the reason why.--YERBLUES--16
Wuh - girl you know the reason why.--YERBLUES--23
Wuh girl - you know the reason why.--YERBLUES--30
... Girl you know the reason why.--YERBLUES--33

RECALL
With lovers and friends I still can recall --
    INMYLIFE--6

RECTIFY
And you've got time to rectify--THINKFORYO--22

RED
If you wear red tonight--YESITIS--1
For red is the colour that my baby wore--YESITIS
    --3
Please don't wear red tonight--YESITIS--14
For red is the colour that will make me blue--
    YESITIS--16
Please don't wear red tonight--YESITIS--23
For red is the colour that will make me blue--
    YESITIS--25
Black, white, green, red --ALLTOGETHE--17

REFRAIN
Hey Jude, refrain --HEYJUDE--10

REFUSE
Time after time you refuse to even listen --
    YOUWONTSEE--13
Time after time you refuse to even listen --
    YOUWONTSEE--22

REGRET
Though he'll regret it someday--THISBOY--2
Still you don't regret a single day.--GIRL--4

REJECT
My love is something you can't reject.--OLDBROWNSH
    --23

RELAX
Turn off your mind, relax and float down-stream--
    TOMORROWNE--1

REMAIN
Some have gone and some remain.--INMYLIFE--4

REMEMBER
Remember that I'll always be in love with you.--
    PSILOVEYOU--2
Remember that I'll always be in love with you.--
    PSILOVEYOU--11
Remember that I'll always, yeah, be in love
    with you.--PSILOVEYOU--18
I'll remember all the little things we've done --
    MISERY--6
I'll remember all the little things we've done --
    MISERY--10
She'll remember and she'll miss her only one,
    lonely one.--MISERY--11
Remember I'll always be true --ALLMYLOVIN--3
Remember I'll always be true --ALLMYLOVIN--17
Then I will remember things we said today.--
    THINGSWESA--5
Then we will remember things we said today.--
    THINGSWESA--10
Then we will remember things we said today.--
    THINGSWESA--21
Then we will remember things we said today.--
    THINGSWESA--32
I remember the first time--EVERYLITTL--4
Remember what I said tonight--YESITIS--2
I would remember all the things we planned--YESITIS
    --7
Please remember how I feel about you--INEEDYOU--16
Please remember how I feel about you--INEEDYOU--26
Last night is the night I will remember you by --
    NIGHTBEFOR--9
Last night is the night I will remember you by --

NIGHTBEFOR--17
There are places I remember --INMYLIFE--1
Remember to let her into your heart --HEYJUDE--3
Remember (hey Jude) to let her into your heart --
    HEYJUDE--17
Remember to let her under your skin (oh) --HEYJUDE
    --28
Please - remember me, Martha my love --MARTHAMYDE
    --2

RENT
Every summer we can rent a cottage--WHENIMSIXT--22
Who finds the money when you pay the rent?--
    LADYMADONN--3
See no future, pay no rent --YOUNEVERGI--8

REPLACING
Replacing every thoughtless frown.--OLDBROWNSH--12

REPLY
NO REPLY.--NOREPLY--Title
No reply--NOREPLY--3
When you gave me no reply.--NOREPLY--21
No reply, no reply.--NOREPLY--30
No reply, no reply.--NOREPLY--30

REPRISE
SGT. PEPPER'S LONELY HEARTS CLUB BAND
    (REPRISE).--SGTPEPPREP--Title

RESERVATION
Roll up (to make a reservation)--MAGICALMYS--7
Roll up (to make a reservation)--MAGICALMYS--25

RESIGN
So you might as well resign yourself to me, oh
    yeah.--ILLGETYOU--18

REST
Wonders how you manage to feed the rest.--
    LADYMADONN--10

RESTING
Resting our head on the seabed--OCTOPUSSGA--11

RESTLESS
Thoughts meander like a restless wind inside a
    letter-box --ACROSSTHEU--13

RETURN
If you must return it you can send it here,
    ((paperback))--PAPERBACKW--23

RETURNING
Little darling, the smiles returning to the faces.
    --HERECOMEST--9

REVIVAL
To help with good Rocky's revival - ah.--ROCKYRACCO
    --39

REVOLUTION
REVOLUTION.--REVOLUTION--Title
You say you wanna revolution --REVOLUTION--2
REVOLUTION ONE.--REVOLUTONE--Title
You say you want a revolution --REVOLUTONE--5
REVOLUTION NINE.--REVOLUNINE--Title

RICE
Eleanor Rigby picks up the rice in the church--
    ELEANORRIG--3

RICH
BABY, YOU'RE A RICH MAN.--BABYYOUREA--Title
Baby, you're a rich man --BABYYOUREA--13
Baby, you're a rich man --BABYYOUREA--14
Baby, you're a rich man too.--BABYYOUREA--15
Baby, you're a rich man --BABYYOUREA--19
Baby, you're a rich man --BABYYOUREA--20

Baby, you're a rich man too.--BABYYOUREA--21
Baby, you're a rich man --BABYYOUREA--28
Baby, you're a rich man --BABYYOUREA--29
Baby, you're a rich man too.--BABYYOUREA--30
Baby, you're a rich man --BABYYOUREA--34
Baby, you're a rich man --BABYYOUREA--35
Baby, you're a rich man too.--BABYYOUREA--36
Oh, baby you're a rich man --BABYYOUREA--37
Baby, you're a rich (baby) man --BABYYOUREA--38
Baby, you're a rich man too.--BABYYOUREA--39
Wuh-oh, baby, you're a rich (oh) man --BABYYOUREA
--40
Baby, you're a rich man --BABYYOUREA--41
Baby, you're a rich man too.--BABYYOUREA--42
Oh, baby, you're a rich man.--BABYYOUREA--43
Baby, you're a rich man.--BABYYOUREA--44

RIDE
TICKET TO RIDE.--TICKETTORI--Title
She's got a ticket to ride--TICKETTORI--5
She's got a ticket to ride--TICKETTORI--6
She's got a ticket to ride--TICKETTORI--7
She's got a ticket to ride--TICKETTORI--13
She's got a ticket to ride--TICKETTORI--14
She's got a ticket to ride--TICKETTORI--15
Oh, she's got a ticket to ride--TICKETTORI--26
She's got a ticket to ride--TICKETTORI--27
She's got a ticket to ride--TICKETTORI--28
Ah, she's got a ticket to ride--TICKETTORI--40
She's got a ticket to ride--TICKETTORI--41
She's got a ticket to ride--TICKETTORI--42
I was alone, I took a ride--GOTTOGETYO--1
I was alone, I took a ride--GOTTOGETYO--25
Sunday mornings go for a ride.--WHENIMSIXT--16
Where I stop and I turn and I go for a ride --
HELTERSKEL--2
And I stop and I turn and I go for a ride--
HELTERSKEL--19

RIDING
I don't know why she's riding so high--TICKETTORI
--17
I don't know why she's riding so high--TICKETTORI
--30
Two of us riding nowhere --TWOOFUS--3

RIGBY
ELEANOR RIGBY.--ELEANORRIG--Title
Eleanor Rigby picks up the rice in the church--
ELEANORRIG--3
Eleanor Rigby died in the church--ELEANORRIG--21

RIGHT
I'll be there to make you feel right --ANYTIMEATA
--6
It's just not right--DONTBOTHER--11
I've got no time for you right now--DONTBOTHER--13
I've got no time for you right now--DONTBOTHER--28
It feels so right now --HOLDMETIGH--1
It feels so right now --HOLDMETIGH--18
It feels so right now --HOLDMETIGH--28
When I'm home everything seems to be right --
HARDDAYSNI--15
When I'm home everything seems to be right --
HARDDAYSNI--28
She ought to do right by me--TICKETTORI--19
She ought to do right by me.--TICKETTORI--22
She ought to do right by me--TICKETTORI--32
She ought to do right by me.--TICKETTORI--35
If I just don't treat you right--YOULIKEMET--4
Is it right that you and I should fight, every
night--ITSONLYLOV--8
Haven't I the right to make it up girl?--ITSONLYLOV
--10
If you don't treat her right my friend--YOUREGONNA
--9
'cos I will treat her right--YOUREGONNA--11
Only time will tell if I am right or I am wrong.--
WECANWORKI--16
Only time will tell if I am right or I am wrong.--
WECANWORKI--25
I told that girl I could start right away --
DRIVEMYCAR--22
Why, tell me why did you not treat me right?--
IMLOOKINGT--9
Why, tell me why did you not treat me right?--
IMLOOKINGT--15
Now that I know what I feel must be right --THEWORD
--23
When I was a boy everything was right,

everything was right.--SHESAIDSHE--9
When I was a boy everything was right,
everything was right.--SHESAIDSHE--9
When I was a boy everything was right,
everything was right.--SHESAIDSHE--15
When I was a boy everything was right,
everything was right.--SHESAIDSHE--15
And it really doesn't matter if I'm wrong I'm
right--FIXINGAHOL--7
Where I belong I'm right where I belong.--
FIXINGAHOL--8
And it really doesn't matter if I'm wrong I'm
right--FIXINGAHOL--15
Where I belong I'm right where I belong.--
FIXINGAHOL--16
Step right this way.--MAGICALMYS--2
So Captain Marvel zapped him right between the
eyes. (Zap!)--CONTINUING--19
All right!--DONTPASSME--1
You may think the band are not quite right --
ONLYANORTH--5
I want a love that's right --OLDBROWNSH--1
But right is only half of what's wrong --OLDBROWNSH
--2
Come together right now over me--COMETOGETH--21
Come together right now over me--COMETOGETH--31
Right!--COMETOGETH--33
Come together right now over me--COMETOGETH--42
She is standing right in front of me --LETITBE/45
--5
You know my name, that's right, look up my
number (hey) --YOUKNOWMYN--10
You know my name - haa, that's right, look up
the number --YOUKNOWMYN--15
That's right (yeah)...--YOUKNOWMYN--42
Oh yeah, oh yeah (that's right).--IVEGOTAFEE--2
She is standing right in front of me --LETITBE/LP
--5
Pick up my bag, run right home --ONEAFTERNI--13
Well - pick up my bag, run right home (run
right home) --ONEAFTERNI--23
Well - pick up my bag, run right home (run
right home) --ONEAFTERNI--23

RIGHTS
If you really like it you can have the rights,
((paperback))--PAPERBACKW--21

RING
I'll buy you a diamond ring my friend --CANTBUYMEL
--3
Man buys ring, woman throws it away --IMDOWN--8
Ring my friend I said you'd call, Dr. Robert --
DRROBERT--1
Ring my friend I said you'd call, Dr. Robert --
DRROBERT--20
Ring my friend I said you'd call, Dr. Robert --
DRROBERT--21
As Mr. Kite flies through the ring - don't be
late.--BEINGFORTH--11
Buys a twenty-carat golden ring (golden ring) --
OBLADIOBLA--10
Buys a twenty-carat golden ring (golden ring) --
OBLADIOBLA--10

RINGING
Let me hear your balalaikas ringing out --
BACKINTHEU--33
Are ringing through my opened ears--ACROSSTHEU
--21

RINGO
Featuring Dennis O'Fell and Ringo.--YOUKNOWMYN--6
Good evening (Ringo).--YOUKNOWMYN--7

RINGS
Say you don't need no diamond rings --CANTBUYMEL
--17
Say you don't need no diamond rings --CANTBUYMEL
--27
He buys her diamond rings, you know, she said so
--IFEELFINE--10
He buys her diamond rings, you know, she said so
--IFEELFINE--18
Wearing rings on every finger --OLDBROWNSH--18

RISE
Sit beside a mountain stream - see her waters rise

--MOTHERNATU--3
Smiles awake you when you rise.--GOLDENSLUM--8

RISK
    Run the risk of knowing that our love may soon be
        gone.--WECANWORKI--4

RITA
    LOVELY RITA.--LOVELYRITA--Title
    Lovely Rita meter maid--LOVELYRITA--2
    Lovely Rita meter maid (aah)--LOVELYRITA--3
    Lovely Rita (oh) meter maid--LOVELYRITA--4
    When I caught a glimpse of Rita--LOVELYRITA--8
    Lovely Rita meter maid--LOVELYRITA--13
    May I inquire discreetly ((lovely Rita))--
        LOVELYRITA--14
    When are you free ((lovely Rita))--LOVELYRITA--15
    Rita!--LOVELYRITA--18
    Got the bill and Rita paid it--LOVELYRITA--23
    Oh, lovely Rita meter maid--LOVELYRITA--26
    Lovely Rita ((lovely meter maid)) meter maid--
        LOVELYRITA--29
    Lovely ((Rita, Rita, Rita)) Rita meter maid--
        LOVELYRITA--30
    Lovely ((Rita, Rita, Rita)) Rita meter maid--
        LOVELYRITA--30
    Lovely ((Rita, Rita, Rita)) Rita meter maid--
        LOVELYRITA--30
    Lovely ((Rita, Rita, Rita)) Rita meter maid--
        LOVELYRITA--30
    Lovely Rita ((oh lovely Rita meter, meter
        maid)) meter maid--LOVELYRITA--31
    Lovely Rita ((oh lovely Rita meter, meter
        maid)) meter maid--LOVELYRITA--31
    Lovely Rita ((da da da da da da)) meter maid--
        LOVELYRITA--32

RIVAL
    To shoot off the legs of his rival.--ROCKYRACCO--12
    His rival it seems had broken his dreams--
        ROCKYRACCO--13

RIVER
    Picture yourself in a boat on a river--LUCYINTHES
        --1

ROAD
    The other day I saw you as I walked along the
        road --WHATGOESON--6
    Another road where maybe I--GOTTOGETYO--3
    Another road where maybe I--GOTTOGETYO--27
    WHY DON'T WE DO IT IN THE ROAD?--WHYDONTWED--Title
    Why don't we do - do it in the road?--WHYDONTWED
        --1
    Why don't we do it in the road? (ah-ha)--WHYDONTWED
        --2
    Why don't we do it in the road? - mmm--WHYDONTWED
        --3
    Why don't we do it in the road?--WHYDONTWED--4
    Why don't we do it in the road?--WHYDONTWED--6
    Why don't we do it in the road?--WHYDONTWED--7
    Why don't we do it in the road?--WHYDONTWED--8
    Why don't we do it in the road?--WHYDONTWED--9
    Why don't we do it in the road?--WHYDONTWED--10
    Why don't we do it in the road?--WHYDONTWED--12
    Well, why don't we do it in the road?--WHYDONTWED
        --13
    Why don't we do it in the road?--WHYDONTWED--14
    Why don't we do - do it, do it in the road?--
        WHYDONTWED--15
    Why don't we do it, yeah, in the road?--WHYDONTWED
        --16
    Why don't you do it in the road?--WHYDONTWED--18
    Sleeps in a hole in the road--MEANMRMUST--4
    Oh I do a road hog--IDIGAPONY--9
    THE LONG AND WINDING ROAD.--LONGANDWIN--Title
    The long and winding road that leads to your door
        --LONGANDWIN--1
    Will never disappear, I've seen that road before.
        --LONGANDWIN--2
    And still they lead me back to the long, winding
        road.--LONGANDWIN--9
    But still they lead me back to the long, winding
        road --LONGANDWIN--12
    Longer than the road that stretches out ahead.--
        TWOOFUS--18
    Longer than the road that stretches out ahead.--
        TWOOFUS--27

ROAM
    Heading for home you start to roam then you're in
        town.--GOODMORNIN--8

ROB
    She could steal but she could not rob.--SHECAMEINT
        --19

ROBERT
    DR. ROBERT.--DRROBERT--Title
    Ring my friend I said you'd call, Dr. Robert --
        DRROBERT--1
    Day or night he'll be there anytime at all, Dr.
        Robert --DRROBERT--2
    Dr. Robert, you're a new and better man --DRROBERT
        --3
    He does everything he can, Dr. Robert.- DRROBERT--5
    If you're down he'll pick you up, Dr. Robert --
        DRROBERT--6
    Take a drink from his special cup, Dr. Robert.--
        DRROBERT--7
    Dr. Robert, he's a man you must believe --DRROBERT
        --8
    No-one can succeed like Dr. Robert.--DRROBERT--10
    Well, well, well, he'll make you, Dr. Robert.--
        DRROBERT--12
    My friend works for the National Health, Dr.
        Robert --DRROBERT--13
    Don't pay money just to see yourself with Dr.
        Robert.--DRROBERT--14
    Dr. Robert, you're a new and better man --DRROBERT
        --15
    He does everything he can, Dr. Robert.-- DRROBERT--17
    Well, well, well, he'll make you, Dr. Robert.--
        DRROBERT--19
    Ring my friend I said you'd call, Dr. Robert --
        DRROBERT--20
    Ring my friend I said you'd call, Dr. Robert --
        DRROBERT--21
    Dr. Robert!--DRROBERT--22

ROCK
    Even hate my rock 'n' roll.--YERBLUES--27

ROCKING-HORSE
    Where rocking-horse people eat marshmallow pies.--
        LUCYINTHES--13

ROCKY
    ROCKY RACCOON.--ROCKYRACCO--Title
    There lived a young boy name of Rocky Raccoon--
        ROCKYRACCO--2
    Hit young Rocky in the eye.--ROCKYRACCO--4
    Rocky didn't like that --ROCKYRACCO--5
    Rocky Raccoon checked into his room - ROCKYRACCO--9
    Rocky had come equipped with a gun--ROCKYRACCO--11
    A - Rocky burst in and grinning a grin--ROCKYRACCO
        --19
    And Rocky collapsed in the corner - ah.--ROCKYRACCO
        --22
    He said, Rocky you met your match--ROCKYRACCO--33
    And Rocky said, Doc it's only a scratch--ROCKYRACCO
        --34
    A - now Rocky Raccoon, he fell back in his room--
        ROCKYRACCO--36
    Gideon checked out and he left it no doubt ((oh
        - Rocky - oh))--ROCKYRACCO--38
    Do do do do - come on Rocky - boy --ROCKYRACCO--45
    Do do do do do - come on Rocky - boy--ROCKYRACCO--46
    The story of Rocky, that's the song.--ROCKYRACCO--48

ROCKY'S
    To help with good Rocky's revival - ah.--
        ROCKYRACCO--39

RODE
    Well you can syndicate any boat you rode/rowed--
        IDIGAPONY--30
    Yeah you can syndicate any boat you rode/rowed--
        IDIGAPONY--31

ROLL
    Roll up, roll up for the Mystery Tour--MAGICALMYS--1
    Roll up, roll up for the Mystery Tour--MAGICALMYS--1
    Roll up, roll up for the Mystery Tour --MAGICALMYS

--3
Roll up, roll up for the Mystery Tour --MAGICALMYS
  --3
Roll up, roll up for the Mystery Tour.--MAGICALMYS
  --4
Roll up, roll up for the Mystery Tour.--MAGICALMYS
  --4
Roll up (and that's an invitation)--MAGICALMYS--5
Roll up for the Mystery Tour --MAGICALMYS--6
Roll up (to make a reservation)--MAGICALMYS--7
Roll up for the Mystery Tour.--MAGICALMYS--8
Roll up, roll up for the Mystery Tour --MAGICALMYS
  --11
Roll up, roll up for the Mystery Tour.--MAGICALMYS
  --11
Roll up, roll up for the Mystery Tour.--MAGICALMYS
  --12
Roll up, roll up for the Mystery Tour.--MAGICALMYS
  --12
Roll up (we've got everything you need)--MAGICALMYS
  --13
Roll up for the Mystery Tour --MAGICALMYS--14
Roll up (satisfaction guaranteed)--MAGICALMYS--15
Roll up for the Mystery Tour.--MAGICALMYS--16
Roll up, roll up for the Mystery Tour--MAGICALMYS
  --22
Roll up, roll up for the Mystery Tour--MAGICALMYS
  --22
Roll up (and that's an invitation)--MAGICALMYS--23
Roll up for the Mystery Tour--MAGICALMYS--24
Roll up (to make a reservation)--MAGICALMYS--25
Roll up for the Mystery Tour.--MAGICALMYS--26
Even hate my rock 'n' roll.--YERBLUES--27
Oh now I roll a stony--IDIGAPONY--19
Oh now I roll a lorry--IDIGAPONY--29

ROLLER
    He one holy roller--COMETOGETH--8

ROLLER-COASTER
    He roller-coaster--COMETOGETH--36

ROLLING
    Like a rolling stone--DIGIT--1
    Like a rolling stone--DIGIT--2
    A - like a rolling stone--DIGIT--3

ROOM
    Well my heart went boom when I crossed that room
      --ISAWHERSTA--11
    Well my heart went boom when I crossed that room
      --ISAWHERSTA--18
    She showed me her room--NORWEGIANW--4
    I'm painting a room in a colourful way--FIXINGAHOL
      --11
    Booked himself a room in the local saloon.--
      ROCKYRACCO--8
    Rocky Raccoon checked into his room --ROCKYRACCO
      --9
    Were in the next room at the hoe-down --ROCKYRACCO
      --18
    A - now Rocky Raccoon, he fell back in his room--
      ROCKYRACCO--36

ROPE
    Bom-pa bom, skip the rope --ALLTOGETHE--11
    Bom-pa bom, skip the rope --ALLTOGETHE--31

ROSE
    Rose and Valerie screaming from the gallery say
      he must go free --MAXWELLSIL--19

ROSETTA
    Rosetta.--GETBACK/LP--1
    Yeah ((Rosetta)).--GETBACK/LP--4

ROUND
    And things you do go round my head--THERESAPLA--6
    I'm gonna break their hearts all round the world
      --ILLCRYINST--16
    'cos I'm gonna break their hearts all round the
      world --ILLCRYINST--25
    And I do appreciate you being round--HELP--16
    And I do appreciate you being round--HELP--26
    And I do appreciate you being round--HELP--36
    Gather round all you clowns--YOUVEGOTTO--17

I can change it round, ((writer))--PAPERBACKW--18
I'll be round, I'll be round.--ANDYOURBIR--9
I'll be round, I'll be round.--ANDYOURBIR--9
I'll be round, I'll be round.--ANDYOURBIR--12
I'll be round, I'll be round.--ANDYOURBIR--12
There's people standing round--LOVEYOUTWO--13
You're holding me down (aah) turning me round
    (aah)--GETTINGBET--5
People running round it's five o'clock--GOODMORNIN--18
And the eyes in his head see the world spinning
    round.--FOOLONTHEH--7
And the eyes in his head see the world spinning
    round.--FOOLONTHEH--14
And the eyes in his head see the world spinning
    round.--FOOLONTHEH--19
Round 'n' round 'n' round 'n' round 'n' round.--
    FOOLONTHEH--21
Round 'n' round 'n' round 'n' round 'n' round.--
    FOOLONTHEH--21
Round 'n' round 'n' round 'n' round 'n' round.--
    FOOLONTHEH--21
Round 'n' round 'n' round 'n' round 'n' round.--
    FOOLONTHEH--21
Round 'n' round 'n' round 'n' round 'n' round.--
    FOOLONTHEH--21
And the eyes in his head see the world spinning
    round.--FOOLONTHEH--26
Oh, round 'n' round 'n' round 'n' round.--
    FOOLONTHEH--27
Oh, round 'n' round 'n' round 'n' round.--
    FOOLONTHEH--27
Oh, round 'n' round 'n' round 'n' round.--
    FOOLONTHEH--27
Oh, round 'n' round 'n' round 'n' round.--
    FOOLONTHEH--27
Oh - show me round the snow-peaked mountains way
    down south --BACKINTHEU--31
At twelve o'clock a meeting round the table --
    CRYBABYCRY--28
Blue mist round my soul --YERBLUES--25
Because the world is round it turns me on--BECAUSE--2
Because the world is round.--BECAUSE--3
All these years I've been wandering round the
    world --IVEGOTAFEE--11
You're only fooling round, only fooling round
    with me.--ONEAFTERNI--7
You're only fooling round, only fooling round
    with me.--ONEAFTERNI--7

ROUNDABOUT
    Behind the shelter in the middle of the roundabout
      --PENNYLANE--20

ROW
    Mr. City policeman sitting pretty little
      policemen in a row--IAMTHEWALR--9

ROWED
    Well you can syndicate any boat you rode/rowed--
      IDIGAPONY--32
    Yeah you can syndicate any boat you rode/rowed--
      IDIGAPONY--33

RUG
    I sat on a rug--NORWEGIANW--11

RUIN
    Everything is closed it's like a ruin--GOODMORNIN

RUINS
    The ruins of the life that you had in mind --
      THINKFORYO--11

RULES
    Filling me up with your rules.--GETTINGBET--6
    Sexy Sadie you broke the rules--SEXYSADIE--5
    Sexy Sadie - oh you broke the rules--SEXYSADIE--8

RUN
    Don't you run and hide, just come on, come on --
      LITTLECHIL--17
    Oh please, don't run and hide --IFIFELL--11
    Run the risk of knowing that our love may soon be
      gone.--WECANWORKI--4
    RUN FOR YOUR LIFE.--RUNFORYOUR--Title
    You better run for your life if you can, little

girl --RUNFORYOUR--5
You better run for your life if you can, little
     girl --RUNFORYOUR--13
You better run for your life if you can, little
     girl --RUNFORYOUR--21
You better run for your life if you can, little
     girl --RUNFORYOUR--29
If the rain comes they run and hide their heads--
     RAIN--1
You didn't run, you didn't lie--GOTTOGETYO--8
Silly people run around they worry me--FIXINGAHOL
     --17
See how they run like pigs from a gun, see how
     they fly--IAMTHEWALR--2
See how they fly like Lucy in the sky, see how
     they run--IAMTHEWALR--10
See how they run.--LADYMADONN--8
See how they run.--LADYMADONN--11
See how they run.--LADYMADONN--17
Pick up my bag, run to the station --ONEAFTERNI--11
Pick up my bag, run right home --ONEAFTERNI--13
Pick up my bag, run to the station --ONEAFTERNI--21
Well - pick up my bag, run right home (run
     right home) --ONEAFTERNI--23
Well - pick up my bag, run right home (run
     right home) --ONEAFTERNI--23

RUNNING
And you'll come running home --ALLIVEGOTT--4
And you'll come running home --ALLIVEGOTT--20
You ((you)) got me running--WHATYOURED--5
Running everywhere at such a speed --IMONLYSLEE--9
There, running my hands through her hair--
     HERETHEREA--5
People running round it's five o'clock--GOODMORNIN
     --18
With a couple of kids running in the yard of
     Desmond and Molly Jones.--OBLADIOBLA--18
With a couple of kids running in the yard of
     Desmond and Molly Jones.--OBLADIOBLA--30

RUSHES
And then the fireman rushes in--PENNYLANE--26

SACK
Fifty acorns tied in a sack.--BALLADOFJO--38
Any jobber got the sack --YOUNEVERGI--10

SACRIFICED
Is leaving (sacrificed most of our lives)--
     SHESLEAVIN--9

SAD
If you're feeling sorry and sad --ANYTIMEATA--7
Don't you be sad, just call me tonight.--ANYTIMEATA
     --9
If I cry it's not because I'm sad --ASKMEWHY--10
I'm so sad and lonely --LITTLECHIL--3
I'm so sad and lonely --LITTLECHIL--7
I'm so sad and lonely --LITTLECHIL--14
I'm so sad and lonely --LITTLECHIL--21
There'll be no sad tomorrow--THERESAPLA--11
And I would be sad --IFIFELL--15
And I would be sad --IFIFELL--22
I'd try to make you sad somehow --ILLCRYINST--9
Though tonight she's made me sad --IDONTWANTT--9
Though tonight she's made me sad --IDONTWANTT--18
I think I'm gonna be sad--TICKETTORI--2
I think I'm gonna be sad--TICKETTORI--23
I know what it is to be sad--SHESAIDSHE--2
I know what it is to be sad (I know what it is
     to be sad).--SHESAIDSHE--21
I know what it is to be sad (I know what it is
     to be sad).--SHESAIDSHE--21
And though the news was rather sad--DAYINTHELI--3
(Are you sad because you're on your own?)--
     WITHALITTL--11
Take a sad song and make it better --HEYJUDE--2
Take a sad song and make it better --HEYJUDE--27
(Take a sad song and make it better)--HEYJUDE--48

SADIE
SEXY SADIE.--SEXYSADIE--Title
Sexy Sadie what have you done?--SEXYSADIE--1
Sexie Sadie - oh what have you done?--SEXYSADIE--4
Sexy Sadie you broke the rules--SEXYSADIE--5
Sexy Sadie - oh you broke the rules--SEXYSADIE--8
One sunny day the world was waiting for the lover

((sexy Sadie))--SEXYSADIE--9
Sexy Sadie (sexy Sadie) the greatest of them
     all ((she's the greatest))--SEXYSADIE--11
Sexy Sadie (sexy Sadie) the greatest of them
     all ((she's the greatest))--SEXYSADIE--11
Sexy Sadie how did you know--SEXYSADIE--12
Sexy Sadie - oh how did you know?--SEXYSADIE--15
Sexy Sadie you'll get yours yet--SEXYSADIE--16
Sexy Sadie - oh you'll get yours yet--SEXYSADIE--19
We gave her everything we owned just to sit at
     her table ((sexy Sadie))--SEXYSADIE--20
Sexy Sadie ((sexy Sadie))--SEXYSADIE--22
Sexy Sadie ((sexy Sadie))--SEXYSADIE--22
(Sexy Sadie she's the latest and the greatest
     of them all)--SEXYSADIE--24
(Sexy Sadie)--SEXYSADIE--27

SAFE
Knowing they're happy and they're safe (happy
     and they're safe).--OCTOPUSSGA--20
Knowing they're happy and they're safe (happy
     and they're safe).--OCTOPUSSGA--20

SAID
Last night I said these words to my girl --
     PLEASEPLEA--1
Last night I said these words to my girl --
     PLEASEPLEA--19
She said she loves you--SHELOVESYO--8
She said you hurt her so--SHELOVESYO--12
She said she loves you--SHELOVESYO--16
The things you said--THERESAPLA--7
If it's something that I said or done --TELLMEWHY
     --13
THINGS WE SAID TODAY.--THINGSWESA--Title
Then I will remember things we said today.--
     THINGSWESA--5
Then we will remember things we said today.--
     THINGSWESA--10
Then we will remember things we said today.--
     THINGSWESA--21
Then we will remember things we said today.--
     THINGSWESA--32
She's happy as can be, you know, she said so --
     IFEELFINE--2
She tells me all the time, you know, she said so
     --IFEELFINE--5
He buys her diamond rings, you know, she said so
     --IFEELFINE--10
Baby said she's mine, you know --IFEELFINE--12
She tells me all the time, you know, she said so
     --IFEELFINE--13
He buys her diamond rings, you know, she said so
     --IFEELFINE--18
They said it wasn't you--NOREPLY--4
They said you were not home--NOREPLY--10
They said you were not home--NOREPLY--23
She said that living with me--TICKETTORI--9
She said that living with me--TICKETTORI--36
Remember what I said tonight--YESITIS--2
This is what I said tonight--YESITIS--15
This is what I said tonight--YESITIS--24
Said you had a thing or two to tell me--INEEDYOU
     --6
We said our goodbyes (aah the night before)--
     NIGHTBEFOR--1
We said our goodbyes (aah the night before)--
     NIGHTBEFOR--1
I said something wrong--YESTERDAY--11
I said something wrong--YESTERDAY--19
She said baby can't you see?--DRIVEMYCAR--2
'n' she said baby it's understood --DRIVEMYCAR--10
And she said listen babe I've got something to
     say --DRIVEMYCAR--23
Did she understand it when they said --GIRL--23
And then she said--NORWEGIANW--15
I mean everything I've said.--RUNFORYOUR--18
Everywhere I go I hear it said --THEWORD--15
Ring my friend I said you'd call, Dr. Robert --
     DRROBERT--1
Ring my friend I said you'd call, Dr. Robert --
     DRROBERT--20
Ring my friend I said you'd call, Dr. Robert --
     DRROBERT--21
She said will fill your head --FORNOONE--22
SHE SAID, SHE SAID.--SHESAIDSHE--Title
SHE SAID, SHE SAID.--SHESAIDSHE--Title
She said I know what it's like to be dead --
     SHESAIDSHE--1
I said who put all those things in your head?--
     SHESAIDSHE--4
She said you don't understand what I said.--

SAID

SHESAIDSHE--7
She said you don't understand what I said.--
  SHESAIDSHE--7
I said no, no, no you're wrong.--SHESAIDSHE--8
I said even though you know what you know --
  SHESAIDSHE--10
She said you don't understand what I said.--
  SHESAIDSHE--13
She said you don't understand what I said.--
  SHESAIDSHE--13
I said no, no, no you're wrong.--SHESAIDSHE--14
I said even though you know what you know --
  SHESAIDSHE--16
She said (she said)--SHESAIDSHE--19
She said (she said)--SHESAIDSHE--19
We'll be over soon they said --BLUEJAYWAY--3
You said that you would be late --DONTPASSME--27
I said that's alright I'm waiting here --DONTPASSME
  --29
He said, I'm gonna get that boy --ROCKYRACCO--6
He said, Danny - Boy this is a showdown.--
  ROCKYRACCO--20
He said, Rocky you met your match--ROCKYRACCO--33
And Rocky said, Doc it's only a scratch--ROCKYRACCO
  --34
The man in the mack said you've got to go back --
  BALLADOFJO--3
The news-people said, say what're you doing in
  bed?--BALLADOFJO--19
I said we're only trying to get us some peace.--
  BALLADOFJO--20
Last night the wife said, oh boy, when you're
  dead --BALLADOFJO--27
The newspapers said, she's gone to his head --
  BALLADOFJO--31
The men from the press said, we wish you success
  --BALLADOFJO--39
PC Thirty-One said, we caught a dirty one,
  Maxwell stands alone --MAXWELLSIL--17
She said she'd always been a dancer --SHECAMEINT
  --12
My baby said she's travelling on the one after
  nine-0-nine --ONEAFTERNI--1
I said, move over honey, I'm travelling on
  that line --ONEAFTERNI--2
I said, move over once, move over twice --
  ONEAFTERNI--3
Said you're travelling on the one after
  nine-0-nine.--ONEAFTERNI--5
I said move over once, move over twice --ONEAFTERNI
  --8
Said you're travelling on the one after
  nine-0-nine.--ONEAFTERNI--10
Railman said, you got the wrong location --
  ONEAFTERNI--12
Well, she said she's travelling on the one after
  nine-0-nine --ONEAFTERNI--15
I said a-move over honey, I'm travelling on
  that line --ONEAFTERNI--16
Said move over once, move over twice --ONEAFTERNI
  --17
Said she's travelling on the one after
  nine-0-nine. (yeah)--ONEAFTERNI--19
Railman said, you got the wrong location --
  ONEAFTERNI--22
She said she's travelling on the one after
  nine-0-nine --ONEAFTERNI--25
Said a - move over honey, I'm travelling on
  that line --ONEAFTERNI--26
I said move over once, move over twice --ONEAFTERNI
  --27
Said we're travelling on the one after nine-0 --
  ONEAFTERNI--29
She said we're travelling on the one after nine-0
  --ONEAFTERNI--30
Said we're travelling on the one after nine-0-nine
  --ONEAFTERNI--31

SAIL

Sail across the Atlantic--HONEYPIE--17
Bom bom bom bom-pa bom, sail the ship --ALLTOGETHE
  --9
Bom bom bom bom-pa bom, ((Oh! boy)), sail the ship--
  ALLTOGETHE--29
Sail me on a silver sun --ITSALLTOOM--21

SAILED

Lived a man who sailed to sea--YELLOWSUBM--2
So we sailed on to the sun--YELLOWSUBM--5

SAILING

Kindly send her sailing back to me--HONEYPIE--27

SAKE

Try thinking more if just for your own sake.--
  THINKFORYO--20

SALOON

Booked himself a room in the local saloon.--
  ROCKYRACCO--8

SAME

And the same goes for me --ALLIVEGOTT--11
And the same goes for me --ALLIVEGOTT--22
It's not the same--DONTBOTHER--3
I know I'll never be the same--DONTBOTHER--15
I know I'll never be the same--DONTBOTHER--30
You're giving me the same old line --NOTASECOND--7
You're giving me the same old line --NOTASECOND--18
Would always feel the same--THISBOY--12
Oh, I can't sleep at night, but just the same --
  ICALLYOURN--9
Oh, I can't sleep at night, but just the same --
  ICALLYOURN--16
Same old thing happen every day.--IMDOWN--9
I'm looking through you, you're not the same.--
  IMLOOKINGT--4
I'm looking through you, you're not the same.--
  IMLOOKINGT--8
You're thinking of me the same old way --IMLOOKINGT
  --11
I'm looking through you, you're not the same.--
  IMLOOKINGT--20
I used to think of no-one else but you were just
  the same --WHATGOESON--22
Everything's the same (when the rain comes down)--
  RAIN--10
Nothing has changed it's still the same--GOODMORNIN
  --15
I will always feel the same.--IWILL--8
It won't be the same now I'm telling you.--
  OLDBROWNSH--8
It won't be the same now that I'm with you.--
  OLDBROWNSH--16
Won't be the same now that I'm with you.--
  OLDBROWNSH--34
It won't be the same now that I'm with you
  (yeah, yeah, yeah)--OLDBROWNSH--36

SAND

Hide your head in the sand, little girl.--
  RUNFORYOUR--6
Hide your head in the sand, little girl.--
  RUNFORYOUR--14
Hide your head in the sand, little girl.--
  RUNFORYOUR--22
Hide your head in the sand, little girl.--
  RUNFORYOUR--30
Me hiding me head in the sand--GETTINGBET--12
Julia sleeping sand silent cloud touch me --JULIA
  --13

SANG

What would you think if I sang outta tune --
  WITHALITTL--1

SAT

I sat on a rug--NORWEGIANW--11

SATISFACTION

Roll up (satisfaction guaranteed)--MAGICALMYS--15

SATISFIED

And keep you satisfied - ooo!--FROMMETOYO--14
And keep you satisfied - ooo!--FROMMETOYO--25
And I'll be satisfied --CANTBUYMEL--18
And I'll be satisfied --CANTBUYMEL--28

SATURDAY

Performs his feat on Saturday at Bishopsgate.--
  BEINGFORTH--9

SAUCE

... Cranberry sauce...--STRAWBERRY--38

SAVE

Nothing to do to save his life call his wife in--
GOODMORNIN--2
We shall scrimp and save ((we shall scrimp and
save)) --WHENIMSIXT--25
We shall scrimp and save ((we shall scrimp and
save)) --WHENIMSIXT--25
We could save the world--WITHINYOUW--14
No-one can save that can't be saved ((love))--
ALLYOUN/YS--9
Trying to save paper.--MEANMRMUST--3

SAVED

No-one was saved.--ELEANORRIG--26
No-one you can save that can't be saved ((love))--
ALLYOUN/YS--9

SAVING

Saving up your money for a rainy day --BALLADOFJO
--25
Saving up to buy some clothes--MEANMRMUST--5

SAVOY

SAVOY TRUFFLE.--SAVOYTRUFF--Title
After the Savoy truffle.--SAVOYTRUFF--5
After the Savoy truffle.--SAVOYTRUFF--10
After the Savoy truffle.--SAVOYTRUFF--18
After the Savoy truffle.--SAVOYTRUFF--27
After the Savoy truffle.--SAVOYTRUFF--29

SAW

I SAW HER STANDING THERE.--ISAWHERSTA--Title
Ooh when I saw her standing there.--ISAWHERSTA--6
Whoa when I saw her standing there.--ISAWHERSTA--10
Whoa since/when I saw her standing there. (hey! aah!)--
ISAWHERSTA--17
Oh since I saw her standing there.--ISAWHERSTA--24
Whoa since I saw her standing there--ISAWHERSTA--25
Yeah, well since I saw her standing there.--
ISAWHERSTA--26
Well I saw her yesterday--SHELOVESYO--5
And if you saw my love --ANDILOVEHE--3
But I saw you peep through your window--NOREPLY--5
I saw the light, I saw the light.--NOREPLY--6
I saw the light, I saw the light.--NOREPLY--6
I know that you saw me--NOREPLY--7
I saw you walk in your door--NOREPLY--13
I saw you walk in your door--NOREPLY--26
The other day I saw you as I walked along the
road --WHATGOESON--6
But when I saw him with you I could feel my
future fold.--WHATGOESON--7
I saw the photograph--DAYINTHELI--5
I saw a film today, oh boy--DAYINTHELI--11
For if I ever saw you --IWILL--5
I've loved you from the moment I saw you --
FORYOUBLUE--13
Everybody saw the sun shine --IVEGOTAFEE--22
Everybody saw the sun shine.--IVEGOTAFEE--31

SAXON

He's the all-American bullet-headed Saxon
mother's son.--CONTINUING--9

SAY

Ask me why, I'll say I love you --ASKMEWHY--14
Ask me why, I'll say I love you --ASKMEWHY--22
Ask me why, I say I'll love you --ASKMEWHY--26
Why do I always have to say love --PLEASEPLEA--8
Say the words you long to hear --DOYOUWANTT--7
Say the words you long to hear --DOYOUWANTT--13
Say the words you long to hear --DOYOUWANTT--21
When I think about you, I can say--ILLGETYOU--11
And she told me what to say.--SHELOVESYO--7
When I say that something--IWANTTOHOL--3
Oh please say to me--IWANTTOHOL--7
And please say to me--IWANTTOHOL--9
When I say that something--IWANTTOHOL--22
If you say you love me too --CANTBUYMEL--10
Say you don't need no diamond rings --CANTBUYMEL
--17
Say you don't need no diamond rings --CANTBUYMEL
--27
I got something to say--YOUCANTDOT--1
And it's worth it just to hear you say --HARDDAYSNI
--10
You're gonna say you love me too, oh.--ISHOULDHAV

--8
You're gonna say you love me too.--ISHOULDHAV--10
You're gonna say you love me too, oh.--ISHOULDHAV
--18
You're gonna say you love me too.--ISHOULDHAV--20
You say you will love me if I have to go --
THINGSWESA--1
You say you'll be mine girl, till the end of time
--THINGSWESA--6
Deep in love, not a lot to say --THINGSWESA--9
Love to hear you say that love is love--THINGSWESA
--12
Deep in love, not a lot to say --THINGSWESA--20
Love to hear you say that love is love--THINGSWESA
--23
Deep in love, not a lot to say --THINGSWESA--31
I got a whole lot of things I gotta say to her.--
WHENIGETHO--6
She is happy just to hear me say that--SHESAWOMAN
--10
One thing I can say girl --EIGHTDAYSA--11
One thing I can say girl --EIGHTDAYSA--31
You're making me say that I've got nobody but you
--ANOTHERGIR--2
I don't wanna say that I've been unhappy with you
--ANOTHERGIR--12
I don't wanna say that I've been unhappy with you
--ANOTHERGIR--18
She wouldn't say--YESTERDAY--10
She wouldn't say--YESTERDAY--18
And I hear them say.--YOUVEGOTTO--8
How could she say to me--YOUVEGOTTO--15
Let me hear you say.--YOUVEGOTTO--18
We can work it out and get it straight or say
good night.--WECANWORKI--9
And she said listen babe I've got something to
say --DRIVEMYCAR--23
When you say she's looking good --GIRL--15
That's all I want to say--MICHELLE--6
I will say the only words I know that you'll
understand.--MICHELLE--8
And I will say the only words I know that
you'll understand --MICHELLE--22
Or should I say--NORWEGIANW--2
To say about the things that you do.--THINKFORYO
--2
Say the word and you'll be free --THEWORD--1
Say the word and be like me --THEWORD--2
Say the word I'm thinking of --THEWORD--3
Say the word and you'll be free --THEWORD--17
Say the word and be like me --THEWORD--18
Say the word I'm thinking of --THEWORD--19
Give the word a chance to say --THEWORD--25
Say the word love --THEWORD--31
Say the word love --THEWORD--32
Say the word love --THEWORD--33
Say the word love --THEWORD--34
I won't want to stay, I don't have much to say --
YOUWONTSEE--9
You say you've seen seven wonders --ANDYOURBIR--4
Say we'll be together every day.--GOTTOGETYO--14
My head is filled with things to say --IWANTTOTEL
--2
Stop and say hello.--PENNYLANE--4
Nothing to say but what a day how's your boy been?
--GOODMORNIN--3
I've got nothing to say but it's OK.--GOODMORNIN
--5
I've got nothing to say but it's OK.--GOODMORNIN
--16
I've got nothing to say but it's OK.--GOODMORNIN
--25
Leaving the note that she hoped would say more.--
SHESLEAVIN--3
And if you say the word--WHENIMSIXT--11
Indicate precisely what you mean to say--WHENIMSIXT
--30
Nothing you can say but you can learn how to play
the game ((love))--ALLYOUN/YS--6
You say yes, I say no --HELLOGOODB--1
You say yes, I say no --HELLOGOODB--1
You say stop and I say go, go, go.--HELLOGOODB--2
You say stop and I say go, go, go.--HELLOGOODB--2
You say goodbye and I say hello - hello, hello.--
HELLOGOODB--4
You say goodbye and I say hello - hello, hello.--
HELLOGOODB--4
I don't know why you say goodbye, I say hello -
hello, hello.--HELLOGOODB--5
I don't know why you say goodbye, I say hello -
hello, hello.--HELLOGOODB--5
I don't know why you say goodbye, I say hello.--
HELLOGOODB--6
I don't know why you say goodbye, I say hello.--

HELLOGOODB--6
I say hi!/high, you say 'lo/low--HELLOGOODB--7
You say why and I say I don't know.--HELLOGOODB--8
You say why and I say I don't know.--HELLOGOODB--8
You say goodbye and I say hello - hello, hello.--
   HELLOGOODB--10
You say goodbye and I say hello - hello, hello.--
   HELLOGOODB--10
I don't know why you say goodbye, I say hello -
   hello, hello--HELLOGOODB--12
I don't know why you say goodbye, I say hello -
   hello, hello--HELLOGOODB--12
I don't know why you say goodbye, I say hello--
   HELLOGOODB--14
I don't know why you say goodbye, I say hello--
   HELLOGOODB--14
Why,why, why, why, why, why do you say --HELLOGOODB
   --16
You say goodbye and I say hello - hello, hello.--
   HELLOGOODB--19
You say goodbye and I say hello - hello, hello.--
   HELLOGOODB--19
I don't know why you say goodbye, I say hello -
   hello, hello --HELLOGOODB--20
I don't know why you say goodbye, I say hello -
   hello, hello --HELLOGOODB--20
I don't know why you say goodbye, I say hello.--
   HELLOGOODB--21
I don't know why you say goodbye, I say hello.--
   HELLOGOODB--21
You say yes, I say no--HELLOGOODB--22
You say yes, I say no--HELLOGOODB--22
((I say yes but I may mean no)) --HELLOGOODB--23
You say stop but I say go, go, go--HELLOGOODB--24
You say stop but I say go, go, go--HELLOGOODB--24
You say goodbye and I say hello - hello, hello.--
   HELLOGOODB--27
You say goodbye and I say hello - hello, hello.--
   HELLOGOODB--27
I don't know why you say goodbye, I say hello -
   hello, hello --HELLOGOODB--28
I don't know why you say goodbye, I say hello -
   hello, hello --HELLOGOODB--28
I don't know why you say goodbye, I say hello -
   hello, hello --HELLOGOODB--29
I don't know why you say goodbye, I say hello -
   hello, hello --HELLOGOODB--29
I don't know why you say goodbye, I say hello -
   hello.--HELLOGOODB--30
I don't know why you say goodbye, I say hello -
   hello.--HELLOGOODB--30
You say you wanna revolution --REVOLUTION--2
You say you got a real solution --REVOLUTION--12
You say you'll change the constitution --REVOLUTION
   --22
You say it's your birthday --BIRTHDAY--1
They say it's your birthday --BIRTHDAY--3
You say it's your birthday --BIRTHDAY--20
You say it's your birthday --BIRTHDAY--22
Now it's time to say good night --GOODNIGHT--1
This is what I'd say:--HONEYPIE--6
You'd say I'm putting you on --IMSOTIRED--9
You'd say I'm putting you on --IMSOTIRED--18
Half of what I say is meaningless --JULIA--1
But I say it just to reach you, Julia.--JULIA--2
I say two--REVOLUTONE--3
You say you want a revolution --REVOLUTONE--5
You say you got a real solution --REVOLUTONE--19
You say you'll change the constitution --REVOLUTONE
   --35
What do you say?--HEYBULLDOG--24
I say woof--HEYBULLDOG--25
What words I say or time of day it is --ONLYANORTH
   --8
All the girls around her say she's got it coming
   --GETBACK/45--18
Peter Brown called to say, you can make it OK --
   BALLADOFJO--11
The news-people said, say what're you doing in
   bed?--BALLADOFJO--19
Not worrying what they or you say --OLDBROWNSH--19
He say I know you, you know me--COMETOGETH--19
He say one and one and one is three--COMETOGETH
   --40
But she doesn't have a lot to say.--HERMAJESTY--2
'n' I say, it's alright.--HERECOMEST--3
'n' I say, it's alright.--HERECOMEST--8
'n' I say, it's alright.--HERECOMEST--12
'n' I say, it's alright.--HERECOMEST--22
Rose and Valerie screaming from the gallery say
   he must go free --MAXWELLSIL--19
Yes, you could say she was attractively built -
   yeah, yeah, yeah.--POLYTHENEP--9
Well I knew what I could not say.--SHECAMEINT--15

All the girls around her say she's got it coming--
   GETBACK/LP--24
I'd like to say thank you on behalf of the group
   and ourselves--GETBACK/LP--38

SAYING
   Before she gets to saying goodbye--TICKETTORI--20
   Before she gets to saying goodbye--TICKETTORI--33
   Think of what you're saying --WECANWORKI--6
   Think of what I'm saying --WECANWORKI--8
   Everyone's saying it --IMEMINE--19
   Everyone's saying it --IMEMINE--32

SAYS
   But now she says she knows--SHELOVESYO--14
   Baby says she's mine, you know --IFEELFINE--4
   When she says her love is dead --FORNOONE--12
   She says that long ago she knew someone --FORNOONE
      --18
   Desmond says to Molly, girl I like your face--
      OBLADIOBLA--3
   And Molly says this as she takes him by the hand:
      --OBLADIOBLA--4
   Queen says no to pot-smoking FBI member.--
      FORYOUBLUE--1

SCARLET
   Scarlet were the clothes she wore--YESITIS--5

SCENE
   Late of Pablo Fanques Fair - what a scene.--
      BEINGFORTH--4
   Man I was mean but I'm changing my scene--
      GETTINGBET--27
   Wishing to avoid an unpleasant scene --MAXWELLSIL
      --9

SCHOOL
   I used to get mad at my school (now I can't
      complain)--GETTINGBET--3
   Then you decide to take a walk by the old school--
      GOODMORNIN--14
   Back in school again, Maxwell plays the fool
      again, teacher gets annoyed --MAXWELLSIL--8

SCIENCE
   Joan was quizzical, studied pataphysical science
      in the home --MAXWELLSIL--1

SCRATCH
   And Rocky said, Doc it's only a scratch--ROCKYRACCO
      --34

SCREAMING
   Rose and Valerie screaming from the gallery say
      he must go free --MAXWELLSIL--19

SCREEN
   I wanna be famous, a star of the screen --
      DRIVEMYCAR--3
   You became a legend of the silver screen--HONEYPIE
      --13

SCREW
   Who'll screw you in the ground--LOVEYOUTWO--14

SCRIMP
   We shall scrimp and save ((we shall scrimp and
      save)) --WHENIMSIXT--25
   We shall scrimp and save ((we shall scrimp and
      save)) --WHENIMSIXT--25

SEA
   Lived a man who sailed to sea--YELLOWSUBM--2
   Till we found a sea of green--YELLOWSUBM--6
   Sky of blue (sky of blue) and sea of green
      (sea of green)--YELLOWSUBM--27
   Sky of blue (sky of blue) and sea of green
      (sea of green)--YELLOWSUBM--27
   Across the sea--HONEYPIE--26
   I'd like to be under the sea--OCTOPUSSGA--1
   I'd like to be under the sea--OCTOPUSSGA--7

I'd like to be under the sea--OCTOPUSSGA--15
I'd like to be under the sea--OCTOPUSSGA--23

SEABED
Resting our head on the seabed--OCTOPUSSGA--11

SEANCE
For a seance in the dark --CRYBABYCRY--29

SEARCHING
So many tears I was searching --LONGLONGLO--7

SEASHELL
Julia seashell eyes windy smile calls me --JULIA
--5

SEAT
If you try to sit, I'll tax your seat, ((sit))--
TAXMAN--12

SECOND
NOT A SECOND TIME.--NOTASECOND--Title
No, no, no, not a second time.--NOTASECOND--10
No, no, no, not a second time.--NOTASECOND--21
Not a second time--NOTASECOND--22
Not a second time--NOTASECOND--23
No, no, no, not a second time--NOTASECOND--24
Well, it's the second time--YOUCANTDOT--9
Their production will be second to none--BEINGFORTH
--13

SECONDS
Made the bus in seconds flat--DAYINTHELI--24

SECRET
DO YOU WANT TO KNOW A SECRET?--DOYOUWANTT--Title
Listen, do you want to know a secret?--DOYOUWANTT
--3
Listen (dodahdo) do you want to know a secret?
(dodahdo)--DOYOUWANTT--9
I've known a secret for the week or two --
DOYOUWANTT--15
Listen (dodahdo) do you want to know a secret?
(dodahdo)--DOYOUWANTT--17

SEE
Well she looked at me, and I, I could see --
ISAWHERSTA--7
I've lost her now for sure, I won't see her no
more --MISERY--4
Can't she see she'll always be the only one,
only one.--MISERY--7
Send her back to me, 'cos everyone can see--
MISERY--8
Send her back to me, 'cos everyone can see--
MISERY--12
It's plain to see--DONTBOTHER--5
I see no use in wondering why --NOTASECOND--2
I see no reason to change mine --NOTASECOND--5
I see no use in wondering why --NOTASECOND--13
I see no reason to change mine --NOTASECOND--16
Can't you see, can't you see?--ISHOULDHAV--6
Can't you see, can't you see?--ISHOULDHAV--6
Can't you see, can't you see?--ISHOULDHAV--16
Can't you see, can't you see?--ISHOULDHAV--16
So I hope you see --IFIFELL--17
So I hope you see --IFIFELL--24
If I could see you now --ILLCRYINST--8
Let's pretend we just can't see his face.--
IMHAPPYJUS--17
Let's pretend we just can't see his face.--
IMHAPPYJUS--25
'cos I'm a - gonna see my baby today --WHENIGETHO
--5
She hates to see me cry--SHESAWOMAN--9
One day you'll look to see I've gone --ILLFOLLOWT
--1
'cos I looked up to see your face.--NOREPLY--8
TELL ME WHAT YOU SEE.--TELLMEWHAT--Title
Tell me what you see--TELLMEWHAT--6
What you see is me--TELLMEWHAT--8
Tell me what you see--TELLMEWHAT--14
What you see is me--TELLMEWHAT--16
Tell me what you see--TELLMEWHAT--17
Can't you try to see that I'm--TELLMEWHAT--20

Tell me what you see--TELLMEWHAT--23
What you see is me--TELLMEWHAT--25
Tell me what you see--TELLMEWHAT--26
Can't you try to see that I'm--TELLMEWHAT--29
Tell me what you see--TELLMEWHAT--32
What you see is me--TELLMEWHAT--34
You tell lies thinking I can't see --IMDOWN--1
So come on back and see--INEEDYOU--18
So come on back and see--INEEDYOU--28
I get high when I see you go by, my oh my--
ITSONLYLOV--1
And I want all the world to see we've met --
IVEJUSTSEE--5
And I want all the world to see we've met --
IVEJUSTSEE--28
I can see them laugh at me --YOUVEGOTTO--7
Try to see it my way --WECANWORKI--1
While you see it your way--WECANWORKI--3
Try to see it my way --WECANWORKI--15
While you see it your way --WECANWORKI--17
Try to see it my way --WECANWORKI--24
While you see it your way --WECANWORKI--26
She said baby can't you see?--DRIVEMYCAR--2
But you see now I'm too much in love.--IFINEEDEDS
--9
But you see now I'm too much in love.--IFINEEDEDS
--19
I need to make you see--MICHELLE--12
Just sees what he wants to see --NOWHEREMAN--11
Nowhere Man can you see me at all?--NOWHEREMAN--12
Well I'd rather see you dead, little girl --
RUNFORYOUR--1
And I'd rather see you dead.--RUNFORYOUR--20
I'd rather see you dead, little girl --RUNFORYOUR
--25
And though you still can't see --THINKFORYO--12
But now the tide is turning I can see that I
was blind.--WHATGOESON--16
YOU WON'T SEE ME.--YOUWONTSEE--Title
If you won't see me (you won't see me) --YOUWONTSEE
--5
If you won't see me (you won't see me) --YOUWONTSEE
--5
You won't see me (you won't see me).--YOUWONTSEE
--6
You won't see me (you won't see me).--YOUWONTSEE
--6
And you won't see me (you won't see me) --
YOUWONTSEE--11
And you won't see me (you won't see me) --
YOUWONTSEE--11
You won't see me (you won't see me).--YOUWONTSEE
--12
You won't see me (you won't see me).--YOUWONTSEE
--12
If you won't see me (you won't see me) --YOUWONTSEE
--20
If you won't see me (you won't see me) --YOUWONTSEE
--20
You won't see me (you won't see me)--YOUWONTSEE--21
You won't see me (you won't see me)--YOUWONTSEE--21
If you won't see me (you won't see me) --YOUWONTSEE
--29
If you won't see me (you won't see me) --YOUWONTSEE
--29
You won't see me (you won't see me).--YOUWONTSEE
--30
You won't see me (you won't see me).--YOUWONTSEE
--30
But you can't see me, you can't see me.--ANDYOURBIR
--6
But you can't see me, you can't see me.--ANDYOURBIR
--6
Don't pay money just to see yourself with Dr.
Robert.--DRROBERT--14
And in her eyes you see nothing --FORNOONE--7
And in her eyes you see nothing --FORNOONE--14
And in her eyes you see nothing --FORNOONE--24
Could see another kind of mind there.--GOTTOGETYO
--4
Ooo then I suddenly see you--GOTTOGETYO--5
Ooo then I suddenly see you--GOTTOGETYO--20
Could see another kind of mind there.--GOTTOGETYO
--28
Then suddenly I see you--GOTTOGETYO--29
They'll fill you in with all their sins, you'll see.
--LOVEYOUTWO--15
That you may see the meaning of within--TOMORROWNE
--5
We see the banker sitting waiting for a trim--
PENNYLANE--25
Misunderstanding all you see--STRAWBERRY--7
See the people standing there who disagree and
never win--FIXINGAHOL--9

Everyone you see is half asleep--GOODMORNIN--11
Everyone you see is full of life--GOODMORNIN--20
Told her I would really like to see her again.--
    LOVELYRITA--22
(What do you see when you turn out the light?)--
    WITHALITTL--21
And to see you're really only very small--
    WITHINYOUW--18
They can't see--WITHINYOUW--26
When you see we're all one--WITHINYOUW--32
Nothing you can see that isn't shown ((love))--
    ALLYOUN/YS--20
Far as the eye can see.--BABYYOUREA--6
What did you see when you were there?--BABYYOUREA
    --11
See how they run like pigs from a gun, see how
    they fly--IAMTHEWALR--2
See how they run like pigs from a gun, see how
    they fly--IAMTHEWALR--2
See how they fly like Lucy in the sky, see how
    they run--IAMTHEWALR--10
See how they fly like Lucy in the sky, see how
    they run--IAMTHEWALR--10
See how they smile, like pigs in a sty, see how
    they snied--IAMTHEWALR--23
See how they smile, like pigs in a sty, see how
    they snied--IAMTHEWALR--23
They can see that he's just a fool--FOOLONTHEH--4
And the eyes in his head see the world spinning
    round.--FOOLONTHEH--7
And the eyes in his head see the world spinning
    round.--FOOLONTHEH--14
And the eyes in his head see the world spinning
    round.--FOOLONTHEH--19
And the eyes in his head see the world spinning
    round.--FOOLONTHEH--26
See all without looking.--INNERLIGHT--16
See how they run.--LADYMADONN--8
See how they run.--LADYMADONN--11
See how they run.--LADYMADONN--17
We'd all love to see the plan.--REVOLUTION--14
Take these sunken eyes and learn to see.--BLACKBIRD
    --6
Dear Prudence, see the sunny skies.--DEARPRUDEN--7
Dear Prudence, let me see you smile --DEARPRUDEN
    --16
So let me see you smile again.--DEARPRUDEN--19
Dear Prudence, won't you let me see you smile?--
    DEARPRUDEN--20
See the hands a - moving --DONTPASSME--12
I don't see you --DONTPASSME--16
How I hate to see you go --DONTPASSME--21
How I hate to see you go --DONTPASSME--34
How I hate to see you go --DONTPASSME--40
To see how the other half live--GLASSONION--6
Till I get to the bottom and I see you again -
    yeah, yeah, yeah.--HELTERSKEL--3
And I get to the bottom and I see you again -
    yeah, yeah, yeah.--HELTERSKEL--20
Now I can see you, be you --LONGLONGLO--9
Take a good look you're bound to see --MARTHAMYDE
    --8
Hold your hand out you silly girl, see what
    you've done --MARTHAMYDE--10
Sit beside a mountain stream - see her waters rise
    --MOTHERNATU--3
You can see them out for dinner--PIGGIES--17
We'd all love to see the plan.--REVOLUTONE--21
You layed it down for all to see--SEXYSADIE--6
You layed it down for all to see--SEXYSADIE--7
I look at you all, see the love there that's
    sleeping --WHILEMYGUI--2
I look at the floor and I see it needs sweeping --
    WHILEMYGUI--4
I look at you all, see the love there that's
    sleeping--WHILEMYGUI--18
The more there is to see.--ITSALLTOOM--7
It's all too much for me to see --ITSALLTOOM--25
When I see your smile --OLDBROWNSH--11
Got to be good-looking 'cos he's so hard to see--
    COMETOGETH--41
I'd ask my friends to come and see--OCTOPUSSGA--5
Well, you should see Polythene Pam.--POLYTHENEP--1
Well, you should see her in drag --POLYTHENEP--3
Yes, you should see Polythene Pam - yeah,
    yeah, yeah.--POLYTHENEP--5
Didn't anybody see?--SHECAMEINT--9
Didn't anybody see?--SHECAMEINT--21
See no future, pay no rent --YOUNEVERGI--8
There is still a chance that they will see --
    LETITBE/45--13
Well you can indicate everything you see--IDIGAPONY
    --27
Yes you can indicate anything you see.--IDIGAPONY
    --28
There is still a chance that they will see --
    LETITBE/LP--13

SEEING
    Hearing them, seeing them--YOUVEGOTTO--13

SEEM
    All those words they seem to slip away.--IWANTTOTEL
        --4
    But if I seem to act unkind--IWANTTOTEL--9

SEEMED
    All my troubles seemed so far away--YESTERDAY--2

SEEMS
    When I'm home everything seems to be right --
        HARDDAYSNI--15
    When I'm home everything seems to be right --
        HARDDAYSNI--28
    These days such a kind girl seems so hard to find
        --THINGSWESA--7
    My independence ((my independence)) seems to
        vanish in the haze--HELP--21
    Yes it seems so long, girl, since you've been gone
        --YOUWONTSEE--18
    Yes it seems so long, girl, since you've been gone
        --YOUWONTSEE--27
    Everybody seems to think I'm lazy.--IMONLYSLEE--7
    And he never seems to notice.--FOOLONTHEH--12
    And nobody seems to like him--FOOLONTHEH--15
    His rival it seems had broken his dreams--
        ROCKYRACCO--13
    Little darling, it seems like years since it's
        been here.--HERECOMEST--10
    Little darling, it seems like years since it's
        been clear.--HERECOMEST--19

SEEN
    Till he's seen you cry.--THISBOY--10
    But if they'd seen--YOUCANTDOT--20
    But if they'd seen--YOUCANTDOT--39
    But as from today well I've seen somebody that's
        new --ANOTHERGIR--13
    But as from today well I've seen somebody that's
        new --ANOTHERGIR--19
    I'VE JUST SEEN A FACE.--IVEJUSTSEE--Title
    I've just seen a face--IVEJUSTSEE--1
    I've just seen a face--IVEJUSTSEE--24
    You say you've seen seven wonders,--ANDYOURBIR--4
    They'd seen his face before--DAYINTHELI--9
    When you've seen beyond yourself--WITHINYOUW--28
    Man you should have seen them kicking Edgar
        Allan Poe--IAMTHEWALR--27
    Have you seen the little piggies--PIGGIES--1
    Have you seen the bigger piggies--PIGGIES--6
    Will never disappear, I've seen that road before.
        --LONGANDWIN--2

SEES
    Till she sees the mistake she has made?--BABYSINBLA
        --15
    Till she sees the mistake she has made?--BABYSINBLA
        --20
    Just sees what he wants to see --NOWHEREMAN--11
    But the fool on the hill sees the sun going down--
        FOOLONTHEH--6
    But the fool on the hill sees the sun going down--
        FOOLONTHEH--13
    But the fool on the hill sees the sun going down--
        FOOLONTHEH--18
    The fool on the hill sees the sun going down--
        FOOLONTHEH--25

SEINE
    Honeymooning down by the Seine.--BALLADOFJO--10

SELF-ASSURED
    I'm not so self-assured--HELP--12
    I'm not so self-assured--HELP--32

SELLING
    The pretty nurse is selling poppies from a tray--
        PENNYLANE--21

SEMOLINA
  Semolina pilchard climbing up the Eiffel Tower--
      IAMTHEWALR--25

SEND
  As I write this letter, send my love to you --
      PSILOVEYOU--1
  As I write this letter, send my love to you --
      PSILOVEYOU--10
  As I write this letter (oh) send my love to you --
      PSILOVEYOU--16
  Send her back to me, 'cos everyone can see--
      MISERY--8
  Send her back to me, 'cos everyone can see--
      MISERY--12
  Just call on me and I'll send it along--FROMMETOYO
      --5
  Just/So call on me and I'll send it along--FROMMETOYO--9
  Just call on me and I'll send it along--FROMMETOYO
      --17
  Just call on me and I'll send it along--FROMMETOYO
      --20
  Just call on me and I'll send it along--FROMMETOYO
      --28
  And I'll send all my lovin' to you.--ALLMYLOVIN--6
  And I'll send all my lovin' to you.--ALLMYLOVIN--12
  All my lovin', I will send to you --ALLMYLOVIN--13
  And I'll send all my lovin' to you.--ALLMYLOVIN--20
  All my lovin', I will send to you --ALLMYLOVIN--21
  All my lovin', I will send to you --ALLMYLOVIN--24
  If you must return it you can send it here,
      ((paperback))--PAPERBACKW--23
  Send me a postcard, drop me a line--WHENIMSIXT--28
  Kindly send her sailing back to me--HONEYPIE--27
  I only send you my invitations--CARRYTHATW--6

SENDING
  Will you still be sending me a valentine--
      WHENIMSIXT--3
  Two of us sending postcards --TWOOFUS--10

SENT
  Did you think that money was heaven sent?--
      LADYMADONN--4

SERMON
  Let this be a sermon --RUNFORYOUR--17
  Father McKenzie writing the words of a sermon--
      ELEANORRIG--11

SET
  I'm so tired, my mind is set on you --IMSOTIRED--6

SEVEN
  You say you've seen seven wonders,--ANDYOURBIR--4
  ... Four, five, six, seven, eight, nine,
      ten...--DAYINTHELI--35
  (... Four, five, six, seven, eight!)--BIRTHDAY--7
  One, two, three, four, five, six, seven,
      eight.--DONTPASSME--36
  Five, six, seven, eight, nine, ten --ALLTOGETHE--3
  One, two, three, four, five, six, seven --
      YOUNEVERGI--24
  One, two, three, four, five, six, seven --
      YOUNEVERGI--26
  One, two, three, four, five, six, seven --
      YOUNEVERGI--28
  One, two, three, four, five, six, seven --
      YOUNEVERGI--30
  One, two, three, four, five, six, seven --
      YOUNEVERGI--32
  One, two, three, four, five, six, seven --
      YOUNEVERGI--34
  One, two, three, four, five, six, seven --
      YOUNEVERGI--36
  One, two, three, four, five, six, seven --
      YOUNEVERGI--38
  One, two, three, four, five, six, seven --
      YOUNEVERGI--40

SEVENTEEN
  Well, she was just seventeen --ISAWHERSTA--2

SEXIE
  Sexie Sadie - oh what have you done?--SEXYSADIE--4

SEXY
  SEXY SADIE.--SEXYSADIE--Title
  Sexy Sadie what have you done?--SEXYSADIE--1
  Sexy Sadie you broke the rules--SEXYSADIE--5
  Sexy Sadie - oh you broke the rules--SEXYSADIE--8
  One sunny day the world was waiting for the lover
      ((sexy Sadie))--SEXYSADIE--9
  Sexy Sadie (sexy Sadie) the greatest of them
      all ((she's the greatest))--SEXYSADIE--11
  Sexy Sadie (sexy Sadie) the greatest of them
      all ((she's the greatest))--SEXYSADIE--11
  Sexy Sadie how did you know--SEXYSADIE--12
  Sexy Sadie - oh how did you know?--SEXYSADIE--15
  Sexy Sadie you'll get yours yet--SEXYSADIE--16
  Sexy Sadie - oh you'll get yours yet--SEXYSADIE--19
  We gave her everything we owned just to sit at
      her table ((sexy Sadie))--SEXYSADIE--20
  Sexy Sadie ((sexy Sadie))--SEXYSADIE--22
  Sexy Sadie ((sexy Sadie))--SEXYSADIE--22
  (Sexy Sadie she's the latest and the greatest
      of them all)--SEXYSADIE--24
  (Sexy Sadie)--SEXYSADIE--27

SGT
  Full speed ahead it is, Sgt.--YELLOWSUBM--21
  SGT. PEPPER'S LONELY HEARTS CLUB BAND.--SGTPEPPERS
      --Title
  That Sgt. Pepper taught the band to play--
      SGTPEPPERS--2
  Sgt. Pepper's Lonely Hearts Club Band.--SGTPEPPERS
      --7
  We're Sgt. Pepper's Lonely Hearts Club Band--
      SGTPEPPERS--8
  Sgt. Pepper's Lonely Hearts Club Band--SGTPEPPERS
      --10
  Sgt. Pepper's Lonely, Sgt. Pepper's Lonely--
      SGTPEPPERS--12
  Sgt. Pepper's Lonely, Sgt. Pepper's Lonely--
      SGTPEPPERS--12
  Sgt. Pepper's Lonely Hearts Club Band.--SGTPEPPERS
      --13
  And Sgt. Pepper's Lonely Hearts Club Band.--
      SGTPEPPERS--25
  SGT. PEPPER'S LONELY HEARTS CLUB BAND
      (REPRISE).--SGTPEPPREP--Title
  We're Sgt. Pepper's Lonely Hearts Club Band --
      SGTPEPPREP--3
  Sgt. Pepper's Lonely Hearts Club Band --SGTPEPPREP
      --5
  Sgt. Pepper's Lonely --SGTPEPPREP--7
  Sgt. Pepper's Lonely --SGTPEPPREP--8
  Sgt. Pepper's Lonely --SGTPEPPREP--9
  Sgt. Pepper's Lonely.--SGTPEPPREP--10
  Sgt. Pepper's Lonely Hearts Club Band --SGTPEPPREP
      --11
  Sgt. Pepper's one and only Lonely Hearts Club
      Band --SGTPEPPREP--13
  Sgt. Pepper's Lonely --SGTPEPPREP--15
  Sgt. Pepper's Lonely --SGTPEPPREP--16
  Sgt. Pepper's Lonely Hearts Club Band.--SGTPEPPREP
      --17

SHADE
  When the sun shines they slip into the shade
      (when the sun shines down)--RAIN--4
  In an octopus's garden in the shade.--OCTOPUSSGA
      --2
  In his octopus's garden in the shade.--OCTOPUSSGA
      --4
  In an octopus's garden in the shade.--OCTOPUSSGA
      --8
  In an octopus's garden in the shade.--OCTOPUSSGA
      --16

SHADES
  Sounds of laughter, shades of life--ACROSSTHEU
      --20

SHADOW
  There's a shadow hanging over me--YESTERDAY--7

SHADY
  Then we lie beneath a shady tree --GOODDAYSUN--10

SHAKE
  Please don't wake me, no, don't shake me --

IMONLYSLEE--5
Please don't wake me, no, don't shake me --
    IMONLYSLEE--25

SHALL
We shall scrimp and save ((we shall scrimp and
    save)) --WHENIMSIXT--25
We shall scrimp and save ((we shall scrimp and
    save)) --WHENIMSIXT--25

SHARE
Knowing that love is to share--HERETHEREA--11
Knowing that love is to share--HERETHEREA--17
About the love we all could share--WITHINYOUW--9

SHAVES
In Penny Lane the barber shaves another customer--
    PENNYLANE--24
Shaves in the dark--MEANMRMUST--2

SHE
Well, she was just seventeen --ISAWHERSTA--2
And the way she looked was way beyond compare.--
    ISAWHERSTA--4
Well she looked at me, and I, I could see --
    ISAWHERSTA--7
She wouldn't dance with another --ISAWHERSTA--9
Can't she see she'll always be the only one,
    only one.--MISERY--7
SHE LOVES YOU.--SHELOVESYO--Title
She loves you yeah, yeah, yeah--SHELOVESYO--1
She loves you yeah, yeah, yeah--SHELOVESYO--2
She loves you yeah, yeah, yeah, yeah.--SHELOVESYO
    --3
And she told me what to say.--SHELOVESYO--7
She said she loves you--SHELOVESYO--8
She said she loves you--SHELOVESYO--8
Yeah, she loves you--SHELOVESYO--10
She said you hurt her so--SHELOVESYO--12
She almost lost her mind--SHELOVESYO--13
But now she says she knows--SHELOVESYO--14
But now she says she knows--SHELOVESYO--14
She said she loves you--SHELOVESYO--16
She said she loves you--SHELOVESYO--16
Yeah, she loves you--SHELOVESYO--18
She loves you, yeah, yeah, yeah--SHELOVESYO--20
She loves you, yeah, yeah, yeah--SHELOVESYO--21
Because she loves you--SHELOVESYO--28
Yeah, she loves you--SHELOVESYO--30
She loves you, yeah, yeah, yeah--SHELOVESYO--32
She loves you, yeah, yeah, yeah--SHELOVESYO--33
That she would leave me on my own--DONTBOTHER--10
She gives me everything --ANDILOVEHE--6
She brings to me --ANDILOVEHE--9
And that she will cry --IFIFELL--19
When she learns we are two.--IFIFELL--20
And that she will cry --IFIFELL--26
When she learns we are two.--IFIFELL--27
She's happy as can be, you know, she said so --
    IFEELFINE--2
She tells me all the time, you know, she said so
    --IFEELFINE--5
She tells me all the time, you know, she said so
    --IFEELFINE--5
He buys her diamond rings, you know, she said so
    --IFEELFINE--10
She tells me all the time, you know, she said so
    --IFEELFINE--13
She tells me all the time, you know, she said so
    --IFEELFINE--13
He buys her diamond rings, you know, she said so
    --IFEELFINE--18
I know she isn't--SHESAWOMAN--7
She don't give boys the eye--SHESAWOMAN--8
She hates to see me cry--SHESAWOMAN--9
She is happy just to hear me say that--SHESAWOMAN
    --10
She don't give boys the eye--SHESAWOMAN--12
She will never make me jealous--SHESAWOMAN--13
I know she isn't--SHESAWOMAN--24
I know she isn't--SHESAWOMAN--34
She thinks of him and so she dresses in black --
    BABYSINBLA--4
She thinks of him and so she dresses in black --
    BABYSINBLA--4
But she thinks only of him --BABYSINBLA--11
She thinks of him.--BABYSINBLA--13
Till she sees the mistake she has made?--BABYSINBLA
    --15
Till she sees the mistake she has made?--BABYSINBLA

--15
Till she sees the mistake she has made?--BABYSINBLA
    --20
Till she sees the mistake she has made?--BABYSINBLA
    --20
She thinks of him and so she dresses in black --
    BABYSINBLA--24
She thinks of him and so she dresses in black --
    BABYSINBLA--24
Every little thing she does--EVERYLITTL--7
She does for me, yeah--EVERYLITTL--8
And you know the thing she does--EVERYLITTL--9
She does for me, ooo.--EVERYLITTL--10
Just to know that she loves me--EVERYLITTL--12
Yes I know that she loves me now.--EVERYLITTL--13
Every little thing she does--EVERYLITTL--17
She does for me, yeah--EVERYLITTL--18
And you know the thing she does--EVERYLITTL--19
She does for me, ooo.--EVERYLITTL--20
Every little thing she does--EVERYLITTL--21
She does for me, yeah--EVERYLITTL--22
And you know the thing she does--EVERYLITTL--23
She does for me, ooo.--EVERYLITTL--24
If she turns up while I'm gone please let me know.
    --IDONTWANTT--4
If she turns up while I'm gone please let me know.
    --IDONTWANTT--16
She was a girl in a million, my friend --IMALOSER
    --5
I should have known she would win in the end.--
    IMALOSER--6
But she don't care.--TICKETTORI--8
She said that living with me--TICKETTORI--9
She would never be free--TICKETTORI--11
But she don't care.--TICKETTORI--16
She ought to think twice--TICKETTORI--18
She ought to do right by me--TICKETTORI--19
Before she gets to saying goodbye--TICKETTORI--20
She ought to think twice--TICKETTORI--21
She ought to do right by me.--TICKETTORI--22
But she don't care.--TICKETTORI--29
She ought to think twice--TICKETTORI--31
She ought to do right by me--TICKETTORI--32
Before she gets to saying goodbye--TICKETTORI--33
She ought to think twice--TICKETTORI--34
She ought to do right by me.--TICKETTORI--35
She said that living with me--TICKETTORI--36
She would never be free--TICKETTORI--38
But she don't care.--TICKETTORI--43
Scarlet were the clothes she wore--YESITIS--5
Nobody in all the world can do what she can do --
    ANOTHERGIR--7
Through thick and thin she will always be my
    friend.--ANOTHERGIR--11
Through thick and thin she will always be my
    friend.--ANOTHERGIR--17
And she keeps calling me back again.--IVEJUSTSEE
    --13
And she keeps calling me back again.--IVEJUSTSEE
    --20
And she keeps calling me back again.--IVEJUSTSEE
    --23
And she keeps calling me back again.--IVEJUSTSEE
    --31
And she keeps calling me back again.--IVEJUSTSEE
    --33
And she keeps calling me back again.--IVEJUSTSEE
    --35
Why she had to go, I don't know--YESTERDAY--9
She wouldn't say--YESTERDAY--10
Why she had to go, I don't know--YESTERDAY--17
She wouldn't say--YESTERDAY--18
How could she say to me--YOUVEGOTTO--15
She was a day tripper --DAYTRIPPER--5
She took me half the way there --DAYTRIPPER--10
She took me half the way there, now.--DAYTRIPPER
    --12
She was a day tripper --DAYTRIPPER--13
She only played one night stands --DAYTRIPPER--19
And she only played one night stands, now.--
    DAYTRIPPER--21
She was a day tripper --DAYTRIPPER--22
Asked a girl what she wanted to be --DRIVEMYCAR--1
She said baby can't you see?--DRIVEMYCAR--2
'n' she said baby it's understood --DRIVEMYCAR--10
And she said listen babe I've got something to
    say --DRIVEMYCAR--23
She will turn to me and start to cry --GIRL--7
And she promises the earth to me and I believe
    her --GIRL--8
She acts as if it's understood --GIRL--17
Was she told when she was young that pain would
    lead to pleasure?--GIRL--22
Was she told when she was young that pain would

      lead to pleasure?--GIRL--22
Did she understand it when they said --GIRL--23
Will she still believe it when he's dead?--GIRL--25
She once had me?--NORWEGIANW--3
She showed me her room--NORWEGIANW--4
She asked me to stay--NORWEGIANW--7
And she told me to sit anywhere--NORWEGIANW--8
And then she said--NORWEGIANW--15
She told me she worked in the morning--NORWEGIANW
      --17
She told me she worked in the morning--NORWEGIANW
      --17
Wearing the face that she keeps in a jar by the door
      --ELEANORRIG--7
When she no longer needs you.--FORNOONE--3
She wakes up, she makes up --FORNOONE--4
She wakes up, she makes up --FORNOONE--4
She takes her time and doesn't feel she has to
      hurry --FORNOONE--5
She takes her time and doesn't feel she has to
      hurry --FORNOONE--5
She no longer needs you.--FORNOONE--6
When she says her love is dead --FORNOONE--12
You think she needs you.--FORNOONE--13
You stay home, she goes out --FORNOONE--17
She says that long ago she knew someone --FORNOONE
      --18
She says that long ago she knew someone --FORNOONE
      --18
But now he's gone, she doesn't need him.--FORNOONE
      --19
She said will fill your head --FORNOONE--22
She feels good (she feels good), she knows
      she's looking fine --GOODDAYSUN--12
She feels good (she feels good), she knows
      she's looking fine --GOODDAYSUN--12
She feels good (she feels good), she knows
      she's looking fine --GOODDAYSUN--12
I'm so proud to know that she is mine.--GOODDAYSUN
      --13
Someone is speaking but she doesn't know he's
      there.--HERETHEREA--7
SHE SAID, SHE SAID.--SHESAIDSHE--Title
SHE SAID, SHE SAID.--SHESAIDSHE--Title
She said I know what it's like to be dead --
      SHESAIDSHE--1
She said you don't understand what I said.--
      SHESAIDSHE--7
She said you don't understand what I said.--
      SHESAIDSHE--13
She said (she said)--SHESAIDSHE--19
She said (she said)--SHESAIDSHE--19
And though she feels as if she's in a play--
      PENNYLANE--22
She is anyway.--PENNYLANE--23
I beat her and kept her apart from the things
      that she loved--GETTINGBET--26
Go to a show you hope she goes--GOODMORNIN--24
In a cap she looked much older--LOVELYRITA--10
Leaving the note that she hoped would say more.--
      SHESLEAVIN--3
She goes downstairs to the kitchen--SHESLEAVIN--4
Stepping outside she is free.--SHESLEAVIN--7
She (we gave her most of our lives)--SHESLEAVIN--8
She breaks down and cries to her husband--
      SHESLEAVIN--16
Why would she treat us so thoughtlessly?--
      SHESLEAVIN--18
How could she do this to me?--SHESLEAVIN--19
She (we never thought of ourselves)--SHESLEAVIN--20
Friday morning at nine o'clock she is far away--
      SHESLEAVIN--25
Waiting to keep the appointment she made--
      SHESLEAVIN--26
She (what did we do that was wrong?)--SHESLEAVIN
      --28
She loves you yeah, yeah, yeah ((love is all,
      love is all))--ALLYOUN/YS--45
Though she was born a long, long time ago --
      YOURMOTHER--4
Though she was born a long, long time ago --
      YOURMOTHER--10
Though she was born a long, long time ago --
      YOURMOTHER--15
Though she was born a long, long time ago --
      YOURMOTHER--23
Look out 'cos here she comes (heh heh heh).--
      HELTERSKEL--17
Yes she is, yes she is.--HELTERSKEL--29
Yes she is, yes she is.--HELTERSKEL--29
She was a working girl--HONEYPIE--1
And if she could only hear me--HONEYPIE--5
Listen to the pretty sound of music as she flies.
      --MOTHERNATU--4

And Molly says this as she takes him by the hand:
      --OBLADIOBLA--4
And as he gives it to her she begins to sing
      (sing):--OBLADIOBLA--12
And in the evening she still sings it with the
      band, yes.--OBLADIOBLA--24
Her name was Magill and she called herself Lil --
      ROCKYRACCO--15
Now she and her man who called himself Dan--
      ROCKYRACCO--17
She came along to turn on everyone--SEXYSADIE--10
She made a fool of everyone--SEXYSADIE--26
Nobody ever loved me like she does --DONTLETMED--5
Ooo she does, yes she does --DONTLETMED--6
Ooo she does, yes she does --DONTLETMED--6
And if somebody loved me like she do me --
      DONTLETMED--7
Ooo she do me, yes she does.--DONTLETMED--8
Ooo she do me, yes she does.--DONTLETMED--8
And from the first time that she really done me --
      DONTLETMED--21
Ooo she done me, she done me good --DONTLETMED--22
Ooo she done me, she done me good --DONTLETMED--22
Ooo she done me, she done me good.--DONTLETMED--24
Ooo she done me, she done me good.--DONTLETMED--24
Sweet Loretta Martin thought she was a woman --
      GETBACK/45--16
But she was another man.--GETBACK/45--17
But she gets it while she can.--GETBACK/45--19
But she gets it while she can.--GETBACK/45--19
But she doesn't have a lot to say.--HERMAJESTY--2
But she changes from day to day.--HERMAJESTY--4
Bang, bang Maxwell's silver hammer made sure
      that she was dead.--MAXWELLSIL--7
She tells Max to stay when the class has gone
      away --MAXWELLSIL--10
But when she turns her back on the boy, he
      creeps up from behind --MAXWELLSIL--12
Bang, bang Maxwell's silver hammer made sure
      that she was dead.--MAXWELLSIL--15
She never stops--MEANMRMUST--9
She's so goodlooking but she looks like a man.--
      POLYTHENEP--2
Yes, you could say she was attractively built -
      yeah, yeah, yeah.--POLYTHENEP--9
SHE CAME IN THROUGH THE BATHROOM WINDOW.--
      SHECAMEINT--Title
She came in through the bathroom window --
      SHECAMEINT--4
But now she sucks her thumb and wonders --
      SHECAMEINT--6
She said she'd always been a dancer --SHECAMEINT
      --12
She worked at fifteen clubs a day--SHECAMEINT--13
And though she thought I knew the answer --
      SHECAMEINT--14
And though she tried her best to help me --
      SHECAMEINT--18
She could steal but she could not rob.--SHECAMEINT
      --19
She could steal but she could not rob.--SHECAMEINT
      --19
Something in the way she moves--SOMETHING--1
Something in the way she woos me --SOMETHING--3
Somewhere in her smile she knows--SOMETHING--6
Something in the way she knows--SOMETHING--15
Something in the things she shows me --SOMETHING
      --17
She is standing right in front of me --LETITBE/45
      --5
Sweet Moretta Fart she thought she was a cleaner--
      GETBACK/LP--2
Sweet Moretta Fart she thought she was a cleaner--
      GETBACK/LP--2
But she was a frying pan ((sweet Loretta
      Martin)).--GETBACK/LP--3
Sweet Loretta Martin thought she was a woman--
      GETBACK/LP--22
But she was another man--GETBACK/LP--23
But she gets it while she can.--GETBACK/LP--25
But she gets it while she can.--GETBACK/LP--25
She is standing right in front of me --LETITBE/LP
      --5
Well, she said she's travelling on the one after
      nine-0-nine --ONEAFTERNI--15
She said she's travelling on the one after
      nine-0-nine --ONEAFTERNI--25
She said we're travelling on the one after nine-0
      --ONEAFTERNI--30

SHE'D
      She said she'd always been a dancer --SHECAMEINT
      --12

SHE'LL

Can't she see she'll always be the only one,
    only one.--MISERY--7
She'll remember and she'll miss her only one,
    lonely one.--MISERY--11
She'll remember and she'll miss her only one,
    lonely one.--MISERY--11
Because I know she'll always be--DONTBOTHER--17
Because I know she'll always be--DONTBOTHER--32

SHE'S

It's you she's thinking of--SHELOVESYO--6
Since she's been gone--DONTBOTHER--1
But till she's here--DONTBOTHER--19
When she's come home--DONTBOTHER--23
But till she's here--DONTBOTHER--34
When she's come home--DONTBOTHER--38
She's happy as can be, you know, she said so --
    IFEELFINE--2
Baby says she's mine, you know --IFEELFINE--4
I'm so glad that she's my little girl --IFEELFINE
    --7
She's so glad she's telling all the world --
    IFEELFINE--8
She's so glad she's telling all the world --
    IFEELFINE--8
She's in love with me and I feel fine (ooo).--
    IFEELFINE--11
Baby said she's mine, you know --IFEELFINE--12
I'm so glad that she's my little girl --IFEELFINE
    --15
She's so glad she's telling all the world --
    IFEELFINE--16
She's so glad she's telling all the world --
    IFEELFINE--16
She's in love with me and I feel fine --IFEELFINE
    --19
She's in love with me and I feel fine.--IFEELFINE
    --20
SHE'S A WOMAN.--SHESAWOMAN--Title
I know that she's no peasant--SHESAWOMAN--2
People tell me that she's only fooling--SHESAWOMAN
    --6
She's a woman who understands--SHESAWOMAN--16
She's a woman who loves her man--SHESAWOMAN--17
I know that she's no peasant--SHESAWOMAN--19
People tell me that she's only fooling--SHESAWOMAN
    --23
She's a woman who understands--SHESAWOMAN--26
She's a woman who loves her man--SHESAWOMAN--27
I know that she's no peasant--SHESAWOMAN--29
People tell me that she's only fooling--SHESAWOMAN
    --33
She's a woman, she's a woman, she's a woman.--
    SHESAWOMAN--35
She's a woman, she's a woman, she's a woman.--
    SHESAWOMAN--35
She's a woman, she's a woman, she's a woman.--
    SHESAWOMAN--35
She's dressed in black.--BABYSINBLA--6
She's dressed in black.--BABYSINBLA--26
There's no fun in what I do when she's not there
    --IDONTWANTT--6
Though tonight she's made me sad --IDONTWANTT--9
Though tonight she's made me sad --IDONTWANTT--18
There's no fun in what I do if she's not there --
    IDONTWANTT--23
She's got a ticket to ride--TICKETTORI--5
She's got a ticket to ride--TICKETTORI--6
She's got a ticket to ride--TICKETTORI--7
She's got a ticket to ride--TICKETTORI--13
She's got a ticket to ride--TICKETTORI--14
She's got a ticket to ride--TICKETTORI--15
I don't know why she's riding so high--TICKETTORI
    --17
Oh, she's got a ticket to ride--TICKETTORI--26
She's got a ticket to ride--TICKETTORI--27
She's got a ticket to ride--TICKETTORI--28
I don't know why she's riding so high--TICKETTORI
    --30
Ah, she's got a ticket to ride--TICKETTORI--40
She's got a ticket to ride--TICKETTORI--41
She's got a ticket to ride--TICKETTORI--42
She's sweeter than all the girls and I met quite
    a few --ANOTHERGIR--6
She's just the girl for me--IVEJUSTSEE--4
She's just the girl for me--IVEJUSTSEE--27
She's gonna change her mind (she's gonna change
    her mind)--YOUREGONNA--4
She's gonna change her mind (she's gonna change
    her mind)--YOUREGONNA--4
She's gonna change her mind (she's gonna change
    her mind)--YOUREGONNA--26

She's gonna change her mind (she's gonna change
    her mind)--YOUREGONNA--26
If she's gone I can't go on --YOUVEGOTTO--3
She's a big teaser --DAYTRIPPER--9
She's a big teaser --DAYTRIPPER--11
She's the kind of girl you want so much it makes
    you sorry --GIRL--3
She's the kind of girl who puts you down--GIRL--11
When you say she's looking good --GIRL--15
She's cool - ooo-ooo-ooo.--GIRL--19
I love her and she's loving me.--GOODDAYSUN--11
She feels good (she feels good), she knows
    she's looking fine --GOODDAYSUN--12
And if she's beside me I know I need never care--
    HERETHEREA--9
And if she's beside me I know I need never care--
    HERETHEREA--15
And she's making me feel like I've never been
    born.--SHESAIDSHE--3
And though she feels as if she's in a play--
    PENNYLANE--22
And she's gone.--LUCYINTHES--8
SHE'S LEAVING HOME.--SHESLEAVIN--Title
She's leaving home after living alone--SHESLEAVIN
    --11
She's leaving home after living alone--SHESLEAVIN
    --23
She's leaving home. ('bye, 'bye)--SHESLEAVIN--33
She's old enough to know better.--CRYBABYCRY--3
She's old enough to know better --CRYBABYCRY--10
She's old enough to know better --CRYBABYCRY--18
She's old enough to know better --CRYBABYCRY--26
She's old enough to know better --CRYBABYCRY--34
She's old enough to know better --CRYBABYCRY--38
She's old enough to know better --CRYBABYCRY--42
She's not a girl who misses much --HAPPINESSI--1
She's well acquainted with the touch of the
    velvet hand --HAPPINESSI--3
She's coming down fast --HELTERSKEL--28
Now she's hit the big time--HONEYPIE--3
And in the evening she's a singer with the band,
    yeah.--OBLADIOBLA--35
Sexy Sadie (sexy Sadie) the greatest of them
    all ((she's the greatest))--SEXYSADIE--11
She's the latest and the greatest (she's the
    greatest) of them all--SEXYSADIE--23
She's the latest and the greatest (she's the
    greatest) of them all--SEXYSADIE--23
(Sexy Sadie she's the latest and the greatest
    of them all)--SEXYSADIE--24
All the girls around her say she's got it coming
    --GETBACK/45--18
The newspapers said, she's gone to his head --
    BALLADOFJO--31
I WANT YOU (SHE'S SO HEAVY).--IWANTYOUSH--Title
She's so - heavy (heavy - heavy - heavy)--
    IWANTYOUSH--25
She's so - heavy--IWANTYOUSH--26
She's so heavy (heavy - heavy)--IWANTYOUSH--27
She's so -.--IWANTYOUSH--41
But as she's getting ready to go, a knock comes
    on the door --MAXWELLSIL--5
She's a go-getter.--MEANMRMUST--10
She's so goodlooking but she looks like a man.--
    POLYTHENEP--2
She's killer-diller when she's dressed to the hilt.
    --POLYTHENEP--7
She's killer-diller when she's dressed to the hilt.
    --POLYTHENEP--7
She's a kind of a girl that makes the News Of
    The World.--POLYTHENEP--8
All the girls around her say she's got it coming--
    GETBACK/LP--24
My baby said she's travelling on the one after
    nine-O-nine --ONEAFTERNI--1
Well, she said she's travelling on the one after
    nine-O-nine --ONEAFTERNI--15
Said she's travelling on the one after
    nine-O-nine. (yeah)--ONEAFTERNI--19
She said she's travelling on the one after
    nine-O-nine --ONEAFTERNI--25

SHEARS

The one and only Billy Shears--SGTPEPPERS--24
Billy Shears!--SGTPEPPERS--26

SHEEP

Sheep dog standing in the rain--HEYBULLDOG--1

SHELTER

Behind the shelter in the middle of the roundabout

--PENNYLANE--20

SHIMMERING
    Her hair of floating sky is shimmering --JULIA--7

SHINE
    I'll try to make it shine.--ANYTIMEATA--14
    Bright are the stars that shine --ANDILOVEHE--15
    Bright are the stars that shine --ANDILOVEHE--20
    When the sun shines, when the sun shines ((sun
        shine)).--RAIN--6
    Shine the weather's fine.--RAIN--8
    Shine the weather's fine.--RAIN--13
    Now the moon begins to shine --GOODNIGHT--9
    Shine on till tomorrow, let it be.--LETITBE/45--23
    Everybody saw the sun shine --IVEGOTAFEE--22
    Everybody saw the sun shine.--IVEGOTAFEE--31
    Shine on till tomorrow, let it be.--LETITBE/LP--23

SHINES
    When the sun shines they slip into the shade
        (when the sun shines down)--RAIN--4
    When the sun shines they slip into the shade
        (when the sun shines down)--RAIN--4
    And sip their lemonade (when the sun shines down)
        --RAIN--5
    When the sun shines, when the sun shines ((sun
        shine)).--RAIN--6
    When the sun shines, when the sun shines ((sun
        shine)).--RAIN--6
    Can you hear me that when it rains and shines
        (when it rains and shines)--RAIN--14
    Can you hear me that when it rains and shines
        (when it rains and shines)--RAIN--14
    It's just a state of mind (when it rains and
        shines)--RAIN--15
    There is still a light that shines on me --
        LETITBE/45--22
    Limitless undying love which shines around me
        like a million suns --ACROSSTHEU--23
    There is still a light that shines on me --
        LETITBE/LP--22

SHINING
    We take a walk, the sun is shining down --
        GOODDAYSUN--7
    It is shining, it is shining.--TOMORROWNE--4
    It is shining, it is shining.--TOMORROWNE--4
    The love that's shining all around you --ITSALLTOOM
        --9
    The love that's shining all around here --
        ITSALLTOOM--17
    The love that's shining all around here --
        ITSALLTOOM--26
    The love that's shining all around you --ITSALLTOOM
        --30

SHIP
    Bom bom bom bom-pa bom, sail the ship --ALLTOGETHE
        --9
    Bom bom bom bom-pa bom, ((Oh! boy)), sail the ship--
        ALLTOGETHE--29

SHIRTS
    In the starched white shirts?--PIGGIES--7
    Always have clean shirts to play around in.--
        PIGGIES--10

SHOE
    OLD BROWN SHOE.--OLDBROWNSH--Title
    Now I'm stepping out this old brown shoe --
        OLDBROWNSH--5

SHOE-SHINE
    He wear no shoe-shine--COMETOGETH--15

SHOES
    Wearing her high-heel shoes --GETBACK/45--33

SHOO-BE-DO-A
    Don't you know it's gonna be ((oh shoo-be-do-a))--
        REVOLUTONE--13
    Alright ((oh shoo-be-do-a))?--REVOLUTONE--14
    Don't you know it's gonna be ((oh shoo-be-do-a))--
        REVOLUTONE--15
    Alright ((oh shoo-be-do-a))?--REVOLUTONE--16
    Don't you know it's gonna be ((oh shoo-be-do-a))--
        REVOLUTONE--17
    Alright ((oh shoo-be-do-a))?--REVOLUTONE--18
    (Oh shoo-be-do-a, oh shoo-be-do-a).--REVOLUTONE--22
    (Oh shoo-be-do-a, oh shoo-be-do-a).--REVOLUTONE--22
    (Oh shoo-be-do-a, oh shoo-be-do-a).--REVOLUTONE--26
    (Oh shoo-be-do-a, oh shoo-be-do-a).--REVOLUTONE--26
    Don't you know it's gonna be ((oh shoo-be-do-a))--
        REVOLUTONE--29
    Alright ((oh shoo-be-do-a))?--REVOLUTONE--30
    Don't you know it's gonna be ((oh shoo-be-do-a))--
        REVOLUTONE--31
    Alright ((oh shoo-be-do-a))?--REVOLUTONE--32
    Don't you know it's gonna be ((oh shoo-be-do-a))--
        REVOLUTONE--33
    Alright ((oh shoo-be-do-a))?--REVOLUTONE--34
    (Oh shoo-be-do-a, oh shoo-be-do-a).--REVOLUTONE--38
    (Oh shoo-be-do-a, oh shoo-be-do-a).--REVOLUTONE--38
    (Oh shoo-be-do-a, oh shoo-be-do-a).--REVOLUTONE--42
    (Oh shoo-be-do-a, oh shoo-be-do-a).--REVOLUTONE--42
    Don't you know it's gonna be ((oh shoo-be-do-a))--
        REVOLUTONE--45
    Alright ((oh shoo-be-do-a))?--REVOLUTONE--46
    Don't you know it's gonna be ((oh shoo-be-do-a))--
        REVOLUTONE--47
    Alright ((oh shoo-be-do-a))?--REVOLUTONE--48
    Don't you know it's gonna be ((oh shoo-be-do-a))--
        REVOLUTONE--49
    Alright ((oh shoo-be-do-a))?--REVOLUTONE--50
    ((Oh)) (oh shoo-be-do-a)--REVOLUTONE--51
    Oh oh (oh shoo-be-do-a)--REVOLUTONE--54
    Oh oh (oh shoo-be-do-a)--REVOLUTONE--56
    Alright (oh shoo-be-do-a)--REVOLUTONE--57
    Alright (oh shoo-be-do-a)--REVOLUTONE--59
    Alright (oh shoo-be-do-a)--REVOLUTONE--61
    Alright (oh shoo-be-do-a)--REVOLUTONE--63
    Alright (oh shoo-be-do-a)--REVOLUTONE--65
    Alright (oh shoo-be-do-a)--REVOLUTONE--67
    Oh-oh-oh-oh-oh-oh ((oh shoo-be-do-a))--REVOLUTONE
        --68
    (Oh shoo-be-do-a)--REVOLUTONE--69
    (Oh shoo-be-do-a)--REVOLUTONE--70
    (Oh shoo-be-do-a) alright --REVOLUTONE--71

SHOOT
    (Bang, bang, shoot, shoot) --HAPPINESSI--19
    (Bang, bang, shoot, shoot) --HAPPINESSI--19
    ((Bang, bang, shoot, shoot)) --HAPPINESSI--21
    ((Bang, bang, shoot, shoot)) --HAPPINESSI--21
    ((Bang, bang, shoot, shoot)) --HAPPINESSI--26
    ((Bang, bang, shoot, shoot)) --HAPPINESSI--26
    ((Bang, bang, shoot, shoot)) --HAPPINESSI--28
    ((Bang, bang, shoot, shoot)) --HAPPINESSI--28
    ((Happiness - bang, bang, shoot, shoot)) --
        HAPPINESSI--30
    ((Happiness - bang, bang, shoot, shoot)) --
        HAPPINESSI--30
    To shoot off the legs of his rival.--ROCKYRACCO--12
    Shoot me--COMETOGETH--1
    Shoot me--COMETOGETH--2
    Shoot me--COMETOGETH--3
    Shoot me--COMETOGETH--4
    Shoot me--COMETOGETH--11
    Shoot me--COMETOGETH--12
    Shoot me--COMETOGETH--13
    Shoot me--COMETOGETH--14
    He shoot Coca-cola--COMETOGETH--18
    Shoot me--COMETOGETH--22
    Shoot me--COMETOGETH--23
    Shoot me--COMETOGETH--24
    Shoot me--COMETOGETH--32
    Shoot me--COMETOGETH--43
    Shoot me--COMETOGETH--44
    Shoot me--COMETOGETH--45

SHOP
    His sister Pam works in a shop--MEANMRMUST--8

SHORE
    Newspaper taxis appear on the shore--LUCYINTHES--16
    Standing on the cast-iron shore - yeah--GLASSONION
        --12

SHORT
    Life is very short and there's no time--WECANWORKI

```
    --11
    Life is very short and there's no time--WECANWORKI
        --20
    A lifetime is so short--LOVEYOUTWO--6


SHORT-HAIRED
    I want a short-haired girl --OLDBROWNSH--3


SHOT
    But Daniel was hot, he drew first and shot--
        ROCKYRACCO--21


SHOULD
    That I - I - I - I should never, never,
        never be blue.--ASKMEWHY--6
    That I - I - I - I should never, never,
        never be blue.--ASKMEWHY--21
    And you know you should be glad.--SHELOVESYO--11
    And you know you should be glad  - ooo!--SHELOVESYO
        --19
    You know you should be glad.--SHELOVESYO--23
    And you know you should be glad - ooo!--SHELOVESYO
        --31
    You know you should be glad--SHELOVESYO--35
    You know you should be glad--SHELOVESYO--37
    You know you should be glad--SHELOVESYO--39
    I'll be good like I know I should (yes,
        you're coming on home)--ITWONTBELO--13
    I'll be good like I know I should (yes,
        you're coming on home)--ITWONTBELO--23
    I should be sleeping like a log --HARDDAYSNI--4
    So why on earth should I moan --HARDDAYSNI--12
    I should be sleeping like a log --HARDDAYSNI--20
    So why on earth should I moan --HARDDAYSNI--25
    I should be sleeping like a log --HARDDAYSNI--33
    I SHOULD HAVE KNOWN BETTER.--ISHOULDHAV--Title
    I should have known better with a girl like you --
        ISHOULDHAV--1
    So - oh, I should have realised a lot of things
        before --ISHOULDHAV--11
    There is one love I should never have crossed.--
        IMALOSER--4
    I should have known she would win in the end.--
        IMALOSER--6
    Why should it be so much to ask of you --WHATYOURED
        --7
    'n' should you need a love that's true, it's me.--
        WHATYOURED--11
    Why should it be so much to ask of you --WHATYOURED
        --14
    'n' should you need a love that's true, it's me.--
        WHATYOURED--18
    Why should it be so much to ask of you --WHATYOURED
        --21
    Why should I feel the way I do?--ITSONLYLOV--5
    Is it right that you and I should fight, every
        night--ITSONLYLOV--8
    Why should I feel the way I do?--ITSONLYLOV--12
    Or should I say--NORWEGIANW--2
    All the things that you should.--THINKFORYO--23
    I don't know why you should want to hide --
        YOUWONTSEE--7
    A love that should have lasted years.--FORNOONE--9
    A love that should have lasted years.--FORNOONE--16
    A love that should have lasted years.--FORNOONE--26
    Should five percent appear too small --TAXMAN--7
    Man you should have seen them kicking Edgar
        Allan Poe--IAMTHEWALR--27
    YOUR MOTHER SHOULD KNOW.--YOURMOTHER--Title
    Your mother should know (your mother should) --
        YOURMOTHER--5
    Your mother should know (your mother should) --
        YOURMOTHER--5
    Your mother should know - aah.--YOURMOTHER--6
    Your mother should know (your mother should) --
        YOURMOTHER--11
    Your mother should know (your mother should) --
        YOURMOTHER--11
    Your mother should know - aah.--YOURMOTHER--12
    Your mother should know (your mother should) --
        YOURMOTHER--16
    Your mother should know (your mother should) --
        YOURMOTHER--16
    Your mother should know - aah.--YOURMOTHER--17
    Your mother should know (your mother should) --
        YOURMOTHER--18
    Your mother should know (your mother should) --
        YOURMOTHER--18
    Your mother should know - aah.--YOURMOTHER--19
    Your mother should know (your mother should) --
        YOURMOTHER--24
```

```
    Your mother should know (your mother should) --
        YOURMOTHER--24
    Your mother should know - yeah ((ooo)).--YOURMOTHER
        --25
    Your mother should know (your mother should) --
        YOURMOTHER--26
    Your mother should know (your mother should) --
        YOURMOTHER--26
    Your mother should know - yeah.--YOURMOTHER--27
    Your mother should know (your mother should) --
        YOURMOTHER--28
    Your mother should know (your mother should) --
        YOURMOTHER--28
    Your mother should know - yeah.--YOURMOTHER--29
    I wonder should I get up and fix myself a drink --
        IMSOTIRED--3
    I wonder should I call you --IMSOTIRED--7
    If you and me should get together --OLDBROWNSH--25
    Well, you should see Polythene Pam.--POLYTHENEP--1
    Well, you should see her in drag --POLYTHENEP--3
    Yes, you should see Polythene Pam - yeah,
        yeah, yeah.--POLYTHENEP--5


SHOULDER
    When you need a shoulder to cry on --ANYTIMEATA--16
    I got a chip on my shoulder that's bigger than my
        feet.--ILLCRYINST--6
    And the bag across her shoulder--LOVELYRITA--11
    Don't carry the world upon your shoulder.--HEYJUDE
        --11
    The movement you need is on your shoulder.--HEYJUDE
        --24


SHOUT
    And Moscow girls make me sing and shout --
        BACKINTHEU--17
    And Moscow girls make me sing and shout --
        BACKINTHEU--29
    You shout aloud.--SAVOYTRUFF--16
    We would shout and swim about--OCTOPUSSGA--17


SHOUTS
    Always shouts out something obscene--MEANMRMUST--13


SHOW
    That it really only goes to show --ASKMEWHY--4
    That it really only goes to show --ASKMEWHY--19
    You don't need me to show the way love --PLEASEPLEA
        --7
    And show you what your loving man can do --
        ILLCRYINST--18
    And show you what your loving man can do --
        ILLCRYINST--27
    This time I will try to show --ILLBEBACK--11
    This time I will try to show --ILLBEBACK--20
    Eight days a week is not enough to show I care.--
        EIGHTDAYSA--18
    Eight days a week is not enough to show I care.--
        EIGHTDAYSA--28
    I would hate my disappointment to show --IDONTWANTT
        --2
    I would hate my disappointment to show --IDONTWANTT
        --14
    But I can show you a better time.--DRIVEMYCAR--12
    I'm here to show everybody the light.--THEWORD--24
    I can show you that when it starts to rain (when
        the rain comes down)--RAIN--9
    I can show you, I can show you ((show you)).--RAIN
        --11
    I can show you, I can show you ((show you)).--RAIN
        --11
    I can show you, I can show you ((show you)).--RAIN
        --11
    There will be a show tonight on trampoline.--
        BEINGFORTH--2
    Go to a show you hope she goes--GOODMORNIN--24
    We hope you will enjoy the show--SGTPEPPERS--9
    I don't really want to stop the show--SGTPEPPERS
        --19
    We hope you have enjoyed the show.--SGTPEPPREP--4
    Nothing that doesn't show.--BABYYOUREA--12
    Well it only goes to show (only, only goes to
        show) --BLUEJAYWAY--8
    Well it only goes to show (only, only goes to
        show) --BLUEJAYWAY--8
    Oh - show me round the snow-peaked mountains way
        down south --BACKINTHEU--31
    Come and show me the magic--HONEYPIE--11
    But can you show me where you are?--SAVOYTRUFF--22
    Show me that I'm everywhere --ITSALLTOOM--23
```

You stick around now it may show --SOMETHING--13

SHOWDOWN
He said, Danny - Boy this is a showdown.--
ROCKYRACCO--20

SHOWED
She showed me her room--NORWEGIANW--4

SHOWING
Penny Lane: there is a barber showing photographs
--PENNYLANE--1

SHOWN
Nothing you can see that isn't shown ((love))--
ALLYOUN/YS--20

SHOWS
And he never shows his feelings.--FOOLONTHEH--17
Something in her style that shows me --SOMETHING
--8
Something in the things she shows me --SOMETHING
--17

SHY
I get shy when they start to stare.--ILLCRYINST--12
I get shy when they start to stare.--ILLCRYINST--21
Why am I so shy when I'm beside you?--ITSONLYLOV
--3

SIDE
And keep you by my side--FROMMETOYO--12
And keep you by my side--FROMMETOYO--23
When you're by my side, you're the only one --
LITTLECHIL--16
I could be happy with you by my side--YESITIS--10
I could be happy with you by my side--YESITIS--19
Wait till I come back to your side --WAIT--3
Wait till I come back to your side --WAIT--7
Wait till I come back to your side --WAIT--15
Wait till I come back to your side --WAIT--23

SIDEBOARD
He got Ono sideboard--COMETOGETH--27

SIGH
When you sigh my my inside just flies, butterfly.
--ITSONLYLOV--2
Make your mother sigh --CRYBABYCRY--2
Make your mother sigh --CRYBABYCRY--9
Make your mother sigh --CRYBABYCRY--17
Make your mother sigh --CRYBABYCRY--25
Make your mother sigh --CRYBABYCRY--33
Make your mother sigh --CRYBABYCRY--37
Make your mother sigh --CRYBABYCRY--41

SIGHT
Just the sight of you makes night-time bright,
very bright.--ITSONLYLOV--9
And kept out of sight--IVEJUSTSEE--16
(Would you believe in a love at first sight?)--
WITHALITTL--19

SIGN
No sign of love behind the tears cried for no-one
--FORNOONE--8
No sign of love behind the tears cried for no-one
--FORNOONE--15
No sign of love behind the tears cried for no-one
--FORNOONE--25
You don't get time to hang a sign on me.--
LOVEYOUTWO--3

SILENT
Julia sleeping sand silent cloud touch me --JULIA
--13

SILENTLY
Silently closing her bedroom door--SHESLEAVIN--2

SILLY
Silly people run around they worry me--FIXINGAHOL--17
Hold your head up you silly girl, look what
you've done--MARTHAMYDE--4
Help yourself to a bit of what is all around you
- silly girl.--MARTHAMYDE--6
That you and me were meant to be for each other -
silly girl.--MARTHAMYDE--9
Hold your hand out you silly girl, see what
you've done --MARTHAMYDE--10
Help yourself to a bit of what is all around you
- silly girl.--MARTHAMYDE--12

SILVER
You became a legend of the silver screen--HONEYPIE
--13
Sail me on a silver sun --ITSALLTOOM--21
MAXWELL'S SILVER HAMMER.--MAXWELLSIL--Title
Bang, bang Maxwell's silver hammer came down
upon her head --MAXWELLSIL--6
Bang, bang Maxwell's silver hammer made sure
that she was dead.--MAXWELLSIL--7
Bang, bang Maxwell's silver hammer came down
upon her head --MAXWELLSIL--13
Bang, bang Maxwell's silver hammer made sure
that she was dead.--MAXWELLSIL--15
Bang, bang Maxwell's silver hammer came down
upon his head --MAXWELLSIL--23
Bang, bang Maxwell's silver hammer made sure
that he was dead.--MAXWELLSIL--25
Silver hammer man!--MAXWELLSIL--28
Protected by a silver spoon --SHECAMEINT--5

SIN
I think it's a sin?--YOUCANTDOT--12
The children asked him if to kill was not a sin --
CONTINUING--27

SINCE
Whoa since/when I saw her standing there. (hey! aah!)--
ISAWHERSTA--17
Oh since I saw her standing there.--ISAWHERSTA--24
Whoa since I saw her standing there--ISAWHERSTA--25
Yeah, well since I saw her standing there.--
ISAWHERSTA--26
Since she's been gone--DONTBOTHER--1
Since you left me I'm so alone (you left me here)
--ITWONTBELO--11
Well since you left me I'm so alone (you left
me here)--ITWONTBELO--21
Oh, I can't sleep at night since you've been
gone --ICALLYOURN--3
And since I lost you it feels like years.--
YOUWONTSEE--17
Yes it seems so long, girl, since you've been gone
--YOUWONTSEE--18
And since I lost you it feels like years.--
YOUWONTSEE--26
Yes it seems so long, girl, since you've been gone
--YOUWONTSEE--27
It's getting better since you've been mine.--
GETTINGBET--10
It's getting better since you've been mine.--
GETTINGBET--19
It's getting better since you've been mine.--
GETTINGBET--32
Little darling, it feels like years since it's
been here.--HERECOMEST--5
Little darling, it seems like years since it's
been here.--HERECOMEST--10
Little darling, it seems like years since it's
been clear.--HERECOMEST--19

SINCERE
When I held you near, you were so sincere--
NIGHTBEFOR--7
When I held you near, you were so sincere --
NIGHTBEFOR--15
When I held you near, you were so sincere --
NIGHTBEFOR--21

SINCERELY
Yours sincerely, wasting away.--WHENIMSIXT--31

SING
AND YOUR BIRD CAN SING.--ANDYOURBIR--Title
And your bird can sing --ANDYOURBIR--2
The Hendersons will dance and sing--BEINGFORTH--10

SING (continued)

That the singer's gonna sing a song--SGTPEPPERS--21
And he wants you all to sing along.--SGTPEPPERS--22
Lend me your ears and I'll sing you a song--
    WITHALITTL--3
And I'll try not to sing outta key.--WITHALITTL--4
Nothing you can sing that can't be sung ((love))--
    ALLYOUN/YS--5
Sing it again.--YOURMOTHER--7
Lift up your hearts and sing me a song--YOURMOTHER
    --13
Sing it again.--YOURMOTHER--20
And Moscow girls make me sing and shout --
    BACKINTHEU--17
And Moscow girls make me sing and shout --
    BACKINTHEU--29
All de children sing:--CONTINUING--10
All de children sing:--CONTINUING--20
All the children sing:--CONTINUING--30
The wind is low, the birds will sing --DEARPRUDEN
    --8
Sing it loud so I can hear you --IWILL--15
So I sing the song of love, Julia.--JULIA--4
So I sing the song of love, Julia.--JULIA--6
So I sing the song of love, Julia.--JULIA--10
When I cannot sing my heart --JULIA--11
So I sing a song of love, Julia.--JULIA--14
So I sing a song of love for Julia --JULIA--16
Swaying daisies sing a lazy song beneath the sun.
    --MOTHERNATU--9
And as he gives it to her she begins to sing
    (sing):--OBLADIOBLA--12
And as he gives it to her she begins to sing
    (sing):--OBLADIOBLA--12
And I will sing a lullaby.--GOLDENSLUM--6
And I will sing a lullaby.--GOLDENSLUM--10
And I will sing a lullaby.--GOLDENSLUM--16
We would sing and dance around--OCTOPUSSGA--13

SINGER

Molly is the singer in a band --OBLADIOBLA--2
And in the evening she's a singer with the band,
    yeah.--OBLADIOBLA--35
If I grow up I'll be a singer --OLDBROWNSH--17

SINGER'S

That the singer's gonna sing a song--SGTPEPPERS--21

SINGING

Make love singing songs.--LOVEYOUTWO--10
Make love singing songs.--LOVEYOUTWO--12
Elementary penguin singing Hare Krishna--IAMTHEWALR
    --26
Blackbird singing in the dead of night --BLACKBIRD
    --1
Blackbird singing in the dead of night --BLACKBIRD
    --5
Blackbird singing in the dead of night --BLACKBIRD
    --13
All day long I'm sitting singing songs for
    everyone.--MOTHERNATU--2

SINGLE

Still you don't regret a single day.--GIRL--4
Every single day of my life?--GOTTOGETYO--7
Every single day of my life?--GOTTOGETYO--22
Every single day...--GOTTOGETYO--31

SINGS

And in the evening she still sings it with the
    band, yes.--OBLADIOBLA--24

SINS

They'll fill you in with all their sins, you'll see.
    --LOVEYOUTWO--16

SIP

And sip their lemonade (when the sun shines down)
    --RAIN--5

SIR

Dear Sir or Madam, will you read my book?--
    PAPERBACKW--2
Aye, Sir, aye.--YELLOWSUBM--23
And curse Sir Walter Raleigh --IMSOTIRED--16

SISTER

Sitting on a sofa with a sister or two.--LOVELYRITA
    --25
His sister Pam works in a shop--MEANMRMUST--8

SIT

And she told me to sit anywhere--NORWEGIANW--8
If you try to sit, I'll tax your seat, ((sit))--
    TAXMAN--12
If you try to sit, I'll tax your seat, ((sit))--
    TAXMAN--12
There beneath the blue suburban skies I sit--
    PENNYLANE--10
There beneath the blue suburban skies I sit--
    PENNYLANE--29
Sit back and let the evening go.--SGTPEPPERS--11
Sit beside a mountain stream - see her waters rise
    --MOTHERNATU--3
We gave her everything we owned just to sit at
    her table ((sexy Sadie))--SEXYSADIE--20

SITTING

Here am I sitting all on my own--ITWONTBELO--6
But you left me sitting on my own --TELLMEWHY--6
Sitting in his nowhere land --NOWHEREMAN--2
Sitting in his nowhere land --NOWHEREMAN--23
We see the banker sitting waiting for a trim--
    PENNYLANE--25
Sitting on a sofa with a sister or two.--LOVELYRITA
    --25
Sitting on a cornflake, waiting for the van to come
    --IAMTHEWALR--4
Mr. City policeman sitting pretty little
    policemen in a row--IAMTHEWALR--9
Sitting in an English garden waiting for the sun--
    IAMTHEWALR--17
Sitting here in Blue Jay Way (way).--BLUEJAYWAY--18
All day long I'm sitting singing songs for
    everyone.--MOTHERNATU--2

SITUATION

I only give you my situation--YOUNEVERGI--5

SIX

The band begins at ten to six--BEINGFORTH--15
... Four, five, six, seven, eight, nine,
    ten...--DAYINTHELI--35
... Four, five, six...--GETTINGBET--1
(... Four, five, six, seven, eight!)--BIRTHDAY--7
One, two, three, four, five, six, seven,
    eight.--DONTPASSME--36
Five, six, seven, eight, nine, ten --ALLTOGETHE--3
One, two, three, four, five, six, seven --
    YOUNEVERGI--24
One, two, three, four, five, six, seven --
    YOUNEVERGI--26
One, two, three, four, five, six, seven --
    YOUNEVERGI--28
One, two, three, four, five, six, seven --
    YOUNEVERGI--30
One, two, three, four, five, six, seven --
    YOUNEVERGI--32
One, two, three, four, five, six, seven --
    YOUNEVERGI--34
One, two, three, four, five, six, seven --
    YOUNEVERGI--36
One, two, three, four, five, six, seven --
    YOUNEVERGI--38
One, two, three, four, five, six, seven --
    YOUNEVERGI--40

SIXTY-FOUR

WHEN I'M SIXTY-FOUR.--WHENIMSIXT--Title
When I'm sixty-four?--WHENIMSIXT--9
When I'm sixty-four?--WHENIMSIXT--21
When I'm sixty-four?--WHENIMSIXT--37

SKIES

There beneath the blue suburban skies I sit--
    PENNYLANE--10
There beneath the blue suburban skies I sit--
    PENNYLANE--29
There beneath the blue suburban skies --PENNYLANE
    --32
With tangerine trees and marmalade skies.--
    LUCYINTHES--2
Dear Prudence, see the sunny skies.--DEARPRUDEN--7

SKIN
    The minute you let her under your skin --HEYJUDE
        --7
    Remember to let her under your skin (oh) --HEYJUDE
        --28

SKIP
    Bom-pa bom, skip the rope --ALLTOGETHE--11
    Bom-pa bom, skip the rope --ALLTOGETHE--31

SKIRTS
    Watching the skirts you start to flirt now you're
        in gear--GOODMORNIN--23

SKY
    Dark is the sky --ANDILOVEHE--16
    Dark is the sky --ANDILOVEHE--21
    My tears are falling like rain from the sky --
        IMALOSER--11
    Sky of blue (sky of blue) and sea of green
        (sea of green)--YELLOWSUBM--27
    Sky of blue (sky of blue) and sea of green
        (sea of green)--YELLOWSUBM--27
    LUCY IN THE SKY WITH DIAMONDS.--LUCYINTHES--Title
    Lucy in the sky with diamonds --LUCYINTHES--9
    Lucy in the sky with diamonds --LUCYINTHES--10
    Lucy in the sky with diamonds - aah.--LUCYINTHES
        --11
    Lucy in the sky with diamonds --LUCYINTHES--20
    Lucy in the sky with diamonds --LUCYINTHES--21
    Lucy in the sky with diamonds - aah.--LUCYINTHES
        --22
    Lucy in the sky with diamonds --LUCYINTHES--27
    Lucy in the sky with diamonds --LUCYINTHES--28
    Lucy in the sky with diamonds - aah.--LUCYINTHES
        --29
    Lucy in the sky with diamonds --LUCYINTHES--30
    Lucy in the sky with diamonds --LUCYINTHES--31
    Lucy in the sky with diamonds - aah.--LUCYINTHES
        --32
    Lucy in the sky with diamonds --LUCYINTHES--33
    Lucy in the sky with diamonds (aah - ooo) --
        LUCYINTHES--34
    Lucy in the sky with diamonds.--LUCYINTHES--35
    See how the fly like Lucy in the sky, see how
        they run--IAMTHEWALR--10
    The sun is up, the sky is blue --DEARPRUDEN--3
    The sun is up, the sky is blue --DEARPRUDEN--23
    Her hair of floating sky is shimmering --JULIA--7
    My mother was of the sky --YERBLUES--10
    Because the sky is blue it makes me cry --BECAUSE
        --10
    Because the sky is blue.--BECAUSE--11

SLAGGERS
    Good evening and welcome to Slaggers --YOUKNOWMYN
        --5

SLEEP
    Oh, I can't sleep at night since you've been
        gone --ICALLYOURN--3
    Oh, I can't sleep at night, but just the same --
        ICALLYOURN--9
    Oh, I can't sleep at night, but just the same --
        ICALLYOURN--16
    And crawled off to sleep in the bath.--NORWEGIANW
        --20
    Good night, sleep tight.--GOODNIGHT--2
    Good night, sleep tight.--GOODNIGHT--4
    Good night, sleep tight.--GOODNIGHT--8
    Good night, sleep tight.--GOODNIGHT--10
    Good night, sleep tight.--GOODNIGHT--15
    Good night, sleep tight.--GOODNIGHT--17
    You know I can't sleep, I can't stop my brain --
        IMSOTIRED--11
    You know I can't sleep, I can't stop my brain --
        IMSOTIRED--20
    Sleep pretty darling do not cry--GOLDENSLUM--5
    Sleep pretty darling do not cry--GOLDENSLUM--9
    Sleep pretty darling do not cry--GOLDENSLUM--15

SLEEPING
    I should be sleeping like a log --HARDDAYSNI--4
    I should be sleeping like a log --HARDDAYSNI--20
    I should be sleeping like a log --HARDDAYSNI--33
    I'M ONLY SLEEPING.--IMONLYSLEE--Title
    Leave me where I am, I'm only sleeping.--IMONLYSLEE
        --6
    And after all, I'm only sleeping.--IMONLYSLEE--12
    And after all, I'm only sleeping.--IMONLYSLEE--18
    Leave me where I am, I'm only sleeping.--IMONLYSLEE
        --26
    Julia sleeping sand silent cloud touch me --JULIA
        --13
    I look at you all, see the love there that's
        sleeping --WHILEMYGUI--2
    I look at you all, see the love there that's
        sleeping--WHILEMYGUI--18

SLEEPS
    Mean Mr. Mustard sleeps in the park--MEANMRMUST--1
    Sleeps in a hole in the road--MEANMRMUST--4

SLEEPY
    Waiting for a sleepy feeling.--IMONLYSLEE--16

SLEPT
    I'm so tired, I haven't slept a wink --IMSOTIRED
        --1

SLIDE
    When I get to the bottom I go back to the top
        of the slide --HELTERSKEL--1
    When I get to the bottom I go back to the top
        of the slide--HELTERSKEL--18

SLING
    A ginger sling with a pineapple heart --SAVOYTRUFF
        --2
    A ginger sling with a pineapple heart --SAVOYTRUFF
        --24

SLIP
    When the sun shines they slip into the shade
        (when the sun shines down)--RAIN--4
    All those words they seem to slip away.--IWANTTOTEL
        --4
    They slither wildly as they slip away across the
        universe.--ACROSSTHEU--2

SLITHER
    They slither wildly as they slip away across the
        universe.--ACROSSTHEU--2

SLOW
    Yellow lorry slow, nowhere to go.--YOUNEVERGI--12

SLOWLY
    Somebody calls you, you answer quite slowly--
        LUCYINTHES--3
    He come grooving up slowly--COMETOGETH--6
    Little darling, I feel that ice is slowly
        melting.--HERECOMEST--18

SLUMBERS
    GOLDEN SLUMBERS.--GOLDENSLUM--Title
    Golden slumbers fill your eyes--GOLDENSLUM--7

SMALL
    Feeling two-foot small.--YOUVEGOTTO--4
    Should five percent appear too small --TAXMAN--7
    And though the holes were rather small--DAYINTHELI
        --30
    And to see you're really only very small--
        WITHINYOUW--18

SMILE
    After a while you start to smile now you feel cool
        --GOODMORNIN--13
    But they're guaranteed to raise a smile.--
        SGTPEPPERS--4
    See how they smile, like pigs in a sty, see how
        they snied--IAMTHEWALR--23
    Dear Prudence, let me see you smile --DEARPRUDEN
        --16
    So let me see you smile again.--DEARPRUDEN--19
    Dear Prudence, won't you let me see you smile?--
        DEARPRUDEN--20
    Julia seashell eyes windy smile calls me --JULIA

--5
Just a smile would lighten everything--SEXYSADIE
   --21
What makes you think you're something special
   when you smile?--HEYBULLDOG--4
When I see your smile --OLDBROWNSH--11
Somewhere in her smile she knows--SOMETHING--6

SMILES
Everyone smiles as you drift past the flowers--
   LUCYINTHES--14
Smiles awake you when you rise.--GOLDENSLUM--8
Little darling, the smiles returning to the faces.
   --HERECOMEST--9

SMILING
The Duchess of Kirkaldy always smiling --CRYBABYCRY
   --20

SMOKE
Found my way upstairs and had a smoke--DAYINTHELI
   --25

SMOKERS
Expert texpert, choking smokers, don't you
   think the joker laughs at you?--IAMTHEWALR--21

SNIED
See how they smile, like pigs in a sty, see how
   they snied--IAMTHEWALR--23

SNORES
Father snores as his wife gets into her
   dressing-gown--SHESLEAVIN--13

SNOW-PEAKED
Oh - show me round the snow-peaked mountains way
   down south --BACKINTHEU--31

SO
So please love me do --LOVEMEDO--4
So please love me do --LOVEMEDO--9
So please love me do --LOVEMEDO--16
So please love me do --LOVEMEDO--21
It's so hard to reason with you, whoa - yeah--
   PLEASEPLEA--17
So how could I dance with another --ISAWHERSTA--5
Like a heart that's oh so true--FROMMETOYO--8
Just/So call on me and I'll send it along--FROMMETOYO--9
So I'm telling you, my friend--ILLGETYOU--13
So you might as well resign yourself to me, oh
   yeah.--ILLGETYOU--18
She said you hurt her so--SHELOVESYO--12
So go away--DONTBOTHER--6
It feels so right now --HOLDMETIGH--1
So hold (hold) me tight (me tight) --HOLDMETIGH--6
So hold (hold) me tight (me tight) --HOLDMETIGH--13
It feels so right now --HOLDMETIGH--18
So hold me tight --HOLDMETIGH--19
So hold (hold) me tight (me tight) --HOLDMETIGH--23
It feels so right now,--HOLDMETIGH--28
So hold me tight --HOLDMETIGH--29
So hold (hold) me tight (me tight) --HOLDMETIGH--33
Since you left me I'm so alone (you left me here)
   --ITWONTBELO--11
Well since you left me I'm so alone (you left
   me here)--ITWONTBELO--21
So every day we'll be happy, I know--ITWONTBELO--25
I'm so sad and lonely --LITTLECHIL--3
I'm so sad and lonely --LITTLECHIL--7
If you want someone to make you feel so fine--
   LITTLECHIL--9
So come on, come on, come on.--LITTLECHIL--11
I'm so sad and lonely --LITTLECHIL--14
I'm so sad and lonely --LITTLECHIL--21
Can't buy me love, oh, everybody tells me so --
   CANTBUYMEL--15
Can't buy me love, oh, everybody tells me so --
   CANTBUYMEL--25
So please listen to me--YOUCANTDOT--23
So please listen to me--YOUCANTDOT--42
Don't you know that it's so?--THERESAPLA--10
Don't you know that it's so?--THERESAPLA--3
So why on earth should I moan --HARDDAYSNI--12
So why on earth should I moan --HARDDAYSNI--25
So - oh, I should have realised a lot of things

before --ISHOULDHAV--11
So I hope you see --IFIFELL--17
So I hope you see --IFIFELL--24
But I can't, so I'll cry instead.--ILLCRYINST--5
But I can't, so I'll cry instead.--ILLCRYINST--10
I'm so happy when you dance with me.--IMHAPPYJUS
   --3
I'm so happy when you dance with me ((oh - oh)).--
   IMHAPPYJUS--15
I'm so happy when you dance with me ((oh - oh)).--
   IMHAPPYJUS--23
Did you have to treat me oh so bad--TELLMEWHY
   --7
I'm so in love with you.--TELLMEWHY--25
I love you so--ILLBEBACK--5
Wishing you weren't so far away --THINGSWESA--4
These days such a kind girl seems so hard to find
   --THINGSWESA--7
I got so many things I gotta do --WHENIGETHO--22
She's happy as can be, you know, she said so --
   IFEELFINE--2
She tells me all the time, you know, she said so
   --IFEELFINE--5
I'm so glad that she's my little girl --IFEELFINE
   --7
She's so glad she's telling all the world --
   IFEELFINE--8
He buys her diamond rings, you know, she said so
   --IFEELFINE--10
She tells me all the time, you know, she said so
   --IFEELFINE--13
I'm so glad that she's my little girl --IFEELFINE
   --15
She's so glad she's telling all the world --
   IFEELFINE--16
He buys her diamond rings, you know, she said so
   --IFEELFINE--18
She thinks of him and so she dresses in black --
   BABYSINBLA--4
She thinks of him and so she dresses in black --
   BABYSINBLA--24
I don't wanna spoil the party so I'll go --
   IDONTWANTT--1
There's nothing for me here so I will disappear --
   IDONTWANTT--3
I don't wanna spoil the party so I'll go --
   IDONTWANTT--13
There's nothing for me here so I will disappear --
   IDONTWANTT--15
For tomorrow may rain so I'll follow the sun.--
   ILLFOLLOWT--2
For tomorrow may rain so I'll follow the sun.--
   ILLFOLLOWT--4
And now the time has come and so my love I must
   go --ILLFOLLOWT--5
For tomorrow may rain so I'll follow the sun.--
   ILLFOLLOWT--8
Yeah, tomorrow may rain so I'll follow the sun.--
   ILLFOLLOWT--9
And now the time has come and so my love I must
   go --ILLFOLLOWT--10
For tomorrow may rain so I'll follow the sun.--
   ILLFOLLOWT--13
And so it's true pride comes before a fall --
   IMALOSER--17
I'm telling you so that you won't lose all.--
   IMALOSER--18
Why should it be so much to ask of you --WHATYOURED
   --7
Why should it be so much to ask of you --WHATYOURED
   --14
Why should it be so much to ask of you --WHATYOURED
   --21
I don't know why she's riding so high--TICKETTORI
   --17
I don't know why she's riding so high--TICKETTORI
   --30
So much younger than today--HELP--9
I'm not so self-assured--HELP--12
In oh so many ways--HELP--20
But ((but)) every now and then ((now and then))
   I feel so insecure--HELP--22
When I was younger, so much younger than today--
   HELP--29
I'm not so self-assured--HELP--32
And so I'm telling you this time you'd better
   stop --ANOTHERGIR--8
So come on back and see--INEEDYOU--18
So come on back and see--INEEDYOU--28
Why am I so shy when I'm beside you?--ITSONLYLOV
   --3
But it's so hard loving you.--ITSONLYLOV--7
But it's so hard loving you.--ITSONLYLOV--14
Yes, it's so hard loving you, loving you - ooo.--

ITSONLYLOV--15
Was I so unwise? (aah the night before)--NIGHTBEFOR
    --6
When I held you near, you were so sincere--
    NIGHTBEFOR--7
When I held you near, you were so sincere --
    NIGHTBEFOR--15
Was I so unwise? (aah the night before)--NIGHTBEFOR
    --20
When I held you near, you were so sincere --
    NIGHTBEFOR--21
All my troubles seemed so far away--YESTERDAY--2
It took me so long to find out --DAYTRIPPER--7
It took me so long to find out --DAYTRIPPER--15
It took me so long to find out --DAYTRIPPER--24
So I will ask you once again.--WECANWORKI--14
So I will ask you once again.--WECANWORKI--23
She's the kind of girl you want so much it makes
    you sorry --GIRL--3
When I think of all the times I tried so hard
    to leave her --GIRL--6
Until I do I'm telling you so you'll understand.--
    MICHELLE--19
So I looked around--NORWEGIANW--9
So I lit a fire--NORWEGIANW--24
When you treat me so unkind.--WHATGOESON--4
It's so easy for a girl like you to lie.--
    WHATGOESON--8
When you treat me so unkind.--WHATGOESON--13
It's so easy for a girl like you to lie.--
    WHATGOESON--17
When you treat me so unkind.--WHATGOESON--29
It's so fine, it's sunshine --THEWORD--5
It's so fine, it's sunshine --THEWORD--13
It's so fine, it's sunshine --THEWORD--21
It's so fine, it's sunshine --THEWORD--29
I have had enough, so act your age.--YOUWONTSEE--2
We have lost the time that was so hard to find--
    YOUWONTSEE--3
Yes it seems so long, girl, since you've been gone
    --YOUWONTSEE--18
Yes it seems so long, girl, since you've been gone
    --YOUWONTSEE--27
So I want to be a paperback writer --PAPERBACKW--6
I'm so proud to know that she is mine.--GOODDAYSUN
    --13
Each day just goes so fast--LOVEYOUTWO--1
A lifetime is so short--LOVEYOUTWO--6
So we sailed on to the sun--YELLOWSUBM--5
Getting so much better all the time.--GETTINGBET
    --20
Getting so much better all the time.--GETTINGBET
    --33
Getting so much better all the time.--GETTINGBET
    --38
That grow so incredibly high (high).--LUCYINTHES
    --15
So may I introduce to you--SGTPEPPERS--5
So let me introduce to you--SGTPEPPERS--23
For so many years. (('bye, 'bye))--SHESLEAVIN--12
Why would she treat us so thoughtlessly?--
    SHESLEAVIN--18
For so many years. (('bye, 'bye))--SHESLEAVIN--24
For so many years. (('bye, 'bye))--SHESLEAVIN--32
About the love that's gone so cold--WITHINYOUW--22
There's so many there to meet.--BLUEJAYWAY--11
So let it out and let it in --HEYJUDE--19
Been away so long I hardly knew the place --
    BACKINTHEU--8
Hey, so look at me --BACKINTHEU--41
So Captain Marvel zapped him right between the
    eyes. (Zap!)--CONTINUING--19
(But when he looked so fierce) his mommy butted
    in --CONTINUING--28
So cry baby cry.--CRYBABYCRY--11
So cry baby cry.--CRYBABYCRY--19
So cry baby cry.--CRYBABYCRY--27
So cry baby cry --CRYBABYCRY--35
So cry baby cry --CRYBABYCRY--39
So cry baby cry.--CRYBABYCRY--43
It's beautiful and so are you.--DEARPRUDEN--4
So let me see you smile again.--DEARPRUDEN--19
It's beautiful and so are you.--DEARPRUDEN--24
You'll never know it hurt me so --DONTPASSME--20
I was so unfair --DONTPASSME--24
You'll never know it hurt me so --DONTPASSME--33
You'll never know it hurt me so --DONTPASSME--39
So come on (come on) come on --EVRBDYMONK--10
So come on (wuh), come on (wuh) --EVRBDYMONK--19
So won't you please come home.--HONEYPIE--9
So won't you please come home.--HONEYPIE--31
Sing it loud so I can hear you --IWILL--15
I'M SO TIRED.--IMSOTIRED--Title
I'm so tired, I haven't slept a wink --IMSOTIRED

--1
I'm so tired, my mind is on the blink --IMSOTIRED
    --2
I'm so tired, I don't know what to do --IMSOTIRED
    --5
I'm so tired, my mind is set on you --IMSOTIRED--6
I'm so tired, I'm feeling so upset --IMSOTIRED--14
I'm so tired, I'm feeling so upset --IMSOTIRED--14
Although I'm so tired, I'll have another
    cigarette--IMSOTIRED--15
So I sing the song of love, Julia.--JULIA--4
So I sing the song of love, Julia.--JULIA--6
So I sing the song of love, Julia.--JULIA--10
So I sing a song of love, Julia.--JULIA--14
So I sing a song of love for Julia --JULIA--16
Now I'm so happy I found you --LONGLONGLO--5
So many tears I was searching --LONGLONGLO--7
So many tears I was wasting - oh, oh!--LONGLONGLO
    --8
So one day he walked into town --ROCKYRACCO--7
But what is sweet now turns so sour.--SAVOYTRUFF
    --20
Feel so suicidal --YERBLUES--19
Feels so suicidal--YERBLUES--26
So take a piece, but not too much.--ITSALLTOOM
    --19
We're so glad you came here --OLDBROWNSH--7
So glad you came here --OLDBROWNSH--15
So glad you came here --OLDBROWNSH--33
I'm so glad you came here --OLDBROWNSH--35
Got to be good-looking 'cos he's so hard to see--
    COMETOGETH--41
I WANT YOU (SHE'S SO HEAVY).--IWANTYOUSH--Title
I want you so bad--IWANTYOUSH--2
I want you so bad--IWANTYOUSH--4
I want you so bad, babe--IWANTYOUSH--8
I want you so bad--IWANTYOUSH--10
I want you so bad, babe--IWANTYOUSH--14
I want you so bad--IWANTYOUSH--16
I want you so bad--IWANTYOUSH--20
I want you so bad--IWANTYOUSH--22
She's so - heavy (heavy - heavy - heavy)--
    IWANTYOUSH--25
She's so - heavy--IWANTYOUSH--26
She's so heavy (heavy - heavy)--IWANTYOUSH--27
I want you so bad--IWANTYOUSH--29
I want you so bad--IWANTYOUSH--31
You know I want you so bad, babe--IWANTYOUSH--35
You know I want you so bad--IWANTYOUSH--37
She's so -.--IWANTYOUSH--41
So he waits behind, writing fifty times I must
    not be so oh - oh oh.--MAXWELLSIL--11
So he waits behind, writing fifty times I must
    not be so oh - oh oh.--MAXWELLSIL--11
The judge does not agree and he tells them so oh
    - oh oh.--MAXWELLSIL--21
We would be so happy you and me--OCTOPUSSGA--21
She's so goodlooking but she looks like a man.--
    POLYTHENEP--2
And so I quit the police department--SHECAMEINT--16
I told you so.--IDIGAPONY--12
I told you so.--IDIGAPONY--22
I told you so.--IDIGAPONY--32
Oh it's so hard.--IVEGOTAFEE--40

SOAP
    A soap impression of his wife which he ate --
        HAPPINESSI--7

SOCKS
    Darning his socks in the night when there's
        nobody there--ELEANORRIG--15
    Everybody pulled their socks up (yeah) --IVEGOTAFEE
        --26
    Everybody pulled their socks up (oh no, no) --
        IVEGOTAFEE--34

SOFA
    Sitting on a sofa with a sister or two.--LOVELYRITA
        --25

SOLD
    They bought and sold you.--WHILEMYGUI--8

SOLID
    Ten somersets he'll undertake on solid ground.--
        BEINGFORTH--18

SOLITUDE

Some kind of solitude is measured out in you--
    HEYBULLDOG--15

SOLO

Standing solo in the sun.--TWOOFUS--20
Standing solo in the sun.--TWOOFUS--29

SOLUTION

You say you got a real solution --REVOLUTION--12
You say you got a real solution --REVOLUTONE--19

SOME

Then we'll have some fun when you're mine, all
    mine --LITTLECHIL--10
But I'll come back again some day.--ILLCRYINST--14
But I'll come back again some day.--ILLCRYINST--23
Some day you'll know I was the one --ILLFOLLOWT--3
If I had some more time to spend,--IFINEEDEDS--4
Had you come some other day --IFINEEDEDS--7
If I had some more time to spend --IFINEEDEDS--14
Had you come some other day --IFINEEDEDS--17
All my life, though some have changed.--INMYLIFE
    --2
Some forever, not for better --INMYLIFE--3
Some have gone and some remain.--INMYLIFE--4
Some have gone and some remain.--INMYLIFE--4
Some are dead and some are living --INMYLIFE--7
Some are dead and some are living --INMYLIFE--7
If you don't want to pay some more (ha ha Mr.
    Heath)--TAXMAN--19
Having been some days in preparation--BEINGFORTH
    --19
To take some tea with me? ((maid))--LOVELYRITA--16
But if you want some fun (ha ha ha) --OBLADIOBLA
    --40
Some kind of happiness is measured out in miles--
    HEYBULLDOG--3
Some kind of innocence is measured out in years--
    HEYBULLDOG--7
Some kind of solitude is measured out in you--
    HEYBULLDOG--15
For some California grass.--GETBACK/45--4
I said we're only trying to get us some peace.--
    BALLADOFJO--20
From where some try to drag me down --OLDBROWNSH
    --10
Saving up to buy some clothes--MEANMRMUST--5
For some California grass.--GETBACK/LP--10

SOMEBODY

Someone to love, somebody new.--LOVEMEDO--11
If you need somebody to love --ANYTIMEATA--4
If somebody tries to take my place --IMHAPPYJUS--16
If somebody tries to take my place --IMHAPPYJUS--24
I need somebody--HELP--2
But as from today well I've got somebody that's
    new --ANOTHERGIR--3
But as from today well I've seen somebody that's
    new --ANOTHERGIR--13
But as from today well I've seen somebody that's
    new,--ANOTHERGIR--19
Leave it all till somebody else lends you a hand.
    --NOWHEREMAN--15
And somebody spoke and I went into a dream--
    DAYINTHELI--26
Somebody needs to know the time glad that I'm here
    --GOODMORNIN--22
Somebody calls you, you answer quite slowly--
    LUCYINTHES--3
I need somebody to love.--WITHALITTL--16
I want somebody to love.--WITHALITTL--18
I want somebody to love.--WITHALITTL--29
And if somebody loved me like she do me --
    DONTLETMED--7
All that I was looking for was somebody who
    looked like you.--IVEGOTAFEE--13

SOMEDAY

Though he'll regret it someday--THISBOY--2
Someday when I'm lonely --THINGSWESA--3
Someday when we're dreaming --THINGSWESA--8
Someday when we're dreaming --THINGSWESA--19
Someday when we're dreaming --THINGSWESA--30
I'll live and love and maybe someday --OLDBROWNSH
    --20
Someday I'm gonna make her mine - oh yeah --
    HERMAJESTY--8
Someday I'm gonna make her mine.--HERMAJESTY--9

SOMEHOW

I'd try to make you sad somehow --ILLCRYINST--9
You'll be thinking of me, somehow I will know --
    THINGSWESA--2
I'll get to you somehow--MICHELLE--18

SOMEONE

Someone to love, somebody new.--LOVEMEDO--11
Someone to love, someone like you.--LOVEMEDO--12
Someone to love, someone like you.--LOVEMEDO--12
If you want someone to make you feel so fine--
    LITTLECHIL--9
I'm a loser and I lost someone who's near to me --
    IMALOSER--7
I'm a loser and I lost someone who's near to me --
    IMALOSER--13
I'm a loser and I lost someone who's near to me --
    IMALOSER--19
You know I need someone--HELP--6
IF I NEEDED SOMEONE.--IFINEEDEDS--Title
If I needed someone to love --IFINEEDEDS--1
If I needed someone.--IFINEEDEDS--3
If I needed someone.--IFINEEDEDS--6
If I needed someone.--IFINEEDEDS--12
If I needed someone.--IFINEEDEDS--16
If I needed someone.--IFINEEDEDS--22
You didn't even think of me as someone with a name.
    --WHATGOESON--23
She says that long ago she knew someone --FORNOONE
    --18
Someone is speaking but she doesn't know he's
    there.--HERETHEREA--7
It's getting hard to be someone--STRAWBERRY--8
Suddenly someone is there at the turnstyle--
    LUCYINTHES--25
I just need someone to love.--WITHALITTL--27
You're waiting for someone to perform with.--
    HEYJUDE--21
I don't know how someone controlled you --
    WHILEMYGUI--7

SOMEONE'S

Spending someone's hard-earned pay.--TWOOFUS--4

SOMERSETS

Ten somersets he'll undertake on solid ground.--
    BEINGFORTH--18

SOMETHING

Oh yeah, I'll tell you something--IWANTTOHOL--1
When I say that something--IWANTTOHOL--3
Yeah, you've got that something--IWANTTOHOL--20
When I say that something--IWANTTOHOL--22
Yeah, you've got that something--IWANTTOHOL--33
When I feel that something--IWANTTOHOL--35
I got something to say--YOUCANTDOT--1
If it's something that I said or done --TELLMEWHY
    --13
I said something wrong--YESTERDAY--11
I said something wrong--YESTERDAY--19
But you can do something in between.--DRIVEMYCAR
    --4
And she said listen babe I've got something to
    say --DRIVEMYCAR--23
When I think of love as something new.--INMYLIFE
    --12
I've got something I can laugh about.--GOODDAYSUN
    --3
Nobody can deny that there's something there.--
    HERETHEREA--4
Something inside that was always denied--SHESLEAVIN
    --31
EVERYBODY'S GOT SOMETHING TO HIDE EXCEPT ME
    AND MY MONKEY.--EVRBDYMONK--Title
Everybody's got something to hide 'cept for me
    and my monkey - wuh.--EVRBDYMONK--7
Everybody's got something to hide 'cept for me
    and my monkey (yeah - wuh).--EVRBDYMONK--16
Everybody's got something to hide 'cept for me
    and my monkey - hey.--EVRBDYMONK--25
In their lives there's something lacking--PIGGIES
    --13
What makes you think you're something special
    when you smile?--HEYBULLDOG--4
My love is something you can't reject.--OLDBROWNSH
    --23
To miss that love is something I'd hate.--
    OLDBROWNSH--28

SOMETHING

Always shouts out something obscene--MEANMRMUST--13
SOMETHING.--SOMETHING--Title
Something in the way she moves--SOMETHING--1
Something in the way she woos me --SOMETHING--3
Something in her style that shows me --SOMETHING
    --8
Something in the way she knows--SOMETHING--15
Something in the things she shows me --SOMETHING
    --17

SOMETIMES

Sometimes I wish I knew you well--IWANTTOTEL--16
Always, no, sometimes, think it's me--STRAWBERRY
    --26
Who sometimes wears it twice as long.--OLDBROWNSH
    --4

SOMEWHERE

Now somewhere in the Black Mountain hills of
    Dakota --ROCKYRACCO--1
Somewhere in her smile she knows--SOMETHING--6

SON

His son is working for the Daily Mail --PAPERBACKW
    --10
He's the all-American bullet-headed Saxon
    mother's son.--CONTINUING--9
MOTHER NATURE'S SON.--MOTHERNATU--Title
Born a poor young country boy - Mother Nature's
    son --MOTHERNATU--1
Find me in my field of grass - Mother Nature's
    son --MOTHERNATU--8
Aah Mother Nature's son.--MOTHERNATU--16

SONG

That the singer's gonna sing a song--SGTPEPPERS--21
Lend me your ears and I'll sing you a song--
    WITHALITTL--3
Let's all get up and dance to a song--YOURMOTHER
    --2
Let's all get up and dance to a song--YOURMOTHER
    --8
Lift up your hearts and sing me a song--YOURMOTHER
    --13
Take a sad song and make it better --HEYJUDE--2
Take a sad song and make it better --HEYJUDE--27
(Take a sad song and make it better)--HEYJUDE--48
Of your Hollywood song.--HONEYPIE--12
Your song will fill the air --IWILL--14
So I sing the song of love, Julia.--JULIA--4
So I sing the song of love, Julia.--JULIA--6
So I sing the song of love, Julia.--JULIA--10
So I sing a song of love, Julia.--JULIA--14
So I sing a song of love for Julia--JULIA--16
Swaying daisies sing a lazy song beneath the sun.
    --MOTHERNATU--9
The story of Rocky, that's the song.--ROCKYRACCO
    --48
ONLY A NORTHERN SONG.--ONLYANORTH--Title
If you're listening to this song --ONLYANORTH--1
As it's only a Northern song.--ONLYANORTH--9
When it's only a Northern song.--ONLYANORTH--12

SONGS

Make love singing songs.--LOVEYOUTWO--10
Make love singing songs.--LOVEYOUTWO--12
All day long I'm sitting singing songs for
    everyone.--MOTHERNATU--2

SONT

Sont des mots qui vont tres bien ensemble, tres
    bien ensemble.--MICHELLE--4
Sont des mots qui vont tres bien ensemble, tres
    bien ensemble.--MICHELLE--10
Sont des mots qui vont tres bien ensemble, tres
    bien ensemble.--MICHELLE--21

SOON

Run the risk of knowing that our love may soon be
    gone.--WECANWORKI--4
We'll be over soon they said --BLUEJAYWAY--3
Soon will be the break of day (day) --BLUEJAYWAY
    --17
And I'll be better, I'll be better Doc as
    soon as I am able.--ROCKYRACCO--35
Soon we'll be away from here --YOUNEVERGI--19

SOOTHING

Your voice is soothing but the words aren't clear.
    --IMLOOKINGT--6

SORROW

In my mind there's no sorrow--THERESAPLA--9
Pools of sorrow, waves of joy--ACROSSTHEU--3

SORRY

If you're feeling sorry and sad --ANYTIMEATA--7
She's the kind of girl you want so much it makes
    you sorry --GIRL--3
We're sorry but it's time to go.--SGTPEPPREP--6
I'm sorry that I doubted you --DONTPASSME--23

SOUL

Who gain the world and lose their soul--WITHINYOUW
    --24
Blue mist round my soul --YERBLUES--25
You don't take nothing with you but your soul -
    think!--BALLADOFJO--28
Oh my soul.--IVEGOTAFEE--39

SOUND

You don't sound different, I've learned the game
    --IMLOOKINGT--7
You tell me that you heard every sound there is --
    ANDYOURBIR--13
When Mr. K. performs his tricks - without a
    sound.--BEINGFORTH--16
Or the sound he appears to make--FOOLONTHEH--11
Listen to the pretty sound of music as she flies.
    --MOTHERNATU--4
I wake up to the sound of music --LETITBE/45--24
I wake up to the sound of music --LETITBE/LP--24

SOUNDS

Sounds of laughter, shades of life--ACROSSTHEU--20

SOUR

But what is sweet now turns so sour.--SAVOYTRUFF
    --20

SOUTH

Oh - show me round the snow-peaked mountains way
    down south --BACKINTHEU--31

SOUTHAMPTON

Standing in the dock at Southampton --BALLADOFJO
    --1

SPACE

About the space between us all--WITHINYOUW--2

SPAIN

You can get married in Gibraltar near Spain.--
    BALLADOFJO--12

SPEAK

Then I could speak my mind and tell you--IWANTTOTEL
    --17
I can only speak my mind, Julia.--JULIA--12

SPEAKING

Someone is speaking but she doesn't know he's
    there.--HERETHEREA--7
Coming down fast (oh I hear my baby speaking -
    ooo)...--HELTERSKEL--30
Speaking words of wisdom, let it be.--LETITBE/45
    --3
Speaking words of wisdom, let it be.--LETITBE/45
    --6
Speaking words of wisdom, let it be.--LETITBE/45
    --26
Speaking words of wisdom, let it be.--LETITBE/LP
    --3
Speaking words of wisdom, let it be.--LETITBE/LP
    --6
Speaking words of wisdom, let it be.--LETITBE/LP
    --26

SPECIAL
    Take a drink from his special cup, Dr. Robert.--
        DRROBERT--7
    I feel good in a special way --GOODDAYSUN--4
    What makes you think you're something special
        when you smile?--HEYBULLDOG--4

SPECIALLY
    Put on specially by the children for a lark.--
        CRYBABYCRY--31

SPEED
    Running everywhere at such a speed --IMONLYSLEE--9
    (Full speed ahead, Mr. Bosun, full speed
        ahead.--YELLOWSUBM--20
    (Full speed ahead, Mr. Bosun, full speed
        ahead.--YELLOWSUBM--20
    Full speed ahead it is, Sgt.--YELLOWSUBM--21

SPEND
    If I had some more time to spend --IFINEEDEDS--4
    If I had some more time to spend --IFINEEDEDS--14
    And I can't spend my whole life trying--RUNFORYOUR
        --11
    Martha my dear, though I spend my days in
        conversation --MARTHAMYDE--1

SPENDING
    Spending someone's hard-earned pay.--TWOOFUS--4

SPENT
    Out of college, money spent --YOUNEVERGI--7

SPINAL
    He one spinal cracker--COMETOGETH--28

SPINNING
    And the eyes in his head see the world spinning
        round.--FOOLONTHEH--7
    And the eyes in his head see the world spinning
        round.--FOOLONTHEH--14
    And the eyes in his head see the world spinning
        round.--FOOLONTHEH--19
    And the eyes in his head see the world spinning
        round.--FOOLONTHEH--26

SPITE
    In spite of you it's true--YESITIS--17
    In spite of you it's true--YESITIS--26

SPLENDID
    A splendid time is guaranteed for all--BEINGFORTH
        --20

SPOIL
    I DON'T WANT TO SPOIL THE PARTY.--IDONTWANTT--Title
    I don't wanna spoil the party so I'll go --
        IDONTWANTT--1
    I don't wanna spoil the party so I'll go --
        IDONTWANTT--13
    Please don't spoil my day, I'm miles away --
        IMONLYSLEE--11
    Please don't spoil my day, I'm miles away --
        IMONLYSLEE--17

SPOKE
    And somebody spoke and I went into a dream--
        DAYINTHELI--26

SPOON
    Protected by a silver spoon --SHECAMEINT--5

SPREAD
    Spread the word and you'll be free --THEWORD--9
    Spread the word and be like me --THEWORD--10
    Spread the word I'm thinking of --THEWORD--11

STAIRS
    Standing alone at the top of the stairs--SHESLEAVIN
        --15

STAND
    'cos I couldn't stand the pain --IFIFELL--14
    'cos I couldn't stand the pain --IFIFELL--21
    'cos I really can't stand it --TELLMEWHY--24
    'cos I couldn't really stand it--YOULIKEMET--17
    'cos I couldn't really stand it--YOULIKEMET--26
    Here I stand head in hand--YOUVEGOTTO--1
    Would you stand up and walk out on me?--WITHALITTL
        --2

STANDING
    I SAW HER STANDING THERE.--ISAWHERSTA--Title
    Ooh when I saw her standing there.--ISAWHERSTA--6
    Whoa when I saw her standing there.--ISAWHERSTA--10
    Whoa since/when I saw her standing there. (hey! aah!)--
        ISAWHERSTA--17
    Oh since I saw her standing there.--ISAWHERSTA--24
    Whoa since I saw here standing there--ISAWHERSTA--25
    Yeah, well since I saw her standing there.--
        ISAWHERSTA--26
    There's people standing round--LOVEYOUTWO--13
    See the people standing there who disagree and
        never win--FIXINGAHOL--9
    Standing by a parking meter--LOVELYRITA--7
    Standing alone at the top of the stairs--SHESLEAVIN
        --15
    If the sun don't come you get a tan from standing
        in the English rain--IAMTHEWALR--18
    Standing on the cast-iron shore - yeah--GLASSONION
        --12
    Sheep dog standing in the rain--HEYBULLDOG--1
    Standing in the dock at Southampton --BALLADOFJO
        --1
    She is standing right in front of me --LETITBE/45
        --5
    She is standing right in front of me --LETITBE/LP
        --5
    Why leave me standing here, let me know the way.--
        LONGANDWIN--6
    You left me standing here a long, long time ago --
        LONGANDWIN--10
    You left me standing here a long, long time ago --
        LONGANDWIN--13
    Standing solo in the sun.--TWOOFUS--20
    Standing solo in the sun.--TWOOFUS--29

STANDS
    She only played one night stands --DAYTRIPPER--19
    And she only played one night stands, now.--
        DAYTRIPPER--21
    PC Thirty-One said, we caught a dirty one,
        Maxwell stands alone --MAXWELLSIL--17

STAR
    I wanna be famous, a star of the screen --
        DRIVEMYCAR--3
    Yes I'm gonna be a star.--DRIVEMYCAR--6
    Yes I'm gonna be a star.--DRIVEMYCAR--14
    Yes I'm gonna be a star.--DRIVEMYCAR--19
    Yes I'm gonna be star.--DRIVEMYCAR--27

STARCHED
    In the starched white shirts?--PIGGIES--7

STARE
    I get shy when they start to stare.--ILLCRYINST--12
    I get shy when they start to stare.--ILLCRYINST--21
    Everywhere people stare --YOUVEGOTTO--5

STARED
    A crowd of people stood and stared--DAYINTHELI--8

STARING
    Lying there and staring at the ceiling --IMONLYSLEE
        --15

STARS
    Bright are the stars that shine --ANDILOVEHE--15
    Bright are the stars that shine --ANDILOVEHE--20

START
    I don't want to start complaining --PLEASEPLEA--13
    I must be sure from the very start --IFIFELL--8

I get shy when they start to stare.--ILLCRYINST--12
I get shy when they start to stare.--ILLCRYINST--21
I told that girl I could start right away --
    DRIVEMYCAR--22
But I've found a driver and that's a start.--
    DRIVEMYCAR--25
She will turn to me and start to cry --GIRL--7
When your prized possessions start to weigh you
    down --ANDYOURBIR--7
Heading for home you start to roam then you're in
    town.--GOODMORNIN--8
After a while you start to smile now you feel cool
    --GOODMORNIN--13
Watching the skirts you start to flirt now you're
    in gear--GOODMORNIN--23
Then you can start to make it better.--HEYJUDE--4
Then you can start to make it better.--HEYJUDE--18
Make an early start --OLDBROWNSH--29

STARTED
    And started to laugh--NORWEGIANW--18

STARTS
    I can show you that when it starts to rain (when
        the rain comes down)--RAIN--9

STATE
    In the state I'm in.--YOUVEGOTTO--14
    It's just a state of mind (when it rains and
        shines)--RAIN--15

STATING
    Stating point of view.--WHENIMSIXT--29

STATION
    Picture yourself on a train in a station--
        LUCYINTHES--23
    Pick up my bag, run to the station --ONEAFTERNI--11
    Pick up my bag, run to the station --ONEAFTERNI--21

STAY
    Just stay away--DONTBOTHER--21
    Just stay away--DONTBOTHER--36
    If you wanna stay mine--YOUCANTDOT--24
    If you wanna stay mine--YOUCANTDOT--43
    Love is here to stay.--THINGSWESA--14
    Love is here to stay.--THINGSWESA--25
    Now it looks as though they're here to stay--
        YESTERDAY--3
    All about the girl who came to stay?--GIRL--2
    She asked me to stay--NORWEGIANW--7
    I won't want to stay, I don't have much to say --
        YOUWONTSEE--9
    Stay in bed, float upstream (float upstream).--
        IMONLYSLEE--4
    Stay in bed, float upstream (float upstream).--
        IMONLYSLEE--24
    You stay home, she goes out --FORNOONE--17
    When I'm with you I want to stay there--GOTTOGETYO
        --17
    I could stay with you.--WHENIMSIXT--12
    ((I can stay till it's time to go)).--HELLOGOODB
        --25
    She tells Max to stay when the class has gone
        away --MAXWELLSIL--10

STAYS
    Molly stays at home and does her pretty face--
        OBLADIOBLA--23
    Desmond stays at home and does his pretty face--
        OBLADIOBLA--34

STEADY
    It's a steady job --PAPERBACKW--11
    And got myself a steady job--SHECAMEINT--17

STEAL
    She could steal but she could not rob.--SHECAMEINT
        --19

STEALING
    By stealing the girl of his fancy --ROCKYRACCO--14

STEP
    Step right this way.--MAGICALMYS--2
    Step on the gas and wipe that tear away.--
        YOUNEVERGI--20

STEPPING
    Stepping outside she is free.--SHESLEAVIN--7
    Now I'm stepping out this old brown shoe --
        OLDBROWNSH--5

STICK
    Umpa, umpa, stick it up your jumper ((joob -
        joob))--IAMTHEWALR--35
    Umpa, umpa, stick it up your jumper.--IAMTHEWALR
        --36
    You stick around now it may show --SOMETHING--13

STIES
    In their sties with all their backing--PIGGIES--11

STILL
    I still love her.--IDONTWANTT--10
    I still love her.--IDONTWANTT--12
    I still love her.--IDONTWANTT--19
    I still love her.--IDONTWANTT--21
    You still moan keep your hands to yourself --IMDOWN
        --17
    You can get it wrong and still you think that
        it's alright.--WECANWORKI--7
    Still you don't regret a single day.--GIRL--4
    Will she still believe it when he's dead?--GIRL--25
    With lovers and friends I still can recall --
        INMYLIFE--6
    And though you still can't see --THINKFORYO--12
    The future still looks good --THINKFORYO--21
    Lift my head, I'm still yawning.--IMONLYSLEE--2
    Lift my head, I'm still yawning.--IMONLYSLEE--22
    And I still go.--FIXINGAHOL--21
    Nothing has changed it's still the same--GOODMORNIN
        --15
    Will you still be sending me a valentine--
        WHENIMSIXT--3
    Will you still need me --WHENIMSIXT--7
    Will you still feed me --WHENIMSIXT--8
    Will you still need me --WHENIMSIXT--19
    Will you still feed me --WHENIMSIXT--20
    A - will you still need me --WHENIMSIXT--35
    Will you still feed me --WHENIMSIXT--36
    The man with the foolish grin is keeping
        perfectly still--FOOLONTHEH--2
    I tell you man he living there still--GLASSONION
        --18
    You know I love you still.--IWILL--2
    And in the evening she still sings it with the
        band, yes.--OBLADIOBLA--24
    Still my guitar gently weeps.--WHILEMYGUI--5
    Still my guitar gently weeps.--WHILEMYGUI--12
    Still my guitar gently weeps ((eee)).--WHILEMYGUI--21
    There is still a chance that they will see --
        LETITBE/45--13
    There is still a light that shines on me --
        LETITBE/45--22
    There is still a chance that they will see --
        LETITBE/LP--13
    There is still a light that shines on me --
        LETITBE/LP--22
    And still they lead me back to the long, winding
        road.--LONGANDWIN--9
    But still they lead me back to the long, winding
        road --LONGANDWIN--12

STINKING
    Now the doctor came in stinking of gin--ROCKYRACCO
        --31

STIRRING
    Stirring up the dirt --PIGGIES--9

STOCKINGS
    Thursday night your stockings needed mending.--
        LADYMADONN--16

STONE
    Like a rolling stone--DIGIT--1
    Like a rolling stone--DIGIT--2
    A - like a rolling stone--DIGIT--3

STONY
    Oh now I roll a stony--IDIGAPONY--19

STOOD
    A crowd of people stood and stared--DAYINTHELI--8

STOP
    Can't stop thinking about her now.--EVERYLITTL--6
    Please ((please)) stop your lying --WHATYOURED--12
    Please ((please)) stop your lying --WHATYOURED--19
    And so I'm telling you this time you'd better
        stop,--ANOTHERGIR--8
    I know I'll often stop and think about them --
        INMYLIFE--15
    I know I'll often stop and think about them --
        INMYLIFE--19
    Stop and say hello.--PENNYLANE--4
    I don't really want to stop the show--SGTPEPPERS
        --19
    You say stop and I say go, go, go.--HELLOGOODB--2
    You say stop but I say go, go, go--HELLOGOODB--24
    Where I stop and I turn and I go for a ride --
        HELTERSKEL--2
    And I stop and I turn and I go for a ride--
        HELTERSKEL--19
    You know I can't sleep, I can't stop my brain --
        IMSOTIRED--11
    You know I can't sleep, I can't stop my brain --
        IMSOTIRED--20

STOPS
    And stops my mind from wandering--FIXINGAHOL--2
    Stops my mind from wandering--FIXINGAHOL--24
    Stops my mind from wandering--FIXINGAHOL--27
    She never stops--MEANMRMUST--9

STORE
    Desmond takes a trolly to the jewellery store --
        OBLADIOBLA--9

STORM
    We would be warm below the storm--OCTOPUSSGA--9

STORY
    Is there anybody going to listen to my story--GIRL
        --1
    It's a dirty story of a dirty man --PAPERBACKW--8
    THE CONTINUING STORY OF BUNGALOW BILL.--CONTINUING
        --Title
    The story of Rocky, that's the song.--ROCKYRACCO
        --48

STRAIGHT
    We can work it out and get it straight or say
        good night.--WECANWORKI--9

STRANGE
    In the pouring rain - very strange.--PENNYLANE--8
    From the pouring rain - very strange.--PENNYLANE
        --27

STRAWBERRY
    STRAWBERRY FIELDS FOREVER.--STRAWBERRY--Title
    'cos I'm going to strawberry fields--STRAWBERRY--2
    Strawberry fields forever.--STRAWBERRY--5
    'cos I'm going to strawberry fields--STRAWBERRY--12
    Strawberry fields forever.--STRAWBERRY--15
    'cos I'm going to strawberry fields--STRAWBERRY--22
    Strawberry fields forever.--STRAWBERRY--25
    'cos I'm going to strawberry fields--STRAWBERRY--32
    Strawberry fields forever.--STRAWBERRY--35
    Strawberry fields forever.--STRAWBERRY--36
    Strawberry fields forever.--STRAWBERRY--37
    I told you about Strawberry Fields--GLASSONION--1

STREAM
    Sit beside a mountain stream - see her waters rise
        --MOTHERNATU--3
    Floating down the stream of time--ITSALLTOOM--12

STREET
    If you drive a car, I'll tax the street,
        ((car))--TAXMAN--11

And you're on your own you're in the street.--
    GOODMORNIN--12
Ask a policeman on the street --BLUEJAYWAY--10

STRETCHES
    Longer than the road that stretches out ahead.--
        TWOOFUS--18
    Longer than the road that stretches out ahead.--
        TWOOFUS--27

STRONG
    And if your heart's strong, hold on, I won't
        delay.--WAIT--6
    And if your heart's strong, hold on, I won't
        delay.--WAIT--22

STRONGER
    Coming off stronger all the time --IMEMINE--7

STRUGGLED
    Home. (we struggled hard all our lives to get by)
        --SHESLEAVIN--22

STUDIED
    Joan was quizzical, studied pataphysical science
        in the home --MAXWELLSIL--1

STUPID
    Corporation T-shirt, stupid bloody Tuesday--
        IAMTHEWALR--5
    He was such a stupid get.--IMSOTIRED--17

STY
    See how they smile, like pigs in a sty, see how
        they snied--IAMTHEWALR--23

STYLE
    I can make it longer if you like the style,
        ((paperback))--PAPERBACKW--17
    They've been going in and out of style--SGTPEPPERS
        --3
    Something in her style that shows me --SOMETHING
        --8

SUBMARINE
    YELLOW SUBMARINE.--YELLOWSUBM--Title
    In our yellow submarine.--YELLOWSUBM--8
    We all live in a yellow submarine --YELLOWSUBM--9
    Yellow submarine, yellow submarine.--YELLOWSUBM--10
    Yellow submarine, yellow submarine.--YELLOWSUBM--10
    We all live in a yellow submarine --YELLOWSUBM--11
    Yellow submarine, yellow submarine.--YELLOWSUBM--12
    Yellow submarine, yellow submarine.--YELLOWSUBM--12
    We all live in a yellow submarine --YELLOWSUBM--16
    Yellow submarine, yellow submarine.--YELLOWSUBM--17
    Yellow submarine, yellow submarine.--YELLOWSUBM--17
    We all live in a yellow submarine --YELLOWSUBM--18
    Yellow submarine, yellow submarine.--YELLOWSUBM--19
    Yellow submarine, yellow submarine.--YELLOWSUBM--19
    In our yellow (in our yellow) submarine
        (submarine - ah ha!)--YELLOWSUBM--28
    In our yellow (in our yellow) submarine
        (submarine - ah ha!)--YELLOWSUBM--28
    We all live in a yellow submarine --YELLOWSUBM--29
    A yellow submarine, a yellow submarine.--YELLOWSUBM
        --30
    A yellow submarine, a yellow submarine.--YELLOWSUBM
        --30
    We all live in a yellow submarine --YELLOWSUBM--31
    A yellow submarine, yellow submarine.--YELLOWSUBM
        --32
    A yellow submarine, yellow submarine.--YELLOWSUBM
        --32
    We all live in a yellow submarine --YELLOWSUBM--33
    Yellow submarine, yellow submarine.--YELLOWSUBM--34
    Yellow submarine, yellow submarine.--YELLOWSUBM--34
    We all live in a yellow submarine --YELLOWSUBM--35
    Yellow submarine, yellow submarine.--YELLOWSUBM--36
    Yellow submarine, yellow submarine.--YELLOWSUBM--36

SUBMARINES
    In the land of submarines.--YELLOWSUBM--4

SUBURBAN
    There beneath the blue suburban skies I sit--
        PENNYLANE--10
    There beneath the blue suburban skies I sit--
        PENNYLANE--29
    There beneath the blue suburban skies --PENNYLANE
        --32

SUCCEED
    No-one can succeed like Dr. Robert.--DRROBERT--10

SUCCESS
    The men from the press said, we wish you success
        --BALLADOFJO--39

SUCH
    It's such a feeling--IWANTTOHOL--15
    It's such a feeling--IWANTTOHOL--28
    These days such a kind girl seems so hard to find
        --THINGSWESA--7
    What have I done to deserve such a fate?--IMALOSER
        --15
    Love was such an easy game to play--YESTERDAY--14
    Love was such an easy game to play--YESTERDAY--22
    Running everywhere at such a speed --IMONLYSLEE--9
    But what you've got means such a lot to me.--
        LOVEYOUTWO--8
    You're such a lovely audience--SGTPEPPERS--16
    Come on is such a joy --EVRBDYMONK--2
    Come on is such a joy --EVRBDYMONK--3
    Come on is such a joy --EVRBDYMONK--11
    Come on is such a joy --EVRBDYMONK--12
    Come on is such a joy --EVRBDYMONK--20
    Come on is such a joy --EVRBDYMONK--21
    He was such a stupid get.--IMSOTIRED--17
    Such a mean old man, such a mean old man.--
        MEANMRMUST--7
    Such a mean old man, such a mean old man.--
        MEANMRMUST--7
    Such a dirty old man, dirty old man.--MEANMRMUST
        --14

SUCKS
    But now she sucks her thumb and wonders --
        SHECAMEINT--6

SUDDENLY
    Suddenly --YESTERDAY--5
    Oh yesterday came suddenly.--YESTERDAY--8
    Ooo then I suddenly see you--GOTTOGETYO--5
    Ooo then I suddenly see you--GOTTOGETYO--20
    Then suddenly I see you--GOTTOGETYO--29
    Suddenly someone is there at the turnstyle--
        LUCYINTHES--25

SUICIDAL
    Feel so suicidal --YERBLUES--19
    Feels so suicidal--YERBLUES--26

SUITCASE
    Friday night arrives without a suitcase --
        LADYMADONN--5

SUMMER
    A four of fish and finger pies in summer--PENNYLANE
        --18
    Every summer we can rent a cottage--WHENIMSIXT--22

SUN
    If the sun has faded away --ANYTIMEATA--13
    I'LL FOLLOW THE SUN.--ILLFOLLOWT--Title
    For tomorrow may rain so I'll follow the sun.--
        ILLFOLLOWT--2
    For tomorrow may rain so I'll follow the sun.--
        ILLFOLLOWT--4
    For tomorrow may rain so I'll follow the sun.--
        ILLFOLLOWT--8
    Yeah, tomorrow may rain so I'll follow the sun.--
        ILLFOLLOWT--9
    For tomorrow may rain so I'll follow the sun.--
        ILLFOLLOWT--13
    When the sun shines they slip into the shade
        (when the sun shines down)--RAIN--4
    When the sun shines they slip into the shade
        (when the sun shines down)--RAIN--4

And sip their lemonade (when the sun shines down)
    --RAIN--5
When the sun shines, when the sun shines ((sun
    shine)).--RAIN--6
When the sun shines, when the sun shines ((sun
    shine)).--RAIN--6
When the sun shines, when the sun shines ((sun
    shine)).--RAIN--6
I need to laugh and when the sun is out --
    GOODDAYSUN--2
We take a walk, the sun is shining down --
    GOODDAYSUN--7
So we sailed on to the sun--YELLOWSUBM--5
Look for the girl with the sun in her eyes--
    LUCYINTHES--7
Sitting in an English garden waiting for the sun--
    IAMTHEWALR--17
If the sun don't come you get a tan from standing
    in the English rain--IAMTHEWALR--18
But the fool on the hill sees the sun going down--
    FOOLONTHEH--6
But the fool on the hill sees the sun going down--
    FOOLONTHEH--13
But the fool on the hill sees the sun going down--
    FOOLONTHEH--18
The fool on the hill sees the sun going down--
    FOOLONTHEH--25
The sun is up, the sky is blue --DEARPRUDEN--3
The sun is up, the sky is blue --DEARPRUDEN--23
Now the sun turns out his light --GOODNIGHT--3
Now the sun turns out his light --GOODNIGHT--16
Glimmering in the sun.--JULIA--8
Swaying daisies sing a lazy song beneath the sun.
    --MOTHERNATU--9
Sail me on a silver sun --ITSALLTOOM--21
HERE COMES THE SUN.--HERECOMEST--Title
Here comes the sun (do-n-do-do) --HERECOMEST--1
Here comes the sun,--HERECOMEST--2
Here comes the sun (do-n-do-do) --HERECOMEST--6
Here comes the sun,--HERECOMEST--7
Here comes the sun, here comes the sun --HERECOMEST
    --11
Here comes the sun, here comes the sun --HERECOMEST
    --11
Sun, sun, sun, here it comes --HERECOMEST--13
Sun, sun, sun, here it comes --HERECOMEST--13
Sun, sun, sun, here it comes --HERECOMEST--13
Sun, sun, sun, here it comes --HERECOMEST--14
Sun, sun, sun, here it comes --HERECOMEST--14
Sun, sun, sun, here it comes --HERECOMEST--14
Sun, sun, sun, here it comes --HERECOMEST--15
Sun, sun, sun, here it comes --HERECOMEST--15
Sun, sun, sun, here it comes --HERECOMEST--15
Sun, sun, sun, here it comes --HERECOMEST--16
Sun, sun, sun, here it comes --HERECOMEST--16
Sun, sun, sun, here it comes --HERECOMEST--16
Sun, sun, sun, here it comes.--HERECOMEST--17
Sun, sun, sun, here it comes.--HERECOMEST--17
Sun, sun, sun, here it comes.--HERECOMEST--17
Here comes the sun (do-n-do-do) --HERECOMEST--20
Here comes the sun --HERECOMEST--21
Here comes the sun (do-n-do-do) --HERECOMEST--23
Here comes the sun --HERECOMEST--24
SUN KING.--SUNKING--Title
Aah - here come the Sun King --SUNKING--1
Here come the Sun King.--SUNKING--2
Here come the Sun King.--SUNKING--5
Everybody saw the sun shine --IVEGOTAFEE--22
Everybody saw the sun shine.--IVEGOTAFEE--31
Standing solo in the sun.--TWOOFUS--20
Standing solo in the sun.--TWOOFUS--29

SUNDAY
    Sunday driver, yeah --DAYTRIPPER--23
    Sunday mornings go for a ride.--WHENIMSIXT--16
    Sunday morning creeping like a nun --LADYMADONN--6
    You and me Sunday driving --TWOOFUS--5

SUNDAYS
    Sundays on the phone to Monday --SHECAMEINT--10
    Sundays on the phone to Monday --SHECAMEINT--22

SUNG
    Nothing you can sing that can't be sung ((love))--
        ALLYOUN/YS--5

SUNKEN
    Take these sunken eyes and learn to see.--BLACKBIRD
        --6

SUNNY
    I'm in love and it's a sunny day.--GOODDAYSUN--5
    Dear Prudence, see the sunny skies.--DEARPRUDEN--7
    One sunny day the world was waiting for the lover
       ((sexy Sadie))--SEXYSADIE--9

SUNS
    Limitless undying love which shines around me
       like a million suns --ACROSSTHEU--23

SUNSHINE
    It's so fine, it's sunshine --THEWORD--5
    It's so fine, it's sunshine --THEWORD--13
    It's so fine, it's sunshine --THEWORD--21
    It's so fine, it's sunshine --THEWORD--29
    GOOD DAY SUNSHINE.--GOODDAYSUN--Title
    Good day sunshine, good day sunshine, good day
       sunshine.--GOODDAYSUN--1
    Good day sunshine, good day sunshine, good day
       sunshine.--GOODDAYSUN--1
    Good day sunshine, good day sunshine, good day
       sunshine.--GOODDAYSUN--1
    Good day sunshine, good day sunshine, good day
       sunshine.--GOODDAYSUN--6
    Good day sunshine, good day sunshine, good day
       sunshine.--GOODDAYSUN--6
    Good day sunshine, good day sunshine, good day
       sunshine.--GOODDAYSUN--6
    Good day sunshine, good day sunshine, good day
       sunshine.--GOODDAYSUN--9
    Good day sunshine, good day sunshine, good day
       sunshine.--GOODDAYSUN--9
    Good day sunshine, good day sunshine, good day
       sunshine.--GOODDAYSUN--9
    Good day sunshine, good day sunshine, good day
       sunshine.--GOODDAYSUN--14
    Good day sunshine, good day sunshine, good day
       sunshine.--GOODDAYSUN--14
    Good day sunshine, good day sunshine, good day
       sunshine.--GOODDAYSUN--14
    Good day sunshine, good day sunshine, good day
       sunshine.--GOODDAYSUN--15
    Good day sunshine, good day sunshine, good day
       sunshine.--GOODDAYSUN--15
    Good day sunshine, good day sunshine, good day
       sunshine.--GOODDAYSUN--15
    Good day sunshine (good day sunshine) (good
       day sunshine) --GOODDAYSUN--16
    Good day sunshine (good day sunshine) (good
       day sunshine) --GOODDAYSUN--16
    Good day sunshine (good day sunshine) (good
       day sunshine) --GOODDAYSUN--16
    (Good day sunshine) (good day...--GOODDAYSUN--17

SUPERIOR
    Mother Superior jump the gun --HAPPINESSI--12
    Mother Superior jump the gun --HAPPINESSI--13
    Mother Superior jump the gun --HAPPINESSI--14
    Mother Superior jump the gun --HAPPINESSI--15
    Mother Superior jump the gun --HAPPINESSI--16
    Mother Superior jump the gun.--HAPPINESSI--17

SURE
    I've lost her now for sure, I won't see her no
       more --MISERY--4
    I must be sure from the very start --IFIFELL--8
    There is one thing I'm sure of--EVERYLITTL--14
    Everybody knows I'm sure--YESITIS--6
    Nobody was really sure if he was from the House
       of Lords--DAYINTHELI--10
    Making sure that I'm not late (hey).--OLDBROWNSH
       --30
    Bang, bang Maxwell's silver hammer made sure
       that she was dead.--MAXWELLSIL--7
    Bang, bang Maxwell's silver hammer made sure
       that she was dead.--MAXWELLSIL--15
    Bang, bang Maxwell's silver hammer made sure
       that he was dead.--MAXWELLSIL--25

SURELY
    With every mistake we must surely be learning --
       WHILEMYGUI--11

SURPRISE
    But I got a big surprise--ILLBEBACK--15
    It is no surprise now--TELLMEWHAT--24

It is no surprise now--TELLMEWHAT--24
It is no surprise now--TELLMEWHAT--33
Bill and his elephants were taken by surprise --
    CONTINUING--18

SURRENDER
    Lay down all thought, surrender to the void--
       TOMORROWNE--3

SWAYING
    Swaying daisies sing a lazy song beneath the sun.
       --MOTHERNATU--9

SWEAT
    The sweat it's gonna fill your head --SAVOYTRUFF
       --14

SWEATER
    You can knit a sweater by the fireside--WHENIMSIXT
       --15
    And a low-neck sweater.--GETBACK/45--34

SWEATY
    Jack-knife in your sweaty hands--HEYBULLDOG--6

SWEEPING
    I look at the floor and I see it needs sweeping --
       WHILEMYGUI--4

SWEET
    Dream sweet dreams for me --GOODNIGHT--5
    Dream sweet dreams for you.--GOODNIGHT--6
    Dream sweet dreams for me --GOODNIGHT--11
    Dream sweet dreams for you.--GOODNIGHT--12
    Dream sweet dreams for me --GOODNIGHT--18
    Dream sweet dreams for you.--GOODNIGHT--19
    In a couple of years they have built a home sweet
       home --OBLADIOBLA--17
    In a couple of years they have built a home sweet
       home--OBLADIOBLA--29
    But what is sweet now turns so sour.--SAVOYTRUFF
       --20
    Sweet Loretta Martin thought she was a woman --
       GETBACK/45--16
    For your sweet top lip I'm in the queue --
       OLDBROWNSH--31
    One sweet dream --YOUNEVERGI--17
    One sweet dream came true today --YOUNEVERGI--21
    Because you're sweet and lovely girl, I love you,
       --FORYOUBLUE--2
    Because you're sweet and lovely girl, it's true --
       FORYOUBLUE--3
    Because you're sweet and lovely girl, I love you
       --FORYOUBLUE--16
    Because you're sweet and lovely girl, it's true --
       FORYOUBLUE--17
    Sweet Moretta Fart she thought she was a cleaner--
       GETBACK/LP--2
    But she was a frying pan ((sweet Loretta
       Martin)).--GETBACK/LP--3
    Sweet Loretta Martin thought she was a woman--
       GETBACK/LP--22

SWEETER
    She's sweeter than all the girls and I met quite
       a few --ANOTHERGIR--6

SWIM
    We would shout and swim about--OCTOPUSSGA--17

SWING
    And your bird can swing --ANDYOURBIR--14

SYMPATHISE
    I'd really sympathise --ANYTIMEATA--8

SYNDICATE
    Well you can syndicate any boat you rode/rowed--
       IDIGAPONY--30
    Yeah you can syndicate any boat you rode/rowed--
       IDIGAPONY--31

T-SHIRT
    Corporation T-shirt, stupid bloody Tuesday--
        IAMTHEWALR--5

TABLE
    At twelve o'clock a meeting round the table --
        CRYBABYCRY--28
    And proceeded to lie on the table --ROCKYRACCO--32
    We gave her everything we owned just to sit at
        her table ((sexy Sadie))--SEXYSADIE--20

TAKE
    Baby take a chance with me.--LITTLECHIL--4
    Baby take a chance with me.--LITTLECHIL--8
    Baby take a chance with me (wuh yeah).--LITTLECHIL
        --15
    Baby take a chance with me, ch yeah --LITTLECHIL
        --22
    Baby take a chance with me, oh yeah --LITTLECHIL
        --23
    Baby take a chance with me, oh yeah --LITTLECHIL
        --24
    Baby take a chance with me, oh yeah.--LITTLECHIL
        --25
    Don't you know I can't take it?--ICALLYOURN--5
    Don't you know I can't take it?--ICALLYOURN--12
    If somebody tries to take my place --IMHAPPYJUS--16
    If somebody tries to take my place --IMHAPPYJUS--24
    Oh how long will it take --BABYSINBLA--14
    Oh how long will it take --BABYSINBLA--19
    I think I'll take a walk and look for her.--
        IDONTWANTT--8
    But I think I'll take a walk and look for her.--
        IDONTWANTT--25
    If you let me take your heart--TELLMEWHAT--1
    I ain't no fool and I don't take what I don't
        want --ANOTHERGIR--4
    I ain't no fool and I don't take what I don't
        want --ANOTHERGIR--14
    I ain't no fool and I don't take what I don't
        want --ANOTHERGIR--20
    If you don't take her out tonight--YOUREGONNA--3
    And I will take her out tonight--YOUREGONNA--5
    If you don't take her out tonight--YOUREGONNA--25
    And I will take her out tonight--YOUREGONNA--27
    Take your time, don't hurry --NOWHEREMAN--14
    It took me years to write, will you take a look?--
        PAPERBACKW--3
    It's a thousand pages, give or take a few,
        ((paperback))--PAPERBACKW--15
    Take a drink from his special cup, Dr. Robert.--
        DRROBERT--7
    We take a walk, the sun is shining down --
        GOODDAYSUN--7
    Be thankful I don't take it all --TAXMAN--8
    If you take a walk, I'll tax your feet.
        ((walk))--TAXMAN--14
    Let me take you down--STRAWBERRY--1
    Let me take you down--STRAWBERRY--11
    Let me take you down--STRAWBERRY--21
    Let me take you down--STRAWBERRY--31
    Then you decide to take a walk by the old school--
        GOODMORNIN--14
    To take some tea with me? ((maid))--LOVELYRITA--16
    Waiting to take you away.--LUCYINTHES--17
    We'd like to take you home with us--SGTPEPPERS--17
    We'd love to take you home.--SGTPEPPERS--18
    The Magical Mystery Tour is waiting to take
        you away--MAGICALMYS--9
    (Waiting to take you away).--MAGICALMYS--10
    The Magical Mystery Tour is hoping to take you
        away --MAGICALMYS--17
    (Hoping to take you away)--MAGICALMYS--18
    The Magical Mystery Tour is coming to take you
        away --MAGICALMYS--27
    (Coming/Hoping to take you away)--MAGICALMYS--28
    The Magical Mystery Tour is dying to take you
        away --MAGICALMYS--29
    (Dying to take you away) --MAGICALMYS--30
    Take you today.--MAGICALMYS--31
    Take a sad song and make it better --HEYJUDE--2
    Take a sad song and make it better --HEYJUDE--27
    (Take it Jude) nah - nah - nah - nah, hey
        Jude.--HEYJUDE--33
    Nah nah nah, nah - nah - nah - nah (take it
        Jude) --HEYJUDE--38
    (Take a sad song and make it better)--HEYJUDE--48
    (Take it Jude) nah - nah - nah - nah, hey
        Jude.--HEYJUDE--65
    Take me to your daddy's farm --BACKINTHEU--32
    Take a cha-cha-cha chance (birthday) --BIRTHDAY--12
    Take a cha-cha-cha chance (birthday) --BIRTHDAY--17

    Take these broken wings and learn to fly.--
        BLACKBIRD--2
    Take these sunken eyes and learn to see.--BLACKBIRD
        --6
    Take these broken wings and learn to fly.--
        BLACKBIRD--14
    Can you take me back where I came from --CRYBABYCRY
        --44
    Can you take me back?--CRYBABYCRY--45
    Can you take me back where I came from --CRYBABYCRY
        --46
    Brother, can you take me back --CRYBABYCRY--47
    Can you take me back?--CRYBABYCRY--48
    Mmm can you take me where I came from --CRYBABYCRY
        --49
    Can you take me back?--CRYBABYCRY--50
    Come on is take it easy --EVRBDYMONK--4
    Come on is take it easy --EVRBDYMONK--5
    Take it easy, take it easy --EVRBDYMONK--6
    Take it easy, take it easy --EVRBDYMONK--6
    Take it easy, take it easy - wuh --EVRBDYMONK--15
    Take it easy, take it easy - wuh --EVRBDYMONK--15
    Take a good look around you --MARTHAMYDE--7
    Take a good look you're bound to see --MARTHAMYDE
        --8
    Take ob-la-di 'b-la-da ((ha ha ha)) --OBLADIOBLA
        --41
    Can I take my friend to bed?--ALLTOGETHE--18
    It's all too much for me to take --ITSALLTOOM--8
    For us to take, it's all too much.--ITSALLTOOM--11
    It's all too much for me to take --ITSALLTOOM--16
    So take a piece, but not too much.--ITSALLTOOM
        --19
    It's all too much for me to take --ITSALLTOOM--29
    For us to take it's all too much.--ITSALLTOOM--32
    You don't take nothing with you but your soul -
        think!--BALLADOFJO--28
    The love you take is equal to the love you make.--
        THEEND--9
    Can I take you out to the pictures, Joan?--
        MAXWELLSIL--4

TAKEN
    Bill and his elephants were taken by surprise --
        CONTINUING--18

TAKES
    She takes her time and doesn't feel she has to
        hurry --FORNOONE--5
    Now they know how many holes it takes--DAYINTHELI
        --32
    And Molly says this as she takes him by the hand:
        --OBLADIOBLA--4
    Desmond takes a trolly to the jewellery store --
        OBLADIOBLA--9
    Takes it back to Molly waiting at the door--
        OBLADIOBLA--11
    Takes him out to look at the Queen--MEANMRMUST--11

TAKING
    I'll make a point of taking her away from you
        (watch what you do), yeah-YOUREGONNA--16
    I'll make a point of taking her away from you
        (watch what you do), yeah--YOUREGONNA--23
    For taking the easy way out --DAYTRIPPER--2
    For taking the easy way out, now.--DAYTRIPPER--4
    Taking my time.--IMONLYSLEE--14
    Taking my time.--IMONLYSLEE--20
    I'm taking the time for a number of things--
        FIXINGAHOL--19

TALK
    I want no one to talk to me--DONTBOTHER--2
    I can't talk to people that I meet.--ILLCRYINST--7
    But when you talk about destruction --REVOLUTION
        --8
    But when you talk about destruction --REVOLUTONE
        --11
    You can talk to me--HEYBULLDOG--9
    You can talk to me--HEYBULLDOG--10
    You can talk to me--HEYBULLDOG--11
    If you're lonely you can talk to me.--HEYBULLDOG
        --12
    You can talk to me--HEYBULLDOG--17
    You can talk to me--HEYBULLDOG--18
    You can talk to me--HEYBULLDOG--19
    If you're lonely you can talk to me - hey!--
        HEYBULLDOG--20

TALKED
    We talked until two--NORWEGIANW--14

TALKING
    If I catch you talking--YOUCANTDOT--3
    I caught you talking to him--YOUCANTDOT--10
    You talking that way--YOUCANTDOT--21
    You talking that way--YOUCANTDOT--40
    Do I have to keep on talking till I can't go on?--
        WECANWORKI--2
    We were talking--WITHINYOUW--1
    We were talking--WITHINYOUW--8
    We were talking--WITHINYOUW--21
    The man of a thousand voices talking perfectly loud
        --FOOLONTHEH--9
    Talking in our beds for a week.--BALLADOFJO--18

TAN
    If the sun don't come you get a tan from standing
        in the English rain--IAMTHEWALR--18

TANGERINE
    With tangerine trees and marmalade skies.--
        LUCYINTHES--2
    Creme tangerine, montelimar --SAVOYTRUFF--1
    Creme tangerine and montelimar --SAVOYTRUFF--23

TANTA
    Questo obrigado tanta mucho cake and eat it
        carousel.--SUNKING--8

TART
    Cool cherry cream, nice apple tart --SAVOYTRUFF--6

TASTE
    I feel your taste all the time we're apart --
        SAVOYTRUFF--7

TAUGHT
    The teachers who taught me weren't cool (now I
        can't complain)--GETTINGBET--4
    That Sgt. Pepper taught the band to play--
        SGTPEPPERS--2

TAX
    If you drive a car, I'll tax the street,
        ((car))--TAXMAN--11
    If you try to sit, I'll tax your seat, ((sit))--
        TAXMAN--12
    If you get too cold, I'll tax the heat,
        ((cold))--TAXMAN--13
    If you take a walk, I'll tax your feet.
        ((walk))--TAXMAN--14

TAXIS
    Newspaper taxis appear on the shore--LUCYINTHES--16

TAXMAN
    TAXMAN.--TAXMAN--Title
    'cos I'm the Taxman --TAXMAN--5
    Yeah, I'm the Taxman.--TAXMAN--6
    'cos I'm the Taxman --TAXMAN--9
    Yeah, I'm the Taxman.--TAXMAN--10
    Taxman.--TAXMAN--15
    'cos I'm the Taxman --TAXMAN--16
    Yeah, I'm the Taxman.--TAXMAN--17
    'cos I'm the Taxman --TAXMAN--20
    Yeah, I'm the Taxman.--TAXMAN--21
    Now my advice for those who die (Taxman)--TAXMAN
        --22
    Declare the pennies on your eyes (Taxman)--TAXMAN
        --23
    'cos I'm the Taxman --TAXMAN--24
    Yeah, I'm the Taxman.--TAXMAN--25
    And you're working for no-one but me (Taxman).--
        TAXMAN--26

TEA
    It's time for tea and meet the wife.--GOODMORNIN
        --21
    To take some tea with me? ((maid))--LOVELYRITA--16
    And arriving late for tea --CRYBABYCRY--21
    Can I bring my friend to tea?--ALLTOGETHE--6

    And get me home for tea.--ITSALLTOOM--24

TEACHER
    Back in school again, Maxwell plays the fool
        again, teacher gets annoyed --MAXWELLSIL--8

TEACHERS
    The teachers who taught me weren't cool (now I
        can't complain)--GETTINGBET--4

TEAR
    Step on the gas and wipe that tear away.--
        YOUNEVERGI--20

TEARING
    You are tearing me apart --WHATGOESON--3
    You are tearing me apart --WHATGOESON--12
    You are tearing me apart --WHATGOESON--28

TEARS
    Every night the tears come down from my eye--
        ITWONTBELO--15
    Holding back these tears in my eyes.--TELLMEWHY--16
    My tears are falling like rain from the sky --
        IMALOSER--11
    We'll forget the tears we've cried.--WAIT--4
    We'll forget the tears we cried.--WAIT--8
    We'll forget the tears we've cried.--WAIT--16
    We'll forget the tears we've cried.--WAIT--24
    Though the days are few, they're filled with tears
        --YOUWONTSEE--16
    Though the days are few they're filled with tears
        --YOUWONTSEE--25
    No sign of love behind the tears cried for no-one
        --FORNOONE--8
    No sign of love behind the tears cried for no-one
        --FORNOONE--15
    No sign of love behind the tears cried for no-one
        --FORNOONE--25
    So many tears I was searching --LONGLONGLO--7
    So many tears I was wasting - oh, oh!--LONGLONGLO
        --8
    Even those tears --IMEMINE--16
    Even those tears --IMEMINE--29
    Has left a pool of tears crying for the day.--
        LONGANDWIN--5

TEASER
    She's a big teaser --DAYTRIPPER--9
    She's a big teaser --DAYTRIPPER--11

TEE
    Tee - tee - tee.--HONEYPIE--28
    Tee - tee - tee.--HONEYPIE--28
    Tee - tee - tee.--HONEYPIE--28

TELEPHONE
    I tried to telephone--NOREPLY--9
    I tried to telephone--NOREPLY--22

TELL
    'cos you tell me things I want to know --ASKMEWHY
        --2
    'cos you tell me things I want to know --ASKMEWHY
        --17
    Do you promise not to tell?--DOYOUWANTT--4
    Do you promise not to tell? (dodahdo)--DOYOUWANTT
        --10
    Do you promise not to tell? (dodahdo)--DOYOUWANTT
        --18
    I could tell the world a thing or two about our love
        --THANKYOUGI--5
    Tell me I'm the only one --HOLDMETIGH--3
    Tell me I'm the only one --HOLDMETIGH--20
    Tell me that you love me baby --IWANNABEYO--13
    Tell me that you love me baby --IWANNABEYO--15
    Oh yeah, I'll tell you something--IWANTTOHOL--1
    Tell me that you want the kind of things --
        CANTBUYMEL--19
    Tell me that you want the kind of things --
        CANTBUYMEL--29
    Do I have to tell you one more time--YOUCANTDOT--11
    That when I tell you that I love you, oh --
        ISHOULDHAV--7
    That when I tell you that I love you, oh --

ISHOULDHAV--17
TELL ME WHY.--TELLMEWHY--Title
Tell me why you cried --TELLMEWHY--1
Tell me why you cried --TELLMEWHY--3
Tell me why you cried --TELLMEWHY--9
Tell me why you cried --TELLMEWHY--11
Tell me what and I'll apologize --TELLMEWHY--14
Tell me why you cried --TELLMEWHY--17
Tell me why you cried --TELLMEWHY--19
Tell me why you cried --TELLMEWHY--26
Tell me why you cried --TELLMEWHY--28
I got a whole lot of things to tell her --
   WHENIGETHO--2
I got a whole lot of things to tell her --
   WHENIGETHO--8
I got a whole lot of things to tell her --
   WHENIGETHO--14
I got a whole lot of things to tell her --
   WHENIGETHO--25
I got a whole lot of things to tell her --
   WHENIGETHO--27
People tell me that she's only fooling--SHESAWOMAN
   --6
People tell me that she's only fooling--SHESAWOMAN
   --23
People tell me that she's only fooling--SHESAWOMAN
   --33
Tell me, oh what can I do?--BABYSINBLA--3
Tell me, oh what can I do?--BABYSINBLA--9
Tell me oh what can I do?--BABYSINBLA--18
Tell me oh what can I do?--BABYSINBLA--23
Tell me oh what can I do?--BABYSINBLA--29
People tell me I'm lucky--EVERYLITTL--2
TELL ME WHAT YOU SEE.--TELLMEWHAT--Title
Tell me what you see--TELLMEWHAT--6
Tell me what you see--TELLMEWHAT--14
Tell me what you see--TELLMEWHAT--17
Tell me what you see--TELLMEWHAT--23
Tell me what you see--TELLMEWHAT--26
Tell me what you see--TELLMEWHAT--32
You tell lies thinking I can't see --IMDOWN--1
Said you had a thing or two to tell me--INEEDYOU
   --6
Only time will tell if I am right or I am wrong.--
   WECANWORKI--16
Only time will tell if I am right or I am wrong.--
   WECANWORKI--25
Why, tell me why did you not treat me right?--
   IMLOOKINGT--9
Why, tell me why did you not treat me right?--
   IMLOOKINGT--15
Tell me why.--WHATGOESON--9
Tell me why (tell me why).--WHATGOESON--18
Tell me why (tell me why).--WHATGOESON--18
Tell me why.--WHATGOESON--25
You tell me that you've got everything you want --
   ANDYOURBIR--1
You tell me that you heard every sound there is --
   ANDYOURBIR--13
Ooo did I tell you I need you--GOTTOGETYO--6
Ooo did I tell you I need you--GOTTOGETYO--21
Did I tell you I need you--GOTTOGETYO--30
I WANT TO TELL YOU.--IWANTTOTEL--Title
I want to tell you--IWANTTOTEL--1
I want to tell you--IWANTTOTEL--12
Then I could speak my mind and tell you--IWANTTOTEL
   --17
I want to tell you--IWANTTOTEL--19
Let me tell you how it will be --TAXMAN--3
I can't tell you but I know it's mine.--WITHALITTL
   --22
They can tell what he wants to do--FOOLONTHEH--16
You tell me that it's evolution --REVOLUTION--5
All I can tell you is brother you have to wait.--
   REVOLUTION--19
You tell me it's the institution --REVOLUTION--25
Oh let me tell you honey --BACKINTHEU--38
I tell you man he living there still--GLASSONION
   --18
Tell me, tell me, tell me, come on tell me the
   answer --HELTERSKEL--6
Tell me, tell me, tell me, come on tell me the
   answer --HELTERSKEL--6
Tell me, tell me, tell me, come on tell me the
   answer --HELTERSKEL--6
Tell me, tell me, tell me, come on tell me the
   answer --HELTERSKEL--6
Tell me, tell me, tell me the answer --HELTERSKEL
   --13
Tell me, tell me, tell me the answer --HELTERSKEL
   --13
Tell me, tell me, tell me the answer --HELTERSKEL
   --13
Tell me, tell me, tell me your answer --HELTERSKEL

--23
Tell me, tell me, tell me your answer --HELTERSKEL
   --23
Tell me, tell me, tell me your answer --HELTERSKEL
   --23
You tell me that it's evolution --REVOLUTONE--8
Well all I can tell you is brother you have to
   wait.--REVOLUTONE--28
You tell me it's the institution --REVOLUTONE--39
One thing I can tell you is you got to be free--
   COMETOGETH--20
I wanna tell her that I love her a lot--HERMAJESTY
   --5
No-one there to tell us what to do.--OCTOPUSSGA--22
Believe me when I tell you, I'll never do you
   no harm.--OHDARLING--2
Believe me when I tell you, I'll never do you
   no harm.--OHDARLING--10
Believe me when I tell you - ooo - I'll never
   do you no harm.--OHDARLING--18
Didn't anybody tell her?--SHECAMEINT--8
Didn't anybody tell her?--SHECAMEINT--20

TELLING
   So I'm telling you, my friend--ILLGETYOU--13
   She's so glad she's telling all the world --
      IFEELFINE--8
   She's so glad she's telling all the world --
      IFEELFINE--16
   I'm telling you so that you won't lose all.--
      IMALOSER--18
   Telling me there'll be no next time--YOULIKEMET--3
   And so I'm telling you this time you'd better
      stop --ANOTHERGIR--8
   Were you telling lies? (aah the night before)--
      NIGHTBEFOR--5
   Were you telling lies? (aah the night before)--
      NIGHTBEFOR--19
   Until I do I'm telling you so you'll understand.--
      MICHELLE--19
   You're telling all those lies--THINKFORYO--3
   It won't be the same now I'm telling you.--
      OLDBROWNSH--8

TELLS
   Can't buy me love, oh, everybody tells me so --
      CANTBUYMEL--15
   Can't buy me love, oh, everybody tells me so --
      CANTBUYMEL--25
   She tells me all the time, you know, she said so
      --IFEELFINE--5
   She tells me all the time, you know, she said so
      --IFEELFINE--13
   She tells Max to stay when the class has gone
      away --MAXWELLSIL--10
   The judge does not agree and he tells them so oh
      - oh oh.--MAXWELLSIL--21

TEN
   The band begins at ten to six--BEINGFORTH--15
   Ten somersets he'll undertake on solid ground.--
      BEINGFORTH--18
   ... Four, five, six, seven, eight, nine,
      ten ...--DAYINTHELI--35
   Five, six, seven, eight, nine, ten --ALLTOGETHE--3
   Keeps a ten bob note up his nose--MEANMRMUST--6

TENDERLY
   And tenderly --ANDILOVEHE--7

TEST-TUBE
   Late nights all alone with a test-tube, oh oh -
      oh oh.--MAXWELLSIL--2

TESTIMONIAL
   Painting testimonial pictures oh oh - oh oh.--
      MAXWELLSIL--18

TEXPERT
   Expert texpert, choking smokers, don't you
      think the joker laughs at you?--IAMTHEWALR--21

THAN
   Than just holding hands.--IFIFELL--6
   That you would love me more than her.--IFIFELL--9
   I got a chip on my shoulder that's bigger than my

feet.--ILLCRYINST--6
Than to break my heart again --ILLBEBACK--10
Than to break my heart again --ILLBEBACK--19
Love you more than any other guy--NOREPLY--18
So much younger than today--HELP--9
When I was younger, so much younger than today--
    HELP--29
She's sweeter than all the girls and I met quite
    a few --ANOTHERGIR--6
Than to be with another man.--RUNFORYOUR--2
Than to be with another man.--RUNFORYOUR--26
Changing faster than the weather --OLDBROWNSH--24
I love you more than ever girl, I do.--FORYOUBLUE
    --4
I love you more than ever girl, I do - really
    love blues.--FORYOUBLUE--18
Flowing more freely than wine --IMEMINE--20
Flowing more freely than wine --IMEMINE--33
Longer than the road that stretches out ahead.--
    TWOOFUS--18
Longer than the road that stretches out ahead.--
    TWOOFUS--27

THANK

THANK YOU GIRL.--THANKYOUGI--Title
And all I gotta do is thank you girl, thank you
    girl.--THANKYOUGI--4
And all I gotta do is thank you girl, thank you
    girl.--THANKYOUGI--4
And all I gotta do is thank you girl, thank you
    girl--THANKYOUGI--7
And all I gotta do is thank you girl, thank you
    girl--THANKYOUGI--7
Thank you girl, for loving me the way that you
    do (way that you do).--THANKYOUGI--8
And all I gotta do is thank you girl, thank you
    girl.--THANKYOUGI--10
And all I gotta do is thank you girl, thank you
    girl.--THANKYOUGI--10
And all I gotta do is thank you girl, thank you
    girl.--THANKYOUGI--14
And all I gotta do is thank you girl, thank you
    girl.--THANKYOUGI--14
We'd like to thank you once again.--SGTPEPPREP--12
Thank you (ooo) (ha ha ha).--OBLADIOBLA--42
I'd like to say thank you on behalf of the group
    and ourselves--GETBACK/LP--38
Thank you, brothers.--IDIGAPONY--37

THANKFUL

Be thankful I don't take it all --TAXMAN--8

THANKS

Thanks folk.--GETBACK/LP--37

THAT

Remember that I'll always be in love with you.--
    PSILOVEYOU--2
Remember that I'll always be in love with you.--
    PSILOVEYOU--11
Remember that I'll always, yeah, be in love
    with you.--PSILOVEYOU--18
That it really only goes to show --ASKMEWHY--4
That I know --ASKMEWHY--5
That I - I - I - I should never, never,
    never be blue.--ASKMEWHY--6
But you're the only love that I've ever had.--
    ASKMEWHY--11
That it really only goes to show --ASKMEWHY--19
That I know --ASKMEWHY--20
That I - I - I - I should never, never,
    never be blue.--ASKMEWHY--21
That before too long I'd fall in love with her.--
    ISAWHERSTA--8
Well my heart went boom when I crossed that room
    --ISAWHERSTA--11
Well my heart went boom when I crossed that room
    --ISAWHERSTA--18
If there's anything that you want--FROMMETOYO--3
I got everything that you want--FROMMETOYO--7
I got arms that long to hold you--FROMMETOYO--11
I got lips that long to kiss you--FROMMETOYO--13
If there's anything that you want--FROMMETOYO--15
I got arms that long to hold you--FROMMETOYO--23
I got lips that long to kiss you--FROMMETOYO--24
If there's anything that you want--FROMMETOYO--26
Thank you girl, for loving me the way that you
    do (way that you do).--THANKYOUGI--8
Thank you girl, for loving me the way that you
    do (way that you do).--THANKYOUGI--8

That's the kind of love that is too good to be true
    --THANKYOUGI--9
That I'll get you, I'll get you in the end--
    ILLGETYOU--14
And you know that can't be bad--SHELOVESYO--9
And you know that can't be bad--SHELOVESYO--17
With a love like that--SHELOVESYO--22
And you know that can't be bad--SHELOVESYO--29
With a love like that--SHELOVESYO--34
With a love like that--SHELOVESYO--36
With a love like that--SHELOVESYO--38
I'll pretend that I'm kissing --ALLMYLOVIN--7
And hope that my dreams will come true --ALLMYLOVIN
    --9
That she would leave me on my own--DONTBOTHER--10
Until that day--DONTBOTHER--24
Until that day--DONTBOTHER--39
Tell me that you love me baby --IWANNABEYO--13
Tell me that you love me baby --IWANNABEYO--15
Now I know that you won't leave me no more--
    ITWONTBELO--26
When I say that something--IWANTTOHOL--3
That my love--IWANTTOHOL--16
Yeah, you've got that something--IWANTTOHOL--20
When I say that something--IWANTTOHOL--22
That my love--IWANTTOHOL--29
Yeah, you've got that something--IWANTTOHOL--33
When I feel that something--IWANTTOHOL--35
That boy took my love away--THISBOY--1
That boy isn't good for you--THISBOY--4
That boy won't be happy--THISBOY--9
Tell me that you want the kind of things --
    CANTBUYMEL--19
That money just can't buy --CANTBUYMEL--20
Tell me that you want the kind of things --
    CANTBUYMEL--29
That money just can't buy --CANTBUYMEL--30
YOU CAN'T DO THAT.--YOUCANTDOT--Title
That might cause you pain--YOUCANTDOT--2
To that boy again.--YOUCANTDOT--4
Oh you can't do that.--YOUCANTDOT--8
Oh you can't do that.--YOUCANTDOT--17
You talking that way--YOUCANTDOT--21
Oh you can't do that - no!--YOUCANTDOT--31
You can't do that--YOUCANTDOT--32
You can't do that--YOUCANTDOT--33
You can't do that--YOUCANTDOT--34
You can't do that--YOUCANTDOT--35
You can't do that.--YOUCANTDOT--36
You talking that way--YOUCANTDOT--40
Oh you can't do that.--YOUCANTDOT--50
I'm not that kinda man.--ICALLYOURN--8
I'm not that kinda man.--ICALLYOURN--15
Don't you know that it's so?--THERESAPLA--10
Don't you know that it's so?--THERESAPLA--12
Bright are the stars that shine --ANDILOVEHE--15
Bright are the stars that shine --ANDILOVEHE--20
I find the things that you do --HARDDAYSNI--6
I find the things that you do --HARDDAYSNI--22
I find the things that you do --HARDDAYSNI--35
That I would love everything that you do --
    ISHOULDHAV--2
That I would love everything that you do --
    ISHOULDHAV--2
That when I tell you that I love you, oh --
    ISHOULDHAV--7
That when I tell you that I love you, oh --
    ISHOULDHAV--7
That when I tell you that I love you, oh --
    ISHOULDHAV--17
That when I tell you that I love you, oh --
    ISHOULDHAV--17
And I found that love was more --IFIFELL--5
That you would love me more than her.--IFIFELL--9
That I would love to love you --IFIFELL--18
And that she will cry --IFIFELL--19
When she learns we are two.--IFIFELL--20
That I would love to love you --IFIFELL--25
And that she will cry --IFIFELL--26
I can't talk to people that I meet.--ILLCRYINST--7
If it's something that I said or done --TELLMEWHY
    --13
That I'm not trying to pretend.--ILLBEBACK--12
I thought that you would realise --ILLBEBACK--13
That if I ran away from you --ILLBEBACK--14
That you would want me too --ILLBEBACK--15
That I'm not trying to pretend.--ILLBEBACK--21
Love to hear you say that love is love--THINGSWESA
    --12
Love to hear you say that love is love--THINGSWESA
    --23
Till I walk out that door again.--WHENIGETHO--20
I'm so glad that she's my little girl --IFEELFINE
    --7

That her baby buys her things, you know --IFEELFINE
--9
I'm so glad that she's my little girl --IFEELFINE
--15
That her baby buys her things, you know --IFEELFINE
--17
I know that she's no peasant--SHESAWOMAN--2
People tell me that she's only fooling--SHESAWOMAN
--6
She is happy just to hear me say that--SHESAWOMAN
--10
I know that she's no peasant--SHESAWOMAN--19
People tell me that she's only fooling--SHESAWOMAN
--23
I know that she's no peasant--SHESAWOMAN--29
People tell me that she's only fooling--SHESAWOMAN
--33
Just to know that she loves me--EVERYLITTL--12
Yes I know that she loves me now.--EVERYLITTL--13
One day you'll find that I have gone --ILLFOLLOWT
--7
One day you'll find that I have gone --ILLFOLLOWT
--12
Is it for her or myself that I cry?--IMALOSER--12
I'm telling you so that you won't lose all.--
IMALOSER--18
I know that you saw me--NOREPLY--7
If I were you I'd realise that I--NOREPLY--17
That I heard before--NOREPLY--20
She said that living with me--TICKETTORI--9
She said that living with me--TICKETTORI--36
For red is the colour that my baby wore--YESITIS
--3
For red is the colour that will make me blue--
YESITIS--16
For red is the colour that will make me blue--
YESITIS--25
Can't you try to see that I'm--TELLMEWHAT--20
Can't you try to see that I'm--TELLMEWHAT--29
Which is all that I deserve--YOULIKEMET--10
I'd admit that I was wrong--YOULIKEMET--18
I'd admit that I was wrong--YOULIKEMET--27
I know that I ((I know that I)) just need
     you like--HELP--23
I know that I ((I know that I)) just need
     you like--HELP--23
You're making me say that I've got nobody but you
     --ANOTHERGIR--2
I don't wanna say that I've been unhappy with you
     --ANOTHERGIR--12
I don't wanna say that I've been unhappy with you
     --ANOTHERGIR--18
It's only love and that is all--ITSONLYLOV--4
It's only love and that is all--ITSONLYLOV--6
Is it right that you and I should fight, every
     night--ITSONLYLOV--8
It's only love and that is all--ITSONLYLOV--11
It's only love and that is all--ITSONLYLOV--13
YOU'RE GOING TO/GONNA LOSE THAT GIRL.--YOUREGONNA--Title
You're gonna lose that girl (yes, yes, you're
     gonna lose that girl)--YOUREGONNA--1
You're gonna lose that girl (yes, yes, you're
     gonna lose that girl)--YOUREGONNA--1
You're gonna lose that girl (yes, yes, you're
     gonna lose that girl)--YOUREGONNA--2
You're gonna lose that girl (yes, yes, you're
     gonna lose that girl)--YOUREGONNA--2
You're gonna lose that girl (yes, yes, you're
     gonna lose that girl)--YOUREGONNA--7
You're gonna lose that girl (yes, yes, you're
     gonna lose that girl)--YOUREGONNA--7
You're gonna lose that girl (yes, yes, you're
     gonna lose that girl)--YOUREGONNA--8
You're gonna lose that girl (yes, yes, you're
     gonna lose that girl)--YOUREGONNA--8
You're gonna lose that girl (yes, yes, you're
     gonna lose that girl)--YOUREGONNA--13
You're gonna lose that girl (yes, yes, you're
     gonna lose that girl)--YOUREGONNA--13
You're gonna lose that girl (yes, yes, you're
     gonna lose that girl)--YOUREGONNA--14
You're gonna lose that girl (yes, yes, you're
     gonna lose that girl)--YOUREGONNA--14
You're gonna lose (yes, yes, you're gonna lose
     that girl)--YOUREGONNA--15
You're gonna lose that girl--YOUREGONNA--18
You're gonna lose that girl--YOUREGONNA--19
You're gonna lose that girl (yes, yes, you're
     gonna lose that girl)--YOUREGONNA--20
You're gonna lose that girl (yes, yes, you're
     gonna lose that girl)--YOUREGONNA--20
You're gonna lose that girl (yes, yes,you're
     gonna lose that girl)--YOUREGONNA--21
You're gonna lose that girl (yes, yes, you're

gonna lose that girl)--YOUREGONNA--21
You're gonna lose (yes, yes, you're gonna lose
     that girl)--YOUREGONNA-22
You're gonna lose that girl (yes, yes, you're
     gonna lose that girl)--YOUREGONNA--29
You're gonna lose that girl (yes, yes, you're
     gonna lose that girl)--YOUREGONNA--29
You're gonna lose that girl (yes, yes, you're
     gonna lose that girl)--YOUREGONNA--30
You're gonna lose that girl (yes, yes, you're
     gonna lose that girl)--YOUREGONNA--30
You're gonna lose (yes, yes, you're gonna lose
     that girl).--YOUREGONNA--31
Run the risk of knowing that our love may soon be
     gone.--WECANWORKI--4
You can get it wrong and still you think that
     it's alright.--WECANWORKI--7
I have always thought that it's a crime--WECANWORKI
--13
There's a chance that we might fall apart before
     too long.--WECANWORKI--18
I have always thought that it's a crime--WECANWORKI
--22
There's a chance that we might fall apart before
     too long.--WECANWORKI--27
I told that girl that my prospects were good --
     DRIVEMYCAR--9
I told that girl that my prospects were good --
     DRIVEMYCAR--9
I told that girl I could start right away --
     DRIVEMYCAR--22
Was she told when she was young that pain would
     lead to pleasure?--GIRL--22
That a man must break his back to earn his day of
     leisure?--GIRL--24
You're the one that I'd be thinking of --IFINEEDEDS
--2
For people and things that went before --INMYLIFE
--14
For people and things that went before --INMYLIFE
--18
These are words that go together well, my
     Michelle.--MICHELLE--2
I will say the only words I know that you'll
     understand.--MICHELLE--8
And I will say the only words I know that
     you'll understand --MICHELLE--22
Well you know that I'm a wicked guy--RUNFORYOUR--9
To say about the things that you do.--THINKFORYO
--2
That we can have if we close our eyes.--THINKFORYO
--5
The ruins of the life that you had in mind --
     THINKFORYO--11
All the things that you should.--THINKFORYO--23
That I've been good, as good as I can be.--WAIT--10
And know that you will wait for me.--WAIT--12
That I've been good, as good as I can be.--WAIT--18
And know that you will wait for me.--WAIT--20
But now the tide is turning I can see that I
     was blind.--WHATGOESON--16
In the good and the bad books that I have read.--
     THEWORD--16
Now that I know what I feel must be right --THEWORD
--23
That the word is just the way --THEWORD--26
We have lost the time that was so hard to find--
     YOUWONTSEE--3
I can show you that when it starts to rain (when
     the rain comes down)--RAIN--9
Can you hear me that when it rains and shines
     (when it rains and shines)--RAIN--14
You tell me that you've got everything you want --
     ANDYOURBIR--1
You tell me that you heard every sound there is --
     ANDYOURBIR--13
Wearing the face that she keeps in a jar by the door
     --ELEANORRIG--7
That no-one will hear--ELEANORRIG--12
You find that all her words of kindness linger on
     --FORNOONE--2
A love that should have lasted years.--FORNOONE--9
A love that should have lasted years.--FORNOONE--16
She says that long ago she knew someone --FORNOONE
--18
A love that should have lasted years.--FORNOONE--26
I'm so proud to know that she is mine.--GOODDAYSUN
--13
Nobody can deny that there's something there.--
     HERETHEREA--4
Knowing that love is to share--HERETHEREA--11
Each one believing that love never dies--HERETHEREA
--12
Knowing that love is to share--HERETHEREA--17

Each one believing that love never dies--HERETHEREA
--18
That is confusing things.--IWANTTOTEL--11
Things that make me feel that I'm mad-SHESAIDSHE
--5
Things that make me feel that I'm mad-SHESAIDSHE
--5
I know that I'm ready to leave --SHESAIDSHE--11
I know that I'm ready to leave --SHESAIDSHE--17
That you may see the meaning of within--TOMORROWNE
--5
That love is all and love is everyone--TOMORROWNE
--7
That ignorance and hate may mourn the dead--
TOMORROWNE--9
And all the people that come and go--PENNYLANE--3
That is you can't, you know, tune in--STRAWBERRY
--18
That is, I think it's not too bad.--STRAWBERRY--20
That is, I think I disagree.--STRAWBERRY--30
He didn't notice that the lights had changed--
DAYINTHELI--7
I'm filling the cracks that ran through the door--
FIXINGAHOL--4
That weren't important yesterday--FIXINGAHOL--20
You're doing the best that I can.--GETTINGBET--15
I beat her and kept her apart from the things
that she loved-GETTINGBET--26
And I'm doing the best that I can.--GETTINGBET--28
Somebody needs to know the time glad that I'm here
--GOODMORNIN--3
That grow so incredibly high (high).--LUCYINTHES
--15
That Sgt. Pepper taught the band to play--
SGTPEPPERS--2
That the singer's gonna sing a song--SGTPEPPERS--21
Leaving the note that she hoped would say more.--
SHESLEAVIN--3
She (what did we do that was wrong?)--SHESLEAVIN
--28
Fun. (fun is the one thing that money can't buy)--
SHESLEAVIN--30
Something inside that was always denied--SHESLEAVIN
--31
Yes I'm certain that it happens all the time.--
WITHALITTL--20
There's nothing you can do that can't be done
((love))--ALLYOUN/YS--4
Nothing you can sing that can't be sung ((love))--
ALLYOUN/YS--5
Nothing you can make that can't be made ((love))--
ALLYOUN/YS--8
No-one you can save that can't be saved ((love))--
ALLYOUN/YS--9
There's nothing you can know that isn't known
((love))--ALLYOUN/YS--19
Nothing you can see that isn't shown ((love))--
ALLYOUN/YS--20
There's nowhere you can be that isn't where
you're meant to be ((love))--ALLYOUN/YS--21
Now that you know who you are--BABYYOUREA--3
Nothing that doesn't show.--BABYYOUREA--12
Happy to be that way.--BABYYOUREA--25
Now that you've found another key--BABYYOUREA--26
They can see that he's just a fool--FOOLONTHEH--4
He knows that they're the fool--FOOLONTHEH--23
That was a hit before your mother was born --
YOURMOTHER--3
That was a hit before your mother was born --
YOURMOTHER--9
That was a hit before your mother was born --
YOURMOTHER--14
Did you think that money was heaven sent?--
LADYMADONN--4
For well you know that it's a fool who plays it
cool --HEYJUDE--12
And don't you know that it's just you --HEYJUDE--22
You tell me that it's evolution --REVOLUTION--5
Don't you know that you can count me out?--
REVOLUTION--9
But if you want money for people with minds that
hate --REVOLUTION--18
That Georgia's always on my my my my my my my my
my mind.--BACKINTHEU--18
That Georgia's always on my my my my my my my my
my mind.--BACKINTHEU--30
That you are part of everything.--DEARPRUDEN--9
I'm sorry that I doubted you --DONTPASSME--23
You said that you would be late --DONTPASSME--27
You know that we're as close as can be - man--
GLASSONION--9
Down to the bits that I left uptown --HAPPINESSI
--10
Well, don't you know that happiness ((happiness)),

--HAPPINESSI--31
... Ah (how was that?)--HELTERSKEL--31
Will the wind that blew her boat--HONEYPIE--25
You know that I need you --LONGLONGLO--13
That you and me were meant to be for each other -
silly girl.--MARTHAMYDE--9
You tell me that it's evolution --REVOLUTONE--8
Don't you know that you can count me out (in)?--
REVOLUTONE--12
But if you want money for people with minds that
hate --REVOLUTONE--27
Rocky didn't like that --ROCKYRACCO--5
He said, I'm gonna get that boy --ROCKYRACCO--6
You know that what you eat you are --SAVOYTRUFF--19
Hey man what's that noise? (woof)--HEYBULLDOG--23
Where I know that I'm free --ITSALLTOOM--22
Show me that I'm everywhere --ITSALLTOOM--23
But they're not, we just wrote it like that.--
ONLYANORTH--3
But they are, they just play it like that.--
ONLYANORTH--6
It's a love that lasts forever --DONTLETMED--15
It's a love that has no past (believe me).--
DONTLETMED--16
And from the first time that she really done me --
DONTLETMED--21
It won't be the same now that I'm with you.--
OLDBROWNSH--16
I want that love of yours --OLDBROWNSH--27
To miss that love is something I'd hate.--
OLDBROWNSH--28
Making sure that I'm not late (hey).--OLDBROWNSH
--30
Won't be the same now that I'm with you.--
OLDBROWNSH--34
It won't be the same now that I'm with you
(yeah, yeah, yeah).--OLDBROWNSH--36
CARRY THAT WEIGHT.--CARRYTHATW--Title
Boy, you're gonna carry that weight--CARRYTHATW--1
Carry that weight a long time.--CARRYTHATW--2
Boy, you're gonna carry that weight--CARRYTHATW--3
Carry that weight a long time.--CARRYTHATW--4
Boy, you're gonna carry that weight--CARRYTHATW--9
Carry that weight a long time.--CARRYTHATW--10
Boy, you're gonna carry that weight--CARRYTHATW--11
Carry that weight a long time.--CARRYTHATW--12
I wanna tell her that I love her a lot--HERMAJESTY
--5
Little darling, I feel that ice is slowly
melting.--HERECOMEST--18
Bang, bang Maxwell's silver hammer made sure
that she was dead.--MAXWELLSIL--7
Bang, bang Maxwell's silver hammer made sure
that she was dead.--MAXWELLSIL--15
Bang, bang Maxwell's silver hammer made sure
that he was dead.--MAXWELLSIL--25
Only place that he's ever been--MEANMRMUST--12
The coral that lies beneath the waves (lies
beneath the ocean waves).--OCTOPUSSGA--18
She's a kind of a girl that makes the News Of
The World.--POLYTHENEP--8
That I don't need no other lover --SOMETHING--7
Something in her style that shows me --SOMETHING
--8
But oh, that magic feeling, nowhere to go --
YOUNEVERGI--13
Oh, that magic feeling --YOUNEVERGI--14
Step on the gas and wipe that tear away.--
YOUNEVERGI--20
There is still a chance that they will see --
LETITBE/45--13
There is still a light that shines on me --
LETITBE/45--22
How about that?--YOUKNOWMYN--47
((That was Can You Dig It? by Georgie
Wood))--DIGIT--11
All that I was looking for was somebody who
looked like you.--IVEGOTAFEE--13
Ooo I've got a feeling that keeps me on my toes --
IVEGOTAFEE--14
I've got a feeling I think that everybody knows --
IVEGOTAFEE--16
There is still a chance that they will see --
LETITBE/LP--13
There is still a light that shines on me --
LETITBE/LP--22
The long and winding road that leads to your door
--LONGANDWIN--1
Will never disappear, I've seen that road before.
--LONGANDWIN--2
The wild and windy night that the rain washed away
--LONGANDWIN--4
I said, move over honey, I'm travelling on
that line --ONEAFTERNI--2

I said a-move over honey, I'm travelling on
   that line --ONEAFTERNI--16
Said a - move over honey, I'm travelling on
   that line --ONEAFTERNI--26
Longer than the road that stretches out ahead.--
   TWOOFUS--18
Longer than the road that stretches out ahead.--
   TWOOFUS--27

THAT'S

Like a heart that's oh so true--FROMMETOYO--8
That's the kind of love that is too good to be true
   --THANKYOUGI--9
Yeah, that's all I gotta do.--ALLIVEGOTT--5
Yeah, that's all I gotta do.--ALLIVEGOTT--21
That's all I do,--ANDILOVEHE--2
I got a chip on my shoulder that's bigger than my
   feet.--ILLCRYINST--6
And that's enough to make you mine girl --
   THINGSWESA--15
And that's enough to make you mine girl --
   THINGSWESA--26
That's a lie--NOREPLY--11
That's a lie--NOREPLY--24
'n' should you need a love that's true, it's me.--
   WHATYOURED--11
'n' should you need a love that's true, it's me.--
   WHATYOURED--18
The girl that's driving me mad is going away.--
   TICKETTORI--4
The girl that's driving me mad is going away,
   yeah.--TICKETTORI--25
But as from today well I've got somebody that's
   new --ANOTHERGIR--3
But as from today well I've seen somebody that's
   new --ANOTHERGIR--13
But as from today well I've seen somebody that's
   new --ANOTHERGIR--19
That's when it hurt me--INEEDYOU--13
That's when it hurt me--INEEDYOU--23
But I've found a driver and that's a start.--
   DRIVEMYCAR--25
That's all I want to say--MICHELLE--6
That's the end'a little girl.--RUNFORYOUR--8
That's the end'a little girl.--RUNFORYOUR--16
That's the end'a little girl.--RUNFORYOUR--24
That's the end'a little girl.--RUNFORYOUR--32
Picks up the letter that's lying there--SHESLEAVIN
   --14
About the love that's gone so cold--WITHINYOUW--22
Roll up (and that's an invitation)--MAGICALMYS--5
Roll up (and that's an invitation)--MAGICALMYS--23
I said that's alright I'm waiting here --DONTPASSME
   --29
The story of Rocky, that's the song.--ROCKYRACCO
   --48
I look at you all, see the love there that's
   sleeping --WHILEMYGUI--2
I look at you all, see the love there that's
   sleeping--WHILEMYGUI--18
You've got it, that's great, you've done it
   ((ha ha ha ha ha))--HEYBULLDOG--28
That's it man (wuh)--HEYBULLDOG--29
That's it, you've got it ((ha ha ha ha))--
   HEYBULLDOG--30
The love that's shining all around you --ITSALLTOOM
   --9
The love that's shining all around here --
   ITSALLTOOM--17
The love that's shining all around here --
   ITSALLTOOM--26
The love that's shining all around you --ITSALLTOOM
   --30
I want a love that's right --OLDBROWNSH--1
You know my name, that's right, look up my
   number (hey) --YOUKNOWMYN--10
You know my name - haa, that's right, look up
   the number --YOUKNOWMYN--15
That's right (yeah)....--YOUKNOWMYN--42
That's all!!--YOUKNOWMYN--46
You looked at me, that's all you had to do --
   FORYOUBLUE--14
Oh yeah, oh yeah (that's right).--IVEGOTAFEE--2

THEIR

I'm gonna break their hearts all round the world
   --ILLCRYINST--16
'cos I'm gonna break their hearts all round the
   world --ILLCRYINST--25
All these places had their moments --INMYLIFE--5
And these memories lose their meaning--INMYLIFE--11
If the rain comes they run and hide their heads--

RAIN--1
And sip their lemonade (when the sun shines down)
   --RAIN--5
They'll fill you in with all their sins, you'll see
   --LOVEYOUTWO--15
Their production will be second to none--BEINGFORTH--13
Who gain the world and lose their soul--WITHINYOUW--24
And my friends have lost their way.--BLUEJAYWAY--2
In their sties with all their backing--PIGGIES--11
In their sties with all their backing--PIGGIES--11
In their lives there's something lacking--PIGGIES
   --13
With their piggy wives --PIGGIES--18
They tumble blindly as they make their way across
   the universe.--ACROSSTHEU--14
Everybody let their hair down --IVEGOTAFEE--25
Everybody pulled their socks up (yeah) --IVEGOTAFEE
   --26
Everybody let their hair down ((a feeling I
   can't hide, oh no)) --IVEGOTAFEE--33
Everybody pulled their socks up (oh no, no) --
   IVEGOTAFEE--34
Everybody put their foot down, oh yeah (yeah).--
   IVEGOTAFEE--35

THEM

I can see them laugh at me --YOUVEGOTTO--7
And I hear them say.--YOUVEGOTTO--8
Hearing them, seeing them--YOUVEGOTTO--13
Hearing them, seeing them--YOUVEGOTTO--13
In my life I've loved them all.--INMYLIFE--8
I know I'll often stop and think about them --
   INMYLIFE--15
I know I'll often stop and think about them --
   INMYLIFE--19
Many more of them live next door--YELLOWSUBM--14
They had to count them all--DAYINTHELI--31
Are you one of them?--WITHINYOUW--27
Man you should have seen them kicking Edgar
   Allan Poe--IAMTHEWALR--27
And I told them where to go.--BLUEJAYWAY--9
He never listens to them--FOOLONTHEH--22
You can see them out for dinner--PIGGIES--17
But you'll have to have them all pulled out--
   SAVOYTRUFF--4
But you'll have to have them all pulled out--
   SAVOYTRUFF--9
But you'll have to have them all pulled out--
   SAVOYTRUFF--17
But you'll have to have them all pulled out--
   SAVOYTRUFF--26
Yes, you'll have to have them all pulled out--
   SAVOYTRUFF--28
Sexy Sadie (sexy Sadie) the greatest of them
   all ((she's the greatest))--SEXYSADIE--11
She's the latest and the greatest (she's the
   greatest) of them all--SEXYSADIE--23
(Sexy Sadie she's the latest and the greatest
   of them all)--SEXYSADIE--24
The judge does not agree and he tells them so oh
   - oh oh.--MAXWELLSIL--21
Them old twelve-bar blues.--FORYOUBLUE--10

THEMSELVES

Who hide themselves behind a wall of illusion--
   WITHINYOUW--4
Now they've lost themselves instead.--BLUEJAYWAY
   --4

THEN

And then while I'm away --ALLMYLOVIN--4
And then while I'm away --ALLMYLOVIN--10
And then while I'm away --ALLMYLOVIN--18
And then I might --HOLDMETIGH--4
And then I might --HOLDMETIGH--21
Then we'll have some fun when you're mine, all
   mine --LITTLECHIL--10
You hurt me then you're back again --NOTASECOND--9
You hurt me then you're back again --NOTASECOND--20
Until then I'll cry instead.--ILLCRYINST--19
Until then I'll cry instead.--ILLCRYINST--28
Then I will remember things we said today.--
   THINGSWESA--5
Then we will remember things we said today.--
   THINGSWESA--10
Then we will remember things we said today.--
   THINGSWESA--21
Then we will remember things we said today.--
   THINGSWESA--32
But ((but)) every now and then ((now and then))
   I feel so insecure--HELP--22

But ((but)) every now and then ((now and then))
    I feel so insecure--HELP--22
And then you'll be the lonely one (you're not
    the only one)--YOUREGONNA--12
Then I guess I'd be with you my friend --IFINEEDEDS
    --5
Then it might not have been like this --IFINEEDEDS
    --8
Then I guess I'd be with you my friend --IFINEEDEDS
    --15
Then it might not have been like this --IFINEEDEDS
    --18
And then she said--NORWEGIANW--15
Then we lie beneath a shady tree --GOODDAYSUN--10
Ooo then I suddenly see you--GOTTOGETYO--5
Ooo then I suddenly see you--GOTTOGETYO--20
Then suddenly I see you--GOTTOGETYO--29
Then I could speak my mind and tell you--IWANTTOTEL
    --17
And then the fireman rushes in--PENNYLANE--26
Heading for home you start to roam then you're in
    town.--GOODMORNIN--8
Then you decide to take a walk by the old school--
    GOODMORNIN--14
Then you may find--WITHINYOUW--29
Then you can start to make it better.--HEYJUDE--4
Then you begin to make it better.--HEYJUDE--8
Then you can start to make it better.--HEYJUDE--18
Then you'll begin ((let it out)) to make it
    better --HEYJUDE--29
Well then nah nah nah, nah - nah - nah - nah
    --HEYJUDE--74
Good evening, you know my name, well then look
    up my number --YOUKNOWMYN--9
Then I find I've got the number wrong.--ONEAFTERNI
    --14
Then I find I got the number wrong - well ((well)).
    --ONEAFTERNI--24

THERE
And I'll be there.--ANYTIMEATA--3
I'll be there to make you feel right --ANYTIMEATA
    --6
And I'll be there.--ANYTIMEATA--12
There is nothing I won't do --ANYTIMEATA--15
And I'll be there.--ANYTIMEATA--21
And I'll be there.--ANYTIMEATA--24
And I'll be there.--ANYTIMEATA--27
I SAW HER STANDING THERE.--ISAWHERSTA--Title
Ooh when I saw her standing there.--ISAWHERSTA--6
Whoa when I saw her standing there.--ISAWHERSTA--10
Whoa since/when I saw her standing there. (hey! aah!)--
    ISAWHERSTA--17
Oh since I saw her standing there.--ISAWHERSTA--24
Whoa since I saw her standing there--ISAWHERSTA--25
Yeah, well since I saw her standing there.--
    ISAWHERSTA--26
I call your name, but you're not there --ICALLYOURN
    --1
There, there's a place where I can go--THERESAPLA
    --1
There, there's a place where I can go--THERESAPLA
    --13
Don't want to cry when there's people there --
    ILLCRYINST--11
Don't want to cry when there's people there --
    ILLCRYINST--20
There is really nothing else I'd rather do --
    IMHAPPYJUS--6
There is one thing I'm sure of--EVERYLITTL--14
There's no fun in what I do when she's not there
    --IDONTWANTT--6
There's no fun in what I do if she's not there --
    IDONTWANTT--23
There is one love I should never have crossed.--
    IMALOSER--4
She took me half the way there --DAYTRIPPER--10
She took me half the way there, now.--DAYTRIPPER
    --12
Is there anybody going to listen to my story--GIRL
    --1
When friends are there, you feel a fool.--GIRL--13
The only difference is you're down there.--
    IMLOOKINGT--13
There are places I remember --INMYLIFE--1
There is no-one compares with you --INMYLIFE--10
And I noticed there wasn't a chair.--NORWEGIANW--10
'cos I won't be there with you.--THINKFORYO--9
'cos I won't be there with you.--THINKFORYO--18
'cos I won't be there with you.--THINKFORYO--27
'cos I won't be there with you.--THINKFORYO--31
'cos I won't be there with you.--THINKFORYO--33
You tell me that you heard every sound there is --

ANDYOURBIR--13
Day or night he'll be there any time at all, Dr.
    Robert --DRROBERT--2
Lying there and staring at the ceiling --IMONLYSLEE
    --15
Darning his socks in the night when there's
    nobody there--ELEANORRIG--15
There will be times when all the things --FORNOONE
    --21
I didn't know what I would find there--GOTTOGETYO
    --2
Could see another kind of mind there.--GOTTOGETYO
    --4
When I'm with you I want to stay there--GOTTOGETYO
    --17
And if I do I know the way there.--GOTTOGETYO--19
I didn't know what I would find there--GOTTOGETYO
    --26
Could see another kind of mind there.--GOTTOGETYO
    --28
HERE, THERE AND EVERYWHERE.--HERETHEREA--Title
Nobody can deny that there's something there.--
    HERETHEREA--4
There, running my hands through her hair--
    HERETHEREA--5
Someone is speaking but she doesn't know he's
    there.--HERETHEREA--7
Watching her eyes and hoping I'm always there.--
    HERETHEREA--13
Watching her eyes and hoping I'm always there.--
    HERETHEREA--19
I will be there and everywhere --HERETHEREA--20
Here, there and everywhere.--HERETHEREA--21
Penny Lane: there is a barber showing photographs
    --PENNYLANE--1
There beneath the blue suburban skies I sit--
    PENNYLANE--10
In Penny Lane there is a fireman with an
    hour-glass--PENNYLANE--12
There beneath the blue suburban skies I sit--
    PENNYLANE--29
There beneath the blue suburban skies --PENNYLANE
    --32
There will be a show tonight on trampoline.--
    BEINGFORTH--2
The Hendersons will all be there--BEINGFORTH--3
See the people standing there who disagree and
    never win--FIXINGAHOL--9
There I will go.--FIXINGAHOL--13
Suddenly someone is there at the turnstyle--
    LUCYINTHES--25
Picks up the letter that's lying there--SHESLEAVIN
    --14
To try our best to hold it there--WITHINYOUW--11
Peace of mind is waiting there--WITHINYOUW--30
How often have you been there?--BABYYOUREA--9
What did you see when you were there?--BABYYOUREA
    --11
There's so many there to meet.--BLUEJAYWAY--11
I tell you man he living there still--GLASSONION
    --18
There lived a young boy name of Rocky Raccoon--
    ROCKYRACCO--2
I look at you all, see the love there that's
    sleeping --WHILEMYGUI--2
I look at you all, see the love there that's
    sleeping--WHILEMYGUI--18
Your love is there for me--ITSALLTOOM--5
The more there is to see.--ITSALLTOOM--7
You're correct, there's nobody there.--ONLYANORTH
    --15
And I told you there's no-one there.--ONLYANORTH
    --16
Once there was a way--GOLDENSLUM--1
Once there was a way--GOLDENSLUM--3
Once there was a way--GOLDENSLUM--11
Once there was a way--GOLDENSLUM--13
No-one there to tell us what to do.--OCTOPUSSGA--22
There will be an answer, let it be.--LETITBE/45--11
There is still a chance that they will see --
    LETITBE/45--13
There will be an answer, let it be.--LETITBE/45--14
Yeah there will be an answer, let it be.--
    LETITBE/45--16
There is still a light that shines on me --
    LETITBE/45--22
Oh there will be an answer, let it be.--LETITBE/45
    --28
There will be an answer, let it be.--LETITBE/LP--11
There is still a chance that they will see --
    LETITBE/LP--13
There will be an answer, let it be.--LETITBE/LP--14
Yeah there will be an answer, let it be.--
    LETITBE/LP--16

THERE

There is still a light that shines on me --
    LETITBE/LP--22
Oh there will be an answer, let it be.--LETITBE/LP
    --28
Oh there will be an answer, let it be.--LETITBE/LP
    --30

THERE'LL

There'll be no sad tomorrow--THERESAPLA--11
Telling me there'll be no next time--YOULIKEMET--3

THERE'S

But you know there's always rain--PLEASEPLEA--14
If there's anything that you want--FROMMETOYO--3
If there's anything I can do--FROMMETOYO--4
If there's anything that you want--FROMMETOYO--15
If there's anything I can do--FROMMETOYO--16
If there's anything that you want--FROMMETOYO--26
If there's anything I can do--FROMMETOYO--27
Well, there's gonna be a time--ILLGETYOU--16
THERE'S A PLACE.--THERESAPLA--Title
There, there's a place where I can go--THERESAPLA
    --1
And it's my mind and there's no time--THERESAPLA
    --3
In my mind there's no sorrow--THERESAPLA--9
There, there's a place where I can go--THERESAPLA
    --13
And it's my mind and there's no time--THERESAPLA
    --15
There's a place, there's a place--THERESAPLA--17
There's a place, there's a place--THERESAPLA--17
There's a place, there's a place.--THERESAPLA--18
There's a place, there's a place.--THERESAPLA--18
Don't want to cry when there's people there --
    ILLCRYINST--11
Don't want to cry when there's people there --
    ILLCRYINST--20
In this world there's nothing I would rather do --
    IMHAPPYJUS--10
In this world there's nothing I would rather do --
    IMHAPPYJUS--18
In this world there's nothing I would rather do --
    IMHAPPYJUS--26
If there's anything I can do --TELLMEWHY--23
There's nothing for me here so I will disappear --
    IDONTWANTT--3
There's no fun in what I do when she's not there
    --IDONTWANTT--6
There's nothing for me here so I will disappear --
    IDONTWANTT--15
There's no fun in what I do if she's not there --
    IDONTWANTT--23
And ((and)) there's no fun in it --WHATYOURED--6
We're all alone and there's nobody else --IMDOWN
    --16
There's a shadow hanging over me--YESTERDAY--7
Life is very short and there's no time--WECANWORKI
    --11
There's a chance that we might fall apart before
    too long.--WECANWORKI--18
Life is very short and there's no time--WECANWORKI
    --20
There's a chance that we might fall apart before
    too long.--WECANWORKI--27
Till they find there's no need (there's no need).
    --IMONLYSLEE--10
Till they find there's no need (there's no need).
    --IMONLYSLEE--10
Darning his sockszin the night when there's
    nobody there--ELEANORRIG--15
Nobody can deny that there's something there.--
    HERETHEREA--4
There's people standing round--LOVEYOUTWO--13
There's one for you, nineteen for me --TAXMAN--4
Everbody knows there's nothing doing--GOODMORNIN
    --9
There's nothing you can do that can't be done
    ((love))--ALLYOUN/YS--4
There's nothing you can know that isn't known
    ((love))--ALLYOUN/YS--19
There's nowhere you can be that isn't where
    you're meant to be ((love))--ALLYOUN/YS--21
There's a fog upon LA --BLUEJAYWAY--1
There's so many there to meet.--BLUEJAYWAY--11
In their lives there's something lacking--PIGGIES
    --13
Everywhere there's lots of piggies--PIGGIES--15
You're correct, there's nobody there.--ONLYANORTH
    --15
And I told you there's no-one there.--ONLYANORTH
    --16

THESE

Treasure ((treasure)) these few words ((words))
    --PSILOVEYOU--3
Treasure ((treasure)) these few words ((words))
    --PSILOVEYOU--12
Last night I said these words to my girl --
    PLEASEPLEA--1
Last night I said these words to my girl --
    PLEASEPLEA--19
Holding back these tears in my eyes.--TELLMEWHY--16
These days such a kind girl seems so hard to find
    --THINGSWESA--7
Look into these eyes now--TELLMEWHAT--13
But now ((but now)) these days are gone
    ((these days are gone))--HELP--11
But now ((but now)) these days are gone
    ((these days are gone))--HELP--11
But now ((now)) these days are gone ((these
    days are gone))--HELP--31
But now ((now)) these days are gone ((these
    days are gone))--HELP--31
All these places had their moments --INMYLIFE--5
But of all these friends and lovers --INMYLIFE--9
And these memories lose their meaning--INMYLIFE--11
These are words that go together well, my
    Michelle.--MICHELLE--2
The act you've known for all these years--
    SGTPEPPERS--6
Take these broken wings and learn to fly.--
    BLACKBIRD--2
Take these sunken eyes and learn to see.--BLACKBIRD
    --6
Take these broken wings and learn to fly.--
    BLACKBIRD--14
All these years I've been wandering round the
    world --IVEGOTAFEE--11

THEY

I get shy when they start to stare.--ILLCRYINST--12
I get shy when they start to stare.--ILLCRYINST--21
They said it wasn't you--NOREPLY--4
They said you were not home--NOREPLY--10
They said you were not home--NOREPLY--23
Did she understand it when they said --GIRL--23
If the rain comes they run and hide their heads--
    RAIN--1
They might as well be dead--RAIN--2
When the sun shines they slip into the shade
    (when the sun shines down)--RAIN--4
Till they find there's no need (there's no need).
    --IMONLYSLEE--10
All the lonely people, where do they all come
    from?--ELEANORRIG--9
All the lonely people, where do they all belong?--
    ELEANORRIG--10
All the lonely people, where do they all come
    from?--ELEANORRIG--17
All the lonely people, where do they all belong?--
    ELEANORRIG--18
All the lonely people, where do they all come
    from?--ELEANORRIG--27
All the lonely people, where do they all belong?--
    ELEANORRIG--29
Burns my feet as they touch the ground.--GOODDAYSUN
    --8
All those words they seem to slip away.--IWANTTOTEL
    --4
They had to count them all--DAYINTHELI--31
Now they know how many holes it takes--DAYINTHELI--32
And wonder why they don't get in my door.--
    FIXINGAHOL--10
Silly people run around they worry me--FIXINGAHOL--17
And never ask me why they don't get past my door.
    --FIXINGAHOL--18
When they pass away.--WITHINYOUW--7
If they only knew.--WITHINYOUW--15
They don't know--WITHINYOUW--25
They can't see--WITHINYOUW--26
See how they run like pigs from a gun, see how
    they fly--IAMTHEWALR--2
See how they run like pigs from a gun, see how
    they fly--IAMTHEWALR--2
I am the eggman (goo) they are the eggmen (goo)
    I am the walrus--IAMTHEWALR--7
See how they fly like Lucy in the sky, see how
    they run--IAMTHEWAL--10
See how they fly like Lucy in the sky, see how
    they run--IAMTHEWAL--10
I am the eggman (goo) they are the eggmen (goo)
    I am the walrus--IAMTHEWALR--15
I am the eggman, they are the eggmen, I am the

walrus--IAMTHEWALR--19
See how they smile, like pigs in a sty, see how
   they snied--IAMTHEWALR--23
See how they smile, like pigs in a sty, see how
   they snied--IAMTHEWALR--23
I am the eggman (goo) they are the eggmen (goo)
   I am the walrus (goo)--IAMTHEWALR--28
We'll be over soon they said --BLUEJAYWAY--3
They can see that he's just a fool--FOOLONTHEH--4
They can tell what he wants to do--FOOLONTHEH--16
They don't like him --FOOLONTHEH--24
See how they run.--LADYMADONN--8
See how they run.--LADYMADONN--11
See how they run.--LADYMADONN--17
They leave the West behind --BACKINTHEU--16
They leave the West behind --BACKINTHEU--28
They say it's your birthday --BIRTHDAY--3
But they don't arrive.--DONTPASSME--5
In a couple of years they have built a home sweet
   home --OBLADIOBLA--17
In a couple of years they have built a home sweet
   home--OBLADIOBLA--29
They don't care what goes on around.--PIGGIES--12
What they need's a damn good whacking.--PIGGIES--14
They bought and sold you.--WHILEMYGUI--8
But they are, they just play it like that.--
   ONLYANORTH--6
But they are, they just play it like that.--
   ONLYANORTH--6
You know they didn't even give us a chance.--
   BALLADOFJO--4
They look just like two gurus in drag.--BALLADOFJO
   --32
Not worrying what they or you say --OLDBROWNSH--19
For though they may be parted --LETITBE/45--12
There is still a chance that they will see --
   LETITBE/45--13
They slither wildly as they slip away across the
   universe.--ACROSSTHEU--2
They slither wildly as they slip away across the
   universe.--ACROSSTHEU--2
They call me on and on across the universe.--
   ACROSSTHEU--12
They tumble blindly as they make their wayzacross
   the universe.--ACROSSTHEU--14
They tumble blindly as they make their way across
   the universe.--ACROSSTHEU--14
For though they may be parted --LETITBE/LP--12
There is still a chance that they will see --
   LETITBE/LP--13
And still they lead me back to the long, winding
   road.--LONGANDWIN--9
But still they lead me back to the long, winding
   road --LONGANDWIN--12

THEY'D
But if they'd seen--YOUCANTDOT--20
They'd laugh in my face.--YOUCANTDOT--22
But if they'd seen--YOUCANTDOT--39
They'd laugh in my face.--YOUCANTDOT--41
They'd seen his face before--DAYINTHELI--9

THEY'LL
They'll fill you in with all their sins, you'll see.
   --LOVEYOUTWO--16

THEY'RE
Now it looks as though they're here to stay--
   YESTERDAY--3
Though the days are few, they're filled with tears
   --YOUWONTSEE--16
Though the days are few they're filled with tears
   --YOUWONTSEE--25
I don't mind, I think they're crazy --IMONLYSLEE
   --8
But they're guaranteed to raise a smile.--
   SGTPEPPERS--4
He knows that they're the fool--FOOLONTHEH--23
But they're not, we just wrote it like that.--
   ONLYANORTH--3
They're gonna crucify me.--BALLADOFJO--8
They're gonna crucify me.--BALLADOFJO--16
They're gonna crucify me.--BALLADOFJO--24
They're gonna crucify me.--BALLADOFJO--36
They're gonna crucify me.--BALLADOFJO--44
They're gonna crucify me.--BALLADOFJO--46
Knowing they're happy and they're safe (happy
   and they're safe).--OCTOPUSSGA--20
Knowing they're happy and they're safe (happy
   and they're safe).--OCTOPUSSGA--20
Knowing they're happy and they're safe (happy

and they're safe).--OCTOPUSSGA--20
Now they're frightened of leaving it --IMEMINE--5

THEY'VE
They've been going in and out of style--SGTPEPPERS
   --3
Now they've lost themselves instead.--BLUEJAYWAY
   --4

THICK
Through thick and thin she will always be my
   friend.--ANOTHERGIR--11
Through thick and thin she will always be my
   friend.--ANOTHERGIR--17
When you find yourself in the thick of it --
   MARTHAMYDE--5
When you find yourself in the thick of it --
   MARTHAMYDE--11

THIN
Through thick and thin she will always be my
   friend.--ANOTHERGIR--11
Through thick and thin she will always be my
   friend.--ANOTHERGIR--17

THING
I could tell the world a thing or two about our love
   --THANKYOUGI--5
One thing I can say girl --EIGHTDAYSA--11
One thing I can say girl --EIGHTDAYSA--31
EVERY LITTLE THING.--EVERYLITTL--Title
Every little thing she does--EVERYLITTL--7
And you know the thing she does--EVERYLITTL--9
There is one thing I'm sure of--EVERYLITTL--14
Every little thing she does--EVERYLITTL--17
And you know the thing she does--EVERYLITTL--19
Every little thing she does--EVERYLITTL--21
And you know the thing she does--EVERYLITTL--23
Every little thing--EVERYLITTL--25
Every little thing--EVERYLITTL--26
Every little thing.--EVERYLITTL--27
Same old thing happen every day.--IMDOWN--9
Said you had a thing or two to tell me--INEEDYOU
   --6
Fun. (fun is the one thing that money can't buy)--
   SHESLEAVIN--30
What a thing to do.--BABYYOUREA--18
What a thing to do (baby).--BABYYOUREA--33
One thing I can tell you is you got to be free--
   COMETOGETH--20

THINGS
'cos you tell me things I want to know --ASKMEWHY
   --2
'cos you tell me things I want to know --ASKMEWHY
   --17
I'll remember all the little things we've done --
   MISERY--6
I'll remember all the little things we've done --
   MISERY--10
Tell me that you want the kind of things --
   CANTBUYMEL--19
Tell me that you want the kind of things --
   CANTBUYMEL--29
And things you do go round my head--THERESAPLA--6
The things you said--THERESAPLA--7
I find the things that you do --HARDDAYSNI--6
To get you money to buy you things --HARDDAYSNI--9
I find the things that you do --HARDDAYSNI--22
I find the things that you do --HARDDAYSNI--35
So - oh, I should have realised a lot of things
   before --ISHOULDHAV--11
You could find better things to do --ILLBEBACK--9
You could find better things to do --ILLBEBACK--18
THINGS WE SAID TODAY.--THINGSWESA--Title
Then I will remember things we said today.--
   THINGSWESA--5
Then we will remember things we said today.--
   THINGSWESA--10
Then we will remember things we said today.--
   THINGSWESA--21
Then we will remember things we said today.--
   THINGSWESA--32
I got a whole lot of things to tell her --
   WHENIGETHO--2
I got a whole lot of things I gotta say to her.--
   WHENIGETHO--6
I got a whole lot of things to tell her --
   WHENIGETHO--8

I got a whole lot of things to tell her --
    WHENIGETHO--14
I got so many things I gotta do --WHENIGETHO--22
I got a whole lot of things to tell her --
    WHENIGETHO--25
I got a whole lot of things to tell her --
    WHENIGETHO--27
That her baby buys her things, you know --IFEELFINE
    --9
That her baby buys her things, you know --IFEELFINE
    --17
I would remember all the things we planned--YESITIS
    --7
I've been alone and I have missed things--
    IVEJUSTSEE--15
When I think of things we did it makes me wanna
    cry.--NIGHTBEFOR--10
When I think of things we did it makes me wanna
    cry.--NIGHTBEFOR--18
For people and things that went before --INMYLIFE
    --14
For people and things that went before --INMYLIFE
    --18
To say about the things that you do.--THINKFORYO
    --2
About the good things--THINKFORYO--4
All the things that you should.--THINKFORYO--23
There will be times when all the things --FORNOONE
    --21
My head is filled with things to say --IWANTTOTEL
    --2
That is confusing things.--IWANTTOTEL--11
I said who put all those things in your head?--
    SHESAIDSHE--4
Things that make me feel that I'm mad--SHESAIDSHE
    --5
I'm taking the time for a number of things--
    FIXINGAHOL--19
I beat her and kept her apart from the things
    that she loved--GETTINGBET--26
I can know all things on earth.--INNERLIGHT--2
You can know all things on earth.--INNERLIGHT--9
For the things you do endear you to me - aah --
    IWILL--17
The way things are going --BALLADOFJO--7
The way things are going --BALLADOFJO--15
The way things are going --BALLADOFJO--23
The way things are going --BALLADOFJO--35
The way things are going --BALLADOFJO--43
The way things are going --BALLADOFJO--45
Something in the things she shows me --SOMETHING
    --17

THINK
I think about you night and day--ILLGETYOU--9
When I think about you, I can say--ILLGETYOU--11
You think you've lost your love--SHELOVESYO--4
I think it's only fair--SHELOVESYO--25
I think you'll understand--IWANTTOHOL--2
I think you'll understand--IWANTTOHOL--21
I think you'll understand--IWANTTOHOL--34
I think it's a sin?--YOUCANTDOT--12
I think I'll let you down (let you down)--
    YOUCANTDOT--13
I think of you--THERESAPLA--5
I think I'll love you too --IMHAPPYJUS--2
I think I'll love you too ((oh)) --IMHAPPYJUS--14
I think I'll love you too ((oh)) --IMHAPPYJUS--22
I think of her --BABYSINBLA--10
I think I'll take a walk and look for her.--
    IDONTWANTT--8
But I think I'll take a walk and look for her.--
    IDONTWANTT--25
I think I'm gonna be sad--TICKETTORI--2
I think it's today, yeah--TICKETTORI--3
She ought to think twice--TICKETTORI--18
She ought to think twice--TICKETTORI--21
I think I'm gonna be sad--TICKETTORI--23
I think it's today, yeah--TICKETTORI--24
She ought to think twice--TICKETTORI--31
She ought to think twice--TICKETTORI--34
When I think of things we did it makes me wanna
    cry.--NIGHTBEFOR--10
When I think of things we did it makes me wanna
    cry.--NIGHTBEFOR--18
Think of what you're saying --WECANWORKI--6
You can get it wrong and still you think that
    it's alright.--WECANWORKI--7
Think of what I'm saying --WECANWORKI--8
When I think of all the times I tried so hard
    to leave her --GIRL--6
When I think of love as something new.--INMYLIFE
    --12

I know I'll often stop and think about them --
    INMYLIFE--15
I know I'll often stop and think about them --
    INMYLIFE--19
I think you know by now--MICHELLE--17
THINK FOR YOURSELF.--THINKFORYO--Title
Think for yourself --THINKFORYO--8
Think for yourself --THINKFORYO--17
Think for yourself --THINKFORYO--26
Think for yourself --THINKFORYO--30
Think for yourself --THINKFORYO--32
I used to think of no-one else but you were just
    the same --WHATGOESON--22
You didn't even think of me as someone with a name.
    --WHATGOESON--23
Everybody seems to think I'm lazy.--IMONLYSLEE--7
I don't mind, I think they're crazy --IMONLYSLEE
    --8
You think she needs you.--FORNOONE--13
No-one, I think, is in my tree--STRAWBERRY--16
That is, I think it's not too bad.--STRAWBERRY--20
Always, no, sometimes, think it's me--STRAWBERRY
    --26
I think I know, I mean, er, yes--STRAWBERRY--28
That is, I think I disagree.--STRAWBERRY--30
Give us a wink and make me think of you.--
    LOVELYRITA--28
What would you think if I sang outta tune --
    WITHALITTL--1
Expert texpert, choking smokers, don't you
    think the joker laughs at you?--IAMTHEWALR--21
Did you think that money was heaven sent?--
    LADYMADONN--4
However big you think you are--SEXYSADIE--17
However big you think you are--SEXYSADIE--18
... However big you think you are.--SEXYSADIE--28
What makes you think you're something special
    when you smile?--HEYBULLDOG--4
You think you know me but you haven't got a clue.
    --HEYBULLDOG--16
You may think the chords are going wrong --
    ONLYANORTH--2
You may think the band are not quite right --
    ONLYANORTH--5
If you think the harmony--ONLYANORTH--13
You don't take nothing with you but your soul -
    think!--BALLADOFJO--28
And all I have to do is think of her --SOMETHING
    --16
I've got a feeling I think that everybody knows --
    IVEGOTAFEE--16

THINKING
And I'm always thinking of you.--ASKMEWHY--15
And I'm always thinking of you.--ASKMEWHY--23
And I'm always thinking of you, you, you.--ASKMEWHY
    --27
It's you she's thinking of--SHELOVESYO--6
You'll be thinking of me, somehow I will know --
    THINGSWESA--2
Can't stop thinking about her now.--EVERYLITTL--6
You tell lies thinking I can't see --IMDOWN--1
You're the one that I'd be thinking of --IFINEEDEDS
    --2
You're thinking of me the same old way --IMLOOKINGT
    --11
Try thinking more if just for your own sake.--
    THINKFORYO--20
Say the word I'm thinking of --THEWORD--3
Spread the word I'm thinking of --THEWORD--11
Say the word I'm thinking of --THEWORD--19
It's the word I'm thinking of --THEWORD--27
Both of us thinking how good it can be--HERETHEREA
    --6

THINKS
She thinks of him and so she dresses in black --
    BABYSINBLA--4
But she thinks only of him --BABYSINBLA--11
She thinks of him.--BABYSINBLA--13
She thinks of him and so she dresses in black --
    BABYSINBLA--24

THIRTY-ONE
PC Thirty-One said, we caught a dirty one,
    Maxwell stands alone --MAXWELLSIL--17

THIS
As I write this letter, send my love to you --
    PSILOVEYOU--1

As I write this letter, send my love to you --
　　PSILOVEYOU--10
As I write this letter (oh) send my love to you --
　　PSILOVEYOU--16
THIS BOY.--THISBOY--Title
But this boy wants you back again.--THISBOY--3
This boy wants you back again.--THISBOY--6
Oh, and this boy would be happy--THISBOY--7
This boy wouldn't mind the pain--THISBOY--11
If this boy gets you back again.--THISBOY--13
This boy, this boy, this boy.--THISBOY--14
This boy, this boy, this boy.--THISBOY--14
This boy, this boy, this boy.--THISBOY--14
I know this love of mine --ANDILOVEHE--17
I know this love of mine --ANDILOVEHE--22
This could only happen to me --ISHOULDHAV--5
If this is love you've got to give me more --
　　ISHOULDHAV--12
This could only happen to me --ISHOULDHAV--15
Before this dance is through --IMHAPPYJUS--1
In this world there's nothing I would rather do --
　　IMHAPPYJUS--10
Before this dance is through ((aah)) --IMHAPPYJUS
　　--13
In this world there's nothing I would rather do --
　　IMHAPPYJUS--18
Before this dance is through ((aah)) --IMHAPPYJUS
　　--21
In this world there's nothing I would rather do --
　　IMHAPPYJUS--26
This time I will try to show --ILLBEBACK--11
This time I will try to show --ILLBEBACK--20
I got no business being here with you this way.--
　　WHENIGETHO--23
Beneath this mask I am wearing a frown.--IMALOSER
　　--10
This happened once before--NOREPLY--1
This is what I said tonight--YESITIS--15
This is what I said tonight--YESITIS--24
Though you've gone away this morning--YOULIKEMET
　　--1
And so I'm telling you this time you'd better
　　stop --ANOTHERGIR--8
And feeling like this--INEEDYOU--14
And feeling like this--INEEDYOU--24
I have never known the like of this--IVEJUSTSEE--14
But other girls were never quite like this --
　　IVEJUSTSEE--17
After all this time I don't know why.--GIRL--9
Then it might not have been like this --IFINEEDEDS
　　--8
Then it might not have been like this --IFINEEDEDS
　　--18
NORWEGIAN WOOD (THIS BIRD HAS FLOWN).--NORWEGIANW
　　--Title
This bird had flown.--NORWEGIANW--23
Let this be a sermon --RUNFORYOUR--17
In this way Mr. K. will challenge the world.--
　　BEINGFORTH--7
How could she do this to me?--SHESLEAVIN--19
Step right this way.--MAGICALMYS--2
You were only waiting for this moment to arise.--
　　BLACKBIRD--4
You were only waiting for this moment to be free.
　　--BLACKBIRD--8
You were only waiting for this moment to arise --
　　BLACKBIRD--16
You were only waiting for this moment to arise --
　　BLACKBIRD--17
You were only waiting for this moment to arise --
　　BLACKBIRD--18
This is what I'd say:--HONEYPIE--6
I like this kinda hot kinda music, hot kinda music
　　--HONEYPIE--22
And Molly says this as she takes him by the hand:
　　--OBLADIOBLA--4
He said, Danny - Boy this is a showdown.--
　　ROCKYRACCO--20
If you're listening to this song --ONLYANORTH--1
Now I'm stepping out this old brown shoe --
　　OLDBROWNSH--5
Got me escaping from this zoo --OLDBROWNSH--13
Elmore James got nothing on this baby - heh.--
　　FORYOUBLUE--12

THOSE
You're telling all those lies--THINKFORYO--3
All those words they seem to slip away.--IWANTTOTEL
　　--4
I said who put all those things in your head?--
　　SHESAIDSHE--4
Now my advice for those who die (Taxman)--TAXMAN
　　--22

Cocoanut fudge really blows down those blues
　　(wuh) --SAVOYTRUFF--8
Even those tears --IMEMINE--16
Even those tears --IMEMINE--29

THOUGH
Though he'll regret it someday--THISBOY--2
Though he may want you too--THISBOY--5
And though we may be blind --THINGSWESA--13
And though we may be blind --THINGSWESA--24
And though he'll never come back --BABYSINBLA--5
And though it's only a whim --BABYSINBLA--12
And/But though he'll never come back --BABYSINBLA--25
Though tonight she's made me sad --IDONTWANTT--9
Though tonight she's made me sad --IDONTWANTT--18
Though I've had a drink or two and I don't care --
　　IDONTWANTT--22
And though I lose a friend in the end you will
　　know, oh.--ILLFOLLOWT--6
And though I lose a friend in the end you will
　　know, oh.--ILLFOLLOWT--11
Though you've gone away this morning--YOULIKEMET
　　--1
Now it looks as though they're here to stay--
　　YESTERDAY--3
All my life, though some have changed.--INMYLIFE
　　--2
Though I know I'll never lose affection --INMYLIFE
　　--13
Though I know I'll never lose affection --INMYLIFE
　　--17
And though you still can't see --THINKFORYO--12
I feel as though you ought to know--WAIT--9
I feel as though you ought to know--WAIT--17
Though the days are few, they're filled with tears
　　--YOUWONTSEE--9
Though the days are few they're filled with tears
　　--YOUWONTSEE--25
I said even though you know what you know --
　　SHESAIDSHE--10
I said even though you know what you know --
　　SHESAIDSHE--16
And though she feels as if she's in a play--
　　PENNYLANE--22
And though the news was rather sad--DAYINTHELI--3
And though the holes were rather small--DAYINTHELI
　　--30
Though she was born a long, long time ago --
　　YOURMOTHER--4
Though she was born a long, long time ago --
　　YOURMOTHER--10
Though she was born a long, long time ago --
　　YOURMOTHER--15
Though she was born a long, long time ago --
　　YOURMOTHER--23
Martha my dear, though I spend my days in
　　conversation,--MARTHAMYDE--1
Though you pick me up,--OLDBROWNSH--9
And though she thought I knew the answer --
　　SHECAMEINT--14
And though she tried her best to help me --
　　SHECAMEINT--18
For though they may be parted --LETITBE/45--12
For though they may be parted --LETITBE/LP--12

THOUGHT
I thought that you would realise--ILLBEBACK--13
I have always thought that it's a crime--WECANWORKI
　　--13
I have always thought that it's a crime--WECANWORKI
　　--22
I thought I knew you, what did I know?--IMLOOKINGT
　　--2
I thought I knew you, what did I know?--IMLOOKINGT
　　--18
Lay down all thought, surrender to the void--
　　TOMORROWNE--3
But I thought you might like to know--SGTPEPPERS
　　--20
She (we never thought of ourselves)--SHESLEAVIN--20
Is leaving (never a thought for our ourselves)--
　　SHESLEAVIN--21
And now the thought of meeting you--HONEYPIE--14
Jojo was a man who thought he was a loner --
　　GETBACK/45--1
Sweet Loretta Martin thought she was a woman --
　　GETBACK/45--16
And though she thought I knew the answer --
　　SHECAMEINT--14
Sweet Moretta Fart she thought she was a cleaner--
　　GETBACK/LP--2
Jojo was a man who thought he was a loner--

THOUGHT

GETBACK/LP--7
Sweet Loretta Martin thought she was a woman--
GETBACK/LP--22

THOUGHTLESS

Replacing every thoughtless frown.--OLDBROWNSH--12

THOUGHTLESSLY

Why would she treat us so thoughtlessly?--
SHESLEAVIN--18

THOUGHTS

Thoughts meander like a restless wind inside a
letter-box --ACROSSTHEU--13

THOUSAND

It's a thousand pages, give or take a few,
((paperback))--PAPERBACKW--15
Four thousand holes in Blackburn, Lancashire--
DAYINTHELI--29
The man of a thousand voices talking perfectly loud
--FOOLONTHEH--9

THREE

One, two, three, four.--ISAWHERSTA--1
One, two, three, four.--TICKETTORI--1
One, two, three, four, one, two.--TAXMAN--1
(One, two, three, four)--TAXMAN--2
One, two (ah yeah), three, four.--SGTPEPPREP--1
If I'd been out till quarter to three--WHENIMSIXT--5
One, two, three, four, five, six, seven,
eight.--DONTPASSME--36
You know it's three weeks, I'm going insane --
IMSOTIRED--12
You know it's three weeks, I'm going insane --
IMSOTIRED--21
Two, three.--YERBLUES--1
One, two, three, four --ALLTOGETHE--1
He say one and one and one is three--COMETOGETH--40
One, two, three, four, five, six, seven --
YOUNEVERGI--24
One, two, three, four, five, six, seven --
YOUNEVERGI--26
One, two, three, four, five, six, seven --
YOUNEVERGI--28
One, two, three, four, five, six, seven --
YOUNEVERGI--30
One, two, three, four, five, six, seven --
YOUNEVERGI--32
One, two, three, four, five, six, seven --
YOUNEVERGI--34
One, two, three, four, five, six, seven --
YOUNEVERGI--36
One, two, three, four, five, six, seven --
YOUNEVERGI--38
One, two, three, four, five, six, seven --
YOUNEVERGI--40
You know my name, you know me number three --
YOUKNOWMYN--34
OK one, two, three, four.--GETBACK/LP--6
A - one, two, three.--IDIGAPONY--2

THRILL

It's certainly a thrill--SGTPEPPERS--15

THROUGH

Well we danced through the night --ISAWHERSTA--13
Oh (wuh!) we danced through the night --ISAWHERSTA
--20
My crying is through, oh.--NOTASECOND--6
My crying is through, oh.--NOTASECOND--17
Before this dance is through,--IMHAPPYJUS--1
Before this dance is through ((aah))--IMHAPPYJUS--13
Before this dance is through ((aah))--IMHAPPYJUS--21
Come on, let me through --WHENIGETHO--21
But I saw you peep through your window--NOREPLY--5
How can I get through--TELLMEWHAT--19
How can I get through--TELLMEWHAT--28
Through thick and thin she will always be my
friend.--ANOTHERGIR--11
Through thick and thin she will always be my
friend.--ANOTHERGIR--17
I'M LOOKING THROUGH YOU.--IMLOOKINGT--Title
I'm looking through you, where did you go?--
IMLOOKINGT--1
I'm looking through you, you're not the same.--
IMLOOKINGT--4

I'm looking through you, you're not the same.--
IMLOOKINGT--8
I'm looking through you and you're nowhere.--
IMLOOKINGT--14
I'm looking through you, where did you go?--
IMLOOKINGT--17
I'm looking through you, you're not the same.--
IMLOOKINGT--20
Aah, I'm looking through you.--IMLOOKINGT--22
Yeah, I'm looking through you.--IMLOOKINGT--23
But I can't get through, my hands are tied.--
YOUWONTSEE--8
There, running my hands through her hair--
HERETHEREA--5
Lastly through a hogshead of real fire--BEINGFORTH--6
As Mr. Kite flies through the ring - don't be
late.--BEINGFORTH--11
I'm filling the cracks that ran through the door--
FIXINGAHOL--4
Looking through the bent-backed tulips--GLASSONION--5
Looking through a glass onion.--GLASSONION--7
Looking through a glass onion.--GLASSONION--14
Looking through a glass onion.--GLASSONION--16
Looking through a glass onion.--GLASSONION--23
When the pain cuts through--SAVOYTRUFF--12
SHE CAME IN THROUGH THE BATHROOM WINDOW.--
SHECAMEINT--Title
She came in through the bathroom window --
SHECAMEINT--4
Are drifting through my opened mind--ACROSSTHEU
--4
Are ringing through my opened ears--ACROSSTHEU
--21
All through the day --IMEMINE--1
All through the night --IMEMINE--3
All through the day --IMEMINE--8
All through the day --IMEMINE--21
All through your life --IMEMINE--34

THROWS

Man buys ring, woman throws it away --IMDOWN--8

THUMB

But now she sucks her thumb and wonders --
SHECAMEINT--6

THURSDAY

Thursday night your stockings needed mending.--
LADYMADONN--16

TICKET

TICKET TO RIDE.--TICKETTORI--Title
She's got a ticket to ride--TICKETTORI--5
She's got a ticket to ride--TICKETTORI--6
She's got a ticket to ride--TICKETTORI--7
She's got a ticket to ride--TICKETTORI--13
She's got a ticket to ride--TICKETTORI--14
She's got a ticket to ride--TICKETTORI--15
Oh, she's got a ticket to ride--TICKETTORI--26
She's got a ticket to ride--TICKETTORI--27
She's got a ticket to ride--TICKETTORI--28
Ah, she's got a ticket to ride--TICKETTORI--40
She's got a ticket to ride--TICKETTORI--41
She's got a ticket to ride--TICKETTORI--42
One way ticket, yeah --DAYTRIPPER--6
One way ticket, yeah --DAYTRIPPER--14
Filling in a ticket in her little white book.--
LOVELYRITA--9

TICKING

I hear the clock a - ticking --DONTPASSME--10

TIDE

But now the tide is turning I can see that I
was blind.--WHATGOESON--16

TIDES

I met you in the morning waiting for the tides of
time --WHATGOESON--15

TIE

Monday's child has learned to tie his bootlace.--
LADYMADONN--7

TIED

But I can't get through, my hands are tied.--
    YOUWONTSEE--8
Fifty acorns tied in a sack.--BALLADOFJO--38

TIES

With plasticine porters with looking-glass ties.--
    LUCYINTHES--24

TIGER

He went out tiger hunting with his elephant and
    gun --CONTINUING--7
Deep in the jungle where the mighty tiger lies --
    CONTINUING--17

TIGHT

And we held each other tight --ISAWHERSTA--14
And we held each other tight --ISAWHERSTA--21
HOLD ME TIGHT.--HOLDMETIGH--Title
Hold me tight --HOLDMETIGH--2
So hold (hold) me tight (me tight) --HOLDMETIGH--6
So hold (hold) me tight (me tight) --HOLDMETIGH--6
Hold me tight,--HOLDMETIGH--9
So hold (hold) me tight (me tight) --HOLDMETIGH--13
So hold (hold) me tight (me tight) --HOLDMETIGH--13
Don't know what it means to hold you tight --
    HOLDMETIGH--16
So hold me tight,--HOLDMETIGH--19
So hold (hold) me tight (me tight) --HOLDMETIGH--23
So hold (hold) me tight (me tight) --HOLDMETIGH--23
Don't know what it means to hold you tight --
    HOLDMETIGH--26
So hold me tight,--HOLDMETIGH--29
So hold (hold) me tight (me tight) --HOLDMETIGH--33
So hold (hold) me tight (me tight) --HOLDMETIGH--33
When I'm home feeling you holding me tight
    tight, yeah.--HARDDAYSNI--16
When I'm home feeling you holding me tight,
    tight, yeah.--HARDDAYSNI--16
When I'm home feeling you holding me tight,
    tight, yeah.--HARDDAYSNI--29
When I'm home feeling you holding me tight,
    tight, yeah.--HARDDAYSNI--29
I don't need to hug or hold you tight --IMHAPPYJUS
    --8
I'm gonna hold her tight --WHENIGETHO--17
Good night, sleep tight.--GOODNIGHT--2
Good night, sleep tight.--GOODNIGHT--4
Good night, sleep tight.--GOODNIGHT--8
Good night, sleep tight.--GOODNIGHT--10
Good night, sleep tight.--GOODNIGHT--15
Good night, sleep tight.--GOODNIGHT--17

TILL

Till we're together ((together)) --PSILOVEYOU--4
And till ((till)) the day I do love ((do love))
    --PSILOVEYOU--8
And till ((till)) the day I do love ((do love))
    --PSILOVEYOU--8
Till we're together ((together)) --PSILOVEYOU--13
And till the day I do love --PSILOVEYOU--20
But till she's here--DONTBOTHER--19
But till she's here--DONTBOTHER--34
Till I belong to you--ITWONTBELO--4
Till I belong to you--ITWONTBELO--10
Till I belong to you--ITWONTBELO--20
Till I belong to you - ooo.--ITWONTBELO--30
Till he's seen you cry.--THISBOY--10
You say you'll be mine girl, till the end of time
    --THINGSWESA--6
I'm gonna love her till the cows come home --
    WHENIGETHO--18
Till I walk out that door again.--WHENIGETHO--20
Till she sees the mistake she has made?--BABYSINBLA--15
Till she sees the mistake she has made?--BABYSINBLA--20
Another girl who will love me till the end --
    ANOTHERGIR--10
Another girl who will love me till the end --
    ANOTHERGIR--16
Do I have to keep on talking till I can't go on?--
    WECANWORKI--2
Leave it all till somebody else lends you a hand.
    --NOWHEREMAN--15
Wait till I come back to your side --WAIT--3
Wait till I come back to your side --WAIT--7
Wait till I come back to your side --WAIT--15
Wait till I come back to your side --WAIT--23
Till they find there's no need (there's no need).
    --IMONLYSLEE--10
Till we found a sea of green--YELLOWSUBM--6
If I'd been out till quarter to three--WHENIMSIXT--5

((I can stay till it's time to go)).--HELLOGOODB--25
Leave it till tomorrow to unpack my case --
    BACKINTHEU--10
Till I get to the bottom and I see you again -
    yeah, yeah, yeah.--HELTERSKEL--3
Shine on till tomorrow, let it be.--LETITBE/45--23
Shine on till tomorrow, let it be.--LETITBE/LP--23

TIME

And in time you'll understand the reason why --
    ASKMEWHY--9
Well, there's gonna be a time--ILLGETYOU--16
I've got no time for you right now--DONTBOTHER--13
I've got no time for you right now--DONTBOTHER--28
NOT A SECOND TIME.--NOTASECOND--Title
No, no, no, not a second time.--NOTASECOND--10
No, no, no, not a second time.--NOTASECOND--21
Not a second time--NOTASECOND--22
Not a second time--NOTASECOND--23
No, no, no, not a second time.--NOTASECOND--24
Well, it's the second time--YOUCANTDOT--9
Do I have to tell you one more time--YOUCANTDOT--11
And it's my mind and there's no time--THERESAPLA--3
And it's my mind and there's no time--THERESAPLA--15
ANY TIME AT ALL.--ANYTIMEATA--Title
Any time at all, any time at all, any time at all--
    ANYTIMEATA--1
Any time at all, any time at all, any time at all--
    ANYTIMEATA--1
Any time at all, any time at all, any time at all--
    ANYTIMEATA--1
Any time at all, any time at all, any time at all--
    ANYTIMEATA--10
Any time at all, any time at all, any time at all--
    ANYTIMEATA--10
Any time at all, any time at all, any time at all--
    ANYTIMEATA--10
Any time at all, any time at all, any time at all--
    ANYTIMEATA--19
Any time at all, any time at all, any time at all--
    ANYTIMEATA--19
Any time at all, any time at all, any time at all--
    ANYTIMEATA--19
Any time at all, any time at all, any time at all--
    ANYTIMEATA--22
Any time at all, any time at all, any time at all--
    ANYTIMEATA--22
Any time at all, any time at all, any time at all--
    ANYTIMEATA--22
Any time at all--ANYTIMEATA--25
This time I will try to show--ILLBEBACK--11
This time I will try to show--ILLBEBACK--20
You say you'll be mine girl, till the end of time
    --THINGSWESA--6
Love me all the time girl --THINGSWESA--17
Love me all the time girl --THINGSWESA--28
I got no time for triviality --WHENIGETHO--11
She tells me all the time, you know, she said so
    --IFEELFINE--5
She tells me all the time, you know, she said so
    --IFEELFINE--13
Gives me all her time as well as loving--SHESAWOMAN--14
Love you all the time.--EIGHTDAYSA--12
Love you all the time.--EIGHTDAYSA--32
I remember the first time--EVERYLITTL--4
And now the time has come and so my love I must
    go --ILLFOLLOWT--5
And now the time has come and so my love I must
    go --ILLFOLLOWT--10
Time will pass away--TELLMEWHAT--10
Listen to me one more time--TELLMEWHAT--18
Listen to me one more time--TELLMEWHAT--27
Telling me there'll be no next time--YOULIKEMET--3
And so I'm telling you this time you'd better
    stop --ANOTHERGIR--8
Love you all the time and never leave you--INEEDYOU--2
I can't forget the time or place--IVEJUSTSEE--2
I can't forget the time or place--IVEJUSTSEE--25
Life is very short and there's no time--WECANWORKI--11
Only time will tell if I am right or I am wrong.--
    WECANWORKI--16
Life is very short and there's no time--WECANWORKI--20
Only time will tell if I am right or I am wrong.--
    WECANWORKI--25
But I can show you a better time.--DRIVEMYCAR--12
After all this time I don't know why.--GIRL--9
If I had some more time to spend --IFINEEDEDS--4
If I had some more time to spend --IFINEEDEDS--14
Biding my time--NORWEGIANW--12
It's time for bed.--NORWEGIANW--16
Take your time, don't hurry --NOWHEREMAN--14
And you've got time to rectify--THINKFORYO--22
It's been a long time, now I'm coming back home --

WAIT--1
It's been a long time, now I'm coming back home --
     WAIT--13
It's been a long time, now I'm coming back home --
     WAIT--25
I met you in the morning waiting for the tides of
     time --WHATGOESON--15
We have lost the time that was so hard to find--
     YOUWONTSEE--3
Time after time you refuse to even listen --
     YOUWONTSEE--13
Time after time you refuse to even listen --
     YOUWONTSEE--13
Time after time you refuse to even listen --
     YOUWONTSEE--22
Time after time you refuse to even listen --
     YOUWONTSEE--22
Day or night he'll be there any time at all, Dr.
     Robert--DRROBERT--2
Taking my time.--IMONLYSLEE--14
Taking my time.--IMONLYSLEE--20
She takes her time and doesn't feel she has to
     hurry --FORNOONE--5
And had you gone, you knew in time--GOTTOGETYO--10
I'll make you maybe next time around.--IWANTTOTEL--8
I've got time.--IWANTTOTEL--15
I've got time.--IWANTTOTEL--22
I've got time.--IWANTTOTEL--23
I've got time.--IWANTTOTEL--24
You don't get time to hang a sign on me.--
     LOVEYOUTWO--3
A splendid time is guaranteed for all--BEINGFORTH--20
I'm taking the time for a number of things--
     FIXINGAHOL--19
It's getting better all the time.--GETTINGBET--2
A little better all the time (it can't get no
     worse)--GETTINGBET--8
A little better all the time (it can't get no
     worse)--GETTINGBET--17
Getting so much better all the time.--GETTINGBET
     --20
It's getting better all the time--GETTINGBET--21
It's getting better all the time--GETTINGBET--23
A little better all the time (it can't get no
     worse)--GETTINGBET--30
Getting so much better all the time.--GETTINGBET--33
It's getting better all the time--GETTINGBET--34
It's getting better all the time--GETTINGBET--36
Getting so much better all the time.--GETTINGBET--38
It's time for tea and meet the wife.--GOODMORNIN--21
Somebody needs to know the time glad that I'm here
     --GOODMORNIN--22
We're sorry but it's time to go.--SGTPEPPREP--6
Yes I'm certain that it happens all the time.--
     WITHALITTL--20
And the time will come--WITHINYOUW--31
Nothing you can do but you can learn how to be
     you in time ((love))--ALLYOUN/YS--10
((I can stay till it's time to go)).--HELLOGOODB
     --25
Though she was born a long, long time ago --
     YOURMOTHER--4
Though she was born a long, long time ago --
     YOURMOTHER--10
Though she was born a long, long time ago --
     YOURMOTHER--15
Though she was born a long, long time ago --
     YOURMOTHER--23
And any time you feel the pain--HEYJUDE--9
We're gonna have a good time.--BIRTHDAY--4
We're gonna have a good time.--BIRTHDAY--23
Now it's time to say good night --GOODNIGHT--1
Now she's hit the big time--HONEYPIE--3
It's been a long, long, long time --LONGLONGLO--1
It took a long, long, long time --LONGLONGLO--4
One more time.--PIGGIES--20
I feel your taste all the time we're apart --
     SAVOYTRUFF--7
Floating down the stream of time--ITSALLTOOM--12
What words I say or time of day it is --ONLYANORTH
     --8
I'm in love for the first time --DONTLETMED--13
And from the first time that she really done me --
     DONTLETMED--21
Carry that weight a long time.--CARRYTHATW--2
Carry that weight a long time.--CARRYTHATW--4
Carry that weight a long time.--CARRYTHATW--10
Carry that weight a long time.--CARRYTHATW--12
Coming off stronger all the time --IMEMINE--7
Everybody had a good time --IVEGOTAFEE--20
Everybody had a hard time ((a feeling deep
     inside, oh yeah)) --IVEGOTAFEE--29
You left me standing here a long, long time ago --
     LONGANDWIN--10

You left me standing here a long, long time ago --
     LONGANDWIN--13

TIMES
Many, many, many times before.--ILLGETYOU--5
Many, many, many times before.--ILLGETYOU--22
When I think of all the times I tried so hard
     to leave her --GIRL--6
There will be times when all the things --FORNOONE--21
So he waits behind, writing fifty times I must
     not be so oh - oh oh.--MAXWELLSIL--11
When I find myself in times of trouble --LETITBE/45
     --1
When I find myself in times of trouble --LETITBE/LP
     --1
Many times I've been alone and many times I've
     cried --LONGANDWIN--7
Many times I've been alone and many times I've
     cried --LONGANDWIN--7

TIRED
I'M SO TIRED.--IMSOTIRED--Title
I'm so tired, I haven't slept a wink--IMSOTIRED--1
I'm so tired, my mind is on the blink--IMSOTIRED--2
I'm so tired, I don't know what to do--IMSOTIRED--5
I'm so tired, my mind is set on you --IMSOTIRED--6
I'm so tired, I'm feeling so upset --IMSOTIRED--14
Although I'm so tired, I'll have another
     cigarette--IMSOTIRED--15

TIT
((Tit, tit, tit, tit, tit))--GIRL--12
((Tit, tit, tit, tit, tit))--GIRL--12
((Tit, tit, tit, tit, tit))--GIRL--12
((Tit, tit, tit, tit, tit))--GIRL--12
((Tit, tit, tit, tit, tit))--GIRL--12
((Tit, tit, tit, tit, tit, tit, tit, tit,
     tit, tit, tit, tit))--GIRL--14
((Tit, tit, tit, tit, tit, tit, tit, tit,
     tit, tit, tit, tit))--GIRL--14
((Tit, tit, tit, tit, tit, tit, tit, tit,
     tit, tit, tit, tit))--GIRL--14
((Tit, tit, tit, tit, tit, tit, tit, tit,
     tit, tit, tit, tit))--GIRL--14
((Tit, tit, tit, tit, tit, tit, tit, tit,
     tit, tit, tit, tit))--GIRL--14
((Tit, tit, tit, tit, tit, tit, tit, tit,
     tit, tit, tit, tit))--GIRL--14
((Tit, tit, tit, tit, tit, tit, tit, tit,
     tit, tit, tit, tit))--GIRL--14
((Tit, tit, tit, tit, tit, tit, tit, tit,
     tit, tit, tit, tit))--GIRL--14
((Tit, tit, tit, tit, tit, tit, tit, tit,
     tit, tit, tit, tit))--GIRL--14
((Tit, tit, tit, tit, tit, tit, tit, tit,
     tit, tit, tit, tit))--GIRL--14
((Tit, tit, tit, tit, tit, tit, tit, tit,
     tit, tit, tit, tit))--GIRL--14
((Tit, tit, tit, tit))--GIRL--16
((Tit, tit, tit, tit))--GIRL--16
((Tit, tit, tit, tit))--GIRL--16
((Tit, tit, tit, tit))--GIRL--16
((Tit, tit, tit, tit))--GIRL--18
((Tit, tit, tit, tit))--GIRL--18
((Tit, tit, tit, tit))--GIRL--18
((Tit, tit, tit, tit))--GIRL--18
((Tit, tit, tit, tit, tit, tit, tit, tit))--GIRL
     --20
((Tit, tit, tit, tit, tit, tit, tit, tit))--GIRL
     --20
((Tit, tit, tit, tit, tit, tit, tit, tit))--GIRL
     --20
((Tit, tit, tit, tit, tit, tit, tit, tit))--GIRL
     --20
((Tit, tit, tit, tit, tit, tit, tit, tit))--GIRL
     --20
((Tit, tit, tit, tit, tit, tit, tit, tit))--GIRL
     --20
((Tit, tit, tit, tit, tit, tit, tit, tit))--GIRL
     --20
((Tit, tit, tit, tit, tit, tit, tit, tit))--GIRL
     --20

TO
Someone to love, somebody new.--LOVEMEDO--11
Someone to love, someone like you.--LOVEMEDO--12
As I write this letter, send my love to you --
     PSILOVEYOU--1

I'll ((I'll)) be coming home ((home)) again
   to you love ((you love)) --PSILOVEYOU--7
As I write this letter, send my love to you --
   PSILOVEYOU--10
As I write this letter (oh) send my love to you --
   PSILOVEYOU--16
You know I want you to --PSILOVEYOU--17
I'll be coming home again to you love--PSILOVEYOU--19
If you need somebody to love --ANYTIMEATA--4
I'll be there to make you feel right--ANYTIMEATA--6
I'll try to make it shine.--ANYTIMEATA--14
When you need a shoulder to cry on --ANYTIMEATA--16
Call me tonight and I'll come to you.--ANYTIMEATA--18
'cos you tell me things I want to know--ASKMEWHY--2
That it really only goes to show --ASKMEWHY--4
I can't believe it's happened to me --ASKMEWHY--12
'cos you tell me things I want to know--ASKMEWHY--17
That it really only goes to show --ASKMEWHY--19
I can't believe it's happened to me --ASKMEWHY--24
Last night I said these words to my girl --
   PLEASEPLEA--1
You don't need me to show the way love --PLEASEPLEA
   --7
Why do I always have to say love --PLEASEPLEA--8
I don't want to start complaining --PLEASEPLEA--13
It's so hard to reason with you, whoa - yeah--
   PLEASEPLEA--17
Last night I said these words to my girl --
   PLEASEPLEA--19
DO YOU WANT TO KNOW A SECRET?--DOYOUWANTT--Title
Listen, do you want to know a secret?--DOYOUWANTT
   --3
Do you promise not to tell?--DOYOUWANTT--4
Say the words you long to hear --DOYOUWANTT--7
Listen (dodahdo) do you want to know a secret?
   (dodahdo)--DOYOUWANTT--9
Do you promise not to tell? (dodahdo)--DOYOUWANTT
   --10
Say the words you long to hear --DOYOUWANTT--13
Listen (dodahdo) do you want to know a secret?
   (dodahdo)--DOYOUWANTT--17
Do you promise not to tell? (dodahdo)--DOYOUWANTT
   --18
Say the words you long to hear --DOYOUWANTT--21
I'm the kind of guy, who never used to cry.--MISERY
   --2
Send her back to me, 'cos everyone can see--
   MISERY--8
Send her back to me, 'cos everyone can see--
   MISERY--12
FROM ME TO YOU.--FROMMETOYO--Title
With love from me to you.--FROMMETOYO--6
With love from me to you.--FROMMETOYO--10
I got arms that long to hold you--FROMMETOYO--11
I got lips that long to kiss you--FROMMETOYO--13
With love from me to you.--FROMMETOYO--18
From me - to you.--FROMMETOYO--19
With love from me to you.--FROMMETOYO--21
I got arms that long to hold you--FROMMETOYO--22
I got lips that long to kiss you--FROMMETOYO--24
With love from me to you.--FROMMETOYO--29
To you, to you, to you.--FROMMETOYO--30
To you, to you, to you.--FROMMETOYO--30
To you, to you, to you.--FROMMETOYO--30
Oh, oh - mmm, you've been good to me--THANKYOUGI
   --1
That's the kind of love that is too good to be true
   --THANKYOUGI--9
Oh, oh - mmm, you've been good to me--THANKYOUGI
   --11
It's not like me to pretend--ILLGETYOU--6
So you might as well resign yourself to me, oh
   yeah.--ILLGETYOU--18
It's not like me to pretend--ILLGETYOU--23
And she told me what to say.--SHELOVESYO--7
You know it's up to you--SHELOVESYO--24
Apologize to her.--SHELOVESYO--27
ALL I'VE GOT TO DO.--ALLIVEGOTT--Title
The words you long to hear --ALLIVEGOTT--9
And I'll send all my lovin' to you.--ALLMYLOVIN--6
And I'll send all my lovin' to you.--ALLMYLOVIN--12
All my lovin', I will send to you --ALLMYLOVIN--13
And I'll send all my lovin' to you.--ALLMYLOVIN--20
All my lovin', I will send to you --ALLMYLOVIN--21
All my lovin', I will send to you --ALLMYLOVIN--24
I want no one to talk to me--DONTBOTHER--2
I want no one to talk to me--DONTBOTHER--2
But I'm to blame--DONTBOTHER--4
It's plain to see--DONTBOTHER--5
Making love to only you.--HOLDMETIGH--12
Don't know what it means to hold you tight --
   HOLDMETIGH--16
Don't know what it means to hold you tight --
   HOLDMETIGH--26

Making love to only you.--HOLDMETIGH--32
Till I belong to you--ITWONTBELO--4
Till I belong to you--ITWONTBELO--10
Till I belong to you--ITWONTBELO--20
Till I belong to you - ooo.--ITWONTBELO--30
If you want someone to make you feel so fine--
   LITTLECHIL--9
I see no reason to change mine --NOTASECOND--5
I see no reason to change mine --NOTASECOND--16
I WANT TO HOLD YOUR HAND.--IWANTTOHOL--Title
Oh please say to me--IWANTTOHOL--7
And please say to me--IWANTTOHOL--9
Just to love you, but oh my!--THISBOY--8
I'll give you all I've got to give --CANTBUYMEL--9
I may not have a lot to give --CANTBUYMEL--11
But what I got I'll give to you --CANTBUYMEL--12
I got something to say--YOUCANTDOT--1
To that boy again.--YOUCANTDOT--4
I caught you talking to him--YOUCANTDOT--10
Do I have to tell you one more time --YOUCANTDOT--11
So please listen to me--YOUCANTDOT--23
So please listen to me--YOUCANTDOT--42
Was I to blame for being unfair?--ICALLYOURN--2
She brings to me --ANDILOVEHE--9
But when I get home to you --HARDDAYSNI--5
To get you money to buy you things --HARDDAYSNI--9
To get you money to buy you things --HARDDAYSNI--9
And it's worth it just to hear you say --HARDDAYSNI
   --10
When I'm home everything seems to be right --
   HARDDAYSNI--15
But when I get home to you --HARDDAYSNI--21
When I'm home everything seems to be right --
   HARDDAYSNI--28
But when I get home to you --HARDDAYSNI--34
This could only happen to me --ISHOULDHAV--5
And when I ask you to be mine --ISHOULDHAV--9
If this is love you've got to give me more --
   ISHOULDHAV--12
This could only happen to me --ISHOULDHAV--15
And when I ask you to be mine --ISHOULDHAV--19
Would you promise to be true --IFIFELL--2
If I give my heart to you --IFIFELL--7
That I would love to love you --IFIFELL--18
That I would love to love you --IFIFELL--25
I got every reason on earth to be mad --ILLCRYINST
   --1
I can't talk to people that I meet.--ILLCRYINST--7
I'd try to make you sad somehow --ILLCRYINST--9
Don't want to cry when there's people there --
   ILLCRYINST--11
I get shy when they start to stare.--ILLCRYINST--12
Don't want to cry when there's people there --
   ILLCRYINST--20
I get shy when they start to stare.--ILLCRYINST--21
I'M HAPPY JUST TO DANCE WITH YOU.--IMHAPPYJUS
   --Title
'cos I'm happy just to dance with you.--IMHAPPYJUS
   --7
I don't need to hug or hold you tight --IMHAPPYJUS
   --8
'cos I'm happy just to dance with you.--IMHAPPYJUS
   --11
Just to dance with you is everything I need (oh)
   --IMHAPPYJUS--12
If somebody tries to take my place --IMHAPPYJUS--16
'cos I'm happy just to dance with you.--IMHAPPYJUS
   --19
Just to dance with you (oh) is everything I
   need (oh) --IMHAPPYJUS--20
If somebody tries to take my place --IMHAPPYJUS--24
'cos I'm happy just to dance with you (oh - oh).--
   IMHAPPYJUS--28
And why you lied to me --TELLMEWHY--2
And why you lied to me.--TELLMEWHY--4
Did you have to treat me oh so bad --TELLMEWHY--7
And why you lied to me --TELLMEWHY--10
And why you lied to me.--TELLMEWHY--12
And why you lied to me --TELLMEWHY--18
And why you lied to me.--TELLMEWHY--20
If you'll only listen to my pleas --TELLMEWHY--22
And why you lied to me --TELLMEWHY--27
And why you lied to me.--TELLMEWHY--29
You could find better things to do --ILLBEBACK--9
Than to break my heart again--ILLBEBACK--10
This time I will try to show--ILLBEBACK--11
That I'm not trying to pretend.--ILLBEBACK--12
You could find better things to do --ILLBEBACK--18
Than to break my heart again --ILLBEBACK--19
This time I will try to show--ILLBEBACK--20
That I'm not trying to pretend.--ILLBEBACK--21
But I hate to leave you--ILLBEBACK--23
You know I hate to leave you --ILLBEBACK--24
You say you will love me if I have to go --

THINGSWESA--1
These days such a kind girl seems so hard to find
   --THINGSWESA--7
Deep in love, not a lot to say --THINGSWESA--9
Love to hear you say that love is love--THINGSWESA
   --12
Love is here to stay.--THINGSWESA--14
And that's enough to make you mine girl --
   THINGSWESA--15
Deep in love, not a lot to say --THINGSWESA--20
Love to hear you say that love is love--THINGSWESA
   --23
Love is here to stay.--THINGSWESA--25
And that's enough to make you mine girl --
   THINGSWESA--26
Deep in love, not a lot to say --THINGSWESA--31
I got a whole lot of things to tell her --
   WHENIGETHO--2
I got a whole lot of things I gotta say to her.--
   WHENIGETHO--6
I got a whole lot of things to tell her --
   WHENIGETHO--8
I got a whole lot of things to tell her --
   WHENIGETHO--14
I got a whole lot of things to tell her --
   WHENIGETHO--25
I got a whole lot of things to tell her --
   WHENIGETHO--27
Baby's good to me, you know --IFEELFINE--1
Only ever has to give me love forever and forever
   --SHESAWOMAN--3
She hates to see me cry--SHESAWOMAN--9
She is happy just to hear me say that--SHESAWOMAN
   --10
Only ever has to give me love forever and forever
   --SHESAWOMAN--20
Only ever has to give me love forever and forever
   --SHESAWOMAN--30
Eight days a week is not enough to show I care.--
   EIGHTDAYSA--18
Eight days a week is not enough to show I care.--
   EIGHTDAYSA--28
Just to know that she loves me--EVERYLITTL--12
I DON'T WANT TO SPOIL THE PARTY.--IDONTWANTT--Title
I would hate my disappointment to show --IDONTWANTT
   --2
I would hate my disappointment to show --IDONTWANTT
   --14
One day you'll look to see I've gone --ILLFOLLOWT
   --1
And I'm not what I appear to be.--IMALOSER--2
I'm a loser and I lost someone who's near to me --
   IMALOSER--7
I'm a loser and I'm not what I appear to be.--
   IMALOSER--8
I'm a loser and I lost someone who's near to me --
   IMALOSER--13
I'm a loser and I'm not what I appear to be.--
   IMALOSER--14
What have I done to deserve such a fate?--IMALOSER
   --15
I'm a loser and I lost someone who's near to me --
   IMALOSER--19
I'm a loser and I'm not what I appear to be.--
   IMALOSER--20
When I came to your door--NOREPLY--2
'cos I looked up to see your face.--NOREPLY--8
I tried to telephone--NOREPLY--9
I tried to telephone--NOREPLY--22
Would it be too much to ask of you --WHATYOURED--3
What you're doing to me?--WHATYOURED--4
Why should it be so much to ask of you --WHATYOURED
   --7
What you're doing to me?--WHATYOURED--8
Why should it be so much to ask of you --WHATYOURED
   --14
What you're doing to me?--WHATYOURED--15
Why should it be so much to ask of you --WHATYOURED
   --21
What you're doing to me?--WHATYOURED--22
What you're doing to me?--WHATYOURED--23
What you're doing to me?--WHATYOURED--24
TICKET TO RIDE.--TICKETTORI--Title
She's got a ticket to ride--TICKETTORI--5
She's got a ticket to ride--TICKETTORI--6
She's got a ticket to ride--TICKETTORI--7
She's got a ticket to ride--TICKETTORI--13
She's got a ticket to ride--TICKETTORI--14
She's got a ticket to ride--TICKETTORI--15
She ought to think twice--TICKETTORI--18
She ought to do right by me--TICKETTORI--19
Before she gets to saying goodbye--TICKETTORI--20
She ought to think twice--TICKETTORI--21
She ought to do right by me.--TICKETTORI--22

Oh, she's got a ticket to ride--TICKETTORI--26
She's got a ticket to ride--TICKETTORI--27
She's got a ticket to ride--TICKETTORI--28
She ought to think twice--TICKETTORI--31
She ought to do right by me-TICKETTORI--32
Before she gets to saying goodbye--TICKETTORI--33
She ought to think twice--TICKETTORI--34
She ought to do right by me.--TICKETTORI--35
Ah, she's got a ticket to ride--TICKETTORI--40
She's got a ticket to ride--TICKETTORI--41
She's got a ticket to ride--TICKETTORI--42
I will prove to you--TELLMEWHAT--2
Listen to me one more time--TELLMEWHAT--18
Can't you try to see that I'm--TELLMEWHAT--20
Trying to get to you--TELLMEWHAT--21
Trying to get to you--TELLMEWHAT--21
Listen to me one more time--TELLMEWHAT--27
Can't you try to see that I'm--TELLMEWHAT--29
Trying to get to you--TELLMEWHAT--30
Trying to get to you--TELLMEWHAT--30
You've tried before to leave me--YOULIKEMET--7
To walk out and make me lonely--YOULIKEMET--9
My independence ((my independence)) seems to
   vanish in the haze--HELP--21
You still moan keep your hands to yourself --IMDOWN
   --17
Please come on back to me--INEEDYOU--3
Said you had a thing or two to tell me--INEEDYOU
   --6
How was I to know you would upset me?--INEEDYOU--7
Just what you mean to me--INEEDYOU--19
Just what you mean to me--INEEDYOU--29
Haven't I the right to make it up girl?--ITSONLYLOV
   --10
And I want all the world to see we've met --
   IVEJUSTSEE--5
And I want all the world to see we've met --
   IVEJUSTSEE--28
Now it looks as though they're here to stay--
   YESTERDAY--3
I'm not half the man I used to be--YESTERDAY--6
Why she had to go, I don't know--YESTERDAY--9
Love was such an easy game to play--YESTERDAY--14
Now I need a place to hide away--YESTERDAY--15
Why she had to go, I don't know--YESTERDAY--17
Love was such an easy game to play--YESTERDAY--22
Now I need a place to hide away--YESTERDAY--23
YOU'RE GOING TO LOSE THAT GIRL.--YOUREGONNA--Title
YOU'VE GOT TO HIDE YOUR LOVE AWAY.--YOUVEGOTTO
   --Title
Turn my face to the wall.--YOUVEGOTTO--2
Hey! you've got to hide your love away.--YOUVEGOTTO
   --9
Hey! you've got to hide your love away.--YOUVEGOTTO
   --10
How could she say to me--YOUVEGOTTO--15
Hey! you've got to hide your love away.--YOUVEGOTTO
   --19
Hey! you've got to hide your love away.--YOUVEGOTTO
   --20
It took me so long to find out --DAYTRIPPER--7
It took me so long to find out --DAYTRIPPER--15
Tried to please her --DAYTRIPPER--18
Tried to please her --DAYTRIPPER--20
It took me so long to find out --DAYTRIPPER--24
Try to see it my way --WECANWORKI--1
Do I have to keep on talking till I can't go on?--
   WECANWORKI--2
Try to see it my way --WECANWORKI--15
Try to see it my way --WECANWORKI--24
Asked a girl what she wanted to be --DRIVEMYCAR--1
And she said listen babe I've got something to
   say --DRIVEMYCAR--23
Is there anybody going to listen to my story--GIRL
   --1
Is there anybody going to listen to my story--GIRL
   --1
All about the girl who came to stay?--GIRL--2
When I think of all the times I tried so hard
   to leave her --GIRL--6
She will turn to me and start to cry --GIRL--7
She will turn to me and start to cry --GIRL--7
And she promises the earth to me and I believe
   her --GIRL--8
Was she told when she was young that pain would
   lead to pleasure?--GIRL--22
That a man must break his back to earn his day of
   leisure?--GIRL--24
If I needed someone to love --IFINEEDS--1
If I had some more time to spend --IFINEEDS--4
If I had some more time to spend --IFINEEDS--14
That's all I want to say--MICHELLE--8
I need to, I need to, I need to--MICHELLE--11
I need to, I need to, I need to--MICHELLE--11

I need to, I need to, I need to--MICHELLE--11
I need to make you see--MICHELLE--12
Oh, what you mean to me--MICHELLE--13
I'll get to you somehow--MICHELLE--18
She asked me to stay--NORWEGIANW--7
And she told me to sit anywhere--NORWEGIANW--8
And started to laugh--NORWEGIANW--19
And crawled off to sleep in the bath.--NORWEGIANW
--20
Knows not where he's going to --NOWHEREMAN--5
Just sees what he wants to see --NOWHEREMAN--11
Knows not where he's going to --NOWHEREMAN--17
Than to be with another man.--RUNFORYOUR--2
Just to make you toe the line.--RUNFORYOUR--12
Than to be with another man.--RUNFORYOUR--26
To say about the things that you do.--THINKFORYO
--2
Do what you want to do --THINKFORYO--6
And go where you're going to --THINKFORYO--7
Do what you want to do --THINKFORYO--15
And go where you're going to --THINKFORYO--16
And you've got time to rectify--THINKFORYO--22
Do what you want to do --THINKFORYO--24
And go where you're going to --THINKFORYO--25
Do what you want to do --THINKFORYO--28
And go where you're going to --THINKFORYO--29
Wait till I come back to your side --WAIT--3
Wait till I come back to your side --WAIT--7
I feel as though you ought to know--WAIT--9
Wait till I come back to your side --WAIT--15
I feel as though you ought to know--WAIT--17
Wait till I come back to your side --WAIT--23
It's so easy for a girl like you to lie.--
WHATGOESON--8
It's so easy for a girl like you to lie.--
WHATGOESON--17
I used to think of no-one else but you were just
the same --WHATGOESON--22
Did you mean to break my heart and watch me die?--
WHATGOESON--24
I'm here to show everybody the light.--THEWORD--24
Give the word a chance to say --THEWORD--25
We have lost the time that was so hard to find--
YOUWONTSEE--3
I don't know why you should want to hide --
YOUWONTSEE--7
I won't want to stay, I don't have much to say --
YOUWONTSEE--9
I won't want to stay, I don't have much to say --
YOUWONTSEE--9
Time after time you refuse to even listen --
YOUWONTSEE--13
Time after time you refuse to even listen --
YOUWONTSEE--22
It took me years to write, will you take a look?--
PAPERBACKW--3
So I want to be a paperback writer --PAPERBACKW--6
But he wants to be a paperback writer.--PAPERBACKW
--12
And I want to be a paperback writer --PAPERBACKW
--19
And I want to be a paperback writer --PAPERBACKW
--25
I can show you that when it starts to rain (when
the rain comes down)--RAIN--9
When your prized possessions start to weigh you
down --ANDYOURBIR--7
He helps you to understand --DRROBERT--4
Don't pay money just to see yourself with Dr.
Robert.--DRROBERT--14
He helps you to understand --DRROBERT--16
Everybody seems to think I'm lazy.--IMONLYSLEE--7
She takes her time and doesn't feel she has to
hurry --FORNOONE--5
I need to laugh and when the sun is out --
GOODDAYSUN--2
I'm so proud to know that she is mine.--GOODDAYSUN
--13
GOT TO GET YOU INTO MY LIFE.--GOTTOGETYO--Title
You knew I wanted just to hold you--GOTTOGETYO--9
Ooo you were meant to be near me--GOTTOGETYO--12
Ooo and I want you to hear me--GOTTOGETYO--13
Got to get you into my life.--GOTTOGETYO--15
When I'm with you I want to stay there--GOTTOGETYO
--17
Got to get you into my life.--GOTTOGETYO--23
I got to get you into my life.--GOTTOGETYO--24
To lead a better life, I need my love to be here.
--HERETHEREA--1
To lead a better life, I need my love to be here.
--HERETHEREA--1
But to love her is to need her everywhere.--
HERETHEREA--10
But to love her is to need her everywhere.--

HERETHEREA--10
Knowing that love is to share--HERETHEREA--11
But to love her is to need her everywhere.--
HERETHEREA--16
But to love her is to need her everywhere.--
HERETHEREA--16
Knowing that love is to share--HERETHEREA--17
I WANT TO TELL YOU.--IWANTTOTEL--Title
I want to tell you--IWANTTOTEL--1
My head is filled with things to say --IWANTTOTEL
--2
All those words they seem to slip away.--IWANTTOTEL
--4
The games begin to drag me down --IWANTTOTEL--6
But if I seem to act unkind--IWANTTOTEL--9
I want to tell you--IWANTTOTEL--12
I want to tell you--IWANTTOTEL--19
LOVE YOU TO/TOO.--LOVEYOUTWO--Title
You don't get time to hang a sign on me.--
LOVEYOUTWO--3
But what you've got means such a lot to me.--
LOVEYOUTWO--8
I'll make love to you,--LOVEYOUTWO--16
If you want me to.--LOVEYOUTWO--17
She said I know what it's like to be dead --
SHESAIDSHE--1
I know what it is to be sad--SHESAIDSHE--2
I know that I'm ready to leave --SHESAIDSHE--11
I know that I'm ready to leave --SHESAIDSHE--17
I know what it's like to be dead (I know what
it's like to be dead) --SHESAIDSHE--20
I know what it's like to be dead (I know what
it's like to be dead) --SHESAIDSHE--20
I know what it is to be sad (I know what it is
to be sad).--SHESAIDSHE--21
I know what it is to be sad (I know what it is
to be sad).--SHESAIDSHE--21
I know what it's like to be dead (I know what
it's like to be dead).--SHESAIDSHE--22
I know what it's like to be dead (I know what
it's like to be dead).--SHESAIDSHE--22
If you try to sit, I'll tax your seat, ((sit))--
TAXMAN--12
If you don't want to pay some more (ha ha Mr.
Heath)--TAXMAN--19
Lay down all thought, surrender to the void--
TOMORROWNE--3
But listen to the colour of your dreams--TOMORROWNE
--11
Or play the game existence to the end--TOMORROWNE
--13
Lived a man who sailed to sea--YELLOWSUBM--2
So we sailed on to the sun--YELLOWSUBM--5
And the band begins to play.--YELLOWSUBM--15
Of every head he's had the pleasure to know--
PENNYLANE--2
He likes to keep his fire-engine clean--PENNYLANE
--14
'cos I'm going to strawberry fields--STRAWBERRY--2
And nothing to get hungabout--STRAWBERRY--4
It's getting hard to be someone--STRAWBERRY--8
It doesn't matter much to me.--STRAWBERRY--10
'cos I'm going to strawberry fields--STRAWBERRY--12
And nothing to get hungabout--STRAWBERRY--14
'cos I'm going to strawberry fields--STRAWBERRY--22
And nothing to get hungabout--STRAWBERRY--24
'cos I'm going to strawberry fields--STRAWBERRY--32
And nothing to get hungabout--STRAWBERRY--34
Their production will be second to none--BEINGFORTH
--13
The band begins at ten to six--BEINGFORTH--15
Well I just had to laugh--DAYINTHELI--4
But I just had to look--DAYINTHELI--14
I'd love to turn you on--DAYINTHELI--16
They had to count them all--DAYINTHELI--31
To fill the Albert Hall--DAYINTHELI--33
I'd love to turn you on--DAYINTHELI--34
I used to get mad at my school (now I can't
complain)--GETTINGBET--3
I've got to admit it's getting better (better)--
GETTINGBET--7
I have to admit it's getting better (better)--
GETTINGBET--9
Me used to be angry young man--GETTINGBET--11
I've got to admit it's getting better (better)--
GETTINGBET--16
I have to admit it's getting better (better)--
GETTINGBET--18
I used to be cruel to my woman--GETTINGBET--25
I used to be cruel to my woman--GETTINGBET--25
Nothing to do to save his life call his wife in--
GOODMORNIN--2
Nothing to do to save his life call his wife in--
GOODMORNIN--2

Nothing to say but what a day how's your boy been?
--GOODMORNIN--3
Nothing to do it's up to you--GOODMORNIN--4
Nothing to do it's up to you--GOODMORNIN--4
I've got nothing to say but it's OK.--GOODMORNIN
--5
Go in to work don't want to go feeling low down--
GOODMORNIN--7
Go in to work don't want to go feeling low down--
GOODMORNIN--7
Heading for home you start to roam then you're in
town.--GOODMORNIN--8
After a while you start to smile now you feel cool
--GOODMORNIN--13
Then you decide to take a walk by the old school--
GOODMORNIN--14
I've got nothing to say but it's OK.--GOODMORNIN
--16
Somebody needs to know the time glad that I'm here
--GOODMORNIN--22
Watching the skirts you start to flirt now you're
in gear--GOODMORNIN--23
Go to a show you hope she goes--GOODMORNIN--24
I've got nothing to say but it's OK.--GOODMORNIN
--25
To take some tea with me? ((maid))--LOVELYRITA--16
Took her out and tried to win her--LOVELYRITA--20
Told her I would really like to see her again.--
LOVELYRITA--22
Follow her down to a bridge by a fountain--
LUCYINTHES--12
Waiting to take you away.--LUCYINTHES--17
That Sgt. Pepper taught the band to play--
SGTPEPPERS--2
But they're guaranteed to raise a smile.--
SGTPEPPERS--4
So may I introduce to you--SGTPEPPERS--5
It's wonderful to be here--SGTPEPPERS--14
We'd like to take you home with us--SGTPEPPERS--17
We'd love to take you home.--SGTPEPPERS--18
I don't really want to stop the show--SGTPEPPERS
--19
But I thought you might like to know--SGTPEPPERS
--20
And he wants you all to sing along.--SGTPEPPERS--22
So let me introduce to you--SGTPEPPERS--23
We're sorry but it's time to go.--SGTPEPPREP--6
We'd like to thank you once again.--SGTPEPPREP--12
She goes downstairs to the kitchen--SHESLEAVIN--4
She breaks down and cries to her husband--
SHESLEAVIN--16
How could she do this to me?--SHESLEAVIN--19
Home. (we struggled hard all our lives to get by)
--SHESLEAVIN--22
Waiting to keep the appointment she made--
SHESLEAVIN--26
If I'd been out till quarter to three--WHENIMSIXT
--5
Indicate precisely what you mean to say--WHENIMSIXT
--30
And I'll try not to sing outta key.--WITHALITTL--4
(Does it worry you to be alone?)--WITHALITTL--9
I need somebody to love.--WITHALITTL--16
I want somebody to love.--WITHALITTL--18
I just need someone to love.--WITHALITTL--27
I want somebody to love.--WITHALITTL--29
To try our best to hold it there--WITHINYOUW--11
To try our best to hold it there--WITHINYOUW--11
Try to realise it's all within yourself--WITHINYOUW
--16
And to see you're really only very small--
WITHINYOUW--18
Nothing you can say but you can learn how to play
the game ((love))--ALLYOUN/YS--6
Nothing you can do but you can learn how to be
you in time ((love))--ALLYOUN/YS--10
There's nowhere you can be that isn't where
you're meant to be ((love))--ALLYOUN/YS--21
How does it feel to be--BABYYOUREA--1
What do you want to be?--BABYYOUREA--4
How does it feel to be--BABYYOUREA--7
Often enough to know.--BABYYOUREA--10
What a thing to do.--BABYYOUREA--18
How does it feel to be--BABYYOUREA--22
Tuned to a natural E--BABYYOUREA--24
Happy to be that way.--BABYYOUREA--25
What are you going to play?--BABYYOUREA--27
What a thing to do (baby).--BABYYOUREA--33
((I can stay till it's time to go))--HELLOGOODB
--25
Sitting on a cornflake, waiting for the van to come
--IAMTHEWALR--4
Well it only goes to show (only, only goes to
show) --BLUEJAYWAY--8

Well it only goes to show (only, only goes to
show) --BLUEJAYWAY--8
And I told them where to go.--BLUEJAYWAY--9
There's so many there to meet.--BLUEJAYWAY--11
And I'd really like to go (go) --BLUEJAYWAY--16
But nobody wants to know him--FOOLONTHEH--3
Or the sound he appears to make--FOOLONTHEH--11
And he never seems to notice.--FOOLONTHEH--12
And nobody seems to like him--FOOLONTHEH--15
They can tell what he wants to do--FOOLONTHEH--16
He never listens to them--FOOLONTHEH--22
Roll up (to make a reservation)--MAGICALMYS--7
The Magical Mystery Tour is waiting to take
you away--MAGICALMYS--9
(Waiting to take you away).--MAGICALMYS--10
The Magical Mystery Tour is hoping to take you
away --MAGICALMYS--17
(Hoping to take you away)--MAGICALMYS--18
Roll up (to make a reservation)--MAGICALMYS--25
The Magical Mystery Tour is coming to take you
away --MAGICALMYS--27
Coming/Hoping to take you away)--MAGICALMYS--28
The Magical Mystery Tour is dying to take you
away--MAGICALMYS--29
(Dying to take you away)--MAGICALMYS--30
Let's all get up and dance to a song--YOURMOTHER
--2
Let's all get up and dance to a song--YOURMOTHER
--8
Wonder how you manage to make ends meet.--
LADYMADONN--2
Monday's child has learned to tie his bootlace.--
LADYMADONN--7
Wonders how you manage to feed the rest.--
LADYMADONN--10
Listen to the music playing in your head.--
LADYMADONN--13
Wonder how you manage to make ends meet.--
LADYMADONN--19
Remember to let her into your heart --HEYJUDE--3
Then you can start to make it better.--HEYJUDE--4
You were made to go out and get her --HEYJUDE--6
Then you begin to make it better.--HEYJUDE--8
Remember (hey Jude) to let her into your heart --
HEYJUDE--17
Then you can start to make it better.--HEYJUDE--18
You're waiting for someone to perform with.--
HEYJUDE--21
Remember to let her under your skin (oh) --HEYJUDE
--28
Then you'll begin ((let it out)) to make it
better --HEYJUDE--29
We all want to change the world.--REVOLUTION--7
We'd all love to see the plan.--REVOLUTION--14
All I can tell you is brother you have to wait.--
REVOLUTION--19
We all want to change your head.--REVOLUTION--24
Didn't get to bed last night --BACKINTHEU--2
Gee, it's good to be back home --BACKINTHEU--9
Leave it till tomorrow to unpack my case --
BACKINTHEU--10
Take me to your daddy's farm --BACKINTHEU--32
Happy birthday to you.--BIRTHDAY--6
Yes, we're going to a party, party --BIRTHDAY--8
Yes, we're going to a party, party --BIRTHDAY--9
Yes, we're going to a party, party.--BIRTHDAY--10
I would like you to dance (birthday) --BIRTHDAY--11
I would like you to dance (birthday) --BIRTHDAY--13
I would like you to dance (birthday) --BIRTHDAY--16
I would like you to dance (birthday) (wuh)--
BIRTHDAY--18
Happy birthday to you.--BIRTHDAY--25
Take these broken wings and learn to fly.--
BLACKBIRD--2
You were only waiting for this moment to arise.--
BLACKBIRD--4
Take these sunken eyes and learn to see.--BLACKBIRD
--6
You were only waiting for this moment to be free.
--BLACKBIRD--8
Take these broken wings and learn to fly.--
BLACKBIRD--14
You were only waiting for this moment to arise --
BLACKBIRD--16
You were only waiting for this moment to arise --
BLACKBIRD--17
You were only waiting for this moment to arise.--
BLACKBIRD--18
The children asked him if to kill was not a sin --
CONTINUING--27
She's old enough to know better.--CRYBABYCRY--3
She's old enough to know better --CRYBABYCRY--10
Picking flowers for a friend who came to play --
CRYBABYCRY--13

She's old enough to know better --CRYBABYCRY--18
She's old enough to know better --CRYBABYCRY--26
She's old enough to know better --CRYBABYCRY--34
She's old enough to know better --CRYBABYCRY--38
She's old enough to know better --CRYBABYCRY--42
Dear Prudence, won't you come out to play?--
  DEARPRUDEN--1
Dear Prudence, won't you come out to play?--
  DEARPRUDEN--5
Dear Prudence, won't you come out to play?--
  DEARPRUDEN--21
Dear Prudence, won't you come out to play?--
  DEARPRUDEN--25
How I hate to see you go --DONTPASSME--21
Just waiting to hear from you.--DONTPASSME--30
How I hate to see you go --DONTPASSME--34
How I hate to see you go --DONTPASSME--40
EVERYBODY'S GOT SOMETHING TO HIDE EXCEPT ME
  AND MY MONKEY.--EVRBDYMONK--Title
Everybody's got something to hide 'cept for me
  and my monkey - wuh.--EVRBDYMONK--7
Everybody's got something to hide 'cept for me
  and my monkey (yeah - wuh).--EVRBDYMONK--16
Everybody's got something to hide 'cept for me
  and my monkey - hey.--EVRBDYMONK--25
To see how the other half live--GLASSONION--6
Lady Madonna trying to make ends meet - yeah--
  GLASSONION--13
Listen to me--GLASSONION--20
Trying to make a dove-tail joint - yeah--GLASSONION
  --22
Now it's time to say good night --GOODNIGHT--1
Now the moon begins to shine --GOODNIGHT--9
And donated to the National Trust.--HAPPINESSI--8
Down to the bits that I left uptown --HAPPINESSI
  --10
When I get to the bottom I go back to the top
  of the slide --HELTERSKEL--1
When I get to the bottom I go back to the top
  of the slide --HELTERSKEL--1
Till I get to the bottom and I see you again -
  yeah, yeah, yeah.--HELTERSKEL--3
A - do you, don't you want me to love you?--
  HELTERSKEL--4
A - will you, won't you want me to make you?--
  HELTERSKEL--11
When I get to the bottom I go back to the top
  of the slide--HELTERSKEL--18
When I get to the bottom I go back to the top
  of the slide--HELTERSKEL--18
And I get to the bottom and I see you again -
  yeah, yeah, yeah.--HELTERSKEL--20
Well, do you, don't you want me to make you?--
  HELTERSKEL--21
To be where you belong.--HONEYPIE--18
Honey Pie come back to me - ooo.--HONEYPIE--19
Play it to me--HONEYPIE--23
Play it to me Hollywood blues.--HONEYPIE--24
Kindly send her sailing back to me--HONEYPIE--27
Come, come back to me Honey Pie--HONEYPIE--32
If you want me to, I will.--IWILL--4
Make it easy to be near you --IWILL--16
For the things you do endear you to me - aah --
  IWILL--17
I'm so tired, I don't know what to do --IMSOTIRED
  --5
But I say it just to reach you, Julia.--JULIA--2
Help yourself to a bit of what is all around you
  - silly girl.--MARTHAMYDE--6
Take a good look you're bound to see --MARTHAMYDE
  --8
That you and me were meant to be for each other -
  silly girl.--MARTHAMYDE--9
Help yourself to a bit of what is all around you
  - silly girl.--MARTHAMYDE--12
Please - be good to me, Martha my love --MARTHAMYDE
  --14
Listen to the pretty sound of music as she flies.
  --MOTHERNATU--4
Desmond says to Molly, girl I like your face--
  OBLADIOBLA--3
Desmond takes a trolly to the jewellery store --
  OBLADIOBLA--9
Takes it back to Molly waiting at the door--
  OBLADIOBLA--11
And as he gives it to her she begins to sing
  (sing):--OBLADIOBLA--12
And as he gives it to her she begins to sing
  (sing):--OBLADIOBLA--12
Always having dirt to play around in.--PIGGIES--5
Always have clean shirts to play around in.--
  PIGGIES--10
Clutching forks and knives to eat the bacon.--
  PIGGIES--19

We all want to change the world.--REVOLUTONE--10
We'd all love to see the plan.--REVOLUTONE--21
Well all I can tell you is brother you have to
  wait.--REVOLUTONE--28
We'd all love to change our head.--REVOLUTONE--37
Only to find Gideon's Bible --ROCKYRACCO--10
To shoot off the legs of his rival.--ROCKYRACCO--12
And proceeded to lie on the table --ROCKYRACCO--32
Only to find Gideon's Bible --ROCKYRACCO--37
To help with good Rocky's revival - ah.--ROCKYRACCO
  --39
But you'll have to have them all pulled out--
  SAVOYTRUFF--4
But you'll have to have them all pulled out--
  SAVOYTRUFF--9
But you'll have to have them all pulled out--
  SAVOYTRUFF--17
But you'll have to have them all pulled out--
  SAVOYTRUFF--26
Yes, you'll have to have them all pulled out--
  SAVOYTRUFF--28
You layed it down for all to see--SEXYSADIE--6
You layed it down for all to see--SEXYSADIE--7
She came along to turn on everyone--SEXYSADIE--10
We gave her everything we owned just to sit at
  her table ((sexy Sadie))--SEXYSADIE--20
I don't know why nobody told you how to unfold
  your love --WHILEMYGUI--15
You were preverted (too/to)--WHILEMYGUI--15
Can I bring my friend to tea?--ALLTOGETHE--6
Can I take my friend to bed?--ALLTOGETHE--18
You don't know what it's like to listen to your
  fears.--HEYBULLDOG--8
You don't know what it's like to listen to your
  fears.--HEYBULLDOG--8
You can talk to me--HEYBULLDOG--9
You can talk to me--HEYBULLDOG--10
You can talk to me--HEYBULLDOG--11
If you're lonely you can talk to me.--HEYBULLDOG
  --12
You can talk to me--HEYBULLDOG--17
You can talk to me--HEYBULLDOG--18
You can talk to me--HEYBULLDOG--19
If you're lonely you can talk to me - hey!--
  HEYBULLDOG--20
To your mother!--ITSALLTOOM--1
The more there is to see.--ITSALLTOOM--7
It's all too much for me to take --ITSALLTOOM--8
For us to take, it's all too much.--ITSALLTOOM--11
From life to life with me --ITSALLTOOM--13
Or where you'd like to be.--ITSALLTOOM--15
It's all too much for me to take --ITSALLTOOM--16
It's all too much for me to see --ITSALLTOOM--25
It's all too much for me to take --ITSALLTOOM--29
For us to take it's all too much.--ITSALLTOOM--32
If you're listening to this song --ONLYANORTH--1
Get back to where you once belonged.--GETBACK/45
  --6
Get back to where you once belonged.--GETBACK/45
  --8
Back to where you once belonged.--GETBACK/45--12
Back to where you once belonged.--GETBACK/45--14
Get back to where you once belonged.--GETBACK/45
  --21
Get back to where you once belonged.--GETBACK/45
  --23
Get back to where you once belonged.--GETBACK/45
  --27
Get back to where you once belonged.--GETBACK/45
  --29
Get back to where you once belonged.--GETBACK/45
  --37
Trying to get to Holland or France.--BALLADOFJO--2
Trying to get to Holland or France.--BALLADOFJO--2
The man in the mack said you've got to go back --
  BALLADOFJO--3
Peter Brown called to say, you can make it OK --
  BALLADOFJO--11
Drove from Paris to the Amsterdam Hilton --
  BALLADOFJO--17
I said we're only trying to get us some peace.--
  BALLADOFJO--20
Giving all your clothes to charity.--BALLADOFJO--26
Made a lightning trip to Vienna --BALLADOFJO--29
The newspapers said, she's gone to his head --
  BALLADOFJO--31
Caught the early plane back to London --BALLADOFJO
  --37
It's good to have the both of you back.--BALLADOFJO
  --40
From where some try to drag me down --OLDBROWNSH
  --10
I may appear to be imperfect --OLDBROWNSH--22
To miss that love is something I'd hate.--

OLDBROWNSH--28
He got hair down to his knee--COMETOGETH--9
Got to be a joker he just do what he please--
COMETOGETH--10
One thing I can tell you is you got to be free--
COMETOGETH--20
Got to be good-looking 'cos he's so hard to see--
COMETOGETH--41
Got to be good-looking 'cos he's so hard to see--
COMETOGETH--41
The love you take is equal to the love you make.--
THEEND--9
To get back homeward.--GOLDENSLUM--2
To get back home.--GOLDENSLUM--4
To get back homeward.--GOLDENSLUM--12
To get back home.--GOLDENSLUM--14
But she doesn't have a lot to say.--HERMAJESTY--2
But she changes from day to day.--HERMAJESTY--4
Little darling, the smiles returning to the faces.
--HERECOMEST--9
Can I take you out to the pictures, Joan?--
MAXWELLSIL--4
But as she's getting ready to go, a knock comes
on the door --MAXWELLSIL--5
Wishing to avoid an unpleasant scene --MAXWELLSIL
--9
She tells Max to stay when the class has gone
away --MAXWELLSIL--10
Trying to save paper.--MEANMRMUST--3
Saving up to buy some clothes--MEANMRMUST--5
Takes him out to look at the Queen--MEANMRMUST--11
I'd get myself to be under the sea--OCTOPUSSGA--1
I'd ask my friends to come and see--OCTOPUSSGA--5
I'd like to be under the sea--OCTOPUSSGA--7
I'd like to be under the sea--OCTOPUSSGA--22
No-one there to tell us what to do.--OCTOPUSSGA--22
No-one there to tell us what to do.--OCTOPUSSGA--22
I'd like to be under the sea--OCTOPUSSGA--23
She's killer-diller when she's dressed to the hilt.
--POLYTHENEP--7
Sundays on the phone to Monday --SHECAMEINT--10
Tuesdays on the phone to me.--SHECAMEINT--11
And though she tried her best to help me --
SHECAMEINT--18
Sundays on the phone to Monday --SHECAMEINT--22
Tuesdays on the phone to me.--SHECAMEINT--23
I don't want to leave her now --SOMETHING--4
I don't want to leave her now --SOMETHING--9
And all I have to do is think of her --SOMETHING
--16
I don't want to leave her now --SOMETHING--18
All the money's gone, nowhere to go.--YOUNEVERGI
--9
Yellow lorry slow, nowhere to go.--YOUNEVERGI--12
But oh, that magic feeling, nowhere to go --
YOUNEVERGI--13
Nowhere to go - nowhere to go.--YOUNEVERGI--15
Nowhere to go - nowhere to go.--YOUNEVERGI--15
All good children go to heaven.--YOUNEVERGI--25
All good children go to heaven.--YOUNEVERGI--27
All good children go to heaven.--YOUNEVERGI--29
All good children go to heaven.--YOUNEVERGI--31
All good children go to heaven.--YOUNEVERGI--33
All good children go to heaven.--YOUNEVERGI--35
All good children go to heaven.--YOUNEVERGI--37
All good children go to heaven.--YOUNEVERGI--39
Mother Mary comes to me --LETITBE/45--2
I wake up to the sound of music,--LETITBE/45--24
Mother Mary comes to me --LETITBE/45--25
Good evening and welcome to Slaggers --YOUKNOWMYN
--5
((And now we'd like to do)) Hark the Angels
Come...--DIGIT--13
Queen says no to pot-smoking FBI member.--
FORYOUBLUE--1
You looked at me, that's all you had to do --
FORYOUBLUE--14
Get back to where you once belonged--GETBACK/LP--12
Get back to where you once belonged--GETBACK/LP--14
Back to where you once belonged--GETBACK/LP--18
Back to where you once belonged--GETBACK/LP--20
Get back to where you once belonged--GETBACK/LP--27
Get back to where you once belonged.--GETBACK/LP
--29
Get back to where you once belonged--GETBACK/LP--33
Get back to where you once belonged--GETBACK/LP--35
I'd like to say thank you on behalf of the group
and ourselves--GETBACK/LP--38
Everything has got to be just like you want it to
--IDIGAPONY--14
Everything has got to be just like you want it to
--IDIGAPONY--14
Everything has got to be just like you want it to
--IDIGAPONY--24

Everything has got to be just like you want it to
--IDIGAPONY--24
Everything has got to be just like you want it to
--IDIGAPONY--34
Everything has got to be just like you want it to
--IDIGAPONY--34
Me hand's getting - a too cold to play a chord now.
--IDIGAPONY--38
Oh please believe me I'd hate to miss the train --
IVEGOTAFEE--6
Mother Mary comes to me --LETITBE/LP--2
I wake up to the sound of music --LETITBE/LP--24
Mother Mary comes to me --LETITBE/LP--25
The long and winding road that leads to your door
--LONGANDWIN--2
It always leads me here, lead me to your door.--
LONGANDWIN--3
And still they lead me back to the long, winding
road.--LONGANDWIN--9
Don't leave me waiting here, lead me to your door.
--LONGANDWIN--11
But still they lead me back to the long, winding
road --LONGANDWIN--12
Don't keep me waiting here (don't keep me
waiting) lead me to your door.--LONGANDWIN--14
I begged her not to go and I begged her on my
bended knee, (oh yeah)--ONEAFTERNI--6
Pick up my bag, run to the station --ONEAFTERNI--11
Pick up my bag, run to the station --ONEAFTERNI--21

TODAY
I'd get myself locked up today --ILLCRYINST--4
THINGS WE SAID TODAY.--THINGSWESA--Title
Then I will remember things we said today.--
THINGSWESA--5
Then we will remember things we said today.--
THINGSWESA--10
Then we will remember things we said today.--
THINGSWESA--21
Then we will remember things we said today.--
THINGSWESA--32
'cos I'm a - gonna see my baby today --WHENIGETHO
--5
I think it's today, yeah--TICKETTORI--3
I think it's today, yeah--TICKETTORI--24
So much younger than today--HELP--9
When I was younger, so much younger than today--
HELP--29
But as from today well I've got somebody that's
new --ANOTHERGIR--3
But as from today well I've seen somebody that's
new --ANOTHERGIR--13
But as from today well I've seen somebody that's
new --ANOTHERGIR--19
Now today I find, you have changed your mind--
NIGHTBEFOR--3
Now today I find you have changed your mind--
NIGHTBEFOR--13
You were above me, but not today.--IMLOOKINGT--12
I read the news today, oh boy--DAYINTHELI--1
I saw a film today, oh boy--DAYINTHELI--11
I read the news today, oh boy--DAYINTHELI--28
It was twenty years ago today-SGTPEPPERS--1
Take you today.--MAGICALMYS--31
One sweet dream came true today --YOUNEVERGI--21
Came true today, came true today.--YOUNEVERGI--22
Came true today, came true today.--YOUNEVERGI--22

TOE
Just to make you toe the line.--RUNFORYOUR--12

TOE-JAM
He got toe-jam football--COMETOGETH--16

TOES
Ooo I've got a feeling that keeps me on my toes --
IVEGOTAFEE--14

TOGETHER
Till we're together ((together)) --PSILOVEYOU--4
Till we're together ((together)) --PSILOVEYOU--5
Till we're together ((together)) --PSILOVEYOU--13
Till we're together ((together)) --PSILOVEYOU--13
These are words that go together well, my
Michelle.--MICHELLE--2
Say we'll be together every day.--GOTTOGETYO--14
All you need is love (all together now) --
ALLYOUN/YS--25
I am he as you are he as you are me and we are

all together--IAMTHEWALR--1
Love you whenever we're together --IWILL--11
ALL TOGETHER NOW.--ALLTOGETHE--Title
All together now (all together now) --ALLTOGETHE
    --13
All together now (all together now) --ALLTOGETHE
    --13
All together now (all together now) --ALLTOGETHE
    --14
All together now (all together now) --ALLTOGETHE
    --14
All together now (all together now) --ALLTOGETHE
    --15
All together now (all together now) --ALLTOGETHE
    --15
All together now (all together now) (all
    together now).--ALLTOGETHE--16
All together now (all together now) (all
    together now).--ALLTOGETHE--16
All together now (all together now) {all
    together now).--ALLTOGETHE--16
All together now (all together now) --ALLTOGETHE
    --21
All together now (all together now) --ALLTOGETHE
    --21
All together now (all together now) --ALLTOGETHE
    --22
All together now (all together now) --ALLTOGETHE
    --22
All together now (all together now) --ALLTOGETHE
    --23
All together now (all together now) --ALLTOGETHE
    --23
All together now (all together now) --ALLTOGETHE
    --24
All together now (all together now) --ALLTOGETHE
    --24
All together now (all together now) --ALLTOGETHE
    --25
All together now (all together now) --ALLTOGETHE
    --25
All together now (all together now) --ALLTOGETHE
    --26
All together now (all together now) --ALLTOGETHE
    --26
All together now (all together now) --ALLTOGETHE
    --27
All together now (all together now) --ALLTOGETHE
    --27
All together now (all together now).--ALLTOGETHE
    --28
All together now (all together now).--ALLTOGETHE
    --28
All together now (all together now) --ALLTOGETHE
    --33
All together now (all together now) --ALLTOGETHE
    --33
All together now (all together now) --ALLTOGETHE
    --34
All together now (all together now) --ALLTOGETHE
    --34
All together now (all together now) --ALLTOGETHE
    --35
All together now (all together now) --ALLTOGETHE
    --35
All together now (all together now) --ALLTOGETHE
    --36
All together now (all together now) --ALLTOGETHE
    --36
All together now (all together now) --ALLTOGETHE
    --37
All together now (all together now) --ALLTOGETHE
    --37
All together now (all together now) --ALLTOGETHE
    --38
All together now (all together now) --ALLTOGETHE
    --38
All together now (all together now) --ALLTOGETHE
    --39
All together now (all together now) --ALLTOGETHE
    --39
All together now (all together now) --ALLTOGETHE
    --40
All together now (all together now) --ALLTOGETHE
    --40
All together now (all together now) --ALLTOGETHE
    --41
All together now (all together now) --ALLTOGETHE
    --41
All together now (all together now) --ALLTOGETHE
    --42
All together now (all together now) --ALLTOGETHE
    --42
All together now (all together now) --ALLTOGETHE

--43
All together now (all together now) --ALLTOGETHE
    --43
All together now --ALLTOGETHE--44
All together now! (wuh, yeah, wahoo!)--ALLTOGETHE
    --45
If you and me should get together --OLDBROWNSH--25
COME TOGETHER.--COMETOGETH--Title
Come together right now over me--COMETOGETH--21
Come together right now over me--COMETOGETH--31
Come together right now over me--COMETOGETH--42
Come together, yeah--COMETOGETH--47
Come together, yeah--COMETOGETH--48
Come together, yeah--COMETOGETH--49
Come together, yeah--COMETOGETH--50
Come together, yeah--COMETOGETH--51
Come together, yeah--COMETOGETH--52
Come together, yeah--COMETOGETH--53
Come together, yeah--COMETOGETH--55
Come together, yeah--COMETOGETH--56
Come together.--COMETOGETH--57

TOLD
And she told me what to say.--SHELOVESYO--7
Because I told you before--YOUCANTDOT--7
Because I told you before--YOUCANTDOT--16
Because I told you before--YOUCANTDOT--30
Because I told you before--YOUCANTDOT--49
'cos I told you once before goodbye --ILLBEBACK--3
You told me--INEEDYOU--10
Oh yes, you told me--INEEDYOU--11
But when you told me--INEEDYOU--21
I told that girl that my prospects were good --
    DRIVEMYCAR--9
I told that girl I could start right away --
    DRIVEMYCAR--22
Was she told when she was young that pain would
    lead to pleasure?--GIRL--22
And she told me to sit anywhere--NORWEGIANW--8
She told me she worked in the morning--NORWEGIANW
    --17
I told her I didn't--NORWEGIANW--19
We'd meet again for I had told you.--GOTTOGETYO--11
And he told us of his life--YELLOWSUBM--3
Told her I would really like to see her again.--
    LOVELYRITA--22
And I told them where to go.--BLUEJAYWAY--9
I told you about Strawberry Fields--GLASSONION--1
I told you about the walrus and me - man--
    GLASSONION--8
I told you about the fool on the hill--GLASSONION
    --17
I don't know why nobody told you how to unfold
    your love --WHILEMYGUI--6
And I told you there's no-one there.--ONLYANORTH--16
When you told me you didn't need me any more --
    OHDARLING--5
A - when you told me you didn't need me any more
    --OHDARLING--7
A - when you told me - ooo - you didn't need me
    any more --OHDARLING--12
A - when you told me you didn't need me any more
    --OHDARLING--14
I told you so.--IDIGAPONY--12
I told you so.--IDIGAPONY--22
I told you so.--IDIGAPONY--32
Wondering really how come nobody told me
    --IVEGOTAFEE--12

TOMORROW
Tomorrow I'll miss you --ALLMYLOVIN--2
Tomorrow I'll miss you --ALLMYLOVIN--16
There'll be no sad tomorrow--THERESAPLA--11
For tomorrow may rain so I'll follow the sun.--
    ILLFOLLOWT--2
For tomorrow may rain so I'll follow the sun.--
    ILLFOLLOWT--4
For tomorrow may rain so I'll follow the sun.--
    ILLFOLLOWT--8
Yeah, tomorrow may rain so I'll follow the sun.--
    ILLFOLLOWT--9
For tomorrow may rain so I'll follow the sun.--
    ILLFOLLOWT--13
TOMORROW NEVER KNOWS.--TOMORROWNE--Title
Leave it till tomorrow to unpack my case --
    BACKINTHEU--10
Shine on till tomorrow, let it be.--LETITBE/45--23
Shine on till tomorrow, let it be.--LETITBE/LP--23

TONIGHT
Don't you be sad, just call me tonight.--ANYTIMEATA

--9
Call me tonight and I'll come to you.--ANYTIMEATA
    --18
Tonight (tonight) tonight (tonight) --HOLDMETIGH
    --7
Tonight (tonight) tonight (tonight) --HOLDMETIGH
    --7
Tonight (tonight) tonight (tonight) --HOLDMETIGH
    --7
Tonight (tonight) tonight (tonight) --HOLDMETIGH
    --7
Tonight tonight --HOLDMETIGH--11
Tonight tonight --HOLDMETIGH--11
Tonight (tonight) tonight (tonight) --HOLDMETIGH
    --14
Tonight (tonight) tonight (tonight) --HOLDMETIGH
    --14
Tonight (tonight) tonight (tonight) --HOLDMETIGH
    --14
Being here alone tonight with you.--HOLDMETIGH--17
Tonight (tonight) tonight (tonight) --HOLDMETIGH
    --24
Tonight (tonight) tonight (tonight) --HOLDMETIGH
    --24
Tonight (tonight) tonight (tonight) --HOLDMETIGH
    --24
Being here alone tonight with you.--HOLDMETIGH--27
Tonight tonight --HOLDMETIGH--31
Tonight tonight --HOLDMETIGH--31
Tonight (tonight) tonight (tonight) --HOLDMETIGH
    --34
Tonight (tonight) tonight (tonight) --HOLDMETIGH
    --34
Tonight (tonight) tonight (tonight) --HOLDMETIGH
    --34
Tonight (tonight) tonight (tonight) --HOLDMETIGH
    --34
I got a girl who's waiting home for me tonight.--
    WHENIGETHO--12
When I getting home tonight --WHENIGETHO--16
Though tonight she's made me sad --IDONTWANTT--9
Though tonight she's made me sad --IDONTWANTT--18
If you wear red tonight--YESITIS--1
Remember what I said tonight--YESITIS--2
Please don't wear red tonight--YESITIS--14
This is what I said tonight--YESITIS--15
Please don't wear red tonight--YESITIS--23
This is what I said tonight--YESITIS--31
You'll be back again tonight--YOULIKEMET--2
But as it is I'll dream of her tonight --IVEJUSTSEE
    --10
If you don't take her out tonight--YOUREGONNA--3
And I will take her out tonight--YOUREGONNA--5
If you don't take her out tonight--YOUREGONNA--25
And I will take her out tonight--YOUREGONNA--27
There will be a show tonight on trampoline.--
    BEINGFORTH--2
And tonight Mr. Kite is topping the bill.--
    BEINGFORTH--21
I wonder where you are tonight --DONTPASSME--14
Are you gonna be in my dreams tonight?--THEEND--2

TOO
That before too long I'd fall in love with her.--
    ISAWHERSTA--8
And before too long I fell in love with her--
    ISAWHERSTA--15
And before too long I fell in love with her.--
    ISAWHERSTA--22
That's the kind of love that is too good to be true
    --THANKYOUGI--9
Pride can hurt you too--SHELOVESYO--26
Though he may want you too--THISBOY--5
'cos I don't care too much for money --CANTBUYMEL
    --7
If you say you love me too --CANTBUYMEL--10
I don't care too much for money --CANTBUYMEL--13
I don't care too much for money --CANTBUYMEL--21
I don't care too much for money --CANTBUYMEL--31
You'd love her too --ANDILOVEHE--4
You're gonna say you love me too, oh.--ISHOULDHAV
    --8
You're gonna say you love me too.--ISHOULDHAV--10
You're gonna say you love me too, oh.--ISHOULDHAV
    --18
You're gonna say you love me too.--ISHOULDHAV--20
You love me too --ISHOULDHAV--21
You love me too --ISHOULDHAV--22
You love me too.--ISHOULDHAV--23

If I love you too --IFIFELL--12
I think I'll love you too --IMHAPPYJUS--2
I think I'll love you too ((oh)) --IMHAPPYJUS--14
I think I'll love you too ((oh)) --IMHAPPYJUS--22
That you would want me too--ILLBEBACK--15
I wonder what went wrong I've waited far too long
    --IDONTWANTT--7
I wonder what went wrong I've waited far too long
    --IDONTWANTT--24
I realise I have left it too late.--IMALOSER--16
Would it be too much to ask of you --WHATYOURED--3
YOU LIKE ME TOO MUCH.--YOULIKEMET--Title
'cos you like me too much and I like you--
    YOULIKEMET--6
'cos you like me too much and I like you--
    YOULIKEMET--12
'cos you like me too much and I like you--
    YOULIKEMET--20
'cos you like me too much and I like you--
    YOULIKEMET--21
'cos you like me too much and I like you--
    YOULIKEMET--29
'cos you like me too much and I like you.--
    YOULIKEMET--30
There's a chance that we might fall apart before
    too long.--WECANWORKI--18
There's a chance that we might fall apart before
    too long.--WECANWORKI--27
But you see now I'm too much in love.--IFINEEDEDS
    --9
But you see now I'm too much in love.--IFINEEDEDS
    --19
LOVE YOU TO/TOO.--LOVEYOUTWO--Title
Should five percent appear too small --TAXMAN--7
If you get too cold, I'll tax the heat,
    ((cold))--TAXMAN--13
That is, I think it's not too bad.--STRAWBERRY--20
You'll be older too--WHENIMSIXT--10
If it's not too dear --WHENIMSIXT--24
When it's far too late--WITHINYOUW--6
Baby, you're a rich man too.--BABYYOUREA--15
Baby, you're a rich man too.--BABYYOUREA--21
Baby, you're a rich man too.--BABYYOUREA--30
Baby, you're a rich man too.--BABYYOUREA--36
Baby, you're a rich man too.--BABYYOUREA--39
Baby, you're a rich man too.--BABYYOUREA--42
Well, it's my birthday too - yeah.--BIRTHDAY--2
Well, it's my birthday too - yeah.--BIRTHDAY--21
When it becomes too much--SAVOYTRUFF--15
You were perverted (too/to)--WHILEMYGUI--15
IT'S ALL TOO MUCH.--ITSALLTOOM--Title
It's all too much --ITSALLTOOM--2
It's all too much.--ITSALLTOOM--3
It's all too much for me to take --ITSALLTOOM--8
For us to take, it's all too much.--ITSALLTOOM--11
It's all too much for me to take --ITSALLTOOM--16
So take a piece, but not too much.--ITSALLTOOM
    --19
It's all too much for me to see --ITSALLTOOM--25
And what I do is all too much.--ITSALLTOOM--28
It's all too much for me to take --ITSALLTOOM--29
For us to take it's all too much.--ITSALLTOOM--32
It's too much - aah.--ITSALLTOOM--33
It's too much.--ITSALLTOOM--34
You're too much - aah.--ITSALLTOOM--37
Too much, too much, too much, too much, too
    much, too much, too much --ITSALLTOOM--39
Too much, too much, too much, too much, too
    much, too much, too much --ITSALLTOOM--39
Too much, too much, too much, too much, too
    much, too much, too much --ITSALLTOOM--39
Too much, too much, too much, too much, too
    much, too much, too much --ITSALLTOOM--39
Too much, too much, too much, too much, too
    much, too much, too much --ITSALLTOOM--39
Too much, too much, too much, too much, too
    much, too much, too much --ITSALLTOOM--39
Too much, too much, too much, too much, too
    much, too much, too much --ITSALLTOOM--39
Too much, too much, too much (wuh!), too
    much, too much, too much --ITSALLTOOM--40
Too much, too much, too much (wuh!), too
    much, too much, too much --ITSALLTOOM--40
Too much, too much, too much (wuh!), too
    much, too much, too much --ITSALLTOOM--40
Too much, too much, too much (wuh!), too
    much, too much, too much --ITSALLTOOM--40
Too much, too much, too much (wuh!), too
    much, too much, too much --ITSALLTOOM--40
Too much, too much, too much (wuh!), too
    much, too much, too much --ITSALLTOOM--40
Too much, too much, too much, too much, too
    much, too much, too much --ITSALLTOOM--41
Too much, too much, too much, too much, too

much, too much, too much --ITSALLTOOM--41
Too much, too much, too much, too much, too
  much, too much --ITSALLTOOM--41
Too much, too much, too much, too much, too
  much, too much --ITSALLTOOM--41
Too much, too much, too much, too much, too
  much, too much --ITSALLTOOM--41
Too much, too much, too much, too much, too
  much, too much --ITSALLTOOM--41
Too much, too much, too much, too much, too
  much, too much --ITSALLTOOM--41
Too much, too much, too much (come on), too
  much, too much, too much.--ITSALLTOOM--42
Too much, too much, too much (come on), too
  much, too much, too much.--ITSALLTOOM--42
Too much, too much, too much (come on), too
  much, too much, too much.--ITSALLTOOM--42
Too much, too much, too much (come on), too
  much, too much, too much.--ITSALLTOOM--42
Too much, too much, too much (come on), too
  much, too much, too much.--ITSALLTOOM--42
Too much, too much, too much (come on), too
  much, too much, too much.--ITSALLTOOM--42
Too much, too much, too much, too much, too
  much, too much --ITSALLTOOM--43
Too much, too much, too much, too much, too
  much, too much --ITSALLTOOM--43
Too much, too much, too much, too much, too
  much, too much --ITSALLTOOM--43
Too much, too much, too much, too much, too
  much, too much --ITSALLTOOM--43
Too much, too much, too much, too much, too
  much, too much --ITSALLTOOM--43
Too much, too much, too much, too much, too
  much, too much --ITSALLTOOM--43
Too much, too much, too much, too much, too
  much, too much --ITSALLTOOM--44
Too much, too much, too much, too much, too
  much, too much --ITSALLTOOM--44
Too much, too much, too much, too much, too
  much, too much --ITSALLTOOM--44
Too much, too much, too much, too much, too
  much, too much --ITSALLTOOM--44
Too much, too much, too much, too much, too
  much, too much --ITSALLTOOM--44
Too much, too much, too much, too much, too
  much, too much --ITSALLTOOM--44
Too much, too much, too much, too much, too
  much, too much --ITSALLTOOM--45
Too much, too much, too much, too much, too
  much, too much --ITSALLTOOM--45
Too much, too much, too much, too much, too
  much, too much --ITSALLTOOM--45
Too much, too much, too much, too much, too
  much, too much --ITSALLTOOM--45
Too much, too much, too much, too much, too
  much, too much --ITSALLTOOM--45
Too much, too much, too much, too much, too
  much, too much --ITSALLTOOM--45
Too much, too much, too much, too much, too
  much, too much.--ITSALLTOOM--46
Too much, too much, too much, too much, too
  much, too much.--ITSALLTOOM--46
Too much, too much, too much, too much, too
  much, too much.--ITSALLTOOM--46
Too much, too much, too much, too much, too
  much, too much.--ITSALLTOOM--46
Too much, too much, too much, too much, too
  much, too much.--ITSALLTOOM--46
Too much, too much, too much, too much, too
  much, too much.--ITSALLTOOM--46
You know my name ((you know)), you know me
  number (too/two)--YOUKNOWMYN--33
You know my name ((you know)), you know me
  number (too/two)--YOUKNOWMYN--37
I feel it now, I hope you feel it too.--FORYOUBLUE
  --15
Me hand's getting - a too cold to play a chord now.
  --IDIGAPONY--38

TOOK
  That boy took my love away--THISBOY--1
  It took me so long to find out --DAYTRIPPER--7
  She took me half the way there --DAYTRIPPER--10
  She took me half the way there, now.--DAYTRIPPER
    --12
  It took me so long to find out --DAYTRIPPER--15
  It took me so long to find out --DAYTRIPPER--24
  It took me years to write, will you take a look?--
    PAPERBACKW--3
  I was alone, I took a ride--GOTTOGETYO--1
  I was alone, I took a ride--GOTTOGETYO--25
  Took her out and tried to win her--LOVELYRITA--20

Took her home I nearly made it--LOVELYRITA--24
In case of accidents he always took his mom --
  CONTINUING--8
It took a long, long, long time --LONGLONGLO--4

TOP
  Standing alone at the top of the stairs--SHESLEAVIN
    --15
  When I get to the bottom I go back to the top
    of the slide --HELTERSKEL--1
  When I get to the bottom I go back to the top
    of the slide--HELTERSKEL--18
  For your sweet top lip I'm in the queue --
    OLDBROWNSH--31
  Here come old flat top--COMETOGETH--5

TOPPING
  And tonight Mr. Kite is topping the bill.--
    BEINGFORTH--21

TOUCH
  And when I touch you--IWANTTOHOL--13
  And when I touch you--IWANTTOHOL--26
  Burns my feet as they touch the ground.--GOODDAYSUN
    --8
  She's well acquainted with the touch of the
    velvet hand --HAPPINESSI--3
  Julia, Julia morning moon touch me --JULIA--9
  Julia sleeping sand silent cloud touch me --JULIA
    --13

TOUR
  MAGICAL MYSTERY TOUR.--MAGICALMYS--Title
  Roll up, roll up for the Mystery Tour --MAGICALMYS
    --1
  Roll up, roll up for the Mystery Tour --MAGICALMYS
    --3
  Roll up, roll up for the Mystery Tour.--MAGICALMYS
    --4
  Roll up for the Mystery Tour --MAGICALMYS--6
  Roll up for the Mystery Tour.--MAGICALMYS--8
  The Magical Mystery Tour is waiting to take
    you away--MAGICALMYS--9
  Roll up, roll up for the Mystery Tour --MAGICALMYS
    --11
  Roll up, roll up for the Mystery Tour.--MAGICALMYS
    --12
  Roll up for the Mystery Tour --MAGICALMYS--14
  Roll up for the Mystery Tour --MAGICALMYS--16
  The Magical Mystery Tour is hoping to take you
    away --MAGICALMYS--17
  The Magical Mystery Tour.--MAGICALMYS--21
  Roll up, roll up for the Mystery Tour--MAGICALMYS
    --22
  Roll up for the Mystery Tour--MAGICALMYS--24
  Roll up for the Mystery Tour.--MAGICALMYS--26
  The Magical Mystery Tour is coming to take you
    away --MAGICALMYS--27
  The Magical Mystery Tour is dying to take you
    away--MAGICALMYS--29

TOW
  When it gets dark I tow your heart away.--
    LOVELYRITA--6

TOWER
  Semolina pilchard climbing up the Eiffel Tower--
    IAMTHEWALR--25

TOWERING
  Towering over your head.--LUCYINTHES--6

TOWN
  In the town where I was born--YELLOWSUBM--1
  Heading for home you start to roam then you're in
    town.--GOODMORNIN--8
  Everywhere in town is getting dark--GOODMORNIN--19
  So one day he walked into town --ROCKYRACCO--7

TRADE
  Meeting a man from the motor trade.--SHESLEAVIN--27

TRAGIC
  Oh, Honey Pie my position is tragic--HONEYPIE--10

TRAIN
>   Picture yourself on a train in a station--
>   LUCYINTHES--23
>   Oh please believe me I'd hate to miss the train --
>   IVEGOTAFEE--6

TRAMPOLINE
>   There will be a show tonight on trampoline.--
>   BEINGFORTH--2

TRAVELLED
>   And have you travelled very far?--BABYYOUREA--5

TRAVELLING
>   Arrive without travelling.--INNERLIGHT--15
>   My baby said she's travelling on the one after
>   nine-0-nine --ONEAFTERNI--1
>   I said, move over honey, I'm travelling on
>   that line --ONEAFTERNI--2
>   Said you're travelling on the one after
>   nine-0-nine.--ONEAFTERNI--5
>   Said you're travelling on the one after
>   nine-0-nine --ONEAFTERNI--10
>   Well, she said she's travelling on the one after
>   nine-0-nine --ONEAFTERNI--15
>   I said a-move over honey, I'm travelling on
>   that line --ONEAFTERNI--16
>   Said she's travelling on the one after
>   nine-0-nine. (yeah)--ONEAFTERNI--19
>   She said she's travelling on the one after
>   nine-0-nine --ONEAFTERNI--25
>   Said a - move over honey, I'm travelling on
>   that line --ONEAFTERNI--26
>   Said we're travelling on the one after nine-0 --
>   ONEAFTERNI--29
>   She said we're travelling on the one after nine-0
>   --ONEAFTERNI--30
>   Said we're travelling on the one after nine-0-nine
>   --ONEAFTERNI--31

TRAVELS
>   The farther one travels --INNERLIGHT--5
>   The farther one travels --INNERLIGHT--12

TRAY
>   The pretty nurse is selling poppies from a tray--
>   PENNYLANE--21

TREASURE
>   Treasure ((treasure)) these few words ((words))
>   --PSILOVEYOU--3
>   Treasure ((treasure)) these few words ((words))
>   --PSILOVEYOU--3
>   Treasure ((treasure)) these few words ((words))
>   --PSILOVEYOU--12
>   Treasure ((treasure)) these few words ((words))
>   --PSILOVEYOU--12

TREAT
>   Did you have to treat me oh so bad --TELLMEWHY--7
>   If I just don't treat you right--YOULIKEMET--4
>   Treat me like you did the night before.--NIGHTBEFOR
>   --4
>   Treat me like you did the night before.--NIGHTBEFOR
>   --8
>   Treat me like you did the night before (yes).--
>   NIGHTBEFOR--14
>   Treat me like you did the night before (yeah).--
>   NIGHTBEFOR--16
>   Treat me like you did the night before.--NIGHTBEFOR
>   --22
>   And I will treat her kind (I'm gonna treat her
>   kind)--YOUREGONNA--6
>   And I will treat her kind (I'm gonna treat her
>   kind)--YOUREGONNA--6
>   If you don't treat her right my friend--YOUREGONNA
>   --9
>   'cos I will treat her right--YOUREGONNA--11
>   The way you treat her what else can I do?--
>   YOUREGONNA--17
>   The way you treat her what else can I do?--
>   YOUREGONNA--24
>   And I will treat her kind (I'm gonna treat her
>   kind)--YOUREGONNA--28
>   And I will treat her kind (I'm gonna treat her
>   kind)--YOUREGONNA--28
>   Why, tell me why did you not treat me right?--

IMLOOKINGT--9
>   Why, tell me why did you not treat me right?--
>   IMLOOKINGT--15
>   When you treat me so unkind.--WHATGOESON--4
>   When you treat me so unkind.--WHATGOESON--13
>   When you treat me so unkind.--WHATGOESON--29
>   Why would she treat us so thoughtlessly?--
>   SHESLEAVIN--18

TREATING
>   The world is treating me bad, misery.--MISERY--1
>   The world is treating me bad, misery.--MISERY--3

TREE
>   Then we lie beneath a shady tree --GOODDAYSUN--10
>   No-one, I think, is in my tree--STRAWBERRY--16
>   Bom-pa bom, chop the tree --ALLTOGETHE--10
>   Bom-pa bom, chop the tree --ALLTOGETHE--30

TREES
>   With tangerine trees and marmalade skies.--
>   LUCYINTHES--2

TRES
>   Sont des mots qui vont tres bien ensemble, tres
>   bien ensemble.--MICHELLE--4
>   Sont des mots qui vont tres bien ensemble, tres
>   bien ensemble.--MICHELLE--4
>   Sont des mots qui vont tres bien ensemble, tres
>   bien ensemble.--MICHELLE--10
>   Sont des mots qui vont tres bien ensemble, tres
>   bien ensemble.--MICHELLE--10
>   Sont des mots qui vont tres bien ensemble, tres
>   bien ensemble.--MICHELLE--21
>   Sont des mots qui vont tres bien ensemble, tres
>   bien ensemble.--MICHELLE--21

TRICKS
>   When Mr. K. performs his tricks - without a
>   sound.--BEINGFORTH--16

TRIED
>   I tried to telephone--NOREPLY--9
>   I tried to telephone--NOREPLY--22
>   You've tried before to leave me--YOULIKEMET--7
>   Tried to please her --DAYTRIPPER--18
>   Tried to please her --DAYTRIPPER--20
>   When I think of all the times I tried so hard
>   to leave her --GIRL--6
>   Took her out and tried to win her--LOVELYRITA--20
>   And though she tried her best to help me --
>   SHECAMEINT--18
>   Anyway you'll never know the many ways I've tried
>   --LONGANDWIN--8

TRIES
>   If somebody tries to take my place --IMHAPPYJUS--16
>   If somebody tries to take my place --IMHAPPYJUS--24

TRIGGER
>   And I feel my finger on your trigger ((oh,
>   yeah)) --HAPPINESSI--23

TRIM
>   We see the banker sitting waiting for a trim--
>   PENNYLANE--25

TRIP
>   The mystery trip.--MAGICALMYS--19
>   Made a lightning trip to Vienna --BALLADOFJO--29

TRIPPER
>   DAY TRIPPER.--DAYTRIPPER--Title
>   She was a day tripper --DAYTRIPPER--5
>   She was a day tripper --DAYTRIPPER--13
>   She was a day tripper --DAYTRIPPER--22
>   Day tripper, yeah --DAYTRIPPER--26
>   Day tripper, yeah --DAYTRIPPER--27
>   Day tripper --DAYTRIPPER--28
>   Day tripper, yeah --DAYTRIPPER--29
>   Day tripper --DAYTRIPPER--30
>   Day tripper.--DAYTRIPPER--31

TRIVIALITY
    I got no time for triviality --WHENIGETHO--11

TROLLY
    Desmond takes a trolly to the jewellery store --
        OBLADIOBLA--9

TROUBLE
    When I find myself in times of trouble --LETITBE/45
        --1
    When I find myself in times of trouble --LETITBE/LP
        --1

TROUBLES
    All my troubles seemed so far away--YESTERDAY--2

TRUE
    I'll always be true --LOVEMEDO--3
    I'll always be true --LOVEMEDO--8
    I'll always be true --LOVEMEDO--15
    I'll always be true --LOVEMEDO--20
    And it's true --ASKMEWHY--3
    And it's true --ASKMEWHY--18
    Like a heart that's oh so true--FROMMETOYO--8
    That's the kind of love that is too good to be true
        --THANKYOUGI--9
    I need you and it's true--ILLGETYOU--10
    Remember I'll always be true --ALLMYLOVIN--3
    And hope that my dreams will come true --ALLMYLOVIN
        --9
    All my lovin', darlin', I'll be true.--ALLMYLOVIN
        --14
    Remember I'll always be true --ALLMYLOVIN--17
    All my lovin', darlin', I'll be true --ALLMYLOVIN
        --22
    Would you promise to be true --IFIFELL--2
    Guess you know it's true --EIGHTDAYSA--2
    Guess you know it's true --EIGHTDAYSA--20
    And so it's true pride comes before a fall --
        IMALOSER--17
    'n' should you need a love that's true, it's me.--
        WHATYOURED--11
    'n' should you need a love that's true, it's me.--
        WHATYOURED--18
    And what's more, it's true, yes it is.--YESITIS--4
    Understand it's true--YESITIS--8
    Yes it is, it's true, yes it is.--YESITIS--9
    In spite of you it's true--YESITIS--17
    Yes it is, it's true, yes it is.--YESITIS--18
    In spite of you it's true--YESITIS--26
    Yes it is, it's true--YESITIS--27
    Yes it is, it's true.--YESITIS--28
    You'll never leave me and you know it's true--
        YOULIKEMET--5
    You'll never leave me and you know it's true--
        YOULIKEMET--11
    I wouldn't let you leave me 'cos it's true--
        YOULIKEMET--19
    I wouldn't let you leave me 'cos it's true--
        YOULIKEMET--28
    If I'm true I'll never leave--GOTTOGETYO--18
    One sweet dream came true today --YOUNEVERGI--21
    Came true today, came true today.--YOUNEVERGI--22
    Came true today, came true today.--YOUNEVERGI--22
    Because you're sweet and lovely girl, it's true --
        FORYOUBLUE--3
    Because you're sweet and lovely girl, it's true --
        FORYOUBLUE--17

TRUFFLE
    SAVOY TRUFFLE.--SAVOYTRUFF--Title
    After the Savoy truffle.--SAVOYTRUFF--5
    After the Savoy truffle.--SAVOYTRUFF--10
    After the Savoy truffle.--SAVOYTRUFF--18
    After the Savoy truffle.--SAVOYTRUFF--27
    After the Savoy truffle.--SAVOYTRUFF--29

TRUST
    If I trust in you --IFIFELL--10
    If you put your trust in me--TELLMEWHAT--11
    And if you do, I'll trust in you --WAIT--11
    And if you do, I'll trust in you --WAIT--19
    And donated to the National Trust.--HAPPINESSI--8

TRUTH
    Never glimpse the truth--WITHINYOUW--5

TRY
    I'll try to make it shine.--ANYTIMEATA--14
    I know you never even try girl --PLEASEPLEA--2
    I know/Why do you never even try girl--PLEASEPLEA--20
    I'd try to make you sad somehow --ILLCRYINST--9
    If it's funny try and understand.--IMHAPPYJUS--5
    This time I will try to show --ILLBEBACK--11
    This time I will try to show --ILLBEBACK--20
    Can't you try to see that I'm--TELLMEWHAT--20
    Can't you try to see that I'm--TELLMEWHAT--29
    How can I even try --YOUVEGOTTO--11
    Try to see it my way --WECANWORKI--1
    Try to see it my way --WECANWORKI--15
    Try to see it my way --WECANWORKI--24
    Try thinking more if just for your own sake.--
        THINKFORYO--20
    If you try to sit, I'll tax your seat, ((sit))--
        TAXMAN--12
    And I'll try not to sing outta key.--WITHALITTL--4
    Mmm gonna try with a little help from my friends.
        --WITHALITTL--7
    Mmm gonna try with a little help from my friends.
        --WITHALITTL--14
    Oh I'm gonna try with a little help from my
        friends.--WITHALITTL--25
    Mmm gonna try with a little help from my friends
        --WITHALITTL--31
    To try our best to hold it there--WITHINYOUW--11
    Try to realise it's all within yourself--WITHINYOUW
        --16
    From where some try to drag me down --OLDBROWNSH
        --10

TRYING
    That I'm not trying to pretend.--ILLBEBACK--12
    That I'm not trying to pretend.--ILLBEBACK--21
    Trying to get to you--TELLMEWHAT--21
    Trying to get to you--TELLMEWHAT--30
    And I can't spend my whole life trying--RUNFORYOUR
        --11
    Lady Madonna trying to make ends meet - yeah--
        GLASSONION--13
    Trying to make a dove-tail joint - yeah--GLASSONION
        --22
    Trying to get to Holland or France.--BALLADOFJO--2
    I said we're only trying to get us some peace.--
        BALLADOFJO--20
    Trying to save paper.--MEANMRMUST--3

TUCSON
    Jojo left his home in Tucson, Arizona--GETBACK/45

    Jojo left his home in Tucson, Arizona--GETBACK/LP
        --9

TUESDAY
    Corporation T-shirt, stupid bloody Tuesday--
        IAMTHEWALR--5
    Tuesday afternoon is never-ending --LADYMADONN--14

TUESDAYS
    Tuesdays on the phone to me.--SHECAMEINT--11
    Tuesdays on the phone to me.--SHECAMEINT--23

TULIPS
    Looking through the bent-backed tulips--GLASSONION
        --5

TUMBLE
    They tumble blindly as they make their way across
        the universe.--ACROSSTHEU--14

TUNE
    That is you can't, you know, tune in--STRAWBERRY
        --18
    What would you think if I sang outta tune --
        WITHALITTL--1

TUNED
    Tuned to a natural E --BABYYOUREA--24

TURN
    Turn me on when I get lonely--SHESAWOMAN--5

Turn me on when I get lonely--SHESAWOMAN--22
Turn me on when I get lonely--SHESAWOMAN--32
Turn my face to the wall.--YOUVEGOTTO--2
She will turn to me and start to cry --GIRL--7
But if your heart breaks, don't wait, turn me
away --WAIT--5
But if your heart breaks, don't wait, turn me
away --WAIT--21
But I can turn away--YOUWONTSEE--10
I turn around, it's past--LOVEYOUTWO--2
Turn off your mind, relax and float down-stream--
TOMORROWNE--1
I'd love to turn you on--DAYINTHELI--16
I'd love to turn you on--DAYINTHELI--34
(What do you see when you turn out the light?)--
WITHALITTL--21
Where I stop and I turn and I go for a ride --
HELTERSKEL--2
And I stop and I turn and I go for a ride--
HELTERSKEL--19
She came along to turn on everyone--SEXYSADIE--10

TURNED
A crowd of people turned away--DAYINTHELI--13

TURNING
But now the tide is turning I can see that I
was blind.--WHATGOESON--16
You're holding me down (aah) turning me round
(aah)--GETTINGBET--5
Quietly turning the backdoor key--SHESLEAVIN--6
I look at the world and I notice it's turning --
WHILEMYGUI--9
Monday morning turning back --YOUNEVERGI--11

TURNS
If she turns up while I'm gone please let me know.
--IDONTWANTT--4
If she turns up while I'm gone please let me know.
--IDONTWANTT--16
Now the sun turns out his light --GOODNIGHT--3
Now the sun turns out his light --GOODNIGHT--16
But what is sweet now turns so sour.--SAVOYTRUFF
--20
Because the world is round it turns me on --BECAUSE
--2
But when she turns her back on the boy, he
creeps up from behind --MAXWELLSIL--12

TURNSTYLE
Suddenly someone is there at the turnstyle--
LUCYINTHES--25

TWELVE
At twelve o'clock a meeting round the table --
CRYBABYCRY--28

TWELVE-BAR
Them old twelve-bar blues.--FORYOUBLUE--10

TWENTY
It was twenty years ago today--SGTPEPPERS--1

TWENTY-CARAT
Buys a twenty-carat golden ring (golden ring) --
OBLADIOBLA--10

TWICE
She ought to think twice--TICKETTORI--18
She ought to think twice--TICKETTORI--21
She ought to think twice--TICKETTORI--31
She ought to think twice--TICKETTORI--34
Who sometimes wears it twice as long.--OLDBROWNSH
--4
I said, move over once, move over twice --
ONEAFTERNI--3
I said move over once, move over twice --ONEAFTERNI
--8
Said move over once, move over twice --ONEAFTERNI
--17
I said, move over once, move over twice --ONEAFTERNI
--27

TWO

I've known a secret for the week or two --
DOYOUWANTT--15
Nobody knows just we two.--DOYOUWANTT--16
One, two, three, four.--ISAWHERSTA--1
I could tell the world a thing or two about our love
--THANKYOUGI--5
When she learns we are two.--IFIFELL--20
When she learns we are two.--IFIFELL--27
Yes, I'm gonna break 'em in two --ILLCRYINST--17
Yes, I'm gonna break 'em in two --ILLCRYINST--26
I've had a drink or two and I don't care --
IDONTWANTT--5
Though I've had a drink or two and I don't care --
IDONTWANTT--22
One, two, three, four.--TICKETTORI--1
Said you had a thing or two to tell me--INEEDYOU
--6
We talked until two--NORWEGIANW--14
I've got a word or two--THINKFORYO--1
I'll be writing more in a week or two. ((writer))
--PAPERBACKW--16
One, two, three, four, one, two.--TAXMAN--1
One, two, three, four, one, two.--TAXMAN--1
(One, two, three, four)--TAXMAN--2
Sitting on a sofa with a sister or two.--LOVELYRITA
--25
One, two (ah yeah), three, four.--SGTPEPPREP--1
One, two - one, two.--WITHINYOUW--20
One, two - one, two.--WITHINYOUW--20
About an hour or two,--DONTPASSME--28
One, two, three, four, five, six, seven,
eight.--DONTPASSME--36
I say two--REVOLUTONE--3
Two, three.--YERBLUES--1
One, two, three, four --ALLTOGETHE--1
They look just like two gurus in drag.--BALLADOFJO
--32
One, two, three, four, five, six, seven --
YOUNEVERGI--24
One, two, three, four, five, six, seven --
YOUNEVERGI--26
One, two, three, four, five, six, seven --
YOUNEVERGI--28
One, two, three, four, five, six, seven --
YOUNEVERGI--30
One, two, three, four, five, six, seven --
YOUNEVERGI--32
One, two, three, four, five, six, seven --
YOUNEVERGI--34
One, two, three, four, five, six, seven --
YOUNEVERGI--36
One, two, three, four, five, six, seven --
YOUNEVERGI--38
One, two, three, four, five, six, seven --
YOUNEVERGI--40
You know my name ((you know)), you know me number
(too/two)--YOUKNOWMYN--33
You know my name ((you know)), you know me number
(too/two)--YOUKNOWMYN--37
OK one, two, three, four.--GETBACK/LP--6
A - one, two, three.--IDIGAPONY--2
A - one, two.--IDIGAPONY--5
TWO OF US.--TWOOFUS--Title
Two of us riding nowhere --TWOOFUS--3
Two of us sending postcards --TWOOFUS--10
Two of us wearing raincoats --TWOOFUS--19
Two of us wearing raincoats --TWOOFUS--28

TWO-FOOT
Feeling two-foot small.--YOUVEGOTTO--4

UH
(Uh) cha, cha--HELLOGOODB--40

UKRAINE
Well, the Ukraine girls really knock me out --
BACKINTHEU--15
Well, the Ukraine girls really knock me out --
BACKINTHEU--27

UMPA
Umpa, umpa, stick it up your jumper ((joob -
joob))--IAMTHEWALR--35
Umpa, umpa, stick it up your jumper ((joob -
joob))--IAMTHEWALR--35
Umpa, umpa, stick it up your jumper.--IAMTHEWALR--36
Umpa, umpa, stick it up your jumper.--IAMTHEWALR--36

UNDER

The minute you let her under your skin --HEYJUDE
--7
Remember to let her under your skin (oh) --HEYJUDE
--28
I'd like to be under the sea--OCTOPUSSGA--1
I'd like to be under the sea--OCTOPUSSGA--7
I'd like to be under the sea--OCTOPUSSGA--15
I'd like to be under the sea--OCTOPUSSGA--23

UNDERSTAND
And in time you'll understand the reason why --
ASKMEWHY--9
Let me understand.--IWANNABEYO--14
I think you'll understand--IWANTTOHOL--2
I think you'll understand--IWANTTOHOL--21
I think you'll understand--IWANTTOHOL--34
And help me understand?--IFIFELL--3
If it's funny try and understand.--IMHAPPYJUS--5
Understand it's true--YESITIS--8
Did she understand it when they said --GIRL--23
I will say the only words I know that you'll
understand.--MICHELLE--8
Until I do I'm telling you so you'll understand.--
MICHELLE--19
And I will say the only words I know that
you'll understand --MICHELLE--22
And his clinging wife doesn't understand.--
PAPERBACKW--9
He helps you to understand --DRROBERT--4
He helps you to understand --DRROBERT--16
Maybe you'd understand.--IWANTTOTEL--18
She said you don't understand what I said.--
SHESAIDSHE--7
She said you don't understand what I said.--
SHESAIDSHE--13

UNDERSTANDS
She's a woman who understands--SHESAWOMAN--16
She's a woman who understands--SHESAWOMAN--26
Childlike, no-one understands--HEYBULLDOG--5

UNDERSTOOD
'n' she said baby it's understood --DRIVEMYCAR--10
She acts as if it's understood --GIRL--17

UNDERTAKE
Ten somersets he'll undertake on solid ground.--
BEINGFORTH--18

UNDYING
Limitless undying love which shines around me
like a million suns --ACROSSTHEU--23

UNFAIR
Was I to blame for being unfair?--ICALLYOURN--2
I was so unfair --DONTPASSME--24

UNFOLD
I don't know why nobody told you how to unfold
your love --WHILEMYGUI--6

UNHAPPY
I don't wanna say that I've been unhappy with you
--ANOTHERGIR--12
I don't wanna say that I've been unhappy with you
--ANOTHERGIR--18

UNIVERSE
But I am of the universe--YERBLUES--12
ACROSS THE UNIVERSE.--ACROSSTHEU--Title
They slither wildly as they slip away across the
universe.--ACROSSTHEU--2
They call me on and on across the universe.--
ACROSSTHEU--12
They tumble blindly as they make their way across
the universe.--ACROSSTHEU--14
It calls me on and on across the universe.--
ACROSSTHEU--24

UNKIND
When you treat me so unkind.--WHATGOESON--4
When you treat me so unkind.--WHATGOESON--13
When you treat me so unkind.--WHATGOESON--29
But if I seem to act unkind--IWANTTOTEL--9

UNPACK
Leave it till tomorrow to unpack my case --
BACKINTHEU--10

UNPLEASANT
Wishing to avoid an unpleasant scene --MAXWELLSIL
--9

UNTIL
Until that day--DONTBOTHER--24
Until that day--DONTBOTHER--39
Until then I'll cry instead.--ILLCRYINST--19
Until then I'll cry instead.--ILLCRYINST--28
Until I find a way--MICHELLE--7
Until I do I'm hoping you will know what I mean.--
MICHELLE--14
Until I do I'm telling you so you'll understand.--
MICHELLE--19
We talked until two--NORWEGIANW--14

UNWISE
Was I so unwise? (aah the night before)--NIGHTBEFOR
--6
Was I so unwise? (aah the night before)--NIGHTBEFOR
--20

UP
You know it's up to you--SHELOVESYO--24
I'd get myself locked up today--ILLCRYINST--4
If she turns up while I'm gone please let me know.
--IDONTWANTT--4
If she turns up while I'm gone please let me know.
--IDONTWANTT--16
'cos I looked up to see your face.--NOREPLY--8
Open up your eyes now--TELLMEWHAT--5
Open up your eyes now--TELLMEWHAT--22
Open up your eyes now--TELLMEWHAT--31
And opened up the doors.--HELP--14
And opened up the doors.--HELP--34
Hurry up John--IMDOWN--24
Haven't I the right to make it up girl?--ITSONLYLOV
--10
I know your mind's made up --THINKFORYO--13
When I call you up your line's engaged.--YOUWONTSEE
--1
If you're down he'll pick you up, Dr. Robert --
DRROBERT--6
When I wake up early in the morning --IMONLYSLEE
--1
When I wake up early in the morning --IMONLYSLEE
--21
Eleanor Rigby picks up the rice in the church--
ELEANORRIG--3
She wakes up, she makes up --FORNOONE--4
She wakes up, she makes up --FORNOONE--4
I feel hung up and I don't know why --IWANTTOTEL
--13
I feel hung up and I don't know why --IWANTTOTEL
--20
Woke up, fell out of bed--DAYINTHELI--18
And looking up I noticed I was late--DAYINTHELI--21
Filling me up with your rules.--GETTINGBET--6
Nothing to do it's up to you--GOODMORNIN--4
Picks up the letter that's lying there--SHESLEAVIN
--14
Would you stand up and walk out on me?--WITHALITTL
--2
Semolina pilchard climbing up the Eiffel Tower--
IAMTHEWALR--25
Umpa, umpa, stick it up your jumper ((joob -
joob))--IAMTHEWALR--35
Umpa, umpa, stick it up your jumper.--IAMTHEWALR
--36
Roll up, roll up for the Mystery Tour --MAGICALMYS
--1
Roll up, roll up for the Mystery Tour --MAGICALMYS
--1
Roll up, roll up for the Mystery Tour --MAGICALMYS
--3
Roll up, roll up for the Mystery Tour --MAGICALMYS
--3
Roll up, roll up for the Mystery Tour.--MAGICALMYS
--4
Roll up, roll up for the Mystery Tour.--MAGICALMYS
--4
Roll up (and that's an invitation)--MAGICALMYS--5
Roll up for the Mystery Tour --MAGICALMYS--6
Roll up (to make a reservation)--MAGICALMYS--7

Roll up for the Mystery Tour.--MAGICALMYS--8
Roll up, roll up for the Mystery Tour --MAGICALMYS
    --11
Roll up, roll up for the Mystery Tour --MAGICALMYS
    --11
Roll up, roll up for the Mystery Tour.--MAGICALMYS
    --12
Roll up, roll up for the Mystery Tour.--MAGICALMYS
    --12
Roll up (we've got everything you need)--MAGICALMYS
    --13
Roll up for the Mystery Tour --MAGICALMYS--14
Roll up (satisfaction guaranteed)--MAGICALMYS--15
Roll up for the Mystery Tour.--MAGICALMYS--16
Roll up, roll up for the Mystery Tour--MAGICALMYS
    --22
Roll up, roll up for the Mystery Tour--MAGICALMYS
    --22
Roll up (and that's an invitation)--MAGICALMYS--23
Roll up for the Mystery Tour--MAGICALMYS--24
Roll up (to make a reservation)--MAGICALMYS--25
Roll up for the Mystery Tour.--MAGICALMYS--26
Let's all get up and dance to a song--YOURMOTHER
    --2
Let's all get up and dance to a song--YOURMOTHER
    --8
Lift up your hearts and sing me a song--YOURMOTHER
    --13
The sun is up, the sky is blue --DEARPRUDEN--3
Dear Prudence, open up your eyes --DEARPRUDEN--6
Dear Prudence, won't you open up your eyes?--
    DEARPRUDEN--10
The sun is up, the sky is blue,--DEARPRUDEN--23
Coming up the drive --DONTPASSME--3
I wonder should I get up and fix myself a drink --
    IMSOTIRED--3
Hold your head up you silly girl, look what
    you've done --MARTHAMYDE--4
Stirring up the dirt --PIGGIES--9
Hey up!--WHILEMYGUI--1
Saving up your money for a rainy day --BALLADOFJO
    --25
Though you pick me up --OLDBROWNSH--9
If I grow up I'll be a singer --OLDBROWNSH--17
He come grooving up slowly--COMETOGETH--6
But when she turns her back on the boy, he
    creeps up from behind --MAXWELLSIL--12
Saving up to buy some clothes--MEANMRMUST--5
Keeps a ten bob note up his nose--MEANMRMUST--6
Pick up the bags, get in the limousine.--YOUNEVERGI
    --18
I wake up to the sound of music --LETITBE/45--24
YOU KNOW MY NAME (LOOK UP MY NUMBER).--YOUKNOWMYN
    --Title
You know my name, look up de number --YOUKNOWMYN
    --1
You know my name, look up de number.--YOUKNOWMYN
    --2
Good evening, you know my name, well then look
    up my number --YOUKNOWMYN--9
You know my name, that's right, look up my
    number (hey) --YOUKNOWMYN--10
Look up the number (heads up boys) --YOUKNOWMYN--14
Look up the number (heads up boys) --YOUKNOWMYN--14
You know my name - haa, that's right, look up
    the number --YOUKNOWMYN--15
You know my name, ba ba ba bum, look up the
    number --YOUKNOWMYN--18
You know my name, look up the number --YOUKNOWMYN
    --19
My name, you know, you know, ((look up the
    number))--YOUKNOWMYN--25
You know my name, look up the number --YOUKNOWMYN
    --29
You know my name, look up the number.--YOUKNOWMYN
    --30
You know, you know my name, look up the number.--
    YOUKNOWMYN--31
You know my name, look up the number --YOUKNOWMYN
    --36
(look up my name)--YOUKNOWMYN--38
You know my number, what's up with you? - ha--
    YOUKNOWMYN--40
Everybody pulled their socks up (yeah) --IVEGOTAFEE
    --26
Everybody pulled their socks up (oh no, no) --
    IVEGOTAFEE--34
I wake up to the sound of music --LETITBE/LP--24
Pick up my bag, run to the station --ONEAFTERNI--11
Pick up my bag, run right home --ONEAFTERNI--13
Pick up my bag, run to the station --ONEAFTERNI--21
Well - pick up my bag, run right home (run
    right home) --ONEAFTERNI--23

UPON
    There's a fog upon LA --BLUEJAYWAY--1
    Don't carry the world upon your shoulder.--HEYJUDE
        --11
    Bang, bang Maxwell's silver hammer came down
        upon her head --MAXWELLSIL--6
    Bang, bang Maxwell's silver hammer came down
        upon her head --MAXWELLSIL--13
    Bang, bang Maxwell's silver hammer came down
        upon his head --MAXWELLSIL--23

UPSET
    How was I to know you would upset me?--INEEDYOU--7
    I'm so tired, I'm feeling so upset --IMSOTIRED--14

UPSIDE
    Upside, upside, upside-down--IMDOWN--42
    Upside, upside, upside-down--IMDOWN--42

UPSIDE-DOWN
    Oh baby, I'm upside-down--IMDOWN--32
    I'm feeling upside-down (I'm really down)--IMDOWN
        --36
    Upside, upside, upside-down--IMDOWN--42

UPSTAIRS
    Found my way upstairs and had a smoke--DAYINTHELI
        --25

UPSTREAM
    Stay in bed, float upstream (float upstream).--
        IMONLYSLEE--4
    Stay in bed, float upstream (float upstream).--
        IMONLYSLEE--4
    Stay in bed, float upstream (float upstream).--
        IMONLYSLEE--24
    Stay in bed, float upstream (float upstream).--
        IMONLYSLEE--24

UPTOWN
    Down to the bits that I left uptown --HAPPINESSI
        --10

US
    Both of us thinking how good it can be--HERETHEREA
        --6
    And he told us of his life--YELLOWSUBM--3
    Everyone of us (everyone of us) has all we need
        (has all we need) --YELLOWSUBM--26
    Everyone of us (everyone of us) has all we need
        (has all we need) --YELLOWSUBM--26
    Nothing can come between us--LOVELYRITA--5
    Give us a wink and make me think of you.--
        LOVELYRITA--28
    We'd like to take you home with us--SGTPEPPERS--17
    Why would she treat us so thoughtlessly?--
        SHESLEAVIN--18
    About the space between us all--WITHINYOUW--2
    Back in the US, back in the US, back in the
        USSR.--BACKINTHEU--14
    Back in the US, back in the US, back in the
        USSR.--BACKINTHEU--14
    If looks could kill it would have been us instead
        of him.--CONTINUING--29
    No-one will be watching us --WHYDONTWED--5
    No-one will be watching us --WHYDONTWED--11
    No-one will be watching us --WHYDONTWED--17
    For us to take, it's all too much.--ITSALLTOOM--11
    For us to take it's all too much.--ITSALLTOOM--32
    You know they didn't even give us a chance.--
        BALLADOFJO--4
    I said we're only trying to get us some peace.--
        BALLADOFJO--20
    He'd let us in, knows where we've been--OCTOPUSSGA
        --3
    No-one there to tell us what to do.--OCTOPUSSGA--22
    TWO OF US.--TWOOFUS--Title
    Two of us riding nowhere --TWOOFUS--3
    Two of us sending postcards --TWOOFUS--10
    Two of us wearing raincoats --TWOOFUS--19
    Two of us wearing raincoats --TWOOFUS--28

USA
    In the USA--HONEYPIE--4

USE
    I see no use in wondering why --NOTASECOND--2
    I see no use in wondering why --NOTASECOND--13

USED
    I'm the kind of guy, who never used to cry.--MISERY
        --2
    I'm not half the man I used to be--YESTERDAY--6
    I used to think of no-one else but you were just
        the same --WHATGOESON--22
    I used to get mad at my school (now I can't
        complain)--GETTINGBET--3
    Me used to be angry young man--GETTINGBET--11
    I used to be cruel to my woman--GETTINGBET--25

USSR
    BACK IN THE USSR.--BACKINTHEU--Title
    I'm back in the USSR --BACKINTHEU--5
    Back in the USSR (yeah).--BACKINTHEU--7
    I'm back in the USSR --BACKINTHEU--12
    Back in the US, back in the US, back in the
        USSR.--BACKINTHEU--14
    Hey, I'm back in the USSR.--BACKINTHEU--24
    Back in the USSR.--BACKINTHEU--26
    I'm back in the USSR (hey!) --BACKINTHEU--35
    Back in the USSR.--BACKINTHEU--37
    I'm back in the USSR --BACKINTHEU--40
    Yeah - back in the USSR.--BACKINTHEU--42

VAIN
    If our new love was in vain.--IFIFELL--16
    If our new love was in vain.--IFIFELL--23

VALENTINE
    Will you still be sending me a valentine--
        WHENIMSIXT--3

VALERIE
    Rose and Valerie screaming from the gallery say
        he must go free --MAXWELLSIL--19

VAN
    Sitting on a cornflake, waiting for the van to come
        --IAMTHEWALR--4

VANISH
    My independence ((my independence)) seems to
        vanish in the haze--HELP--21

VELVET
    She's well acquainted with the touch of the
        velvet hand --HAPPINESSI--3

VERA
    Vera, Chuck and Dave.--WHENIMSIXT--27

VERY
    I must be sure from the very start --IFIFELL--8
    Just the sight of you makes night-time bright,
        very bright.--ITSONLYLOV--9
    Life is very short and there's no time--WECANWORKI
        --11
    Life is very short and there's no time--WECANWORKI
        --20
    Working for peanuts is all very fine --DRIVEMYCAR
        --11
    In the pouring rain - very strange.--PENNYLANE--8
    From the pouring rain - very strange.--PENNYLANE
        --27
    It's getting very near the end.--SGTPEPPREP--14
    And to see you're really only very small--
        WITHINYOUW--18
    And have you travelled very far?--BABYYOUREA--5
    Please don't you be very long --BLUEJAYWAY--6
    Please don't you be very long (don't be long) --
        BLUEJAYWAY--13
    Please don't you be very long (don't be long) --
        BLUEJAYWAY--20
    Please don't you be very long--BLUEJAYWAY--23
    Please don't you be very long --BLUEJAYWAY--26
    Please don't you be very long --BLUEJAYWAY--29

VIENNA
    Made a lightning trip to Vienna --BALLADOFJO--29

VIEW
    Doesn't have a point of view --NOWHEREMAN--4
    Doesn't have a point of view --NOWHEREMAN--16
    Stating point of view.--WHENIMSIXT--29

VOICE
    Your voice is soothing but the words aren't clear.
        --IMLOOKINGT--6

VOICES
    The man of a thousand voices talking perfectly loud
        --FOOLONTHEH--9
    With voices out of nowhere --CRYBABYCRY--30

VOID
    Lay down all thought, surrender to the void--
        TOMORROWNE--3

VONT
    Sont des mots qui vont tres bien ensemble, tres
        bien ensemble.--MICHELLE--4
    Sont des mots qui vont tres bien ensemble, tres
        bien ensemble.--MICHELLE--10
    Sont des mots qui vont tres bien ensemble, tres
        bien ensemble.--MICHELLE--21

WAH
    Wah!--IMDOWN--23
    Nah - nah - nah - nah, hey Jude (Jude, hey
        Jude, wah!).--HEYJUDE--49

WAHOO
    All together now! (wuh, yeah, wahoo!)--ALLTOGETHE
        --45

WAIT
    WAIT.--WAIT--Title
    Wait till I come back to your side --WAIT--3
    But if your heart breaks, don't wait, turn me
        away --WAIT--5
    Wait till I come back to your side --WAIT--7
    And know that you will wait for me.--WAIT--12
    Wait till I come back to your side --WAIT--15
    And know that you will wait for me.--WAIT--20
    But if your heart breaks, don't wait, turn me
        away --WAIT--21
    Wait till I come back to your side --WAIT--23
    I don't mind, I could wait forever--IWANTTOTEL--14
    I don't mind, I could wait forever--IWANTTOTEL--21
    All I can tell you is brother you have to wait.--
        REVOLUTION--19
    Will I wait a lonely lifetime?--IWILL--3
    Well all I can tell you is brother you have to
        wait.--REVOLUTONE--28

WAITED
    I wonder what went wrong I've waited far too long
        --IDONTWANTT--7
    I wonder what went wrong I've waited far too long
        --IDONTWANTT--24

WAITING
    I got a girl who's waiting home for me tonight.--
        WHENIGETHO--12
    I've been waiting here for you --WHATYOURED--9
    I've been waiting here for you --WHATYOURED--16
    I met you in the morning waiting for the tides of
        time --WHATGOESON--15
    Waiting for a sleepy feeling.--IMONLYSLEE--16
    We see the banker sitting waiting for a trim--
        PENNYLANE--25
    Waiting to take you away.--LUCYINTHES--17
    Waiting to keep the appointment she made--
        SHESLEAVIN--26
    Peace of mind is waiting there--WITHINYOUW--30
    Sitting on a cornflake, waiting for the van to come
        --IAMTHEWALR--4
    Sitting in an English garden waiting for the sun--
        IAMTHEWALR--17
    The Magical Mystery Tour is waiting to take
        you away--MAGICALMYS--9

(Waiting to take you away).--MAGICALMYS--10
You're waiting for someone to perform with.--
  HEYJUDE--21
You were only waiting for this moment to arise.--
  BLACKBIRD--4
You were only waiting for this moment to be free.
  --BLACKBIRD--8
You were only waiting for this moment to arise --
  BLACKBIRD--16
You were only waiting for this moment to arise --
  BLACKBIRD--17
You were only waiting for this moment to arise.--
  BLACKBIRD--18
Waiting for your knock, dear --DONTPASSME--6
I said that's alright I'm waiting here --DONTPASSME
  --29
Just waiting to hear from you.--DONTPASSME--30
Takes it back to Molly waiting at the door--
  OBLADIOBLA--11
One sunny day the world was waiting for the lover
  ((sexy Sadie))--SEXYSADIE--9
The world was waiting just for you?--SEXYSADIE--13
The world was waiting just for you?--SEXYSADIE--14
Your mommy's waiting for you,--GETBACK/45--32
Don't leave me waiting here, lead me to your door.
  --LONGANDWIN--11
Don't keep me waiting here (don't keep me
  waiting) lead me to your door.--LONGANDWIN--14
Don't keep me waiting here (don't keep me
  waiting) lead me to your door.--LONGANDWIN--14

WAITS
    Waits at the window--ELEANORRIG--6
    So he waits behind, writing fifty times I must
      not be so oh - oh oh.--MAXWELLSIL--11

WAKE
    When I wake up early in the morning --IMONLYSLEE
      --1
    Please don't wake me, no, don't shake me --
      IMONLYSLEE--5
    When I wake up early in the morning --IMONLYSLEE
      --21
    Please don't wake me, no, don't shake me --
      IMONLYSLEE--25
    I wake up to the sound of music --LETITBE/45--24
    I wake up to the sound of music --LETITBE/LP--24

WAKES
    She wakes up, she makes up --FORNOONE--4

WALK
    Till I walk out that door again.--WHENIGETHO--20
    I think I'll take a walk and look for her.--
      IDONTWANTT--8
    But I think I'll take a walk and look for her.--
      IDONTWANTT--25
    I saw you walk in your door--NOREPLY--13
    I saw you walk in your door--NOREPLY--26
    To walk out and make me lonely--YOULIKEMET--9
    We take a walk, the sun is shining down --
      GOODDAYSUN--7
    If you take a walk, I'll tax your feet.
      ((walk))--TAXMAN--14
    If you take a walk, I'll tax your feet.
      ((walk))--TAXMAN--14
    Then you decide to take a walk by the old school--
      GOODMORNIN--14
    Would you stand up and walk out on me?--WITHALITTL
      --2

WALKED
    'cos you walked hand in hand--NOREPLY--15
    'cos you walked hand in hand--NOREPLY--28
    The other day I saw you as I walked along the
      road --WHATGOESON--6
    So one day he walked into town --ROCKYRACCO--7

WALKING
    When I'm walking beside her--EVERYLITTL--1
    Big man (yeah?) walking in the park--HEYBULLDOG--13

WALKS
    As he walks from the grave --ELEANORRIG--25

WALL

Turn my face to the wall.--YOUVEGOTTO--2
Carve your number on my wall --IFINEEDEDS--10
Carve your number on my wall --IFINEEDEDS--20
Who hide themselves behind a wall of illusion--
  WITHINYOUW--4
Writing letters on my wall.--TWOOFUS--11

WALRUS
    I AM THE WALRUS.--IAMTHEWALR--Title
    I am the eggman (goo) they are the eggmen (goo)
      I am the walrus--IAMTHEWALR--7
    I am the eggman (goo) they are the eggmen (goo)
      I am the walrus--IAMTHEWALR--15
    I am the eggman, they are the eggmen, I am the
      walrus--IAMTHEWALR--19
    I am the eggman (goo) they are the eggmen (goo)
      I am the walrus (goo)--IAMTHEWALR--28
    I told you about the walrus and me - man--
      GLASSONION--8
    The walrus was Paul--GLASSONION--11
    He got walrus gumboot--COMETOGETH--26

WALTER
    And curse Sir Walter Raleigh --IMSOTIRED--16

WALTZ
    And of course Henry the Horse dances the waltz.--
      BEINGFORTH--14

WANDERING
    And stops my mind from wandering--FIXINGAHOL--2
    And kept my mind from wandering--FIXINGAHOL--5
    And when my mind is wandering--FIXINGAHOL--12
    Stops my mind from wandering--FIXINGAHOL--24
    Stops my mind from wandering--FIXINGAHOL--27
    All these years I've been wandering round the
      world --IVEGOTAFEE--11

WANNA
    And when I, I wanna kiss you, yeah --ALLIVEGOTT--6
    And when I, I wanna kiss you, yeah --ALLIVEGOTT--17
    I WANNA BE YOUR MAN.--IWANNABEYO--Title
    I wanna be your lover baby --IWANNABEYO--1
    I wanna be your man.--IWANNABEYO--2
    I wanna be your lover baby --IWANNABEYO--3
    I wanna be your man.--IWANNABEYO--4
    I wanna be your man--IWANNABEYO--9
    I wanna be your man--IWANNABEYO--10
    I wanna be your man--IWANNABEYO--11
    I wanna be your man.--IWANNABEYO--12
    I wanna be your man--IWANNABEYO--16
    I wanna be your lover baby --IWANNABEYO--17
    I wanna be your man.--IWANNABEYO--18
    I wanna be your lover baby --IWANNABEYO--19
    I wanna be your man--IWANNABEYO--20
    I wanna be your man--IWANNABEYO--21
    I wanna be your man--IWANNABEYO--22
    I wanna be your man.--IWANNABEYO--23
    I wanna be your man.--IWANNABEYO--24
    I wanna be your lover baby --IWANNABEYO--30
    I wanna be your man.--IWANNABEYO--31
    I wanna be your lover baby --IWANNABEYO--32
    I wanna be your man.--IWANNABEYO--33
    I wanna be your man--IWANNABEYO--38
    I wanna be your man--IWANNABEYO--39
    I wanna be your man--IWANNABEYO--40
    I wanna be your man.--IWANNABEYO--41
    I wanna be your man (oh)--IWANNABEYO--43
    I wanna be your man (come on!)--IWANNABEYO--44
    I wanna be your man (wuh - wuh)--IWANNABEYO--45
    I wanna be your man.--IWANNABEYO--46
    I wanna hold your hand--IWANTTOHOL--4
    I wanna hold your hand--IWANTTOHOL--5
    I wanna hold your hand.--IWANTTOHOL--6
    I wanna hold your hand.--IWANTTOHOL--12
    I wanna hold your hand--IWANTTOHOL--23
    I wanna hold your hand--IWANTTOHOL--24
    I wanna hold your hand.--IWANTTOHOL--25
    I wanna hold your hand--IWANTTOHOL--36
    I wanna hold your hand--IWANTTOHOL--37
    I wanna hold your hand--IWANTTOHOL--38
    I wanna hold your hand--IWANTTOHOL--39
    If you wanna stay mine--YOUCANTDOT--24
    If you wanna stay mine--YOUCANTDOT--43
    I don't wanna kiss or hold your hand --IMHAPPYJUS
      --4
    I just wanna dance with you all night --IMHAPPYJUS
      --9
    I wanna go--ILLBEBACK--22

I don't wanna spoil the party so I'll go --
    IDONTWANTT--1
I don't wanna spoil the party so I'll go --
    IDONTWANTT--13
I don't wanna say that I've been unhappy with you
    --ANOTHERGIR--12
I don't wanna say that I've been unhappy with you
    --ANOTHERGIR--18
When I think of things we did it makes me wanna
    cry.--NIGHTBEFOR--10
When I think of things we did it makes me wanna
    cry.--NIGHTBEFOR--18
I wanna be famous, a star of the screen --
    DRIVEMYCAR--3
You say you wanna revolution --REVOLUTION--2
We all wanna change the world.--REVOLUTION--4
We all wanna change the world.--REVOLUTONE--7
Yes I'm lonely - wanna die --YERBLUES--2
Yes I'm lonely - wanna die --YERBLUES--3
In the morning - wanna die --YERBLUES--6
In the evening - wanna die --YERBLUES--7
I'm lonely - wanna die --YERBLUES--14
Lonely - wanna die --YERBLUES--21
Wanna die, yeah wanna die --YERBLUES--28
Wanna die, yeah wanna die --YERBLUES--28
Yes I'm lonely - wanna die --YERBLUES--31
Yes I'm lonely - wanna die --YERBLUES--32
... Wanna die --YERBLUES--34
I wanna tell her that I love her a lot--HERMAJESTY
    --5

WANT

You know I want you to --PSILOVEYOU--17
'cos you tell me things I want to know --ASKMEWHY
    --2
'cos you tell me things I want to know --ASKMEWHY
    --17
I don't want to start complaining --PLEASEPLEA--13
DO YOU WANT TO KNOW A SECRET?--DOYOUWANTT--Title
Listen, do you want to know a secret?--DOYOUWANTT
    --3
Listen (dodahdo) do you want to know a secret?
    (dodahdo)--DOYOUWANTT--9
Listen (dodahdo) do you want to know a secret?
    (dodahdo)--DOYOUWANTT--17
If there's anything that you want--FROMMETOYO--3
I got everything that you want--FROMMETOYO--7
If there's anything that you want--FROMMETOYO--15
If there's anything that you want--FROMMETOYO--26
Whenever I want you around, yeah --ALLIVEGOTT--1
Whenever you want me at all --ALLIVEGOTT--12
Whenever you want me at all --ALLIVEGOTT--23
I want no one to talk to me--DONTBOTHER--2
If you want someone to make you feel so fine--
    LITTLECHIL--9
I WANT TO HOLD YOUR HAND.--IWANTTOHOL--Title
Though he may want you too--THISBOY--5
Tell me that you want the kind of things --
    CANTBUYMEL--19
Tell me that you want the kind of things --
    CANTBUYMEL--29
Don't want to cry when there's people there --
    ILLCRYINST--11
Don't want to cry when there's people there --
    ILLCRYINST--20
That you would want me too--ILLBEBACK--15
I DON'T WANT TO SPOIL THE PARTY.--IDONTWANTT--Title
I ain't no fool and I don't take what I don't
    want --ANOTHERGIR--4
I ain't no fool and I don't take what I don't
    want --ANOTHERGIR--14
I ain't no fool and I don't take what I don't
    want --ANOTHERGIR--20
You don't want my loving any more--INEEDYOU--12
You don't want my loving any more--INEEDYOU--22
And I want all the world to see we've met --
    IVEJUSTSEE--5
And I want all the world to see we've met --
    IVEJUSTSEE--28
She's the kind of girl you want so much it makes
    you sorry --GIRL--3
That's all I want to say--MICHELLE--6
I want you, I want you, I want you--MICHELLE--16
I want you, I want you, I want you--MICHELLE--16
I want you, I want you, I want you--MICHELLE--16
Do what you want to do --THINKFORYO--6
Do what you want to do --THINKFORYO--15
Do what you want to do --THINKFORYO--24
Do what you want to do --THINKFORYO--28
I don't know why you should want to hide --
    YOUWONTSEE--7
I won't want to stay, I don't have much to say --
    YOUWONTSEE--9

So I want to be a paperback writer --PAPERBACKW--6
And I want to be a paperback writer --PAPERBACKW
    --19
And I want to be a paperback writer --PAPERBACKW
    --25
You tell me that you've got everything you want --
    ANDYOURBIR--1
You want her, you need her --FORNOONE--10
Ooo and I want you to hear me--GOTTOGETYO--13
When I'm with you I want to stay there--GOTTOGETYO
    --17
I want her everywhere--HERETHEREA--8
I want her everywhere--HERETHEREA--14
I WANT TO TELL YOU.--IWANTTOTEL--Title
I want to tell you--IWANTTOTEL--1
I want to tell you--IWANTTOTEL--12
I want to tell you--IWANTTOTEL--19
If you want me to.--LOVEYOUTWO--17
Don't ask me what I want it for (ha ha Mr.
    Wilson)--TAXMAN--18
If you don't want to pay some more (ha ha Mr.
    Heath)--TAXMAN--19
Go in to work don't want to go feeling low down--
    GOODMORNIN--7
I don't really want to stop the show--SGTPEPPERS
    --19
I want somebody to love.--WITHALITTL--18
I want somebody to love.--WITHALITTL--29
What do you want to be?--BABYYOUREA--4
We all want to change the world.--REVOLUTION--7
But if you want money for people with minds that
    hate --REVOLUTION--18
We all want to change your head.--REVOLUTION--24
A - do you, don't you want me to love you?--
    HELTERSKEL--4
A - will you, won't you want me to make you?--
    HELTERSKEL--11
Well, do you, don't you want me to make you?--
    HELTERSKEL--21
If you want me to, I will.--IWILL--4
How I want you.--LONGLONGLO--11
But if you want some fun (ha ha ha) --OBLADIOBLA
    --40
You say you want a revolution --REVOLUTONE--5
We all want to change the world.--REVOLUTONE--10
But if you want money for people with minds that
    hate --REVOLUTONE--27
I want a love that's right --OLDBROWNSH--1
I want a short-haired girl --OLDBROWNSH--3
I want that love of yours --OLDBROWNSH--27
I WANT YOU (SHE'S SO HEAVY).--IWANTYOUSH--Title
I want you--IWANTYOUSH--1
I want you so bad--IWANTYOUSH--2
I want you--IWANTYOUSH--3
I want you so bad--IWANTYOUSH--4
I want you--IWANTYOUSH--7
I want you so bad, babe--IWANTYOUSH--8
I want you--IWANTYOUSH--9
I want you so bad--IWANTYOUSH--10
I want you--IWANTYOUSH--13
I want you so bad, babe--IWANTYOUSH--14
I want you--IWANTYOUSH--15
I want you so bad--IWANTYOUSH--16
I want you--IWANTYOUSH--19
I want you so bad--IWANTYOUSH--20
I want you--IWANTYOUSH--21
I want you so bad--IWANTYOUSH--22
I want you--IWANTYOUSH--28
I want you so bad--IWANTYOUSH--29
I want you so bad--IWANTYOUSH--30
I want you so bad--IWANTYOUSH--31
I want you--IWANTYOUSH--34
You know I want you so bad, babe--IWANTYOUSH--35
I want you--IWANTYOUSH--36
You know I want you so bad--IWANTYOUSH--37
I don't want to leave her now --SOMETHING--4
I don't want to leave her now --SOMETHING--9
I don't want to leave her now --SOMETHING--18
I want you in the morning girl, I love you --
    FORYOUBLUE--5
I want you at the moment I feel blue --FORYOUBLUE
    --6
Well you can celebrate anything you want--IDIGAPONY
    --7
Yes you can celebrate anything you want.--IDIGAPONY
    --8
All I want is you--IDIGAPONY--13
Everything has got to be just like you want it to
    --IDIGAPONY--14
All I want is you--IDIGAPONY--23
Everything has got to be just like you want it to
    --IDIGAPONY--24
I want is you--IDIGAPONY--33
Everything has got to be just like you want it to

--IDIGAPONY--34

WANTED
    Asked a girl what she wanted to be --DRIVEMYCAR--1
    You knew I wanted just to hold you--GOTTOGETYO--9

WANTS
    But this boy wants you back again.--THISBOY--3
    This boy wants you back again.--THISBOY--6
    I'm the one who wants you--ILLBEBACK
        --5
    Yes I'm the one who wants you--ILLBEBACK--7
    Just sees what he wants to see --NOWHEREMAN--11
    But he wants to be a paperback writer--PAPERBACKW
        --12
    And he wants you all to sing along.--SGTPEPPERS--22
    But nobody wants to know him--FOOLONTHEH--3
    They can tell what he wants to do--FOOLONTHEH--16

WAR
    The English Army had just won the war--DAYINTHELI
        --12

WARM
    Come and keep your comrade warm.--BACKINTHEU--34
    HAPPINESS IS A WARM GUN.--HAPPINESSI--Title
    Happiness ((happiness)) is a warm gun--HAPPINESSI
        --18
    Happiness ((happiness)) is a warm gun, momma--
        HAPPINESSI--20
    Because - (happiness) is a warm gun, momma--
        HAPPINESSI--25
    Happiness ((happiness)) is a warm gun, yes it is--
        HAPPINESSI--27
    Happiness is a warm, yes it is - gun--HAPPINESSI
        --29
    Is a warm gun, momma ((is a warm gun, yeah)).--
        HAPPINESSI--32
    Is a warm gun, momma ((is a warm gun, yeah)).--
        HAPPINESSI--32
    We would be warm below the storm--OCTOPUSSGA--9

WARNING
    He got early warning--COMETOGETH--37

WAS
    Well, she was just seventeen --ISAWHERSTA--2
    And the way she looked was way beyond compare.--
        ISAWHERSTA--4
    You made me glad when I was blue--THANKYOUGI--2
    You made me glad when I was blue--THANKYOUGI--12
    Was I to blame for being unfair?--ICALLYOURN--2
    And I found that love was more --IFIFELL--5
    If our new love was in vain.--IFIFELL--16
    If our new love was in vain.--IFIFELL--23
    I was lonely without her--EVERYLITTL--5
    Some day you'll know I was the one --ILLFOLLOWT--3
    She was a girl in a million, my friend --IMALOSER
        --5
    Was bringing her down, yeah--TICKETTORI--10
    When I was around.--TICKETTORI--12
    Was bringing her down, yeah--TICKETTORI--37
    When I was around.--TICKETTORI--39
    I'd admit that I was wrong--YOULIKEMET--18
    I'd admit that I was wrong--YOULIKEMET--27
    When ((when)) I was younger ((when I was
        young))--HELP--8
    When ((when)) I was younger ((when I was
        young))--HELP--8
    When I was younger, so much younger than today--
        HELP--29
    How was I to know you would upset me?--INEEDYOU--7
    Love was in your eyes (aah the night before)--
        NIGHTBEFOR--2
    Was I so unwise? (aah the night before)--NIGHTBEFOR
        --6
    Love was in your eyes (aah the night before)--
        NIGHTBEFOR--12
    Was I so unwise? (aah the night before)--NIGHTBEFOR
        --20
    Love was such an easy game to play--YESTERDAY--14
    Love was such an easy game to play--YESTERDAY--22
    She was a day tripper --DAYTRIPPER--5
    She was a day tripper --DAYTRIPPER--13
    She was a day tripper --DAYTRIPPER--22
    Was she told when she was young that pain would
        lead to pleasure?--GIRL--22
    Was she told when she was young that pain would

lead to pleasure?--GIRL--22
I was alone--NORWEGIANW--22
And I was born with a jealous mind --RUNFORYOUR--10
But now the tide is turning I can see that I
    was blind.--WHATGOESON--16
We have lost the time that was so hard to find--
    YOUWONTSEE--3
I wouldn't mind if I knew what I was missing.--
    YOUWONTSEE--14
I wouldn't mind if I knew what I was missing.--
    YOUWONTSEE--23
And was buried along with her name--ELEANORRIG--22
No-one was saved.--ELEANORRIG--26
I was alone, I took a ride--GOTTOGETYO--1
I was alone, I took a ride--GOTTOGETYO--25
When I was a boy everything was right,
    everything was right.--SHESAIDSHE--9
When I was a boy everything was right,
    everything was right.--SHESAIDSHE--9
When I was a boy everything was right,
    everything was right.--SHESAIDSHE--9
When I was a boy everything was right,
    everything was right.--SHESAIDSHE--15
When I was a boy everything was right,
    everything was right.--SHESAIDSHE--15
When I was a boy everything was right,
    everything was right.--SHESAIDSHE--15
In the town where I was born--YELLOWSUBM--1
And though the news was rather sad--DAYINTHELI--3
Nobody was really sure if he was from the House
    of Lords--DAYINTHELI--10
Nobody was really sure if he was from the House
    of Lords--DAYINTHELI--10
And looking up I noticed I was late--DAYINTHELI--21
Man I was mean but I'm changing my scene--
    GETTINGBET--27
It was twenty years ago today--SGTPEPPERS--1
She (what did we do that was wrong?)--SHESLEAVIN
    --28
Is having (we didn't know it was wrong)--SHESLEAVIN
    --29
Something inside that was always denied--SHESLEAVIN
    --31
That was a hit before your mother was born --
    YOURMOTHER--3
That was a hit before your mother was born --
    YOURMOTHER--3
Though she was born a long, long time ago --
    YOURMOTHER--4
That was a hit before your mother was born --
    YOURMOTHER--9
That was a hit before your mother was born --
    YOURMOTHER--9
Though she was born a long, long time ago --
    YOURMOTHER--10
That was a hit before your mother was born --
    YOURMOTHER--14
That was a hit before your mother was born --
    YOURMOTHER--14
Though she was born a long, long time ago --
    YOURMOTHER--15
Though she was born a long, long time ago --
    YOURMOTHER--23
Did you think that money was heaven sent?--
    LADYMADONN--4
On the way the paper bag was on my knee --
    BACKINTHEU--3
The children asked him if to kill was not a sin --
    CONTINUING--27
The King of Marigold was in the kitchen --
    CRYBABYCRY--4
The Queen was in the parlour --CRYBABYCRY--6
The King was in the garden --CRYBABYCRY--12
The Queen was in the playroom --CRYBABYCRY--14
The Duke was having problems --CRYBABYCRY--22
I was so unfair --DONTPASSME--24
The walrus was Paul--GLASSONION--11
... Ah (how was that?)--HELTERSKEL--31
She was a working girl--HONEYPIE--1
He was such a stupid get.--IMSOTIRED--17
So many tears I was searching --LONGLONGLO--7
So many tears I was wasting - oh, oh!--LONGLONGLO
    --8
Her name was Magill and she called herself Lil --
    ROCKYRACCO--15
But Daniel was hot, he drew first and shot--
    ROCKYRACCO--21
One sunny day the world was waiting for the lover
    ((sexy Sadie))--SEXYSADIE--9
The world was waiting just for you?--SEXYSADIE--13
The world was waiting just for you?--SEXYSADIE--14
My mother was of the sky --YERBLUES--10
My father was of the earth --YERBLUES--11
Jojo was a man who thought he was a loner --

GETBACK/45--1
Jojo was a man who thought he was a loner --
  GETBACK/45--1
Sweet Loretta Martin thought she was a woman --
  GETBACK/45--16
But she was another man.--GETBACK/45--17
Once there was a way--GOLDENSLUM--1
Once there was a way--GOLDENSLUM--3
Once there was a way--GOLDENSLUM--11
Once there was a way--GOLDENSLUM--13
Joan was quizzical, studied pataphysical science
  in the home --MAXWELLSIL--1
Bang, bang Maxwell's silver hammer made sure
  that she was dead.--MAXWELLSIL--7
Bang, bang Maxwell's silver hammer made sure
  that she was dead.--MAXWELLSIL--15
Bang, bang Maxwell's silver hammer made sure
  that he was dead.--MAXWELLSIL--25
Yes, you could say she was attractively built -
  yeah, yeah, yeah.--POLYTHENEP--9
((That was Can You Dig It? by Georgie
  Wood))--DIGIT--11
Sweet Moretta Fart she thought she was a cleaner--
  GETBACK/LP--2
But she was a frying pan ((sweet Loretta
  Martin)).--GETBACK/LP--3
Jojo was a man who thought he was a loner--
  GETBACK/LP--7
Jojo was a man who thought he was a loner--
  GETBACK/LP--7
Sweet Loretta Martin thought she was a woman--
  GETBACK/LP--22
But she was another man--GETBACK/LP--23
All that I was looking for was somebody who
  looked like you.--IVEGOTAFEE--13
All that I was looking for was somebody who
  looked like you.--IVEGOTAFEE--13

WASHED
The wild and windy night that the rain washed away
  --LONGANDWIN--4

WASN'T
They said it wasn't you--NOREPLY--4
And I noticed there wasn't a chair.--NORWEGIANW--10

WASTING
Yours sincerely, wasting away.--WHENIMSIXT--31
So many tears I was wasting - oh, oh!--LONGLONGLO
  --8

WATCH
I'll make a point of taking her away from you
  (watch what you do), yeah--YOUREGONNA--16
I'll make a point of taking her away from you
  (watch what you do), yeah--YOUREGONNA--23
Did you mean to break my heart and watch me die?--
  WHATGOESON--24

WATCHING
Watching her eyes and hoping I'm always there.--
  HERETHEREA--13
Watching her eyes and hoping I'm always there.--
  HERETHEREA--19
Watching the skirts you start to flirt now you're
  in gear--GOODMORNIN--23
No-one will be watching us --WHYDONTWED--5
No-one will be watching us --WHYDONTWED--11
No-one will be watching us --WHYDONTWED--17

WATER
He got Muddy Water--COMETOGETH--38

WATERS
Sit beside a mountain stream - see her waters rise
  --MOTHERNATU--3

WAVE
Changing my life with a wave of her hand--
  HERETHEREA--3

WAVES
And we lived beneath the waves--YELLOWSUBM--7
In our little hideaway beneath the waves.--
  OCTOPUSSGA--10

The coral that lies beneath the waves (lies
  beneath the ocean waves).--OCTOPUSSGA--18
The coral that lies beneath the waves (lies
  beneath the ocean waves).--OCTOPUSSGA--18
Pools of sorrow, waves of joy--ACROSSTHEU
  --3

WAY
You don't need me to show the way love --PLEASEPLEA
  --7
And the way she looked was way beyond compare.--
  ISAWHERSTA--4
And the way she looked was way beyond compare.--
  ISAWHERSTA--4
Thank you girl, for loving me the way that you
  do (way that you do).--THANKYOUGI--8
Thank you girl, for loving me the way that you
  do (way that you do).--THANKYOUGI--8
You talking that way--YOUCANTDOT--21
You talking that way--YOUCANTDOT--40
If I could get my way --ILLCRYINST--3
Come on, out my way --WHENIGETHO--4
I got no business being here with you this way.--
  WHENIGETHO--23
I never needed ((never needed)) anybody's help
  in any way--HELP--10
I never needed anybody's help in any way--HELP--30
Why should I feel the way I do?--ITSONLYLOV--5
Why should I feel the way I do?--ITSONLYLOV--12
I might have looked the other way--IVEJUSTSEE--8
The way you treat her what else can I do?--
  YOUREGONNA--17
The way you treat her what else can I do?--
  YOUREGONNA--24
Love will find a way?--YOUVEGOTTO--16
For taking the easy way out --DAYTRIPPER--2
For taking the easy way out, now.--DAYTRIPPER--4
One way ticket, yeah --DAYTRIPPER--6
She took me half the way there --DAYTRIPPER--10
She took me half the way there, now.--DAYTRIPPER
  --12
One way ticket, yeah --DAYTRIPPER--14
Try to see it my way --WECANWORKI--1
While you see it your way--WECANWORKI--3
Try to see it my way --WECANWORKI--15
While you see it your way --WECANWORKI--17
Try to see it my way --WECANWORKI--24
While you see it your way --WECANWORKI--26
You're thinking of me the same old way --IMLOOKINGT
  --11
Until I find a way--MICHELLE--7
That the word is just the way --THEWORD--26
I feel good in a special way --GOODDAYSUN--4
And if I do I know the way there.--GOTTOGETYO--19
In this way Mr. K. will challenge the world.--
  BEINGFORTH--7
Found my way downstairs and drank a cup--DAYINTHELI
  --20
Found my way upstairs and had a smoke--DAYINTHELI
  --25
I'm painting a room in a colourful way--FIXINGAHOL
  --11
Happy to be that way.--BABYYOUREA--25
BLUE JAY WAY.--BLUEJAYWAY--Title
And my friends have lost their way.--BLUEJAYWAY--2
Sitting here in Blue Jay Way (way).--BLUEJAYWAY--18
Sitting here in Blue Jay Way (way).--BLUEJAYWAY--18
Well on the way, head in a cloud--FOOLONTHEH--8
Step right this way.--MAGICALMYS--
On the way the paper bag was on my knee --
  BACKINTHEU--3
Oh - show me round the snow-peaked mountains way
  down south --BACKINTHEU--31
North of England way--HONEYPIE--2
The way things are going --BALLADOFJO--7
The way things are going --BALLADOFJO--15
The way things are going --BALLADOFJO--23
The way things are going --BALLADOFJO--35
The way things are going --BALLADOFJO--43
The way things are going --BALLADOFJO--45
Once there was a way--GOLDENSLUM--1
Once there was a way--GOLDENSLUM--3
Once there was a way--GOLDENSLUM--11
Once there was a way--GOLDENSLUM--13
Something in the way she moves--SOMETHING--1
Something in the way she woos me --SOMETHING--3
Something in the way she knows--SOMETHING--15
They tumble blindly as they make their way across
  the universe.--ACROSSTHEU--14
Why leave me standing here, let me know the way.--
  LONGANDWIN--6
Not arriving on our way back home.--TWOOFUS--6
We're on our way home --TWOOFUS--7

We're on our way home --TWOOFUS--8
Lifting latches on our way back home.--TWOOFUS--13
We're on our way home --TWOOFUS--14
We're on our way home --TWOOFUS--15
Getting nowhere on our way back home.--TWOOFUS--22
We're on our way home --TWOOFUS--23
We're on our way home --TWOOFUS--24
Getting nowhere on our way back home.--TWOOFUS--31
We're on our way home --TWOOFUS--32
We're on our way home --TWOOFUS--33

WAYS

In oh so many ways--HELP--20
I could know the ways of heaven.--INNERLIGHT--4
You can know the ways of heaven.--INNERLIGHT--11
Anyway you'll never know the many ways I've tried
    --LONGANDWIN--8

WE

Nobody knows just we two.--DOYOUWANTT--16
Well we danced through the night --ISAWHERSTA--13
And we held each other tight --ISAWHERSTA--14
Oh (wuh!) we danced through the night --ISAWHERSTA
    --20
And we held each other tight--ISAWHERSTA--21
When she learns we are two.--IFIFELL--20
When she learns we are two.--IFIFELL--27
Let's pretend we just can't see his face.--
    IMHAPPYJUS--17
Let's pretend we just can't see his face.--
    IMHAPPYJUS--25
THINGS WE SAID TODAY.--THINGSWESA--Title
Then I will remember things we said today.--
    THINGSWESA--5
Then we will remember things we said today.--
    THINGSWESA--10
Then we will remember things we said today.--
    THINGSWESA--10
And though we may be blind --THINGSWESA--13
Then we will remember things we said today.--
    THINGSWESA--21
Then we will remember things we said today.--
    THINGSWESA--21
And though we may be blind --THINGSWESA--24
Then we will remember things we said today.--
    THINGSWESA--32
Then we will remember things we said today.--
    THINGSWESA--32
I would remember all the things we planned--YESITIS
    --7
We will never be apart--TELLMEWHAT--3
Where we just met--IVEJUSTSEE--3
Where we just met--IVEJUSTSEE--26
We said our goodbyes (aah the night before)--
    NIGHTBEFOR--1
When I think of things we did it makes me wanna
    cry.--NIGHTBEFOR--10
We said our goodbyes (aah the night before)--
    NIGHTBEFOR--11
When I think of things we did it makes me wanna
    cry.--NIGHTBEFOR--18
WE CAN WORK IT OUT.--WECANWORKI--Title
We can work it out, we can work it out.--WECANWORKI
    --5
We can work it out, we can work it out.--WECANWORKI
    --5
We can work it out and get it straight or say
    good night.--WECANWORKI--9
We can work it out, we can work it out.--WECANWORKI
    --10
We can work it out, we can work it out.--WECANWORKI
    --10
There's a chance that we might fall apart before
    too long.--WECANWORKI--18
We can work it out, we can work it out.--WECANWORKI
    --19
We can work it out, we can work it out.--WECANWORKI
    --19
There's a chance that we might fall apart before
    too long.--WECANWORKI--27
We can work it out, we can work it out.--WECANWORKI
    --28
We can work it out, we can work it out.--WECANWORKI
    --28
We talked until two--NORWEGIANW--14
That we can have if we close our eyes.--THINKFORYO
    --5
That we can have if we close our eyes.--THINKFORYO
    --5
We'll forget the tears we cried.--WAIT--8
We have lost the time that was so hard to find--

YOUWONTSEE--3
We take a walk, the sun is shining down --
    GOODDAYSUN--7
Then we lie beneath a shady tree --GOODDAYSUN--10
So we sailed on to the sun--YELLOWSUBM--5
Till we found a sea of green--YELLOWSUBM--6
And we lived beneath the waves--YELLOWSUBM--7
We all live in a yellow submarine --YELLOWSUBM--9
We all live in a yellow submarine --YELLOWSUBM--11
We all live in a yellow submarine --YELLOWSUBM--16
We all live in a yellow submarine --YELLOWSUBM--18
As we live a life of ease--YELLOWSUBM--25
Everyone of us (everyone of us) has all we need
    (has all we need) --YELLOWSUBM--26
Everyone of us (everyone of us) has all we need
    (has all we need) --YELLOWSUBM--26
We all live in a yellow submarine --YELLOWSUBM--29
We all live in a yellow submarine --YELLOWSUBM--31
We all live in a yellow submarine --YELLOWSUBM--33
We all live in a yellow submarine --YELLOWSUBM--35
We see the banker sitting waiting for a trim--
    PENNYLANE--25
We hope you will enjoy the show--SGTPEPPERS--9
We hope you have enjoyed the show.--SGTPEPPREP--4
She (we gave her most of our lives)--SHESLEAVIN--8
Home. (we gave her everything money could buy)--
    SHESLEAVIN--10
She (we never thought of ourselves)--SHESLEAVIN--20
Home. (we struggled hard all our lives to get by)
    --SHESLEAVIN--22
She (what did we do that was wrong?)--SHESLEAVIN
    --28
Is having (we didn't know it was wrong)--SHESLEAVIN
    --29
Every summer we can rent a cottage--WHENIMSIXT--22
We shall scrimp and save ((we shall scrimp and
    save)) --WHENIMSIXT--25
We shall scrimp and save ((we shall scrimp and
    save)) --WHENIMSIXT--25
We were talking--WITHINYOUW--1
We were talking--WITHINYOUW--8
About the love we all could share--WITHINYOUW--9
When we find it--WITHINYOUW--10
We could save the world--WITHINYOUW--14
We were talking--WITHINYOUW--21
I am he as you are he as you are me and we are
    all together--IAMTHEWALR--1
We all wanna change the world.--REVOLUTION--4
We all want to change the world.--REVOLUTION--7
We're all doing what we can.--REVOLUTION--17
We all want to change your head.--REVOLUTION--24
We all wanna change the world.--REVOLUTONE--7
We all want to change the world.--REVOLUTONE--10
We're all doing what we can.--REVOLUTONE--25
We all know ob-la-di 'b-la-da --SAVOYTRUFF--21
We gave her everything we owned just to sit at
    her table ((sexy Sadie))--SEXYSADIE--20
We gave her everything we owned just to sit at
    her table ((sexy Sadie))--SEXYSADIE--20
With every mistake we must surely be learning --
    WHILEMYGUI--11
WHY DON'T WE DO IT IN THE ROAD?--WHYDONTWED--Title
Why don't we do - do it in the road?--WHYDONTWED
    --1
Why don't we do it in the road? (ah-ha)--WHYDONTWED
    --2
Why don't we do it in the road? - mmm--WHYDONTWED
    --3
Why don't we do it in the road?--WHYDONTWED--4
Why don't we do it in the road?--WHYDONTWED--6
Why don't we do it in the road?--WHYDONTWED--7
Why don't we do it in the road?--WHYDONTWED--8
Why don't we do it in the road?--WHYDONTWED--9
Why don't we do it in the road?--WHYDONTWED--10
Why don't we do it in the road?--WHYDONTWED--12
Well, why don't we do it in the road?--WHYDONTWED
    --13
Why don't we do it in the road?--WHYDONTWED--14
Why don't we do - do it, do it in the road?--
    WHYDONTWED--15
Why don't we do it, yeah, in the road?--WHYDONTWED
    --16
We are dead.--ITSALLTOOM--38
But they're not, we just wrote it like that.--
    ONLYANORTH--3
The men from the press said, we wish you success
    --BALLADOFJO--39
PC Thirty-One said, we caught a dirty one,
    Maxwell stands alone --MAXWELLSIL--17
We would be warm below the storm--OCTOPUSSGA--9
We would sing and dance around--OCTOPUSSGA--13
Because we know we can't be found.--OCTOPUSSGA--14
Because we know we can't be found.--OCTOPUSSGA--14
We would shout and swim about--OCTOPUSSGA--17

We would be so happy you and me--OCTOPUSSGA--21
And I hope we passed the audition.--GETBACK/LP--39

WE'D
We'd meet again for I had told you.--GOTTOGETYO--11
We'd like to take you home with us--SGTPEPPERS--17
We'd love to take you home.--SGTPEPPERS--18
We'd like to thank you once again.--SGTPEPPREP--12
We'd all love to see the plan.--REVOLUTION--14
We'd all love to see the plan.--REVOLUTONE--21
We'd all love to change our head.--REVOLUTONE--37
((And now we'd like to do)) Hark the Angels
   Come...--DIGIT--13

WE'LL
So every day we'll be happy, I know--ITWONTBELO--25
Then we'll have some fun when you're mine, all
   mine --LITTLECHIL--10
We'll go on and on.--THINGSWESA--18
We'll go on and on.--THINGSWESA--29
We'll forget the tears we've cried.--WAIT--4
We'll forget the tears we cried.--WAIT--8
We'll forget the tears we've cried.--WAIT--16
We'll forget the tears we've cried.--WAIT--24
Say we'll be together every day.--GOTTOGETYO--14
We'll be over soon they said --BLUEJAYWAY--3
Soon we'll be away from here --YOUNEVERGI--19

WE'RE
Till we're together ((together)) --PSILOVEYOU--4
Till we're together ((together)) --PSILOVEYOU--13
Someday when we're dreaming --TH1NGSWESA--8
Someday when we're dreaming --THINGSWESA--19
Someday when we're dreaming --THINGSWESA--30
We're all alone and there's nobody else--IMDOWN--16
We're Sgt. Pepper's Lonely Hearts Club Band--
   SGTPEPPERS--8
We're Sgt. Pepper's Lonely Hearts Club Band --
   SGTPEPPREP--3
We're sorry but it's time to go.--SGTPEPPREP--6
When you see we're all one--WITHINYOUW--32
We're all doing what we can.--REVOLUTION--17
We're gonna have a good time.--BIRTHDAY--4
Yes, we're going to a party, party --BIRTHDAY--8
Yes, we're going to a party, party --BIRTHDAY--9
Yes, we're going to a party, party --BIRTHDAY--10
We're gonna have a good time.--BIRTHDAY--23
You know that we're as close as can be - man--
   GLASSONION--9
Love you whenever we're together --IWILL--11
Love you when we're apart.--IWILL--12
We're all doing what we can.--REVOLUTONE--25
I feel your taste all the time we're apart --
   SAVOYTRUFF--7
I said we're only trying to get us some peace.--
   BALLADOFJO--20
We're so glad you came here --OLDBROWNSH--7
Said we're travelling on the one after nine-0 --
   ONEAFTERNI--29
She said we're travelling on the one after nine-0
   --ONEAFTERNI--30
Said we're travelling on the one after nine-0-nine
   --ONEAFTERNI--31
We're on our way home --TWOOFUS--7
We're on our way home --TWOOFUS--8
We're going home.--TWOOFUS--9
We're on our way home --TWOOFUS--14
We're on our way home --TWOOFUS--15
We're going home.--TWOOFUS--16
We're on our way home --TWOOFUS--23
We're on our way home --TWOOFUS--24
We're going home.--TWOOFUS--25
We're on our way home --TWOOFUS--32
We're on our way home --TWOOFUS--33
We're going home.--TWOOFUS--34
We're going home.--TWOOFUS--35

WE'VE
I'll remember all the little things we've done --
   MISERY--6
I'll remember all the little things we've done --
   MISERY--10
And I want all the world to see we've met --
   IVEJUSTSEE--5
And I want all the world to see we've met --
   IVEJUSTSEE--28
We'll forget the tears we've cried.--WAIT--4
We'll forget the tears we've cried.--WAIT--16
We'll forget the tears we've cried.--WAIT--24
Roll up (we've got everything you need)--MAGICALMYS

--13
He'd let us in, knows where we've been--OCTOPUSSGA
   --3

WEAK
Makes me weak in the knee.--HONEYPIE--15

WEAR
If you wear red tonight--YESITIS--1
Please don't wear red tonight--YESITIS--14
Please don't wear red tonight--YESITIS--23
It doesn't really matter what clothes I wear --
   ONLYANORTH--10
He wear no shoe-shine--COMETOGETH--15

WEARING
Beneath this mask I am wearing a frown.--IMALOSER
   --10
Wearing the face that she keeps in a jar by the door
   --ELEANORRIG--7
Wearing her high-heel shoes --GETBACK/45--33
Wearing rings on every finger --OLDBROWNSH--18
Two of us wearing raincoats --TWOOFUS--19
Two of us wearing raincoats --TWOOFUS--28

WEARS
And the banker never wears a mack--PENNYLANE--7
Who sometimes wears it twice as long.--OLDBROWNSH
   --4

WEATHER
Changing faster than the weather --OLDBROWNSH--24

WEATHER'S
Shine the weather's fine.--RAIN--8
Shine the weather's fine.--RAIN--13

WEAVING
Everyone's weaving it --IMEMINE--6

WEDDING
Where a wedding has been--ELEANORRIG--4

WEDNESDAY
Wednesday morning at five o'clock as the day begins
   --SHESLEAVIN--1
Wednesday morning papers didn't come --LADYMADONN
   --15

WEEDS
Doing the garden, digging the weeds--WHENIMSIXT--17

WEEK
I've known a secret for the week or two --
   DOYOUWANTT--15
EIGHT DAYS A WEEK.--EIGHTDAYSA--Title
Eight days a week.--EIGHTDAYSA--8
Eight days a week.--EIGHTDAYSA--16
Eight days a week I love you --EIGHTDAYSA--17
Eight days a week is not enough to show I care.--
   EIGHTDAYSA--18
Eight days a week.--EIGHTDAYSA--26
Eight days a week I love you --EIGHTDAYSA--27
Eight days a week is not enough to show I care.--
   EIGHTDAYSA--28
Eight days a week --EIGHTDAYSA--36
Eight days a week --EIGHTDAYSA--37
Eight days a week.--EIGHTDAYSA--38
I'll be writing more in a week or two. ((writer))
   --PAPERBACKW--6
Talking in our beds for a week.--BALLADOFJO--18

WEEKS
You know it's three weeks, I'm going insane --
   IMSOTIRED--12
You know it's three weeks, I'm going insane --
   IMSOTIRED--21

WEEP
I never weep at night, I can't go on.--ICALLYOURN
   --4

I never weep at night, I call your name.--
    ICALLYOURN--10
I never weep at night, I call your name --
    ICALLYOURN--17

WEEPS

WHILE MY GUITAR GENTLY WEEPS.--WHILEMYGUI--Title
While my guitar gently weeps.--WHILEMYGUI--3
Still my guitar gently weeps.--WHILEMYGUI--5
While my guitar gently weeps.--WHILEMYGUI--10
Still my guitar gently weeps.--WHILEMYGUI--12
While my guitar gently weeps.--WHILEMYGUI--19
Still my guitar gently weeps ((eee)).--WHILEMYGUI--21

WEIGH

When your prized possessions start to weigh you
    down --ANDYOURBIR--7

WEIGHT

CARRY THAT WEIGHT.--CARRYTHATW--Title
Boy, you're gonna carry that weight--CARRYTHATW--1
Carry that weight a long time.--CARRYTHATW--2
Boy, you're gonna carry that weight--CARRYTHATW--3
Carry that weight a long time.--CARRYTHATW--4
Boy, you're gonna carry that weight--CARRYTHATW--9
Carry that weight a long time.--CARRYTHATW--10
Boy, you're gonna carry that weight--CARRYTHATW--11
Carry that weight a long time.--CARRYTHATW--12

WELCOME

Good evening and welcome to Slaggers --YOUKNOWMYN
    --5

WELL

Well, she was just seventeen --ISAWHERSTA--2
Well she looked at me, and I, I could see --
    ISAWHERSTA--7
Well my heart went boom when I crossed that room
    --ISAWHERSTA--11
Well we danced through the night --ISAWHERSTA--13
Well my heart went boom when I crossed that room
    --ISAWHERSTA--18
Yeah, well since I saw her standing there.--
    ISAWHERSTA--26
Well, there's gonna be a time--ILLGETYOU--16
So you might as well resign yourself to me, oh
    yeah.--ILLGETYOU--18
Well I saw her yesterday--SHELOVESYO--5
Well since you left me I'm so alone (you left
    me here)--ITWONTBELO--21
Well, it's the second time--YOUCANTDOT--9
Well I gave you everything I had --TELLMEWHY--5
Well I beg you on my bended knees --TELLMEWHY--21
Gives me all her time as well as loving--SHESAWOMAN
    --14
Well baby, I'm down (I'm really down)--IMDOWN--41
But as from today well I've got somebody that's
    new --ANOTHERGIR--3
But as from today well I've seen somebody that's
    new --ANOTHERGIR--13
But as from today well I've seen somebody that's
    new --ANOTHERGIR--19
These are words that go together well, my
    Michelle.--MICHELLE--2
Well I'd rather see you dead, little girl --
    RUNFORYOUR--1
Well you know that I'm a wicked guy--RUNFORYOUR--9
They might as well be dead--RAIN--2
Well, well, well, you're feeling fine --DRROBERT
    --11
Well, well, well, you're feeling fine --DRROBERT
    --11
Well, well, well, you're feeling fine --DRROBERT
    --11
Well, well, well, he'll make you, Dr. Robert.--
    DRROBERT--12
Well, well, well, he'll make you, Dr. Robert.--
    DRROBERT--12
Well, well, well, he'll make you, Dr. Robert.--
    DRROBERT--12
Well, well, well, you're feeling fine --DRROBERT
    --18
Well, well, well, you're feeling fine --DRROBERT
    --18·
Well, well, well, you're feeling fine --DRROBERT
    --18
Well, well, well, he'll make you, Dr. Robert.--
    DRROBERT--19
Well, well, well, he'll make you, Dr. Robert.--

DRROBERT--19
Well, well, well, he'll make you, Dr. Robert.--
    DRROBERT--19
Sometimes I wish I knew you well--IWANTTOTEL--16
Well I just had to laugh--DAYINTHELI--4
Well it only goes to show (only, only goes to
    show) --BLUEJAYWAY--8
Well on the way, head in a cloud--FOOLONTHEH--8
For well you know that it's a fool who plays it
    cool --HEYJUDE--12
(Well you know you can make it, Jude, you've
    just gotta break it.)--HEYJUDE--46
Well then nah nah nah, nah - nah - nah - nah
    --HEYJUDE--74
Well you know --REVOLUTION--3
Well you know --REVOLUTION--6
Well you know --REVOLUTION--13
Well you know --REVOLUTION--16
Well you know --REVOLUTION--23
Well you know --REVOLUTION--26
Well, the Ukraine girls really knock me out --
    BACKINTHEU--15
Well, the Ukraine girls really knock me out --
    BACKINTHEU--27
Well, it's my birthday too - yeah.--BIRTHDAY--2
Well, it's my birthday too - yeah.--BIRTHDAY--21
Well here's another place you can go--GLASSONION
    --3
Well here's another clue for you all:--GLASSONION
    --10
Well here's another place you can be--GLASSONION
    --19
She's well acquainted with the touch of the
    velvet hand --HAPPINESSI--3
Well, don't you know that happiness ((happiness))
    --HAPPINESSI--31
Well, you may be a lover, but you ain't no
    dancer.--HELTERSKEL--7
Well, do you, don't you want me to make you?--
    HELTERSKEL--21
Well, look out helter-skelter.--HELTERSKEL--27
Well you know --REVOLUTONE--6
Well you know --REVOLUTONE--9
Well you know --REVOLUTONE--20
Well you know --REVOLUTONE--24
Well all I can tell you is brother you have to
    wait.--REVOLUTONE--28
Well you know --REVOLUTONE--36
Well you know --REVOLUTONE--40
Well, why don't we do it in the road?--WHYDONTWED
    --13
Well you know I nearly broke down and cried.--
    OHDARLING--6
A - well you know, I nearly broke down and died.--
    OHDARLING--8
A - well you know I nearly broke down and cried.--
    OHDARLING--13
A - well you know, I nearly broke down and died.--
    OHDARLING--15
Well, you should see Polythene Pam.--POLYTHENEP--1
Well, you should see her in drag --POLYTHENEP--3
Well I knew what I could not say.--SHECAMEINT--15
Good evening, you know my name, well then look
    up my number --YOUKNOWMYN--9
Well you can celebrate anything you want--IDIGAPONY
    --7
Well you can penetrate any place you go--IDIGAPONY
    --10
Well you can radiate everything you are--IDIGAPONY
    --17
Well you can imitate everyone you know--IDIGAPONY
    --20
Well you can indicate everything you see--IDIGAPONY
    --27
Well you can syndicate any boat you rode/rowed--
    IDIGAPONY--30
Well, she said she's travelling on the one after
    nine-0-nine --ONEAFTERNI--15
Well - pick up my bag, run right home (run
    right home) --ONEAFTERNI--23
Then I find I got the number wrong - well
    --ONEAFTERNI--24
Then I find I got the number wrong - well
    --ONEAFTERNI--24

WENT

Well my heart went boom when I crossed that room
    --ISAWHERSTA--11
Well my heart went boom when I crossed that room
    --ISAWHERSTA--18
I wonder what went wrong I've waited far too long
    --IDONTWANTT--7
I wonder what went wrong I've waited far too long

--IDONTWANTT--24
For people and things that went before --INMYLIFE
  --14
For people and things that went before --INMYLIFE
  --18
And somebody spoke and I went into a dream--
  DAYINTHELI--26
He went out tiger hunting with his elephant and
  gun --CONTINUING--7

WERE

They said you were not home--NOREPLY--10
If I were you I'd realise that I--NOREPLY--17
They said you were not home--NOREPLY--23
Scarlet were the clothes she wore--YESITIS--5
But other girls were never quite like this --
  IVEJUSTSEE--17
Were you telling lies? (aah the night before)--
  NIGHTBEFOR--5
When I held you near, you were so sincere--
  NIGHTBEFOR--7
When I held you near, you were so sincere --
  NIGHTBEFOR--15
Were you telling lies? (aah the night before)--
  NIGHTBEFOR--19
When I held you near, you were so sincere --
  NIGHTBEFOR--21
I told that girl that my prospects were good --
  DRIVEMYCAR--9
You were above me, but not today.--IMLOOKINGT--12
I used to think of no-one else but you were just
  the same --WHATGOESON--22
Ooo you were meant to be near me--GOTTOGETYO--12
And though the holes were rather small--DAYINTHELI
  --30
We were talking--WITHINYOUW--1
We were talking--WITHINYOUW--8
We were talking--WITHINYOUW--21
What did you see when you were there?--BABYYOUREA
  --11
You were made to go out and get her --HEYJUDE--6
You were only waiting for this moment to arise.--
  BLACKBIRD--4
You were only waiting for this moment to be free.
  --BLACKBIRD--8
You were only waiting for this moment to arise --
  BLACKBIRD--16
You were only waiting for this moment to arise --
  BLACKBIRD--17
You were only waiting for this moment to arise.--
  BLACKBIRD--18
Bill and his elephants were taken by surprise --
  CONTINUING--18
You were in a car crash --DONTPASSME--25
That you and me were meant to be for each other -
  silly girl.--MARTHAMYDE--9
Were in the next room at the hoe-down --ROCKYRACCO
  --18
I don't know how you were diverted --WHILEMYGUI--14
You were perverted (too/to)--WHILEMYGUI--15
I don't know how you were inverted--WHILEMYGUI--16

WEREN'T

Wishing you weren't so far away --THINGSWESA--4
That weren't important yesterday--FIXINGAHOL--20
The teachers who taught me weren't cool (now I
  can't complain)--GETTINGBET--4

WEST

They leave the West behind --BACKINTHEU--16
They leave the West behind --BACKINTHEU--28

WET

Everybody had a wet dream --IVEGOTAFEE--21
Everybody had a wet dream (oh yeah) --IVEGOTAFEE
  --30

WHACKING

What they need's a damn good whacking.--PIGGIES--14

WHAO-HO

Whao-ho love me do.--LOVEMEDO--5

WHAT

You know what I mean --ISAWHERSTA--3
And she told me what to say.--SHELOVESYO--7
Don't know what it means to hold you tight --

HOLDMETIGH--16
Don't know what it means to hold you tight --
  HOLDMETIGH--26
But what I got I'll give to you --CANTBUYMEL--12
Whoa, whoa, I never realised what a kiss could
  be --ISHOULDHAV--4
Whoa, whoa, I never realised what a kiss could
  be --ISHOULDHAV--14
And show you what your loving man can do --
  ILLCRYINST--18
And show you what your loving man can do --
  ILLCRYINST--27
Tell me what and I'll apologize --TELLMEWHY--14
Oh dear, what can I do?--BABYSINBLA--1
Tell me, oh what can I do?--BABYSINBLA--3
Oh dear, what can I do?--BABYSINBLA--7
Tell me, oh what can I do?--BABYSINBLA--9
Dear what can I do?--BABYSINBLA--16
Tell me oh what can I do?--BABYSINBLA--18
Dear what can I do?--BABYSINBLA--21
Tell me oh what can I do?--BABYSINBLA--23
Oh dear, what can I do?--BABYSINBLA--27
Tell me oh what can I do?--BABYSINBLA--29
There's no fun in what I do when she's not there
  --IDONTWANTT--6
I wonder what went wrong I've waited far too long
  --IDONTWANTT--7
There's no fun in what I do if she's not there --
  IDONTWANTT--23
I wonder what went wrong I've waited far too long
  --IDONTWANTT--24
And I'm not what I appear to be.--IMALOSER--2
I'm a loser and I'm not what I appear to be.--
  IMALOSER--8
I'm a loser and I'm not what I appear to be.--
  IMALOSER--14
What have I done to deserve such a fate?--IMALOSER
  --15
I'm a loser and I'm not what I appear to be.--
  IMALOSER--20
WHAT YOU'RE DOING.--WHATYOURED--Title
Look ((look)) what you're doing --WHATYOURED--1
What you're doing to me?--WHATYOURED--4
What you're doing to me?--WHATYOURED--8
Wondering what you're gonna do --WHATYOURED--10
What you're doing to me?--WHATYOURED--15
Wondering what you're gonna do --WHATYOURED--17
What you're doing to me?--WHATYOURED--22
What you're doing to me?--WHATYOURED--23
What you're doing to me?--WHATYOURED--24
Remember what I said tonight--YESITIS--2
This is what I said tonight--YESITIS--15
This is what I said tonight--YESITIS--24
TELL ME WHAT YOU SEE.--TELLMEWHAT--Title
Tell me what you see--TELLMEWHAT--6
What you see is me--TELLMEWHAT--8
Tell me what you see--TELLMEWHAT--14
What you see is me--TELLMEWHAT--16
Tell me what you see--TELLMEWHAT--17
Tell me what you see--TELLMEWHAT--23
What you see is me--TELLMEWHAT--25
Tell me what you see--TELLMEWHAT--26
Tell me what you see--TELLMEWHAT--32
What you see is me--TELLMEWHAT--34
I ain't no fool and I don't take what I don't
  want --ANOTHERGIR--6
Nobody in all the world can do what she can do --
  ANOTHERGIR--7
I ain't no fool and I don't take what I don't
  want --ANOTHERGIR--14
I ain't no fool and I don't take what I don't
  want --ANOTHERGIR--20
Just what you mean to me--INEEDYOU--19
Just what you mean to me--INEEDYOU--29
I'll make a point of taking her away from you
  (watch what you do), yeah--YOUREGONNA--16
The way you treat her what else can I do?--
  YOUREGONNA--17
I'll make a point of taking her away from you
  (watch what you do), yeah--YOUREGONNA--23
The way you treat her what else can I do?--
  YOUREGONNA--24
Think of what you're saying --WECANWORKI--6
Think of what I'm saying --WECANWORKI--8
Asked a girl what she wanted to be --DRIVEMYCAR--1
I thought I knew you, what did I know?--IMLOOKINGT
  --2
I thought I knew you, what did I know?--IMLOOKINGT
  --18
Oh, what you mean to me--MICHELLE--13
Until I do I'm hoping you will know what I mean.--
  MICHELLE--14
You don't know what you're missing --NOWHEREMAN--8
Just sees what he wants to see --NOWHEREMAN--11

You don't know what you're missing --NOWHEREMAN--20
Do what you want to do --THINKFORYO--6
Do what you want to do --THINKFORYO--15
Do what you want to do --THINKFORYO--24
Do what you want to do --THINKFORYO--28
WHAT GOES ON?--WHATGOESON--Title
What goes on in your heart? (wuh)--WHATGOESON--1
What goes on in your mind?--WHATGOESON--2
What goes on in your mind?--WHATGOESON--5
What goes on in your heart?--WHATGOESON--10
What goes on in your mind?--WHATGOESON--11
What goes on in your mind?--WHATGOESON--14
What goes on in your heart?--WHATGOESON--19
(What goes on in your mind?)--WHATGOESON--21
What goes on in your heart?--WHATGOESON--26
What goes on in your mind?--WHATGOESON--27
What goes on in your mind?--WHATGOESON--30
Now that I know what I feel must be right --THEWORD
    --23
I wouldn't mind if I knew what I was missing.--
    YOUWONTSEE--14
I wouldn't mind if I knew what I was missing.--
    YOUWONTSEE--23
What does he care?--ELEANORRIG--16
I didn't know what I would find there--GOTTOGETYO
    --2
What can I do, what can I be?--GOTTOGETYO--16
What can I do, what can I be?--GOTTOGETYO--16
I didn't know what I would find there--GOTTOGETYO
    --26
But what you've got means such a lot to me.--
    LOVEYOUTWO--8
She said I know what it's like to be dead --
    SHESAIDSHE--1
I know what it is to be sad--SHESAIDSHE--2
She said you don't understand what I said.--
    SHESAIDSHE--7
I said even though you know what you know --
    SHESAIDSHE--10
She said you don't understand what I said.--
    SHESAIDSHE--13
I said even though you know what you know --
    SHESAIDSHE--16
I know what it's like to be dead (I know what
    it's like to be dead) --SHESAIDSHE--20
I know what it's like to be dead (I know what
    it's like to be dead) --SHESAIDSHE--20
I know what it is to be sad (I know what it is
    to be sad).--SHESAIDSHE--21
I know what it is to be sad (I know what it is
    to be sad).--SHESAIDSHE--21
I know what it's like to be dead (I know what
    it's like to be dead).--SHESAIDSHE--22
I know what it's like to be dead (I know what
    it's like to be dead).--SHESAIDSHE--22
Don't ask me what I want it for (ha ha Mr.
    Wilson)--TAXMAN--18
Late of Pablo Fanques Fair - what a scene.--
    BEINGFORTH--4
Nothing to say but what a day how's your boy been?
    --GOODMORNIN--3
She (what did we do that was wrong?)--SHESLEAVIN
    --28
Indicate precisely what you mean to say--WHENIMSIXT
    --30
What would you think if I sang outta tune --
    WITHALITTL--1
What do I do when my love is away?--WITHALITTL--8
(What do you see when you turn out the light?)--
    WITHALITTL--21
What do you want to be?--BABYYOUREA--4
What did you see when you were there?--BABYYOUREA
    --11
What a thing to do.--BABYYOUREA--18
What are you going to play?--BABYYOUREA--27
What a thing to do (baby).--BABYYOUREA--33
They can tell what he wants to do--FOOLONTHEH--16
We're all doing what we can.--REVOLUTION--17
What did you kill --CONTINUING--2
What did you kill --CONTINUING--5
What did you kill --CONTINUING--12
What did you kill --CONTINUING--15
What did you kill --CONTINUING--22
What did you kill --CONTINUING--25
What did you kill --CONTINUING--32
What did you kill --CONTINUING--35
What did you kill --CONTINUING--38
What did you kill --CONTINUING--41
What did you kill --CONTINUING--44
What did you kill --CONTINUING--47
What did you kill --CONTINUING--50
What did you kill --CONTINUING--53
This is what I'd say:--HONEYPIE--6
I'm so tired, I don't know what to do --IMSOTIRED

    --5
But I know what you would do.--IMSOTIRED--8
Half of what I say is meaningless --JULIA--1
Hold your head up you silly girl, look what
    you've done --MARTHAMYDE--4
Help yourself to a bit of what is all around you
    - silly girl.--MARTHAMYDE--6
Hold your hand out you silly girl, see what
    you've done --MARTHAMYDE--10
Help yourself to a bit of what is all around you
    - silly girl.--MARTHAMYDE--12
They don't care what goes on around.--PIGGIES--12
What they need's a damn good whacking.--PIGGIES--14
We're all doing what we can.--REVOLUTONE--25
You know that what you eat you are --SAVOYTRUFF--19
But what is sweet now turns so sour.--SAVOYTRUFF
    --20
Sexy Sadie what have you done?--SEXYSADIE--1
Sexie Sadie - oh what have you done?--SEXYSADIE--4
And you know what it's worth.--YERBLUES--13
What makes you think you're something special
    when you smile?--HEYBULLDOG--4
You don't know what it's like to listen to your
    fears.--HEYBULLDOG--8
What do you say?--HEYBULLDOG--24
Everywhere it's what you make --ITSALLTOOM--10
And what I do is all too much.--ITSALLTOOM--28
Everywhere it's what you make --ITSALLTOOM--31
It doesn't really matter what chords I play --
    ONLYANORTH--7
What words I say or time of day it is --ONLYANORTH
    --8
It doesn't really matter what clothes I wear --
    ONLYANORTH--10
Not worrying what they or you say --OLDBROWNSH--19
Got to be a joker he just do what he please--
    COMETOGETH--10
Oh, what joy for every girl and boy--OCTOPUSSGA--19
No-one there to tell us what to do.--OCTOPUSSGA--22
Well I knew what I could not say.--SHECAMEINT--15

WHAT'RE
    The news-people said, say what're you doing in
        bed?--BALLADOFJO--19

WHAT'S
    And what's more, it's true, yes it is.--YESITIS--4
    Hey man what's that noise? (woof)--HEYBULLDOG--23
    But right is only half of what's wrong --OLDBROWNSH
        --2
    You know my number, what's up with you? - ha--
        YOUKNOWMYN--40

WHEN
    When you need a shoulder to cry on --ANYTIMEATA--16
    Ooh when I saw her standing there.--ISAWHERSTA--6
    Ooh when I saw her standing there.--ISAWHERSTA--10
    Well my heart went boom when I crossed that room
        --ISAWHERSTA--11
    When I saw her standing there. (hey! aah!)--
        ISAWHERSTA--17
    Well my heart went boom when I crossed that room
        --ISAWHERSTA--18
    You made me glad when I was blue--THANKYOUGI--2
    You made me glad when I was blue--THANKYOUGI--12
    When I think about you, I can say--ILLGETYOU--11
    When I'm gonna change/make your mind--ILLGETYOU--17
    And when I, I wanna kiss you, yeah --ALLIVEGOTT--6
    And when I, I wanna kiss you, yeah --ALLIVEGOTT--17
    When every night I'm all alone--DONTBOTHER--12
    When she's come home--DONTBOTHER--23
    When she's come home--DONTBOTHER--38
    Every night when everybody has fun--ITWONTBELO--5
    Then we'll have some fun when you're mine, all
        mine --LITTLECHIL--10
    When you're by my side, you're the only one --
        LITTLECHIL--16
    When I say that something--IWANTTOHOL--3
    And when I touch you--IWANTTOHOL--13
    When I say that something--IWANTTOHOL--22
    And when I touch you--IWANTTOHOL--26
    When I feel that something--IWANTTOHOL--35
    When I feel low, when I feel blue--THERESAPLA--2
    When I feel low, when I feel blue--THERESAPLA--2
    When I'm alone.--THERESAPLA--4
    When I feel low, when I feel blue--THERESAPLA--14
    When I feel low, when I feel blue--THERESAPLA--14
    When I'm alone.--THERESAPLA--16
    But when I get home to you --HARDDAYSNI--5
    'cos when I get you alone --HARDDAYSNI--13
    When I'm home everything seems to be right --

HARDDAYSNI--15
When I'm home feeling you holding me tight,
    tight, yeah.--HARDDAYSNI--16
But when I get home to you --HARDDAYSNI--21
'cos when I get you alone --HARDDAYSNI--26
When I'm home everything seems to be right --
    HARDDAYSNI--28
When I'm home feeling you holding me tight,
    tight, yeah.--HARDDAYSNI--29
But when I get home to you --HARDDAYSNI--34
That when I tell you that I love you, oh --
    ISHOULDHAV--7
And when I ask you to be mine --ISHOULDHAV--9
That when I tell you that I love you, oh --
    ISHOULDHAV--17
And when I ask you to be mine --ISHOULDHAV--19
When she learns we are two.--IFIFELL--20
When she learns we are two.--IFIFELL--27
Don't want to cry when there's people there --
    ILLCRYINST--11
I get shy when they start to stare.--ILLCRYINST--12
And when I do you'd better hide all the girls --
    ILLCRYINST--15
Don't want to cry when there's people there --
    ILLCRYINST--20
I get shy when they start to stare.--ILLCRYINST--21
And when I do you'd better hide all the girls --
    ILLCRYINST--24
I'm so happy when you dance with me.--IMHAPPYJUS
    --3
I'm so happy when you dance with me ((oh - oh)).--
    IMHAPPYJUS--15
I'm so happy when you dance with me ((oh - oh)).--
    IMHAPPYJUS--23
Someday when I'm lonely --THINGSWESA--3
Someday when we're dreaming --THINGSWESA--8
Someday when we're dreaming --THINGSWESA--19
Someday when we're dreaming --THINGSWESA--30
WHEN I GET HOME.--WHENIGETHO--Title
When I get home.--WHENIGETHO--3
When I get home.--WHENIGETHO--9
When I get home.--WHENIGETHO--15
When I getting home tonight --WHENIGETHO--16
When I get home, yeah.--WHENIGETHO--26
When I get home.--WHENIGETHO--28
Turn me on when I get lonely--SHESAWOMAN--5
Turn me on when I get lonely--SHESAWOMAN--22
Turn me on when I get lonely--SHESAWOMAN--32
When I'm walking beside her--EVERYLITTL--1
When I'm with her I'm happy--EVERYLITTL--11
There's no fun in what I do when she's not there
    --IDONTWANTT--6
When I came to your door--NOREPLY--2
When you gave me no reply.--NOREPLY--21
When I was around.--TICKETTORI--12
When I was around.--TICKETTORI--39
And it's nice when you believe me--YOULIKEMET--14
And it's nice when you believe me--YOULIKEMET--23
When ((when)) I was younger ((when I was
    young))--HELP--8
When ((when)) I was younger ((when I was
    young))--HELP--8
When ((when)) I was younger ((when I was
    young))--HELP--8
When I was younger, so much younger than today--
    HELP--29
How can you laugh when you know I'm down?--IMDOWN
    --6
(How can you laugh) when you know I'm down?--IMDOWN
    --7
How can you laugh when you know I'm down?--IMDOWN
    --13
(How can you laugh) when you know I'm down?--IMDOWN
    --14
How can you laugh when you know I'm down?--IMDOWN
    --21
(How can you laugh) when you know I'm down?--IMDOWN
    --22
That's when it hurt me--INEEDYOU--13
But when you told me--INEEDYOU--21
That's when it hurt me--INEEDYOU--23
I get high when I see you go by, my oh my--
    ITSONLYLOV--1
When you sigh my my inside just flies, butterfly.
    --ITSONLYLOV--2
Why am I so shy when I'm beside you?--ITSONLYLOV
    --3
When I held you near, you were so sincere--
    NIGHTBEFOR--7
When I think of things we did it makes me wanna
    cry.--NIGHTBEFOR--10
When I held you near, you were so sincere --
    NIGHTBEFOR--15
When I think of things we did it makes me wanna

cry.--NIGHTBEFOR--18
When I held you near, you were so sincere --
    NIGHTBEFOR--21
When I think of all the times I tried so hard
    to leave her --GIRL--6
When friends are there, you feel a fool.--GIRL--13
When you say she's looking good --GIRL--15
Was he told when she was young that pain would
    lead to pleasure?--GIRL--22
Did she understand it when they said --GIRL--23
Will she still believe it when he's dead?--GIRL--25
When I think of love as something new.--INMYLIFE
    --12
And when I awoke--NORWEGIANW--21
When you treat me so unkind.--WHATGOESON--4
But when I saw him with you I could feel my
    future fold.--WHATGOESON--7
When you treat me so unkind.--WHATGOESON--13
When you treat me so unkind.--WHATGOESON--29
When I call you up your line's engaged.--YOUWONTSEE
    --1
When the sun shines they slip into the shade
    (when the sun shines down)--RAIN--4
When the sun shines they slip into the shade
    (when the sun shines down)--RAIN--4
And sip their lemonade (when the sun shines down)
    --RAIN--5
When the sun shines, when the sun shines ((sun
    shine)).--RAIN--6
When the sun shines, when the sun shines ((sun
    shine)).--RAIN--6
I can show you that when it starts to rain (when
    the rain comes down)--RAIN--9
I can show you that when it starts to rain (when
    the rain comes down)--RAIN--9
Everything's the same (when the rain comes down)--
    RAIN--10
Can you hear me that when it rains and shines
    (when it rains and shines)--RAIN--14
Can you hear me that when it rains and shines
    (when it rains and shines)--RAIN--14
It's just a state of mind (when it rains and
    shines)--RAIN--15
When your prized possessions start to weigh you
    down --ANDYOURBIR--7
When your bird is broken will it bring you down?--
    ANDYOURBIR--10
When I wake up early in the morning --IMONLYSLEE
    --1
When I'm in the middle of a dream --IMONLYSLEE--3
When I wake up early in the morning --IMONLYSLEE
    --21
When I'm in the middle of a dream --IMONLYSLEE--23
Darning his socks in the night when there's
    nobody there--ELEANORRIG--15
When she no longer needs you.--FORNOONE--3
When she says her love is dead --FORNOONE--12
There will be times when all the things --FORNOONE
    --21
I need to laugh and when the sun is out --
    GOODDAYSUN--2
When I'm with you I want to stay there--GOTTOGETYO
    --17
When you're here--IWANTTOTEL--3
When I get near you--IWANTTOTEL--5
When I was a boy everything was right,
    everything was right.--SHESAIDSHE--9
When I was a boy everything was right,
    everything was right.--SHESAIDSHE--15
But, you know, I know when it's a dream--STRAWBERRY
    --27
When Mr. K. performs his tricks - without a
    sound.--BEINGFORTH--16
And when my mind is wandering--FIXINGAHOL--12
When it gets dark I tow your heart away.--
    LOVELYRITA--6
When I caught a glimpse of Rita--LOVELYRITA--8
When are you free ((lovely Rita))--LOVELYRITA--15
WHEN I'M SIXTY-FOUR.--WHENIMSIXT--Title
When I get older losing my hair--WHENIMSIXT--1
When I'm sixty-four?--WHENIMSIXT--9
When your lights have gone.--WHENIMSIXT--14
When I'm sixty-four?--WHENIMSIXT--21
When I'm sixty-four?--WHENIMSIXT--37
What do I do when my love is away?--WITHALITTL--8
(What do you see when you turn out the light?)--
    WITHALITTL--21
When it's far too late--WITHINYOUW--6
When they pass away.--WITHINYOUW--7
When we find it--WITHINYOUW--10
When you've seen beyond yourself--WITHINYOUW--28
When you see we're all one--WITHINYOUW--32
What did you see when you were there?--BABYYOUREA
    --11

Who finds the money when you pay the rent?--
    LADYMADONN--3
But when you talk about destruction --REVOLUTION
    --8
(But when he looked so fierce) his mommy butted
    in --CONTINUING--28
Your inside is out when your outside is in --
    EVRBDYMONK--17
Your outside is in when your inside is out --
    EVRBDYMONK--18
When I hold you in my arms ((oh, yeah)) --
    HAPPINESSI--22
When I get to the bottom I go back to the top
    of the slide --HELTERSKEL--1
When I get to the bottom I go back to the top
    of the slide--HELTERSKEL--18
Love you when we're apart.--IWILL--12
And when at last I find you --IWILL--13
When I cannot sing my heart --JULIA--11
When I loved you?--LONGLONGLO--3
When you find yourself in the thick of it --
    MARTHAMYDE--5
When you find yourself in the thick of it --
    MARTHAMYDE--11
But when you talk about destruction --REVOLUTONE
    --11
When the pain cuts through--SAVOYTRUFF--12
When it becomes too much--SAVOYTRUFF--15
What makes you think you're something special
    when you smile?--HEYBULLDOG--4
When I look into your eyes --ITSALLTOOM--4
When you're listening late at night --ONLYANORTH
    --4
When it's only a Northern song.--ONLYANORTH--12
Last night the wife said, oh boy, when you're
    dead --BALLADOFJO--27
When I see your smile --OLDBROWNSH--11
Smiles awake you when you rise.--GOLDENSLUM--8
She tells Max to stay when the class has gone
    away --MAXWELLSIL--10
But when she turns her back on the boy, he
    creeps up from behind --MAXWELLSIL--12
Believe me when I tell you, I'll never do you
    no harm.--OHDARLING--2
Believe me when I beg you - ooo - don't ever
    leave me alone.--OHDARLING--4
When you told me you didn't need me any more --
    OHDARLING--5
A - when you told me you didn't need me any more
    --OHDARLING--7
Believe me when I tell you, I'll never do you
    no harm.--OHDARLING--10
A - when you told me - ooo - you didn't need me
    any more --OHDARLING--12
A - when you told me you didn't need me any more
    --OHDARLING--14
Believe me when I tell you - ooo - I'll never
    do you no harm.--OHDARLING--18
She's killer-diller when she's dressed to the hilt.
    --POLYTHENEP--7
When I find myself in times of trouble --LETITBE/45
    --1
And when the broken-hearted people--LETITBE/45--9
And when the night is cloudy --LETITBE/45--21
When I find myself in times of trouble --LETITBE/LP
    --1
And when the broken-hearted people--LETITBE/LP--9
And when the night is cloudy --LETITBE/LP--21

WHENEVER
Whenever I want you around, yeah --ALLIVEGOTT--1
Whenever you want me at all --ALLIVEGOTT--12
Whenever you call --ALLIVEGOTT--14
Whenever you want me at all --ALLIVEGOTT--23
Whenever you call --ALLIVEGOTT--25
Love you whenever we're together --IWILL--11

WHERE
There, there's a place where I can go--THERESAPLA
    --1
There, there's a place where I can go--THERESAPLA
    --13
'cos I know where you've been--NOREPLY--12
'cos I know where you've been--NOREPLY--25
And bring you back where you belong--YOULIKEMET--16
And bring you back where you belong--YOULIKEMET--25
Where we just met--IVEJUSTSEE--3
Where we just met--IVEJUSTSEE--26
I'm looking through you, where did you go?--
    IMLOOKINGT--1
I'm looking through you, where did you go?--
    IMLOOKINGT--17

Knows not where he's going to --NOWHEREMAN--5
Knows not where he's going to --NOWHEREMAN--17
Or I won't know where I am.--RUNFORYOUR--4
Or you won't know where I am.--RUNFORYOUR--28
And go where you're going to --THINKFORYO--7
And go where you're going to --THINKFORYO--16
And go where you're going to --THINKFORYO--25
And go where you're going to --THINKFORYO--29
Leave me where I am, I'm only sleeping.--IMONLYSLEE
    --6
Leave me where I am, I'm only sleeping.--IMONLYSLEE
    --26
Where a wedding has been--ELEANORRIG--4
All the lonely people, where do they all come
    from?--ELEANORRIG--9
All the lonely people, where do they all belong?--
    ELEANORRIG--10
All the lonely people, where do they all come
    from?--ELEANORRIG--17
All the lonely people, where do they all belong?--
    ELEANORRIG--18
All the lonely people, where do they all come
    from?--ELEANORRIG--27
All the lonely people, where do they all belong?--
    ELEANORRIG--29
Another road where maybe I--GOTTOGETYO--3
Another road where maybe I--GOTTOGETYO--27
In the town where I was born--YELLOWSUBM--1
I'm fixing a hole where the rain gets in--
    FIXINGAHOL--1
Where it will go.--FIXINGAHOL--3
Where it will go.--FIXINGAHOL--6
Where I belong I'm right where I belong.--
    FIXINGAHOL--8
Where I belong I'm right where I belong.--
    FIXINGAHOL--8
Where I belong I'm right where I belong.--
    FIXINGAHOL--16
Where I belong I'm right where I belong.--
    FIXINGAHOL--16
I'm fixing a hole where the rain gets in--
    FIXINGAHOL--23
Where it will go, where it will go.--FIXINGAHOL--25
Where it will go, where it will go.--FIXINGAHOL--25
I'm fixing a hole where the rain gets in--
    FIXINGAHOL--26
Where it will go.--FIXINGAHOL--28
Where would I be without you?--LOVELYRITA--27
Where rocking-horse people eat marshmallow pies.--
    LUCYINTHES--13
There's nowhere you can be that isn't where
    you're meant to be ((love))--ALLYOUN/YS--21
And I told them where to go.--BLUEJAYWAY--9
Deep in the jungle where the mighty tiger lies --
    CONTINUING--17
Can you take me back where I came from --CRYBABYCRY
    --44
Can you take me back where I came from --CRYBABYCRY
    --46
Mmm can you take me where I came from --CRYBABYCRY
    --49
I wonder where you are tonight --DONTPASSME--14
You know the place where nothing is real--
    GLASSONION--2
Where everything flows--GLASSONION--4
Where I stop and I turn and I go for a ride --
    HELTERSKEL--2
To be where you belong.--HONEYPIE--18
But can you show me where you are?--SAVOYTRUFF--22
Makes no difference where you are--ITSALLTOOM--14
Or where you'd like to be.--ITSALLTOOM--15
Where I know that I'm free --ITSALLTOOM--22
Get back to where you once belonged.--GETBACK/45
    --6
Get back to where you once belonged.--GETBACK/45
    --8
Back to where you once belonged.--GETBACK/45--12
Back to where you once belonged.--GETBACK/45--14
Get back to where you once belonged.--GETBACK/45
    --21
Get back to where you once belonged.--GETBACK/45
    --23
Get back to where you once belonged.--GETBACK/45
    --27
Get back to where you once belonged.--GETBACK/45
    --29
Get back to where you once belonged.--GETBACK/45
    --37
From where some try to drag me down --OLDBROWNSH
    --10
He'd let us in, knows where we've been--OCTOPUSSGA
    --3
Get back to where you once belonged--GETBACK/LP--12
Get back to where you once belonged--GETBACK/LP--14

Back to where you once belonged--GETBACK/LP--18
Back to where you once belonged--GETBACK/LP--20
Get back to where you once belonged--GETBACK/LP--27
Get back to where you once belonged.--GETBACK/LP--29
Get back to where you once belonged--GETBACK/LP--33
Get back to where you once belonged--GETBACK/LP--35

WHICH
Which is all that I deserve--YOULIKEMET--10
A soap impression of his wife which he ate --
HAPPINESSI--7
Images of broken light which dance before me like
a million eyes --ACROSSTHEU--11
Limitless undying love which shines around me
like a million suns --ACROSSTHEU--23
Phase one in which Doris gets her oats.--TWOOFUS--2

WHILE
And then while I'm away --ALLMYLOVIN--4
And then while I'm away --ALLMYLOVIN--10
And then while I'm away --ALLMYLOVIN--18
If she turns up while I'm gone please let me know.
--IDONTWANTT--4
If she turns up while I'm gone please let me know.
--IDONTWANTT--16
While you see it your way--WECANWORKI--3
While you see it your way --WECANWORKI--17
While you see it your way --WECANWORKI--26
Love me while you can--LOVEYOUTWO--4
After a while you start to smile now you feel cool
--GOODMORNIN--13
Lying with his eyes while his hands are busy
working overtime --HAPPINESSI--6
WHILE MY GUITAR GENTLY WEEPS.--WHILEMYGUI--Title
While my guitar gently weeps.--WHILEMYGUI--3
While my guitar gently weeps.--WHILEMYGUI--10
While my guitar gently weeps.--WHILEMYGUI--19
But she gets it while she can.--GETBACK/45--19
But she gets it while she can.--GETBACK/LP--25

WHIM
And though it's only a whim --BABYSINBLA--12

WHISPER
Let me whisper in your ear --DOYOUWANTT--6
Let me whisper in your ear, (dodahdo)--DOYOUWANTT
--12
Let me whisper in your ear, (dodahdo)--DOYOUWANTT
--20
Is whisper in your ear --ALLIVEGOTT--8
Whisper words of wisdom, let it be.--LETITBE/45--8
Whisper words of wisdom, let it be.--LETITBE/45--18
Whisper words of wisdom, let it be.--LETITBE/45--20
Whisper words of wisdom, let it be.--LETITBE/45--30
Whisper words of wisdom, let it be.--LETITBE/LP--8
Whisper words of wisdom, let it be.--LETITBE/LP--18
Whisper words of wisdom, let it be.--LETITBE/LP--20
Whisper words of wisdom, let it be.--LETITBE/LP--32

WHITE
Filling in a ticket in her little white book.--
LOVELYRITA--9
In the starched white shirts?--PIGGIES--7
Black, white, green, red --ALLTOGETHE--17

WHO
I'm the kind of guy, who never used to cry.--MISERY
--2
'cos I'm the one who won your love--YOUCANTDOT--19
'cos I'm the one who won your love--YOUCANTDOT--38
I don't know who can --ICALLYOURN--6
I don't know who can --ICALLYOURN--13
I love you so, I'm the one who wants you --
ILLBEBACK--5
Yes I'm the one who wants you--ILLBEBACK--7
She's a woman who understands--SHESAWOMAN--16
She's a woman who loves her man--SHESAWOMAN--17
She's a woman who understands--SHESAWOMAN--26
She's a woman who loves her man--SHESAWOMAN--27
Another girl who will love me till the end --
ANOTHERGIR--10
Another girl who will love me till the end --
ANOTHERGIR--16
All about the girl who came to stay?--GIRL--2
She's the kind of girl who puts you down--GIRL--11
Who is it for?--ELEANORRIG--8
I said who put all those things in your head?--
SHESAIDSHE--4

Now my advice for those who die (Taxman)--TAXMAN--22
Lived a man who sailed to sea--YELLOWSUBM--2
About a lucky man who made the grade--DAYINTHELI--2
See the people standing there who disagree and
never win--FIXINGAHOL--9
The teachers who taught me weren't cool (now I
can't complain)--GETTINGBET--4
Who could ask for more?--WHENIMSIXT--18
Who hide themselves behind a wall of illusion--
WITHINYOUW--4
Who gain the world and lose their soul--WITHINYOUW--24
Now that you know who you are--BABYYOUREA--3
Who finds the money when you pay the rent?--
LADYMADONN--3
For well you know that it's a fool who plays it
cool --HEYJUDE--12
Picking flowers for a friend who came to play --
CRYBABYCRY--13
She's not a girl who misses much --HAPPINESSI--1
Who knows how long I've loved you?--IWILL--1
Now she and her man who called himself Dan--
ROCKYRACCO--17
Jojo was a man who thought he was a loner --
GETBACK/45--1
Who sometimes wears it twice as long.--OLDBROWNSH--4
Who knows baby, you may comfort me (hey).--
OLDBROWNSH--21
Who knows baby, you may comfort me (hey).--
OLDBROWNSH--26
Jojo was a man who thought he was a loner--
GETBACK/LP--7
All that I was looking for was somebody who
looked like you.--IVEGOTAFEE--13

WHO'LL
Who'll screw you in the ground--LOVEYOUTWO--14

WHO'S
I got a girl who's waiting home for me tonight.--
WHENIGETHO--12
I'm a loser and I lost someone who's near to me --
IMALOSER--7
I'm a loser and I lost someone who's near to me --
IMALOSER--13
I'm a loser and I lost someone who's near to me --
IMALOSER--19

WHOA
Please please me, whoa - yeah--PLEASEPLEA--5
Please please me, whoa - yeah--PLEASEPLEA--11
It's so hard to reason with you, whoa - yeah--
PLEASEPLEA--17
Please please me, whoa - yeah--PLEASEPLEA--23
Please me, whoa - yeah--PLEASEPLEA--25
Please me, whoa - yeah--PLEASEPLEA--27
Whoa closer --DOYOUWANTT--5
Whoa closer, (dodahdo)--DOYOUWANTT--11
Whoa closer, (dodahdo)--DOYOUWANTT--19
Whoa when I saw her standing there--ISAWHERSTA
--10
Whoa since/when I saw her standing there.
(hey! aah!)--ISAWHERSTA--17
Whoa since I saw her standing there--ISAWHERSTA
--25
Oh yeah, oh yeah, whoa - yeah.--ILLGETYOU--26
Whoa!--IWANNABEYO--29
Whoa, whoa, I never realised what a kiss could
be --ISHOULDHAV--4
Whoa, whoa, I never realised what a kiss could
be --ISHOULDHAV--4
Whoa, whoa, I never realised what a kiss could
be --ISHOULDHAV--14
Whoa, whoa, I never realised what a kiss could
be --ISHOULDHAV--14
(Whoa, whoa, whoa)--MAXWELLSIL--26
(Whoa, whoa, whoa)--MAXWELLSIL--26
(Whoa, whoa, whoa)--MAXWELLSIL--26

WHOA-HO
Whoa-ho love me do.--LOVEMEDO--10
Whoa-ho love me do (hey hey).--LOVEMEDO--17
Whoa-ho love me do.--LOVEMEDO--22
Whoa-ho love me do --LOVEMEDO--24

WHOA-OH-AAH
Whoa-oh-aah, whoa-oh-aah --WHENIGETHO--1
Whoa-oh-aah, whoa-oh-aah --WHENIGETHO--1
Whoa-oh-aah, whoa-oh-aah --WHENIGETHO--7
Whoa-oh-aah, whoa-oh-aah --WHENIGETHO--7

WHOA—OH—AAH

Whoa-oh-aah, whoa-oh-aah --WHENIGETHO--13
Whoa-oh-aah, whoa-oh-aah --WHENIGETHO--13
Whoa-oh-aah, whoa-oh-aah --WHENIGETHO--24
Whoa-oh-aah, whoa-oh-aah --WHENIGETHO--24

WHOLE

I got a whole lot of things to tell her --
WHENIGETHO--2
I got a whole lot of things I gotta say to her.--
WHENIGETHO--6
I got a whole lot of things to tell her --
WHENIGETHO--8
I got a whole lot of things to tell her --
WHENIGETHO--14
I got a whole lot of things to tell her --
WHENIGETHO--25
I got a whole lot of things to tell her --
WHENIGETHO--27
And I can't spend my whole life trying--RUNFORYOUR
--11

WHY

ASK ME WHY.--ASKMEWHY--Title
And in time you'll understand the reason why --
ASKMEWHY--9
Ask me why, I'll say I love you --ASKMEWHY--14
Ask me why, I'll say I love you --ASKMEWHY--22
Ask me why, I'll say I love you--ASKMEWHY--26
Why do I always have to say love --PLEASEPLEA--8
Why do you make me blue?--PLEASEPLEA--18
Why do you never even try girl --PLEASEPLEA--21
I see no use in wondering why --NOTASECOND--2
I'm wondering why --NOTASECOND--8
I see no use in wondering why --NOTASECOND--13
I'm wondering why --NOTASECOND--19
So why on earth should I moan --HARDDAYSNI--12
So why on earth should I moan --HARDDAYSNI--25
TELL ME WHY.--TELLMEWHY--Title
Tell me why you cried --TELLMEWHY--1
And why you lied to me --TELLMEWHY--2
Tell me why you cried --TELLMEWHY--3
And why you lied to me.--TELLMEWHY--4
Tell me why you cried --TELLMEWHY--9
And why you lied to me --TELLMEWHY--10
Tell me why you cried --TELLMEWHY--11
And why you lied to me.--TELLMEWHY--12
Tell me why you cried --TELLMEWHY--17
And why you lied to me --TELLMEWHY--18
Tell me why you cried --TELLMEWHY--19
And why you lied to me.--TELLMEWHY--20
Tell me why you cried --TELLMEWHY--26
And why you lied to me.--TELLMEWHY--27
Tell me why you cried --TELLMEWHY--28
And why you lied to me.--TELLMEWHY--29
Don't ask me why--SHESAWOMAN--15
Why should it be so much to ask of you --WHATYOURED
--7
Why should it be so much to ask of you --WHATYOURED
--14
Why should it be so much to ask of you --WHATYOURED
--21
I don't know why she's riding so high--TICKETTORI
--17
I don't know why she's riding so high--TICKETTORI
--30
Why am I so shy when I'm beside you?--ITSONLYLOV
--3
Why should I feel the way I do?--ITSONLYLOV--5
Why should I feel the way I do?--ITSONLYLOV--12
Why she had to go, I don't know--YESTERDAY--9
Why she had to go, I don't know--YESTERDAY--17
After all this time I don't know why.--GIRL--9
Why, tell me why did you not treat me right?--
IMLOOKINGT--9
Why, tell me why did you not treat me right?--
IMLOOKINGT--9
Why, tell me why did you not treat me right?--
IMLOOKINGT--15
Why, tell me why did you not treat me right?--
IMLOOKINGT--15
Tell me why.--WHATGOESON--9
Tell me why (tell me why).--WHATGOESON--18
Tell me why (tell me why).--WHATGOESON--18
Tell me why.--WHATGOESON--25
I don't know why you should want to hide --
YOUWONTSEE--7
I feel hung up and I don't know why --IWANTTOTEL
--13
I feel hung up and I don't know why --IWANTTOTEL
--20
And wonder why they don't get in my door.--
FIXINGAHOL--10

And never ask me why they don't get past my door.
--FIXINGAHOL--18
Why would she treat us so thoughtlessly?--
SHESLEAVIN--18
I don't know why you say goodbye, I say hello -
hello, hello.--HELLOGOODB--5
I don't know why you say goodbye, I say hello.--
HELLOGOODB--6
You say why and I say I don't know.--HELLOGOODB--8
I don't know why you say goodbye, I say hello -
hello, hello--HELLOGOODB--12
I don't know why you say goodbye, I say hello--
HELLOGOODB--14
Why,why, why, why, why, why do you say --HELLOGOODB
--16
Why,why, why, why, why, why do you say --HELLOGOODB
--16
Why,why, why, why, why, why do you say --HELLOGOODB
--16
Why,why, why, why, why, why do you say --HELLOGOODB
--16
Why,why, why, why, why, why do you say --HELLOGOODB
--16
Why,why, why, why, why, why do you say --HELLOGOODB
--16
I don't know why you say goodbye, I say hello -
hello, hello--HELLOGOODB--20
I don't know why you say goodbye, I say hello.--
HELLOGOODB--21
I don't know why you say goodbye, I say hello -
hello, hello--HELLOGOODB--28
I don't know why you say goodbye, I say hello -
hello, hello--HELLOGOODB--29
I don't know why you say goodbye, I say hello -
hello.--HELLOGOODB--30
And why I'm by myself --DONTPASSME--15
I don't know why nobody told you how to unfold
your love --WHILEMYGUI--6
WHY DON'T WE DO IT IN THE ROAD?--WHYDONTWED--Title
Why don't we do - do it in the road?--WHYDONTWED
--1
Why don't we do it in the road? (ah-ha)--WHYDONTWED
--2
Why don't we do it in the road? - mmm--WHYDONTWED
--3
Why don't we do it in the road?--WHYDONTWED--4
Why don't we do it in the road?--WHYDONTWED--6
Why don't we do it in the road?--WHYDONTWED--7
Why don't we do it in the road?--WHYDONTWED--8
Why don't we do it in the road?--WHYDONTWED--9
Why don't we do it in the road?--WHYDONTWED--10
Why don't we do it in the road?--WHYDONTWED--12
Well, why don't we do it in the road?--WHYDONTWED
--13
Why don't we do it in the road?--WHYDONTWED--14
Why don't we do - do it, do it in the road?--
WHYDONTWED--15
Why don't we do it, yeah, in the road?--WHYDONTWED
--16
Why don't you do it in the road?--WHYDONTWED--18
Ooo - girl you know the reason why.--YERBLUES--5
Wuh - girl you know the reason why.--YERBLUES--9
Wuh - girl you know the reason why.--YERBLUES--16
Wuh - girl you know the reason why.--YERBLUES--23
Wuh girl - you know the reason why.--YERBLUES--30
... Girl you know the reason why.--YERBLUES--33
Why leave me standing here, let me know the way.--
LONGANDWIN--6

WICKED

Well you know that I'm a wicked guy--RUNFORYOUR--9

WIFE

And his clinging wife doesn't understand.--
PAPERBACKW--9
Nothing to do to save his life call his wife in--
GOODMORNIN--2
It's time for tea and meet the wife.--GOODMORNIN
--21
Father snores as his wife gets into her
dressing-gown--SHESLEAVIN--13
A soap impression of his wife which he ate --
HAPPINESSI--7
Last night the wife said, oh boy, when you're
dead --BALLADOFJO--27

WIGHT

In the Isle of Wight --WHENIMSIXT--23

WIGWAM

Wigwam frightened of the dark--HEYBULLDOG--14

WILD

WILD HONEY PIE.--WILDHONEYP--Title
The wild and windy night that the rain washed away
   --LONGANDWIN--4

WILDLY

They slither wildly as they slip away across the
   universe.--ACROSSTHEU--2

WILL

I hope it will be mine --ANYTIMEATA--17
Without her I will be in misery.--MISERY--9
Without her I will be in misery.--MISERY--13
Yes I will I'll get you in the end, oh yeah,
   oh yeah.--ILLGETYOU--8
Yes I will, I'll get you in the end, oh yeah,
   oh yeah.--ILLGETYOU--15
Yes I will, I'll get you in the end, oh yeah,
   oh yeah--ILLGETYOU--25
I'll be here, yes I will --ALLIVEGOTT--13
I'll be here, yes I will --ALLIVEGOTT--24
And hope that my dreams will come true --ALLMYLOVIN
   --9
All my lovin', I will send to you --ALLMYLOVIN--13
All my lovin', I will send to you --ALLMYLOVIN--21
All my lovin', I will send to you.--ALLMYLOVIN--24
Will never die --ANDILOVEHE--18
Will never die --ANDILOVEHE--23
Will make me feel alright.--HARDDAYSNI--7
Will make me feel alright.--HARDDAYSNI--23
Will make me feel alright.--HARDDAYSNI--36
And that she will cry --IFIFELL--19
And that she will cry --IFIFELL--26
This time I will try to show --ILLBEBACK--11
This time I will try to show --ILLBEBACK--20
You say you will love me if I have to go --
   THINGSWESA--1
You'll be thinking of me, somehow I will know --
   THINGSWESA--2
Then I will remember things we said today.--
   THINGSWESA--5
Then we will remember things we said today.--
   THINGSWESA--10
Then we will remember things we said today.--
   THINGSWESA--21
Then we will remember things we said today.--
   THINGSWESA--32
I will never leave her--SHESAWOMAN--11
She will never make me jealous--SHESAWOMAN--13
Oh how long will it take --BABYSINBLA--14
Oh how long will it take --BABYSINBLA--19
I will love her forever--EVERYLITTL--15
For I know love will never die.--EVERYLITTL--16
There's nothing for me here so I will disappear --
   IDONTWANTT--3
There's nothing for me here so I will disappear --
   IDONTWANTT--15
And though I lose a friend in the end you will
   know, oh.--ILLFOLLOWT--6
And though I lose a friend in the end you will
   know, oh.--ILLFOLLOWT--11
For red is the colour that will make me blue--
   YESITIS--16
For red is the colour that will make me blue--
   YESITIS--25
I will prove to you--TELLMEWHAT--2
We will never be apart--TELLMEWHAT--3
Time will pass away--TELLMEWHAT--10
If you leave me I will follow you--YOULIKEMET--15
If you leave me I will follow you--YOULIKEMET--24
Another girl who will love me till the end --
   ANOTHERGIR--10
Through thick and thin she will always be my
   friend.--ANOTHERGIR--11
Another girl who will love me till the end --
   ANOTHERGIR--16
Through thick and thin she will always be my
   friend.--ANOTHERGIR--17
Last night is the night I will remember you by --
   NIGHTBEFOR--9
Last night is the night I will remember you by --
   NIGHTBEFOR--17
And I will take her out tonight--YOUREGONNA--5
And I will treat her kind (I'm gonna treat her
   kind)--YOUREGONNA--6
'cos I will treat her right--YOUREGONNA--11
And I will take her out tonight--YOUREGONNA--27
And I will treat her kind (I'm gonna treat her
   kind)--YOUREGONNA--28

Love will find a way?--YOUVEGOTTO--16
So I will ask you once again.--WECANWORKI--14
Only time will tell if I am right or I am wrong.--
   WECANWORKI--16
So I will ask you once again.--WECANWORKI--23
Only time will tell if I am right or I am wrong.--
   WECANWORKI--25
She will turn to me and start to cry --GIRL--7
Will she still believe it when he's dead?--GIRL--25
And maybe you will get a call from me --IFINEEDEDS
   --11
And maybe you will get a call from me --IFINEEDEDS
   --21
I will say the only words I know that you'll
   understand.--MICHELLE--8
Until I do I'm hoping you will know what I mean.--
   MICHELLE--14
And I will say the only words I know that
   you'll understand --MICHELLE--22
And know that you will wait for me.--WAIT--12
And know that you will wait for me.--WAIT--20
And I will lose my mind--YOUWONTSEE--4
Dear Sir or Madam, will you read my book?--
   PAPERBACKW--2
It took me years to write, will you take a look?--
   PAPERBACKW--3
When your bird is broken will it bring you down?--
   ANDYOURBIR--10
That no-one will hear--ELEANORRIG--12
There will be times when all the things --FORNOONE
   --21
She said will fill your head --FORNOONE--22
I will be there and everywhere --HERETHEREA--20
Let me tell you how it will be --TAXMAN--3
There will be a show tonight on trampoline.--
   BEINGFORTH--2
The Hendersons will all be there--BEINGFORTH--3
In this way Mr. K. will challenge the world.--
   BEINGFORTH--7
The Hendersons will dance and sing--BEINGFORTH--10
Their production will be second to none--BEINGFORTH
   --13
And Mr. H. will demonstrate--BEINGFORTH--17
Where it will go.--FIXINGAHOL--3
Where it will go.--FIXINGAHOL--6
There I will go.--FIXINGAHOL--13
Where it will go, where it will go.--FIXINGAHOL--25
Where it will go, where it will go.--FIXINGAHOL--25
Where it will go.--FIXINGAHOL--28
We hope you will enjoy the show--SGTPEPPERS--9
Will you still be sending me a valentine--
   WHENIMSIXT--3
Will you still need me --WHENIMSIXT--7
Will you still feed me --WHENIMSIXT--8
Will you still need me --WHENIMSIXT--19
Will you still feed me --WHENIMSIXT--20
A - will you still need me --WHENIMSIXT--35
Will you still feed me --WHENIMSIXT--36
And the time will come--WITHINYOUW--31
Soon will be the break of day (day) --BLUEJAYWAY
   --17
The wind is low, the birds will sing --DEARPRUDEN
   --8
The clouds will be a daisy chain --DEARPRUDEN--18
A - will you, won't you want me to make you?--
   HELTERSKEL--11
Will the wind that blew her boat--HONEYPIE--25
I WILL.--IWILL--Title
Will I wait a lonely lifetime?--IWILL--3
If you want me to, I will.--IWILL--4
I will always feel the same.--IWILL--8
Your song will fill the air --IWILL--14
You know I will - I will.--IWILL--18
You know I will - I will.--IWILL--18
You will find the bigger piggies--PIGGIES--8
No-one will be watching us --WHYDONTWED--5
No-one will be watching us --WHYDONTWED--11
No-one will be watching us --WHYDONTWED--17
And I will sing a lullaby.--GOLDENSLUM--6
And I will sing a lullaby.--GOLDENSLUM--10
And I will sing a lullaby.--GOLDENSLUM--16
You're asking me will my love grow?--SOMETHING--11
There will be an answer, let it be.--LETITBE/45--11
There is still a chance that they will see --
   LETITBE/45--13
There will be an answer, let it be.--LETITBE/45--14
Yeah there will be an answer, let it be.--
   LETITBE/45--16
Oh there will be an answer, let it be.--LETITBE/45
   --28
There will be an answer, let it be.--LETITBE/LP--11
There is still a chance that they will see --
   LETITBE/LP--13
There will be an answer, let it be.--LETITBE/LP--14

Yeah there will be an answer, let it be.--
    LETITBE/LP--16
Oh there will be an answer, let it be.--LETITBE/LP
    --28
Oh there will be an answer, let it be.--LETITBE/LP
    --30
Will never disappear, I've seen that road before.
    --LONGANDWIN--2

WILSON
Don't ask me what I want it for (ha ha Mr.
    Wilson)--TAXMAN--18

WIN
I should have known she would win in the end.--
    IMALOSER--6
I can never win --YOUVEGOTTO--12
See the people standing there who disagree and
    never win--FIXINGAHOL--9
Took her out and tried to win her--LOVELYRITA--20

WIND
The wind is low, the birds will sing --DEARPRUDEN
    --8
Will the wind that blew her boat--HONEYPIE--25
Because the wind is high it blows my mind --BECAUSE
    --5
Because the wind is high.--BECAUSE--6
Thoughts meander like a restless wind inside a
    letter-box --ACROSSTHEU--13
Oh now I feel the wind blow--IDIGAPONY--26

WINDING
THE LONG AND WINDING ROAD.--LONGANDWIN--Title
The long and winding road that leads to your door
    --LONGANDWIN--1
And still they lead me back to the long, winding
    road.--LONGANDWIN--9
But still they lead me back to the long, winding
    road --LONGANDWIN--12

WINDOW
But I saw you peep through your window--NOREPLY--5
Keeping an eye on the world going by my window --
    IMONLYSLEE--13
Keeping an eye on the world going by my window --
    IMONLYSLEE--19
Waits at the window--ELEANORRIG--6
Without looking out of my window --INNERLIGHT--3
Without looking out of your window --INNERLIGHT--10
SHE CAME IN THROUGH THE BATHROOM WINDOW.--
    SHECAMEINT--Title
She came in through the bathroom window --
    SHECAMEINT--4

WINDOW-PANE
Like a lizard on a window-pane.--HAPPINESSI--4

WINDY
Julia seashell eyes windy smile calls me --JULIA
    --5
The wild and windy night that the rain washed away
    --LONGANDWIN--4

WINE
Drinking her wine.--NORWEGIANW--13
Birthday greetings, bottle of wine?--WHENIMSIXT--4
But I gotta get a bellyfull of wine.--HERMAJESTY
    --6
Flowing more freely than wine --IMEMINE--20
Flowing more freely than wine --IMEMINE--33

WINGS
Take these broken wings and learn to fly.--
    BLACKBIRD--2
Take these broken wings and learn to fly.--
    BLACKBIRD--14

WINK
Give us a wink and make me think of you.--
    LOVELYRITA--28
I'm so tired, I haven't slept a wink --IMSOTIRED
    --1

WINTER
Little darling, it's been a long, cold lonely
    winter.--HERECOMEST--4

WIPE
Step on the gas and wipe that tear away.--
    YOUNEVERGI--20

WIPING
Father McKenzie wiping the dirt from his hands--
    ELEANORRIG--24

WISDOM
Speaking words of wisdom, let it be.--LETITBE/45
    --3
Speaking words of wisdom, let it be.--LETITBE/45
    --6
Speaking words of wisdom, let it be.--LETITBE/45--8
Whisper words of wisdom, let it be.--LETITBE/45--18
Whisper words of wisdom, let it be.--LETITBE/45--20
Speaking words of wisdom, let it be.--LETITBE/45
    --26
Whisper words of wisdom, let it be.--LETITBE/45--30
Speaking words of wisdom, let it be.--LETITBE/LP
    --3
Speaking words of wisdom, let it be.--LETITBE/LP
    --6
Whisper words of wisdom, let it be.--LETITBE/LP--8
Whisper words of wisdom, let it be.--LETITBE/LP--18
Whisper words of wisdom, let it be.--LETITBE/LP--20
Speaking words of wisdom, let it be.--LETITBE/LP
    --26
Whisper words of wisdom, let it be.--LETITBE/LP--32

WISH
Sometimes I wish I knew you well--IWANTTOTEL--16
The men from the press said, we wish you success
    --BALLADOFJO--39

WISHING
Wishing you weren't so far away --THINGSWESA--4
Wishing to avoid an unpleasant scene --MAXWELLSIL
    --9

WITH
Remember that I'll always be in love with you.--
    PSILOVEYOU--2
Remember that I'll always be in love with you.--
    PSILOVEYOU--11
Remember that I'll always, yeah, be in love
    with you.--PSILOVEYOU--18
I do all the pleasing with you --PLEASEPLEA--16
It's so hard to reason with you, whoa - yeah--
    PLEASEPLEA--17
I'm in love with you - ooo.--DOYOUWANTT--8
I'm in love with you - ooo.--DOYOUWANTT--14
I'm in love with you - ooo,--DOYOUWANTT--22
So how could I dance with another --ISAWHERSTA--5
That before too long I'd fall in love with her.--
    ISAWHERSTA--8
She wouldn't dance with another --ISAWHERSTA--9
And before too long I fell in love with her--
    ISAWHERSTA--15
Now I'll never dance with another --ISAWHERSTA--16
And before too long I fell in love with her.--
    ISAWHERSTA--22
Now I'll never dance with another--ISAWHERSTA--23
With love from me to you.--FROMMETOYO--6
With love from me to you.--FROMMETOYO--10
With love from me to you.--FROMMETOYO--18
With love from me to you.--FROMMETOYO--21
With love from me to you--FROMMETOYO--29
And eternally I'll always be in love with you--
    THANKYOUGI--3
And eternally I'll always be in love with you--
    THANKYOUGI--13
Imagine I'm in love with you--ILLGETYOU--2
I've imagined I'm in love with you--ILLGETYOU--4
Imagine I'm in love with you--ILLGETYOU--19
I've imagined I'm in love with you--ILLGETYOU--21
With a love like that--SHELOVESYO--22
With a love like that--SHELOVESYO--34
With a love like that--SHELOVESYO--36
With a love like that--SHELOVESYO--38
Being here alone tonight with you.--HOLDMETIGH--17
Being here alone tonight with you.--HOLDMETIGH--27
Little child, won't you dance with me?--LITTLECHIL

--2
Baby take a chance with me.--LITTLECHIL--4
Little child, won't you dance with me?--LITTLECHIL
--6
Baby take a chance with me.--LITTLECHIL--8
Little child, won't you dance with me?--LITTLECHIL
--13
Baby take a chance with me (wuh yeah).--LITTLECHIL
--15
Little child, won't you dance with me?--LITTLECHIL
--20
Baby take a chance with me, oh yeah --LITTLECHIL
--22
Baby take a chance with me, oh yeah --LITTLECHIL
--23
Baby take a chance with me, oh yeah --LITTLECHIL
--24
Baby take a chance with me, oh yeah.--LITTLECHIL
--25
I should have known better with a girl like you --
ISHOULDHAV--1
If I fell in love with you --IFIFELL--1
If I fell in love with you.--IFIFELL--28
I'M HAPPY JUST TO DANCE WITH YOU.--IMHAPPYJUS
--Title
I'm so happy when you dance with me.--IMHAPPYJUS
--3
'cos I'm happy just to dance with you.--IMHAPPYJUS
--7
I just wanna dance with you all night --IMHAPPYJUS
--9
'cos I'm happy just to dance with you.--IMHAPPYJUS
--11
Just to dance with you is everything I need (oh)
--IMHAPPYJUS--12
I'm so happy when you dance with me ((oh - oh)).--
IMHAPPYJUS--15
'cos I'm happy just to dance with you.--IMHAPPYJUS
--19
Just to dance with you (oh) is everything I
need (oh) --IMHAPPYJUS--20
I'm so happy when you dance with me ((oh - oh)).--
IMHAPPYJUS--23
I've discovered I'm in love with you (oh - oh).--
IMHAPPYJUS--27
'cos I'm happy just to dance with you (oh - oh).--
IMHAPPYJUS--28
I'm so in love with you.--TELLMEWHY--25
I got no business being here with you this way.--
WHENIGETHO--23
I'm in love with her and I feel fine.--IFEELFINE
--3
I'm in love with her and I feel fine.--IFEELFINE
--6
She's in love with me and I feel fine (ooo).--
IFEELFINE--11
I'm in love with her and I feel fine.--IFEELFINE
--14
She's in love with me and I feel fine --IFEELFINE
--19
She's in love with me and I feel fine.--IFEELFINE
--20
When I'm with her I'm happy--EVERYLITTL--11
With another man in my place.--NOREPLY--16
With another man in my place.--NOREPLY--29
She said that living with me--TICKETTORI--9
She said that living with me--TICKETTORI--36
I could be happy with you by my side--YESITIS--10
I could be happy with you by my side--YESITIS--19
I don't wanna say that I've been unhappy with you
--ANOTHERGIR--12
I don't wanna say that I've been unhappy with you
--ANOTHERGIR--18
Then I guess I'd be with you my friend --IFINEEDS
--5
Then I guess I'd be with you my friend --IFINEEDS
--15
With lovers and friends I still can recall --
INMYLIFE--6
There is no-one compares with you --INMYLIFE--10
Than to be with another man --RUNFORYOUR--2
Catch you with another man --RUNFORYOUR--7
And I was born with a jealous mind --RUNFORYOUR--10
Catch you with another man --RUNFORYOUR--15
Catch you with another man --RUNFORYOUR--23
Than to be with another man --RUNFORYOUR--26
Catch you with another man --RUNFORYOUR--31
'cos I won't be there with you.--THINKFORYO--9
'cos I won't be there with you.--THINKFORYO--18
'cos I won't be there with you.--THINKFORYO--27
'cos I won't be there with you.--THINKFORYO--31
'cos I won't be there with you.--THINKFORYO--33z
But when I saw him with you I could feel my
future fold.--WHATGOESON--7

You didn't even think of me as someone with a name.
--WHATGOESON--23
Though the days are few, they're filled with tears
--YOUWONTSEE--16
Though the days are few they're filled with tears
--YOUWONTSEE--25
Don't pay money just to see yourself with Dr.
Robert.--DRROBERT--14
And was buried along with her name--ELEANORRIG--22
When I'm with you I want to stay there--GOTTOGETYO
--17
Changing my life with a wave of her hand--
HERETHEREA--3
My head is filled with things to say --IWANTTOTEL
--2
They'll fill you in with all the sins, you'll see.
--LOVEYOUTWO--15
On the corner is a banker with a motorcar--
PENNYLANE--5
In Penny Lane there is a fireman with an
hour-glass--PENNYLANE--12
Living is easy with eyes closed--STRAWBERRY--6
Filling me up with your rules.--GETTINGBET--6
To take some tea with me? ((maid))--LOVELYRITA--16
Sitting on a sofa with a sister or two.--LOVELYRITA
--25
LUCY IN THE SKY WITH DIAMONDS.--LUCYINTHES--Title
With tangerine trees and marmalade skies.--
LUCYINTHES--2
A girl with kaleidoscope eyes.--LUCYINTHES--4
Look for the girl with the sun in her eyes--
LUCYINTHES--7
Lucy in the sky with diamonds --LUCYINTHES--9
Lucy in the sky with diamonds --LUCYINTHES--10
Lucy in the sky with diamonds - aah.--LUCYINTHES
--11
Climb in the back with your head in the clouds--
LUCYINTHES--18
Lucy in the sky with diamonds --LUCYINTHES--20
Lucy in the sky with diamonds --LUCYINTHES--21
Lucy in the sky with diamonds - aah.--LUCYINTHES
--22
With plasticine porters with looking-glass ties.--
LUCYINTHES--24
With plasticine porters with looking-glass ties.--
LUCYINTHES--24
The girl with kaleidoscope eyes.--LUCYINTHES--26
Lucy in the sky with diamonds --LUCYINTHES--27
Lucy in the sky with diamonds --LUCYINTHES--28
Lucy in the sky with diamonds - aah.--LUCYINTHES
--29
Lucy in the sky with diamonds --LUCYINTHES--30
Lucy in the sky with diamonds --LUCYINTHES--31
Lucy in the sky with diamonds - aah.--LUCYINTHES
--32
Lucy in the sky with diamonds --LUCYINTHES--33
Lucy in the sky with diamonds (aah - ooo) --
LUCYINTHES--34
Lucy in the sky with diamonds.--LUCYINTHES--35
We'd like to take you home with us--SGTPEPPERS--17
I could stay with you.--WHENIMSIXT--12
WITH A LITTLE HELP FROM MY FRIENDS.--WITHALITTL
--Title
Oh I get by with a little help from my friends --
WITHALITTL--5
Mmm I get high with a little help from my friends
--WITHALITTL--6
Mmm gonna try with a little help from my friends.
--WITHALITTL--7
No I get by with a little help from my friends --
WITHALITTL--12
Mmm get high with a little help from my friends --
WITHALITTL--13
Mmm gonna try with a little help from my friends.
--WITHALITTL--14
Oh I get by with a little help from my friends --
WITHALITTL--23
Mmm get high with a little help from my friends --
WITHALITTL--24
Oh I'm gonna try with a little help from my
friends.--WITHALITTL--25
Oh I get by with a little help from my friends --
WITHALITTL--30
Mmm gonna try with a little help from my friends
--WITHALITTL--31
Oh I get high with a little help from my friends
--WITHALITTL--32
Yes I get by with a little help from my friends --
WITHALITTL--33
With a little help from my friends.--WITHALITTL--34
With our love--WITHINYOUW--12
With our love--WITHINYOUW--13
The man with the foolish grin is keeping
perfectly still--FOOLONTHEH--2

You're waiting for someone to perform with.--
    HEYJUDE--21
But if you want money for people with minds that
    hate --REVOLUTION--18
You ain't gonna make it with anyone anyhow.--
    REVOLUTION--29
He went out tiger hunting with his elephant and
    gun --CONTINUING--7
With a message at the local bird and bee.--
    CRYBABYCRY--23
With voices out of nowhere --CRYBABYCRY--30
She's well acquainted with the touch of the
    velvet hand --HAPPINESSI--3
The man in the crowd with the multicoloured
    mirrors on his hobnail boots --HAPPINESSI--5
Lying with his eyes while his hands are busy
    working overtime --HAPPINESSI--6
Love you with all my heart --IWILL--10
With a couple of kids running in the yard of
    Desmond and Molly Jones.--OBLADIOBLA--18
And in the evening she still sings it with the
    band, yes.--OBLADIOBLA--24
With a couple of kids running in the yard of
    Desmond and Molly Jones.--OBLADIOBLA--30
And in the evening she's a singer with the band,
    yeah.--OBLADIOBLA--35
In their sties with all their backing--PIGGIES--11
With their piggy wives --PIGGIES--18
But if you want money for people with minds that
    hate --REVOLUTONE--27
You ain't gonna make it with anyone anyhow.--
    REVOLUTONE--44
And one day his woman ran off with another guy --
    ROCKYRACCO--3
Rocky had come equipped with a gun--ROCKYRACCO--11
To help with good Rocky's revival - ah.--ROCKYRACCO
    --39
A ginger sling with a pineapple heart --SAVOYTRUFF
    --2
A ginger sling with a pineapple heart --SAVOYTRUFF
    --24
With every mistake we must surely be learning --
    WHILEMYGUI--11
From life to life with me --ITSALLTOOM--13
With your long blonde hair and your eyes of blue
    --ITSALLTOOM--35
With your long blonde hair and your eyes of blue
    --ITSALLTOOM--36
You don't take nothing with you but your soul -
    think!--BALLADOFJO--28
Baby, I'm in love with you --OLDBROWNSH--6
Baby, I'm in love with you --OLDBROWNSH--14
It won't be the same now that I'm with you.--
    OLDBROWNSH--16
Baby, I'm in love with you.--OLDBROWNSH--32
Won't be the same now that I'm with you.--
    OLDBROWNSH--34
It won't be the same now that I'm with you
    (yeah, yeah, yeah)--OLDBROWNSH--36
Late nights all alone with a test-tube, oh oh -
    oh oh.--MAXWELLSIL--2
An octopus's garden with me.--OCTOPUSSGA--6
In an octopus's garden with you --OCTOPUSSGA--24
In an octopus's garden with you --OCTOPUSSGA--25
In an octopus's garden with you.--OCTOPUSSGA--26
You know my number, what's up with you? - ha--
    YOUKNOWMYN--40
You're only fooling round, only fooling round
    with me.--ONEAFTERNI--7

WITHIN
    That you may see the meaning of within--TOMORROWNE
        --5
    WITHIN YOU, WITHOUT YOU.--WITHINYOUW--Title
    Try to realise it's all within yourself--WITHINYOUW
        --16
    And life flows on within you and without you.--
        WITHINYOUW--19
    And life flows on within you and without you.--
        WITHINYOUW--33

WITHOUT
    Without her I will be in misery.--MISERY--9
    Without her I will be in misery.--MISERY--13
    I was lonely without her--EVERYLITTL--5
    I could never really live without you--INEEDYOU--17
    I could never really live without you--INEEDYOU--27
    When Mr. K. performs his tricks - without a
        sound.--BEINGFORTH--16
    Where would I be without you?--LOVELYRITA--27
    WITHIN YOU, WITHOUT YOU.--WITHINYOUW--Title
    And life flows on within you and without you.--

WITHINYOUW--19
And life flows on within you and without you.--
    WITHINYOUW--33
Without going out of my door --INNERLIGHT--1
Without looking out of my window --INNERLIGHT--3
Without going out of your door --INNERLIGHT--8
Without looking out of your window --INNERLIGHT--10
Arrive without travelling.--INNERLIGHT--15
See all without looking.--INNERLIGHT--16
Do all without doing.--INNERLIGHT--17
Friday night arrives without a suitcase --
    LADYMADONN--5

WIVES
    With their piggy wives --PIGGIES--18

WOKE
    Woke up, fell out of bed--DAYINTHELI--18

WOMAN
    SHE'S A WOMAN.--SHESAWOMAN--Title
    She's a woman who understands--SHESAWOMAN--16
    She's a woman who loves her man--SHESAWOMAN--17
    She's a woman who understands--SHESAWOMAN--26
    She's a woman who loves her man--SHESAWOMAN--27
    She's a woman, she's a woman, she's a woman.--
        SHESAWOMAN--35
    She's a woman, she's a woman, she's a woman.--
        SHESAWOMAN--35
    She's a woman, she's a woman, she's a woman.--
        SHESAWOMAN--35
    Man buys ring, woman throws it away --IMDOWN--8
    I used to be cruel to my woman--GETTINGBET--25
    And one day his woman ran off with another guy --
        ROCKYRACCO--3
    Sweet Loretta Martin thought she was a woman --
        GETBACK/45--16
    Sweet Loretta Martin thought she was a woman--
        GETBACK/LP--22

WON
    'cos I'm the one who won your love--YOUCANTDOT--19
    'cos I'm the one who won your love--YOUCANTDOT--38
    Of all the love I have won or have lost --IMALOSER
        --3
    The English Army had just won the war--DAYINTHELI
        --12

WON'T
    There is nothing I won't do --ANYTIMEATA--15
    I've lost her now for sure, I won't see her no
        more --MISERY--4
    IT WON'T BE LONG.--ITWONTBELO--Title
    It won't be long yeah (yeah) yeah (yeah) yeah
        (yeah)--ITWONTBELO--1
    It won't be long yeah (yeah) yeah (yeah) yeah
        (yeah)--ITWONTBELO--2
    It won't be long yeah (yeah)--ITWONTBELO--3
    It won't be long yeah (yeah) yeah (yeah) yeah
        (yeah)--ITWONTBELO--7
    It won't be long yeah (yeah) yeah (yeah) yeah
        (yeah)--ITWONTBELO--8
    It won't be long yeah (yeah)--ITWONTBELO--9
    It won't be long yeah (yeah) yeah (yeah) yeah
        (yeah)--ITWONTBELO--17
    It won't be long yeah (yeah) yeah (yeah) yeah
        (yeah)--ITWONTBELO--18
    It won't be long yeah (yeah)--ITWONTBELO--19
    Now I know that you won't leave me no more--
        ITWONTBELO--26
    It won't be long yeah (yeah) yeah (yeah) yeah
        (yeah)--ITWONTBELO--27
    It won't be long (yeah) yeah (yeah) yeah
        (yeah)--ITWONTBELO--28
    It won't be long yeah (yeah)--ITWONTBELO--29
    Little child, won't you dance with me?--LITTLECHIL--2
    Little child, won't you dance with me?--LITTLECHIL
        --6
    Little child, won't you dance with me?--LITTLECHIL
        --13
    Little child, won't you dance with me?--LITTLECHIL
        --20
    That boy won't be happy--THISBOY--9
    I'm telling you so that you won't lose all.--
        IMALOSER--18
    Won't you please please help me?--HELP--18
    Won't you please please help me?--HELP--28
    Won't you please please help me?--HELP--38
    Or I won't know where I am.--RUNFORYOUR--4

Or you won't know where I am.--RUNFORYOUR--28
'cos I won't be there with you.--THINKFORYO--9
'cos I won't be there with you.--THINKFORYO--18
'cos I won't be there with you.--THINKFORYO--27
'cos I won't be there with you.--THINKFORYO--31
'cos I won't be there with you.--THINKFORYO--33
And if your heart's strong, hold on, I won't
    delay.--WAIT--6
And if your heart's strong, hold on, I won't
    delay.--WAIT--22
YOU WON'T SEE ME.--YOUWONTSEE--Title
If you won't see me (you won't see me) --YOUWONTSEE
    --5
If you won't see me (you won't see me) --YOUWONTSEE
    --5
You won't see me (you won't see me).--YOUWONTSEE
    --6
You won't see me (you won't see me).--YOUWONTSEE
    --6
I won't want to stay, I don't have much to say --
    YOUWONTSEE--9
And you won't see me (you won't see me) --
    YOUWONTSEE--11
And you won't see me (you won't see me) --
    YOUWONTSEE--11
You won't see me (you won't see me).--YOUWONTSEE
    --12
You won't see me (you won't see me).--YOUWONTSEE
    --12
If you won't see me (you won't see me) --YOUWONTSEE
    --20
If you won't see me (you won't see me) --YOUWONTSEE
    --20
You won't see me (you won't see me)--YOUWONTSEE--21
You won't see me (you won't see me)--YOUWONTSEE--21
If you won't see me (you won't see me) --YOUWONTSEE
    --29
If you won't see me (you won't see me) --YOUWONTSEE
    --29
You won't see me (you won't see me).--YOUWONTSEE
    --30
You won't see me (you won't see me).--YOUWONTSEE
    --30
You won't forget her.--FORNOONE--23
Dear Prudence, won't you come out to play?--
    DEARPRUDEN--1
Dear Prudence, won't you come out to play?--
    DEARPRUDEN--5
Dear Prudence, won't you open up your eyes?--
    DEARPRUDEN--10
Dear Prudence, won't you let me see you smile?--
    DEARPRUDEN--20
Dear Prudence, won't you come out to play?--
    DEARPRUDEN--21
Dear Prudence, won't you come out to play?--
    DEARPRUDEN--25
A - will you, won't you want me to make you?--
    HELTERSKEL--11
So won't you please come home.--HONEYPIE--9
So won't you please come home.--HONEYPIE--31
It won't be the same now I'm telling you.--
    OLDBROWNSH--8
It won't be the same now that I'm with you.--
    OLDBROWNSH--16
Won't be the same now that I'm with you.--
    OLDBROWNSH--34
It won't be the same now that I'm with you
    (yeah, yeah, yeah).--OLDBROWNSH--36
And if you leave me I won't be late again --
    IVEGOTAFEE--8

WONDER
    I wonder what went wrong I've waited far too long
        --IDONTWANTT--7
    I wonder what went wrong I've waited far too long
        --IDONTWANTT--24
    And wonder why they don't get in my door.--
        FIXINGAHOL--10
    Wonder how you manage to make ends meet.--
        LADYMADONN--2
    Wonder how you manage to make ends meet.--
        LADYMADONN--19
    I wonder where you are tonight --DONTPASSME--14
    I wonder should I get up and fix myself a drink --
        IMSOTIRED--3
    I wonder should I call you --IMSOTIRED--7

WONDERFUL
    It's wonderful to be here--SGTPEPPERS--14

WONDERING

I see no use in wondering why --NOTASECOND--2
I'm wondering why --NOTASECOND--8
I see no use in wondering why --NOTASECOND--13
I'm wondering why --NOTASECOND--19
Wondering what you're gonna do --WHATYOURED--10
Wondering what you're gonna do --WHATYOURED--17
Wondering really how come nobody told me--IVEGOTAFEE
    --12

WONDERS
    You say you've seen seven wonders --ANDYOURBIR--4
    Wonders how you manage to feed the rest.--
        LADYMADONN--10
    But now she sucks her thumb and wonders --
        SHECAMEINT--6

WONKY
    He got wonky finger--COMETOGETH--17

WOOD
    NORWEGIAN WOOD (THIS BIRD HAS FLOWN).--NORWEGIANW
        --Title
    Norwegian wood?--NORWEGIANW--6
    Norwegian wood?--NORWEGIANW--26
    ((That was Can You Dig It? by Georgie
        Wood))--DIGIT--11

WOOF
    Woof!--HEYBULLDOG--21
    Hey bulldog (woof), hey bulldog, hey bulldog,
        hey bulldog.--HEYBULLDOG--22
    Hey man what's that noise? (woof)--EHYBULLDOG
        --23
    I say woof--HEYBULLDOG--25
    Woof - aah! ha ha ha--HEYBULLDOG--27

WOOS
    Something in the way she woos me--SOMETHING
        --3

WORD
    I've got a word or two--THINKFORYO--1
    THE WORD.--THEWORD--Title
    Say the word and you'll be free --THEWORD--1
    Say the word and be like me --THEWORD--2
    Say the word I'm thinking of --THEWORD--3
    Have you heard the word is love?--THEWORD--4
    It's the word love.--THEWORD--6
    But now I've got it the word is good.--THEWORD
        --8
    Spread the word and you'll be free--THEWORD--9
    Spread the word and be like me --THEWORD--10
    Spread the word I'm thinking of --THEWORD--11
    Have you heard the word is love?--THEWORD--12
    It's the word love.--THEWORD--14
    Say the word and you'll be free --THEWORD--17
    Say the word and be like me --THEWORD--18
    Say the word I'm thinking of --THEWORD--19
    Have you heard the word is love?--THEWORD
        --20
    It's the word love.--THEWORD--22
    Give the word a chance to say --THEWORD--25
    That the word is just the way --THEWORD--26
    It's the word I'm thinking of --THEWORD--27
    And the only word is love.--THEWORD--28
    It's the word love.--THEWORD--30
    Say the word love --THEWORD--31
    Say the word love --THEWORD--32
    Say the word love --THEWORD--33
    Say the word love.--THEWORD--34
    You gave me the word--GETTINGBET--13
    And if you say the word--WHENIMSIXT--11

WORDS
    Treasure ((treasure)) these few words ((words))
        --PSILOVEYOU--3
    Treasure ((treasure)) these few words ((words))
        --PSILOVEYOU--3
    Treasure ((treasure)) these few words ((words))
        --PSILOVEYOU--12
    Treasure ((treasure)) these few words ((words))
        --PSILOVEYOU--12
    Last night I said these words to my girl --
        PLEASEPLEA--1
    Last night I said these words to my girl --
        PLEASEPLEA--19
    Say the words you long to hear --DOYOUWANTT--7
    Say the words you long to hear --DOYOUWANTT--13

WORDS

Say the words you long to hear --DOYOUWANTT--21
The words you long to hear --ALLIVEGOTT--9
Your voice is soothing but the words aren't clear.
   --IMLOOKINGT--6
These are words that go together well, my
   Michelle.--MICHELLE--2
I will say the only words I know that you'll
   understand.--MICHELLE--8
And I will say the only words I know that
   you'll understand --MICHELLE--22
Father McKenzie writing the words of a sermon--
   ELEANORRIG--11
You find that all her words of kindness linger on
   --FORNOONE--2
All those words they seem to slip away.--IWANTTOTEL
   --4
What words I say or time of day it is --ONLYANORTH
   --8
But as the words are leaving his lips, a noise
   comes from behind --MAXWELLSIL--22
Speaking words of wisdom, let it be.--LETITBE/45
   --3
Speaking words of wisdom, let it be.--LETITBE/45
   --6
Whisper words of wisdom, let it be.--LETITBE/45--8
Whisper words of wisdom, let it be.--LETITBE/45--18
Whisper words of wisdom, let it be.--LETITBE/45--20
Speaking words of wisdom, let it be.--LETITBE/45
   --26
Whisper words of wisdom, let it be.--LETITBE/45--30
Words are flowing out like endless rain into a
   paper cup --ACROSSTHEU--1
Speaking words of wisdom, let it be.--LETITBE/LP
   --3
Speaking words of wisdom, let it be.--LETITBE/LP
   --6
Whisper words of wisdom, let it be.--LETITBE/LP--8
Whisper words of wisdom, let it be.--LETITBE/LP--18
Whisper words of wisdom, let it be.--LETITBE/LP--20
Speaking words of wisdom, let it be.--LETITBE/LP
   --26
Whisper words of wisdom, let it be.--LETITBE/LP--32

WORE

For red is the colour that my baby wore--YESITIS
   --3
Scarlet were the clothes she wore--YESITIS--5

WORK

You know I work all day --HARDDAYSNI--8
WE CAN WORK IT OUT.--WECANWORKI--Title
We can work it out, we can work it out.--WECANWORKI
   --5
We can work it out, we can work it out.--WECANWORKI
   --5
We can work it out and get it straight or say
   good night.--WECANWORKI--9
We can work it out, we can work it out.--WECANWORKI
   --10
We can work it out, we can work it out.--WECANWORKI
   --10
We can work it out, we can work it out.--WECANWORKI
   --19
We can work it out, we can work it out.--WECANWORKI
   --19
We can work it out, we can work it out.--WECANWORKI
   --28
We can work it out, we can work it out.--WECANWORKI
   --28
Go in to work don't want to go feeling low down--
   GOODMORNIN--7

WORKED

She told me she worked in the morning--NORWEGIANW
   --17
She worked at fifteen clubs a day--SHECAMEINT--13

WORKING

And I been working like a dog --HARDDAYSNI--2
And I been working like a dog --HARDDAYSNI--18
And I been working like a dog --HARDDAYSNI--31
Working for peanuts is all very fine --DRIVEMYCAR
   --11
His son is working for the Daily Mail --PAPERBACKW
   --10
Look at him working--ELEANORRIG--14
And you're working for no-one but me (Taxman).--
   TAXMAN--26
Lying with his eyes while his hands are busy
   working overtime --HAPPINESSI--6

She was a working girl--HONEYPIE--1

WORKS

My friend works for the National Health, Dr.
   Robert --DRROBERT--13
But it all works out--STRAWBERRY--9
His sister Pam works in a shop--MEANMRMUST--8

WORLD

The world is treating me bad, misery.--MISERY--1
The world is treating me bad, misery.--MISERY--3
I could tell the world a thing or two about our love
   --THANKYOUGI--5
I'm gonna break their hearts all round the world
   --ILLCRYINST--16
'cos I'm gonna break their hearts all round the
   world --ILLCRYINST--25
In this world there's nothing I would rather do --
   IMHAPPYJUS--10
In this world there's nothing I would rather do --
   IMHAPPYJUS--18
In this world there's nothing I would rather do --
   IMHAPPYJUS--26
She's so glad she's telling all the world --
   IFEELFINE--8
She's so glad she's telling all the world --
   IFEELFINE--16
Nobody in all the world can do what she can do --
   ANOTHERGIR--7
And I want all the world to see we've met --
   IVEJUSTSEE--5
And I want all the world to see we've met --
   IVEJUSTSEE--28
Nowhere Man the world is at your command.--
   NOWHEREMAN--9
Nowhere Man the world is at your command.--
   NOWHEREMAN--21
Keeping an eye on the world going by my window --
   IMONLYSLEE--13
Keeping an eye on the world going by my window --
   IMONLYSLEE--19
In this way Mr. K. will challenge the world.--
   BEINGFORTH--7
We could save the world--WITHINYOUW--14
Who gain the world and lose their soul--WITHINYOUW
   --24
And the eyes in his head see the world spinning
   round.--FOOLONTHEH--7
And the eyes in his head see the world spinning
   round.--FOOLONTHEH--14
And the eyes in his head see the world spinning
   round.--FOOLONTHEH--19
And the eyes in his head see the world spinning
   round.--FOOLONTHEH--26
Don't carry the world upon your shoulder.--HEYJUDE
   --11
By making his world a little colder.--HEYJUDE--13
We all wanna change the world.--REVOLUTION--4
We all want to change the world.--REVOLUTION--7
We all wanna change the world.--REVOLUTONE--10
We all want to change the world.--REVOLUTONE--10
One sunny day the world was waiting for the lover
   ((sexy Sadie)--SEXYSADIE--9
The world was waiting just for you?--SEXYSADIE--13
The world was waiting just for you?--SEXYSADIE--14
I look at the world and I notice it's turning --
   WHILEMYGUI--9
All the world is birthday cake --ITSALLTOOM--18
Because the world is round it turns me on --BECAUSE
   --2
Because the world is round.--BECAUSE--3
She's a kind of a girl that makes the News Of
   The World.--POLYTHENEP--8
Living in the world agree --LETITBE/45--10
Nothing's gonna change my world --ACROSSTHEU--7
Nothing's gonna change my world --ACROSSTHEU--8
Nothing's gonna change my world --ACROSSTHEU--9
Nothing's gonna change my world.--ACROSSTHEU--10
Nothing's gonna change my world --ACROSSTHEU--16
Nothing's gonna change my world --ACROSSTHEU--17
Nothing's gonna change my world --ACROSSTHEU--18
Nothing's gonna change my world.--ACROSSTHEU--19
Nothing's gonna change my world --ACROSSTHEU--26
Nothing's gonna change my world --ACROSSTHEU--27
Nothing's gonna change my world --ACROSSTHEU--28
Nothing's gonna change my world.--ACROSSTHEU--29
All these years I've been wandering round the
   world --IVEGOTAFEE--11
Living in the world agree --LETITBE/LP--10

WORM

The worm he licks my bone --YERBLUES--18

WORRY

Nowhere Man don't worry --NOWHEREMAN--13
Silly people run around they worry me--FIXINGAHOL
--17
(Does it worry you to be alone?)--WITHALITTL--9

WORRYING

Not worrying what they or you say --OLDBROWNSH--19

WORSE

A little better all the time (it can't get no
worse)--GETTINGBET--8
A little better all the time (it can't get no
worse)--GETTINGBET--17
A little better all the time (it can't get no
worse)--GETTINGBET--30
Life is getting worse --PIGGIES--4

WORTH

And it's worth it just to hear you say --HARDDAYSNI
--10
And you know what it's worth.--YERBLUES--13

WOULD

I know, little girl, only a fool would doubt
our love--THANKYOUGI--6
That she would leave me on my own--DONTBOTHER--10
Oh, and this boy would be happy--THISBOY--7
Would always feel the same--THISBOY--12
That I would love everything that you do --
ISHOULDHAV--2
Would you promise to be true --IFIFELL--2
That you would love me more than her.--IFIFELL--9
And I would be sad --IFIFELL--15
That I would love to love you --IFIFELL--18
And I would be sad --IFIFELL--22
That I would love to love you --IFIFELL--25
In this world there's nothing I would rather do --
IMHAPPYJUS--10
In this world there's nothing I would rather do --
IMHAPPYJUS--18
In this world there's nothing I would rather do --
IMHAPPYJUS--26
I thought that you would realise --ILLBEBACK--13
That you would want me too --ILLBEBACK--15
I would hate my disappointment to show --IDONTWANTT
--2
I would hate my disappointment to show --IDONTWANTT
--14
I should have known she would win in the end.--
IMALOSER--6
Would it be too much to ask of you --WHATYOURED--3
She would never be free--TICKETTORI--11
She would never be free--TICKETTORI--38
I would remember all the things we planned--YESITIS
--7
How was I to know you would upset me?--INEEDYOU--7
Was she told when she was young that pain would
lead to pleasure?--GIRL--22
I didn't know what I would find there--GOTTOGETYO
--2
I didn't know what I would find there--GOTTOGETYO
--26
Told her I would really like to see her again.--
LOVELYRITA--22
Where would I be without you?--LOVELYRITA--27
Leaving the note that she hoped would say more.--
SHESLEAVIN--3
Why would she treat us so thoughtlessly?--
SHESLEAVIN--18
Would you lock the door?--WHENIMSIXT--6
What would you think if I sang outta tune --
WITHALITTL--1
Would you stand up and walk out on me?--WITHALITTL
--2
(Would you believe in a love at first sight?)--
WITHALITTL--19
I would like you to dance (birthday) --BIRTHDAY--11
I would like you to dance (birthday) --BIRTHDAY--13
I would like you to dance (birthday) --BIRTHDAY--16
I would like you to dance (birthday) (wuh)--
BIRTHDAY--18
If looks could kill it would have been us instead
of him.--CONTINUING--29
You said that you would be late --DONTPASSME--27
But I know what you would do.--IMSOTIRED--8
Just a smile would lighten everything--SEXYSADIE

--21
We would be warm below the storm--OCTOPUSSGA--9
We would sing and dance around--OCTOPUSSGA--13
We would shout and swim about--OCTOPUSSGA--17
We would be so happy you and me--OCTOPUSSGA--21

WOULDN'T

She wouldn't dance with another --ISAWHERSTA--9
This boy wouldn't mind the pain--THISBOY--11
I wouldn't let you leave me 'cos it's true--
YOULIKEMET--19
I wouldn't let you leave me 'cos it's true--
YOULIKEMET--28
She wouldn't say--YESTERDAY--10
She wouldn't say--YESTERDAY--18
I wouldn't mind if I knew what I was missing.--
YOUWONTSEE--14
((No I wouldn't, no I wouldn't))--YOUWONTSEE--15
((No I wouldn't, no I wouldn't))--YOUWONTSEE--15
I wouldn't mind if I knew what I was missing.--
YOUWONTSEE--23
((No I wouldn't, no I wouldn't))--YOUWONTSEE--24
((No I wouldn't, no I wouldn't))--YOUWONTSEE--24

WOW

Wow (ow) - oh--IWANNABEYO--25

WRITE

As I write this letter, send my love to you --
PSILOVEYOU--1
As I write this letter, send my love to you --
PSILOVEYOU--10
As I write this letter (oh) send my love to you --
PSILOVEYOU--16
I'll write home every day --ALLMYLOVIN--5
I'll write home every day --ALLMYLOVIN--11
I'll write home every day --ALLMYLOVIN--19
It took me years to write, will you take a look?--
PAPERBACKW--3

WRITER

PAPERBACK WRITER.--PAPERBACKW--Title
Paperback writer ((paperback writer)) paperback
writer.--PAPERBACKW--1
Paperback writer ((paperback writer)) paperback
writer.--PAPERBACKW--1
Paperback writer ((paperback writer)) paperback
writer.--PAPERBACKW--1
So I want to be a paperback writer --PAPERBACKW--6
Paperback writer.--PAPERBACKW--7
But he wants to be a paperback writer--PAPERBACKW
--12
Paperback writer.--PAPERBACKW--13
Paperback writer ((paperback writer)) paperback
writer.--PAPERBACKW--14
Paperback writer ((paperback writer)) paperback
writer.--PAPERBACKW--14
Paperback writer ((paperback writer)) paperback
writer.--PAPERBACKW--14
I'll be writing more in a week or two. ((writer))
--PAPERBACKW--16
I can change it round, ((writer))--PAPERBACKW--18
And I want to be a paperback writer --PAPERBACKW
--19
Paperback writer.--PAPERBACKW--20
It could make a million for you overnight.
((writer))--PAPERBACKW--22
But I need a break, ((writer))--PAPERBACKW--24
And I want to be a paperback writer --PAPERBACKW
--25
Paperback writer.--PAPERBACKW--26
Paperback writer ((paperback writer)) paperback
writer.--PAPERBACKW--27
Paperback writer ((paperback writer)) paperback
writer.--PAPERBACKW--27
Paperback writer ((paperback writer)) paperback
writer.--PAPERBACKW--27
(Paperback writer) paperback writer.--PAPERBACKW
--29
(Paperback writer) paperback writer.--PAPERBACKW
--29
(Paperback writer) paperback writer.--PAPERBACKW
--30
(Paperback writer) paperback writer.--PAPERBACKW
--30
(Paperback writer) paperback writer.--PAPERBACKW
--31
(Paperback writer) paperback writer.--PAPERBACKW
--31
(Paperback writer) paperback writer.--PAPERBACKW

WRITER

--32
(Paperback writer) paperback writer.--PAPERBACKW
--32

WRITING
I'll be writing more in a week or two. ((writer))
--PAPERBACKW--16
Father McKenzie writing the words of a sermon--
ELEANORRIG--11
So he waits behind, writing fifty times I must
not be so oh - oh oh.--MAXWELLSIL--11
Writing letters on my wall.--TWOOFUS--11

WRONG
I wonder what went wrong I've waited far too long
--IDONTWANTT--7
I wonder what went wrong I've waited far too long
--IDONTWANTT--24
I'd admit that I was wrong--YOULIKEMET--18
I'd admit that I was wrong--YOULIKEMET--27
I said something wrong--YESTERDAY--11
I said something wrong--YESTERDAY--19
You can get it wrong and still you think that
it's alright.--WECANWORKI--7
Only time will tell if I am right or I am wrong.--
WECANWORKI--16
Only time will tell if I am right or I am wrong.--
WECANWORKI--25
I said no, no, no you're wrong.--SHESAIDSHE--8
I said no, no, no you're wrong.--SHESAIDSHE--14
But it's all wrong--STRAWBERRY--29
And it really doesn't matter if I'm wrong I'm
right--FIXINGAHOL--7
And it really doesn't matter if I'm wrong I'm
right--FIXINGAHOL--15
She (what did we do that was wrong?)--SHESLEAVIN
--28
Is having (we didn't know it was wrong)--SHESLEAVIN
--29
You may think the chords are going wrong --
ONLYANORTH--2
But right is only half of what's wrong --OLDBROWNSH
--2
Railman said, you got the wrong location --
ONEAFTERNI--12
Then I find I've got the number wrong.--ONEAFTERNI
--14
Railman said, you got the wrong location --
ONEAFTERNI--22
Then I find I got the number wrong - well ((well)).
--ONEAFTERNI--24

WROTE
But they're not, we just wrote it like that.--
ONLYANORTH--3

WUH
Oh (wuh!) we danced through the night --ISAWHERSTA
--20
Ow! - wuh!--IWANNABEYO--42
I wanna be your man (wuh - wuh)--IWANNABEYO--45
I wanna be your man (wuh - wuh)--IWANNABEYO--45
Baby take a chance with me (wuh yeah).--LITTLECHIL
--15
Wuh!--NOTASECOND--11
I call your name, I call your name, (wuh) I
call your name.--ICALLYOURN--18
Ooo (wuh - wuh, wuh - wuh, wuh).--IFEELFINE--22
Ooo (wuh - wuh, wuh - wuh, wuh).--IFEELFINE--22
Ooo (wuh - wuh, wuh - wuh, wuh).--IFEELFINE--22
Ooo (wuh - wuh, wuh - wuh, wuh).--IFEELFINE--22
Ooo (wuh - wuh, wuh - wuh, wuh).--IFEELFINE--22
(Wuh)--SHESAWOMAN--25
Hey! - wuh!--IDONTWANTT--17
Wuh!--IMDOWN--25
Ow - ow - ow - wuh!--IMDOWN--27
What goes on in your heart? (wuh)--WHATGOESON--1
(Wuh)--WHATGOESON--20
Da da da - da - da - da - wuh - oh--LOVELYRITA--34
Wuh!--SGTPEPPREP--2
Wuh!--SGTPEPPREP--18
All you need is love, (wuh) all you need is
love (hey) --ALLYOUN/YS--17
Love is all you need (wuh) (love is all you
need)--ALLYOUN/YS--32
Wuh - yeah --BACKINTHEU--20
(Wuh oh)--BIRTHDAY--15
I would like you to dance (birthday) (wuh)--
BIRTHDAY--18
Everybody's got something to hide 'cept for me

and my monkey - wuh.--EVRBDYMONK--7
Come on is make it easy - wuh.--EVRBDYMONK--14
Take it easy, take it easy - wuh --EVRBDYMONK--15
Everybody's got something to hide 'cept for me
and my monkey (yeah - wuh).--EVRBDYMONK--16
So come on (wuh), come on (wuh) --EVRBDYMONK--19
So come on (wuh), come on (wuh) --EVRBDYMONK--19
Make it easy (wuh), make it easy (wuh) --EVRBDYMONK
--24
Make it easy (wuh), make it easy (wuh) --EVRBDYMONK
--24
(Hey - yeah, wuh, yeah - wuh!)--EVRBDYMONK--26
(Hey - yeah, wuh, yeah - wuh!)--EVRBDYMONK--26
Wuh!--HELTERSKEL--10
Cocoanut fudge really blows down those blues
(wuh) --SAVOYTRUFF--8
Coffee dessert - yes you know it's good news
(wuh) --SAVOYTRUFF--25
Oh - wuh... ((eee))--WHILEMYGUI--26
I love you, yeah, Honey Pie, wuh!--WILDHONEYP--4
Wuh - girl you know the reason why.--YERBLUES--9
Wuh - girl you know the reason why.--YERBLUES--16
Wuh - girl you know the reason why.--YERBLUES--23
Wuh girl - you know the reason why.--YERBLUES--30
All together now! (wuh, yeah, wahoo!)--ALLTOGETHE
--45
That's it man (wuh)--HEYBULLDOG--29
(Wuh!)--ITSALLTOOM--20
Too much, too much, too much (wuh!), too
much, too much, too much --ITSALLTOOM--40
Get back Loretta (wuh - wuh).--GETBACK/45--24
Get back Loretta (wuh - wuh).--GETBACK/45--24
Get back Loretta (wuh - wuh).--GETBACK/LP--30
Get back Loretta (wuh - wuh).--GETBACK/LP--30

WUH-OH
Wuh-oh, baby, you're a rich (oh) man --BABYYOUREA
--40

WUHOO
Love is all you need (wuhoo)--ALLYOUN/YS--47
Love is all you need (wuhoo)--ALLYOUN/YS--48

YA
All ya gotta do is call --ANYTIMEATA--20
All ya gotta do is call --ANYTIMEATA--26
Ya just gotta call on me, yeah --ALLIVEGOTT--15
Ya just gotta call on me.--ALLIVEGOTT--16
Ya just gotta call on me, yeah --ALLIVEGOTT--26
Ya just gotta call on me --ALLIVEGOTT--27
(Ooh) ya just gotta call on me --ALLIVEGOTT--28

YAHOO
Love is all you need (yahoo) (eee - hi)--
ALLYOUN/YS--38
I only have grandchildren (yahoo ha ha ha ha ha
ha ha)--HEYBULLDOG--32
You know my name, ba ba ba ba ba ba ba ba
((yahoo)) --YOUKNOWMYN--13

YARD
With a couple of kids running in the yard of
Desmond and Molly Jones.--OBLADIOBLA--18
With a couple of kids running in the yard of
Desmond and Molly Jones.--OBLADIOBLA--30

YAWNING
Lift my head, I'm still yawning.--IMONLYSLEE--2
Lift my head, I'm still yawning.--IMONLYSLEE--22

YEAH
Remember that I'll always, yeah, be in love
with you.--PSILOVEYOU--18
Please please me, whoa - yeah--PLEASEPLEA--5
Please please me, whoa - yeah--PLEASEPLEA--11
It's so hard to reason with you, whoa - yeah--
PLEASEPLEA--17
Please please me, whoa - yeah--PLEASEPLEA--24
Please me, whoa - yeah--PLEASEPLEA--25
Please me, whoa - yeah--PLEASEPLEA--27
Yeah, well since I saw her standing there.--
ISAWHERSTA--26
Oh yeah, oh yeah, oh yeah, oh yeah.--ILLGETYOU--1
Oh yeah, oh yeah, oh yeah, oh yeah.--ILLGETYOU--1
Oh yeah, oh yeah, oh yeah, oh yeah.--ILLGETYOU--1
Oh yeah, oh yeah, oh yeah, oh yeah.--ILLGETYOU--1
Yes I will I'll get you in the end, oh yeah,

oh yeah.--ILLGETYOU--8
Yes I will I'll get you in the end, oh yeah,
    oh yeah.--ILLGETYOU--8
Yes I will, I'll get you in the end, oh yeah,
    oh yeah.--ILLGETYOU--15
Yes I will, I'll get you in the end, oh yeah,
    oh yeah.--ILLGETYOU--15
So you might as well resign yourself to me, oh
    yeah.--ILLGETYOU--18
Yes I will, I'll get you in the end, oh yeah,
    oh yeah--ILLGETYOU--25
Yes I will, I'll get you in the end, oh yeah,
    oh yeah--ILLGETYOU--25
Oh yeah, oh yeah, whoa - yeah.--ILLGETYOU--26
Oh yeah, oh yeah, whoa - yeah.--ILLGETYOU--26
Oh yeah, oh yeah, whoa - yeah.--ILLGETYOU--26
She loves you yeah, yeah, yeah--SHELOVESYO--1
She loves you yeah, yeah, yeah--SHELOVESYO--1
She loves you yeah, yeah, yeah--SHELOVESYO--1
She loves you yeah, yeah, yeah--SHELOVESYO--2
She loves you yeah, yeah, yeah--SHELOVESYO--2
She loves you yeah, yeah, yeah, yeah.--SHELOVESYO
    --3
She loves you yeah, yeah, yeah, yeah.--SHELOVESYO
    --3
She loves you yeah, yeah, yeah, yeah.--SHELOVESYO
    --3
She loves you yeah, yeah, yeah, yeah.--SHELOVESYO
    --3
Yeah, she loves you--SHELOVESYO--10
Yeah, she loves you--SHELOVESYO--18
She loves you, yeah, yeah, yeah--SHELOVESYO--20
She loves you, yeah, yeah, yeah--SHELOVESYO--20
She loves you, yeah, yeah, yeah--SHELOVESYO--21
She loves you, yeah, yeah, yeah--SHELOVESYO--21
She loves you, yeah, yeah, yeah--SHELOVESYO--21
Yeah, she loves you--SHELOVESYO--30
She loves you, yeah, yeah, yeah--SHELOVESYO--32
She loves you, yeah, yeah, yeah--SHELOVESYO--32
She loves you, yeah, yeah, yeah--SHELOVESYO--32
She loves you, yeah, yeah, yeah--SHELOVESYO--33
She loves you, yeah, yeah, yeah--SHELOVESYO--33
She loves you, yeah, yeah, yeah--SHELOVESYO--33
Yeah, yeah, yeah--SHELOVESYO--40
Yeah, yeah, yeah--SHELOVESYO--40
Yeah, yeah, yeah--SHELOVESYO--40
Yeah, yeah, yeah, yeah.--SHELOVESYO--41
Yeah, yeah, yeah, yeah.--SHELOVESYO--41
Yeah, yeah, yeah, yeah.--SHELOVESYO--41
Yeah, yeah, yeah, yeah.--SHELOVESYO--41
Whenever I want you around, yeah --ALLIVEGOTT--1
Yeah, that's all I gotta do.--ALLIVEGOTT--5
And when I, I wanna kiss you, yeah --ALLIVEGOTT--6
Ya just gotta call on me, yeah --ALLIVEGOTT--15
And when I, I wanna kiss you, yeah --ALLIVEGOTT--17
Yeah, that's all I gotta do.--ALLIVEGOTT--21
Ya just gotta call on me, yeah --ALLIVEGOTT--26
It won't be long yeah (yeah) yeah (yeah) yeah
    (yeah)--ITWONTBELO--1
It won't be long yeah (yeah) yeah (yeah) yeah
    (yeah)--ITWONTBELO--1
It won't be long yeah (yeah) yeah (yeah) yeah
    (yeah)--ITWONTBELO--1
It won't be long yeah (yeah) yeah (yeah) yeah
    (yeah)--ITWONTBELO--1
It won't be long yeah (yeah) yeah (yeah) yeah
    (yeah)--ITWONTBELO--1
It won't be long yeah (yeah) yeah (yeah) yeah
    (yeah)--ITWONTBELO--1
It won't be long yeah (yeah) yeah (yeah) yeah
    (yeah)--ITWONTBELO--2
It won't be long yeah (yeah) yeah (yeah) yeah
    (yeah)--ITWONTBELO--2
It won't be long yeah (yeah) yeah (yeah) yeah
    (yeah)--ITWONTBELO--2
It won't be long yeah (yeah) yeah (yeah) yeah
    (yeah)--ITWONTBELO--2
It won't be long yeah (yeah) yeah (yeah) yeah
    (yeah)--ITWONTBELO--2
It won't be long yeah (yeah)--ITWONTBELO--3
It won't be long yeah (yeah)--ITWONTBELO--3
It won't be long yeah (yeah) yeah (yeah) yeah
    (yeah)--ITWONTBELO--7
It won't be long yeah (yeah) yeah (yeah) yeah
    (yeah)--ITWONTBELO--7
It won't be long yeah (yeah) yeah (yeah) yeah
    (yeah)--ITWONTBELO--7
It won't be long yeah (yeah) yeah (yeah) yeah

(yeah)--ITWONTBELO--7
It won't be long yeah (yeah) yeah (yeah) yeah
    (yeah)--ITWONTBELO--7
It won't be long yeah (yeah) yeah (yeah) yeah
    (yeah)--ITWONTBELO--8
It won't be long yeah (yeah) yeah (yeah) yeah
    (yeah)--ITWONTBELO--8
It won't be long yeah (yeah) yeah (yeah) yeah
    (yeah)--ITWONTBELO--8
It won't be long yeah (yeah) yeah (yeah) yeah
    (yeah)--ITWONTBELO--8
It won't be long yeah (yeah) yeah (yeah) yeah
    (yeah)--ITWONTBELO--8
It won't be long yeah (yeah)--ITWONTBELO--9
It won't be long yeah (yeah)--ITWONTBELO--9
It won't be long yeah (yeah) yeah (yeah) yeah
    (yeah)--ITWONTBELO--17
It won't be long yeah (yeah) yeah (yeah) yeah
    (yeah)--ITWONTBELO--17
It won't be long yeah (yeah) yeah (yeah) yeah
    (yeah)--ITWONTBELO--17
It won't be long yeah (yeah) yeah (yeah) yeah
    (yeah)--ITWONTBELO--17
It won't be long yeah (yeah) yeah (yeah) yeah
    (yeah)--ITWONTBELO--17
It won't be long yeah (yeah) yeah (yeah) yeah
    (yeah)--ITWONTBELO--18
It won't be long yeah (yeah) yeah (yeah) yeah
    (yeah)--ITWONTBELO--18
It won't be long yeah (yeah) yeah (yeah) yeah
    (yeah)--ITWONTBELO--18
It won't be long yeah (yeah) yeah (yeah) yeah
    (yeah)--ITWONTBELO--18
It won't be long yeah (yeah) yeah (yeah) yeah
    (yeah)--ITWONTBELO--18
It won't be long yeah (yeah)--ITWONTBELO--19
It won't be long yeah (yeah)--ITWONTBELO--19
It won't be long yeah (yeah) yeah (yeah) yeah
    (yeah)--ITWONTBELO--27
It won't be long yeah (yeah) yeah (yeah) yeah
    (yeah)--ITWONTBELO--27
It won't be long yeah (yeah) yeah (yeah) yeah
    (yeah)--ITWONTBELO--27
It won't be long yeah (yeah) yeah (yeah) yeah
    (yeah)--ITWONTBELO--27
It won't be long yeah (yeah) yeah (yeah) yeah
    (yeah)--ITWONTBELO--27
It won't be long (yeah) yeah (yeah) yeah
    (yeah)--ITWONTBELO--28
It won't be long (yeah) yeah (yeah) yeah
    (yeah)--ITWONTBELO--28
It won't be long (yeah) yeah (yeah) yeah
    (yeah)--ITWONTBELO--28
It won't be long (yeah) yeah (yeah) yeah
    (yeah)--ITWONTBELO--28
It won't be long (yeah) yeah (yeah) yeah
    (yeah)--ITWONTBELO--28
It won't be long yeah (yeah)--ITWONTBELO--29
It won't be long yeah (yeah)--ITWONTBELO--29
Baby take a chance with me (wuh yeah).--LITTLECHIL
    --15
Yeah come on, come on, come on.--LITTLECHIL--18
Baby take a chance with me, oh yeah --LITTLECHIL
    --22
Baby take a chance with me, oh yeah --LITTLECHIL
    --23
Baby take a chance with me, oh yeah --LITTLECHIL
    --24
Baby take a chance with me, oh yeah.--LITTLECHIL
    --25
I've cried for you, yeah.--NOTASECOND--14
Oh yeah, I'll tell you something--IWANTTOHOL--1
Yeah, you've got that something--IWANTTOHOL--20
Yeah, you've got that something--IWANTTOHOL--33
When I'm home feeling you holding me tight,
    tight, yeah.--HARDDAYSNI--16
When I'm home feeling you holding me tight,
    tight, yeah.--HARDDAYSNI--29
When I get home, yeah.--WHENIGETHO--26
She does for me, yeah--EVERYLITTL--8
She does for me, yeah--EVERYLITTL--18
She does for me, yeah--EVERYLITTL--22
Yeah, tomorrow may rain so I'll follow the sun.--
    ILLFOLLOWT--9
I think it's today, yeah--TICKETTORI--3
Was bringing her down, yeah--TICKETTORI--10

I think it's today, yeah--TICKETTORI--24
The girl that's driving me mad is going away,
    yeah.--TICKETTORI--25
Was bringing her down, yeah--TICKETTORI--37
Yes it is, yes it is, oh yes it is, yeah.--YESITIS
    --13
Yes it is, yes it is, oh yes it is, yeah.--YESITIS
    --22
Oh yeah, yeah, yeah, yeah, yeah--IMDOWN--33
Oh yeah, yeah, yeah, yeah, yeah--IMDOWN--33
Oh yeah, yeah, yeah, yeah, yeah--IMDOWN--33
Oh yeah, yeah, yeah, yeah, yeah--IMDOWN--33
Oh yeah, yeah, yeah, yeah, yeah--IMDOWN--33
Baby, I'm down, yeah--IMDOWN--38
Oh baby, I'm down, yeah--IMDOWN--39
Yeah, aah - ooo I'm down (down on the ground)--
    IMDOWN--45
Treat me like you did the night before (yeah).--
    NIGHTBEFOR--16
I'll make a point of taking her away from you
    (watch what you do), yeah--YOUREGONNA--17
I'll make a point of taking her away from you
    (watch what you do), yeah--YOUREGONNA--24
One way ticket, yeah --DAYTRIPPER--6
One way ticket, yeah --DAYTRIPPER--14
Sunday driver, yeah --DAYTRIPPER--23
Day tripper, yeah --DAYTRIPPER--26
Day tripper, yeah --DAYTRIPPER--27
Day tripper, yeah --DAYTRIPPER--29
Beep beep mmm beep beep yeah.--DRIVEMYCAR--17
Beep beep mmm beep beep yeah --DRIVEMYCAR--30
Beep beep mmm beep beep yeah --DRIVEMYCAR--31
Beep beep mmm beep beep yeah --DRIVEMYCAR--32
Beep beep mmm beep beep yeah --DRIVEMYCAR--33
Beep beep mmm beep beep yeah --DRIVEMYCAR--34
Yeah, oh baby you've changed.--IMLOOKINGT--21
Yeah, I'm looking through you.--IMLOOKINGT--23
(Yeah) ooo (come on) la la la--YOUWONTSEE--31
(Oh yeah) ooo - la la la--YOUWONTSEE--32
Yeah, I'm the Taxman.--TAXMAN--6
Yeah, I'm the Taxman.--TAXMAN--10
Yeah, I'm the Taxman.--TAXMAN--17
Yeah, I'm the Taxman.--TAXMAN--21
Yeah, I'm the Taxman.--TAXMAN--25
One, two (ah yeah), three, four.--SGTPEPPREP--1
Love is all you need (oh yeah)--ALLYOUN/YS--42
Loves you yeah, yeah, yeah ((love is all, love
    is all))--ALLYOUN/YS--44
Loves you yeah, yeah, yeah ((love is all, love
    is all))--ALLYOUN/YS--44
Loves you yeah, yeah, yeah ((love is all, love
    is all))--ALLYOUN/YS--44
She loves you yeah, yeah, yeah ((love is all,
    love is all))--ALLYOUN/YS--45
She loves you yeah, yeah, yeah ((love is all,
    love is all))--ALLYOUN/YS--45
She loves you yeah, yeah, yeah ((love is all,
    love is all))--ALLYOUN/YS--45
Your mother should know - yeah ((ooo)).--YOURMOTHER
    --25
Your mother should know - yeah.--YOURMOTHER--27
Your mother should know - yeah.--YOURMOTHER--29
Nah nah nah nah nah, nah nah nah nah, yeah.--
    HEYJUDE--25
Oh yeah - nah nah nah, nah - nah - nah - nah--
    HEYJUDE--31
((yeah yeah yeah yeah yeah yeah)) --HEYJUDE--32
((yeah yeah yeah yeah yeah yeah)) --HEYJUDE--32
((yeah yeah yeah yeah yeah yeah)) --HEYJUDE--32
((yeah yeah yeah yeah yeah yeah)) --HEYJUDE--32
((yeah yeah yeah yeah yeah yeah)) --HEYJUDE--32
((yeah yeah yeah yeah yeah yeah)) --HEYJUDE--32
Nah nah nah, nah - nah - nah - nah (yeah, yeah,
    yeah) --HEYJUDE--44
Nah nah nah, nah - nah - nah - nah (yeah, yeah,
    yeah) --HEYJUDE--44
Nah nah nah, nah - nah - nah - nah (yeah, yeah,
    yeah) --HEYJUDE--44
(Jude Jude Jude Jude Jude Jude - yeah yeah
    yeah yeah yeah)--HEYJUDE--54
(Jude Jude Jude Jude Jude Jude - yeah yeah
    yeah yeah yeah)--HEYJUDE--54
(Jude Jude Jude Jude Jude Jude - yeah yeah
    yeah yeah yeah)--HEYJUDE--54
(Jude Jude Jude Jude Jude Jude - yeah yeah
    yeah yeah yeah)--HEYJUDE--54
(Jude Jude Jude Jude Jude Jude - yeah yeah
    yeah yeah yeah)--HEYJUDE--54
Nah - nah - nah - nah, hey Jude (yeah).--HEYJUDE
    --61
((Yeah - yeah yeah yeah yeah yeah yeah - yeah
    yeah ---HEYJUDE--66
((Yeah - yeah yeah yeah yeah yeah yeah - yeah
    yeah ---HEYJUDE--66

((Yeah - yeah yeah yeah yeah yeah yeah - yeah
    yeah ---HEYJUDE--66
((Yeah - yeah yeah yeah yeah yeah yeah - yeah
    yeah ---HEYJUDE--66
((Yeah - yeah yeah yeah yeah yeah yeah - yeah
    yeah ---HEYJUDE--66
((Yeah - yeah yeah yeah yeah yeah yeah - yeah
    yeah ---HEYJUDE--66
((Yeah - yeah yeah yeah yeah yeah yeah - yeah
    yeah ---HEYJUDE--66
((Yeah - yeah yeah yeah yeah yeah yeah - yeah
    yeah ---HEYJUDE--66
yeah yeah yeah - ha ha ha ha ha))--HEYJUDE--67
yeah yeah yeah - ha ha ha ha ha))--HEYJUDE--67
yeah yeah yeah - ha ha ha ha ha))--HEYJUDE--67
Back in the USSR (yeah).--BACKINTHEU--7
Wuh - yeah --BACKINTHEU--20
Ooo yeah --BACKINTHEU--21
Ooo yeah --BACKINTHEU--22
Yeah.--BACKINTHEU--23
Yeah - back in the USSR.--BACKINTHEU--42
Well, it's my birthday too - yeah.--BIRTHDAY--2
Dance! (dance!) (yeah)--BIRTHDAY--14
Well, it's my birthday too - yeah.--BIRTHDAY--21
Everybody's got something to hide 'cept for me
    and my monkey (yeah - wuh).--EVRBDYMONK--16
(Hey - yeah, wuh, yeah - wuh!)--EVRBDYMONK--26
(Hey - yeah, wuh, yeah - wuh!)--EVRBDYMONK--26
Standing on the cast-iron shore - yeah--GLASSONION
    --12
Lady Madonna trying to make ends meet - yeah--
    GLASSONION--13
Oh yeah, oh yeah, oh yeah! (yeah)--GLASSONION--15
Oh yeah, oh yeah, oh yeah! (yeah)--GLASSONION--15
Oh yeah, oh yeah, oh yeah! (yeah)--GLASSONION--15
Oh yeah, oh yeah, oh yeah! (yeah)--GLASSONION--15
Trying to make a dove-tail joint - yeah--GLASSONION
    --22
Do do do do do, oh yeah.--HAPPINESSI--2
When I hold you in my arms ((oh, yeah)) --
    HAPPINESSI--22
And I feel my finger on your trigger ((oh,
    yeah)) --HAPPINESSI--23
I know nobody can do me no harm ((oh, yeah)) --
    HAPPINESSI--24
Is a warm gun, momma ((is a warm gun, yeah)).--
    HAPPINESSI--32
Till I get to the bottom and I see you again -
    yeah, yeah, yeah.--HELTERSKEL--3
Till I get to the bottom and I see you again -
    yeah, yeah, yeah.--HELTERSKEL--3
Till I get to the bottom and I see you again -
    yeah, yeah, yeah.--HELTERSKEL--3
Helter-skelter, helter-skelter, helter-skelter
    - yeah.--HELTERSKEL--9
And I get to the bottom and I see you again -
    yeah, yeah, yeah.--HELTERSKEL--20
And I get to the bottom and I see you again -
    yeah, yeah, yeah.--HELTERSKEL--20
And I get to the bottom and I see you again -
    yeah, yeah, yeah.--HELTERSKEL--20
Yeah!--HONEYPIE--20
I light the light - yeah, ooo - ha.--HONEYPIE--21
Do do do do do - yeah yeah yeah.--MOTHERNATU--12
Do do do do do - yeah yeah yeah.--MOTHERNATU--12
Do do do do do - yeah yeah yeah.--MOTHERNATU--12
La-la how the life goes on - yeah.--OBLADIOBLA--16
(Ah - yeah)--OBLADIOBLA--22
And in the evening she's a singer with the band,
    yeah.--OBLADIOBLA--35
La-la how the life goes on - yeah --OBLADIOBLA--37
Oh yeah yeah --ROCKYRACCO--40
Oh yeah yeah --ROCKYRACCO--40
Yeah, yeah, yeah, yeah, yeah, yeah, yeah,
    yeah, yeah ((eee))--WHILEMYGUI--25
Yeah, yeah, yeah, yeah, yeah, yeah, yeah
    yeah, yeah ((eee))--WHILEMYGUI--25
Yeah, yeah, yeah, yeah, yeah, yeah, yeah,
    yeah, yeah ((eee))--WHILEMYGUI--25
Yeah, yeah, yeah, yeah, yeah, yeah, yeah,
    yeah, yeah ((eee))--WHILEMYGUI--25
Yeah, yeah, yeah, yeah, yeah, yeah, yeah,
    yeah, yeah ((eee))--WHILEMYGUI--25
Yeah, yeah, yeah, yeah, yeah, yeah, yeah,yeah,
    yeah, yeah ((eee))--WHILEMYGUI--25
Yeah, yeah, yeah, yeah, yeah, yeah, yeah,
    yeah, yeah ((eee))--WHILEMYGUI--25
Yeah, yeah, yeah, yeah, yeah, yeah, yeah,
    yeah, yeah ((eee))--WHILEMYGUI--25
Yeah, yeah, yeah, yeah, yeah, yeah, yeah,
    yeah, yeah ((eee))--WHILEMYGUI--25
Why don't we do it, yeah, in the road?--WHYDONTWED

--16
I love you, yeah, Honey Pie, wuh!--WILDHONEYP--4
Wanna die, yeah wanna die --YERBLUES--28
All together now! (wuh, yeah, wahoo!)--ALLTOGETHE
   --45
Big man (yeah?) walking in the park--HEYBULLDOG--13
Eee - (yeah) aah --DONTLETMED--29
Oh get back, yeah get back --GETBACK/45--26
Yeah get back, get back --GETBACK/45--28
Oh get back, get back, yeah --GETBACK/45--38
Oh get back, get back yeah, yeah --GETBACK/45--38
Get back - oh yeah.--GETBACK/45--39
It won't be the same now that I'm with you
   (yeah, yeah, yeah).--OLDBROWNSH--36
It won't be the same now that I'm with you
   (yeah, yeah, yeah).--OLDBROWNSH--36
It won't be the same now that I'm with you
   (yeah, yeah, yeah).--OLDBROWNSH--36
Come together, yeah--COMETOGETH--47
Come together, yeah--COMETOGETH--48
Come together, yeah--COMETOGETH--49
Come together, yeah--COMETOGETH--50
Come together, yeah--COMETOGETH--51
Come together, yeah--COMETOGETH--52
Come together, yeah--COMETOGETH--53
Come together, yeah--COMETOGETH--55
Come together, yeah--COMETOGETH--56
Oh yeah, alright --THEEND--1
Someday I'm gonna make her mine - oh yeah --
   HERMAJESTY--8
Yeah!--IWANTYOUSH--40
Yes, you should see Polythene Pam - yeah,
   yeah, yeah.--POLYTHENEP--5
Yes, you should see Polythene Pam - yeah,
   yeah, yeah.--POLYTHENEP--5
Yes, you should see Polythene Pam - yeah,
   yeah, yeah.--POLYTHENEP--5
Yes, you could say she was attractively built -
   yeah, yeah, yeah.--POLYTHENEP--9
Yes, you could say she was attractively built -
   yeah, yeah, yeah.--POLYTHENEP--9
Yes, you could say she was attractively built -
   yeah, yeah, yeah.--POLYTHENEP--9
(Yeah)--POLYTHENEP--10
Oh yeah.--SHECAMEINT--24
Yeah there will be an answer, let it be.--
   LETITBE/45--16
Let it be, let it be, let it be, yeah let it
   be.--LETITBE/45--19
Yeah let it be, let it be, let it be, yeah let
   it be.--LETITBE/45--27
Yeah let it be, let it be, let it be, yeah let
   it be.--LETITBE/45--27
Let it be, let it be, let it be, yeah let it be.--
   LETITBE/45--29
That's right (yeah)...--YOUKNOWMYN--42
Yeah ((Rosetta)).--GETBACK/LP--4
Oh get back, yeah, get back --GETBACK/LP--32
Yeah, get back, get back --GETBACK/LP--34
Yeah OK.--IDIGAPONY--1
Yeah you can syndicate any boat you rode/rowed
   --IDIGAPONY--31
Oh yeah, oh yeah (that's right).--IVEGOTAFEE--2
Oh yeah, oh yeah (that's right).--IVEGOTAFEE--2
Yes, yeah, I've got a feeling, yeah.--IVEGOTAFEE
   --5
Yes, yeah, I've got a feeling, yeah.--IVEGOTAFEE
   --5
Oh yeah, (yeah) oh yeah --IVEGOTAFEE--7
Oh yeah, (yeah) oh yeah --IVEGOTAFEE--7
Oh yeah, (yeah) oh yeah --IVEGOTAFEE--7
Oh no, oh no, oh no, yeah, yeah!--IVEGOTAFEE--9
Oh no, oh no, oh no, yeah, yeah!--IVEGOTAFEE--9
I've got a feeling, yeah, I've got a feeling.--
   IVEGOTAFEE--10
Oh yeah, oh yeah ((oh yeah)) --IVEGOTAFEE--15
Oh yeah, oh yeah ((oh yeah)) --IVEGOTAFEE--15
Oh yeah, oh yeah ((oh yeah)) --IVEGOTAFEE--15
Oh yeah, oh yeah ((oh yeah)), oh yeah - yeah,
   yeah!--IVEGOTAFEE--17
Oh yeah, oh yeah ((oh yeah)), oh yeah - yeah,
   yeah!--IVEGOTAFEE--17
Oh yeah, oh yeah ((oh yeah)), oh yeah - yeah,
   yeah!--IVEGOTAFEE--17
Oh yeah, oh yeah ((oh yeah)), oh yeah - yeah,
   yeah!--IVEGOTAFEE--17
Oh yeah, oh yeah ((oh yeah)), oh yeah - yeah,
   yeah!--IVEGOTAFEE--17
Oh yeah, oh yeah ((oh yeah)), oh yeah - yeah,
   yeah!--IVEGOTAFEE--17
I've got a feeling yeah - (yeah).--IVEGOTAFEE--18
I've got a feeling yeah - (yeah).--IVEGOTAFEE--18
Oh yeah (oh yeah), oh yeah, oh yeah.--IVEGOTAFEE
   --23

Oh yeah (oh yeah), oh yeah, oh yeah.--IVEGOTAFEE
   --23
Oh yeah (oh yeah), oh yeah, oh yeah.--IVEGOTAFEE
   --23
Oh yeah (oh yeah), oh yeah, oh yeah.--IVEGOTAFEE
   --23
(Yeah) everybody had a good year --IVEGOTAFEE--24
Everybody pulled their socks up (yeah) --IVEGOTAFEE
   --26
Everybody put the fool down, oh yeah - (yeah).--
   IVEGOTAFEE--27
Everybody put the fool down, oh yeah - (yeah).--
   IVEGOTAFEE--27
Everybody had a hard time ((a feeling deep
   inside, oh yeah)) --IVEGOTAFEE--29
Everybody had a wet dream (oh yeah) --IVEGOTAFEE
   --30
Everybody put their foot down, oh yeah (yeah).--
   IVEGOTAFEE--35
Everybody put their foot down, oh yeah (yeah).--
   IVEGOTAFEE--35
I've got a feeling ((oh yeah)) --IVEGOTAFEE--36
I've got a feeling (oh yeah) --IVEGOTAFEE--37
I've got a feeling, yeah, yeah, yeah, yeah.--
   IVEGOTAFEE--38
I've got a feeling, yeah, yeah, yeah, yeah.--
   IVEGOTAFEE--38
I've got a feeling, yeah, yeah, yeah, yeah.--
   IVEGOTAFEE--38
I've got a feeling, yeah, yeah, yeah, yeah.--
   IVEGOTAFEE--38
Yeah there will be an answer, let it be.--
   LETITBE/LP--16
Let it be, let it be, let it be, yeah let it be --
   LETITBE/LP--19
Yeah let it be, let it be, let it be, yeah let
   it be --LETITBE/LP--27
Yeah let it be, let it be, let it be, yeah let
   it be --LETITBE/LP--27
Let it be, let it be, let it be, yeah let it be --
   LETITBE/LP--29
Let it be, let it be, oh let it be, yeah let
   it be --LETITBE/LP--31
Yeah, yeah, yeah, yeah.--LONGANDWIN--15
Yeah, yeah, yeah, yeah.--LONGANDWIN--15
Yeah, yeah, yeah, yeah.--LONGANDWIN--15
Yeah, yeah, yeah, yeah.--LONGANDWIN--15
I begged her not to go and I begged her on my
   bended knee, (oh yeah)--ONEAFTERNI--6
Said she's travelling on the one after
   nine-0-nine. (yeah)--ONEAFTERNI--19

YEAR
Here, making each day of the year--HERETHEREA--2
Everybody had a hard year --IVEGOTAFEE--19
(Yeah) everybody had a good year --IVEGOTAFEE--24
Ooo - hu, everybody had a good year ((I've got
   a feeling)) --IVEGOTAFEE--28
Everybody had a good year ((I've got a feeling))
   --IVEGOTAFEE--32

YEARS
And since I lost you it feels like years.--
   YOUWONTSEE--17
And since I lost you it feels like years.--
   YOUWONTSEE--26
It took me years to write, will you take a look?--
   PAPERBACKW--3
A love that should have lasted years.--FORNOONE--9
A love that should have lasted years.--FORNOONE--16
A love that should have lasted years.--FORNOONE--26
It was twenty years ago today--SGTPEPPERS--1
The act you've known for all these years--
   SGTPEPPERS--6
For so many years. (('bye, 'bye))--SHESLEAVIN--12
For so many years. (('bye, 'bye))--SHESLEAVIN--24
For so many years. (('bye, 'bye))--SHESLEAVIN--32
Many years from now --WHENIMSIXT--2
In a couple of years they have built a home sweet
   home --OBLADIOBLA--17
In a couple of years they have built a home sweet
   home--OBLADIOBLA--29
Some kind of innocence is measured out in years--
   HEYBULLDOG--7
Little darling, it feels like years since it's
   been here.--HERECOMEST--5
Little darling, it feels like years since it's
   been here.--HERECOMEST--10
Little darling, it seems like years since it's
   been clear.--HERECOMEST--19
All these years I've been wandering round the
   world --IVEGOTAFEE--11

YELLOW
```
    YELLOW SUBMARINE.--YELLOWSUBM--Title
    In our yellow submarine.--YELLOWSUBM--8
    We all live in a yellow submarine.--YELLOWSUBM--9
    Yellow submarine, yellow submarine.--YELLOWSUBM--10
    Yellow submarine, yellow submarine.--YELLOWSUBM--10
    We all live in a yellow submarine --YELLOWSUBM--11
    Yellow submarine, yellow submarine.--YELLOWSUBM--12
    Yellow submarine, yellow submarine.--YELLOWSUBM--12
    We all live in a yellow submarine --YELLOWSUBM--16
    Yellow submarine, yellow submarine.--YELLOWSUBM--17
    Yellow submarine, yellow submarine.--YELLOWSUBM--17
    We all live in a yellow submarine --YELLOWSUBM--18
    Yellow submarine, yellow submarine.--YELLOWSUBM--19
    Yellow submarine, yellow submarine.--YELLOWSUBM--19
    In our yellow (in our yellow) submarine
        (submarine - ah ha!)--YELLOWSUBM--28
    In our yellow (in our yellow) submarine
        (submarine - ah ha!)--YELLOWSUBM--28
    We all live in a yellow submarine --YELLOWSUBM--29
    A yellow submarine, a yellow submarine.--YELLOWSUBM
        --30
    A yellow submarine, a yellow submarine.--YELLOWSUBM
        --30
    We all live in a yellow submarine --YELLOWSUBM--31
    A yellow submarine, yellow submarine.--YELLOWSUBM
        --32
    A yellow submarine, yellow submarine.--YELLOWSUBM
        --32
    We all live in a yellow submarine --YELLOWSUBM--33
    Yellow submarine, yellow submarine.--YELLOWSUBM--34
    Yellow submarine, yellow submarine.--YELLOWSUBM--34
    We all live in a yellow submarine --YELLOWSUBM--35
    Yellow submarine, yellow submarine.--YELLOWSUBM--36
    Yellow submarine, yellow submarine.--YELLOWSUBM--36
    Cellophane flowers of yellow and green--LUCYINTHES
        --5
    Yellow matter custard, dripping from a dead
        dog's eye--IAMTHEWALR--12
    Pink, brown, yellow, orange and blue --ALLTOGETHE
        --19
    Yellow lorry slow, nowhere to go.--YOUNEVERGI--12
```

YER
```
    YER BLUES.--YERBLUES--Title
```

YES
```
    Yes, love me do --LOVEMEDO--23
    Yes, love me do.--LOVEMEDO--25
    Yes I will I'll get you in the end, oh yeah,
        oh yeah.--ILLGETYOU--8
    Yes I will, I'll get you in the end, oh yeah,
        oh yeah.--ILLGETYOU--15
    Yes I will, I'll get you in the end, oh yeah,
        oh yeah--ILLGETYOU--25
    I'll be here, yes I will --ALLIVEGOTT--13
    I'll be here, yes I will --ALLIVEGOTT--24
    I'll be good like I know I should (yes,
        you're coming on home)--ITWONTBELO--13
    I'll be good like I know I should (yes,
        you're coming on home)--ITWONTBELO--23
    Yes, I'm gonna break 'em in two --ILLCRYINST--17
    Yes, I'm gonna break 'em in two --ILLCRYINST--26
    Yes I'm the one who wants you--ILLBEBACK--7
    Yes I know I'm a lucky guy.--EVERYLITTL--3
    Yes I know that she loves me now.--EVERYLITTL--13
    YES IT IS.--YESITIS--Title
    And what's more, it's true, yes it is.--YESITIS--4
    Yes it is, it's true, yes it is.--YESITIS--9
    Yes it is, it's true, yes it is.--YESITIS--9
    Yes it is, yes it is, oh yes it is, yeah.--YESITIS
        --13
    Yes it is, yes it is, oh yes it is, yeah.--YESITIS
        --13
    Yes it is, yes it is, oh yes it is, yeah.--YESITIS
        --13
    Yes it is, it's true, yes it is.--YESITIS--18
    Yes it is, it's true, yes it is.--YESITIS--18
    Yes it is, yes it is, oh yes it is, yeah.--YESITIS
        --22
    Yes it is, yes it is, oh yes it is, yeah.--YESITIS
        --22
    Yes it is, yes it is, oh yes it is, yeah.--YESITIS
        --22
    Yes it is, it's true--YESITIS--27
    Yes it is, it's true.--YESITIS--28
    Oh yes, I'm down (I'm really down)--IMDOWN--29
    Oh yes, you told me--INEEDYOU--11
    Yes, it's so hard loving you, loving you - ooo.--
        ITSONLYLOV--15
    Falling, yes I am falling--IVEJUSTSEE--12
    Falling, yes I am falling--IVEJUSTSEE--19
```

```
    Falling, yes I am falling--IVEJUSTSEE--22
    Falling, yes I am falling--IVEJUSTSEE--30
    Falling, yes I am falling--IVEJUSTSEE--32
    (Oh) falling, yes I am falling--IVEJUSTSEE--34
    Treat me like you did the night before (yes).--
        NIGHTBEFOR--14
    You're gonna lose that girl (yes, yes, you're
        gonna lose that girl)--YOUREGONNA--1
    You're gonna lose that girl (yes, yes, you're
        gonna lose that girl)--YOUREGONNA--1
    You're gonna lose that girl (yes, yes, you're
        gonna lose that girl)--YOUREGONNA--2
    You're gonna lose that girl (yes, yes, you're
        gonna lose that girl)--YOUREGONNA--2
    You're gonna lose that girl (yes, yes, you're
        gonna lose that girl)--YOUREGONNA--7
    You're gonna lose that girl (yes, yes, you're
        gonna lose that girl)--YOUREGONNA--7
    You're gonna lose that girl (yes, yes, you're
        gonna lose that girl)--YOUREGONNA--8
    You're gonna lose that girl (yes, yes, you're
        gonna lose that girl)--YOUREGONNA--8
    You're gonna lose that girl (yes, yes, you're
        gonna lose that girl)--YOUREGONNA--13
    You're gonna lose that girl (yes, yes, you're
        gonna lose that girl)--YOUREGONNA--13
    You're gonna lose that girl (yes, yes, you're
        gonna lose that girl)--YOUREGONNA--14
    You're gonna lose that girl (yes, yes, you're
        gonna lose that girl)--YOUREGONNA--14
    You're gonna lose (yes, yes, you're gonna lose
        that girl)--YOUREGONNA--15
    You're gonna lose (yes, yes, you're gonna lose
        that girl)--YOUREGONNA--15
    You're gonna lose that girl (yes, yes, you're
        gonna lose that girl)--YOUREGONNA--20
    You're gonna lose that girl (yes, yes, you're
        gonna lose that girl)--YOUREGONNA--20
    You're gonna lose that girl (yes, yes, you're
        gonna lose that girl)--YOUREGONNA--21
    You're gonna lose that girl (yes, yes, you're
        gonna lose that girl)--YOUREGONNA--21
    You're gonna lose (yes, yes, you're gonna lose
        that girl)--YOUREGONNA--22
    You're gonna lose (yes, yes, you're gonna lose
        that girl)--YOUREGONNA--22
    You're gonna lose that girl (yes, yes, you're
        gonna lose that girl)--YOUREGONNA--29
    You're gonna lose that girl (yes, yes, you're
        gonna lose that girl)--YOUREGONNA--29
    You're gonna lose that girl (yes, yes, you're
        gonna lose that girl)--YOUREGONNA--30
    You're gonna lose that girl (yes, yes, you're
        gonna lose that girl)--YOUREGONNA--30
    You're gonna lose (yes, yes, you're gonna lose
        that girl).--YOUREGONNA--31
    You're gonna lose (yes, yes, you're gonna lose
        that girl).--YOUREGONNA--31
    Yes I'm gonna be a star.--DRIVEMYCAR--6
    Yes I'm gonna be a star.--DRIVEMYCAR--14
    Yes I'm gonna be a star.--DRIVEMYCAR--19
    Yes I'm gonna be star.--DRIVEMYCAR--27
    Yes it seems so long, girl, since you've been gone
        --YOUWONTSEE--18
    Yes it seems so long, girl, since you've been gone
        --YOUWONTSEE--27
    I think I know, I mean, er, yes--STRAWBERRY--28
    Yes I admit it's getting better (better)--
        GETTINGBET--31
    Yes I'm certain that it happens all the time.--
        WITHALITTL--20
    Yes I get by with a little help from my friends --
        WITHALITTL--33
    You say yes, I say no --HELLOGOODB--1
    You say yes, I say no--HELLOGOODB--22
    ((I say yes but I may mean no))--HELLOGOODB--23
    Yes, we're going to a party, party --BIRTHDAY--8
    Yes, we're going to a party, party --BIRTHDAY--9
    Yes, we're going to a party, party.--BIRTHDAY--10
    Happiness ((happiness)) is a warm gun, yes it is--
        HAPPINESSI--27
    Happiness is a warm, yes it is - gun--HAPPINESSI
        --29
    Yes she is, yes she is.--HELTERSKEL--29
    Yes she is, yes she is.--HELTERSKEL--29
    And in the evening she still sings it with the
        band, yes.--OBLADIOBLA--24
    Oh yes--REVOLUTONE--2
    Coffee dessert - yes you know it's good news --
        SAVOYTRUFF--3
    Coffee dessert - yes you know it's good news
        (wuh) --SAVOYTRUFF--25
    Yes, you'll have to have them all pulled out--
        SAVOYTRUFF--28
```

Yes I'm lonely - wanna die --YERBLUES--2
Yes I'm lonely - wanna die --YERBLUES--3
Yes I'm lonely - wanna die --YERBLUES--31
Yes I'm lonely - wanna die --YERBLUES--32
Ooo she does, yes she does --DONTLETMED--6
Ooo she do me, yes she does.--DONTLETMED--8
Yes, you should see Polythene Pam - yeah,
    yeah, yeah.--POLYTHENEP--5
Yes, you could say she was attractively built -
    yeah, yeah, yeah.--POLYTHENEP--9
Yes it did, nah nah nah nah nah nah nah - nah--
    YOUNEVERGI--23
Yes, you know, ((you know my name)) --YOUKNOWMYN--32
Yes you can celebrate anything you want.--IDIGAPONY
    --8
Yes you can penetrate any place you go--IDIGAPONY
    --11
Yes you can radiate everything you are.--IDIGAPONY
    --18
Yes you can imitate everyone you know--IDIGAPONY
    --21
Yes you can indicate anything you see.--IDIGAPONY
    --28
Yes, yeah, I've got a feeling, yeah.--IVEGOTAFEE
    --5

YESTERDAY
    Well I saw her yesterday--SHELOVESYO--5
    YESTERDAY.--YESTERDAY--Title
    Yesterday --YESTERDAY--1
    Oh I believe in yesterday.--YESTERDAY--4
    Oh yesterday came suddenly.--YESTERDAY--8
    Now I long for yesterday.--YESTERDAY--12
    Yesterday --YESTERDAY--13
    Oh I believe in yesterday.--YESTERDAY--16
    Now I long for yesterday.--YESTERDAY--20
    Yesterday --YESTERDAY--21
    Oh I believe in yesterday.--YESTERDAY--24
    That weren't important yesterday--FIXINGAHOL--20
    (Love is all you need) Yesterday (love is all
        you need)--ALLYOUN/YS--40

YET
    And yet you don't believe her --FORNOONE--11
    Sexy Sadie you'll get yours yet--SEXYSADIE--16
    Sexy Sadie - oh you'll get yours yet--SEXYSADIE--19

YOKO
    THE BALLAD OF JOHN AND YOKO.--BALLADOFJO--Title

YOU
    You know I love you.--LOVEMEDO--2
    You know I love you.--LOVEMEDO--2
    You know I love you.--LOVEMEDO--7
    You know I love you.--LOVEMEDO--7
    Someone to love, someone like you.--LOVEMEDO--12
    You know I love you.--LOVEMEDO--14
    You know I love you.--LOVEMEDO--14
    You know I love you.--LOVEMEDO--19
    You know I love you.--LOVEMEDO--19
    PS I LOVE YOU.--PSILOVEYOU--Title
    As I write this letter, send my love to you --
        PSILOVEYOU--1
    Remember that I'll always be in love with you.--
        PSILOVEYOU--2
    PS I love you, you, you, you.--PSILOVEYOU--6
    PS I love you, you, you, you.--PSILOVEYOU--6
    PS I love you, you, you, you.--PSILOVEYOU--6
    PS I love you, you, you, you.--PSILOVEYOU--6
    I'll ((I'll)) be coming home ((home)) again
        to you love ((you love)) --PSILOVEYOU--7
    I'll ((I'll)) be coming home ((home)) again
        to you love ((you love)) --PSILOVEYOU--7
    PS I love you, you, you, you.--PSILOVEYOU--9
    PS I love you, you, you, you.--PSILOVEYOU--9
    PS I love you, you, you, you.--PSILOVEYOU--9
    PS I love you, you, you, you.--PSILOVEYOU--9
    As I write this letter, send my love to you --
        PSILOVEYOU--10
    Remember that I'll always be in love with you.--
        PSILOVEYOU--11
    PS I love you, you, you, you.--PSILOVEYOU--15
    PS I love you, you, you, you.--PSILOVEYOU--15
    PS I love you, you, you, you.--PSILOVEYOU--15
    PS I love you, you, you, you.--PSILOVEYOU--15
    As I write this letter (oh) send my love to you --
        PSILOVEYOU--16
    You know I want you to --PSILOVEYOU--17
    You know I want you to --PSILOVEYOU--17
    Remember that I'll always, yeah, be in love

with you.--PSILOVEYOU--18
I'll be coming home again to you love --PSILOVEYOU
    --19
PS I love you, you, you, you --PSILOVEYOU--21
PS I love you, you, you, you --PSILOVEYOU--21
PS I love you, you, you, you --PSILOVEYOU--21
PS I love you, you, you, you --PSILOVEYOU--21
You, you, you --PSILOVEYOU--22
You, you, you --PSILOVEYOU--22
You, you, you --PSILOVEYOU--22
I love you.--PSILOVEYOU--23
All you gotta do is call --ANYTIMEATA--2
If you need somebody to love --ANYTIMEATA--4
I'll be there to make you feel right --ANYTIMEATA
    --6
Don't you be sad, just call me tonight.--ANYTIMEATA
    --9
All you gotta do is call --ANYTIMEATA--11
When you need a shoulder to cry on --ANYTIMEATA--16
Call me tonight and I'll come to you.--ANYTIMEATA
    --18
All you gotta do is call --ANYTIMEATA--23
I love you --ASKMEWHY--1
'cos you tell me things I want to know --ASKMEWHY
    --2
Ask me why, I'll say I love you --ASKMEWHY--14
And I'm always thinking of you.--ASKMEWHY--15
I love you --ASKMEWHY--16
'cos you tell me things I want to know --ASKMEWHY
    --17
Ask me why, I'll say I love you --ASKMEWHY--22
And I'm always thinking of you.--ASKMEWHY--23
Ask me why, I'll say I love you--ASKMEWHY--26
And I'm always thinking of you, you, you.--ASKMEWHY
    --27
And I'm always thinking of you, you, you.--ASKMEWHY
    --27
And I'm always thinking of you, you, you.--ASKMEWHY
    --27
I know you never even try girl --PLEASEPLEA--2
Like I please you.--PLEASEPLEA--6
You don't need me to show the way love --PLEASEPLEA
    --7
Like I please you.--PLEASEPLEA--12
But you know there's always rain--PLEASEPLEA--14
I do all the pleasing with you --PLEASEPLEA--16
It's so hard to reason with you, whoa - yeah--
    PLEASEPLEA--17
Why do you make me blue?--PLEASEPLEA--18
I know/Why do you never even try girl--PLEASEPLEA--2(
Like I please you.--PLEASEPLEA--24
Like I please you--PLEASEPLEA--26
Like I please you.--PLEASEPLEA--28
DO YOU WANT TO KNOW A SECRET?--DOYOUWANTT--Title
You'll never know how much I really love you --
    DOYOUWANTT--1
Listen, do you want to know a secret?--DOYOUWANTT
    --3
Do you promise not to tell?--DOYOUWANTT--4
Say the words you long to hear --DOYOUWANTT--7
I'm in love with you - ooo.--DOYOUWANTT--8
Listen (dodahdo) do you want to know a secret?
    (dodahdo)--DOYOUWANTT--9
Do you promise not to tell? (dodahdo)--DOYOUWANTT
    --10
Say the words you long to hear --DOYOUWANTT--13
I'm in love with you - ooo.--DOYOUWANTT--14
Listen (dodahdo) do you want to know a secret?
    (dodahdo)--DOYOUWANTT--17
Do you promise not to tell? (dodahdo)--DOYOUWANTT
    --18
Say the words you long to hear --DOYOUWANTT--21
I'm in love with you - ooo --DOYOUWANTT--22
You know what I mean --ISAWHERSTA--3
FROM ME TO YOU.--FROMMETOYO--Title
If there's anything that you want--FROMMETOYO--3
With love from me to you.--FROMMETOYO--6
I got everything that you want--FROMMETOYO--7
With love from me to you.--FROMMETOYO--10
I got arms that long to hold you--FROMMETOYO--11
And keep you by my side--FROMMETOYO--12
I got lips that long to kiss you--FROMMETOYO--13
And keep you satisfied - ooo!--FROMMETOYO--14
If there's anything that you want--FROMMETOYO--15
With love from me to you.--FROMMETOYO--18
From me - to you.--FROMMETOYO--19
With love from me to you.--FROMMETOYO--21
I got arms that long to hold you--FROMMETOYO--22
And keep you by my side--FROMMETOYO--23
I got lips that long to kiss you--FROMMETOYO--24
And keep you satisfied - ooo!--FROMMETOYO--25
If there's anything that you want--FROMMETOYO--26
With love from me to you--FROMMETOYO--29
To you, to you, to you.--FROMMETOYO--30

To you, to you, to you.--FROMMETOYO--30
To you, to you, to you.--FROMMETOYO--30
THANK YOU GIRL.--THANKYOUGI--Title
You made me glad when I was blue--THANKYOUGI--2
And eternally I'll always be in love with you--
   THANKYOUGI--3
And all I gotta do is thank you girl, thank you
   girl.--THANKYOUGI--4
And all I gotta do is thank you girl, thank you
   girl.--THANKYOUGI--4
And all I gotta do is thank you girl, thank you
   girl.--THANKYOUGI--7
And all I gotta do is thank you girl, thank you
   girl--THANKYOUGI--7
Thank you girl, for loving me the way that you
   do (way that you do).--THANKYOUGI--8
Thank you girl, for loving me the way that you
   do (way that you do).--THANKYOUGI--8
Thank you girl, for loving me the way that you
   do (way that you do).--THANKYOUGI--8
And all I gotta do is thank you girl, thank you
   girl.--THANKYOUGI--10
And all I gotta do is thank you girl, thank you
   girl.--THANKYOUGI--10
You made me glad when I was blue--THANKYOUGI--12
And eternally I'll always be in love with you--
   THANKYOUGI--13
And all I gotta do is thank you girl, thank you
   girl.--THANKYOUGI--14
And all I gotta do is thank you girl, thank you
   girl.--THANKYOUGI--14
I'LL GET YOU.--ILLGETYOU--Title
Imagine I'm in love with you--ILLGETYOU--2
I've imagined I'm in love with you--ILLGETYOU--4
But I'll get you, I'll get you in the end--
   ILLGETYOU--7
But I'll get you, I'll get you in the end--
   ILLGETYOU--7
Yes I will I'll get you in the end, oh yeah,
   oh yeah.--ILLGETYOU--8
I think about you night and day--ILLGETYOU--9
I need you and it's true--ILLGETYOU--10
When I think about you, I can say--ILLGETYOU--11
So I'm telling you, my friend--ILLGETYOU--13
That I'll get you, I'll get you in the end--
   ILLGETYOU--14
That I'll get you, I'll get you in the end--
   ILLGETYOU--14
Yes I will, I'll get you in the end, oh yeah,
   oh yeah.--ILLGETYOU--15
So you might as well resign yourself to me, oh
   yeah.--ILLGETYOU--18
Imagine I'm in love with you--ILLGETYOU--19
I've imagined I'm in love with you--ILLGETYOU--21
But I'll get you, I'll get you in the end--
   ILLGETYOU--24
But I'll get you, I'll get you in the end--
   ILLGETYOU--24
Yes I will, I'll get you in the end, oh yeah,
   oh yeah--ILLGETYOU--25
SHE LOVES YOU.--SHELOVESYO--Title
She loves you yeah, yeah, yeah--SHELOVESYO--1
She loves you yeah, yeah, yeah--SHELOVESYO--2
She loves you yeah, yeah, yeah, yeah.--SHELOVESYO
   --3
You think you've lost your love--SHELOVESYO--4
It's you she's thinking of--SHELOVESYO--6
She said she loves you--SHELOVESYO--8
And you know that can't be bad--SHELOVESYO--9
Yeah, she loves you--SHELOVESYO--10
And you know you should be glad.--SHELOVESYO--11
And you know you should be glad.--SHELOVESYO--11
She said you hurt her so--SHELOVESYO--12
She said she loves you--SHELOVESYO--16
And you know that can't be bad--SHELOVESYO--17
Yeah, she loves you--SHELOVESYO--18
And you know you should be glad - ooo!--SHELOVESYO
   --19
And you know you should be glad - ooo!--SHELOVESYO
   --19
She loves you, yeah, yeah, yeah--SHELOVESYO--20
She loves you, yeah, yeah, yeah--SHELOVESYO--21
You know you should be glad.--SHELOVESYO--23
You know you should be glad.--SHELOVESYO--23
You know it's up to you--SHELOVESYO--24
You know it's up to you--SHELOVESYO--24
Pride can hurt you too--SHELOVESYO--26
Because she loves you--SHELOVESYO--28
And you know that can't be bad--SHELOVESYO--29
Yeah, she loves you--SHELOVESYO--30
And you know you should be glad - ooo!--SHELOVESYO
   --31
And you know you should be glad - ooo!--SHELOVESYO
   --31

She loves you, yeah, yeah, yeah--SHELOVESYO--32
She loves you, yeah, yeah, yeah--SHELOVESYO--33
You know you should be glad--SHELOVESYO--35
You know you should be glad--SHELOVESYO--35
You know you should be glad--SHELOVESYO--37
You know you should be glad--SHELOVESYO--37
You know you should be glad--SHELOVESYO--39
You know you should be glad--SHELOVESYO--39
Whenever I want you around, yeah --ALLIVEGOTT--1
Is call you on the phone --ALLIVEGOTT--3
And when I, I wanna kiss you, yeah --ALLIVEGOTT--6
The words you long to hear --ALLIVEGOTT--9
And I'll be kissing you.--ALLIVEGOTT--10
Whenever you want me at all --ALLIVEGOTT--12
Whenever you call --ALLIVEGOTT--14
And when I, I wanna kiss you, yeah --ALLIVEGOTT--17
Is call you on the phone --ALLIVEGOTT--19
Whenever you want me at all --ALLIVEGOTT--23
Whenever you call --ALLIVEGOTT--25
Close your eyes and I'll kiss you --ALLMYLOVIN--1
Tomorrow I'll miss you --ALLMYLOVIN--2
And I'll send all my lovin' to you.--ALLMYLOVIN--6
And I'll send all my lovin' to you.--ALLMYLOVIN--12
All my lovin', I will send to you --ALLMYLOVIN--13
Close your eyes and I'll kiss you --ALLMYLOVIN--15
Tomorrow I'll miss you --ALLMYLOVIN--16
And I'll send all my lovin' to you.--ALLMYLOVIN--20
All my lovin', I will send to you --ALLMYLOVIN--21
All my lovin', I will send to you.--ALLMYLOVIN--24
I've got no time for you right now--DONTBOTHER--13
I'll let you know--DONTBOTHER--22
I've got no time for you right now--DONTBOTHER--28
I'll let you know--DONTBOTHER--37
It's you, you, you, you - ooo-ooo.--HOLDMETIGH--8
It's you, you, you, you - ooo-ooo.--HOLDMETIGH--8
It's you, you, you, you - ooo-ooo.--HOLDMETIGH--8
It's you, you, you, you - ooo-ooo.--HOLDMETIGH--8
Let me go on loving you --HOLDMETIGH--10
Making love to only you.--HOLDMETIGH--12
It's you, you, you, you - ooo-ooo.--HOLDMETIGH--15
It's you, you, you, you - ooo-ooo.--HOLDMETIGH--15
It's you, you, you, you - ooo-ooo.--HOLDMETIGH--15
It's you, you, you, you - ooo-ooo.--HOLDMETIGH--15
Don't know what it means to hold you tight --
   HOLDMETIGH--16
Being here alone tonight with you.--HOLDMETIGH--17
It's you, you, you, you - ooo-ooo.--HOLDMETIGH--25
It's you, you, you, you - ooo-ooo.--HOLDMETIGH--25
It's you, you, you, you - ooo-ooo.--HOLDMETIGH--25
It's you, you, you, you - ooo-ooo.--HOLDMETIGH--25
Don't know what it means to hold you tight --
   HOLDMETIGH--26
Being here alone tonight with you.--HOLDMETIGH--27
Let me go on loving you --HOLDMETIGH--30
Making love to only you.--HOLDMETIGH--32
It's you, you, you, you - ooo-ooo --HOLDMETIGH--35
It's you, you, you, you - ooo-ooo --HOLDMETIGH--35
It's you, you, you, you - ooo-ooo --HOLDMETIGH--35
It's you, you, you, you - ooo-ooo --HOLDMETIGH--35
You - ooo.--HOLDMETIGH--36
Love you like no other baby --IWANNABEYO--5
Love you like no other baby --IWANNABEYO--7
Tell me that you love me baby --IWANNABEYO--13
Tell me that you love me baby --IWANNABEYO--15
Love you like no other baby --IWANNABEYO--34
Love you like no other baby --IWANNABEYO--36
Till I belong to you--ITWONTBELO--4
Till I belong to you--ITWONTBELO--10
Since you left me I'm so alone (you left me here)
   --ITWONTBELO--11
Since you left me I'm so alone (you left me here)
   --ITWONTBELO--11
Till I belong to you--ITWONTBELO--20
Well since you left me I'm so alone (you left
   me here)--ITWONTBELO--21
Well since you left me I'm so alone (you left
   me here)--ITWONTBELO--21
Now I know that you won't leave me no more--
   ITWONTBELO--26
Till I belong to you - ooo.--ITWONTBELO--30
Little child, won't you dance with me?--LITTLECHIL
   --2
Little child, won't you dance with me?--LITTLECHIL
   --6
If you want someone to make you feel so fine--
   LITTLECHIL--9
If you want someone to make you feel so fine--
   LITTLECHIL--9
Little child, won't you dance with me?--LITTLECHIL
   --13
Don't you run and hide, just come on, come on --
   LITTLECHIL--17
Little child, won't you dance with me?--LITTLECHIL
   --20

You know you made me cry --NOTASECOND--1
You know you made me cry --NOTASECOND--1
I've cried for you.--NOTASECOND--3
You hurt me then you're back again --NOTASECOND--9
You know you made me cry --NOTASECOND--12
You know you made me cry --NOTASECOND--12
I've cried for you, yeah.--NOTASECOND--14
You hurt me then you're back again --NOTASECOND--20
Oh yeah, I'll tell you something--IWANTTOHOL--1
And when I touch you--IWANTTOHOL--13
And when I touch you--IWANTTOHOL--26
But this boy wants you back again.--THISBOY--3
That boy isn't good for you--THISBOY--4
Though he may want you too--THISBOY--5
This boy wants you back again.--THISBOY--6
Just to love you, but oh my!--THISBOY--8
Till he's seen you cry.--THISBOY--11
If this boy gets you back again.--THISBOY--13
I'll buy you a diamond ring my friend --CANTBUYMEL--3
If it makes you feel alright --CANTBUYMEL--4
I'll get you anything my friend --CANTBUYMEL--5
If it makes you feel alright --CANTBUYMEL--6
I'll give you all I've got to give --CANTBUYMEL--9
If you say you love me too --CANTBUYMEL--10
If you say you love me too --CANTBUYMEL--10
But what I got I'll give to you --CANTBUYMEL--12
Say you don't need no diamond rings --CANTBUYMEL--17
Tell me that you want the kind of things --CANTBUYMEL--19
Say you don't need no diamond rings --CANTBUYMEL--27
Tell me that you want the kind of things --CANTBUYMEL--29
YOU CAN'T DO THAT.--YOUCANTDOT--Title
That might cause you pain--YOUCANTDOT--2
If I catch you talking--YOUCANTDOT--3
I'm gonna let you down--YOUCANTDOT--5
And leave you flat--YOUCANTDOT--6
Because I told you before--YOUCANTDOT--7
Oh you can't do that.--YOUCANTDOT--8
I caught you talking to him--YOUCANTDOT--10
Do I have to tell you one more time--YOUCANTDOT--11
I think I'll let you down (let you down)--YOUCANTDOT--13
I think I'll let you down (let you down)--YOUCANTDOT--13
And leave you flat--YOUCANTDOT--14
(Gonna let you down and leave you flat)--YOUCANTDOT--15
(Gonna let you down and leave you flat)--YOUCANTDOT--15
Because I told you before--YOUCANTDOT--16
Oh you can't do that.--YOUCANTDOT--17
You talking that way--YOUCANTDOT--21
If you wanna stay mine--YOUCANTDOT--24
I'm gonna let you down (let you down)--YOUCANTDOT--27
I'm gonna let you down (let you down)--YOUCANTDOT--27
And leave you flat--YOUCANTDOT--28
(Gonna let you down and leave you flat)--YOUCANTDOT--29
(Gonna let you down and leave you flat)--YOUCANTDOT--29
Because I told you before--YOUCANTDOT--30
Oh you can't do that - no!--YOUCANTDOT--31
You can't do that--YOUCANTDOT--32
You can't do that--YOUCANTDOT--33
You can't do that--YOUCANTDOT--34
You can't do that--YOUCANTDOT--35
You can't do that.--YOUCANTDOT--36
You talking that way--YOUCANTDOT--40
If you wanna stay mine--YOUCANTDOT--43
I'm gonna let you down (let you down)--YOUCANTDOT--46
I'm gonna let you down (let you down)--YOUCANTDOT--46
And leave you flat--YOUCANTDOT--47
(Gonna let you down and leave you flat)--YOUCANTDOT--48
(Gonna let you down and leave you flat)--YOUCANTDOT--48
Because I told you before--YOUCANTDOT--49
Oh you can't do that.--YOUCANTDOT--50
Don't you know I can't take it?--ICALLYOURN--5
Don't you know I can't take it?--ICALLYOURN--12
I think of you--THERESAPLA--5
And things you do go round my head--THERESAPLA--6
The things you said--THERESAPLA--7
Like I love only you.--THERESAPLA--8
Don't you know that it's so?--THERESAPLA--10
Don't you know that it's so?--THERESAPLA--12

And if you saw my love --ANDILOVEHE--3
Have you near me.--ANDILOVEHE--14
But when I get home to you --HARDDAYSNI--5
I find the things that you do --HARDDAYSNI--6
You know I work all day --HARDDAYSNI--8
To get you money to buy you things --HARDDAYSNI--9
To get you money to buy you things --HARDDAYSNI--9
And it's worth it just to hear you say --HARDDAYSNI--10
'cos when I get you alone --HARDDAYSNI--13
You know I feel OK.--HARDDAYSNI--14
When I'm home feeling you holding me tight, tight, yeah.--HARDDAYSNI--16
But when I get home to you --HARDDAYSNI--21
I find the things that you do --HARDDAYSNI--22
'cos when I get you alone --HARDDAYSNI--26
You know I feel OK.--HARDDAYSNI--27
When I'm home feeling you holding me tight, tight, yeah.--HARDDAYSNI--29
But when I get home to you --HARDDAYSNI--34
I find the things that you do --HARDDAYSNI--35
You know I feel alright --HARDDAYSNI--37
You know I feel alright.--HARDDAYSNI--38
I should have known better with a girl like you --ISHOULDHAV--1
That I would love everything that you do --ISHOULDHAV--2
Can't you see, can't you see?--ISHOULDHAV--6
Can't you see, can't you see?--ISHOULDHAV--6
That when I tell you that I love you, oh --ISHOULDHAV--7
That when I tell you that I love you, oh --ISHOULDHAV--7
You're gonna say you love me too, oh.--ISHOULDHAV--8
And when I ask you to be mine --ISHOULDHAV--9
You're gonna say you love me too.--ISHOULDHAV--10
Can't you see, can't you see?--ISHOULDHAV--16
Can't you see, can't you see?--ISHOULDHAV--16
That when I tell you that I love you, oh --ISHOULDHAV--17
That when I tell you that I love you, oh --ISHOULDHAV--17
You're gonna say you love me too, oh.--ISHOULDHAV--18
And when I ask you to be mine --ISHOULDHAV--19
You're gonna say you love me too.--ISHOULDHAV--20
You love me too --ISHOULDHAV--21
You love me too.--ISHOULDHAV--22
You love me too.--ISHOULDHAV--23
If I fell in love with you --IFIFELL--1
Would you promise to be true --IFIFELL--2
If I give my heart to you --IFIFELL--7
That you would love me more than her.--IFIFELL--9
If I trust in you --IFIFELL--10
If I love you too --IFIFELL--12
So I hope you see --IFIFELL--17
That I would love to love you --IFIFELL--18
So I hope you see --IFIFELL--24
That I would love to love you --IFIFELL--25
If I fell in love with you.--IFIFELL--28
If I could see you now --ILLCRYINST--8
I'd try to make you sad somehow --ILLCRYINST--9
And show you what your loving man can do --ILLCRYINST--18
And show you what your loving man can do --ILLCRYINST--27
I'M HAPPY JUST TO DANCE WITH YOU.--IMHAPPYJUS--Title
I think I'll love you too --IMHAPPYJUS--2
I'm so happy when you dance with me.--IMHAPPYJUS--3
'cos I'm happy just to dance with you.--IMHAPPYJUS--7
I don't need to hug or hold you tight --IMHAPPYJUS--8
I just wanna dance with you all night --IMHAPPYJUS--9
'cos I'm happy just to dance with you.--IMHAPPYJUS--11
Just to dance with you is everything I need (oh) --IMHAPPYJUS--12
I think I'll love you too ((oh)) --IMHAPPYJUS--14
I'm so happy when you dance with me ((oh - oh)).--IMHAPPYJUS--15
'cos I'm happy just to dance with you.--IMHAPPYJUS--19
Just to dance with you (oh) is everything I need (oh) --IMHAPPYJUS--20
I think I'll love you too ((oh)) --IMHAPPYJUS--22
I'm so happy when you dance with me ((oh - oh)).--IMHAPPYJUS--23
I've discovered I'm in love with you (oh - oh).--IMHAPPYJUS--27

'cos I'm happy just to dance with you (oh - oh).--
    IMHAPPYJUS--28
Tell me why you cried --TELLMEWHY--1
And why you lied to me --TELLMEWHY--2
Tell me why you cried --TELLMEWHY--3
And why you lied to me.--TELLMEWHY--4
Well I gave you everything I had --TELLMEWHY--5
But you left me sitting on my own --TELLMEWHY--6
Did you have to treat me oh so bad --TELLMEWHY--7
Tell me why you cried --TELLMEWHY--9
And why you lied to me --TELLMEWHY--10
Tell me why you cried --TELLMEWHY--11
And why you lied to me.--TELLMEWHY--12
If you don't I really can't go on --TELLMEWHY--15
Tell me why you cried --TELLMEWHY--17
And why you lied to me --TELLMEWHY--18
Tell me why you cried --TELLMEWHY--19
And why you lied to me.--TELLMEWHY--20
Well I beg you on my bended knees --TELLMEWHY--21
I'm so in love with you.--TELLMEWHY--25
Tell me why you cried --TELLMEWHY--26
And why you lied to me.--TELLMEWHY--27
Tell me why you cried --TELLMEWHY--28
And why you lied to me.--TELLMEWHY--29
You know if you break my heart, I'll go --ILLBEBACK
    --1
You know if you break my heart, I'll go --ILLBEBACK
    --1
'cos I told you once before goodbye --ILLBEBACK--3
1 love you so--ILLBEBACK--4
I'm the one who wants you--ILLBEBACK--6
Yes I'm the one who wants you--ILLBEBACK--7
You could find better things to do --ILLBEBACK--9
I thought that you would realise --ILLBEBACK--13
That if I ran away from you --ILLBEBACK--14
That you would want me too --ILLBEBACK--15
You could find better things to do --ILLBEBACK--17
But I hate to leave you --ILLBEBACK--23
You know I hate to leave you --ILLBEBACK--24
You know I hate to leave you --ILLBEBACK--24
You if you break my heart, I'll go--ILLBEBACK
    --26
You if you break my heart, I'll go--ILLBEBACK
    --26
You say you will love me if I have to go--
    THINGSWESA--1
You say you will love me if I have to go --
    THINGSWESA--1
Wishing you weren't so far away --THINGSWESA--4
You say you'll be mine girl, till the end of time
    --THINGSWESA--6
Love to hear you say that love is love--THINGSWESA
    --12
And that's enough to make you mine girl --
    THINGSWESA--15
Love to hear you say that love is love--THINGSWESA
    --23
And that's enough to make you mine girl --
    THINGSWESA--26
Come on if you please --WHENIGETHO--10
I got no business being here with you this way.--
    WHENIGETHO--23
Baby's good to me, you know --IFEELFINE--1
She's happy as can be, you know, she said so --
    IFEELFINE--2
Baby says she's mine, you know --IFEELFINE--4
She tells me all the time, you know, she said so
    --IFEELFINE--5
That her baby buys her things, you know --IFEELFINE
    --9
He buys her diamond rings, you know, she said so
    --IFEELFINE--10
Baby said she's mine, you know --IFEELFINE--12
She tells me all the time, you know, she said so
    --IFEELFINE--13
That her baby buys her things, you know --IFEELFINE
    --17
He buys her diamond rings, you know, she said so
    --IFEELFINE--18
Guess you know it's true --EIGHTDAYSA--2
Hope you need my love babe --EIGHTDAYSA--3
Just like I need you.--EIGHTDAYSA--4
Love you every day girl --EIGHTDAYSA--9
Love you all the time.--EIGHTDAYSA--12
Eight days a week I love you --EIGHTDAYSA--17
Guess you know it's true --EIGHTDAYSA--20
Hope you need my love babe --EIGHTDAYSA--21
Just like I need you, oh - oh.--EIGHTDAYSA--22
Eight days a week I love you --EIGHTDAYSA--27
Love you every day girl --EIGHTDAYSA--29
Love you all the time.--EIGHTDAYSA--32
And you know the thing she does--EVERYLITTL--9
And you know the thing she does--EVERYLITTL--19
And you know the thing she does--EVERYLITTL--23

And though I lose a friend in the end you will
    know, oh.--ILLFOLLOWT--6
And though I lose a friend in the end you will
    know, oh.--ILLFOLLOWT--11
I'm telling you so that you won't lose all.--
    IMALOSER--18
I'm telling you so that you won't lose all.--
    IMALOSER--18
They said it wasn't you--NOREPLY--4
But I saw you peep through your window--NOREPLY--5
I know that you saw me--NOREPLY--7
They said you were not home--NOREPLY--10
I saw you walk in your door--NOREPLY--13
'cos you walked hand in hand--NOREPLY--15
If I were you I'd realise that I--NOREPLY--17
Love you more than any other guy--NOREPLY--18
When you gave me no reply.--NOREPLY--21
They said you were not home--NOREPLY--23
I saw you walk in your door--NOREPLY--26
'cos you walked hand in hand--NOREPLY--28
Would it be too much to ask of you,--WHATYOURED--3
You ((you)) got me running--WHATYOURED--5
You ((you)) got me running--WHATYOURED--5
Why should it be so much to ask of you --WHATYOURED
    --7
I've been waiting here for you --WHATYOURED--9
'n' should you need a love that's true, it's me.--
    WHATYOURED--11
Why should it be so much to ask of you --WHATYOURED
    --14
I've been waiting here for you --WHATYOURED--16
'n' should you need a love that's true, it's me.--
    WHATYOURED--18
Why should it be so much to ask of you --WHATYOURED
    --21
If you wear red tonight--YESITIS--1
I could be happy with you by my side--YESITIS--10
In spite of you it's true--YESITIS--17
I could be happy with you by my side--YESITIS--19
In spite of you it's true--YESITIS--26
TELL ME WHAT YOU SEE.--TELLMEWHAT--Title
If you let me take your heart--TELLMEWHAT--1
I will prove to you--TELLMEWHAT--2
If I'm part of you--TELLMEWHAT--4
Tell me what you see--TELLMEWHAT--6
What you see is me--TELLMEWHAT--8
If you put your trust in me--TELLMEWHAT--11
Tell me what you see--TELLMEWHAT--14
Don't you realise now--TELLMEWHAT--15
What you see is me--TELLMEWHAT--16
Tell me what you see--TELLMEWHAT--17
Can't you try to see that I'm--TELLMEWHAT--20
Trying to get to you--TELLMEWHAT--21
Tell me what you see--TELLMEWHAT--23
What you see is me--TELLMEWHAT--25
Tell me what you see--TELLMEWHAT--26
Can't you try to see that I'm--TELLMEWHAT--29
Trying to get to you--TELLMEWHAT--30
Tell me what you see--TELLMEWHAT--32
What you see is me--TELLMEWHAT--34
YOU LIKE ME TOO MUCH.--YOULIKEMET--Title
If I just don't treat you right--YOULIKEMET--4
You'll never leave me and you know it's true--
    YOULIKEMET--5
'cos you like me too much and I like you--
    YOULIKEMET--6
'cos you like me too much and I like you--
    YOULIKEMET--6
But you haven't got the nerve--YOULIKEMET--8
,You'll never leave me and you know it's true--
    YOULIKEMET--11
'cos you like me too much and I like you--
    YOULIKEMET--12
'cos you like me too much and I like you--
    YOULIKEMET--12
And it's nice when you believe me--YOULIKEMET--14
If you leave me I will follow you--YOULIKEMET--15
If you leave me I will follow you--YOULIKEMET--15
And bring you back where you belong--YOULIKEMET--16
And bring you back where you belong--YOULIKEMET--16
I wouldn't let you leave me 'cos it's true--
    YOULIKEMET--19
'cos you like me too much and I like you--
    YOULIKEMET--20
'cos you like me too much and I like you--
    YOULIKEMET--20
'cos you like me too much and I like you--
    YOULIKEMET--21
'cos you like me too much and I like you--
    YOULIKEMET--21
And it's nice when you believe me--YOULIKEMET--23
If you leave me I will follow you--YOULIKEMET--24
If you leave me I will follow you--YOULIKEMET--24
And bring you back where you belong--YOULIKEMET--25

And bring you back where you belong--YOULIKEMET--25
I wouldn't let you leave me 'cos it's true--
    YOULIKEMET--28
'cos you like me too much and I like you--
    YOULIKEMET--29
'cos you like me too much and I like you--
    YOULIKEMET--29
'cos you like me too much and I like you.--
    YOULIKEMET--30
'cos you like me too much and I like you.--
    YOULIKEMET--30
You know I need someone--HELP--6
Help me if you can, I'm feeling down--HELP--15
And I do appreciate you being round--HELP--16
Won't you please please help me?--HELP--18
I know that I ((I know that I)) just need
    you like--HELP--23
Help me if you can, I'm feeling down--HELP--25
And I do appreciate you being round--HELP--26
Won't you please please help me?--HELP--28
Help me if you can, I'm feeling down--HELP--35
And I do appreciate you being round--HELP--36
Won't you please please help me?--HELP--38
You tell lies thinking I can't see --IMDOWN--1
You can't cry 'cos you're laughing at me --IMDOWN
    --2
How can you laugh when you know I'm down?--IMDOWN
    --6
How can you laugh when you know I'm down?--IMDOWN
    --6
(How can you laugh) when you know I'm down?--IMDOWN
    --7
(How can you laugh) when you know I'm down?--IMDOWN
    --7
How can you laugh when you know I'm down?--IMDOWN
    --13
How can you laugh when you know I'm down?--IMDOWN
    --13
(How can you laugh) when you know I'm down?--IMDOWN
    --14
(How can you laugh) when you know I'm down?--IMDOWN
    --14
You still moan keep your hands to yourself --IMDOWN
    --17
How can you laugh when you know I'm down?--IMDOWN
    --21
How can you laugh when you know I'm down?--IMDOWN
    --21
(How can you laugh) when you know I'm down?--IMDOWN
    --22
(How can you laugh) when you know I'm down?--IMDOWN
    --22
Can you hear me?--IMDOWN--26
Baby you know I'm down (I'm really down)--IMDOWN
    --28
Ooo, you know I'm....--IMDOWN--46
You're making me say that I've got nobody but you
    --ANOTHERGIR--2
And so I'm telling you this time you'd better
    stop --ANOTHERGIR--8
I don't wanna say that I've been unhappy with you
    --ANOTHERGIR--12
I don't wanna say that I've been unhappy with you
    --ANOTHERGIR--18
I NEED YOU.--INEEDYOU--Title
You don't realise how much I need you--INEEDYOU--1
You don't realise how much I need you--INEEDYOU--1
Love you all the time and never leave you--INEEDYOU
    --2
Love you all the time and never leave you--INEEDYOU
    --2
I need you.--INEEDYOU--5
Said you had a thing or two to tell me--INEEDYOU
    --6
How was I to know you would upset me?--INEEDYOU--7
You told me--INEEDYOU--10
Oh yes, you told me--INEEDYOU--11
You don't want my loving any more--INEEDYOU--12
Please remember how I feel about you--INEEDYOU--16
I could never really live without you--INEEDYOU--17
Just what you mean to me--INEEDYOU--19
I need you.--INEEDYOU--20
But when you told me--INEEDYOU--21
You don't want my loving any more--INEEDYOU--22
Please remember how I feel about you--INEEDYOU--26
I could never really live without you--INEEDYOU--27
Just what you mean to me--INEEDYOU--29
I need you--INEEDYOU--30
I need you--INEEDYOU--31
I need you.--INEEDYOU--32
I get high when I see you go by, my oh my--
    ITSONLYLOV--1
When you sigh my my inside just flies, butterfly.
    --ITSONLYLOV--2

Why am I so shy when I'm beside you?--ITSONLYLOV
    --3
But it's so hard loving you.--ITSONLYLOV--7
Is it right that you and I should fight, every
    night--ITSONLYLOV--8
Just the sight of you makes night-time bright,
    very bright.--ITSONLYLOV--9
But it's so hard loving you.--ITSONLYLOV--14
Yes, it's so hard loving you, loving you - ooo.--
    ITSONLYLOV--15
Yes, it's so hard loving you, loving you - ooo.--
    ITSONLYLOV--15
Now today I find, you have changed your mind--
    NIGHTBEFOR--3
Treat me like you did the night before.--NIGHTBEFOR
    --4
Were you telling lies? (aah the night before)--
    NIGHTBEFOR--5
When I held you near, you were so sincere--
    NIGHTBEFOR--7
When I held you near, you were so sincere--
    NIGHTBEFOR--7
Treat me like you did the night before.--NIGHTBEFOR
    --8
Last night is the night I will remember you by --
    NIGHTBEFOR--9
Now today I find you have changed your mind--
    NIGHTBEFOR--13
Treat me like you did the night before (yes).--
    NIGHTBEFOR--14
When I held you near, you were so sincere --
    NIGHTBEFOR--15
When I held you near, you were so sincere --
    NIGHTBEFOR--15
Treat me like you did the night before (yeah).--
    NIGHTBEFOR--16
Last night is the night I will remember you by --
    NIGHTBEFOR--17
Were you telling lies? (aah the night before)--
    NIGHTBEFOR--19
When I held you near, you were so sincere --
    NIGHTBEFOR--21
When I held you near, you were so sincere --
    NIGHTBEFOR--21
Treat me like you did the night before.--NIGHTBEFOR
    --22
If you don't take her out tonight--YOUREGONNA--3
If you don't treat her right my friend--YOUREGONNA
    --9
I'll make a point of taking her away from you
    (watch what you do), yeah--YOUREGONNA--16
I'll make a point of taking her away from you
    (watch what you do), yeah--YOUREGONNA--16
The way you treat her what else can I do?--
    YOUREGONNA--17
I'll make a point of taking her away from you
    (watch what you do), yeah--YOUREGONNA--23
I'll make a point of taking her away from you
    (watch what you do), yeah--YOUREGONNA--23
The way you treat her what else can I do?--
    YOUREGONNA--24
If you don't take her out tonight--YOUREGONNA--25
Gather round all you clowns--YOUVEGOTTO--17
Let me hear you say.--YOUVEGOTTO--18
While you see it your way--WECANWORKI--3
You can get it wrong and still you think that
    it's alright.--WECANWORKI--7
You can get it wrong and still you think that
    it's alright.--WECANWORKI--14
So I will ask you once again.--WECANWORKI--17
While you see it your way --WECANWORKI--17
So I will ask you once again.--WECANWORKI--23
While you see it your way --WECANWORKI--26
She said baby can't you see?--DRIVEMYCAR--2
But you can do something in between.--DRIVEMYCAR
    --4
Baby you can drive my car --DRIVEMYCAR--5
Baby you can drive my car --DRIVEMYCAR--7
And maybe I'll love you.--DRIVEMYCAR--8
But I can show you a better time.--DRIVEMYCAR--12
Baby you can drive my car --DRIVEMYCAR--13
Baby you can drive my car --DRIVEMYCAR--15
And maybe I'll love you.--DRIVEMYCAR--16
Baby you can drive my car --DRIVEMYCAR--18
Baby you can drive my car --DRIVEMYCAR--20
And maybe I'll love you.--DRIVEMYCAR--21
Baby you can drive my car --DRIVEMYCAR--26
Baby you can drive my car --DRIVEMYCAR--28
And maybe I'll love you.--DRIVEMYCAR--29
She's the kind of girl you want so much it makes
    you sorry --GIRL--3
She's the kind of girl you want so much it makes
    you sorry --GIRL--3
Still you don't regret a single day.--GIRL--4

She's the kind of girl who puts you down--GIRL--11
When friends are there, you feel a fool.--GIRL--13
When you say she's looking good --GIRL--15
Then I guess I'd be with you my friend --IFINEEDEDS
--5
Had you come some other day --IFINEEDEDS--7
But you see now I'm too much in love.--IFINEEDEDS
--9
And maybe you will get a call from me --IFINEEDEDS
--11
Then I guess I'd be with you my friend --IFINEEDEDS
--15
Had you come some other day --IFINEEDEDS--17
But you see now I'm too much in love.--IFINEEDEDS
--19
And maybe you will get a call from me --IFINEEDEDS
--21
I'M LOOKING THROUGH YOU.--IMLOOKINGT--Title
I'm looking through you, where did you go?--
IMLOOKINGT--1
I'm looking through you, where did you go?--
IMLOOKINGT--1
I thought I knew you, what did I know?--IMLOOKINGT
--2
You don't look different, but you have changed --
IMLOOKINGT--3
You don't look different, but you have changed --
IMLOOKINGT--3
I'm looking through you, you're not the same.--
IMLOOKINGT--4
You don't sound different, I've learned the game
--IMLOOKINGT--7
I'm looking through you, you're not the same.--
IMLOOKINGT--8
Why, tell me why did you not treat me right?--
IMLOOKINGT--9
You were above me, but not today.--IMLOOKINGT--12
I'm looking through you and you're nowhere.--
IMLOOKINGT--14
Why, tell me why did you not treat me right?--
IMLOOKINGT--15
I'm looking through you, where did you go?--
IMLOOKINGT--17
I'm looking through you, where did you go?--
IMLOOKINGT--17
I thought I knew you, what did I know?--IMLOOKINGT
--18
You don't look different, but you have changed --
IMLOOKINGT--19
You don't look different, but you have changed --
IMLOOKINGT--19
I'm looking through you, you're not the same.--
IMLOOKINGT--20
Aah, I'm looking through you.--IMLOOKINGT--22
Yeah, I'm looking through you.--IMLOOKINGT--23
There is no-one compares with you --INMYLIFE--10
In my life I love you more.--INMYLIFE--16
In my life I love you more.--INMYLIFE--20
In my life I love you more.--INMYLIFE--21
I love you, I love you, I love you--MICHELLE--5
I love you, I love you, I love you--MICHELLE--5
I love you, I love you, I love you--MICHELLE--5
I need to make you see--MICHELLE--12
Oh, what you mean to me--MICHELLE--13
Until I do I'm hoping you will know what I mean.--
MICHELLE--14
I love you.--MICHELLE--15
I want you, I want you, I want you--MICHELLE--16
I want you, I want you, I want you--MICHELLE--16
I want you, I want you, I want you--MICHELLE--16
I think you know by now--MICHELLE--17
I'll get to you somehow--MICHELLE--18
Until I do I'm telling you so you'll understand.--
MICHELLE--19
Isn't he a bit like you and me?--NOWHEREMAN--6
You don't know what you're missing --NOWHEREMAN--8
Nowhere Man can you see me at all?--NOWHEREMAN--12
Leave it all till somebody else lends you a hand.
--NOWHEREMAN--15
Isn't he a bit like you and me?--NOWHEREMAN--18
You don't know what you're missing --NOWHEREMAN--20
Well I'd rather see you dead, little girl --
RUNFORYOUR--1
You better keep your head, little girl --RUNFORYOUR
--3
You better run for your life if you can, little
girl --RUNFORYOUR--5
You better run for your life if you can, little
girl --RUNFORYOUR--5
Catch you with another man --RUNFORYOUR--7
Well you know that I'm a wicked guy--RUNFORYOUR--9
Just to make you toe the line.--RUNFORYOUR--12
You better run for your life if you can, little
girl --RUNFORYOUR--13

You better run for your life if you can, little
girl --RUNFORYOUR--13
Catch you with another man --RUNFORYOUR--15
And I'd rather see you dead.--RUNFORYOUR--20
You better run for your life if you can, little
girl --RUNFORYOUR--21
You better run for your life if you can, little
girl --RUNFORYOUR--21
Catch you with another man --RUNFORYOUR--23
I'd rather see you dead, little girl --RUNFORYOUR
--25
You better keep your head, little girl --RUNFORYOUR
--27
Or you won't know where I am.--RUNFORYOUR--28
You better run for your life if you can, little
girl --RUNFORYOUR--29
You better run for your life if you can, little
girl --RUNFORYOUR--29
Catch you with another man --RUNFORYOUR--31
To say about the things that you do.--THINKFORYO
--2
Do what you want to do --THINKFORYO--6
'cos I won't be there with you.--THINKFORYO--9
I left you far behind--THINKFORYO--10
The ruins of the life that you had in mind --
THINKFORYO--11
And though you still can't see --THINKFORYO--12
Do what you want to do --THINKFORYO--15
'cos I won't be there with you.--THINKFORYO--18
All the things that you should.--THINKFORYO--23
Do what you want to do --THINKFORYO--24
'cos I won't be there with you.--THINKFORYO--27
Do what you want to do --THINKFORYO--28
'cos I won't be there with you.--THINKFORYO--31
'cos I won't be there with you.--THINKFORYO--33
I feel as though you ought to know--WAIT--9
And if you do, I'll trust in you --WAIT--11
And if you do, I'll trust in you --WAIT--11
And know that you will wait for me.--WAIT--12
I feel as though you ought to know--WAIT--17
And if you do, I'll trust in you --WAIT--19
And if you do, I'll trust in you --WAIT--19
And know that you will wait for me.--WAIT--20
You are tearing me apart --WHATGOESON--3
When you treat me so unkind.--WHATGOESON--4
The other day I saw you as I walked along the
road --WHATGOESON--6
But when I saw him with you I could feel my
future fold.--WHATGOESON--7
It's so easy for a girl like you to lie.--
WHATGOESON--8
You are tearing me apart --WHATGOESON--12
When you treat me so unkind.--WHATGOESON--13
I met you in the morning waiting for the tides of
time --WHATGOESON--15
It's so easy for a girl like you to lie.--
WHATGOESON--17
I used to think of no-one else but you were just
the same --WHATGOESON--22
You didn't even think of me as someone with a name.
--WHATGOESON--23
Did you mean to break my heart and watch me die?--
WHATGOESON--24
You are tearing me apart --WHATGOESON--28
When you treat me so unkind.--WHATGOESON--29
Have you heard the word is love?--THEWORD--4
Have you heard the word is love?--THEWORD--12
Have you heard the word is love?--THEWORD--20
YOU WON'T SEE ME.--YOUWONTSEE--Title
When I call you up your line's engaged.--YOUWONTSEE
--1
If you won't see me (you won't see me) --YOUWONTSEE
--5
If you won't see me (you won't see me) --YOUWONTSEE
--5
You won't see me (you won't see me).--YOUWONTSEE
--6
You won't see me (you won't see me).--YOUWONTSEE
--6
I don't know why you should want to hide --
YOUWONTSEE--7
And you won't see me (you won't see me) --
YOUWONTSEE--11
And you won't see me (you won't see me) --
YOUWONTSEE--11
You won't see me (you won't see me).--YOUWONTSEE
--12
You won't see me (you won't see me).--YOUWONTSEE
--12
Time after time you refuse to even listen --
YOUWONTSEE--13
And since I lost you it feels like years.--
YOUWONTSEE--17
If you won't see me (you won't see me) --YOUWONTSEE

--20
If you won't see me (you won't see me) --YOUWONTSEE
--20
You won't see me (you won't see me)--YOUWONTSEE--21
You won't see me (you won't see me)--YOUWONTSEE--21
Time after time you refuse to even listen --
YOUWONTSEE--22
And since I lost you it feels like years.--
YOUWONTSEE--26
If you won't see me (you won't see me) --YOUWONTSEE
--29
If you won't see me (you won't see me) --YOUWONTSEE
--29
You won't see me (you won't see me).--YOUWONTSEE
--30
You won't see me (you won't see me).--YOUWONTSEE
--30
Dear Sir or Madam, will you read my book?--
PAPERBACKW--2
It took me years to write, will you take a look?--
PAPERBACKW--3
I can make it longer if you like the style,
((paperback))--PAPERBACKW--17
If you really like it you can have the rights,
((paperback))--PAPERBACKW--21
If you really like it you can have the rights,
((paperback))--PAPERBACKW--21
It could make a million for you overnight.
((writer))--PAPERBACKW--22
If you must return it you can send it here,
((paperback))--PAPERBACKW--23
If you must return it you can send it here,
((paperback))--PAPERBACKW--23
I can show you that when it starts to rain (when
the rain comes down)--RAIN--9
I can show you, I can show you ((show you)).--RAIN
--11
I can show you, I can show you ((show you)).--RAIN
--11
I can show you, I can show you ((show you)).--RAIN
--11
Can you hear me that when it rains and shines
(when it rains and shines)--RAIN--14
Can you hear me, can you hear me? ((hear me))--
RAIN--16
Can you hear me, can you hear me? ((hear me))--
RAIN--16
You tell me that you've got everything you want --
ANDYOURBIR--1
You tell me that you've got everything you want --
ANDYOURBIR--1
But you don't get me, you don't get me.--ANDYOURBIR
--3
But you don't get me, you don't get me.--ANDYOURBIR
--3
You say you've seen seven wonders --ANDYOURBIR--4
But you can't see me, you can't see me.--ANDYOURBIR
--6
But you can't see me, you can't see me.--ANDYOURBIR
--6
When your prized possessions start to weigh you
down --ANDYOURBIR--8
When your bird is broken will it bring you down?--
ANDYOURBIR--10
You may be awoken --ANDYOURBIR--11
You tell me that you heard every sound there is --
ANDYOURBIR--13
You tell me that you heard every sound there is --
ANDYOURBIR--13
But you can't hear me, you can't hear me.--
ANDYOURBIR--15
But you can't hear me, you can't hear me.--
ANDYOURBIR--15
He helps you to understand --DRROBERT--4
If you're down he'll pick you up, Dr. Robert --
DRROBERT--6
Dr. Robert, he's a man you must believe --DRROBERT
--8
Well, well, well, he'll make you, Dr. Robert.--
DRROBERT--12
He helps you to understand --DRROBERT--16
Well, well, well, he'll make you, Dr. Robert.--
DRROBERT--19
You find that all her words of kindness linger on
--FORNOONE--2
When she no longer needs you.--FORNOONE--3
She no longer needs you.--FORNOONE--6
And in her eyes you see nothing --FORNOONE--7
You want her, you need her --FORNOONE--10
You want her, you need her --FORNOONE--10
And yet you don't believe her --FORNOONE--11
You think she needs you.--FORNOONE--13
You think she needs you.--FORNOONE--13
And in her eyes you see nothing --FORNOONE--14

You stay home, she goes out --FORNOONE--17
You won't forget her.--FORNOONE--23
And in her eyes you see nothing --FORNOONE--24
GOT TO GET YOU INTO MY LIFE.--GOTTOGETYO--Title
Ooo then I suddenly see you--GOTTOGETYO--5
Ooo did I tell you I need you--GOTTOGETYO--6
Ooo did I tell you I need you--GOTTOGETYO--6
You didn't run, you didn't lie--GOTTOGETYO--8
You didn't run, you didn't lie--GOTTOGETYO--8
You knew I wanted just to hold you--GOTTOGETYO--9
You knew I wanted just to hold you--GOTTOGETYO--9
And had you gone, you knew in time--GOTTOGETYO--10
And had you gone, you knew in time--GOTTOGETYO--10
We'd meet again for I had told you.--GOTTOGETYO--11
Ooo you were meant to be near me--GOTTOGETYO--12
Ooo and I want you to hear me--GOTTOGETYO--13
Got to get you into my life.--GOTTOGETYO--15
When I'm with you I want to stay there--GOTTOGETYO
--17
Ooo then I suddenly see you--GOTTOGETYO--20
Ooo did I tell you I need you--GOTTOGETYO--21
Ooo did I tell you I need you--GOTTOGETYO--21
Got to get you into my life.--GOTTOGETYO--23
I got to get you into my life.--GOTTOGETYO--24
Then suddenly I see you--GOTTOGETYO--29
Did I tell you I need you--GOTTOGETYO--30
Did I tell you I need you--GOTTOGETYO--30
I WANT TO TELL YOU.--IWANTTOTEL--Title
I want to tell you--IWANTTOTEL--1
When I get near you--IWANTTOTEL--5
I'll make you maybe next time around.--IWANTTOTEL
--8
I want to tell you--IWANTTOTEL--12
Sometimes I wish I knew you well--IWANTTOTEL--16
Then I could speak my mind and tell you--IWANTTOTEL
--17
I want to tell you--IWANTTOTEL--19
LOVE YOU TO/TOO.--LOVEYOUTWO--Title
You don't get time to hang a sign on me.--
LOVEYOUTWO--3
Love me while you can --LOVEYOUTWO--4
Who'll screw you in the ground--LOVEYOUTWO--14
They'll fill you in with all their sins, you'll see.
--LOVEYOUTWO--15
I'll make love to you--LOVEYOUTWO--16
If you want me to.--LOVEYOUTWO--17
She said you don't understand what I said.--
SHESAIDSHE--7
I said even though you know what you know --
SHESAIDSHE--10
I said even though you know what you know --
SHESAIDSHE--10
She said you don't understand what I said.--
SHESAIDSHE--13
I said even though you know what you know --
SHESAIDSHE--16
I said even though you know what you know --
SHESAIDSHE--16
Let me tell you how it will be --TAXMAN--3
There's one for you, nineteen for me --TAXMAN--4
If you drive a car, I'll tax the street,
((car))--TAXMAN--11
If you try to sit, I'll tax your seat, ((sit))--
TAXMAN--12
If you get too cold, I'll tax the heat,
((cold))--TAXMAN--13
If you take a walk, I'll tax your feet.
((walk))--TAXMAN--14
If you don't want to pay some more (ha ha Mr.
Heath)--TAXMAN--19
That you may see the meaning of within--TOMORROWNE
--5
Let me take you down--STRAWBERRY--1
Misunderstanding all you see--STRAWBERRY--7
Let me take you down--STRAWBERRY--11
That is you can't, you know, tune in--STRAWBERRY
--18
That is you can't, you know, tune in--STRAWBERRY
--18
Let me take you down--STRAWBERRY--21
But, you know, I know when it's a dream--STRAWBERRY
--27
Let me take you down--STRAWBERRY--31
I'd love to turn you on--DAYINTHELI--16
I'd love to turn you on--DAYINTHELI--34
You gave me the word--GETTINGBET--13
Nothing to do it's up to you--GOODMORNIN--4
Heading for home you start to roam then you're in
town.--GOODMORNIN--8
Everyone you see is half asleep--GOODMORNIN--11
After a while you start to smile now you feel cool
--GOODMORNIN--13
After a while you start to smile now you feel cool
--GOODMORNIN--13

Then you decide to take a walk by the old school--
  GOODMORNIN--14
Everyone you see is full of life--GOODMORNIN--20
Watching the skirts you start to flirt now you're
  in gear--GOODMORNIN--23
Go to a show you hope she goes--GOODMORNIN--24
When are you free ((lovely Rita))--LOVELYRITA--15
Where would I be without you?--LOVELYRITA--27
Give us a wink and make me think of you.--
  LOVELYRITA--28
Somebody calls you, you answer quite slowly--
  LUCYINTHES--3
Somebody calls you, you answer quite slowly--
  LUCYINTHES--3
Everyone smiles as you drift past the flowers--
  LUCYINTHES--14
Waiting to take you away.--LUCYINTHES--17
So may I introduce to you--SGTPEPPERS--5
We hope you will enjoy the show--SGTPEPPERS--9
We'd like to take you home with us--SGTPEPPERS--17
We'd love to take you home.--SGTPEPPERS--18
But I thought you might like to know--SGTPEPPERS
  --20
And he wants you all to sing along.--SGTPEPPERS--22
So let me introduce to you--SGTPEPPERS--23
We hope you have enjoyed the show.--SGTPEPPREP--4
We'd like to thank you once again.--SGTPEPPREP--12
Will you still be sending me a valentine--
  WHENIMSIXT--3
Would you lock the door?--WHENIMSIXT--6
Will you still need me --WHENIMSIXT--7
Will you still feed me --WHENIMSIXT--8
And if you say the word--WHENIMSIXT--11
I could stay with you.--WHENIMSIXT--12
You can knit a sweater by the fireside--WHENIMSIXT
  --15
Will you still need me --WHENIMSIXT--19
Will you still feed me --WHENIMSIXT--20
Indicate precisely what you mean to say--WHENIMSIXT
  --30
A - will you still need me --WHENIMSIXT--35
Will you still feed me --WHENIMSIXT--36
What would you think if I sang outta tune --
  WITHALITTL--1
Would you stand up and walk out on me?--WITHALITTL
  --2
Lend me your ears and I'll sing you a song--
  WITHALITTL--3
(Does it worry you to be alone?)--WITHALITTL--9
(Are you sad because you're on your own?)--
  WITHALITTL--11
(Do you need anybody?)--WITHALITTL--15
(Would you believe in a love at first sight?)--
  WITHALITTL--19
(What do you see when you turn out the light?)--
  WITHALITTL--21
(What do you see when you turn out the light?)--
  WITHALITTL--21
I can't tell you but I know it's mine.--WITHALITTL
  --22
(Do you need anybody?)--WITHALITTL--26
WITHIN YOU, WITHOUT YOU.--WITHINYOUW--Title
WITHIN YOU, WITHOUT YOU.--WITHINYOUW--Title
No-one else can make you change--WITHINYOUW--17
And life flows on within you and without you.--
  WITHINYOUW--19
And life flows on within you and without you.--
  WITHINYOUW--19
Are you one of them?--WITHINYOUW--27
Then you may find--WITHINYOUW--29
When you see we're all one--WITHINYOUW--32
And life flows on within you and without you.--
  WITHINYOUW--33
And life flows on within you and without you.--
  WITHINYOUW--33
ALL YOU NEED IS LOVE.--ALLYOUN/YS--Title
There's nothing you can do that can't be done
  ((love))--ALLYOUN/YS--4
Nothing you can sing that can't be sung ((love))--
  ALLYOUN/YS--5
Nothing you can say but you can learn how to play
  the game ((love))--ALLYOUN/YS--6
Nothing you can say but you can learn how to play
  the game ((love))--ALLYOUN/YS--6
Nothing you can make that can't be made ((love))--
  ALLYOUN/YS--8
No-one you can save that can't be saved ((love))--
  ALLYOUN/YS--9
Nothing you can do but you can learn how to be
  you in time ((love))--ALLYOUN/YS--10
Nothing you can do but you can learn how to be
  you in time ((love))--ALLYOUN/YS--10
Nothing you can do but you can learn how to be
  you in time ((love))--ALLYOUN/YS--10

All you need is love, all you need is love --
  ALLYOUN/YS--12
All you need is love, all you need is love --
  ALLYOUN/YS--12
All you need is love, love, love is all you need.
  --ALLYOUN/YS--13
All you need is love, love, love is all you need.
  --ALLYOUN/YS--13
All you need is love, (wuh) all you need is
  love (hey) --ALLYOUN/YS--17
All you need is love, (wuh) all you need is
  love (hey) --ALLYOUN/YS--17
All you need is love, love, love is all you need.
  --ALLYOUN/YS--18
All you need is love, love, love is all you need.
  --ALLYOUN/YS--18
There's nothing you can know that isn't known
  ((love))--ALLYOUN/YS--19
Nothing you can see that isn't shown ((love))--
  ALLYOUN/YS--20
There's nowhere you can be that isn't where
  you're meant to be ((love))--ALLYOUN/YS--21
All you need is love, all you need is love --
  ALLYOUN/YS--23
All you need is love, all you need is love --
  ALLYOUN/YS--23
All you need is love, love, love is all you need.
  --ALLYOUN/YS--24
All you need is love, love, love is all you need.
  --ALLYOUN/YS--24
All you need is love (all together now) --
  ALLYOUN/YS--25
All you need is love (everybody)--ALLYOUN/YS
  --26
All you need is love, love, love is all you need.
  --ALLYOUN/YS--27
All you need is love, love, love is all you need.
  --ALLYOUN/YS--27
Love is all you need (love is all you need)--
  ALLYOUN/YS--28
Love is all you need (love is all you need)--
  ALLYOUN/YS--28
Love is all you need (love is all you need)--
  ALLYOUN/YS--29
Love is all you need (love is all you need)--
  ALLYOUN/YS--29
Love is all you need (love is all you need)--
  ALLYOUN/YS--30
Love is all you need (love is all you need)--
  ALLYOUN/YS--30
Love is all you need (love is all you need)--
  ALLYOUN/YS--31
Love is all you need (love is all you need)--
  ALLYOUN/YS--31
Love is all you need (wuh) (love is all you
  need)--ALLYOUN/YS--32
Love is all you need (wuh) (love is all you
  need)--ALLYOUN/YS--32
Love is all you need (love is all you need)--
  ALLYOUN/YS--33
Love is all you need (love is all you need)--
  ALLYOUN/YS--33
Love is all you need (love is all you need)--
  ALLYOUN/YS--34
Love is all you need (love is all you need)--
  ALLYOUN/YS--34
Love is all you need (love is all you need)--
  ALLYOUN/YS--35
Love is all you need (love is all you need)--
  ALLYOUN/YS--35
Love is all you need (love is all you need)--
  ALLYOUN/YS--36
Love is all you need (love is all you need)--
  ALLYOUN/YS--36
Love is all you need (love is all you need)--
  ALLYOUN/YS--37
Love is all you need (love is all you need)--
  ALLYOUN/YS--37
Love is all you need (yahoo) (eee - hi)
  --ALLYOUN/YS-38
Love is all you need (love is all you need)--
  ALLYOUN/YS--39
Love is all you need (love is all you need)--
  ALLYOUN/YS--39
(Love is all you need) Yesterday (love is all
  you need)--ALLYOUN/YS--40
(Love is all you need) Yesterday (love is all
  you need)--ALLYOUN/YS--40
(Oh) love is all you need--ALLYOUN/YS--41
Love is all you need (oh yeah)--ALLYOUN/YS
  --42
Love is all you need--ALLYOUN/YS--43
Loves you yeah, yeah, yeah ((love is all, love
  is all))--ALLYOUN/YS--44

She loves you yeah, yeah, yeah ((love is all,
  love is all))--ALLYOUN/YS--45
Love is all you need--ALLYOUN/YS--46
Love is all you need (wuhoo)--ALLYOUN/YS--47
Love is all you need (wuhoo)--ALLYOUN/YS--48
Love is all you need (oh)--ALLYOUN/YS--49
Love is all you need--ALLYOUN/YS--50
Love is all you need.--ALLYOUN/YS--51
Now that you know who you are--BABYYOUREA--3
Now that you know who you are--BABYYOUREA--3
What do you want to be?--BABYYOUREA--4
And have you travelled very far?--BABYYOUREA--5
How often have you been there?--BABYYOUREA--9
What did you see when you were there?--BABYYOUREA--11
What did you see when you were there?--BABYYOUREA--11
You keep all your money in a big brown bag --
  BABYYOUREA--16
What are you going to play?--BABYYOUREA--27
You keep all your money in a big brown bag --
  BABYYOUREA--31
You say yes, I say no --HELLOGOODB--1
You say stop and I say go, go, go.--HELLOGOODB--2
You say goodbye and I say hello - hello, hello.--
  HELLOGOODB--4
I don't know why you say goodbye, I say hello -
  hello, hello.--HELLOGOODB--5
I don't know why you say goodbye, I say hello.--
  HELLOGOODB--6
I say hi!/high, you say 'lo/low--HELLOGOODB--7
You say why and I say I don't know.--HELLOGOODB--8
You say goodbye and I say hello - hello, hello.--
  HELLOGOODB--10
I don't know why you say goodbye, I say hello -
  hello, hello--HELLOGOODB--12
I don't know why you say goodbye, I say hello--
  HELLOGOODB--14
Why,why, why, why, why do you say --HELLOGOODB
  --16
You say goodbye and I say hello - hello, hello.--
  HELLOGOODB--19
I don't know why you say goodbye, I say hello -
  hello, hello--HELLOGOODB--20
I don't know why you say goodbye, I say hello.--
  HELLOGOODB--21
You say yes, I say no--HELLOGOODB--22
You say stop but I say go, go, go--HELLOGOODB--24
You say goodbye and I say hello - hello, hello.--
  HELLOGOODB--27
I don't know why you say goodbye, I say hello -
  hello, hello--HELLOGOODB--28
I don't know why you say goodbye, I say hello -
  hello, hello--HELLOGOODB--29
I don't know why you say goodbye, I say hello -
  hello.--HELLOGOODB--30
I am he as you are he as you are me and we are
  all together--IAMTHEWALR--1
I am he as you are he as you are me and we are
  all together--IAMTHEWALR--1
Man you been a naughty boy, you let your face
  grow long--IAMTHEWALR--6
Man you been a naughty boy, you let your face
  grow long--IAMTHEWALR--6
Boy, you been a naughty girl, you let your
  knickers down--IAMTHEWALR--14
Boy, you been a naughty girl, you let your
  knickers down--IAMTHEWALR--14
If the sun don't come you get a tan from standing
  in the English rain--IAMTHEWALR--18
Expert texpert, choking smokers, don't you
  think the joker laughs at you?--IAMTHEWALR--21
Expert texpert, choking smokers, don't you
  think the joker laughs at you?--IAMTHEWALR--21
Man you should have seen them kicking Edgar
  Allan Poe--IAMTHEWALR--27
Please don't you be very long --BLUEJAYWAY--6
Please don't you be very long (don't be long) --
  BLUEJAYWAY--13
Please don't you be very long--BLUEJAYWAY--19
Please don't you be very long (don't be long)--
  BLUEJAYWAY--20
Please don't you be very long--BLUEJAYWAY--23
Please don't you be very long--BLUEJAYWAY--26
The Magical Mystery Tour is waiting to take
  you away--MAGICALMYS--9
(Waiting to take you away).--MAGICALMYS--10
Roll up (we've got everything you need)--MAGICALMYS
  --13
The Magical Mystery Tour is hoping to take you
  away --MAGICALMYS--17
(Hoping to take you away)--MAGICALMYS--18
The Magical Mystery Tour is coming to take you
  away --MAGICALMYS--27
(Coming/Hoping to take you away)--MAGICALMYS--28
The Magical Mystery Tour is dying to take you

away--MAGICALMYS--29
Dying to take you away)--MAGICALMYS--30
Take you today.--MAGICALMYS--31
You can know all things on earth.--INNERLIGHT--9
You can know the ways of heaven.--INNERLIGHT--11
Wonder how you manage to make ends meet.--
  LADYMADONN--2
Who finds the money when you pay the rent?--
  LADYMADONN--3
Did you think that money was heaven sent?--
  LADYMADONN--4
Wonders how you manage to feed the rest.--
  LADYMADONN--10
Wonder how you manage to make ends meet.--
  LADYMADONN--19
Then you can start to make it better.--HEYJUDE--4
You were made to go out and get her --HEYJUDE--6
The minute you let her under your skin --HEYJUDE
  --7
Then you begin to make it better.--HEYJUDE--8
And any time you feel the pain--HEYJUDE--9
For well you know that it's a fool who plays it
  cool --HEYJUDE--12
You have found her, now go and get her (let it
  out and let it in) --HEYJUDE--16
Then you can start to make it better.--HEYJUDE--18
And don't you know that it's just you --HEYJUDE--22
And don't you know that it's just you --HEYJUDE--22
The movement you need is on your shoulder.--HEYJUDE
  --24
(Well you know you can make it, Jude, you've
  just gotta break it.)--HEYJUDE--46
(Well you know you can make it, Jude, you've
  just gotta break it.)--HEYJUDE--46
You say you wanna revolution,--REVOLUTION--2
You say you wanna revolution,--REVOLUTION--2
Well you know --REVOLUTION--3
You tell me that it's evolution,--REVOLUTION--5
Well you know --REVOLUTION--6
But when you talk about destruction --REVOLUTION
  --8
Don't you know that you can count me out?--
  REVOLUTION--9
Don't you know that you can count me out?--
  REVOLUTION--9
Don't you know it's gonna be alright, alright,
  alright?--REVOLUTION--10
You say you got a real solution --REVOLUTION--12
You say you got a real solution --REVOLUTION--12
Well you know --REVOLUTION--13
You ask me for a contribution --REVOLUTION--15
Well you know --REVOLUTION--16
But if you want money for people with minds that
  hate --REVOLUTION--18
All I can tell you is brother you have to wait.--
  REVOLUTION--19
All I can tell you is brother you have to wait.--
  REVOLUTION--19
Don't you know it's gonna be alright, alright
  ((alright)), alright?--REVOLUTION--20
You say you'll change the constitution --REVOLUTION
  --22
Well you know --REVOLUTION--23
You tell me it's the institution --REVOLUTION--25
Well you know --REVOLUTION--26
You better free your mind instead.--REVOLUTION--27
But if you go carrying pictures of Chairman Mao --
  REVOLUTION--28
You ain't gonna make it with anyone anyhow.--
  REVOLUTION--29
Don't you know it's gonna be alright, alright,
  alright ((alright))?--REVOLUTION--30
You don't know how lucky you are boys --BACKINTHEU
  --6
You don't know how lucky you are boys --BACKINTHEU
  --6
You don't know how lucky you are boy --BACKINTHEU
  --13
You don't know how lucky you are boy --BACKINTHEU
  --13
You don't know how lucky you are boys --BACKINTHEU
  --25
You don't know how lucky you are boys --BACKINTHEU
  --25
You don't know how lucky you are boy --BACKINTHEU
  --36
You don't know how lucky you are boy --BACKINTHEU
  --36
Oh let me tell you honey --BACKINTHEU--38
You say it's your birthday --BIRTHDAY--1
Happy birthday to you.--BIRTHDAY--6
I would like you to dance (birthday) --BIRTHDAY--11
I would like you to dance (birthday) --BIRTHDAY--13
I would like you to dance (birthday) --BIRTHDAY--16

I would like you to dance (birthday) (wuh)--
    BIRTHDAY--18
You say it's your birthday --BIRTHDAY--20
You say it's your birthday --BIRTHDAY--22
Happy birthday to you.--BIRTHDAY--25
You were only waiting for this moment to arise.--
    BLACKBIRD--4
You were only waiting for this moment to be free.
    --BLACKBIRD--8
You were only waiting for this moment to arise --
    BLACKBIRD--16
You were only waiting for this moment to arise --
    BLACKBIRD--17
You were only waiting for this moment to arise.--
    BLACKBIRD--18
What did you kill --CONTINUING--2
What did you kill --CONTINUING--5
What did you kill --CONTINUING--12
What did you kill --CONTINUING--15
What did you kill --CONTINUING--22
What did you kill --CONTINUING--25
What did you kill --CONTINUING--32
What did you kill --CONTINUING--35
What did you kill --CONTINUING--38
What did you kill --CONTINUING--41
What did you kill --CONTINUING--44
What did you kill --CONTINUING--47
What did you kill --CONTINUING--50
What did you kill --CONTINUING--53
Can you take me back where I came from --CRYBABYCRY
    --44
Can you take me back?--CRYBABYCRY--45
Can you take me back where I came from --CRYBABYCRY
    --46
Brother, can you take me back --CRYBABYCRY--47
Can you take me back?--CRYBABYCRY--48
Mmm can you take me where I came from --CRYBABYCRY
    --49
Can you take me back?--CRYBABYCRY--50
Dear Prudence, won't you come out to play?--
    DEARPRUDEN--1
It's beautiful and so are you.--DEARPRUDEN--4
Dear Prudence, won't you come out to play?--
    DEARPRUDEN--5
That you are part of everything.--DEARPRUDEN--9
Dear Prudence, won't you open up your eyes?--
    DEARPRUDEN--10
Dear Prudence, let me see you smile --DEARPRUDEN
    --16
So let me see you smile again.--DEARPRUDEN--19
Dear Prudence, won't you let me see you smile?--
    DEARPRUDEN--20
Dear Prudence, won't you let me see you smile?--
    DEARPRUDEN--20
Dear Prudence, won't you come out to play?--
    DEARPRUDEN--21
It's beautiful and so are you.--DEARPRUDEN--24
Dear Prudence, won't you come out to play?--
    DEARPRUDEN--25
Does it mean you don't love me any more?--
    DONTPASSME--9
I wonder where you are tonight --DONTPASSME--14
I don't see you --DONTPASSME--16
Does it mean you don't love me any more?--
    DONTPASSME--17
'cos you know, darling, I love only you --
    DONTPASSME--19
'cos you know, darling, I love only you --
    DONTPASSME--19
How I hate to see you go --DONTPASSME--21
I'm sorry that I doubted you --DONTPASSME--23
You were in a car crash --DONTPASSME--25
And you lost your hair.--DONTPASSME--26
You said that you would be late --DONTPASSME--27
You said that you would be late --DONTPASSME--27
Just waiting to hear from you.--DONTPASSME--30
'cos you know, darling, I love only you --
    DONTPASSME--32
'cos you know, darling, I love only you --
    DONTPASSME--32
How I hate to see you go --DONTPASSME--34
'cos you know, darling, I love only you --
    DONTPASSME--38
'cos you know, darling, I love only you --
    DONTPASSME--38
How I hate to see you go --DONTPASSME--40
The deeper you go, the higher you fly --EVRBDYMONK
    --8
The deeper you go, the higher you fly --EVRBDYMONK
    --8
The higher you fly, the deeper you go --EVRBDYMONK
    --9
The higher you fly, the deeper you go --EVRBDYMONK
    --9

I told you about Strawberry Fields--GLASSONION--1
You know the place where nothing is real--
    GLASSONION--2
Well here's another place you can go--GLASSONION
    --3
I told you about the walrus and me - man--
    GLASSONION--8
You know that we're as close as can be - man--
    GLASSONION--9
Well here's another clue for you all:--GLASSONION
    --10
I told you about the fool on the hill--GLASSONION
    --17
I tell you man he living there still--GLASSONION
    --18
Well here's another place you can be--GLASSONION
    --19
Dream sweet dreams for you.--GOODNIGHT--6
Dream sweet dreams for you.--GOODNIGHT--12
Dream sweet dreams for you.--GOODNIGHT--19
When I hold you in my arms ((oh, yeah)) --
    HAPPINESSI--22
Well, don't you know that happiness ((happiness))
    --HAPPINESSI--31
Till I get to the bottom and I see you again -
    yeah, yeah, yeah.--HELTERSKEL--3
A - do you, don't you want me to love you?--
    HELTERSKEL--4
A - do you, don't you want me to love you?--
    HELTERSKEL--4
A - do you, don't you want me to love you?--
    HELTERSKEL--4
I'm coming down fast but I'm miles above you --
    HELTERSKEL--5
Well, you may be a lover, but you ain't no
    dancer.--HELTERSKEL--7
Well, you may be a lover, but you ain't no
    dancer.--HELTERSKEL--7
A - will you, won't you want me to make you?--
    HELTERSKEL--11
A - will you, won't you want me to make you?--
    HELTERSKEL--11
A - will you, won't you want me to make you?--
    HELTERSKEL--11
I'm coming down fast but don't let me break you --
    HELTERSKEL--12
'cos you may be a lover, but you ain't no dancer.
    --HELTERSKEL--14
'cos you may be a lover, but you ain't no dancer.
    --HELTERSKEL--14
And I get to the bottom and I see you again -
    yeah, yeah, yeah.--HELTERSKEL--20
Well, do you, don't you want me to make you?--
    HELTERSKEL--21
Well, do you, don't you want me to make you?--
    HELTERSKEL--21
Well, do you, don't you want me to make you?--
    HELTERSKEL--21
I'm coming down fast but don't let me break you --
    HELTERSKEL--22
'cos you may be a lover, but you ain't no dancer.
    --HELTERSKEL--24
'cos you may be a lover, but you ain't no dancer.
    --HELTERSKEL--24
Honey Pie you are making me crazy--HONEYPIE--7
So won't you please come home.--HONEYPIE--9
You became a legend of the silver screen--HONEYPIE
    --13
And now the thought of meeting you--HONEYPIE--14
Oh, Honey Pie you are driving me frantic--HONEYPIE
    --16
To be where you belong.--HONEYPIE--18
Now Honey Pie you are making me crazy--HONEYPIE--29
So won't you please come home.--HONEYPIE--31
Who knows how long I've loved you?--IWILL--1
You know I love you still.--IWILL--2
You know I love you still.--IWILL--2
If you want me to, I will.--IWILL--4
For if I ever saw you --IWILL--5
Love you forever and forever --IWILL--9
Love you with all my heart --IWILL--10
Love you whenever we're together --IWILL--11
Love you when we're apart.--IWILL--12
And when at last I find you --IWILL--13
Sing it loud so I can hear you --IWILL--15
Make it easy to be near you --IWILL--16
For the things you do endear you to me - aah,--
    IWILL--17
For the things you do endear you to me - aah --
    IWILL--17
You know I will - I will.--IWILL--18
I'm so tired, my mind is set on you --IMSOTIRED--6
I wonder should I call you --IMSOTIRED--7
But I know what you would do.--IMSOTIRED--8

You'd say I'm putting you on --IMSOTIRED--9
You know I can't sleep, I can't stop my brain --
   IMSOTIRED--11
You know it's three weeks, I'm going insane --
   IMSOTIRED--12
You know I'd give you everything I've got for a
   little peace of mind.--IMSOTIRED--13
You know I'd give you everything I've got for a
   little peace of mind.--IMSOTIRED--13
You'd say I'm putting you on --IMSOTIRED--18
You know I can't sleep, I can't stop my brain --
   IMSOTIRED--20
You know it's three weeks, I'm going insane --
   IMSOTIRED--21
You know I'd give you everything I've got for a
   little peace of mind.--IMSOTIRED--22
You know I'd give you everything I've got for a
   little peace of mind.--IMSOTIRED--22
I'd give you everything I've got for a little
   peace of mind --IMSOTIRED--23
I'd give you everything I've got for a little
   peace of mind.--IMSOTIRED--24
But I say it just to reach you, Julia.--JULIA--2
How could I ever have lost you --LONGLONGLO--2
When I loved you?--LONGLONGLO--3
Now I'm so happy I found you --LONGLONGLO--5
How I love you.--LONGLONGLO--6
Now I can see you, be you --LONGLONGLO--9
Now I can see you, be you --LONGLONGLO--9
How can I ever misplace you?--LONGLONGLO--10
How I want you.--LONGLONGLO--11
Oh I love you --LONGLONGLO--12
You know that I need you --LONGLONGLO--13
You know that I need you --LONGLONGLO--13
Oh I love you.--LONGLONGLO--14
Hold your head up you silly girl, look what
   you've done --MARTHAMYDE--4
When you find yourself in the thick of it --
   MARTHAMYDE--5
Help yourself to a bit of what is all around you
   - silly girl.--MARTHAMYDE--6
Take a good look around you --MARTHAMYDE--7
That you and me were meant to be for each other -
   silly girl.--MARTHAMYDE--9
Hold your hand out you silly girl, see what
   you've done --MARTHAMYDE--10
When you find yourself in the thick of it --
   MARTHAMYDE--11
Help yourself to a bit of what is all around you
   - silly girl.--MARTHAMYDE--12
Martha my dear, you have always been my
   inspiration --MARTHAMYDE--13
But if you want some fun (ha ha ha) --OBLADIOBLA
   --40
Thank you (ooo) (ha ha ha).--OBLADIOBLA--42
Have you seen the little piggies--PIGGIES--1
Have you seen the bigger piggies--PIGGIES--6
You will find the bigger piggies--PIGGIES--8
You can see them out for dinner--PIGGIES--17
You say you want a revolution --REVOLUTONE--5
You say you want a revolution --REVOLUTONE--5
Well you know --REVOLUTONE--6
You tell me that it's evolution --REVOLUTONE--8
Well you know --REVOLUTONE--9
But when you talk about destruction --REVOLUTONE
   --11
Don't you know that you can count me out (in)?--
   REVOLUTONE--12
Don't you know that you can count me out (in)?--
   REVOLUTONE--12
Don't you know it's gonna be ((oh shoo-be-do-a))--
   REVOLUTONE--13
Don't you know it's gonna be ((oh shoo-be-do-a))--
   REVOLUTONE--15
Don't you know it's gonna be ((oh shoo-be-do-a))--
   REVOLUTONE--17
You say you got a real solution --REVOLUTONE--19
You say you got a real solution --REVOLUTONE--19
Well you know --REVOLUTONE--20
You ask me for a contribution --REVOLUTONE--23
Well you know --REVOLUTONE--24
But if you want money for people with minds that
   hate --REVOLUTONE--27
Well all I can tell you is brother you have to
   wait.--REVOLUTONE--28
Well all I can tell you is brother you have to
   wait.--REVOLUTONE--28
Don't you know it's gonna be ((oh shoo-be-do-a))--
   REVOLUTONE--29
Don't you know it's gonna be ((oh shoo-be-do-a))--
   --REVOLUTONE--31
Don't you know it's gonna be ((oh shoo-be-do-a))--
   REVOLUTONE--33
You say you'll change the constitution --REVOLUTONE

--35
Well you know --REVOLUTONE--36
You tell me it's the institution --REVOLUTONE--39
Well you know --REVOLUTONE--40
If you go carrying pictures of Chairman Mao --
   REVOLUTONE--43
You ain't gonna make it with anyone anyhow.--
   REVOLUTONE--44
Don't you know it's gonna be ((oh shoo-be-do-a))--
   REVOLUTONE--45
Don't you know it's gonna be ((oh shoo-be-do-a))--
   REVOLUTONE--47
Don't you know it's gonna be ((oh shoo-be-do-a))--
   REVOLUTONE--49
He said, Rocky you met your match--ROCKYRACCO--33
Coffee dessert - yes you know it's good news --
   SAVOYTRUFF--3
You might not feel it now --SAVOYTRUFF--11
You shout aloud.--SAVOYTRUFF--16
You know that what you eat you are --SAVOYTRUFF--19
You know that what you eat you are --SAVOYTRUFF--19
You know that what you eat you are --SAVOYTRUFF--19
But can you show me where you are?--SAVOYTRUFF--22
But can you show me where you are?--SAVOYTRUFF--22
Coffee dessert - yes you know it's good news
   (wuh) --SAVOYTRUFF--25
Sexy Sadie what have you done?--SEXYSADIE--1
You made a fool of everyone--SEXYSADIE--2
You made a fool of everyone--SEXYSADIE--3
Sexie Sadie - oh what have you done?--SEXYSADIE--4
Sexy Sadie you broke the rules--SEXYSADIE--5
You layed it down for all to see--SEXYSADIE--6
You layed it down for all to see--SEXYSADIE--7
Sexy Sadie - oh you broke the rules--SEXYSADIE--8
Sexy Sadie how did you know--SEXYSADIE--12
The world was waiting just for you?--SEXYSADIE--13
The world was waiting just for you?--SEXYSADIE--14
Sexy Sadie - oh how did you know?--SEXYSADIE--15
However big you think you are--SEXYSADIE--17
However big you think you are--SEXYSADIE--17
However big you think you are--SEXYSADIE--18
However big you think you are--SEXYSADIE--18
... However big you think you are.--SEXYSADIE--28
... However big you think you are.--SEXYSADIE--28
I look at you all, see the love there that's
   sleeping --WHILEMYGUI--2
I don't know why nobody told you how to unfold
   your love --WHILEMYGUI--6
I don't know how someone controlled you --
   WHILEMYGUI--7
They bought and sold you.--WHILEMYGUI--8
I don't know how you were diverted --WHILEMYGUI--14
You were perverted (too/to)--WHILEMYGUI--15
I don't know how you were inverted,--WHILEMYGUI--16
No-one alerted you.--WHILEMYGUI--17
I look at you all, see the love there that's
   sleeping--WHILEMYGUI--18
Look, look at you all --WHILEMYGU1--20
Why don't you do it in the road?--WHYDONTWED--18
I love you, yeah, Honey Pie, wuh!--WILDHONEYP--4
Ooo - girl you know the reason why.--YERBLUES--5
Wuh - girl you know the reason why.--YERBLUES--9
And you know what it's worth.--YERBLUES--13
Wuh - girl you know the reason why.--YERBLUES--16
Wuh - girl you know the reason why.--YERBLUES--23
Wuh girl - you know the reason why.--YERBLUES--30
... Girl you know the reason why.--YERBLUES--33
I love you.--ALLTOGETHE--4
I love you.--ALLTOGETHE--8
I love you.--ALLTOGETHE--20
ALL YOU NEED IS LOVE.--ALLYOU/MMT--Title
Love is all you need--ALLYOU/MMT--1
(Oh) love is all you need--ALLYOU/MMT--2
Love is all you need--ALLYOU/MMT--3
Love is all you need--ALLYOU/MMT--4
Love is all you need--ALLYOU/MMT--5
Love is all you need.--ALLYOU/MMT--6
What makes you think you're something special
   when you smile?--HEYBULLDOG--4
What makes you think you're something special
   when you smile?--HEYBULLDOG--4
You don't know what it's like to listen to your
   fears.--HEYBULLDOG--8
You can talk to me--HEYBULLDOG--9
You can talk to me--HEYBULLDOG--10
You can talk to me--HEYBULLDOG--11
If you're lonely you can talk to me.--HEYBULLDOG
   --12
Some kind of solitude is measured out in you--
   HEYBULLDOG--15
You think you know me but you haven't got a clue.
   --HEYBULLDOG--16
You think you know me but you haven't got a clue.
   --HEYBULLDOG--16

You think you know me but you haven't got a clue.
    --HEYBULLDOG--16
You can talk to me--HEYBULLDOG--17
You can talk to me--HEYBULLDOG--18
You can talk to me--HEYBULLDOG--19
If you're lonely you can talk to me - hey!--
    HEYBULLDOG--20
What do you say?--HEYBULLDOG--24
Do you know any more?--HEYBULLDOG--26
The love that's shining all around you --ITSALLTOOM
    --9
Everywhere it's what you make --ITSALLTOOM--10
Makes no difference where you are--ITSALLTOOM--14
The love that's shining all around you --ITSALLTOOM
    --30
Everywhere it's what you make --ITSALLTOOM--31
You may think the chords are going wrong --
    ONLYANORTH--2
You may think the band are not quite right --
    ONLYANORTH--5
If you think the harmony--ONLYANORTH--13
And I told you there's no-one there.--ONLYANORTH
    --16
Don't you know it's gonna last --DONTLETMED--14
Can you dig it?--DONTLETMED--32
Get back to where you once belonged.--GETBACK/45
    --6
Get back to where you once belonged.--GETBACK/45
    --8
Back to where you once belonged.--GETBACK/45--12
Back to where you once belonged.--GETBACK/45--14
Get back to where you once belonged.--GETBACK/45
    --21
Get back to where you once belonged.--GETBACK/45
    --23
Get back to where you once belonged.--GETBACK/45
    --27
Get back to where you once belonged.--GETBACK/45
    --29
Your mommy's waiting for you --GETBACK/45--32
Get back to where you once belonged.--GETBACK/45
    --37
You know they didn't even give us a chance.--
    BALLADOFJO--4
Christ! you know it ain't easy --BALLADOFJO--5
You know how hard it can be --BALLADOFJO--6
Peter Brown called to say, you can make it OK --
    BALLADOFJO--11
You can get married in Gibraltar near Spain.--
    BALLADOFJO--12
Christ! you know it ain't easy --BALLADOFJO--13
You know how hard it can be --BALLADOFJO--14
The news-people said, say what're you doing in
    bed?--BALLADOFJO--19
Christ! you know it ain't easy --BALLADOFJO--21
You know how hard it can be --BALLADOFJO--22
You don't take nothing with you but your soul -
    think!--BALLADOFJO--28
You don't take nothing with you but your soul -
    think!--BALLADOFJO--28
Christ! you know it ain't easy --BALLADOFJO--33
You know how hard it can be --BALLADOFJO--34
The men from the press said, we wish you success
    --BALLADOFJO--39
It's good to have the both of you back.--BALLADOFJO
    --40
Christ! you know it ain't easy --BALLADOFJO--41
You know how hard it can be.--BALLADOFJO--42
Baby, I'm in love with you --OLDBROWNSH--6
We're so glad you came here --OLDBROWNSH--7
It won't be the same now I'm telling you.--
    OLDBROWNSH--8
Though you pick me up --OLDBROWNSH--9
Baby, I'm in love with you --OLDBROWNSH--14
So glad you came here --OLDBROWNSH--15
It won't be the same now that I'm with you.--
    OLDBROWNSH--16
Not worrying what they or you say --OLDBROWNSH--19
Who knows baby, you may comfort me (hey).--
    OLDBROWNSH--21
My love is something you can't reject.--OLDBROWNSH
    --23
If you and me should get together --OLDBROWNSH--25
Who knows baby, you may comfort me (hey).--
    OLDBROWNSH--26
Baby, I'm in love with you.--OLDBROWNSH--32
So glad you came here --OLDBROWNSH--33
Won't be the same now that I'm with you.--
    OLDBROWNSH--34
I'm so glad you came here --OLDBROWNSH--35
It won't be the same now that I'm with you.
    (yeah, yeah, yeah).--OLDBROWNSH--36
Love is all, love is you.--BECAUSE--9
I never give you my pillow --CARRYTHATW--5

I only send you my invitations--CARRYTHATW--6
He say I know you, you know me--COMETOGETH--19
He say I know you, you know me--COMETOGETH--19
One thing I can tell you is you got to be free--
    COMETOGETH--20
One thing I can tell you is you got to be free--
    COMETOGETH--20
Hold you in his armchair you can feel his disease
    --COMETOGETH--30
Hold you in his armchair you can feel his disease
    --COMETOGETH--30
Are you gonna be in my dreams tonight?--THEEND--2
Love you, love you, love you, love you, love
    you --THEEND--3
Love you, love you, love you, love you, love
    you --THEEND--3
Love you, love you, love you, love you, love
    you --THEEND--3
Love you, love you, love you, love you, love
    you --THEEND--3
Love you, love you, love you, love you, love
    you --THEEND--3
Love you, love you, love you, love you, love
    you --THEEND--4
Love you, love you, love you, love you, love
    you --THEEND--4
Love you, love you, love you, love you, love
    you --THEEND--4
Love you, love you, love you, love you, love
    you --THEEND--4
Love you, love you, love you, love you, love
    you --THEEND--4
Love you, love you, love you, love you, love
    you --THEEND--5
Love you, love you, love you, love you, love
    you --THEEND--5
Love you, love you, love you, love you, love
    you --THEEND--5
Love you, love you, love you, love you, love
    you --THEEND--5
Love you, love you, love you, love you, love
    you --THEEND--5
Love you, love you, love you, love you, love
    you --THEEND--6
Love you, love you, love you, love you, love
    you --THEEND--6
Love you, love you, love you, love you, love
    you --THEEND--6
Love you, love you, love you, love you, love
    you --THEEND--6
Love you, love you, love you, love you, love
    you --THEEND--6
Love you, love you, love you, love you.--THEEND--7
Love you, love you, love you, love you.--THEEND--7
Love you, love you, love you, love you.--THEEND--7
Love you, love you, love you, love you.--THEEND--7
The love you take is equal to the love you make.--
    THEEND--9
The love you take is equal to the love you make.--
    THEEND--9
Smiles awake you when you rise.--GOLDENSLUM--8
Smiles awake you when you rise.--GOLDENSLUM--8
I WANT YOU (SHE'S SO HEAVY).--IWANTYOUSH--Title
I want you--IWANTYOUSH--1
I want you so bad--IWANTYOUSH--2
I want you--IWANTYOUSH--3
I want you so bad--IWANTYOUSH--4
I want you--IWANTYOUSH--7
I want you so bad, babe--IWANTYOUSH--8
I want you--IWANTYOUSH--9
I want you so bad--IWANTYOUSH--10
I want you--IWANTYOUSH--13
I want you so bad, babe--IWANTYOUSH--14
I want you--IWANTYOUSH--15
I want you so bad--IWANTYOUSH--16
I want you--IWANTYOUSH--19
I want you so bad--IWANTYOUSH--20
I want you--IWANTYOUSH--21
I want you so bad--IWANTYOUSH--22
I want you--IWANTYOUSH--28
I want you so bad--IWANTYOUSH--29
I want you--IWANTYOUSH--30
I want you so bad--IWANTYOUSH--31
I want you--IWANTYOUSH--34
You know I want you so bad, babe--IWANTYOUSH--35
You know I want you so bad, babe--IWANTYOUSH--35
I want you--IWANTYOUSH--36
You know I want you so bad--IWANTYOUSH--37
You know I want you so bad--IWANTYOUSH--37
Can I take you out to the pictures, Joan?--
    MAXWELLSIL--4
We would be so happy you and me--OCTOPUSSGA--21
In an octopus's garden with you --OCTOPUSSGA--24
In an octopus's garden with you --OCTOPUSSGA--25

In an octopus's garden with you.--OCTOPUSSGA--26
Oh darling, please believe me, I'll never do
  you no harm.--OHDARLING--1
Believe me when I tell you, I'll never do you
  no harm.--OHDARLING--2
Believe me when I tell you, I'll never do you
  no harm.--OHDARLING--2
Oh darling, if you leave me I'll never make it
  alone --OHDARLING--3
Believe me when I beg you - ooo - don't ever
  leave me alone.--OHDARLING--4
When you told me you didn't need me any more --
  OHDARLING--5
When you told me you didn't need me any more --
  OHDARLING--5
Well you know I nearly broke down and cried.--
  OHDARLING--6
A - when you told me you didn't need me any more
  --OHDARLING--7
A - when you told me you didn't need me any more
  --OHDARLING--7
A - well you know, I nearly broke down and died.--
  OHDARLING--8
Oh darling, if you leave me, I'll never make
  it alone.--OHDARLING--9
Believe me when I tell you, I'll never do you
  no harm.--OHDARLING--10
Believe me when I tell you, I'll never do you
  no harm.--OHDARLING--10
A - when you told me - ooo - you didn't need me
  any more --OHDARLING--12
A - when you told me - ooo - you didn't need me
  any more --OHDARLING--12
A - well you know I nearly broke down and cried.--
  OHDARLING--13
A - when you told me you didn't need me any more
  --OHDARLING--14
A - when you told me you didn't need me any more
  --OHDARLING--14
A - well you know, I nearly broke down and died.--
  OHDARLING--15
Oh darling, please believe me, I'll never let
  you down.--OHDARLING--16
Believe me when I tell you - ooo - I'll never
  do you no harm.--OHDARLING--18
Believe me when I tell you - ooo - I'll never
  do you no harm.--OHDARLING--18
Well, you should see Polythene Pam.--POLYTHENEP--1
Well, you should see her in drag --POLYTHENEP--3
Yes, you should see Polythene Pam - yeah,
  yeah, yeah.--POLYTHENEP--5
Yes, you could say she was attractively built -
  yeah, yeah, yeah.--POLYTHENEP--9
You know I believe 'n' how.--SOMETHING--5
You know I believe 'n' how.--SOMETHING--10
You stick around now it may show --SOMETHING--13
You know I believe 'n' how.--SOMETHING--19
YOU NEVER GIVE ME YOUR MONEY.--YOUNEVERGI--Title
You never give me your money --YOUNEVERGI--1
You only give me your funny paper--YOUNEVERGI--2
And in the middle of negotiations you break down.
  --YOUNEVERGI--3
I never give you my number --YOUNEVERGI--4
I only give you my situation--YOUNEVERGI--5
YOU KNOW MY NAME (LOOK UP MY NUMBER).--YOUKNOWMYN
  --Title
You know my name, look up de number.--YOUKNOWMYN
  --1
You know my name, look up de number.--YOUKNOWMYN
  --2
You, you know, you know my name --YOUKNOWMYN--3
You, you know, you know my name --YOUKNOWMYN--3
You, you know, you know my name --YOUKNOWMYN--3
You, you know, you know my name.--YOUKNOWMYN--4
You, you know, you know my name.--YOUKNOWMYN--4
You, you know, you know my name.--YOUKNOWMYN--4
Good evening, you know my name, well then look
  up my number --YOUKNOWMYN--9
You know my name, that's right, look up my
  number (hey) --YOUKNOWMYN--10
You, you know, you know my name ((you know my
  name)) --YOUKNOWMYN--11
You, you know, you know my name ((you know my
  name)) --YOUKNOWMYN--11
You, you know, you know my name ((you know my
  name)) --YOUKNOWMYN--11
You, you know, you know my name ((you know my
  name)) --YOUKNOWMYN--11
You, you know, you know my name (brrrrrr - ha,
  hey!) --YOUKNOWMYN--12
You, you know, you know my name (brrrrrr - ha,
  hey!) --YOUKNOWMYN--12
You, you know, you know my name (brrrrrr - ha,
  hey!) --YOUKNOWMYN--12

You know my name, ba ba ba ba ba ba ba ba
  ((yahoo)) --YOUKNOWMYN--13
You know my name - haa, that's right, look up
  the number --YOUKNOWMYN--15
(Oh) oh, you know, you know, you know my
  name (come on Dennis) --YOUKNOWMYN--16
(Oh) oh, you know, you know, you know my
  name (come on Dennis) --YOUKNOWMYN--16
(Oh) oh, you know, you know, you know my
  name (come on Dennis) --YOUKNOWMYN--16
You know, you know, you know my name, ha ha ha
  ha --YOUKNOWMYN--17
You know, you know, you know my name, ha ha ha
  ha --YOUKNOWMYN--17
You know, you know, you know my name, ha ha ha
  ha --YOUKNOWMYN--17
You know my name, ba ba ba bum, look up the
  number --YOUKNOWMYN--18
You know my name, look up the number --YOUKNOWMYN
  --19
You, you know, you know my name, baby --YOUKNOWMYN
  --20
You, you know, you know my name, baby --YOUKNOWMYN
  --20
You, you know, you know my name, baby --YOUKNOWMYN
  --20
You, you know, you know my name --YOUKNOWMYN--21
You, you know, you know my name --YOUKNOWMYN--21
You, you know, you know my name --YOUKNOWMYN--21
You know, you know my name --YOUKNOWMYN--22
You know, you know my name --YOUKNOWMYN--22
You know, you know my name ((oh, let's hear it,
  come on Dennis)) --YOUKNOWMYN--23
You know, you know my name ((oh, let's hear it,
  come on Dennis)) --YOUKNOWMYN--23
My name, you know, you know, ((look up the
  number))--YOUKNOWMYN--25
My name, you know, you know, ((look up the
  number))--YOUKNOWMYN--25
You know my name (you know my number).--YOUKNOWMYN
  --26
You know my name (you know my number).--YOUKNOWMYN
  --26
You know, ((you know my name))--YOUKNOWMYN--27
You know, ((you know my name))--YOUKNOWMYN--27
You know, you know my name. ((you know my
  number))--YOUKNOWMYN--28
You know, you know my name. ((you know my
  number))--YOUKNOWMYN--28
You know, you know my name. ((you know my
  number))--YOUKNOWMYN--28
You know my name, look up the number --YOUKNOWMYN
  --29
You know my name, look up the number.--YOUKNOWMYN
  --30
You know, you know my name, look up the number.--
  YOUKNOWMYN--31
You know, you know my name, look up the number.--
  YOUKNOWMYN--31
Yes, you know, ((you know my name))--YOUKNOWMYN--32
Yes, you know, ((you know my name))--YOUKNOWMYN--32
You know my name ((you know)), you know me
  number (too/two)--YOUKNOWMYN--33
You know my name ((you know)), you know me
  number (too/two)--YOUKNOWMYN--33
You know my name ((you know)), you know me
  number (too/two)--YOUKNOWMYN--33
You know my name, you know me number three --
  YOUKNOWMYN--34
You know my name, you know me number three --
  YOUKNOWMYN--34
You know my name, you know me number four --
  YOUKNOWMYN--35
You know my name, you know me number four --
  YOUKNOWMYN--35
You know my name, look up the number --YOUKNOWMYN
  --36
You know my name ((you know)), you know me
  number (too/two)--YOUKNOWMYN--37
You know my name ((you know)), you know me
  number (too/two)--YOUKNOWMYN--37
You know my name ((you know)), you know me
  number (too/two)--YOUKNOWMYN--37
You know my name ((you know my name)) --YOUKNOWMYN
  --39
You know my name ((you know my name)) --YOUKNOWMYN
  --39
You know my number, what's up with you? - ha--
  YOUKNOWMYN--40
You know my number, what's up with you? - ha--
  YOUKNOWMYN--40
You know my name.--YOUKNOWMYN--41
((That was Can You Dig It? by Georgie
  Wood))--DIGIT--11

FOR YOU BLUE.--FORYOUBLUE--Title
Because you're sweet and lovely girl, I love you
     --FORYOUBLUE--2
I love you more than ever girl, I do.--FORYOUBLUE
     --4
I want you in the morning girl, I love you --
     FORYOUBLUE--5
I want you in the morning girl, I love you --
     FORYOUBLUE--5
I want you at the moment I feel blue --FORYOUBLUE
     --6
I'm living every moment girl for you.--FORYOUBLUE
     --7
I've loved you from the moment I saw you --
     FORYOUBLUE--13
I've loved you from the moment I saw you --
     FORYOUBLUE--13
You looked at me, that's all you had to do --
     FORYOUBLUE--14
You looked at me, that's all you had to do --
     FORYOUBLUE--14
I feel it now, I hope you feel it too.--FORYOUBLUE
     --15
Because you're sweet and lovely girl, I love you
     --FORYOUBLUE--16
I love you more than ever girl, I do - really
     love blues.--FORYOUBLUE--18
Get back to where you once belonged--GETBACK/LP--12
Get back to where you once belonged--GETBACK/LP--14
Back to where you once belonged--GETBACK/LP--18
Back to where you once belonged--GETBACK/LP--20
Get back to where you once belonged--GETBACK/LP--27
Get back to where you once belonged.--GETBACK/LP
     --29
Get back to where you once belonged--GETBACK/LP--33
Get back to where you once belonged--GETBACK/LP--35
I'd like to say thank you on behalf of the group
     and ourselves--GETBACK/LP--38
Well you can celebrate anything you want--IDIGAPONY
     --7
Well you can celebrate anything you want--IDIGAPONY
     --7
Yes you can celebrate anything you want.--IDIGAPONY
     --8
Yes you can celebrate anything you want.--IDIGAPONY
     --8
Well you can penetrate any place you go--IDIGAPONY
     --10
Well you can penetrate any place you go--IDIGAPONY
     --10
Yes you can penetrate any place you go--IDIGAPONY
     --11
Yes you can penetrate any place you go--IDIGAPONY
     --11
I told you so.--IDIGAPONY--12
All I want is you--IDIGAPONY--13
Everything has got to be just like you want it to
     --IDIGAPONY--14
Well you can radiate everything you are--IDIGAPONY
     --17
Well you can radiate everything you are--IDIGAPONY
     --17
Yes you can radiate everything you are.--IDIGAPONY
     --19
Yes you can radiate everything you are.--IDIGAPONY
     --18
Well you can imitate everyone you know--IDIGAPONY
     --18
Well you can imitate everyone you know--IDIGAPONY
     --20
Yes you can imitate everyone you know--IDIGAPONY
     --20
Yes you can imitate everyone you know--IDIGAPONY
     --21
I told you so.--IDIGAPONY--22
All I want is you--IDIGAPONY--23
Everything has got to be just like you want it to
     --IDIGAPONY--24
Well you can indicate everything you see--IDIGAPONY
     --27
Well you can indicate everything you see--IDIGAPONY
     --27
Yes you can indicate anything you see.--IDIGAPONY
     --28
Yes you can indicate anything you see.--IDIGAPONY
     --28
Well you can syndicate any boat you rode/rowed
     --IDIGAPONY--30
Well you can syndicate any boat you rode/rowed
     --IDIGAPONY--30
Yeah you can syndicate any boat you rode/rowed
     --IDIGAPONY--31
Yeah you can syndicate any boat you rode/rowed
     --IDIGAPONY--31

I told you so.--IDIGAPONY--32
All I want is you--IDIGAPONY--33
Everything has got to be just like you want it to
     --IDIGAPONY--34
Thank you, brothers.--IDIGAPONY--37
And if you leave me I won't be late again --
     IVEGOTAFEE--8
All that I was looking for was somebody who
     looked like you.--IVEGOTAFEE--13
You left me standing here a long, long time ago --
     LONGANDWIN--10
You left me standing here a long, long time ago --
     LONGANDWIN--13
Railman said, you got the wrong location --
     ONEAFTERNI--12
Railman said, you got the wrong location --
     ONEAFTERNI--22
You and me Sunday driving --TWOOFUS--5
You and me burning matches --TWOOFUS--12
You and I have memories --TWOOFUS--17
You and me chasing paper --TWOOFUS--21
You and I have memories --TWOOFUS--26
You and me chasing paper --TWOOFUS--30
You better believe it.--TWOOFUS--36

YOU'D
     You'd love her too --ANDILOVEHE--4
And when I do you'd better hide all the girls --
     ILLCRYINST--15
And when I do you'd better hide all the girls --
     ILLCRYINST--24
And so I'm telling you this time you'd better
     stop --ANOTHERGIR--8
Ring my friend I said you'd call, Dr. Robert --
     DRROBERT--1
Ring my friend I said you'd call, Dr. Robert --
     DRROBERT--20
Ring my friend I said you'd call, Dr. Robert --
     DRROBERT--21
Maybe you'd understand.--IWANTTOTEL--18
You'd say I'm putting you on --IMSOTIRED--9
You'd say I'm putting you on --IMSOTIRED--18
You'd better free your mind instead.--REVOLUTONE
     --41
Or where you'd like to be.--ITSALLTOOM--15

YOU'LL
     And in time you'll understand the reason why --
     ASKMEWHY--9
You'll never know how much I really love you --
     DOYOUWANTT--1
You'll never know how much I really care.--
     DOYOUWANTT--2
And you'll come running home --ALLIVEGOTT--4
And you'll come running home --ALLIVEGOTT--20
I think you'll understand--IWANTTOHOL--2
And/You'll let me be your man--IWANTTOHOL--8
You'll let me hold your hand--IWANTTOHOL--10
And/You'll let me hold your hand--IWANTTOHOL--11
I think you'll understand--IWANTTOHOL--23
I think you'll understand--IWANTTOHOL--34
If you'll only listen to my pleas --TELLMEWHY--22
You'll be thinking of me, somehow I will know --
     THINGSWESA--2
You say you'll be mine girl, till the end of time
     --THINGSWESA--6
One day you'll look to see I've gone --ILLFOLLOWT
     --1
Some day you'll know I was the one --ILLFOLLOWT--3
One day you'll find that I have gone --ILLFOLLOWT
     --7
One day you'll find that I have gone --ILLFOLLOWT
     --12
You'll be back again tonight--YOULIKEMET--2
You'll never leave me and you know it's true--
     YOULIKEMET--5
You'll never leave me and you know it's true--
     YOULIKEMET--11
And then you'll be the lonely one (you're not
     the only one)--YOUREGONNA--12
I will say the only words I know that you'll
     understand.--MICHELLE--8
Until I do I'm telling you so you'll understand.--
     MICHELLE--19
And I will say the only words I know that
     you'll understand --MICHELLE--22
Say the word and you'll be free --THEWORD--1
Spread the word and you'll be free --THEWORD--9
Say the word and you'll be free --THEWORD--17
They'll fill you in with all their sins, you'll see.
     --LOVEYOUTWO--15
You'll be older too--WHENIMSIXT--10

Hey Jude, you'll do --HEYJUDE--23
Then you'll begin ((let it out)) to make it
    better --HEYJUDE--29
You say you'll change the constitution --REVOLUTION
    --22
You'll never know it hurt me so --DONTPASSME--20
You'll never know it hurt me so --DONTPASSME--33
You'll never know it hurt me so --DONTPASSME--39
You say you'll change the constitution --REVOLUTONE
    --35
But you'll have to have them all pulled out--
    SAVOYTRUFF--4
But you'll have to have them all pulled out--
    SAVOYTRUFF--9
But you'll have to have them all pulled out--
    SAVOYTRUFF--17
But you'll have to have them all pulled out--
    SAVOYTRUFF--26
Yes, you'll have to have them all pulled out--
    SAVOYTRUFF--28
Sexy Sadie you'll get yours yet--SEXYSADIE--16
Sexy Sadie - oh you'll get yours yet--SEXYSADIE--19
Anyway you'll never know the many ways I've tried
    --LONGANDWIN--8

YOU'RE
If you're feeling sorry and sad --ANYTIMEATA--7
Now you're mine --ASKMEWHY--7
But you're the only love that I've ever had.--
    ASKMEWHY--11
You're not the hurting kind.--SHELOVESYO--15
Now you're coming, you're coming on home (now
    you're coming on home)--ITWONTBELO--12
Now you're coming, you're coming on home (now
    you're coming on home)--ITWONTBELO--12
Now you're coming, you're coming on home (now
    you're coming on home)--ITWONTBELO--12
I'll be good like I know I should (yes,
    you're coming on home)--ITWONTBELO--13
You're coming home, you're coming home--ITWONTBELO
    --14
You're coming home, you're coming home--ITWONTBELO
    --14
Now you're coming, you're coming on home (now
    you're coming on home)--ITWONTBELO--22
Now you're coming, you're coming on home (now
    you're coming on home)--ITWONTBELO--22
Now you're coming, you're coming on home (now
    you're coming on home)--ITWONTBELO--22
I'll be good like I know I should (yes,
    you're coming on home)--ITWONTBELO--23
You're coming home, you're coming home--ITWONTBELO
    --24
You're coming home, you're coming home--ITWONTBELO
    --24
Then we'll have some fun when you're mine, all
    mine --LITTLECHIL--10
When you're by my side, you're the only one --
    LITTLECHIL--16
When you're by my side, you're the only one --
    LITTLECHIL--16
You're giving me the same old line --NOTASECOND--7
You hurt me then you're back again --NOTASECOND--9
You're giving me the same old line --NOTASECOND--18
You hurt me then you're back again --NOTASECOND--20
I call your name, but you're not there --ICALLYOURN
    --1
You're gonna give me everything --HARDDAYSNI--11
You're gonna say you love me too, oh.--ISHOULDHAV
    --8
You're gonna say you love me too.--ISHOULDHAV--10
You're gonna say you love me too, oh.--ISHOULDHAV
    --18
You're gonna say you love me too.--ISHOULDHAV--20
WHAT YOU'RE DOING.--WHATYOURED--Title
Look ((look)) what you're doing --WHATYOURED--1
What you're doing to me?--WHATYOURED--4
What you're doing to me?--WHATYOURED--8
Wondering what you're gonna do --WHATYOURED--10
What you're doing to me?--WHATYOURED--15
Wondering what you're gonna do --WHATYOURED--17
What you're doing to me?--WHATYOURED--22
What you're doing to me?--WHATYOURED--23
What you're doing to me?--WHATYOURED--24
You can't cry 'cos you're laughing at me --IMDOWN
    --2
You're making me say that I've got nobody but you
    --ANOTHERGIR--2
YOU'RE GOING TO/GONNA LOSE THAT GIRL.--YOUREGONNA--Title
You're gonna lose that girl (yes, yes, you're
    gonna lose that girl)--YOUREGONNA--1
You're gonna lose that girl (yes, yes, you're
    gonna lose that girl)--YOUREGONNA--1

You're gonna lose that girl (yes, yes, you're
    gonna lose that girl)--YOUREGONNA--2
You're gonna lose that girl (yes, yes, you're
    gonna lose that girl)--YOUREGONNA--2
You're gonna lose that girl (yes, yes, you're
    gonna lose that girl)--YOUREGONNA--7
You're gonna lose that girl (yes, yes, you're
    gonna lose that girl)--YOUREGONNA--7
You're gonna lose that girl (yes, yes, you're
    gonna lose that girl)--YOUREGONNA--8
You're gonna lose that girl (yes, yes, you're
    gonna lose that girl)--YOUREGONNA--8
You're gonna find her gone (you're gonna find
    her gone)--YOUREGONNA--10
You're gonna find her gone (you're gonna find
    her gone)--YOUREGONNA--10
And then you'll be the lonely one (you're not
    the only one)--YOUREGONNA--12
You're gonna lose that girl (yes, yes, you're
    gonna lose that girl)--YOUREGONNA--13
You're gonna lose that girl (yes, yes, you're
    gonna lose that girl)--YOUREGONNA--13
You're gonna lose that girl (yes, yes, you're
    gonna lose that girl)--YOUREGONNA--14
You're gonna lose that girl (yes, yes, you're
    gonna lose that girl)--YOUREGONNA--14
You're gonna lose (yes, yes, you're gonna lose
    that girl)--YOUREGONNA--15
You're gonna lose (yes, yes, you're gonna lose
    that girl)--YOUREGONNA--15
You're gonna lose that girl--YOUREGONNA--18
You're gonna lose that girl--YOUREGONNA--19
You're gonna lose that girl (yes, yes, you're
    gonna lose that girl)--YOUREGONNA--20
You're gonna lose that girl (yes, yes, you're
    gonna lose that girl)--YOUREGONNA--20
You're gonna lose that girl (yes, yes, you're
    gonna lose that girl)--YOUREGONNA--21
You're gonna lose that girl (yes, yes, you're
    gonna lose that girl)--YOUREGONNA--21
You're gonna lose (yes, yes, you're gonna lose
    that girl)--YOUREGONNA--22
You're gonna lose (yes, yes, you're gonna lose
    that girl)--YOUREGONNA--22
You're gonna lose that girl (yes, yes, you're
    gonna lose that girl)--YOUREGONNA--29
You're gonna lose that girl (yes, yes, you're
    gonna lose that girl)--YOUREGONNA--29
You're gonna lose that girl (yes, yes, you're
    gonna lose that girl)--YOUREGONNA--30
You're gonna lose that girl (yes, yes, you're
    gonna lose that girl)--YOUREGONNA--30
You're gonna lose (yes, yes, you're gonna lose
    that girl).--YOUREGONNA--31
You're gonna lose (yes, yes, you're gonna lose
    that girl).--YOUREGONNA--31
Think of what you're saying --WECANWORKI--6
You're the one that I'd be thinking of --IFINEEDEDS
    --2
I'm looking through you, you're not the same.--
    IMLOOKINGT--4
I'm looking through you, you're not the same.--
    IMLOOKINGT--8
You're thinking of me the same old way --IMLOOKINGT
    --11
The only difference is you're down there.--
    IMLOOKINGT--13
I'm looking through you and you're nowhere.--
    IMLOOKINGT--14
I'm looking through you, you're not the same.--
    IMLOOKINGT--20
You don't know what you're missing --NOWHEREMAN--8
You don't know what you're missing --NOWHEREMAN--20
You're telling all those lies--THINKFORYO--3
And go where you're going to --THINKFORYO--7
You're gonna cause more misery.--THINKFORYO--14
And go where you're going to --THINKFORYO--16
And go where you're going to --THINKFORYO--25
And go where you're going to --THINKFORYO--29
Dr. Robert, you're a new and better man --DRROBERT
    --3
If you're down he'll pick you up, Dr. Robert --
    DRROBERT--6
Well, well, well, you're feeling fine --DRROBERT
    --11
Dr. Robert, you're a new and better man --DRROBERT
    --15
Well, well, well, you're feeling fine --DRROBERT
    --18
When you're here --IWANTTOTEL--3
And you're making me feel like I've never been
    born.--SHESAIDSHE--6
I said no, no, no you're wrong.--SHESAIDSHE--8
'cos you're making me feel like I've never been

born.--SHESAIDSHE--12
I said no, no, no you're wrong.--SHESAIDSHE--14
'cos you're making me feel like I've never been
    born.--SHESAIDSHE--18
And you're working for no-one but me. (Taxman)--
    TAXMAN--26
You're holding me down (aah) turning me round
    (aah)--GETTINGBET--5
You're doing the best that I can.--GETTINGBET--15
Heading for home you start to roam then you're in
    town.--GOODMORNIN--8
And you're on your own you're in the street.--
    GOODMORNIN--12
And you're on your own you're in the street.--
    GOODMORNIN--12
Watching the skirts you start to flirt now you're
    in gear--GOODMORNIN--23
And you're gone.--LUCYINTHES--19
You're such a lovely audience--SGTPEPPERS--16
(Are you sad because you're on your own?)--
    WITHALITTL--11
And to see you're really only very small--
    WITHINYOUW--18
There's nowhere you can be that isn't where
    you're meant to be ((love))--ALLYOUN/YS--21
BABY, YOU'RE A RICH MAN.--BABYYOUREA--Title
Baby, you're a rich man --BABYYOUREA--13
Baby, you're a rich man --BABYYOUREA--14
Baby, you're a rich man too.--BABYYOUREA--15
Baby, you're a rich man --BABYYOUREA--19
Baby, you're a rich man --BABYYOUREA--20
Baby, you're a rich man too.--BABYYOUREA--21
Baby, you're a rich man --BABYYOUREA--28
Baby, you're a rich man --BABYYOUREA--29
Baby, you're a rich man too.--BABYYOUREA--30
Baby, you're a rich man --BABYYOUREA--34
Baby, you're a rich man --BABYYOUREA--35
Baby, you're a rich man too.--BABYYOUREA--36
Oh, baby you're a rich man --BABYYOUREA--37
Baby, you're a rich (baby) man --BABYYOUREA--38
Baby, you're a rich man too.--BABYYOUREA--39
Wuh-oh, baby, you're a rich (oh) man --BABYYOUREA
    --40
Baby, you're a rich man --BABYYOUREA--41
Baby, you're a rich man too.--BABYYOUREA--42
Oh, baby, you're a rich man.--BABYYOUREA--43
Baby, you're a rich man.--BABYYOUREA--44
Baby, you're a...--BABYYOUREA--45
You're waiting for someone to perform with.--
    HEYJUDE--21
Take a good look you're bound to see --MARTHAMYDE
    --8
You're gonna know and how.--SAVOYTRUFF--13
What makes you think you're something special
    when you smile?--HEYBULLDOG--4
If you're lonely you can talk to me.--HEYBULLDOG
    --12
If you're lonely you can talk to me - hey!--
    HEYBULLDOG--20
You're too much - aah.--ITSALLTOOM--37
If you're listening to this song --ONLYANORTH--1
When you're listening late at night --ONLYANORTH
    --4
You're correct, there's nobody there.--ONLYANORTH
    --15
Last night the wife said, oh boy, when you're
    dead --BALLADOFJO--27
Boy, you're gonna carry that weight--CARRYTHATW--1
Boy, you're gonna carry that weight--CARRYTHATW--3
Boy, you're gonna carry that weight--CARRYTHATW--9
Boy, you're gonna carry that weight--CARRYTHATW--11
You're asking me will my love grow?--SOMETHING--11
Because you're sweet and lovely girl, I love you
    --FORYOUBLUE--2
Because you're sweet and lovely girl, it's true --
    FORYOUBLUE--3
Because you're sweet and lovely girl, I love you
    --FORYOUBLUE--16
Because you're sweet and lovely girl, it's true --
    FORYOUBLUE--17
Said you're travelling on the one after
    nine-0-nine.--ONEAFTERNI--5
You're only fooling round, only fooling round
    with me.--ONEAFTERNI--7
Said you're travelling on the one after
    nine-0-nine.--ONEAFTERNI--10

YOU'VE
Oh, oh - mmm, you've been good to me--THANKYOUGI
    --1
Oh, oh - mmm, you've been good to me--THANKYOUGI
    --11
You think you've lost your love--SHELOVESYO--4

And now you've changed your mind--NOTASECOND--4
And now you've changed your mind --NOTASECOND--15
Yeah, you've got that something--IWANTTOHOL--20
Yeah, you've got that something--IWANTTOHOL--33
Oh, I can't sleep at night since you've been
    gone --ICALLYOURN--3
If this is love you've got to give me more --
    ISHOULDHAV--12
'cos I know where you've been--NOREPLY--12
'cos I know where you've been--NOREPLY--25
You've ((you've)) got me crying, girl --WHATYOURED
    --13
You've ((you've)) got me crying, girl --WHATYOURED
    --13
You've ((you've)) got me crying, girl --WHATYOURED
    --20
You've ((you've)) got me crying, girl --WHATYOURED
    --20
Though you've gone away this morning--YOULIKEMET
    --1
You've tried before to leave me--YOULIKEMET--7
YOU'VE GOT TO HIDE YOUR LOVE AWAY.--YOUVEGOTTO
    --Title
Hey! you've got to hide your love away.--YOUVEGOTTO
    --9
Hey! you've got to hide your love away.--YOUVEGOTTO
    --10
Hey! you've got to hide your love away.--YOUVEGOTTO
    --19
Hey! you've got to hide your love away.--YOUVEGOTTO
    --20
Yeah, oh baby you've changed.--IMLOOKINGT--21
You've changed.--IMLOOKINGT--24
You've changed.--IMLOOKINGT--25
You've changed.--IMLOOKINGT--26
You've changed.--IMLOOKINGT--27
And you've got time to rectify--THINKFORYO--22
Yes it seems so long, girl, since you've been gone
    --YOUWONTSEE--18
Yes it seems so long, girl, since you've been gone
    --YOUWONTSEE--27
You tell me that you've got everything you want --
    ANDYOURBIR--1
You say you've seen seven wonders --ANDYOURBIR--4
But what you've got means such a lot to me.--
    LOVEYOUTWO--8
It's getting better since you've been mine.--
    GETTINGBET--10
It's getting better since you've been mine.--
    GETTINGBET--19
It's getting better since you've been mine.--
    GETTINGBET--32
The act you've known for all these years--
    SGTPEPPERS--6
When you've seen beyond yourself--WITHINYOUW--28
Now that you've found another key--BABYYOUREA--26
(Well you know you can make it, Jude, you've
    just gotta break it.)--HEYJUDE--46
Hold your head up you silly girl, look what
    you've done --MARTHAMYDE--4
Hold your hand out you silly girl, see what
    you've done --MARTHAMYDE--10
You've got it, that's great, you've done it
    ((ha ha ha ha ha))--HEYBULLDOG--28
You've got it, that's great, you've done it
    ((ha ha ha ha ha))--HEYBULLDOG--28
That's it, you've got it ((ha ha ha ha))--
    HEYBULLDOG--30
The man in the mack said you've got to go back --
    BALLADOFJO--3

YOUNG
When ((when)) I was younger ((when I was
    young))--HELP--8
Was she told when she was young that pain would
    lead to pleasure?--GIRL--22
Me used to be angry young man--GETTINGBET--11
Born a poor young country boy - Mother Nature's
    son --MOTHERNATU--1
There lived a young boy name of Rocky Raccoon--
    ROCKYRACCO--2
Hit young Rocky in the eye.--ROCKYRACCO--4

YOUNGER
When ((when)) I was younger ((when I was
    young))--HELP--8
So much younger than today--HELP--9
When I was younger, so much younger than today--
    HELP--29
When I was younger, so much younger than today--
    HELP--29

YOUR

Let me whisper in your ear --DOYOUWANTT--6
Let me whisper in your ear, (dodahdo)--DOYOUWANTT--12
Let me whisper in your ear, (dodahdo)--DOYOUWANTT--20
When I'm gonna change/make your mind--ILLGETYOU--17
You think you've lost your love--SHELOVESYO--4
Is whisper in your ear --ALLIVEGOTT--8
Close your eyes and I'll kiss you --ALLMYLOVIN--1
Close your eyes and I'll kiss you --ALLMYLOVIN--15
I WANNA BE YOUR MAN.--IWANNABEYO--Title
I wanna be your lover baby --IWANNABEYO--1
I wanna be your man.--IWANNABEYO--2
I wanna be your lover baby --IWANNABEYO--3
I wanna be your man.--IWANNABEYO--4
I wanna be your man--IWANNABEYO--9
I wanna be your man--IWANNABEYO--10
I wanna be your man.--IWANNABEYO--11
I wanna be your man.--IWANNABEYO--12
I wanna be your man.--IWANNABEYO--16
I wanna be your lover baby --IWANNABEYO--17
I wanna be your man.--IWANNABEYO--18
I wanna be your lover baby --IWANNABEYO--19
I wanna be your man.--IWANNABEYO--20
I wanna be your man.--IWANNABEYO--21
I wanna be your man.--IWANNABEYO--22
I wanna be your man.--IWANNABEYO--23
I wanna be your man.--IWANNABEYO--24
I wanna be your lover baby --IWANNABEYO--30
I wanna be your man.--IWANNABEYO--31
I wanna be your lover baby --IWANNABEYO--32
I wanna be your man.--IWANNABEYO--33
I wanna be your man.--IWANNABEYO--38
I wanna be your man.--IWANNABEYO--39
I wanna be your man.--IWANNABEYO--40
I wanna be your man.--IWANNABEYO--41
I wanna be your man (oh)--IWANNABEYO--43
I wanna be your man (come on!)--IWANNABEYO--44
I wanna be your man (wuh - wuh)--IWANNABEYO--45
I wanna be your man.--IWANNABEYO--46
And now you've changed your mind--NOTASECOND--4
And now you've changed your mind--NOTASECOND--15
I WANT TO HOLD YOUR HAND.--IWANTTOHOL--Title
I wanna hold your hand--IWANTTOHOL--4
I wanna hold your hand--IWANTTOHOL--5
I wanna hold your hand.--IWANTTOHOL--6
And/You'll let me be your man--IWANTTOHOL--8
You'll let me hold your hand--IWANTTOHOL--10
And/You'll let me be your man--IWANTTOHOL--11
I wanna hold your hand.--IWANTTOHOL--12
I wanna hold your hand--IWANTTOHOL--23
I wanna hold your hand--IWANTTOHOL--24
I wanna hold your hand.--IWANTTOHOL--25
I wanna hold your hand--IWANTTOHOL--36
I wanna hold your hand--IWANTTOHOL--37
I wanna hold your hand--IWANTTOHOL--38
I wanna hold your hand.--IWANTTOHOL--39
'cos I'm the one who won your love--YOUCANTDOT--19
'cos I'm the one who won your love--YOUCANTDOT--38
I CALL YOUR NAME.--ICALLYOURN--Title
I call your name, but you're not there --ICALLYOURN--1
I never weep at night, I call your name.--ICALLYOURN--10
I never weep at night, I call your name --ICALLYOURN--17
I call your name, I call your name, (wuh) I call your name.--ICALLYOURN--18
I call your name, I call your name, (wuh) I call your name.--ICALLYOURN--18
I call your name, I call your name, (wuh) I call your name.--ICALLYOURN--18
And show you what your loving man can do --ILLCRYINST--18
And show you what your loving man can do --ILLCRYINST--27
I don't wanna kiss or hold your hand --IMHAPPYJUS--4
Ooo I need your love babe --EIGHTDAYSA--1
Ooo I need your love babe --EIGHTDAYSA--19
When I came to your door--NOREPLY--2
But I saw you peep through your window--NOREPLY--5
'cos I looked up to see your face.--NOREPLY--8
I saw you walk in your door--NOREPLY--13
I saw you walk in your door--NOREPLY--26
Please ((please)) stop your lying --WHATYOURED--12
Please ((please)) stop your lying --WHATYOURED--19
If you let me take your heart--TELLMEWHAT--1
Open up your eyes now--TELLMEWHAT--5
If you put your trust in me--TELLMEWHAT--11
I'll make bright your day--TELLMEWHAT--12
Open up your eyes now--TELLMEWHAT--22

Open up your eyes now--TELLMEWHAT--31
You still moan keep your hands to yourself --IMDOWN--17
As I looked in your eyes--INEEDYOU--9
Love was in your eyes (aah the night before)--NIGHTBEFOR--2
Now today I find, you have changed your mind--NIGHTBEFOR--3
Love was in your eyes (aah the night before)--NIGHTBEFOR--12
Now today I find you have changed your mind--NIGHTBEFOR--13
YOU'VE GOT TO HIDE YOUR LOVE AWAY.--YOUVEGOTTO--Title
Hey! you've got to hide your love away.--YOUVEGOTTO--9
Hey! you've got to hide your love away.--YOUVEGOTTO--10
Hey! you've got to hide your love away.--YOUVEGOTTO--19
Hey! you've got to hide your love away.--YOUVEGOTTO--20
While you see it your way--WECANWORKI--3
While you see it your way --WECANWORKI--17
While you see it your way --WECANWORKI--26
Carve your number on my wall --IFINEEDEDS--10
Carve your number on my wall --IFINEEDEDS--20
Your lips are moving, I cannot hear --IMLOOKINGT--5
Your voice is soothing but the words aren't clear.--IMLOOKINGT--6
Nowhere Man the world is at your command.--NOWHEREMAN--9
Take your time, don't hurry --NOWHEREMAN--14
Nowhere Man the world is at your command.--NOWHEREMAN--21
RUN FOR YOUR LIFE.--RUNFORYOUR--Title
You better keep your head, little girl --RUNFORYOUR--3
You better run for your life if you can, little girl --RUNFORYOUR--5
Hide your head in the sand, little girl.--RUNFORYOUR--6
You better run for your life if you can, little girl --RUNFORYOUR--13
Hide your head in the sand, little girl.--RUNFORYOUR--14
You better run for your life if you can, little girl --RUNFORYOUR--21
Hide your head in the sand, little girl.--RUNFORYOUR--22
You better keep your head, little girl --RUNFORYOUR--27
You better run for your life if you can, little girl --RUNFORYOUR--29
Hide your head in the sand, little girl.--RUNFORYOUR--30
I know your mind's made up --THINKFORYO--13
Although your mind's opaque --THINKFORYO--19
Try thinking more if just for your own sake.--THINKFORYO--20
Wait till I come back to your side --WAIT--3
But if your heart breaks, don't wait, turn me away --WAIT--5
And if your heart's strong, hold on, I won't delay.--WAIT--6
Wait till I come back to your side --WAIT--7
Wait till I come back to your side --WAIT--15
But if your heart breaks, don't wait, turn me away --WAIT--21
And if your heart's strong, hold on, I won't delay.--WAIT--22
Wait till I come back to your side --WAIT--23
What goes on in your heart? (wuh)--WHATGOESON--1
What goes on in your mind?--WHATGOESON--2
What goes on in your mind?--WHATGOESON--5
What goes on in your heart?--WHATGOESON--10
What goes on in your mind?--WHATGOESON--11
What goes on in your mind?--WHATGOESON--14
What goes on in your heart?--WHATGOESON--19
(What goes on in your mind?)--WHATGOESON--21
What goes on in your heart?--WHATGOESON--26
What goes on in your mind?--WHATGOESON--27
What goes on in your mind?--WHATGOESON--30
In your mind.--WHATGOESON--31
In your mind.--WHATGOESON--32
When I call you up your line's engaged.--YOUWONTSEE--1
I have had enough, so act your age.--YOUWONTSEE--2
AND YOUR BIRD CAN SING.--ANDYOURBIR--Title
And your bird can sing --ANDYOURBIR--2
And your bird is green --ANDYOURBIR--5
When your prized possessions start to weigh you down --ANDYOURBIR--7

When your bird is broken will it bring you down?--
    ANDYOURBIR--10
And your bird can swing --ANDYOURBIR--14
Your day breaks, your mind aches --FORNOONE--1
Your day breaks, your mind aches --FORNOONE--1
Your day breaks, your mind aches --FORNOONE--20
Your day breaks, your mind aches --FORNOONE--20
She said will fill your head --FORNOONE--22
I said who put all those things in your head?--
    SHESAIDSHE--4
If you try to sit, I'll tax your seat, ((sit))--
    TAXMAN--12
If you take a walk, I'll tax your feet.
    ((walk))--TAXMAN--14
Declare the pennies on your eyes (Taxman)--TAXMAN
    --23
Turn off your mind, relax and float down-stream--
    TOMORROWNE--7
But listen to the colour of your dreams--TOMORROWNE
    --11
Filling me up with your rules.--GETTINGBET--6
Nothing to say but what a day how's your boy been?
    --GOODMORNIN--3
And you're on your own you're in the street.--
    GOODMORNIN--12
When it gets dark I tow your heart away.--
    LOVELYRITA--6
Towering over your head.--LUCYINTHES--6
Climb in the back with your head in the clouds--
    LUCYINTHES--18
When your lights have gone.--WHENIMSIXT--14
Grandchildren on your knee --WHENIMSIXT--26
Give me your answer--WHENIMSIXT--32
Lend me your ears and I'll sing you a song--
    WITHALITTL--9
(Are you sad because you're on your own?)--
    WITHALITTL--11
You keep all your money in a big brown bag --
    BABYYOUREA--16
You keep all your money in a big brown bag --
    BABYYOUREA--31
Man you been a naughty boy, you let your face
    grow long--IAMTHEWALR--6
Boy, you been a naughty girl, you let your
    knickers down--IAMTHEWALR--14
Umpa, umpa, stick it up your jumper ((joob-
    joob))--IAMTHEWALR--35
Umpa, umpa, stick it up your jumper.--IAMTHEWALR
    --36
YOUR MOTHER SHOULD KNOW.--YOURMOTHER--Title
That was a hit before your mother was born --
    YOURMOTHER--3
Your mother should know (your mother should) --
    YOURMOTHER--5
Your mother should know (your mother should) --
    YOURMOTHER--5
Your mother should know - aah.--YOURMOTHER--6
That was a hit before your mother was born --
    YOURMOTHER--9
Your mother should know (your mother should) --
    YOURMOTHER--11
Your mother should know (your mother should) --
    YOURMOTHER--11
Your mother should know - aah.--YOURMOTHER--12
Lift up your hearts and sing me a song--YOURMOTHER
    --13
That was a hit before your mother was born --
    YOURMOTHER--14
Your mother should know (your mother should) --
    YOURMOTHER--16
Your mother should know (your mother should) --
    YOURMOTHER--16
Your mother should know - aah.--YOURMOTHER--17
Your mother should know (your mother should) --
    YOURMOTHER--18
Your mother should know (your mother should) --
    YOURMOTHER--18
Your mother should know - aah.--YOURMOTHER--19
Your mother should know (your mother should) --
    YOURMOTHER--24
Your mother should know (your mother should) --
    YOURMOTHER--24
Your mother should know - yeah ((ooo)).--YOURMOTHER
    --25
Your mother should know (your mother should) --
    YOURMOTHER--26
Your mother should know (your mother should) --
    YOURMOTHER--26
Your mother should know - yeah.--YOURMOTHER--27
Your mother should know (your mother should) --
    YOURMOTHER--28
Your mother should know (your mother should) --
    YOURMOTHER--28
Your mother should know - yeah.--YOURMOTHER--29

Without going out of your door --INNERLIGHT--8
Without looking out of your window --INNERLIGHT--10
Lady Madonna, children at your feet --LADYMADONN
    --1
Lady Madonna, baby at your breast --LADYMADONN--9
Listen to the music playing in your head.--
    LADYMADONN--13
Thursday night your stockings needed mending.--
    LADYMADONN--16
Lady Madonna, children at your feet --LADYMADONN
    --18
Remember to let her into your heart --HEYJUDE--3
The minute you let her under your skin --HEYJUDE
    --7
Don't carry the world upon your shoulder.--HEYJUDE
    --11
Remember (hey Jude) to let her into your heart --
    HEYJUDE--17
The movement you need is on your shoulder.--HEYJUDE
    --24
Remember to let her under your skin (oh) --HEYJUDE
    --28
We all want to change your head.--REVOLUTION--24
You better free your mind instead.--REVOLUTION--27
Take me to your daddy's farm --BACKINTHEU--32
Let me hear your balalaikas ringing out --
    BACKINTHEU--33
Come and keep your comrade warm.--BACKINTHEU--34
You say it's your birthday --BIRTHDAY--1
They say it's your birthday --BIRTHDAY--3
I'm glad it's your birthday --BIRTHDAY--5
You say it's your birthday --BIRTHDAY--20
You say it's your birthday --BIRTHDAY--22
I'm glad it's your birthday --BIRTHDAY--24
All your life --BLACKBIRD--3
All your life --BLACKBIRD--7
All your life --BLACKBIRD--15
Make your mother sigh --CRYBABYCRY--2
Make your mother sigh --CRYBABYCRY--9
Make your mother sigh --CRYBABYCRY--17
Make your mother sigh --CRYBABYCRY--25
Make your mother sigh --CRYBABYCRY--33
Make your mother sigh --CRYBABYCRY--37
Make your mother sigh --CRYBABYCRY--41
Dear Prudence, open up your eyes --DEARPRUDEN--6
Dear Prudence, won't you open up your eyes?--
    DEARPRUDEN--10
I listen for your footsteps --DONTPASSME--2
Listen for your footsteps --DONTPASSME--4
Waiting for your knock, dear --DONTPASSME--6
And you lost your hair.--DONTPASSME--26
Your inside is out when your outside is in --
    EVRBDYMONK--17
Your inside is out when your outside is in --
    EVRBDYMONK--17
Your outside is in when your inside is out --
    EVRBDYMONK--18
Your outside is in when your inside is out --
    EVRBDYMONK--18
Close your eyes and I'll close mine --GOODNIGHT--7
Close your eyes and I'll close mine --GOODNIGHT--14
And I feel my finger on your trigger ((oh,
    yeah)) --HAPPINESSI--23
Tell me, tell me, tell me your answer --HELTERSKEL
    --23
Of your Hollywood song.--HONEYPIE--12
I didn't catch your name --IWILL--6
Your song will fill the air --IWILL--14
Hold your head up you silly girl, look what
    you've done --MARTHAMYDE--4
Hold your hand out you silly girl, see what
    you've done --MARTHAMYDE--10
Desmond says to Molly, girl I like your face--
    OBLADIOBLA--3
You'd better free your mind instead.--REVOLUTONE
    --41
He said, Rocky you met your match--ROCKYRACCO--33
I feel your taste all the time we're apart --
    SAVOYTRUFF--7
The sweat it's gonna fill your head --SAVOYTRUFF
    --14
I don't know why nobody told you how to unfold
    your love --WHILEMYGUI--6
Jack-knife in your sweaty hands--HEYBULLDOG--6
You don't know what it's like to listen to your
    fears.--HEYBULLDOG--8
To your mother!--ITSALLTOOM--1
When I look into your eyes --ITSALLTOOM--4
Your love is there for me--ITSALLTOOM--5
So take your piece, but not too much.--ITSALLTOOM
    --19
With your long blonde hair and your eyes of blue
    --ITSALLTOOM--35
With your long blonde hair and your eyes of blue

--ITSALLTOOM--35
With your long blonde hair and your eyes of blue
   --ITSALLTOOM--35
With your long blonde hair and your eyes of blue
   --ITSALLTOOM--36
Your mommy's waiting for you --GETBACK/45--32
Saving up your money for a rainy day --BALLADOFJO
   --25
Giving all your clothes to charity.--BALLADOFJO--26
You don't take nothing with you but your soul -
   think!--BALLADOFJO--28
When I see your smile --OLDBROWNSH--11
For your sweet top lip I'm in the queue --
   OLDBROWNSH--31
Golden slumbers fill your eyes--GOLDENSLUM--7
YOU NEVER GIVE ME YOUR MONEY.--YOUNEVERGI--Title
You never give me your money --YOUNEVERGI--1
You only give me your funny paper--YOUNEVERGI--2
All through your life --IMEMINE--34
The long and winding road that leads to your door
   --LONGANDWIN--1
It always leads me here, lead me to your door.--
   LONGANDWIN--3
Don't leave me waiting here, lead me to your door.
   --LONGANDWIN--11
Don't keep me waiting here (don't keep me
   waiting) lead me to your door.--LONGANDWIN--14

YOURS
Yours sincerely, wasting away.--WHENIMSIXT--31
Sexy Sadie you'll get yours yet--SEXYSADIE--16
Sexy Sadie - oh you'll get yours yet--SEXYSADIE--19
I want that love of yours --OLDBROWNSH--27

YOURSELF
So you might as well resign yourself to me, oh
   yeah.--ILLGETYOU--18
You still moan keep your hands to yourself --IMDOWN
   --17

THINK FOR YOURSELF.--THINKFORYO--Title
Think for yourself --THINKFORYO--8
Think for yourself --THINKFORYO--17
Think for yourself --THINKFORYO--26
Think for yourself --THINKFORYO--30
Think for yourself --THINKFORYO--32
Don't pay money just to see yourself with Dr.
   Robert.--DRROBERT--14
Picture yourself in a boat on a river--LUCYINTHES
   --1
Picture yourself on a train in a station--
   LUCYINTHES--23
Try to realise it's all within yourself--WITHINYOUW
   --16
When you've seen beyond yourself--WITHINYOUW--28
When you find yourself in the thick of it --
   MARTHAMYDE--5
Help yourself to a bit of what is all around you
   - silly girl.--MARTHAMYDE--6
When you find yourself in the thick of it --
   MARTHAMYDE--11
Help yourself to a bit of what is all around you
   - silly girl.--MARTHAMYDE--12

ZAP
So Captain Marvel zapped him right between the
   eyes. (Zap!)--CONTINUING--19

ZAPPED
So Captain Marvel zapped him right between the
   eyes. (Zap!)--CONTINUING--19

ZOO
Inside a zoo --BABYYOUREA--17
Inside a zoo --BABYYOUREA--32
Got me escaping from this zoo --OLDBROWNSH--13

Ah, look at all the lonely people

Eleanor Rigby, picks up the rice
in the church where a wedding
has been
lives in a dream.
Waits at the window, wearing the face
that she keeps in a jar by the door
who is it for?
All the lonely. - - - - - etc.

Father McKenzie, writing the words of a
sermon that no-one will hear
no-one comes near.
Look at him working, darning his
socks in the night, when there's
nobody there, what does he care?
All the lonely people . . . . . .

Ah look at all the lonely people

Paul McCartney

Appendix One: Contractions

'B—LA—DA

Take ob-la-di 'b-la-da ((ha ha ha)) --OBLADIOBLA
--41
We all know ob-la-di 'b-la-da --SAVOYTRUFF--21

'BYE

For so many years. (('bye, 'bye))--SHESLEAVIN--12
For so many years. (('bye, 'bye))--SHESLEAVIN--12
For so many years. (('bye, 'bye))--SHESLEAVIN--24
For so many years. (('bye, 'bye))--SHESLEAVIN--24
For so many years. (('bye, 'bye))--SHESLEAVIN--32
For so many years. (('bye, 'bye))--SHESLEAVIN--32
She's leaving home. ('bye, 'bye)--SHESLEAVIN--33
She's leaving home. ('bye, 'bye)--SHESLEAVIN--33
Goodbye, goodbye, 'bye, 'bye, 'bye?--HELLOGOODB--17
Goodbye, goodbye, 'bye, 'bye, 'bye?--HELLOGOODB--17
Goodbye, goodbye, 'bye, 'bye, 'bye?--HELLOGOODB--17

'CEPT

Everybody's got something to hide 'cept for me
and my monkey - wuh.--EVRBDYMONK--7
Everybody's got something to hide 'cept for me
and my monkey (yeah - wuh).--EVRBDYMONK--16
Everybody's got something to hide 'cept for me
and my monkey - hey.--EVRBDYMONK--25

'COS

'cos you tell me things I want to know --ASKMEWHY
--2
'cos you tell me things I want to know --ASKMEWHY
--17
Send her back to me, 'cos everyone can see--
MISERY--8
Send her back to me, 'cos everyone can see--
MISERY--12
It's easy 'cos I know--ILLGETYOU--3
It's easy 'cos I know--ILLGETYOU--20
'cos I don't care too much for money --CANTBUYMEL
--7
'cos I'm the one who won your love--YOUCANTDOT--19
'cos I'm the one who won your love--YOUCANTDOT--38
'cos when I get you alone --HARDDAYSNI--13
'cos when I get you alone --HARDDAYSNI--26
'cos I've been in love before --IFIFELL--4
'cos I couldn't stand the pain --IFIFELL--14
'cos I couldn't stand the pain --IFIFELL--21
'cos I've just lost the only girl I had.--
ILLCRYINST--2
'cos I'm gonna break their hearts all round the
world --ILLCRYINST--25
'cos I'm happy just to dance with you.--IMHAPPYJUS
--7
'cos I'm happy just to dance with you.--IMHAPPYJUS
--11
'cos I'm happy just to dance with you.--IMHAPPYJUS
--19
'cos I'm happy just to dance with you (oh - oh).--
IMHAPPYJUS--28
'cos I really can't stand it --TELLMEWHY--24
'cos I told you once before goodbye --ILLBEBACK--3
'cos I'm a - gonna see my baby today --WHENIGETHO
--5
'cos I looked up to see your face.--NOREPLY--8
'cos I know where you've been--NOREPLY--12
'cos you walked hand in hand--NOREPLY--15
'cos I know where you've been--NOREPLY--25
'cos you walked hand in hand--NOREPLY--28
'cos you like me too much and I like you--
YOULIKEMET--6
'cos you like me too much and I like you--
YOULIKEMET--12
'cos I couldn't really stand it--YOULIKEMET--17
I wouldn't let you leave me 'cos it's true--
YOULIKEMET--19
'cos you like me too much and I like you--
YOULIKEMET--20
'cos you like me too much and I like you--
YOULIKEMET--21
'cos I couldn't really stand it--YOULIKEMET--26
I wouldn't let you leave me 'cos it's true--
YOULIKEMET--28
'cos you like me too much and I like you--
YOULIKEMET--29

'cos you like me too much and I like you.--
YOULIKEMET--30
You can't cry 'cos you're laughing at me --IMDOWN
--2
'cos I will treat her right--YOUREGONNA--11
'cos I won't be there with you.--THINKFORYO--9
'cos I won't be there with you.--THINKFORYO--18
'cos I won't be there with you.--THINKFORYO--27
'cos I won't be there with you.--THINKFORYO--31
'cos I won't be there with you.--THINKFORYO--33
'cos you're making me feel like I've never been
born.--SHESAIDSHE--12
'cos you're making me feel like I've never been
born.--SHESAIDSHE--18
'cos I'm the Taxman --TAXMAN--5
'cos I'm the Taxman --TAXMAN--9
'cos I'm the Taxman --TAXMAN--16
'cos I'm the Taxman --TAXMAN--20
'cos I'm the Taxman --TAXMAN--24
'cos I'm going to strawberry fields--STRAWBERRY--2
'cos I'm going to strawberry fields--STRAWBERRY--12
'cos I'm going to strawberry fields--STRAWBERRY--22
'cos I'm going to strawberry fields--STRAWBERRY--32
'cos you know, darling, I love only you --
DONTPASSME--19
'cos you know, darling, I love only you --
DONTPASSME--32
'cos you know, darling, I love only you --
DONTPASSME--38
I need a fix 'cos I'm going down --HAPPINESSI--9
I need a fix 'cos I'm going down.--HAPPINESSI--11
'cos you may be a lover, but you ain't no dancer.
--HELTERSKEL--14
Look out 'cos here she comes (heh heh heh).--
HELTERSKEL--17
'cos you may be a lover, but you ain't no dancer.
--HELTERSKEL--24
Got to be good-looking 'cos he's so hard to see--
COMETOGETH--41

'EM

Yes, I'm gonna break 'em in two --ILLCRYINST--17
Yes, I'm gonna break 'em in two --ILLCRYINST--26

'LO

I say hi!/high, you say 'lo/low--HELLOGOODB--7

'ROUND

Look around, 'round --DEARPRUDEN--11
('round, 'round, 'round, 'round, 'round,
'round, 'round, 'round)--DEARPRUDEN--12
('round, 'round, 'round, 'round, 'round,
'round, 'round, 'round)--DEARPRUDEN--12
('round, 'round, 'round, 'round, 'round,
'round, 'round, 'round)--DEARPRUDEN--12
('round, 'round, 'round, 'round, 'round,
'round, 'round, 'round)--DEARPRUDEN--12
('round, 'round, 'round, 'round, 'round,
'round, 'round, 'round)--DEARPRUDEN--12
('round, 'round, 'round, 'round, 'round,
'round, 'round, 'round)--DEARPRUDEN--12
('round, 'round, 'round, 'round, 'round,
'round, 'round, 'round)--DEARPRUDEN--12
('round, 'round, 'round, 'round, 'round,
'round, 'round, 'round)--DEARPRUDEN--12
Look around, 'round, 'round --DEARPRUDEN--13
Look around, 'round, 'round --DEARPRUDEN--13
('round, 'round, 'round, 'round, 'round,
'round, 'round)--DEARPRUDEN--14
('round, 'round, 'round, 'round, 'round,
'round, 'round)--DEARPRUDEN--14
('round, 'round, 'round, 'round, 'round,
'round, 'round)--DEARPRUDEN--14
('round, 'round, 'round, 'round, 'round,
'round, 'round)--DEARPRUDEN--14
('round, 'round, 'round, 'round, 'round,
'round, 'round)--DEARPRUDEN--14
('round, 'round, 'round, 'round, 'round,
'round, 'round)--DEARPRUDEN--14
('round, 'round, 'round, 'round, 'round,
'round, 'round)--DEARPRUDEN--14
Look around (('round)).--DEARPRUDEN--15

Appendix Two: Prefixed Words

A–DO

A - DO
    A - do you, don't you want me to love you?
      --HELTERSKEL--4

A - GONNA
    'cos I'm gonna see my baby today--WHENIGETHO
      --5

A - LIKE
    A - like a rolling stone--DIGIT--3

A - MOVE
    I said a - move over honey, I'm travelling on
      that line--ONEAFTERNI--16
    Said a - move over honey, I'm travelling on
      that line--ONEAFTERNI--26

A - MOVING
    See the hands a - moving--DONTPASSME--12

A - NOW
    A - now Rocky Raccoon, he fell back in his room--
      ROCKYRACCO--36

A - ONE
    A - one, two, three.--IDIGAPONY--2
    A - one, two.--IDIGAPONY--5

A - ROCKY
    A - Rocky burst in and grinning a grin--ROCKYRACCO
      --19

A - TICKING
    I hear the clock a - ticking--DONTPASSME--10

A - WELL
    A - well you know, I nearly broke down and died--
      OHDARLING--8
    A - well you know I nearly broke down and cried--
      OHDARLING--13
    A - well you know, I nearly broke down and died--
      OHDARLING--15

A - WHEN
    A - when you told me you didn't need me any more
      --OHDARLING--7
    A - when you told me - ooo - you didn't need me any more
      --OHDARLING--12
    A - when you told me you didn't need me any more
      --OHDARLING--14

A - WILL
    A - will you still need me--WHENIMSIXT--35
    A - will you, won't you want me to make you?--
      HELTERSKEL--11

In the town where I was born
Lived a man who sailed to sea,
And he told us of his life,
In the land of Submarines

So we sailed into the sun,
Till we found the sea of green
And we live beneath the waves
in our Yellow Submarine

We all live in a Yellow Submarine
look out   Yellow Submarine
Yellow Submarine

Paul McCartney

Alphabetical Word-frequency List

Words are listed alphabetically, including articles, contractions and prefixed words. Capitalization of letters does not necessarily indicate capitalization in all cases of word use. Asterisks (*) identify words with frequencies that vary (homophones, etc.), usually by only one or two uses of the word.

643 a	27 around	2 bended	1 bull-frog	2 chords
77 aah	2 arrive	10 beneath	6 bulldog	5 Christ
1 able	1 arrives	2 benefit	1 bullet-headed	1 Chuck
1 aboard	2 arriving	1 bent-backed	1 bum	2 church
24 about	58 as	5 beside	29 Bungalow	1 CIA
2 above	20 ask	4 best	1 buried	1 cigarette
1 accidents	3 asked	1 bet	1 burning	1 city
2 aches	1 asking	81 better	1 burns	1 class
1 acorns	4 asleep	4 between	1 burst	3 clean
1 acquainted	1 assure	2 beyond	1 bus	1 cleaner
9 across	75 at	2 Bible	1 Busby	2 clear
4 act	1 ate	1 biding	1 business	1 climb
1 acts	2 a-ticking	6 bien	1 busy	1 climbing
8 admit	1 Atlantic	11 big	168 but	1 clinging
1 a-do	1 attractively	3 bigger	1 butted	1 clock
1 advice	1 attracts	32 Bill	1 butterfly	8 close
2 affection	1 audience	2 Billy	20 buy	2 closed
1 afraid	1 audition	8 bird	6 buys	3 closer
26 after	1 avoid	1 birds	47 by	1 closing
1 afternoon	1 awake	19 birthday	11 'bye	4 clothes
39 again	1 aware	1 Bishopsgate	1 c	3 cloud
1 age	56 away	4 bit	2 cable	3 clouds
8 ago	2 away-hey	1 bits	3 cake	2 cloudy
1 a-gonna	3 a-well	16 black	2 California	1 clown
3 agree	3 a-when	8 blackbird	37 call	1 clowns
22 ah	2 a-will	1 Blackburn	3 called	12 club
1 ah-ha	1 awoke	2 'b-la-da	7 calling	1 clubs
1 ah-hey	1 awoken	2 blame	6 calls	2 clue
5 ahead	2 aye	2 blew	23 came	2 clutching
1 Aids	1 b	4 blind	195 can	1 coat
22 ain't	11 ba	1 blindly	102 can't	1 Coca-cola
1 air	11 babe	1 blink	2 cannot	1 cocoanut
1 Albert	103 baby	1 blisters	1 cap	1 coffee
1 alerted	8 baby's	2 blonde	3 captain	9 cold
1 a-like	157 back	1 bloody	14 car	1 colder
381 all	1 backdoor	1 blow	1 carathon	1 collapsed
1 all-American	1 backing	2 blows	22 care	1 college
1 Allan	1 bacon	36 blue	1 caressing	4 colour
1 almost	23 bad	5 blues	1 carousel	1 colourful
31 alone	11 bag	1 BOAC	10 carry	1 comb
9 along	1 bags	4 boat	2 carrying	151 come
1 aloud	1 balalaikas	1 bob	2 carve	30 comes
5 already	1 Ballad	14 bom	2 case	2 comfort
62 alright	19 band	8 bom-pa	1 cast-iron	28 coming
3 although	22 bang	1 bone	1 cat	2 command
41 always	3 banker	3 book	6 catch	1 compare
30 am	1 banks	1 booked	4 caught	2 compares
2 amore	2 barber	1 books	2 cause	2 complain
2 a-move	1 barrow	2 boom	1 cave	1 complaining
2 a-moving	1 based	1 bootlace	1 ceiling	1 comrade
1 Amsterdam	1 bath	1 boots	2 celebrate	2 conceive
29 an	2 bathroom	3 bop	1 celebrated	1 confusing
626 and	1 BB	14 born	1 celebrations	1 constitution
1 angels	1 BBC	1 bosun	1 cellophane	1 continuing
1 angry	426 be	2 both	3 'cept	2 contribution
1 annoyed	1 beach	10 bother	1 certain	1 controlled
38 another	1 beat	1 bottle	1 certainly	1 conversation
1 a-now	5 beautiful	4 bottom	10 cha	1 cooking
16 answer	1 became	2 bought	2 cha-cha-cha	5 cool
36 any	25 because	1 bound	1 chain	1 coral
10 anybody	1 becomes	38 boy	1 chair	2 corner
2 anybody's	9 bed	5 boys	2 Chairman	1 cornflake
2 anyhow	1 bedroom	8 bra	1 challenge	1 corporation
3 anyone	1 beds	2 brain	15 chance	1 correct
11 anything	1 bee	2 brand	29 change*	65 'cos
2 anyway	66 been	18 break	18 changed	1 cottage
2 anywhere	24 beep	1 breakfast	1 changes	44 could
2 a-one	48 before	1 breaking	3 changing	6 couldn't
9 apart	2 beg	5 breaks	1 charity	3 count
1 apologize	2 begged	1 breast	1 Charles	1 country
7 appear	4 begin	1 bridge	2 chasing	4 couple
1 appears	8 beginning	5 bright	2 checked	1 course
1 apple	5 begins	4 bring	1 cherry	1 cows
1 appointment	1 behalf	2 bringing	1 chicka	1 crabalocker
3 appreciate	12 behind	2 brings	15 child	1 cracker
70 are	10 being	6 broke	1 childlike	1 cracks
1 aren't	27 believe	5 broken	20 children	1 cranberry
4 arise	4 believing	2 broken-hearted	1 childrens'	1 crash
2 Arizona	4 belle	3 brother	1 chip	1 crawled
1 armchair	1 bellyfull	1 brothers	1 chocolate	1 crawling
3 arms	16 belong	7 brown	1 choking	3 crazy
1 army	17 belonged	1 brrrrr	2 chop	1 cream
1 a-Rocky	2 below	3 built	1 chord	1 creeping

1	creeps	1	dock	18	ever	1	folk	2	greet		
2	creme	1	doctor	1	everybody	9	follow	1	greetings		
20	cried	10	dodahdo	1	evermore	19	fool	2	grin		
1	cries	28	does	34	every	5	fooling	1	grinning		
2	crime	13	doesn't	26	everybody	1	foolish	1	grooving		
4	crossed	5	dog	8	everybody's	1	foot	11	ground		
3	crowd	1	dog's	16	everyone	1	football	1	group		
6	crucify	19	doing	3	everyone's	2	footsteps	4	grow		
1	cruel	286	don't	34	everything	197	for	3	guaranteed		
63	cry	1	donated	1	everything's	22	forever	5	guess		
11	crying	18	done	16	everywhere	11	forget	7	guitar		
3	cup	20	door	2	evolution	1	forgive	1	gumboot		
1	curse	2	doors	1	except	1	forks	17	gun		
1	custard	2	Doris	1	existence	1	form	9	Guru		
1	customer	1	dose	1	expert	13	found	1	gurus		
1	cut	2	doubt	9	eye	1	fountain	5	guy		
1	cuts	1	doubted	1	eyeball	24	four	4	h		
1	d	1	dove-tail	43	eyes	1	France	76	ha		
87	da	10	dow	1	f	1	frantic	1	ha-ha-ha		
1	da-da	154	down	15	face	14	free	1	haa		
1	da-da-da-da-da	1	down-stream	1	faces	2	freely	2	habit		
1	daddy	2	downstairs	1	faded	2	Friday	41	had		
1	daddy's	18	Dr.	2	fair	20	friend	10	hair		
1	daily	5	drag	4	fall	21	friends	7	half		
1	daisies	1	dragged	13	falling	4	frightened	1	hall		
1	daisy	1	drank	1	famous	69	from	8	hammer		
1	Dakota	1	dreadful	1	fancy	3	front	29	hand		
1	damn	16	dream	1	Fanques	2	frown	1	hand's		
1	Dan	3	dreaming	9	far	1	frying	1	handkerchief		
35	dance	10	dreams	1	fare	1	fudge	8	hands		
2	danced	4	dressed	1	farm	4	full	1	handy		
4	dancer	2	dresses	1	fart	8	fun	2	hang		
1	dances	1	dressing-gown	2	farther	2	funny	1	hanging		
1	Daniel	1	drew	6	fast	1	fuse	3	happen		
2	Danny	1	drift	1	faster	2	fussing	3	happened		
10	dark	1	drifting	1	fate	3	future	3	happens		
2	darkness	4	drink	4	father	1	g	14	happiness		
2	darlin'	1	drinking	2	FBI	4	g'goo	28	happy		
19	darling	1	dripping	1	fears	8	g'joob	25	hard		
1	darning	11	drive	1	feat	1	gain	1	hard-earned		
1	Dave	2	driver	1	featuring	1	gallery	1	hardly		
97	day	16	driving	4	feed	5	game	1	hare		
7	day's	2	drop	62	feel	1	games	1	hark		
20	days	1	drove	43	feeling	13	garden	7	harm		
4	de	1	Duchess	3	feelings	1	garters	1	harmony		
28	dead	1	Duke	10	feels	1	gas	27	has		
1	Deaf	4	dum	9	feet	1	gather	1	hat		
26	dear	4	dying	7	fell	6	gave	13	hate		
1	decide	1	Dylan's	1	ferde	1	gear	1	hates		
1	declare	2	e	6	few	1	gee	93	have		
6	deep	8	each	1	field	7	gently	4	haven't		
2	deeper	1	eagle	12	fields	2	Georgia's	5	having		
1	defeliche	4	ear	1	fierce	1	Georgie	1	Hawtrey		
2	delay	5	early	1	fifteen	164	get	1	haze		
1	demonstrate	1	earn	2	fifty	12	gets	82	he		
1	denied	6	ears	1	fight	26	getting	1	he'd		
5	Dennis	7	earth	2	fighting	1	getting-a	8	he'll		
1	deny	1	ease	7	fill	11	Gibraltar	15	he's		
1	department	30	easy	3	filled	1	Gideon	34	head		
3	des	4	eat	3	filling	2	Gideon's	1	heading		
2	deserve	1	eating	1	film	1	gin	2	heads		
7	Desmond	1	Edgar	1	filter	2	ginger	1	health		
2	dessert	1	Edison	2	finally	154	girl	33	hear		
2	destruction	8	eee	41	find	10	girls	6	heard		
1	determined	4	eggman	1	finds	36	give	1	hearing		
9	Deva	4	eggmen	18	fine	4	gives	1	hears		
5	diamond	1	Eiffel	4	finger	3	giving	26	heart		
16	diamonds	15	eight	2	fingers	22	glad	2	heart's		
39	did	3	Eleanor	2	fire	5	glass	15	hearts		
22	didn't	1	elementary	1	fire-engine	1	glimmering	1	heat		
17	die	1	elephant	2	fireman	2	glimpse	1	Heath		
7	died	1	elephants	1	fireside	102	go	11	heaven		
2	dies	1	Elmore	5	first	1	go-getter	14	heavy		
2	difference	7	else	1	fish	39	goes	7	heh		
3	different	2	'em	1	fishwife	43	going	10	helà		
18	dig*	17	end	18	five	4	golden	7	held		
1	digging	4	end'a	3	fix	29	gone	50	hello		
2	dinner	1	endear	5	fixing	121	gonna	40	help		
1	direction	1	endless	9	flat	21	goo	1	helping		
4	dirt	3	ends	1	flew	124	good	2	helps		
5	dirty	1	engaged	3	flies	1	good-looking	17	helter-skelter		
2	disagree	1	England	1	flight	27	goodbye	2	Hendersons		
3	disappear	3	English	1	flirt	2	goodbyes	1	Henry		
2	disappearing	1	enjoy	5	float	1	goodlooking	193	her		
2	disappointment	1	enjoyed	2	floating	138	got	65	here		
1	disconnect	13	enough	1	floor	23	gotta	3	here's		
1	discovered	6	ensemble	3	flowers	1	grabbed	1	herself		
1	discreetly	1	equal	3	flowing	1	grade	101	hey		
1	disease	1	equipped	2	flown	2	grandchildren	1	hey-hey-hey		
1	diverted	1	er	3	flows	3	grass	2	hi*		
374	do	1	escaping	10	fly	1	grave	32	hide		
1	do-do-do	2	eternally	1	flying	2	great	1	hideaway		
4	do-n-do-do	12	even	1	fog	5	greatest	1	hiding		
2	Doc	8	evening	1	fold	8	green	13	high*		

1 high-heel	1 j	2 learns	24 made	1 moments
2 higher	1 jack-knife	42 leave	6 Madonna	3 momma
7 hill	1 jackboots	9 leaving	3 magic	1 mommy
1 hills	9 Jai	14 left	6 magical	1 mommy's
1 hilt	1 James	1 legend	1 Magill	3 Monday
1 Hilton	1 jar	1 legs	12 maid	1 Monday's
18 him	2 Jay	1 leisure	1 mail	24 money
2 himself	2 jealous	1 lemonade	1 Majesty	1 money's
63 his	1 jewellery	3 lend	3 Majesty's	4 monkey
6 hit	2 Jo	1 lends	1 majoring	2 montelimar
3 hmm	2 Joan	5 less	96 make*	3 moon
19 ho	3 job	160 let	13 makes	47 more
1 hobnail	1 jobber	7 let's	16 making	1 Moretta
1 hoe-down	2 John	2 lets	109 man	42 morning
1 hog	1 Johnny	4 letter	3 manage	1 mornings
1 hogshead	7 joint	1 letter-box	1 mantelshelf	2 Moscow
52 hold	7 Jojo	1 letters	20 many	2 most
5 holding	2 joke	1 licks	2 Mao	48 mother
6 hole	2 joker	7 lie	1 Marigold	1 mother's
3 holes	3 Jones	8 lied	2 market	1 motor
1 holiday	12 joob	8 lies	1 market-place	1 motorcar
1 Holland	8 joy	56 life	1 marmalade	3 mots
2 Hollywood	1 ju-ju	2 lifetime	1 married	2 mountain
1 holy	50 Jude	3 lift	7 Martha	1 mountains
92 home	1 judge	1 lifting	3 Martin	1 mourn
2 homeward	5 Judy	14 light	1 Marvel	10 move
24 honey	16 Julia	1 lighten	4 Mary	1 movement
1 honeymooning	6 jump	1 lightning	1 mask	1 moves
1 hoo	2 jumper	2 lights	1 match	2 moving
1 hoops	1 jungle	137 like	1 matches	15 Mr.
11 hope	90 just	1 likes	1 Matt	95 much
1 hoped	4 k	1 Lil	6 matter	1 mucho
6 hoping	2 kaleidoscope	1 limitless	1 mattered	1 muddy
1 horse	17 keep	1 limousine	1 Max	1 multicoloured
1 horses	3 keeping	7 line	4 Maxwell	1 mundo
3 hot	9 keeps	1 line's	7 Maxwell's	6 music
3 hour	3 kept	1 linger	32 may	12 must
1 hour-glass	4 key	1 lip	11 maybe	2 Mustard
1 house	1 kicking	5 lips	2 McKenzie	374 my
85 how	2 kids	21 listen	825 me	10 myself
1 how's	16 kill	2 listening	18 mean	19 mystery
3 however	1 killer-diller	1 listens	1 meander	2 n
1 hu	1 kilt	1 lit	2 meaning	18 'n'
4 huh	20 kind	80 little	1 meaningless	257 nah
1 hug	5 kinda	14 live	3 means	49 name
2 hung	1 kindly	3 lived	3 meant	1 named
4 hungabout	1 kindness	6 lives	3 meanwhile	1 Nancy
1 hunting	8 King	13 living	3 measured	2 nasty
3 hurry	1 Kirkaldy	1 lizard	1 medicine	2 national
10 hurt	10 kiss	1 'lo*	7 meet	1 natural
1 hurting	2 kissing	2 local	3 meeting	4 nature's
1 husband	2 kitchen	2 location	1 melting	2 naughty
290 I*	4 Kite	1 lock	1 member	17 near
32 I'd	6 knee	1 locked	3 memories	9 nearly
147 I'll	1 knees	3 log	2 men	126 need
327 I'm	15 knew	1 London	2 mending	1 need's
90 I've	1 knickers	58 lonely	1 message	11 needed
5 ice	1 knit	2 loner	1 Messrs	5 needs
151 if	1 knives	109 long	7 met	1 negotiations
1 ignorance	4 knock	5 longer	13 meter	1 nerve
1 illusion	384 know	60 look	2 mi	91 never
1 images	6 knowing	10 looked	1 Miami	1 never-ending
2 imagine	7 known	21 looking	7 Michelle	13 new
2 imagined	20 knows	1 looking-glass	6 middle	6 news
2 imitate	1 Krishna	4 looks	12 might	1 news-people
1 imperfect	19 la	1 Lords	1 mighty	1 newspaper
1 important	8 la-la	8 Loretta	4 miles	1 newspapers
1 impression	1 lacking	2 lorry	1 military	4 next
410 in	6 lady	36 lose	4 million	6 nice
1 inciting	1 lagoon	9 loser	68 mind	72 night
1 incredibly	1 Lancashire	1 losing	2 mind's	1 night-time
2 independence	3 land	15 lost	2 minds	1 nights
3 indicate	9 Lane	14 lot	59 mine	4 nine
1 inner	1 lark	1 lots	1 minute	2 nine-o
1 innocence	10 last	2 loud	1 mirrors	8 nine-o-nine
1 inquire	3 lasted	485 love	12 misery	1 nineteen
2 insane	1 lastly	7 loved	1 misplace	130 no
1 insecure	1 lasts	19 lovely	5 miss	21 no-one
12 inside	1 latches	13 lover	1 missed	2 no-one's
1 inspiration	11 late	2 lovers	1 misses	21 nobody
9 instead	2 latest	20 loves	5 missing	2 noise
2 institution	16 laugh	10 lovin'	1 mist	1 none
18 into	2 laughing	14 loving	3 mistake	1 North
2 introduce	1 laughs	6 low*	1 misunderstanding	3 Northern
1 inverted	1 laughter	1 low-neck	1 misunderstood	3 Norwegian
1 investigation	1 lay	9 lucky	43 mmm	1 nose
2 invitation	2 layed	17 Lucy	2 mmm-mmm	77 not
1 invitations	4 lazy	3 lullaby	1 mmm-mmm-mmm	2 note
1 inviting	7 lead	6 lying	4 moan	43 nothing
317 is	2 leads	10 ma	1 mojo	12 nothing's
1 Isle	1 Lear	1 machine	8 Molly	3 notice
11 isn't	6 learn	2 mack	1 mom	2 noticed
422 it	2 learned	15 mad	8 moment	1 novel
241 it's	1 learning	1 Madam		165 now
				26 nowhere

27 number
1 nun
1 nurse
4 o'clock
2 O'Fell
1 oats
9 ob-la-da
11 ob-la-di
1 obrigado
1 obscene
2 ocean
1 oceanchild
10 octopus's
1 odes
268 of
5 off
4 often
348 oh
1 oh-oh
1 oh-oh-oh
1 oh-oh-oh-oh-oh-
10 OK
23 old
3 older
3 OM
273 on
32 once
101 one
5 onion
82 only
1 Ono
2 ooh
1 ooho
77 ooo
1 ooo-mmm
5 ooo-ooo
1 ooo-ooo-aah
1 ooo-ooo-ooo
1 ooo-ooo-ooo-oh
1 opaque
5 open
4 opened
37 or
1 orange
20 other
10 ought
36 our
1 ours
3 ourselves
84 out
3 outside
4 outta
19 over
3 overnight
1 overtime
17 ow
7 own
1 owned
1 Pablo
1 pages
1 paid
7 pain
3 painting
4 Pam
2 pan
1 paparatsi
6 paper
32 paperback
1 papers
1 paramucho
1 parasol
2 Paris
2 park
1 parking
1 parlour
2 part
2 parted
9 party
9 pass
1 passed
5 past
1 pataphysical
1 Paul
5 pay
1 PC
6 peace
1 peanuts
3 peasant
1 peep
2 penetrate
1 penguin
1 pennies
9 penny
39 people

1 pepper
20 Pepper's
1 percent
2 perfectly
1 perform
2 performs
1 perverted
1 Peter
1 phase
8 phone
1 photograph
1 photographs
1 piano
8 pick
2 picker
1 picking
3 picks
3 picture
5 pictures
19 pie
1 piece
2 pies
6 piggies
2 piggy
2 pigs
1 pilchard
1 pillow
2 pineapple
1 pink
24 place
2 places
1 plain
2 plan
2 plane
1 planned
4 plans
1 plasticine
20 play
2 played
4 playing
1 playroom
2 plays
1 pleas
80 please
1 pleasing
2 pleasure
1 pocket
1 Poe
5 point
1 police
2 policeman
1 policemen
4 Polythene
1 pony
1 pool
1 pools
1 poor
1 poppies
1 pornographic
1 porters
1 portrait
1 position
1 possessing
1 possessions
1 postcard
1 postcards
1 pot-smoking
2 pouring
1 precisely
1 preparation
6 presents
1 press
7 pretend
11 pretty
5 pride
1 priestess
1 prized
1 problems
1 proceeded
2 production
4 promise
1 promises
1 prospects
1 protected
1 proud
1 prove
13 Prudence
5 PS
1 public
7 pulled
5 put
1 puts
2 putting
1 pygmy

1 quando
1 quarter
6 queen
1 questo
1 queue
3 qui
3 quiet
1 quietly
1 quit
4 quite
1 quizzical
4 Raccoon
2 radiate
2 railman
28 rain
2 raincoats
3 rains
1 rainy
1 raise
1 Raleigh
3 ran
9 rather
1 reach
5 read
3 ready
10 real
7 realise
3 realised
51 really
13 reason
1 recall
1 rectify
7 red
1 refrain
2 refuse
2 regret
1 reject
1 relax
1 remain
24 remember
3 rent
1 replacing
5 reply
1 reprise
2 reservation
1 resign
1 rest
1 resting
1 restless
1 return
1 returning
1 revival
5 revolution
1 rice
21 rich
18 ride
3 riding
3 Rigby
51 right
1 rights
8 ring
2 ringing
2 Ringo
5 rings
2 rise
1 risk
19 Rita
2 rival
1 river
28 road
1 roam
1 rob
18 Robert
1 rock
1 rocking-horse
15 Rocky
1 Rocky's
2 rode*
27 roll
1 roller
1 roller-coaster
3 rolling
8 room
2 rope
1 rose
2 Rosetta
36 round
19 'round
1 roundabout
1 row
2 rowed*
1 rug
1 ruin
1 ruins

3 rules
21 run
8 running
1 rushes
2 sack
1 sacrificed
23 sad
17 Sadie
2 safe
89 said
4 sail
2 sailed
1 sailing
1 sake
1 saloon
23 same
6 sand
1 sang
1 sat
1 satisfaction
4 satisfied
1 Saturday
1 sauce
6 save
2 saved
2 saving
6 Savoy
23 saw
1 Saxon
149 say
6 saying
7 says
1 scarlet
3 scene
3 school
1 science
1 scratch
1 screaming
2 screen
1 screw
2 scrimp
9 sea
1 seabed
1 seance
1 searching
1 seashell
1 seat
8 second
1 seconds
5 secret
158 see
1 seeing
2 seem
1 seemed
12 seems
15 seen
7 sees
1 Seine
2 self-assured
1 selling
1 semolina
20 send
2 sending
1 sent
2 sermon
1 set
14 seven
1 seventeen
1 Sexie
16 sexy
22 Sgt
5 shade
1 shades
1 shadow
1 shady
2 shake
3 shall
3 share
2 shaves
244 she
1 she'd
5 she'll
111 she's
2 shears
1 sheep
1 shelter
1 shimmering
11 shine
11 shines
7 shining
2 ship
2 shirts
2 shoe
1 shoe-shine

1 shoes
39 shoo-be-do-a
27 shoot
1 shop
2 shore
3 short
1 short-haired
1 shot
65 should
5 shoulder
4 shout
1 shouts
30 show
1 showdown
1 showed
1 showing
1 shown
3 shows
3 shy
9 side
1 sideboard
8 sigh
3 sight
4 sign
1 silent
1 silently
6 silly
11 silver
2 sin
18 since
3 sincere
1 sincerely
31 sing
3 singer
1 singer's
7 singing
4 single
1 sings
1 sins
1 sip
3 sir
2 sister
8 sit
11 sitting
1 situation
15 six
4 sixty-four
5 skies
2 skin
2 skip
1 skirts
28 sky
1 Slaggers
15 sleep
11 sleeping
2 sleeps
1 sleepy
1 slept
2 slide
2 sling
3 slip
1 slither
1 slow
3 slowly
2 slumbers
4 small
11 smile
3 smiles
1 smiling
1 smoke
1 smokers
1 snied
1 snores
1 snow-peaked
216 so
1 soap
3 socks
1 sofa
1 sold
1 solid
1 solitude
2 solo
2 solution
26 some
17 somebody
8 someday
3 somehow
23 someone
1 someone's
1 somersets
31 something
3 sometimes
2 somewhere
6 son

21 song	2 Sunday's	24 three	3 understands	7 weeps
3 songs	1 sung	1 thrill	2 understood	1 weigh
3 sont	1 sunken	42 through	1 undertake	9 weight
5 soon	3 sunny	1 throws	1 undying	1 welcome
1 soothing	1 suns	1 thumb	2 unfair	85 well
2 sorrow	24 sunshine	1 Thursday	1 unfold	8 went
4 sorry	6 superior	16 ticket	2 unhappy	32 were
4 soul	9 sure	1 ticking	6 universe	3 weren't
7 sound	1 surely	1 tide	4 unkind	2 West
1 sounds	5 surprise	1 tides	1 unpack	2 wet
1 sour	1 surrender	1 tie	1 unpleasant	1 whacking
1 South	1 swaying	2 tied	8 until	1 whao-ho
1 Southampton	1 sweat	1 ties	2 unwise	169 what
1 space	2 sweater	2 tiger	100 up	1 what're
1 Spain	1 sweaty	29 tight	5 upon	4 what's
2 speak	1 sweeping	33 till	2 upset	198 when
8 speaking	20 sweet	127 time	2 upside	6 whenever
3 special	1 sweeter	9 times	3 upside-down	78 where
1 specially	1 swim	7 tired	1 upstairs	5 which
4 speed	1 swing	33 tit	4 upstream	17 while
4 spend	1 sympathise	763 to*	1 uptown	1 whim
1 spending	2 syndicate	25 today	26 us	12 whisper
1 spent	1 t-shirt	1 toe	1 USA	3 white
1 spinal	3 table	1 toe-jam	2 use	38 who
4 spinning	86 take	1 toes	6 used	1 who'll
2 spite	1 taken	74 together	11 USSR	4 who's
1 splendid	6 takes	32 told	2 vain	21 whoa
5 spoil	7 taking	12 tomorrow	1 valentine	4 whoa-ho
1 spoke	12 talk	44 tonight	1 Valerie	8 whoa-oh-aah
1 spoon	1 talked	124 too*	1 van	7 whole
3 spread	10 talking	13 took	1 vanish	98 why
1 stairs	1 tan	5 top	1 velvet	1 wicked
7 stand	3 tangerine	1 topping	1 Vera	6 wife
22 standing	1 tanta	6 touch	16 very	1 Wight
3 stands	1 tart	18 tour	1 Vienna	1 wigwam
5 star	1 taste	1 tow	3 view	2 wild
1 starched	2 taught	1 tower	1 voice	1 wildly
3 stare	4 tax	1 towering	2 voices	131 will
1 stared	1 taxis	4 town	1 void	1 Wilson
1 staring	15 taxman	1 trade	3 vont	4 win
2 stars	5 tea	1 tragic	2 wah	6 wind
14 start	1 teacher	2 train	1 wahoo	4 winding
1 started	1 teachers	1 trampoline	14 wait	8 window
1 starts	1 tear	1 travelled	2 waited	1 window-pane
2 state	3 tearing	13 travelling	30 waiting	2 windy
1 stating	17 tears	2 travels	2 waits	5 wine
3 station	2 teaser	1 tray	6 wake	2 wings
17 stay	3 tee	4 treasure	1 wakes	2 wink
2 stays	2 telephone	21 treat	11 walk	1 winter
2 steady	96 tell	2 treating	4 walked	1 wipe
1 steal	11 telling	4 tree	2 walking	1 wiping
1 stealing	6 tells	1 trees	1 walks	14 wisdom
2 step	5 ten	6 tres	5 wall	2 wish
2 stepping	1 tenderly	1 tricks	8 walrus	2 wishing
3 stick	1 test-tube	9 tried	1 Walter	191 with
1 sties	1 testimonial	2 tries	1 waltz	5 within
35 still	1 texpert	1 trigger	6 wandering	18 without
1 stinking	18 than	1 trim	70 wanna	1 wives
1 stirring	14 thank	2 trip	117 want	1 woke
1 stockings	1 thankful	10 tripper	2 wanted	13 woman
3 stone	1 thanks	1 triviality	9 wants	4 won
1 stony	332 that	1 trolly	1 war	67 won't
1 stood	47 that's	2 trouble	10 warm	8 wonder
14 stop	1027 the	1 troubles	1 warning	1 wonderful
4 stops	20 their	38 true	112 was	7 wondering
1 store	24 them	6 Truffle	1 washed	3 wonders
1 storm	2 themselves	5 trust	2 wasn't	1 wonky
4 story	39 then	1 truth	2 wasting	4 wood
1 straight	98 there	23 try	3 watch	5 woof
2 strange	2 there'll	10 trying	6 watching	1 woos
12 strawberry	51 there's	2 Tucson	1 water	29 word
2 stream	20 these	2 Tuesday	1 waters	34 words
3 street	69 they	2 Tuesdays	1 wave	2 wore
2 stretches	5 they'd	1 tulips	5 waves	12 work
2 strong	1 they'll	1 tumble	76 way	2 worked
1 stronger	17 they're	2 tune	4 ways	9 working
1 struggled	2 they've	1 tuned	116 we	3 works
1 studied	4 thick	16 turn	8 we'd	53 world
2 stupid	20 thin	1 turned	11 we'll	1 worm
1 sty	55 thing	5 turning	39 we're	3 worry
3 style	65 things	7 turns	9 we've	1 worrying
28 submarine	15 thinking	1 turnstyle	1 weak	4 worse
1 submarines	4 thinks	1 twelve	5 wear	2 worth
3 suburban	1 thirty-one	1 twelve-bar	6 wearing	47 would
1 succeed	58 this	1 twenty	2 wears	12 wouldn't
1 success	7 those	1 twenty-carat	1 weather	1 wow
19 such	37 though	9 twice	2 weather's	7 write
1 sucks	16 thought	47 two	1 weaving	30 writer
6 suddenly	1 thoughtless	1 two-foot	1 wedding	4 writing
2 suicidal	1 thoughtlessly	1 uh	1 Wednesday	22 wrong
1 suitcase	1 thoughts	2 Ukraine	1 weeds	1 wrote
1 summer	3 thousand	4 umpa	14 week	53 wuh
64 sun		6 under	2 weeks	1 wuh-oh
4 Sunday		18 understand	3 weep	2 wuhoo

7	ya	19	years	3	yet	156	you're	4	yours
3	yahoo	32	yellow	1	Yoko	46	you've	17	yourself
2	yard	1	yer	731	you	6	young	1	zap
2	yawning	105	yes	12	you'd	4	younger	1	zapped
359	yeah	13	yesterday	45	you'll	283	your	3	zoo
5	year								

Numerical Word-frequency List

Words are listed in descending order, from the most to the least frequently used. Capitalization of letters does not necessarily indicate capitalization in all cases of word use. Frequencies for articles, contractions and prefixed words also appear. Asterisks (*) identify words with frequencies that vary (homophones, etc.), usually by only one or two uses of the word.

1027 the	85 well	37 or	23 same	17 Lucy
825 me	84 out	37 through	23 saw	17 near
763 to*	82 he	36 any	23 someone	17 ow
731 you	82 only	36 blue	23 try	17 Sadie
643 a	81 better	36 give	22 ah	17 somebody
626 and	80 little	36 lose	22 ain't	17 stay
485 love	80 please	36 our	22 bang	17 tears
426 be	78 where	36 round	22 care	17 they're
422 it	77 aah	35 dance	22 didn't	17 while
410 in	77 not	35 still	22 forever	17 yourself
384 know	77 ooo	34 every	22 glad	16 answer
381 all	76 ha	34 everything	22 Sgt	16 belong
374 do	76 way	34 head	22 standing	16 black
374 my	75 at	34 words	22 wrong	16 diamonds
359 yeah	74 together	33 hear	21 friends	16 dream
348 oh	72 night	33 till	21 goo	16 driving
332 that	70 are	33 tit	21 listen	16 everyone
327 I'm	70 wanna	32 Bill	21 looking	16 everywhere
317 is	69 from	32 hide	21 no-one	16 Julia
290 I*	69 they	32 I'd	21 nobody	16 kill
296 don't	68 mind	32 may	21 rich	16 laugh
283 your	67 won't	32 once	21 run	16 making
273 on	66 been	32 paperback	21 song	16 sexy
268 of	65 'cos	32 told	21 treat	16 thought
257 nah	65 here	32 were	21 whoa	16 ticket
244 she	65 should	32 yellow	20 ask	16 turn
241 it's	65 think	31 alone	20 buy	16 very
216 so	64 sun	31 sing	20 children	15 chance
198 when	63 cry	31 something	20 cried	15 child
197 for	63 his	30 am	20 days	15 eight
195 can	62 alright	30 comes	20 door	15 face
193 her	62 feel	30 easy	20 friend	15 he's
191 with	60 look	30 show	20 kind	15 hearts
169 what	59 mine	30 waiting	20 knows	15 knew
168 but	58 as	30 writer	20 loves	15 lost
165 now	58 lonely	29 an	20 many	15 mad
164 get	58 this	29 Bungalow	20 other	15 Mr.
160 let	56 away	29 change*	20 Pepper's	15 Rocky
158 see	56 life	29 gone	20 play	15 seen
157 back	55 things	29 hand	20 send	15 six
156 you're	53 world	29 tight	20 sweet	15 sleep
154 down	53 wuh	29 word	20 their	15 taxman
154 girl	52 hold	28 coming	20 these	15 thinking
151 come	51 really	28 dead	20 thing	14 bom
151 if	51 right	28 does	19 band	14 born
149 say	51 there's	28 happy	19 birthday	14 car
147 I'll	50 hello	28 rain	19 darling	14 free
138 got	50 Jude	28 road	19 doing	14 happiness
137 like	49 name	28 sky	19 fool	14 heavy
131 will	48 before	28 submarine	19 ho	14 left
130 no	48 mother	27 around	19 la	14 light
127 time	47 by	27 believe	19 lovely	14 live
126 need	47 more	27 goodbye	19 mystery	14 lot
124 good	47 that's	27 has	19 over	14 loving
124 too*	47 two	27 number	19 pie	14 seven
121 gonna	47 would	27 roll	19 Rita	14 start
117 want	46 you've	27 shoot	19 round	14 stop
116 we	45 you'll	26 after	19 such	14 thank
112 was	44 could	26 dear	19 years	14 wait
111 she's	44 tonight	26 everybody	18 break	14 week
109 long	43 eyes	26 getting	18 changed	14 wisdom
109 man	43 feeling	26 heart	18 dig*	13 doesn't
105 yes	43 going	26 nowhere	18 done	13 enough
103 baby	43 mmm	26 some	18 Dr.	13 falling
102 can't	43 nothing	26 us	18 ever	13 found
102 go	42 leave	25 because	18 fine	13 garden
101 hey	42 morning	25 hard	18 five	13 hate
101 one	42 through	25 today	18 him	13 high*
100 up	41 always	24 about	18 into	13 living
98 there	41 find	24 beep	18 mean	13 lover
98 why	41 had	24 four	18 'n'	13 makes
97 day	40 help	24 honey	18 ride	13 meter
96 make*	39 again	24 made	18 Robert	13 new
96 tell	39 did	24 money	18 since	13 Prudence
95 much	39 goes	24 place	18 than	13 reason
93 have	39 people	24 remember	18 tour	13 took
92 home	39 shoo-be-do-a	24 sunshine	18 understand	13 travelling
91 never	39 then	24 them	18 without	13 woman
90 I've	39 we're	24 three	17 belonged	13 yesterday
90 just	38 another	23 bad	17 die	12 behind
89 said	38 boy	23 came	17 end	12 club
87 da	38 true	23 gotta	17 gun	12 even
86 take	38 who	23 old	17 helter-skelter	12 fields
85 how	37 call	23 sad	17 keep	12 gets

12 inside	9 nearly	7 red	5 drag	4 finger
12 joob	9 ob-la-da	7 says	5 early	4 frightened
12 maid	9 party	7 sees	5 first	4 full
12 might	9 pass	7 shining	5 fixing	4 g'goo
12 misery	9 Penny	7 singing	5 float	4 gives
12 must	9 rather	7 sound	5 fooling	4 golden
12 nothing's	9 sea	7 stand	5 game	4 grow
12 seems	9 side	7 taking	5 glass	4 h
12 strawberry	9 sure	7 those	5 greatest	4 haven't
12 talk	9 times	7 tired	5 guess	4 huh
12 tomorrow	9 tried	7 turns	5 guy	4 hungabout
12 whisper	9 twice	7 weeps	5 having	4 k
12 work	9 wants	7 whole	5 holding	4 key
12 wouldn't	9 weight	7 wondering	5 ice	4 Kite
12 you'd	9 we've	7 write	5 Judy	4 knock
11 anything	9 working	7 ya	5 kinda	4 lazy
11 ba	8 admit	6 bien	5 less	4 letter
11 babe	8 ago	6 broke	5 lips	4 looks
11 bag	8 baby's	6 bulldog	5 longer	4 Mary
11 big	8 beginning	6 buys	5 miss	4 Maxwell
11 'bye	8 bird	6 calls	5 missing	4 miles
11 crying	8 blackbird	6 catch	5 needs	4 million
11 drive	8 bom-pa	6 couldn't	5 off	4 moan
11 forget	8 bra	6 crucify	5 onion	4 monkey
11 ground	8 close	6 deep	5 ooo-ooo	4 nature's
11 heaven	8 each	6 ears	5 open	4 next
11 hope	8 eee	6 ensemble	5 past	4 nine
11 isn't	8 evening	6 fast	5 pay	4 o'clock
11 late	8 everybody's	6 few	5 pictures	4 often
11 maybe	8 fun	6 gave	5 point	4 opened
11 needed	8 g'joob	6 heard	5 pride	4 outta
11 ob-la-di	8 green	6 hit	5 PS	4 Pam
11 pretty	8 hammer	6 hole	5 put	4 plans
11 shine	8 hands	6 hoping	5 read	4 playing
11 shines	8 he'll	6 jump	5 reply	4 Polythene
11 silver	8 joy	6 knee	5 revolution	4 promise
11 sitting	8 King	6 knowing	5 rings	4 quite
11 sleeping	8 la-la	6 lady	5 secret	4 Raccoon
11 smile	8 lied	6 learn	5 shade	4 sail
11 telling	8 lies	6 lives	5 she'll	4 satisfied
11 USSR	8 Loretta	6 low*	5 shoulder	4 shout
11 walk	8 Molly	6 lying	5 skies	4 sign
11 we'll	8 moment	6 Madonna	5 soon	4 single
10 anybody	8 nine-o-nine	6 magical	5 spoil	4 sixty-four
10 being	8 phone	6 matter	5 star	4 small
10 beneath	8 pick	6 middle	5 surprise	4 sorry
10 bother	8 ring	6 music	5 tea	4 soul
10 carry	8 room	6 news	5 ten	4 speed
10 cha	8 running	6 nice	5 they'd	4 spend
10 dark	8 second	6 paper	5 top	4 spinning
10 dodahdo	8 sigh	6 peace	5 trust	4 stops
10 dow	8 sit	6 piggies	5 turning	4 story
10 dreams	8 someday	6 presents	5 upon	4 Sunday
10 feels	8 speaking	6 queen	5 wall	4 tax
10 fly	8 until	6 sand	5 waves	4 thick
10 girls	8 walrus	6 save	5 wear	4 thinks
10 hair	8 we'd	6 Savoy	5 which	4 town
10 hela	8 went	6 saying	5 wine	4 treasure
10 hurt	8 whoa-oh-aah	6 silly	5 within	4 tree
10 kiss	8 window	6 son	5 woof	4 umpa
10 last	8 wonder	6 suddenly	5 year	4 unkind
10 looked	7 appear	6 superior	4 act	4 upstream
10 lovin'	7 brown	6 takes	4 arise	4 walked
10 ma	7 calling	6 tells	4 asleep	4 ways
10 move	7 day's	6 touch	4 begin	4 what's
10 myself	7 Desmond	6 tres	4 believing	4 who's
10 octopus's	7 died	6 truffle	4 belle	4 whoa-ho
10 OK	7 earth	6 under	4 best	4 win
10 ought	7 else	6 universe	4 between	4 winding
10 real	7 fell	6 used	4 bit	4 won
10 talking	7 fill	6 wake	4 blind	4 wood
10 tripper	7 gently	6 wandering	4 boat	4 worse
10 trying	7 guitar	6 watching	4 bottom	4 writing
10 warm	7 half	6 wearing	4 bring	4 younger
9 across	7 harm	6 whenever	4 caught	4 yours
9 along	7 heh	6 wife	4 clothes	3 agree
9 apart	7 held	6 wind	4 colour	3 although
9 bed	7 hill	6 young	4 couple	3 anyone
9 cold	7 Jojo	5 ahead	4 crossed	3 appreciate
9 Deva	7 known	5 already	4 dancer	3 arms
9 eye	7 lead	5 beautiful	4 de	3 asked
9 far	7 let's	5 begins	4 dirt	3 a-well
9 feet	7 lie	5 beside	4 do-n-do-do	3 a-when
9 flat	7 line	5 blues	4 dressed	3 banker
9 follow	7 loved	5 boys	4 drink	3 bigger
9 Guru	7 Martha	5 breaks	4 dum	3 book
9 instead	7 Maxwell's	5 bright	4 dying	3 bop
9 Jai	7 meet	5 broken	4 ear	3 brother
9 keeps	7 met	5 Christ	4 eat	3 built
9 Lane	7 Michelle	5 cool	4 eggman	3 cake
9 leaving	7 own	5 Dennis	4 eggmen	3 called
9 loser	7 pain	5 diamond	4 end'a	3 captain
9 lucky	7 pretend	5 dirty	4 fall	3 'cept
	7 pulled	5 dog	4 father	
	7 realise		4 feed	

376

3 changing
3 clean
3 closer
3 cloud
3 clouds
3 count
3 crazy
3 crowd
3 cup
3 des
3 different
3 disappear
3 dreaming
3 Eleanor
3 ends
3 English
3 everyone's
3 feelings
3 filled
3 filling
3 fix
3 flies
3 flowers
3 flowing
3 flows
3 front
3 future
3 giving
3 grass
3 guaranteed
3 happen
3 happened
3 here's
3 hmm
3 holes
3 hot
3 hour
3 however
3 hurry
3 indicate
3 job
3 Jones
3 keeping
3 kept
3 land
3 lasted
3 lend
3 lift
3 lived
3 log
3 lullaby
3 magic
3 Majesty's
3 manage
3 Martin
3 means
3 meant
3 meanwhile
3 measured
3 meeting
3 memories
3 mistake
3 momma
3 Monday
3 moon
3 mots
3 Northern
3 Norwegian
3 notice
3 older
3 OM
3 ourselves
3 outside
3 overnight
3 painting
3 peasant
3 picks
3 picture
3 qui
3 quiet
3 rains
3 ran
3 ready
3 realised
3 rent
3 riding
3 Rigby
3 rolling
3 rules
3 scene
3 school
3 share
3 short

3 shows
3 shy
3 sight
3 sincere
3 singer
3 sir
3 slip
3 slowly
3 smiles
3 socks
3 somehow
3 sometimes
3 songs
3 sont
3 special
3 spread
3 stands
3 stare
3 station
3 stick
3 stone
3 street
3 style
3 suburban
3 sunny
3 table
3 tangerine
3 tearing
3 tee
3 thousand
3 understands
3 upside-down
3 view
3 vont
3 watch
3 weep
3 weren't
3 white
3 wonders
3 works
3 worry
3 yahoo
3 yet
3 zoo
2 above
2 aches
2 affection
2 amore
2 a-move
2 anybody's
2 anyhow
2 anyway
2 a-one
2 apologize
2 Arizona
2 arrive
2 arriving
2 away-hey
2 a-will
2 aye
2 barber
2 bathroom
2 beg
2 begged
2 below
2 bended
2 benefit
2 beyond
2 Bible
2 Billy
2 'b-la-da
2 blame
2 blew
2 blonde
2 blows
2 boom
2 both
2 bought
2 brain
2 brand
2 bringing
2 brings
2 broken-hearted
2 cable
2 California
2 cannot
2 carrying
2 carve
2 case
2 cause
2 celebrate
2 cha-cha-cha
2 Chairman
2 chasing

2 checked
2 chop
2 chords
2 church
2 clear
2 closed
2 cloudy
2 clue
2 clutching
2 coffee
2 comfort
2 command
2 complain
2 conceive
2 constitution
2 contribution
2 corner
2 creme
2 crime
2 danced
2 Danny
2 darkness
2 darlin'
2 deeper
2 delay
2 deserve
2 dessert
2 destruction
2 dies
2 difference
2 dinner
2 disagree
2 disappearing
2 disappointment
2 Doc
2 doors
2 Doris
2 doubt
2 downstairs
2 dresses
2 driver
2 drop
2 e
2 'em
2 eternally
2 evolution
2 fair
2 farther
2 FBI
2 fifty
2 fighting
2 finally
2 fingers
2 fire
2 fireman
2 floating
2 flown
2 footsteps
2 freely
2 Friday
2 frown
2 funny
2 fussing
2 Georgia's
2 Gideon's
2 ginger
2 glimpse
2 goodbyes
2 grandchildren
2 great
2 greet
2 grin
2 habit
2 hang
2 heads
2 heart's
2 helps
2 Hendersons
2 hi*
2 higher
2 himself
2 Hollywood
2 homeward
2 hung
2 imagine
2 imagined
2 imitate
2 independence
2 insane
2 institution
2 introduce
2 invitation
2 Jay
2 jealous
2 Jo

2 Joan
2 John
2 joke
2 joker
2 jumper
2 kaleidoscope
2 kids
2 kissing
2 kitchen
2 latest
2 laughing
2 layed
2 leads
2 learned
2 learns
2 lets
2 lifetime
2 lights
2 listening
2 local
2 location
2 loner
2 lorry
2 loud
2 lovers
2 mack
2 Mao
2 market
2 McKenzie
2 meaning
2 men
2 mending
2 mi
2 mind's
2 minds
2 mmm-mmm
2 montelimar
2 Moscow
2 most
2 mountain
2 moving
2 Mustard
2 n
2 nasty
2 national
2 naughty
2 nine-o
2 no-one's
2 noise
2 note
2 noticed
2 ocean
2 O'Fell
2 ooh
2 pan
2 Paris
2 park
2 part
2 parted
2 penetrate
2 perfectly
2 performs
2 picker
2 pies
2 piggy
2 pigs
2 pineapple
2 places
2 plan
2 plane
2 played
2 plays
2 pleasure
2 policeman
2 pouring
2 production
2 putting
2 radiate
2 railman
2 raincoats
2 refuse
2 regret
2 reservation
2 ringing
2 Ringo
2 rise
2 rival
2 rode*
2 rope
2 Rosetta
2 rowed*
2 sack
2 safe
2 sailed
2 saved

2 saving
2 screen
2 scrimp
2 seem
2 self-assured
2 sending
2 sermon
2 shake
2 shall
2 shaves
2 shears
2 ship
2 shirts
2 shoe
2 shore
2 sin
2 sister
2 skin
2 skip
2 sleeps
2 slide
2 sling
2 slumbers
2 solo
2 solution
2 somewhere
2 sorrow
2 speak
2 spite
2 stars
2 state
2 stays
2 steady
2 step
2 stepping
2 strange
2 stream
2 stretches
2 strong
2 stupid
2 suicidal
2 summer
2 Sundays
2 sweater
2 syndicate
2 taught
2 teaser
2 telephone
2 themselves
2 there'll
2 they've
2 thin
2 tied
2 tiger
2 train
2 travels
2 treating
2 tries
2 trip
2 trouble
2 Tucson
2 Tuesday
2 Tuesdays
2 tune
2 Ukraine
2 understood
2 unfair
2 unhappy
2 unwise
2 upset
2 upside
2 use
2 vain
2 voices
2 wah
2 waited
2 waits
2 walking
2 wanted
2 wasn't
2 wasting
2 wears
2 weather's
2 Wednesday
2 weeks
2 West
2 wet
2 wild
2 windy
2 wings
2 wink
2 wish
2 wishing
2 wore

2 worked	1 bone	1 crabalocker	1 except	1 he'd
2 worth	1 booked	1 cracker	1 existence	1 heading
2 wuhoo	1 books	1 cracks	1 expert	1 health
2 yard	1 bootlace	1 cranberry	1 eyeball	1 hearing
2 yawning	1 boots	1 crash	1 f	1 hears
1 able	1 bosun	1 crawled	1 faces	1 heat
1 aboard	1 bottle	1 crawling	1 faded	1 Heath
1 accidents	1 bound	1 cream	1 famous	1 helping
1 acorns	1 breakfast	1 creeping	1 fancy	1 Henry
1 acquainted	1 breaking	1 creeps	1 Fanques	1 herself
1 acts	1 breast	1 cries	1 fare	1 hey-hey-hey
1 a-do	1 bridge	1 cruel	1 farm	1 hideaway
1 advice	1 brothers	1 curse	1 fart	1 hiding
1 afraid	1 brrrrrr	1 custard	1 faster	1 high-heel
1 afternoon	1 bull-frog	1 customer	1 fate	1 hills
1 age	1 bullet-headed	1 cut	1 fears	1 hilt
1 a-gonna	1 bum	1 cuts	1 feat	1 Hilton
1 ah-ha	1 buried	1 d	1 featuring	1 hobnail
1 ah-hey	1 burning	1 da-da	1 ferde	1 hoe-down
1 Aids	1 burns	1 da-da-da-da-da	1 field	1 hog
1 air	1 burst	1 daddy	1 fierce	1 hogshead
1 Albert	1 bus	1 daddy's	1 fifteen	1 holiday
1 alerted	1 Busby	1 daily	1 fight	1 Holland
1 a-like	1 business	1 daisies	1 film	1 holy
1 all-American	1 busy	1 daisy	1 filter	1 honeymooning
1 Allan	1 butted	1 Dakota	1 finds	1 hoo
1 almost	1 butterfly	1 damn	1 fire-engine	1 hoops
1 aloud	1 c	1 Dan	1 fireside	1 hoped
1 a-moving	1 cap	1 dances	1 fish	1 horse
1 Amsterdam	1 carathon	1 Daniel	1 fishwife	1 horses
1 angels	1 caressing	1 darning	1 flew	1 hour-glass
1 angry	1 carousel	1 Dave	1 flight	1 house
1 annoyed	1 cast-iron	1 Deaf	1 flirt	1 how's
1 a-now	1 cat	1 decide	1 floor	1 hu
1 anywhere	1 cave	1 declare	1 flying	1 hug
1 appears	1 ceiling	1 defeliche	1 fog	1 hunting
1 apple	1 celebrated	1 demonstrate	1 fold	1 hurting
1 appointment	1 celebrations	1 denied	1 folk	1 husband
1 aren't	1 cellophane	1 deny	1 foolish	1 ignorance
1 armchair	1 certain	1 department	1 foot	1 illusion
1 army	1 certainly	1 determined	1 football	1 images
1 a-Rocky	1 chain	1 digging	1 forgive	1 imperfect
1 arrives	1 chair	1 direction	1 forks	1 important
1 asking	1 challenge	1 disconnect	1 form	1 impression
1 assure	1 changes	1 discovered	1 fountain	1 inciting
1 ate	1 charity	1 discreetly	1 France	1 incredibly
1 a-ticking	1 Charles	1 disease	1 frantic	1 inner
1 Atlantic	1 cherry	1 diverted	1 frying	1 innocence
1 attractively	1 chicka	1 do-do-do	1 fudge	1 inquire
1 attracts	1 childlike	1 dock	1 fuse	1 insecure
1 audience	1 childrens'	1 doctor	1 g	1 inspiration
1 audition	1 chip	1 dog's	1 gain	1 inverted
1 avoid	1 chocolate	1 donated	1 gallery	1 investigation
1 awake	1 choking	1 dose	1 games	1 invitations
1 aware	1 chord	1 doubted	1 garters	1 inviting
1 awoke	1 Chuck	1 dove-tail	1 gas	1 Isle
1 awoken	1 CIA	1 down-stream	1 gather	1 j
1 b	1 cigarette	1 dragged	1 gear	1 jack-knife
1 backdoor	1 city	1 drank	1 gee	1 jackboots
1 backing	1 class	1 dreadful	1 Georgie	1 James
1 bacon	1 cleaner	1 dressing-gown	1 getting-a	1 jar
1 bags	1 climb	1 drew	1 Gibraltar	1 jewellery
1 balalaikas	1 climbing	1 drift	1 Gideon	1 jobber
1 Ballad	1 clinging	1 drifting	1 gin	1 Johnny
1 banks	1 clock	1 drinking	1 glimmering	1 joint
1 barrow	1 closing	1 dripping	1 go-getter	1 ju-ju
1 based	1 clown	1 drove	1 good-looking	1 judge
1 bath	1 clowns	1 Duchess	1 goodlooking	1 jungle
1 BB	1 clubs	1 Duke	1 grabbed	1 kicking
1 BBC	1 coat	1 Dylan's	1 grade	1 killer-diller
1 beach	1 Coca-cola	1 eagle	1 grave	1 kilt
1 beat	1 cocoanut	1 earn	1 greetings	1 kindly
1 became	1 colder	1 ease	1 grinning	1 kindness
1 becomes	1 collapsed	1 eating	1 grooving	1 Kirkaldy
1 bedroom	1 college	1 Edgar	1 group	1 knees
1 beds	1 colourful	1 Edison	1 gumboot	1 knickers
1 bee	1 comb	1 Eiffel	1 gurus	1 knit
1 behalf	1 compare	1 elementary	1 ha-ha-ha	1 knives
1 bellyfull	1 compares	1 elephant	1 haa	1 Krishna
1 bent-backed	1 complaining	1 elephants	1 hall	1 lacking
1 bet	1 comrade	1 Elmore	1 hand's	1 lagoon
1 biding	1 confusing	1 endear	1 handkerchief	1 Lancashire
1 birds	1 continuing	1 endless	1 handy	1 lark
1 Bishopsgate	1 controlled	1 engaged	1 hanging	1 lastly
1 bits	1 conversation	1 England	1 happens	1 lasts
1 Blackburn	1 cooking	1 enjoy	1 hard-earned	1 latches
1 blindly	1 coral	1 enjoyed	1 hardly	1 laughs
1 blink	1 cornflake	1 equal	1 hare	1 laughter
1 blisters	1 corporation	1 equipped	1 hark	1 lay
1 bloody	1 correct	1 er	1 harmony	1 Lear
1 blow	1 cottage	1 escaping	1 hat	1 learning
1 BOAC	1 country	1 everbody	1 hates	1 legend
1 bob	1 course	1 evermore	1 Hawtrey	1 legs
	1 cows	1 everything's	1 haze	1 leisure

1 lemonade	1 newspapers	1 proud	1 showing	1 teachers
1 lends	1 night-time	1 prove	1 shown	1 tear
1 letter-box	1 nights	1 public	1 sideboard	1 tenderly
1 letters	1 nineteen	1 puts	1 silent	1 test-tube
1 licks	1 none	1 pygmy	1 silently	1 testimonial
1 lifting	1 North	1 quando	1 sincerely	1 texpert
1 lighten	1 nose	1 quarter	1 singer's	1 thankful
1 lightning	1 novel	1 questo	1 sings	1 thanks
1 likes	1 nun	1 queue	1 sins	1 they'll
1 Lil	1 nurse	1 quietly	1 sip	1 thirty-one
1 limitless	1 oats	1 quit	1 situation	1 thoughtless
1 limousine	1 obrigado	1 quizzical	1 skirts	1 thoughtlessly
1 line's	1 obscene	1 rainy	1 Slaggers	1 thoughts
1 linger	1 oceanchild	1 raise	1 sleepy	1 thrill
1 lip	1 odes	1 Raleigh	1 slept	1 throws
1 listens	1 oh-oh	1 reach	1 slither	1 thumb
1 lit	1 oh-oh-oh	1 recall	1 slow	1 Thursday
1 lizard	1 oh-oh-oh-oh-oh-	1 rectify	1 smiling	1 ticking
1 'lo*	1 Ono	1 refrain	1 smoke	1 tide
1 lock	1 ooho	1 reject	1 smokers	1 tides
1 locked	1 ooo-mmm	1 relax	1 snied	1 tie
1 London	1 ooo-ooo-aah	1 remain	1 snores	1 ties
1 looking-glass	1 ooo-ooo-ooo	1 replacing	1 snow-peaked	1 toe
1 Lords	1 ooo-ooo-ooo-oh	1 reprise	1 soap	1 toe-jam
1 losing	1 opaque	1 resign	1 sofa	1 toes
1 lots	1 orange	1 rest	1 sold	1 topping
1 low-neck	1 ours	1 resting	1 solid	1 tow
1 machine	1 overtime	1 restless	1 solitude	1 tower
1 Madam	1 owned	1 return	1 someone's	1 towering
1 Magill	1 Pablo	1 returning	1 somersets	1 trade
1 mail	1 pages	1 revival	1 soothing	1 tragic
1 Majesty	1 paid	1 rice	1 sounds	1 trampoline
1 majoring	1 paparatsi	1 rights	1 sour	1 travelled
1 mantelshelf	1 papers	1 risk	1 South	1 tray
1 Marigold	1 paramucho	1 river	1 Southampton	1 trees
1 market-place	1 parasol	1 roam	1 space	1 tricks
1 marmalade	1 parking	1 rob	1 Spain	1 trigger
1 married	1 parlour	1 rock	1 specially	1 trim
1 marshmallow	1 passed	1 rocking-horse	1 spending	1 triviality
1 Marvel	1 pataphysical	1 Rocky's	1 spent	1 trolly
1 mask	1 Paul	1 roller	1 spinal	1 troubles
1 match	1 PC	1 roller-coaster	1 splendid	1 truth
1 matches	1 peanuts	1 rose	1 spoke	1 tulips
1 Matt	1 peep	1 roundabout	1 spoon	1 tumble
1 mattered	1 penguin	1 row	1 stairs	1 tuned
1 Max	1 pennies	1 rug	1 starched	1 turned
1 meander	1 Pepper	1 ruin	1 stared	1 turnstyle
1 meaningless	1 percent	1 ruins	1 staring	1 twelve
1 medicine	1 perform	1 rushes	1 started	1 twelve-bar
1 melting	1 perverted	1 sacrificed	1 starts	1 twenty
1 member	1 Peter	1 sailing	1 stating	1 twenty-carat
1 message	1 phase	1 sake	1 steal	1 two-foot
1 Messrs	1 photograph	1 saloon	1 stealing	1 uh
1 Miami	1 photographs	1 sang	1 sties	1 undertake
1 mighty	1 piano	1 sat	1 stinking	1 undying
1 military	1 picking	1 satisfaction	1 stirring	1 unfold
1 minute	1 piece	1 Saturday	1 stockings	1 unpack
1 mirrors	1 pilchard	1 sauce	1 stony	1 unpleasant
1 misplace	1 pillow	1 Saxon	1 stood	1 upstairs
1 missed	1 pink	1 scarlet	1 store	1 uptown
1 misses	1 plain	1 science	1 storm	1 USA
1 mist	1 planned	1 scratch	1 straight	1 valentine
1 misunderstanding	1 plasticine	1 screaming	1 stronger	1 Valerie
1 misunderstood	1 playroom	1 screw	1 struggled	1 van
1 mmm-mmm-mmm	1 pleas	1 seabed	1 studied	1 vanish
1 mojo	1 pleasing	1 seance	1 sty	1 velvet
1 mom	1 pocket	1 searching	1 submarines	1 Vera
1 moments	1 Poe	1 seashell	1 succeed	1 Vienna
1 mommy	1 police	1 seat	1 success	1 voice
1 mommy's	1 policemen	1 seconds	1 sucks	1 void
1 Monday's	1 pony	1 seeing	1 suitcase	1 wahoo
1 money's	1 pool	1 seemed	1 sung	1 wakes
1 Moretta	1 pools	1 Seine	1 sunken	1 walks
1 mornings	1 poor	1 selling	1 suns	1 Walter
1 mother's	1 poppies	1 semolina	1 surely	1 waltz
1 motor	1 pornographic	1 sent	1 surrender	1 war
1 motorcar	1 porters	1 set	1 swaying	1 warning
1 mountains	1 portrait	1 seventeen	1 sweat	1 washed
1 mourn	1 position	1 Sexie	1 sweaty	1 water
1 movement	1 possessing	1 shades	1 sweeping	1 waters
1 moves	1 possessions	1 shadow	1 sweeter	1 wave
1 mucho	1 postcard	1 shady	1 swim	1 weak
1 muddy	1 postcards	1 she'd	1 swing	1 weather
1 multicoloured	1 pot-smoking	1 sheep	1 sympathise	1 weaving
1 mundo	1 precisely	1 shelter	1 t-shirt	1 wedding
1 named	1 preparation	1 shimmering	1 taken	1 weeds
1 Nancy	1 press	1 shoe-shine	1 talked	1 weigh
1 natural	1 priestess	1 shoes	1 tan	1 welcome
1 need's	1 prized	1 shop	1 tanta	1 whacking
1 negotiations	1 problems	1 short-haired	1 tart	1 whao-ho
1 nerve	1 proceeded	1 shot	1 taste	1 what're
1 never-ending	1 promises	1 shouts	1 taxis	1 whim
1 news-people	1 prospects	1 showdown	1 teacher	1 who'll
1 newspaper	1 protected	1 showed		1 wicked

1	Wight	1	winter	1	wonderful	1	worrying	1	yer
1	wigwam	1	wipe	1	wonky	1	wow	1	Yoko
1	wildly	1	wiping	1	woos	1	wrote	1	zap
1	Wilson	1	wives	1	worm	1	wuh-oh	1	zapped
1	window-pane	1	woke						

Listener's Guide to Songs

As an aid in locating the songs covered by this work for listening purposes, a song index to 49 long-playing recordings (LPs) released in the United Kingdom, Canada and the United States follows. This index is limited to commercially released *studio* recordings; live albums, extended-play recordings (EPs), and singles (45rpm) are not referenced.

Only albums of the EMI/Capitol organization have been indexed (Capitol, Parlophone and Apple labels), except in the case of the United Artists' **A Hard Day's Night** album.

Country of release is noted in the song index only when albums with identical titles vary in content; otherwise, the song is understood to appear on the one or more albums with that title regardless of country of release.

Differences in the contents of the recently released **Beatles Rarities** albums are more musical than lyrical, so they are also indexed here despite such things as the rearrangement of two verses in one song (*I'm Only Sleeping*) on the US album, and other slight variations.

Albums Indexed

ABBEY ROAD
    Apple PCS 7088 (UK)
    Apple SO 383 (US)

BEATLEMANIA WITH THE BEATLES
    Capitol of Canada ST 6051

THE BEATLES (2 LPs)
    Apple PCS 7067/8 (UK)
    Apple SWBO 101 (US)

THE BEATLES COLLECTION (14 LPs)
    Parlophone BC 13 (UK)
    Capitol BC 13 (US)

BEATLES FOR SALE
    Parlophone PCS 3062 (UK)

THE BEATLES 1962--1966 (2 LPs)
    Apple PCSP 717 (UK)
    Apple SKBO 3403 (US)

THE BEATLES 1967--1970 (2 LPs)
    Apple PCSP 718 (UK)
    Apple SKBO 3404 (US)

THE BEATLES RARITIES
    Parlophone SPSLP 261 (UK)
    Capitol SHAL-12060 (US)

THE BEATLES SECOND ALBUM
    Capitol ST 2080 (US)

BEATLES VI
    Capitol ST 2358 (US)

BEATLES '65
    Capitol ST 2228 (US)

THE BEST OF GEORGE HARRISON
    Parlophone PAS 10011 (UK)
    Capitol ST 11578 (US)

A COLLECTION OF BEATLES OLDIES...
    BUT GOLDIES
    Parlophone PCS 7016 (UK)

THE EARLY BEATLES
    Capitol ST 2309 (US)

A HARD DAY'S NIGHT
    Parlophone PCS 3058 (UK)
    United Artists UAS 6366 (US)

HELP!
    Parlophone PCS 3071 (UK)
    Capitol SMAS 2386 (US)

HEY JUDE
    Apple SW385/SO385 (US)

LET IT BE
    Apple PXS 1 (UK)
    Apple AR 34001 (US)

LONG TALL SALLY
    Capitol of Canada ST 6063

LOVE SONGS (2 LPs)
    Parlophone PCSP 721 (UK)
    Capitol SKBL 11711 (US)

MAGICAL MYSTERY TOUR
    Parlophone PCTC 255 (UK)
    Capitol SMAL 2835 (US)

MEET THE BEATLES
    Capitol ST 2047 (US)

PLEASE PLEASE ME
    Parolphone PCS 3043 (UK)

REVOLVER
    Parlophone PCS 7009 (UK)
    Capitol ST 2576 (US)

ROCK 'N' ROLL MUSIC (2 LPs)
    Parlophone PCSP 719 (UK)
    Capitol SKBO 11537 (US)

RUBBER SOUL
    Parlophone PCS 3075 (UK)
    Capitol ST 2442

SGT. PEPPER'S LONELY HEARTS
    CLUB BAND
    Parlophone PCS 7027 (UK)
    Capitol SMAS 2653 (US)

SOMETHING NEW
    Capitol ST 2018 (US)

TWIST AND SHOUT
    Capitol of Canada ST 6054

WITH THE BEATLES
    Parlophone PCS 3045 (UK)

YELLOW SUBMARINE
    Apple PCS 7070 (UK)
    Apple SW 153 (US)

YESTERDAY...AND TODAY
    Capitol ST 2553 (US)

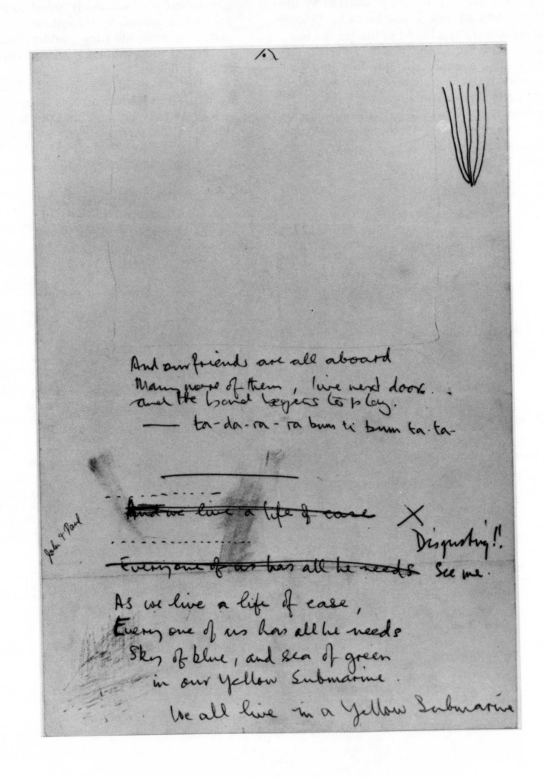

Song Index to Albums

ACROSS THE UNIVERSE
   The Beatles Collection
   The Beatles 1967--1970
   The Beatles Rarities
   Let It Be
ALL I'VE GOT TO DO
   Beatlemania With The Beatles
   The Beatles Collection
   Meet The Beatles
   With The Beatles
ALL MY LOVING
   Beatlemania With The Beatles
   The Beatles Collection
   The Beatles 1962--1966
   With The Beatles
ALL TOGETHER NOW
   The Beatles Collection
   Yellow Submarine
ALL YOU NEED IS LOVE (MMT)
   Magical Mystery Tour (US)
ALL YOU NEED IS LOVE (YS)
   The Beatles Collection
   The Beatles 1967--1970
   Magical Mystery Tour (UK)
   Yellow Submarine
AND I LOVE HER
   The Beatles Collection
   The Beatles 1962--1966
   The Beatles Rarities (US)
   A Hard Day's Night
   Love Songs
   Something New
AND YOUR BIRD CAN SING
   The Beatles Collection
   Revolver (UK)
   Yesterday...And Today
ANOTHER GIRL
   The Beatles Collection
   Help!
ANY TIME AT ALL
   The Beatles Collection
   A Hard Day's Night (UK)
   Rock 'n' Roll Music
   Something New
ASK ME WHY
   The Beatles Collection
   The Early Beatles
   Please Please Me
   Twist And Shout
BABY, YOU'RE A RICH MAN
   Magical Mystery Tour
BABY'S IN BLACK
   The Beatles Collection
   Beatles For Sale
   Beatles '65
BACK IN THE USSR
   The Beatles
   The Beatles Collection
   The Beatles 1967--1970
   Rock 'n' Roll Music
THE BALLAD OF JOHN AND YOKO
   The Beatles 1967--1970
   Hey Jude
BECAUSE
   Abbey Road
   The Beatles Collection
BEING FOR THE BENEFIT OF
    MR. KITE
   The Beatles Collection
   Sgt. Pepper's
BIRTHDAY
   The Beatles
   The Beatles Collection
   Rock 'n' Roll Music

BLACKBIRD
   The Beatles
   The Beatles Collection
BLUE JAY WAY
   Magical Mystery Tour
CAN'T BUY ME LOVE
   The Beatles Collection
   The Beatles 1962--1966
   A Collection of Beatles...
   A Hard Day's Night
   Hey Jude
CARRY THAT WEIGHT
   Abbey Road
   The Beatles Collection
COME TOGETHER
   Abbey Road
   The Beatles Collection
   The Beatles 1967--1970
THE CONTINUING STORY OF
    BUNGALOW BILL
   The Beatles
   The Beatles Collection
CRY BABY CRY
   The Beatles
   The Beatles Collection
A DAY IN THE LIFE
   The Beatles Collection
   The Beatles 1967--1970
   Sgt. Pepper's
DAY TRIPPER
   The Beatles 1962--1966
   A Collection of Beatles...
   Yesterday...And Today
DEAR PRUDENCE
   The Beatles
   The Beatles Collection
DIG IT
   The Beatles Collection
   Let It Be
DO YOU WANT TO KNOW A SECRET?
   The Beatles Collection
   The Early Beatles
   Please Please Me
   Twist And Shout
DR. ROBERT
   The Beatles Collection
   Revolver (UK)
   Yesterday...And Today
DON'T BOTHER ME
   Beatlemania With The Beatles
   The Beatles Collection
   Meet The Beatles
   With The Beatles
DON'T LET ME DOWN
   The Beatles 1967--1970
   Hey Jude
DON'T PASS ME BY
   The Beatles
   The Beatles Collection
   The Beatles Rarities
DRIVE MY CAR
   The Beatles Collection
   The Beatles 1962--1966
   Rock 'n' Roll Music
   Rubber Soul (UK)
   Yesterday...And Today
EIGHT DAYS A WEEK
   The Beatles Collection
   Beatles For Sale
   The Beatles 1962--1966
   Beatles VI
ELEANOR RIGBY
   The Beatles Collection
   The Beatles 1962--1966

   A Collection of Beatles...
   Revolver
THE END
   Abbey Road
   The Beatles Collection
EVERY LITTLE THING
   The Beatles Collection
   Beatles For Sale
   Beatles VI
   Love Songs
EVERYBODY'S GOT SOMETHING TO
    HIDE EXCEPT ME AND MY
    MONKEY
   The Beatles
   The Beatles Collection
FIXING A HOLE
   The Beatles Collection
   Sgt. Pepper's
FLYING
   Magical Mystery Tour
THE FOOL ON THE HILL
   The Beatles 1967--1970
   Magical Mystery Tour
FOR NO ONE
   The Beatles Collection
   Love Songs
   Revolver
FOR YOU BLUE
   The Beatles Collection
   The Best of George Harrison
   Let It Be
FROM ME TO YOU
   The Beatles 1962--1966
   A Collection of Beatles...
   Twist And Shout
GET BACK (45)
   The Beatles 1967--1970
GET BACK (LP)
   The Beatles Collection
   Let It Be
   Rock 'n' Roll
GETTING BETTER
   The Beatles Collection
   Sgt. Pepper's
GIRL
   The Beatles Collection
   The Beatles 1962--1966
   Love Songs
   Rubber Soul
GLASS ONION
   The Beatles
   The Beatles Collection
GOLDEN SLUMBERS
   Abbey Road
   The Beatles Collection
GOOD DAY SUNSHINE
   The Beatles Collection
   Revolver
GOOD MORNING GOOD MORNING
   The Beatles Collection
   Sgt. Pepper's
GOOD NIGHT
   The Beatles
   The Beatles Collection
GOT TO GET YOU INTO MY LIFE
   The Beatles Collection
   Revolver
   Rock 'n' Roll Music
HAPPINESS IS A WARM GUN
   The Beatles
   The Beatles Collection
A HARD DAY'S NIGHT
   The Beatles Collection
   The Beatles 1962--1966

A Collection of Beatles...
A Hard Day's Night
HELLO GOODBYE
    The Beatles 1967--1970
    Magical Mystery Tour
HELP!
    The Beatles Collection
    The Beatles 1962--1966
    The Beatles Rarities (US)
    A Collection of Beatles...
    Help!
HELTER-SKELTER
    The Beatles
    The Beatles Collection
    The Beatles Rarities (US)
    Rock 'n' Roll Music
HER MAJESTY
    Abbey Road
    The Beatles Collection
HERE COMES THE SUN
    Abbey Road
    The Beatles Collection
    The Beatles 1967--1970
    The Best of George Harrison
HERE THERE AND EVERYWHERE
    The Beatles Collection
    Love Songs
    Revolver
HEY BULLDOG
    The Beatles Collection
    Rock 'n' Roll Music
    Yellow Submarine
HEY JUDE
    The Beatles 1967--1970
    Hey Jude
HOLD ME TIGHT
    Beatlemania With The Beatles
    The Beatles Collection
    Meet The Beatles
    With The Beatles
HONEY PIE
    The Beatles
    The Beatles Collection
I AM THE WALRUS
    The Beatles 1967--1970
    The Beatles Rarities (US)
    Magical Mystery Tour
I CALL YOUR NAME
    The Beatles Collection
    The Beatles Rarities (UK)
    The Beatles Second Album
    Long Tall Sally
    Rock 'n' Roll Music
(I) DIG A PONY
    The Beatles Collection
    Let It Be
I DON'T WANT TO SPOIL THE PARTY
    The Beatles Collection
    Beatles For Sale
    Beatles VI
I FEEL FINE
    The Beatles 1962--1966
    Beatles '65
    A Collection of Beatles...
I ME MINE
    The Beatles Collection
    Let It Be
I NEED YOU
    The Beatles Collection
    Help!
    Love Songs
I SAW HER STANDING THERE
    The Beatles Collection
    Long Tall Sally
    Meet The Beatles
    Please Please Me
    Rock 'n' Roll Music
I SHOULD HAVE KNOWN BETTER
    The Beatles Collection
    A Hard Day's Night

Hey Jude
I WANNA BE YOUR MAN
    Beatlemania With The Beatles
    The Beatles Collection
    Meet The Beatles
    Rock 'n' Roll Music
    With The Beatles
I WANT TO HOLD YOUR HAND
    The Beatles Collection (US)
    The Beatles 1962--1966
    A Collection of Beatles...
    Long Tall Sally
    Meet The Beatles
I WANT TO TELL YOU
    The Beatles Collection
    Revolver
I WANT YOU (SHE'S SO HEAVY)
    Abbey Road
    The Beatles Collection
I WILL
    The Beatles
    The Beatles Collection
    Love Songs
IF I FELL
    The Beatles Collection
    A Hard Day's Night
    Love Songs
    Something New
IF I NEEDED SOMEONE
    The Beatles Collection
    The Best of George Harrison
    Rubber Soul (UK)
    Yesterday...And Today
I'LL BE BACK
    The Beatles Collection
    Beatles '65
    A Hard Day's Night (UK)
    Love Songs
I'LL CRY INSTEAD
    The Beatles Collection
    A Hard Day's Night
    Something New
I'LL FOLLOW THE SUN
    The Beatles Collection
    Beatles For Sale
    Beatles '65
    Love Songs
I'LL GET YOU
    The Beatles Collection
    The Beatles Rarities (UK)
    The Beatles Second Album
    Long Tall Sally
I'M A LOSER
    The Beatles Collection
    Beatles For Sale
    Beatles '65
I'M DOWN
    The Beatles Collection
    The Beatles Rarities (UK)
    Rock 'n' Roll Music
I'M HAPPY JUST TO DANCE WITH YOU
    The Beatles Collection
    A Hard Day's Night
    Something New
I'M LOOKING THROUGH YOU
    The Beatles Collection
    Rubber Soul
I'M ONLY SLEEPING
    The Beatles Collection
    The Beatles Rarities (US)
    Revolver (UK)
I'M SO TIRED
    The Beatles
    The Beatles Collection
IN MY LIFE
    The Beatles Collection
    The Beatles 1962--1966
    Love Songs
    Rubber Soul
THE INNER LIGHT

The Beatles Collection
The Beatles Rarities
IT WON'T BE LONG
    Beatlemania With The Beatles
    The Beatles Collection
    Meet The Beatles
    With The Beatles
IT'S ALL TOO MUCH
    The Beatles Collection
    Yellow Submarine
IT'S ONLY LOVE
    The Beatles Collection
    Help! (UK)
    Love Songs
    Rubber Soul (US)
I'VE GOT A FEELING
    The Beatles Collection
    Let It Be
I'VE JUST SEEN A FACE
    The Beatles Collection
    Help! (UK)
    Rubber Soul (US)
JULIA
    The Beatles
    The Beatles Collection
LADY MADONNA
    The Beatles 1967--1970
    Hey Jude
LET IT BE (45)
    The Beatles 1967--1970
    Hey Jude
LET IT BE (LP)
    The Beatles Collection
    Let It Be
LITTLE CHILD
    Beatlemania With The Beatles
    The Beatles Collection
    Meet The Beatles
    With The Beatles
THE LONG AND WINDING ROAD
    The Beatles Collection
    The Beatles 1967--1970
    Let It Be
    Love Songs
LONG, LONG, LONG
    The Beatles
    The Beatles Collection
LOVE ME DO
    The Beatles Collection
    The Beatles 1962--1966
    The Beatles Rarities (US)
    The Early Beatles
    Please Please Me
    Twist And Shout
LOVE YOU TO/TOO
    The Beatles Collection
    Revolver
LOVELY RITA
    The Beatles Collection
    Sgt. Pepper's
LUCY IN THE SKY WITH DIAMONDS
    The Beatles Collection
    The Beatles 1967--1970
    Sgt. Pepper's
MAGICAL MYSTERY TOUR
    The Beatles 1967--1970
    Magical Mystery Tour
MARTHA MY DEAR
    The Beatles
    The Beatles Collection
MAXWELL'S SILVER HAMMER
    Abbey Road
    The Beatles Collection
MEAN MR. MUSTARD
    Abbey Road
    The Beatles Collection
MICHELLE
    The Beatles Collection
    The Beatles 1962--1966
    A Collection of Beatles...

Love Songs
Rubber Soul
MISERY
    The Beatles Collection
    The Beatles Rarities (US)
    Long Tall Sally
    Please Please Me
MOTHER NATURE'S SON
    The Beatles
    The Beatles Collection
THE NIGHT BEFORE
    The Beatles Collection
    Help!
    Rock 'n' Roll Music
NO REPLY
    The Beatles Collection
    Beatles For Sale
    Beatles '65
NORWEGIAN WOOD (THIS BIRD HAS
    FLOWN)
    The Beatles Collection
    The Beatles 1962--1966
    Love Songs
    Rubber Soul
NOT A SECOND TIME
    Beatlemania With The Beatles
    The Beatles Collection
    Meet The Beatles
    With The Beatles
NOWHERE MAN
    The Beatles Collection
    The Beatles 1962--1966
    Rubber Soul (UK)
    Yesterday...And Today
OB-LA-DI, OB-LA-DA
    The Beatles
    The Beatles Collection
    The Beatles 1967--1970
OCTOPUS'S GARDEN
    Abbey Road
    The Beatles Collection
    The Beatles 1967--1970
OH! DARLING
    Abbey Road
    The Beatles Collection
OLD BROWN SHOE
    The Beatles 1967--1970
    Hey Jude
ONE AFTER NINE-O-NINE
    The Beatles Collection
    Let It Be
ONLY A NORTHERN SONG
    The Beatles Collection
    Yellow Submarine
PS I LOVE YOU
    The Beatles Collection
    The Early Beatles
    Love Songs
    Please Please Me
    Twist And Shout
PAPERBACK WRITER
    The Beatles Collection
    The Beatles 1962--1966
    A Collection of Beatles...
    Hey Jude
PENNY LANE
    The Beatles 1967--1970
    The Beatles Rarities (US)
    Magical Mystery Tour
PIGGIES
    The Beatles
    The Beatles Collection
PLEASE PLEASE ME
    The Beatles Collection
    The Beatles 1962--1966
    The Early Beatles
    Please Please Me
    Twist And Shout
POLYTHENE PAM
    Abbey Road

The Beatles Collection
RAIN
    The Beatles Collection
    The Beatles Rarities (UK)
    Hey Jude
REVOLUTION
    The Beatles 1967--1970
    Hey Jude
    Rock 'n' Roll Music
REVOLUTION ONE
    The Beatles
    The Beatles Collection
REVOLUTION NINE
    The Beatles
    The Beatles Collection
ROCKY RACCOON
    The Beatles
    The Beatles Collection
RUN FOR YOUR LIFE
    The Beatles Collection
    Rubber Soul
SAVOY TRUFFLE
    The Beatles
    The Beatles Collection
SGT. PEPPER'S LONELY HEARTS
    CLUB BAND
    The Beatles Collection
    The Beatles 1967--1970
    Sgt. Pepper's
SGT. PEPPER'S LONELY HEARTS
    CLUB BAND (REPRISE)
    The Beatles Collection
    Sgt. Pepper's
SEXY SADIE
    The Beatles
    The Beatles Collection
SHE CAME IN THROUGH THE
    BATHROOM WINDOW
    Abbey Road
    The Beatles Collection
SHE LOVES YOU
    The Beatles Collection (US)
    The Beatles 1962--1966
    The Beatles Second Album
    A Collection of Beatles...
    Twist And Shout
SHE SAID SHE SAID
    The Beatles Collection
    Revolver
SHE'S A WOMAN
    The Beatles Collection
    The Beatles Rarities (UK)
    Beatles '65
SHE'S LEAVING HOME
    The Beatles Collection
    Love Songs
    Sgt. Pepper's
SOMETHING
    Abbey Road
    The Beatles Collection
    The Beatles 1967--1970
    The Best of George Harrison
    Love Songs
STRAWBERRY FIELDS FOREVER
    The Beatles 1967--1970
    Magical Mystery Tour
SUN KING
    Abbey Road
    The Beatles Collection
TAXMAN
    The Beatles Collection
    The Beatles Rarities (UK)
    The Best of George Harrison
    Revolver
    Rock 'n' Roll Music
TELL ME WHAT YOU SEE
    The Beatles Collection
    Beatles VI
    Help! (UK)
    Love Songs

TELL ME WHY
    The Beatles Collection
    A Hard Day's Night
    Something New
THANK YOU GIRL
    The Beatles Collection
    The Beatles Second Album
THERE'S A PLACE
    The Beatles Collection
    The Beatles Rarities (US)
    Please Please Me
    Twist And Shout
THINGS WE SAID TODAY
    The Beatles Collection
    A Hard Day's Night (UK)
    Something New
THINK FOR YOURSELF
    The Beatles Collection
    The Best of George Harrison
    Rubber Soul
THIS BOY
    The Beatles Collection
    The Beatles Rarities (UK)
    Long Tall Sally
    Love Songs
TICKET TO RIDE
    The Beatles Collection
    The Beatles 1962--1966
    A Collection of Beatles...
    Help!
TOMORROW NEVER KNOWS
    The Beatles Collection
    Revolver
TWO OF US
    The Beatles Collection
    Let It Be
WAIT
    The Beatles Collection
    Rubber Soul
WE CAN WORK IT OUT
    The Beatles 1962--1966
    A Collection of Beatles...
    Yesterday...And Today
WHAT GOES ON?
    The Beatles Collection
    Rubber Soul (UK)
    Yesterday...And Today
WHAT YOU'RE DOING
    The Beatles Collection
    Beatles For Sale
    Beatles VI
WHEN I GET HOME
    The Beatles Collection
    A Hard Day's Night (UK)
    Something New
WHEN I'M SIXTY-FOUR
    The Beatles Collection
    Sgt. Pepper's
WHILE MY GUITAR GENTLY WEEPS
    The Beatles
    The Beatles Collection
    The Beatles 1967--1970
    The Best of George Harrison
WHY DON'T WE DO IT IN THE ROAD
    The Beatles
    The Beatles Collection
WILD HONEY PIE
    The Beatles
    The Beatles Collection
WITH A LITTLE HELP FROM MY
    FRIENDS
    The Beatles Collection
    The Beatles 1967--1970
    Sgt. Pepper's
WITHIN YOU, WITHOUT YOU
    The Beatles Collection
    Sgt. Pepper's
THE WORD
    The Beatles Collection
    Rubber Soul

YELLOW SUBMARINE
    The Beatles Collection
    The Beatles 1962--1966
    A Collection of Beatles...
    Revolver
    Yellow Submarine
YER BLUES
    The Beatles
    The Beatles Collection
YES IT IS
    The Beatles Collection
    The Beatles Rarities (UK)
    Beatles VI
    Love Songs
YESTERDAY
    The Beatles Collection
    The Beatles 1962--1966
    A Collection of Beatles...

Help! (UK)
Love Songs
Yesterday...And Today
YOU CAN'T DO THAT
    The Beatles Collection
    The Beatles Second Album
    A Hard Day's Night (UK)
    Long Tall Sally
    Rock 'n' Roll Music
YOU KNOW MY NAME (LOOK UP MY
        NUMBER)
    The Beatles Collection
    The Beatles Rarities
YOU LIKE ME TOO MUCH
    The Beatles Collection
    Beatles VI
    Help! (UK)
YOU NEVER GIVE ME YOUR MONEY

Abbey Road
    The Beatles Collection
YOU WON'T SEE ME
    The Beatles Collection
    Rubber Soul
YOUR MOTHER SHOULD KNOW
    Magical Mystery Tour
YOU'RE GOING TO/GONNA LOSE THAT
        GIRL
    The Beatles Collection
    Help!
    Love Songs
YOU'VE GOT TO HIDE YOUR LOVE
        AWAY
    The Beatles Collection
    The Beatles 1962--1966
    Help!
    Love Songs

One of the most famous of early Beatles songs — *She loves you* — is also quintessential. It is simply an affirmation, epitomised in its 'Yeah yeah yeah' refrain; and it exists in the moment, without before or after. For although its key signature is the E flat beloved of Tin Pan Alley, the opening phrase is pentatonic, or perhaps an aeolian C which veers towards E flat; and although some of the effect depends on contrast between upward tending sharp sevenths and the blue flat sevenths of folk tradition, no conflict is generated, and the song has little sense of beginning, middle and end. The final guitar chord looks like a triad of E flat major with added sixth; yet the melody suggests that C, not E flat, is the root. The timeless, present-affirming modality is instinctive; and the words, if still perfunctorily vacuous, are no longer *merely* magic talisman, abracadabra.

–Wilfrid Mellers
Twilight of the Gods

Who put the "yeah"s on 'She Loves You'?
John and I wrote it into the song. 'She love you, yeah, yeah, yeah.' But the idea of having the sixth chord when it finishes was George's. George Harrison's. And George Martin said "That's funny. That's very old fashioned." And we said "Yes, but it's nice, isn't it?" He said "Yes, OK,"

–Paul McCartney
(quoted in *Paul McCartney In His Own Words*
by Paul Gambaccini)

(*She Loves You* was written while
travelling on a bus in Yorkshire in 1963)

THINGS WE SAID TODAY

WITHDRAWN